D1075378

NOVELL'S ®

CNE Study Guide for NetWare 4.1

DAVID JAMES CLARKE, IV

NOVELL
PRESS ®

Novell Press, San Jose

Novell's CNE Study Guide for NetWare 4.1
Published by
Novell Press
2180 Fortune Drive
San Jose, CA 95131

Library of Congress Catalog Card No.: 95-81551

ISBN: 1-56884-734-3

Printed in the United States of America

10 9 8 7 6 5 4 3 2 1

1A/SZ/RR/ZV

Distributed in the United States by IDG Books Worldwide, Inc.

Distributed by Macmillan Canada for Canada; by Computer and Technical Books for the Caribbean Basin; by Contemporantea de Ediciones for Venezuela; by Distribuidora Cuspide for Argentina; by CITFC for Brazil; by Ediciones ZETA S.C.R. Ltda. for Peru; by Editorial Limusa SA for Mexico; by Transworld Publishers Limited in the United Kingdom and Europe; by Al-Maiman Publishers & Distributors for Saudi Arabia; by Simron Pty. Ltd. for South Africa; by IDG Communications (IIK) Ltd. for Hong Kong; by Toppan Company Ltd. for Japan; by Addison Wesley Publishing Company for Korea; by Longman Singapore Publisher Ltd. for Singapore, Malaysia, Thailand, and Indonesia; by Unalis Corporation for Taiwan; by WS Computer Publishing Company, Inc. for the Philippines; by WoodsLane Enterprises Ltd. for New Zealand.

For general information on Novell Press books in the U.S., including information on discounts and premiums, contact IDG Books at 800-434-3422 or 415-655-3000.

For information on where to purchase Novell Press books outside the U.S., contact IDG Books International at 415-655-3021 or fax 415-655-3295.

For information on translations, contact Waterside Productions, Inc., 2191 San Elijo Avenue, Cardiff, CA 92007-1839, at 619-632-9190.

For sales inquiries and special prices for bulk quantities, call IDG Books Worldwide at 415-655-3000.

For information on using Novell Press books in the classroom, or for ordering examination copies, contact Jim Kelly at 800-434-2086.

John Kilcullen, *President & CEO*
Brenda McLaughlin, *Senior Vice President & Group Publisher*

The IDG Books Worldwide logo is a trademark of IDG Books Worldwide, Inc.

Rosalie Kearsley, *Publisher, Novell Press, Inc.*

Novell Press and the Novell Press logo are trademarks of Novell, Inc.

Welcome to Novell Press

Novell Press, the world's leading provider of networking books, is the premier source for the most timely and useful information in the networking industry. Novell Press books cover fundamental networking issues as they emerge—from today's Novell and third-party products to the concepts and strategies that will guide the industry's future. The result is a broad spectrum of titles for the benefit of those involved in networking at any level: end-user, department administrator, developer, systems manager, or network architect.

Novell Press books are written by experts with the full participation of Novell's technical, managerial, and marketing staff. The books are exhaustively reviewed by Novell's own technicians and are published only on the basis of final released software, never on prereleased versions.

Novell Press at IDG is an exciting partnership between two companies at the forefront of the knowledge and communications revolution. The Press is implementing an ambitious publishing program to develop new networking titles centered on the current version of NetWare and on Novell's GroupWise and other popular groupware products.

Novell Press books are translated into 12 languages and are available at bookstores around the world.

Rosalie Kearsley, *Publisher, Novell Press, Inc.*
David Kolodney, *Associate Publisher, IDG Books Worldwide, Inc.*

Novell Press

Publisher
Rosalie Kearsley

Associate Publisher
David Kolodney

Market Development Manager
Colleen Bluhm

Associate Acquisitions Editor
Anne Hamilton

Communications Project Specialist
Marcy Shanti

Managing Editor
Terry Somerson

Associate Developmental Editor
Amy Marks

Project Manager
Susan Davis

Copy Editors
Luann Rouff
Kevin Shafer
Carolyn Welch

Technical Editor
Gamal Herbon

Editorial Assistant
Jean Leitner

Production Director
Beth Jenkins

**Supervisor of
Project Coordination**
Cindy L. Phipps

Supervisor of Page Layout
Kathie S. Schnorr

Production Systems Specialist
Steve Peake

Pre-Press Coordination
Tony Augsburger
Patricia R. Reynolds
Theresa Sánchez-Baker

Media/Archive Coordination
Leslie Popplewell
Kerri Cornell
Michael Wilkey

Associate Project Coordinator
J. Tyler Connor

Graphics Coordination
Shelley Lea
Gina Scott
Carla Radzikinas

Production Staff
Shawn Aylsworth
Cameron Booker
Kerri Cornell
Dominique DeFelice
Jill Lyttle
Mark C. Owens
Kate Snell

Proofreaders
Christine Sabooni
Christine Meloy Beck
Gwenette Gaddis
Dwight Ramsey
Carl Saff
Rob Springer

Indexer
Sherry Massey

Illustrator
David Puckett

Cartoonist
Mike Kim

Cover Designer
Archer Design

Cover Photographer
Sandra Wavrick

About the Author

David James Clarke, IV, is the author of the best-selling books *Novell's CNE Study Guide* and *Novell's CNA Study Guide*. He is also the developer of The Clarke Tests v2.0, an interactive learning system, and the producer of the D.J.C. video series *So You Wanna Be a CNE?!* Clarke is a Certified Novell Instructor (CNI), Engineer (CNE), and Administrator (CNA). He speaks at numerous national conferences and currently serves as the president and CEO of Clarke Industries, Inc. He lives in Avila Beach, California.

I dedicate this book to the human race for never ceasing to amaze me...and since you're a human, I guess that in some strange way, I dedicate this book to you!

Foreword

Novell recognized very early that networking calls for a different kind of company and a different type of approach to dealing with computer systems. We know we need partners, and we regard the CNEs as being among the most important partners of all. The CNE program creates the pervasive expertise that will be needed to be of service to pervasive computing as it develops. Intelligent networking requires trained technicians on the spot, who can deal with the myriad configurations and platforms that Novell networking seeks to seamlessly connect. That in turn fosters openness, fosters freedom of choice. None of that would be well served if Novell tried to impose a one-size-fits-all networking system. So the CNE is essential right there on the ground. CNEs can go for the best answers, including those produced by other companies. They are practical, expert, and creative in fitting the technology to particular business needs. We are proud to be their partners in this unfolding enterprise.

The opportunities for CNEs have never been greater. Networking is more and more in demand; it is the solution virtually every company is turning to. A CNE understands business issues and networking capabilities, and combines them in such a way as to create and deliver effective solutions.

From a broader perspective, networking is also becoming ever more pervasive in the activities of our daily lives. The whole thing is exploding and will continue to explode in the foreseeable future. Change is happening, and the technician's skills will also need to evolve at a rapid rate. The CNE program is very conscious of the need to keep up with real world developments and future directions. So much more innovation is in store; so much more is going to be connected to computer networks—we have only begun to imagine the possibilities! All that change spells growing opportunities for everyone who participates in moving to better, more powerful solutions for our customers. In all of this, it is the CNE who will be on the front lines of progress.

Novell's CNE Study Guide for NetWare 4.1 by David Clarke is a great example of the Novell partnership philosophy: human, open, precise, and expert. It is an extraordinarily welcome resource to help students join with Novell in the amazing and ever-changing future of computer networking.

Drew Major
V.P. & Chief Scientist, Operating Systems
Novell, Inc.

Acknowledgments

Where do I start? This has been a monumental effort—the most ambitious project I've ever worked on—partly because NetWare 4 is so sophisticated and partly because the CNE program has evolved tremendously, but mostly because I wanted to blow your socks off. Of course, I couldn't have done it without the help of a fantastic group of professionals (who were supported by very understanding families and friends).

I know it sounds corny, but my family is everything. I gained a new respect for them while writing this book, mostly because I continued to test the envelope of sanity. Crazy hours, crazy requests, crazy trips. Mary, my wife, deserves the most credit for supporting my work and bringing a great deal of happiness into my life. She is my anchor. Then there's Leia, my daughter. She knew when to interrupt me. She somehow knew just when I needed a break—daughter's intuition. Most of all, they both have brought much needed perspective into my otherwise one-dimensional life. For that, I owe them everything.

I also owe a great deal to my parents for their unending support and devotion. They are the architects of my life and I couldn't have accomplished anything without their guidance and love. In addition, my sister Athena and her new family, Ralph and Taylor, deserve kudos for standing by me through thick and thin.

In addition, thanks to my second family for opening their hearts to me. Don and Diane have been wonderfully generous to me, Mary, and their precious granddaughter, Leia. Also, Keith and Bob have been great brothers to me, and Lisa and Pam have been great sisters to Mary. Finally, Jessica has been a creative and fun influence on Leia.

Before I close my family circle, I must thank two important "extended family" members—Dr. James Buxbaum and Rene Mendoza. They are life-friends who have always supported my writing. Together we are works-in-progress—a novel with James and a screenplay with Rene. Someday we'll finish....

Now let's meet the professional "Dream Team" behind this book. At center, my partner in vocabulary, is Cathy Ettelson. She has been instrumental in all aspects of this book—research, the mad scientist's laboratory, exercises, and the list goes on. I owe a great deal to this brilliant woman, and I truly couldn't have done it without her. Next, at forward, is Lori Ficklin, who was responsible for bringing my words to life—literally. At the other forward position is Gamal Herbon, the technical eyes and ears of this team. Next, at guard, are David Puckett, the master of the beautiful illustrations in this book, and Mike Kim, a gifted cartoonist with a pipeline to our collective funny bone.

Behind every great book is an incredible production team. It all started with Susan Davis. If she wasn't hunting down lost tapes or mediating conference calls, she was sketching posters 'til all hours of the night—not to mention that her voice has a mystical, soothing quality to it. Speaking of mystical, I don't know how Amy Marks pulled it off. Her legendary organization, quick wit, and patience were instrumental in getting this book out the door.

Tyler Connor, Cameron Booker, Mark Owens, Shelley Lea, Carla Radzikinas, and Gina Scott deserve a lot of the credit for finishing this book on time. They all performed above and beyond the call of duty in every aspect of production. I would also like to thank Luann Rouff, Kevin Shafer, Carolyn Welch, Zephyr Albright, and all the proof-readers, typesetters, artists, and management who made this book possible. Finally, thanks to Brenda McLaughlin for assembling such a talented group of professionals and for having an amazing standard of quality herself.

I'd like to thank all the magicians who have mastered the magic of NetWare 4—starting with Drew Major. Not only did Drew invent NetWare, he continues to evolve it. Thanks for finding time out of your busy schedule to share a few thoughts with us in the foreword. Next, I'd like to acknowledge two of the smartest guys I've ever met—Jeff Hughes and Blair Thomas of Novell Consulting Services. They were great allies in navigating the labyrinth of NDS design and NetWare 4 trickery.

Thanks to Kristin Marks and Steve Kalman for their magic touch in NetWare 4 optimization. Also, thanks for helping with the "road show." You're both great friends. When I think of printing magic, I immediately think of J.D. Marymee and Sandy Stevens. I was lucky enough to get a tour of their printing world and learn to appreciate the sophistication and complexity of NetWare 4 printing. You'll get a similar tour in Chapter 14. Also, thanks to Eric Burkholder for expanding my mind to the ideas of Schema extension and NDS on the Internet. Finally, thanks to Ken Neff for providing *Novell Application Notes* references.

This is the future of network publishing, and this book wouldn't be possible without the insight, guidance, hard work, and dedication of Rose Kearsley and David Kolodney—they *are* Novell Press. Rose has been a wonderful friend and supportive publisher throughout the past four years. I can only hope for greater things in the future. The dramatic revolution of *Novell's CNE Study Guide* is due in part to David Kolodney's almost clairvoyant insight—not to mention his uncanny ability to convince people they need to give us stuff. And, of course, all of this wouldn't have been possible without Anne Hamilton.

Also at Novell Press, Marcy Shanti has been a wonderful friend through thick and thin—always e-mailing, calling, or popping up at just the right time. Marcy was also my eyes and ears to Novell Education, an invaluable resource. And Colleen Bluhm was a stabilizing force through the white-water rapids that were this book. I really needed your help, and you came through for me time and time again.

In addition, I'd like to thank Novell Education for evolving the CNE curriculum to an exceptionally high level. Thanks to K.C. Sue, Russ Clark, Adnan Kandah, and everyone else for supporting this book and setting a very high quality standard. Also, thanks to all the NAECs and NEAPs for continuing the standard of excellence and providing a nurturing learning environment for NetWare 4 CNE candidates everywhere. You are truly the core of the CNE program.

I must thank all of my NetWare Users International (NUI) friends for being there with me "on the road." You're all wonderful people, and you're doing great things for NetWare users everywhere. Thanks to Daryl Alder for your wisdom, Midge Johnson for your organization, and Shelly Moore for your guidance. I would be lost without all of you.

Life is not one-dimensional. There's more to it than NetWare 4 and NDS—although it doesn't seem like it at times. Fortunately, I have my friends to remind me of this. First, there's Paul Wildrick, my friend and business partner. Thanks for making my life even more complicated than it already is. Thanks to Ted Lloyd for being, well, Ted Lloyd. How can you always be right? Isn't there a law against that? Thanks to Lisa and Brian Smith for being friends and keeping the ship afloat. You both have a calming influence. Which is more than I can say for Brent Sharp—although your particular type of chaos I both like and admire.

Finally, thanks to Billy Gibbs for life on the links, Tears for Fears for inspiration, and Mall of America for somewhere to shop when I'm in town. Thanks to Marcus Kaufman for being, well, Marcus Kaufman, The Tick for being a superhero role model, and The Walt Disney Company for teaching me everything I know about networking.

I saved the best for last. Thanks to *YOU* for caring enough about NetWare 4 and your education to buy this book. You deserve a great deal of credit for your enthusiasm and dedication. Thanks again, and I hope this education changes your life. Good luck, and welcome to your new exciting life! Enjoy the show.

(IDG Books Worldwide would like to give special thanks to Patrick J. McGovern, founder of International Data Group, who made this book possible.)

Contents at a Glance

Table of Contents

Chapter 4   •   NDS Design   **253**

Preface

Hi! I'm baaaaack!

It seems like just yesterday we were frolicking through the life of a CNE in *Novell's CNE Study Guide for Netware 3.12*. Well, the world's changed and CNEship has entered a new frontier—NetWare 4! It's unlike anything you've ever seen. There are clouds, trees, gardeners, and leaf objects. It's a plethora of permaculture; a virtual cornucopia of chlorophyll. And that's not all. NetWare 4 introduces a whole new dimension in networking—NDS. You're in for the ride of your life. Green thumb required.

So, do you still want to be a CNE? The "007" of cyberworld? Good. Don't worry, you still get to traverse the obstacle course of unpredictable network challenges. It's just that the course has gotten a little bigger and the obstacles have gotten a little more unpredictable. The good news is the rewards still greatly outweigh the pain. You'll be more competitive in today's job market and maybe even save the world along the way. Life as a CNE has never been more exciting! Ready, set, go.

Wait! You don't have to travel alone. I'll be by your side every step of the way—your trusted CNE tour guide. And, I've brought along a few other friends to help. Heroes from our unspoiled history—before instant popcorn, talking cars, and daytime television. There's Albert Einstein, Sherlock Holmes, Gandhi, and Mother Teresa, just to name a few—the NetWare 4 dream team. With friends like these, you can't but succeed. Ready, set, go.

Wait! How about a quick preview? This is the Preface after all. Ready, set, preview!

ZEN

"I don't pretend to understand the universe; it's a great deal bigger than I am."

Thomas Carlyle

The journey begins with a "seed of thought." Before you know it, you'll have a huge NDS tree growing out of your head. Chapter 1 explores the next generation of NetWare 4. It is a preview of NetWare 4 and the entire book. The main new feature is NDS (NetWare Directory Services)—that's covered in Chapter 2. Next, you'll learn the basic fundamentals of NDS—it's a whole new ballgame. Once you're done with NDS, it's time to attack the NetWare 4 CNE obstacle course—design, installation, and management.

NetWare 4 CNEs have three main tasks in NetWare 4—design, installation, and management. First, you design the NDS tree—as a superhero. Second, you install the servers using an established design—as a doctor. And, third, you get to configure and manage it—as an NDS gardener. Talk about your split personalities! CNEs must excel in all three jobs, although each is very different. Fortunately, this book will help you every step of the way.

In Chapter 3, we introduce the pseudo-fictitious organization ACME. ACME is a group of world-famous heroes from the past who have banded together to save the world. We will be using them throughout the book in examples, exercises, and case studies. In Chapter 3, we will create the team responsible for ACME's NDS tree design and provide a large list of design inputs, including WAN layouts, an organization chart, and a workflow diagram. Good luck, and by the way, thanks for saving the world!

Then, you're in for the ride of your life. Chapter 4 explores the nuts and bolts of NDS design—a very important CNE task. Once again, we'll use ACME as an example. You will learn about tree design, partitioning, time sychronization, and most important, accessibility design. This is where the fun begins! Finally, in Chapter 5 you get to start NDS implementation. It all starts with a small seed. Then with water, sunlight, and love, the seedling grows into a fruitful, majestic tree. In Chapter 5 we learn how to bring our design to life and provide a transition to the next part—NetWare 4 installation.

In Chapter 6, the network is born. This is the true implementation of NDS design. During NetWare 4 installation, you follow six stages and 23 steps toward NetWare 4 Nirvana. It's a great place to start. Next, in Chapter 7, you will explore the miracle of NetWare 4 migration. NetWare 4 is so different from earlier versions, upgrading is really migrating. It's a whole new frontier of networking. This chapter outlines the steps of migrating from NetWare 2 or 3 all the way to NetWare 4. It seems like a breeze next to installation.

Once the tree has been designed and installed, it's time to take care of it. Chapter 8, NDS Management, deals with the daily tasks of gardening. We cover object naming, NWADMIN, object types, and Bindery Services. Try to keep the dirt out from under your fingernails. As we learn in Chapter 9, the tree also needs to be pruned periodically. This provides better health and efficiency (distributed databases) as well as tree stability and longevity (fault tolerance). Also, we'll explore time synchronization for better access to sunlight.

In Chapter 10, we learn that the file system represents NetWare life "within" the server. All of our focus so far has been "above" the server. Now we get a chance to work with a big, electronic filing cabinet. Chapter 11 continues this journey with a look at security. Information is now the new commodity—more valuable than money. We need to take new measures to protect our information. NetWare 4 includes a five-layered security model including login/password authentication, login restrictions, NDS rights, file system access rights, and attributes. Think of it as your impenetrable network armor.

Once the LAN has been installed (born) it enters the second and third phases of its lifespan—configuration (childhood) and management (adulthood). In Chapter 12, the first of two related chapters, I'll walk you through the five steps of configuration using Leia as an example. Then, in Chapter 13, we're introduced to the final phase of LAN lifespan—adulthood. Here the network gets married, has children of her own, plans for retirement, and finally retires. There are five steps in this chapter.

That leaves the last two topics: printing and optimization. Printing (Chapter 14) is "the great challenge." NetWare 4 printing is simple and works great until...you add users. It's their fault. In this chapter, we will explore some proven methods for successful NetWare 4 printing installation, management, and troubleshooting. In addition, we'll get a peek at printing's future—NDPS. Then we complete the journey with Chapter 15—the final frontier. Once you've lived through the LAN lifespan and set up NetWare 4 printing, only one task is left—optimization. Put the pedal to the metal and enter the new frontier at the speed of light. Your life will never be the same.

That pretty much sums it up—five courses in one book. Wow! These chapters cover everything there is to know about NetWare 4, life as a CNE, and saving the world. Of course, we couldn't survive our journey without three great appendices. Appendix A is an overview of Novell Education. Appendix B is a great cross-reference of CNE course objectives. It points you in the right direction—course by course. And finally, Appendix C has all the answers—literally. It has answers for case studies, exercises, and quizzes.

Speaking of answers, I have a few life puzzles I could use answered. How about you?

Life Puzzles

ZEN

"Next, when you are describing,
A shape, or sound, or tint;
Don't state the matter plainly,
But put it in a hint;
And learn to look at all things,
With a sort of mental squint."

Lewis Carroll

There is a difference between puzzles and problems. Life puzzles allow you to stretch your mind and explore parts of your brain you didn't even know you had. Also, they usually have one answer—or so it seems. Life problems, on the other hand, arise through the everyday process of getting out of bed and putting on your clothes. Also, there is never a "right" answer—just shades of grey. So the moral is—read this book in bed, and enjoy the life puzzles.

In addition to life puzzles, there are a myriad of other informational tidbits scattered throughout the book. These quips provide instant information in the form of Zen, Quizzes, Tips, Real World, and The Brain. Check them out:

ZEN

Words of wisdom from people more enlightened than I am. Plus, they make you look really smart in front of your friends.

QUIZ

These brain puzzlers help bring much needed perspective into your difficult and absorbing journey. It's a great idea to come up for "mental air" every now and then. And these quizzes will appear at just the right time—before you mentally suffocate.

TIP

Highlights time-proven management techniques and action-oriented ideas. These tips are great ways of expanding your horizons beyond just CNEship—they're your ticket to true nerd-om.

REAL WORLD

Welcome to the real world. I don't want you to be a two-dimensional CNE in a three-dimensional world. These icons represent the other dimension. In an attempt to bring this book to life, I've included various real-world scenarios, case studies, and situational walk throughs.

THE BRAIN

In case yours turns to Jell-O. These are great context-sensitive references to supplemental brains. Brains-for-hire, like NetWare 4 documentation, Application Notes, Albert Einstein, and so on. Enjoy them, and give yours a rest.

Inevitably, at some point you're going to want to apply all this great NetWare 4 knowledge to some physical structure—a LAN perhaps. One assumes you will *act* on this book's CNE concepts, theories, exercises, and examples. One assumes at some point, you'll need to scream! That's OK, I'm here for you. I care.

ZEN

"All the animals except man know that the principle business of life is to enjoy it."

Samuel Butler

The main goal of this book is to take you on a magic carpet ride through the next generation of NetWare—NetWare 4. Nobody said it couldn't be fun! As a matter of fact, I've worked overtime to make this the most painless, and even enjoyable, NetWare 4 experience of your life. I've even included a life-size poster of NDS and the ACME tree.

It would be irresponsible of me to abandon you at the very moment you need the most help—real life! I'm here for you—every step of the way. I'm only a cybercall away. Also, in an effort to provide you with the most complete education possible, we have gathered an all-star collection of additional learning tools on the CD-ROM bound into this book—The Clarke Tests v2.0, World Wire, Cyber State University, NSEPro, and DS Standard. See Appendix D for complete details on the CD-ROM contents.

In addition, I spend most of the year traveling around the globe—meeting you! I speak at NetWare Users International conferences, Networld + Interop, Networks Expo, and others. But if none of that works for you, I'm always available to chat. Really! I'm sitting by the cyperphone waiting for it to cyberring. Find me:

- ▸ Internet: dciv@garnet.berkeley.edu

- ▸ The Web: Hot Link from NOVELL.COM

- ▸ CompuServe: 71700,403

- ▸ World Wire: DAVID CLARKE, IV

    - ▸ Sign up at 1-510-254-1194 (on-line)
    - ▸ Phone: 1-510-254-7283

- ▸ The Clarke Tests: 1-800-684-8858

- ▸ Cyber State University: 1-510-253-TREK

- ▸ NUI Conferences: 1-800-228-4NUI

NetWare 4 CNE—A New Frontier

ZEN

"As knowledge increases, wonder deepens."

Charles Morgan

There's a whole galaxy of NetWare 4 knowledge nuggets out there—and we will explore every last one of them. Our mission is to boldly go where no one has gone before—or at least get through this book without losing our marbles. Our first stop— the twilight zone. Take a quick look at this mind-twisting crossword puzzle. Welcome to your life! Scary, huh? Whatever you do, don't attempt the puzzle now, it could cause irreparable damage to your brain cells. On second thought—go ahead! You'll like it— really. And when you've had enough, the answers are in Appendix C. Ciao.

NETWARE 4 CNE—A NEW FRONTIER

Across

1. Where the World Health Index is calculated
4. NetWare 4 server startup directory
6. Default server installation method
8. A "global village"
9. Prehistoric file sharing
11. Perpetuating the filing myth

13. Scrawling signatures
15. Just do it!
19. Dynamic bad block remapping
20. Most reliable external time source
24. The rules of NDS
25. Not up
26. The MONITOR.NLM washing machine
27. Top of the world
29. Where orphan files go to live
32. Characteristics of each network resource
33. ASCII, by default
34. A whole new world above the WAN
36. Dinosaur of NDS security
37. When lightening strikes
38. Mobile users
40. Etch-a-Sketch for NDS
41. More than 64 entries
42. First NetWare 4 volume
43. Defines country code, character code set, and keyboard mapping
44. The new server superhero
45. Layout of the LANd

Down

1. Your friend for NDS gardening
2. Are you really AEinstein?
3. Storing and forwarding MHS messages
5. A measure of our future
7. Pruning in the non-GUI world
10. A Cure for Mother Earth
12. General layout of NDS tree design
14. "Elder" partitions
16. They turn colors in the fall
17. "On," by default
18. The new home of Sherlock Holmes and Dr. Watson
21. NetWare 4 context navigation tool
22. The goal

23. Gathering unused RAM in NetWare 4
25. The new BINDFIX
28. I'm just not your_____
29. Virtual reality ACME
30. Physical network resources in the NDS tree
31. "I've deleted my file and can't get up!"
33. Server installation with all the bells and whistles
35. _____comic, paper bag optional
38. Your friend for NDS gardening
39. NetWare in German

See Appendix C for answers.

NetWare 4 CNE Basics

To NetWare 4, or not to NetWare 4—that is the question.
Whether tis nobler in the mind to suffer
The slings and arrows of previous NetWare versions,
Or to take arms against a sea of troubles, and by opposing end them.

To Upgrade, To Migrate.
No more bindery—and by a migration to say we end the heartache,
And the thousand natural shocks that the bindery is heir to!
Tis a consummation devoutly to be wished.

To Upgrade, To Migrate.
To Migrate—perchance to plan poorly.
Aye, there's the rub.
For in that poor planning, what problems may arise.
When we have shuffled off this earlier version, must give us mortal pause.
There's the respect that makes calamity of staying with an earlier version.

William Shakespeare (as told by Richard Rosdal)

Welcome to NetWare 4—the next generation of computing. Not since *Romeo and Juliet* has there been so much network synergy. Not since *Hamlet* has a company been so driven. Not since *The Tempest* has a product been so compelling. Even William Shakespeare saw it coming.

You are in for the ride of your life. Like a roller coaster, it starts with a deep breath and seatbelt (Chapter 1). Then, you make the nerve-racking ascent toward the sky (Chapter 2). Finally, in Chapter 3, we'll let you loose on the most exhilarating 1,600 pages you've ever read. Truly an "E" ticket ride!

The portal to a new frontier has been opened up for you today...warp speed ahead.

Introduction to NetWare 4

"We've come halfway across the galaxy to see NetWare 4!"

So you think you know NetWare. Well, I have a surprise for you! Not even Bo knows NetWare. Novell's fourth generation of the NetWare operating system is a completely new ball game—and fortunately nobody is on strike.

Welcome to NetWare 4!

NetWare 4 is the big kahuna. It represents Novell's tenth try at the NetWare network operating system. The original architects of NetWare—Drew Major and Superset—returned to the proverbial drawing board and completely redesigned the interface, communications, and functionality of NetWare. The result is a powerful, flexible, and fast wide area network operating system. There's a mouthful.

NetWare 4 epitomizes transparent connectivity. It unobtrusively provides the user with simultaneous access to multiple network resources from one login—whatever that means. Simply stated, users no longer belong to servers—they belong to the *network* as a whole. All resources of the wide area network (WAN) are created as objects in a hierarchical tree, much like files in a directory structure. Users, servers, printers, volumes, and groups are treated equally and given simultaneous access to each other's resources. It's been a long and winding road, but we've finally achieved NetWare Nirvana in true form. This is all made possible through NetWare 4's newest wonder—NetWare Directory Services (NDS).

NDS is an object-oriented database that organizes network resources into a *hierarchical* tree—there's that fancy word again. The global NDS tree is fully replicated and distributed throughout the network, providing efficient connectivity and network fault tolerance—which is easier said than done. NDS also features a single login and hidden security system that makes access to any server, volume, or network resource completely transparent to the user. NDS takes care of the complexities of network topology, communications, protocol translation, and authentication in the background far away from the user.

Think of NDS as a friendly cloud of joy overlooking your network! NDS is simplicity through sophistication.

TIP

NDS enables you to manage network resources (such as servers, users, and printers) and services, but it does not control the file system (directories and files). NetWare 4 provides a variety of non-NDS utilities for managing the file system.

In addition to NetWare Directory Services, NetWare 4 offers myriad additional features and benefits. We will explore these in just a moment.

THE BRAIN

For an introduction to NetWare Directory Services, see Chapter I ("Understanding NetWare Directory Services") of the *Novell NetWare 4 Introduction to NetWare Directory Services* manual.

NetWare 4 is not an upgrade of NetWare 3.1x—it requires a system *migration*. NetWare 4 is a completely different way of approaching networking. It splits the role of networking into two halves—logical and physical. The logical half defines organizations and workgroups. The physical half defines users and servers. The beauty of this approach is that NetWare 4 can be as simple or complex as you want it to be. In addition, it includes a feature called *bindery emulation* that enables a NetWare 4 server to look like a NetWare 3.12 server. This is a whole new twist on backward compatibility. All in all, NetWare 4 is a great solution for small-, medium-, and large-size local area networks (LANs), metropolitan area networks (MANs), and wide area networks (WANs). Also, you better get used to it, because NetWare 4 is the foundation of Novell's new Enterprise approach to networking. Before you know it, NetWare 3 will be long gone and you'll be reading *Novell's CNE Study Guide for NetWare 5*.

TIP

NetWare 3.12 is actually more similar to NetWare 4 than you might think. NetWare 3.12 was originated because users of NetWare 3.11 were complaining that NetWare 4.0 had all the cool features. To satisfy these users, Novell released a special version of NetWare 3.11 that included some of the new advanced NetWare 4.0 features such as VLMs, SMS, a new menu system, on-line documentation, and better Windows support. In reality, NetWare 3.12 is a subset of NetWare 4 without NDS.

If all of this seems a little overwhelming, have no fear, Uncle David is here. NetWare 4 actually isn't as alien as you might think. As a matter of fact, Novell hasn't made any dramatic changes to the fundamental architecture of the core operating system (OS).

The Novell designers simply built on top of what exists in NetWare 3.12. As you can see in Figure 1.1, NetWare 3.12 consists of the core OS and some supplemental services. All of the services shown in this figure are mostly unchanged in NetWare 4.1. These services include

FIGURE 1.1

The Foundation of NetWare 3.12

Inter-national	Dyna-Text	Client Services (VLMs)	Core OS	Message Handling Services (MHS)	Storage Management Services (SMS)	Menu System

▶ Core OS—Of course, the core operating system has been "tweaked" a little in NetWare 4.1, but the fundamental 32-bit architecture remains unchanged from NetWare 3.12. NetWare 4 still relies on the console prompt and uses NetWare Loadable Modules (NLMs) to provide additional functionality.

TIP

One of the most exciting enhancements in the NetWare 4.1 core OS is the elimination of overhead instruction sets. The NetWare 4.1 core uses a reduced number of instructions to accomplish the same things it did in NetWare 3.12. This elimination of overhead enables the operating system to run a little bit faster even with the CPU overhead caused by NDS. In addition to cooptimization, the NetWare 4.1 core OS includes UniCode support (with a conversion table for direct multiple languages), CONFIG.NLM, support for the Pentium 4 MB page (ON by default), as well as the ability to automatically detect PCI and PCMCIA bus systems.

▶ Internationalization—Both NetWare 3.12 and 4 are designed to support numerous international languages and utilities. By default, NetWare 4 supports English, French, German, Italian, and Spanish.

THE BRAIN

For further information on using NetWare 4 in languages other than English, refer to the "International Use of NetWare 4.1" section of the *Novell NetWare 4 Concepts* manual.

▶ DynaText—The DynaText viewer included with NetWare 4 offers all the
functionality of the Novell ElectroText viewer provided in NetWare 3.12,
plus a quicker response time, enhanced graphical user interface (GUI),
Macintosh and UnixWare support, and compatibility for public or private
notes in on-line manuals.

▶ Client services (VLMs)—Both NetWare 3.12 and 4 offer better workstation
connectivity through the NetWare DOS Requester. The Requester uses
Virtual Loadable Modules (VLMs) to provide enhanced workstation support
for NDS, NCP packet signing, and advanced user authentication. The latest
version also supports connection timeout optimization, auto-reconnect, and
much better extended memory management.

▶ Message Handling Services (MHS)—Novell now includes a sophisticated
e-mail engine with NetWare 3.12 and 4. In NetWare 3.12 this engine is
implemented as Basic MHS; in NetWare 4, it is termed MHS Services for
NetWare 4. Both versions provide a background engine for storing and
forwarding NetWare messages. In addition, they provide a starter e-mail
application called FirstMail, which includes both DOS and Windows
versions. In addition, the NetWare 4 version of MHS provides full integration
with NDS and NetWare 4 administration utilities. Furthermore, it takes
advantage of specific mail-oriented NDS objects and includes SFT III
compatibility.

▶ Storage Management Services (SMS)—Like MHS, both NetWare 3.12
and 4 include a background engine for backing up and restoring server data.
SMS enables data to be stored and retrieved using a variety of front-end
applications. Also, these applications can call on numerous independent
storage devices attached directly to the NetWare server. In addition, SMS can
back up all file systems—including DOS, OS/2, Macintosh, MS Windows,
and UNIX. Another exciting feature of SMS is workstation backup. This
might seem a little backwards for those of you who are used to backing up
servers from the workstation—now we're backing up workstations from the
server. NetWare 4's SMS adds support for NDS backup and the System
Independent Data Format (SIDF).

▸ Menu System—Since NetWare 3.11, Novell has dedicated itself to providing a better integrated menu system. NetWare 3.12 and 4 use the new Saber-like menu system for building a consistent user interface. It includes better memory management, a higher level of workstation security, and user input options.

ZEN

"The guy who invented headcheese must have been really hungry."

Jerry Seinfeld

As I mentioned earlier, NetWare 4 builds on the foundation of NetWare 3. Now let's take a look at the evolution of NetWare from a server-centric OS to a network-centric OS. As you can see in Figure 1.2, there are five main features that make NetWare 4 the operating system of the next generation. These features build on top of the NetWare 3 foundation and reach to the sky. The most pervasive of these features is NDS:

FIGURE 1.2

The Evolution of NetWare 4

▸ NetWare Directory Services (NDS)—NDS is also known as the "Cloud." It oversees all facets of network operation—from logging in to multiprotocol routing. In short, NetWare 4 is NetWare 3.12 with NDS. It's that simple—or not. Life in the NDS universe is a little more complicated than you might think. The price for user transparency is your blood, sweat, and tears. NDS generates a great deal more administrative overhead than you might be used to. But all of your hard work is worth it. NDS will ultimately increase user productivity and add more value to the network. Some customers are projecting a 300 percent return on their NetWare 4 investment. We'll take a much closer look at NDS in just a moment and then spend all of Chapter 2 learning its hidden secrets. Welcome to the X-Files.

▶ Better File System—NetWare 4 optimizes the server disk with three new features: file compression, data migration, and block suballocation. File compression automatically reduces the size of infrequently used files by up to 63 percent. Data migration offloads these files to near-line storage devices. Finally, block suballocation decreases storage inefficiencies by allowing multiple files to share a single disk block. More details to come.

▶ Enhanced GUI Utilities—NetWare 4 has vastly improved the interface for both user and administrator utilities. At the forefront of the new utility revolution is NetWare Administrator (NWADMIN)—a fully integrated Windows-based graphical administrator tool. The NetWare Administrator centralizes all NetWare 4 tasks in one graphical NDS structure. NetWare 4 also offers a text-based menu version of NetWare Administrator, enhanced console commands, server NLMs, and new user command line utilities. All in all, NetWare 4 not only works better, it also looks better.

ZEN

"Image is everything."

Andre Agassi

▶ NDS Security and Auditing—NetWare 4 security is controlled by a five-layer security model. This model looks very similar to the NetWare 3.12 four-layer model, except that it includes an additional layer of login security—NDS security. This layer defines security above the server by controlling movement throughout the NDS tree. NDS access rights apply to both the object and property levels. In addition to NDS security, NetWare 4 includes a comprehensive and powerful auditing feature. Independent auditors can track network transactions according to a variety of strategies, including logins/logouts, trustee modifications, file access and modification, NDS activity, queue management, and object management. The beauty of NetWare 4 auditing is that independent auditors can track network resources without having any other rights to the WAN. You will learn more about NetWare 4 NDS security later in this chapter.

▸ Improved Memory Management—NetWare 4 manages file server RAM in a completely different way than NetWare 3.12 did. Earlier versions of NetWare allocated memory to multiple pools that served specific purposes. These pools were so inefficient that server applications could run out of RAM even if there was plenty of memory available in the main pool. NetWare 4 has consolidated all server RAM into one central pool and memory is reallocated as needed. In addition, NetWare 4 includes memory protection that allows NLMs to run in a protected area of RAM. This ensures the safety of the core OS while you are testing third-party NLMs. Shields up!

As you can see from this discussion, NetWare 4 represents the peak of OS evolution. It builds on the foundation of NetWare 3.12 to create a more powerful platform for the next generation of networking. For an even more detailed comparison of the NetWare 3 and NetWare 4 features, refer to Table 1.1.

THE BRAIN

For a quick overview of new features in NetWare 4, refer to the *Novell NetWare 4 New Features* manual.

So you bought NetWare 4 and now what do you do with it? How do you design your NDS tree? Where do you put your user accounts? What steps should you take to optimize performance, transparency, and system fault tolerance? Who shot Mr. Burns? What did you get yourself into? Don't panic—these are good questions.

This book is dedicated to *YOU*. I hope to get you through NetWare 4 with the least amount of pain. Who knows—you might even enjoy yourself along the way. We're going to start this first chapter with a brief snapshot of what NetWare 4 is all about.

T A B L E   I.I

NetWare 4 and NetWare 3 Features Comparison

FEATURE	NETWARE 4	NETWARE 3
ARCHITECTURE		
Maximum number of user connections per server	1,000	250
Nondedicated server	Yes (NetWare 4 for OS/2)	No
Single login to network	Yes	No
Additive licensing	Yes	No
Memory protection	Yes	No
Global directory services	Yes	No
FILE SYSTEM AND STORAGE		
File compression	Yes	No
Data migration	Yes	No
Block suballocation	Yes	No
NETWORK SECURITY		
RSA public/private key encryption	Yes	No
Restrict login to specific Macintosh addresses	Yes	No
Security auditing	Yes	No

(continued)

1.1 CONTINUED

NetWare 4 and NetWare 3 Features Comparison

FEATURE	NETWARE 4	NETWARE 3
NETWORK MANAGEMENT		
GUI utility with view of entire network	Yes	No
Remote console session security	Yes	No
Remote console modem callback	Yes	No
Maximum shared printers	256 per print server	16 per print server
RAM used with remote printer	4.6 to 5.4 KB	4 to 20 KB
Integrated messaging	Yes	No
Network Link Services Protocol (NLSP)	Yes	Yes (add-on required)
CLIENT SUPPORT AND INTEROPERABILITY		
LPT ports on client	LPT-1 to LPT-9	LPT-1 to LPT-3
NetWare 4 Macintosh user licenses included	Matches the number of NetWare user licenses	5
GUI user tools	Yes	Yes
NetWare DOS Requester support	Yes	Yes

You will get a glimpse of the features and benefits that make Novell's fourth-generation operating system the *next generation* of networking. Here's what's in store:

- ▸ NetWare Directory Services

- ▸ NetWare 4 Enhanced File System

- ▸ NetWare 4 Security

- ▸ NetWare 4 Utility Management

- ▸ NetWare 4 Configuration

- ▸ NetWare 4 Management

- ▸ NetWare 4 Printing

In the next chapter, we'll expand on the heart of NetWare 4—NDS. But this is only the beginning. Once you've been introduced to the technology, you must learn what to do with it. Imagine what could happen if this power falls into the wrong hands. Imagine what Napoleon could have done with a turbocharged water cannon! No, we must harness the power of NetWare 4 by learning how to design, install, and manage it. That's the true focus of *Novell's CNE Study Guide for NetWare 4.1*. Aah, but let's not get ahead of ourselves. It all begins with an introduction to NetWare 4, and I can't think of a better place to start than with NetWare Directory Services.

QUIZ

I'm in a giving mood; it must be your birthday. I have three gifts for you— small, medium, and large. Each gift is wrapped with a different color paper that is red, green, or silver. In addition, I've placed a different color bow on each package, either red, green, or gold. In order to earn your gifts, describe the wrapping and bow combination for each present. Here are some clues:

- ▸ *The small gift has a green bow.*

- ▸ *The large gift is the only one that matches.*

Remember, puzzles help stretch your imagination. But whatever you do, don't pull a frontal lobe!

(Q1-1)
(See Appendix C for all quiz answers.)

NetWare Directory Services

The most significant feature of NetWare 4 is the introduction of NetWare Directory Services (NDS). NDS is a distributed hierarchical database of network information that replaces the bindery in earlier versions of NetWare. NDS is a combination of features from OSI X.500, Banyan StreeTalk, and some other stuff nobody has ever heard of. The result is an object-oriented hierarchical directory structure with complex access rights and distributed WAN partitions. Wow! Just think of it as a huge network phone-book.

NDS classifies all network resources into objects. These objects can be organized by function, location, size, type, or color—it doesn't matter. The point is that the NDS tree organizes objects independently from their physical location. When a user logs into the network, he/she can access any object in the tree to which they have rights, regardless of its location. This type of openness, however, does not come without a price. One obvious problem is security—which is why user access to network resources is controlled by a complex system of NDS security.

So what does this all mean? The bottom line is this—users don't access physical resources anymore. Instead, they access logical objects in the NDS tree.

This means users don't need to know which NetWare server provides a particular resource. All they need to know is where it exists in the logical NDS world. We're going to start our discussion of NDS by introducing its fundamental components. We'll talk about NDS objects, NDS management, and bindery services. Then, in the next chapter, we will delve more deeply into the NDS world, learning all there is to know before Part II (NetWare 4 Design). Let's start with a brief peek inside the NDS Cloud.

THE "CLOUD"

NDS has many names:

▸ The Directory

▸ The Tree

▸ The Cloud

▸ The StayPuf Marshmallow Man

In reality, it's all of these things. But the best description is the "Cloud." NDS oversees physical network resources and provides users with a logical world to live in. This differs dramatically from what we're used to in NetWare 3.12. As you can see in Figure 1.3, the NetWare 3.12 bindery is server-centric. This means that every physical resource exists within or around the server. If user Guinevere wants to access files or printers on multiple servers, she must have a login account and security access on each one. This system makes access and management both repetitive and time-consuming. Also, note that nothing exists *above* the server. The server itself represents the highest level of the network organizational structure. Users, volumes, files, and printers all exist *on* each server.

F I G U R E   1.3

*The NetWare 3.12 Flat
Server-Centric Bindery*

NDS, on the other hand, creates a whole new world *above* the server. As you can see in Figure 1.4, each network resource exists only once as a logical object above the server. Suddenly, the server has gone from being at the top of the network organizational chart to being a physical object in the NDS tree. The beauty of this system is that Guinevere only logs in once and has instant access to all network resources. She doesn't log into each server; she logs into the NDS tree and it tracks where her files and printers are. All logins, attaches, and access rights are handled in the background by NDS.

TIP

NDS epitomizes user transparency. To the user, resource access seems like magic. To the administrator, it requires hours of NetWare 4.1 design, installation, and management work. Fortunately, you have *Novell's CNE Study Guide for NetWare 4.1* **to guide the way.**

F I G U R E 1.4

The Network-Centric NDS Cloud and Hierarchical Tree

The main lesson to learn from the accompanying graphics is the direction of the arrows. In Figure 1.3, the arrows of communication are horizontal. This means that all communication exists within and among NetWare 3.12 servers. If Guinevere wants access to another resource, she must follow the horizontal communication path to another server and either re-login or attach. In contrast, Figure 1.4 shows the communication arrows running vertically. This means that communication occurs within and between the NDS Cloud and physical resources. The NDS Cloud handles the problem of locating resources and transparently grabs whatever Guinevere needs. This vertical communication structure makes finding and using network resources much easier for the user. In addition, it provides a single point of central network management for administrators.

ZEN

"Never keep up with the Joneses. Drag them down to your level. It's cheaper."

Quentin Crisp

The NDS tree is stored in a fully replicated, globally distributed, object-oriented database called the Directory. The Directory consists of multiple hidden system files in a hidden directory in the root of the SYS: volume on each server. These files can be replicated and distributed throughout the LAN to provide fault tolerance and increased connectivity. Although all NetWare 4 servers use NDS, they don't have to contain their own Directory database. If a server contains a portion of the database, that portion is called a *partition*. If a server doesn't have a copy of the database, it must access it from some other server. The bottom line is, a NetWare 4 server can contain the entire Directory database, pieces of it (partitions), or none at all.

In addition, NetWare Directory Services requires a temporal assurance system called *time synchronization*. This means that everybody has to agree on what time it is. Time is critical to NDS because NetWare uses *time stamps* for synchronization, auditing, and NDS security. Time synchronization is implemented using a variety of time server types.

Finally, NetWare Directory Services is fully backward compatible. That is to say, it supports bindery emulation, so that previous versions of NetWare can peacefully coexist with NetWare 4 NDS. In addition, a new feature called NETSYNC allows NetWare 3.12 binderies to be uploaded and distributed with NetWare 4 NDS to other NetWare 3.12 binderies. We'll take a closer look at these features in the next chapter. For now, let's continue our discussion of NDS with a brief look at objects and properties.

NDS OBJECTS

The Directory consists of objects, properties, and values. Even though NDS replaces earlier NetWare binderies, it is organized in much the same way. NDS objects define logical or physical entities that provide organizational or technical function to the network. NDS objects come in three flavors: [Root], container objects, and leaf objects. As you can see, the tree analogy is alive and well. The [Root] is the very top of the NDS tree. Container objects define the organizational boundaries of the NDS tree and house other container objects and/or leaf objects. Leaf objects are the physical network resources that provide technical services and WAN functionality. Leaf objects define the lowest level of the NDS structure.

Each NDS object consists of categories of information called *properties*. Properties are similar to fields in a database record that categorize types of information. User objects, for example, have properties such as Login name, Password, Postal Address, and Description. Although the same type of object may have the same properties, the information within those properties may change. For example, two user objects both have a login name property, but one has a value of Guinevere and the other has a value of Gilligan.

As you learned earlier, NDS objects come in three flavors: [Root], container objects, and leaf objects. Now let's take a closer look.

[Root]

The [Root] object defines the top of the NDS organizational structure. Each Directory can only have one [Root]; it is created during installation. The [Root] cannot be deleted, renamed, or moved. The NDS [Root] object is exceptional in that it begins the boundaries of the NDS world. It behaves much like a container object, in that it houses other container objects. The main difference is the [Root] cannot contain leaf objects.

TIP

Each NDS object has a specific icon that graphically depicts its purpose. The [Root] object's icon is particularly interesting. Because it represents the opening porthole to the NDS world, its icon is, appropriately, a picture of the earth.

Container Objects

Container objects are logical organizers. They are the Tupperware™ bowls of our NDS kitchen. Actually, the analogy works well—work with me here. The nature of storing Tupperware is that larger containers enclose smaller containers, which, in turn, house even smaller ones. Of course, the biggest Tupperware container in the world is the [Root]. Also, Tupperware containers are used to store fruits and vegetables. In NDS, our Tupperware containers store lettuce "leaf" objects. Sorry.

Here's a quick list of the three types of NetWare 4 NDS container objects available as of this writing:

- Country—Designates the country where certain parts of the organization reside.

- Organization—Represents a company, university, or department. NDS only supports one layer of Organization objects. Therefore, these containers can only hold Organizational Units and leaf objects.

- Organizational Unit—Represents a division, business unit, or project team. Organizational Units hold other Organizational Units or leaf objects.

Leaf Objects

Leaf objects are logical or physical network resources. Most of your life will be spent designing, installing, and managing leaf objects—you'll quickly become a vegetarian. These are the ultimate entities that NetWare 4 users seek. Because leaf objects reside at the bottom of the NDS tree, they cannot hold other leaf objects. They represent the proverbial end of the road. Here's a brief list of some of the most common NDS leaf objects. A more comprehensive list can be found in Chapter 2.

- User—Represents any user in the NDS tree. This would be Guinevere.

- NetWare Server—Represents any NetWare server providing file or other services.

- Volume—Exists as a logical pointer to any physical volume on a NetWare server. This object enables administrators to organize volumes independently from the physical servers they are attached to.

- Group—Defines an unrelated list of users for the purpose of assigning access rights and other management strategies.

- Print Server—Represents any network print server.

- Printer—Represents any physical printing device on the network.

▸ Computer—Represents any network computer that is not providing file or print services, such as gateways, routers, and workstations.

THE BRAIN

For an overview of NDS objects (including a list of the most common container and leaf objects), refer to the Object section of the *Novell NetWare 4 Concepts* manual.

This completes our brief discussion of NDS objects. You'll want to get to know them well because all future discussions center around how to organize and manage these cute little logical network entities. Speaking of which, let's take a quick look at some general strategies for NDS management.

ZEN

"I was a vegetarian until I started leaning towards the sun."

Anonymous

NDS MANAGEMENT

Once you understand the relationships of NDS objects, it's time to start building your tree. As in nature, it starts with the [Root] and builds from there. Figure 1.5 represents each container object as a specific graphical icon. Here's a quick summary:

▸ —[Root]

▸ —Organization

▸ —Organizational Unit

F I G U R E I.5

The Start of a Simple NDS
Tree

Each leaf object is represented by a graphic that depicts its purpose. For example, printers are represented by printer icons, servers are represented by computer icons, and users by people icons. Refer to Chapter 2 for a more detailed list of NDS object icons.

These icons are used throughout this book and in graphical NDS utilities. NetWare Administrator (NWADMIN), for example, uses icons to provide a snapshot of the entire NDS tree. This feature makes it easier for administrators and users to locate and use NetWare 4 resources.

Once you've begun your tree by planting container objects, it's time to organize the physical and logical resources—leaf objects. Remember, Leaf objects are stored in specific NetWare 4 Tupperware containers. From there, they can either be managed, accessed, or eaten—it's your choice. Later in Part II (NetWare 4 Design) you'll learn a variety of guidelines for designing and building NDS trees. For now, it's important to understand how the tree is organized and what it looks like once it's been built.

Once the NDS tree has been designed and installed, you get to move on to the third phase of CNE life—management. NDS management consists of three topics:

▸ NDS naming

▸ NDS partitioning

▸ Time synchronization

NDS naming defines rules for locating leaf objects. One of the most important aspects of a leaf object is its position in the NDS tree. Proper naming is required when users log in, access NDS utilities, print, and when you perform most other management tasks, as well.

The next management topic is NDS partitioning. Because the tree houses all your network resources, it can grow large very quickly. As with any database, size can decrease performance and reliability. For this reason, NetWare 4 has a built-in database distribution feature called *partitioning and replication*. Partitioning breaks the database tree into small pieces, and replication places those pieces on multiple servers. This strategy increases database performance and provides distributed fault tolerance.

The final management topic is time synchronization. As you learned earlier, this is a temporal assurance scheme that forces all NetWare 4 servers to agree on the time. This is particularly important because all NDS background operations and security strategies rely on a *time stamp*. Time synchronization is accomplished through the use of four time server types.

Now let's take a closer look at each of these NDS management topics in a little more depth, beginning with NDS naming.

NDS Naming

Your name identifies you as a truly unique individual. In much the same way, an NDS object's name identifies its location in the hierarchical tree. The whole NDS naming strategy relies on *context*. Context defines the position of an object within the Directory tree structure. When you request a particular network resource, you must identify the object's context so that NDS can find it. NetWare 4 uses specific naming guidelines for creating an object's context. You must follow these rules carefully:

- An object's *context* is identified by listing all of the container objects leading *from* the object *to* the [Root].

- A leaf object's *common name (CN)* specifically identifies it within a given context. User objects, for example, have a login name that identifies them for login purposes. In this case, the login name is the common name. It is possible for two user objects in the same NDS tree to have the same common name—provided, however, that they have different contexts.

> ▶ A leaf object's *distinguished name (DN)* is a combination of its common name
> and its context. Distinguished names begin with a leading period and use
> periods to separate container objects within the context. A distinguished
> name identifies an object exactly. Although two objects within the NDS tree
> may have the same common name, they must have unique distinguished
> names.

Refer to Figure 1.6 for an example of these NDS naming concepts. In this example,
the user Albert Einstein exists within the container LABS under the Organization ACME.
Albert's context is OU=LABS.O=ACME. In addition, his common name is CN=AEinstein.
Finally, his distinguished name is a combination of his common name and context:

`.CN=AEINSTEIN.OU=LABS.O=ACME`

F I G U R E 1.6

*NDS Naming for
AEINSTEIN*

In the unlikely event there were another AEinstein within the ACME tree, he would have to be identified within a different context. For example, a Mr. Einstein living in the ADMIN container would have a different distinguished name:

```
.CN=AEINSTEIN.OU=ADMIN.O=ACME
```

Believe it or not, NDS naming is even more complicated than this. In Chapter 2 we will discuss some exceptions to these guidelines, specifically, current context, relative, distinguished name, and typeless name. For now, suffice it to say that naming is important and you'll get the hang of it with practice. It's safe to say you'll become a great scientist of NDS nomenclature.

NDS Partitioning

As you will quickly come to appreciate, the NDS tree grows and grows and grows. Before you know it, you'll have a huge monstrosity on your hands—the size of Jupiter. Fortunately, NetWare 4 includes a segmentation strategy known as NDS partitioning. As I mentioned earlier, *partitioning* breaks up the NDS tree into two or more pieces, which can be separated and distributed. Because the NDS tree is stored in a database, pieces of the database can be distributed on multiple file servers. This strategy, *replication*, is used to increase network performance and fault tolerance.

TIP

NDS partitions have nothing to do with the logical disk partitions you're used to on the server disk. NDS partitions are logical pieces of the database that can be distributed on multiple servers. Hard disk partitions are physical divisions of the internal disks that separate the NetWare operating system from DOS or another OS. Although these two concepts are unrelated, they work together in an odd way—one is stored on top of the other. If you really want to mess up your users, point out that logical NDS partitions are stored on internal disk partitions—brain drain!

As you can see in Figure 1.7, NDS partitioning simply breaks the ACME Organization into two pieces:

▸ Partition A—Known as the [Root] Partition because it is the only one that contains the [Root].

▶ Partition B—Known as the LABS Partition because it's the highest container object. In addition, Partition B is termed a "child" of Partition A because LABS is a subset of the ACME Organization.

F I G U R E 1.7

Breaking the NDS Tree into
Two Partitions

This feature has many advantages because it enables you to separate the tree into smaller communities. Because 90 percent of all the resources accessed by users are within their own partition, administrators can increase efficiency by segregating users near their resources. We can also increase network fault tolerance by placing copies of other partitions on local servers (by the process of replication).

NetWare 4 enables you to create four types of NDS replicas:

▶ Master—A Read/Write copy of the original partition. Each partition has only one master replica.

▶ Read/Write—A Read/Write copy of a partition. Each partition may have multiple Read/Write replica copies. When you change objects in a Read/Write replica, those changes are propagated to all other replicas of the same partition. This process, known as replica synchronization, creates background traffic over WAN communication lines.

▸ Read-Only—A Read-Only copy of a partition. These replicas are used for searching and viewing objects only. You cannot make any changes.

▸ Subordinate References—A special replica created and maintained by NDS. A subordinate reference is created automatically on a server when it contains a parent replica but not any of the children. In simpler terms, subordinate references are created on servers "where parent is but child is not." Think of it as NDS baby-sitting.

Figure 1.8 shows a sample replica distribution strategy for ACME. In this graphic, the server in Partition A has a master of that partition and a Read/Write replica of the B partition. Similarly, the server in the B partition has a master of that information and a Read/Write replica of the A partition. This way, users in both locations can access NDS information from their local server. In addition, if either server goes down, NDS can still operate from replicas placed on the other server.

Although this is a relatively simple example, I'm sure you can imagine that NDS partitioning gets hairy when organizations get large. We'll discuss this topic many more times throughout the book, beginning again in Chapter 2 and continuing in Chapter 9.

QUIZ

A statistician is someone who can put his head in an oven and his feet in the freezer, and then tell you, "On Average: I feel fine!" Let's see if you have what it takes.
A roulette wheel has the numbers 0 to 36. From the information below, which number have I bet on?

1. *It is divisible by 3.*
2. *When the digits are added together, the total lies between 4 and 8.*
3. *It is an odd number.*
4. *When the digits are multiplied together, the total lies between 4 and 8.*

(Q1-2)

FIGURE 1.8

*Replicating Two Partitions
on Distributed Servers*

REPLICAS
A—Master
B—Read/Write

REPLICAS
A—Read/Write
B—Master

Time Synchronization

To keep track of replica synchronization and other critical NDS events, NetWare 4 relies on a complex system of *time synchronization*. Time synchronization is a method of ensuring that all NDS objects report the same time stamp. In addition to NDS, other NetWare 4 services requiring time stamps include the file system, security, and messaging.

Time stamps report time according to the Universal Time Coordinated (UTC) equivalent. This is a time system that adjusts to the local time zone and Daylight Savings Time. It is also equivalent to Greenwich Mean Time (GMT). UTC is calculated using three values for each time server:

- Local time

- +/- time zone offset from UTC

> ‣ - Daylight Savings Time offset

For example, the NORAD, Colorado, time is seven hours behind GMT. Therefore, if the time in NORAD is 12:00 noon and there is no Daylight Savings Time, UTC is 19:00.

All NetWare 4 servers are *time servers* of some type. Time servers provide a consistent source for the time stamps that NDS and other features use. Each time you install a NetWare 4 server, you must provide it with specific time configuration parameters, including time server type and the above three UTC values. NetWare 4 includes four types of time servers:

> ‣ Single Reference server—This is the default configuration for most small WANs. It provides time to Secondary servers only and cannot coexist with Primary or other Reference servers.

> ‣ Reference server—Provides a central point of time control for the entire network. These servers get their time from an external source, such as an atomic clock.

> ‣ Primary servers—Work together with other Primary servers to "vote" on the correct time. This voting procedure determines network UTC in combination with values received from Reference servers.

> ‣ Secondary servers—Part of the default configuration. These servers do not participate in voting and are told what the time is by other time servers.

NetWare 4 provides administrators with two methods for accomplishing time synchronization—default and custom. The default method assumes that only two types of time servers are necessary: Single-Reference servers and Secondary servers. This method is simple and efficient but does not provide the flexibility required by large NDS implementations. The custom method, on the other hand, requires administrative planning. It uses Reference, Primary, and Secondary servers to minimize a single point of failure. In addition, the custom configuration method cuts down on network traffic by minimizing unneeded synchronization chatter.

Later in the book you'll learn how to determine which time configuration method is best for you. In addition, we'll explore design guidelines for distributing each of the types of time servers. For now, let's wallow in our ignorance and enjoy the simplicity of NetWare 4 in its infancy. Speaking of simplicity, I wonder how NetWare 4 coexists with bindery-based servers like NetWare 3.12's?

BINDERY SERVICES

One of the biggest concerns with NetWare 4's radical new approach is compatibility with earlier stuff—that is, bindery-based servers. Fortunately, NetWare 4 contains a sophisticated *bindery emulation* system. Bindery emulation provides backward compatibility with bindery-based servers by making the NetWare 4 Directory look like a flat-file bindery to NetWare 2.2 and 3.12 servers in the correct context. Because the bindery database is a flat-file structure, bindery emulation can only exist within one container at a time. Think of it as taking a two-dimensional slice of a three-dimensional object. For example, if you sliced a three-dimensional orange in half and took a two-dimensional view of it, the orange would appear to be a circle. In much the same way, if you isolate a particular container in the three-dimensional NDS tree, the objects in that container will appear to be a flat-file bindery.

The lucky container object where you set a server's bindery emulation is called the *bindery context*. You can change a server's bindery context by using the SET command at the console. For example, in Figure 1.9, the bindery context for SALES-SRV1 is

```
OU=SALES.OU=MARKETING.O=ACME
```

In this case, any user logging into SALES-SRV1 with NETx will have access to only Cathy and HP5. This user will not see any other objects in the NDS tree, including PR-PS1 and Doug.

TIP

Although NetWare 4.1 bindery services may seem a little restricting, consider that you're asking a highly evolved operating system to emulate an unsophisticated flat bindery. There is one consolation, however. NetWare 4.1 enables you to define up to 16 bindery contexts for each server. This means users logging into a specific server from a NetWare 3.12 server can, in fact, see all the objects from 16 containers. The objects are all clumped together into one *superbindery*.

FIGURE 1.9

Bindery Services for a
NetWare 3.12 User

[Root]

O=ACME

OU=ADMIN   OU=MARKETING   OU=LABS

OU=SALES   OU=PR

Bindery
Context for
SALES-SRV1

CN=HP5   CN=HP4SI
CN=Cathy   CN=Doug
CN=SALES-SRV 1   CN=PR-PSI

By default, bindery services is enabled during installation. The bindery services context is automatically set to the context in which the NetWare server is installed. If you find that additional clients outside of this context need resources through bindery services, determine where access is needed and set the bindery context for those containers. Objects and properties that are unique to NDS are not available through bindery services. These include container login scripts, profile login scripts, some print services, and messaging.

Bindery services will work for you if any of the following is true:

▶ TRUE: You need to provide a migration period for users who have not upgraded their workstation software yet. This means the VLMs have not been loaded and users are still using the old NETx software.

▶ TRUE: If you are still running applications and utilities that rely on Bindery Services to operate properly. This includes many printer-based print server chips, old versions of NetWare for Macintosh, and old versions of NetWare SAA.

▶ TRUE: If you need to administer NetWare 4 user accounts, group accounts, and print services from a NetWare 3.12 client using SYSCON and PCONSOLE.

▶ TRUE: If you just can't take the three-dimensional world anymore, and you want to live in a two-dimensional picture world. Or you like circles better than oranges.

In addition to bindery emulation, NetWare 4 Bindery Services includes an advanced NDS management tool known as *NetSync*. NetSync is an NLM that enables you to copy the binderies of multiple NetWare 3.1x servers into an NDS container on a NetWare 4 server. You can then manage the users, groups, and print services of the NetWare 3.1x servers as part of the NDS Directory tree using NWADMIN or NETADMIN.

Another exciting aspect of NetSync is that it enables you to integrate existing NetWare 3.1x objects without having to upgrade all their host servers. In addition, NetSync enables you to create a "cluster" of NetWare 3.1x servers that can be updated any time a change is made inside the NetWare 4 container. This feature enables administrators to centrally manage multiple binderies (known as a superbindery) and synchronize those changes to a cluster of servers. It may sound fascinating, but NetSync is not very easy to use. We'll discuss it in more detail in Chapter 8.

ZEN

"If a man wishes to be sure of the road he treads on, he must close his eyes and walk in the dark."

Anonymous

Well, that does it for NetWare Directory Services—for now. This section was designed to simply whet your appetite for the 12-course meal to come. Obviously, NDS has a lot more complexity and internal features. But of course, there's no reason to start with the entree. I've provided you with a general overview of the "Cloud," NDS objects, NDS management, and finally, Bindery Services. Although this represents NDS in a nutshell, it's not an easy nut to crack. As you'll learn in Chapter 2, NDS has many idiosyncrasies that can make it challenging to deal with on a daily basis. Also, in Chapter 8 you'll learn about NDS management, and finally, in Chapter 9, we'll discuss partition management and synchronization.

On the other side of the coin, the beauty of NDS is that it can be as simple or complex as you make it. I think there's a life lesson in there somewhere. In the meantime, let's take a look at the rest of NetWare 4 and see what else it has to offer, starting with its enhanced file system.

NetWare 4 Enhanced File System

When NetWare 4 was rolled out, one of its key selling points was *improved disk management*. As a matter of fact, Novell still uses complex ROI (return on investment) calculations to justify your investment in NetWare 4. These ROI formulas are based on two major assumptions:

▸ You will save hundreds of hours managing NetWare 4 because of its centralized NDS administration format.

▸ You will save thousands of dollars in disk storage because of block suballocation, file compression, and data migration.

So here we are: the major file system enhancements in NetWare 4. These three impressive disk usage strategies were designed to solve serious disk space management problems in earlier versions of NetWare. Once again, they are

▸ Block suballocation

▸ File compression

▸ Data migration

Block suballocation solves the problem of wasted space with medium to large block sizes. *Data migration* solves the problem of disk cram by providing an efficient method for near-line storage. *File compression* eases the pain of purchasing expensive on-line disks by automatically compressing inactive files. All of these features are exciting and new, but they probably shouldn't be the basis for purchasing NetWare 4. Take a long, hard look at NDS before you make a life-changing decision like that.

Let's take a closer look at NetWare 4's file system enhancement strategies.

BLOCK SUBALLOCATION

A *block* is a discrete allocation unit of disk space. In less technical terms, it's a chunk of hard disk. A file is made up of one or more chunks of data, as needed. Each NetWare 4 volume has a predefined block size. These blocks range in size from 4 KB all the way up to 64 KB. The problem arises when you use medium to large block sizes and store numerous small files. As you can see in Figure 1.10, a 64 KB block is fully occupied by a 5 KB or 63 KB file—it can't tell the difference. The problem is that the 5 KB file results in 59 KB of unusable wasted disk space. A couple thousand 5 KB files later, and you've wasted more than 100 megabytes of internal server disk—not a good thing.

TIP

A friend of mine thought it would be cool to install NetWare 3.12 on a 120 MB hard disk using a 64 KB block size. (I have strange friends.) Much to his surprise, the server ran out of disk space before the SYSTEM and PUBLIC files were ever loaded! NetWare 4's block suballocation feature would have solved this problem.

Block suballocation solves the problem of wasted disk space by dividing partially used disk blocks into 512-byte suballocation blocks. These suballocation blocks can be used by multiple files. For example, a 5 KB file would still take the first 5 KB of a 64 KB block—as shown in Figure 1.11. But the remaining 59 KB becomes available for leftovers from other full blocks. A second 100 KB file, for example, would take up another 64 KB block and send the remaining 36 KB over to the first block (as shown in Figure 1.11). Without block suballocation, the remaining 36 KB would occupy another entire 64 KB block—therefore wasting another 28 KB of space in addition to the 59 KB already wasted from the 5 KB file.

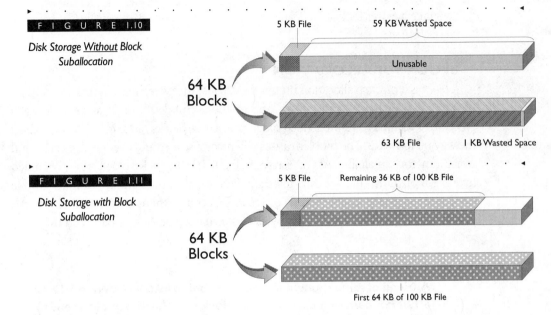

F I G U R E 1.10

*Disk Storage <u>Without</u> Block
Suballocation*

F I G U R E 1.11

*Disk Storage with Block
Suballocation*

Bottom line:

▸ Without block suballocation—The two files totaling 105 KB would occupy three 64 KB blocks and waste 87 KB of server disk space.

▸ With block suballocation—The two files totaling 105 KB would occupy two suballocated blocks, leaving 23 KB of server disk space to be used by a third file.

The most important thing to remember about block suballocation is that it only works when files exceed the block size. Files always start at the beginning of a new block. You cannot start a new file within an already-occupied suballocation block. You can, however, store the remainder of large files within the suballocation area. Finally, block suballocation is activated at the volume level within NetWare 4. You'll learn more about how to optimize it in Chapter 15.

FILE COMPRESSION

One of the flashiest sales features of NetWare 4 is file compression, mainly because most people can relate to it. The idea of more than doubling your server disk space is exciting and easy to grasp. Unfortunately, many early users ignored the true value of NetWare 4—NDS. The idea of improving your network by adding a big nebulous cloud didn't excite too many users. Of course, now that you understand the internal workings of NDS, its value becomes more apparent.

File compression enables NetWare 4 volumes to hold more on-line data by automatically compressing inactive files. Users can save up to 63 percent of the server's disk space by activating file compression—that's 1 GB of files in 370 MB of space. File compression is activated in one of two ways:

▸ By flagging directories and files as IC (Immediate Compress)

▸ By using the SET command at the server console to configure various inactivity delay parameters

By default, file compression is turned ON and the inactivity delay is set to seven days. This means that if a file is not accessed within seven days, it will automatically be compressed. Users can avoid having their files compressed by flagging specific files as DC (Don't Compress). Finally, files are automatically decompressed when users access them. Decompression occurs much faster than compression, at a rate of 100 KB per second.

Compressing files on NetWare 4 server disks occurs in five steps:

1 • A timer goes off and file compression begins. By default, all files are compressed just before midnight on the day at which the inactivity delay expires. Once file compression is activated, NetWare reads and analyzes each file.

2 • NetWare builds a temporary file describing the original file. This feature ensures that the original file is not at risk if data is corrupted during the compression process. In addition, if a disk error or power failure occurs during compression, the original, uncompressed file is retained.

3 • NetWare determines whether any disk sectors can be saved by compressing the file. A gain of at least 2 percent (by default) is required before a file is compressed. This parameter is configurable using the SET console command.

4 • NetWare begins creation of the compressed file.

5 • NetWare replaces the original with the compressed file after an error-free compressed version has been created.

THE BRAIN

For more information on file compression, refer to the "File Compression" section of the *Novell NetWare 4 Concepts* manual.

There are 10 SET parameters for managing file compression. In addition, CNEs can use the IC and DC attributes to activate and deactivate compression on specific files. Both of these strategies will be discussed as part of optimization in Chapter 15.

TIP

Wouldn't it be cool if you could activate file compression on this book before shoving it into your brain? That way you could only decompress the topics you needed at appropriate times. The only danger with this scenario is the chance of filling up your brain with uncompressed knowledge, thereby eliminating important childhood memories such as swimming pools, "Gilligan's Island," summer break, and your first kiss.

DATA MIGRATION

Data migration solves the problem of disk cram by providing an efficient method for "near-line" storage. "What is near-line?" you ask. Near-line storage is somewhere between on-line (hard disks) and off-line (tape backup)—I know you probably saw that coming.

As you can see in Figure 1.12, on-line storage is provided by fast, internal server disks. The problem with on-line storage is that it's finite in capacity. On the other extreme, we have off-line storage in the form of tape backups. This storage is infinite in size because multiple tapes can be used. In addition, off-line storage can be placed off-site for disaster recovery and better system fault tolerance. The problem with off-line storage is human intervention—somebody has to stroll over to the backup device and place the tape in the correct place, which takes time and effort. As I'm sure you've already figured out, these are two luxuries CNEs don't have.

So what are our options? Fortunately, NetWare 4 includes a form of near-line storage that solves both problems. Near-line storage is much faster than off-line tape but has the potential for infinite storage capacities and therefore outperforms on-line disks. Data migration provides near-line storage by automatically transferring inactive data to a tape drive or optical disk without actually removing the data's entries from the server's DET or file allocation table (FAT). The data still appear to be on the volume and users can transparently access the data without having to worry about which tape it's on or where the file exists.

TIP

Near-line data migration is still much slower than on-line disks, so the system must have a way of informing users that the file is on its way. Many near-line tape manufacturers provide terminate-and-stay-resident programs (TSRs) that display a message while NetWare is searching for the near-line file, something like, "Hold your horses, we're working over here!"

Data migration is part of a new NetWare 4 storage system known as the High Capacity Storage System (HCSS). HCSS extends the storage capacity of a NetWare server by integrating an optical disk library or *jukebox*. HCSS uses rewritable optical disks to move files between faster low-capacity storage devices (the server's hard disk) and slower high-capacity storage devices (jukebox). HCSS is fully integrated into NetWare 4 and activated using special drivers on the server. Once it has been activated, migration is performed on a file-by-file basis, according to two criteria:

▶ Capacity threshold—The percentage of the server's hard disk that can be used before HCSS starts migrating files from the hard disk to the jukebox.

▶ Least Recently Used (LRU)—A series of guidelines that determines which files are moved from the server's hard disk to the jukebox. These guidelines move the least active files first.

Data migration and HCSS are exciting parts of NetWare 4 and should be looked at closely. Because there are performance sacrifices for installing HCSS, you should only consider it if you need real-time access to archived files. Some sample implementations include law libraries, financial information, and medical records. For a more detailed discussion of optimizing data migration, refer to Chapter 15.

QUIZ

This time we're looking for a common arithmetic symbol, which, when it is placed between 4 and 5, results in a number that is greater than 4, but less than 6. Hmmmm, I bet you thought you had escaped math in high school— nope. You're gonna need it for NetWare 4 security.

(Q1-3)

Well, that completes our discussion of the NetWare 4 enhanced file system. As you can see, Novell has added some pretty exciting disk management strategies to an already impressive 32-bit file system. The good news is nothing else has changed. NetWare 4 still uses a DOS-like command line and drives are mapped in exactly the same way as they were in NetWare 3.12. There's no reason to fix something that isn't broken. If this section just tantalizes your appetite for more, have no fear, we'll return to the NetWare 4 file system in Chapter 10. For now, let's continue our introduction with a quick look at a new and improved NetWare security model.

NetWare 4 Security

Security in the information age poses an interesting challenge. Computers and communications have made it possible to collect volumes of data about you and me—from our last purchase at the five-and-dime to our detailed medical records. Privacy has become a commodity that is exchanged on the open market. Information is no longer the fodder of afternoon talk shows; it has become *the* unit of exchange for the 21st century—more valuable than money.

I'll bet you thought you left cops and robbers behind in childhood. Well, this is a variation on the game and the stakes are quite high. As a CNE, it is your responsibility to design, install, and manage the NetWare 4 network. But most important, you must protect it. You need a brain filled with sophisticated security strategies and a utility belt full of advanced protection tools. Think of these as your impenetrable network armor.

NetWare security, in general, is pretty good. But for many of today's WANs, it's not good enough. A truly *secure* network protects more than just user data; it protects everything! So what is "everything"? The definition of everything has changed in NetWare 4. Now the world exists in a nebulous cloud full of Tupperware containers and user objects. As the NetWare universe becomes more open and interconnected, security becomes more and more important. Fortunately, NetWare 4 has a dramatically improved security model for creating and maintaining your impenetrable network armor. Let's take a closer look.

ZEN

"Nothing in life is to be feared. It is only to be understood."

Marie Curie

THE NETWARE 4 SECURITY MODEL

NetWare 4 improves on the earlier security model by adding supplemental front-end barriers for filtering unauthorized users. Once again, the same security principle applies: *Goal—Let the good guys in and keep the bad guys out!*

As you can see in Figure 1.13, the NetWare 4 security model consists of five layers. They are

1 • Login/password authentication

2 • Login restrictions

3 • NDS security

4 • File system access rights

5 • Directory/file attributes

F I G U R E 1.13

The NetWare 4 Security Model

It all starts with login/password authentication. Remember, users don't log into NetWare servers anymore; they log into the Cloud. Once Guinevere issues her login name, the network authenticates it and asks for a password. NetWare 4 uses the password to decrypt a session-specific private key. Once this has been accomplished, the system matches the user name against a list of global and personal login restrictions. These login restrictions allow for conditional access according to a variety of criteria, including password expiration, time of day, station restrictions, and intruder lockout.

Now that Guinevere has passed layers one and two, she is officially logged into the NDS tree. Her ability to access any object in the tree is determined by a complex NDS security structure. At the heart of NDS security is the Access Control List (ACL). The ACL defines who can access an object and what the user can do with it. In this case, Guinevere can only use objects that she has rights to.

The fourth layer of the NetWare 4 security model involves file system security. If Guinevere has the Supervisor right to any NetWare 4 server object, she is granted unlimited access to the file system. File system security is almost identical to previous versions of NetWare and includes access rights, the inherited rights filter (IRF), and effective rights. Finally, directories and files themselves are protected via attribute security. NetWare 4 uses many of the same attributes as NetWare 3.12 as well as some additional attributes for file compression and data migration. Attribute security is the final line of defense and should be implemented only as a last resort.

Now let's take a closer look at the five layers of the NetWare 4 security model and learn a little bit more about how you can use them as the foundation of your impenetrable network armor.

LAYER 1: LOGIN/PASSWORD AUTHENTICATION

When logging into a NetWare 4 system, users do not log into the server—they log into the *network*. First, the user requests access by typing **login** followed by a valid user name. Once this occurs, authentication begins. There are two phases:

1 • Initialization—The server and workstation authenticate the session with an encrypted key. Guinevere is required to enter a valid password to decrypt the key.

2 • Background—NetWare continues to attach the key to all messages to ensure data integrity. This process is known as background NCP (NetWare Core Protocol) Packet Signing.

In addition to authentication, NetWare 4 accepts passwords up to 127 characters. This is a substantial improvement over earlier versions. The limit is significantly decreased, though, for Macintosh clients. They are limited to no more than 11 characters. In fact, one way of locking out Macintosh clients is to set the minimum password length to 12. However tempting this may be, I am not endorsing this treacherous behavior. Attention Macintosh users: Stay tuned for ways of getting even.

LAYER 2: LOGIN RESTRICTIONS

Once Guinevere provides a valid login name and password, she is authenticated. The network responds with conditional access and NDS rights take over. At this point, I stress the word *conditional access*. Permanent access is made possible by a variety of login restrictions:

- Account restrictions—anything from Account Locked to Force Periodic Password Changes

- Password restrictions—including Minimum Password Length and Force Unique Passwords

- Station Restrictions—limits users to specific workstation node IDs

- Time Restrictions—determines when users can and cannot use the system

- Intruder Detection/Lockout—a global feature that detects incorrect password attempts and locks bad guys out

Each of these restrictions are configured by the administrator using a variety of NetWare 4 tools, including NWADMIN and NETADMIN. We will learn all the details of how and why in Chapter 11.

LAYER 3: NDS SECURITY

Once Guinevere enters the Cloud, her ability to access leaf and container objects is determined by a sophisticated NDS security structure. The heart of NDS security, the ACL, is a property of every NDS object. It defines who can access the object (trustees) and what each trustee can do (rights). The ACL is divided into two types of rights:

- Object rights—define an object's trustees and control what the trustees can do with the object

▶ Property rights—limit the trustees' access to only specific properties of the object

Figure 1.14 shows a great example: Let's say the group object Admin has rights to the user object Leia. ADMIN has the Browse object right, which means any member of the group can see Leia and view information about her. But Leia is shy (yeah, right). She wants to limit what the administrators can see (reasonable enough). She only wants them to see her last name, postal address, and telephone number. So Leia limits the group's rights by assigning the Read property right to only these three properties: Last Name, Postal Address, and Telephone Number. No sweat.

F I G U R E 1.14

Understanding NDS Security

Admin Group

Leia

Object Rights	Property Rights
Browse	Read — Last Name
	Postal Address
	Telephone

FIRST NAME: ▮▮▮
LAST NAME: Clarke
PASSWORD: ▮▮▮

POSTAL ADDRESS: California
TELEPHONE: 510-555-1212

ACL: ▮▮▮

Object and Property rights are designed to provide efficient access to NDS objects without making it an administrative nightmare. You be the judge.

Users can acquire object rights in one of three ways: trustee assignment, inheritance, or ancestral inheritance. Global property rights can be inherited, but rights to specific properties must be assigned explicitly. *Trustee assignments* occur when an object is given explicit access to any other object or its properties. The administrator handles trustee assignments by adding the user to a host object's ACL property through use of the NWADMIN or NETADMIN utilities.

Inheritance is a little simpler. If rights are granted at the container level, they are inherited for all container and leaf objects within. This means that rights assigned to the [Root] object, for example, are inherited by every object in the NDS tree. Be very careful. Fortunately, NetWare 4 includes the IRF, which blocks inherited rights. Finally, there's *ancestral inheritance*. This means objects can inherit rights by being associated with other objects. Sometimes the associations are obvious; most of the time they're not. The types of objects that you can ancestrally inherit rights from include Groups, Organizational Roles, and [Public]. This is a type of security equivalence.

Regardless of how you acquire object and property rights, the concept of *effective rights* still applies. This means the actual rights you can exercise with a given object are the combination of explicit trustee assignments, inheritance, and the IRF. The mathematical product of this mess is known as effective NDS rights. That effectively ends our discussion of NDS security and moves us onto the fourth layer of the NetWare 4 security model—file system access rights.

QUIZ

So, you think you're good at math? Here's a doozy. Using the figure 7 seven times, write out a calculation that gives the answer 7777.

(Q1-4)

LAYER 4: FILE SYSTEM ACCESS RIGHTS

Well, here we are. Congratulations! You've finally made it to NetWare Nirvana. You've passed through three difficult barriers of network armor and the search is over—your files await you. Aah, but not so fast! Before you can access any files on the NetWare server, you must have the appropriate file system access rights. Following is a list of the eight rights that control access to NetWare 4 files (they almost spell a word):

▸ W—Write: Grants the right to open and change the contents of files.

▸ (O)—Doesn't exist but is needed to spell a word.

▸ R—Read: Grants the right to open files in the directory and read their contents or run applications.

▸ M—Modify: Grants the right to change the attributes or name of a file or directory.

▸ F—File Scan: Grants the right to see files and directories.

▸ A—Access Control: Grants the right to change trustee assignments and the IRF.

▸ C—Create: Grants the right to create new files and subdirectories.

▸ E—Erase: Grants the right to delete a directory, its files, and subdirectories.

▸ S—Supervisor: Grants all rights to a directory and files and subdirectories. This right cannot be blocked by the IRF.

Holy anatomical nematoids, Batman! That spells WORMFACES. It's not a pretty sight, but certainly a name you will not forget. NetWare 4 file system access rights are administered in much the same way as NDS object rights. They are granted with the help of trustee assignments, inheritance, and ancestral inheritance. In addition, file system rights are subject to the same rules as NDS effective rights. All in all, NDS and file system security parallel one another—one operating in the clouds (NDS) and one with its feet firmly planted on the ground (file system).

TIP

NDS security and file system access rights behave almost identically—I emphasize the word "almost." There is only one simple difference—the NDS IRF *can* block the Supervisor NDS right while the file system IRF *cannot* block S (Supervisor). This has some interesting effects on distributed administration. Check out Chapter 11.

Well, that completes the majority of NetWare 4's security model. There's only one layer left and it is seldom used—directory/file attributes.

LAYER 5: DIRECTORY/FILE ATTRIBUTES

Directory and file attributes provide the final and most sophisticated layer of the NetWare 4 security model. These attributes are rarely used but provide a powerful tool for specific security solutions. If all else fails, you can always turn to attribute security to save the day.

Chapter 11 gives an exhaustive list, but following is a brief list of some of the most interesting NetWare 4 directory and file attributes:

Directory Attributes

▸ Hidden—Hides the directory from DOS or OS/2 DIR commands. It also prevents the directory from being deleted or copied.

▸ Normal—Not extraordinary.

▸ Purge—Tells NetWare to purge the directory and any files in it when they are deleted. This inhibits the FILER utility from salvaging deleted files.

▸ System—Marks directories used only by the operating system. These directories and their files are also hidden when using DOS or OS/2 DIR commands.

File Attributes

▸ Immediate Compress—Marks the file so that it is compressed on disk as soon as the operating system can find the time.

▸ Compressed—A status flag set by NetWare that indicates that the file is in compressed form.

▸ Can't Compress—A status flag set by NetWare that indicates that the file cannot be compressed because of insignificant space savings. This parameter is SETtable.

▸ Don't Compress—Marks the file so that it is never compressed.

- Migrated—A status flag set by NetWare that indicates that the file has been migrated to near-line storage.

- Don't Migrate—Marks the file so that it is never migrated to an HCSS device.

- Don't Suballocate—Prevents an individual file from being suballocated. This is a good idea for large and active database files.

- Read/Write—Allows users to change the contents of the file.

- Read Only—Indicates that no one can write to the file.

- Shareable—Allows the file to be accessed by more than one user at a time.

- Execute Only—Allows the file to be executed only. It cannot be copied, and the attribute cannot be removed. Also note that backup utilities don't back up files marked "Execute Only."

That's enough fun for now. We will explore all five layers of the NetWare 4 security model in much more depth later in Chapter 11. For now, please appreciate the sophistication and complexity of NetWare 4 security. Once again, the goal is to create an impenetrable network armor. Of course, should somebody get lucky and break through your network armor, it would be nice to know what they're doing there. That's where NetWare 4 auditing comes in. Let's take a closer look.

NETWARE 4 AUDITING

An additional feature of NetWare 4 security is auditing. This functionality provides a sophisticated suite of auditing services that acts independently of traditional network management. The key to auditing is its password strategy. Unique passwords are required at multiple stages throughout the auditing process. These passwords are kept independently from Admin (NetWare 4's special supervisor) and other administrative users. Auditors can track network transactions according to a variety of activities.

NetWare 4 auditing is made possible through the AUDITCON menu utility. The beauty of NetWare 4 auditing is that AUDITCON auditors can track network resources without actually having any other rights to the resources. Auditors can only audit! This functionality is analogous to the independent auditors who audit banks—assuming, of course, that the bank is not a savings and loan.

So how does it work? The network supervisor (Admin) begins by enabling auditing on specific volumes and containers. During this process, he/she creates a variety of auditing passwords. Admin then notifies the auditor of each password. The beauty of this strategy is that different auditors can track different types of network resources. The first AUDITCON task the auditor performs is setting a new audit password. This now restricts the network supervisor from interfering with any of the auditing services. The auditor can then flag specific resources to be tracked, and the system automatically creates reports. These reports can be customized by the auditor to provide numerous details to network supervisors. Once again, the beauty of this system is that auditors can only audit—they have no special access to other NetWare 4 resources. Where was this feature in the late 1980s? In addition, all auditing files are flagged open and cannot be accessed by nonauditors without serious corruption.

NetWare 4 auditors can track resources and events according to three criteria:

- File and directory events—These settings allow you to audit the opening, closing, modifying, deleting, and salvaging of NetWare 4 files and directories.

- Server events—These settings let you audit the downing of servers, mounting and dismounting of volumes, and the modification of security rights.

- NDS events—These settings help you track specific directory services events such as adding, deleting, moving, and modifying objects. In addition, NDS auditing allows you to track user object logins and logouts.

ZEN

"An elephant—a mouse built to government specifications."

Robert Heinlein

Well, there you go. That's NetWare 4 security in a nutshell. Remember:
Goal—Let the good guys in and keep the bad guys out.

This is accomplished by creating a series of barriers and trap doors. Also, a full set of impenetrable network armor couldn't hurt. Fortunately, NetWare 4 gives you all the tools you need to create a maximum security network.

Speaking of tools. . .

NetWare 4 Utility Management

To do the job right, you have to use the correct tool. Just ask Batman what life would be like without his utility belt. Well, now it's your turn to explore a personalized NetWare utility belt—thanks to NetWare 4.

One of the most dramatic improvements in NetWare 4 utility management is the introduction of GUI (graphical user interface) utilities. These cute little graphical guys provide a friendly user interface for one consolidated utility—NWADMIN. In addition, the supervisor functionality and user functionality have been separated into two distinct utilities—NWADMIN and NWUSER.

In addition to GUI utilities, many of the command line and menu utilities from NetWare 3.12 have been integrated and consolidated into new NetWare 4 DOS-based tools. Also, the number of command line utilities has dropped dramatically, even with the introduction of four or five completely new CLUs (command line utilities).

Finally, at the server, new NLMs and console commands have been integrated to support NDS and the enhanced file and memory management of NetWare 4. The most dramatic improvement has been the integration of all SET parameters into one central management NLM—SERVMAN, a new Saturday-morning superhero rivaling The Tick.

Let's take a closer look at all the cool toys included in NetWare 4. After all, remember:
MOTTO—To do the job right, you have to use the correct tool.

GUI UTILITIES

The NetWare 4 GUI utilities are supported by Microsoft Windows or OS/2's Presentation Manager. These utilities provide a central Windows interface for consolidated management tasks. In addition, NetWare 4 has separated the supervisor functionality from the user functionality. Supervisors use the NetWare Administrator (NWADMIN); users hang out with NWUSER. NetWare 4 also offers DOS-based versions of these utilities that we'll look at in just a moment. For now, let's concentrate on the GUI tools—and we're not talking cookie dough here.

NWADMIN

NWADMIN, the NetWare Administrator, runs as a multiple document interface (MDI) application. The primary NWADMIN window is a browser that displays the NDS tree from your current context down. You can switch the tree view to the [Root] by using the Set Context choice from within NWADMIN's Options menu. In addition, you can view the complete file system within any server by double-clicking on the appropriate volume object. All in all, administrators can open a total of nine Browser windows at one time.

Figure 1.15 shows a sample of the NWADMIN browser. This utility integrates four main menu tools—FILER, NETADMIN, PARTMGR, and PCONSOLE. With NetWare Administrator, you can perform the following tasks:

- ▸ Create user and group accounts

- ▸ Create and delete NDS objects

- ▸ Move and rename NDS objects

- ▸ Create and manage NDS and file system security

- ▸ Set up printing services

- ▸ Create and manage NDS partitions and replicas

- ▸ Use the Remote Management Facility

- ▸ Access on-line graphical help

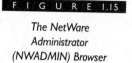

FIGURE 1.15

The NetWare
Administrator
(NWADMIN) Browser

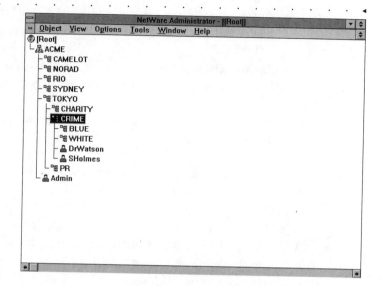

We will explore all the intricacies of NWADMIN throughout this book. Who knows? You might even learn to like it.

TIP

If you break out in hives every time you use Windows, you had better see a doctor. Unfortunately, it's not going away anytime soon. As a matter of fact, the DOS-based equivalent of NWADMIN is an inadequate substitute, to say the least. I suggest some anti-Windows ointment—distributed freely by Novell.

NWUSER

NetWare 4 also includes a graphical user utility—NWUSER. This GUI tool runs in Microsoft Windows or OS/2 Presentation Manager and enables users to perform simple network tasks from within a consolidated friendly interface. NWUSER consists of icons across the top of two split Browser windows. The left window lists connected servers; the right lists NDS resources available in your current context.

Icons across the top of NWUSER enable users to perform five tasks:

▸ Printing—Users can capture ports to printers and manage print jobs after they've been sent.

▸ Attachments—Users can manage network attachments, access a specific file server, and view configuration information about it.

▸ Drives—Users can manage network and search drive mappings as well as view effective rights on selected drives.

▸ Messages—Users can send and receive messages as well as disable incoming notes.

▸ Configuration—Users can customize their NWUSER settings.

DynaText

In addition to the above administrative and user utilities, NetWare 4 includes a GUI interface for on-line documentation. DynaText uses an advanced Windows-based searching engine for access to more than 3,000 pages of NetWare 4 documentation. The DynaText Browser includes a library window, book display, and sophisticated searching capabilities. As seen in Figure 1.16, the library window offers the opportunity for Novell to integrate a variety of documents in multimedia form. In fact, *Novell's CNE Study Guide for NetWare 4.1* may be available in DynaText form—someday. This GUI on-line tool is currently available from your DOS, Microsoft Windows, Macintosh, UNIX, or OS/2 workstation. Get one while it's hot.

F I G U R E 1.16

NetWare 4 DynaText On-line Documentation

That completes our discussion of GUI utilities. Now let's take a closer look at their boring DOS-based counterparts.

DOS-BASED UTILITIES

For those of you who just can't deal with the GUI universe, NetWare 4 includes DOS-based versions of all the GUI utilities. In the case of NWADMIN, it takes four DOS-based menu utilities to cover the same features. NWUSER, on the other hand, has an identical counterpart—NETUSER. In addition to these menu utilities, NetWare 4 uses command line utilities for quick-and-dirty management tasks. Let's take a quick look at some of the key DOS-based menu and command line utilities.

NETADMIN

NETADMIN is the DOS-based version of NWADMIN. Well, that's not entirely true, because NETADMIN only covers a portion of the administrative capabilities of our GUI friend. Some of the things NETADMIN can't do include partition management, file system management, and printing services. Some of the things NETADMIN *can* do include:

- ▸ Manage objects—This NETADMIN option enables administrators to create and manage NDS objects, properties, and security.

- ▸ Manage according to search pattern—You can select individual objects to view or manage. Administrators can only view objects within one container at a time. This is particularly restrictive when compared with NWADMIN's ability to view the entire tree in one snapshot.

- ▸ Change context—Enables you to move your current position in the NDS tree.

- ▸ Search—Administrators can search for any NDS object or object class using wildcards.

NETADMIN includes a Browser with the same functionality as the main NWADMIN screen. The key difference is NETADMIN browses one container at a time. As you can see in Figure 1.17, the NETADMIN Browser doesn't give you the same graphical NDS snapshot that NWADMIN does. You'll find this to be pretty annoying over time.

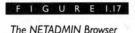

F I G U R E I.17

The NETADMIN Browser

```
NetAdmin  4.55                          Monday  November  22, 1999  12:50pm
Context: white.crime.tokyo.acme
Login Name: Admin.acme
                              Object, Class

  ..                                    (parent)
                                        (current context)
  FTuck                                 (User)
  LJohn                                 (User)
  MMarion                               (User)
  RHood                                 (User)
  User_Template                         (User)
  WHITE-SRV1                            (NetWare Server)
  WHITE-SRV1_SYS                        (Volume)




Press <F10> to select the parent object, <Enter> to change the context.
Enter=Change context/Select   F10=View or edit   F5=Mark   Ins=Add   Alt+F1=More
```

PARTMGR

DOS-based partitioning and replication management are accomplished using the PARTMGR menu utility. In the GUI world, this functionality is integrated into NWADMIN. In the less-flashy DOS world, PARTMGR enables administrators to create and merge partitions and add, delete, modify, and synchronize replicas. Once again, you can only view one container at a time. Also, PARTMGR doesn't provide the same graphical icon look that NWADMIN does. As with most DOS-based utilities, you really need to know what you're doing in order to be productive with PARTMGR. Take a tip from Uncle David—use NWADMIN.

TIP

Working in NETADMIN and PARTMGR is like being in a two dimensional ship traveling through three-dimensional space. All you get are small snapshots of the whole picture. Earlier, we used the analogy of slicing through an orange to reveal a circle. This is how it works in the DOS-based menu world. Although these tools are not for everybody, some administrators find them to be quick and efficient. Others think they're confusing and clumsy. It's your call. Warp speed ahead.

PCONSOLE

DOS-based administrators can create, configure, and manage printing services from within PCONSOLE. In the GUI world, these tasks are integrated into NWADMIN. They can also monitor, modify, pause, and delete print jobs. Finally, PCONSOLE includes a Quick Setup option that allows you to avoid time-consuming customization.

Other Menu Utilities

In addition to the DOS-based menu utilities we've just discussed, there are a few other important tools in NetWare 4 you should be aware of:

- NETUSER—The DOS-based menu version of NWUSER. This utility performs all the same tasks as NWUSER in a simpler text-based menu.

- AUDITCON—This is NetWare 4's auditing console utility. It provides all auditing functionality to special network auditors. In order to access the different levels of AUDITCON, NetWare auditors must use incremental passwords. AUDITCON also enables auditors to generate detailed custom reports.

- FILER—This utility provides access to all file system management tasks. In addition, it includes a salvaging function for undeleting lost files.

Command Line Utilities

NetWare 4 command line utilities enable users and administrators to perform various basic network tasks from the workstation command line. These tasks include accessing network resources, mapping drives, setting up printing, and sending messages. Although there are almost 100 command line utilities in NetWare 4, 90 percent of the functionality is accomplished by fewer than 10. Here's a quick look at some of the most important ones:

- NLIST—This is the most versatile NetWare 4 command line utility. It provides the functionality for intelligent NDS searching. NLIST enables users and administrators to search the NDS database for object information and properties. There are numerous NLIST options that you'll learn as we go along. Learn it, use it, be it.

- CX—This command line utility enables users and administrators to change their current context. CX performs the same task in NDS as CD does in the NetWare file system. In order to move to a certain container in the tree, you simply type **CX** followed by the appropriate distinguished name.

TIP

A special version of CX enables you to view the entire NDS tree—CX /RAT. I can't help but think that this is a hidden reference to Mickey Mouse.

▶ NDIR—This utility provides the same type of functionality as NLIST, except it operates on the NetWare file system instead of NDS. NDIR also includes valuable volume information analogous to earlier CHKVOL, CHKDIR, and LISTDIR utilities.

▶ LOGIN—This all-important NDS access utility allows users and administrators to attach to NetWare 2, 3, and 4 servers.

QUIZ

How far in the future does the Star Wars saga take place?

(Q1-5)

That concludes our quick trip through the DOS-based utility universe. It's not as pretty and cheery as GUI happyland, but many users find the DOS-based world to be more efficient and down-to-earth. Now, let's complete our discussion of NetWare 4 utility management with a look inside the server.

SERVER UTILITIES

Look out, there's a new superhero in Gotham. He is faster than a speedy processor, has more storage than a CD-ROM, and is able to search huge databases in a single second. He's SERVMAN!

SERVMAN is at the core of NetWare 4's new server utility strategy. In addition to SERVMAN, NetWare 4 provides numerous powerful console commands and a variety of improved NLMs. The goal is to create a sophisticated administrative platform without making it too difficult to use. The most important thing to note about NetWare 4 server utilities is that they can cause serious damage if not handled correctly. As a CNE, it is your responsibility to ensure that these tools are kept out of the reach of small children and NetWare users. Fortunately, they're protected with a "childproof cap" in the form of Supervisor rights and file server access protection.

Let's take a quick look at what NetWare 4 has to offer at the server console.

Console Commands

Console commands enable CNEs to interact directly with the NetWare 4 operating system core. These commands are internal to SERVER.EXE and do not require any other support commands. Console commands enable you to perform various administrative tasks, including controlling file servers, printers, and disk drives; sending messages; setting the server clock; performing general LAN maintenance; managing external optical drives; and setting international languages.

One of the most powerful NetWare 4 console commands is SET. Using this utility, you can customize the OS core with almost 100 advanced parameters. These parameters are organized into 11 categories, ranging from communications to file system to time synchronization. Warning: Don't mess around with SET unless you've been adequately trained and you're wearing protective gloves.

NetWare Loadable Modules

NLMs are Lego™ pieces that attach to the core OS and provide additional functionality. The modular architecture of NLMs enables you to load and unload them without adversely affecting the WAN. NetWare 4 NLMs provide internal disk communications, protocol support, name space, and management capabilities. The management tasks are what we're interested in.

Of course, at the heart of the new NetWare 4 NLM management strategy is SERVMAN—our superhero. Let's take a closer look.

> ► SERVMAN—NetWare 4's new SERVer MANager is the most exciting and versatile new server utility. SERVMAN provides a menu interface for SET parameters and displays valuable NetWare configurations. As you can see in Figure 1.18, SERVMAN includes two windows—Server General Information and Available Options. Of course, this is only the beginning.

ZEN

"Wait 'till they get a load of me!"

The Joker (Batman)

F I G U R E 1.18

*SERVMAN, Our New
NetWare 4 Superhero*

```
NetWare 4.10 Server Manager  4.14            NetWare Loadable Module
                 ┌─────────────────────────────────────────┐
                 │     Server General Information           │
                 │                                          │
                 │ Server uptime:          1:23:17:33       │
                 │ Processor utilization:         71%       │
                 │ Processor speed:             6,576       │
                 │ Server processes:                6       │
                 │ Loaded NLMs:                    23       │
                 │ Mounted volumes:                 1       │
                 │ Active queues:                   0       │
                 │ Logged-in users:                 2       │
                 │ Loaded name spaces:              1       │
                 └─────────────────────────────────────────┘

               ┌────────────────────────┐
               │   Available Options     │
               │ ┌────────────────────┐  │
               │ │Server parameters   │  │
               │ │Storage information │  │
               │ │Volume information  │  │
               │ │Network information │  │
               │ └────────────────────┘  │
               └────────────────────────┘

  Enter=Select option   Tab=Next window   Alt+F10=Exit        F1=Help
```

▸ DSREPAIR—This is a new server NLM utility used to repair and correct problems in the NDS database. When you run DSREPAIR, all NDS database files are locked until you exit the utility. DSREPAIR runs from the SYS:SYSTEM directory and checks all NDS objects and their property references. Only run DSREPAIR as a last resort and definitely keep it out of the reach of children and NetWare users.

▸ CDROM—This NLM is an improved NetWare 4 module that enables you to load CD-ROM devices as NetWare volumes. This is particularly valuable because NetWare on-line documentation is available primarily on CD-ROM. In addition, CNEs can make other multimedia resources available to users, including Novell's *NSEPro Encyclopedia* and *Myst*.

This completes our discussion of NetWare 4 utility management. As you can see, we've only tried on your new NetWare 4 utility belt for size. As times get tougher, we must acquire new tools to take on the world. Fortunately, NetWare 4 is chock full of exciting new utilities. We will be exploring these tools in greater depth throughout the book. Also, refer to Chapter 13 for a more detailed discussion of server-based utilities. Be forewarned—you never know when SERVMAN might pop into your life.

Speaking of life, do you remember when yours started? Have you ever experienced the miracle of birth? How about the birth of a LAN? After all, networks are alive, aren't they?

NetWare 4 Configuration

The birth of a LAN. If you take a close look at the definition of life, your NetWare 4 LAN might just be alive. With this in mind, your LAN must also evolve from infant to adult. As you and I have grown (or are still growing) from childhood to adulthood, so must the NetWare 4 LAN. In simple terms, there are three phases of life—birth, childhood, and adulthood.

During birth, the NetWare 4 server is installed. In the grand scheme of things, this event is quick and painless (although I don't know about that latter part). Once the server has been installed, you are left with a simple directory structure, some workstations, and a cute little baby—um, I mean ADMIN user.

Over time, this adorable little baby will learn to walk, learn to talk, and start getting along with others. He/she will go to school and learn some very valuable skills. Finally, at some point, he/she will make an abrupt transition into adulthood.

In NetWare 4, childhood is dominated by the LAN configuration. Your server undergoes five important modifications during configuration:

1 • Workstation connectivity

2 • Login scripts

3 • Menu system

4 • Network applications

5 • E-mail

The third and final phase of life is adulthood. At this point, your LAN is secure and pretty well established in its new purpose. The goal shifts from guiding the infant to "keeping it going." These are the golden years. During adulthood, your LAN will get married, have children, plan for the future, and finally retire. This phase of LAN adulthood is controlled by NetWare 4 management. It goes like this:

► Server management

► Workstation management

> ▸ Storage Management Services (SMS)

> ▸ Remote Management Facility (RMF)

Wow, I bet you didn't think becoming a CNE would be such a life-changing experience. In Chapter 12, we'll take a closer look at the five steps of NetWare configuration. Next, in Chapter 13, we'll break down the four components of LAN adulthood. But for now, let's take a quick peek at these two critical phases of life development—starting with NetWare 4 configuration. NetWare management will be covered in the next section. Also, don't forget NetWare 4 installation (birth!)—that's covered in Chapters 6 and 7.

STEP 1: WORKSTATION CONNECTIVITY

Workstation connectivity is where it all begins. During this step, the client computer boots and activates a variety of configuration files. These configuration files establish the client environment and attach users to the network. All of this magic occurs with the help of just four simple files:

> ▸ CONFIG.SYS—The first configuration file loaded during the boot process.

> ▸ AUTOEXEC.BAT—This autoexecuting batch file is modified to activate the SERVER.EXE file.

> ▸ STARTNET.BAT—A NetWare 4 connectivity file that automates the workstation connection.

> ▸ NET.CFG—The final workstation configuration file. It is used to customize ODI and VLM settings.

Once the first step of configuration has been completed, each user is well on his/her way to NetWare Nirvana. The next step is login scripts.

STEP 2: LOGIN SCRIPTS

NetWare 4 supports four login scripts that are executed in systematic progression. These scripts automate critical user configurations. Here's a quick look:

▸ Container Login Scripts—Properties of Organization and Organizational Unit containers. They replace the earlier system login scripts.

▸ Profile Login Scripts—Properties of Profile objects. These scripts customize environmental parameters for groups of users.

▸ User Login Scripts—Properties of User objects. They provide a tool for user-specific login customization.

▸ Default Login Script—Executed for any user who does not have an individual user script.

Once the Container, Profile, and/or User login scripts have been executed, the system automatically loads a user menu—Step 3. Hmmm, this childhood thing is moving along soooo smoothly—something must be wrong.

STEP 3: MENU SYSTEM

Junior goes to preschool.

In order for your users to get anything done, they need a friendly menu interface. The menu should act as a central access point for user applications and e-mail. Fortunately, NetWare 4 has a built-in menu system that provides custom NetWare-looking menus. The system uses a simple script format and is versatile enough to support large groups of users with a single menu file.

The NetWare 4 menu syntax is based on two simple command types:

▸ Organizational Commands—They provide the menu's look and feel: MENU and ITEM.

▸ Control commands—They execute menu instructions and allow branching to submenus: EXEC, SHOW, LOAD, and GETx.

Once you have established a central, caring menu system, it's time to develop some applications and e-mail to go with it. Let's take a look.

STEP 4: NETWORK APPLICATIONS

NetWare 4 provides excellent support for network applications. Their configuration is accomplished through a seven-step approach for installation and customization. It goes something like this:

1 • Make sure the application is NetWare compatible *before* you buy it.

2 • Make sure the software is truly multiuser.

3 • Determine an appropriate directory structure for the program files and all their support components.

4 • Install the software.

5 • Create file attributes for the sharable or nonsharable network application.

6 • Create user rights for access to network application directories.

7 • Configure the workstations for specific application needs.

Once the application software has been installed and users have proper access rights, the menu environment can be used as a friendly front end. All of this extra effort really pays off by dramatically increasing network transparency and user productivity. It's amazing how far you can get with a little TLC (tender loving computing).

STEP 5: E-MAIL

The final step in NetWare 4 configuration focuses on tying all the other components together. E-mail has become one of the most critical LAN components, next to file and printing services. That's because it improves communication, increases productivity, and maximizes the use of existing resources.

E-mail in NetWare 4 relies on an integrated messaging platform called *MHS Services for NetWare 4*. MHS (Message Handling Service) stores, forwards, and routes user messages. These messages include text, binary graphics, digitized video, and audio data. MHS services is integrated with NDS and uses various NDS objects to accomplish these messaging tasks.

NetWare 4 MHS services relies on three important pieces:

▶ MHS engine—Accepts data from a variety of user e-mail software packages and delivers it to any type of mailbox.

▶ Mailboxes—Physical locations on a messaging server where messages are delivered.

▶ MHS applications—Provide the user interface for creating and reading NetWare 4 messages.

This completes the final step of NetWare 4 configuration. That wasn't so bad. During this phase, we struggled through LAN childhood together. You learned about the five steps of NetWare configuration and prepared the network for its final and most difficult challenge—adulthood.

QUIZ

David Letterman once said, "Fall is my favorite season in Los Angeles, watching the birds change colors and fall from the trees." Along those lines, here's a little mind bender for you:

There is a field with a number of trees in it. There are a number of birds (more than one) in each tree. There is more than one tree in the field, and each tree has the same number of birds in it. If you knew the total number of birds in the field, you would know the total number of trees. If there are between 200 and 300 birds, how many trees are there?

(Q1-6)

NetWare 4 Management

So you have a new car, a new job, and a new apartment. Welcome to adulthood. It's funny how we continually yearn for these days during childhood. Now that we're here, we just want to be young again. Go figure.

Once you reach adulthood, your focus shifts from "getting started" to keeping things going. As a CNE, your system moves right from childhood into LAN adulthood with a focus on NetWare management. Now your focus shifts to the long term. Suddenly, your mind is filled with thoughts of a family (servers and workstations), a pension (SMS), and retirement (RMF). Aah, adulthood!

NetWare 4 management is the most time-consuming aspect of being a CNE. If you figure that configuration occurs only once, management dominates your life forever. In NetWare 4, this is accomplished through four strategies:

- ▸ Server management

- ▸ Workstation management

- ▸ Storage Management Services (SMS)

- ▸ Remote Management Facility (RMF)

Server management involves daily tasks for protecting and maintaining the NetWare 4 server. This also includes management and maintenance of the NDS database.

Workstation management can be even more challenging, because it involves the NetWare user. Workstation management focuses on connectivity strategies as well as virus prevention and diskless workstations.

As the old adage goes, "You never miss anything until it's gone." This holds especially true for NetWare data. One of the most important things you can do as a NetWare 4 CNE is plan for the future—backups. SMS is a NetWare 4 backup engine that provides data storage and retrieval *from* a variety of front-end applications *to* numerous back-end storage devices.

Finally, RMF enables you to manage the server console from anywhere in the world—including the Happy Acres Retirement Home. RMF can become the cornerstone of your server maintenance schedule. In addition, it's particularly useful as part of your server security model. Remember: "The NetWare 4 file server must be locked away in a cabinet with no user or CNE access." RMF enables you to access the server console from a remote workstation.

In Chapter 13 we're going to take a detailed look at these four strategies for NetWare 4 management. But for now, let's take a quick look at some of the key components of LAN adulthood—starting with marriage.

SERVER MANAGEMENT

At some point, your focus must shift from users to server management. After all, the entire network will suffer if your servers aren't running correctly. Server management consists of five components:

▸ Startup Management—You must separate the server startup tasks that occur once during installation from those that occur every time the server is turned on.

▸ NDS Management—You must learn to protect and manage the NDS database through various server tasks including NDS repair, partitioning, database replication, server time synchronization, and database maintenance.

▸ Server Protection—Because the server is at the heart of your LAN, you want to use any means possible to protect it. This includes locking up the server, preventing access to the keyboard with MONITOR.NLM, using the SECURE CONSOLE command, and adding a password for RMF.

▸ Console Commands—Most of your server management duties will take place at the server console. The colon (:) prompt accepts two kinds of commands: console commands and NetWare Loadable Modules (NLMs). NetWare 4 includes numerous console commands for a variety of server management and maintenance tasks.

▸ NLMs—NetWare Loadable Modules represent the other server command type. NLMs are modular Legos that provide supplemental functionality to the NetWare 4 server.

As you can see, marriage takes work. Fortunately, most of the time the rewards greatly outweigh the pain. As a CNE, you must also work very hard to keep the server running. In both cases, communication is the key.

ZEN

"By all means marry. If you get a good spouse, you will be happy. And, if you get a bad one, you will become a philosopher."

Socrates

WORKSTATION MANAGEMENT

So you're cruising along through life, minding your own business, and wham—it hits you. Suddenly, your family is twice as big as it was a few years ago. It's an abrupt wake-up call when you finally realize you're not the child anymore. Now your focus shifts to the other children in your life—the workstations.

As a CNE, you will spend just as much time managing the workstations as you do managing the server. In addition, managing workstations can be even more challenging, because they encompass a much more diverse collection of users, applications, and operating systems. In order to fully optimize the client connection and keep things running smoothly, you'll have to employ a stern, yet caring, workstation management strategy. Following are a few important things to think about.

ODI

ODI stands for *Open Datalink Interface*. ODI enables the workstation to send and receive network files through its internal network interface card (NIC). As you can see in Figure 1.19, this is accomplished using three important pieces:

▶ *Multiple Link Interface Driver (MLID)*—This component interfaces with the internal NIC. One example, 3C5X9.COM.

▶ *Link Support Layer (LSL)*—It acts as a switchboard to route packets between MLID and the Protocol Stack. One example, LSL.COM.

▶ *Protocol Stack*—One of three protocol-specific files used to translate and negotiate network communications. The default file is IPXODI.COM for IPX/SPX and TCPIP.EXE for TCP/IP.

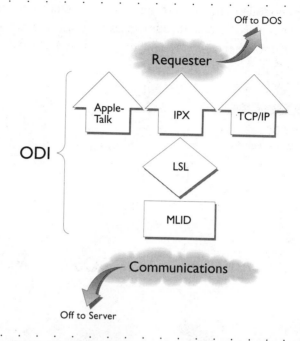

*ODI Client Services in
NetWare 4*

REAL WORLD

ODI loading at the workstation works a little bit differently from the way the figure shows it. Although the MLID layer is at the bottom and is the first point of contact for incoming packets, it is not the first ODI driver loaded. Here's the actual order:

1. LSL.COM
2. 3C5X9.COM *(or other MLID)*
3. IPXODI.COM *(or other protocol stack)*

That does it for communications; now let's take a look at the second major component of the client connection—the NetWare DOS Requester.

NetWare DOS Requester

The NetWare DOS Requester is a connection point between your workstation operating system (WOS) and the NetWare 4 LAN. As you can see in Figure 1.20, it's a marshmallow-looking thing that surrounds DOS and provides transparent connectivity between user applications and the network. Think of it as a traffic cop at the workstation—

it takes requests from the user and decides whether they should be handled by the WOS or the NetWare server. If your request is destined for the server, the Requester sends it down through the ODI layers. If not, it enables DOS to process the request and sends it back to the user.

F I G U R E I.20

NetWare DOS Requester
for NetWare 4

The Requester functionality is made possible through a variety of modular files called *Virtual Loadable Modules (VLMs)*. Each VLM performs a specific function, including PRINT.VLM for printer redirection, CONN.VLM for connectivity, FIO.VLM for file services, and NETX.VLM for backward compatibility to NETX. All of this is made possible with the VLM manager—VLM.EXE.

To activate the NetWare 4 VLMs and attach to NDS, you must first start with VLM.EXE. Because VLMs are load order-dependent, the manager makes sure children are loaded before their parents. In addition, the manager tries to load all VLMs in extended memory first and only uses expanded and conventional RAM if necessary.

Well, that does it for the NetWare DOS Requester and ODI. Both of these workstation connectivity strategies rely on workstation-specific configuration files for implementation and customization. As you will see in Chapter 13, these configuration files enable CNEs to increase user transparency and pinpoint communication problems.

In addition to the workstation connectivity strategies already described, you should be aware of additional management issues, including non-DOS support, virus prevention, and diskless workstations. Let's take a quick look:

▶ Non-DOS Support—In addition to DOS, NetWare 4 supports Windows 95 (Windows 95 Requester), OS/2 (NetWare Client for OS/2), Macintosh (NetWare for Macintosh and MacNDS), and finally, UNIX (NetWare NFS). In addition, DOS workstations can share non-DOS files through an internal server naming scheme—name space. The bottom line is that any happy family is made up of many types of children. Look at the Brady Bunch, for example.

▶ Virus Prevention—There will come a day when your child gets his/her first cold. While it may seem like the end of the world, the little one will be just fine if you give him/her chicken soup and some TLC (tender loving computing). Similarly, workstations can get hit by a virus that creates chaos on your LAN. It's paramount in network security to implement standard procedures for protection against network viruses.

▶ Diskless Workstations—Diskless workstations are clients without a floppy or hard disk. They can dramatically improve your quality of life by enhancing virus prevention, saving money, and, of course, centralizing NetWare administration.

Children aren't so bad. Once you get the hang of it, I think you might even enjoy parenthood. Having servers and workstations enables you to relive a little bit of your own childhood and adds years to your life. Of course, all the while, you need to be thinking about the future and what happens when your children get children of their own. Planning for the future and retirement are important aspects of adulthood. Let's take a closer look.

ZEN

"So near, and yet . . . so what?"

Anonymous

STORAGE MANAGEMENT SERVICES

Fortunately, NetWare 4 includes a versatile new backup feature called Storage Management Services (SMS). SMS is a combination of related services that enables you to store and retrieve data from various targets—Target Service Agents (TSAs). SMS is a backup engine that operates independently from the front-end application and back-end device. As you can see in Figure 1.21, SMS supports a variety of TSA front-ends, including NetWare File Systems, NDS, DOS, and OS/2 file systems, and BTRIEVE databases. Any or all of these resources can be backed up to a variety of back-end devices, including DOS Read/Write disks, and tape and optical drives.

FIGURE 1.21

The Architecture of Storage Management Services

So how does it work? At the heart of the SMS model is the backup application. NetWare 4 includes a starter program called SBACKUP. SBACKUP is an NLM that operates at the NetWare 4 server and communicates directly with the host backup device. SBACKUP works within the SMS architecture to route data requests among TSAs and the backup device. This process consists of seven simple steps:

1 • Load the backup device driver on the host server.

2 • Load TSA software on all target devices. This includes the host server, if you plan to back it up.

3 • Load SBACKUP.NLM at the host server.

4 • Select a target to be backed up from the menu. The available options within SBACKUP should reflect all devices that have loaded the appropriate TSA.

5 • Select the backup device from an available options list. This list should reflect all devices attached to the host server.

6 • Back up the data from all loaded targets.

7 • Unload SBACKUP files in reverse order.

That completes our discussion of NetWare 4 backup—so how's your nest egg doing? Remember, you never know what little surprises life has in store for you; it's best to be prepared.

REMOTE MANAGEMENT FACILITY (RMF)

The final step in our life journey is retirement—RMF. Our life's been a very exciting adventure and now it's time to kick back and put it in cruise control. Welcome to Happy Acres!

RMF is the final step in NetWare 4 configuration and management. It enables you to manage all your NetWare file servers from one location. This is particularly useful because file server security states that the machine should be locked away in a cabinet with no monitor and keyboard. Also, NetWare 4 prides itself on multiple servers spanning wide geographic boundaries. In both cases, you'll spend more time trying to access the servers than doing the important stuff—maintaining and managing them.

So, how does it work? RMF supports CNE access from both a workstation and a modem. In either case, it consists of two main components:

▸ REMOTE.NLM

▸ RCONSOLE.EXE

The RMF server NLMs are broken into two functions—REMOTE facility and connection services. The REMOTE facilities are provided by one NLM—REMOTE.NLM. This module manages the information exchange to and from the workstation and the server. In addition, REMOTE.NLM enables a CNE to specify an RMF password.

Connection services are a little bit trickier. As you remember from our earlier discussion, RMF supports access from both a direct workstation and a modem. In either case, the connection NLM is different. When you access RMF from a direct workstation, the connection NLM is RSPX.NLM. This module provides communication support and advertises the server's availability for remote access. On the other hand, when you're accessing RMF from an asynchronous modem, the connection NLM is RS232.NLM.

This module initializes the server modem port and transfers screen and keystroke information to REMOTE.NLM. Check out Table 1.2 for a quick summary.

T A B L E 1.2	DIRECT WORKSTATION	ASYNCHRONOUS MODEM
Understanding the RMF NLMs	REMOTE.NLM	REMOTE.NLM
	RSPX.NLM	RS232.NLM

Whether you're accessing RMF from a direct workstation or asynchronous modem, you're going to need RCONSOLE.EXE. RCONSOLE is a supervisor utility stored in the SYS:SYSTEM subdirectory. RCONSOLE provides direct access to the NetWare server console screen and enables you to perform any task as if you were sitting right in front of it. In addition, RCONSOLE provides an Available Options menu with supplemental tasks, including changing screens, scanning server directories, and performing a remote install. All in all, RCONSOLE is your friend, because it enables you to enjoy the good life without having to run around like a chicken with your head cut off.

ZEN

"Finally, science has discovered a cure for baldness. Although it's not quite what you'd think. Instead of growing hair, they shrink your head to fit what hair you've got left."

Anonymous

Well, that does it. Your life in a nutshell. We've brought our LAN from birth through childhood and the rewards of adulthood. Through NetWare 4 configuration and management, we've transformed a relatively limp and lifeless LAN into a powerful and productive business tool. Remember, as a CNE, you can't just set up the server and walk away. Your life is irrevocably bound to the childhood and adulthood of your LAN.

NetWare 4 Printing

The final major topic of NetWare 4 is printing. We always save printing for last because it's the most troublesome aspect of the LAN. Not that printing is inherently flawed; it actually works quite well under "normal conditions." The problem is that you rarely experience normal conditions. NetWare printing breaks down pretty quickly when things get hairy. And as I'm sure you know, things are always hairy!

In this section we take a quick look at the fundamental printing components of NetWare 4 and explore some configuration strategies and management utilities. Later, in Chapter 14, we'll learn everything there is to know about this strange animal, but for now—let's get on with the show.

PRINTING COMPONENTS

Like previous versions of NetWare, NetWare 4 does not have built-in printing services. These services are not available until you add them. In order to add NetWare 4 printing, you work with all three main NDS printing objects:

- ▸ Print queues

- ▸ Print servers

- ▸ Printers

So how does it work? As you can see in Figure 1.22, it all starts at the NetWare workstation. Somehow, users print their documents from a client application to the print queue. The print queue is a shared area on the file server disk that stores print jobs in the order in which they are received. The print queue then lines up the various users' documents and sends them to the appropriate printer when the time is right. The print server keeps track of print job priority and directs them from the queue to the appropriate network printer. Voilà!

NetWare 4 Printing

In a transparent NetWare printing environment, users print directly from their network application and the output magically appears on the printer down the hall. While this level of magic seems trivial to them, it's a nightmare for you, the CNE. In earlier versions of NetWare, it was worse, because users had to be aware of which print queue serviced "their" printer. Redirection commands were complex, and they had to redirect print jobs from local workstation ports to specific network print queues. Now you can see why it all breaks down.

NetWare 4 has dramatically simplified printing by introducing background queue management. This means users no longer print to queues; they can print directly to printer objects. As a matter of fact, they don't even need to know where the objects are stored, just the ones to which they want to print. Wow!

Now let's take a quick look at how these three fundamental printing components become NDS objects.

Print Queue

Print queues hold user jobs in line until they are ready to be sent off to the correct network printer. These jobs are stored as binary or text files and prioritized on a first-come, first-served basis. In NetWare 4, the print queue is a subdirectory of the QUEUES directory off the root of any selected volume.

In NDS, the print queue object makes the resource available to users in the same container. If a user wants to print, he/she needs to have access to the print queue object.

Print Server

The *print server* is a device that monitors print queues and printers. It understands the relationship between the two and sends print jobs to the appropriate printer when the time is right. In NetWare 4, the print server exists as PSERVER.NLM running on the file server.

In NDS, a print server object contains information about printers and print queues. In addition, this object supports a password for printing security.

TIP

In addition to PSERVER.NLM, NetWare 4 supports third-party printing devices as print servers. HP, for example, has an NIC called the Jet Direct card that plugs into any HP LaserJet printer and makes it act as a print server. It's important to note that this functionality must coexist with NDS, and therefore, use advanced technology. Many of the third-party printing devices that operated in the NetWare 3 world don't work in NetWare 4. Make sure yours does.

Printers

Almost any printer can be used for network printing. This represents the ultimate star of our printing show. The printer can be attached to the print server, any NetWare server, a workstation, or directly to the network cable.

In NetWare 4, special software is needed to make the printer available for network printing—NPRINTER. At a NetWare file or print server, NPRINTER runs as an NLM. At the workstation, NPRINTER runs as an .EXE file. In NDS, a printer object contains valuable configuration information about print job formats.

Also, the printer object takes on new meaning with NetWare 4's background queue management. Users can now print directly to objects within their home container without having to worry about queues and print servers. This is probably one of the most important improvements to the NetWare 4 printing system.

PRINTING CONFIGURATIONS

Printing configuration in NetWare 4 is simplified, but it takes some getting used to. Print queues, print servers, and printers are implemented differently than in earlier versions. It may not seem like it now, but take my word for it—this *is* an improvement.

NetWare 4 print queues lie under the QUEUES subdirectory on volumes distributed throughout the NDS tree. You're no longer restricted to the SYS:SYSTEM subdirectory. In addition, users no longer need to print to a NetWare queue—they simply print directly to printers. Any user in the WAN can print to any printer to which he/she has sufficient rights. NetWare 4 handles all of the connectivity functions in the background.

Next, print servers exist only as PSERVER.NLM on the NetWare 4 server. One of the properties of the Print Server object is Printers. This property lists the printers that are serviced by this print server—all 256 of them! In order for the printer to broadcast itself as a network device, the server must be running a special program—NPRINTER.NLM. In addition, printers can be attached to nondedicated workstations running NPRINTER.EXE. The loop is completed through the Print Queue property of the Printer object. This lists all independent print queues that are servicing the printer.

ZEN

"You think printing is bad? I know a guy with a really bad office job. He cleans windows—not the big ones—the little ones inside envelopes. Count your blessings."

Anonymous

Although all of this theory is very interesting, the real mystery is how you make it work in the "real world." Two words: printing setup. Here's the setup process:

1 • Create and configure printing objects. It all starts when you create the three NDS printing objects using NWADMIN or PCONSOLE. Begin by creating the Print Queue object and identifying the volume on which it will reside. Next, create the Printer object and configure its printer type, location, interrupt, and port; then assign a print queue. Finally, create the Print Server object and add new printers and an optional password to be used to load PSERVER.NLM.

2 • Initialize the print server. Next, you must choose a network server to act as the print server. Remember, NetWare 4 printing only works with PSERVER.NLM, unless, of course, you're using a third-party print server device. Choose the server and load PSERVER.NLM with the correct NDS context.

3 • Connect the printer to the network. Finally, you must identify your network printers and decide whether they'll be attached to workstations or servers. Printers attached to servers require NPRINTER.NLM; printers attached to workstations use NPRINTER.EXE.

4 • Customize printing. This optional step enables you to deal with life's little surprises. If all goes well, you can spend the rest of your life using NetWare 4's simple printing architecture and relying on application print servers for fancy fonts and document layout. Unfortunately, life doesn't always work that way and sometimes you're forced to create customized print forms and configurations. All of this exciting customization can be accomplished using NWADMIN, PRINTCON, or PRINTDEF.

PRINTING MANAGEMENT

So everything's working fine and your users are happily printing along. Then zowie—the printer breaks! Oops, what now? Printing management is your life. More than any other network resource, printing services requires constant attention. You'll need to learn how to manage print queues, print servers, and printers. Fortunately, NetWare 4 provides a variety of powerful tools for just this type of emergency. Here's how printing management works:

▸ Managing Print Queues—During your stint as a CNE, you'll have to learn to manage a variety of print queue tasks, including controlling print queue workflow, managing print jobs in the queue, and controlling access to the print queue. Many of these tasks can be accomplished by using NWADMIN or PCONSOLE. I recommend NWADMIN, because it enables you to manage queues from within a graphical utility. One of the most important aspects of print queue management is what you do with the jobs once they're there. NWADMIN provides two windows for this task—Print Queue Job List and Print Job Detail. More to come in Chapter 14.

▸ Managing the Print Server—While dealing with the print server on a daily basis, you'll have to perform a variety of tasks, including viewing print server status, bringing down the print server, and assigning print server users and operators. Once again, these tasks can be accomplished using NWADMIN or PCONSOLE. Be careful when you assign print server operators, because they're given power to control things any mortal user shouldn't have access to.

▸ Managing the Printer—Logically, the printer is at the end of the road. When you perform routine printer management tasks, consider viewing and controlling the printer status and responding to printer error messages. The Printer Status window in NWADMIN or PCONSOLE enables you to perform numerous maintenance tasks, including changing service mode, mounting forms, stop/starting printers, selecting form feed, and stopping jobs. I predict you'll spend a lot of time here.

So, there you have it. NetWare 4 printing configuration and management. The only thing left is *to print*. Believe it or not, this is the easiest part of NetWare 4 print services. To print, you just need two things—a print job at the workstation and a way to redirect it to the printer. If your application is network aware, it can send print jobs directly to a network printer. If the application is not network aware, it prints only to local devices through DOS. That's where redirection comes in.

You can configure clients so that print jobs sent to LPT1, for example, find their way to a specific network printer. This can be done using one of three NetWare tools: CAPTURE, NetWare User Tools for Windows, and NETUSER. *CAPTURE* sets up print job redirection before a user opens an application. CAPTURE is a utility that assigns a specific NetWare 4 queue or printer to each local port. *NetWare User Tools for Windows* sets up print job redirection using a GUI interface. With this tool, users can modify the resource parameters at any time. Once again, the goal is to assign a specific network printer to each local device. Finally, *NETUSER* is a menu utility that sets up the print job resource before the user opens an application. Unfortunately, NETUSER does not enable you to customize any print options; it just uses the defaults.

So there you are. NetWare 4 printing. That wasn't so bad, was it—YES!

ZEN

"Oh, oh, oh . . . the things you've got to know."

Anonymous

Wouldn't life in the NetWare 4 universe be great without printing? Of course, without printers, there wouldn't be paperwork, and without paperwork, you wouldn't be reading this book. And without this book, you wouldn't be a great CNE. Without CNEship, you would be stuck in a musty office somewhere generating copious paperwork. So after all, printing is a good thing. I guess in some strange way, printing conquers bureaucracy.

I have a treat in store for you in Chapter 14 when we get to spend much more time scouring every detail of NetWare 4 printing. For now, just be glad you're using NetWare 4 because its printing architecture has been dramatically improved.

ZEN

"The trouble with life in the fast lane is that you get to the end in an awful hurry!"

Anonymous

We sure could learn an important lesson from this quote. Take a moment to relax. Unwind. Go for a peaceful walk. Clear your mind.

Welcome back. That completes our discussion of the major NetWare 4 technologies. So far, we've introduced NDS, the NetWare 4 enhanced file system, security, utility management, client services, NetWare 4 configuration, management, and finally printing. Wow, that's quite an introduction. Of course, NetWare 4 is quite an impressive operating system. Remember, we're talking the peak of OS evolution here. I bet you can't wait to dive into the nitty gritty of NetWare 4 design, installation, and management. But, wait, before I let you get away, we need to take a quick look at a few additional NetWare 4 features—namely, memory management, internationalization, and DynaText.

Other NetWare 4 Features

At the beginning of this chapter, we outlined the two types of services in NetWare 4—the "core" services and the "evolved" services. The core services of NetWare 4 establish a foundation upon which to build. These services are relatively unchanged from NetWare 3.12. Two important core services we haven't discussed yet are internationalization and DynaText.

Evolved services, on the other hand, build on the foundation of NetWare 4 and define the evolution of this amazing OS. At the forefront of evolved services is NDS. Additional services include a better file system, enhanced GUI utilities, NDS security and auditing, and improved memory management. It's the latter we're interested in now.

Let's take a moment to explore these three services and see what impact they'll have on your life as a CNE and your journey through the NetWare 4 universe.

MEMORY MANAGEMENT

NetWare 4 manages file server RAM more efficiently than did NetWare 3.12. Earlier versions of NetWare allocated memory to multiple pools that served specific purpose. In NetWare 3.12, these pools expanded as needed, but rarely returned unused memory. Occasionally, a server application ran out of RAM even if there was plenty of memory in the main pool.

NetWare 4 has consolidated all server RAM into one main pool and memory is reallocated as needed. The server operates much more efficiently and applications rarely run out of valuable file server RAM. In addition, NetWare 4 includes memory protection. Memory protection defines the OS's ability to run NLMs in a protected memory area on the server. NetWare 4 memory protection provides CNEs with a tool to test NLMs within a protected ring of memory without bringing down the server or corrupting other applications.

Protected rings of memory are less efficient than nonprotected rings, but shield the operating system core from harmful NLMs. Ring protection provides a logical means to segment memory and provide protection for processes such as disk/LAN drivers and the operating system. These segments are limited in size and are granted privilege levels. As you can see in Figure 1.23, ring zero maintains the highest privilege level and includes the NetWare 4 OS files. In addition, the proven disk drivers and LAN drivers hang out there.

NetWare 4 Memory
Protection

Ring three, on the other hand, is the lowest privilege and is defined as the protected ring. Even though it appears as though rings one and two are available, only two rings can coexist at one time—typically ring zero (OS) and ring three (protected).

NetWare 4's memory management features are made possible through a new management scheme that uses the Intel-based paging mechanism. This strategy provides the foundation for memory protection and efficient memory allocation. In addition, NetWare 4 includes server console commands and NLMs for managing memory protection. At the heart of this strategy is the DOMAIN server NLM utility. For more detail regarding NetWare 4 memory management, refer to Chapter 15.

ZEN

"The search is what anyone would undertake if he were not sunk in the everydayness of his own life. To become aware of the possibility of the search is to be onto something. Not to be onto something is to be in despair."

Walter Percy

INTERNATIONALIZATION

NetWare 4's internationalization strategy offers support for multiple languages. NetWare 4 provides utility and installation capability for a variety of simultaneous languages. By default, English is used for the operating system NLMs and all utilities. Other languages can be set at installation and when utilities and services are requested. Differences in date, time, and number formats are also supported.

The most amazing of NetWare 4's international features is the ability for multiple workstations to access the same resources while simultaneously using different languages. This is made possible through the use of the NetWare DOS Requester and client SET parameters. By default, NetWare 4 supports English, French, German, Italian, and Spanish languages.

Keep in mind that although most languages support the standard microcomputer hardware, some languages require special consideration. To use Japanese, for example, the keyboard must support double-byte characters. If a user with this hardware sends a message to a user with a single-byte character language, the recipient will see garbage characters on the screen. There's an important lesson here. The hardware cannot interpret the double-byte characters. In addition, software will not act as a translator, either. It will simply display the information in the native workstation language. This means if you send a German message to someone working in English, it will appear as German. NetWare 4 is not yet intelligent enough to translate from German to English—nor does it want to.

DYNATEXT

NetWare 4 provides electronic versions of all its product documentation. The DynaText utility enables you to choose a manual, browse its contents, search for topics, and print. As you can see in Figure 1.24, the DynaText window is broken into two halves. The left half provides an outline of all the major topics while the right half provides the book text and graphics. Scroll bars and menu icons round out the interface. DynaText supports any of the major client operating systems: Microsoft Windows 95, OS/2, Macintosh, and UnixWare. In addition, it supports two operating modes: stand-alone or networked. Wait, that's not all. Novell on-line documentation is also available in several languages. All you have to do is set the NWLANGUAGE parameter at the workstation and voilà, different users are viewing on-line documentation in different languages—simultaneously! What will they think of next?

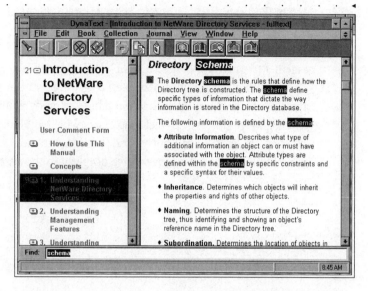

*NetWare 4 DynaText
On-line Documentation*

To install on-line documentation on the NetWare server, simply use the INSTALL.NLM utility and NetWare 4 DynaText CD-ROM. Later in the book, we'll take a closer look at on-line documentation and provide some exercises for practicing with it on your own.

QUIZ

Let's say you're going for a Sunday drive to Podunk and back. I don't know why, let's just say that you are! It's 120 miles from here, and you average 60 MPH on the trip out. On the return trip, you take it easy and average 40 MPH. What was your average speed for the round-trip? Don't worry, it's not as easy as it sounds.

(Q1-7)

Well, there you have it. NetWare 4 *is* the big kahuna. If you're not in awe by now, you must be a very hard person to impress. As we mentioned earlier, the goal of NetWare 4 is transparent connectivity. The NDS Cloud surely helps the situation by enabling us to represent physical network devices as logical objects. Also, this NDS Cloud concept permeates all aspects of NetWare 4 configuration, management, and printing.

On the other hand, I hope you've come to appreciate that NetWare 4 can also be down-to-earth. It's not quite as alien as you might think. Many of NetWare 4's dramatic changes have been built on top of NetWare 3. Both the core and evolved services work together to provide a cohesive, cool WAN architecture.

Remember, this book is dedicated to getting you through NetWare 4 with the least amount of pain. Who knows, you might even enjoy yourself along the way. In this first chapter, we've given you a brief snapshot of what NetWare 4 is all about. In the remaining 14 chapters, we'll round out your education with some in-depth understanding. Get those neurons firing. It's time to dive deeper into the *next generation* of networking.

EXERCISE 1.1: GETTING TO KNOW DYNATEXT

This exercise assumes that you have access to the NetWare 4 DynaText program using *one* of the following methods:

▸ DynaText installed on the server

▸ DynaText installed to run on a server CD-ROM drive that is set up as a shared network device

▸ DynaText installed on your workstation

▸ DynaText installed to run on your workstation CD-ROM drive

See Chapter 6 for further information regarding DynaText installation.

1 • Execute the DynaText application in MS Windows

a. Load MS Windows on your workstation by typing **WIN** and pressing Enter. Find the group icon that contains the DynaText icon and double-click on it. Then, double-click on the DynaText icon to start the application.

b. The screen will be divided into two main sections: Collection and Title. The NetWare 4.1 option should be highlighted in the Collection window on the left. The Master Index option should be highlighted in the Title window on the right.

2 • Look up an item in the DynaText Master Index

a. Double-click on the Master Index option in the Title window to open the Master Index. This will display a list on the left side of the screen containing letters of the alphabet (each letter will be repeated three times, such as AAA).

b. Use the Outline scroll bar to the right of the alphabet list to scroll down to "TTT." You'll notice an expand button (it will have a + symbol) in front of

"TTT." Click on the expand button to display topics that begin with the letter *T*. Using the Outline scroll bar again, scroll down until you see the words "time stamp, explained," and then double-click on them. This will cause references to that topic to be displayed on the right side of the screen.

c. If you look on the right side of the screen, you'll notice that there is a reference to "time stamp, explained" in the *Concepts* manual. Click on the blue cross-reference button to the right of the word "Concepts" to display the reference indicated.

d. An explanation of the term "time stamp" will then be displayed on the right side of the screen. Read the explanation, using the right scroll bar to view the entire reference. When you are finished reading, double-click on the close button next to the File menu on the menu bar.

e. The Master Index full-text screen will be displayed. Use the Outline scroll bar to view "TTT," and then click the collapse button in front of it (it will have a – symbol) to collapse the list of topics beginning with *T*. Double-click on the close button next to the File menu on the menu bar to return to the main Master Index menu.

3 • Search for an item across books

a. If you want to search for a topic across all manuals, make sure you're on the main screen. (You should see all of the manuals listed on the right side of the screen.) Click on the Find field that is near the bottom left of the screen, and then type **COUNTRY** and press Enter to find all occurrences of the word *COUNTRY* in the manuals listed. If you look in the Hits column, you'll see the number of times the word(s) you searched for occurred in each manual. If you want to view the occurrences of the word(s) you selected in a particular manual, double-click on that manual, and then use the forward (rightward pointing triangle) button on the top of the screen to scroll through each occurrence in that manual. Double-click on the close button next to the File menu on the menu bar to return to the main Master Index menu.

4 • Search for an item with a book

    a. The method for searching within a book is essentially the same as searching across books, except that you double-click on the book in question before indicating the text string to search in the Find field. When you are finished searching, you will then need to double-click on the close button next to the File menu on the menu bar to return to the main DynaText screen.

5 • Research assignment

    a. Using whatever method you want, use DynaText to answer the questions that follow. Search all books each time unless otherwise indicated. (The answers are listed in Appendix C.)

        (1) What was the former name of UTC?

        (2) Determine whether a user can modify a subordinate reference. (Note: A subordinate reference replica is another name for a subordinate reference.)

        (3) How many characters can a distinguished name contain?

        (4) Search the *Introduction to NetWare Directory Services* manual only to determine what an ACL contains.

        (5) Search the *Concepts* manual only to determine if some properties enable you to indicate more than one value.

        (6) Search the *Building and Auditing a Trusted NetWare 4 Environment* Research Report only to determine how many properties exist in the Directory Services schema.

Match each of the following NDS terms with its description:

1 • ___ DynaText

2 • ___ GUI

3 • ___ SMS

4 • ___ File compression

5 • ___ Internationalization

6 • ___ MHS

7 • ___ Ring zero

8 • ___ Data migration

9 • ___ VLMs

10 • ___ AUDITING

11 • ___ 1000

12 • ___ Block suballocation

13 • ___ 256

14 • ___ IRF

15 • ___ Inheritance

16 • ___ Profile

17 • ___ ODI

18 • ___ MLID

19 • ___ IPX

20 • ___ Print queue

A. Maximum number of connections per server

B. E-mail engine

C. Holds print jobs waiting to be printed

D. On-line documentation

E. Rights flowing down from above

F. Increases disk space up to 63 percent

G. Modular programs that run on theworkstation

H. Maximum number of printers per print server

I. NetWare OS runs here

J. Type of user interface

K. Useful with large disk allocation blocks

L. Transfers inactive data to near-term storage

M. LAN driver written to ODI specifications

N. Allows protocols to coexist on same network board

O. Backup engine

P. Type of login script

Q. Filters inherited rights

R. Provides choice of language

S. Security feature that can be activated at the volume or container level

T. Default NetWare 4 communications protocol

See Appendix C for answers.

EXERCISE 1.3: GETTING TO KNOW NDS

PART I:

Write **C** for container or **L** for leaf next to each of the following objects:

1 • ___ Volume

2 • ___ Country

3 • ___ User

4 • ___ Group

5 • ___ Organizational Unit

6 • ___ Server

7 • ___ Print Queue

8 • ___ Organizational Role

9 • ___ Computer

10 • ___ Organization

See Appendix C for answers.

PART II:

Indicate whether you think each item below would be a container or a leaf object. If you think it would be a Container object, indicate what type of container (i.e., Country, Organization, or Organizational Unit).

1 • _____ The Human Resources department

2 • _____ Guinevere

3 • _____ A database server

4 • _____   The PAYCHECK print queue

5 • _____   ACME, Inc.

6 • _____   The Administrator Organizational Role

7 • _____   UK (i.e., United Kingdom)

8 • _____   A dot matrix printer

9 • _____   The Tokyo office

10 • _____   The SYS: volume

See Appendix C for answers.

Understanding NDS

Every cloud has a silver lining. Even Daisy-Head Mayzie had 15 minutes of fame. But she let it go to her head—literally. One sunny afternoon, sweet little Mayzie sprouted a Daisy out of her head! How odd.

After she got over the initial shock, Mayzie got a "big head." She left her family and friends to become a star in Hollywood. But all the money and fame didn't change the fact that she had a plant growing out of her cranium. And what's money worth anyway without somebody to share it with? So Daisy-Head Mayzie realized her mistake and left the afternoon talk shows to return home. Yes, HOME. Not a SYS:USERS directory, not a base in baseball. No, this home is where everybody loves her for who she is, not what she has growing out of her head. Everybody lived happily ever after.

This could happen to you. You could become "NDS-Head Fred!" As a matter of fact, you can probably feel a slight "twinge" even as you read this. You knew that your new life as a NetWare 4 CNE would be exciting, but nobody prepared you for this. The more you learn about NDS, the faster your tree will sprout. Until one day you'll be as rich and famous as Daisy-Head Mayzie. But don't make the same mistakes that she did. Don't abandon the people who got you here—your family, your friends, Novell, and Ortho Weed Killer. Keep your head out of the clouds and your two feet planted firmly *in the* ground.

ZEN

"Congratulations! Today is your day. You're off to great places! You're off and away!"

Dr. Seuss

I'm here to help you deal with this whole cranial gardening thing. As we learned in the last chapter, NDS is a virtual tree structure that helps you organize network resources. It's also referred to as the "Cloud" because it floats above physical resources—servers, printers, and users. In the next chapter, we begin our examination of the three phases of life as a CNE with a discussion of NDS design. But before we get there, you'll need an NDS tree growing out of your head to make sense of it all. That's the goal of this chapter. We hope to generate enough neurokinetic energy to stimulate cranial growth. In other words, we're going to make you think until it hurts. So, without any further ado, let's start at the beginning — with the NDS database.

THE BRAIN

As a NetWare 4 CNE, you'll have two main **NDS responsibilities**—
design and management. **NDS** design focuses on the structural
organization of objects, partitions, and time servers. This material is
covered in excruciating detail in Chapter 4. **NDS** management takes
over from there. It deals with sophisticated utilities and daily
management tasks, including naming context, troubleshooting,
partition management, and time synchronization. These topics are
tackled in Chapters 8 and 9. So what are we doing here? In this chapter,
we're going to build a conceptual framework for all the fun to come.
This is just a general introductory discussion. The real meat-and-
potatoes happens later. So, open your mind and have fun. It'll be easier
on you if you don't fight it.

Getting to Know NDS

NDS is your friend. It may seem a little intimidating at first, but when you get to
know NDS, it's actually pretty fun. Really. NDS is a big Sta-Puff marshmallow man that
keeps track of your network's resources. In more technical terms, it's a distributed object-
oriented hierarchical database of physical network objects. Huh? Just think of it as a
huge WAN phone book. NDS classifies all network resources into 24 different objects.
These objects can be organized by function, location, size, type, or color—it doesn't
matter. The point is, NDS organizes network resources independently from their physical
location. When a user logs into the network, he/she can access any object in the tree
regardless of its location. This type of openness, however, does not come without a
price. One obvious problem is security—which is why NDS is controlled by a complex
impenetrable armor known as *NDS access rights*.

So what does NDS look like? From the outside, it looks like a big cloud hovering over
your network. On the inside, however, it's a hierarchical tree similar to the DOS file
system. As you can see in Figure 2.1, NDS organizes resources into logical groups called
containers. This is like Tupperware gone mad. In Figure 2.1, servers are organized
according to function. Then users are placed in the same container to simplify connectivity.
In addition, productivity increases because users are near the resources they use. NDS

also creates a global method of interconnectivity for all servers, users, groups, and other resources throughout the WAN. The bottom line is this—users don't access physical resources anymore. Instead, they access logical objects in the NDS tree. This means they don't need to know which NetWare server provides a particular resource. All they need to know is where the server exists in the logical NDS world.

A Tree in a Cloud

So is NDS worth it? Well, you have to make that decision for yourself. But here are some of its benefits:

- ▸ Global database providing central access to and management of network information, resources, and services.

- ▸ Standard method of managing, viewing, and accessing network information, resources, and services.

▶ Logical organization of network resources that is independent of the physical characteristics or layout of the network.

▶ Dynamic mapping between an object and the physical resource to which it refers.

So what do you think? Is NDS for you? Before you answer, let's take a moment to get to know NDS. Who knows—you might even like it.

THE "CLOUD"

NDS has many different names—the Directory, the tree, the "Cloud," the Sta-Puff marshmallow man. In reality, it's all of these things. But the most appropriate description is the "Cloud." NDS oversees physical network resources and provides users with a logical world to live in. This differs dramatically from what you're used to— NetWare 3.12. As you can see in Figure 2.2, the NetWare 3.12 bindery is *server-centric*. This means that every physical resource exists within and/or around the server. If Leia wants to access files or printers on multiple servers, she must have a log in account and security access on every one. This system makes access and management both repetitive and time consuming. Also note that nothing exists *above* the server. The server itself represents the highest level of the network organization structure. Users, volumes, files, and printers all exist within each server.

NDS, on the other hand, creates a whole new world *above* the server. As you can see in Figure 2.3, each network resource exists only once as a logical object in the "Cloud." NDS is *network-centric* in the sense that everything happens in the NDS hierarchy. Suddenly the server has gone from being at the top of the network organizational chart to being a physical object at the bottom. The beauty of this system is that Leia only logs in once and has instant access to all network resources. She doesn't log in to each server— she logs in to the NDS tree, and it tracks where her files and printers are. All log ins, attaches, and access rights are handled in the background by NDS. This is the epitome of user transparency. The beauty is that they don't need to see inside the "Cloud"; all they need to know is that their stuff is there.

F I G U R E 2.2

The NetWare 3.12 Flat
Server-Centric Bindery

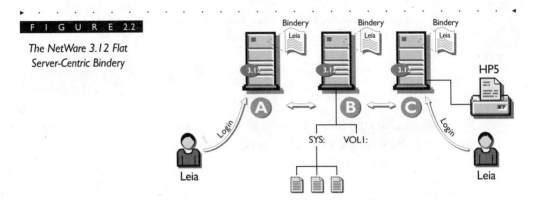

F I G U R E 2.2

The NetWare 3.12 Flat
Server-Centric Bindery

The main lesson to learn from the accompanying graphics is the direction of the arrows. In Figure 2.2, the arrows of communication are horizontal. This means that all communication exists within and between NetWare 3.12 servers. If Leia wants access to another resource, she must follow the horizontal communication path to another server by either re-logging in or attaching. In contrast, Figure 2.3 shows the communication arrows running vertically. This means that communication occurs from within and between the NDS Cloud and its physical resources. The NDS Cloud handles the problem of locating resources and transparently grabs whatever Leia wants. This vertical communication structure makes finding and using network resources much easier for the user. In addition, and this is the part you'll like, it provides a single point of central network management for CNEs.

Let's take a closer look at the difference between NDS and the NetWare 3 bindery.

F I G U R E 2.3

*The NetWare 4.1
Hierarchical Network-
Centric NDS Cloud*

QUIZ

Let me tell you a little story. Maybe you've heard it before. It's about
this little girl named Alice, who traveled through the "looking glass."
Are you with me, here? When Alice entered the Forest of Forgetfulness,
she didn't forget *everything*—only certain things. She often forgot her
name, and the one thing she was most likely to forget was the day of
the week.

Now, the Lion and the Unicorn were frequent visitors to the forest—
strange creatures. The Lion lies on Mondays, Tuesdays, and Wednesdays
and tells the truth on the other days of the week. The Unicorn, on the
other hand, lies on Thursdays, Fridays, and Saturdays, but tells the truth
on the other days of the week. One day Alice met the Lion and the
Unicorn resting under a tree. They made the following statements:

(continued)

Lion: Yesterday was one of my lying days.

Unicorn: Yesterday was one of my lying days.

From these two statements, Alice (who was a very bright girl) was able to deduce the day of the week. Can you?

(Q2-1)
(see Appendix C for quiz answers.)

NDS VERSUS THE BINDERY

The bindery is a flat-file database that tracks network resources on each server. It's stored as the files NET$OBJ.SYS, NET$PROP.SYS, and NET$VAL.SYS in the SYS:SYSTEM directory. The bindery uses these three files to track network objects, properties, and values. When users need to access a server's resources, they must log in and register with its respective bindery. If the server doesn't recognize them, it disallows access. Then the administrator must create a special entry with different access security for this user. This is painstaking and dumb.

NDS, on the other hand, stores information about network resources in a global database, called the Directory. This database is distributed on all servers in the WAN so that users can instantly get access to what they need. Suddenly you've been escalated from a lowly bindery user to the top of the NDS food chain. As an object, you exist at the same level as the NetWare 4 server. How does it feel?

Following is a brief comparison of NDS and the NetWare bindery. In each case, focus on NDS's network-centric approach.

- ▸ Database—The bindery is a flat-file database consisting of three files in the SYS:SYSTEM directory. Each server retains its own database. NDS, on the other hand, is an object-oriented hierarchical database, called the Directory. The Directory encompasses all objects in the WAN and is distributed across servers. It also consists of database files on the SYS: volume. These files are, however, protected in a system-owned special directory.

REAL WORLD

The Sta-Puff marshmallow man has to come down to earth sometimes. With all this flowery talk of clouds and trees, this simple fact remains—NDS is a database with parts of it stored on the SYS: volume of every NetWare 4 server. More specifically, the database is made up of four protected files in SYS:_NETWARE:

- ▸ BLOCK.NDS
- ▸ ENTRY.NDS
- ▸ PARTITIO.NDS
- ▸ VALUE.NDS

All these files are very hard to find. Take my word for it, they are there. If you need to see them yourself, use the Directory Scan option of RCONSOLE. See Chapter 13 (Netware 4 Management) for more details.

▸ Server—In NetWare 3, the server is king of the hill. It houses the bindery and controls all network resources. In NetWare 4, however, the server's importance diminishes quite a bit. It's simply another logical object in the global NDS tree. Network resources are accessed through the "Cloud"— independently from the physical server. But don't get caught up in the logical insignificance of the NetWare 4 server. In the physical realm, it's still king of the hill. After all, NetWare 4 has to be installed somewhere, files have to be stored somewhere, and users have to log into something.

▸ Users—In NetWare 3, users are defined as objects in the server-based bindery. You must maintain a user entry for every server to which a user needs access. In NDS, however, users are logical objects in the NDS Cloud. Each user is defined only once. The system takes care of tracking the resources to which they need access. This is made possible using a concept called *context,* which we'll explain a little bit later.

▶ Log in—Bindery log ins are server-centric. This means that users must log in or attach to every server they use a resource from—files, printing, or applications. NDS log ins are network-centric. This means that users issue one log in statement for access to the entire "Cloud." Once they're in, the world is at their fingertips.

TIP

In order for NDS to identify you, you must provide your "full NDS name" at context. This includes your log in name and user "context." There's that word again. A user's full name is a combination of who they are and where they live. My log in name, for example, would be DAVID in CALIFORNIA in the USA. We'll talk about this later in the NDS naming section in this chapter.

▶ Network Resources—In a bindery network, resources are owned by the server. Volumes and printers, for example, are tracked according to the server to which they're attached. User access to these resources requires log in or attachment to the host server. NDS, on the other hand, distributes network resources independently from the server to which they're attached. It might seem strange, but volumes can be organized across the tree from their host servers. It's possible for users to have access to the NetWare 4 file system without logical access to its host server. Very cool. But don't get too carried away. Physical volumes still reside inside NetWare 4 servers. We haven't figured out how to separate the two yet—that's NetWare 5!

As you can see, NDS is a huge improvement over the NetWare 3 bindery. NDS is actually not even an improvement—it's a complete revolution. Nothing is as it appears. So if NDS isn't what you think it is, what is it? Let's take a closer look.

ZEN

"The truth is out there."

The X-Files

COMPOSITION OF THE TREE

Plant a tree in a Cloud—it's good for the environment.

As in nature, the NDS tree starts with the [Root] and builds from there. Next, it sprouts container objects, which are branches reaching toward the sky. Finally, leaf objects flutter in the wind and provide network functionality to users, servers, and the file system. As you can see in Figure 2.4, the tree analogy is alive and well.

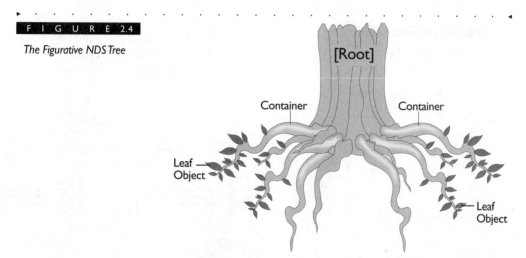

FIGURE 2.4

The Figurative NDS Tree

The real NDS tree is made up of special logical objects. NDS objects define logical or physical entities that provide organizational or technical function to the network. As you can see in Figure 2.5, they come in three different flavors:

- [Root]

- Container objects

- Leaf objects

The [Root] is the very top of the NDS tree. Because it represents the opening porthole to our NDS world, its icon is appropriately a picture of the earth. Container objects define the organizational boundaries of the NDS tree and house other container objects and/or leaf objects. In Figure 2.5, we use container objects to define the ACME organization and its two divisions—ADMIN and LABS. Finally, leaf objects are the physical network resources that provide technical services and WAN functionality. Leaf objects define the lowest level of the NDS structure. In Figure 2.5, leaf objects represent users, printers, servers, and a group. NDS supports 21 different leaf object types. We'll discuss these types in detail in the next section.

F I G U R E 2.5

The Real NDS Tree

The tree can be organized any way you want as long as it makes sense. AEinstein, for example, is placed near the resources he uses—the HP5 printer and LABS-SRV1 file server. In Chapter 4 (NDS Design), we'll learn more about the ACME organization and rules for tree design. For now, just focus on the conceptual framework of NDS and its tree structure.

On a more fundamental level, the NDS tree is stored in a fully replicated, globally distributed object-oriented database, called the Directory. The Directory consists of multiple hidden system files in the SYS:_NETWARE directory on each server. These files are replicated and distributed throughout the WAN to provide fault tolerance and increased connectivity. Although all NetWare 4 servers use NDS, they don't have to contain their own directory database. If a server contains a portion of the database, that portion is called a *partition*. If a server doesn't have a copy of the database, then it must access it from some other server—this is less efficient. The bottom line is that a NetWare 4 server can contain the entire directory database, pieces of it (partitions), or none at all.

In addition, NDS requires a temporal assurance system, called *time synchronization*. This means that everybody has to agree on what time it is. Time is critical to NDS because NetWare uses time stamps for synchronization, auditing, and NDS security. Time synchronization is implemented using a variety of different time server types, as you'll see later in this chapter.

Typically, a single network has only one directory. Although it's possible for a WAN to have multiple NDS trees, users can only be logged into one at a time. Also, resources cannot be shared between multiple trees. For this reason, Novell is pushing toward a single tree for the whole world. We'll see, but it sure explains the world icon for the [Root].

ZEN

"So be sure when you step, step with care and great tact. And remember that life's a great balancing act. Just never forget to be dexterous and deft. And never mix up your right foot with your left."

Dr. Seuss

Now that you understand the fundamental architecture of NDS, let's take a closer look at its different container and leaf objects. Remember, plant a tree in a Cloud—it's good for the environment.

NDS Objects

When you sprout a cranial conifer and become NDS-Head Fred, leaf objects and the [Root] will become important to you. I'd like to take this opportunity to help you out a little and explain them more. After all, even Daisy-Head Mayzie studied botany.

As we just learned, the NDS tree consists of three different objects—[Root], container, and leaf objects. What we didn't learn is that these objects have specific properties and values. Remember, NDS is, after all, a database. An object is similar to a record or row of information in a database table. The property is a field in each database record. For example, the properties of a sales database may be Name, Phone Number, and Last Item Purchased. Finally, values are data strings stored in each object property. These values define the information around which the database is built. Let's take a closer look.

UNDERSTANDING NDS OBJECTS

As we learned earlier, NDS objects define logical or physical entities that provide organizational or technical functionality to the network. They come in three different flavors:

▸ [Root]

▸ Container objects

▸ Leaf objects

As you can see, the tree analogy is alive and well. Figure 2.5 shows that objects come in many different shapes and sizes. They can be physical resources (printers and servers), NDS resources (groups), users or a logical tree organizer (containers). We'll take a closer look at each of NetWare 4's 24 different object types in just a moment.

Each NDS object consists of categories of information called *properties*. Properties are similar to fields in a database record which categorize types of information. User objects, for example, have properties such as Log in Name, Password, Postal Address, and Description. While the same type of object may have the same properties, the information within those properties can change. For example, two user objects both have a log in Name property but one has a value of Leia and the other has a value of AEinstein.

In addition, a unique collection of properties define the class of an object. For example, a Printer object differs from a User object in that it has different properties. The Printer object needs to track the default queue, for example, whereas users are more interested in generational qualifiers. NDS uses two different types of properties:

▸ Required properties—The NDS object cannot be created until these properties are completed. When creating an object, you are prompted for required values (for example, last name for users and host server/host volume for the Volume object).

▸ Multivalued properties—These properties support more than one entry. For example, the user properties' Telephone Number can hold multiple numbers that apply to a single user. Other user multivalued properties include Location and Fax Number.

Finally, values are the data stored in object properties. Refer to Table 2.1 for an illustration of the relationship between NDS objects, properties, and values.

TABLE 2.1	OBJECT	PROPERTY	VALUE
NDS Objects, Properties, and Values	User	Log in Name	AEinstein
		Title	Super smart scientist
		Location	NORAD
		Password	Relativity
	Printer	Common Name	HP5
		Default Queue	HP5-PQ1
		Print Server	LABS-PS1
	NCP Server	Full Name	LABS-SRV1
		Version	NetWare 4.10
		Operator	Admin
		Status	Running just fine

Now let's explore each of the 24 NDS objects in detail starting with [Root]. You never know which objects you're going to have sprouting from your cerebellum.

[ROOT]

The [Root] object defines the top of the NDS organizational structure. Each directory can only have one [Root], which is created during installation. The [Root] cannot be deleted, renamed, or moved. The NDS [Root] object is exceptional in that it begins the boundaries of your NDS world. It behaves very much like a container object in that it houses other container objects. The main difference is that the [Root] cannot contain leaf objects.

Each NDS object has a specific icon that depicts its purpose graphically. The [Root] object's icon is particularly interesting. Because the [Root] object represents the opening porthole to the NDS world, its icon is appropriately a picture of the earth. As you can see in Figure 2.6, the [Root] defines the top of our tree and houses the ACME container object.

FIGURE 2.6

Understanding NDS Objects

The [Root] can hold only these specific container objects:

- ▸ Country—An optional container object that designates the country where your network resides.

- ▸ Organization—A one-dimensional container that typically represents your company.

- ▸ Alias—A logical NDS pointer to any other object existing elsewhere in the tree. In this case, the Alias can only point to Country and Organization objects.

The [Root] object is exceptional in one other way. It's the only NDS object without any properties. It simply exists as a placeholder for the top of the tree structure. It can have trustees, however. As we'll see in Chapter 11 (Netware 4 Security), any rights you assign to the [Root] are inherited ancestrally by all objects in the tree—this is a bad thing. All in all, the [Root] is a cool object, but you can't do much with it. Most of your design and management tasks will involve container and leaf objects.

REAL WORLD

You might notice the square brackets ([ ]) surrounding the [Root] object. These brackets designate the object as a special NDS entity. NetWare 4 supports two other such entities— [Public] and [Supervisor]. [Public] is a special trustee that applies security to all other objects in the tree. Users can inherit the rights of [Public] without having to log in. They simply need to attach. As we'll see in Chapter 11, this creates a serious NDS security loophole.

[Supervisor] is a special superuser for bindery emulation. Users from the NetWare 3 world can log in to NDS using [Supervisor] and inherit all its special rights. [Supervisor] has other important properties that allow you to manage NetWare 3 and 4 coexistence.

CONTAINER OBJECTS

Container objects are logical organizers. They are the Tupperware bowls of our NDS kitchen. Actually the analogy works well—work with me here. The nature of Tupperware is that larger containers enclose smaller containers, which in turn house even smaller ones. Of course, the biggest Tupperware container in the world is the [Root]. Maybe in the future, when NDS takes over the world, we'll all be enclosed in a pale green airtight plastic bowl. Finally, Tupperware containers are used to store fruits and vegetables. In NDS, our Tupperware container objects store lettuce "leaf" objects. Sorry.

Here's a quick list of the three types of NetWare 4 NDS container objects:

- Country—designates the country where certain parts of the organization reside.

- Organization—represents a company, university, or department. NDS only supports one layer of Organization objects, hence, the term "one-dimensional."

> ▸ Organizational Unit—represents a division, business unit, or project team within the Organization. Organizational Units hold other Organizational Units or leaf objects. They are multidimensional.

Refer to Figure 2.6 for an illustration of the relationship between the [Root] and container objects. The ACME Organization houses other Organizational Units (including LABS), which in turn house leaf objects (like AEinstein). Let's take a closer look at these three different container objects.

ZEN

"I yelled for help. I screamed. I shrieked. I howled. I jowled. I cried, 'Oh save me from these pale green pants with nobody inside!'"

Dr. Seuss

Country Objects

The Country object is optional. It designates the country where your network resides and organizes other objects within the country. You can use a Country object to designate the country where your organization headquarters is or, if you have a multinational WAN, to designate each country that is part of your network. The Country object is also useful if you plan on cruising across the information superhighway.

As I said a moment ago, the Country object is optional. It is not created as part of the default NetWare 4 installation. You must specifically configure the Country object during installation of the very first server or it can never be used. Also, this object must be a valid two-character country abbreviation. These abbreviations are defined as part of the ISO X.500 standard. Most trees don't use the Country object. Finally, Country objects can only house NDS containers—Locality, Organization, and/or Organizational Units. They cannot support leaf objects. Leafs must be stored within Organization or Organizational Unit containers.

REAL WORLD

NDS supports a secret fourth container object type—Locality. The Locality object is like the Country object in that it's optional and not created as part of the default NetWare 4 installation. You can use a Locality object to designate the region where your organization headquarters resides. Unlike Country objects, Locality objects can reside either under Country, Organization, or Organizational Unit containers.

Organization Objects

If you don't use a Country object, the next layer in the tree is typically an Organization. As you can see in Figure 2.6, ACME is represented as an "O." You can use the Organization object to designate a company, a division of a company, a university or college with various departments, and so on. Every directory tree must contain at least one Organization object. Therefore, it is required. Many small implementations use only the Organization object and place all their resources directly underneath it. Organization objects must be placed directly below the [Root], unless a Country or Locality object is used.

Earlier we defined the Organization as a one-dimensional object. This means the tree can only support one layer of organizations. If you look at the icon closer, you'll see a box with multiple horizontal boxes underneath. Additional vertical hierarchy is defined by Organizational Units—they are multidimensional. We'll describe them in just a moment.

Figure 2.7 illustrates the Details screen of the ACME Organization. On the right side are the many page buttons, which identify categories of NDS properties. Associated with each page button is an input screen for a specific set of information. The Identification page button (shown here) allows you to define the following Organization properties:

- Name

- Other Name

- Description

- ▸ Location

- ▸ Telephone

- ▸ Fax Number

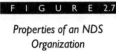

FIGURE 2.7

Properties of an NDS Organization

Similar page buttons allow you to configure important Organization parameters, including postal information, print job configurations, trustee assignments, and so on. As far as ACME is concerned, the Organization container defines the top of the functional tree.

Organizational Unit Objects

The Organizational Unit object is a "natural group." It allows you to organize users with the leaf objects they use. You can create group log in scripts, a user template for security, trustee assignments, security equivalences, and distributed administrators. All in all, Organizational Units are your friends.

Organizational Units represent a division, a business unit, or a project team. In Figure 2.6, the LABS OU represents a division within the ACME Organization. In this container, AEinstein works with his printers and servers. Organizational Units use the exact same properties as Organizations but in a slightly different way (see Figure 2.7). Organizational Units are multidimensional in that you can have many hierarchical levels of containers within containers. Remember, the Organization can only exist at one level.

Organizational Units are the most flexible Tupperware containers because they contain other OUs or leaf objects. Now let's take a look at the real stars of our NDS world—the leafs.

LEAF OBJECTS

Leaf objects represent logical or physical network resources. Most of your CNE life will be spent designing, installing, and managing leaf objects—you'll become a vegetarian very quickly. These are the ultimate entities that NetWare 4 users seek. Because leaf objects reside at the bottom of the NDS tree, they cannot hold other leafs. They represent the proverbial "end of the road." As we learned earlier, each type of leaf object has certain properties that hold information about it. This collection of properties differentiates the various leaf object classes. NetWare 4 supports six different categories for leaf object functionality:

- ▶ User leaf objects

- ▶ Server leaf objects

- ▶ Printer leaf objects

- ▶ Messaging leaf objects

- ▶ Informational leaf objects

- ▶ Miscellaneous leaf objects

QUIZ

Look, there's that mischievious Alice again. She's trying to figure out when to believe the Lion. He says he'll help her escape from this crazy world. On what days of the week is it possible for the Lion to make the following two statements:

1 • **I lied yesterday.**
2 • **I will lie again tomorrow.**

Please help Alice find her way home.

(Q2-2)

In this section, we'll explore each of these six categories and identify the key properties of all 21 NDS leaf objects. So what's stopping you? Let's get going.

User Leaf Objects

Users are the center of your universe. After all, they are the ones that "use" the network. NDS supports four different leaf objects that help users do what they do. Let's check them out:

▶ User—Represents a person who uses the network. The user can be a beginner, a gardener, or NDS-Head Fred. The only requirement is that every person who logs into the WAN must be represented by a unique User object. When you create a User object, you can create a home directory for that user, who then has default rights to the file system. In addition, you can define default log in restrictions using the special USER_TEMPLATE object. In Figure 2.6, AEinstein is a User object in the LABS Organizational Unit. Notice the name designator—"CN." This represents Albert's log in name or *common name*. As you can see in Figure 2.8, AEinstein has a plethora of user-related properties—55, to be exact. The page buttons on the right-hand side identify property categories such as identification, security restrictions, mailbox, print job configurations, log in script, and so on.

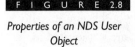

Properties of an NDS User
Object

TIP

NDS is a very powerful database with a lot of valuable user information. Consider using it as a central company database of employee data. If you can't find what you need in the 55 default properties, you can always create your own. The NetWare 4 SDK (Software Developers Kit) provides interface tools for modifying and adding NDS properties.

▶ Group—Defines an unrelated list of users for the purpose of assigning access rights and other management strategies. Remember, containers create "natural groups" for objects within the same Organization or Organizational Unit. The Group object, on the other hand, allows you to organize users from anywhere in the NDS tree. This is a great management strategy for assigning unrelated trustee rights or log in restrictions.

▶ Organizational Role—Defines a position or role within the Organization. If you want to assign security to a "position" instead of an "employee," consider creating an Organizational Role. The occupant can change frequently, but the responsibilities of the position will not. Whenever a user occupies the Organizational Role, they "absorb" its security. Some sample Organizational Roles include Postmaster, Chief Scientist, Administrative Assistant, and Coffee Jockey.

▸ Profile—NetWare 4's group log in script. The Profile object is a log in script that can be shared by a group of unrelated users. If you have users who need to share common log in script commands but are not located in the same portion of the tree, consider assigning them a profile. As we'll see in Chapter 12 the Profile log in script executes after the system log in script and before the user script.

Server Leaf Objects

The NetWare 4 server is still king of the physical hill. Even though it loses a lot of its significance in the logical realm, NetWare still resides on it, users still log in to it, and printers still attach to it. NDS supports three different leaf objects that apply to the logical server. Let's take a closer look:

▸ NCP Server—Represents any server running NetWare on your network. The server can be running NetWare 2, 3, 4, or 5 (although I'd be surprised by the latter). The NDS Server object is created automatically during installation. The only way to insert a logical object is to actually install NetWare and place it in the tree. You can, however, create virtual servers using the Alias object. We'll take a look at this strategy a little later. If you create a bindery-based server (NetWare 2 or 3), you'll need to manually create a logical NCP server object to make its file systems available. Some of the Server object properties can be seen in Figure 2.9. The page buttons provide some interesting informational categories including Identification, Error Log, Blocks Read, Blocks Written, Connect Time, and other dynamic statistics.

▸ Volume—Points to a physical volume installed somewhere on the WAN. A logical Volume object is created automatically for every physical volume installed during server creation. NWAdmin will allow you to browse the file system using an NDS Volume object. You can create other volumes as logical pointers from different parts of the tree. Otherwise, consider using the Alias object. In the Volume object's properties, you can store identification information such as the host server, volume location, and so on. You can also set restrictions for use of the volume such as disk space restrictions and attribute security. Interestingly, the NDS logical volume is stored independently from the physical server to which it's attached.

FIGURE 2.9

*Properties of an NDS
Server Object*

► Directory Map—Represents a logical pointer to a physical directory in the
NetWare 4 file system. Directory Map objects are an excellent tool for
centralizing file system management. Instead of creating drive mappings to
physical directories, you can create them to logical Directory Map objects.
Then when the physical location changes, you only have to change the one
central object. All drive mappings will then be updated immediately. Pretty
cool, huh?

ZEN

*"We see them come. We see them go.
Some are fast, and some are slow.
Some are high, and some are low.
Not one of them is like another.
Don't ask us why; go ask your mother."*

Dr. Seuss

Printer Leaf Objects

Like previous versions, NetWare 4 printing relies on three main elements—print queue, print server, and printer. Each of these printing elements is represented in the NDS tree as a leaf object. Users print to print queues where jobs are stored until the printer is ready. Once a job gets to the top of the queue, the print server redirects it to the appropriate printer. Sounds pretty simple to me—you be the judge. Here's a quick look at these three critical printer NDS objects:

▸ Printer—Represents a physical printing device on the network. This logical object allows users to find the printers they need. Every printer must be represented by a corresponding NDS object and placed in the same container as the users who print to it. Some of the critical printer properties can be seen in Figure 2.10. These include Location, Department, Organization, Assignments, Configuration, Notification, and Features.

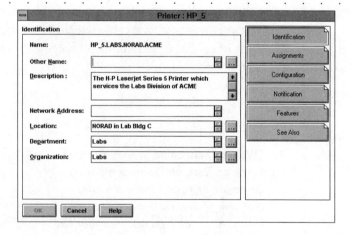

F I G U R E 2.10

*Properties of an NDS
Printer Object*

▸ Print Queue—Represents a logical print queue on the WAN. Every print queue must have a corresponding NDS object. Also, the location of the object in the tree directly impacts users' ability to print. Typically, the queues are stored in the same container as the users and printers to which they relate. NetWare 4 gives you the flexibility to assign print queues to any volume, not just SYS:. It's about time.

▸ Print Server—Represents a NetWare 4 or third-party print server. Once again, the print server should be placed in the same container as the printers and print queues it uses. Also, make sure your third-party print server software is NDS compatible. If not, you'll need to create Print Server objects manually for each of your different machines. This is especially important if your users are accessing the network through bindery emulation.

Messaging Leaf Objects

NetWare 4 includes an impressive messaging engine called MHS Services for NetWare 4. It utilizes the Message Handling Service (MHS) standard. When you install and configure MHS, a variety of messaging objects are created. These objects allow you to control communications between users throughout the WAN. For a complete discussion of MHS Services, consult Chapter 12 (Netware 4 Configuration). For now, here's what they look like:

▸ Messaging Server—Represents a messaging server residing on any NetWare 4 server. This object is created automatically during MHS Services installation. The messaging server sends, receives, and manages user e-mail.

▸ Message Routing Group—Represents a group of messaging servers that can transfer e-mail directly among each other. If users need to send e-mail to opposite sides of the tree, a Message Routing Group will bridge the gap.

▸ Distribution List—Represents a list of mail recipients for MHS Services. Instead of sending a message to every user individually, you can send it to the Distribution List. The MHS will then copy the message to each member individually. Using a Distribution List increases sending efficiency and cuts down on WAN traffic.

▸ External Entity—Represents a non-native NDS object that is imported for e-mail purposes. MHS Services uses this object to represent users from bindery-based directories or external e-mail. This way, other non-MHS users could participate in e-mail Distribution Lists and other NDS activities.

Informational Leaf Objects

Most of the leaf objects so far have performed an obvious network function. Two other objects, however, exist for one purpose only—to store information. The AFP Server and Computer objects allow you to categorize information about non-critical physical resources such as AppleTalk servers and workstations. Let's take a closer look:

▸ AFP Server—Represents an AFP-based server running the AppleTalk file protocol. This service can be running on a NetWare server or native Macintosh machine. The point is that this object provides NetWare services to Apple Macintosh workstations. The AFP Server object has no effect on network operations—it only stores information about the AFP server including Description, Location, and Network Address.

▸ Computer—Represents a non-server network computer, including workstations, routers, and notebooks. Once again, this object has no effect on network operations; it only stores information about computers. This is, however, an excellent opportunity to integrate NDS and your inventory database. A plethora of computer properties are available to you, including Description, Network Address, Serial Number, Server, Owner, and Status.

Miscellaneous Leaf Objects

No list would be complete without the final category—miscellaneous. There are four NDS leaf objects that don't fall into any other category. They're dominated by the Alias object, which points to any of the 23 previous resources. In addition, there are Bindery objects, Bindery Queues, and, of course, the Unknown leaf object—whose icon, interestingly enough, is a user with a paper bag over its head. Let's check them out:

▸ Alias—A logical pointer to any other leaf or container object in the NDS tree. Think of it as an NDS "chameleon." When you create an Alias, it assumes the icon form of its host object. Although it may look like there are two AEinstein users, only one really exists in the tree. The other is a fake pointer. The beauty of the Alias is that it allows you to distribute objects outside of their parent container. If, for example, users in Admin need access to information about AEinstein, you can place an Alias of him in the Admin container. This way, he appears to live there, but in reality it's simply a logical pointer to the real Albert Einstein in OU=LABS (see Figure 2.11).

Understanding the Alias Object

Be very careful with the Alias object. In many cases, you can't tell an Alias from the real Albert Einstein. If you delete or rename an Alias, nothing happens to the host. But if you accidentally mistake the host for the Alias and delete it, all of its Alias objects disappear into Never-Never Land. Actually, they become Unknown leaf objects.

▶ Unknown—Represents an NDS object that has been invalidated or cannot be identified as belonging to any of the other 23 classes (for example, when an Alias becomes invalidated because the user deleted the Alias's host). If you have any Unknown objects, you may want to research where they came from: It's probably a bad sign.

▶ Bindery—Represents an object placed in the NDS tree by an upgrade or migration utility. Bindery objects are used by NDS to provide backward compatibility with bindery-based utilities. This way users can access the resource from NetWare 3 workstations.

▸ Bindery Queue—Represents a print queue placed in the NDS tree by an upgrade or migration utility. This is a special type of Bindery object that points to older NetWare 3 print queues. Users accessing the tree through Bindery Services can print to bindery-based queues. Otherwise, you'll need to create a true print queue NDS object for everybody else.

That's all of them. We've discussed every NDS object supported by NetWare 4. You'll want to get to know them well because all future discussions center around how to organize, design, and manage these cute little network entities. Once you understand the relationships between NDS objects, you can start building your tree. As you've seen in this discussion, every leaf and container object is represented by an icon graphic that depicts its purpose. For example, printers are printers, servers are computers, and users are people. These icons are used throughout this book and in graphical NDS utilities. NWADMIN, for example, uses icons to provide a snapshot of the entire NDS tree in a hierarchical structure. This feature makes it easier for administrators and users to locate and use NetWare 4 resources.

ZEN

"Look what we found in the park in the dark. We will take him home, we will call him Clarke. He will live at our house, he will grow and grow. Will our mother like this? We don't know."

Dr. Seuss

Overview of NDS Design and Management

Now that you understand what the NDS tree is made of, we need to explore how it works. Three main topics dominate NDS design and management:

▸ NDS naming

▸ NDS partitioning

▸ Time synchronization

NDS naming defines rules for locating leaf objects. One of the most important aspects of a leaf object is its position in the NDS tree. Proper naming is required when logging in, accessing NDS utilities, printing, and for most other management tasks.

NDS partitioning deals with database performance and reliability. Since the tree houses all your network resources, it can grow large very quickly. As with any database, size can decrease performance and reliability. For this reason, NetWare 4 has a built-in database distribution feature called partitioning and replication. Partitioning breaks the database tree into small pieces and replication places those pieces on multiple servers. This strategy increases database performance and provides distributed fault tolerance.

Time synchronization is a temporal assurance scheme that forces all NetWare 4 servers to agree on what time it is. This is particularly important because all NDS background operations and security strategies rely on a time stamp. Time synchronization is accomplished through the use of four different time server types. We'll explore these types a little later in this chapter.

In Part II (NetWare 4 Design) we're going to explore naming, partitioning, and time synchronization from a design point of view. There's a lot you need to understand about how these concepts work *before* you install the very first server. Then, in Part IV (NetWare 4 Management), we'll dedicate two chapters to managing these key NDS elements. But, for now, let's take an introductory look at how NDS naming, partitioning, and time synchronization work. Keep in mind that the real meaningful discussions will occur in later parts of this book.

NDS Naming

Your name identifies you as a truly unique individual. Let's take NDS-Head Fred, for example. This name says "Hi, I'm Fred, and I have an NDS tree growing out of my head!" In much the same way, an NDS object's name identifies its location in the hierarchical tree. NDS naming impacts two important NetWare 4 tasks:

- Log in—You need to identify your exact location in the NDS tree in order for NetWare 4 to authenticate you during log in.

- Resource Access—NDS naming exactly identifies the type and location of NetWare 4 resources including file servers, printers, log in scripts, and files.

The whole NetWare 4 NDS naming scheme is much more complicated than "Hi, I'm Fred." It requires both your name and location. For example, a proper NDS name would be "Hi, I'm Fred in the ADMIN division of ACME." As you can see in Figure 2.12, Fred's NDS name identifies who he is and where he works. This naming scheme relies on a concept called *context*.

FIGURE 2.12

Getting to Know the Real "Fred"

"...of ACME"

O=ACME

"...in the Admin division ..."

OU=ADMIN

"I'm Fred ..."

CN=Fred

CN=ADMIN-SRV1

Context defines the position of an object within the directory tree structure. When you request a particular network resource, you must identify the object's context so that NDS can find it. NetWare 4 uses very specific naming guidelines for creating an object's context, and we'll review these in just a moment. For now, let's explore why naming standards are so important.

ZEN

"Who am I? My name is Ned. I do not like my little bed. This is no good. This is not right. My feet stick out of bed all night."

Dr. Seuss

Novell recommends that before you implement NDS, you create a document that describes your naming standards. The NDS naming rules we're going to learn here only work if object names are consistent across the WAN. A naming standards document provides guidelines for naming key container and leaf objects including users, printers, servers, volumes, print queues, and Organizational Units. In addition, it identifies standard properties and value formats. Consistency, especially in the naming scheme used for objects, provides several benefits:

► Consistent naming schemes provide a guideline for network administrators who will add, modify, or move objects within the directory tree.

► Having the naming standards eliminates redundant planning. The standards give CNEs an efficient model to meet their needs but leave implementation of resource objects open and flexible.

► Consistent naming schemes help users identify resources quickly, and this maximizes users' productivity.

► Consistent naming allows users to identify themselves easily during log in.

In Chapter 4 (NDS Design) we'll explore NDS naming standards in great detail. In addition, you'll get an opportunity to create a naming standards document for ACME. For now, let's focus on NetWare 4 rules for using NDS names. I can't think of a better place to start than context.

CONTEXT

As we learned above, the whole NDS naming strategy hinges on the concept of context. Context defines the position of an object within the directory tree structure. When you request a particular network resource, you must identify the object's context so that NDS can find it.

In Figure 2.12, Fred's context is "...in the ADMIN division of ACME." This context identifies where Fred lives in the NDS tree structure. It identifies all container objects leading from him to the [Root]. In addition to context, Figure 2.12 identifies Fred's common name (CN). A leaf object's common name specifically identifies it within a given container. In this example, the user object's common name is "Fred."

Two objects in the same NDS tree may have the same common name—provided, however, that they have different contexts. This is why naming is so important. As you can see in Figure 2.13, our NDS tree has two "Fred"s, but each has a different context.

F I G U R E 2.13

Understanding NDS
Context

Each NDS object has a naming type associated with it. This naming type is identified with a one- or two-character abbreviation:

- ▸ O=Organization container

- ▸ OU=Organizational Unit container

- ▸ CN=common name of leaf object

Also notice the syntax used to create an object's context. In Figure 2.13, Fred's context is created by identifying each of his containers in reverse order leading to the [Root]. Each container is separated by a period.

There are two types of NDS context:

- ▸ Current context

- ▸ Object context

Let's take a closer look.

Current Context

Current context defines "where you are" in the NDS tree at any given time. This is *not* "where you live." This is a very important distinction. In Figure 2.13, for example, Fred "lives" in OU=ADMIN.O=ACME. But at any given time, he can hang out in O=ACME or OU=LABS.O=ACME.

This is all made possible by *tree walking.* Tree walking allows users to navigate anywhere within the NDS tree structure. Fred's current context impacts the utilities he uses and the resources he can access. In technical terms, current context is a logical pointer in the NetWare DOS Requester, which identifies the NDS default container for your workstation. Simply stated, it's where you are, not where you live.

A user's current context can be set in one of the following ways:

▶ During login, using the NAME CONTEXT statement in NET.CFG.

▶ With the CONTEXT log in script command.

▶ At any time, using the CX utility.

As we'll see in just a moment, current context also impacts how you approach object naming. As a matter of fact, it is the foundation of *distinguished naming.*

Object Context

In contrast to current context, object context defines "where you live." In Figure 2.13, for example, Fred's object context is OU=ADMIN.O=ACME or OU=LABS.O=ACME, depending on which Fred you're talking about. Context is identified by listing all containers starting from Fred and moving back toward the [Root]. Object context is used for two important purposes:

▶ Logging in

▶ Accessing resources

When logging in, users must provide their complete object context. In Figure 2.13, for example, Fred would type:

```
LOG IN .CN=FRED.OU=ADMIN.O=ACME
```

In addition to logging in, you'll need a resource's object context when trying to access it. This is particularly important for file servers, printers, Profile log in scripts, Directory Map objects, volumes, and groups. The server in Figure 2.12, for example, has the same object context as Fred, that is, OU=ADMIN.O=ACME. Since Fred and the server have the same object context, they can refer to each other by their common names. Isn't that friendly?

You can view information about an object's context or change your own current context by using the CX command line utility. Let's take a closer look.

Using CX

CX is the key NetWare 4 utility for dealing with NDS context. It allows you to perform two important tasks:

▶ Change your workstation's current context

▶ View information about any resource's object context

CX is a relatively straightforward command with a great deal of versatility. As a matter of fact, it's similar to the file system CD command in its general approach. If you type CX by itself, the system displays your workstation's current context. This is marginally interesting at best. CX really excels when you combine it with one or more command line switches. Here are some of the more interesting ones:

▶ CX—View your workstation's current context.

▶ CX /T—View the directory tree structure below your current context.

▶ CX /A /T—View all objects in the directory tree structure below your current context.

▶ CX /R /A /T—Change your current context to the [Root] and view all objects in the directory tree.

▶ CX /CONT—List containers only below the current context in a vertical list with no directory structure.

- CX /C—Scroll continuously through output.

- CX .OU=ADMIN.O=ACME—Change your current context to the ADMIN container of ACME.

- CX /?—View on-line help and all CX options.

- CX /VER—View the version number of the CX utility and the list of files it executes.

Probably the most useful CX option is

- CX /R /A /T

I'm sure there's a hidden meaning somewhere in the rodent reference. Regardless, the CX /R /A /T option displays the relative location of all objects in the NDS tree (see Figure 2.14).

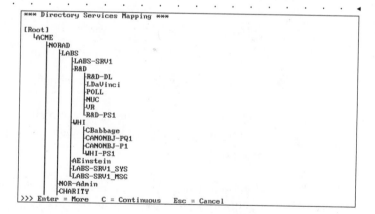

FIGURE 2.14

Using CX /R/A/T in the ACME Tree

```
*** Directory Services Mapping ***

[Root]
  ᴸACME
     ┣NORAD
     ┗LABS
        ┣LABS-SRV1
        ┣R&D
        ┃  ┣R&D-DL
        ┃  ┣LDaVinci
        ┃  ┣POLL
        ┃  ┣NUC
        ┃  ┣UR
        ┃  ┗R&D-PS1
        ┣WHI
        ┃  ┣CBabbage
        ┃  ┣CANONBJ-PQ1
        ┃  ┣CANONBJ-P1
        ┃  ┗WHI-PS1
        ┣AEinstein
        ┣LABS-SRV1_SYS
        ┗LABS-SRV1_MSG
     ┣NOR-Admin
     ┗CHARITY
>>> Enter = More    C = Continuous    Esc = Cancel
```

ZEN

"My alphabet starts with this letter called YUZZ. It's the letter I use to spell YUZZ-A-MA-TUZZ. You'll be sort of surprised what there is to be found once you go beyond 'Z' and start poking around!"

Dr. Seuss

If you don't remember where you live, the CX utility can be your guide. You can use it before logging in to find your home context if you are in the F:\LOG IN directory. It can also be used by administrators to print out the complete NDS tree structure every Friday afternoon. Of course, this can be a valuable asset to your NetWare 4 log book. All in all, CX is a very useful utility for dealing with NDS navigation and object naming.

Now that you've discovered the importance of *context*, it's time to review how it impacts NDS naming rules. Knowing where you live is only half of the equation. Now we have to discover exactly who you are.

NAMING RULES

Home is where the heart is. Similarly, your network productivity is defined by the container you live in—your context. To access resources efficiently, you must be in proximity to them. Otherwise, security and naming gets more difficult. Context is the key.

Now that we understand how NDS context works, let's review the naming rules associated with it:

► Current context defines your workstation's current position in the directory tree.

► An object's context defines its home container.

► Each object has an identifier abbreviation that defines it for naming purposes (O=Organization, OU=Organizational Unit, and CN=common name of leaf objects).

► Context is defined by listing all containers from the object in reverse order to the [Root]. Each object is separated by a period.

► Context is important for logging in and accessing NDS resources.

So there you have it. That's how context works. With this in mind, it's time to explore the two main types of NDS names:

- ► Distinguished names

- ► Typeful names

Distinguished Names

An object's distinguished name is its complete NDS path. It is a combination of common name and object context. Each object in the NDS tree has a unique distinguished name that identifies it as an individual from all other objects in the tree. In Figure 2.12, Fred's distinguished name would be "I'm Fred in the ADMIN division of ACME."

Notice how the distinguished name identifies Fred as an individual and the context in which he lives. Similarly, in Figure 2.13, Fred's NDS distinguished name would be .CN=Fred.OU=ADMIN.O=ACME. Once again, Fred's distinguished name is a combination of his common name and his context.

Here's another example (refer to AEinstein in Figure 2.15). AEinstein's context is OU=R&D.OU=LABS.O=ACME. His common name is CN=AEinstein. Therefore, his distinguished name as a simple mathematical addition of the two: .CN= AEinstein.OU=R&D.OU=LABS.O=ACME.

Elementary, my dear Einstein, elementary. There's no "new math" here; only simple addition. If you want complex calculations, refer to Chapter 11 (Netware 4 Security).

Notice the use of periods. Neither the context nor the common name started with a period but the distinguished name did. The leading period identifies the name as a complete distinguished one. Otherwise, it is assumed to be an incomplete, or *relative*, distinguished name. A relative distinguished name lists an object's path from itself up to the current context—not the [Root]. The relativity part refers to how NDS builds the distinguished name. Remember, all objects must have a unique distinguished name. The relative distinguished name is simply a short cut.

It seems appropriate to demonstrate the relative distinguished name concept with the help of Albert Einstein.

FIGURE 2.15

Building AEinstein's Distinguished Name

ZEN

"The Scientific Theory I like best is that the rings of Saturn are composed entirely of lost airline luggage."

Mark Russell

Again, refer to Figure 2.15. If AEinstein's current context was the same as his object context OU=R&D.OU=LABS.O=ACME, then his relative distinguished name would be the same as his common name CN=AEinstein. But life is rarely this simple. What if Albert Einstein used the CX command to change his current context to

OU=LABS.O=ACME? What would his relative distinguished name be now? See Figure 2.16. Correct! His relative distinguished name would become CN=AEinstein.OU=R&D. When you add this to his current context of OU=LABS.O=ACME, you get the correct distinguished name:

.CN=AEinstein.OU=R&D.OU=LABS.O=ACME

Piece of cake. Once again, notice the use of periods. The relative distinguished name does not use a leading period. This identifies it as a relative, not complete distinguished name.

Building AEinstein's Relative Distinguished Name

Current Context=OU=LABS.O=ACME
Relative=CN=AEinstein.OU=R&D

Therefore ....

Distinguished Name=.CN=AEinstein.OU=R&D.OU=LABS.O=ACME

As you can see, object and current context play a very important role in distinguished and relative distinguished naming. Whether it's fair or not, you are defined by the place you live. Of course, it can get even weirder. NDS supports trailing periods, which allow you to change the current context while using relative distinguished naming...as if that wasn't hard enough already. The bottom line is that each trailing period moves the current context up one container.

It seems simple at first, but it can get crazy very quickly. Let's take Leia, for example. She lives in the ADMIN container. If we were in LABS, she couldn't use a relative distinguished name to identify herself—or could she? A single trailing period would move her current context up to O=ACME. Then she could use a relative distinguished name to move down the ADMIN side of the tree (see Figure 2.17). Her current context would be OU=LABS.O=ACME, and her relative distinguished name would be:

CN=Leia.OU=ADMIN.

The resulting distinguished name would be Leia's relative name plus her new current context (remember, the trailing period moved the current context from OU=LABS.O=ACME up to O=ACME). That is, her distinguished name would be:

.CN=Leia.OU=ADMIN.O=ACME

Piece of cake. It gets even weirder if Leia's current context is:

OU=R&D.OU=LABS.O=ACME

In this case, her relative distinguished name would be:

CN=Leia.OU=ADMIN..

Are we having fun yet? Just like anything in life, it's very important where you place your dots. Here's a quick summary:

▶ All objects in the NDS name are separated by dots.

▶ Distinguished names are preceded by a dot. This identifies them as complete.

▸ Relative distinguished names are *not* preceded by a dot. This identifies them as incomplete.

▸ Trailing dots can only be used in relative distinguished names, and they modify the current context. Each dot moves the context up one container.

FIGURE 2.17

Using Trailing Periods

New Current Context

Relative

O=ACME

OU=ADMIN   OU=LABS

CN=Fred
CN=Leia   OU=R&D
CN=HP5
                          CN=AEinstein
                          CN=Fred
Original Current Context=OU=LABS.O=ACME   CN=R&D-SRV1
Relative=CN=Leia.OU=ADMIN .
New Current Context=O=ACME

Therefore ....

Distinguished Name=.CN=Leia.OU=ADMIN.O=ACME

For a complete summary of NDS distinguished naming rules, refer to Table 2.2. Now let's step back in reality for a moment and explore the other NDS naming category—typeful names.

T A B L E 2.2		DISTINGUISHED NAMES	RELATIVE DISTINGUISHED NAMES
Getting to Know Distinguished Naming	What it is	Complete unique name	Incomplete name based on current context
	How it works	Lists complete path from object to [Root]	Lists relative path from object to current context
	Abbreviation	DN	RDN
	Leading period	Leading periods required	No leading periods allowed
	Trailing periods	No trailing periods allowed	Trailing periods optional

Typeful Names

Typeful names use attribute type abbreviations to distinguish between the different container types and leaf objects in NDS names. In all the examples to this point, we've used these abbreviations to help clarify context, distinguished, and relative distinguished names. The most popular abbreviations are:

- ▶ C: Country container

- ▶ O: Organization container

- ▶ OU: Organizational Unit container

- ▶ CN: common name of leaf objects

These attribute types help to avoid confusion that can occur when creating complex distinguished and relative distinguished names. I highly recommend that you use them. Of course, like most things in life—they are optional! You can imagine how crazy NDS naming gets when you choose not to use these attribute abbreviations. This insanity is known as *typeless naming*.

Typeless names operate the same as typeful names, but they don't include the object attribute type. In these cases, NDS has to "guess" what object types you're using. Take the following typeless name, for example:

.Admin.ACME

Is this the Admin Organizational Unit under ACME? Or is this the Admin user under ACME? In both cases, it's a valid distinguished name, except one identifies an Organizational Unit container and the other identifies a user leaf object (see Figure 2.18). Well, here's the bottom line—which one is it? It's up to NDS.

F I G U R E 2.18

Getting Confused with Typeless Naming

Fortunately, NetWare 4 has some guidelines for "guessing" what the object type should be.

1 • The leftmost object is a common name (leaf object).

2 • The rightmost object is an Organization (container object).

3 • All middle objects are Organizational Units (container objects).

QUIZ

Once again, we return to the Land of Forgetfulness and find Alice in cranial combat with the Lion. She still hasn't figured him out. Here's the question on the table: When can the Lion say, "I lied yesterday and I will lie again tomorrow."? *Warning!* **The answer is *not* the same as that of the preceding problem!**

Hmmm

(Q2-3)

Although this works for most cases, it's only a general guideline. Many times, typeless names are more complex. Take our example in Figure 2.18, for instance. We know now that the rightmost object is an Organization, but what about "Admin?" Is it a common name or an Organizational Unit? We still don't know. Fortunately, NetWare 4 includes numerous exceptions to deal with complex typeless scenarios. Here's how it works:

> ► Exception Rule 1: Container objects—NetWare 4 utilities are intelligent enough to resolve their own typeless names depending on what they are trying to accomplish. CX, for example, is used primarily for changing context. If you apply the CX command to a typeless name, it assumes the leftmost object is an Organization or Organizational Unit. This is because you can't change context to a leaf object. Other utilities that allow you to change context include NETADMIN and NWAdmin. In summary, here's how our example from Figure 2.18 would look with the CX utility:

CX .ADMIN.ACME—.OU=ADMIN.O=ACME

▶ Exception Rule 2: Leaf objects—Similarly, resource-based utilities recognize the leftmost object of a typeless name as a leaf object. Many of these utilities are expecting to see a common name. The most prevalent are LOG IN, MAP, and CAPTURE. Here's how it works for our example in Figure 2.18:

LOG IN .Admin.ACME—.CN=Admin.O=ACME

▶ Exception Rule 3: Mixed naming schemes—It is possible to generate an NDS name that mixes both typeless and typeful naming. In this case, the typeful abbreviation is used as a reference point for resolving the typeless portion of the name. NDS simply focuses on the typeful portion and moves to the left. All subsequent typeless objects are assigned one less abbreviation. Here's an example from Figure 2.18:

.ADMIN.O=ACME—.OU=ADMIN.O=ACME

Of course, this mixed NDS name would be resolved differently if CX or LOG IN were involved. Some exception rules take precedence over others.

▶ Exception Rule 4: Using current context—If all else fails, NDS uses the current context as an example of NDS naming. If your typeless name has the same number of objects as the current context, it assigns attribute abbreviations accordingly. For example, if your current context was .OU=LABS.O=ACME, the typeless name in Figure 2.18 would become .OU=ADMIN.O=ACME.

In another example, let's assume the Country object is involved. If your current context was OU=LABS.O=ACME.C=US, then .ADMIN.ACME.US would become .OU=ADMIN.O=ACME.C=US.

If, however, the typeless name has a different number of objects as the current context, the default NDS naming rules apply. That is, rightmost Organization, leftmost common name, and all intervening Organizational Units.

> ▶ Exception Rule 5: Country object—The Country object messes up NDS defaults in almost all cases. Naming is no exception. The Country object is a special circumstance and is assumed *not* to exist. If you introduce the Country object in either the current context or a typeful portion of the name, you'll run into trouble. In this case, NDS tries to resolve the name using any of the exception rules above. If they don't apply, it isolates the Country object and applies the defaults to the rest of the typeless name. Pretty weird, huh?

There you have it. This completes our discussion of typeless names and NDS naming in general. As you can see, this is a very important topic because it impacts all aspects of NDS design, installation, and management. No matter what you do, you're going to have to use the correct name to log in or access NDS resources. As we've learned, an object's name is a combination of "who they are" (common name) and "where they live" (context).

Congratulations! You are now a professor of NDS nomenclature. And nomenclature is important. After all, where would we be without names for all of our stuff. Here are a few important ones:

> ▶ Biochip—A computer chip that relies on the biological function of proteins and enzymes to send signals rather than on the flow of electrons, theoretically producing faster computers, often called biocomputers or organic CPUs. Also, the foundation of NetWare 4 NDS.

> ▶ Butterfly effect—The major impact resulting from a minor force left unchecked over a long time such as the multiplying of a draft from a butterfly's wings in Beijing to a hurricane in Rio. This is the foundation of chaos theory. And we all know that chaos theory impacts a CNE's existence more than anything.

> ▶ Cocktail diplomacy—Verbal persuasion and discussion rather than warfare, terrorism, or other forceful tactics of international political procedure. Also, the preferred way of dealing with NetWare 4 users.

> ▶ Cyberphilia—The love of computers and anything to do with computers. In extreme cases, this is said to lead to "CNE widow"—a person who has lost their spouse to the fascinations of NetWare 4.

▸ Electropollution—Excessive amounts of electromagnetic waves in the environment resulting from the increasingly widespread use of electricity and the electronic equipment it powers. Many believe it will eventually lead to EMI overload and an innate propensity to feel blades of wet grass between one's toes.

▸ Faddict—A person who compulsively follows a temporary fashion. This condition has been described as *faddiction*. Of course, we know the latest fad is NetWare 4 CNE-ism.

As you can see, there's a lot to NDS nomenclature. Stay tuned throughout the book for more fascinating "neo-words." For now, let's shift our focus from naming to partition management. NDS partitioning is the second of our three NDS management concepts. Don't forget your seat belt.

NDS Partitioning

As you will quickly come to appreciate, the NDS tree grows and grows and grows. Before you know it, you'll have a huge monstrosity on your hands—the size of Jupiter. Fortunately, NetWare 4 includes a segmentation strategy known as NDS partitioning. *Partitioning* breaks up the NDS tree into two or more pieces that can be separated and distributed, which makes dealing with NDS objects more manageable.

Since the NDS tree is stored in a database, pieces of the database can be distributed on multiple file servers. This strategy is known as *replication*. NDS replicas provide two important benefits to the "Cloud":

▸ Replicas increase network performance by decreasing the size of database files and placing resources closest to the users who need them.

▸ Replicas increase fault tolerance because extra copies of the database are distributed on multiple servers throughout the WAN.

NDS partitions have nothing to do with the logical disk partitions you're used to on the server disk. NDS partitions are logical pieces of the "Cloud," which can be distributed on multiple servers. Hard disk partitions are physical divisions of the internal disks that separate the NetWare operating system from DOS. Although these two concepts are unrelated, they work together in an odd way—one is stored on top of the other. To really mess up your mind, note that logical NDS partitions are stored on internal disk partitions—brain drain!

ZEN

"Oh, the thinks you can think up if only you try!"

Dr. Seuss

As you can see in Figure 2.19, NDS partitioning simply breaks the ACME organization into two pieces:

- ▸ Partition A—Known as the [Root] partition because it is the only one that contains the [Root] global object.

- ▸ Partition B—Known as the LABS partition because OU=LABS is the highest container object in that segment. In addition, Partition B is termed a *child* of Partition A because LABS is a subset of the ACME Organization.

Partitioning has many advantages because it allows you to separate the tree into smaller segments. Since 90 percent of all the resources accessed by users are within their own partitions, CNEs can increase efficiency by locating users near the resources they use the most. We can also increase network fault tolerance by placing copies of other partitions on local servers. This is known as replication. NetWare 4 allows you to create four different types of NDS replicas:

- ▸ Master

- ▸ Read/Write

- ▸ Read-Only

- ▸ Subordinate Reference

But I digress. Let's not get ahead of ourselves. To understand the distribution of NDS replicas, we first need to explore the concept of partitioning. More specifically, we need to understand why partitions are important and what they do for us. Granted, NDS replication is more important to you—as a CNE. But you have to start somewhere. And we're going to start with partitions.

UNDERSTANDING NDS PARTITIONS

To understand partitioning, we need to review the characteristics of our NDS Cloud:

▸ It is a database that replaces the bindery.

▸ It contains data on all objects in the Directory tree including their names, security rights, and property values. All network information except the file system comes from the Directory.

▶ It is network-centric, not server-centric, like the older bindery. This allows the Directory to track *all* network resources throughout the WAN.

▶ NDS uses the Directory for access control to other objects in the WAN. NDS checks the Directory to make sure that you can view, manipulate, create, or delete resource objects.

▶ NDS uses the Directory for authentication—an important part of logging in.

▶ Except for the Server and Volume objects, the Directory does *not* contain information about the file system. NetWare 4 data is still restricted to internal server volumes.

Partitioning is the process of dividing the Directory into smaller, more manageable pieces. These pieces can then be distributed near the users that need them. As you can see in Figure 2.19, the ACME tree has been partitioned into two segments—the [Root] partition and the LABS partition. Notice that partitioning occurs along the boundaries of container objects. All the leaf objects in a container are included in the same partition as their parent. Also notice that a partition is named for the container closest to the [Root]. In the case of Partition B, this would be OU=LABS. The topmost container object in the partition is termed the *partition root object*. I know this is confusing, but it serves an important purpose. This container is the parent of all other child partitions in this segment of the tree. And, as we all know, parents know best. If you get confused, remember this one simple rule: [Root] with square brackets ([Root]) describes the top of the world. There is only one [Root] partition. On the other hand, Root without square brackets (root) simply describes the topmost container in a given partition. Every partition must have a partition root object; therefore, there can be many of them.

Once again, returning to Figure 2.19, Partition A is the [Root] partition and Partition B is the LABS partition, with OU=LABS as the partition root object. No sweat.

ZEN

"Did I ever tell you how lucky you are?
Thank goodness for all the things you are not!
Thank goodness you're not something someone forgot
and left all alone in some punkerish place.
Like a rusty tin coat hanger hanging in space."

Dr. Seuss

As a CNE, you have total control over NDS partitioning. You can decide how, when, and where they are created. To simplify things, NDS gives you two simple choices:

▸ Centralized

▸ Distributed

In small network environments, centralizing the Directory makes it easier to manage the information in its database. The response time for users is adequate as long as the number of users and devices in the partition remains small. In this context, the term *small* means a network with roughly one to ten servers or 100 to 5000 objects, all in the same location and not connected by WAN links. If your network meets this criteria, you probably will not partition the NDS database at all. Instead, you'll leave the tree as a single database and replicate it on each of your servers. This strategy is simple and employs the NetWare 4 defaults.

On the other hand, if your network is large or has several sites with many servers, you may want to partition the Directory. Partitioning also implies distributed replication. By distributing the database, you will increase the availability of the information and provide quicker access for users. In addition, distributed replication increases fault tolerance because extra copies of the database are available throughout the WAN.

Assuming you choose the distributed approach, NDS partitioning is inevitable. Unfortunately, NetWare 4 doesn't help you out at all. By default, only the [Root] partition is created during initial server installation. All subsequent servers are added to this partition. It's up to you, as a NetWare 4 CNE, to create a new partition for each new server. In partitioning, the server is the key. Remember, partitions are replicated as portions of the database on distributed NetWare 4 servers. For this reason, you want to create new partitions for each new server. Well, maybe not every new server. Here are a few guidelines to think about:

▸ Each time the first server is installed in a new container, consider creating a partition at that container level. All subsequent servers in the same container should then receive replicas of the existing partition.

▸ Every time you add a new location to the NDS WAN, consider creating a container for the new location and defining a partition around it. It's assumed that new locations will bring along their own servers.

▸ For organizational purposes, consider creating a partition for each new container object even if it doesn't have its own server. This helps segment Organization-based NDS information. Also, it allows you to plan ahead in case servers are ever added to the new container.

▸ Try to create a pyramid shape when creating NDS partitions. The top level of the tree should have fewer partitions than the lower layers. This triangular design allows you to distribute the partitions relatively close to leaf objects (particularly users). This encourages you to create small partitions and distribute them closer to the users who access resources. In addition, it also increases fault tolerance by distributing many multiple segments of the database.

Keep in mind, though, that size and number of partitions can significantly affect the synchronization and responsiveness of your network. Avoid creating partitions that are too large (greater than 5000 objects) or with too many servers (more than ten) because they take too long to synchronize, and managing all replicas becomes more complex. On the other hand, avoid partitions that are too small (fewer than 100 objects). If a partition contains only a few objects, the access and fault tolerance benefits may not be worth the time you invest in managing it.

As you can see in Figure 2.20, we've installed a new server (R&D-SRV1) in the new OU=R&D subcontainer of OU=LABS. By default, this container and all its objects (particularly the server) will be added to the existing LABS partition. According to our new philosophy, we should create an additional partition for the new container and its objects (particularly the server). Using PARTMGR or NWADMIN, we create Partition C at the OU=R&D container. This becomes the R&D partition. Now we can distribute replicas of each of the three partitions to each of the three servers in our ACME NDS tree.

Replicas are good! They allow us to increase resource access and fault tolerance by distributing copies of partitions to multiple servers throughout the WAN. Now that we've created our partitions, it's time to distribute copies (replicas) of them to strategic servers. That's NDS replication. Don't worry—this is only an appetizer. We will revisit NDS partitioning in much more detail later in Chapter 4 (NDS Design) and Chapter 9 (Partition Management and Synchronization). For now, let's introduce replication.

FIGURE 2.20

Creating a New R&D Partition

NDS REPLICATION

If you build the partitions...they will come!

Earlier we learned that NDS partitioning provides two key advantages—resource access and fault tolerance. Well, actually partitioning doesn't do anything. It only breaks up the database into little pieces. It's how we distribute these pieces to NetWare 4 servers that provides the advantages. So it's more accurate to say that NDS replication provides two key advantages:

► Resource access—Replication allows you to place resources closest to the users who access them. This decreases the time needed for authentication, modification, and information queries. It also increases the probability that information will be retrieved from the nearest available server. This limits the amount of traffic sent over slow and expensive WAN links. In addition, replication allows for faster *name resolution*. Name resolution is an NDS process that allows you to access information outside your current partition. Every partition stores pointers to servers containing parent and child information. An organized replication strategy allows NDS to find remote objects more quickly.

► Fault tolerance—Replication distributes exact copies of database segments to multiple servers throughout the WAN. If your local copy becomes unavailable or corrupted, another copy can be used for authentication or resource access. With replication, users can access the network even when their local server, router, or WAN link goes down. The goal is to never have a single point of failure in the NetWare 4 Cloud.

It sounds too good to be true. Well, in many cases, it is. There's a cost associated with replication—synchronization delays. Since replicas need to be updated constantly, synchronization becomes an important issue. As you add more replicas, you create more synchronization traffic. This background overhead slows down critical data traffic—especially over WAN links. Also, replica management can be a nightmare as you continue to build up and modify the NDS tree. So the real trick becomes, How do I optimize replica distribution and minimize synchronization delays? Just like any puzzle, the solution is staring you in the face. You just need to figure out where all the little pieces go. Fortunately, NetWare 4 includes four different replica types for dealing with this crazy puzzle. Let's take a closer look.

ZEN

"My shoe is off, my foot is cold.
I have a bird, I like to hold.
My hat is old, my teeth are gold.
And now my story is all told."

Dr. Seuss

Replica Types

As we learned earlier, NetWare 4 includes four different replica types. Each has its own advantages and disadvantages. Some are created by default and others apply only to specific circumstances. Before you get excited about distributing NDS replicas, learn what each of the four types can do. Here's a quick look:

- ▶ Master—A Read/Write copy of the original partition. Each partition has only one Master replica. When you first define a partition, the Master is created by default. If you would like to redefine a partition boundary or join it with another, you must be able to access the server that holds the Master replica of that partition. This is the key difference between the Master and other replica types. If the Master replica becomes unavailable for any reason, you can upgrade any Read/Write replica using PARTMGR or NWADMIN.

- ▶ Read/Write—A Read/Write copy of any partition. Each partition may have multiple Read/Write replica copies. When you change objects in a Read/Write replica, those changes are propagated to all other replicas of the same partition. This process, known as *replica synchronization*, creates background traffic over WAN communication lines. Both Master and Read/Write replicas generate synchronization traffic. Be careful how many of these replicas you distribute. Finally, Read/Write replicas cannot be used to redefine partition boundaries—that requires a Master.

- ▶ Read-Only—A Read-Only copy of any partition. These replicas are used for searching and viewing objects only. You cannot make any changes to a Read-Only replica. These replicas receive synchronization changes from Read/Write and Master copies. They do not generate any replica synchronization traffic.

▸ Subordinate References—A special replica created and maintained by NDS. A Subordinate Reference is created automatically on a server when it contains a parent replica but not any of the children. In simpler terms, Subordinate References are created on servers "where parent is but child is not." Think of it as NDS babysitting. The key difference is Subordinate References do not contain object data—they point to the replica that does. This facilitates tree connectivity. The good news is that if you eventually add a child replica to the server, the Subordinate Reference is removed automatically.

There you have it: The four NDS replica types. In general, Read/Write replicas are the most popular for CNE management. Master replicas are created automatically during partitioning, and Subordinate References flourish throughout the tree as needed. Read-Only replicas, however, can be very effective if you have many servers and few containers. Now that you understand the different replica types, it's time to distribute and manage them.

Before we learn how to manage these four different replica types, let's revisit Subordinate References. I sensed a blank stare when we came across that bullet. The bottom line is, that Subordinate References increase tree connectivity by providing bridges to partitions you don't have. In Figure 2.20, for example, the ADMIN-SRV1 server gets a Master replica of the [Root] Partition. That's all! Initially it is cut off from all other portions of the tree—namely Partitions B and C. This is where Subordinate References come in. NetWare 4 bridges the gap by placing a Subordinate Reference of Partition B on the ADMIN-SRV1 server. This way, Leia can access information about AEinstein by pointing to the OU=LABS container. In turn, LABS-SRV1 has a Subordinate Reference of Partition C. This allows AEinstein to manage the R&D Group. Hopefully, you can see how Subordinate References bridge the gap by providing pointers to partitions you don't have. Without them, you'd be isolated in your own little private Idaho.

Now that we've cleared that up, let's take a closer look at managing default and new NDS replicas.

Managing NDS Replicas

As we learned earlier, partitioning itself doesn't accomplish anything productive. It simply breaks the NDS database into little pieces. Replication is where the real action is. Replication allows us to distribute these pieces among strategically placed servers. We also learned that NetWare 4 doesn't partition by default. It does, however, include a simple default replication strategy: *Every partition should be replicated at least three times.*

When you install a new NetWare 4 server, its host partition expands. No new partition is created. Replication of the partition depends on how many servers already exist. The first server on a partition gets the Master replica. The second and third new servers receive a Read/Write replica. All other servers in the same partition are replica-deprived. Remember, the basic premise is that every partition should be replicated at least three times.

When you merge directory trees, source servers with [Root] replicas receive Read/Write replicas of the new [Root] Partition. They also receive Subordinate Reference replicas to the [Root]'s child partitions. Next, target servers with [Root] replicas receive Subordinate References of the top-level partition of the source tree. This allows both source and target servers to share information about one another's objects—both new and old. Finally, a NetWare 3 upgraded to NetWare 4 receives a Read/Write replica of all partitions containing the server's bindery context.

So those are the defaults. It's a great place to start, but don't think of it as the end-all. As a matter of fact, it's only the beginning. As a NetWare 4 CNE, you should take NDS partitions and replication very seriously. Once a new server has been installed, you should consider creating a new partition around its parent container. This strategy is illustrated in Figure 2.20 with the addition of R&D-SRV1.

Also consider placing Read/Write replicas of other partitions on the new server. In Figure 2.21, we've demonstrated a strategy known as *saturated replication.* This means that every server has either a Master or Read/Write replica of every partition in the tree.

FIGURE 2.21

Saturated Replication in the ACMENDS Tree

Saturated replication works fine when there's a small number of servers. In large environments, however, it's not very practical because of synchronization delays. Replica updates take place automatically at specific intervals. Some updates, such as changing a user's password, are immediate (within 10 seconds). Other updates, such as log in updates, are synchronized every five minutes. Changes made to Figure 2.21, for example, would generate 27 replica updates—that's 3^3. This is manageable. But consider what background traffic would look like with 50 servers and 20 different partitions—that's 9,536,743,164,062,000,000,000,000,000,000,000 updates every few minutes. Wow!

QUIZ

Numbers can be challenging, fascinating, confusing, and frustrating, but once you have developed an interest in them, a whole new world is opened up as you discover their many characteristics and patterns. Numbers can be divided into many different categories, including amicable, abundant, deficient, perfect, and delectable numbers.

Amicable numbers are pairs that are mutually equal to the sum of all their aliquot parts: for example, 220 and 284. The aliquot parts of 220 are 1, 2, 4, 5, 10, 11, 20, 22, 44, 55, and 110, the sum of which is 284, while the aliquot parts of 284 are 1, 2, 4, 71 and 142, the sum of which is 220. There are seven known pairs of amicable numbers, the largest of which are 9,437,056 and 7,363,584.

Abundant, deficient, and perfect numbers can be linked together because all numbers fit into these categories. An *abundant number* is one such that the sum of all its divisors (except itself) is greater than the number itself: for example, 12, because its divisors (1, 2, 3, 4, and 6) total 16. The opposite of this is a *deficient number*, where the divisors total less than the number itself: for example, 10, whose divisors (1, 2 and 5) total 8. If a number is not abundant or deficient, then it must be a *perfect number*, which means that it equals the sum of its aliquot parts: for example, 6, where its divisors (1, 2, 3) also total 6. Perfect numbers were first named in Ancient Greece by the Pythagoreans around 500 BC and to date, only 30 have been discovered. The first four perfect numbers were discovered before AD 100, and they include 6 and 496. However, the next (33,550,336) was not found until the fifteenth century. With the help of computer technology, the process of discovering new perfect numbers has been speeded up and the latest to be found has no fewer than 240 digits. One fact that has emerged is that all the perfect numbers now known are even numbers. However, no one from the time of Euclid to the present day has been able to prove that it is mathematically impossible for a perfect odd number to exist.

So, having dealt with amicable, abundant, deficient, and perfect numbers, what, may you ask, is a *delectable number*? The answer is that a nine-digit number is delectable if (a) it contains the digits 1 to 9 exactly once each (no zero) and (b) the numbers created by taking the first *n* digits (*n* runs from 1 to 9) are each divisible by *n*, so that the first digit is divisible by 1 (it always will be), the first two digits form a number divisible by 2, the first three digits form a number divisible by 3, and so on. Only one delectable number is known. Can you find out what it is?

Matching:

A) Abundant	1) 10
B) Perfect	2) 220
C) Deficient	3) 381654729
D) Amicable	4) 12
E) Delectable	5) 8128
	6) 284
	7) 386451729
	8) 28

(Q2-4)

All of this synchronization magic is accomplished within a group of servers known as a *replica ring*. A replica ring is an internal system group that includes all servers with replicas of a given partition. In Figure 2.21, the replica ring for Partition A includes:

▸ A—Master: CN=ADMIN-SRV1.

▸ A—R/W: CN=LABS-SRV1.

▸ A—R/W: CN=R&D-SRV1.

All synchronization takes place within the replica ring. The synchronization delay is greater when servers within a replica ring are separated by slow WAN links. Therefore, you'll want to keep track of replica rings and organize their distribution accordingly.

We will explore some time-proven replica distribution strategies in Chapter 4 (NDS Design). Then, in Chapter 9 (Partition Management and Synchronization), we'll dive more deeply into key facets of replication management, including fault tolerance, traffic efficiency, unsynchronized replicas, and DSTRACE. But first, let's finish off with a few general guidelines for managing NDS replicas:

► Fault tolerance—To meet fault tolerance needs, plan for three or more strategically placed replicas of each partition. You should also plan for possible WAN link failures whenever necessary. Don't place the entire replica ring in a single portion of the global network. This creates a single point of WAN link failure.

► Traffic efficiency—Generally only the information that's updated (Delta) gets sent across the network; however, when you place a new replica, the entire file is copied. Each object takes up roughly 3 KB of space. So large replicas can be in excess of 10 MB in size. Consider placing large replicas during low-traffic time periods.

► Work groups—Create partitions that follow the boundaries of functional work groups. Then place replicas of each partition on the servers that are physically close to the users within that work group. This balances productivity and traffic efficiency.

► Logging in—Users need access to a Master or Read/Write replica for log in authentication. In addition, NDS updates all appropriate replicas when the user logs in. For these reasons, consider distributing local Read/Write replicas closest to the servers users attach to. Let's return to Figure 2.21 as an example. Consider what happens when all ACME directors return to ADMIN headquarters for the annual meeting. AEinstein attaches to the ADMIN-SRV1 server. Since this server is part of his home partition's replica ring, he can authenticate locally. This increases log in speed and decreases background synchronization traffic.

► [Root]—The [Root] partition is the most important segment of the entire NDS tree. Replicate it often. Consider creating a Read/Write replica of the [Root] partition on all geographically distributed servers. If you lose this partition, the entire network becomes inaccessible. There is a caveat, however. In the pyramid replica design, the [Root] partition has many children. Each server that receives replicas of the [Root] partition also receives Subordinate References for all of its child partitions. This may create more synchronization traffic than you initially intended. Be careful.

▶ Bindery Services—Make sure to follow a server's *bindery context* when distributing replicas. As we'll learn a little later, a server's bindery context lists all containers available to non-NDS users from this server. To work properly, the bindery server must have a Master or Read/Write replica of all containers in its bindery context. Don't worry—we'll revisit this topic multiple times later in the book.

▶ Moving containers—Because moving a container object directly affects partitions, it is considered a partitioning operation. You'll have to use the Partition Manager tool in NWADMIN to move a container. Before you do so, the container must be the highest object in its local partition. As you remember from our earlier discussion, this is called the partition root object. If you try to move the container without making it a partition root, an error message will appear. Once you've moved the container, give NDS a few minutes to resynchronize itself and update all objects with their new distinguished names. In addition, you may have to change the NAME CONTEXT statement in NET.CFG to reflect name changes. Finally, remind your users that they now have a new identity—since their home has moved.

Well, there you have it. That's partitioning and replication in a nutshell. In Chapter 4 (NDS Design), we'll explore partitioning design in more detail. And you'll get a chance to create a replication strategy for ACME. Then we'll carry our discussion further in Chapter 9 (Partition Management and Synchronization), where we'll explore NetWare 4 partitioning tools and some special strategies for managing and troubleshooting NDS replicas.

For now, sit back, relax, and wallow in your newfound knowledge. There's time for only one more NDS management topic—time synchronization.

ZEN

"Waiting for the fish to bite or waiting for wind to fly a kite. Or waiting around for Friday night or waiting perhaps for their Uncle Jake or a pot to boil or a better break or a string of pearls or a pair of pants or a wig with curls or another chance. Everyone is just waiting."

Dr. Seuss

Time Synchronization

"Does anybody really know what time it is; does anybody really care?"

NDS does. As a matter of fact, NDS has to! Every aspect of NDS existence relies on time. Sound familiar? Time synchronization is a method of ensuring that all NDS objects report the same *time stamp*. Time stamps are important for:

▸ Replica synchronization

▸ Messaging

▸ Log in authentication and time-based security

▸ File and directory operations

Time stamps report time according to the Universal Time Coordinated (UTC) equivalent. This is a time system that adjusts to the local time zone and Daylight Savings Time. It is also equivalent to Greenwich Mean Time (GMT). UTC is calculated using three values for each time server:

▸ Local time

▸ +/– time zone offset from UTC

▸ – Daylight Savings Time offset

For example, the San Francisco, California, time is eight hours behind GMT. Therefore, if the time in San Francisco is 12:00 noon and there is no Daylight Savings Time, UTC is 20:00.

All of this fancy temporal footwork is accomplished during server installation with the Time Configuration Parameters Worksheet (see Figure 2.22). With this worksheet, you can define your new NetWare server as one of four different *time servers*. Time servers provide a consistent source for the time stamps that NDS and other features use. Each time you install a NetWare 4 server, you must provide it with specific time configuration parameters, including time server type and the above three UTC values.

► · ◄

F I G U R E 2.22

*Time Configuration
Parameters Worksheet in
INSTALL.NLM*

```
┌──────────────────────────────────────────────────────────────────────────┐
│ NetWare Server Installation  4.1                     NetWare Loadable Module│
│ Verify/Enter Time Configuration Information For This Server                │
│ ┌────────────────────────────────────────────────────────────────────────┐│
│ │ Time server type:                            Single Reference            ││
│ │                                                                          ││
│ │ Standard time zone abbreviation:             MST                         ││
│ │ Standard time offset from UTC:               7:00:00  BEHIND             ││
│ │                                                                          ││
│ │ Does your area have daylight saving time (DST): YES                      ││
│ │ DST time zone abbreviation:                  MDT                         ││
│ │ DST offset from standard time:               1:00:00  AHEAD              ││
│ │ DST Start: First Sunday of April at  2:00:00 am                          ││
│ │ DST End:   Last Sunday of October at  2:00:00 am                         ││
│ └────────────────────────────────────────────────────────────────────────┘│
│ ┌────────────────────────────────────────────────────────────────────────┐│
│ │ Standard Time Zone Abbreviation Help                                     ││
│ │                                                                          ││
│ │ Enter the abbreviation for your time zone (standard time).  This string is││
│ │ mainly for display and formatting purposes and may be changed later in your││
│ │ AUTOEXEC.NCF configuration file.   For example, if this server is being  ▼││
│ │                 ─(To scroll, <F7>-up <F8>-down)─                         ││
│ └────────────────────────────────────────────────────────────────────────┘│
│ Continue and save time parameters <F10>       Previous screen      <Esc>   │
│ Help                               <F1>        Abort INSTALL <Alt><F10>     │
└──────────────────────────────────────────────────────────────────────────┘
```

Let's explore the four different time server types and discuss the advantages and disadvantages of each.

TIME SERVER TYPES

All NetWare 4 servers are *time servers* of some type. Time servers create and manage time stamps. There are two general categories of time servers: time providers and time consumers. *Time providers* provide time and are categorized as Primary, Reference or Single-Reference servers. *Time consumer servers* request their time from a provider and are categorized as Secondary servers.

Regardless, all time servers have the same fundamental responsibilities. First, they provide time to any requesting time provider, time consumer, or workstation. Second, they manage time synchronization and make sure everybody agrees what time it is. And, finally, they all adjust their internal clocks to correct discrepancies and maintain a consistent time across all NetWare 4 servers.

QUIZ

**If my three were a four,
And my one were a three,
What I am would be nine less
Than half what I'd be.
I'm only three digits,
Just three in a row,
So what in the world must I be?
Do you know?**

Hint: Synergy.

(Q2-5)

So which time server are you?

- Single-Reference—A time provider. This is the default configuration for most small WANs. It provides time to Secondary servers and cannot coexist with Primary or other Reference servers.

- Reference—A time provider. These servers act as a central point of time control for the entire network. They get their time from an external source such as the Internet or an atomic clock.

- Primary—A time provider or time consumer. These servers work together with other Primary servers to "vote" on the correct time. This voting procedure determines network UTC in combination with values received from Reference servers.

> ▸ Secondary—A time consumer. This is part of the default configuration. These servers do not participate in voting and are told what the time is by other time providers.

Let's take a closer look.

Single-Reference Time Servers

As we learned above, this is the default configuration for most small WANs. If used, it stands alone as the only time provider on the entire network. Therefore, it cannot coexist with Primary or Reference time providers (see Figure 2.23). All other NetWare 4 servers in the same tree default to the Secondary time server type.

F I G U R E 2.23

Default Time Configuration with Single-Reference and Secondary Servers

It's important to note that time servers never send out their time automatically. They must be asked to report their time. This only happens when a server's *synchronization flag* has been activated. The synchronization flag occurs when the server is confident that its internal clock is within a *synchronization radius* of accepted time. The synchronization radius defaults to 2000 milliseconds (two seconds). You can adjust this value through SERVMAN. The key point here is that Single-Reference servers always activate their synchronization flag because they're the only ones on the network that matter.

Finally, Single-Reference time servers typically get their time from their own internal clock. You can, however, connect the server to a more reliable external time source such as the Internet, a radio clock, or atomic time provider.

REAL WORLD

It is possible for a Single-Reference time server to coexist with other time providers; however, it's not recommended. The Single-Reference time server will not check with the other time providers when sending out NDS time stamps. As far as it's concerned, the Single-Reference server is always right.

Reference Time Servers

Reference time servers are like Single-Reference servers in that they provide a central point of time control for the entire network. These time providers almost always get their time from an external source including the Internet, radio clocks, and/or atomic providers.

Reference time servers differ from Single-Reference servers in one important area—they CAN coexist with Primary servers. As you can see in Figure 2.24, Reference time servers provide time to primaries. Primaries then vote on what time they think it should be and eventually provide time to Secondary time consumers. Even though voting occurs with Reference time servers, it's important to note that *they always win*! No matter what time the primaries decide it is, they eventually agree with the Reference server. It's like saying, "Go ahead and argue about the time as long as your answer eventually matches mine." The Reference server is given higher priority because it's thought to be more reliable. This is because of its external time source. If you use the internal server clock, you're defeating the purpose of Reference and Primary voting.

FIGURE 2.24

Custom Time Configuration with Reference and Primary Servers

If you have a Reference server, why bother with primaries at all? It's simple—fault tolerance. If the Reference server ever goes down, the primaries can take over and negotiate time for all the Secondary time consumers.

ZEN

"Today you don't have to be tidy or neat. If you wish, you may eat with both hands and both feet. So get in there and munch. Have a big munch-er-oo! Today is your birthday! Today you are you!"

Dr. Seuss

Primary Time Servers

Primary time servers work together to vote on the correct time. This voting procedure can operate with or without the help of a Reference server. In either case, Primary servers vote every five minutes and adjust their internal time 50 percent of the time value discrepancy. They do not correct 100 percent because of oscillation errors. The 50 percent correction allows all the time servers to eventually converge on a single time stamp. This convergence is made easier with the presence of a Reference server since it provides an ultimate goal. Without a Reference server, multiple primaries continue to vote until two of them agree. At this point, both synchronization flags are set and Secondary servers receive the new time stamp.

There are a few important configurations in this scenario. First, there's the *polling interval*. This is the waiting period between votes. By default, it's five minutes. Next, there's the question of who votes with whom. In one configuration method, all primaries vote with everybody, whereas in another, you can specify exactly who votes with whom. We'll explore these options a little later. Finally, there's the *offset threshold*—that is, by how much should a Primary be allowed to change its clock during voting? The default is two seconds. The offset threshold is also a configurable parameter. Refer to Chapters 4 and 9 for more detailed information concerning Primary time server configuration.

Refer to Figure 2.24 for a review of Primary and Reference server voting. Notice that Secondary consumers ultimately get their time stamp from Primary servers. Again, this increases fault tolerance by creating redundant time providers.

Secondary Time Servers

Secondary time servers are part of the default configuration. These are the ultimate *time consumers*. They do not participate in voting and are told exactly what time it is by any of the other three time providers. Remember, time providers only give time stamps when they're asked for them. This puts the responsibility on the shoulders of Secondary time servers. Every five minutes they poll a specific time source for the correct time. If there's a discrepancy, the Secondary server changes its internal clock by 100 percent. By default, this time polling occurs every five minutes. (Of course, this is configurable.)

Probably 90 percent of your NetWare 4 servers will be Secondary time consumers. In a generic configuration with 100 servers, you may have seven primaries, a Reference, and 92 Secondary time servers. It sure puts things in perspective.

For a summary of these four different time server types, refer to Table 2.3. Now that you're a time-server pro, let's take a closer look at the two different methods for accomplishing time synchronization—default and custom.

T A B L E   2.3

Getting to Know NetWare 4 Time Servers

FIRST SERVER TYPE	TIME PROVIDER	DESCRIPTION	GETS TIME FROM	ADJUSTS CLOCK	GIVES TIME TO
Single-Reference	Yes	Default configuration. Only services Secondary time servers.	Internal clock mostly	No	Secondary
Reference	Yes	Same as Single-Reference except it participates in Primary voting.	External source mostly	No	Primary and Secondary
Primary	Yes	Participates in voting to determine correct time stamp.	Voting procedure or Reference server	Yes. 50 percent correction per polling interval	Secondary
Secondary	No	Default configuration. Consumes time stamp from other time providers.	Single-Reference, Reference, or Primary	Yes. 100 percent correction per polling interval	Clients only

TIME CONFIGURATION

NetWare 4 provides you with two methods for accomplishing time synchronization:

▸ Default

▸ Custom

The default method assumes that only two types of time servers are necessary—Single-Reference time providers and Secondary time consumers. This method is simple and efficient but does not provide the flexibility required by large NDS implementations. The custom method, on the other hand, requires administrative planning. It uses Reference, Primary, and Secondary servers to minimize a single point of failure. In addition, the custom configuration method cuts down on network traffic by minimizing unneeded synchronization chatter. This is accomplished with the help of TIMESYNCH.CFG—a custom time configuration file. Let's take a quick look at how it works. Remember, there will be a lot more time for in-depth design issues in Chapter 4 and detailed management issues in Chapter 9.

Default Time Configuration

The default NetWare 4 installation assumes only two types of time servers are necessary—Single-Reference and Secondary. This default method is simple and efficient. It also doesn't require any special time synchronization reconfiguration when new servers are added to the network. They're just defined as Secondary time consumers.

The default method uses the Service Advertising Protocol (SAP) to advertise time from Single-Reference to Secondary servers. Although SAP is fast over a single network segment, it can overburden slow WAN links. Be careful not to set too many time providers (no more than two) on either side of a slow link. The time synchronization traffic might adversely affect network performance. Also ensure that SAP filters around the network do not impede SAP traffic. Remember, NDS doesn't require SAP, and many administrators choose to turn it off. If this is the case, you'll have to use TIMESYNC.CFG and the custom method.

The default method may not be ideal for large NDS implementations with many sites connected by WAN links. If you decide to add Primary servers, the voting process could involve more network traffic than necessary. All in all, the default time configuration method is a good choice for small to medium implementations. It has the following advantages:

▸ It is easy to understand and requires no planning.

▸ It does not require a special custom configuration file. You don't have to provide any configuration information to time providers because the default method relies on SAP for time stamp advertisement.

▸ SAP is fast and dynamic. If you add or delete services from the server, the updates happen quickly.

▸ The chance of synchronization error is reduced because time consumers only talk to specific time providers. They never negotiate with other Secondary servers.

On the other hand, the default time configuration has its shortcomings—it's not the cat's meow. Here're some disadvantages:

▸ The Single-Reference server must be contacted by every other Secondary on the network. If a WAN link goes down, Secondary time servers are left wandering in temporal space. This can cause a time/space continuum anomaly—that's bad.

▸ Using SAP means that a misconfigured server may disrupt the network. Some of the Secondary servers may synchronize to an unsynchronized time provider rather than to the authorized Single-Reference server. If NDS events occur with improper time stamps, you'll run into real trouble.

▸ One time source means a single point of failure. However, should a Single-Reference server go down, a Secondary time consumer can easily be set as the Single-Reference server using SERVMAN.

Custom Time Configuration

The custom configuration method is not difficult, but it requires some planning. It uses Reference and Primary servers as time providers to minimize a single point of failure. You'll need to know the physical layout of your network before using the custom configuration method. This helps you to distribute time providers (see Chapter 4). To use the custom configuration method, you'll need to determine which servers are time providers and where Secondary servers should go for synchronization.

For the custom configuration method to work, each server is given a special configuration file—TIMESYNCH.CFG. This file provides an internal listing for time-server guidance. For Reference and Primary servers, TIMESYNC.CFG provides a voting list; for Secondary servers, TIMESYNC.CFG defines a *time provider group*.

The custom configuration method cuts down on network traffic but requires a great deal of administration. It is appropriate for networks with more than 30 servers in distributed geographic locations. Here are some of its advantages:

▸ As a NetWare 4 CNE, you have complete control of the time synchronization hierarchy. You can control who votes with whom and tell Secondary servers where to get their time.

▸ You can optimize network traffic and distribute time sources around the world.

▸ You can provide redundant time synchronization paths and alternate time providers in case of network failures.

But the custom configuration method is not the cat's meow, either. There are many circumstances when its additional administrative overhead is not justified. Here are a couple of disadvantages:

▸ Customization requires careful planning, especially on a large network. Imagine reconfiguring numerous TIMESYNC.CFG files when the tree has changed or the company moves locations. No thanks!

▸ Network expansion involves too much work and reconfiguration.

It's pretty easy to see that the default configuration works well for small networks (fewer than 30 servers), and the custom configuration method works well for large networks (greater than 30 servers). If you choose the custom configuration method, try to create a pyramid hierarchy structure for time providers and time consumers (see Figure 2.24). Also, keep the number of time providers as small as possible to reduce network traffic. You can further enhance network performance by making sure time consumers get their time stamp from local servers—not over WAN links.

We're all out of time! (Pun intended.)

ZEN

"Oh! The places you'll go! You'll be on your way up! You'll be seeing great sights! You'll join the high fliers who soar to high heights!"

Dr. Seuss

That's everything you need to know about the "Cloud." Well, not really, but it's a very good start. Remember, every cloud has a silver lining and this chapter has been yours. Can you feel the *twinge* in the crown of your cranium? Has your NDS tree begun to sprout? Pretty soon, you'll be NDS-Head Fred!

The goal of this chapter was to make you think until it hurt—to generate enough neurokinetic energy to stimulate cranial growth. Have we succeeded? You be the judge. It all started with an NDS getting-familiar period. Once you were comfortable with the concept of a tree in a cloud, we learned about the 24 different objects that live there—including the [Root] and leaves. We learned that NDS objects come in two different flavors: Tupperware containers and physical leaf resources. We learned about Countries, Users, Distribution Lists, and the Alias object (if that's what it's really called).

With objects come names. Names uniquely identify "who we are" and "where we live." It works much the same way in NDS. NDS naming was the first of three important management topics we covered. We learned about the common name (who) and context (where). And we learned how these two are combined to create the distinguished name.

Then we explored partitioning—the second NDS management topic. NDS partitions are small pieces of the larger NetWare 4 puzzle. We can distribute these pieces on servers throughout the WAN for increased fault tolerance and better resource access. This process is known as replication. We learned about the four different NDS replica types and how and when they can be used. By now, the [Root] should have been forming around your cerebellum.

The final NDS management topic is time synchronization. NDS has to know what time it is: Time stamps are required for logging in, NDS replication, and many other important network tasks. This is accomplished with the help of three different time providers (Single-Reference, Reference, and Primary) and one special time consumer server (Secondary). We not only learned about servers, we explored two different configuration methods (default and custom). That's just about when we ran out of time!

So here we are—NDS-Head Fred! So far, we've explored the basics of NetWare 4 and the intricacies of NetWare Directory Services. That completes our discussion of CNE basics. Now you're ready to start the *real* journey:

- ▸ NetWare 4 Design

- ▸ NetWare 4 Installation

- ▸ NetWare 4 Management

Don't be scared—I'll be with you every step of the way. And we'll return to these topics many times again. This is only the beginning and I can't wait for you to become a full-fledged superhero....

ZEN

"Today is gone. Today was fun. Tomorrow is another one. Every day from here to there funny things are everywhere."

Dr. Seuss

To complete this exercise, you will need Admin-level access to a NetWare 4 NDS tree. You will explore the NDS tree structure using three different utilities: NetWare Administrator (NWADMIN), NETADMIN, and CX. Before beginning this exercise, you'll need to make sure that your network administrator has set up the NetWare Administrator icon in MS Windows on your workstation.

NETWARE ADMINISTRATOR

The NetWare Administrator (NWADMIN) utility is undoubtedly the most versatile utility available in NetWare 4. It can be used to perform a variety of functions, including the type of network administrator tasks that are available in FILER, NETADMIN, PARTMGR, and PCONSOLE.

During NetWare 4 installation, the files for the MS Windows version of this utility are stored in the SYS:PUBLIC directory. The files for the OS/2 version are stored in the SYS:PUBLIC\OS2 directory. Before you run the NetWare Administrator in MS Windows or OS/2 on a workstation for the first time, you'll need to create an NWADMIN icon. From then on, you can select the icon to activate the utility. As stated earlier, this exercise assumes that your network administrator has already set up the NetWare Administrator icon for you in MS Windows on your workstation.

In this exercise, we are going to use NWADMIN to explore the NDS tree.

1 • Exploring the browser window. Execute the NetWare Administrator (NWADMIN) utility in MS Windows by double-clicking on its icon. At least one NDS container object should be displayed. If not, select the Browse option from the Tools menu to open a browser window.

a. What container and its objects are displayed when you activate the NetWare Administrator utility? How can you determine what your current context is? How was your current context determined? Is it the same current context that would be displayed using the CX command at the DOS prompt?

b. How many containers are displayed? What type of containers are represented? How many leaf objects, if any, are displayed? What type of leaf objects are represented?

2 • Changing context

a. Keying in a new context. Keying in the name of a new context is one of the two methods available for changing your current context. Change your context to the [Root] by selecting Set Context... from the View menu. Type [Root] and press Enter. The [Root] icon should then be displayed at the top of the screen.

b. Walking the tree. Next, let's try the "walking the tree" method to change your current context. Select Set Context... from the View menu.

(1) Click on the Browser button to the right of the New Context field to display the Select Object window.

(2) To navigate the tree, double-click on a container in the Directory Context list box on the right side of the screen to move down one level in the tree or double-click on the double-dot (..) to move up one level in the tree. The objects that are located in each container that you select will be displayed in the Objects list box on the left side of the screen. Practice walking up and down the tree. When you are done, walk all the way up the tree, so that the [Root] icon is displayed at the top of the Object list box on the left side of the screen.

(3) The Name Filter field in the middle of the main NWADMIN browser screen allows you to restrict the objects that are listed in the Object list box on the left side of the screen by using wildcard characters or object names. The Directory Context filter field allows you to restrict the containers that are displayed on the right side of the screen by using wildcard characters or container names. Practice using these filters to limit what is displayed on the screen. When you are done, delete any filters in either field.

(4)   When the container you want to select as the current context is displayed in the Objects list box (which in this case is the [Root] object), click on it, then click on the OK button at the bottom of the window. The container that you have selected will appear in the New Context field in the Set Current Context window. Click on the OK button at the bottom of the Set Current Context window to return to the main NWADMIN browser screen.

3 • Opening a container object and viewing its contents. There are two methods available for opening a container and viewing its contents:

a. Double-clicking on the container's object name or icon.

b. Clicking on the container object to select it, then selecting the Expand option from the View menu.

Practice using both of these methods to view the contents of various containers. Determine the type of containers that are in each container, as well as the type of leaf objects.

4 • Viewing the object dialog (object details) of a container object. The object dialog lets you display and edit information relating to an object's properties. When you open an object dialog, you'll notice that there is a column of page buttons along the right side of the screen. You can click on each button, one at a time, to view the category of information indicated on the button. There two methods available for viewing the information relating to a container object:

a. Clicking on the container object with the left mouse button to select it, then selecting the Details option from the Object menu.

b. Clicking on the container object with the right mouse button to select it, then selecting Details from the menu pull-down that appears on the screen.

Practice using both of these methods to look at the information available for various types of container objects, including the [Root], a Country object (if one exists), an Organization object, and Organizational Unit objects.

5 • Viewing the object dialog (object details) of a leaf object. There are three methods for viewing the information relating to a leaf object:

a. Double-clicking on the leaf object.

b. Clicking on the leaf object with the left mouse button to select it, then selecting the Details option from the Object menu.

c. Clicking on the leaf object with the right mouse button to select it, then selecting Details from the menu that appears on the screen.

Practice using all three of these methods to look at the information available for various types of leaf objects, including Users, Groups, Print Servers, Printers, Print Queues, etc.

When you are ready to exit the NetWare Administrator utility, select the Exit option from the File menu.

NETADMIN

The NETADMIN utility is a menu utility that can be used to manage NDS objects and their properties. It is much more limited in scope than the NetWare Administrator Utility.

1 • Changing context. In order to change your current context for purposes of the NETADMIN utility, choose the Change context option from the NetAdmin Options menu. There are two methods of changing your context for the purposes of this utility. (When you exit the utility, you will return to the current context that was set before you ran the utility.) One is keying in the name of a new context in the field provided; the other is pressing the Insert key and walking the tree.

a. Press Insert. The contents of the current directory will be displayed, as well as a dot (.) representing the current directory and a double-dot (..) representing the parent directory. You will *not* need to select the dot (.) for purposes of this exercise.

b. Practice walking up and down the tree by double-clicking on the double-dot (..) to move up one level in the tree and double-clicking on a container to move down one level in the tree. You'll notice that the current context is displayed at the top of the screen. Go ahead and walk all the way up the tree by double-clicking on the double-dot (..) until the [Root] is listed as your current context, then walk down the tree by double-clicking on a container object, then double-clicking on a container object below that container object, and so on.When the current context you want is selected, press F10 to return to the NetAdmin Options menu.

2 • Managing objects. In order to view and manage objects and their properties, select the Manage objects option from the Netadmin Options menu. You'll notice that you can walk the tree from this screen as well.

a. In order to display information about an object, select the object using the up and down arrow keys, then press F10 to select it. You'll notice that the name and type of the object that you selected will be listed at the top of the menu that appears. Select the View or edit properties of this object menu option and press Enter. A list of categories will be displayed. Select the category desired and press Enter. Review the information displayed for this category, then press Esc to return to the previous menu. Use this method to display the various properties of this object, then press Esc to return to the Object, Class menu.

b. Practice using this technique to display the properties of various types of container and leaf objects. When you're ready to exit the NETADMIN utility, press Esc twice when the Object, Class menu is displayed, then select Yes and press Enter when asked if you want to exit.

CX

The NetWare 4 CX command line utility can be used to display or modify your context, or to view containers and leaf objects in your Directory tree. Open a DOS window in MS Windows (or exit MS Windows) and perform the following steps at the DOS prompt:

1 • Change to the F: drive:

```
F:
```

2 • Display your current context:

```
CX
```

3 • Display online help for the CX command.

```
CX /?
```

4 • Display containers in the current context.

```
CX /CONT
```

5 • Display containers and objects in the current context.

```
CX /A /CONT
```

6 • Display containers at or below the current context.

```
CX /T
```

7 • Display containers and objects at or below the current context.

```
CX /A /T
```

8 • Display all of the containers and objects in the Directory tree, starting at the [Root], without changing your current context.

```
CX /R /A /T
```

9 • Create and display a file that contains a visual representation of the NDS tree structure.

```
CX /R /A /T > TREE.NDS
TYPE TREE.NDS
```

10 • Change your current context to the [Root].

```
CX /R
```

11 • Display containers in the [Root].

```
CX /CONT
```

12 • Move down one level in the NDS tree.

```
CX context
```
(where context is the name of a container that was listed in Step 11)

13 • Move up one level in the NDS tree (which in this case happens to be the [Root]).

```
CX .
```

14 • Display all containers below the [Root].

```
CX /T
```

15 • Move to a container several levels below the [Root].

```
CX context
```
(where context is a context such as .WHITE.CRIME.TOKYO.ACME)

16 • Move up four levels in the NDS tree.

```
CX ....
```
(where you indicate one dot for each level you want to move up in the NDS tree)

See Appendix C for answers.

EXERCISE 2-2: UNDERSTANDING NDS NAMING

Answer the following questions using the directory structure listed below.

FIGURE 2.25

*Understanding NDS
Naming for Tokyo*

1 • Indicate a typeless distinguished name for BMasterson.

2 . Provide a typeful distinguished name for RHood.

3 • List a typeless relative distinguished name for the CRIME Organizational Unit, assuming that your current context is the [Root].

4 • Show a typeful relative distinguished name for the BLUE-SRV1 server object from the default current context.

5 • If your current context is .CRIME.TOKYO.ACME, what is the shortest name that accurately references the SHolmes User object?

6 • Assume your current context is .TOKYO.ACME. Indicate a typeless relative distinguished name for the LJohn User object.

7 • If your current context is .PR.TOKYO.ACME, what would be a typeful relative distinguished name for SirKay?

8 • Assume your current context is .WHITE.CRIME.TOKYO.ACME. Provide a typeless relative distinguished name for Admin.

9 • If your current context is .BLUE.CRIME.TOKYO.ACME, what would be a typeful relative distinguished name for BThomas?

10 • Assume your current context is .WHITE.CRIME.TOKYO.ACME. What is the longest possible typeful relative distinguished name for the SYS: volume on the BLUE-SRV1 server?

11 • If DHolliday attaches to the BLUE-SRV1 server by default, what's his current context after login? Give two LOGIN commands for DHolliday.

12 • How would MMarion visit SirKay?

13 • How can you make sure that SirKay's workstation drops him into his home context when he attaches to the "Cloud"?

14 • Provide 10 LOGIN commands for SHolmes from
.BLUE.CRIME.TOKYO.ACME:

15 • What is the easiest way to move above ACME from the .PR.TOKYO.ACME
context?

See Appendix C for answers.

EXERCISE 2-3: PLANT A TREE IN A CLOUD

Circle the 20 NDS terms hidden in this word search puzzle using the hints provided.

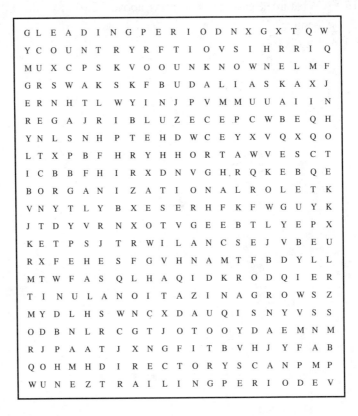

```
G L E A D I N G P E R I O D N X G X T Q W
Y C O U N T R Y R F T I O V S I H R R I Q
M U X C P S K V O O U N K N O W N E L M F
G R S W A K S K F B U D A L I A S K A X J
E R N H T L W Y I N J P V M M U U A I I N
R E G A J R I B L U Z E C E P C W B E Q H
Y N L S N H P T E H D W C E Y X V Q X Q O
L T X P B F H R Y H H O R T A W V E S C T
I C B B F H I R X D N V G H R Q K E B Q E
B O R G A N I Z A T I O N A L R O L E T K
V N Y T L Y B X E S E R H F K F W G U Y K
J T D Y V R N X O T V G E E B T L Y E P X
K E T P S J T R W I L A N C S E J V B E U
R X F E H E S F G V H N A M T F B D Y L L
M T W F A S Q L H A Q I D K R O D Q I E R
T I N U L A N O I T A Z I N A G R O W S Z
M Y D L H S W N C X D A U Q I S N Y V S S
O D B N L R C G T J O T O O Y D A E M N M
R J P A A T J X N G F I T B V H J Y F A B
Q O H M H D I R E C T O R Y S C A N P M P
W U N E Z T R A I L I N G P E R I O D E V
```

Hints:

1 • Object that represents a logical NDS pointer to another object in the tree.

2 • Container object that uses predetermined two-character names.

3 • The context that would be displayed if you issued the CX command with no options.

4 • Command line utility used to view or change your current context.

5 • Object that represents a logical pointer to a physical directory in the NetWare 4 file system.

6 • RCONSOLE menu option that can be used to display the four main files that comprise the NetWare 4 NDS database.

7 • An object that represents a set of users and is used for assigning rights.

8 • Identifies a name as a distinguished name.

9 • Similar to a Country object, except that it can exist in a Country, Organization, or Organizational Unit container.

10 • Command that can be used in NET.CFG to set the current context.

11 • Item that represents a resource in the NDS database.

12 • Container object that is often used to represent a company, university, or association.

13 • Object that represents a position or role with an organization.

14 • Container object that is considered a "natural group."

15 • Object that represents a login script that is used by a group of users who reside in the same or different containers.

16 • Special superuser used for bindery emulation.

17 • Allows you to change the current context while using relative distinguished naming.

18 • Name that contains object attribute abbreviations.

19 • Name that does not contain object attribute abbreviations.

20 • NDS object that has been invalidated or cannot be identified as belonging to any of the other object classes.

See Appendix C for answers.

NETWARE 4 BASICS

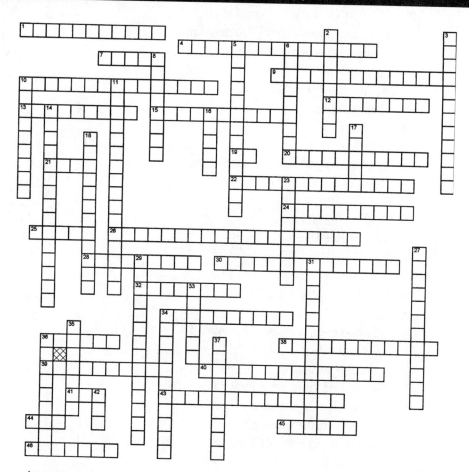

Across

1. A two-dimensional slice of 3-D NDS
3. No more wasted space
5. Your name and address combined
7. A two-dimensional tool in a three-dimensional world
11. Multiple layers of Tupperware
12. It's time to vote
14. Where am I?
15. Tupperware

16. Entrance to the "Cloud"
18. Getting to know the workstation NIC
20. Off-loading out-of-date files to near-line
21. The mysterious object class
24. A global view
25. You, me, Albert Einstein
27. Where you live
30. Everybody
32. The "Cloud"
34. Only one per partition, the king of replication
35. A piece of the "Cloud"
36. The old way of storing users
37. ACME in the NDS tree
39. The new NetWare 4 approach
40. The old NetWare 3 approach
42. The other NetWare 4 directory tree
43. The time keepers of NetWare 4

Down

1. Backward compatibility to NetWare 3
2. Creating a superbindery
4. NetWare 4 incognito
6. Does anyone know what time it is?
7. NDS details at the command line
8. The new e-mail engine
9. Somewhere between "off" and "on"
10. Saving space
11. You, me, printers
13. A small town in the NetWare 4 global village
15. Who you are, not where you live
17. A revolving job
19. Also GMT
20. "Red books" in electronic form
22. Login interrogation in NetWare 4
23. A beginner MHS application
26. The last word in time voting

27. A two-letter container
28. They "haggle" over the time
29. When
31. Security flows down the tree
33. The new backup engine
35. A Group login script object
38. Really big hard drives
41. Life at the new NetWare 4 workstation

See Appendix C for answers.

NetWare 4 Design

I am MIGHTY!

I have a glow you cannot see,
I have a heart as big as the moon...
as warm as bath water.

We're superheroes, man
We don't have time to be charming.
The boots of good were made for walking.
We're watching the big picture, friend.
We know the score.

We are a public service, not glamor boys!
Not captains of industry,
Not makers of things.
Keep your vulgar monies.

We are a justice sandwich,
no toppings necessary.
Living rooms of America,
do you catch my drift?

Do you dig?!!!

The Tick

You are a superhero.

You are a doctor.

You are a gardener.

As a NetWare 4 CNE, you are three people in one.

Today, you are a superhero. Probably the most exciting experience for anyone is the realization of a dream. For some, a dream may be as simple as more money, a better job, or pickles on ham and cheese. For others, dreaming is serious business—to be President of the United States, a cure for cancer, peace on Earth. Reality should never get in the way of your dreams. Do you have any?

Superheroes are in the dream-making business. As a NetWare 4 superhero, you have one simple task—build an NDS tree and save the world. No pressure. It all starts with NDS design. You'll learn about naming standards, tree design, partitioning, replication, and time synchronization. And as if that's not enough, you'll have to implement them in a testing lab and pilot program first. Steps you take today could decide the fate of humanity. No pressure.

Wow! NDS design is serious business. Is the world in very good hands? Sure, you can handle it—you're a NetWare 4 superhero!

Step 1: NDS Preparation

The world is in a lot of trouble. If we keep abusing the Planet Earth at our current pace, there'll be nothing left in a few decades.

As a matter of fact, the Alpha Centurions have discovered this and decided to do something about it. As it turns out, they are great fans of the Planet Earth and would hate to see us destroy it. They have given us until January 1, 2000, to clean up our act—or else. It's safe to say the fate of the human race is in your hands.

To save the world, we have created an organization called ACME (A Cure for Mother Earth). ACME is staffed by the greatest heroes from our unspoiled history. They are the founding mothers and fathers of Earth's Golden Age—before instant popcorn, talking cars, and daytime television. It's clear that somewhere along the human timeline, progress went amuck.

We've used the OTO (Oscillating Temporal Overthruster) prototype to vortex back in time and grab the ACME management. They're a little disoriented but more than happy to help. Now it's your turn to step up to the plate—as ACME's MIS department. You will build a pervasive internetwork for ACME using NetWare 4. The clock is ticking and connectivity is the key.

ZEN

"Knock on the sky and listen to the sound."

M'Tau Zen

As a NetWare 4 CNE, you come highly recommended. Your mission—should you choose to accept it—is to build the ACME WAN and NDS tree. You will need courage, design experience, NDS know-how, and this book. If you succeed, you will save the world and become a CNE! All in a day's work.

Actually, you have a daunting task ahead of you. A project of this magnitude requires sharp thinking and a very organized approach. All the fancy footwork and LAN lexicon in the world isn't going to help you if you don't have a game plan. That's where Figure 3.1 comes in—it's your ACME game plan. As you can see, saving the world falls into four simple steps:

- ▸ Step 1: NDS Preparation

- ▸ Step 2: Design

▸ Step 3: Implementation

▸ Step 4: Management

NDS Preparation   **1**   Chapter 3

Design   **2**   Chapter 4

Implementation   **3**   Chapters 5-7

Management   **4**   Chapters 8-15

[Root]

In Step 1, the project starts rolling with NDS preparation. The primary focus of this phase is the project team. These are the men and women who will carry you through the triumphs and pitfalls of saving the world. The project team consists of many networking experts, including management, server specialists, NDS experts, and connectivity specialists. The team's first task is systems analysis and data gathering. Once you've gathered all pertinent project information, you can develop a project scope and move on to Step 2. All of this fun will be outlined in the pages to follow.

Step 2 is the first of the three main project phases—design, implementation, and management. NDS design begins with the formation of a tree framework. This framework is further refined with the help of three important NDS concepts:

▸ Partitioning

▸ Time synchronization

▸ Resource accessibility

These design components have a dramatic effect on the success or failure of your WAN. Unfortunately, NDS design is one of the least understood of the three main project phases. Design is especially crucial in NetWare 4 because network productivity relies on the availability of resources. These resources must be organized logically. Please don't underestimate the importance and sophistication of NDS design. This phase is covered in excruciating detail in Chapter 4.

Things really start hopping in Step 3—implementation. You're probably getting a little stir-crazy by now because NDS preparation and design don't involve much *action*. Don't worry, there's more than enough action to go around in Steps 3 and 4. The goal of NDS implementation is NetWare 4 installation and migration. But before you can get there, you must get all your ducks in a row. This is the purpose of a testing lab and pilot program. The testing lab allows you to implement the design in a nonproduction environment. Then you can further test your design in a controlled segment of the larger network—a pilot program. Once all the kinks have been worked out, you can create an implementation schedule and start installing and migrating NetWare 4 resources—servers, workstations, users, printers, and so on. The testing portions of Step 3 are covered in Chapter 5 (NDS Implementation). The real action takes place in Chapter 6 (NetWare 4 Installation) and Chapter 7 (NetWare 4 Migration). I bet you can't wait.

Once your network's in place, it's time to make it shine. Welcome to Step 4. Management is the ongoing process of fiddling with and tweaking your NetWare 4 WAN. This is where we get to earn our money as ACME superheroes!

NetWare 4 management hinges on NDS. It involves partitioning, the file system, security, printing, and optimization. But none of this is useful without configuration and management. Configuration is a five-step process that brings the users on-line and offers them a productive networking environment. Additional management allows you to keep the servers running, make daily backups, and perform routine maintenance tasks from remote locations. This is where you'll spend most of your life as a NetWare 4 CNE. Fortunately, we've devoted half of this book to NetWare 4 Management (Chapters 8 through 15). Boy, do we have fun in store for you!

ZEN

"Don't Panic!"

The Hitchhiker's Guide to the Galaxy

That's all it takes to save the world and become a NetWare 4 CNE. Don't hyperventilate—breathe slowly. It's going to be all right. I'm here to walk with you every step of the way. And there's a great poster in the back of this book that outlines your mission. But be careful not to let these facts fall into the wrong hands. Believe it or not, there are forces at work that do not share our love for the human race—especially the Alpha Centurions. Let's start our life-or-death journey with a closer look at the "Process."

The Process

There's more to saving the world than you might think—as we just saw. When a company makes an investment in a NetWare 4 network, someone has the responsibility of implementing it. Similarly, when the Alpha Centurions decide to destroy the human race, someone has the responsibility of stopping them—you!

You weren't born with this responsibility—it was given to you. Do you feel lucky? As the director of the Labs division, Albert Einstein chose you as the head MIS consultant.

In this scenario, Albert Einstein takes on the role of Information Services (IS) Manager. The IS Manager starts your project with three simple questions:

- What is the Process you will use for implementing NetWare 4 in our organization?

- What resources (such as people, computers, and money) will the Process require?

- How much time will planning and implementation take?

Your answers to these questions set you on a path of wonder, intrigue, and very late nights. Your ability to complete the project (and save the world) depends entirely on the Process.

So what is the Process? The Process is a systematic methodology for designing, implementing, and managing NetWare 4. In most cases, it consists of the four simple steps shown in Figure 3.1:

- Step 1: NDS Preparation

- Step 2: Design

- Step 3: Implementation

- Step 4: Management

Having a systematic approach like this reduces the time it takes to design the network, which gives you a head start on implementation and management. It also ensures that the needs of Albert Einstein are met and all critical requirements are addressed. This results ultimately in an efficient NetWare 4 WAN for today and tomorrow (assuming there is a tomorrow).

Let's take a closer look at the Process and learn a little more about "saving the world."

TIP

Programmers and IS professionals sometimes call the Process a System Design Life Cycle (SDLC); others call it an Information Systems

Development Methodology; or better yet, a Software Engineering Process Model. Regardless of what you call it, the Process is a structured approach toward designing, implementing, and managing an information system.

In addition to different names, there are many different approaches to the Process, including linear, structured, incremental, and/or spiral:

▶ The linear approach handles each step one at a time in order. It is used in traditional bottom-up software and systems development efforts.

▶ The structured model, on the other hand, allows all activities to take place simultaneously. This approach is used in top-down development that involves nonlinear efforts.

▶ The incremental approach is a variation on the structured model used with rapid prototyping.

▶ Finally, the spiral model allows you to modify certain requirements during the life of the project. This approach is used in inherently risky, costly, or unstable environments—kind of like saving the world.

The Process is an interesting mix of all four approaches.

NDS PREPARATION PHASE

It all begins with NDS preparation. During this phase, we create the project team and outline the Process. As you can see in Figure 3.2, we're just getting things started.

Your project team is the center of attention. It consists of seven or eight different specialists who fall into three categories:

▶ Management

▶ Hardware Specialists

▶ Software Specialists

FIGURE 3.2

Step 1: NDS Preparation

NDS Preparation

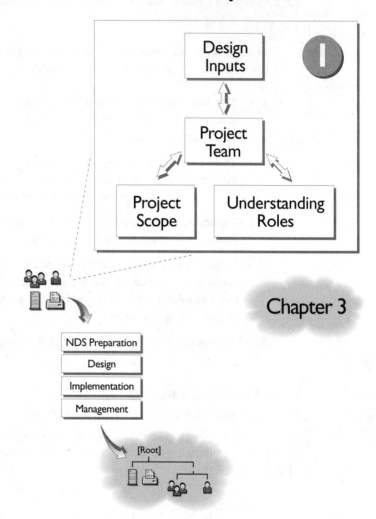

Each project team member has a specific role that needs to be outlined clearly. Once you've assembled the team, you must train them—not in the technological aspects of NetWare 4 but in the intricacies of the Process. Once you've trained the team members, they can begin the two most important tasks of Step 1: gathering NDS information and determining the project scope.

Data gathering is the process of determining *who* is doing *what* to *whom* and *why*. In other words, it's "just the facts, ma'am." Objectivity is crucial in data gathering. All sorts of distortion effects have been found to alter data as it is gathered. The *Hawthorne Effect* states that individuals who know they are part of a study behave differently from those who are not part of a study or who don't know they are part of a study. In addition, the *Learning Curve* shows that data gathered early in an experiment is not always as accurate as data gathered later. The members of your project team can use a variety of methods for data gathering: observation, conversation, research, questionnaires, and random sampling. Eventually they will settle on a few key design inputs:

- ▸ The Company's Organizational Chart

- ▸ Physical WAN Layout Map

- ▸ Network Resource Lists

- ▸ A World Location Map

- ▸ Background Information and a Workflow Diagram

Later in this chapter, we will explore data gathering for ACME. We will discover each of these design inputs and learn the role they play in the Process and NDS design.

Once you've established your project team and gathered all of ACME's information, it's time to determine the project's scope. Establishing the scope of a project is critical for keeping things under control. Scope provides physical boundaries for the network as well as financial and personnel limitations. After defining the problem accurately, you must explore the system resources and determine how far they can be stretched. In many cases, the scope acts as a restraint to keep unworkable solutions from expanding too far. If the scope is too broad, the network will never be finished. If the scope is too narrow, the network surely will not meet ACME's needs. Albert Einstein is looking for the bottom line — "How much will it cost me and how long will it take?" These questions can be answered by determining the project's scope.

QUIZ

Part of NDS preparation is "seeing what isn't there." Use the following rhyme to test your perceptivity skills:

A CNE came to the riverside,

With a donkey bearing an obelisk,

But he did not venture to ford the tide,

For he had too good an *.

What is the missing word?

(Q3-1)

(See Appendix C for all quiz answers.)

That's the gist of NDS preparation. With your team all fueled up and ready to go, it's time to launch into the three main phases of the Process:

- ▸ Design

- ▸ Implementation

- ▸ Management

DESIGN PHASE

It has been my experience that all the factors, details, and lexicon in the world of networking can be narrowed down into two very important classifications: people and performance. During the design phase, you only have to concern yourself with these two categories. Analyze the ACME information and prioritize the results with respect to their influence over the people in the office and the performance of the network. It's that simple. The ultimate goal is to develop an effective balance of NDS components that creates a design synergy.

Yes, there's that word again—*synergy*. Synergy states that "the whole is greater than the sum of its parts." Synergy in networking is the product of well-orchestrated software and hardware components. In the best scenario, these resources complement each other to create a WAN that exceeds the productivity and performance of individual systems. In NetWare 4, these resources must be designed according to three important criteria (see Figure 3.3):

▶ NDS tree—Designing the upper and lower layers of the Directory tree. This design helps you optimize NDS so that it's productive for users and easy to manage. It also lays the foundation for partitioning and time synchronization.

▶ Partitioning—Next, your design must outline partition boundaries and replica placement. These procedures help provide scaleability, fault tolerance, and resource access.

▶ Time synchronization—The design must include guidelines for both default and customized time synchronization strategies. For customized trees, you'll need to offer setup models for TIMESYNC.CFG and efficient guidelines for time-server placement. These procedures help provide accurate synchronized time to all servers on the ACME WAN. Remember, time stamps are critical to all NDS events.

These design criteria rely on a *naming standards document* as a central point of control. After all, if you're going to save the world, everybody must speak the same language. The NDS tree relies on naming standards for container organization, partitioning, and replica placement. Time servers also rely on standardization for both default and custom configurations.

The final step in the design phase deals with accessibility. This is where synergy comes in. The system must be designed so that both physical and logical resources are easily accessible to users. Once again, this step impacts all three design criteria—NDS tree, partitioning, and time synchronization. Accessibility design should also account for the needs of non-NetWare 4 users—Bindery Services.

Okay, with the ACME design in place, you're ready for *action*—literally!

Step 2: Design

Design

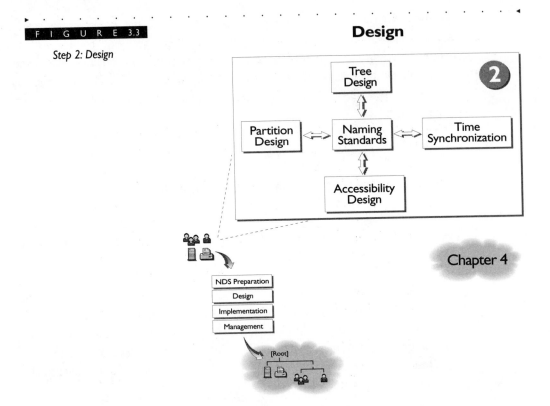

IMPLEMENTATION PHASE

This is where the fun begins. If you're feeling a little restless from the first two phases, you'll get plenty of action in the final two. As you can see in Figure 3.4, all of your initial action centers around the implementation schedule. This schedule outlines the rollout of NetWare 4 installation and migration. But before you can implement NetWare 4 in the ACME production environment, we'll need to test it in more controlled pilot programs.

It all starts in your off-line testing lab. Here you can be creative and brave without causing system-wide crashes. While you are in the lab, you should consider installing NetWare 4 multiple times and creating diverse NDS trees. Then test partitioning, replication, time synchronization, and common network applications. Finally, make sure backup and restore procedures operate correctly. All of this extra work should help you avoid major pitfalls during the pilot program.

F I G U R E 3.4

Step 3: Implementation

Implementation

Once you're comfortable with each individual piece, consider putting them together in a controlled pilot program. The pilot system involves installing your first production NetWare 4 server. Each production application can be tested in a more real-life environment. You can also test user compatibility with NDS and Bindery Services. A pilot system is your bridge between the lab and a full implementation of NetWare 4 across the entire ACME WAN. You might consider the Labs division in NORAD as your pilot implementation. The scientists who work there are more likely to understand what you're going through.

Once you've scheduled, tested, and piloted the implementation, you're ready for Prime Time!

- ▶ NetWare 4 Installation

- ▶ NetWare 4 Migration

NetWare 4 Installation creates new servers and places them in the existing NDS tree. The very first installation is significant because it outlines the boundaries of NDS. Furthermore, NetWare 4 Migration allows you to integrate NetWare 3 servers into the new system. Migration retains the existing file system and translates the bindery into NDS objects.

During this entire phase, you should always keep design *synergy* in mind.

ZEN

Wogging—Jogging interspersed with periods of walking at a brisk pace especially as a form of aerobic exercise. Also used to describe the dizzying feeling most CNEs experience prior to NDS management.

MANAGEMENT PHASE

Welcome to the "Real World." The first three phases of the Process were packed with questions, answers, intrigue, mystery, knowledge, decisions, and shopping. Here's where the adventure begins. NetWare 4 management is the adventure of dealing with the WAN once it has been built. The project team has gathered a plethora of ACME information and prioritized it into a synergistic design. The implementation team has spent lots of time and money fusing network components into a functional skeleton—now it's your turn.

In NetWare 4 management, it is your responsibility to take this unsophisticated network skeleton and develop a thriving, dynamic, breathing NetWare WAN. It is your system to configure, manage, maintain, and troubleshoot. In addition, it is your responsibility to work in conjunction with other CNEs to expand this WAN into the realm of interconnectivity—*if you build it, they will come.*

Your role, as a NetWare 4 CNE, is probably the most excruciating and the most rewarding. The project team dissembles at this point but you stay around to keep things running on a daily basis. You are the ruler of your own kingdom—mapping out boundaries, filling it with users, adding security, and laying down the laws. This is a huge responsibility. And your success or failure hinges on three important characteristics: network knowledge, management skills, and fire containment. To be successful, you must fully understand the intricacies of your WAN, be sensitive to the needs of your users, and develop precautionary guidelines for network crashes. Nobody said it was going to be easy, but then again, the rewards will greatly outweigh the pain.

As you can see in Figure 3.5, NetWare 4 management centers around NDS. Five key management components directly impact the success or failure of ACME:

▸ Security—laying down the law

▸ Partitioning—breaking the kingdom into functional regions

▸ File system—currency

▸ Printing—your kingdom's industry

▸ Optimization—keeping things running smoothly

F I G U R E 3.5

Step 4: Management

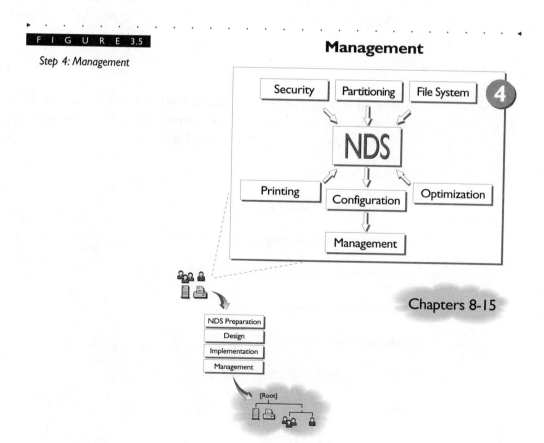

Of course, to keep peace in your kingdom, you must have a military and bureaucratic government—that's NDS. These management aspects rely on NetWare 4 configuration and management. During configuration, you establish a productive user environment with workstation connectivity, login scripts, a menu system, network applications, and e-mail. In addition, a series of management tasks help you proactively maintain file servers, workstations, backup, and the Remote Management Facility (RMF). This is a snapshot of your daily life. This is what you signed up for!

NetWare 4 management dominates the majority of your life as a CNE. The first three phases typically occur once. Management occurs every day. That's why we've dedicated more than half of this book to the final phase of the Process. As a matter of fact, this book is a road map to saving the world. Refer to Table 3.1 for more details.

Now that you understand the overall Process, let's get started with Step 1 (NDS preparation). Fortunately, you don't have to do it alone. Let's get some help. Let's build a project team.

QUIZ

Just another example of "seeing what isn't there." The same hero claims all these famous phrases. As a matter of fact, his or her name is an anagram of one of them. Who is our hero?

"The world's mine oyster"

"The better part of valor is discretion"

"Be to yourself as you would to your friend"

"If money go before, all ways do lie open"

"I'll make a wise phrase"

"All that glisters is not gold"

"I'll blow the wind that profits nobody"

(Q3-2)

PHASE	TASK	NOVELL'S CNE STUDY GUIDE FOR NETWARE 4.1
NDS Preparation	Project team	Chapter 3
	Understand roles	Chapter 3
	Design inputs	Chapter 3
	Project scope	Chapter 3
Design	Naming standards	Chapter 4
	Tree design	Chapter 4
	Partition design	Chapter 4
	Time synchronization	Chapter 4
	Accessibility design	Chapter 4
Implementation	Testing lab	Chapter 5
	Pilot program	Chapter 5
	Implementation schedule	Chapter 5
	Installation	Chapter 6
	Migration	Chapter 7
Management	NDS	Chapter 8
	Partitioning	Chapter 9
	File system	Chapter 10
	Security	Chapter 11
	Configuration	Chapter 12
	Management	Chapter 13
	Printing	Chapter 14
	Optimization	Chapter 15

The Project Team

Never underestimate the value of a friend—especially when you're trying to save the world. That's why we've used the OTO (Oscillating Temporal Overthruster) prototype to go back in time and recruit heroes from our unspoiled past. These heroes will not only fill the roles of ACME management—a few lucky ones will become members of your project team. It doesn't matter how many people are on the team as long as the concerns and tasks for each role are represented. You can have members performing multiple roles or specific subtasks within a role. It all depends on the size of your organization. Typically the most efficient balance employs a one-to-one relationship. That is, one team member for each design role. So how do you find these people? Just like any scientific method—draw straws. Asking yourself the following questions might help, too:

- Does ACME have an IS organization? If so, how is it organized?

- Who manages ACME servers? Who manages ACME workstations?

- Who understands the complexities of internetworking protocols? Does anybody within ACME have a handle on the physical WAN layout?

- Who will train the network administrators and users?

- Who handles software upgrades and network management?

- Who manages other network resources such as printers and file storage?

- Who can help test the networking software and applications? Do they use valid scientific methods?

As you can see, these are primarily technical questions. The majority of the project team should be made up of scientists and technically minded individuals. This isn't to say, however, that you should ignore bureaucrats. It's always a good idea to balance scientists with managerial expertise. That's also part of your job as the team leader.

Once you've established the team, make sure each member has a clear understanding of his or her responsibilities and priorities. They should also have clear expectations of how to interact with each other. Each team member has specific expertise and comes from a different area of management. Make sure that they understand the interdependency between team members. Try to avoid fostering hierarchy. Each team member has a job to do and no one member is more important than another—except you, of course. You're the most important! Finally, be sensitive to team member concerns. Everybody has something unique to add, and you should keep an open mind to their input. You never know when they might teach you something.

Most project teams are separated into three functional areas:

- Management

- Hardware Specialists

- Software Specialists

Management includes ACME's IS Manager, the Testing Lab Coordinator, the Education/Training Coordinator, and you (aka the MIS department). Hardware Specialists focus on servers, workstations, and NetWare 4 printing. Finally, Software Specialists deal with NDS concerns, network applications, and general connectivity. Let's take a closer look at each of these nine ACME team members and focus on their priorities, expectations, and concerns.

MANAGEMENT

Of course, *you* are running the show. It's a good thing you're a NetWare 4 CNE, or the world wouldn't have any chance at all. But you can't do everything alone. Three specialized managers can help you keep the Hardware and Software Specialists in line. They are:

- IS Manager

- Testing Lab Coordinator

- Education/Training Coordinator

IS Manager

The IS Manager is the central contact point for ACME staff and management. He or she is most likely the head of the IS department and understands the ramifications of the Process. ACME's IS Manager is Albert Einstein. Following is a list of his responsibilities and concerns:

- Coordinate with the NDS Expert to ensure an efficient transition from NetWare 3 to NetWare 4.

- Acquire the appropriate resources and funding to proceed with all phases of the Process.

- Act as a liaison between the project team and ACME management.

- Give direction to the project.

- Manage costs and estimates; organize and schedule management meetings.

- Create an efficient and effective network design.

- Coordinate evaluation of software and licensing issues.

- Coordinate design, implementation, and management timelines.

- Ensure user productivity and adequate training.

- Oversee the testing lab, pilot implementation, and ACME-wide rollout.

Testing Lab Coordinator

The Testing Lab Coordinator performs tests on the new NetWare 4 operating system with current applications. He or she should run diagnostics, provide statistics on performance, and ensure network hardware and software stability. The Testing Lab represents the first aspect of implementation. The Coordinator must be precise and systematic in his or her testing methodologies. For this reason, we've chosen Sherlock Holmes as the ACME Testing Lab Coordinator. Following is a list of his responsibilities and concerns:

▸ Test the compatibility between NetWare 4 and current applications.

▸ Create network performance benchmarks.

▸ Set up the Lab environment to emulate ACME production.

▸ Provide test results about network performance and software compatibility.

▸ Obtain current versions of application software.

▸ Get resources for the Lab from the IS Manager.

▸ Coordinate pilot rollout with the IS Manager.

Education/Training Coordinator

The Education/Training Coordinator analyzes the new skills required by team members. He or she then arranges for training sessions and materials to help the team attain a high level of network proficiency. In addition, the Education/Training Coordinator deals with training issues for distributed administrators and users. He or she ensures that all administrators get the opportunity to become CNEs and that ACME users feel comfortable with the new global WAN. He or she must be wise yet firm, sensitive yet diligent. For these reasons, we've chosen Buddha as the ACME Education/Training Coordinator. Following is a list of his responsibilities and concerns:

▸ Identify and provide implementation and administration guidelines.

▸ Train the project team.

▸ Train network administrators.

▸ Train users.

▸ Work closely with you and the IS Manager to continually evaluate team members.

> ▸ Research information affecting users and administrators, then provide on-the-job training.

> ▸ Lobby the IS Manager for education and training budgets.

> ▸ Set up the education and training lab with the help of the Testing Lab Coordinator and other specialists.

> ▸ Identify appropriate timing for training sessions and integrate sessions into the overall project time line.

> ▸ Get members prepared for meetings and serve Cafe Latte.

As you can see, the project management staff has a lot on their plate. Albert Einstein, Sherlock Holmes, and Buddha work closely with you to foster team synergy and keep the project on course.

ZEN

Karmarker's algorithm — a technique of solving a complex mathematical problem quickly by eliminating groups of possible solutions with the aid of solid geometry. Also thought to be a method of choosing the ACME Project Team.

Now let's take a look at the non-management team members: Hardware and Software Specialists.

HARDWARE SPECIALISTS

The ACME Hardware Specialists tweak computers all day. They are the ultimate gigabyte gurus who purchase, set up, and troubleshoot the network hardware. The Hardware Specialists are an important part of the project team because they understand the intricacies of LAN-based computers. They also understand the strain NetWare 4 can place on servers and workstations.

There are three Hardware Specialists on our team:

> ▸ Server Specialist

▸ Workstation Specialist

▸ Printing Specialist

Server Specialist

In earlier versions of NetWare, the server was the heart and soul of the LAN. Even though it takes a logical back seat in NetWare 4, its importance should never be underestimated. Regardless of what the tree looks like, it exists as three or four database files within your network server. In addition, the server plays an important role in system-wide time synchronization. As I'm sure you can imagine, the Server Specialist is invaluable in choosing the correct hardware initially and then keeping it running. We've chosen Marie Curie as the Server Specialist because of her excellent reputation as a nuclear scientist. Just draw your own conclusions. Following is a list of her responsibilities and concerns:

▸ Determine and plan the pilot implementation.

▸ Install, upgrade, and migrate all NetWare 4 servers.

▸ Ensure effective time synchronization strategies.

▸ Assist the Testing Lab Coordinator.

▸ Develop an effective management strategy for centralized and distributed administrators.

▸ Establish protocol standardization. This includes standards for frame type usage. Don't forget to register your IPX addresses.

▸ Design server placement in the NDS tree. This should be coordinated with the NDS Expert.

▸ Calculate needed disk space and memory for new and existing servers.

▸ Plan and implement a NetWare 4–compatible data backup system.

▸ Establish disaster recovery options.

▶ Determine backward compatibility.

▶ Identify and install appropriate Bindery Services technology for non-NetWare 4 users.

▶ Determine performance overhead created by new operating system utilities and additional NLMs.

Workstation Specialist

The Workstation Specialist spends his or her day working with users and their workstations. This is probably the most challenging job because it entails "user interface." We all know what a hurdle that can be. For this reason, the Workstation Specialist should be a counselor as well as a technical innovator. The goal here is to keep both the workstations and users "humming" with minimal fuss. The challenge is great but not insurmountable. For this reason, we've chosen Sir Isaac Newton as ACME's Workstation Specialist. He's never been the same since that apple incident. Maybe it will help him understand the user's plight. Following is a list of his responsibilities and concerns:

▶

Upgrade all workstations with VLMs and the NetWare DOS Requester.

▶ Automate workstation connectivity as outlined in Step 1 of NetWare 4 configuration.

▶ Identify and solve problems with workstation hardware.

▶ Determine and implement changes to existing client procedures. Also perform any client updates necessary.

▶ Create an efficient implementation schedule for upgrading workstations.

▶ Determine memory requirements to run client software and existing network applications.

▶ Maintain consistent configuration files across all workstations.

▶ Identify performance overhead related to the new VLMs.

- Investigate and solve possible storage issues (for example, the 10 MB necessary for client software installation).

- Work with the Testing Lab Coordinator to determine the compatibility of VLMs with existing Windows 95 environments.

- Coordinate Profile and User login scripts with the NDS Expert.

- Determine and solve problems with specialized bindery and traveling users.

- Determine a method for user login and connection—establishing correct name context.

Printing Specialist

Aah, printers. They can be even more challenging than workstations. The Printing Specialist provides access to printers, determines printer location, and upgrades printing software. Of course, all users want their own printers—but this defeats the purpose of a network. It's also an ineffective use of ACME's resources. After all, we're trying to save the world here. The Printing Specialist has to understand the needs of his or her users and their "evolution" as NetWare 4 users. For his unique and overwhelming understanding in this area, we've chosen Charles Darwin as ACME's Printing Specialist. Following is a list of his responsibilities and concerns:

- Provide users with access to appropriate printers (this is the tricky part).

- Work with the IS Manager to determine budgets for printer acquisition.

- Upgrade printing software and workstation drivers.

- Create a well-defined migration strategy for existing and new printers.

- Enable Bindery Services for direct connection to non-NetWare 4 printers.

- Configure and administer new printing utilities.

- Coordinate CAPTURE statements in Profile and User login scripts with the NDS Expert.

▸ Provide interconnectivity for printing for Macintosh and UNIX machines. Also provide user access to specialized Macintosh- and UNIX-type printers.

The Hardware Specialists are the true *geeks* of your project team. But they have important responsibilities with the users as well. Both the Workstation and Printing Specialists have their own user challenges to deal with. As the NetWare 4 CNE, consider supporting them as they try to foster a productive user environment.

ZEN

"It's a well-known fact that any man would rather drill a hole in his hand than admit, especially to his wife, that he cannot handle a hardware problem by himself. Put an ordinary husband on the Space Shuttle, and within minutes he'll be attempting to repair the retro thruster modules himself. After all, if you call in NASA, they'll charge you an arm and a leg!"

Dave Barry

Now let's take a look at the final three members of our project team—the Software Specialists.

SOFTWARE SPECIALISTS

On the outside, the Software Specialists may appear to be a little less nerdy than their hardware counterparts. Don't let that fool you! The Software Specialists are just as technical as the Hardware Specialists but in a slightly different way. Software Specialists deal with the *inner* workings of the system, not the outer hardware. These heroes have a very important role in ensuring a smooth transition from NetWare 3 LANs to a global NetWare 4 WAN.

There are three Software Specialists on the ACME project team. They are:

▸ NDS Expert

▸ Application Specialist

▸ Connectivity Specialist

NDS Expert

If you thought NDS was strange, wait until you meet the NDS Expert. In order to truly understand NDS, you have to think like a "cloud"—a scary proposition. Since NDS impacts all facets of the system, this expert needs to have a firm grasp on the big picture. This is one of the most valuable members of your project team. For his intellectual spark and wizardry, we've chosen Merlin as the ACME NDS Expert. Somehow, it seems appropriate. Following is a list of his responsibilities and concerns:

▸ Lead the project team through most of the NDS design phase.

▸ Create directory tree design and organize the upper and lower portions of the tree.

▸ Design and implement NDS security.

▸ Design and implement NDS management components, including partitions, replica placement, time synchronization, and accessibility.

▸ Participate in choosing the team members. Also, communicate NDS concerns to the IS Manager and you.

▸ Ensure that the design is thorough and meets all department needs at key points throughout the Process. Also ensure that each project team member participates in data gathering and that the design phase meets established time lines.

▸ Coordinate System, Profile, and User login scripts with other team members, including Workstation and Printing Specialists.

▸ Oversee the creation and maintenance of a detailed design and implementation log book. This will also be the cornerstone of WAN expansion.

▸ Know NDS inside and out.

Application Specialist

The Application Specialist maintains network and user applications. He or she also oversees software upgrades and coordinates the installation of specialized database and application servers. He or she also participates in certain aspects of NetWare 4 configuration, including menu systems, e-mail, and workstation connectivity. Since network applications are the true productivity tools of the WAN, this specialist must be fully aware of the impact of all WAN influences on them—including NDS, synchronization, name context, distributed printers, and security. For this reason, we've chosen Gandhi as ACME's Application Specialist. He also seems to have a grasp on the big picture. Following is a list of his responsibilities and concerns:

- Migrate existing applications into the new NetWare 4 WAN.

- Install new applications.

- Ensure stability of existing and new applications.

- Provide user access to applications through connectivity and security.

- Update menu systems.

- Work with the Testing Lab Coordinator to ensure application compatibility with NetWare 4.

- Coordinate System, Profile, and User login scripts with the NDS Expert.

- Work with the Server Specialist to ensure availability of specialized application servers.

Connectivity Specialist

The Connectivity Specialist works with the physical network, Internet backbone, telecommunications, WAN design, and router placement. He or she must understand the technical aspects of internetworking. In addition, the Connectivity Specialist must understand traffic concerns caused by replicas, time synchronization, and NDS overhead. For this reason, he/she must work very closely with the other project team members to optimize router placement. Maid Marion is the best woman for the job. She understands connectivity. Following is a list of her responsibilities and concerns:

▸ Determine the effect of routing, protocols, telecommunications, and WAN structure on the directory tree design.

▸ Make decisions regarding single or multiple protocols on the network. Also coordinate with the Server Specialist to ensure protocol compatibility.

▸ Deliver better internetwork traffic throughput.

▸ Advise the project team about routing, protocols, and WAN structure.

▸ Determine the efficiency of LAN/WAN bandwidth issues. This involves determining which protocol to use on the LAN versus the WAN.

▸ Determine the need to include specialized products, including NetWare IP. This should include identifying current utilization figures.

▸ Maintain seamless connectivity to hosts and other non-NetWare 4 operating systems.

There you have it. That's your project team. Nine of the greatest minds in history—plus *you*! It's nice to know the world is in such good hands.

Now that you have the team in place, you can get them rolling. The first task is data gathering—and it's a doozy! In the next section, we'll learn everything there is to know about ACME and discover some very detailed NDS design inputs. It's amazing what you can find when you go digging around. So without any further ado, let's get to know ACME.

ZEN

"Peanuts and pineapples. Noses and grapes. Everything comes in different shapes."

Dr. Seuss

Gathering NDS Information

As we learned earlier, data gathering is the process of determining *who* is doing *what* to *whom* and *why*. In other words, "just the facts, ma'am." In our case, it breaks out like this:

- Who —ACME

- What—Trying to make the world a better place and increase the *World Health Index.*

- Whom—All living creatures on the earth.

- Why—To save the human race from Alpha Centurion annihilation.

Objectivity is crucial in data gathering. Sometimes it's harder than you might think—like now. All sorts of distortions have a profound effect on the data as it is gathered. The *Hawthorne Effect* states that individuals who know they have to save the earth shrivel up and crawl into caves under the influence of immense pressure. But that's not going to happen to us, because we are CNE superheroes!

The process of data gathering for NDS design is interesting. You have a specific purpose—building a WAN infrastructure using NetWare 4 and NDS. With this purpose in mind, you need to view the company through *rose-colored glasses*. This means seeing things from a specific point of view, that is, Novell's point of view. As I'm sure you've experienced, data changes as you draw it into focus. When you approach ACME, view the data from two unique points of view:

- Organizational—How does the company operate and what's its purpose?

- Technical—What technical devices are in place to facilitate the exchange of information?

It's a pretty tricky balancing act. Organizational design inputs are more subjective in nature. They deal with the company as a business unit and ignore the means for exchanging information. Technical design inputs, on the other hand, are objective in nature. They involve the physical WAN infrastructure and ignore the content of the message. Obviously, both are equally important, but since we're designing an NDS infrastructure, you may want to give more weight to the technical inputs (see Figure 3.6).

FIGURE 3.6

Balancing Organizational
and Technical Design
Inputs

There are four organizational design inputs. They are represented as a reverse pyramid in Figure 3.6 because information narrows as you move down the model. Here's a quick list:

- Company overview

- Organizational chart

- *Chronicles*

- Workflow

Organizational design inputs start with a company overview and snapshot of its mission statement. These items are usually detailed in the organizational chart, which also helps you identify the players and their relationships to each other. The *Chronicles* is a detailed study of each division and its key players. A careful study of the in-depth *Chronicles* helps you to create a workflow diagram. The workflow document and its accompanying diagram describe the daily operations of the company and each key player's task-oriented responsibilities. It also describes the daily or weekly movement of data from one location to another. Along with the organizational chart, the workflow document is probably the most important organizational design input.

There are also four technical design inputs. These inputs concentrate more on the delivery of information than its content. Technical inputs typically are already in place and need to be redesigned to accommodate NetWare 4 and NDS. Here's a quick list:

▸ World Location Map

▸ WAN Layout

▸ Campus Maps

▸ Resource Lists

Technical design inputs start with the world location map—a global view of the company's geography. From a connectivity point of view, the world location map quickly becomes a WAN layout. The WAN layout is one of the most important technical design inputs because it summarizes the movement of data between company locations. Next, you should zero in on each location and create detailed campus maps. Each campus map identifies the distribution of buildings, LANs, routers, and existing WAN backbones. Finally, the resource list, which is the most nerdy technical design input, breaks out each campus into its physical network resources—users, file servers, print servers, print queues, and printers.

Each of these organizational and technical design inputs will play a key role in saving the world. As you'll learn in following chapters, technical design inputs help define the upper layers of the NDS tree. They also play an important role in NDS naming, partitioning, replica distribution, and time synchronization. Finally, in Chapter 8 (Managing NDS), we'll use the resource list to create a plethora of NDS objects and place them in the new tree. It's important to note that object placement plays a key role in resource accessibility and WAN productivity.

The organizational design inputs, on the other hand, define the bottom layers of the NDS tree. With them, we can add flexibility and purpose to the WAN infrastructure. Organizational inputs play an important role in security, configuration, management, and application design. They also help us refine our NDS objects and ensure their productive placement in the tree.

We have a lot to look forward to in the next 12 chapters. But before we can go anywhere, we need to explore ACME in depth and develop our eight critical design inputs. It's a good thing we have our project team to help. On the count of three, let them loose. 1, 2,....

GETTING TO KNOW ACME

In the social hierarchy of needs, the world is pretty screwed up. The Pyramid of Needs states that basic fundamental needs, like food and shelter, preclude us from enjoying higher needs, like art, education, and corn dogs. This pyramid exists at many different levels throughout the world. Almost two-thirds of our population doesn't have sufficient resources to satisfy the lowest basic needs—medicine, food, shelter, and peace—while a smaller percentage takes higher needs—like digital watches—for granted. Something needs to change.

As a matter of fact, the Alpha Centurions have discovered this and have decided to do something about it. As it turns out, they are great fans of the Planet Earth and would hate to see us destroy it. The good news is they are a benevolent and intelligent race. They understand the Pyramid of Needs and recognize that everyone should be able to enjoy digital watches. They have discovered that the top 1 percent of the Earth's population is destroying the world at an alarming pace, while the other 99 percent are just trying to survive. In an effort to save the world, they have issued an ultimatum:

Clean up your act or find another planet to exploit!

They have given us until January 1, 2000, to clean up our act—or else! It's safe to say that the fate of the human race is in your hands. To help measure our progress, the Alpha Centurions have developed a World Health Index (WHI). The WHI is a balanced calculation of seven positive and seven negative factors that determine how good or bad we're treating the Earth. They've decided that 100 is a good number to shoot for. It represents a good balance between basic and higher needs. Once the world achieves a

WHI of 100, almost everyone will be able to afford a digital watch. Here's a quick list of the 14 positive and negative WHI factors:

WHI Positive	WHI Negative
Charity	Crime
Love	Pollution
Birth	Starvation
Education	Disease
Health	War
Laughing	Poverty
Sports	Corruption

Bottom line: The Alpha Centurions have given us a little over three years to increase our WHI from its current level (–2) to 100. We have until January 1, 2000. If we don't clean up our act by then, they will mercifully eradicate all humans and let the animals and plants live peacefully on the Planet Earth.

ZEN

"This magnificent butterfly finds a little heap of dirt and sits still on it. But man will never on his heap of mud keep still."

Joseph Conrad

ACME has been designed as "A Cure for Mother Earth." It is staffed by the greatest heroes from our unspoiled history. These are the founding mothers and fathers of Earth's golden age—before instant popcorn, talking cars, and daytime television. It's clear that somewhere along the human timeline, progress went amuck. We need help from heroes before that time. In order to vortex back in history and grab the ACME management, we've used the prototype Oscillating Temporal Overthruster (OTO). We've hand-chosen only the brightest and most resourceful characters, then meticulously trained each one of them for special tasks. They're a little disoriented but more than happy to help.

These historical heroes have been placed in an innovative organizational structure. As you can see in Figure 3.7 (see poster bound into this book as well), ACME is organized around five main divisions. They are:

- Human Rights (Gandhi)—Taking care of the world's basic needs, including medicine, food, shelter, and peace. These tasks are handled jointly by Albert Schweitzer, Mother Teresa, Florence Nightingale, and Buddha. This division's work has the most positive impact on the WHI.

- Labs (Albert Einstein)—Putting technology to good use. This division is the technical marvel of ACME. In addition to research and development (R&D) efforts, the Labs division is responsible for the WHI tracking center in NORAD. This division is staffed by the wizardry of Leonardo da Vinci, Sir Isaac Newton, Charles Darwin, Marie Curie, Charles Babbage, and A.d.a., "The Countess of Lovelace."

- Operations (King Arthur)—Saving the world can be a logistical nightmare. Fortunately, we have King Arthur and the Knights of the Round Table to help us out. In this division, ACME routes money from caring contributors (Charity) to those who need it most (Financial)—there's a little Robin Hood in there somewhere. Also, with the help of Merlin, we distribute all the Human Rights and Labs material to the four corners of the globe.

- Crime Fighting (Sherlock Holmes and Dr. Watson)—Making the world a safer place. This division tackles the almost insurmountable task of eradicating world crime. It's a good thing we have the help of Sherlock Holmes and some of our greatest crime-fighting superheroes, including Robin Hood, Maid Marion, Wyatt Earp, and Wild Bill Hickok. These heroes deal with the single most negative factor in WHI calculations—crime. This is very important work.

- Admin (George Washington)—Keeping the rest of ACME running smoothly. It's just like a well-oiled machine with the help of America's Founding Fathers—George Washington, Thomas Jefferson, Abraham Lincoln, FDR, and James Madison. Their main job is public relations under the command of one of our greatest orators, Franklin Delano Roosevelt (FDR). In addition to getting the word out, Admin tracks ACME activity (auditing) and keeps the facilities operating at their best.

*ACME Organizational
Chart*

Now it's your turn. You are the final piece in our globe-trotting puzzle. You are ACME's MIS department. We have recruited you as the architect of our communications strategy. As a NetWare 4 CNE, you come highly recommended. Your mission—should you choose to accept it—is to build the ACME WAN. You will need courage, design experience, NDS know-how, and this book. If you succeed, you will save the world and become a CNE! All in a day's work.

ACME has a daunting task ahead of it, so we don't have any time to mess around. I'd like to begin by thanking you for choosing to accept this mission. Now you'll find some design inputs included with this book. They are *for your eyes only*. Once you have read the inputs, eat them! There's other good news—you don't have to save the world alone. The project team is here to help you. Following is a list of our eight ACME design inputs and the respective roles of each project team member. Remember, we're counting on you. Be careful not to let these facts fall into the wrong hands. Believe it or not, there are forces at work that don't share our love for the human race.

ACME Overview

- ▶ IS Manager—Provide an in-depth tour of the ACME facilities.

- ▶ All project team members—Absorb ACME's mission and integrate it into everything they do.

ACME Organizational Chart

▸ IS Manager—Identify upper management.

▸ Education/Training Coordinator—Determine which groups need training and who to contact for scheduling.

▸ NDS Expert—Identify major divisions and potential ACME work groups.

ACME *Chronicles*

▸ IS Manager—Identify ACME management tasks and the relationships between employees.

▸ Education/Training Coordinator—Identify individuals for managerial and technology training. Determine who will be the most affected by updated technology.

▸ All project team members—Grasp the daily routine of ACME and identify communication paths.

ACME Workflow

▸ IS Manager—Learn how ACME's workflow affects the big picture. Determine better communication paths.

▸ Testing Lab Coordinator—Identify what applications are being used and test them with NetWare 4 and NDS.

▸ Education/Training Coordinator—Discover how ACME can make the most of updated networking technology to better facilitate workflow.

▸ NDS Expert—Learn how information flows throughout the company. Isolate data flow to help design the bottom layers of the NDS tree. Finally, associate workflow tasks with new NDS objects.

▸ Application Specialist—Identify what new and existing applications are needed to facilitate work and data flow.

▸ Connectivity Specialist—Follow the flow of data over the existing network communications path. Determine whether to include remote sites in the directory tree.

ACME World Location Map

▸ Server Specialist—Determine how many servers are at each location. Track which version of NetWare each of the servers is running, and then document these servers in a Global Location Map to help the NDS Expert build the top levels of the tree.

▸ NDS Expert—Use server information to plan the upper layers of the NDS tree. Begin to sketch partitioning and replication strategies. Finally, decide whether regional containers are necessary.

▸ Connectivity Specialist—Determine how information is flowing throughout the main ACME locations.

ACME WAN Layout

▸ Testing Lab Coordinator—Determine a method of simulating typical bandwidth scenarios over existing ACME WAN links.

▸ Server Specialist—Identify key servers performing routing functions in the ACME WAN topology.

▸ NDS Expert—Count the WAN sites and measure throughput across all WAN links. This will help define the upper layers of the NDS tree. It also impacts replication and time synchronization.

▸ Connectivity Specialist—Identify the fastest and slowest WAN links. Determine a need for remote dial-in.

ACME Campus Maps

▶ Testing Lab Coordinator—Learn to simulate typical LAN traffic.

▶ Server Specialist—Determine how many servers are in each LAN segment. Identify requirements for special services such as NetWare for Macintosh and supplemental protocols.

▶ NDS Expert—Determine the major resources in each LAN. Discover how they are grouped, and build appropriate NDS objects.

▶ Application Specialist—Learn where applications are stored and how they are used. Discover more efficient alternatives.

▶ Connectivity Specialist—Learn how data is routed within LAN segments. Discover more efficient alternatives.

ACME Resource List

▶ IS Manager—Identify the resources that will require special management. Budget for upgrading existing hardware and buying new equipment.

▶ Testing Lab Coordinator—Obtain samples of all physical resources and test them under the stresses of NetWare 4 and NDS.

▶ Education/Training Coordinator—Determine needs for specialized training for particular workstations and/or printers.

▶ Server Specialist—Track NetWare 3 and NetWare 4 servers in each location. Determine the diversity of clients and special networking products such as SAA, NFS, Macintosh, and TCP/IP. Plan for expansion.

▶ Workstation Specialist—Identify the status of existing clients and determine how many workstations need to be upgraded.

▶ NDS Expert—Convert existing and new resources to the new NDS naming standard, then use this list to create and place NDS objects in the tree.

▸ Application Specialist—Determine how many software licenses need to be supported for each platform. Explore the prospect of upgrading user applications.

▸ Connectivity Specialist—Identify existing protocols and plan for the addition of new ones. Propose a strategy for connecting these physical resources in local- and wide-area environments.

There you have it. The eight ACME design inputs and all of your helpers. There's a lot more to this design stuff than meets the eye. Now let's take a closer look at the remaining six ACME inputs and begin sketching out a strategy for saving the world. Sounds like fun!

QUIZ

One last time, let's test your ability to "see what isn't there." The man from the country at the top of the Himalayas came by plane to meet the man from the Far East who was wearing a chain around his neck. What was the weather when they met the man from the Middle East?

(Q3-3)

ACME *CHRONICLES*
A day in the life...
What you're about to read is for your eyes only. This is extremely confidential information. The ACME *Chronicles* is a detailed look at the life and times of ACME. This is an exceptional organization created for a singular purpose—to save the world. As you can see in Figure 3.7, ACME is organized around five main divisions:

▸ Human Rights

▸ Labs

▸ Operations

▸ Crime Fighting

▶ Admin

Let's go inside and see what makes them tick.

Human Rights—Gandhi in Sydney

This is the "heart" of ACME's purpose. Human Rights has the most profound positive effect on the WHI. Efforts here can save lives and increase our chances of surviving into the next century. The goal of Human Rights is to raise people from the bottom of the Pyramid of Needs. By satisfying their basic needs (medicine, food, shelter, and peace), we hope to give humans the strength to fight for higher needs (equality, justice, education, and digital watches). This makes the world a better place and dramatically improves the WHI.

All Human Rights materials developed here are distributed every day through 10 different distribution centers around the world. This is ACME's manufacturing facility for food, shelter, and medical aid. In addition, the peacekeepers use any means necessary to thwart global wars. Let's take a closer look at the four different departments of Human Rights.

▶ Medical (Albert Schweitzer)—This department is collecting basic medical materials and training doctors and nurses for field work. Also, ACME is eagerly developing vaccines and working overtime to cure serious diseases. Finally, their medical staff is taking steps to clean up the sanitation of "dirty" countries. This is all accomplished with the help of Albert Schweitzer and his dedicated staff.

▶ Food (Mother Teresa)—With the help of her country-trained culinary heroes, Mother Teresa will determine how much Opossum Stew the whole world can eat. In addition, they are developing a series of genetically engineered organisms that will transform inedible materials into food stock. Finally, ACME's Food department has teamed up with R&D to create virtual reality (V/R) programming that teaches people how to grow food of their own. After all, if you give a person a fish, they eat for a day; but if you teach them to fish, they eat for a lifetime (and get a guest spot on ESPN's *Outdoor World*).

▶ Shelter (Florence Nightingale)—With all the new healthier and happier people in the world, our attention shifts to shelter. Fortunately, Florence Nightingale and her crack construction team have developed a cheap recyclable geodesic dome called a Permaculture. It has central heating, air conditioning, water, plumbing, and computer-controlled maid service. The most amazing thing about the dome is that it can be constructed from any native materials—that's cacti and sand in the desert, lily pads in the marsh, and snow in the Arctic. If all else fails, they're edible.

▶ Peace (Buddha)—One of the most overlooked basic needs is peace. All the other stuff doesn't mean a hill of beans if you're living in a war zone. Buddha's job is to somehow settle the 101 wars currently plaguing our Earth. He relies on a combination of wisdom, diplomacy, military presence, and fortune cookies.

That completes our discussion of Human Rights. Now let's take a look at the ACME Labs division.

Labs—Albert Einstein in NORAD

Albert Einstein is one of the greatest minds in our history, but how far can he push technology? The U.S. Military has loaned us the NORAD facility in Colorado as a base for technical wizardry. In addition to Research & Development (R&D), this is the central point of a vast WHI data-collection network.

ACME's R&D efforts are controlled by Leonardo da Vinci and his dream team of scientists. They use technology and a little bit of magic to save the Earth. Current projects include alternative power sources, V/R programming, anti-pollutants, NDS, and a cure for bad hair days. Let's take a closer look:

▶ V/R (Sir Isaac Newton)—V/R programming is being developed to convince the world that a cure is necessary. The V/R devices will be sold as video games and will help ACME tap the minds of the world. This borders on mind control but in a good way (if that's possible). There's nothing that brain power and a little bit of magic can't cure.

- Pollution (Charles Darwin)—This department is developing anti-pollutants and methods of transforming garbage into fuel. Also, this group is working to eradicate the world's largest scourge—ElectroPollution. Currently Leonardo da Vinci and Charles Darwin are working on airplanes powered by pencil erasure grit.

- Nuclear (Marie Curie)—Cybernetic soldiers (Nuclear Disarmament Squads or NDS) are being designed to infiltrate and neutralize nuclear weapons facilities. Finally, somebody's splitting atoms for good.

In addition to R&D, NORAD is the central point of a vast WHI data-collection network. This network is the pulse of ACME. Collection of world data and calculation of the WHI occur here every day. Currently, the WHI sits at –2. And as we all know, it must climb to over 100 by January 1, 2000. Charles Babbage and Ada diligently guard the computers and make daily adjustments to WHI calculations. Ada's sacrifice is particularly notable because she used to be the "Countess of Lovelace." But fortunately for us, she had a soft spot in her heart for mathematics and Mr. Babbage.

Distributed world data–collection centers are scattered to all four corners of the Earth. There are 10 ACME WHI hubs—one in every divisional headquarters—and 5 more scattered to strategic points around the Earth. From each of these sites, world data is sent to NORAD and calculated on a daily basis. The results are distributed to every major newspaper so the world can chart ACME's progress. In addition to the 10 WHI hubs, there are hundreds of collection clusters distributed around each hub. Each cluster sends data directly to the closest hub (via dial-up lines) and eventually back to the central site at NORAD. See Figure 3.8 for an illustration of the 10 data-collection hubs.

ZEN

Techno-hip—comfortable with the use of the modern jargon of computers and other recent technological developments. Just think—all you have to do is memorize all the CNE nomenclature in this book and you will be a "techno-hipster." An unexpected side effect of becoming a CNE.

That completes our journey through ACME technology. Now let's take a look at the Operations division.

Operations—King Arthur in Camelot

King Arthur and his court will keep ACME financed through charity drives and financial spending. After all, "money makes the world go 'round." Never before has it been more true. In addition, the Operations division handles the arduous task of distributing ACME aid to all the people who need it. Here's how it works:

- ▶ Distribution (Merlin)—We're going to need all the magic we can get. This department handles the distribution of human rights materials, medical supplies, doctors, nurses, food, hardware, building supplies, and pre-fabricated geodesic domes. No guns! It also handles implementation of WHI devices from R&D, such as anti-pollutants, Nuclear Disarmament Squads (NDS), anti-hacking viruses, and V/R programming. The latter is handled through satellite TV transmissions and video games. ACME distribution takes place through the same 10 hubs as WHI. Once again, refer to Figure 3.8. Think of it as data in (WHI) and aid out (Distribution).

- ▶ Financial (Guinevere)—This is the money-out department. Guinevere handles the distribution of charity contributions, including the purchase of human rights material, bailing-out of bankrupt nations, and the funding of internal ACME activities. For a more detailed discussion of Financial operations, refer to the ACME Workflow section below.

- ▶ Charity (Knights of the Round Table)—This is the money-in department. The Knights collect charity from world organizations and distribute it to the Financial department for disbursement. Each of the five major Knights oversees one of five charity centers—in each of the divisional headquarters. Sir Lancelot is in Sydney, Sir Gawain is in NORAD, Sir Galahad handles Camelot, Sir Percival oversees Rio, and Sir Kay is in Tokyo. I haven't seen such dedication since the medieval ages.

Well, that's how ACME's Operations work. Now let's take a look at Crime Fighting.

Crime Fighting—Sherlock Holmes in Tokyo

Crime has one of the most negative effects on the WHI. Fortunately, we have history's greatest crime-fighting mind to help us out—Sherlock Holmes. With the help of Dr. Watson, he has identified two major categories of world crime:

▸ White Collar

▸ Blue Collar

White-collar crimes include cyberhacking and political espionage. Robin Hood and his Band of Superheroes direct white-collar crime-fighting efforts from Tokyo. Here are some of the different types of crimes they're concerned with:

▸ Cyber (Friar Tuck)—With the help of the *Cyberphilia* underground, Friar Tuck attempts to thwart cyber crime. Most cyber crimes occur on The Net, so ACME must constantly monitor global communications. Tuck also has the help of an off-shoot group of guardian angels known as the Cyber Angels.

▸ Political (Maid Marion)—She can charm her way through any politically tense situation. Political crimes are especially rampant in emerging nations, so Maid Marion enlists the help of the United Nations.

▸ Financial (Little John)—With some creative financing and the help of ex-IRS agents, Little John thwarts financial crimes throughout the world. These crimes especially hurt the middle class, so he has recruited some key Yuppies as undercover agents.

Blue-collar crimes are a little more obvious—such as violence and theft. This is familiar ground for Wyatt Earp and his band of western heroes. They're not glamorous, but they're effective. Here's a look at ACME Crime Fighting from the blue-collar point of view:

▸ Violent (Bat Masterson)—This cowboy is in his own element. He thwarts violent crime by getting inside the criminal's mind—literally.

▸ Environmental (Wild Bill Hickok)—A great fan of the environment, Mr. Hickok uses his country charm to thwart environmental crimes such as excessive deforestation, toxic waste, whaling, oil spills, ElectroPollution, and forced extinction.

▸ Theft (Doc Holliday)—With his legendary sleight of hand, Doc Holliday stays one step ahead of the world's thieves.

So that's what's happening on the crime fighting front. Now let's take a close look at the final ACME division—Admin.

Admin—George Washington in Rio

Ever since the beginning of time, humans have quested for wisdom and knowledge. Now we'll need to put all of our enlightenment to good use—or else. A few centuries ago, the United States' Founding Fathers joined a growing group of men and women called Illuminoids. These people were dissatisfied with everyday life on Planet Earth and began to reach above, within, and everywhere else for a better way. The Illuminoids formed a variety of organizations dedicated to creating a New World Order including the Masons, Trilateral Commission, Council on Foreign Relations (CFR), and the Bilderberg Group.

Regardless of their ultimate motivation, the Illuminoids' hearts were in the right place—"let's make the world a better place." The founder of the Trilateral Commission has always claimed they are just *a group of concerned citizens interested in fostering greater understanding and cooperation among international allies.* Whether or not it's true, it sounds like a great fit for ACME. Once again, we've used the OTO to grab some of the earliest Illuminoids and solicit their help for ACME administration.

George Washington keeps the ACME ship afloat. Along with FDR, he keeps things running smoothly and makes sure the world hears about our plight. In addition, James Madison keeps the facilities running, while Abraham Lincoln makes sure ACME is held accountable for all its work. For years, the Trilateral Commission has been rumored to covertly run the world. Now they get a chance to overtly save it!

Now let's take a look at the four departments that make up ACME's administration:

▶ Public Relations (Franklin Delano Roosevelt)—This department solicits help from the rest of the world by enlisting the help of heroes from our own age—the 1990s. We're not going to be able to save the world alone. The PR department is responsible for communicating our plight to the four corners of the Earth. Department members inform everyday citizens about the Alpha Centurion ultimatum, daily WHI quotes, and requests for charity. There is a local PR office in each major location. See the organizational chart in Figure 3.7 for more details.

▸ Marketing (Thomas Jefferson)—Educating the rest of the world and soliciting help is another Marketing department responsibility. In addition to advertising, this department develops materials for distributed PR offices. Its goal is to rally all nations around ACME and our cause in order to save the Earth. They also bake really good apple pies and chocolate chip cookies.

▸ Auditing (Abraham Lincoln)—He makes sure that everyone stays in line. Financial trails for all charity moneys and complete records of all changes to the WHI are tracked by the Auditing department. Although it's part of the internal ACME organization, Auditing is an independent tracking company that generates bonded reports.

▸ Facilities (James Madison)—This department keeps everyone working, happy, and fed. The Facilities department also organizes field trips and ACME parties. Imagine the doozy they're going to have when we finally succeed!

Well, there you have it. That's everything there is to know about ACME. I hope these *Chronicles* have helped you and the project team better understand what ACME is up against. This is no normal organization. If ACME goes out of business, the world is either lost or saved—it's up to you.

ACME WORKFLOW

Although it may look complicated, the daily grind at ACME is really pretty simple. It's a combination of workflow and dataflow. *Workflow* describes the daily operations of ACME staff and their task-oriented responsibilites. *Dataflow* describes the daily or weekly movement of data from one location to another. Although the two are not always the same, they should be compatible. This is the goal of ACME synergy.

In this section, we're going to take a detailed look at how work and data flow through the ACME organization. This data has a dramatic impact on NDS design. Afterall, work and data flow over the WAN infrastructure. Refer to Figure 3.8 as you follow along. Here's how it works:

ACME Workflow Diagram

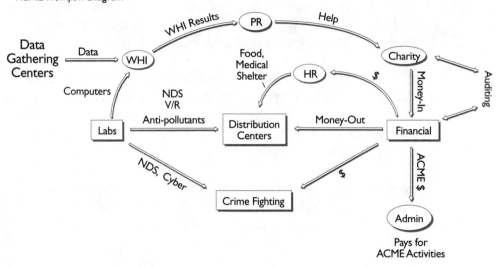

Financial—Money-Out

Of course, money makes the world go 'round! The Financial department has two main responsibilities:

- Money-in

- Money-out

Money-in focuses on funding ACME activities and distributing charities to needy people. In funding ACME activities, Guinevere pays for Human Rights materials, Admin work, and Crime Fighting tools. Next, she disburses charity money through distribution centers. Money-in comes from the various Charity activities. All financial activity is audited by the internal Auditing organization.

Technically, this is accomplished from a central database at the Financial headquarters in Camelot. No money changes hands. Quarterly budgets are developed in Camelot and distributed to local banks for Human Rights, Crime Fighting, Distribution, and Admin. Each of these distributed sites sends weekly updates to the central database with the help of local servers.

Distribution Centers

The Distribution department is the hub of ACME achievements. Distribution centers disburse three kinds of aid:

- Human Rights materials (such as food, medicine, and shelter)

- Money from the Financial department

- Exciting inventions from Labs

Each of the 10 distribution centers maintains its own distributed database. They move material to local warehouses for delivery to needy people. Weekly summary updates are sent to the central inventory management database in Camelot. The central database oversees the big picture of aid distribution.

If a center runs out of a particular resource, one of two things happens:

1 • Camelot updates the center's budget, and they purchase the resource locally.

2 • Camelot orders the movement of resources from another distribution center. This option makes sense for finite materials such as special inventions from Labs or medical supplies.

Labs and Their Inventions

This is where the brainiacs hang out. Scientists in the Labs division develop world-saving toys for:

- Crime Fighting—NDS and cyberviruses

- Distribution—V/R programming and anti-pollutants

The Labs division supports WHI and all its technical needs. New product updates are sent to Distribution and Crime Fighting for internal consumption. This is secure information.

WHI Calculations

Labs is also where the WHI (World Health Index) is calculated. Charles Babbage and Ada collect data from data-gathering centers (DGCs) throughout the world. These DGCs are housed in divisional headquarters and distribution centers throughout the ACME WAN. They are:

NORAD	Seattle
Rio	Cairo
Camelot	New York
Sydney	Moscow
Tokyo	St. Andrews

Ironically, the distribution centers send aid *out* and the DGCs pull data *in*—from the same 10 locations. Daily WHI summary calculations are sent to NORAD each day so the final WHI calculation can be made. Results are distributed to PR daily for inclusion in global periodicals—including the ACME *Chronicles* (an hourly interactive newsletter).

Public Relations

This is the voice of ACME. In addition to distributing daily WHI reports, Public Relations (PR) educates the world and helps solicit money for Charity. PR pulls the daily WHI results from NORAD twice a day. They're also the on-line editors of the ACME *Chronicles*, which gives them some great financial leads for Charity.

Charity—Money-In Charity is ACME's open door. It is the funnel for ACME contributions. There is a charity center in each of the five divisional headquarters. This is how the top 1 percent helps the rest of us. Their motto is:

Spread the Wealth, or the Alpha Centurions will eat you!

All money collected by Charity is sent to the Financial department for disbursement. Two of the most important uses for this money are Crime Fighting and Admin. Note that the money doesn't actually change hands. It is deposited in local divisional banks, and daily updates are sent to the central financial database in Camelot.

Crime Fighting

Remember, crime has one of the greatest negative effects on the WHI. The Crime Fighting department relies on the following sources:

- Labs' inventions (NDS and cyberviruses)

- Money from the Financial department

- The guile of Robin Hood, Wyatt Earp, and their respective heroes

ACME Administration

The ACME staff has to eat. Admin relies on money from Financial to keep things running smoothly. You can't fight bureaucracy. In addition, the Auditing department needs audit-level access to the central financial database in Camelot. They are responsible for tracking money-in from Charity and money-out from Financial.

ZEN

Chaos theory—the systematic approach to describing very complex events in mathematics and science by rounding off numerical data to reveal very general patterns. This theory can be used to describe the irregular patterns of a dripping water faucet, fluctuations in insect populations, stock-market price changes, or the daily grind of a CNE. In all cases, chaos theory relies on the strange attractor, which is a complex and unpredictable pattern of movement—much like a user's interface with NetWare workstations or your understanding of ACME.

That's all there is to it. No sweat. As you can see, ACME runs like a well-oiled machine. Somebody sure put a lot of effort into designing its organizational structure—and it shows! We're in good hands with ACME.

Now let's shift gears from organizational inputs to technical design inputs. These include:

- ACME World Location Map

- ACME WAN Layout

- ACME Campus Maps

- ACME Resource List

Remember, you need to create a design synergy that properly balances organizational and technical design inputs. Think *balance!*

ACME WAN MAPS

The world is a pretty big place. It takes a truly global organization to save it. ACME is this organization. Now we shift our focus from organizational design inputs to more technical data. These four inputs play an important role in designing the upper layers of the NDS tree. In addition, they affect NDS naming, partitioning, replica distribution, time synchronization, and object placement. In this section, we'll explore the first three technical design inputs:

- ▶ ACME World Location Map

- ▶ ACME WAN Layout

- ▶ ACME Campus Maps

ACME World Location Map

ACME's global structure is shown in Figure 3.9. This structure includes the five main divisional headquarters and five more distribution/WHI data-collection centers. The ACME organization has been distributed to all four corners of the globe to ensure cultural diversity. Five different continents are represented as well as most of the world's major countries. This is truly an organization for the world.

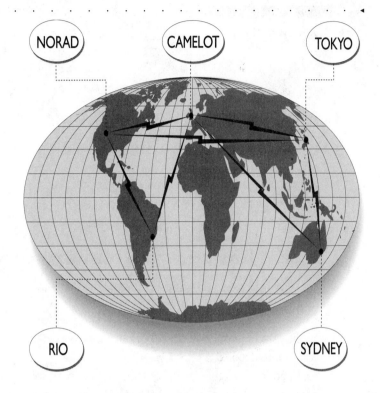

F I G U R E 3.9

ACME World Location Map

ACME WAN Layout

As you can see in Figure 3.10, ACME organizes its five main hubs in a *ring/star redundant design.* This structure provides multiple redundant paths from each location. Even if the center of the star (Camelot) goes down, all other sites remain connected. This is accomplished with the help of sophisticated WAN hubs and high-bandwidth lines.

FIGURE 3.10

ACME WAN Layout

Note the bandwidth measurements on each WAN link. These values are important to the NDS Expert as he attempts to design the upper layers of the tree. It also affects replica placement and the distribution of time providers. Refer to Chapter 4 (NDS Design) for a more detailed discussion.

In addition to the ACME organizational chart, WAN layout is probably one of the most important design inputs. The WAN layout represents how ACME shares network resources. Your NDS tree should model it very closely.

ACME Campus Maps

The ACME campus maps allow you to zero in on specific details about primary WAN hubs. You'll need to better understand ACME's local area networks in order to refine the NDS tree. The campus maps show server distribution, router placement, remote access points, and the backbone topology. Each location within the hub provides more insight into how ACME uses its existing network resources. These campus maps can be further enhanced by adding newer technology.

In this case, we've identified three important campuses:

▸ Tokyo—headquarters for the Crime Fighting division (see Figure 3.11).

▸ Camelot—headquarters for ACME Operations (see Figure 3.12).

▸ NORAD—headquarters for ACME Labs and technical wizardry (see Figure 3.13).

FIGURE 3.11

ACME Campus Map for Tokyo

FIGURE 3.12

ACME Campus Map for Camelot

FIGURE 3.13

ACME Campus Map for NORAD

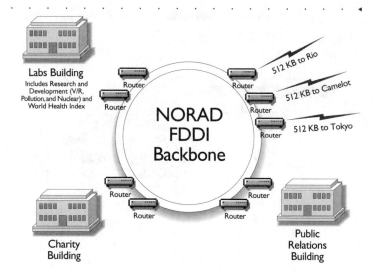

Study these campus maps very closely because they represent a graphical organization of ACME's network resources. This should help you better understand the final technical design input—ACME's resource list.

QUIZ

The value of certain NDS resources isn't always apparent until you look at them very closely. Study the following statement and tell me what it spells:

"Three straight lines joined together so that they are rotated symmetric; four straight lines of three different lengths joined together so that they are vertically symmetric and then repeated later on; a semi-circle repeated later on; three straight lines joined together so that they are vertically symmetric; two straight lines joined together to form a right-angle; and three straight lines joined together so that they are laterally symmetric.

(Q3-4)

ACME RESOURCE LIST

Resources are the life-blood of your network. Let's be honest. A network is simply a bunch of resources connected together. Although this oversimplifies your work at ACME, it is a fair summary of your purpose. As a NetWare 4 CNE, you are chartered with the role of connecting ACME's resources—both old and new.

Before you connect the resources, you must bring them all up to the same level. This involves upgrading NetWare 3 servers to NetWare 4, installing the NetWare DOS Requester client software, testing and upgrading network applications, and improving printer hardware. In addition to upgrading, you'll need to buy some new equipment.

The upgrade process should be reflected in your resource lists. The first list you'll get is existing equipment. Once you've analyzed it, you should create a resource wish list. This list includes all the equipment (old and new) you'll need to accomplish your goal. The wish list can become your road map. It identifies all the areas where you'll need to upgrade or purchase new equipment. Of course, you'll need help from the IS Manager and Guinevere to make this happen.

When you're creating ACME's wish list, focus on these key resources:

- Administrators

- File servers

- Print servers

- Print queues

- Printers

A naming standard is critical to resource organization. Typically, existing naming standards are haphazard at best. Few organizations use naming standards at all. You'll find even less continuity when you attempt to connect dissimilar LANs from geographically separated organizations. In Chapter 4, we'll create a naming standards document and reorganize our resource list. But for now, let's take a look at the resources you'll need in each ACME division.

Human Rights Division

In the Human Rights division, there's one main user (Gandhi) and three department heads. The main division has two file servers, a global print server, and one HP4SI printer. The Medical department is run by Albert Schweitzer. He also has two file servers and one HP4SI printer. Next, the Food department relies on Mother Teresa and her network resources: one file server and one HP4SI printer. The Shelter department has Florence Nightingale at the helm and uses two file servers and an HP4SI printer. Finally, the Peace department is managed by Buddha, who has one file server and an HPIIISI printer.

Labs Division

The Labs division is under the quality tutelage of Albert Einstein. He relies on one main division-oriented file server. In the R&D department, Leonardo da Vinci shares one file server with his three departments. The main print server is also located in the R&D building. Charles Darwin (Pollution), Sir Isaac Newton (V/R), and Marie Curie (Nuclear) each have their own HP4SI printers.

The WHI department is run by Charles Babbage and Ad.a. They need three file servers for index calculations and data storage. They also rely on a print server for output to their Canon BubbleJet printer.

Operations Division

King Arthur runs the Operations division with one file server and a lot of guile. He uses a single print server to service his Canon BubbleJet printer. The Financial department, however, is a lot more technically demanding. Guinevere needs three file servers, two print servers, and two HP4SI printers. In addition, Merlin runs the Distribution department with the help of two file servers, a print server, and an HP III LaserJet printer.

Network resources for the Charity department are much more difficult to track because they're spread across the five global hubs. Each charity center is different depending on the needs of its network administrator. Here's a quick breakdown:

- NORAD—Sir Gawain uses one file server, a print server, and one HP4SI printer.

- Rio—Sir Percival also uses one file server, one print server, and an HP4SI printer.

▶ Camelot—Sir Galahad relies on one file server, a print server, and a new HP5 LaserJet printer.

▶ Sydney—Sir Lancelot needs one file server, a print server, and one HP4SI printer.

▶ Tokyo—Sir Kay is a little busier than the other locations. He needs two file servers, a print server, and an HP4SI LaserJet printer.

ZEN

Flexiplace—a place at home set aside for working that is connected by computer to an office, thereby enabling the worker to avoid commuting to an office. Also called an "electronic cottage," which allows for telecommuting. This is the preferable way of dealing with troubled NetWare 4 users and ACME Operations.

Crime Fighting Division

Sherlock Holmes and Dr. Watson rely on the latest technology to help their crime-fighting efforts. They use two file servers, a print server, and an HP5 LaserJet printer. Each of their Crime Fighting departments follows suit and takes advantage of new technology.

The Blue-Collar department is run by Wyatt Earp. He needs one file server, a print server, and a single HP III LaserJet printer. In addition, each of his crime-fighting units needs its own file server and HP4SI printer. As a matter of fact, Bat Masterson needs two file servers for the Violent Crimes Unit.

Robin Hood runs the White-Collar Crime Fighting department. His criminals are a little more sophisticated. Therefore, he needs two file servers, a print server, and a Canon BubbleJet printer. In addition, each of his crime-fighting units requires its own file server and LaserJet printer. Friar Tuck uses an HP LaserJet III, Maid Marion has an HP4SI, and Little John needs two HP4SI printers to fight financial crime.

Admin Division

George Washington heads up the Admin division. He uses two file servers, a print server, and a Canon BubbleJet printer. Each of his department heads uses a similar configuration. James Madison of Facilities uses one file server, a print server, and an HP4SI printer. Abraham Lincoln has a file server and an HP4SI printer for the Auditing department, and Thomas Jefferson uses a file server and two HP III LaserJet printers.

Network resource tracking for the PR department is a bit trickier because the department is spread across all five ACME locations. Here's a quick breakdown:

- ▸ NORAD—David James Clarke, IV, uses one file server, a print server, and two printers: an HP4SI and a Canon BubbleJet.

- ▸ Rio—Jeff Hughes uses one file server and two printers: an HP4SI and a Canon BubbleJet.

- ▸ Camelot—Cathy Ettelson doesn't print as much as do David and Jeff. She uses a file server, a print server, and one HP4SI printer.

- ▸ Sydney—Mary Clarke requires the same configuration as Cathy, that is, a single file server, a print server, and an HP4SI printer.

- ▸ Tokyo—Blair Thomas follows suit with a single file server, a print server, and an HP4SI printer.

In addition to these resources, ACME has a special NDS file server in each of its five main locations: NORAD, Tokyo, Sydney, Rio, and Camelot.

That completes our detailed discussion of the ACME resource wish list. For a complete summary, refer to Table 3.2. In Chapter 4 (NDS Design), we'll develop a naming standards document and rename these resources. Then in Chapter 8 (Managing NDS), we'll learn all about object placement and create associated NDS objects.

TABLE 3.2			
The ACME Resource Wish List	**DIVISION**	**DEPARTMENT**	**RESOURCES**
	Human Rights		
		Headquarters	Gandhi Two file servers One print server One HP4SI printer
		Medical	Albert Schweitzer Two file servers One HP4SI printer
		Food	Mother Teresa One file server One HP4SI printer
		Shelter	Florence Nightingale Two file servers One HP4SI printer
		Peace	Buddha One file server One HPIII printer
	Labs		
		Headquarters	Albert Einstein One file server
		R&D	Leonardo Da Vinci Charles Darwin Sir Isaac Newton Marie Curie One file server One print server Three HP4SI printers
		WHI	Charles Babbage Ada Three file servers One print server One Canon BubbleJet printer

(continued)

DIVISION	DEPARTMENT	RESOURCES
Operations		
	Headquarters	King Arthur
		One file server
		One print server
		One Canon BubbleJet printer
	Distribution	Merlin
		Two file servers
		One print server
		One HPIII LaserJet printer
	Financial	Guinevere
		Three file servers
		Two print servers
		Two HP4SI printers
	Charity	Sir Percival
		Sir Lancelot
		Sir Gawain
		Sir Galahad
		Sir Kay
		Six file servers
		Five print servers
		Three HP4SI printers
		Two HP5 printers
Crime Fighting		
	Headquarters	Sherlock Holmes
		Dr. Watson
		Two file servers
		One print server
		One HP5 printer
	Blue Collar	Wyatt Earp
		Bat Masterson
		Wild Bill Hickok
		Doc Holliday
		Five file servers
		One print server
		Three HP4SI printers
		One HPIII LaserJet printer

DIVISION	DEPARTMENT	RESOURCES
Crime Fighting		
	White Collar	Robin Hood
		Friar Tuck
		Maid Marion
		Little John
		Five file servers
		One print server
		Three HP4SI printers
		One HPIII LaserJet printer
		One Canon BubbleJet printer
Admin		
	Headquarters	George Washington
		Franklin Delano Roosevelt
		Two file servers
		One print server
		One Canon BubbleJet printer
	Facilities	James Madison
		One file server
		One print server
		One HP4SI printer
	Auditing	Abraham Lincoln
		One file server
		One HP4SI printer
	Marketing	Thomas Jefferson
		One file server
		Two HPIII LaserJet printers
	Public Relations	Mary Clarke
		David James Clarke, IV
		Cathy Ettelson
		Jeff Hughes
		Blair Thomas
		Five file servers
		Five print servers
		Five HP4SI printers
		Two Canon BubbleJet printers

(continued)

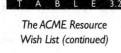

DIVISION	DEPARTMENT	RESOURCES
Locations		
	Camelot	One file server
	NORAD	One file server
	Rio	One file server
	Sydney	One file server
	Tokyo	One file server

T A B L E 3.2

The ACME Resource Wish List (continued)

This completes our discussion of gathering NDS information. In this section, we put ACME under the NDS microscope. This is a critical part of Step 1. All the information you've gathered here will act as raw material for ACME design, installation, and management. It's impossible to create a WAN for ACME until you get inside its collective heads and see what makes them tick. Remember, this is highly confidential information so please make sure it doesn't fall into the wrong hands. Once you've memorized the facts that appear here, you must eat the pages!

I'm ready for NDS design now—how about you? But before we can move on to Step 2, we'll need to explore the final aspect of NDS preparation—the project scope.

The Project Scope

The final task in NDS preparation is establishing the project scope. This task is critical for keeping the WAN under control. Scope provides physical boundaries for the network as well as financial and personnel limitations. After gathering the information, you must explore the system resources and determine how far they can be stretched. In many cases, the scope acts as a restraint to keep unworkable solutions from expanding too far. If the scope is too broad, the WAN will never be finished. If the scope is too narrow, the WAN will surely not meet ACME's needs.

It is critical to establish a WAN scope early in the Process. This is because it has a strong influence on costs, expectations, environment, and implementation time. ACME management is always looking for the bottom line:

How much will it cost us and how long will it take?

In our example, it's important to establish scope right away. How many locations are there? What's it going to take to improve the WHI from –2 to 100? How do my current resources match up with the resource wish list? All of these are good questions that need to be answered before you move on to NDS design. Three components help you establish a project scope. Here's how they work:

▸ Determine project complexity—You will need to analyze certain aspects of the project to determine whether it calls for a simple or complex network. If there are 15 or more servers, for example, you'll need to design custom partitions. If there are 30 or more servers, you'll need to use the customized time configuration method. You'll also need a test lab. Other criteria that impact a project's complexity include multiple sites connected by a WAN, and expected network growth. Further analysis of ACME tells me it's going to be a very complex project.

▸ Developing a schedule—You'll need to develop a process time line in order to coordinate project team activities. This time line also helps ACME management assess the WAN's impact on daily business operations. Once you've developed a schedule, make sure to reevaluate it at key points along the way.

▸ Implementation check points—This component fits with the implementation schedule by providing a mechanism for reevaluating progress. You'll need to use a proactive approach toward keeping the project on time.

ZEN

"I have one last request. Don't use embalming fluid on me. I want to be stuffed with crabmeat."

Woody Allen

If that doesn't sum it up, I don't know what does. On that note, we've completed our discussion of project scope and NDS preparation in general. It has been a wild ride, and the fun has only just begun. In this chapter, we learned about the Process and its four important steps:

▸ Step 1: NDS Preparation

▸ Step 2: Design

▸ Step 3: Implementation

▸ Step 4: Management

In Step 1, we created the project team and gathered filing cabinets full of ACME information. This information will become the foundation of Steps 2, 3, and 4. And who's going to accomplish them? The project team.

As you can see, preparation is crucial. If you think like a Boy Scout, you'll be okay. Please don't try to approach a project of this magnitude without being prepared. Study the information in this chapter carefully, and when you're ready, move on to Step 2— NDS Design.

Good luck; and by the way, thanks for saving the world!

Step 2: NDS Design

The most fascinating thing about roller coasters is the dramatic *ups* and *downs*—literally. Not just the exceptional vertical transitions, but the emotional highs and lows, as well. It all starts with a slow, gentle climb to the highest peak of the ride. Your stomach churns as you anticipate the mind-shattering thrill that awaits. Then, as if for centuries, you pause at the apex, contemplating certain doom.

The fall is the best part. You know you're going to survive, of course, but that doesn't seem to diminish the altitude of the experience. No matter how you slice it—it's straight down, and you love it!

The rest of the ride is great, but nothing compares to the initial thrill. It transcends the rest of the experience. Each new surprise, each hairpin turn, each gut-wrenching twirl is enhanced by the dizzying effect of the very first fall. The ups make the downs that much better.

Welcome to the Apex of NetWare 4. I don't know if you noticed, but the first three chapters were setups—for this very moment. The slow, gentle ascension of NDS and ACME have brought you to the brink of the greatest ride of your CNE life—NDS design.

ZEN

"The greatest thrill known to man isn't flying—it's landing!"

Anonymous

NDS design is one of the most remarkable (and misunderstood) aspects of NetWare 4. You can't really understand it until you've done it, but you can't do it until you understand it—I think this is called a paradox. Fortunately, my friends and I have done *a lot* of design all over the world (and throughout time), so we'll teach you everything you need to know. It starts with four key tree (that rhymes) components:

- ▸ NDS Naming Standards

- ▸ NDS Tree Design

- ▸ Partition and Replica Design

- ▸ Time Synchronization Design

Objects and their names are the foundation of NDS. A complete naming standard is important so that you can design an NDS database that is flexible, easy to use, and meets your business needs. Also, there's so much diversity in NDS "object-ology" that a naming standard is required for most design and management tasks.

Once you've created a naming standards document, it's time to roll up your sleeves and get to work. NDS tree design is a great place to start. At this point, you convert the design inputs into a "rough" NDS tree. The *top* layers of the tree are geographic and the *bottom* layers are organizational. In addition, the container structure should resemble a pyramid in design. It's important to note that most object placement occurs later— during the NDS management phase (see Chapter 8). NDS tree design is primarily concerned with the branches of the tree and a few key leaves, like servers and administrators.

Next, you get to partition the new tree into small little pieces and scatter them around the world (replica placement). At this point, you don't actually perform any partitioning operations, you simply *design* the partition boundaries. Once the boundaries have been designed, you must give serious thought to where they'll go—*replica placement*. Replica placement is one of the most important aspects of NDS design because it directly affects your network's performance, accessibility, and fault tolerance. Remember, you won't actually *place* anything until later—during the NDS management phase (see Chapter 8).

Finally, Time Synchronization Design ensures that all our servers agree on the time. You can choose to accept the NetWare 4 defaults, or institute a customized time synchronization strategy of your own. The important thing is that you consider WAN performance and synchronization traffic when you build your design. Time is of the essence.

What next? Well, that completes the four main aspects of NDS design, but it doesn't end our lesson. One related topic remains, and it almost always gets overlooked— Accessibility Design. Accessibility transcends everything you do in NetWare 4. It is the sole purpose for the WAN's existence—so users can have access to stuff! If you ignore accessibility during the NDS design phase, some users will invariably get left out in the cold. You'll need to address special NDS accessibility considerations (such as mobile users, remote users, login scripts, Bindery Services, connections, and non-DOS workstations). Believe me, it'll make your life much easier if you try to be a little more accessible to your users. Give it a try.

So much to learn, and so little time. Let's start with a closer look at the fundamentals of object naming, and explore a naming standards document for ACME. Ready, set, go.

ZEN

"What's in a name? A rose by any other name would smell as sweet!"

William Shakespeare

NDS Naming Standards

Naming is very closely tied to everything we do. It uniquely identifies us ("Hi. I'm Bob"), it describes our stuff ("I have lots of computers"), and it helps us classify the diversity of mankind ("Bob's a Nerd"). Similarly, NDS naming is fundamental to the "Cloud," because it describes the interrelationships between network resources. In addition, resource searching, a key functionality of the NDS database, relies on naming for objects *types* and *locations*. Good naming implies improved search capabilities now and in the future when more applications take advantage of the Directory's capabilities. You must always think to the future.

NetWare 4 uses a mechanism called the *schema* to define the NDS naming structure for all network resources. The schema is distributed to all NetWare 4 servers, and it follows very specific rules. Contrary to the NetWare 3 Bindery, NDS is a special-purpose naming service that stores objects in a hierarchical format and service up to 16 million objects per server. Your understanding of the schema will help you manage the internal structure of NDS naming. Also, it will help you plan for the future through supplemental object types, add-on products, or third-party applications. After all, once you understand the schema, nobody says you can't change it.

Let's start our discussion of NDS naming standards with a brief stroll through the land of NetWare 4 schema. Then, we'll take a quick-and-dirty look at NDS naming rules, distinguished names, relative distinguished names, context, typeful, and finally, typeless naming. Refer to Chapter 2 for a more comprehensive discussion of these critical naming concepts. Then, the *pièce de résistance*—ACME's NDS Naming Standard. In the final section, we'll explore naming standards in general, and build a doozy for ACME.

So, sit tight, hold onto the person next to you, and enjoy this gut-wrenching, heart-in-your-throat, spine-tingling roller coaster. Truly, an "E" ticket ride.

NDS SCHEMA

NetWare Directory Services (NDS) is an object-oriented name service, and all objects and properties are defined by a set of rules called the *schema*. The schema rules dictate the relationships of all objects and their associated properties. It is automatically stored on every NetWare 4 server, even if it doesn't contain NDS replicas. The schema consists of the following three major components:

- ▸ Object Class

- ▸ Property Definitions

- ▸ Property Syntaxes

These three components work together to establish the set of rules that control the creation of a particular object class in the Directory. In Figure 4.1, you can see the relationship between these components. For instance, each object class is defined in terms of its property definitions. The property definitions, in turn, are defined in terms of certain property syntaxes. The property syntaxes determine data types for property values.

F I G U R E 4.1

Relationship Between the Three Components of the NDS Schema

TIP

Probably the coolest thing about the NDS schema is its flexibility. With special tools, you can enhance and modify the object classes and their definitions. This allows you to create a myriad of exciting new NDS objects (including Picture ID, Credit Card Number, Voice Recognition Pattern, and/or Hat Size). You can even cross-link NDS to the World Wide Web by altering certain aspects of the schema. Of course, these modifications are performed by professionals. Whatever you do, don't try this at home. Also, be sure to account for new object types when you're building your naming standards document.

The *object class* defines the types of NDS objects that can be stored in the Directory. The object class is used as the template for creating individual objects and determining their set of characteristics. This means that every object in the tree belongs to an object class that specifies what properties it can use. This is how NDS tracks the different sets of properties for each object. As you can see in Figure 4.1, object classes are constructed from property definitions.

The default NetWare 4 Schema contains 32 object classes. We discussed 24 of them in Chapter 2. These object classes cannot be removed or deleted. Each of the object classes in the Schema is defined by its relationship to other objects. This relationship is based on the object's name type.

Every NDS object is defined by its *name type* (also referred to as its naming property) and a *value*. The value is assigned by you (the CNE) during the object's creation. As we learned previously, an object's name type determines how it is used in the tree. Some objects are containers, while others are leaf objects. Table 4.1 lists the object name types that are assigned to many of the object classes.

T A B L E 4.1	NAME TYPE	NAME VALUE
Getting to Know Object Name Types	C	Country
	L	Locality
	S	State or Province Name
	O	Organization
	OU	Organizational Unit
	CN	Common Name (includes all leaf objects)

The first five name types (C=Country, L=Locality, S=State, O=Organization, and OU=Organizational Unit) are all container objects. The final name type, CN=Common Name, includes all leaf object classes. This is how NDS deals with non-containers—users, printers, servers, and so on. Table 4.2 lists most of the leaf object classes that use CN as their name type.

TIP

As you may have noticed, not all of the container name types are available to you when building the NDS tree. For example, L=Locality and S=State do not show up in the current versions of NetWare 4 utilities. These name types are found in the schema, but have not been implemented in the utilities. The name type L=Locality was placed in the schema for compatibility with the X.500 standard. When building the structure of your NDS tree, you will use the other container name types (namely, O=Organization and OU=Organizational Unit), which provide you with all the functionality you will need. The L=Locality may be implemented in future releases of NetWare and NDS.

T A B L E 4.2		
Leaf Object Classes and CN	CN=AFP Server	CN=Organization Role
	CN=Bindery	CN=Print Queue
	CN=Bindery Queue	CN=Print Server
	CN=Computer	CN=Printer
	CN=Directory Map	CN=Profile
	CN=Group	CN=User
	CN=NetWare Server	CN=Volume

THE BRAIN

For more information regarding the NDS Schema and its internal structures, check out *Novell's Guide to NetWare 4.1 Networks* by Novell Press.

That's enough schema for now. We'll revisit this concept throughout the remainder of the book. Also, you'll undoubtedly run across in-depth schema discussions at cocktail parties and other social gatherings. Remember, you saw it here first.

ZEN

"Frankly, I don't believe people think of their office as a workplace anymore. I think they think of it as a stationery store with Danish. You want to get your pastry, your envelopes, your supplies, your toilet paper, six cups of coffee, and then go home."

Jerry Seinfeld

Now, let's continue our naming discussion with a quick review of the NDS naming rules. Then, we'll dive into the real meat and potatoes of NDS design—the naming standards document.

NDS NAMING RULES

Your name identifies you as a truly unique individual. In much the same way, an NDS object's name identifies its object class and location in the hierarchical tree. As we learned in Chapter 2, NDS naming impacts two important NetWare 4 tasks:

▸ Login—You must identify your exact location in the NDS tree in order for NetWare 4 to authenticate you during login.

▸ Resource Access—NDS naming exactly identifies the type and location of NetWare 4 resources, including file servers, printers, login scripts, and files.

Before we create ACME's naming standards document, we must learn a few more things about NDS naming rules. In Chapter 2, we discussed a variety of naming issues, including

- ▶ Distinguished Names

- ▶ Relative Distinguished Names

- ▶ Typeful Names

- ▶ Typeless Names

- ▶ Context

- ▶ Leading Periods

- ▶ Trailing Periods

In this section, we will review these concepts and provide some additional insight into how they affect NDS design. Then, we'll jump into a naming standards document for ACME. So, without any further ado, let's start with distinguished names.

Distinguished Names

Each object in the tree is given a distinguished name during creation. This determines the object's name type and its location in the NDS tree. Distinguished names provide a global, complete, and unique identity for objects in the tree. In summary, it consists of three things:

- ▶ The name type

- ▶ The object's name value

- ▶ A list of each container between itself and the [Root]

For example, in Figure 4.2, the distinguished name for George Washington is his object name plus the names of all the containers between him and the [Root]. It begins with his common name, CN=GWashington, followed by each of his containers, OU=ADMIN.OU=RIO.O=ACME.

FIGURE 4.2

George Washington's Distinguished Name is .CN=GWashington.OU =ADMIN.OU=RIO.O=ACME.

Here's what it looks like together:

```
.CN=GWashington.OU=ADMIN.OU=RIO.O=ACME
```

TIP

The proper order for writing an object's distinguished name is *least-significant* (object deepest in the tree) to the *most-significant* (object closest to the [Root]). The distinguished name is written left-to-right. Also, **NDS** will resolve distinguished names regardless of their case. For

instance, in the previous example, the use of **GWashington's**
distinguished name could also be written as
**cn=gwashington.ou=admin.ou=rio.o=acme. We are, however, using
upper/lower case for user objects as part of our NDS naming standard.**

Figure 4.3 illustrates another example of NDS distinguished naming. It includes two
NDS server objects:

```
CN=LABS-SRV1.OU=LABS.OU=NORAD.O=ACME
CN=WHITE-SRV1.OU=WHITE.OU=CRIME.OU=TOKYO.O=ACME
```

▶ • ◀

FIGURE 4.3

*More NDS Distinguished
Names (LABS-SRVI and
WHITE-SRVI)*

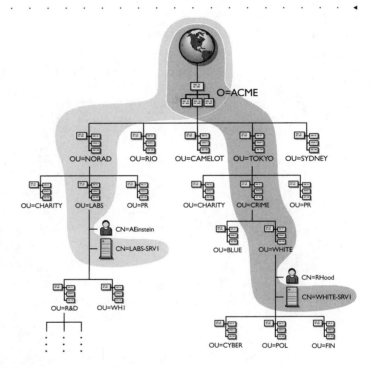

Relative Distinguished Names

A *relative distinguished name* (RDN) makes assumptions about an object's location in
the tree—its context. It must be unique only in relation to the object's parent container.
It is cumbersome to use distinguished names all the time, because they are long and
redundant. You should become familiar with the use of the relative distinguished name

because it allows you to identify objects in relation to their context. These names are shorter and easier to deal with.

For example, Figure 4.4 shows that objects in the PR department in the NORAD location of the ACME tree have unique relative distinguished names in relation to their parent object—OU=PR. Some of the objects are CN=DClarke (user), CN=NOR-PR-SRV1 (server), CN=NOR-PR-SRV1_SYS (volume), and CN=HP4SI-P1 (printer).

F I G U R E 4.4

Relative Distinguished
Names for Two HP4SI
Printers

The relative distinguished name must be unique, but only in the object's parent container. Two objects can share the same name, as long as they live in different containers. This is because objects in different containers are said to be distinguished relative to their parents. Check out the two HP4SI-P1 printers in Figure 4.4. Even though they share the same *relative* name, they each have a unique *distinguished* name:

```
CN=HP4mSI-P1 (in container OU=PR.OU=NORAD.O=ACME)
CN=HP4SI-P1 (in container OU=CHARITY.OU=TOKYO.O=ACME)
```

REAL WORLD

If you are migrating from NetWare 3, then you must create a unique relative distinguished name for each of the objects that you are passing to NetWare 4 and NDS. The NetWare 3 bindery permits you to create the objects with the same name, as long as the object types are different. This rule does not apply to NetWare 4 and NDS.

For example, it is very common for an administrator in NetWare 3 to create a Print Queue object and the group that will use the print queue with the same name. This is an easy method to administer the printing setup, and it is legal in the bindery. However, in NetWare 4, each leaf object is treated the same and must have a unique relative distinguished name within its home container.

During the preparation of your migration from NetWare 3 to NetWare 4, you must clean up or resolve any of these duplicate names. If you do not resolve the naming conflicts, then the migration program will migrate the first object, but not the second object with the same name. For more complete information about migration, refer to Chapter 5 (Step 3: NDS Implementation) and Chapter 7 (NetWare 4 Migration).

Relative distinguished names are not just reserved for leaf objects. All objects in the NDS tree have relative distinguished names in relationship to their parents. For example, you can't create two OU=NORAD containers under the O=ACME Organization. On the other hand, you can create containers with the same name, provided that they are spread throughout the tree. For example, in Figure 4.5, notice that there is a container called CHARITY and PR under each of the locations. This is legal because each instance of the OU=CHARITY and OU=PR containers are unique within each of the location OUs.

Remember, combining each of the relative distinguished names with its parent container creates a distinguished name. Also, both relative distinguished names and the distinguished names can be referenced with (*typeful*) or without (*typeless*) name types. Let's see how that works.

TIP

Although users *can* share relative distinguished names in different containers, we highly recommend that you create a naming standard for usernames that makes them unique across the entire NDS tree. Having a global naming standard for users reduces the chance of a name conflict when the users are created or moved. Also, it simplifies NDS management, login, and resource access for you. These are all good things.

Typeful Names

When you place an object's name type in its name, it's referred to as *typeful naming*. Here are a couple of examples:

```
.CN=SirKay.OU=CHARITY.OU=TOKYO.O=ACME
.CN=TOK-CHR-PS1.OU=CHARITY.OU=TOKYO.O=ACME
```

You can also refer to each of these objects independently as CN=SirKay, CN=TOK-CHR-PS1, OU=CHARITY, OU=TOKYO, and O=ACME. Each object has its own object type plus a unique object name. This type of naming allows NDS to resolve the object's identity in a segmented fashion—one piece at a time. You're not required, however, to provide the name type for each segment (or at all). However, if you start mixing typeful and typeless segments, you're asking for trouble.

TIP

Using typeful names can get cumbersome for users. Consider using typeless naming at the command line, and especially for LOGIN.EXE.

Typeless Names

Typeless names are simply names without types. Makes sense. In these cases, NDS has to "guess" what object types you're using. Here are typeless versions of the names shown previously:

```
.SirKay.CHARITY.TOKYO.ACME
.TOK-CHR-PS1.CHARITY.TOKYO.ACME
```

Notice that we removed the object name type from each segment. You can now refer to the Knight as simply SirKay instead of CN=SirKay. The other leaf and container objects are similarly stripped of their typeness—TOK-CHR-PS1, CHARITY, TOKYO, and ACME. Like the typeful naming method, typeless naming is not case-sensitive. Again, using the previous examples, you can see that .siRKay.charITY.Tokyo.ACME is equivalent to .SIRKAY.ChaRIty.TOKyo.ACMe.

TIP

Typeless names are easier to use for both administrators and users because they are shorter and more intuitive. You should use typeless naming during your day-to-day operations, and become very familiar with it. You can also use this method of typeless naming for indicating either a relative distinguished name or a distinguished name.

The real tricky part of typeless names is guessing which name type to attribute to each object segment. Fortunately, NetWare 4 has some guidelines for determining this:

1 • The leftmost object is a common name (leaf object).

2 • The rightmost object is an Organization (container object).

3 • All middle objects are Organizational Units (container objects).

ZEN

"Diplomacy is the art of saying 'Nice Doggie' until you can find a stick!"

Will Rogers

While this works for most cases, it's only a general guideline. Many times, typeless names are more complex. Things get especially crazy when you mix typeless and typeful names, such as .SirKay.OU=CHARITY.TOKYO.O=ACME. NetWare 4 uses five exception rules for resolving complex typeless names:

1 • Container Objects—Context utilities such as CX are intelligent enough to assume the leftmost object is an OU.

2 • Leaf Objects—Similarly, resource-based utilities such as CAPTURE recognize the leftmost object of a typeless name as a leaf object.

3 • Mixed Names—If both naming schemes are used in the same name, the typeful abbreviation is used as a reference point for resolving the typeless portion of the name.

4 • Current Context—If all else fails, NDS uses the current context to resolve typeless names.

5 • Country Object—If you introduce the Country object in either the current context or a typeful portion of the name, all heck breaks loose. In this case, NDS tries to resolve the name by using any of the previous exception rules. If they don't apply, it isolates the Country object and applies the defaults to the remainder of the typeless name.

Context

Context defines an object's position in the NDS tree. If two objects are in the same container, they have the same context. In NDS design terms, *context* is defined as the name of an object's parent container. As you can see in Figure 4.6, Charles Darwin (CDarwin) is working on Pollution research (OU=POLL), in the R&D department

(OU=R&D) of LABS (OU=LABS) located at the NORAD office (OU=NORAD) of ACME (O=ACME). His context is

`OU=POLL.OU=R&D.OU=LABS.OU=NORAD.O=ACME.`

FIGURE 4.6

Charles Darwin's (CDARWIN) Context

TIP

The best analogy for context in NDS is the DOS PATH command. The path statement in DOS helps you quickly and automatically find files stored in specific subdirectories. In the same fashion, the context in NDS helps you quickly and automatically find resources in specific NDS containers.

Current context defines your workstation's current position in the NDS tree. By controlling your users' current contexts, you can make resource access and tree navigation much easier. From there, they only must reference an object's relative distinguished name—much shorter. For example, Figure 4.7 shows several contexts within the ACME tree. If you're current context was OU=OPS.OU=CAMELOT.O=ACME, then you could reference the BubbleJet printer as CN=CANNONBJ-P1—much easier than the long distinguished name.

Contexts in the ACME Tree

There are many different ways to set a user's current context. The two most popular are

▸ NAME CONTEXT statement in the NET.CFG file

▸ CX

The NAME CONTEXT statement in NET.CFG allows you to set a user's context before logging in. For example, KingArthur could login with his relative distinguished (LOGIN KingArthur) if you put the following statement in his NET.CFG configuration file:

```
Name Context = "OU=OPS.OU=CAMELOT.O=ACME"
```

He could also use the CX (Change conteXt) command to manually set his current context prior to logging in. It goes something like this:

```
CX .OU=OPS.OU=CAMELOT.O=ACME
```

Context does one other thing for you. It allows you to support users from previous versions of NetWare (NetWare 2 and/or NetWare 3). NetWare 4 includes a backward-compatibility feature called Bindery Services. This feature allows bindery users and bindery-based applications to access the NDS tree as if it were the bindery. Bindery Services relies on a special context known as the *bindery context*. Users and bindery applications can only see the NDS objects in their server's bindery context. It's a two-dimensional view of the three-dimensional NDS universe.

TIP

In order to set the bindery context on a server, you can enter SET BINDERY CONTEXT = "OU=OPS.OU=CAMELOT.O=ACME" at the server console, or use SERVMAN.NLM.

Stop for a moment and ask yourself one simple question: "What if I were King Arthur?" Among other things, you'd live in the OU=OPS division of OU=CAMELOT. If you were a bindery user and you attached to the OPS-SRV1 server, your view of the NDS world would be severely diminished (see Figure 4.7). All King Arthur would see is a server (OPS-SRV1), its volume (OPS-SRV1_SYS), a print server (OPS-PS1), a print queue (CANONBJ-PQ1), and a printer (CANONBJ-P1).

A server's default bindery context is set to the container where it was originally installed. The context can be changed to include up to 16 different containers in a sort of "superbindery." It is important to note that previous versions of NetWare 4 (up to and including NetWare 4.02) only allowed you to set a single bindery context for your server. How restricting.

TIP

In terms of bindery context on the server, NDS will only see the objects that previously existed in a NetWare 3 bindery. These objects are limited to user, group, print queue, and print server. In addition, NetWare 4 has added the profile object to assist with migrations from NetWare Name Services (NNS).

Leading Periods

A period (.) is used to separate individual name segments in distinguished names, relative distinguished names, and context. NetWare 4 also supports leading and trailing periods.

A name with a leading period instructs the client software to ignore the current context and start the search at the [Root]. This means that any object name with a leading period will be treated as a distinguished name starting at the [Root].

The leading period is simply a shortcut for navigating the tree, and there can be only one leading period in the object name. Trailing periods, on the other hand, are a completely different kettle of fish.

Trailing Periods

Trailing periods alter the current context. Weird, huh? A single trailing period will move the current context up one container in the tree. For instance, you can use the following CX command to switch to the parent container:

CX .

Unlike leading periods, you can have as many trailing periods as you want. If you want to move up two layers in the tree, simply supply two trailing periods. Simple. For example, in Figure 4.7, if you were King Arthur and you wanted to move to the O=ACME container, you would type:

CX ..

Trailing periods can only be used with relative distinguished names—that is, without leading periods. For example, in Figure 4.7, if King Arthur were at home and he wanted to access the LABS server, he would reference it as:

LABS-SRV1.LABS.NORAD..

In the previous example, NDS bounced King Arthur's current context one layer for each trailing period. He starts at OU=OPS and ends up at O=ACME. This resolves the server's distinguished name as .LABS-SRV1.LABS.NORAD.ACME. Correct!

ZEN

"If a wheel turns, and nothing else moves with it, I should say it was not a part of the machinery."

Ludwig Wittgenstein

OK, that's eNough Naming NoNsense for Now—lots of N's. If you need more explanation, refer to the "NDS Naming" section of Chapter 2. Our focus here is NDS design. Now that we've explored the fundamentals of NDS naming, and discovered some name-related design caveats, it's time to dive into the real star of this show—the NDS naming standards document. I promise that we'll put all your naming knowledge to good use.

NDS NAMING STANDARD GUIDELINES

An NDS naming standards document is crucial. It provides guidelines for naming key container and leaf objects (including users, printers, servers, volumes, print queues, and Organizational Units). In addition, it identifies standard properties and value formats. Consistency (especially in the naming scheme used for objects) provides several benefits, including the following:

▶ Consistent naming schemes provide a guideline for network administrators who will add, modify, or move objects within the directory tree.

▶ Naming standards eliminate redundant planning. The standards give CNEs an efficient model to meet their needs, but leave implementation of resource objects open and flexible.

▶ Consistent naming schemes help users identify resources quickly, and this maximizes user productivity.

▶ Finally, consistent naming allows users to easily identify themselves during login.

As I previously stated, the naming standards document is required—but it doesn't have to be difficult or time-consuming to create. The first step is to ask yourself a few questions:

▶ How can I provide a Directory structure for my employees that is flexible, easy to use, and meets today's business needs?

▶ How can I ensure that I provide a consistent Directory structure within all our divisions, locations, and, perhaps, operating companies?

▶ How can I communicate and implement a consistent standard across an entire company, one that will be followed by everyone?

The answers can be found in your naming standards document. The process of creating naming guidelines forces you to deal with these critical issues and tackle them head-on. Before you can do anything, however, you'll need to create some naming standard guidelines. And, even more importantly, you'll want to do it before installing your very first NetWare 4 server. Once an installation has begun, it becomes more difficult to implement a standard. At a minimum, you should define how Organizational Units, Servers, and User objects are going to look. These are the most popular NDS objects.

So where do you start? Many companies already have some standard in place for defining their users. This is usually based on an e-mail standard. Review the standard and make modifications where necessary to improve the current standard. If your company's network is small, you still should create naming guidelines, because it will most likely grow to include more users and resources—then naming becomes *very* important.

Your naming guidelines must be global in nature. You should strive to implement your naming standards consistently across the entire network so that all users and all departments can readily and easily access resources anywhere on the WAN. Global naming guidelines also can help you and your distributed administrators. It clarifies the identity and purpose of all objects in the tree.

ZEN

"When you look at actual children, no matter how they are raised, you notice immediately that little girls are, in fact, smaller versions of real human beings, whereas little boys are Pod People from the Planet Destructo!"

Dave Barry

You will probably need the input from others at ACME in order to create effective naming guidelines. These individuals may include input from e-mail administrators, network administrators, and mainframe personnel. Also, you'll need information from each division.

Usually, an established host environment has user naming standards in place. Review these standards as a basis for your NetWare 4 user naming guidelines. Some customers prefer to maintain their host usernames on the LAN rather than create a new standard at the network level. Others can't wait to change their host usernames.

Consider all other naming guidelines that are in place from a NetWare 3 environment when creating your NDS standard. Your NetWare 3 printers and servers may already have names defined that will work just fine after migration to the NetWare 4 tree. If you have sufficient or acceptable guidelines (for your organization), then there is no need to change them.

OK, that's enough advice. Now get off the couch and let's take a closer look at the five main objectives in creating NDS naming guidelines:

1 • Make browsing and navigation of the NDS tree easier for the users.

2 • Make maintenance of the NDS tree easier for the network administration staff.

3 • Make merging separate NDS trees easier.

4 • Keep the NDS object names unique as required by certain services.

5 • Avoid special characters reserved by the WAN's many operating systems.

NDS Browsing and Navigation

Your primary objective for creating naming guidelines is to provide your users with a simple view of their network resources. You may not see the immediate need for good naming guidelines. However, as more applications are written to take advantage of NDS and its searching capabilities, you'll quickly change your tune. Soon, an uncomplicated naming standard will be required.

Objects should be named with purpose and consistency. This will eventually provide you with a solid foundation for NDS browsing, navigation, and resource access. Other dividends will be recognized as applications make more use of the Directory and its services. You will see that the system is much more efficient if the users can quickly identify the network resources available to them and minimize the impact on searching NDS.

You should also keep the names of all the objects short and simple. Yet, these names should be descriptive enough so that users can easily identify what the object is and the services it provides. For example, the object name HP4SI-P1 is short yet descriptive and lets the user know that this object is an HP4SI LaserJet printer. Another example, HP4SI-PQ1, is also short, yet descriptive. In this case, the PQ1 suffix lets the user know that the object is the print queue that supports the HP4SI printer (P1).

Throughout this book, there have been countless cases when we've relied on efficient ACME naming. In all cases, it has been helpful to have clear and simple names. Some examples of the naming guidelines for ACME are shown in Table 4.3.

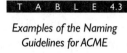

Examples of the Naming
Guidelines for ACME

OBJECT	NAME	STANDARD
[Root]	Tree Name	ACME_TREE
O=Organization	A Cure for Mother Earth	ACME
OU=Organizational Unit	Rio de Janeiro, Brazil	RIO
	Tokyo, Japan	TOKYO
	Sydney, Australia	SYDNEY
	Research and Development	R&D
	World Health Index	WHI
	Facilities	FAC
	Public Relations	PR
CN=Users	George Washington	GWashington
	Thomas Jefferson	TJefferson
	Leonardo DaVinci	LDaVinci
	Albert Einstein	AEinstein
CN=Servers	Server in Labs	LABS-SRVI
	Server in White	WHITE-SRVI
	Server in NORAD/PR	NOR-PR-SRVI
CN=Printers	HP4SI in NORAD/PR	HP4SI-PI
CN=Print Queues	Queue in NORAD/PR	HP4SI-PQI

Easier Administration

Consistent naming also provides a framework for NetWare 4 administration, monitoring, and optimization. You and your distributed administrators will be installing file servers, creating users and printers, modifying existing objects, and moving objects throughout the NDS tree. You will also set up numerous workstation configuration files, and control the user's friendly WAN interface. In all these cases, your job is going to be much easier if efficient naming guidelines are in place.

Merging NDS Trees

The ability to merge multiple NDS trees together is a dominant feature of NetWare 4.1. This is pruning at its finest. This miracle relies on a shared naming standard between the two merging trees. The tree merge will be seamless to the users because their workstation configuration files will not change, even though the NDS trees are merged.

Naming has the largest negative impact on merging two disparate NDS trees. It impacts every facet of NDS management and resource accessibility. The effort to reconfigure each affected workstation and printer, for example, could slow down the overall process or may be prohibitive altogether.

QUIZ

Now's a good time for another little "brain stretcher." Try this one on for size:

Eight bingo balls numbered from one to eight are placed into a bag then drawn out at random, one by one, and the numbers written down to form an eight-figure number. What are the odds that the eight-figure number will divide by nine exactly?

(Q4-1)
(See Appendix C for quiz answers.)

Unique NDS Object Names

Some NDS objects have unusual requirements for naming exclusivity. File and Print servers, for example, broadcast their services using the Service Advertising Protocol (SAP). SAP and RIP (Routing Information Protocol) will not tolerate two different devices "SAPing" the same name. Therefore, your naming standard must identify these devices and handle them appropriately.

Also, you'll want to distribute the naming guidelines to all administrators on the WAN, which will ensure object naming exclusivity where appropriate. In addition, we recommend that user objects have unique names throughout the tree. This way, users can be moved or added without conflict. Keep in mind, though, that not all objects in the NDS tree need naming exclusivity—just the finicky ones.

Avoid Special Characters

"Special" is good, but in NDS it's reserved for the tree only. NDS needs a slew of special characters for its own operations. Avoid using any of the following characters in your naming standards document:

- ▸ Period (.)—Used by NDS to separate the name segments of distinguished names. For example, the distinguished name for the user George Washington is CN=GWashington.OU=ADMIN.OU=RIO.O=ACME. Wow, check out all those periods.

- ▸ Plus (+)—Used by NDS to represent objects with multiple naming attributes (such as bindery objects). A common use of the plus sign is for bindery object naming. For example, a bindery object with the plus sign in the name is seen as CN=Bindery Name + Object. In the case of an AppleTalk print server it might appear as CN=AtpsQuser+83.

- ▸ Equals (=)—Used by NDS to tie name types and object names together. For example the object type O=Organization would appear as O=ACME.

- ▸ Backslash (\)—Precedes the previous special characters, if they are used as part of an object name. For example, if you want to use the name "ACME Inc." (which has a period at the end), you would need to type **ACME Inc\.**

Here's another tip from Uncle David: Avoid using spaces in any object names. You should use the dash (-) or underscore (_) characters instead. Spaces are used as delimiters for all command line parameters. If you use spaces in an NDS object name, you'll need to enclose it in quotation marks—too much work. For example, if the user George Washington is named "George Washington" in NDS with a space separating the first and last name, when George logs in, he would have to type

```
LOGIN "George Washington"
```

If he was required to provide the full distinguished name during login, he would type

```
LOGIN "George Washington.ADMIN.RIO.ACME"
```

If he used the underscore instead, it would be a little easier:

```
LOGIN George_Washington
```

You should also avoid the forward slash (/) in naming container or leaf objects. The Windows-based NWUSER utility, for example, will fail if you MAP permanent drives to, or CAPTURE a print queue to, an object with a forward slash in it. This is a Windows issue—figures.

ZEN

"Your children need your presence more than your presents."

Jesse Jackson

Well, there you go. That's everything you need to know about NDS naming guidelines. Now, I think we're ready to attack the ACME naming standards document. I can barely contain my excitement. How about you?!

ACME'S NAMING STANDARDS DOCUMENT

Here we are—finally. The first 10 feet of "the Great Drop." We've reached the Apex of NetWare 4, and we're looking straight down at a 100-foot drop. The first 10 feet are the most interesting, because you still don't know what to expect. Your stomach has not quite reached your throat yet. Wait until you get to NDS tree design. Producing ACME's naming standards document is not very glamorous work, but it's critical. And you would realize this if you'd been awake during the last 25 pages or so. Fortunately, it's not brain surgery. Once you understand the impact of the previous NDS naming guidelines, the rest is a piece of cake. As a matter of fact, it's as easy as 1-2-3:

- ▸ Step 1: Document the naming standard for each object class in the ACME tree.

- ▸ Step 2: Provide an example for each object class.

- ▸ Step 3: Specify properties for each object class selected.

ACME's naming standards document is simply a manifestation of these guidelines. Now that you understand the rules, you just have to apply them to ACME (or some other organization). Let's take a closer look at these three simple steps, and build a naming standard for ACME. Cool.

Step 1: Document the Naming Standard for Each Object Class in the ACME Tree

It all starts here—*review*. Begin by taking a long hard look at ACME and the network resources it uses. Consider the impact of naming on these resources, and come up with some simple guidelines for standardizing the names. This review will also help prepare you for the second phase of NDS design—NDS tree design. But let's not get ahead of ourselves.

The good news is that most of your effort is focused on a few leaf and container objects, namely:

- Users

- Organization

- Organizational Units

- Servers

- Printers and Print Queues

Object Class: Users

When creating a naming standard, the first step is to decide what to do with the users. NetWare 4 allows usernames up to 64 characters long. However, a 64-character user name is ridiculous. Consider limiting it to eight characters or less. This is appropriate in many cases, but not ACME. The eight-character rule makes file system management much easier, but it hinders the identity and exclusivity of key users.

In our case, we're going to use the first character of the first name and the *entire* last name. This helps differentiate people and simplifies identity. Also, if there are duplicate names within a single container, then the middle initial is added to resolve the name conflict.

As I said previously, some companies choose to limit the username to eight characters. This naming convention matches the username to the DOS home directory. Since DOS subdirectories are limited to just eight characters, this design will automatically match the name of the DOS subdirectory to the appropriate username. For example, Thomas Jefferson, becomes

TJEFFERS

In other cases, you may want to use the first six characters of a user's last name and the first two characters of the user's first name. This name would appear as

JEFFERTH

> **TIP**
>
> **Remember, object names within the same container must be unique. Duplicate names are only allowed if objects are distributed to different containers. However, it is recommended that you keep object names unique across the entire tree.**

Object Class: Organization

Your Organization should reflect your company name. In our case, "A Cure for Mother Earth" becomes ACME, and the Organization name becomes O=ACME. With the Organization restricted to the company's name, it frees up the Organizational Units to become the true Tupperware containers of NDS logic.

Object Class: Organizational Units

Organizational Units can span multiple container depths. With this flexibility, they can be used for "geography" and "organization." As you'll learn in the next section, geography defines the upper layers of the NDS tree. So, the first few layers of Organizational Units should be reserved for locations—OU=SYDNEY and OU=TOKYO. They could have been abbreviated to SYD and TOK, but their names are already short. Remember, the names must be *both* short and descriptive ("SYD" isn't very descriptive).

The next OU layers are dedicated to divisions and departments—OU=R&D for the Research and Development department and OU=MRKT for Marketing. Remember, be short, but descriptive.

TIP

The tree name should be named with the company name plus "_TREE". You should not use the same name that you used for the O=Organization. We are using ACME_TREE and O=ACME for our NDS tree.

Object Class: Servers

Servers are very finicky. Their names must be unique across the entire WAN because of SAP and RIP broadcasting. You may wish to consider a server name that incorporates both its location and department. For ACME, a NetWare server in the CHARITY department of NORAD is called NOR-CHR-SRV1 and a print server is called NOR-CHR-PS1. On the other hand, a file server in the R&D department of NORAD is called R&D-SRV1. Why?

You may wonder why the naming standards seem different for different departments—let me explain. R&D is a unique department within the ACME tree and, therefore, it doesn't need any special location designator. However, the CHARITY and PR departments are not unique departments—they exist in each location throughout the ACME tree. Therefore, the servers in those containers should use the location designator to uniquely identify them.

TIP

A printer that connects directly to the network and services a print queue on the file server is called a *Queue Server*. A Queue Server is a special-purpose print server that must have a unique name to broadcast using SAP. All Queue Servers use SAP to advertise their services on the network. The HP JetDirect card is an example of a Queue Server device.

Object Class: Printers and Print Queues

Unlike servers, printers and print queues don't require naming exclusivity. The department and location information is obtained through the object's NDS context. This means that an HP LaserJet 4SI in R&D can share the same name as an HP LaserJet 4SI in WHITE—they have different distinguished names because they are in different parent containers. In summary, a printer's distinguished name identifies its location and department. Therefore, printer and print queue names should reflect functionality, not location.

For example, an ACME HP4SI printer is named HP4SI-P1 and its associated print queue is called HP4SI-PQ1—regardless of where they live. A Canon BubbleJet printer is named CANONBJ-P2 and its print queue is named CANONBJ-PQ2. This type of naming provides the user with fundamental information about the printer and its associated print queue. Remember, function over location.

That completes our discussion of the main NDS object classes. In addition, you might want to consider naming standards for groups, organizational roles, directory map objects, and profiles.

ZEN

"Do what you do best; if you're a runner, run; if you're a bell, ring."

Ignas Berstein

Naming standards for ACME's object classes are outlined in Table 4.4. Check it out.

T A B L E 4.4	NDS OBJECT CLASS	STANDARD
Naming Standards for ACME Object Classes	Users	First character of the first name, plus the entire last name. All titles are spelled out.
	Organization	Abbreviation of the company name.
	Organizational Unit	Location, division, or department name. Abbreviate the name if there are more than eight characters.

TABLE 4.4	NDS OBJECT CLASS	STANDARD
Naming Standards for ACME Object Classes (continued)	NetWare Server	Department-SRV#. Exception for the CHARITY and PR departments which require geographic information as well (that is, Location-Department-SRV#).
	Volumes	ServerName_VolumeName.
	Print Server	Department-PS#. Exception for the CHARITY and PR departments as above (that is, Location-Department-PS#).
	Printer	PrinterType-P#.
	Print Queue	PrinterType-PQ#.
	Computer	No standard because it is not used.

Step 2: Provide an Example for Each Object Class

A picture is worth a thousand words. So far, ACME's naming standard is relatively one-dimensional—that is, all rules and no application. As a matter of fact, you'll find Table 4.4 is only marginally useful. That's because it doesn't have any examples. One example can convey the meaning of an entire written page. Therefore, include some brief examples in your naming standards document. It helps illustrate your reasoning. Examples also ensure that distributed administrators will stay on track.

Table 4.5 is simply a reprint of Table 4.4, but with examples for each of the object classes. Notice how everything suddenly falls into place—just like magic. Now all you need are some property guidelines, and the naming standard is done!

TABLE 4.5

Using Examples in Your
NDS Naming Standard

NDS OBJECTS	STANDARD	EXAMPLES
Users	First character of the first name, plus the entire last name. All titles are spelled out.	GWashington, SirGawain
Organization	Abbreviation of the company name which is "A Cure for Mother Earth."	ACME
Organizational Unit	Location, division, or department name. Abbreviate the name if there are over eight characters.	NORAD, R&D, ADMIN
NetWare Server	Department-SRV#. Exception for the CHARITY and PR departments, which is Location-Department-SRV#.	LABS-SRV1, NOR-CHR-SRV1
Volumes	ServerName_VolumeName.	LABS-SRV1_SYS, NOR-CHR-SRV1_SYS
Print Server	Department-PS#. Exception for the CHARITY and PR departments, which is Location-Department-PS#.	FAC-PS1, TOK-PR-PS1
Printer	PrinterType-P#.	HP4SI-P1, CANONBJ-P2
Print Queue	PrinterType-PQ#	HP4SI-PQ1, CANONBJ-PQ2
Computer	No standard because it is not used.	

Step 3: Specify Properties for Each Object Class Selected

The final step is to put your naming guidelines under the microscope. Now, you must focus in on each object class and provide rules for Required, Optional, and System properties.

First, determine which properties should be required. Start with the mandatory NDS properties and expand from there. For example, NDS won't allow you to create a user object without Login Name and Last Name properties. In ACME's case, we're also requiring Given Name, Full Name, Middle Initial, Title, Location, Telephone Number, Fax Number, Home Directory, and Require Password.

Next, determine which properties will be optional. Finally, identify system properties (such as Network Address and so on). In addition, you'll want to provide naming rules for how the properties look. Refer to Table 4.6 for an example of ACME's User Class property standard.

TABLE 4.6	PROPERTY	REQ/OPT/SYSTEM	STANDARD
NDS Property Standards of the ACME User Class	Login Name	Required	First character of the first name, plus the entire last name. Add a middle initial to resolve name conflicts.
	Given Name	Required	First name of the user.
	Last Name	Required	Last name of the user.
	Full Name	Required	First and last name of the user.
	Generational Qual.	Optional	
	Middle Initial	Required	Middle initial of the user, if known.
	Other Name	Optional	
	Title	Required	Job title.
	Description	Optional	
	Location	Required	City or site location (NORAD, RIO, and so on)

PROPERTY	REQ/OPT/SYSTEM	STANDARD
Department	Optional	
Telephone Number	Required	Business phone number with area code.
Fax Number	Required	Fax phone number with area code.
Language	Optional	Preferred language of the user.
Network Address	System	
Default Server	Optional	Enter the same server as the home directory.
Home Directory	Required	Enter the volume: subdirectory\user path.
Require Password	Required	Force the user to have a password.
Account Balance	Optional	
Login Script	Optional	Determined by site administrators.
Print Job Config.	Optional	Determined by site administrators.
Post Office Box	Optional	
Street	Optional	
City	Optional	
State or Province	Optional	
Zip Code	Optional	
See Also	Optional	

TIP

Currently the NetWare 4 utilities can't enforce additional required properties. The user object, for example, is only required to have a Login Name and Last Name. Your standard, however, may be different. You will need to enforce required user properties at the management level—in your naming guidelines. Also, it helps if you explain the reasoning for including the property. This helps distributed administrators buy into it.

Once you've completed the naming guidelines and examples, there's only one more set of rules to complete your naming standards document—Syntax. Table 4.7 shows a simple, but effective, syntax standard. Notice that we've also included examples. In the most basic sense, this is a summary of the entire naming standards document. As a matter of fact, small organizations could probably get away with just the Naming Syntax guidelines.

Whatever you do, don't skimp on naming standards—they're too important to the productivity and survival of your NDS design. More is better in this case.

TABLE 4.7	OBJECT TYPE	SYNTAX	EXAMPLE
ACME's Naming Standard Syntax	[Root] or Tree Name	AAAA_TREE	ACME_TREE
	Organization	AAAA	O=ACME
	Organizational Units	XXXXX or YYYYY	OU=NORAD, OU=LABS
	NetWare Servers	XXX-YYYYY-SRV#	LABS-SRV1
	Print Servers	XXX-YYYYY-PS#	NOR-CHR-PS4
	Printers	<Prn Type>-P#	HP4SI-P1
	Print Queues	<Prn Type>-PQ#	HP4SI-PQ1
	Volume Names	<Server>_<Volume>	LABS-SRV1_SYS

The legend:
AAAA = Company Name
XXX = Location (NOR, RIO, CAM, TOK, SYD)
YYYYY = Department (LABS, CHR, PR, ADM, OPS, FIN)
SRV = File Server
PS = Print Server
CS=Communications Server
# = Quantity (1, 2, 3, ... , 9)

(Volumes are SYS, VOL1, DATA, USERS, SHARE)
Note: File and print servers only use the location attribute if the parent container is not unique (that is, OU=CHARITY or OU=PR). Also, printers and print queues increment according to their print server, not container.

Congratulations! You've completed the ACME naming standards document. What an accomplishment. It wasn't easy, but now you should feel much more comfortable about the future of ACME's design. At the very least, we know what to call stuff.

The next step is Tree Design. This is when you get a chance to show off your famous CNE creativity. But don't get too creative. There are established rules for tree design, just as there are for naming standards. Sorry, sometimes I can be such a stick in the mud—not!

ZEN

"Philosophy begins in Wonder."

Aristotle

NDS Tree Design

Somewhere near the top of the fall, you'll begin to feel your stomach in your throat. This is probably the most popular roller coaster sensation—it epitomizes The Fall. Then, the wind grabs your hair (real or otherwise) with great force and tugs it in the opposite direction. Your face turns to rubber, and your knees buckle under the force of 3Gs. Aren't roller coasters a blast?

With the naming standards document in place, you're halfway down the "Great NDS Dipper." Now it's time to shift gears and begin accelerating to full speed (3Gs). In ACME's case this means it's time to come up with the

- NDS Tree Design

- Partition and Replica Design

- Time Synchronization Design

If you build it (NDS tree design), they will come. Then, we can break the tree into little pieces (partition design), and scatter the pieces around (replica placement). Once they're there, we'll buy them all digital watches (time synchronization design). So, what are you waiting for? Let's build the NDS tree.

DESIGN GOALS

Before you get too excited about designing ACME's tree, we must review some important NDS design goals. After all, what are we trying to accomplish here? A well-designed NDS tree will

▸ Organize the network resources in your company.

▸ Provide a blueprint for the rollout of NetWare 4.

▸ Be flexible to allow for corporate changes.

If your tree doesn't accomplish these three goals, then it's not a well-designed tree. Let's take a closer look.

Organize the Network Resources in Your Company

The primary goal of your NDS tree is *to organize network resources*. Your NDS tree structure should reflect the location and placement of network resources throughout your WAN. It should also provide easy resource access to both users and distributed administrators. To accomplish this, you must focus on both the location of resources and their purpose—balance is the key. Figure 4.8 shows how the OPS resources are grouped near the users who need them. This increases accessibility.

For example, some users need access to a particular printer or server, while a larger group may need access to an e-mail server. The e-mail server would be grouped higher in the tree so that all users needing the resource have common access. In Figure 4.8, for example, Guinevere is placed in the same container as her CAM-FIN-SRV1 server. But her printer (HP4SI-P2) may rely on a print server (OPS-PS1) higher in the tree—a different container. We'll revisit this strategy later. The bottom line is that department-specific resources should be placed lower in the tree, and shared resources should be placed higher in the tree.

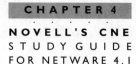
FIGURE 4.8

*Grouping Users and Their
Network Resources*

Provide a Blueprint for the Rollout of NetWare 4

After the NDS tree has been designed, it will provide a blueprint for the installation of all your NetWare 4 servers. For example, the tree design will give you the location where an NDS server should be installed. Also, some companies may be forced to implement multiple trees during the rollout of NetWare 4. This is because of geographical or political pressures. Regardless, they should share the same basic tree design. This will make merging much easier when the time comes—and it will.

Additionally, your NDS blueprint provides a clear map of how to migrate the entire corporation to NetWare 4. Initially, your migration will begin with a few servers and may eventually involve hundreds of machines (52 for ACME). After you gain the experience of tree design, naming standards, lab testing, and server installation, you'll be ready to repeat this process at all locations throughout the WAN. You will be successful at each installation because your blueprint will be well-understood.

Be Flexible to Allow for Corporate Changes

The final goal is flexibility. Your tree design must be flexible enough to allow for future corporate changes. This simply means that, as the corporation changes both organizationally and physically, you will be able to represent those changes easily without large modifications to the tree structure. This objective can be met by designing a tree that is rigid at the top and flexible at the bottom. You'll see what I mean in just a second.

TIP

Today's corporations are constantly shifting and changing. Some are being purchased by others, while others are undergoing mergers. The likelihood that this will decrease is very slight. Therefore, you can make your job easier by planning ahead and building in enough flexibility to anticipate these changes. How do you do that? You must not only learn, but truly understand, the rules for a successful tree design. Once you understand the rules, every design question and circumstance has an answer and can be factored into your design.

These goals may seem obvious, even trivial, but don't underestimate them. You will always encounter other "forces" that want to gravitate the tree in wrong directions. *Political pressure* is one classic example. Certain individuals want the tree to reflect their personal needs (power, or whatever). The best way to deal with these individuals is to ask them one simple question, "How does this help us organize our network resources?" In other words, if you have specific goals on which you can fall back, you can deal with the political design issues by applying each issue against your design goals. Keep in mind that the network is installed to serve a business purpose, and that the tree is not a mechanism for displaying superiority in your company. If you design with this intent in mind, many of the political pressures can be easily dissipated.

REAL WORLD

Politics should not get in the way of your tree design, but sometimes they do. Not long ago, an agency was in the process of designing its NetWare 4 tree. During the design, some individuals insisted that they should be represented as their own Organizational Units in the tree because of where they appeared organizationally in their agency. They incorrectly assumed that managerial positions or positions of authority should receive special attention in the design of the tree. As important as these individuals were, they were not containers for the organization of network resources. Regardless of their titles, they were users nonetheless, and shared resources with other individuals on the same floor or building. Sorry, power mongers, you're the same as everyone else in the eyes of NDS.

Now that we've got that straight, you're ready to design ACME's NDS tree. Fortunately, I have a simple four-step plan for you—don't I always. Ready, set, design.

QUIZ

Things are not always as they appear. What's the next logical number in this sequence?

3, 7, 10, 11, 12, ?

Where's my naming standard when I need it?

(Q4-2)

ACME'S NDS TREE DESIGN

Here we are—tree design. You're prepped and ready to begin organizing ACME's resources. Just don't get any dirt under your fingernails. Today we start down a path that irrevocably defines the future of ACME, and the fate of humanity. But there's no pressure. Decisions you make here, today, will form the foundation of ACME's network, and the platform for their purpose—sounds heavy. In other words, don't mess up the tree design.

The four-step process to follow looks something like this:

- ▸ Step 1: Design Inputs—Gather your company's design inputs (WAN layout, organizational chart, and so on).

- ▸ Step 2: Pyramid—Design the NDS tree in the shape of a pyramid.

- ▸ Step 3: Top Layers—Design the top layers of the tree according to geography.

- ▸ Step 4: Bottom Layers—Design the bottom layers of the tree according to organization.

It starts with the design inputs you gathered in the last chapter. These will help identify ACME's geography, resources, and organizational structure. Next, sketch the tree in the shape of a pyramid using geography (WAN layouts) at the top and departments (organizational chart) at the bottom. Once you have a rough design, fill it in with all the organizations and resources identified in the ACME Resource List. But don't get too carried away. Remember, tree design focuses on branches, servers, administrators, and printers. All the other resources will be placed in the "NDS Management" section of Chapter 8.

This four-step model is the best way to proceed, but it's certainly not the only way. The methods presented here have been developed by Novell Consulting Services and have been implemented by hundreds of their large and small customers with great success. Although each company's network will have different requirements, the tree design guidelines in this section will give you a great head start regardless of the size of your company.

So what does size have to do with it? It does make a difference. The line between "small" and "large" companies is very subjective, so we must establish a distinction between the two. The easiest approach is to define what we mean by a "small" company. In most cases, a small company is 5 servers or less, with no wide area network (WAN) connections, and less than 500 users. Certainly there is no written law that this is true. However, a network of this size has many less design ramifications than a network with thousands of users and a very complicated network infrastructure.

A "large" network, then, is anything greater than 5 servers *with* a WAN connection, *and* greater than 500 users. As you follow through this chapter, you will be able to determine into which category (small or large) you fall. So, let's begin the design.

STEP 1: DESIGN INPUTS

In chapter 3, we explored the first step of NDS design—NDS Preparation. One of the most important preparation tasks was Data Gathering. We discovered eight different design inputs in two different categories (organizational and technical). In this section, NDS tree design, we're very interested in five of those ACME inputs, namely:

- ACME WAN Layout

- ACME Campus Maps

- ACME World Map

- ACME Resource List

- ACME Organizational Chart

Notice that all four technical inputs are represented here and only one organizational input. That's because NDS tree design is primarily a technical activity. After all, what are we organizing—technical resources, not people. However, we can't totally ignore people, either. They sneak in toward the bottom.

Now, let's review these five design inputs and learn a little more about their roles in NDS tree design.

ACME WAN Layout

Figure 4.9 shows ACME's WAN layout map. The WAN layout consists of all your major hub locations and their interconnected routers and bridges. Notice in ACME's WAN layout map that all five main sites are shown with their router connections and the speed of these links in kilobits per second. Your WAN layout map may look similar and it may additionally include the link speeds of your satellite offices (or distribution centers in our case).

Your WAN documentation may be more than one, nice, compact diagram. Don't worry if your documentation consists of several pages of information. The key here is to understand how your infrastructure is organized and where the major locations are. These documents are necessary for the upper layer design of your tree, as we will explain in Step 3. Most companies have some sort of WAN map, but you may have to draw a new one. Try to consolidate all of the important interconnectivity information in a single overview.

FIGURE 4.9

ACME WAN Layout Map

ACME Campus Maps

The WAN layout provides a great interconnectivity overview, but it's not enough. You'll need campus maps for each major hub site. This type of documentation varies from company to company. Some companies show the entire hub and campus diagrams together, while others separate the information because of its complexity. Regardless, the campus maps should show the type of information illustrated in Figure 4.10. This is ACME's campus map for the CAMELOT hub.

FIGURE 4.10

ACME Campus Map for CAMELOT

The ACME campus map for CAMELOT shows an FDDI ring and routers connecting the distributed buildings. The campus diagram may also show building structures and their addresses. For example, the ACME WAN layout shows a network in CAMELOT. Further research however produces a list of sites within the Camelot area, such as an operations center (OPS) located at the south end of the city and a public relations office (PR) located in the downtown district. An office for charitable contributions (CHR) is also found at the north end of the city. Figure 4.10 shows a list of these sites.

Campus maps are important because they refine ACME's WAN/LAN infrastructure. We need the campus maps to organize the second tier of ACME's TOP layers—that's Step 3.

ZEN

"Flying doesn't make me nervous. Driving to the airport can make me nervous. Because, if you miss that plane, there's no alternative. On the ground, you have options. You have buses, you have taxis, you have trains. But when you're taking a flight, if you miss it—that's it. No airline goes, 'Well, you missed the flight. We do have a cannon leaving in about ten minutes. Would you be interested in that?'"

Jerry Seinfeld

ACME World Map

The last map is a big one. It provides a global view of ACME and its distributed locations. Each hub site, building, and distribution center should be integrated into one ACME World Map. This provides a snapshot of the ACME geography and becomes the foundation of the top layers of ACME's tree. In addition, this information combines with the ACME WAN layout to determine if regional containers are necessary. Refer to the poster in the back of this book, or Figure 3.9 in Chapter 3, for a picture of ACME's World Map.

ACME Resource List

The final technical input is a doozy—the ACME Resource List. This list gives valuable information about the servers and printers found in each region, site, building, or department. Table 4.8 shows the resource list for ACME with its locations, organizations, administrators, servers, printers, and print queues. These are the only resources we're interested in during NDS tree design. Later, in Chapter 8, we'll focus on all the ACME resources and place them in appropriate containers. Today, we're more interested in the branches of the tree.

Also, notice that the ACME Resource List has undergone a significant change. The original wish list can be found in Table 3.2 in Chapter 3. This list has been updated to include the naming standards discussed previously. Additionally, appropriate administrator, servers, and printers have been distributed to their proper locations—as per the WAN layout and campus maps. Don't you just love it when a plan comes together.

T A B L E   4.8

ACME's Updated Resource List

LOC	ORG	ADMINISTRATOR	SERVERS	PRINTER/QUEUES
NORAD				
	CHARITY	SirGawain	NOR-SRV1	
			NOR-CHR-SRV1	HP4SI-P1/PQ1
			NOR-CHR-PS1	
	LABS	AEinstein	LABS-SRV1	
	R&D.LABS	LDaVinci	R&D-SRV1	
			R&D-PS1	
	POLL.R&D.LABS	CDarwin		HP4SI-P1/PQ1
	NUC.R&D.LABS	MCurie		HP4SI-P2/PQ2
	VR.R&D.LABS	INewton		HP4SI-P3/PQ3
	WHI.LABS	CBabbage	WHI-SRV1	CANONBJ-P1/PQ1
		Ada	WHI-SRV2	
			WHI-SRV3	
			WHI-PS1	
	PR	DClarke	NOR-PR-SRV1	HP4SI-P1/PQ1
			NOR-PR-PS1	CANONBJ-P1/PQ1
RIO			RIO-SRV1	
	CHARITY	SirPercival	RIO-CHR-SRV1	HP4SI-P1/PQ1
			RIO-CHR-PS1	
	ADMIN	GWashington	ADMIN-SRV1	CANONBJ-P1/PQ1
		FDR	ADMIN-SRV2	
			ADMIN-PS1	

T A B L E 4.8

ACME's Updated Resource List (continued)

LOC	ORG	ADMINISTRATOR	SERVERS	PRINTER/QUEUES
	FAC.ADMIN	JMadison	FAC-SRV1	HP4SI-P1/PQ1
			FAC-PS1	
	AUDIT.ADMIN	ALincoln	AUD-SRV1	HP4SI-P2/PQ2
	MRKT.ADMIN	TJefferson	MRKT-SRV1	HPIII-P1/PQ1
				HPIII-P2/PQ2
	PR	JHughes	RIO-PR-SRV1	HP4SI-P1/PQ1
			RIO-PR-PS1	CANONBJ-P1/PQ1
CAMELOT				
	CHARITY	SirGalahad	CAM-SRV1	
			CAM-CHR-SRV1	HP5-P1/PQ1
			CAM-CHR-PS1	
	OPS	KingArthur	OPS-SRV1	CANONBJ-P1/PQ1
			OPS-PS1	
	FIN.OPS	Guinevere	CAM-FIN-SRV1	HP4SI-P1/PQ1
			CAM-FIN-SRV2	HP4SI-P2/PQ2
			CAM-FIN-SRV3	
			CAM-FIN-PS1	
			CAM-FIN-PS2	
	DIST.OPS	Merlin	DIST-SRV1	HPIII-P1/PQ1
			DIST-SRV2	
			DIST-PS1	

TABLE 4.8

ACME's Updated Resource List (continued)

LOC	ORG	ADMINISTRATOR	SERVERS	PRINTER/QUEUES
SYDNEY	PR	CEttelson	CAM-PR-SRVI, CAM-PR-PSI	HP4SI-P1/PQI
	CHARITY	SirLancelot	SYD-SRVI, SYD-CHR-SRVI, SYD-CHR-PSI	HP5-P1/PQI
	HR	Gandhi	HR-SRVI, HR-SRV2, HR-PSI	HP4SI-P1/PQI
	MEDICAL.HR	ASchweitzer	MED-SRVI, MED-SRV2	HP4SI-P2/PQ2
	FOOD.HR	MTeresa	FOOD-SRVI	HP4SI-P3/PQ3
	SHELTER.HR	FNightengale	SHELT-SRVI, SHELT-SRV2	HP4SI-P4/PQ4
	PEACE.HR	Buddha	PEACE-SRVI	HPIII-P1/PQI
	PR	MClarke	SYD-PR-SRVI, SYD-PR-PSI	HP4SI-P1/PQI
TOKYO	CHARITY	SirKay	TOK-SRVI, TOK-CHR-SRVI, TOK-CHR-SRV2, TOK-CHR-PSI	HP4SI-P1/PQI

LOC	ORG	ADMINISTRATOR	SERVERS	PRINTER/QUEUES
	CRIME	SHolmes	CRIME-SRV1	HP5-P1/PQ1
		Dr Watson	CRIME-SRV2	
			CRIME-PS1	
	BLUE.CRIME	WEarp	BLUE-SRV1	HPIII-P1/PQ1
			BLUE-PS1	
	VIO.BLUE. CRIME	BMasterson	VIO-SRV1	HP4SI-P1/PQ1
			VIO-SRV2	
	ENV.BLUE. CRIME	WBHickok	ENV-SRV1	HP4SI-P2/PQ2
	THEFT.BLUE. CRIME	DHoliday	THEFT-SRV1	HP4SI-P3/PQ3
	WHITE.CRIME	RHood	WHITE-SRV1	CANONBJ-P1/PQ1
			WHITE-SRV2	
			WHITE-PS1	
	CYBER.WHITE. CRIME	FrTuck	CYBER-SRV1	HPIII-P1/PQ1
	POL.WHITE. CRIME	MMarion	POL-SRV1	HP4SI-P1/PQ1
	FIN.WHITE. CRIME	LJohn	TOK-FIN-SRV1	HP4SI-P2/PQ2
				HP4SI-P3/PQ3
	PR	BThomas	TOK-PR-SRV1	HP4SI-P1/PQ1
			TOK-PR-PS1	

T A B L E   4.8

ACME's Updated Resource List (continued)

Wow! That's quite a list. Study it carefully, because everything we do from now on will center around these critical resources. Our sole purpose in life is to organize these network resources productively—well maybe not our *sole* purpose for living, but a pretty important one. Anyway, keep this list handy, you'll need it during Steps 3 and 4.

ACME Organizational Chart

That brings us to the final design input—ACME's Organizational Chart (see Figure 4.11). Some companies have pages of organizational charts. Try not to get too wrapped up in them. Your main purpose here is to identify divisions, departments, or other organizational workgroups. Also, use the Work Flow Diagram (see Figure 3.8 in Chapter 3) to identify auxiliary workgroups throughout the WAN. These divisions, departments, and workgroups will become the foundation of ACME's bottom layers—that's Step 4.

FIGURE 4.11

ACME's Organizational Chart

TIP

Resist the temptation to design your tree around the Organizational Chart. This is more common than you think, mostly because it's the only design input people understand. It's also the *only* design input available in many cases. I know it's more work, but develop technical inputs for your organization and use them for your tree design. You'll thank me in the long run, especially when it comes time to design partitions and replica placement.

That completes Step 1. Many times it's the most difficult of the four steps. Very few companies document their WAN to this extent. You might even have to create a few inputs yourself. But it's worth it. Nothing's harder than trying to design the tree without them. These documents are the driving forces of the entire NDS design process.

Speaking of the process, let's move on to Step 2—Pyramid.

ZEN

"Make your plans as fantastic as you like, because 25 years from now they will seem mediocre. Make your plans 10 times as great as you first planned, and 25 years from now you will wonder why you did not make them 50 times as great."

Henry Curtis

STEP 2: PYRAMID

Now that you've gathered all the design inputs, it's time to put them to good use. The overall tree design should take the shape of a pyramid, or inverted tree. This places most of the objects at the bottom of the structure with the fewest containers at the top. Furthermore, the pyramid design should be split into two sections:

- ▸ Top

- ▸ Bottom

First, you will design the top of the tree. It should be organized according to the geography of ACME. Then, the bottom layers can rest on top. They are organized according to ACME's organization. Figure 4.12 illustrates how the pyramid design splits the top and bottom sections of the tree.

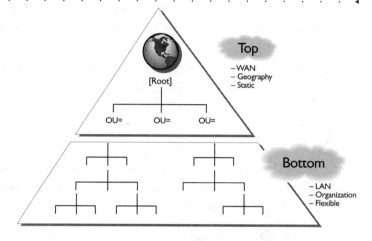

FIGURE 4.12

The Pyramid Design of ACME's Tree

The advantage of a pyramid design is the top layers become the foundation or (static layers) where upon the bottom layers can be established. The bottom layers of the tree are the layers that will be more dynamic and give your tree the flexibility it requires to change when your company changes.

Another advantage of the pyramid design is *natural partitioning*. This means that partition boundaries flow naturally and Subordinate Reference replicas are minimized. We'll discuss this later.

An alternative to our pyramid design is a flat tree that places all NDS objects in the top layers (see Figure 4.13).

TIP

An efficient NDS tree will have more Organizational Units at the bottom layers of the tree. No matter what, try not to exceed 60–70 Organizational Units per layer. Even the largest companies with many branch offices can meet this requirement.

The FLAT Design of
ACME's Tree

[Root]

O=ACME

OU=LOC1   OU=LOC2   OU=LOC3   · · ·   OU=LOC149   OU=LOC150

With all NDS objects in the top of the tree, our ACME design becomes rigid and inefficient. A flat tree is not recommended because of the way it must be partitioned and replicated. Synchronization traffic is increased considerably, and a very large number of Subordinate Reference replicas may appear.

As seen in Figure 4.12, the tree always starts with the [Root] object on top, followed by the O=Organization container. After the O=ACME Organization, we start distributing OU=Organization Unit(s). The top of the tree should reflect the physical structure of your WAN. This top section builds a solid foundation for the bottom layers. Typically, only a selected set of users and network resources are located in the top layers of the tree. For example, the Admin user is located in the O=ACME Organization because INSTALL automatically put it there. He or she is also the central administrator for the entire WAN, so he or she belongs there. As we stated previously, place globally shared resources only in the top layers.

The bottom of the tree is defined by the local area network (LAN) and is based on the functional organization of your company. See Figure 4.12 above. This can be accomplished by using the divisions, departments, workgroups, and teams in the corporation. These bottom layer OU's will hold the majority of ACME's objects, including users, file servers, printers, queues, and other network resources.

QUIZ

ACME recently sponsored an international chess tournament. Sherlock Holmes introduced you to the four semifinalists: Zena Le Vue, Dr. A. Glebe, Rob E. Lumen, and Ann Ziata. Was he being polite or testing your cognitive skills? Both. As it turns out, each semifinalist represented one of four continents: Europe, Africa, the Americas, and Australia. Can you correctly match each of the four chess masters with their home continent?

Good show Mr. Holmes.

(Q4-3)

Now that we understand the rough pyramid shape of ACME's tree, let's take a closer look at the top and bottom layers. Remember, each half serves a unique and special purpose.

STEP 3: TOP LAYERS

As in most things, the top is the most important half. It is the foundation of ACME's NDS tree design. The rest of the tree branches downward from there.

The top layer starts at the [Root]. Then, the O=Organization defines the company— ACME. And finally, the first tier of OU=Organization Units defines distributed WAN hubs. As you can see in Figure 4.14, ACME's top layers are organized around three main container objects:

- ▶ [Root]

- ▶ O=Organization

- ▶ OU=Organizational Units

Let's explore these three containers and learn how they "magically" appeared in ACME's top layers. Also, we'll throw in the C=Country object for good measure.

FIGURE 4.14

ACME's Top Layers

(ACME_TREE)

O=ACME

OU=NORAD   OU=RIO   OU=CAMELOT   OU=TOKYO   OU=SYDNEY

The Top Layers Reflect
ACME's WAN Layout

[Root] Object

First, you must name the tree itself. The tree name is represented by the [Root] object and is placed at the very top of the pyramid. Your tree name should represent the company name plus _TREE. For example, our company is called ACME so we chose to name the tree ACME_TREE. Check out Figure 4.14.

The tree name must be unique, because trees use SAP to broadcast themselves. SAP enables all applications requiring NDS to find the database very efficiently. If you must install more than one logical tree on the same physical WAN, be sure that the trees have different names. The company name plus _TREE guideline works because it clearly identifies the SAP broadcast as an NDS tree. Otherwise, we'll get an identity crisis where tree SAPs are confused with server SAPs. Bad news.

TIP

The NDS tree always starts with the [Root] container object. In most discussions, the [Root] object is not counted as a layer in the tree. Also, the schema defines the [Root] as the object class TOP. The [Root] object is the only instance of the object class TOP and for this reason TOP is known as an *effective* class. Cool.

Once you've named the [Root], it's time to move on. The next container can be either a C=Country or O=Organization. Novell Consulting Services recommends that you use the O=Organization next. The C=Country object causes all sorts of problems. And, of course, we're going to talk about it next.

C=Country Object

The C=Country designator is used to specify a particular country based on the X.500 standard. Public network providers, such as NetWare Connect Services (NCS), will make use of the Country object. The question is often asked, "If a company wants to connect to a public service provider, must I use the C=Country object?" Fortunately, the answer is "no." But they will add it for you. Also fortunately, the gateways that establish the connection between your private corporate tree and the public trees will be able to translate the country codes as needed. So, you don't have to worry about it.

Of course it's a free country (pun intended) and you can use the C=Country container if you wish to. If you do choose to use the Country object, it will add an additional layer to your NDS tree and create some rather interesting naming problems. Consider the example in Figure 4.15.

If we add a C=Country object to the ACME tree, the first question is, "Which country do we choose?" Do we use multiple country codes? For our example, ACME is headquartered primarily in Camelot; therefore, our Country object will be C=UK (United Kingdom). Just for fun, let's look at some of the user's contexts that would be created in other locations. Abraham Lincoln resides in the RIO location, and so his name would be

```
.CN=ALincoln.OU=AUDIT.OU=ADMIN.OU=RIO.O=ACME.C=UK
```

ACME Gets a C=Country
Object

In addition, Sherlock Holmes in the TOKYO location would have the following name:

`.CN=SHolmes.OU=CRIME.OU=TOKYO.O=ACME.C=UK`

Now, these are some ugly names. In addition to being longer, these names are confusing. If Mr. Lincoln resides in RIO, why is his C object "UK"? Also for users who work in both the UK and the United States, it is difficult (if not impossible) to determine where in the tree they belong. Finally, consider the problems that will be created with typeless or relative distinguished names. Now everybody will have to specify whether they're using the C=Country attribute.

Nah, too much work. But, if you've already implemented the C=Country object in your tree, don't worry. It doesn't cause any serious connectivity problems. It's just a pain in the neck. For the rest of us, the second container under [Root] should be O=Organization.

O=Organization Object

After the [Root], you can start your "real" tree with at least one O=Organization object. This tier defines the company and its purpose. All other geographic and organizational function is provided by lower OU=Organizational Units.

You should name the O=Organization the same as your company. Also, most companies use an abbreviation to alleviate long object names. For example, our company is named "A Cure for Mother Earth," which is abbreviated to ACME. In almost every case, this layer contains only a single O=Organization container, and all other structure is handled below—with OU's. Sometimes, however, this is not the case. Some multinational conglomerates include many different companies, and each operates independently. In this case, you may want to create an O=Organization for each corporation. In Figure 4.16, we've combined ACME and the UN into a single NDS tree.

*ACME and the UN Share
an NDS Tree*

TIP

It is recommended that you do not name the O=Organization the same as the [Root]. The ACME tree, for example uses the company name plus _TREE for the tree name. Our corporation would therefore be named O=ACME, with a tree name of ACME_TREE.

TIP

A single NDS tree with two or more O=Organization objects is extremely rare and not usually recommended. The reason that this configuration is not often used is because there is not a single object at the top of the tree that represents the entire conglomerate company. This makes merging and partition management a little bit trickier.

On the other extreme, some companies are so small that they only need a single O=Organization and no other containers. In Figure 4.17, for example, we've created a "smaller" ACME with all the users, servers, volumes, and printers in a single O=ACME container. This design is simple, easy to use, and very easy to manage.

FIGURE 4.17

A Single O=Organization at ACME

Chances are, you don't fall into either of these extreme categories. Chances are, you're just like the rest of us and you need OU=Organizational Units to define the majority of your tree. Now, let's explore the final tier of the TOP layers—Organizational Units.

ZEN

"Be what you wish to seem."

Socrates

OU=Organizational Units

The final top layers are defined by Organizational Unit containers. These are the most important layers in the tree, because they represent a transition point between the inflexible upper layers and the flexible bottom layers. These OUs also define the layout of the rest of the tree. In summary, this is where your tree begins to take shape.

You can choose one of three approaches for the final tier of the top layers:

▶ Geographical—Organize the upper layers according to ACME's WAN Layout Map and distributed sites.

▶ Regional—Insert regional containers to further organize numerous distributed sites.

▶ Departmental—Organize the upper layers according to ACME's Organizational Chart and departmental workgroups.

These three top layer strategies should be prioritized in the order shown. Try the geographical approach first, it's the best one—trust me. OK, so you don't trust me. Well, at least give me a chance to convince you. Here's a detailed discussion of each of the three approaches, and an explanation of why ACME chose the geographical approach.

Geographical Top Layers

The first OU=Organizational Unit approach is based on the geographic boundaries of your WAN. Remember, the sole purpose of the NDS tree is to productively organize network resources. These resources are geographically distributed and rely on slow WAN links for interconnectivity. To optimize partitioning, replica placement, and time synchronization, you should design the first OU's along these WAN boundaries.

The geographical approach relies on your WAN Layout Map. As you can see in Figure 4.9, ACME is organized around five main hubs—CAMELOT, RIO, SYDNEY, TOKYO, and NORAD. These hubs become the foundation of ACME's OU structure, as shown in Figure 4.14. Once you've established the geographic top of the tree, you can zero in on each location with an organizational design—at the bottom layers.

Of course, life is full of exceptions. And the geographical approach is not *always* the answer (just most of the time). Here are two exceptions:

▸ **Exception 1**—Companies with a single site or local campus network are not dependent upon the geographical design approach. Since there's very little geography with which to work, you should skip the geographical layers and go straight to organization. Some companies with few servers and users may not need to create additional containers at all. Rather, they can place all the NDS objects under a single O=Organization (see Figure 4.17).

▸ **Exception 2**—Companies with WAN sites or local campuses connected with very high speed links (such as T-3 or greater). The location OU's are less important because the limiting slow WAN links have been removed. In this case, the very high bandwidths nullify geographic considerations.

REAL WORLD

Many companies still choose to use geographical designators even though they have very high speed WAN links. One such company, for example, has a metropolitan area network (MAN) running FDDI between 12 buildings across a city. The basis of their decision to stick with geographic sites was twofold. First, for administrative purposes, they wanted to have each building supported by a single administrator. The distributed OU sites gave the tree a good place to break out security administration. Second, certain local applications worked best with the geographic design at the top of the tree.

If you're using a campus layout (such as a research park or university), first consider the speed of the links between buildings or floors. The geographical approach could still be used with buildings representing minor OU sites within the network infrastructure. Even in ACME's case, the distributed campus buildings could be useful second-tier container objects—as long as they help organize the network resources.

As a matter of fact, the second-tier OU's in NORAD server *both* purposes. As you can see in Figure 4.18, the NORAD campus connects three buildings—Labs, Charity, and PR. It so happens that these are also the organizational workgroups located there. Interestingly, regardless of how we design the second-tier NORAD OU's (geographical or organizational), they will turn out the same—OU=LABS, OU=CHARITY, and OU=PR. What an interesting coincidence. This type of design overlapping occurs only in special circumstances. It's also a sign of a wonderfully designed WAN infrastructure.

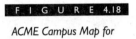

FIGURE 4.18

ACME Campus Map for NORAD

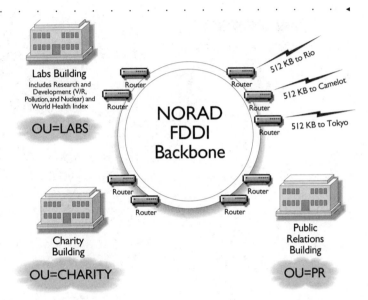

Regional Top Layers

The second OU=Organizational Unit approach relies on the introduction of regional containers above the geographic OUs. This is necessary if the total number of locations is high. Adding an intermediate "regional" layer helps to ensure a balanced pyramid design.

Consider what happens when ACME decides to expand. Let's say they decide to integrate more offices throughout the world. In this example only, ACME's WAN infrastructure would look something like Figure 4.19. Notice that the distributed offices connect together via 56 KB links, while the hubs still use 512 KB lines. Also, each city is added to the WAN layout through their appropriate regional hub.

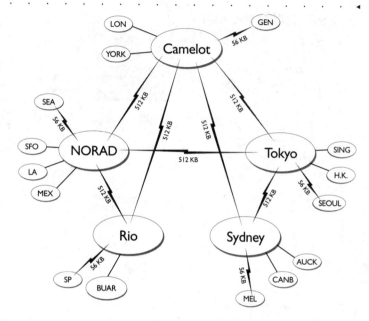

F I G U R E 4.19

ACME'S New WAN Layout
with Expanded Cities

Using the WAN infrastructure, we have designed a new tree that includes regional OUs named North America (NA), South America (SA), Europe (EUR), Asia(ASIA), and Australia (AUST). These regional OUs group the appropriate cities and help keep the NDS tree design looking like a pyramid (see Figure 4.20).

Departmental Top Layers

The final OU=Organizational Unit option is based on the organizational workgroups throughout your company. This departmental approach should only be used in two cases:

1 • Your company doesn't have a WAN infrastructure or other locations to consider. If your company operates over a LAN or high-speed WAN, then you can skip the geographical design and go directly to the organizational bottom layer design. This approach is based solely on the Organization Chart.

FIGURE 4.20

Regional Top Layers for
ACME

2 •   If you're a rebel, and you really want to design your tree according to the company's Organizational Chart. This approach is justified if there is something "very special" about your company—all resources are organized according to workgroup function. It happens.

In either of these cases, you can place your departments, divisions, and workgroups at the top of the tree and physical locations at the bottom. This is a little less efficient because any change to the organizational structure ripples down the entire NDS tree design.

Consider the example in Figure 4.21. We have swapped the ACME design and put their workgroups at the top. The first question is, "Where do most network changes occur?" Most changes occur at the organizational level. That's not to say that changes don't occur to geographic sites as well, but they are less frequent. Therefore, when you make changes to the tree, you want to impact the least number of people. Not in this case. Remember, flexibility at the bottom, rigidity at the top. Also, when considering other design requirements (such as administration, partitions, replicas, network resource placement, login scripts, and Bindery Services), it is apparent that the organization layers of the NDS tree more adequately consider these elements.

*ACME's Alter-Ego Tree—
Departmental Top Layers*

That completes Step 3. We're well on our way to NDS Nirvana. There's only one step left, and it's a doozy. Check it out.

ZEN

Three o'clock syndrome—The tendency of office employees to become drowsy in the mid-afternoon. Or, the tendency on the part of working mothers to feel guilty about being away from home when their children arrive there from school. Or, finally, the tendency of anyone to feel anything at 3:00 a.m. or p.m.

STEP 4: BOTTOM LAYERS

With ACME's top layers in place, it's time to add organizational functionality to our tree. Then, we'll begin resource placement with the administrators, servers, printers, and print queues. These are the two functions of the bottom layers:

▸ Organizational Function

▸ Resource Placement

Organizational Function

Throughout the book, we've been harping on the tree as a framework for network resources. It's true. But what *is* ACME doing with the resources? Working! And how does ACME work? According to their organizational chart! So, it looks as though organizational function matters after all.

The bottom layers should be designed according to the organizational boundaries of your company. The bottom OU=Organizational Units should be based on ACME's divisions, departments, and workgroups. This information is detailed in Figure 4.11 (ACME's Organizational Chart). Further refinement can be found in ACME's WorkFlow analysis (see Chapter 3).

Another interesting thing happens as you move down the tree—resources get closer to users. Also, the communication lines shorten. Most bottom layer OUs are separated by LAN links, not slow WAN lines. This means synchronization isn't such a problem, and the design becomes very flexible. Refer to Figure 4.22 for an illustration of ACME's bottom layers.

FIGURE 4.22

ACME's Bottom Layers

During the design of the bottom layers, ensure that there's a place for every user and network resource. Also, distribute shared departments, if necessary. For example, ACME's Charity and PR departments have an office in each major location. Furthermore, each office has at least one server and shares information with a central database in CAMELOT. For this reason, we've decided to create an OU=CHARITY and OU=PR container in every location. This might seem repetitive, but it's the only way to handle distributed shared departments.

Also, notice in Figure 4.22 that the top layers of the ACME tree are based completely on the WAN infrastructure—they will remain fairly stable. Once the WAN infrastructure has been taken care of, your design effort should switch to the bottom of the tree. The bottom of ACME's tree is based on its organizational chart. Almost all of ACME's network resources will be placed in the bottom of the tree—close to its users.

Resource Placement

Resource placement considerations also will affect how you design the bottom layers of your tree. At this point you may want to consider the networking needs of your users. How are they organized? If the resources are organized according to workgroups, they should be placed in the same container as users. However, if the network resources offer services to multiple departments, you should place the resources higher in the tree— possibly at the location container.

Remember, there should be a logical place for every network resource and user. At this point you should review ACME's updated resource list (see Table 4.8). It includes functional containers, servers, administrators, printers, and print queues. These are the only resources that will have any significant design impact. All other NDS resources (such as groups, login scripts, and directory map objects) will be placed during the NDS Management phase (see Chapter 8).

QUIZ

Let's play a game. You, me, and Albert Einstein will each toss a coin in succession. The winner will be the first to throw a head. What are each of our respective chances?

(Q4-4)

Congratulations! You're the proud parent of a baby NDS tree. It may seem innocent now, but wait until your users get hold of it. Now wasn't that easy. Let's review—pyramid, geography, organization—all done. Well, at least with the rough draft. Next, there are a few external design factors you should consider before finalizing the design. It's time for some fine-tuning.

DESIGN CONSIDERATIONS

Some CNEs try to design the NDS tree all in one step—simultaneously juggling five design inputs and four external pressures. Not a good idea. First, create the top layers according to geography. Next, create the bottom layers according to organization. Now you're finished with the rough draft.

Next, fine-tune the tree with any of the following design considerations:

▶ Administration

▶ NDS partitions and replicas

▶ Login scripts

▶ Bindery Services

Interestingly, these design considerations only affect the bottom layers of the tree. Fortunately, this is the flexible half. This is because they mostly deal with user resources, and most of them live in the bottom layers of the tree—although this is not a social commentary. Let's explore these four external design pressures in a little more depth.

Administration

Tree Administration is one of the most important design considerations—mostly because it involves *you*! There are two choices: centralized and distributed. *Centralized administration* relies on a single IS (Information Services) staff for all portions of the tree. *Distributed administration*, on the other hand, distributes branch control to container administrators—typically at the departmental or geographic level. Here's how it works.

Centralized Administration

In this case, the entire NDS tree is controlled by one IS group. This group manages all the additions and deletions of NDS objects, partitioning, replication, and everything else related to the NDS database. In Chapter 11 we'll learn how to create central administrators by giving them Supervisor rights to the top of the tree—[Root].

If the NDS tree is to be managed centrally, the IS staff will build the entire tree. They have control over all NDS objects throughout the tree. This also helps standardize naming and object placement.

Distributed Administration

With distributed administration, on the other hand, control over portions of the NDS tree is delegated to individuals or independent groups. These individuals may be departmental administrators, or they may be responsible for all the network resources in a particular location. In this scenario, you'll still need a central IS staff to handle the top layers of the tree. We'll also explore decentralized administration in Chapter 11.

If the NDS tree will be decentrally managed, each container administrator will decide independently how that portion of the tree is organized. The IS department handles the top layers and then relinquishes control to distributed individuals. This is difficult for many IS managers, especially with the higher learning curve associated with NDS. Just make sure your container administrators know what they're doing. If you care, you'll give them each a copy of this book (hint, hint).

In addition to this book, here are a few more gifts for container administrators:

1 • They should have sufficient security over their containers to create, delete, or change all their objects.

2 • They should carefully determine (and justify) if more levels must be created beneath their containers before making changes.

3 • They should actively participate in creating and using the naming standards document.

4 • They should not partition their OUs without the assistance of the central IS department.

5 • They should inform the central IS staff before adding a new server into the corporate tree.

The depth of the tree can also impact your administration choices. Remember, the recommendation is to build the NDS tree like a pyramid with fewer layers at the top and more layers at the bottom. Centralized administration dictates that a flat and wide tree is easier to administer. If your company has only a few servers and users, you can build a shallow tree that is good for centralized administration.

On the other hand, distributed administrators can determine the depth of their portion of the tree. But don't let them go wild. The NDS tree is much easier to deal with if it's three to five layers deep. Even the largest companies can design a productive NDS tree with five layers or less. Check out ACME, they use five—and that includes the [Root].

TIP

There is no physical limit to the number of layers in the NDS tree. There is, however, a logical limit to the total number of layers you can access. For instance, NDS has a limit of 255 characters for a distinguished name. Thus, the actual limit for the number of layers is dependent on the number of characters in the name of each container. If your OU names are long, you will not be able to have as many layers as with shorter names. For example, if all the OU names are just two characters long, then you can have 127 layers. But, if your OU's average 20 characters in length, you can only have 12 layers.

NDS Partitions and Replicas

The next external pressure comes from NDS partitions. The tree design should reflect a variety of partitioning factors, including the size of the partition (total number of objects), the total number of replicas, and where in the tree the partitions are created.

A container object is required for the creation of a partition. In addition, it is designated the "root-most" object of the partition. Figure 4.23 shows a number of partitions, and in two cases we've identified the partition root—the NORAD partition and the TOKYO partition.

FIGURE 4.23

Partitioning ACME's
Locations

When you're creating NDS partitions, always follow the physical network infrastructure. Like the top layers of the tree, partitions typically follow the WAN layout map—creating a partition at each location. This strategy has many advantages, but the most apparent is accessibility. Network resources are always available to local users. In Figure 4.23, we've partitioned all five ACME hubs.

The size of your partitions and the total number of replicas is a design consideration for the bottom of the tree. Typically, partitions range in size from 50 to 5000 objects. If the partition grows to be significantly larger than 5000 objects, you should probably split the partition in two. Therefore, in Figure 4.24 we create a new partition called OPS under CAMELOT because that location's partition has grown beyond the 5000 object limit. More partitions, in the right places, provide greater efficiency in your tree design. Remember, a partition contains information about all the objects in a specific subtree, not just the objects in a single container.

The New OPS Partition

REAL WORLD

We are not suggesting that NDS will not work in partitions with more than 5000 objects. However, based on experience, partitions work most efficiently in the 50- to 5000-object range. Therefore, when your partitions reach this size, begin assessing the need to split the partition. Check your user's performance and synchronization performance, and use that as a guide.

The next design consideration is the total number of replicas in a partition. If the number of replicas is greater than 10 to 15, consider splitting the partition to reduce the total number of replicas. Novell recommends three replicas for each partition. The primary reason you would need more than a couple of replicas for any partition is Bindery Services. Bindery Services requires a copy of the replica. We'll discuss Bindery Services considerations in just a moment.

Decide who is responsible for the partitioning of the NDS tree. If you manage the tree centrally, then all the partitioning decisions should be made by the central IS department. If tree administration is distributed, then you may turn over partitioning control to each container administrators. Whichever way you handle partitioning make sure that you decide who's going to do it *before* you start installing servers.

We will discuss partitioning design in greater depth later in this chapter and in Chapter 9 (NDS Partition Management and Synchronization).

ZEN

"My children always had an unusual diet .... In general, they refused to eat anything that hadn't danced on TV."

Erma Bombeck

Login Scripts

The third NDS tree design consideration deals with login scripts. Login scripts impact the bottom layers of the tree and indirectly control how users access certain resources. In general, users need login scripts to MAP network drives, CAPTURE print queues, and set other environmental variables. Therefore, the login scripts become a very important design consideration.

Typically, users needing the same login script will be grouped together in the same OU container. You can then use the Container login script to provide access to NDS resources. Figure 4.25 shows two Container login scripts—one for OU=FIN (shared by Guinevere, *et al.*) and one for OU=DIST (shared by Merlin, *et al.*). You should separate the users who need different login scripts for the same reason. As you design the login scripts for your users, you are, in fact, designing the organizational structure of the bottom level of the tree.

Another approach is to create a single login script and copy it to multiple containers. In this case, user placement is not affected. However, this strategy requires that you (the NetWare 4 CNE) keep track of all the scripts and make sure they're the same. Too much work. I have a solution.

You can also make use of the Profile login script. It enables you to span a single login script across multiple OU containers. For example, the SYDNEY location has a profile script for the HR department. It spans across the following three OU's: OU=MEDICAL, OU=FOOD, and OU=SHELTER. Check out Figure 4.26.

F I G U R E 4.25

*Understanding Container
Login Scripts*

F I G U R E 4.26

*A Profile Login Script for
the OU=HR Containers*

We'll discuss login scripts in much greater depth in Chapter 12. For now, let's explore the final tree design consideration—Bindery Services.

Bindery Services

NDS provides backward compatibility to NetWare 2 and NetWare 3 users with a feature called *Bindery Services*. This feature allows bindery versions of NetWare and other third-party software to access the NDS database as if it were the bindery. For example, a client can use the NETX shell (NetWare 3 client) to login to a NetWare 4 server and run any bindery-based application that exists there.

Bindery Services is enabled on any NetWare 4 server through the SET Server Bindery Context command. The server can select one OU container or many containers as the bindery context. The *server bindery context* is simply the containers the bindery user sees as the bindery. Only the leaf objects in bindery context container(s) appear to bindery users. In Figure 4.27, we've used SERVMAN.NLM to create a bindery context for the CAM-SRV1 server—OU=OPS.OU=CAMELOT.O=ACME. This means that bindery users in Camelot will only see the NDS objects within the OU=OPS container.

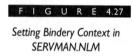

F I G U R E 4.27

Setting Bindery Context in SERVMAN.NLM

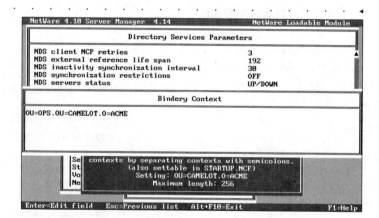

If you're concerned about your server's bindery context, use the SET Bindery Context command as shown in Figure 4.28. It tells you what's going on. If you want to change your server's bindery context, use the SET Server Bindery Context command at the file server console.

NetWare 4 Bindery Services allows you to select up to 16 OU containers as a "superbindery." Here's the kicker: In order for Bindery Services to work, the host server must have a Master or Read/Write replica of bindery context partition. If the server has 16 bindery containers, it must hold 16 separate replicas.

FIGURE 4.28

Understanding the SET
Bindery Context Command

```
CAM-SRV1:SET BINDERY CONTEXT
Bindery Context:  OU=OPS.OU=CAMELOT.O=ACME
Maximum length:  255
    Can be set in the startup ncf file
    Description: The NetWare Directory Services container where bindery
                 services are provided.  Set multiple contexts by separating
                 contexts with semicolons.
CAM-SRV1:
```

As you can see, placing bindery replicas can increase the total number of replicas for each partition. This will affect the tree design because you may be forced to split a partition to reduce the number of replicas. Bindery Services is the only reason you want to maintain more than a few replicas of any partition.

Finally, what about bindery resource placement? You must place all bindery users and their appropriate users in the same bindery context container. If you plan on using many NetWare 3 users, this can get quite cumbersome. It will also affect your NDS tree design because it requires that you combine users and resources from multiple departments into a single OU—this defeats the purpose of bottom layer organization. I don't like it. Only use Bindery Services if you have to, and refer to the "NDS Accessibility Design" section at the end of this chapter for more details.

TIP

Before you change the bottom of your tree design to accommodate Bindery Services, determine whether you even need Bindery Services at all. Remember, Bindery Services is an optional feature that does not have to be enabled at each server. You should determine if the clients are using NETX or applications that require Bindery Services. You could also identify the users and key applications, and force them to use Bindery Services on specific servers.

REAL WORLD

Here is a brief list of some the applications you may encounter that make bindery calls. This is a brief list, and you need to check all your applications to determine if they require the bindery.

- ▸ Print services
- ▸ Menuing systems
- ▸ Backup utilities
- ▸ Host connectivity products
- ▸ Network management utilities
- ▸ Other NetWare 3–based applications and utilities

Congratulations again! The tree has been built *and* refined. Now we're really finished. As you can see, there are many more external design pressures to consider than just geography and organization. It's a good thing you stayed awake during those last few pages.

ZEN

"Are you having trouble in saying this stuff? It's really quite easy for me. I just look in my mirror and see what I say. And then I just say what I see."

Dr. Seuss

Now it's time to move forward. The tree has been designed, and we're ready for more. You are ready for more—aren't you? Good, because Partition and Replica Design are next. I wonder how the roller coaster ride is going....

Partition and Replica Design

"whooooa!"

"aaaaaah!"

"heeeelp!"

These are all great examples of how the roller coaster ride is going—it's going *fast*! We're halfway down "The Great Fall" now, and my stomach is officially in my throat. The exhilaration can only be eclipsed by free-falling from an airplane (now, there's an idea). We can't do that yet. That's NetWare 5—Novell hasn't announced it yet.

Our third stop along the NDS design tour is partition and replica design. Once the tree has been designed, we get to break it into small little pieces (partitioning) and scatter them around the WAN (replica placement). At this point, you don't actually perform any partitioning operations, you simply *design* the partition boundaries. Once the boundaries have been designed, you must give serious thought to where they'll go—replica placement.

Replica placement is one of the most important aspects of NDS design because it directly affects your network's performance, accessibility, and fault tolerance. Remember, you won't actually *place* anything until later—during the NDS Management phase (Chapter 9).

In the next few pages we're going to explore ACME's partition boundaries and replica placement design. But before we do, we should take a moment to review NDS partitioning and replication. We discussed these topics in depth previously in Chapter 2. Now we'll take the story a little bit farther—into the realm of design. Here's what's in store for us in this section:

- ▸ Understanding NDS Partitions

- ▸ Designing ACME's Partitions

- ▸ Understanding NDS Replicas

- ▸ Placing ACME's Replicas

Think of this discussion as Genetics 101, and we're learning how to clone NDS containers. Ready, set, clone.

UNDERSTANDING NDS PARTITIONS

NDS partitions are logical pieces of the NDS tree (see Figure 4.29). This process effectively splits the NDS database into subtrees. The subtrees can then be distributed to NetWare 4 servers throughout your WAN. Partitioning the NDS tree provides you with the ability to selectively distribute the NDS tree information to the areas in your network that need the information—near the users.

FIGURE 4.29

Understanding ACME Partitioning

The purpose of partitioning is to give you the ability to scale the NDS database across NetWare 4 servers. Splitting up the database and storing its pieces on separate servers distributes the workload for both NDS and the server. In addition, NetWare 4 partitioning tools allow you to choose which partitions go on which servers.

For example, in Figure 4.29, you can see that the NORAD partition and its object information is placed on the NOR-SRV1 server in NORAD. The same is true for all the other locations. By partitioning the NDS tree, you can keep the local information in each location, and yet still have access to the rest of the global database. Life is good.

Partitioning is hierarchical—meaning that the root-most partition is parent to its subordinate children. When all partitions are taken together, they form a hierarchical map back to the [Root] object. Figure 4.30 illustrates the hierarchical partition map formed by ACME's distributed locations. It also shows the parent/child relationship between OU=CAMELOT and its subcontainers.

F I G U R E 4.30

Hierarchical Partition Map for ACME

As in life, partition parents must manage their subordinate children. This is ensured in NDS through a concept known as *subordinate references*. When new partitions are created under an existing container, their parent must maintain pointers to the new partitions. This concept is shown in Figure 4.31. NDS requires these pointers so that all partitions are linked together to form a common database of information.

Subordinate references create and maintain the fragile link between parent and child partitions. Therefore, any server holding a partition can end up with a large number of subordinate reference pointers to children of that container. For example, check out the CAM-SRV1 server in Figure 4.31. It gets a copy of every location OU, because they are all children of the [Root] Partition.

Understanding Subordinate
References

As a matter of fact, the [Root] is a very sensitive partition. Let us emphasize that NDS creates a subordinate reference pointer automatically when a server holding a parent partition creates a link to its child partitions. However, for greatest efficiency we recommend that you keep the number of separately partitioned containers to 60 to 70 per layer. For these reasons, we also recommend that the [Root] partition be kept small with only the [Root] and an Organization container below it.

With all of this "family tree" stuff in mind, let's explore some more important partitioning rules. Then, we'll learn how to create partition boundaries. Cool.

Partitioning Rules

NDS partitioning follows these simple rules:

1 • Each partition must be named and requires a single container object as the top (or root) of the partition (not to be confused with the [Root] partition). The container object that is used as the start of the partition is called the *partition root object*. Only one partition root object exists for each partition, and it is the topmost container object. Check out Figure 4.23.

2 • Two containers at the same level cannot share a partition without a parent watching over them. Play nicely children. This rule is illustrated in Figure 4.32.

3 • Partitions cannot overlap with any other part of the NDS tree. This means that one object will never reside in two partitions.

4 • Each partition contains all the information for the connected subtree, unless another subordinate partition is created underneath.

Now that we know the rules, let's get busy creating partition boundaries. Here's a quick lesson.

Creating Partition Boundaries

During installation of the very first NetWare 4 server, the [Root] partition is created and a Master copy (replica) of it is placed on this server. In NetWare 4.1, the [Root] partition is the only partition the installation program creates. There is no default partitioning beyond this—it's all up to you. See Figure 4.33 for an illustration of the [Root] partition. Since this [Root] partition is the only partition that is created during installation, it is often called the *default partition*. The [Root] partition cannot be removed unless you remove NDS from all the NetWare 4 servers—which is really removing the entire tree.

F I G U R E 4.33

The Default [Root]
Partition for ACME

Child partitions can be created under the [Root] partition by selecting a subordinate container object (typically an OU) as the top of the new partition. A partition can only have one topmost container object (referred to as the *partition root object*).

When the partition is created, it takes its name from the top most container object. All the objects in the tree that are under the partition root container are contained within the new partition. This is always true, unless there is a previously defined partition lower in the tree. The partition defined previously is not affected. Figure 4.34 shows how the NORAD partition is created underneath and to the side of the [Root] Partition. All the NDS objects in the NORAD location are suddenly part of the NORAD Partition.

Creating a new partition under an existing parent is sometimes referred to as a *partition split*. This is because the child simple splits away from underneath the parent's control. In Figure 4.34 above, the NORAD child simply splits away from the [Root] partition. This operation is extremely fast because it doesn't generate any traffic on your WAN. We're simply dividing one database into two with all the information staying on the same server that contained the original partition. This split operation will create a new child subordinate reference pointer on all the servers that had a copy of the parent partition.

F I G U R E 4.34

The New NORAD Partition

ZEN

"One of the disadvantages of having children is that they eventually get old enough to give you presents they make at school."

Robert Byrne

Now you're ready for ACME. This has been a great preview, but I want to get my hands dirty. I want to feel mud under my fingernails. I want to prune the ACME tree! (I really need to get a hobby.)

DESIGNING ACME'S PARTITIONS

Where do we start? Partition design is very simple if you follow this one cardinal rule: Partition to distribute the NDS database across ACME servers—if it doesn't need to be partitioned, then don't!

The number one design criteria for partitioning is the physical layout of your network infrastructure—mostly the location of network servers. Using this criteria, your main task is to partition the NDS database so that it localizes NDS information. The bottom line is keep the NORAD information in NORAD, the RIO information in RIO, and so on. Figure 4.29 shows how the ACME tree has been partitioned along the lines of WAN communications. Note that in our example the [Root] partition is very small and includes only the [Root] and O=ACME. This is recommended and will be discussed later when we address replication.

Before you start tearing apart the top and bottom layers of ACME's tree design, consider the following partitioning guidelines:

1 • **Don't span a WAN link or physical locations with a partition**—This design guideline rule is very important and should not be ignored. If you span a WAN link, it creates unnecessary NDS synchronization traffic between two or more locations. Spanning a WAN link is shown in Figure 4.35 and should be avoided.

F I G U R E 4.35

*Don't Span WAN Links
with Partitions*

2 • **Keep the [Root] partition small**—Typically, this should include only the [Root] object and the O=Organization container. Do not include any other subordinate container OUs in the partition with the [Root] object—this creates unnecessary subordinate references.

3 • **The top layers of the tree should be partitioned according to location**—Again, remember guideline number 1, do not span a WAN link with the same partition. Partition locally wherever possible.

TIP

These guidelines do not suggest that you partition every Organizational Unit in your tree. There is also such a thing as overpartitioning. Partition locally, and further partition at that site only if necessary.

4 • **The bottom layers of the tree should be partitioned in special cases only**—The bottom layers of the tree should be partitioned only if there is a special requirement. The special requirements are either size of the partition (total number of objects is greater than 5000), too many replicas of the same partition, or the need to break out an administrative domain.

5 • **Use the pyramid design for partitioning as well**—You will want a small number of partitions at the top layers of the tree and possibly more partitions as you move toward the bottom. If you have designed the tree based on a pyramid shape, as recommended, then your partition design will naturally follow the tree design. Remember, one of the advantages of the pyramid tree design was natural partitioning. Now you know what we were talking about.

6 • **Do not create a partition unless there's a local server**—Do not create a partition (even if it includes a WAN link) if there is not a server locally on which to store it. This situation is common only with small remote offices that do not have servers at their local sites. The users would currently access all the network services across the WAN infrastructure anyway. The access to NDS is not any different. Figure 4.36 shows how the remote users in the OU=DIST container would still be part of its partition even though they don't have a server of their own.

*Don't Partition for Remote
Sites Unless They Have
Their Own Server*

Partitioning the Top Layers of ACME's Tree

It all starts at the top. As I'm sure you've guessed by now, the top layers should be partitioned according to the WAN infrastructure. What a surprise! Since the top layers have already been designed according to the WAN layout, the partition boundaries should follow naturally.

The NDS database will not scale as well if you try to combine multiple geographical sites into one partition. If you try to span more than one location in a partition, then the information in the partition will synchronize with the other copies across the slower WAN links. This reduces the efficiency of the network and destroys the purpose of trying to create a partition in the first place.

If you have implemented regional OU containers, then you should create a partition for each of the regional OUs and store that partition on a server separate from its parent partition. After the regional partitions are defined, you'll need to create a child partition at each location. This will distribute subordinate references to location-based servers.

That was easy. Now for the tricky part. Let's see what's going on at the bottom layers of ACME's tree.

Partitioning the Bottom Layers of ACME's Tree

As I'm sure you remember, the bottom layers are designed according to ACME organizational structure. Does organization have a big impact on partitioning? Not really. We've already partitioned ACME according to location, so what do we do with the bottom layers? Nothing...in most cases. But, of course, the world is full of exceptions, and here are three:

- Partition size

- Number of replicas

- Partition administration

Partition Size

As the partition size grows, you should consider creating another partition to help distribute the workload to other servers. A normal-sized partition is approximately 5000 objects. If the partition grows to be significantly larger, you might consider splitting it into new children. Remember, a partition contains all the objects in a defined subtree, not just the objects in a single container.

Figure 4.37 shows how the CAMELOT partition is split into two partitions—one parent and one new child. The OU=OPS container object becomes a new child partition to CAMELOT. We created the new OPS Partition, because CAMELOT got too big—more than 5000 objects. Those Knights sure are busy!

FIGURE 4.37

Splitting the CAMELOT
Partition in Two

Number of Replicas

Another exception revolves around the total number of replicas of a single partition. If the total number of replicas goes beyond 10 to 15, then you should consider splitting the partition just to reduce the number of replicas that must be synchronized. Again, that's too much work for the server. The only reason you'll want more than three replicas of any partition is to support Bindery Services.

Also, keep in mind that more replicas mean more management—especially if a partition breaks and needs repairing. Replica repair can be difficult if you have a large number of replicas because each one may need to be repaired separately.

Partition Administration

NDS allows you to distribute partition administration as well. Lucky you. If a department manager wants the responsibility of managing his or her own partitioning, then you must plan the superior partitions accordingly. For example, the rights needed to partition the NDS tree are either the Supervisor object right at the OU, or the Write right to its ACL. Also, if there is a need to create a new partition from the parent then the individual creating the child also needs full rights to the parent. For more information on NDS security, refer to Chapter 11.

That completes our partition design for ACME. If you follow these partitioning guidelines at both the top and bottom layers, the NDS information always will remain close to the user and other leaf objects. Remember, location is the key when creating partition boundaries.

THE BRAIN

For more information about creating NDS partitions refer to Chapter 9 (Partition Management and Synchronization). In that chapter, you'll get an opportunity to create "real" ACME partitions using NWADMIN's Partition Manager. Design is theory, management is *action*.

Very good. Now that we have ACME's partition design in place, it's time to spread them out—replica placement. This is the fun part. We get to distribute all the little pieces to ACME servers everywhere. And why do we do this? Because we can!

ZEN

Designer genes—Genetic material that has been altered through genetic engineering for use in agricultural, medical, and networking experiments. Thought to be the foundation of NetWare 4 replication.

UNDERSTANDING NDS REPLICAS

The next step in NDS design is *replica placement*. Once the pieces have been created, you can distribute them. Why?

- ▶ Because replicas increase NDS fault tolerance.

- ▶ Because replicas enhance network performance.

- ▶ Because replicas simplify name resolution.

First of all, replication increases the availability of partitions—it spreads them around. This also increases reliability. For example, if a server holding a replica of your partition goes down, then you can simply use another copy for authentication and updates.

Second, distributed replicas increase NDS performance. Replication enables you to distribute partition copies to local servers throughout the WAN. Having a local replica decreases the time needed for certain NDS tasks (such as authentication, NDS changes, searches, and data gathering). This does not imply that replicas should be used for mobile users. Having a replica locally means on the server where the majority of the users need the information.

Finally, replication enhances name resolution, because users requesting NDS information first must locate a server with the data's information on it. Replication spreads the data around. If the requested information is not found on the server to which the user is already authenticated, then NDS automatically will connect the user to the proper server through the process of name resolution. This connection process is simplified when there are more replicas from which to choose. It also happens faster and more reliably.

TIP

For improved speed, you can replicate the [Root] partition in strategic locations (such as hub sites). This allows users to walk the tree faster. The [Root] partition should be kept small for the purpose of keeping NDS traffic to a minimum.

In order to truly understand replica placement, you must learn what makes them tick. Here's a list of some basic replica rules:

1 • **A partition can have multiple replicas**—Multiple copies of a partition are known as *replicas* and can be stored on separate servers across the WAN.

2 • **Only one master replica per partition**—A partition can only have one replica designated as the Master. The other partitions will have Read/Write and/or Read-Only replicas. Refer to Chapter 2 for more detail.

3 • **Only one replica of a given partition can be stored on an single server**—A NetWare 4 server can hold multiple replicas from different partitions. It cannot hold two replicas of the same partition.

4 • **All replicas will participate in the replica synchronization for a partition**— All replicas (regardless of their type) are part of their partition's synchronization list (or replica ring) and, therefore, participate in synchronization operations. Again, refer to Chapter 2 for more details.

These rules are important because they describe the characteristics of replication. You must understand how replicas behave before you start copying ACME's partitions. If you feel you're ready, we'll move on to "Placing ACME's Replicas." If not, refer to Chapter 2 for a more detailed replica review. Ready, set, replicate.

PLACING ACME'S REPLICAS

Welcome to phase 2 of partition design—replica placement. The partitions we created in the previous section aren't going to do us any good until we clone them. As a matter of fact, replica placement is one of your most important design responsibilities—for the three reasons outlined previously. Here's how it works:

- ▸ Fault Tolerance—Eliminate any single point of failure in ACME's NDS tree.

- ▸ Local Distribution—Place replicas on local servers for efficiency and speed.

- ▸ Bindery Services—Bindery users and applications need Master or Read/Write replicas of their server's bindery context.

- ▸ Improved Name Resolution—Distribute replicas strategically to create "bridges" between separated containers.

Let's take a closer look at replica placement for ACME. And, who knows, we may learn a thing or two along the way.

Fault Tolerance

The primary goal of replication is to eliminate any single point of failure in the entire NDS tree. Distributing multiple replicas of a partition increases the availability of object information if one of the servers should become unavailable. In Figure 4.38, the NORAD and CAMELOT partitions have been replicated to multiple servers within their locations. This provides fault tolerance for each partition. If one of the servers in the partition goes down, the information isn't lost—it's available from the other server.

F I G U R E 4.38

Replication for NORAD and CAMELOT

The NetWare 4 server installation program automatically creates up to three NDS replicas for each partition—for fault tolerance. When you install additional servers into the NDS tree, NetWare places a replica of the server's home partition on the first three servers. After that, you're on your own.

For example, in Figure 4.39, the NORAD partition is automatically replicated as new servers are added. It starts with NOR-SRV1, then NOR-CHR-SRV1, and finally LABS-SRV1. Also, notice that NOR-SRV1 gets a Master replica. That's because it was the first server installed into the NORAD partition. The others receive Read/Write replicas. Then, one sunny day in June, you decide to install a fourth server (R&D-SRV1) into the

NORAD partition—nothing happens! Remember, NetWare 4 only replicates the first *three* servers by default. The first thing you should do is place a Read/Write NORAD replica on the new R&D-SRV1 server. Check out Chapter 9 for the correct procedures.

F I G U R E 4.39

Default Replication for NORAD

This strategy only applies to the new server's home partition. It doesn't have any affect on other partitions in the tree. This is done for one simple purpose—fault tolerance of the NDS database. If you are comfortable with where the three automatic replicas are placed, then you don't need to place any of your own.

As a general guideline, you should have at least a Master and two Read/Write replicas of every partition. If you don't have three servers in the same site, replicate the partition elsewhere. Just make sure the NDS information is available somewhere.

Local Distribution

Always replicate locally—if you can. It makes your life much easier if you place all replicas of a partition on local servers. Local to who? Local to the users who need the resources defined in the host partition. Don't place replicas on servers across the WAN if a local one is available. If you follow this guideline, you can be guaranteed that the users will retrieve their personal information from the nearest available server. This is faster, more efficient, more reliable.

Ideally, you should place the replica that contains a user's NDS information on the same server that stores the user's home directory. This may not always be possible, but it does improve the user's access to the NDS objects and the file system. For example, during the login, any given user will MAP drives to volumes, CAPTURE to print queues, and access several of their user properties. NDS will execute each of these requests regardless of where the replicas are stored. However, the login speed for the user will be increased if the user finds the requested information on the first attached server—the local one.

TIP

Always try to place all three replicas of any given partition on local servers—within the same WAN hub. If you are forced to place the third replica across a WAN link because there are only two servers at the location, consider not creating the third replica. The cost in WAN traffic efficiency is not worth the gain in NDS fault tolerance.

Here's the $64,000 question: "What happens if the site only has one server? Do I still partition and replicate locally? How do I replicate for fault tolerance?" In the case of a remote site with just one server, you should still partition at that site and place the Master replica on that server. A second Read/Write replica should be placed at the nearest WAN location.

Figure 4.40 illustrates how a small remote office should be replicated. For this example only, assume that there is a small remote site called OU=SLC connected to the NORAD hub. There is only one server in the remote site—it's called SLC-SRV1. You should create a small partition and Master replicate it to SLC-SRV1. You should also place a Read/Write replica of OU=SLC in the NORAD location—possibly on the Master NOR-SRV1 server.

F I G U R E 4.40

Replicating a Remote Site for NORAD

Typically, remote sites contain a small number of user objects anyway. Therefore, replicating across the WAN doesn't become such a big deal. You really don't have any choice. It's better to replicate a small partition across a WAN than to lose the NDS information altogether if the server ever goes down. And, by the way, the server *will* go down—it's the way of life.

ZEN

"Prehistory was a very difficult time for humans. Hostile, vicious, person-eating predators roamed the Earth. Disease was rampant. Mortality rates were horrific. The automatic bank teller was still only a dream."

Dave Barry

Bindery Services

As mentioned previously, Bindery Services has a big impact on replica placement. Each bindery user or application requires a Master or Read/Write replica of its server's bindery context in order to work. The server bindery context can be set at the server console by typing the following:

```
SET SERVER BINDERY CONTEXT = OU=PR.OU=NORAD.O=ACME
```

In the Figure 4.41, the bindery users attached to NOR-PR-SRV1 only see the NDS objects in the OU=PR.OU=NORAD.O=ACME container. Actually, they can't see *all* the NDS objects, just the bindery-equivalent objects (such as servers, users, groups, printers, print queues, print servers, and profiles). In case you were wondering, the Profile NDS object was added to NetWare 4 as a bindery-equivalent. Unfortunately some really cool, new NDS objects aren't available to bindery users (such as directory maps, organizational roles, computers, and aliases).

FIGURE 4.41

Bindery Services in the NORAD Container

In order for a NetWare 4 server to support Bindery Services, it must hold either a Master or Read/Write replica of the partition in which the users are interested. In our case, the OU=PR users are OK, because the NOR-PR-SRV1 server has a Read/Write replica of the NORAD Partition. And, it just so happens that the OU=PR container exists within the NORAD Partition. Did I mention that the bindery context doesn't need to be its own partition? True.

REAL WORLD

Bindery Services is also required during a NetWare 3 to NetWare 4 server upgrade. For example, when you upgrade a NetWare 3 server, a Read/Write replica of its home partition is placed on the new NetWare 4 server. This happens regardless of whether there are already three replicas of the partition. Interesting.

Improved Name Resolution

Name resolution is the mechanism NDS uses to find object information not stored on the local server. It is also referred to as *tree walking*. If the NDS information you need is not stored locally, the server must walk the directory tree to find a server with a replica. Every replica maintains a set of pointers to all the other replicas of the same partition—this is called a *replica ring*. Using these pointers NDS can locate the partitions that are above and below any container in the tree. Think of them as logical bridges between containers.

The [Root] is probably the most troublesome name resolution replica because it stores information about everybody. Replicas of the [Root] partition bridge to every container in the tree. For this reason, you should replicate the [Root] partition to all major hub sites in your WAN. But remember, the [Root] partition must be small. You don't want the subordinate references getting out of hand.

Figure 4.42 illustrates replica placement for ACME's [Root] partition. In this case, we've distributed the small partition to three strategic locations—in NORAD on the NOR-SRV1 server, in CAMELOT on the CAM-SRV1 server, and in TOKYO on the TOK-SRV1 server. Don't go hog-wild on [Root] replication—three or four replicas are fine. Finally, you probably don't need to replicate any other partitions for name resolution. The [Root] partition should take care of all your tree walking needs.

FIGURE 4.42

*Replica Placement for
ACME's [Root] Partition*

That's it! You've taken another step toward NDS Nirvana. Three down, and only one more design step to go. So far, we've created a naming standards document, designed the top and bottom layers of the tree, and outlined partition boundaries. In the last section, we scattered the partitions to all four corners of ACME. So what's left? Time!

Time Synchronization Design

Time is an interesting phenomenon. Albert Einstein learned that time changes in relation to your speed. This is especially true when you're rocketing down a Big Dipper at Mach 3. Some moments seem to last forever (pausing at the Apex), while others occur in the blink of an eye (The Fall). Which of these choices describes your experience with this chapter—eternity or the blink of an eye?

No matter how you look at it, time controls everything. This is especially true in NDS. Time impacts every aspect of your NetWare 4 life—NDS operations, resource access, and security, just to name a few. For this reason, time synchronization becomes a priority. And it only works properly if it's been designed efficiently.

The final step in NDS design focuses on time synchronization. Time synchronization coordinates and maintains consistent time for all of the servers in your NDS tree. Time synchronization design relies on one of two time configuration strategies: default (small trees) and custom (large trees).

The *default* time synchronization option works best for small networks with only a few servers in a single location. This configuration is commonly referred to as the *single reference* configuration because it uses a Single Reference time provider.

The *custom* time synchronization option provides more flexibility for larger networks with multiple servers in distributed locations. It uses a special time provider group. The *time provider* group is designed to provide greater fault tolerance and efficiency for communicating time across multiple servers and wide area networks.

Once NetWare time has been configured there's very little left to do. It simply runs. Later we'll explore both of these configuration options in detail. But before we do, let's start with a quick review of NetWare 4 time synchronization in general.

QUIZ

I need a vacation, how about you? Let's take a little train trip....

A train traveling at the speed of 50 m.p.h. enters a tunnel which is 1 1/2 miles long. The length of the train is 1/4 mile. How long does it take for all of the train to pass through the tunnel, from the moment the front enters to the moment the rear emerges?

(Q4-5)

UNDERSTANDING TIME SYNCHRONIZATION

Time synchronization provides NetWare 4 servers with a mechanism for coordinating NDS time stamps. NetWare 4 uses the TIMESYNC NLM to coordinate time stamps between all servers on the WAN. TIMESYNC.NLM maintains each server's Universal Time Coordinate (UTC)—a fancy name for Greenwich Mean Time (GMT).

TIP

The TIMESYNC NLM is automatically loaded each time the server is started. Time synchronization is active only when the TIMESYNC NLM is loaded. You should not unload this module.

Local time for each server is calculated by applying (adding) the time zone and daylight savings time settings to the server's UTC value. For example, if a server is located in the Mountain Standard Time zone (NORAD), its UTC offset would be +7. This value is applied (along with subtracting one hour for Daylight Savings Time, if in effect) as an offset to standardize the server's time to UTC. Therefore, each server regardless of its geographic location can be standardized to UTC time. Once again, the calculation is:

Local time +/- *time zone offset from UTC-* Daylight Savings Time offset

As you can see in Figure 4.43, you can type **TIME** to display these time statistics at the NetWare 4 file server console.

FIGURE 4.43

The NetWare 4 TIME Command

```
CAM-SRV1:TIME
   Time zone string: "GMT0BST"
   DST status:  OFF
   DST start:   Sunday, 26 March 2000   2:00:00 am GMT
   DST end:     Sunday, 29 October 2000   2:00:00 am BST
   Time synchronization is active.
   Time is synchronized to the network.
Wednesday,  1 December 1999   4:56:35 am UTC
Wednesday,  1 December 1999   4:56:35 am GMT
CAM-SRV1:
```

The TIME command displays the time zone string, status of daylight savings time (DST), if time synchronization is active, time synchronization status (synchronized or not), and the current server time (in both UTC and local format). Use this command periodically to check the status of your time servers. They must be synchronized in order to maintain accurate time stamps.

All NetWare 4 servers are time servers of some type—either *providers* or *consumers*. Time providers provide time to time consumers—makes sense. As you can see in Figure 4.44, NetWare 4 supports three different time providers—*Primary server, Reference server,* and *Single Reference server*. On the other hand, there's only one type of time consumer: *Secondary server*. The majority of your NetWare 4 servers will be time consumers.

F I G U R E 4.44

Time Providers and Time Consumers

TIME PROVIDERS	TIME CONSUMERS
Primary Reference Single Reference	Secondary

All NetWare 4 time servers perform three functions in relation to time synchronization:

1 • Provide UTC time to any NLM or requesting client workstation.

2 • Provide status information regarding the synchronization of UTC time.

3 • Adjust their clock rate to correct for time discrepancies and maintain UTC synchronization.

Now, let's take a closer look at each of the four time server types. In this section, we will expand on what you learned in Chapter 2—we're mostly interested in time design issues. You may want to review time synchronization in Chapter 2 before proceeding. See you on the other side.

Secondary Time Servers

Secondary time consumers rely on other sources to provide them with network time. A Secondary server can contact a Single Reference, Reference, or Primary server for the network time. The Secondary server will be the most prevalent type of time server on your network because most servers do not need to participate in time providing. By default, all servers except the first server are designated as Secondary servers when they're installed. The first server is defined as a Single Reference time provider.

The Secondary server will try to make up any difference between its clock and the time it receives from the network. The network time comes from any of the time providers during each polling interval. Therefore, any discrepancies in the Secondary's time will be resolved during each polling interval. Secondary servers can provide time to requesting clients or server applications.

TIP

Secondary time servers do not participate in time providing. These servers do not vote with any other time server. They simply get the network time from other time providers.

Primary Time Servers

Primary time servers are the first time providers. They are time providers because they distribute time to other requesting Secondary servers. The interesting part is how they determine the time.

Primary servers poll. This voting process determines the "official time" for your WAN. Polling is accomplished by contacting all other time providers and identifying any discrepancies between the Primary server's local clock and the calculated network time. If there is a difference, then the Primary server adjusts its clock to 50 percent during each polling loop.

Like all time servers, Primary time providers are obsessed with their internal *synchronization radius*. This is the allowable timing discrepancy within each server. If the Primary server is within its synchronization radius, it raises its time synchronization flag. This indicates that synchronization has occurred and everything is fine.

During the polling process, each Primary time server has one vote. This could be a problem if Primaries are your only time providers. In this case, there will never be a single source of time convergence. This problem is resolved by integrating a Reference server into your time provider group.

Reference Time Server

A Reference time server adds important stability to a Primary time provider group. Both time providers vote on network time, but Reference servers get the last word. During each polling interval, all the Primary time servers converge their internal clocks to the time of the Reference server. On the other hand, the Reference time server will never adjust its clock. This naturally makes the Reference time server the point of reference for convergence—hence the name.

TIP

During the voting process, the reference time server has 16 votes. This means that the Reference server will always win the vote. You should only have one Reference server in your tree. The best balance is one Reference server and a few Primary servers. This is called a *time provider group*, and it's the topic of discussion in the next section.

In this scenario, the primary servers provide fault tolerance. If the Reference server should fail, multiple Primary servers can average their time together to provide consistent network time. Therefore, the Reference server is the supreme authority of time except when it is not accessible.

The most significant difference between Primary and Reference servers is that the Reference server does *not* adjust its internal clock. As long as it's operational, it is the center of the temporal universe. All other time servers converge to the Reference server's time. Because the Reference server is the only server that adjusts its internal clock, you should connect it to an external time source.

External clocks accomplish several important things. First, they provide an accurate and automated mechanism to check time. Some of your applications may require accurate time of day, if they initiate a process (such as a backup) in the middle of the night. Second, automated time sources fight temporal drift—it happens to the best of us. They ensure that the Reference server's clock stays within its synchronization radius by constantly updating it. There are various products available that connect PCs to external time sources (such as a radio clock, modem, the Internet, or the atomic clock in NORAD).

Only one Reference time server is usually needed on the network. Multiple Reference servers can be placed on the network, but they will not synchronize with each other. Some companies with large, worldwide networks prefer to use multiple Reference servers to provide fault tolerance or have the Reference closer to a particular group of servers.

Single Reference Time Servers

The Single Reference time server is a stand-alone time provider for the entire network. This is the default configuration and requires no intervention during installation. The main difference between a Reference server and a Single Reference server is that the Single Reference server can raise its synchronization flag without confirming its time with any other time sources—it has *total* control. The Single Reference server should only be used in small sites with less than 30 servers and no WAN connections.

TIP

Regardless of the size of your network, you can initially accept the Single Reference default until your installation grows beyond 30. Also, if you choose the Single Reference server option, do not use any other time providers. A Single Reference is the only time source required under this configuration.

With the Single Reference time configuration, all other servers are Secondaries. This means they all converge to the Single Reference's time during each polling cycle. A Single Reference time server can be connected to an external source, or use its own internal clock, it doesn't matter. Occasionally, it may be necessary to check the server's time against a reliable source (for example, try dialing "POPCORN") just to make sure.

ZEN

Minibang—An explosion involving much smaller amounts of energy and matter than that of the Big Bang—thought to be the origin of the universe in its current state. Also, the sound heard from a user's head when he or she finally logs in to NDS.

That completes our general time synchronization overview. Now it's time to explore two critical time synchronization design issues:

▸ Time Configur ation

▸ Time Communication

Time configuration design outlines a strategy for time server definitions and placement. There are two options: default and custom. Then, *time communication design* deals with how the time servers talk to each other—SAP or Configured Lists. Let's start with time configuration design.

TIME CONFIGURATION DESIGN

Time configuration defines how your time servers are distributed. In addition, it outlines which servers are providers and which servers are consumers. As we learned previously, NetWare 4 supports two basic time configuration designs:

▸ Default: Single Reference

▸ Custom: Time Provider Group

Whatever you do, be sure to choose the correct configuration method for your WAN. First, ask yourself, "Is my network distributed over multiple sites? Are there WAN links to consider?" If so, definitely use the custom method. A time provider group gives your network greater fault tolerance by distributing the time servers to multiple locations. Next, determine if your network has less than 30 servers. If so, use the default configuration method.

This sounds simple, and it is. However, these are just a few of the many factors you must consider in choosing a time configuration approach. Let's take a closer look at each.

Default: Single Reference Time Server

The first NetWare 4 server is automatically configured as a Single Reference server. All other servers are Secondary time servers.

On the up side, the default configuration method is simple and requires absolutely no advanced planning. Additionally, no configuration files are needed and the possibility of errors during time synchronization is considerably minimized. This works best if you have less than 30 servers in your tree and no distributed locations. Refer to Figure 4.45 for an example of the default time configuration method.

▸ · ◄

F I G U R E 4.45

Default Time Configuration

Single Reference Time Server

Secondary Time Servers

The default configuration method relies on a central file server with a trusted hardware clock. This becomes the sole time provider, and you should monitor its time frequently. If you're unhappy with your first time provider, you can always redesignate another server as the Single Reference by using the SERVMAN utility.

On the down side, the default time configuration creates a single point of failure. If the Single Reference time server fails, all network time is lost. Even if this happens for a short period of time (a day or less), it can have a dramatic effect on NDS synchronization and security. When the sole time provider drops off, all Secondary servers continue to maintain their own time. Even worse, they continue to stamp NDS events—with the wrong time! Fortunately, they all resynchronize when the time provider wakes up.

If the default time configuration method isn't for you, consider using a time provider group. That's the other option—custom.

Custom: Time Provider Group

The custom time configuration method provides more fault tolerance, efficiency, and flexibility to large interconnected WANs. The time provider group requires one Reference time server and a minimum of two other Primary time servers. These three or more time providers form a *time provider group* that in turn provides time to the rest of the NetWare 4 servers—Secondaries.

As you can see in Figure 4.46, ACME organizes its time providers according to geography—one in each WAN hub. This configuration requires simple adjustments to the servers in the time provider group. One server will be designated as the Reference and two to seven servers may be designated as Primary time servers.

The selection of your Reference server should be based on a centralized location within your WAN infrastructure. For example, the ACME WAN uses a hub and spoke design. CAMELOT is the central hub, so it will be the home of the Reference server. The Primary servers are then distributed across the WAN links to each of the spoke locations. If your network is a large WAN, place a few extra Primary servers in strategic locations. The remainder of the installed file servers will be Secondary servers— by default. Figure 4.47 illustrates the placement of ACME time providers and time consumers. This design maximizes traffic efficiency and temporal fault tolerance.

F I G U R E 4.46

ACME's Time Provider
Group

F I G U R E 4.47

ACME's Custom Time
Configuration Design

CHAPTER 4

NOVELL'S CNE
STUDY GUIDE
FOR NETWARE 4.1

In addition, you should connect the Reference Server to an external time source to ensure highly accurate time. Notice the satellite configuration in Figure 4.47.

Some companies may consider using multiple time provider groups. This increases redundancy in worldwide operations. For example, ACME could implement this approach by creating three independent time provider groups—one in NORAD, CAMELOT, and RIO for example. This way, time is determined locally, instead of traversing the WAN links every polling interval. There's one caveat though. Be sure that the Reference server in each group is going to the same external clock as the others. This will ensure a single (yet external) source of time convergence.

QUIZ

When I was a kid in school I memorized the following phrase in math class. Why?

"Now I know a super utterance to assist maths."

(Q4-6)

That's all there is to know about time configuration design. Once you've configured time, you have to decide how the time servers are going to communicate with each other. That's phase two—time communication design.

TIME COMMUNICATION DESIGN

With the time providers and time consumers in place, it's time to decide how they're going to talk to each other. Once again, you have two choices:

- Default: SAP Method

- Custom: Configured Lists

Time communication occurs in two instances. First, when time providers "vote" with each other about the network's correct time. And second, when Secondary time servers "poll" time providers for the correct time. This occurs at regular polling intervals. Let's take a closer look at each of the two time communication designs—starting with the default method.

Default: SAP Method

The SAP method is the default time communication design and it requires no intervention. Both time providers and time consumers communicate using the Service Advertising Protocol (SAP) by default. You should be aware that SAP causes a small amount of additional traffic on your WAN lines during time synchronization polling cycles. Also, SAP is self-configuring. This means there's no protection against a misconfigured time server. If someone messes up a local time server, everyone will feel it in a matter of minutes. This could disrupt your entire NDS time synchronization system.

REAL WORLD

SAP traffic is not required for NDS. It is the communications protocol of choice for NetWare 3 servers. As a matter of fact, you can turn SAP off in NetWare 4 with the help of built-in multiprotocol tools—called *SAP Filtering*. Refer to Chapter 13 for more details.

If you decide to filter SAP, be sure not to filter time synchronization packets. They use type "h26B."

Custom: Configured Lists

Configured Lists provide much more flexibility for your time synchronization communications. The Configured List allows you to specify exactly who talks to whom. You can tell time providers where to vote, and time consumers from whom to get their time. I love control.

For ACME, we've decided to use the Configured Lists design in coordination with our time provider groups. The communication design is distributed to all time servers using the TIMESYNC.CFG file.

Each server's Configured List is created using the Time Parameters option of SERVMAN. The first step is to enable the Configured List option as shown in Figure 4.48. Once you've turned it ON, you can start customizing the list.

F I G U R E 4.48

Activating Time Configured Lists in SERVMAN

The Configured List is primarily a tool for defining with which providers this server interacts. Figure 4.48 is the Time Parameters screen for NOR-SRV1. The next step is to list all the Time Providers with whom NOR-SRV1 will vote. Remember, CAMELOT is ACME's Reference server, and all other locations have at least one Primary time server. The Configured List entries shown in Figure 4.49 include CAM-SRV1, RIO-SRV1, SYD-SRV1, and TOK-SRV1. With this design, NOR-SRV1 will always communicate with the CAMELOT Reference server first.

F I G U R E 4.49

ACME's Configure List for the NOR-SRV1 Primary Time Server

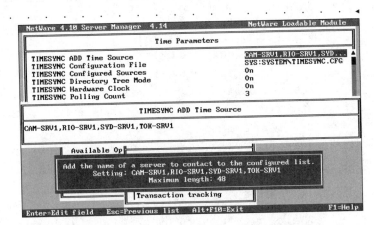

The Configured Lists time communication design provides you with complete control of the time synchronization hierarchy. It also reduces SAP traffic on your network and provides direct server-to-server contact. Refer to Chapter 9 for more details about using SERVMAN as a time-management tool.

ZEN

Joygerm fever—A mental condition characterized by happiness, kindness, and courtesy. Also attributed to CNEs at the point just before mental breakdown.

You're time is up! Congratulations, you've really finished ACME's NDS design. Wow, it's been a long and tough journey, but we made it to the end. Let's review.

It all started with ACME's naming standards document. A complete naming standard is important so that you design an NDS database that is flexible, easy to use, and meets your business needs. Also, there's so much diversity in NDS "object-ology," that a naming standard is required for most design and management tasks. As a matter of fact, ACME's naming standard is the center of the NDS design.

After we created the naming standards document, we move onto the real action—NDS tree design. We started with a rough pyramid design outlining the geographic top and organizational bottom layers of the tree. Then, we further refined the design with respect to administration, partitioning, login scripts, and Bindery Services.

With the tree in place, we moved on to partitioning and replication. We started by breaking the tree into small little pieces (NDS partitioning). This occurred along the geographic boundaries of the ACME. Then, we scattered the pieces around the world (replica placement). Replica placement is one of the most important aspects of NDS design because it directly affects your network's performance, accessibility, and fault tolerance.

Finally, Time Synchronization Design ensures that all our servers agree on the time. We explored the four different time server types and learned how to design them according to two important factors: time configuration and time communication. We determined that ACME needs five Time Providers (one in each location) with a Reference server in CAMELOT. Furthermore, all time servers will communicate with each other using custom Configured Lists.

So what's next? Well, that completes the four main aspects of NDS design, but it doesn't end our lesson. There's one related topic remaining and it almost always gets overlooked—NDS Accessibility Design. NDS accessibility transcends everything you do in NetWare 4. It is the sole purpose for the WAN's existence—so users can have access to stuff! If you ignore accessibility during the NDS design phase, some users will invariably get left out in the cold.

In the next section, we will explore NDS accessibility with respect to diverse clients, connection types, login scripts, and nomads. Yes, nomads. So, without any further ado, let's end this "Fall" and get on with the rest of the Roller Coaster.

QUIZ

A hand in bridge in which all 13 cards are a 9 or below is called a Yarborough, after the Second Earl of Yarborough (d. 1897), who is said to have bet 1000 to 1 against the dealing of such a hand. What, however, are the actual odds against such a hand? Was the noble Lord onto a good thing?

(Q4-7)

NDS Accessibility Design

Users use resources. Their life depends on it. A user's accessibility to resources hinges on your NDS design. Therefore, each user's life balances on the accessibility of your NDS design. But there's no pressure.

NDS accessibility is important because it defines all access points to NetWare 4 resources. The following access points make or break user productivity:

- ▸ Diverse Clients

- ▸ Connection Types

- ▸ Login Scripts

- ▸ Nomads

NDS accessibility starts at the client workstation. NetWare 4 supports a variety of clients, including DOS, Windows NT, OS/2, Macintosh, and UNIX. The NetWare 4 client accesses the NDS tree in one of two ways: through an NDS connection or Bindery Services. Either way, this connection is managed by NetWare 4 and distributed servers.

When users finally attach to the tree, their productivity is controlled by a series of automatic configuration files called *login scripts*. These are your tools for ensuring productive NDS accessibility. Then there're *nomads*—those crazy migrating users who travel around the world each day. Logging in from the strangest places, always demanding resources. Nomads are the biggest challenge in NDS accessibility design.

So, you wanna be a NetWare 4 CNE? OK, let's see what kind of Accessibility Engineer (AE) you are.

DIVERSE CLIENTS

NDS accessibility design starts at the client. This is the user's interface to our NDS world. And there are many different types of users—diverse clients.

Desktop support is key to NetWare 4. A server cannot serve the user community unless access is provided for the client. This access requires speed and reliability for all users and must make good use of limited memory at each workstation. Following is a discussion of NetWare 4's currently supported clients with the latest version of software.

NetWare DOS Requester

NetWare 4 uses the NetWare DOS Requester for workstations running the DOS/Windows operating system. This software is currently a replacement for the older NetWare shell known as NETX.EXE. The NetWare DOS Requester is fully backward-compatible, including previous versions of NetWare 4, NetWare 3, NetWare 2, and Personal NetWare. The DOS/Windows client supports both an NDS and bindery connection, and is explained in detail in Chapter 13.

NetWare Client for OS/2

The NetWare Client for OS/2 supports a connection from an OS/2 workstation to a NetWare 4 server. The current version of client software is NetWare Client 2.11 for OS/2.

With this client software, an OS/2 user can connect and log in to a NetWare 4 server with full NDS capability, file and print, management, and security. Additionally, the NetWare Client for OS/2 will allow you to run enhanced mode MS-Windows applications in a NetWare 4.1 environment. The NetWare Client for OS/2 supports connectivity to NetWare 4 through IPX/SPX, NetBIOS, and Named Pipes.

NetWare Client for Windows NT 3.5

The NetWare Client for Windows NT 3.5 provides an NDS connection from a Windows NT workstation to a NetWare 4 tree. Also provided with this client is an NT workstation version of Novell's NWADMIN utility. With these two products, you can manage your NetWare 4 network with an NT workstation running NT version 3.5 and Novell's NetWare Client for Windows NT version 3.5.

You can access NetWare services and browse authorized NDS information including files and directories through mapping drives, configuring print queues, and attaching to other servers. The NetWare Client for Windows NT 3.5 supports services over IPX or IP transport protocols. IP services are offered through NetWare IP over Microsoft's Windows NT TCP/IP protocol stack. This client also provides synchronized login to the Mircrosoft Windows NT desktop and the NetWare 4.1 network with use of a single username and password.

Windows NT does have its moments, and here are a few to consider:

▶ Autoreconnect service for client-side fault tolerance.

▶ 32-bit ODI or NDIS drivers for a greater degree of protocol and network adapter choices.

▶ Windows NT long file names support through the NetWare server HPFS name space.

▶ Win32 application and backward-compatibility support for running 16-bit applications.

▶ DOS box support for running many standard NetWare utilities such as NETADMIN.

NetWare Client for Mac

The NetWare Client for Mac is supported as an NDS connection to a NetWare 4 server. The current version is 5.1 and allows Mac clients to communicate via IPX to NetWare 4. File and print services as well as NDS connections are provided with this client—known as MacNDS. We'll learn more about Macintosh support in Chapter 13.

NetWare UNIX Client

The NetWare for Unix Client (NUC) is currently at version 2.02 and supports a bindery-based connection to a NetWare 4 server. Users running UnixWare clients can connect and access NetWare 4 file and print services, as well as attach to other servers on the WAN. Each NetWare 4 server that supports UnixWare clients must load the NUC.NLM.

The state of the client lightly impacts NDS accessibility design. For the most part, you must ensure two things. First, be sure the client software supports NDS. Second, be sure the client software provides all the NetWare 4 services in a native environment. If you can accomplish these two goals, you're well on your way to achieving cultural diversity.

ZEN

"You cannot step in the same river twice, for new waters are ever flowing in upon you."

Heraclitus

Next, let's learn how these clients attach to the tree and explore the two different connection types that NetWare 4 supports.

CONNECTION TYPES

Next, we must understand the different ways of accessing NDS. Remember, the user's life depends on it. If the user can't get a report out on time, it could be curtains. So, be sure you manage the user connection types so nobody gets kicked off the WAN.

NetWare 4 supports two different types of network connections:

- Bindery Services connection

- NDS connection

The basic difference between these types of connections is the fact that the Bindery Services connection is server-centric. This means that multiple connections require multiple user names and passwords, and the login process must be repeated at every server.

On the other hand, the NDS connection provides you with the ability to have a single login to multiple NetWare 4 servers. A single login allows the user to enter the username and password once. Any additional drive mappings to other NetWare 3 and NetWare 4 servers will be handled in the background.

In addition, NetWare 4 supports *additive licensing*. This is the ability to increase the total number of licenses on any given NetWare 4 server. This enhancement allows administrators the opportunity to more closely match the number of licensed users to their actual needs. A company that currently has a 100-user license can add a 25-user license to the NetWare 4 server to accommodate increased growth. NetWare 4 supports 5-, 10-, 25-, 50-, 100-, 250-, 500-, and 1000-user versions in any combination.

Let's explore the two NetWare 4 connection types—starting with NDS connections.

NDS Connections

An NDS connection requires the NetWare DOS Requester for authentication to a NetWare 4 server. An NDS connection provides a security mechanism known as RSA encryption between the client and server and also provides background authentication. We'll explore these concepts in Chapter 11. NDS supports three connectivity states:

▸ Connected, but not logged in

▸ Authenticated

▸ Licensed

Connected, But Not Logged In

In this state, the user is attached to a NetWare 4 server either through the NETX shell or the VLM client. A "connected, but not logged in" state can exist for either NetWare 3 or NetWare 4 users to the first attached server. You're standing on the front porch. The good news is this is not a "licensed" connection. A NetWare 4 attachment doesn't decrement your server license count as it did in NetWare 3. In NetWare 4, only authenticated connections are licensed.

Authenticated

This type of connection indicates that a NetWare 4 server has established a user's identity and he or she is in the door. Authentication occurs for both NetWare 3 and NetWare 4 users, but NetWare 4 offers much more security. In either case, the Authenticated connection is also licensed. This means the host server's license count drops by one. Also, the authenticating server tracks the user whether he or she uses any local resources. All other servers only count the user while he or she is using the resources. For this reason, you'll want to pay attention to which servers are authenticating which users.

Authentication is invisible to the user. During the login sequence, the user will enter a password when prompted, and the remaining process occurs behind the scenes. All sensitive data is never transmitted across the wire for security purposes. Authentication relies on encryption algorithms based on a public/private key system.

After successful authentication has occurred, a process known as *background authentication* may occur if the user's login script specifies connections to other servers. A connection to another NetWare 4 server, for example, does not require the user to reenter his or her password.

Licensed

A connection is said to be licensed when a user has mapped a drive or captured to a printer. Each user will decrement the user license by one after a connection has been licensed. Only an authenticated connection can be licensed. Also, the license count returns to its previous level when the user stops accessing the resource (that is, "unmaps" the drive or "uncaptures" the printer).

A combination of these states determines what level a user currently has in NetWare 4 connectivity. For example, when a connection is neither authenticated or licensed, the user can navigate the NDS tree through the use of the CX (Change conteXt) command. This doesn't cost anything. The user has attached to a server, but has not yet authenticated. If a user is licensed and authenticated, he or she can access NDS and file system information to the extent allowed by his or her rights. This costs licenses on all servers the user accesses.

That was enlightening. Now, what about Bindery Services connections? They're much simpler.

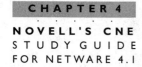

Bindery Services Connections

NDS provides compatibility to previous versions of NetWare through the use of Bindery Services connections. This type of connection does not provide the capability of a single login to the network. For example, a client using the NETX shell to log in to a NetWare 4 server must enter a username and password for each server. Additional connections to other NetWare 4 servers would require the user to enter another username and password.

Bindery Services can be enabled on any NetWare 4 server through the SET Server Bindery Context command. The server can select one container or multiple containers in the NDS tree to set as the bindery context. All the leaf objects in the NDS container(s) that are also objects in the NetWare 3 bindery (that is, users, groups, queues, and print servers) are seen as the bindery.

Bindery Services in NetWare 4 enable you to select up to 16 OU containers as the server bindery context. The requirement for Bindery Services is that the server stores at least a Read/Write replica of the partition where the bindery context is set.

I feel "connected" to you in some way. This NDS accessibility stuff must be going to my head. Login scripts are next.

LOGIN SCRIPTS

The next step in accessibility design involves login scripts. These are special NDS configuration files that execute automatically when users log in to the tree. They can save you hours of work and increase NDS accessibility—if done right.

Traditionally, login scripts were used to establish the users network environment. The login scripts for NetWare 4 are used to map network drives, map to applications, capture to printers and print queues, and set other important environment variables. The login scripts become the center of user access and need careful consideration. Fortunately, we explore them in excruciating depth in Chapter 12. For now, let's explore some important login script design considerations.

NetWare 4 supports two types of login scripts:

- Bindery-based login scripts

- NDS login scripts

TIP

It is recommended that you execute the login scripts before launching Windows. If there are users who go into Windows immediately after they boot their workstations, then you must have them log in to the network and let it run the login scripts before launching Windows.

Bindery-Based Login Scripts

Bindery-based login scripts in NetWare 4 operate in the same manner as system, user, and default scripts in NetWare 2 and NetWare 3. These login scripts should be preserved on NetWare 4 servers to provide Bindery Services to NETX clients. For example, a bindery user attaching to a NetWare 4 server will need bindery login scripts from specific places on the server file system. In addition, NDS clients using the /B option also attach with a bindery connection.

The System login script supports commands that affect all the bindery-based users on that server. These commands display messages, map network drives, map search drives, and set environmental variables. The System login script is the best place to manage the mapping and CAPTURE statements for all the bindery users. After a user successfully attaches to the server, the System login script executes from SYS:PUBLIC\NET$LOG.DAT, if it exists. If the User login script is present, it will execute from the SYS:MAIL\USERID subdirectory. If the User login script does not exist, then the Default login script is executed. The Default login script is hard-coded into the LOGIN.EXE program.

Figure 4.50 shows the order of execution for bindery-based login scripts. If you are familiar with NetWare 3, notice that the bindery-based login scripts for NetWare 4 are executed in the same order.

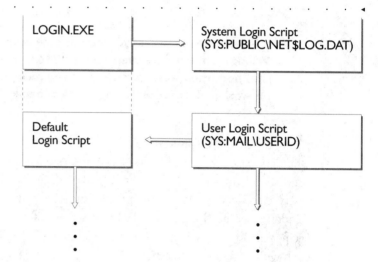

*Bindery-based Login Scripts
in NetWare 4*

Bindery-based login scripts are server-centric. This means that they only affect bindery users who attach to a specific server. They have no impact on the NDS tree. Since these login scripts are server-centric, there aren't a lot of design issues. However, you should try to move all your users to NDS login scripts as soon as possible.

You can make changes to both the System and User login scripts by using the NetWare 3 SYSCON.EXE utility. You can also edit the NET$LOG.DAT file directly with any text-editing program. Although the bindery-based login scripts can be edited, any changes made are not automatically synchronized to the corresponding NDS login scripts. Speaking of NDS scripts—let's see what they have in store for us.

ZEN

Barbecue mode—A maneuver that slowly rotates a spacecraft in order to distribute the sun's heat evenly over the craft's surface. Or, the state of a NetWare 4 CNE when the network is broken.

NDS Login Scripts

NDS login scripts are properties of container, profile, and user objects. They are only accessible through an authenticated NDS connection. Users execute Container scripts from their parent container only. This is roughly equivalent to the NetWare 3 system login script. After the Container login script, a Profile login script can be used. If no Profile exists, the User script is executed. As in the bindery-based scenario, the default login script activates only if there's no User script. Again, the default login script is hard-coded into the LOGIN.EXE program.

Refer to Figure 5.51 for an illustration of NetWare 4's NDS login scripts. Notice the order of execution.

FIGURE 5.51

NDS Login Scripts in NetWare 4

As we've seen, NetWare 4 supports four different NDS login scripts. We will discuss each of them in depth in Chapter 12. For now, let's discover how they impact your NDS accessibility design:

▶ Container Login Script—A property of O=Organization or OU=Organizational Unit containers. Users *only* execute their parent's container script. If one doesn't exist, tough. This is an important accessibility issue. Make sure the Container scripts exist at the bottom layers of the tree—where the users are.

▸ Profile Login Scripts—A property of the special Profile leaf object. These login scripts can be shared by any group of users, anywhere in the tree. Typically, the Profile script provides three accessibility advantages: login script sharing for the entire company, login script sharing for each location, or login script sharing for a special group. This special object solves the accessibility problem created by restricting container scripts.

▸ User Login Script—A property of each User object. Don't use them. It's too much work. Accomplish all accessibility configurations in the container or Profile scripts.

▸ Default Login Script—Hard-coded into LOGIN.EXE. It only runs if there's no User script. You don't want it to run, and you don't want User scripts—oops! Now what? Simple, use the NO_DEFAULT command in the Container or Profile scripts.

That's enough of that. Are you ready for some fun? Well, this might qualify—nomads.

NOMADS

Finally, there're *nomads*. The greatest challenge to accessibility design. Nomads are remote or mobile users who insist on logging in from "other places." You must make certain adjustments to your design to accommodate nomadic users. You can do it, you're a CNE.

NetWare 4 allows the user to access resources from anywhere in the tree. Isn't that nice. This feature helps you manage nomadic users, but it also encourages user migration. Let's face it, we live in a TV-dinner, drive-through world. Users are on the go, and you must accommodate them. Start by asking yourself a few simple questions:

▸ "Self, does this user carry a laptop computer?"

▸ "Self, where is the user geographically located?"

▸ "Self, what is the user's home office?"

As users wander throughout the WAN, they access the network and its resources in different ways. Knowing what kind of access each user wants will help you set up the user environments. For example, some users just want dial-in access to the network from remote locations. These locations can range from their homes, hotel rooms, and even airplanes. This type of user, typically, dials in to the network from a laptop or home computer.

Some users may travel from one office to another and need full access to all the local network resources of the office they are visiting. Although the users need full access to the local resources, they still want the data from their home directory and server. Essentially, the definition of a traveling user is broken into two types:

▸ *Remote users* access the tree through dial-in connections.

▸ *Mobile users* access the tree from a variety of distributed locations and from a variety of different machines.

Remote Users

Remote users travel a lot and need network access from their laptop computer through dial-in lines. These Road Warriors are usually self-contained (that is, their laptops are configured with all the necessary applications software). The user can continue to work when on the road and merely dials into the network to transfer e-mail messages, download files, or get other resources.

The remote user requires less accessibility design considerations because he or she only accesses the tree for login authentication. There's very little NDS browsing and management going on. Fortunately, remote users will not impact the tree design or force you to create any special NDS objects. They simply dial into specific predetermined access points in the WAN and use their normal NDS context.

Some remote users dial-in just to transfer their e-mail messages. Typically, there are special phone lines dedicated for just the remote e-mail users. These lines may have their own security and access methods and would not affect the Directory tree design.

If a remote user travels to another office and plugs a laptop computer into the network, he or she suddenly becomes a mobile user. Now that's a completely different kettle of fish. Check it out.

ZEN

"The fly that was buzzing around the house had once been her loving husband."

From the movie *The Fly*

Mobile Users

Mobile users are a more challenging breed. They travel from one office to another and from computer to computer. They don't care, they're just cyber-scavangers. Even worse, they expect full access to all local resources while maintaining the ability to get data from their home server. Yeah, right!

Mobile users may not carry laptops with them. Instead, they expect to have a computer available at the other site. Some mobile users, however, carry laptops and plug them into the network when they arrive. Thus, the best definition of a mobile user is "a nomadic individual who uses someone else's computer at someone else's site—a cyber-scavenger."

Whether the user travels thousands of miles or across the building, the issues are the same. The users want simultaneous access to local network applications and remote personal data. It's your job to make this as seamless as possible.

TIP

Users who carry laptop computers to a new location are not considered mobile users if they do not need access to the local network resources. If the users are content to access their home resources across the network, then they are simply remote users. There are no special considerations for remote users. Remember, NetWare 4 will let the users log in from anywhere in the ACME world.

In order to support mobile users, you must answer two of the previous three questions: "Where is the user geographically located?" and "What is the user's home office?" There are several mechanisms for supporting mobile users, and here's a list of the most useful ones:

- Manually changing the NDS name context

> ▶ Using an alias object to change the NDS name context

> ▶ Using workstation configuration files to change the NDS name context

> ▶ Special nomadic login scripts

Most of these mechanisms focus on the user's name context. The name context helps identify who the user is and where the user should be. While a mobile user's physical location may change, the user's context won't.

If the mobile user has traveled without a laptop computer, he or she expects to use any available computer in the office to log into the network. The main issue with this scenario is how to determine the user's name context for login purposes. There are several ways to work around this problem. The mobile user can manually enter the context at the computer console before login, you can create alias objects that point to the user in his or her normal context, and/or the name context can be set in the workstation configuration file. Let's check them out.

Manually Changing the NDS Name Context

The first option requires user intervention. This can be troublesome to say the least. In this case, the mobile user manually enters his or her name context into the computer before login. This implies that the user understands how to use the CX (Change conteXt) command. For example, the ACME user JMadison would need to set his/her name context by typing:

```
CX .FAC.ADMIN.RIO.ACME
```

Notice the leading period. That forces NDS to start at the [Root] and resolves JMadison's name from there. This overwrites any effect from the local current context. You never now what it's going to be.

Using an Alias Object to Change the NDS Name Context

The second option doesn't require user intervention. This is a good thing. In this case, the mobile user's context can be changed automatically with the help of an Alias User object. If you have a small number of mobile users, you can create an Alias object below the O=Organization for each mobile user. The alias would point to the user's primary object in his or her parent container.

The value of this strategy is that it creates a simple context for each of the mobile users. The users do not need to know what their context is, or even how to set it. The user simply would enter the name of the alias during the login process.

For example, there has been an alias object created for the user JMadison in the ACME tree. As you can see in Figure 4.52, the alias object (called JMadison) was created directly under O=ACME. The alias object points to the real object in the OU=FAC department at RIO. When JMadison wants to login to the network from any site, he uses the name of the alias object as follows:

```
LOGIN .JMadison.ACME
```

FIGURE 4.52

Using an Alias for JMadison
in ACME

Once again, notice the leading period. It forces LOGIN to start at the [Root] object, and, therefore, ignores the workstation's unpredictable current context. This method works well if you have a small number of mobile users. This method may not work if your nomad population is high.

Using Workstation Configuration Files to Change the NDS Name Context

The third option also doesn't require any user intervention. In this case, we can set the user's name context with a special workstation configuration file called NET.CFG. The NET.CFG file is read during the loading of the workstation client. Following is an example of JMadison's NET.CFG. Notice the section called "NetWare DOS Requester," and the line where the NAME CONTEXT ="OU=FAC.OU=ADMIN.OU=RIO.O=ACME".

In order for this to work, the user must run his or her own NET.CFG file. This could exist on a laptop, or a special login diskette. When the user arrives on site and connects to the network, the user's name context is resolved from the setting in his or her personal NET.CFG file. Here's an example of JMadison's configuration file:

```
Personal NET.CFG for JMadison

LINK SUPPORT
    MEMPOOL 6192
    BUFFERS 10 1580
    MAX STACKS 8

LINK DRIVER NE2000
    INT 5
    PORT 300
    MEM D0000
    FRAME Ethernet_802.2

NETWARE DOS REQUESTER
    NAME CONTEXT = "OU=FAC.OU=ADMIN.OU=RIO.O=ACME"
    PREFERRED SERVER = FAC-SRV1
    FIRST NETWORK DRIVE = F
    NETWARE PROTOCOL = NDS,BIND
    SHOW DOTS = ON
    USE DEFAULTS = ON
    PB BUFFERS = 10
```

You can also use the PREFERRED SERVER variable in NET.CFG to connect JMadison to his bindery context server. This provides support for both newer and older clients.

Special Nomadic Login Scripts

The final nomadic configuration option deals with special login scripts. Once the name context issue has been resolved, it's time to turn our attention toward drive mappings and CAPTURE statements. Remember, mobile users want simultaneous access to local applications and remote data. This can only be accomplished with sophisticated login script variables and a special environment variable called NW_SITE.

The following is JMadison's special mobile login script. With this script, he can log in from any of ACME's five major sites. The script demonstrates how he can be mapped to the local e-mail and application server, while maintaining a background connection to his home file system. This is his container login script in .OU=FAC.OU=ADMIN.OU=RIO.O=ACME. (Note: It also requires the NW_SITE DOS environment variable be set in his personal CONFIG.SYS workstation file.)

```
;***********************************************************
; MOBILE CONTAINER LOGIN SCRIPT
;     for OU=FAC.OU=ADMIN.OU=RIO.O=ACME
; Creation Date: 11/8/99
; Revisions:
;***********************************************************
REM Do not execute default script
NO_DEFAULT
Write "Good %GREETING_TIME, %LOGIN_NAME"
REM Map PUBLIC drive to local server
MAP S16:=SYS:PUBLIC
REM  Map F: drive to the user's home server
MAP F:="HOME_DIRECTORY"
REM Map NetWare Drives according to the NW_SITE variable

IF <NW_SITE> == "NORAD" THEN BEGIN
     MAP ROOT M:= NOR-SRV1\SYS:MAIL
     MAP ROOT W:= NOR-SRV1\SYS:APPS\WP
     MAP ROOT Q:= NOR-SRV1\SYS:APPS\QPRO
     END
IF <NW_SITE> == "RIO" THEN BEGIN
     MAP ROOT M:= RIO-SRV1\SYS:MAIL
     MAP ROOT W:= RIO-SRV1\SYS:APPS\WP
```

```
            MAP ROOT Q:= RIO-SRV1\SYS:APPS\QPRO
            END
IF <NW_SITE> == "CAMELOT" THEN BEGIN
            MAP ROOT M:= CAM-SRV1\SYS:MAIL
            MAP ROOT W:= CAM-SRV1\SYS:APPS\WP
            MAP ROOT Q:= CAM-SRV1\SYS:APPS\QPRO
            END
IF <NW_SITE> == "TOKYO" THEN BEGIN
            MAP ROOT M:= TOK-SRV1\SYS:MAIL
            MAP ROOT W:= TOK-SRV1\SYS:APPS\WP
            MAP ROOT Q:= TOK-SRV1\SYS:APPS\QPRO
            END
IF <NW_SITE> == "SYDNEY" THEN BEGIN
            MAP ROOT M:= SYD-SRV1\SYS:MAIL
            MAP ROOT W:= SYD-SRV1\SYS:APPS\WP
            MAP ROOT Q:= SYD-SRV1\SYS:APPS\QPRO
            END
EXIT
```

The End.

Wow, what a chapter! Wow, what a ride! No matter how you slice it, NDS design is a wild time. And just think, this is just the first part of the NetWare 4 Roller Coaster. There's more gut-wrenching, spine-tingling, hair-tugging fun to come. In Chapter 5, we'll explore Step 3: NDS Implementation (*swoosh!*). Then, in Chapters 6 and 7, we'll dive into NetWare 4 installation (*whoooa!*). But the real fun begins with Chapter 8— NDS management (*heeeeelp!*).

Look, if you can make it through The Fall, then you can accomplish anything. There's an exciting world of NetWare 4 out there—waiting for you. Let's attack it together....

Step 3: NDS Implementation

As a NetWare 4 CNE, you come highly recommended. Your mission—should you choose to accept it—is to build the ACME WAN and NDS tree. You will need courage, design experience, NDS know-how, and this book. If you succeed, you will save the world and become a CNE! All in a day's work.

Actually, you have a daunting task ahead of you. A project of this magnitude requires sharp thinking and a very organized approach. All the fancy footwork and LAN lexicon in the world isn't going to help you if you don't have a game plan. That's where Figure 5.1 comes in—it's your ACME game plan. As you can see, saving the world falls into four simple steps:

- ▶ Step 1: NDS Preparation

- ▶ Step 2: Design

- ▶ Step 3: Implementation

- ▶ Step 4: Management

FIGURE 5.1

How to Save the World in 4 Easy Steps!

NDS Preparation   **1**   Chapter 3

Design   **2**   Chapter 4

Implementation   **3**   Chapters 5-7

Management   **4**   Chapters 8-15

[Root]

Welcome to Step 3! This is Prime Time.

If you're feeling a little restless from the first two steps, you'll get plenty of action in Steps 3 and 4. As you can see in Figure 5.2, all of your initial action centers around the implementation schedule. This schedule outlines the rollout of NetWare 4 installation and migration. But before you can implement NetWare 4 in the production ACME environment, you'll need to test it in a more controlled pilot program.

Implementation

It all starts in your off-line testing lab. Here you can be creative and brave without causing system-wide crashes. While you are in the lab, you should consider installing NetWare 4 multiple times and creating diverse NDS trees. Then test partitioning, replication, time synchronization, and common network applications. Finally, make sure backup and restore procedures operate correctly.

Once you're comfortable with each individual piece, consider putting them together in a controlled pilot program. The pilot system involves installing your first production NetWare 4 server and then testing each production application in a realistic environment. You can also test user compatibility with NDS and Bindery Services. A pilot system is your bridge between the lab and a full implementation of NetWare 4 across the entire ACME WAN. You might consider the Labs division in NORAD as your pilot implementation. The scientists who work there are more likely to understand what you're going through.

Once you've scheduled, tested, and piloted the implementation, you're ready for prime time—NetWare 4 installation and migration—but not today. That's for tomorrow (Chapters 6 and 7). So, let's see where we're going today:

▸ ACME testing lab—Involves five different experiments, including hardware installation, NDS implementation, testing login scripts, testing applications, and testing backup and restore procedures.

▸ ACME pilot program—A bridge between the testing controlled testing lab and uncontrolled production environment. Remember, take it slowly.

▸ ACME implementation schedule—The heart and soul of NDS implementation. The implementation schedule defines 10 important tasks and becomes a blueprint for ACME success. Remember, the whole world is counting on you—no pressure.

That's Step 3 in a nutshell. Well, not entirely. I have a surprise for you—a present actually. I'm going to take you an a tour through "Virtual Reality ACME." Yes, VR. Sir Isaac Newton and Preferred Systems, Inc., have worked long and hard to develop a new off-line modeling tool called DS Standard. This product allows you to create the ACME tree from the comfort of your own sofa, tent, igloo, hut, or whatever. And it looks a lot like NetWare 4's main on-line management tool—NWADMIN. To top it off, we've included a full-blown copy of DS Standard on the CD-ROM bound into this book. It must be your birthday. Later in this chapter, we'll explore DS Standard and then use it in the case study at the end to build ACME's tree.

So, without any further ado, let's get on with Step 3—NDS implementation: Let's build a testing lab.

ZEN

Quipstering—Using clever or witty remarks in one's conversation or writing...like in this book! Oh, I'm such a "quipster."

ACME Testing Lab

It all starts in the mad scientist's laboratory. This is where all great science is made. The testing lab is a completely open environment where you can get comfortable and creative with NDS implementation. For example, you can:

▸ Install NetWare 4 a bunch of times

▸ Design and build the ACME NDS tree

▸ Test the NDS compatibility of existing and new applications

▸ Run login scripts

▸ Invent a new hair dryer/PDA device

This kind of experience is invaluable—and it can't be taught. The lessons you learn in the lab will help you avoid major mistakes during the pilot and full-blown implementations. The lab experience allows you to learn how NetWare 4 operates within a subset of ACME. More important, the lab is a safe haven where you can experiment with strange modifications and view the impact of these changes on the NDS tree. Let's start our whirlwind tour of NDS implementation with a view inside ACME's Lab, and a hands-on demonstration of their strange new experiments. Remember to wear your protective clothing.

UNDERSTANDING THE LAB

The decision to have a lab depends entirely on your circumstances. Even though most small sites don't have the resources to install a lab, they can still benefit by getting some hands-on experience at their local education center. If you're responsible for a small site and plan to use the default configurations, the lab isn't as crucial, but it can provide you with some valuable administrative experience. And if your site is small and you *do* have a lab, you really should consider a brief testing period in the lab to familiarize yourself with NetWare 4—especially from an administrative standpoint. Besides, setting up a lab and installing NetWare 4 in this environment will instill confidence in your project team as they learn about the features and capabilities of NetWare 4. Plus, it will give you time to work with the operating system, perform diagnostics, and test utilities and applications.

If your site will install or migrate more than 30 NetWare 4 servers, an implementation of a NetWare 4 lab is strongly recommended. Many customers will move from the default settings of NetWare 4 to configurable parameters at approximately this number of servers. The lab gives you the opportunity to adjust and test the configuration parameters you're likely to change.

For larger sites with a Wide Area Network (WAN) in place, we recommend that you follow, where applicable, the lab procedures presented throughout this book. Network administrators of large sites should be completely familiar with the functions and features of NetWare 4 before beginning a full-scale migration to NetWare 4.

For the ACME site, lab testing is being handled at the NORAD facility in the Labs division. This facility evaluates all new software and hardware before deploying it onto the production network, so the new operating system being deployed in the ACME tree has already gone through the lab process.

Many large organizations have a permanent lab for testing new software and hardware at their site. Others may consider creating a temporary lab for this project. Either way, you will need to dedicate some hardware for use as NetWare 4 servers and workstations during your lab project.

Your lab should consist of at least four nodes: two NetWare 4 servers and two workstations. The servers and adapter cards should be similar to the hardware that will be used in your network environment. If you're planning to upgrade your hardware, then use the new hardware in your lab environment. Each NetWare 4 server should exceed, if possible, the minimum hardware requirements provided by Novell. The bottom line is that you want to duplicate your LAN topology and your actual environment as closely as possible.

Figure 5.3 shows the ACME lab for testing NetWare 4 for the entire ACME tree installation. This lab has four dedicated NetWare 4 servers and three workstations for running the Novell and third-party utilities. Also, because the ACME network is primarily Token Ring, we have a Token Ring concentrator in the lab to connect the servers and workstations. All file servers have a CD-ROM drive as well as sufficient disk and memory capacity. The lab ring also has a connection to the corporate backbone located in the Labs division at NORAD.

FIGURE 5.3

The ACME Lab

Workstation

NetWare 4.1   NetWare 4.1

Connection to
Corporate backbone

16 MB
Token Ring

Workstation

CD-ROM

NetWare 4.1   NetWare 4.1

Workstation

Your lab can be smaller but should contain at least three nodes. A three-node network would consist of two NetWare 4 file servers and a single workstation. One of the servers must have a CD-ROM device for installing NetWare 4. You should also try to have a network connection to your backbone so that you have access to any servers currently in operation on your network. Figure 5.4 shows a minimal configuration.

Minimal Lab Configuration

UNDERSTANDING THE EXPERIMENTS

The purpose of any lab is to run experiments. ACME's testing lab is no different. There are five interesting new experiments going on even as we speak:

- ► Experiment 1—Hardware Installation

- ► Experiment 2—NDS Implementation

- ► Experiment 3—Testing Login Scripts

- ► Experiment 4—Testing Applications

- ► Experiment 5—Testing backup and Restore Procedures

ZEN

Hawking radiation—The telltale particles that in theory escape the gravity of a black hole in space. Also thought to orbit the NetWare 4 NDS tree during periods of high activity.

Experiment I—Hardware Installation

If your site already has a lab in place, you can simply designate a group of servers and workstations for your test. Follow the installation procedures found inChapter6. If your company is creating a lab from scratch, follow the set of procedures outlined below.

Perhaps the most difficult aspect of installing NetWare 4 is installing and connecting a CD-ROM drive. Your job will be a lot easier if you obtain the latest CD-ROM drivers from Novell and/or third-party manufacturers. You'll save yourself hours of frustration— trust me. For most hardware products, you can obtain the latest drivers from the vendor's bulletin board. All drivers on the Novell NetWare 4.1 CD-ROM have been tested with NetWare 4.1.

The following steps will help you install your CD-ROM as a NetWare volume:

► Step 1: Access the NETWARE.40_____\DISKDRV directory on the NetWare 4.1 CD-ROM.

► Step 2: Download the .DSK files to your SYS:\SYSTEM directory and load the following files:

  ► Appropriate driver or

  ► ASPICD.DSK or CDNASPI.DSK

► Step 3: From the server console, type:

```
LOAD <.DSK driver>
LOAD CDROM.NLM
```

► Step 4: After loading the previous drivers, type the following at the console:

```
CD DEVICE LIST
CD VOLUME LIST
```

► Step 5: At the command prompt, type **CD MOUNT** *<volume name>* to mount the CD-ROM as a NetWare volume. You can then map a drive to this volume and access the CD-ROM device.

Experiment 2—NDS Implementation

Refer to the section "Task 6—Server Migration" for detailed information on installation procedures. To continue with the lab exercise, install the NetWare 4 operating system on each of your lab servers. Although loading the software isn't difficult, you should become familiar with the install options such as the Simple install and Custom Install.

Practice removing NDS from the server, too. Occasionally you may have to remove a server from the tree to allow for hardware repairs or shipment to another location, and you should follow the appropriate steps for removing a server from the tree.

Familiarize yourself with the install utility and its features. You may have to add new NLMs or additional licenses, and the INSTALL utility handles these procedures.

If you are migrating from NetWare 3 to NetWare 4 and you have the hardware, you can perform an Across-the-Wire migration of a current NetWare 3 server to a lab NetWare 4 server. This approach allows you to upgrade your hardware to a new platform for NetWare 4 and does not endanger your current NetWare 3 server.

Refer to Chapter 4 for valuable design strategies. For modeling you can use Preferred Systems' DS Standard product to simplify the experimenting process (see "Getting Started with DS Standard" section).

Whether you use DS Standard or Novell's NWADMIN utility, the lab tree you design will eventually become your production tree. So take your time defining the appropriate levels and placement of resources. If you have a successful and functioning lab tree, you do not need to create another tree unless you want to maintain separate trees for testing purposes.

The first partition you'll create is the default [Root]. After your lab servers are up and running you can use the NWADMIN or PARTMGR utilities to make additional partitions. Each of your sites should be separate partitions subordinate to [Root]. Use your lab to learn how to create replicas as well. Although your lab may be somewhat limited in size, you should still become familiar with how the partition utilities place replicas on servers.

Time synchronization on your lab servers will initially be set up with the defaults. Your first NetWare 4 server is installed as a Single-Reference server and all others are Secondary servers.

Check out the timesync parameters available through the various SET commands as well as the SERVMAN utility. Use the SERVMAN utility if you want to change the defaults. For example, you can create a small time provider group by changing your Single-Reference server to a Reference server. Then change the other two or three lab servers to

Primary servers. With a LANalyzer or other equipment you can view the packets sent and received during your timesync interval.

Use other commands such as SET TIMESYNC DEBUG=7 to enable the time synchronization screen on your NetWare 4 server. This screen will show you the status of time synchronization and will show you the adjustments that are being made if this server's time is not synchronized.

Experiment 3—Testing Login Scripts

The lab is a great place to design and test your Container login scripts. Populate one of your containers with User objects from your company. Test the Container login script for errors and to verify that all necessary environment variables have been defined.

If you are planning to use Profile login scripts as well, the lab is the perfect place to test the functionality of these scripts.

Experiment 4—Testing Applications

Not all applications need to be tested for NetWare 4 compatibility. However, some applications, especially those written by internal staff, may need some testing. Here are a few important questions to ask yourself:

1 • Is the application bindery based? Bindery-based applications require Bindery Services to be enabled on that server as well as a Read/Write replica of the defined context.

2 • Were these applications written for the NETX client of some other operating system? If so, they should be tested on a workstation with the VLMs loaded. Some basic and easy tests you can perform are listed below:

   a. Run the application to completion or proper termination.

   b. Print a document with the application.

   c. Use the application to do a file save of your work onto the NetWare 4 server.

   d. Test your tape backup system support for NetWare 4 and NDS.

You should try to keep your application testing short and simple. You will never be able to test for every feature and function of every product. Concentrate your efforts on the specialty applications that are not in the mainstream.

Experiment 5—Testing Backup and Restore Procedures

Perform a full backup and restore of a NetWare 4 server. This backup includes files as well as NDS tree information. Always have a clear understanding of how your planned backup procedures work with the specific backup product you're using. The lab is the best place to gain experience in backup and recovery procedures.

ZEN

Permaculture—An alternative lifestyle based on agriculture in which each of the related activities is located to help conserve energy. Many members of ACME believe we should gravitate toward permaculture to help save the planet Earth. Of course, I'm doing my part by making this book only 1600 pages long.

ACME Pilot Program

Now, you're almost ready for prime time. Before you can attack the ACME implementation head-on, you should consider testing your lab results on a small segment of the overall tree. The pilot program serves as a dress rehearsal before you move into full-scale migration. In ACME's case, the pilot program will accomplish the following:

- ▶ Give the project team a chance to practice its implementation procedures.

- ▶ Provide a "live" blueprint for full-scale client and server migration.

- ▶ Provide more accurate feedback for application compatibility.

- ▶ Give insight into how users react to NDS and the "new" logical network resources.

- ▶ Gather valuable performance data for fine-tuning partitioning, replica, and time synchronization designs.

We will start in the OU=LABS container, because the scientists are more sympathetic to our experiments. Who knows? They might even offer to help. In this case, we will migrate three pilot servers (LABS-SRV1, R&D-SRV1, and WHI-SRV1), two HP4SI printers, a print server (R&D-PS1), and all the administrative users under OU=LABS. That includes AEinstein, LDaVinci, CDarwin, MCurie, INewton, CBabbage, and Ada.

Refer to Task 9 of the ACME implementation schedule for more details. Speaking of schedules, let's stay on track and move forward to the center of NDS implementation—the schedule!

ACME Implementation Schedule

The ACME implementation schedule is where all the action is. It is the center of attention, a blueprint for success—another roadmap for saving the world. More important, it's your friend. Make one, learn it, use it.

The implementation schedule should provide detailed, measurable tasks that you can perform during the life of the ACME implementation. The main focus of the implementation schedule is the tasks and their associated subtasks. You should also include a detailed timeline with key milestones. In addition, the schedule will establish the proper timing and help to order all the NDS implementation tasks.

The schedule also helps you track the status of the project and can provide immediate feedback to your staff and management. A well-planned implementation schedule will not only help you manage and track the status of the NetWare 4 project, but it can be used to set deadlines for each task. Let's be honest, these things can go on forever.

The implementation schedule consists primarily of a set of charts—each with a task description, its subtasks, guidelines, duration, start and end dates, percent completion, and task lead (person). If possible, the schedule should also show the interdependencies of the tasks, measure the progress, review the work, and produce reports for management. Finally, make sure to update the chart daily, weekly, and monthly—until the project is finished.

Here's a quick preview of the 10 tasks in ACME's implementation schedule:

▸ Task 1—Project Scope

▸ Task 2—Training

▸ Task 3—NDS Implementation

▸ Task 4—Security and Auditing

▸ Task 5—Client Migration

▸ Task 6—Server Migration

▸ Task 7—Printing Migration

▸ Task 8—Application Migration

▸ Task 9—Pilot Program

▸ Task 10—Rollout

Now, let's build ACME's implementation schedule together. We will discuss each task in depth, and create a task-oriented timing chart. Remember, these charts are the roadmaps for ACME's success. Please take them very seriously—we have!

ZEN

Pi wars—The competition among computer experts to refine the value of the mathematical constant pi (3.14159...). As we all know, it is the number expressing the constant relationship of the diameter of any circle to its circumference—or the number of CNEs it takes to screw in a lightbulb.

TASK 1—PROJECT SCOPE

It all starts with the project scope. This establishes the boundaries of ACME's NDS implementation. This is strictly a planning stage—it doesn't involve any action. It does, however, continue throughout the first half of the project.

You need to continually assess the scope of your implementation and make subtle adjustments as needed. This involves scheduling, task orientation, documentation, and acceptance testing. ACME's project scope implementation schedule is shown in Table 5.1. But, before we explore this first schedule, let's review some of its key components:

- ▸ Task and Description—A detailed description of each task and its associated subtasks. It's usually in outline form.

- ▸ Duration—The actual time it takes to complete the task. The duration is calculated according to an 8-hour workday and 5-day workweek and is always less than the difference between the start and end dates. This is because of organizational concerns, scheduling conflicts, and Murphy's Laws.

- ▸ Start Date—When the task begins according to the calendar. This shows interdependencies between tasks because some start after others. But most are staggered; that is, they happen at the same time.

- ▸ End Date—When the task finishes. This is usually greater than the start date plus duration.

- ▸ %Complete—An on-going meter of task progress.

- ▸ Person—Whoever is in charge of the task and accountable for the schedule.

Table 5.1 is a template for your implementation schedule. Fill in the information as needed.

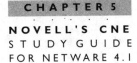

T A B L E   5.1

ACME's Project Scope Schedule

TASK	DESCRIPTION	DURATION	START DATE	END DATE	%COMPLETE	PERSON
Main Task: Project Scope		12 weeks	1/1/97			
1.1 Determine Milestones						
1.2 Determine Critical Path						
1.3 Determine Success Factors						
1.4 Risk Analysis						
1.5 Establish Reporting and Tracking						
1.6 Documentation						
1.7 Acceptance Testing						

ZEN

Croissantization—The popularization of croissants as part of peoples' diet in a trendy society. This is an example of junk-food imperialism. The aggressive international marketing of food that is high in calories but low in nutritional value such as candy and most fast foods. Typically, the only nourishment allowed for busy CNEs.

TASK 2—TRAINING

"Knowledge is nourishment for the mind," and it's never been more obvious than with ACME and NDS implementation. Please don't skimp on training. This is one of the most critical tasks in the entire process. Like project scope, training occurs throughout the life of the project. As a matter of fact, training occurs before, during, and after the ACME implementation.

Because some later tasks are dependent on training, we will start this task first—on January 1, 1997. During the training phase, you need to train your administrators, users, and the project team. The training task also involves lab testing.

Here are some excellent sources for NetWare 4 training:

- ▸ Novell Authorized Education Centers—Five courses are available for NetWare 4 alone.

- ▸ NetWare Users International (NUI)—This user group offers regular meetings and conferences.

- ▸ Novell Press books—*Novell's CNE Study Guide for NetWare 4.1* and *Novell's Guide to NetWare 4.1 Networks* are just a few of the titles you'll find useful.

- ▸ Vendor Workshops—These workshops are often held at NUI meetings and conferences.

- ▸ *Novell Application Notes*—Novell's monthly technical journal for network design, implementation, administration, and integration.

- ▸ Colleges and Universities—Many of these institutions now offer NetWare training courses.

Refer to Table 5.2 for ACME's training schedule.

ACME's Training Schedule

TASK	DESCRIPTION	DURATION	START DATE	END DATE	%COMPLETE	PERSON
Main Task: Training		20 weeks	1/1/97			
2.1 Determine Training Needs						
2.2 Training Strategies						
2.3 Obtain Training						
2.4 Set Up the Lab						

ZEN

Language pollution—The use of many new expressions, slang terms, or foreign words when viewed as unnecessary. Otherwise known as NDS nomenclature. Get the hint?

TASK 3—NDS IMPLEMENTATION

NDS implementation transcends all the other tasks in the sense that it occurs continually. Once you have designed the NDS tree (see Chapter 4), you must install the servers (Chapters 6 and 7), and finally, put the resources in place and manage the tree (Chapters 8 and 9).

Following are some estimated time frames for each of ACME's NDS implementation subtasks:

1 • Create NDS Naming Standard—4 days

2 • Design NDS Tree—2 days

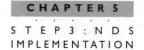

3 • Design and Implement Partitions and Replicas—3 days

4 • Design and Implement Time Synchronizaton—2 days

5 • Develop NDS Accessibility Plan—7 days

Remember, these aren't consecutive calendar days—they are actual duration. The real calendar time will be much longer. Refer to Chapter 4 for an in-depth discussion of these subtasks. For now, refer to Table 5.3 for ACME's NDS implementation schedule. Notice that it occurs one month after training begins. You have to learn this stuff before you can schedule it.

T A B L E 5.3

ACME's NDS Implementation Schedule

TASK	DESCRIPTION	DURATION	START DATE	END DATE	%COMPLETE	PERSON
Main Task: NDS Implementation		**5 weeks**	**2/1/97**			
3.1 NDS Naming Standard (4 days)						
3.11 Identify Existing Standards						
3.12 Create NDS Naming Documents						
3.13 Deliver NDS Naming Documents						
3.2 NDS Tree (2 days)						
3.21 Gather Corporate Documents						

(continued)

T A B L E 5.3

ACME's NDS Implementation Schedule (continued)

TASK	DESCRIPTION	DURATION	START DATE	END DATE	%COMPLETE	PERSON
Main Task: NDS Implementation		**5 weeks**	**2/1/97**			
3.22 Review WAN Maps						
3.23 Review Campus Maps						
3.24 Design Top of the Tree						
3.25 Review Organization						
3.26 Review Resource List						
3.27 Design Bottom of the Tree						
3.28 Place Resources in Containers						
3.29 Design Considerations						
3.29.1 Administration						
3.29.2 Partitioning						
3.29.3 Login Scripts						
3.29.4 Bindery Services						
3.29.5 Test NDS Tree Design						

T A B L E 5.3

ACME's NDS Implementation Schedule

TASK	DESCRIPTION	DURATION	START DATE	END DATE	%COMPLETE	PERSON
Main Task: NDS Implementation		**5 weeks**	**2/1/97**			
3.3 Design and Implement Partitions and Replicas (3 days)						
3.31 Review WAN Map						
3.32 Partition Top of the Tree						
3.33 Replica Strategy						
3.33.1 Replicate Locality						
3.33.2 Replicate for Fault Tolerance						
3.34 Partition Bottom as Needed						
3.35 Develop Partition and Replica Guidelines						
3.36 Test Partitions and Replica Strategy						
3.4 Design and Implement Time Synchronization (2 days)						

(continued)

ACME's NDS Implementation Schedule (continued)

TASK	DESCRIPTION	DURATION	START DATE	END DATE	%COMPLETE	PERSON
Main Task: NDS Implementation		**5 weeks**	**2/1/97**			
3.41 Evaluate TimeSync Options						
3.41.1 Single-Reference (Default)						
3.41.2 Time Provider Group						
3.42 Choose Option Based on WAN						
3.43 Evaluate TimeSync Communications						
3.43.1 Service Advertising Protocol (SAP)						
3.43.2 Configured List						
3.44 Develop Time Synchronization Strategy						
3.45 Test Time Synchronization Strategy						
3.5 NDS Accessibility Plan (7 days)						

T A B L E   5.3

ACME's NDS Implementation Schedule

TASK	DESCRIPTION	DURATION	START DATE	END DATE	%COMPLETE	PERSON
Main Task: NDS Implementation		**5 weeks**	**2/1/97**			
3.51 Analyze Existing Login Scripts						
3.52 Move System Login Script to Container Login Script						
3.53 Test Login Scripts						
3.53.1 Container Login Scripts						
3.53.2 Profile Login Scripts						
3.54 Develop Mobile User Strategy						
3.55 Test Mobile User Access						
3.56 Deliver Accessibility Plan						

ZEN

Offenders' tag—An electronic device worn by a person under house arrest that monitors his/her movements and alerts police to violations of restrictions of movement. Or the second layer of NetWare 4's five-layered security model—login restrictions.

TASK 4—SECURITY AND AUDITING

Security and auditing is a very important part of the NDS implementation. Once you've established the tree guidelines, you need to concentrate on securing it. See Chapter 11 for more details.

Note that migrating users don't have to worry about file system security—it should already be in place. You should, however, test it first. Refer to Table 5.4 for ACME's security and auditing schedule.

TABLE 5.4

ACME Security and Auditing System

TASK	DESCRIPTION	DURATION	START DATE	END DATE	%COMPLETE	PERSON
Main Task: Security and Auditing		1 week	3/1/97			
4.1 Server Security						
4.11 Server Settings						
4.2 NDS Security						
4.21 Object Security						
4.22 Property Security						
4.23 Develop NDS Security Strategy						
4.24 Test Security Strategy						

T A B L E 5.4

ACME Security and Auditing System

TASK	DESCRIPTION	DURATION	START DATE	END DATE	%COMPLETE	PERSON
Main Task: Security and Auditing		**I week**	**3/1/97**			
4.3 File System Security						
4.31 Develop File System Strategy						
4.32 Test File System Strategy						
4.4 Audit						
4.41 Define Audit Procedures						
4.42 Understand Audit Utilities						
4.43 Develop Audit Strategy						
4.44 Test Audit Strategy						

ZEN

Sniglet—A word made-up for something without a name or concise description. It is based on a pun or a clever combination of existing words. I guess it's safe to say this book is one big "sniglet."

The next two tasks represent the Big Two of the implementation tasks: client migration and server migration. After all, users depend on NetWare 4 clients and the NDS tree depends on NetWare 4 servers. In these two sections, we explain the details of client and server migration in a little more depth. Remember, these are two critical phases.

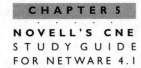
TASK 5—CLIENT MIGRATION

We'll get a chance to install and migrate client resources in Chapters 6 and 7. For starters, let's take a look at NetWare 4's client migration strategy.

Client Migration Strategy

If most of your users are using the NETX shell in DOS for connectivity to the network servers, then you should upgrade these workstations as soon as possible to the NetWare DOS Requester (or VLMs). The VLMs support connectivity to both NetWare 3 and NetWare 4. They also provide users with the following benefits:

▶ Full NDS connection to NetWare 4 servers.

▶ Full backward compatibility to existing NetWare 3 servers.

▶ Efficient use of workstation resources by optimizing the memory of the workstation. This is accomplished by loading the NetWare DOS Requester into the high- or extended-memory space. This provides the user with more conventional memory.

▶ Support for up to 50 concurrent server connections. This is an increase over the eight previously supported in the NETX shell.

▶ Support for multiple languages at the workstation—enabling the user to receive screen messages in his/her native language.

▶ Performance increase during the workstation-to-server communication—thanks to Packet Burst and Large Internet Packet features, which are enabled automatically at the client.

▶ Automatic increased security during workstation-to-server communication, as a result of RSA encryption.

▶ Modularity architecture of the NetWare DOS Requester, which allows you to choose the VLM modules you want to load at each workstation.

TIP

Consider moving the client team and other IS staff to the NetWare DOS Requester first. This will enable them to become familiar with the technology. Then, when you migrate the users, your administrators will already have personal experience with the system.

The client team should migrate the workstations to the latest client software before any servers are migrated to NetWare 4. For example, the NetWare DOS Requester (VLM) software can provide your workstation with more conventional memory. Once the server is migrated to NetWare 4, the user will have immediate support for single login and other services unique to the NetWare 4 operating system.

The OS/2 Requester for NDS also provides many of the same benefits as the NetWare DOS Requester such as full backward compatibility. The Mac client for NetWare 4 also provides you with the benefit of single login to any NetWare 4 servers.

The client team should plan for about 15 minutes per workstation to complete the installation of the latest client software. The team should also combine all necessary changes into a single visit to each workstation. Following are some things you should consider while planning your client migration strategy:

1 • Determine and define the contents for each of the configuration files on the workstation. These configuration files include CONFIG.SYS, AUTOEXEC.BAT, NET.CFG, and STARTNET.BAT. You should define a standardized set of files across all workstations in the network.

2 • During the migration or installation of the new client software, the fastest method of installation method is to download from a server rather than using floppy disks. This method is only possible if you are migrating from NETX workstations.

3 • Consider upgrading other system software for the workstations. For example, you could take this opportunity to upgrade the workstations to the latest version of Windows or to perform other upgrades.

4 • Schedule the migration of your workstations during a period that is long enough to migrate your selected set of users. You may need to schedule this process during a weekend. Obviously, the more people involved in the migration of workstations, the faster this will go.

5 • The client team could also consider an automated strategy for upgrades from the server. For instance, when the user logs into a NetWare 4 server, the automated program would download the required programs to the workstations. This implies that the workstations are standardized in their file structure.

QUIZ

A friend of yours is tossing a coin and you are betting him on the outcome. You bet on heads every time. Your unit stake is $1.00 per toss. You begin by betting $1.00 on the first toss. If you win, you again place $1.00 on the second toss but if you lose, you double the stake to $2.00, then $4.00, and continue to double after every loss. After every win, you revert to the $1.00 stake. After 100 tosses of the coin, heads has come down 59 times. How much profit are you making, assuming that the one hundredth toss was heads?

(Q5-1)
(See Appendix C for all quiz answers.)

Client Migration Methods

The first step in migrating your clients is to determine what type of clients you will need to migrate. The most prevalent client upgrade will be to Novell's DOS/Windows client, which is also known as the DOS Requester client. The second step is to determine which migration approach is best for your organization. For example, you could use diskettes, load the client from a NetWare 4 server, or use an automated approach.

NetWare 4 supports three different client migration methods:

▸ Diskette Method

▸ Server Method

▸ CD-ROM Method

If your site will be using the NetWare DOS Requester or the OS/2 Requester, you can create client installation diskettes from your NetWare server utility INSTALL.NLM. The diskette method is fairly slow and is recommended only for small sites with a few workstations.

For sites where you have more workstations, you should run the client installation from the NetWare 4 server. With this option, the installation utility will need to be run from every workstation. Individual users can run the utility or your network administrator may need to help out.

Regardless of your site's size, if you are moving from a non-NetWare operating system to NetWare 4, you will most likely need to visit each workstation. To load the DOS/Windows client, you'll have to unload the previous operating system and then load the NetWare 4 client in its place. Because this process cannot be automated easily, you will have to work on each workstation individually.

Now let's take a closer look at each of the client migration methods.

Diskette Method The diskette method is the slowest. However, it may be your only option if the workstation being upgraded does not currently have the NETX shell or if you are migrating from another LAN operating system.

The migration process will take approximately 15–20 minutes per workstation if you are loading the client software from diskettes. This time estimate doesn't account for any additional work you may be performing on a workstation at the same time. Also, the more standardized your workstations are before you begin, the less time the migration process will take.

If you are migrating a workstation from another operating system, you will need to remove or disable the other operating system from loading at start-up. Once the other operating system has been disabled, you can run the client install utility and begin your upgrade process.

You can create the client install diskettes from any NetWare 4 server by performing the following steps:

1 • At your NetWare 4 server console type **LOAD INSTALL.** Select Product Options and press Enter. You will see the screen shown in Figure 5.5.

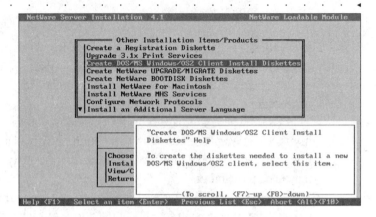

FIGURE 5.5

Product Options Screen in
INSTALL .NLM

2 • Select Create DOS/MS Windows/OS2 Client Install Diskettes and press Enter.

3 • Select the size of diskettes you wish to create and press Enter. You'll need five blank, formatted diskettes for the DOS/Windows client and seven for the OS/2 client.

You can also use the MAKEDISK.BAT utility to create your client diskettes. This utility is found in your SYS:PUBLIC\CLIENT directory. There is a MAKEDISK.BAT utility for both DOS/Windows clients and OS/2 clients. Both utilities will create diskettes for you at a workstation rather than at the server, which may be more convenient for your administrators.

Server Method   The server installation method requires that you have a client running the NETX shell or an earlier version of the NetWare DOS Requester so that the workstation can access a NetWare 4 server. The workstation simply logs into the NetWare 4 server and runs the INSTALL utility from the F:\PUBLIC\CLIENT\DOSWIN subdirectory.

A screen will appear, similar to the one shown in Figure 5.6. Once the configuration information has been entered, the utility will begin the installation process.

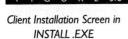

F I G U R E 5.6

*Client Installation Screen in
INSTALL .EXE*

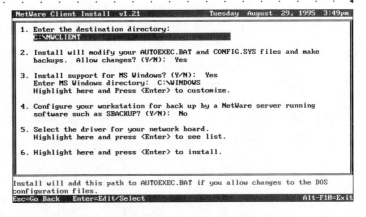

This method is faster than the diskette method and many of your users will be able to do it themselves with little assistance. You will still need to answer the questions contained in the installation parameter screen (see Figure 5.6), but your users should be able to handle the rest.

CD-ROM Method   The CD-ROM method is similar to the server method except that you will access the INSTALL utility from a CD-ROM. The CD-ROM must first be mounted as a NetWare volume. This method is faster than installing from diskettes, but it's not as fast as installing from the server. You'll find the CD-ROM version INSTALL.EXE in the D:NW410\CLIENTS\DOSWIN (or OS2) directory.

QUIZ

What is the five-digit number, no zeros, in which the last digit is five times the first, the second digit is twice the first, the third is the sum of the first and second, and the fourth is the sum of the first, second, and third?

(Q5-2)

Client Migration Preparation

Because INSTALL.EXE copies and modifies files, this utility may be replaced with your own custom-designed batch files to install the client based on your specific needs. This section provides information on creating .BAT files that can replace or work with the INSTALL utility to automate the process.

For large installations with many workstations that are currently running NETX, this is the recommended approach. For sites not using NetWare, a batch file approach is more difficult.

The automated process basically gives a Container login script the ability to query the workstation for the existence of the NetWare DOS Requester. If the current DOS Requester is not found, the Container login script can be designed to launch a set of batch files that will perform the functions of the INSTALL.EXE utility on that workstation. A scripting language such as Novell's Navigator can be used to simplify this process.

If you have plans to perform other work on workstations, such as upgrading the version of DOS or bringing in new hardware, your best option is to use the INSTALL utility off a current NetWare 4 server. You can create a series of batch files that will upgrade your DOS version and load the DOS/Windows client in a semi-automated fashion.

The NET.CFG file contains network parameters that are read while network software is being loaded. This file can be compared to the boot parameters found in a workstation's CONFIG.SYS file. Once you have loaded a workstation with the client software, a default NET.CFG is placed in the C:\NWCLIENT directory. The default NET.CFG contains the startup information needed for that workstation to connect to the network. A sample NET.CFG is shown here:

```
NetWare DOS Requester
    FIRST NETWORK DRIVE = F
    NETWARE PROTOCOL = NDS, BIND
    NAME CONTEXT = "OU=LABS.OU=NORAD.O=ACME"
    PREFERRED SERVER = LABS-SRV1
Link Driver PCMDMCS
    MEM D9000
    FRAME ETHERNET_802.2
```

A standardized NET.CFG file is highly recommended for any size company. The NET.CFG file is read at the time the VLM.EXE software is loaded at your workstation.

Here's your chance to put your lab environment to work again, testing your NET.CFG file. If you have standardized your workstation hardware, all workstations will have the same NIC card and driver, which simplifies maintenance of this file. For example, you won't have to make exceptions for other drivers.

You can use the following sequence to define your migration strategy:

1 • Determine your workstation types.

2 • Create Install Diskettes for your workstations (regardless of the migration method you choose). See Novell's documentation for Macintosh and Unix workstations.

3 • Choose your migration method:

▸ Diskette method

▸ Server method

▸ CD-ROM method

4 • Load workstation software according to your chosen method and consider doing the following:

▸ Load standard NET.CFG that you have created.

▸ Upgrade your DOS version if necessary.

▸ Take inventory of the PC hardware.

5 • Reboot the workstation and login as an NDS user to verify that the workstation is operational.

Refer to Table 5.5 for ACME's client migration schedule. You will need a little training to get the client migration started, so you'll see that we're waiting a month after the training time line. This process could start at the same time as NDS implementation, because the NetWare DOS Requester supports both NetWare 3 and NetWare 4. It's a great place to start.

So how long will it take? Consider the following calculation for ACME:

2000 workstations × 15 minutes per workstation = 30,000 minutes
30,000 minutes = 500 hours = 62.5 workdays = 12.5 weeks

Even though we've calculated a duration of 12.5 weeks, it could take up to 4 calendar months to visit every workstation.

T A B L E 5.5

ACME's Client Migration Schedule

TASK	DESCRIPTION	DURATION	START DATE	END DATE	%COMPLETE	PERSON
Main task: Client Migration		12 weeks	2/1/97			
5.1 Functional testing for each desktop						
5.2 Evaluate Client Migration Options						
5.3 Determine Client Migration Strategy						
5.4 Test Client Migration Strategy						

ZEN

Hundredth-monkey phenomenom—A controversial theory proposed as an explanation for the supposed spontaneous spread of behavior when a population of animals reaches a certain high number. In one experiment, the hundredth monkey learned to wash sweet potatoes. In another experiment, the hundredth user learned how to use VLMs.

TASK 6—SERVER MIGRATION

The second of the Big Two implementation tasks focuses on the NetWare 4 server. This is the big kahuna. The server houses NDS, stores the user's files, and provides a gateway to the cyber frontier. For all of these reasons, you should take great care in server migration.

Following is a detailed introduction to server migration methods and preparation tasks. Follow this discussion closely, and then refer to Chapters 6 and 7 for excrutiating server detail. Ready, set, serve!

Server Migration Methods

NetWare 4 supports four different server migration methods:

- ▸ File Copy Method

- ▸ In-place Method

- ▸ Across-the-Wire Method

- ▸ Same-Server Method

Each of these options has its own advantages and disadvantages. The method you use will depend on your current operating system, available hardware, and available time. Some methods are faster than others and some offer more configuration options. Let's take a closer look.

File Copy Method   Perhaps the simplest migration method you can use is copying the files and data from your current operating system to the Netware 4 file system. This is a very dynamic migration method because you can choose which files and subdirectories you want to move. You can move an entire volume, a group of subdirectories, or a single file.

There are a few requirements you'll need to meet before you can perform a File Copy:

- ▸ Your new NetWare 4 server must be installed and running on the network along with the server you intend to migrate.

- ▸ You will need to choose a workstation and establish a concurrent connection to both servers.

▶ You'll need to use login accounts with rights that allow you to read and write the data to and from the appropriate source and destination servers.

▶ Your workstation must have enough memory to support the concurrent login to both servers.

▶ In a mixed operating system environment, the workstation performing the migration will have to be loaded with two protocols to support both operating systems.

▶ Both the source and destination servers must be visible to the workstation performing the copy.

Check out Figure 5.7 to see how the File Copy method works. In this figure, a user logs into a NetWare 3.12 server called NETWARE_312 and a NetWare 4.1 server called NETWARE_410. After connecting to both servers from a DOS workstation, the user maps drives to the source server and to the destination server. Then the user issues an XCOPY command with appropriate parameters and copies the data from the VOL1 volume to the DATA directory or a similar volume on the destination server.

The drive mappings for the workstations are as follows:

```
MAP F:=SERVER_312\VOL1:
MAP G:=SERVER_410\VOL1:DATA
```

The copy command would appear as:

```
XCOPY F:*.* G: /S /E
```

This command copies all files from the F: drive to the G: drive, including all subdirectories (/S) even if empty (/E).

FIGURE 5.7

*Server Migration with the
File Copy Method*

Although the File Copy migration method is the simplest and quickest way to move information from one server to another, it may not be practical for those who require information other than just data (for example, trustee assignments). But for some migrations, it is currently the only option. For example, migrating a network from DEC Pathworks users to NetWare 4 requires the COPY command. There is no other mechanism currently available. The advantages and disadvantages of the File Copy migration method are listed below.

Advantages:

▸ Restricts the copy of the source server to Read-only on the data files. The copy procedure provides fault tolerance because the source server is only being read and not altered in any way.

▸ Selects volumes, directories, or files that you wish to be moved. For example, the entire drive does not need to be copied to the other server, which means you can do migrations in stages.

▶ Allows you to move different types of name spaces. This method supports Macintosh, NFS, and other native desktops if the workstation is already attached with active name space.

▶ Supports file transfers between popular network operating systems. For example, DEC Pathworks or LANtastic files can be copied.

▶ Data files can be moved at any time because the procedure is nondisruptive to the user. However, the increased network traffic may affect users' performance.

▶ You can use several utilities to perform the File Copy (for example, COPY, XCOPY, NCOPY, File Manager in Windows, Norton Utilities, XTREE, and other third-party products).

Disadvantages:

▶ Does not move the bindery in NetWare 2 and NetWare 3. This means that users, groups, and print services are not migrated to the new server.

▶ Does not maintain existing source file trustee assignments. After the migration, these assignments need to be redefined.

▶ Requires additional server hardware. Both the source and destination server need to be installed and running on the network. This method also requires availability of a workstation.

▶ Requires a concurrent connection to both the source and destination server. Both servers need to be visible to the workstation. The only way around this is to attach to the source server to move the data files to a temporary storage device and then move the files to the destination server in stages.

▶ Could be slow because it moves the data files across the network from one server to another.

TIP

If the servers are not visible or you have problems communicating with the network, you should check to see if your workstation is set up with the same frame types as the servers. With the release of NetWare 4.1, Novell changed the default Ethernet frame type from Ethernet 802.3 to Ethernet 802.2.

The File Copy migration method is valuable to companies that are performing file server data restructuring. If you need to change the layout of the server significantly or apply large changes in naming then you may choose to simply copy the files from server to server.

In-place Method   The In-place method uses a NetWare 4 installation program called INSTALL.EXE, which loads the corresponding INSTALL.NLM as the server loads. In-place migration provides you with a path to upgrade from a NetWare 3 server to NetWare 4—all in the same box. Figure 5.8 illustrates how you can upgrade a NetWare 3.12 server to NetWare 4.1 within the same physical machine.

F I G U R E 5.8

Server Migration with the In-place Method

Since the file server hardware stays the same, the data volumes remain the same. Only new files are added to the SYS: volume in the system subdirectories. The data files on the other volumes on the server will not be moved or changed.

The In-place migration method is the fastest method for migration because it does not move the data files. The other migration methods are slower because all the data has to be migrated across the LAN or WAN network. This method is recommended when you are upgrading an existing NetWare 3 server to NetWare 4 on the same hardware device. To use this utility to migrate a NetWare 2 server, you'll have to upgrade the server to NetWare 3 first.

The NetWare 4 installation program can be started in DOS from the NetWare 4.1 CD-ROM. Then from the NetWare 4 Install main menu, you would select Upgrade a NetWare 3 Server to NetWare 4.

The In-place migration method is excellent for situations in which you do not have the luxury of migrating from one server hardware to other. The advantages and disadvantages of this method are listed below.

Advantages:

▸ Uses the same physical server hardware. This eliminates the cost of a new server hardware system just to perform the migration.

▸ Passwords are maintained or kept. The user will not change passwords.

▸ Migrates the existing bindery information with full NDS compatibility. All the users, groups, and trustee assignments are migrated or maintained.

▸ User login scripts will be placed directly into the corresponding NDS property for the user.

▸ Preserves all the user print configuration databases. The PRINTCON.DAT and PRINTDEF.DAT databases are written directly into the NDS property for each user.

▸ Migrates all the servers faster. The data in the file system or volumes remain unmodified. The bindery files are the only information that needs to be converted. They are moved to NDS.

▶ The name spaces are maintained. Since the data files are not changing, the name space (MAC, NFS, and so on) are fully supported.

Disadvantages:

▶ Does not allow the volume block size to be changed. We recommend that each NetWare 4 server have 64 KB volume blocks. But, since the file system remains intact from before the upgrade, you will have the original volume block size set for your server (probably 4 KB blocks). To change the volume block size, follow these steps:

1 • Back up data to tape.

2 • Delete the volume.

3 • Create the new volume using the correct volume block size.

4 • Restore data from tape.

▶ Does not allow you to turn on suballocation for the file system. Suballocation can be turned on after the upgrade, but the suballocation will affect only subsequent writes to the disks.

▶ May require a restoration from a tape backup if a failure occurs during the upgrade process. Although the In-place upgrade method is restartable if a failure occurs, there are other windows of vulnerability that may require you to do a tape restore.

ZEN

Fax hacker—A person who uses a fax machine to send messages that have not been requested by the recipient, usually in large numbers or too many people. Welcome to junk mail in the 21st century.

Across-the-Wire Method The Across-the-Wire migration utility (AMU) allows you to migrate network servers from a different network operating system including NetWare. This method supports migration from NetWare 2, NetWare 3, LAN Server, LAN Manager, and Banyan Vines.

With this method, the physical server hardware is going to be replaced. The utility migrates the bindery or administrative information and data files from the original server to the NetWare 4 server. The Across-the-Wire utility runs on a DOS workstation that should be logged into both the source and destination servers. The workstation will read the administrative information and data files from the source server and write them to the NetWare 4 server (see Figure 5.9).

*Server Migration with the
Across-the-Wire Method*

SOURCE

DESTINATION

NetWare
3.12

NetWare
4.1

READ

WRITE

DOS Workstation

MIGRATE.EXE

Because this method runs at the workstation and has to move all the data, it is very important that you choose a fast workstation. As a minimum, we recommend a 66 Mhz 486 workstation with at least 480 KB of free memory. The workstation needs at least a 16- or 32-bit LAN card. Although a slower workstation with an 8-bit LAN card will work, it will increase the time needed to complete the migration. You should find the fastest PC possible and place it on the same network segment as the server being migrated.

To start the migration process at the DOS workstation, you first need to connect and login to both the source and destination servers as a Supervisor or someone with the necessary access rights. This method uses the MIGRATE.EXE utility (see Figure 5.10).

Main Menu of
MIGRATE.EXE

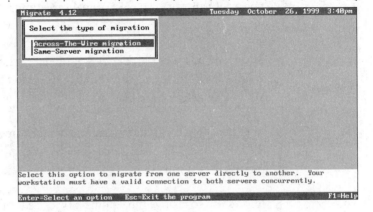

The Across-the-Wire migration utility tracks and logs all of the actions of the migration. The log file is written on the hard drive of the workstation. The log file requires approximately 1 MB for every 1GB of data migrated. Following is a list of the advantages and disadvantages of this method.

Advantages:

▸ Migrates previous NetWare versions as well as other network operating systems (for example, NetWare 2, NetWare 3, LAN Server, LAN Manager, or Banyan Vines). This utility does not support migration from previous versions of NetWare 4 (v4.0x) to NetWare 4.1.

▸ Migrates all the bindery information into NDS (Bindery Services mode). The users, groups, and trustee assignments are maintained.

▸ The server being migrated is Read-only and the data files and bindery remain the same. In the event of a network crash, the server being migrated is unmodified.

▸ Allows consolidation of multiple source servers into a single NetWare 4 server. The source servers can be from different operating systems.

▸ Gives you the chance to replace or upgrade the server to newer, more powerful hardware. The NetWare 4 server must be up and running on the network.

▸ Selectively migrates the data files or bindery information. You can select a volume from the source server to be moved to the new NetWare 4 as a new Volume:Directory combination.

▸ Multiple DOS workstations can migrate the same server, different volumes at the same time. This means that you can have more than one workstation process the information.

▸ Allows you to change the volume block size for the file system. You can select the volume block size during the installation of the NetWare 4 server or destination server. You should always select a volume block size of 64 KB.

▸ Allows you to turn on file suballocation before the migration of the data files.

Disadvantages:

▸ Requires that the DOS workstation be connected concurrently to both the source and destination servers in order to migrate the data files. This could cause a problem if you have to support different network operating systems. You must then load both protocol stacks for each operating system.

▸ Limits the connection to the NetWare 4 destination server as Bindery Service access. This will cause a problem when you try to migrate information (for example, login scripts) that needs to be placed in NDS.

▸ The migration procedure is slow because the DOS workstation is transferring all the data files across the network. The data being copied could be disruptive to the network traffic and may require you to execute the migration process during off-peak hours.

▸ Passwords are maintained because the workstation doing the migration cannot read the password. You can migrate either with no passwords or with random passwords.

▸ DOS name space or files are the only name space supported. The Mac, NFS, and others are not supported through the DOS workstation. You can do a File Copy using a native desktop machine to move the files.

Same-Server Method   You can also use a modified version of the Across-the-Wire utility to migrate other network operating systems, even if you are not replacing the server hardware. You'll need to choose Same-Server migration from the MIGRATE.EXE main menu (see Figure 5.10). The Same-Server method allows an upgrade without requiring a new server. This option migrates the bindery or bindery-like information from the source server to the DOS workstation.

The Same-Server method does not copy or migrate any data files. To keep your data files, you'll need to back up them before doing the migration. After you have rebuilt the physical hardware device and loaded NetWare 4, you can restore the data files. Then you can restore the bindery information from the DOS workstation.

If you want to consolidate hardware, you should also use the Same-Server version of MIGRATE.EXE. It allows you to move the information from several existing servers into one NetWare 4 server.

Server Migration Preparation

The server team should also consider performing the following functions in preparation for the migration of each NetWare 4 server:

I • Apply the corporate NDS naming standard while the objects are still in the bindery. NDS does not support different object types having the same name. By contrast, the binderies in previous versions of NetWare do support different object types with the same name. For example, in NetWare 3, a Group object called HP4SI and a print queue called HP4SI have the same name because they are different object types. In NetWare 4 you cannot have any leaf object with the same name in the same container. This conflict needs to be resolved before the migration of the server to NetWare 4. If there is a duplicate, the migration utilities will not migrate the second occurrence of a duplicate object name. A Novell utility called DUPBIND (found on NetWire) displays the duplicate object names in the binderies so that they can be changed before a migration begins.

2 • Clean up the binderies and delete users and other objects that are no longer in use. Take this opportunity to remove security and access privileges that are no longer required. The SECURITY.EXE program in NetWare 3 will help you find and expose the detailed security information for each of the objects in the bindery. Users that have left the company or are no longer using that server should be removed.

3 • Make a complete backup of your servers before beginning a migration. Some companies have individuals in an operations group that are responsible for backups. The server team should work with this group to ensure that a recent backup has been performed on any server that is about to be migrated.

4 • Run the BINDFIX utility in NetWare 3 to remove any objects that are corrupted in the bindery.

5 • If you are migrating multiple NetWare 2 or NetWare 3 servers into a single NetWare 4 server, the server team should check for users with accounts on the multiple servers. Migrating multiple servers and duplicate users will present you with several challenges during migration to NetWare 4. First, the MIGRATE utility prompts you to change the username on the second and subsequent servers. Second, the migrate utility will merge the User objects that have the same name into a single NDS object with cumulative rights. This may not be what you had intended.

6 • If each of the multiple NetWare 2 or NetWare 3 servers are migrated into different containers in the NDS tree (OUs), the duplicate username will be migrated to each individual container with the same name but a different context. In most cases, you do not want to manage the same user twice in the tree.

7 • Delete old files and applications from the file system. This will free up disk space for other purposes. You may discover many old, unused, and duplicated applications that are wasting disk space.

8 • If you are using Ethernet, ensure that your network uses the NetWare 4 default Ethernet frame type of 802.2. Although NetWare 4 will support both the 802.3 raw and IEEE 802.2 frame types, 802.2 provides automatic check summing of packets to ensure greater communication reliability and is the preferred standard.

TIP

Always try to use the Ethernet 802.2 frame type and begin phasing out the 802.3 raw frame type if in use at your site. Choosing just one frame type will eliminate additional network traffic considerably.

Refer to Table 5.6 for ACME's server migration schedule. This is the most time-consuming aspect of NDS implementation, because it involves most of the other implementation tasks. At ACME, we will be migrating 52 total servers, but 3 of them will be part of the earlier pilot program—so that leaves us with 49 total servers. It takes about 1.5 days per server, once you know what you're doing. So, here's the math:

49 servers × 1.5 days = 74 days = 15 weeks

Also, notice that the server migration starts 1.5 months after the client migration. This is because of two factors. First, the NDS implementation must be completed before we can begin (4 weeks after 2/1/97). Second, we have to wait for the procedures from the pilot program (15 days more). That puts us at 3/15/97.

T A B L E 5.6

ACME's Server Migration Schedule

TASK	DESCRIPTION	DURATION	START DATE	END DATE	%COMPLETE	PERSON
Main Task: Server Migration		15 weeks	3/15/97			
6.1 Evaluate In-place Utility						
6.2 Evaluate Across-the-Wire Utility						
6.3 Determine Strategy for Server Migrations						
6.4 Perform Mock Migration in the Lab						
6.5 Test Server Migration Strategy						
6.6 Develop Backup and Restore Strategy						

ZEN

U-turn worker—A professional or skilled worker who returns from unemployment in a big city to work in the nonurban locality from which he/she originally came. Or the propensity of CNEs to return back to the comfortable confines of DOS.

TASK 7—PRINTING MIGRATION

This printing team is responsible for designing the printing strategies for NetWare 4. All the print software and hardware should be tested for compatibility. This includes connections greater than 250 users. The printing strategies should also encompass printing in a mixed environment—NetWare 3 and NetWare 4. This team should address the following issues for both a pure NetWare 4 printing strategy and a mixed NetWare 3 and NetWare 4 environment.

Setup for a pure NetWare 4 printing strategy:

- ▶ Quick Setup

- ▶ Default print queue for printers

- ▶ Workstations running VLMs

- ▶ Workstations running NETX

Setup for a mixed NetWare 3 and NetWare 4 printing strategy:

- ▶ Queues on NetWare 4, with the print servers on NetWare 3

- ▶ Queues on NetWare 3, with the print servers on NetWare 4

- ▶ Queues and print servers on NetWare 3, with client on NetWare 4 and VLMs

Refer to Table 5.7 for ACME's printing migration schedule. This process depends entirely on the server migration tasks. Printing implementation takes roughly 2 hours per server:

52 servers × 2 hours per server = 104 hours = 13 days = 2.5 weeks

We will begin implementing printing with the very first pilot server; therefore, this process starts on 3/1/97.

T A B L E 5.7

ACME's Printing Migration Schedule

TASK	DESCRIPTION	DURATION	START DATE	END DATE	%COMPLETE	PERSON
Main Task: Printing Migration		**5 weeks**	**3/1/97**			
7.1 Identify Existing Printing Environment						
7.2 Evaluate Proposed Printing Layout						
7.3 Evaluate Direct Print Cards and Printers						
7.4 Determine Printing Migration Strategy						
7.5 Test Printing Migration Strategy						

ZEN

Neoism—An old policy or idea presented in a way that makes it appear new or innovative such as NetWare 4 printing.

TASK 8—APPLICATION MIGRATION

This application project team is responsible for accomplishing compatibility testing for applications running on both NetWare 4 servers and clients. There are several issues to deal with during the compatibility testing, including:

- Bindery-based software programs

- NDS-aware applications

- Connections greater than 250 users

- VLM compatibility

This group is also responsible for the migration and implementation of existing applications in the new NetWare 4 production environment. Not all applications need to be tested for compatibility—primarily because NetWare 4 has been around for a few years and also because mainstream applications are already known to be completely compatible. Applications written by internal staff should be tested.

Refer to Table 5.8 for ACME's application migration schedule. Note that the actual migration of the applications occurs during the server migration phase—the duration is included in the 15 week estimate for Task 6. In this section, we will estimate the duration for compatibility pretesting. This task also occurs before client and server migration. It takes roughly 1 day to test each application, and ACME has 24 different applications. Therefore, compatibility pretesting will take approximately five weeks. We better start as soon as we can. Note, the client migration may overlap with application pretesting.

T A B L E 5.8

ACME's Application Migration Schedule

TASK	DESCRIPTION	DURATION	START DATE	END DATE	%COMPLETE	PERSON
Main Task: Application Migration		**5 weeks**	**2/1/97**			
8.1 Identify all Applications						
8.2 For Internally Written Applications						
8.21 Install						
8.22 Test on a Desktop						
8.23 Test on Server						
8.24 Test Printing						
8.25 Document Compatibility						
8.3 Deliver Applications into Production						

ZEN

Reversible raincoat sentence—A statement that, with a minor change as in word order or word substitution, produces a cleverly expressed idea. Here's a great example:"Ask not what your country can do for you; ask what you can do for your country."

TASK 9—PILOT PROGRAM

The pilot program is a very important precursor to server migration. It allows you to test the implementation procedures on a few "live" production servers. The goal here is to establish procedures and blueprints for the rest of the server migrations.

It usually takes twice as much time to perform a pilot migration as a regular migration. This is because you're working on your first couple of servers and you're documenting every step. This means that it will take us two weeks to adequately migrate the three Labs pilot servers. Refer to Table 5.9 for ACME's pilot program schedule.

T A B L E 5.9

ACME's Pilot Program Schedule

TASK	DESCRIPTION	DURATION	START DATE	END DATE	%COMPLETE	PERSON
Main Task: Pilot Program		**2 weeks**	**3/1/97**			
9.1 Pilot Preparation						
9.11 Clean Up (Objects and Files)						
9.12 Apply Naming Standards on NetWare 3 Servers						
9.13 Run BINDFIX						
9.14 Back Up Servers						
9.2 Pilot Installation or Migration						
9.21 Upgrade Server to NetWare 4						

(continued)

T A B L E 5.9

ACME's Pilot Program Schedule
(continued)

TASK	DESCRIPTION	DURATION	START DATE	END DATE	%COMPLETE	PERSON
Main Task: Pilot Program		**2 weeks**	**3/1/97**			
9.22 Test Server (Production-like)						
9.23 Document any Problems						
9.24 Modify Procedures Based on Results						
9.3 Acceptance Testing						
9.31 Provide Daily Support to User						

ZEN

Gridlock—A massive traffic jam in which vehicles are unable to move in a network of intersections. Also can be applied to a variety of nonautomotive situations, including speaking (vocal gridlock), bureaucracy (corporate gridlock), or networking (bindery gridlock).

TASK 10—ROLLOUT

Well, we finally made it! This is the last leg of a very exhausting race. The rollout schedule is an overview of the entire project. In includes project scope, training, NDS, resource migration, and the pilot program.

As you can see in Table 5.10, we've included a significant cushion in the rollout schedule. Even though the project will only take 21 weeks, that's not factoring in scheduling conflicts, traveling, and Murphy's Laws. So, add another 25 percent to the total duration, and we should finish the ACME implementation on September 28, 1997. No sweat, now all we have to do is—just do it! Ready, set, rollout.

T A B L E 5.10

ACME's Final Rollout Schedule

TASK	DESCRIPTION	DURATION	START DATE	END DATE	%COMPLETE	PERSON
Main Task: Rollout		**21 weeks**	**2/1/97**	**9/28/97**		
10.1 Just Do It!						

ZEN

Workquake—An upheaval in the way workers pursue their assignments in the workplace especially as a result of computerization—and NetWare 4 is at the epicenter. Now you can better understand the general feeling of WANphobia among users.

Wow, that's a lot of work! I can feel a very large "workquake" approaching. We're going to be very busy over the next eight months. It's a good thing we're attacking this ACME WAN together.

That completes Step 3. As you can see, NDS implementation centers on the implementation schedule. It is truly a roadmap for ACME success. The remaining 10 chapters of this book are dedicated to getting you through the ACME implementation schedule—and beyond. But before we roll up our sleeves and attack this thing head-on, I have a little present for you—remember, I care.

I know how much you like virtual reality, so here it is...Virtual Reality ACME. Knock yourself out!

Getting Started with DS Standard

Welcome to Virtual Reality ACME. You're going to love this tool. DS Standard allows you to create an NDS tree from the comfort of your own sofa, tree house, airplane, hot tub, golf course—you get the idea. It's an amazing off-line modeling tool that incorporates many of the same features as NWADMIN—NetWare 4's main on-line NDS management tool. And that's not all. We've included a full-blown version of DS Standard on the CD-ROM bound into this book. Why? Because we care! Use it or lose it.

DS Standard was developed by Preferred Systems, Inc., with a lot of help from Novell. It is a Windows-based design tool that allows you to model, analyze, and manage your NDS tree *before* moving it into production. Using this tool, you can practice all this great design stuff without threatening the viability of your company's NDS tree. Please use it to practice everything you've learned in Chapters 3–5. Also, you'll get a chance to build ACME's tree with DS Standard at the end of this chapter. Check out the case study.

Here's how it works:

▸ Phase 1—Discover

▸ Phase 2—Model/Analyze/Manage

▸ Phase 3—Configure

As with most things, it all starts with discovery. The discover phase searches your current network for available resources—they will populate the DS Standard database. If you are running on a NetWare 3 network, the discovery process will read your bindery information. If you are currently running on a NetWare 4 WAN, DS Standard will read the entire NDS database. Keep in mind that the current version doesn't discover any extensions made to the NDS database. It just sees the standard NDS objects—about 24 of them.

The modeling and management phase is where you get to design your NDS tree. You can either build a tree from scratch or manipulate the objects DS Standard found during discovery. In addition, DS Standard provides tree design templates and previously discovered views to get you started. As a matter of fact, the entire ACME tree is included on the CD-ROM bound into this book. No cheating though, you should really build it yourself first.

The configure phase takes your NDS model and actually implements it on your real NetWare 4 WAN. This takes the virtual out of virtual reality. Imagine if you could bring virtual characters to life with the press of a button. Well, that's what we're accomplishing here. Suddenly, DS Standard isn't just a modeling tool anymore. Now it's a full-fledged configuration tool.

I'm excited to get my hands on this technological marvel, how about you? Let's first learn how to install it, then build the ACME tree using DS Standard. Ready, set, model.

INSTALLING DS STANDARD

Remember, DS Standard is an off-line modeling tool. This means it runs on any standalone computer. Well, almost any.... Here's the minimum workstation configuration for running DS Standard:

▸ IBM PC or compatible, 80386 or higher. For best performance, use an 80486/33 or higher.

▸ Minimum of 8 MB of RAM, preferably 16 MB.

▸ 10 MB of available disk space for DS Standard and 17 MB with The Assistant (an artificially intelligent DS Standard buddy).

▸ 3 MB additional space for each server discovered.

▸ MS Windows, Version 3.1 or higher. Your CONFIG.SYS file should contain the line FILES=40.

Once Windows is running on your workstation, begin the installation by inserting the diskette labeled *disk 1 of 4* and typing **A: SETUP** from the Program Manager's Run option. If you are installing the product from a CD-ROM, type **D:\DSINST\SETUP.EXE** where D is the letter of your CD-ROM drive. Choose OK at the Run dialog to begin the DS Standard installation.

The installation program will then ask if you want to install DS Standard, The Assistant, or both. For our purposes we are installing both. Follow the installation screens and enter your registration information to proceed. The installation takes about 10 minutes.

You must also apply a DS Standard NDS license to every NetWare 4 server you want to discover. In addition, you'll need appropriate NDS security. For our purposes, we have installed the product as a single-user application. In a multiple server production environment, you'll need to purchase a separate license for each NetWare 4 server.

OK, now we're ready to attack the ACME tree. But first, let's explore some DS Standard nomenclature: projects and views. A *project* is a collection of views that can be obtained from either a bindery query or an NDS query. A *view* is a smaller subset of a project and consists of objects and their properties. These values can be discovered or placed in the DS Standard database manually. Speaking of manually, let's do some tree building. Ready, set, construct.

QUIZ

The plumber left the taps running in the bath with the plug out. The hot water tap would fill the bath in 54 seconds. The cold water tap would fill the bath in 48 seconds. The plug out would release a bath full of water in 30 seconds. Would the bath ever fill up?

(Q5-3)

USING DS STANDARD WITH ACME

This is a great opportunity for you to build ACME's tree without having to fly to NORAD. In this discussion, and the subsequent case study, we will build the ACME tree from scratch. No discovering here. If you need to discover something, read the documentation.

DS Standard is a very friendly tool. It includes numerous Help windows and The Assistant to guide us along. It all starts with the DS Standard main screen view (see Figure 5.11). There's not much to it. Nothing like a clean, empty slate to stimulate your creativity.

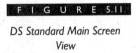

F I G U R E 5.11

DS Standard Main Screen
View

Your first task is to create an ACME project. To create a project, select the File, New Project option. You will be presented with a dialog as shown in Figure 5.12. Fill in the project information and continue. We will name the project ACME Tree Design and use the tree design staff as our project authors.

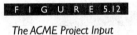

F I G U R E 5.12

The ACME Project Input
Screen

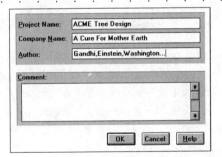

With the ACME project in place, you can start building the tree. But first, you'll need a new view. From the main screen, choose File and New View. Suddenly, more choices. An intermediate pull-down menu appears with three options (see Figure 5.13):

▶ Bindery View—A discovery option for bindery searches of NetWare 2 or NetWare 3 servers. You can also import Bindery Services information from NetWare 4 servers with this option.

▸ NDS View—A discovery option that will build your tree based on information collected from NetWare 4 NDS servers throughout the WAN.

▸ Empty View—A manual option for creating NDS designs from scratch. That's us.

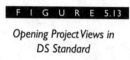

F I G U R E 5.13

Opening Project Views in DS Standard

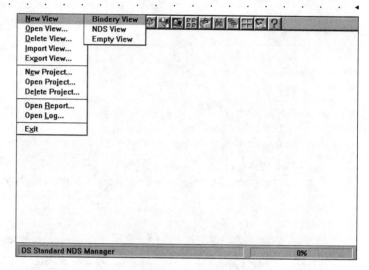

When you select a project view, DS Standard prompts you for a View Name and Author(s). We will use ACME Tree and "Gandhi," respectively. After you enter this information, an empty tree appears with one single NDS object—you guessed it, the [Root] (see Figure 5.14). Welcome to the beginning of life. This view can be closed, opened, saved, deleted, imported, exported, and so on. The good news is that you can start adding objects now. Yeah!

Not really. I'm sorry, there's more beaucracy. But we're almost there, I promise. Before we can start building the tree, we need to associate the ACME Tree view with our ACME Tree Design project. These two steps are interchangeable. In other words, you can create multiple views first and then assign them to a project or you can create a project and assign it to multiple views.

FIGURE 5.14

The Beginning of ACME's Tree

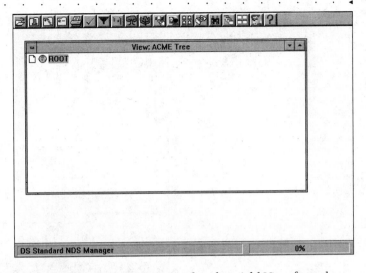

To add our view to the ACME Tree Design project, simply select Add View from the Project menu. Note: Your project must be already open in order to add a view. Finally, DS Standard provides some tree design templates at this point. You can choose a small, medium, or large tree. These templates are designed to speed up the process of creating your tree. We don't need any templates.

Now, we can start—really. To begin the ACME tree, choose Add Object from the Edit menu. Another intermediate pull-down window appears (see Figure 5.15). This is the DS Standard object creation window. Notice there are 19 object types to choose from, but only 3 of them are highlighted—Country, Organization, and Alias. Why? Correct, these are the only objects allowed directly underneath the [Root]. Incidentally, the Alias object only supports the Country and Organization containers at this point. Choose Organization and click that mouse.

FIGURE 5.15

Adding Objects in DS
Standard

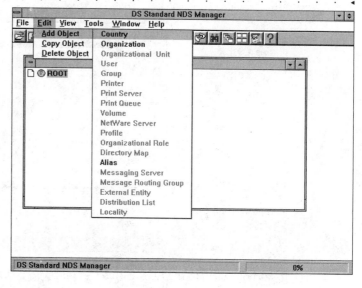

The DS Standard Organization input screen contains the same property information as NWADMIN. As a matter of fact, it even looks the same. This VR modeling tool has become less V and more R. The ACME Organization window is shown in Figure 5.16. We will, of course, call it ACME.

FIGURE 5.16

Organization Input Screen
in DS Standard

Now, follow the same procedure and create Organizational Unit objects for each of the five ACME locations. The NDS tree is beginning to take shape, as shown in Figure 5.17. Remember, the top layers will be geographic and the bottom layers will be organizational. We learned all this great stuff in Chapter 4.

The Top Geographic Layers of ACME's NDS Tree

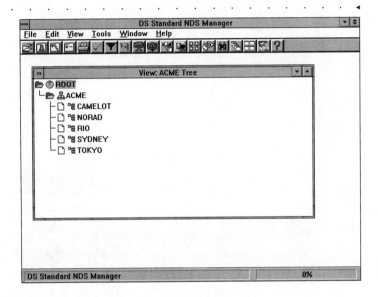

The fun continues as we create the rest of the container skeleton. The bottom OU layers define the departmental boundaries of ACME. See Figure 5.18 for an illustration of all four layers of ACME's NDS tree. It's so beautiful.

FIGURE 5.18

The Bottom Organizational Layers of ACME's NDS Tree

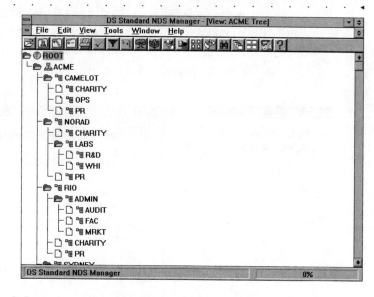

Once the container skeleton is in place, we can distribute the rest of ACME's leaf objects according to the resource list in Chapter 4. These objects define servers, printers, print queue, and so on. Be careful, there are tons of rules governing the placement of NDS leaf objects. We will explore them in great depth in Chapter 8. But what the heck, try it yourself. Now's the time to practice. You can't hurt anything. If you want, you can protect the skeleton by saving it to a different view. This way you can always come back to it if necessary.

Once you have completed ACME's basic tree design, you can run some basic design tests on it—check out the View option. For example, you can run the Verify Directory Tree option. It checks your NDS design for tree depth, number of objects per container, and other useful information. This option will also check your tree for objects that contain unresolved references (that is, name conflicts and so on). The feature is called Resolve References for Selected Objects.

You can also create a DS Standard Report for selected objects in your view. The object report provides detailed information about the object's properties. You can print a report on multiple objects or just a single server—it's up to you. In Figure 5.19, you can see the detailed object report for OU=LABS. This is a wonderful way of documenting your NDS tree. It sure beats NWADMIN.

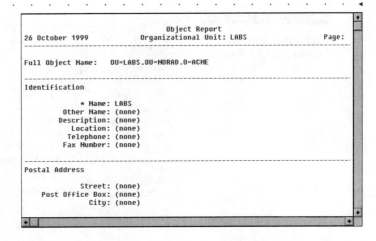

FIGURE 5.19

A DS Standard Report for OU=LABS

```
                                          Object Report
         26 October 1999          Organizational Unit: LABS              Page:
         --------------------------------------------------------------------------

         Full Object Name:    OU=LABS.OU=NORAD.O=ACME

         --------------------------------------------------------------------------

         Identification

                      * Name: LABS
                  Other Name: (none)
                 Description: (none)
                    Location: (none)
                   Telephone: (none)
                  Fax Number: (none)

         --------------------------------------------------------------------------

         Postal Address

                      Street: (none)
             Post Office Box: (none)
                        City: (none)
```

Congratulations! You've completed the ACME tree design—in virtual reality at least. Now comes the tricky part. You can use the DS Standard Configure option to transfer your "fake" tree to a "real" NDS WAN. You can also use the Configure option to make changes to existing NDS objects. Very cool. Here's how it works.

During the first configuration phase, DS Standard must run a consistency check on your current NDS tree. This check will ensure that all changes can be implemented successfully—such as the assignment of mandatory attributes and the cross-referencing of users and print queues, for example. The Preconfigure Verify option will display a log file with all your NDS information. Simply choose Options, Preconfigure Verify from the Tools menu. The log parameter screen appears (see Figure 5.20).

FIGURE 5.20

*Preconfigure Verify Log
Option in DS Standard*

Interestingly, the Verify Metrics can be preconfigured to monitor the implementation of your tree. In this case, we are limiting the total number of objects per container to 1000 with only 6 levels of depth. Once you are satisfied with the metrics, you can run the Verify Directory Tree option again to test your tree design. Notice in Figure 5.21 how the metrics control the size and propagation of the tree. Pretty cool, huh?

FIGURE 5.21

*Verifying ACME's NDS Tree
Design*

```
------------------------- Verify 10-26-1999 12:04AM -------------------------

Checking fully distinguished names of deepest leaf objects
for names over the maximum of 127 characters.
No fully distinguished names are too long.
Checking for number of objects in containers and number of containers in cont
Maximum number of objects in a container is 1000.
Maximum number of containers in a container is 100.
No containers hold too many leaf and container objects.
No containers hold too many container objects.
Checking maximum tree depth.
Depth is O.K.
Checking objects for names over the specified maximums.
Maximum object name length for object of type User is 15.
Maximum object name length for object of type External Entity is 15.
Maximum object name length for object of type Directory Map is 15.
Maximum object name length for object of type Group is 15.
Maximum object name length for object of type Distribution List is 15.
Maximum object name length for object of type Messaging Server is 15.
Maximum object name length for object of type Message Routing Group is 15.
Maximum object name length for object of type NetWare Server is 15.
Maximum object name length for object of type Organization is 15.
Maximum object name length for object of type Organizational Role is 15.
Maximum object name length for object of type Organizational Unit is 15.
Maximum object name length for object of type Printer is 15.
Maximum object name length for object of type Print Server is 15.
```

You can also add, delete, search and replace objects during the configure phase. As the final step, you use the Configure option to write your NDS tree, or portions of the tree, to the actual NDS database. You can select all the objects in the view or only a certain container, for example. To initiate the writing process, select Configure Selected Objects from the View menu. You'll be prompted with a confirmation screen before proceeding. Boom! It's done—how exciting. You've not only modeled the tree, you've actually brought it to life. Great work.

REAL WORLD

In addition to being used as a migration tool, DS Standard can be used as a disaster recovery tool. After you have discovered your NDS tree, you can save the information to a set of files that can serve as an NDS backup. With this backup you will be able to recover a full NDS tree or repair a partial tree.

For example, a customer may have multiple sites with a single server at each site. These sites are not yet connected by a WAN link and yet they want the benefits of NetWare 4. The remote sites can install NetWare 4 on their servers—each as a separate tree. They can use DS Standard to discover their trees and save the information. When the site has a WAN link in place, they can remove NDS from each server and reinstall it into the corporate tree. Because you are not reinstalling the operating system, this process is quick and can be accomplished in about 10 minutes.

The last step is to use DS Standard and your previously discovered tree information to restore your server's objects and attributes. You can use the Configure option to place the DS Standard database back onto the production tree. This method could be used if you did not want to use the DSMERGE utility, which actually merges NDS trees together. You can also use DS Standard to restore selected portions of the NDS tree. If a portion of your tree has become corrupted, you can use DS Standard to restore that portion of the tree based on your last discovery and saved view. The restoration includes the objects as well as the trustee information associated with those objects.

ZEN

Blipvert—Any advertisement that has been greatly compressed from many seconds to just a few seconds while containing the same amount of information. Probably what you're hoping for with this book.

Congratulations! You've survived Virtual Reality ACME. Sometimes the fine line between real and unreal gets a little fuzzy. DS Standard walks that line. At times it seems as though we're really implementing ACME's NDS, and then it hits us.... This is just a modeling tool, it's not real. Then, when we least expect it, bam! We press the Configure Selected Objects button, and the tree comes alive. I didn't expect that.

Life is this way sometimes. It's like *strange luck*—not good, not bad, but both somehow. Welcome to Step 3—NDS implementation. This has been an interesting, almost strange, journey through ACME's testing lab, pilot program, and implementation schedule.

We started in the testing lab. It provided us with a nonproduction environment for five ACME experiments: hardware installation, NDS implementation, testing login scripts, testing applications, and testing backup and restore procedures. With success, we set our sights a little higher and implemented a small segment of the ACME WAN—a pilot program.

If all goes well in the first two testing phases, you're ready for a full-blown NetWare 4 NDS implementation. Of course, you'll need a schedule. The schedule is the cornerstone of the entire implementation process. It defines 10 important tasks and provides a blueprint for ACME success.

So, here we are. It's time to bring the implementation schedule to life. It's time to install NetWare 4. We're on the brink of something amazing here—I can feel it. How about you? Good luck, and by the way, thanks for saving the world!

CASE STUDY: BUILDING THE ACME TREE WITH DS STANDARD

In this exercise, we're going to build the ACME tree using DS Standard—a Windows-based off-line NDS modeling tool. A copy of DS Standard is included on the CD-ROM bound into this book.

Before you begin this exercise, make sure that you have read the DS Standard section in this chapter and installed DS Standard on your workstation. Also, make sure you have reviewed (and understand) the ACME Resource List shown in Table 4.8 of Chapter 4. We are going to use the information it contains to build the ACME tree.

Here's how it works:

1 • Create the top layers of the tree.

2 • Create the NORAD subtree, creating container and leaf objects one layer at a time, moving from the top of the tree to the bottom.

3 • Create the other four subtrees, one subtree at a time, creating container and objects one layer at a time, from the top of the tree to the bottom.

If you're ready to go, let's get started!

1 • **Execute DS Standard.** Execute the DS Standard NDS Manager utility by double-clicking on its icon in Windows.

2 • **Create a project.** Create a new project in DS Standard by selecting the New Project option from the File menu. A New Project dialog box will appear. Type **ACME Tree Design** in the Project Name field, **ACME** in the Company Name field, and your name in the Author field, then click on the OK button to continue. A Project: ACME View screen will then be displayed.

3 • **Create a view.** Next, create a new view for this project by selecting the New View option from the File Menu, then selecting the Empty View option from the pull-down menu. When you do this, you will be presented with a New Empty View dialog box. Type **Initial ACME Tree Design** in the View Name field and your name in the Author field, then click on the OK button

to continue. An empty tree will be displayed consisting of only one object—the [Root]. Click on the Maximize button in the upper right corner of the View: Initial ACME Tree Design window to maximize the size of the window and give yourself more room to work.

4 • **Create the ACME Organization object.** You are now ready to start adding objects to the tree. Whenever you want to create an object in the tree, you need to click on the parent container with the right mouse button, then select the appropriate type of object from the pull-down menu that appears. In this case, we want to create an Organization object under the [Root]. Therefore, you need to click on the [Root] with the right mouse button, then select Add Organization from the pull-down menu. When you make this selection, you will be presented with an Organization dialog box. As you can see, the Identification page button is selected by default. The asterisk (*) in front of the Name field indicates that the field is required (that is, the object cannot be created unless a value is supplied for this field). Type **ACME** in the Name field and click on the OK button. An ACME Organization object will then be created under the [Root].

5 • **Create the CAMELOT, NORAD, RIO, SYDNEY, and TOKYO Organizational Units.** Now that you've created the ACME Organization object, you're ready to create the five Organizational Unit objects under it, corresponding to the five ACME locations.

a. Create the CAMELOT Organizational Unit. To create the CAMELOT Organizational Unit, click on the ACME container with the right mouse button and select the Add Organizational Unit option from the pull-down menu. An Organizational Unit dialog box will appear. As you can see, the Name field has an asterisk in front of it, indicating that it is a required field. Type **CAMELOT** in this field and click on the OK button. When you do this, a CAMELOT Organizational Unit will be created under the ACME Organization object.

b. Create the NORAD Organizational Unit. To create the NORAD Organizational Unit, click on the ACME Organization object with the right mouse button and select the Add Organizational Unit option from the pull-down menu. An Organizational Unit dialog box will be displayed. Type **NORAD** in the Name field and click on the OK button. A NORAD Organizational Unit will be created under the ACME Organization object.

c. Create the RIO, SYDNEY, and TOKYO Organizational Units. Create an Organizational Unit for each of the three remaining ACME locations (that is, Rio, Sydney, and Tokyo) using the same procedure listed in Step 5b. In each case, make sure that you click on the container under which you want the new object created (in this case, the ACME Organization) rather than the object that is highlighted. (If you accidentally create an object in the wrong location, highlight the incorrect object and press Delete.) Refer to Figure 5.22 for an example of what the ACME tree should look like at this point.

FIGURE 5.22

Upper Layers of the ACME Tree Created in DS Standard

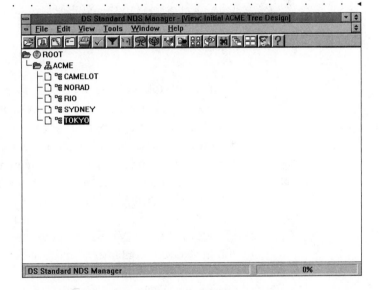

6 • **Create the container and leaf objects in the NORAD container.**
Now that we've created the top levels of the tree, let's concentrate on the NORAD subtree. As you can see in Table 4.8 of Chapter 4, there are three Organizational Units in the NORAD container (CHARITY, PR, and LABS) as well as one Server object (NOR-SRV1) and a Volume object (NOR-SRV1_SYS).

a. Create the CHARITY Organizational Unit. Click on the NORAD Organizational Unit with the right mouse button and select Add Organizational Unit from the pull-down menu. An Organizational Unit dialog box will appear. Type **CHARITY** in the Name field and click on the OK button. When you do this, the CHARITY Organizational Unit will be created under the NORAD container.

b. Create the PR Organizational Unit. Use the same method to create a PR Organizational Unit under the NORAD container.

c. Create the LABS Organizational Unit. Use the same method to create a LABS Organizational Unit under the NORAD container.

d. Create the leaf objects in the NORAD container. Now that you've created the container objects in the NORAD container, let's create the leaf objects as well.

(1) Create the NOR-SRV1 Server object. To create this object, click on the NORAD container with the right mouse button, then select Add NetWare Server from the pull-down menu. A NetWare Server dialog box will be displayed. You'll notice that the Name field is preceded by an asterisk (*), indicating that it is a required field. Type **NOR-SRV1** in this field, then click on the OK button. The NOR-SRV1 Server object will be created in the NORAD container.

(2) Create the NOR-SRV1_SYS Volume object. To create this object, click on the NORAD container with the right mouse button, then select Add Volume from the pull-down menu. A Volume dialog box will be displayed. You'll notice that there are three required fields for a volume: Name, Host Server, and Host Volume. Type **NOR-CHR-SRV1_SYS** in both the Name and Host Volume fields, then click on the browse button to the right of the Host Server field. Next, click on the NOR-CHR-SRV1 Server object, then click on the OK button. The NOR-SRV1_SYS volume will then be created in the NORAD container. Refer to Figure 5.23 for an example of what the container and leaf objects in the NORAD Organization should look like.

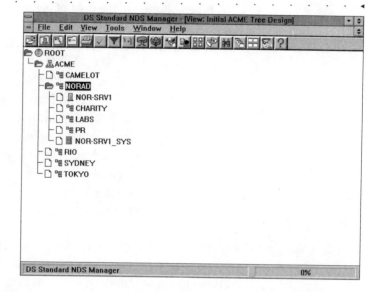

FIGURE 5.23

*Container and Leaf Objects
in the NORAD
Organizational Unit
Created in DS Standard*

7 • **Create the container and leaf objects in the CHARITY, PR, and LABS
containers.**

a. Create objects in the CHARITY container.

(1)   Create the NOR-CHR-SRV1 NetWare Server object. To create this
object, click on the CHARITY container with the right mouse button,
then select Add NetWare Server from the pull-down menu. A
NetWare Server dialog box will be displayed. You'll notice that the
Name field is preceded by an asterisk (*), indicating that it is a
required field. Type **NOR-CHR-SRV1** in this field, then click on the
OK button. The NOR-CHR-SRV1 Server object will then be created in
the CHARITY container.

(2)   Create the NOR-CHR-SRV1_SYS Volume object. To create this object,
click on the CHARITY container with the right mouse button, then
select Add Volume from the pull-down menu. A Volume dialog box
will be displayed. You'll notice that there are three required fields for a
volume: Name, Host Server, and Host Volume. Type **NOR-CHR-
SRV1_SYS** in both the Name and Host Volume fields. Next, click on

the browse button to the right of the Host Server field, click on the
NOR-CHR-SRV1 Server object, then click on the OK button. The
NOR-CHR-SRV1_SYS volume will then be created in the CHARITY
container.

(3) Create the NOR-CHR-PS1 Print Server object. To create this object,
click on the CHARITY container with the right mouse button, then
select Add Print Server from the pull-down menu. A Print Server
dialog box will be displayed. As you can see, the Name field is a
required field. Type **NOR-CHR-PS1** in this field, then click on the OK
button. The NOR-CHR-PS1 Print Server object will then be created in
the CHARITY container.

(4) Create the HP4SI-P1 Printer object. To create this object, click on the
CHARITY container with the right mouse button, then select Add
Printer from the pull-down menu. A Print Server dialog box will
appear. You'll notice that the Name field is a required field. Type
HP4SI-P1 in this field, then click on the OK button. The HP4SI-P1
Printer object will be created in the CHARITY container.

(5) Create the HP4SI-PQ1 Print Queue object. To create this object, click
on the CHARITY container with the right mouse button, then select
Add Print Queue from the pull-down menu. A Print Queue dialog
box will be displayed. You'll notice that the Name field and Volume
field are required fields. Type **HP4SI-PS1** in the Name field. Next,
click on the browse button to the right of the Volume field. Select the
NOR-CHR-SRV1_SYS volume and click on the OK button. The
HP4SI-PQ1 Print QUEUE object will then be created in the CHARITY
container.

(6) Create the SirGawain User object. To create this object, click on the
CHARITY container with the right mouse button, then select Add
User from the pull-down menu. A User dialog box will be displayed.
You'll notice that the Login Name field and the Last Name field are

required fields. Type **SirGawain** in the Login Name field and **Gawain** in the Last Name field, then click on the OK button. The SirGawain User object will then be created in the CHARITY container

b. Create objects in the PR container.

   (1) Create the NOR-PR-SRV1 Server object.

   (2) Create the NOR-PR-SRV1_SYS object.

   (3) Create the NOR-PR-PS1 Print Server object

   (4) Create the CANONBJ-P1 and HP4SI-P1 Printer objects.

   (5) Create the CANONBJ-PQ1 and HP4SI-PQ1 Print Queue objects.

   (6) Create the DClarke User object.

c. Refer to Figure 5.24 for an example of what the leaf objects in the CHARITY and PR Organizational Units should look like.

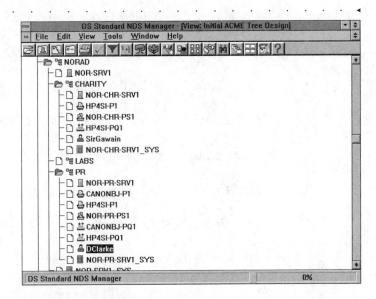

FIGURE 5.24

Leaf Objects in the CHARITY and PR Organizational Units Created in DS Standard

    d. Create container and leaf objects in the LABS container.

       (1)   Create the R&D Organizational Unit.

       (2)   Create the WHI Organizational Unit.

       (3)   Create the LABS-SRV1 Server object.

       (4)   Create the LABS-SRV1_SYS Volume object.

       (5)   Create the AEinstein User object.

8 • Create the container and leaf objects in the WHI and R&D containers.

    a. Create the leaf objects in the WHI container.

       (1)   Create the WHI-SRV1, WHI-SRV2, and WHI-SRV3 Server objects.

       (2)   Create the WHI-SRV1_SYS, WHI-SRV2_SYS, and WHI-SRV3_SYS Volume objects.

       (3)   Create the WHI-PS1 Printer Server object.

       (4)   Create the CANONBJ-P1 Printer object.

       (5)   Create the CANONBJ-PQ1 Print Queue object.

       (6)   Create the CBabbage and ADA User objects.

    b. Create container and leaf objects in the R&D container.

       (1)   Create the NUC Organizational Unit.

       (2)   Create the POLL Organizational Unit.

       (3)   Create the VR Organizational Unit.

       (4)   Create the R&D-SRV1 Server object.

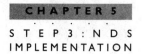
(5)   Create the R&D-SRV1_SYS Volume object.

(6)   Create the R&D-PS1 Print Server object.

(7)   Create the LDaVinci User object.

c. Refer to Figure 5.25 for a sample of what the container and leaf objects in the R&D and WHI Organizational Units should look like.

F I G U R E 5.25

Containers and Leaf Objects in R&D and WHI Containers Created in DS Standard

9 •   Create the leaf objects in the NUC, POLL, and VR containers.

a. Create the leaf objects in the NUC container.

(1)   Create the MCurie User object.

(2)   Create the HP4SI-P2 Printer object.

(3)   Create the HP4SI-PQ2 Print Queue object.

b. Create the leaf objects in the POLL container.

    (1)   Create the HP4SI-P1 Printer object.

    (2)   Create the HP4SI-PQ1 Print Queue object.

    (3)   Create the CDarwin User object.

c. Create the leaf objects in the VR container.

    (1)   Create the HP4SI-P3 Printer object.

    (2)   Create the HP4SI-PQ3 Print Queue object.

    (3)   Create the INewton User object.

d. See Figure 5.26 for an example of what the leaf objects in the POLL, NUC, and VR Organizational Units should look like.

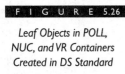

F I G U R E 5.26

Leaf Objects in POLL, NUC, and VR Containers Created in DS Standard

10 • Build the containers and leaf objects in the CAMELOT subtree using the information found in Table 4.8 in Chapter 4.

11 • Build the containers and leaf objects in the RIO subtree using the information found in Table 4.8 in Chapter 4.

12 • Build the containers and leaf objects in the SYDNEY subtree using the information found in Table 4.8 in Chapter 4.

13 • Build the containers and leaf objects in the TOKYO subtree using the information found in Table 4.8 in Chapter 4.

Congratulations! You've built the ACME tree—well, at least in "Virtual Reality" land. A sample of the completed DS Standard file can be found on the World Wire information service (see Appendix D for more information). Take a long, hard look at your accomplishment, because later in Chapter 8 we're going to do it for real. It's exciting when VR becomes a little less virtual and a little more real. See you in the new frontier.

EXERCISE 5-1: NEXT GENERATION OF NETWORKING

```
N  B  X  E  T  X  E  T  N  O  C  Y  R  E  D  N  I  B  E  S  L
G  D  I  R  E  C  T  O  R  Y  G  Y  R  W  N  N  R  I  X  L  O
Y  I  S  I  N  G  L  E  R  E  F  E  R  E  N  C  E  N  E  B  L
N  S  D  X  V  J  R  B  F  P  K  S  T  E  C  X  Y  D  J  T  C
T  T  G  S  B  Q  P  X  V  E  L  E  A  F  O  B  J  E  C  T  F
B  I  D  U  X  M  L  D  L  T  E  E  N  U  B  Q  C  R  O  K  I
H  N  U  U  E  E  I  X  U  E  S  R  Z  E  T  T  E  Y  N  Z  L
G  G  A  U  T  H  E  N  T  I  C  A  T  I  O  N  U  Z  T  V  H
I  U  O  W  T  I  M  E  S  E  R  V  E  R  F  R  M  N  A  F  B
S  I  H  Y  D  C  O  L  M  U  F  X  E  Q  G  B  C  F  I  W  R
S  S  U  B  O  R  D  I  N  A  T  E  R  E  F  E  R  E  N  C  E
Y  H  Y  R  N  F  J  M  I  L  X  B  J  T  C  O  N  T  E  X  T
T  E  F  V  Z  S  U  O  O  Y  T  R  E  P  O  R  P  G  R  T  J
K  D  D  F  C  F  C  L  F  O  D  C  H  V  M  O  A  B  K  P  G
Z  N  G  C  D  V  U  J  M  D  X  H  B  S  M  N  R  L  B  Q  H
C  A  T  W  P  H  Z  W  U  J  X  W  P  L  O  E  T  W  W  L  E
J  M  K  C  Q  V  I  K  P  G  K  K  G  S  N  V  I  T  L  P  E
F  E  E  R  M  S  J  V  X  I  F  O  G  W  N  D  T  H  Y  H  O
T  I  M  E  S  Y  N  C  H  R  O  N  I  Z  A  T  I  O  N  K  L
S  W  V  I  N  E  X  J  Y  W  H  E  G  E  M  D  O  P  E  W  V
E  O  N  Q  S  G  R  S  I  G  M  J  Q  Z  E  N  N  O  E  E  Y
```

Using the hints provided, circle the 20 Netware 4 terms hidden in this word search puzzle.

HINTS

1 • Provides global access to network resources.

2 • Container where bindery context is set.

3 • Item in tree that holds information about a resource.

4 • Topmost object in the NDS tree.

5 • Logical division of the NDS database.

6 • Distributed NDS database.

7 • Object that can hold other objects.

8 • Ensures that all network servers report the same time.

9 • Object that cannot contain other objects.

10 • Object's leaf name.

11 • Hierarchical representation of the NDS structure.

12 • Default type of time server.

13 • Describes an object's location in the database.

14 • Created if parent partition exists but no children.

15 • Complete name of an object.

16 • System for representing the correct time.

17 • Provides time to other servers.

18 • Flat file database.

19 • Background process that verifies authorization.

20 • Characteristic of an object.

See Appendix C for answers.

NETWARE 4 DESIGN

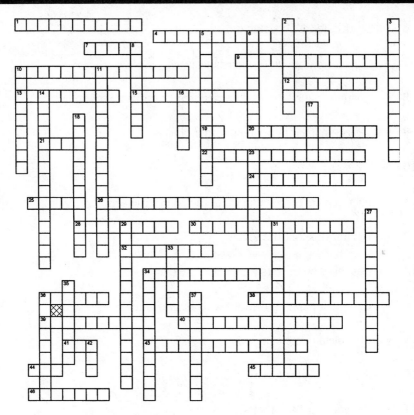

Across

1. One of three reasons to replicate
4. The bad guys
7. Creating more children partitions
9. Step 3 of NDS design
10. A graphical look at ACME's *Chronicles*
12. The heart and soul of NDS implementation
13. Specialist who leads the design team
15. Setting context in NET.CFG
19. NDS navigation at the command line
20. Step 1 of NDS design

21. The divisional headquarters of ACME's greatest minds
22. Changes context in relative distinguished names
24. "A day in the life of ACME"
25. Building a bigger parent partition
26. Input for bottom layers of the NDS tree
28. In charge of the project team
30. One of three reasons to replicate
32. Creating client migration diskettes
34. A great place for NDS experiments
36. Specialist who plans the pilot program
38. Foundation of the bottom layers of the NDS tree
39. Focusing in on ACME's WAN layout
40. Customized time communication
41. The center of ACME's New World Order
43. One of three reasons to replicate
44. Server-to-server communication
45. The home of ACME permaculture
46. Including object class

Down
2. Connection type while accessing MAPped drives and CAPTUREd printers
3. Specialist who gathers WAN layout data
5. Connection type when host server identifies user
6. When
8. The second (and longest) implementation task
10. Design input for top layers of NDS tree
11. "Global" design input
14. Very first time server
16. "Young" subordinate partitions
17. Minimum number of replicas per partition
18. Design input for leaf objects
23. An invisible, often-misunderstood NDS object
27. A bridge between NDS design and full-blown implementation
29. Describes and classifies ACME's stuff
31. Establishes distinguished name

33. Step 2 of NDS design

34. Customized time configuration file

35. They "haggle" for time

36. Most popular time server type

37. Foundation for top layers of NDS tree

42. The ACME time machine

See Appendix C for answers.

Doctor

NetWare 4 Installation

▶ · ◀

Is your network alive?

> ▶ *It's a carbon-based organic life-form—silicon is close enough.*

> ▶ *It consumes food—your LAN processes valuable information.*

> ▶ *It propagates—most NetWare 4 WANs include multiple servers.*

> ▶ *It's self-aware—many times your network has a mind of its own.*

There you go—your LAN must be alive.
And as a living, breathing life-form, it must be born.
This evolution is both painful and rewarding.
But there's nothing more exciting than being involved from Day One.
That's today!

You are a superhero.

You are a doctor.

You are a gardener.

As a NetWare 4 CNE, you are three people in one.

Today, you are a doctor. Not an ordinary human mechanic—no. You are a "Silicon Surgeon." Today, you will deliver an exciting new form of life—an NDS-enhanced newborn. But it won't be an ordinary delivery—no. The birth will involve optical disks (backbone), UTP (circulatory system), a CPU (brain), workstations (limbs), and of course, a birth certificate (license).

Your network will be born today, thanks to NetWare 4 installation and migration. But this is only the beginning. Actions you take today will begin the lifespan of a LAN! Later, in Chapters 12 and 13, you'll learn more about LAN childhood and adulthood. But let's not get ahead of ourselves.

Enjoy the moment.

Today, you'll help deliver one of the most exciting forms of life—an NDS-enhanced newborn. And it's only Monday.

NetWare 4 Installation

If you build it, they will come!

There's something terrible about Mondays. First you seem to wake up on the "wrong side" of the bed. Then you burn the toast, pop a shirt button, and hit every red light on the way to work. Well, it can't possibly get any worse. Fortunately, you made it to the office without killing yourself or causing a tsunami to hit Central Park.

You settle into your comfy leather chair and let out a great sigh of relief. All is well. Then it happens again! This time your boss dumps a menacing red box on your desk labeled "Novell NetWare 4—High-Performance NetWare Operating System." You have to install it. Where do you begin? You look inside the box, hoping that the installation media consists of a single 3.5-inch diskette and are horrified to find two CD-ROMs *and* two diskettes. You're sure this can't be a good sign. You quickly review your options:

- ▸ Filing a request for an immediate medical leave due to stress

- ▸ Pawning off the job to some other unsuspecting victim

- ▸ Giving the installation a shot

Being the weekday warrior that you are, you decide to give the installation a shot. Of course, you keep the other options open in case this proves to be a poor choice.

ZEN

And now for your Monday morning exercises. Ready?
"Up, down—Up, down—Up, down."
That's it. And now, the other eyelid.

Welcome to NetWare 4 installation. This is the second of the "three faces of a CNE." Now that you've designed the LAN, it's time to build it. Think of this as "NetWare Resuscitation"—you're breathing life into an otherwise limp and lifeless LAN. Once the server is "born," you can move into the daily grind of managing it—"childhood" and "adulthood."

NetWare 4 installation is dominated by SERVER.EXE, NLMs, and AUTOEXEC.NCF. It can be a little intimidating at first, especially if you've never installed NetWare before. But have no fear, Dr. David is here. In this chapter, we will traverse every installation obstacle together—all 23 of them. We'll learn about disk partitions, IPX internal network numbers, and NDS context. In addition, there are two extensive installation case studies (walkthroughs) at the end of the chapter. So sit back, relax, and enjoy the rest of your Monday. After all, it can only get better.

Before You Begin

Installing NetWare 4 consists of two main tasks:

▸ Installation of the NetWare 4 operating system on the server

▸ Installation of the client software on distributed workstations

Also, you can install a number of optional products for added functionality. Some of these products are bundled with NetWare, including NetWare for Macintosh, MPR, and DynaText. Some others are available at additional cost.

The purpose of this chapter is to guide you through the basic steps of the server and workstation installation process. In addition, we'll explore some optional products: DynaText and NetWare for Macintosh. Wow, we're gonna be busy.

But before you begin, you'll need to install various LAN hardware components, such as

▸ Network interface cards

▸ Cabling and hubs

▸ Uninterruptible power supplies

The main concern is to make sure there are no hardware conflicts with your LAN components or server/workstation machines. You'll also need to make sure that your "computer room" meets recommended power and operating environment requirements.

You should consult your hardware documentation to determine applicable temperature, humidity, heat dissipation, and power consumption requirements. Novell recommends that you use dedicated power lines for all hardware components (such as servers, workstations, printers, and so on). This is a good idea, especially in lightning high-risk zones.

To protect your network servers from power surges and voltage spikes, it's important that you connect each server to an appropriate uninterruptible power supply (UPS). Novell also recommends that you provide UPS protection for network workstations and other peripherals. (If this is not feasible, you should protect your workstations and peripherals with surge suppressers and ferro-resonant isolation transformers.)

THE BRAIN

Refer to the Site Equipment Preparation section in Chapter 1 of the *Novell NetWare 4 Installation* manual for information on how to protect network equipment from static electricity.

Before purchasing LAN hardware, you should confirm that it is NetWare compatible by looking for one of the following NetWare symbols:

▶ The "Yes, It runs with NetWare" symbol indicates that the manufacturer of the product claims that the product runs with NetWare. Products of this type have been tested only by the manufacturer and thus are not certified by Novell.

▶ The "Yes, NetWare Tested and Approved" symbol means that the product has passed rigorous testing by Novell Labs™ and meets Novell's strict quality standards. Bulletins containing the test results for such products are available from Novell.

▶ The "NetWare Ready" symbol indicates that the product is certified by Novell Labs and is bundled with NetWare. This is done to simplify the installation process for products from participating OEMs by either bundling them or preinstalling them with the NetWare operating system, Personal NetWare™, or NetWare client software.

The really hard-core CNEs have these graphics tattooed on their bodies. Get a life.

MINIMUM HARDWARE REQUIREMENTS

Before you purchase your server hardware, make sure that it meets the following minimum hardware requirements:

- An IBM-compatible architecture with an 80386, 80486 (SX or DX), or Pentium processor.

- 8 MB of RAM for the basic NetWare 4 operating system (OS) if it is installed from either CD-ROM or diskette; 10 MB if installing NetWare 4 using the server-to-server method. (The additional 2 MB of RAM is used for loading STREAMS and CLIB NLMs.)

- 90 MB of free disk space on the hard disk: 15 MB for the DOS partition and 75 MB for the NetWare partition (SYS: volume). If you copy all of the optional NetWare file groups to the server, you'll need an additional 25 MB for the SYS: volume.

- An additional 60 MB of free disk space to install the DynaText viewer and NetWare 4.1 documentation. Additional space will be necessary if you want to install the documentation in more than one language. If you are low on disk space, you can view DynaText directly from the CD-ROM, rather than storing it on the server hard disk.

- One network interface card (NIC).

- The appropriate network cabling and related components (hubs, UPS, and so on).

- A CD-ROM drive that can read ISO 9660-formatted CD-ROM disks—if NetWare 4 is being installed from CD-ROM.

REAL WORLD

The hardware requirements just listed are minimums, not recommended standards. Realistically, you'll want a fast processor, more RAM, and a larger hard disk.

You'll need to add additional memory, based on the following:

▸ NetWare Loadable Modules (NLMs) used. You'll need to add an additional 2 MB of RAM (total) if you use any of the following NLMs on this server: optional NetWare products (such as NetWare for Macintosh or NetWare NFS), print server software (PSERVER.NLM), or management NLMs such as BTRIEVE, INSTALL, MONITOR, or SERVMAN.

▸ The RAM required for disk caching (1 MB minimum, with 4 MB to 8 MB is preferable).

▸ RAM that is calculated on the basis of disk size (total disk size in MB multiplied by 0.008).

In terms of hard disk size, you'll need a disk that is large enough for all of your network needs, including the network operating system, optional network products, applications, documentation, and the file system. Finally, if your server contains more than 16 MB of RAM, you'll need to use 32-bit AT busmastering or DMA boards (unless the driver supports more than 16 MB of RAM). Contact the computer manufacturer for additional information.

THE BRAIN

For a more accurate method for calculating the amount of server RAM required, see the article titled "Server Memory—Calculating Memory Requirements for NetWare 3 and 4" in the January 1995 issue of the *Novell Application Notes*.

There is a method to our madness. As a matter of fact, there are three methods for installing NetWare 4:

- CD-ROM

- Floppy diskettes

- Server-to-server (called "remote installation area" by Novell)

NetWare 4 ships on CD-ROM by default. You can order diskettes from Novell's NetWare Fulfillment Center, but the installation process would involve swapping numerous diskettes and this could possibly be the last straw for your Monday. The final method, server-to-server, is typically used if your CD-ROM is installed on a computer other than the server or if you are installing a number of servers at one time. It involves copying the installation files to an existing server, and then logging into that machine from the "wannabe" server. In this chapter, we'll cover the CD-ROM method—it's the most common.

THE BRAIN

You'll find a comparison of the three types of installation media in the Choose an Installation Medium sections in Chapter 2 and Chapter 3 of the *Novell NetWare 4 Installation* manual.

CHOOSING AN INSTALLATION TYPE

Okay. We've set up our hardware and chosen our poison (CD-ROM); now it's time to get down to business. NetWare 4 offers two basic types of server installation:

- Simple installation—The faster and easier of the two methods. It makes a number of assumptions and uses default settings for most configurable parameters.

- Custom installation—You specify configurable parameters, such as the IPX internal network number, disk mirroring or duplexing, and the enabling or disabling of file compression, block suballocation, and data migration features.

Let's take a closer look.

ZEN

"When making your choice in life, do not neglect to live."

Samuel Jackson

Simple Installation

The simple installation approach should be used if your server meets *all* of the following criteria:

- A DOS partition of 15+ MB exists on the server.

- DOS is installed on the server's DOS partition.

- The server boots from a DOS partition rather than from diskette.

- No disk mirroring, disk duplexing, or disk subsystem is required.

- All free disk space not allocated to the DOS partition is available for a NetWare partition.

- Each disk will contain only one NetWare volume.

- A randomly generated IPX number is acceptable.

- AUTOEXEC.BAT and CONFIG.SYS startup files can be used without modification.

- IPX is the only communications protocol that will be installed (although TCP/IP and/or AppleTalk can be installed manually at a later date).

- NetWare Directory Services (NDS) will be installed with a single Organization per tree containing all objects.

Custom Installation

The custom installation method should be used if your server does not meet the requirements for a simple installation—duh! Some of the configuration options that you can specify in a custom installation include

- Determine whether to boot the server from the DOS partition or a boot diskette

- Assign a nonrandom IPX internal network number

- Partition hard disks

- Mirror or duplex hard disks

- Specify volume names

- Span volumes across multiple drives

- Modify time zone parameters for NDS

- Edit the STARTUP.NCF and AUTOEXEC.NCF startup files

- Choose nonrouting TCP/IP or AppleTalk protocols in addition to IPX

Well, there you have it. We've installed the LAN components, plugged in the NetWare 4 CD-ROM, and chosen a simple or custom installation method—can we finally get started? No! It must be Monday. The last order of business is to walk down the "before you begin" checklist. It looks something like this:

❑ The name of the Directory tree (you'll need to think of one if this is the first server in the tree)

❑ The detailed NDS design (remember Chapters 3, 4, and 5)

❑ A password for the Admin user (if this is the first server in the tree, you'll need to make one up)

❏ A unique server name

❏ A unique IPX internal network number (applicable to a custom installation only)

❏ The type and configuration of the disk controller, as well as the appropriate driver(s), if they are not contained on the NetWare 4 Installation CD-ROM

❏ The type and configuration of the network board(s), as well as the appropriate driver(s), if they are not contained on the NetWare 4 Installation CD-ROM

Now, we're finally ready to roll.

NETWARE 4 INSTALLATION PREVIEW

In this chapter, we'll explore the detailed steps of both the simple and custom installation types. They both traverse the same 23 steps, but the simple install automates a few of them. In either case, the installation process occurs through six stages:

1 • Preparing the server hard disk

2 • Running SERVER.EXE

3 • Loading the NetWare drivers

4 • Loading INSTALL.NLM

5 • Installing NetWare Directory Services (NDS)

6 • Creating server startup files

The actual process of creating the server occurs during Stages 1 and 2. When SERVER.EXE is run, the NetWare 4 operating system is loaded into memory and a colon prompt (:) is displayed. It's alive! At this point, the server is alive, but you can't do anything with it. The server's on life support. The remaining four stages add more and more functionality. Stage 3 adds connectivity by loading LAN and disk drivers. Stage 4 creates a NetWare partition on the hard disk, and then defines one or more volumes with cool SYSTEM and PUBLIC files. Stage 5 installs NDS. And finally, Stage 6 enables you to create/modify the AUTOEXEC.NCF and STARTUP.NCF server startup files.

THE BRAIN

If you encounter problems during the installation process, refer to Appendix G of the *Novell NetWare 4 Installation* manual for tips on troubleshooting.

NetWare 4 Simple Installation

I know how you feel. It's been a looooong day already, and it's only 9:30 a.m. I feel your pain—because I care. Together we can get through this thing. Together we can conquer the NetWare 4 install.

Let's start out slowly (simple), and then work our way into the really hard parts (custom). Fortunately, the NetWare 4 simple installation is essentially a subset of the custom installation. It's faster and easier than the custom method, because it asks a minimum of questions and uses defaults for most configurable parameters. Detailed, step-by-step instructions for performing a Simple NetWare 4 installation can be found in the case study at the end of the chapter (entitled Simple Installation for the U.N.).

QUIZ

Just to keep things simple and warm up the old noodle, here's one of my favorites: A train leaves from Boston to New York. An hour later, a train leaves from New York to Boston. The second train is traveling 15 MPH faster than the first, but the first has a 7.5 MPH tailwind. Which train will be nearer to Boston when they meet?

(Q6-1)
(See Appendix C for quiz answers.)

Listed here is a brief description of what happens during a simple installation. We're just trying to get your feet wet. Refer to the NetWare 4 Custom Installation section for more detailed information on how each of these 23 steps works.

STAGE 1: PREPARE THE SERVER HARD DISK

During Stage 1, the focus is on the DOS operating system. The first step is to boot the server machine with DOS. This is because NetWare 4 doesn't have its own "cold boot loader," and thus is loaded on the server by executing the SERVER.EXE file from the DOS partition. The simple install does not give you the option of booting the server from a diskette.

After you boot DOS, the next step is to configure the DOS partition. This consists of making at least two full backups, creating a temporary boot diskette, using the DOS FDISK utility to delete existing server disk partitions, creating a new DOS partition of 15+ MB, and using the DOS FORMAT utility to format the new partition as bootable. Wow, that was a mouthful.

Next, you'll need to configure the CD-ROM drive as a DOS device. This is because NetWare 4 is shipped on CD-ROM, and you just blew away the CD-ROM drivers on the hard disk. Make sure to use the manufacturer's instructions for this part. Then, you'll probably have to reboot the computer to activate the changes made to the AUTOEXEC.BAT and CONFIG.SYS by the CD-ROM installation program.

To begin the automated installation process, insert the NetWare 4 Installation CD-ROM disk in the CD-ROM drive and switch to that drive (typically D:). Execute the INSTALL.BAT file found in the root directory. You will be asked to choose a language—your choices are Deutsch, English, Español, Français, and Italiano. If you have a CD-ROM that is set up for English-only, you will not be given this choice. After you select your language, you will be asked several questions about the type of installation desired. Make the following menu choices, in order:

1 • NetWare Server Installation (see Figure 6.1)

2 • NetWare 4.1

3 • Simple Installation of NetWare 4.1

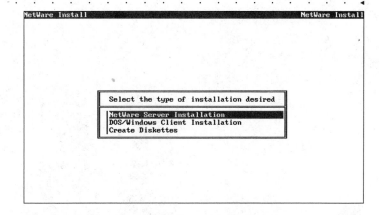

NetWare Install

FIGURE 6.1

NetWare 4 Server Installation Screen

> Select the type of installation desired
>
> NetWare Server Installation
> DOS/Windows Client Installation
> Create Diskettes

We're cruising now! You will then be prompted for a unique server name. You will *not* be prompted for an IPX internal network number. NetWare will automatically generate a random eight-digit hexadecimal IPX number for you—without even asking (how rude). If you were performing a custom install, you would be given the option of overriding this default (and so you should). The system then copies a number of server boot files from the CD-ROM to the C:\NWSERVER directory on your DOS partition.

During a simple install, the system automatically selects the locale configuration (country code, character code set, and keyboard mapping) and filename format for you. The defaults provided assume that you reside in the United States and want to use the DOS filename format. Of course, in a custom install, you are given the option of overriding these defaults.

There you have it. The DOS partition is ready to go. Next stop, SERVER.EXE.

STAGE 2: RUN SERVER.EXE

During Stage 2, the focus shifts from the DOS operating system to NetWare 4. The installation program automatically executes SERVER.EXE and loads NetWare 4 into memory. This process transfers control of the server from DOS to NetWare (see Figure 6.2). At this point, the server is up and running, but you can't do anything with it. In the next step you'll load the NetWare drivers and establish connectivity between NetWare 4 and the hard disk(s) and NIC(s).

FIGURE 6.2

SERVER.EXE—From DOS
to NetWare 4

REAL WORLD

If your server is an 80386 that was manufactured in 1987, you may find that it doesn't execute certain 32-bit instructions correctly. This could negatively affect the way NetWare 4 functions. If a message is displayed indicating that this problem has occurred, you may be able to solve the problem by replacing a ROM chip on the board. Contact the computer manufacturer for further details.

If you were performing a custom installation, you would be given the option of customizing startup file SET parameters. Because this is a simple install, NetWare does it for you. If your server contains a hard disk, CD-ROM, or other device that uses ASPI, the installation program automatically inserts the following line in your STARTUP.NCF file:

```
SET RESERVED BUFFERS BELOW 16 MB = 200
```

STAGE 3: LOAD THE NETWARE DRIVERS

During Stage 3, we jump-start our barely functioning server. We load and configure various NetWare drivers, including

▸ Disk drivers for the internal hard disk

▸ LAN drivers for internal NICs

▸ Binding IPX to the LAN driver

When you load drivers, it's important to make sure that there are no interrupt or address conflicts with other hardware. So, what about additional protocols? During the custom install, you are given the option of installing TCP/IP and/or AppleTalk in addition to IPX. But in a simple install, you have to add them manually—afterward.

ZEN

"Though we often live unconsciously, 'on automatic pilot,' every one of us can learn to be awake. It just takes vision."

Anonymous

That's more like it. Now that the server is functioning normally, we shift our focus to INSTALL.NLM. This is where the real fun begins.

STAGE 4: LOAD INSTALL.NLM

Now that you've established connectivity, we're ready to activate the NetWare partition(s). At this point, NetWare 4 automatically loads INSTALL.NLM. Also, you may be prompted with a warning saying that there is a potential conflict with the DOS CD-ROM driver (see Figure 6.3). If this message is displayed, ignore the warning and continue with the installation. No worries.

F I G U R E 6.3

CD-ROM Warning in
INSTALL NLM

```
 NetWare Server Installation  4.1                    NetWare Loadable Module

 Warning:

 There is a slight chance that you may be using a NetWare
 driver that conflicts with the DOS CD-ROM driver.  INSTALL
 cannot determine this for you.  See <F1> for more information.

 If there is a driver conflict and INSTALL accesses the CD-ROM
 via DOS, the KEYBOARD WILL LOCK-UP.  You will then need to
 reboot your computer, restart the installation, and try to
 mount the CD-ROM as a NetWare volume the second time.




                          ┌──────────────────────────────────────┐
                          │         Select an action:            │
                          ├──────────────────────────────────────┤
                          │ Continue accessing the CD-ROM via DOS │
                          │ Try to mount the CD-ROM as a NetWare volume│
                          └──────────────────────────────────────┘

 Help <F1>            Previous screen <Esc>           Abort INSTALL <Alt><F10>
```

Next, the installation program automatically creates a NetWare partition on the internal server disk. By default, it occupies the entire disk except for the DOS partition. Then, it creates the SYS: volume using the entire NetWare partition. Finally, NetWare 4 mounts the new SYS: volume.

During a custom installation, you are given the opportunity to create additional volumes. Also, you can specify a plethora of manual disk options, including the size of NetWare partitions, mirroring or duplexing, and changing the size of the Hot Fix redirection area. Finally, you are given the option of changing the default settings for file compression (default is ON), block suballocation (default is ON), and data migration (default is OFF).

In the simple install, you are then prompted to insert the NetWare 4 License diskette (as shown in Figure 6.4). Make sure that this is a unique server disk that is not being used on any other server. If you attempt to use the same license on more than one server, you'll get a copyright violation warning. When a message is displayed indicating that the license has been installed successfully, remove the diskette and store it in a safe place—like on the refrigerator door in the lunchroom. Make sure to use a "certified" broccoli magnet for support.

FIGURE 6.4

*Inserting the Unique Server
Connection License
Diskette*

```
NetWare Server Installation 4.1                     NetWare Loadable Module



            The license file will be installed from drive A:. Insert the
            disk labeled, "SERVER CONNECTION LICENSE", (which contains
            the file "SERVER.MLS") into the drive. Licenses currently
            installed on this server allow a total of 0 connections.

            Warning:  Do not try to install this same license on any
            other server.  Doing so will cause a copyright violation
            warning to be issued.

                Press <F3> to specify a different path;
                Press <Enter> to continue.



Continue                                   <Enter>
Specify a different source drive/directory <F3>
Continue without installing a license      <F9>        Delete last license <F8>
Help                                       <F1>        Abort INSTALL <Alt><F10>
```

TIP

If you were installing NetWare 4 from a network volume rather than CD-ROM, you would be given the opportunity to reestablish the server-to-server connection at this point.

The final step in Stage 4 involves optional NetWare files. These are the beginning of your default SYS: file system. During the simple install, NetWare 4 will automatically begin copying optional files from the CD-ROM to the SYS:SYSTEM and SYS:LOGIN directories on the NetWare partition. Later, in Stage 6, you'll copy the rest of the required SYSTEM and PUBLIC files. For now, we'll move on to Stage 5.

THE BRAIN

Only some of the NetWare 4 file sets are copied to the server during a simple installation. For a list of these, refer to the File Sets Copied During Installation section in Chapter 2 of the *Novell NetWare 4 Installation* manual.

STAGE 5: INSTALL NETWARE DIRECTORY SERVICES (NDS)

Once the SYSTEM and PUBLIC files have been copied to the default SYS: volume, it's time to begin building our tree. Don't forget your protective gloves.

At this point, NetWare 4 searches the WAN for any existing Directory trees. If it doesn't find one, it responds with a simple question:

```
Is this the first NetWare 4 server?
```

If it is, you'll need to create the very first tree and give it a name (see Figure 6.5). If it's not the first server, you'll need to select an existing tree. Once you've selected a tree, NetWare 4 adds this server to it and configures time synchronization.

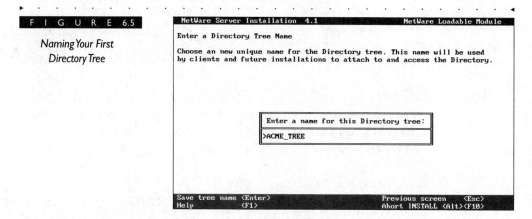

FIGURE 6.5

Naming Your First
Directory Tree

We start with time synchronization. First, NetWare asks you to specify a time zone for this server. For instance, if we're at ACME's Admin headquarters in Rio, you would select Latin America.

Next, we move on to NDS Context. We have to tell NetWare 4 where in the tree to put this server. Remember, we're using the simple installation method. Therefore, the server is placed in a single Organization container. First, you are prompted for the name of the Organization. Second, you must supply a password for the special Admin user. If this is the first server in this tree, you'll make this stuff up. If you're adding this server to an existing tree, you'll have to use established Organization names and passwords.

After you provide the Admin password, NetWare displays a summary screen with the following information: Directory tree name, Directory context, and Admin username (see Figure 6.6). Make sure to write down this information, and keep it in a safe place. Maybe next to the License diskette!

F I G U R E 6.6

*Important NDS Context
Information*

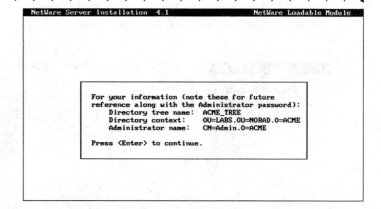

```
NetWare Server Installation  4.1                    NetWare Loadable Module




          ┌──────────────────────────────────────────────────┐
          │ For your information (note these for future        │
          │ reference along with the Administrator password):  │
          │      Directory tree name:   ACME_TREE              │
          │      Directory context:     OU=LABS.OU=NORAD.O=ACME│
          │      Administrator name:    CN=Admin.O=ACME        │
          │                                                    │
          │ Press <Enter> to continue.                         │
          └──────────────────────────────────────────────────┘
```

Voilà, we're done. That wasn't so bad. Now you have a living, breathing server. But, in order to automate this process during server startup, we need to create the following two configuration files: STARTUP.NCF and AUTOEXEC.NCF. That's Stage 6.

STAGE 6: CREATE SERVER STARTUP FILES

Once NetWare Directory Services has been installed, the system automatically creates STARTUP.NCF and AUTOEXEC.NCF for you. These two files help automate the server startup process. During the custom install, you're allowed to modify these files. NetWare then copies these files to the SYSTEM and PUBLIC directories on the default SYS: volume.

All is done. Now, you're given an opportunity to install other installation items/products, such as:

▶ A Registration diskette

▶ DOS/MS Windows/OS2 client install diskettes

▶ NetWare Upgrade/Migration diskettes

▶ DynaText on-line documentation and viewers

All of these options and more are shown in Figure 6.7. Once you're done with these options, you'll choose Continue Installation.

F I G U R E   6.7

Other Installation Items/ Products in INSTALL.NLM

```
NetWare Server Installation  4.1                    NetWare Loadable Module

Other Installation Options

Choose any of the following optional installation items or products.

                 ┌──── Other Installation Items/Products ────┐
                 │ Create a Registration Diskette             │
                 │ Upgrade 3.1x Print Services                │
                 │ Create DOS/MS Windows/OS2 Client Install Diskettes │
                 │ Create NetWare UPGRADE/MIGRATE Diskettes   │
                 │ Create NetWare BOOTDISK Diskettes          │
                 │▼Install NetWare for Macintosh              │
                 └────────────────────────────────────────────┘

                 ┌──────── Other Installation Actions ────────┐
                 │                                             │
                 │ Choose an item or product listed above      │
                 │ Install a product not listed                │
                 │ View/Configure/Remove installed products    │
                 │ Continue installation                       │
                 └────────────────────────────────────────────┘

Help <F1>   Previous screen <Esc>   Change Lists <Tab>   Abort <Alt><F10>
```

Now, we're REALLY done. Congratulations! As a safety measure, you should down the server by typing DOWN, and then restart it by typing RESTART SERVER. Your NetWare 4 server is alive!

Here's a quick review of the major stages involved in a NetWare 4 simple installation:

1 • Prepare the server hard disk.

2 • Run SERVER.EXE.

3 • Load the NetWare drivers.

4 • Load INSTALL.NLM.

5 • Install NDS.

6 • Create server startup files.

Wow, wasn't that fun? Suddenly Mondays aren't so bad anymore. The simple installation is a breeze. But remember, it makes a lot of assumptions for you. This is not for everyone. If you need more flexibility or you're feeling a little more daring, you should consider tackling the custom install. That's the true CNE obstacle course.

Ready, set, go.

ZEN

"You'll laugh. You'll cry. You'll hurl!"

Wayne's World

NetWare 4 Custom Installation

Welcome to the big show. This is where we separate the men from the boys or the women from the girls. The NetWare 4 custom installation gives you total control over all 23 steps. This is good for you—especially if you're a control freak. But, be forewarned. In order to make it through the custom install, you need to know what you're doing. There's no one there to hold your hand.

So, in the spirit of goodwill, and to increase your chances of making it through the install in one piece, I offer the following in-depth discussion. Hold onto your hats. And, if this discussion isn't enough for you, there's a detailed, step-by-step walkthrough of the ACME custom installation at the end of the chapter.

Now that we've warmed up with the simple install, let's start the custom process at the beginning: preparing the server hard disk.

STAGE 1: PREPARE THE SERVER HARD DISK

The NetWare 4 core operating system (OS) consists of a single file called SERVER.EXE. In order to load NetWare 4, you must first boot the server using DOS, and then execute SERVER.EXE. This transfers server control from DOS to the NetWare 4 partition. Refer again to Figure 6.2.

Before you can install NetWare 4, you need to set up the DOS partition. Here's what happens during Stage 1 of the custom installation process:

- ► Step 1— Configure the DOS partition. This consists of booting the server using DOS, making at least two full backups on tape or other media, making a temporary boot diskette, using the DOS FDISK utility to delete existing server disk partitions and create a new DOS partition of 15+ MB, and then using the DOS FORMAT utility to format the new partition.

▸ Step 2— Configure the CD-ROM drive as a DOS device.

▸ Step 3— Run the INSTALL.BAT installation program.

▸ Step 4— Assign a server name and IPX internal network number to uniquely identify your server on the WAN.

▸ Step 5— Copy server boot files to the DOS partition (C:\NWSERVER directory).

▸ Step 6— Select server locale information (which assigns the country code, character code set, and keyboard mapping to be used) and filename format (which identifies whether filenames will be restricted to only those characters allowed by DOS naming conventions).

As you can see, we're pretty busy in Stage 1—let's get started. Remember, there's a detailed walkthrough case study at the end of the chapter.

Step 1: Configure the DOS Partition

Unlike other operating systems such as NetWare 2.x, OS/2, and UNIX, NetWare 4 doesn't have its own cold-boot loader. In order to start the server, you need to boot from a DOS partition. It is also possible, although not preferable, to boot the server from a diskette.

You should complete the following hard disk preparation tasks prior to installation:

▸ Boot DOS on the server.

▸ Make at least two full system backups (including network security information, if applicable).

▸ Create a temporary boot diskette.

▸ Use FDISK to delete existing partitions and create a new DOS partition of 15 MB or more.

▸ Use FORMAT to format the DOS partition and make it bootable.

The first task in preparing your hard disk is to boot the server using the version of DOS supplied with your computer.

Next, make at least two full server backups on tape or other storage media. Remember, all of the data on the server will be destroyed during the installation process. If the computer is currently being used as a server, make sure to back up the network security information as well as the file system.

The third task is to create a temporary boot diskette. Interestingly, this is a task that is often overlooked. Because the FDISK and FORMAT utilities (used later) wipe out existing data, you'll find yourself in the unenviable position of trying to make a boot diskette on a computer with no data. If this happens, you'll either need to find an identically configured computer or restore the data from tape.

To make the diskette bootable, insert a blank diskette in drive A and type

```
FORMAT A: /S
```

This procedure formats the diskette and copies COMMAND.COM and two hidden system files to the root directory. After the diskette is formatted, you'll need to use the DOS COPY or XCOPY commands to copy two important utilities to the boot diskette: FDISK.EXE and FORMAT.COM. Also, don't forget the CD-ROM drivers and configuration files. In addition, you may want to copy a few other DOS programs such as EDIT.COM (to edit ASCII files), QBASIC.EXE (which is required by EDIT.COM), MEM.EXE (to display information about available RAM), and MSD.EXE (to confirm which interrupts and memory addresses are in use).

TIP

Instead of making a temporary boot diskette, you can use the NetWare 4 License diskette that comes with your system. It is a bootable diskette that contains a limited version of Novell DOS 7 as well as the FDISK and FORMAT utilities. If you use this approach, you'll need to make sure that you have your CD-ROM installation program available, so that you can reinstall the CD-ROM drivers after you reformat the DOS partition. Another disadvantage of this approach is that you may run into DOS version mismatch problems if you try to use DOS utilities from your original version of DOS. Aah, it's not worth the trouble. Use a clean boot diskette.

The fourth task involves using the DOS FDISK utility to delete existing partitions and create a DOS partition of 15 to 35 MB, depending on your needs. Typically, your server machine will have a DOS partition occupying the entire internal disk—unless it is currently being used as a server. If so, it will probably contain a DOS partition and a NetWare partition.

You're going to need a large-enough DOS partition to support disk drivers, LAN drivers, name space modules, the SERVER.EXE boot file, and repair utilities. If you plan to store additional utilities on the DOS partition—such as diagnostic software, mouse drivers, SCSI drivers, and antivirus software—you'll need even more space. Although Novell recommends a minimum of 15 MB for the DOS partition, you may want to increase it to 35 MB to accommodate miscellaneous drivers and utilities. You'd hate to run out of DOS space at this point.

To execute the FDISK utility, make sure your temporary boot disk is in Drive A, and then type

    A:
    FDISK

The main FDISK screen will be displayed, as shown in Figure 6.8. Follow the appropriate menu options to delete any existing partitions, and then create a new DOS partition of 15 to 35 MB and designate it as "active." Leave the rest of the hard disk as free space, so that it can be converted into a NetWare partition later, in Stage 4.

FIGURE 6.8

The Main Menu of FDISK

```
                        MS-DOS Version 6
                     Fixed Disk Setup Program
                (C)Copyright Microsoft Corp. 1983 - 1993

                          FDISK Options

     Current fixed disk drive: 1

     Choose one of the following:

     1. Create DOS partition or Logical DOS Drive
     2. Set active partition
     3. Delete partition or Logical DOS Drive
     4. Display partition information

     Enter choice: [1]




     Press Esc to exit FDISK
```

REAL WORLD

In some cases, it's easier to troubleshoot server problems if you increase the size of the DOS partition 1 MB for every 1 MB of server RAM. For instance, if your server has 16 MB of RAM, you might want to increase your DOS partition to 31 MB (15 MB + 16 MB), plus additional space for miscellaneous drivers and utilities.

Refer to either of the case studies at the end of the chapter for a detailed, step-by-step discussion of how to use FDISK to create and delete DOS partitions. You can also consult the DOS manual that came with your computer for further information.

When you exit the FDISK program, the computer will reboot. Key in the correct date and time when you are prompted. If this is your only server and the date or time is incorrect, you will probably want to change the "hardware" date and time using the CMOS setup program built into your computer. See the manual that came with your computer for further information.

The fifth task involves formatting the DOS partition and making it bootable. This can be accomplished by typing

```
FORMAT C: /S
```

After you have formatted the DOS partition, remove the temporary boot diskette from drive A and reboot the server. Then, move on to Step 2.

Step 2: Configure the CD-ROM Drive

At this point, you might want to use the DOS COPY command to copy the files from the temporary boot diskette to the DOS partition. You don't need to install the full version of DOS unless it tickles your fancy. Next, you'll need to update the CONFIG.SYS and AUTOEXEC.BAT files to automatically load any device drivers necessary—such as the ones needed to make your CD-ROM function as a DOS device. An alternate method would be to use the installation program that came with the CD-ROM drive.

Here's a typical example. The following two lines are required in CONFIG.SYS for the Adaptec 1542 SCSI CD-ROM adapter:

```
DEVICE=A:\ADAPTEC\ASPI4DOS.SYS /D
DEVICE=A:\ADAPTEC\ASPI CD:SYS /D:ASPICD0
```

In addition, the following line is required in the AUTOEXEC.BAT file:

```
A: \DOS\MSCDEX.EXE /D:ASPICD0 /M:12 /S
```

TIP

Make sure to copy any and all CD-ROM drivers from the server disk before you run FDISK or FORMAT. Doing so afterward doesn't help you because the drivers are gone.

After you have updated AUTOEXEC.BAT and CONFIG.SYS with the appropriate device drivers, remove any diskettes from drive A and boot the computer for the changes you made to take effect. You then need to switch to the root of the CD-ROM drive by typing

`D:` *(or the appropriate drive letter)*
`CD \`

TIP

When you purchase a CD-ROM drive, make sure that it can also be used as a NetWare device. This is made possible using the CD-ROM NLM from NetWare 4. Make sure that the CD-ROM is installed on a separate SCSI adapter from that being used by the hard drive, because NetWare 4 sometimes hangs if the CD-ROM drive and hard disk are attached to the same adapter.

Step 3: Run INSTALL.BAT and select the server language

The INSTALL.BAT program automates most of your early NetWare 4 install steps. To begin, access INSTALL.BAT from the CD-ROM directory by typing

```
INSTALL
```

TIP

You can abort the installation process at nearly any point by pressing Alt+F10. You can continue the installation at a later time by rebooting the server, executing SERVER.EXE from the DOS prompt, loading INSTALL.NLM, and executing each installation step manually. Alternately, you can restart the installation from the beginning by executing the INSTALL.BAT program found in the root of the NetWare 4 Installation CD-ROM.

When you execute INSTALL.BAT, it starts by asking you a rather strange question:

Which language do you want?

A screen similar to Figure 6.9 appears. Choose the Select this line to install in English option from the NetWare Install menu if you want the installation instructions to be displayed in English. Choose one of the other four options (Deutsch, Español, Français, or Italiano) if you want the installation instructions to be displayed in another language.

QUIZ

To them, "mutual intelligibility" is a necessity. To many of us, it's a mystery. Who are they?

(Q6-2)

F I G U R E 6.9

Selecting a Language in INSTALL.BAT

▶ · ◀

REAL WORLD

If you happen to have one of the early releases of the NetWare 4 Installation CD-ROM, you won't get an opportunity to select alternative languages. CD-ROMs of this vintage display installation instructions only in English. If you want to use a language other than English, make sure the front of your NetWare 4 Installation CD-ROM disk lists Deutsch, English, Español, Français, and Italiano.

Next, you will be asked several questions about the type of installation you want. When you are prompted, choose NetWare Server Installation.

When you are asked what product you want to install, select NetWare 4.1.

Finally, when you are asked what type of installation you want to perform, as shown in Figure 6.10, select Custom Installation of NetWare 4.1.

▶ · ◀

F I G U R E 6.10

*Simple and Custom
Installation Options in
INSTALL.BAT*

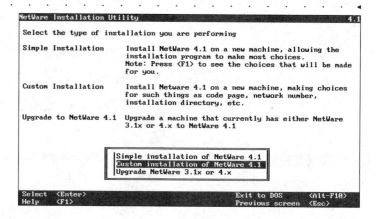

Before proceeding, NetWare checks your server to see if it contains a DOS partition of 15 MB or more and enough free space to perform a NetWare 4 installation. If not, the installation program displays a warning and asks if you still want to continue. If you receive this error message, press Alt+F10 to exit the installation program, and then fix the problem before you begin again.

Now, we're really making progress. I'm starting to get goose bumps; how about you?

Step 4: Assign the Server Name and IPX Internal Network Number

Next, you will be prompted for the server name. It can be 2 to 47 characters long. You should choose a name that's brief and easily recognizable—such as the department name, the location, the primary purpose of the server, or an abbreviated concatenation of such information. Characters that are not allowed include spaces, " * + , \ / : ; = ? [and]. Also, the first character in the server name cannot be a period.

A fairly sophisticated server-naming scheme recommended by Novell includes the use of a set of three three-character codes separated by hyphens (representing the location, division, and server number, respectively). You can use whatever standard you wish for designating these codes, as long as they're consistent. For instance, if your company only has servers in major cities with commercial airports, you could use the three-character airline city code (such as LAX) to designate the location, because all commercial airports in the world have distinct codes. The first server installed in the Small Consumer Electronics Division office in Los Angeles, for instance, could be designated as LAX-SCE-001.

As you saw in Chapter 4, it is wise to plan for future growth when you design a naming scheme. For instance, just because the company only has offices in major cities at the present time doesn't mean this will always be the case.

One disadvantage of this approach is the difficulty in specifying clear standards with only three-character codes. For instance, does the code "IRV" represent Irvine, California, or Irving, Texas? Also, don't forget that you may have network administrators in a number of countries speaking various languages. What might seem like an obvious choice to one person might make no sense whatsoever to someone else. Another disadvantage is that an 11-character server name might prove to be very inconvenient if you're not a good typist. Refer to Chapter 4 for details on ACME's naming standards.

Once you enter the server name, you will be prompted for a one- to eight-digit IPX *internal network number*. This is an eight-digit hexadecimal number used to uniquely identify this server on the internetwork. You can either accept the randomly generated IPX internal network number displayed on the screen or enter a new one. You'll probably want to designate a number that is recognizable, because many troubleshooting tools represent servers by their IPX numbers (TRACK ON, for example). The numbers 0 and FFFFFFFF are reserved by NetWare and cannot be used. Darn.

As a final check, you'll need to make sure that both the server name and IPX internal network number are unique. In other words, if you have a server named SALES at one location, you can't have another server with that same name anywhere else on the WAN.

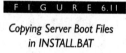

TIP

It's a good idea to develop a documented naming convention for server names and IPX internal network numbers. This will help you to quickly identify a server when necessary. When you're asked to supply a server name, press F1 to display suggested server naming rules.

Step 5: Copy the Server Boot Files to the DOS Partition

Next, the system will display the default source and destination paths for copying server boot files—this is shown in Figure 6.11. You'll notice that the default destination path is C:\NWSERVER. The defaults should be just fine in this case. Press F4 if you need to change the default destination path. As soon as you make your selection, the system will automatically copy a number of server boot files from the CD-ROM to the directory you indicated (typically, C:\NWSERVER).

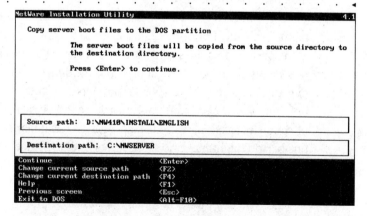

F I G U R E 6.11

Copying Server Boot Files in INSTALL.BAT

These files enable you to activate the server from the DOS partition and get things started. They include SERVER.EXE, disk drivers, and special LAN drivers. In addition, NetWare 4 copies disk and volume utilities to this directory, including VREPAIR.NLM. Once INSTALL is done copying files, we move on to the final step in Stage 1: entering the server's locale and filename information.

Step 6: Select the Server Locale and Filename Format

Once the server boot files have been copied to the C:\NWSERVER directory, INSTALL displays the default locale information (see Figure 6.12). Locale information is used to customize server language and keyboard settings. These parameters include

▸ Country code—a three-character code that designates the server's physical country

▸ Code page—a three-character code that designates the character code set for ASCII

▸ Keyboard mapping—a country-specific keyboard mapping for non-U.S. keyboards (such as Japanese Kanji)

You'll notice that the default values are set up for the United States, so you'll need to change them if your server is located elsewhere. When the locale configuration is correct, select the Press <Enter> here to continue field and press Enter.

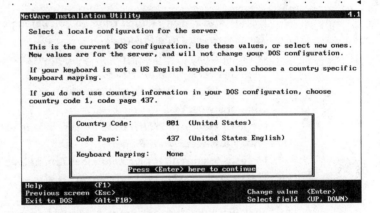

F I G U R E   6.12

Locale Configuration Screen in INSTALL.BAT

Next, you'll be asked to select the filename format. The DOS Filename Format enforces DOS naming restrictions as set forth by your country code and code page. The NetWare Filename Format allows you to use uppercase and lowercase letters as well as graphics. You should probably choose the DOS Filename Format because it prevents NETx workstations from creating non-DOS filenames. When you're asked to choose a filename format, select DOS Filename Format.

TIP

If you choose the DOS Filename Format, you can still use OS/2 or Macintosh filenames. You'll just have to rely on NetWare 4's built-in name space feature.

Well, that does it for the DOS partition. Now, you'll need to transfer server control from DOS to the NetWare partition. This is accomplished using SERVER.EXE. This is where the ride gets really thrilling. Hold on to your lunch.

QUIZ

Speaking of thrills, let's take a trip to the "Island of Imperfection." There are three tribes there—the Pukkas, who always tell the truth; the Wotta-Woppas, who never tell the truth; and the Shilli-Shallas, who make statements that are alternatively true and false or false and true.

An explorer lands on the island and questions three natives—Tom, Dick, and Harry—as follows:

Explorer asks Tom: *Which tribe do you belong to?*
Tom answers: *I'm a Pukka.*
He asks Dick: *(i) Which tribe do you belong to?*
Dick answers: *I'm a Wotta-Woppa.*
He asks Dick: *(ii) Was Tom telling the truth?*
Dick answers: *Yes.*
He asks Harry: *(i) Which tribe do you belong to?*
Harry answers: *I'm a Pukka.*
He asks Harry: *(ii) Which tribe does Tom belong to?*
Harry answers: *He's a Shilli-Shalla.*

To which tribe does each man belong? Hmmmm.

(Q6-3)

STAGE 2: RUN SERVER.EXE

Your purpose in Stage 1 was to prepare the server hard disk for installation. Most of the first few steps dealt with setting up the DOS partition for booting. During Stage 1, you booted the system to DOS, backed up existing data, deleted existing partitions, configured the CD-ROM as a DOS device, executed INSTALL.BAT, assigned a server name and IPX internal network number, copied server boot files to the DOS partition, and selected the locale information and filename format. No wonder you're already tired.

During Stage 2, the focus shifts from DOS to the NetWare 4 operating system. This is accomplished in three easy steps:

▸ Step 7—Start the server. The NetWare 4 operating system is loaded into memory when SERVER.EXE is executed. These happen automatically.

▸ Step 8—Determine whether to customize startup file SET parameters.

▸ Step 9—Indicate whether you want the AUTOEXEC.BAT file to automatically execute SERVER.EXE whenever the server is booted.

It's as easy as 1-2-3. Let's take a closer look at the quick and easy steps of Stage 2.

Step 7: Start the Server (Happens Automatically)

SERVER.EXE is the main NetWare 4 operating system file—that's what you paid for. When SERVER is automatically executed by INSTALL.BAT, the batch file loads NetWare 4 into server memory and kicks out COMMAND.COM. Now your server is up and running, but you can't do anything with it. It's barely functioning on life support. This is because connectivity has not yet been established between NetWare 4 and internal resources, such as hard disk(s) and NIC(s). To jump-start the server, you'll need to load disk and LAN drivers. But not so fast; that's Stage 3. We're not done with Stage 2 yet. Patience, patience.

TIP

SERVER.EXE runs from the DOS prompt. When you execute it, the server reboots and flushes all DOS programs from memory. This represents a dramatic shift in power from the conservative DOS operating system to liberal NetWare 4. You can tell the system is rebooting because the lights on the computer flash. Is this a political statement? Who knows?

Refer to Figure 6.13 for a snapshot of the console when SERVER.EXE is loaded. Notice the time, date, and SPEED index. Also, note how the server name is displayed with the colon prompt (:). Pretty clever. Now let's breathe life into this otherwise lifeless hunk of silicon—onward to disk and LAN drivers. Not so fast. There are a few more optional steps left in Stage 2.

▶ . . . . ◀

FIGURE 6.13

The SERVER.EXE Console Prompt

```
Loading OS at 00310000

Loading . . .
System Console
Novell NetWare 4.10 November 8, 1994
Processor speed: 5476
(Type SPEED at the command prompt for an explanation
of the speed
rating)
LCONFIG.SYS file exists, overriding default locale
values

LABS-SRV1:
```

Step 8: Customize SET Commands for STARTUP.NCF

Speaking of optional steps—this one fits the bill. INSTALL gives you the option of adding special SET commands to the server startup files. If you select Yes, an edit box will be displayed in which you can specify customized startup commands. For example, if you have disk, CD-ROM, or other devices that use ASPI, add the following line to your STARTUP.NCF file:

```
SET RESERVED BUFFERS BELOW 16MB = 200
```

To determine if a particular device uses ASPI, consult the documentation from the manufacturer. Press F10 when you're finished.

If you don't want to specify any customized SET commands, select No instead.

THE BRAIN

Refer to the Modify the STARTUP.NCF File and Modify the AUTOEXEC.NCF File sections in Chapter 3 of the *Novell NetWare 4 Installation* manual for information on updating NetWare 4 startup files. Also, refer to the SET command section in the *Novell NetWare 4 Utilities* manual for detailed information about NetWare 4 SET commands.

Step 9: Customize Server AUTOEXEC.BAT

Next, you'll be asked whether you'd like the AUTOEXEC.BAT file to automatically execute SERVER.EXE whenever the server is booted. If you choose Yes, INSTALL will add SERVER to the top of your AUTOEXEC.BAT file. If you choose No, you'll have to switch to the directory containing the server boot files (typically C:\NWSERVER) and type SERVER whenever you want to load NetWare 4—too much work.

QUIZ

I've got a great word for ya: **Mukluk.** *But what does it mean?*

(Q6-4)

After you traverse the final two options, INSTALL.BAT moves on to Stage 3. Now you finally get to breathe life into your stagnant server by loading the NetWare drivers.

STAGE 3: LOAD THE NETWARE DRIVERS

In Stage 2, INSTALL.BAT loaded the core NetWare 4 OS into server RAM with SERVER.EXE. It also gave you the option of customizing startup file SET parameters and determining whether the AUTOEXEC.BAT file should automatically load SERVER.EXE. Even though our server is alive [as shown by the colon prompt (:)], we can't do anything with it.

Stage 3 jump-starts the server by loading and configuring server disk and LAN drivers. It also binds the LAN driver to IPX or other communications protocol(s). Here's how it works:

- ▸ Step 10—Load the server disk and CD-ROM driver(s). Disk drivers control communication between the server's CPU and the internal disk controller. CD-ROM drivers control communication between the server's CPU and the internal CD-ROM drive.

- ▸ Step 11—Load the server LAN driver(s). A LAN driver is used as an interface between the file server and the internal NIC. Choosing the appropriate LAN driver enables communications to occur between the internal network board and external cabling system. Also, we'll need to bind IPX (or another communications protocol) to the LAN driver at this point.

With all this in mind, let's continue with "NetWare Resuscitation."

Step 10: Load the Server Disk and CD-ROM Driver(s)

Disk drivers control communication between the server's CPU and internal disk controllers. CD-ROM drivers control communication between the server's CPU and internal CD-ROM drives. In many cases, you'll need to select both a disk driver and a CD-ROM driver—otherwise they will conflict.

NetWare 4 includes an extensive list of internal drivers, as Figure 6.14 shows. Select the appropriate disk driver from the list and configure it with correct hardware parameters. You can usually accept the default settings unless the switches on your drive have been changed. If the hardware settings have been changed, refer to the manufacturer's documentation for further information.

If your server has more than one hard disk and they're connected to the same controller, you'll only need to load one driver. If the hard disks are connected to different controllers, you'll need to load multiple drivers.

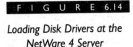

F I G U R E 6.14

Loading Disk Drivers at the NetWare 4 Server

TIP

If you're installing NetWare 4 from a CD-ROM that is sharing a SCSI adapter with another internal or external device (such as a hard disk or tape unit), you may find that the system hangs when you are loading drivers or copying files. If this happens, obtain updated drivers from the manufacturer of the SCSI adapter.

Earlier versions of NetWare employed an architecture called *monolithic architecture.* It used a single disk driver with a .DSK filename extension as the interface between NetWare and the disk controller. NetWare 4 uses a newer architecture, called *NetWare Peripheral Architecture (NPA),* in which two drivers share this responsibility: a Host Adapter Module (with—what else?—a .HAM filename extension) and a Custom Device Module (with a .CDM filename extension).

The advantage of the monolithic architecture is that it's been around much longer than NPA and individual drivers have been more thoroughly tested by Novell and third parties. A disadvantage of the monolithic architecture is that the driver selected must support all connected devices.

NPA, on the other hand, provides better scalability, because each hardware device uses an individual CDM. Also, NPA will be the primary disk driver architecture used in future releases of NetWare. Table 6.1 lists Novell's monolithic disk drivers, and Table 6.2 lists Novell's newer NPA disk drivers, HAMS, and CDMs.

T A B L E   6.1

Novell's Monolithic Disk Drivers

COMPUTER ARCHITECTURE	CONTROLLER	DISK DRIVER
Industry Standard Architecture (ISA)	AT class	ISADISK
	IDE (ATA)	IDE
Extended Industry Standard Architecture (EISA)	AT	ISADISK
	IDE (ATA)	IDE
	EISA (vendor proprietary)	See vendor
MicroChannel Architecture (MCA)	ESDI	PS2ESDI
	IBM SCSI	PS2SCSI

T A B L E   6.2

Novell's Newer NPA Disk Drivers

COMPUTER ARCHITECTURE	CONTROLLER	HAM	CDM
Industry Standard Architecture (ISA)	AT class		
	IDE (ATA)	IDEATA.HAM	IDEHD.CDM (hard disk)
	Adaptec 154X	SCSI154X.HAM	SCSIHD.CDM (hard disk)
			SCSICD.CDM (CD-ROM drive)
			SCSIMO.CDM (magneto-optical drive)
			SCSI2TP.CDM (tape drive)

COMPUTER ARCHITECTURE	CONTROLLER	HAM	CDM
Extended Industry Architecture (EISA)	AT class IDE (ATA)	IDEATA.HAM	IDEHD.CDM (hard disk)
	Adaptec 154X	SCSI154X.HAM	SCSIHD.CDM (hard disk)
			SCSICD.CDM (CD-ROM drive)
			SCSIMO.CDM (magneto-optical drive)
			SCSI2TP.CDM (tape drive)
EISA vendor proprietary		See vendor data	See vendor data
MicroChannel Architecture (hard [MCA] disk)	IBM SCSI	SCSIPS2.HAM	SCSIHD.CDM
			SCSICD.CDM (CD-ROM drive)
			SCSIMO.CDM (magneto-optical drive)
			SCSI2TP.CDM (tape drive)

THE BRAIN

For a more detailed discussion of **NPA**, refer to the **NetWare Peripheral Architecture (NPA)** section in **Chapter 3** of the *Novell NetWare 4 Installation* manual.

Step 11: Load the Server LAN Driver(s)

The NetWare 4 LAN driver serves as an interface between the server and its internal NIC. Activating the appropriate LAN driver enables you to communicate between the internal network board and external cabling system. Once again, NetWare 4 includes an extensive list of internal LAN drivers, as you can see in Figure 6.15.

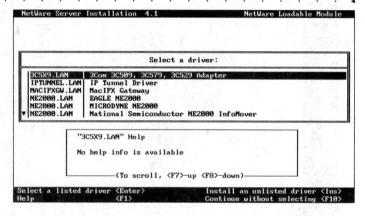

F I G U R E 6.15

Loading Disk Drivers at the NetWare 4 Server

After choosing the correct NIC, you'll be prompted for various configuration parameters, including the communication protocol(s) you wish to use, interrupts, a port address, node address, and frame type. IPX is the default protocol for NetWare and will be chosen automatically.

TIP

The protocols selected at this stage are, by definition, nonrouting protocols. If you require routing protocols, you will need to configure them after the server is installed by loading the **INSTALL.NLM** utility and choosing the **Configure Network Protocols** option.

In addition, a screen will pop up for each frame type bound to IPX. *Binding* is the process of attaching a protocol to a specific server NIC and starting communications. When you bIND IPX to a LAN driver, you must specify the *external network address*. This is a unique hexadecimal number that distinguishes the physical LAN cabling. Unlike the IPX internal network number, the external network address can be the same for two servers as long as they are attached to the same physical cabling trunk. Many times the internal address is alphabetic (using A–F) and the external address is numeric. This differentiates the two.

TIP

Novell provides a new service called The IPX Registry that keeps track of IPX internal network numbers for you. This ensures that no two servers in your organization share the same number. It also ensures that no two servers *in the world* share the same number. Remember, Novell's goal is to have a private, secure Internet running around the world by the year 2000. What will all the machines be running? NetWare 7.21?

Next, each NIC can support multiple *frame types*. The frame type identifies the packet architecture for LAN communications. It's kind of confusing, but a single cabling trunk can support multiple frame types simultaneously—but they have to use different external network addresses. Weird, huh? Anyway, NetWare 4 defaults to Ethernet_802.2, whereas NetWare 3.11 defaults to Ethernet_802.3. Be careful.

Refer to Table 6.3 for a list of commonly used Novell LAN drivers.

STAGE 4: LOAD INSTALL.NLM

In Stage 3, we established server connectivity by loading and configuring disk drivers and LAN drivers. In addition, we bound IPX [(or other communication protocol(s)] to the internal NIC and established an external network address for each frame type. Now it's time to shift control over to INSTALL.NLM and get serious about NetWare partitions, the SYS: volume, and SYSTEM and PUBLIC files.

ZEN

"History is about to be rewritten by two guys that can't spell."

Bill & Ted's Excellent Adventure

T A B L E 6.3

Some Common Novell LAN Drivers

CABLING SYSTEM	NETWORK BOARD	LAN DRIVER
ARCnet	RX-Net	TRXNET.LAN
	RX-NET II	
	RX-NET/2	
Ethernet	NE/2	NE2.LAN
	NE/2T	NE2_32 LAN
	NE/2-32	NE1000.LAN
	NE1000 ASSY 950–054401	NE2000.LAN
	NE1000 ASSY 810–160–001	NE2100.LAN
	NE2000 ASSY 810–149	NE1500T.LAN
	NE2000T ASSY 810–000220	
	NE2100 ASSY 810–000209	
	NE1500T ASSY 810–000214	
	NE3200	
	NE32HUB	NE32HUB.LAN
Token Ring	NTR2000	NTR2000.LAN

Here's what we have to look forward to in Stage 4:

- ▸ Step 12—Determine whether to configure the CD-ROM drive as a DOS or NetWare device. You may be warned about a potential conflict with the CD-ROM driver.

- ▸ Step 13—Create NetWare disk partition(s). By default, NetWare 4 creates a single NetWare partition occupying all available server space. Also, you will get the opportunity to configure disk mirroring and the hot fix redirection area.

- ▸ Step 14—Create NetWare volume(s). By default, NetWare 4 creates a single SYS: volume occupying the entire disk partition. You will also have a chance to configure other file system options, such as data migration, file compression, and block suballocation.

- ▸ Step 15—License the NetWare OS. At this point, you will be prompted for a valid, unique License diskette.

- ▸ Step 16—Reestablish a server-to-server connection (only applicable with the "server-to-server" installation method).

- ▸ Step 17—Copy SYSTEM and PUBLIC files to the default SYS: volume and determine whether to install optional file groups.

The server is finally starting to wake up. This is our opportunity to pump some serious muscle. INSTALL.NLM is our friend.

Step 12: Configure the CD-ROM as a DOS or NetWare Device

In some cases, an error message such as the one shown earlier in Figure 6.3 will be displayed. This indicates a chance that there is a conflict with the active CD-ROM driver. If the message appears, try selecting the following option: Continue accessing the CD-ROM via DOS.

Step 13: Create NetWare Disk Partition(s)

Every NetWare 4 server requires at least one disk partition. Only one NetWare partition is allowed per hard disk, but each partition can consist of up to eight volume segments. You'll be given two options for creating NetWare partitions: manual or automatic.

If you choose to create disk partitions automatically, NetWare 4 will create a single partition using all free disk space beyond the DOS partition — as seen in Figure 6.16. With this method, you will not be given the option of mirroring or duplexing server disk(s).

► . . . . ◄

F I G U R E 6.16

Creating NetWare Disk Partitions in INSTALL.NLM

On the other hand, you should choose to partition the disk manually if

► You wish to selectively delete existing disk partitions.

► You want to specify the size of the NetWare partition.

► You need other operating systems to reside on the same disk.

► You need to mirror or duplex disks.

► You want to change the size of the hot fix redirection area.

TIP

If your disk size seems smaller than anticipated, it may be because NetWare lists the true size in megabytes (that is, 1,048,576 rather than 1 million). Also, the disk size listed by NetWare does not show the disk space that has been allocated for the hot fix redirection area.

After creating the NetWare partitions on each server drive, you can optionally choose to mirror or duplex them—if you have a server with two or more hard disks. With *mirroring,* data is duplicated on two disks using the same controller. With *duplexing,* NetWare duplicates the data on two disks using different controllers. Duplexing, which is the more expensive of the two options, offers greater safety because the likelihood of losing two disk controllers at the same time is lower than that of losing two hard drives.

You're halfway there. Before you can store files on the new disk partition, you need to define at least one volume on it. Look out, that's Step 14.

Step 14: Create NetWare Volume(s)

By default, NetWare 4 allocates all available disk space (beyond the DOS partition) to a single volume called SYS: (see Figure 6.17). You can create additional volumes by reducing the size of the SYS: volume and allocating that space to other segments. For servers with multiple hard disks, NetWare automatically creates one volume per disk.

You can assign whatever name you want to any volume other than SYS:. The SYS: volume is required because it houses all the NetWare 4 SYSTEM and PUBLIC files. Chapter 10 takes a closer look at volumes. Also, the SYS: volume is given a "logical" name in the NDS tree: "*server*_SYS." For example, the first ACME volume is named LABS-SRV1_SYS.

After you create the server volumes, you have the chance to modify various volume parameters. These are shown in Figure 6.17. They include block size, volume segments, file compression, block suballocation, and data migration. The defaults for these last three parameters are

- File compression: ON

- Block suballocation: ON

- Data migration: OFF

FIGURE 6.17

*Modifying Volume
Parameters in
INSTALL.NLM*

Chapter 1 of this book gives additional information on file compression, block suballocation, and data migration. Also, if you plan to use Novell's High Capacity Storage System (HCSS), you'll want to press the Enter key twice on each of these fields to toggle them to the opposite of the default values.

THE BRAIN

Novell's High Capacity Storage System (HCSS) extends the storage capability of a NetWare server by moving files between a faster low-capacity system (the hard disk) and a slower high-capacity system (rewritable optical disks in a jukebox). This process is transparent to the user. Users (and programs) use the same NetWare commands and function calls to access directories and files in both systems.

See the High Capacity Storage System section of the *Novell NetWare 4 Concepts* manual for an overview of HCSS. For an in-depth exploration of this topic, refer to the article titled "Inside Novell's High Capacity Storage System (HCSS)" beginning on page 1 of the February 1995 issue of the *Novell Application Notes* publication.

Step 15: License the NetWare Operating System

Next, you will be asked to insert the NetWare 4 License diskette into drive A: (A:). This was shown earlier in Figure 6.4. Make sure to use a unique License diskette— NetWare is kind of picky about these things. If you use the same License diskette on two different servers, NetWare 4 will display a license violation warning. And that's not all. It will also cut the user connection number down to 1. This gives you just enough maneuvering room to revalidate the license. Nice try.

ZEN

"If you can't find the truth right where you are, where else do you think you will find it?"

Anonymous

NetWare 4 licensing works a bit differently than in previous versions of NetWare. In NetWare 3, licensing was built into SERVER.EXE. This meant Novell had to manufacture 5 million different SERVER.EXE files—too much work. So, in NetWare 4 designers developed a way of "validating" a server and "binding" the license information to a generic SERVER.EXE file. This is accomplished using the Server Connection License diskette. Just think of it: $47,995 for a single 3.5-inch floppy diskette. Now that's a serious markup.

After you've successfully licensed your NetWare 4 server, make sure to store the License diskette in a safe place (on your refrigerator). You may even want to make a copy of the diskette and store it off-site as part of your disaster-recovery strategy.

Step 16: Reestablish Server-to-Server Connection (If Needed)

If you are using the "server-to-server" installation method, you'll need to reestablish your remote server connection at this point. This involves identifying the previously used username and password. Here's why: Earlier, when the LAN driver was loaded, we lost our background connection to the other server. IPX can only handle one type of communication at a time, per NIC. Fortunately, INSTALL is smart enough to recognize what has happened. It automatically recalls the source server path from memory, but you have to reenter the password.

Now it's time to move on.

Step 17: Copying Optional NetWare Files

After you've licensed your destination server and reconnected to the source server (if applicable), a new screen pops up. This one lists the default source and destination paths for copying NetWare 4 optional files (see Figure 6.18). If you're installing from the server's CD-ROM, you can probably accept the default—that's from the D: drive to the SYS: volume. Press F3 if you want to change the defaults.

Initially, all of the file groups are selected. To deselect a file group, select it and press Enter. Later in Step 20, we'll copy the required SYSTEM and PUBLIC files to the SYS:SYSTEM and SYS:PUBLIC directories.

F I G U R E 6.18

*Copying Optional
NetWare 4 File Groups*

We are well on our way to NetWare 4 Nirvana. Just a couple more Zen icons, and we'll be there. Also, for those of you out there in NetWare 3 land—this completes the "familiar" part of our show. Please exit to the rear of the cabin. Now, we're going to explore something radically different—installation of "the Cloud."

QUIZ

Speaking of "radically different," here's one for the record books: George, John, Arthur, and David are married, but not necessarily respectively, to Christine, Eve, Dana, and Rose. They remember that at a party years ago various predictions had been made. George had said that John would not marry Christine. John had said that Arthur would marry Dana. Arthur predicted that whoever David married, it would not be Eve. David, who at that time was more interested in horses than matrimony, had predicted that Gallant Dancer would win the Kentucky Derby. The only one to predict correctly was the man who later married Dana.

Who married whom? Did Gallant Dancer win the race? Who shot Mr. Burns?

(Q6-5)

STAGE 5: INSTALL NETWARE DIRECTORY SERVICES (NDS)

In Stage 4, we set up the NetWare partition. This involved six steps: CD-ROM configuration, NetWare partition creation, volume definition, licensing, reestablishment of the server-to-server connection, and finally, the copying of optional NetWare files. Now our server is alive and well.

The most important stage remains. In Stage 5 we finally get to install "the Cloud"— NetWare Directory Services (NDS). This involves tree names, server context, and time zone information. And all of this activity in only *one* step—think of it as a "leap." Let's take a closer look.

Step 18: Install NetWare Directory Services (NDS)

Have you ever watched cloud seeding? It helps build bigger clouds to quench the thirst of Mother Earth. Well, in Step 18 we get to do some cloud seeding of our own. It all starts with a simple question (Figure 6.19):

```
Is this the first NetWare 4 server?
```

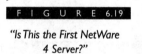

F I G U R E 6.19

"Is This the First NetWare 4 Server?"

If Yes, you'll be asked to input a tree name. Use something creative such as "Elm" or "Redwood." If No, you'll need to choose from a list of existing trees. This will be the new home of this server. Also, we'll tell NetWare 4 where to put the server in the tree at a later time.

Next, INSTALL.NLM will shift over to time zone information. Remember, every NetWare 4 server has to be a time server of some type—most are Secondary time servers. The Time Zone Information screen prompts you to choose among 18 different time zones. This helps automate the input of parameters into the Time Configuration window (see Figure 6.20). As you can see, there's a ton of complex time parameters required for every server: Time server type (Single Reference, Reference, Primary, or Secondary); Standard time offset from UTC (Universal Time Coordinated); Daylight savings time (DST); and DST offset.

F I G U R E   6.20

NetWare 4 Time Configuration Window in INSTALL.NLM

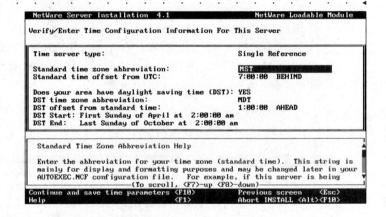

```
NetWare Server Installation  4.1                    NetWare Loadable Module

Verify/Enter Time Configuration Information For This Server

 Time server type:                                 Single Reference

 Standard time zone abbreviation:                  MST
 Standard time offset from UTC:                    7:00:00   BEHIND

 Does your area have daylight saving time (DST):   YES
 DST time zone abbreviation:                       MDT
 DST offset from standard time:                    1:00:00   AHEAD
 DST Start: First Sunday of April at  2:00:00 am
 DST End:   Last Sunday of October at 2:00:00 am

 Standard Time Zone Abbreviation Help

 Enter the abbreviation for your time zone (standard time).  This string is
 mainly for display and formatting purposes and may be changed later in your
 AUTOEXEC.NCF configuration file.   For example, if this server is being
                    (To scroll, <F7>-up <F8>-down)
Continue and save time parameters <F10>          Previous screen     <Esc>
Help                              <F1>           Abort INSTALL <Alt><F10>
```

THE BRAIN

Refer to Chapter 3 of the *Novell NetWare 4 Getting Started* manual or Chapter 7 of the *Supervising the Network II* manual for further information.

TIP

Entering incorrect time synchronization information can cause major problems. Don't change the default values unless you know what you're doing.

Next, we get to define the "Cloud." You will be asked for the server's Directory tree context, as shown in Figure 6.21. The context is composed of an optional Country code (example: C=US), an Organization name (example: O=ACME), and optionally, up to three levels of Organizational Units (for example, OU=NORAD and OU=LABS). In most cases, Novell doesn't recommend the use of Country containers. They are reserved for public service providers.

As a matter of fact, the only way to define a Country container is to manually add it to the Server Context field. Notice that there's no option for it.

Also, you'll be asked for an Admin password. If this is the first server in the tree, you get to make one up. Otherwise, you'll need to input the "real" Admin password. This controls who adds servers to *your* tree.

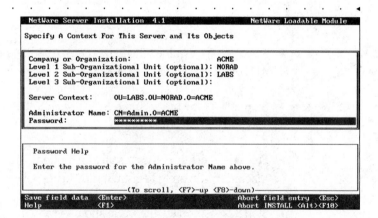

F I G U R E   6.21

NDS Server Context Screen in INSTALL.NLM

Once you have provided all of the requested information, you'll be asked to save the directory information and continue. A summary window will be displayed listing the Directory tree name, Directory context, and Admin username. You should write down this information and keep it in a safe place. Don't forget the Admin password.

Well, there you have it. All done! The server is alive and well, and walking in the clouds. I couldn't be happier for you! Now, we will end the installation process with a little "housekeeping"—creating server startup files, copying SYSTEM and PUBLIC files, and installing optional products. That's Stage 6.

ZEN

"Everything in moderation, including moderation."

Anonymous

STAGE 6: CREATE SERVER STARTUP FILES

In Stage 5, you installed NDS. As part of that step, you were asked to supply a tree name, the server context, and time zone information. You were also asked for an Admin password—new or used.

Now, it's time to finish off the custom installation with some general housekeeping tasks, including

- ▸ Step 19—Determine whether to create/modify the STARTUP.NCF and AUTOEXEC.NCF server startup files.

- ▸ Step 20—Copy the required SYSTEM and PUBLIC files to the SYS:SYSTEM and SYS:PUBLIC directories.

- ▸ Step 21—Perform other installation options, such as installing NetWare for Macintosh, Creating Registration Diskettes, Client Install, and DynaText Install.

- ▸ Step 22—Complete the installation—yeah!

- ▸ Step 23—Boot the server using the new startup files.

These steps are your life in a nutshell. Let's take a look.

Step 19: Create/Modify STARTUP.NCF and AUTOEXEC.NCF

The first housekeeping task involves two server startup files—STARTUP.NCF and AUTOEXEC.NCF. These two files automate the startup process so you don't have to perform these 23 steps every time the server is booted.

It starts with STARTUP.NCF (see Figure 6.22). STARTUP.NCF contains commands to load disk drivers, name space modules, and special SET parameters. The STARTUP.NCF file is stored in the C:\NWSERVER directory and is called by SERVER.EXE. When the system displays the proposed STARTUP.NCF file, you'll notice that it includes the disk driver and SET parameter information that you supplied earlier. How kind. Accept the defaults and continue by pressing F10.

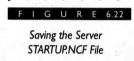

FIGURE 6.22

*Saving the Server
STARTUP.NCF File*

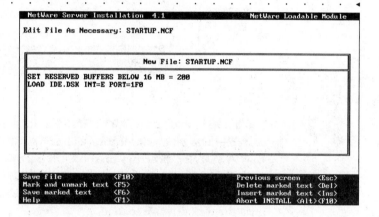

```
NetWare Server Installation  4.1                    NetWare Loadable Module
Edit File As Necessary: STARTUP.NCF


┌──────────────────────────────────────────────────────────────────────────┐
│                        New File: STARTUP.NCF                               │
├──────────────────────────────────────────────────────────────────────────┤
│SET RESERVED BUFFERS BELOW 16 MB = 200                                      │
│LOAD IDE.DSK INT=E PORT=1F0                                                 │
│                                                                            │
│                                                                            │
│                                                                            │
│                                                                            │
│                                                                            │
│                                                                            │
└──────────────────────────────────────────────────────────────────────────┘
Save file              <F10>            Previous screen      <Esc>
Mark and unmark text   <F5>             Delete marked text   <Del>
Save marked text       <F6>             Insert marked text   <Ins>
Help                   <F1>             Abort INSTALL <Alt><F10>
```

TIP

The SYS: volume is automatically mounted when the corresponding disk driver is loaded by STARTUP.NCF.

Next it's AUTOEXEC.NCF's turn (as shown in Figure 6.23). AUTOEXEC.NCF, on the other hand, contains information such as the server name, IPX internal network number, time zone information, commands to load and bind the LAN driver(s), and so on. It is stored in the SYS:SYSTEM directory and is called by the STARTUP.NCF file. Once again, you'll notice that the proposed AUTOEXEC.NCF file in Figure 6.23 includes the values we specified earlier.

F I G U R E 6.23

Saving the Server
AUTOEXEC.NCF File

TIP

You'll notice that the STARTUP.NCF and AUTOEXEC.NCF files are stored in two different locations: The STARTUP.NCF file is stored in the C:\NWSERVER directory on the DOS partition and the AUTOEXEC.NCF file is stored in the SYS:SYSTEM directory on the NetWare partition. This is because the NetWare partition doesn't exist until the disk driver is loaded.

If you need to modify the STARTUP.NCF or AUTOEXEC.NCF files at a later date, you can do so by loading the INSTALL.NLM utility and choosing NCF files options from the Install Options menu, as shown in Figure 6.24. If you choose not to create these files, you'll have to load these statements and SET parameters every time the server is booted—major drag!

F I G U R E 6.24

Configuring NCF Files with
INSTALL.NLM

Step 20: Copy the NetWare 4 SYSTEM and PUBLIC Files to SYS:

Now you finally get to copy the required NetWare 4 files to the SYS:SYSTEM and SYS:PUBLIC directories. This is the third time you have copied files to the server disk:

▶ Step 5: Copy the server boot files to the DOS partition—C:\NWSERVER.

▶ Step 17: Copy the optional NetWare 4 files to the SYS: volume.

▶ Step 20: Copy the required SYSTEM and PUBLIC files to the SYS: volume— SYS:SYSTEM and SYS:PUBLIC.

Once it's done, INSTALL returns with the Other Installation Options screen. That's Step 21.

Step 21: Perform Other Installation Options

After the SYSTEM and PUBLIC files have been copied to the SYS: volume, a list of additional options will be displayed. This was shown earlier in Figure 6.7. Any of these options can be installed now or at a later date via INSTALL.NLM (see Figure 6.24). Later in this chapter, we're going to explore three very important "Other Options:"

▶ Client Installation

▶ DynaText

▶ NetWare for Macintosh

Try to control your excitement.

Step 22: Complete the Installation

CONGRATULATIONS!

I bet you thought you'd never make it! The last two steps mark the end of a long and rewarding journey. At this point you choose Continue Installation from the Other Installation Options menu. Then, INSTALL returns with the congratulatory message in Figure 6.25.

Step 23: Boot the Server Using the Startup Files

Once you've completed the NetWare 4 custom installation, you'll need to reboot the server to make sure that it is operating properly. First type DOWN, and then RESTART SERVER to restart it.

CUSTOM INSTALLATION ROAD MAP

In case you got lost anywhere along the way, here's a road map to get you on the right track.

- ▸ Step 1— Configure the DOS partition.

- ▸ Step 2— Configure the CD-ROM drive.

- ▸ Step 3— Run INSTALL.BAT and select the server language.

- ▸ Step 4— Assign the server name and IPX internal network number.

- ▸ Step 5— Copy the server boot files to the DOS partition.

- ▸ Step 6— Select the server locale and filename format.

- ▸ Step 7— Start the server (happens automatically).

▶ Step 8— Customize SET commands for STARTUP.NCF.

▶ Step 9—Customize the server AUTOEXEC.BAT.

▶ Step 10 —Load the server disk and CD-ROM driver(s).

▶ Step 11—Load the server LAN driver(s).

▶ Step 12—Configure the CD-ROM as a DOS or NetWare device.

▶ Step 13—Create NetWare disk partition(s).

▶ Step 14—Create NetWare volume(s).

▶ Step 15—License the NetWare operating system.

▶ Step 16—Reestablish server-to-server connection (if needed).

▶ Step 17—Copy optional NetWare files.

▶ Step 18— Install NDS.

▶ Step 19—Create/modify AUTOEXEC.NCF and STARTUP.NCF.

▶ Step 20—Copy the NetWare 4 SYSTEM and PUBLIC files to SYS:.

▶ Step 21—Perform other installation options.

▶ Step 22—Complete the installation.

▶ Step 23—Boot the server using the new startup files.

ZEN

"He was 98 lbs of solid nerd until he became ..."

The Toxic Avenger

Installing Other Stuff

Okay, put down the champagne. You're not done yet! There's always other stuff that needs to be installed, namely

- Client installation

- DynaText installation

- NetWare for Macintosh

Near the end of the NetWare 4 server installation, you were given the option of performing Other Installation Items/Options. The list is pretty exhaustive (refer again to Figure 6.7):

- Create a Registration diskette.

- Upgrade 3.1*x* Print Services.

- Create DOS/MS Windows/OS2 Client Install diskettes.

- Create NetWare Upgrade/Migrate diskettes.

- Create NetWare Bookdisk diskettes.

- Install NetWare for Macintosh.

- Install NetWare MHS.

- Configure NetWare protocols.

- Install an additional server language.

- Change the server language.

- Install on-line documentation and viewers.

You can access these options at anytime by loading INSTALL.NLM and choosing Product Options.

This section will discuss three additional installation options in detail, including NetWare 4 DOS/MS Windows/OS2 client software, DynaText on-line documentation, and NetWare for Macintosh. Let's start with the client.

CLIENT INSTALLATION

Earlier versions of NetWare used a program such as WSGEN or SHGEN to generate an IPX.COM file that implemented the IPX/SPX stack and was linked to the appropriate network driver. In NetWare 4, Open Data Link Interface (ODI) drivers eliminate the need for static linking by providing a flexible way of binding a protocol stack (such as IPXODI.COM) to the driver.

The NETX.COM shell found in earlier version of NetWare has been replaced by VLM.EXE, which is a Virtual Loadable Module (VLM) manager that loads a number of other VLMs (see Chapter 13). These VLMs together form the NetWare DOS Requester, which provides support for DOS and MS Windows client workstations.

THE BRAIN

For further information on the NetWare DOS Requester, consult the NetWare DOS Requester section in the *Novell NetWare 4 Concepts* manual.

Before you begin the client installation, you'll need to install all of the appropriate network hardware (such as NIC boards, cabling, and related components) and make sure there are no hardware conflicts. Refer to Table 6.4 for some client install-related action items.

T A B L E 6.4	TYPE OF BOARD	ACTION REQUIRED
Network Board Configuration	ISA network boards	Look at the network board to determine the settings. The documentation that came with the board should describe where each setting is located.
	EISA or MCA network board	Run the workstation's reference or setup program. The program will list the settings for your network board.
	PCI local bus network boards	Run the workstation's reference or setup program. The program will list the settings for your network board.

NOTE: If you already have a network connection established, switch to the SYS:PUBLIC directory and type **NVER**, and then press Enter.

In NetWare 4, you'll use INSTALL.EXE to install the NetWare 4 DOS/Windows client software. The client software is designed so that it can simultaneously support access to NetWare 2.2, 3.1x, and 4.1 servers. During the client install, you'll be given the opportunity of designating Deutsch, English, Español, Français, or Italiano support.

The installation program creates a batch file called STARTNET.BAT that loads the appropriate software for connecting workstations to the LAN (see Chapter 12). It then gives you the option of calling this batch file from the AUTOEXEC.BAT file—automation is a good thing.

The client software can be installed from three different places:

▸ The NetWare 4 Installation CD-ROM—switch to the \CLIENT\DOSWIN directory and type INSTALL.

▸ Diskettes that you make using the CD-ROM—you can create a set of diskettes using the MAKEDISK command found in the \CLIENT\DOSWIN directory on the CD-ROM. In order to create these diskettes, you will need to type MAKEDISK A: *language* (where *language* is English, French, German, Italian, or Spanish).

▸ An existing server—you'll need to copy the appropriate directories from the NetWare 4 Installation CD-ROM, making sure that the directory structure matches the one on the CD-ROM. Then, type **INSTALL**.

Finally, here are the workstation hardware and software requirements for installing DOS and Windows client support:

- ▸ IBM PC or compatible with 8088, 80286, 80386, 80486 (SX, SLC, DX, and so on) or Pentium processor

- ▸ DOS and MS Windows (optional)

- ▸ 4 MB of hard disk space (5 MB if MS Windows software is installed)

The NetWare 4 client install places client software in the directory of your choice (the default is C:\NWCLIENT). It also configures a few workstation files for you. When you run INSTALL.EXE, it displays a data entry screen asking for all sorts of information (shown in Figure 6.26):

FIGURE 6.26

The NetWare 4 Client Installation Configuration Screen

```
NetWare Client Install   v1.21                    Tuesday  August  29, 1995  3:49pm
1. Enter the destination directory:
   C:\NWCLIENT
2. Install will modify your AUTOEXEC.BAT and CONFIG.SYS files and make
   backups.  Allow changes? (Y/N):  Yes
3. Install support for MS Windows? (Y/N):  Yes
   Enter MS Windows directory:  C:\WINDOWS
   Highlight here and Press <Enter> to customize.
4. Configure your workstation for back up by a NetWare server running
   software such as SBACKUP? (Y/N):  No
5. Select the driver for your network board.
   Highlight here and press <Enter> to see list.
6. Highlight here and press <Enter> to install.

Install will add this path to AUTOEXEC.BAT if you allow changes to the DOS
configuration files.
Esc=Go Back    Enter=Edit/Select                              Alt-F10=Exit
```

- ▸ The destination directory for the client files

- ▸ Whether to update your AUTOEXEC.BAT and CONFIG.SYS files

- ▸ Whether to install MS Windows support

- ▸ Workstation backup configuration

- ▸ LAN driver information

After you supply this information, the NetWare 4 client install performs the following functions:

▸ Creates a directory for the client files (the default is C:\NWCLIENT) and copies ODI drivers and VLMs to it

▸ Creates a NET.CFG file with the settings you have indicated

▸ Creates a STARTNET.BAT file that loads the ODI drivers and the NetWare DOS Requester

▸ Updates the AUTOEXEC.BAT and CONFIG.SYS files (if requested)

▸ Copies special DLL files, INI files, and utilities to the appropriate Windows directories (only if you request MS Windows support).

For detailed instructions on installing DOS/Windows client software, refer to the case study at the end of this chapter titled "Client and DynaText Installation for ACME." More detailed information is available in Chapters 4 and 5 of the *Novell NetWare Client for DOS and MS Windows User Guide* manual.

QUIZ

Who invented the "Swivel Chair"?

The answer may surprise you. Or not.

(Q6-6)

Now you can log in to your new server and install the documentation. Interesting how the documentation isn't available until *after* you install the server and client. Hmmmm. I guess you're lucky to have a copy of *Novell's CNE Study Guide for NetWare 4.1*.

DYNATEXT INSTALLATION

"What's a Subordinate Reference?"

"List the DSTRACE switches!"

"How many NDS access rights are there?"

These are all great questions, and I know just the place to find the answers: DynaText. The NetWare 4 on-line documentation (also called DynaText) enables you to electronically access the information found in NetWare 4 manuals. Too bad it's not available *before* you install the server and workstation. Well, actually it is—we've included a copy of DynaText on the CD-ROM in this book. And the case study at the end of this chapter provides instructions for installing it on your stand-alone MS Windows machine.

The NetWare 4 on-line documentation consists of two main parts:

▸ Documentation database—This contains the technical information from the NetWare 4 manuals and can be installed in one or more languages.

▸ DynaText viewer—This enables you to view, search, annotate, and print on-line documentation.

The on-line documentation can be accessed using three different methods:

1 • From the network—Once the on-line documentation and DynaText viewer have been installed on the network, they can be accessed by any user (with the appropriate rights) from any workstation.

2 • From a stand-alone workstation—If the documentation database and DynaText viewer are installed on a workstation, they can only be accessed by a user on that workstation. This method is faster and more convenient, and the documentation is available when the network is down. A disadvantage is the amount of hard disk space required on the workstation—about 60 MB.

3 • From the Installation CD-ROM—NetWare 4 offers the option of accessing the documentation database from a CD-ROM. But you must install the DynaText viewer on a local or network disk. This way, you can mount the server's CD-ROM as a NetWare volume and allow users to run the documentation right off the central server CD-ROM. This conserves disk space but negatively impacts DynaText performance.

Prerequisites

The following are the prerequisites for installing NetWare 4 on-line documentation:

- A minimum of 60 MB of free server hard disk space if you plan to install both the documentation database and DynaText viewer. Each additional language requires approximately 40 to 60 MB of additional hard disk space.

- A minimum of 6 MB of free server hard disk space if you plan to install the DynaText viewer only. If you install more than one viewer language, each additional viewer language will require an extra 2 MB of hard disk space.

- A CD-ROM drive that can read ISO 9660-formatted CD-ROM disks.

- A minimum of 4 MB of RAM (although 8 MB is recommended) for any workstation using the MS Windows viewer. Plus, you need MS Windows 3.11 (or Windows 95) and/or OS/2 v2.1x, and a VGA or Super VGA display.

Planning for the On-line Documentation

On-line documentation can be accessed from any NetWare 4 GUI client, including

- Microsoft (MS) Windows

- IBM OS/2 running WIN-OS/2

- Apple Macintosh

- Novell's UnixWare

If you want DynaText to be accessible by all users, you'll need to reference the documentation from the SYSDOCS.CFG file. This is created during the on-line documentation installation process. You'll also need to make sure that users have access to the SYS:DOC (documentation) and SYS:DOCVIEW (viewer) directories.

On the other hand, if you want the documentation restricted to only a few people, you should reference the documentation from a platform-specific configuration file and install the software on a local hard disk or secure network directory.

NetWare 4 on-line documentation can be installed in the following languages: English, French, German, Italian, and Spanish. The command for installing different languages depends on the type of workstation.

THE BRAIN

Refer to the *NetWare 4 Installing and Using Novell On-line Documentation* manual for further information about installing DynaText.

You can install DynaText during or after the NetWare 4 custom installation. During the NetWare 4 install, you would choose the Other Installation Items/Products choice from within INSTALL.NLM (refer again to Figure 6.7). Otherwise, there are two methods for installing DynaText at a later date:

- INSTALL.NLM

- NCOPY.EXE

The easiest way to is to use INSTALL.NLM (refer again to Figure 6.24). This server tool provides an automated procedure for installing the on-line documentation using a default directory structure. The NCOPY command line utility, on the other hand, should be used if you want to store the MS Windows or OS/2 documentation database and DynaText viewer files in nondefault directories. NCOPY cannot be used to install Macintosh or UnixWare DynaText viewers.

QUIZ

Here's a doozy to finish off what's left of your brain—Andy, Brad, Cole, and Doug all live in different houses on River Road.

By a curious coincidence, the age of each man is either seven greater or seven less than the number of his house. All of them are more than 15 years old and less than 90; all their ages are different.

Andy said that the number of Brad's house was even and Brad remarked that the number of his house was greater than that of Doug's. "My age," he added proudly, "is a perfect cube."

Cole said that the number of his house was greater by three than Andy's, and that Doug's age was an exact multiple of Andy's age.

Doug, who has an unfortunate habit of complicating things, said that Brad's age was either 27 or an even number other than 64. "Furthermore," he commented, "Cole does not live at number 19."

Unfortunately, these remarks were not all true. It was interesting to note that remarks made by those who lived in even-numbered houses were false, and remarks made by those who lived in odd-numbered houses were true.

What are their ages and the numbers of their houses? Why do you care?

(Q6-7)

DynaText Installation Steps

Now it's time for the "nuts and bolts" of DynaText installation. Also reference the appropriate case study at the end of the chapter. Here's a quick snapshot of the major installation steps:

1 • Mount the CD-ROM as a NetWare device.

2 • Load INSTALL.NLM.

3 • Specify the source path, platform(s), language(s), and destination directory for the documentation.

4 • Supply the Admin password.

The first task is to mount the CD-ROM as a NetWare device. In order to do so, make sure the following drivers and NLMs have been loaded on the server: SCSI drivers (if applicable), ASPI drivers for the controller card (if applicable), NWPA.NLM, and CDROM.NLM.

THE BRAIN

If you're interested in information on CD-ROM drivers and their load order for the purposes of enabling a CD-ROM drive to be mounted as a NetWare 4 volume, consult Appendix F of the *Novell NetWare 4 Installation* manual.

As soon as you've loaded all of the relevant drivers and NLMs into server memory, type

`CD DEVICE LIST`

to display the volume name and device number for the currently mounted CD-ROM drive. Write down both the volume name and the device number for future reference.

If you do not have an existing CD-ROM disk in the drive, insert the NetWare 4 documentation CD-ROM and type

`CD MOUNT n`

to mount the CD-ROM disk, where *n* is the CD-ROM device number from above. Wait for the CD-ROM drive to "spin up," and then press Enter.

If you have a CD-ROM disk other than the NetWare 4 documentation CD-ROM disk in the CD-ROM drive, type

`CD CHANGE n`

to enable you to change CD-ROM disks. Once again, *n* represents the CD-ROM device number from above. Wait for the CD-ROM drive to "spin down," and then replace the existing CD-ROM disk with the NetWare 4 documentation. Wait for the CD-ROM drive to "spin up," and then press Enter. The server will begin to index the CD-ROM. When it's finished, you're ready to go.

The second task is to load the INSTALL.NLM utility by typing

`LOAD INSTALL`

If a message is displayed saying that INSTALL.NLM is already loaded, press Alt+Esc until the Installation Options menu is displayed on the screen. If you are using the RCONSOLE utility, press F3 until this screen is displayed.

THE BRAIN

You will find instructions for using RCONSOLE to install a server in Appendix E of the *Novell NetWare 4 Installation* manual.

The next step is to choose the product to be installed. First, select Product Options from the Install Options screen. Next, select the Choose an item or product option from the Other Installation Actions menu. Finally, select the Online Documentation Database and Viewers option from the Other Installation Actions menu.

The third task involves changing the source path. You'll notice that the default source path lists drive A:. This is because the INSTALL.NLM utility assumes that additional products will be shipped on diskette—wrong! When you're asked to specify a directory path, press F3, and then type the name of the volume associated with the CD-ROM. I hope you wrote this down when you entered the "CD DEVICE LIST" command in the first task. Don't forget to put a colon (:) after the volume name. When you enter the correct source path, the "File Groups" screen will appear.

During the fourth task, you choose the database(s) and viewer(s) that need to be installed. You'll notice that databases can be installed in different languages. Select the specific databases and viewers you want installed, and then press F10 to continue.

The fifth task involves updating the SYSDOCS.CFG and DYNATEXT.INI configuration files that point to the location of executable and data files. This task is only necessary if you change the destination paths.

The sixth, and final, task is to configure the workstations. Remember, we can use different workstations, including MS Windows 3.11 (or Windows 95), OS/2 running WIN-OS/2, Macintosh, and UnixWare. Here's how you do it:

1 • Update the SET NWLANGUAGE command in AUTOEXEC.BAT.

2 • Create a program icon for DynaText in MS Windows.

Voilà, you're done!

Here's a quick review of the individual steps involved in installing NetWare 4 on-line documentation:

1 • Mount the CD-ROM as a NetWare device.

2 • Load INSTALL.NLM at the console prompt.

3 • Select the source path for the documentation.

4 • Select the documentation and viewer groups you want to install.

5 • Select the destination directory for the documentation database.

6 • Select the documentation and viewer groups you want to install.

7 • Copy the selected documentation databases and viewers to the server.

8 • Select the documentation and viewer groups you want to install.

9 • Manually configure the configuration files (if you chose not to use the default directories).

THE BRAIN

If you'd like additional information on planning, installing, and configuring the DynaText documentation database and viewers, refer to Chapters 3 through 5 of the *Novell NetWare 4 Installing and Using Novell On-line Documentation* manual. Also, check out the DynaText case study at the end of this chapter.

ZEN

"What happens to the hole when the cheese is gone?"

Bertolt Brecht

INSTALLING NETWARE FOR MACINTOSH

NetWare 4 supports Macintosh workstations through the optional NetWare for Macintosh server product. Fortunately it is bundled on the NetWare 4 CD-ROM. It provides NetWare file services, print services, and routing services to Macintosh computers through native AFP (AppleTalk Filing Protocol).

TIP

The "free" NetWare for Macintosh product bundled with NetWare 4 matches the user connection limit of your native server license. For example, a 1000-user license of NetWare 4 would include a 1000-user version of NetWare for Macintosh. This is a dramatic improvement over earlier NetWare products, which included only a five-user version of NetWare for Macintosh.

NetWare for Macintosh allows Macintosh users to share files with each other and with DOS, Windows, OS/2, or UnixWare clients. It also allows them to print to NetWare print queues, as well as provide AppleTalk printing access to non-Macintosh users.

The three basic stages in the NetWare for Macintosh installation process are

▶ Stage 1—Installing NetWare for Macintosh on the server

▶ Stage 2—Configuring NetWare for Macintosh on the server

▶ Stage 3—Installing Macintosh client software on workstations

You can install NetWare for Macintosh during a custom NetWare 4 server installation, or at a later date using INSTALL.NLM (see Figure 6.7). Let's quickly review these three stages. Also, refer to the case study at the end of this chapter for more details.

Stage 1: Installing NetWare for Macintosh on the Server

To begin the NetWare for Macintosh installation, type the following at the server console:

`LOAD INSTALL`

The Installation Options menu will be displayed. Select Product Options from this menu. Next, select the Choose an item or product listed above option from the Other Installation Actions menu. Then, choose Install NetWare for Macintosh.

After you've navigated Sherwood Forest, you'll be asked to provide a source path for the NetWare for Macintosh files. Press F3 if you need to change the default. You'll notice that the default path is the one you used during the last product installation—it should work. A small number of files will be copied to the server.

If you are connected to a remote server, a screen will pop up requesting your username and password. At this point, you may receive a warning of a potential conflict with the DOS CD-ROM driver—no worries.

Finally, select the Install NW-MAC option. A message displays informing you that files are being copied to the SYS: volume on the host server. After the files have been copied, a Final Installation Options window appears asking for the following information:

▸ The volume to add Macintosh name space to

▸ Whether NetWare for Macintosh File Services should be loaded from AUTOEXEC.NCF

▸ Whether NetWare for Macintosh Print Services should be loaded from AUTOEXEC.NCF

▸ Whether to install Macintosh client support files

After you've completed the server stage, the NetWare for Macintosh Configuration window shows up. That's Stage 2.

THE BRAIN

For further information on the NetWare for Macintosh installation procedure, refer to Chapter 1 of the *Novell NetWare 4 NetWare for Macintosh File and Print Services* manual.

Stage 2: Configuring NetWare for Macintosh Services

Once you have installed the NetWare for Macintosh software, you must configure and activate it. In order to enable file and print services, you'll need to perform the following tasks using the NetWare for Macintosh Configuration window:

1 • Configure and enable AppleTalk. In order for Macintosh clients to communicate with the NetWare 4 server, you'll need to do the following using INET.CFG: Identify the network board, enable the AppleTalk protocol, and bind the AppleTalk protocol to the LAN driver.

2 • Customize file services. NetWare file services are available to Macintosh clients as soon as NetWare for Macintosh is installed. The AFPCON utility, however, can be used to customize Macintosh file services to maximize the network's capabilities and enhance performance. Some of the custom file services provided by AFPCON are allowing Guest logins, allowing users to save passwords for auto logins, restarting the AFP server, setting the maximum number of AFP connections, shutting down the AFP server, and volume information. Unlike DOS, Macintosh files have both a resource fork and a data fork. NetWare can support Macintosh filenames with a maximum of 32 characters, using name space. The Macintosh name space must be loaded on the volume(s) that will store Macintosh files. This can be done during server installation or at a later date using the INSTALL.NLM utility.

3 • Next, you can set up print services with ATPSCON: change context, configure printer services, configure spoolers, define printer models, log options, management options, and quick configuration.

4 • Finally, you should configure and enable print services using ATPSCON.

TIP

NetWare for Macintosh print services provides bidirectional print communication with printers. This makes AppleTalk a preferred protocol for managing advanced printing environments.

When you choose an option from the NetWare for Macintosh Configuration window, the installation program loads the appropriate NLMs or enables you to install additional files and name space. Each of these NLMs can be loaded from the server prompt or the NetWare for Macintosh Configuration window. Table 6.5 lists NLMs that are loaded from the NetWare for Macintosh Configuration window.

TABLE 6.5	OPTION	NLM
NetWare for Macintosh Configuration NLMs	Configure File Services	AFPCON.NLM
	Configure Print Services	ATPSCON.NLM
	Configure CD-ROM Services	HFSCDCON.NLM
	Configure AppleTalk Stack	INETCFG.NLM

THE BRAIN

If you'd like more information on configuring and enabling the NetWare for Macintosh product, refer to Chapter 1 of the *Novell NetWare 4 NetWare for Macintosh File and Print Services* manual.

Stage 3: Installing Macintosh Client Software

The final installation stage involves the Macintosh workstation. The MacNDS client software is used to provide NDS access to Macintosh clients running the System 7 operating system. As soon as NetWare for Macintosh is installed on the server, Macintosh workstations can obtain limited access to network services by using AppleShare. They simply log in to the server under Bindery Services. In order to log in as an NDS client, you'll need to install the NetWare 4 MacNDS client software on each Macintosh workstation.

The MacNDS client files are typically copied to the server during the NetWare for Macintosh installation. You should find them in a self-extracting archive file called MacNDS.SEA. In order to install the Macintosh client, you'll need to enable Bindery Services on the server containing the installation files. Next, you'll connect to the server and log in as Supervisor. Then, you'll access the volume containing the client installation files and double-click on the MacNDS.SEA file in the PUBLIC\MAC folder. A dialog box will be displayed asking you to identify the destination directory for the files. If you accept the default, the installation program creates a MacNDS folder within your language folder.

THE BRAIN

More information on the NetWare for Macintosh client installation procedure can be found in Chapter 2 of the *Novell NetWare 4 NetWare for Macintosh File and Print Services* manual.

Just to summarize, the basic stages in the NetWare for Macintosh installation process are

1 • Install NetWare for Macintosh on the server

2 • Configure NetWare for Macintosh on the server

3 • Install Macintosh client software on the workstations

You've done it. The Macintosh and DOS clients can now access our new, exciting server and read electronic documentation. Isn't technology wonderful?

ZEN

"Goodnight stars. Goodnight air."

Margaret Wise Brown

That's it. Mondays aren't so bad! Look, you made it through two server installs and three optional products, and it's not even time to go. It's only 4:59 p.m. I wonder who needs "resuscitation" now—you or the server?

We have been through a lot together today. We created a life—the NetWare 4 server. It all started with a review of the NetWare 4 Installation prerequisites and some hardware and software requirements. Then we got our feet wet with the easier simple installation method. We strolled through the six stages of server installation with the guidance of INSTALL.BAT and INSTALL.NLM. It was kind of nice letting the server make all the tough decisions.

Unfortunately life isn't always so simple; sometimes it needs to be "customized"! In the second NetWare 4 install, we explored all 23 steps in excruciating detail—ouch! You probably learned more about SERVER.EXE, HAM drivers, License diskettes, and time zones than you ever wanted to. But that's the price for knowledge. Besides, who else is going to save the Earth?

That's not all. You also learned about three important installation "options," namely Client Installation, DynaText, and NetWare for Macintosh.

Well, that just about does it. It's 5:00 p.m. and time to go home. You should feel proud about what you accomplished today. I wonder what tomorrow has in store for you?

EXERCISE 6.1: CHOOSING THE CORRECT INSTALLATION METHOD

Read each of the scenarios listed here and indicate which NetWare 4 installation method (simple or custom) you would recommend.

SCENARIO 1

A CAD/CAM software developer wants to install NetWare 4 on a 133-MHz Pentium that has 64 MB of RAM and four 1.2 gigabyte (GB) hard disks. The network designers use Ethernet thick cabling as a backbone and Ethernet thin cabling between workstations. The development firm has Silicon Graphics and Sun workstations as well as PCs. Which installation method would you recommend for this company?

SCENARIO 2

A dentist's office has a 486/66 server with 8 MB of RAM and a 510-MB disk. The office is wired for Ethernet 10Base-T and uses 386- and 486-based PCs. Which installation method would you recommend for this office?

SCENARIO 3

A busy medical corporation with multiple hospital and medical clinic locations wants to install a series of NetWare 4 servers at its various locations. The corporate office needs to communicate with each of the hospital and clinic locations as well as with its major suppliers. Because hard disk reliability is important, each of the hard disks will be mirrored. Which installation method would you recommend for this corporation?

See Appendix C for answers.

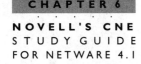

CASE STUDY: SIMPLE INSTALLATION FOR THE U.N.

As you know, saving the world is a challenging task. Fortunately, ACME isn't alone. We've recruited world leaders from the United Nations (U.N.) to help out. Currently, they operate using their own independent LAN in Geneva. But soon they'll become part of the ACME electronic family (Chapter 8).

In the meantime, you need to get them started with a server of their own. You've decided that the simple installation method should work fine for such a simple organization. Have fun and refer back to the U.N. NDS tree periodically for reference.

I. PREPARE THE SERVER HARD DISK

a. Configure the server's DOS partition.

(1) Back up existing data. Choose a computer to be used as the server and make at least two backup copies of all data. (Remember that all existing data on this computer's hard disk will be destroyed during the server installation process!)

(2) Create a boot diskette. Insert a blank diskette in drive A:. Make it bootable by typing FORMAT A: /S. After it is formatted, copy the following files to it:

(a) Required files: C:\DOS\FDISK.EXE, C:\DOS\FORMAT.COM, the appropriate CD-ROM drivers, plus any other drivers that your computer needs in order to operate properly. (Make sure that you make a printout of your AUTOEXEC.BAT and CONFIG.SYS so that you can see the proper syntax for executing each driver.)

(b) Optional files: C:\DOS\EDIT.COM, C:\DOS\QBASIC.EXE (required by EDIT.COM), C:\DOS\MEM.EXE, and C:\DOS\MSD.EXE.

(3) Use FDISK to delete existing partitions and create a 15 MB DOS partition. (The directions listed here were designed for use with MS-DOS v6.2. The steps required for your version of DOS may differ.)

(a) Delete the primary DOS partition. Make sure the bootable disk you made in the previous step is in drive A:. Type **A:** and press Enter to switch to the floppy drive. Type **FDISK** and press Enter to execute the FDISK command. Type **4** and press Enter to select the Display partition information option. Take note of the number and type of partitions that exist on your hard disk. Type **3** and press Enter to select the Delete partition or Logical DOS Drive option. Type **1** and press Enter to select the Delete Primary DOS partition option.

When you are asked what primary DOS partition to delete, type the number of the Primary DOS partition (which should be listed near the top of the screen) and press Enter. When you are asked for the volume label of the Primary DOS partition, type the volume label (which should be listed near the top of the screen) and press Enter. (Press Enter alone if the partition has no volume label.) When you are asked whether you are sure, type **Y** and press Enter. Press Esc to return to the FDISK Options screen.

(b) Delete the non-DOS partition. (Skip this step if there are no more partitions left on the hard disk.) To delete a non-DOS partition, type 3 and press Enter to choose the Delete partition or Logical DOS Drive option. Type **4** and press Enter to choose the Delete Non-DOS Partition option. When you are prompted, key in the number of the non-DOS partition to be deleted and press Enter. Type **Y** and press Enter when you are asked if you wish to continue. Press Esc to return to the FDISK options menu. At this point, there will probably be no partitions remaining. If there are partitions remaining, repeat this procedure, choosing the appropriate menu choices for the type of partitions involved.

(c) Create a 15-MB DOS partition. Type **1** and press Enter to select the Create DOS partition or Logical DOS drive option. Type **1** and press Enter to select the Create Primary DOS Partition option. Type **N** and press Enter when you are asked whether you wish to use the maximum available size for a Primary DOS Partition. Type **15** and press Enter when you are asked to enter a partition size in megabytes or percentage of disk space. (It will assume that you are entering the number in megabytes if you don't use a percent sign.)

You may notice that the installation program creates a partition that is slightly larger than 15 MB. Press Esc to return to the FDISK options screen. Type **2** and press Enter to select the Set active partition option. Type **1** and press Enter when you are prompted for the number of the partition you want to make active. Press Esc to return to the FDISK Options screen. Press Esc again to exit the FDISK utility.

When you are prompted to insert a system diskette into drive A: and strike a key, just press any key. This will cause the computer to reboot. When you are prompted for the correct date, key in the correct date if an incorrect one is displayed and press Enter. (Press Enter alone to accept the default.) When you are prompted for the correct time, key in the correct time if an incorrect one is displayed and press Enter. (Press Enter alone to accept the default.) If this is your only server and the date and/or time listed is incorrect, this would be a good time to change the "hardware" date and time using the CMOS setup program built into your computer. See the manual that came with your computer for the exact procedure.

(4) Format the DOS partition and make it bootable. Type **FORMAT C: /S** and press Enter to format the DOS partition and install system files. Type **Y** and press Enter when you are asked whether to proceed with the format. Type **LABS-SRV1** and press Enter when you are asked for a volume label.

b. Install and configure the CD-ROM drive as a DOS device. Copy the CD-ROM drivers (plus other drivers, if any) from your boot diskette to the C: drive, and then create an AUTOEXEC.BAT file to automatically load the drivers into memory. Make sure the CD-ROM is set up to function as a DOS device. (You can look at the AUTOEXEC.BAT and CONFIG.SYS that you printed out earlier for assistance. Alternately, you can use the software installation procedure that was supplied with your CD-ROM drive.) Next, type **D:** (or the appropriate drive letter) and press Enter to switch to the CD-ROM drive.

c. Run INSTALL.BAT and select the installation type desired. Type **INSTALL** and press Enter to execute the INSTALL.BAT file on the CD-ROM. A menu will display from which you select the language to use during the installation process. Choose the Select this line to install in English option from the NetWare Install menu if you want to display the installation instructions in English. Choose one of the other four options (Deutsch, Español, Français, or Italiano) if you want the installation instructions to be displayed in another language. Next, choose the NetWare Server Installation option from the Select the Type of Installation Desired menu and press Enter. Then select the NetWare 4.1 option from the Choose the Product You Want to Install menu and press Enter. Finally, select the Simple Installation of NetWare 4.1 option from the Select the Type of Installation You Are Performing menu and press Enter.

d. Indicate the server name. Type **UN001** as the server name and press Enter.

e. Copy the server boot files to the DOS partition. The system will automatically copy a number of server boot files from the CD-ROM to the C:\NWSERVER directory on the DOS partition.

2. RUN SERVER.EXE

a. Start the server. The SERVER.EXE file will be executed automatically. (The system essentially does a warm boot as it flushes the DOS operating system from server RAM and replaces it with the NetWare 4 operating system.)

3. LOAD THE NETWARE DRIVERS

a. Load and configure the appropriate server disk and CD-ROM driver(s). Select the appropriate NetWare disk driver for your hard disk and press Enter. (If you have an enhanced IDE hard disk, for instance, try using IDE.DSK.) Review the disk driver parameters listed to make sure they are correct, and then select the Save parameters and continue option and press Enter. When you are asked if you want to select an additional disk driver, select No and press Enter.

b. Load and configure the appropriate server LAN driver(s). When you are prompted, select the appropriate LAN driver for the NIC installed in your server and press Enter. Carefully review the LAN driver parameters listed. (It's important that you use interrupts and addresses that do not conflict with other hardware.) If you need to change any parameters, choose the Select/Modify driver parameters option and press Enter. Use the arrow keys on your keyboard to move to each parameter to be changed. After you make the necessary changes, press F10 or Esc to save the changes. Next, select the Save parameters and load driver option and press Enter. Select No and press Enter when you are asked if you want to select an additional network driver. Finally, select the Continue installation option and press Enter.

4. LOAD INSTALL.NLM

a. If you are prompted, determine whether to continue accessing the CD-ROM via DOS or to attempt to mount the CD-ROM as a NetWare volume. The system will automatically load the INSTALL.NLM utility. If you are prompted with a warning that there may be a conflict with the DOS CD-ROM driver, ignore the warning, and then select the Continue accessing the CD-ROM via DOS option and press Enter. (You will probably be able to continue normally despite the warning.)

b. Mount the SYS: volume. The system automatically creates a NetWare partition on the hard disk, creates a SYS: volume within that partition, and mounts the SYS: volume.

c. License the NetWare operating system. When you are prompted, insert the NetWare 4 License disk in drive A: and press Enter to continue. The system will automatically copy "preinstallation" files from the CD-ROM to the SYS:SYSTEM and SYS:LOGIN directories.

d. If you are installing across the network, reconnect server-to-server. Ignore this step, because in this exercise you are installing from CD-ROM.

5. INSTALL NETWARE DIRECTORY SERVICES (NDS)

a. Install NDS. When you are asked whether this is the first NetWare 4 server, select Yes, this is the first NetWare 4 server and press Enter. Next, select the appropriate time zone for where the server will be located ("Geneva") and press Enter. (This is most likely "Netherlands, Mid-European Time"). When you are prompted for the Organization name, type **UN** and press Enter. When you are prompted for the Admin password, type in the password and press Enter, and then key it in again and press Enter when you are prompted to retype it for verification. (Make sure you choose a password you will remember!) At this point, NDS will be installed on the server. When the directory tree name, directory context, and administrator name are displayed on the screen, write them down (along with the Admin password chosen earlier) and press Enter.

6. CREATE SERVER STARTUP FILES

a. Copy the NetWare SYSTEM and PUBLIC files to the SYS: volume. The system will automatically copy files from the CD-ROM to the SYS:SYSTEM and SYS:PUBLIC directories.

b. Perform other installation options. Ignore this step.

c. Complete the installation. Select the Continue installation option from the Other Installation Actions menu and press Enter. Press Enter again to exit to the system console screen.

d. Boot the server using the STARTUP.NCF and AUTOEXEC.NCF files. Remove the NetWare 4 License disk from drive A:. Type **DOWN** to down the server, and then type **EXIT** to exit to the DOS prompt. Reboot the server.

There you have it. The U.N. is now in business. But what about ACME? It's next.

CASE STUDY: CUSTOM INSTALLATION FOR ACME

Now that you've warmed up with the U.N. installation, it's time to move on to ACME. ACME's needs are obviously much more complex, and so the Custom Installation method seems justified. As its resident CNE, it's your responsibility to install all 51 of ACME's servers. Happy, happy, joy, joy!

I know it seems like a daunting task, but just like anything, we'll take it one step at a time. After all, this is why they pay you the big bucks. Let's start with the first server in NORAD at the Labs division. Albert Einstein will be proud.

I. PREPARE THE SERVER HARD DISK

a. Configure the server's DOS partition.

(1) Back up existing data. Choose a computer to be used as the server and make at least two backup copies of all data. (Remember that all existing data on this computer's hard disk will be destroyed during the server installation process!)

(2) Create a boot diskette. Insert a blank diskette in drive A:. Make it bootable by typing **FORMAT A: /S**. After it is formatted, copy the following files to it.

(a) Required files: C:\DOS\FDISK.EXE, C:\DOS\FORMAT.COM, the appropriate CD-ROM drivers, plus any other drivers that your computer needs in order to operate properly. (Make sure that you make a printout of your AUTOEXEC.BAT and CONFIG.SYS so that you can see the proper syntax for executing each driver.)

(b) Optional files: C:\DOS\EDIT.COM, C:\DOS\QBASIC.EXE (required by EDIT.COM), C:\DOS\MEM.EXE, and C:\DOS\MSD.EXE.

(3) Use FDISK to delete existing partitions and create a 15-MB DOS partition. (The directions listed below were designed for use with MS-DOS V6.2. The steps required for your version of DOS may differ.)

(a) Delete the primary DOS partition. Make sure the bootable disk you made in the previous step is in drive A:. Type **A:** and press Enter to switch to the floppy drive. Type **FDISK** and press Enter to execute the FDISK command. Type **4** and press Enter to select the Display partition information option. Take note of the number and type of partitions that exist on your hard disk. Type **3** and press Enter to select the Delete partition or Logical DOS Drive option. Type **1** and press Enter to select the Delete Primary DOS partition option.

When you are asked what primary DOS partition to delete, type the number of the Primary DOS partition (which should be listed near the top of the screen) and press Enter. When you are asked for the volume label of the Primary DOS partition, type the volume label (which should be listed near the top of the screen) and press Enter. (Press Enter alone if the partition has no volume label.) When you are asked if you are sure, type **Y** and press Enter. Press Esc to return to the FDISK Options screen.

(b) Delete the non-DOS partition. (Skip this step if there are no more partitions left on the hard disk.) To delete a non-DOS partition, type **3** and press Enter to choose the Delete partition or Logical DOS Drive option. Type **4** and press Enter to choose the Delete Non-DOS Partition option. When you are prompted, key in the number of the non-DOS partition to be deleted and press Enter. Type **Y** and press Enter when you are asked if you wish to continue. Press Esc to return to the FDISK Options menu. At this point, there will probably be no partitions remaining. If there are any partitions remaining, repeat this procedure, choosing the appropriate menu choices for the type of partitions involved.

(c) Create a 15-MB DOS partition. Type **1** and press Enter to select the Create DOS partition or Logical DOS drive option. Type **1** and press Enter to select the Create Primary DOS Partition option. Type **N** and press Enter when you are asked if you wish to use the maximum available size for a Primary DOS Partition. Type **15** and press Enter when you are asked to enter a partition size in megabytes or percentage of disk space. (It will assume that you are entering the number in megabytes if you don't use a percent sign.)

You may notice that the installation program creates a partition that is slightly larger than 15 MB. Press Esc to return to the FDISK options screen. Type **2** and press Enter to select the Set active partition option. Type **1** and press Enter when you are prompted for the number of the partition you want to make active. Press Esc to return to the FDISK Options screen. Press Esc again to exit the FDISK utility. When you are prompted to insert a system diskette into drive A: and strike a key, just press any key. This will cause the computer to reboot.

When you are prompted for the correct date, key in the correct date if an incorrect one is displayed and press Enter. (Press Enter alone to accept the default.) When you are prompted for the correct time, key in the correct time if an incorrect one is displayed and press Enter. (Press Enter alone to accept the default.) If this is your only server and the date and/or time listed is incorrect, this would be a good time to change the "hardware" date and time using the CMOS setup program built into your computer. See the manual that came with your computer for the exact procedure.

(3) Format the DOS partition and make it bootable. Type **FORMAT C: /S** and press Enter to format the DOS partition and install system files. Type Y and press Enter when you are asked whether to proceed with the format. Type **UN001** and press Enter when you are asked for a volume label.

b. Install and configure the CD-ROM drive as a DOS device. In the previous simple installation, you should have updated the AUTOEXEC.BAT file to automatically load the CD-ROM drivers into memory and make the CD-ROM a DOS device. Reboot the server. Next, type **D:** (or the appropriate drive letter) and press Enter to switch to the CD-ROM drive.

c. Run INSTALL.BAT and select the installation type desired. Type **INSTALL** and press Enter to execute the INSTALL.BAT file on the CD-ROM. A menu will display from which you select the language to use during the installation process. Choose the Select this line to install in English option from the NetWare Install menu if you want to display the installation instructions in English. Choose one of the other four options (Deutsch, Español, Français, or Italiano) if you want the installation instructions to be displayed in another language. Next, choose the NetWare Server Installation option from the Select the Type of Installation Desired menu and press Enter. Then select the NetWare 4.1 option from the Choose the Product You Want to Install menu and press Enter. Finally, select the Custom Installation of NetWare 4.1 option from the Select the Type of Installation You Are Performing menu and press Enter.

d. Assign the server name and internal IPX network number. Type **LABS-SRV1** as the server name and press Enter. A randomly generated internal IPX network number will be displayed. To replace it, type **BADCAFE** and press Enter.

e. Copy the server boot files to the DOS partition. When the default source and destination paths for the server boot files are displayed, press Enter to accept the defaults. The system will then automatically copy a number of server boot files from the CD-ROM to the C:\NWSERVER directory on the DOS partition.

f. Select the locale information and file format. Default locale information will be displayed for the United States. If you reside outside of the United States, modify the country code, code page, and keyboard mapping parameters. Press Enter to continue. When you are asked to choose a filename format, select the DOS filename format and press Enter.

2. RUN SERVER.EXE

a. Start the server. The SERVER.EXE file will be executed automatically. (The system essentially does a warm boot as it flushes the DOS operating system from server RAM and replaces it with the NetWare 4 operating system.)

b. Indicate any SET commands to be included in STARTUP.NCF. Do not select any special startup commands at this time. Select No and press Enter when you are asked if you want to include any special startup commands.

c. Confirm that AUTOEXEC.BAT should execute SERVER.EXE. When the system asks you whether it's okay to have AUTOEXEC.BAT automatically execute SERVER.EXE, choose No and press Enter.

3. LOAD THE NETWARE DRIVERS

a. Load and configure the appropriate server disk and CD-ROM driver(s). Select the appropriate NetWare disk driver for your hard disk and press Enter. (If you have an enhanced IDE hard disk, for instance, try using IDE.DSK.) Review the disk driver parameters listed to make sure they are correct, andthen select the Save parameters and continue option and press Enter. When you are asked whether you want to select an additional disk driver, select No and press Enter.

b. Load and configure the appropriate server LAN driver(s). When you are prompted, select the appropriate LAN driver for the NIC installed in your server and press Enter. Carefully review the LAN driver parameters listed. (It's important that you use interrupts and addresses that do not conflict with other hardware.) If you need to change any parameters, choose the Select/Modify driver parameters option and press Enter. Use the arrow keys on your keyboard to move to each parameter to be changed.

After making the necessary changes, press F10 or Esc to save the changes. Next, select the Save parameters and Continue option and press Enter. When you are asked whether you want to select an additional network driver, select No and press Enter. Finally, select the Continue installation option and press Enter. Note the protocol, frame type, and address information listed on the screen, and then press Enter to continue.

4. LOAD INSTALL.NLM

a. If you are prompted, determine whether to continue accessing the CD-ROM via DOS or to attempt to mount the CD-ROM as a NetWare volume. The system will automatically load the INSTALL.NLM utility. If you are prompted with a warning that there may be a conflict with the DOS CD-ROM driver, ignore the warning, and then select the Continue accessing the CD-ROM as a NetWare volume option and press Enter. (You will probably be able to continue normally despite the warning.)

b. Create NetWare disk partition(s). Select the Manually option from the Create NetWare disk partitions menu and press Enter. Select the Create NetWare disk partition option from the Disk Partition Options menu and press Enter. Press F10 or Esc to accept the default values. When you are asked whether to create the NetWare partition, select Yes and press Enter. Select Continue with Installation from the Disk Partition Options menu and press Enter. Read the information on the screen and press Enter.

c. Create the NetWare volume(s):

(1) Create the SYS: volume. Press F3 or Ins to be given the opportunity to modify the size of the SYS: volume. Select the SYS: volume and press Enter. Type **75 MB** for the new disk segment size and press Enter. Press F10 or Esc to save the new disk segment size.

(2) Create the VOL1: volume. Select the (free space) parameter from the Volume Disk Segment List and press Enter. When you are asked what you'd like to do with the new segment, select Make this segment a new volume and press Enter. Type **VOL1** in the disk segment volume name field and press Enter. Press F10 or Esc to save the changes and accept the disk segment size displayed on the screen. (This will assign all remaining free disk space to the VOL1: volume.) Press F10 or Esc to return to the Manage NetWare Volumes screen.

(3) Configure file compression, block suballocation, and data migration. (This case study assumes that you will be using Novell's High Capacity Storage System [HCSS] in the future. If so, it is recommended that you turn block suballocation and file compression off and data migration on.) Select the SYS: volume and press Enter. Select the File Compression field and press Enter twice to toggle the field to OFF. Select the Block Suballocation field and press Enter twice to toggle the field to OFF. Select the Data Migration field and press Enter twice to toggle the field to ON. Press Esc to return to the Manage NetWare Volumes screen. Press F10 to save volume changes and continue. Select Yes and press Enter when you are asked whether to save volume changes.

d. License the NetWare operating system. When you are prompted, insert the NetWare 4 License disk in drive A: and press Enter. The system will automatically copy "preinstallation" files from the CD-ROM to the SYS:SYSTEM and SYS:LOGIN directories. Press Enter when a message is displayed saying that the Server Connection License was successfully installed. A default path for installing files from the CD-ROM will be displayed. Press Enter to accept the default.

e. If you are installing across the network, reconnect server-to-server. Ignore this step, because in this case study you are installing from a CD-ROM.

f.   Install optional NetWare files. A list of optional NetWare files that can be installed will be displayed on the screen. Scroll down and make sure that only the following groups are selected:

(1)   NetWare DOS Utilities

(2)   NetWare MS Windows Utilities

To deselect a group that should not be selected, arrow down to that line and press the Spacebar. When the correct groups are marked, press F10 to continue. The system will then automatically copy files from the CD-ROM to the SYS: volume.

5. INSTALL NDS

a.   Install NetWare Directory Services (NDS). When you are asked whether this is the first NetWare 4 server, select Yes, this is the first NetWare 4 server and press Enter. When you are asked to enter the name for this Directory tree, type **ACME_TREE** and press Enter. Next, select the appropriate time zone for where the server is located and press Enter. (For instance, this server is located in Colorado, so we'll select United States of America, Mountain Time.) When you are prompted for the Organization name, type **ACME** and press Enter. Review the information on the Time Configuration Information screen and modify any parameters, if necessary. Press F10 to save the time parameters and continue.

The server context screen will be displayed. Type **ACME** in the Company or Organization field and press Enter. Type **NORAD** in the Level1 Sub-Organizational Unit (optional) field and press Enter. Type **LABS** in the Level2 Sub-Organizational Unit (optional) field and press Enter. Type a password you are sure you will remember in the password field and press Enter. When you are prompted, type the password a second time for verification and press Enter. Select Yes and press Enter when you are asked whether to save directory information and continue.

At this point, NDS will automatically be installed on the server. When the Directory tree name, directory context, and administrator name are displayed on the screen, note them for future reference (along with the Admin password chosen earlier) and press Enter.

6. CREATE SERVER STARTUP FILES

a. Create/Modify AUTOEXEC.NCF and STARTUP.NCF. The proposed STARTUP.NCF file will be displayed on the screen. Review the file, and then press F10 to accept the default values. Select Yes and press Enter when you are asked whether to save the new STARTUP.NCF file. The proposed AUTOEXEC.NCF file will be displayed next. Review the file, and then press F10 to accept the default values. Select Yes and press Enter when you are asked whether to save the new AUTOEXEC.NCF file.

b. Copy the NetWare SYSTEM and PUBLIC files to the SYS: volume. The system will then automatically copy files from the CD-ROM to the SYS:SYSTEM and SYS:PUBLIC directories.

c. Perform other installation options. Ignore this step. Select the Continue installation option from the Other Installation Actions menu and press Enter.

d. Complete the installation. Read the information screen and press Enter to exit to the system console screen.

e. Boot the server using the STARTUP.NCF and AUTOEXEC.NCF files. Remove the NetWare 4 license disk from drive A:. Type **DOWN** to down the server, and then type **EXIT** to exit to the DOS prompt. Reboot the server. Finally, type **C:\NWSERVER\SERVER** to reload the NetWare 4 operating system.

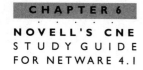
CASE STUDY: CUSTOM INSTALLATION FOR AN EXISTING SERVER

Good work. That's one down and 50 to go. Well, not really. Fortunately, some of the ACME scientists brought their own NetWare 4 servers with them. So, instead of installing all of them from scratch, you've got a little bit of a head start.

Of course, it's still Monday, so you can't expect too many miracles. The servers still need to be reinstalled (wrong NDS tree), but you can skip a few early steps. Following is a detailed walkthrough for the first "new, yet used" NetWare 4 server.

I. PREPARE THE SERVER HARD DISK

a. Configure the server's DOS partition.

(1) Remove Directory Services from the server. At the server console, type LOAD INSTALL and press Enter. Select the Directory Services option from the Installation Options menu and press Enter. Select the Remove Directory Services from this server option from the Directory Services Option menu. Read the warning displayed on the screen, and then press Enter to continue. Select Yes and press Enter to remove Directory Services. Press Esc to abort the login, and then press Esc to return to the Installation Options menu. Press Alt+Esc to return to the server console.

(2) Delete the SYS: volume. Type DISMOUNT SYS at the server prompt. Press Alt+Esc to toggle to the Installation Options menu. Select Volume options from the Installation Options menu and press Enter. Select the SYS: volume and press Del to delete it. Read the warning and press Enter to continue. Select the Yes option and press Enter when you are asked whether to delete the SYS: volume. Press Enter to continue. Select the Yes option and press Enter when you are asked whether to save the volume configuration option.

(3)   Delete the NetWare partition. Select Disk options from the Installation
       Options menu and press Enter. Select the Modify disk partitions and
       Hot Fix from the Available Disk Options menu and press Enter. Select
       the Delete any disk partition option from the Disk Partition Options
       menu and press Enter. Select the NetWare Partition option from the
       Available Disk Partition menu and press Enter. *Do not delete your DOS
       partition!* Select Yes and press Enter when you are asked whether to
       delete the disk partition. Press Esc three times to exit the INSTALL
       utility.

(4)   Bring down the server. Type **DOWN** and press Enter to bring down
       the server. Type **EXIT** and press Enter to return to the DOS prompt.

(5)   Delete the NetWare 4.1 boot files from the DOS partition. Type
       CD \NWSERVER to switch to the C:\NWSERVER directory. Type
       DEL *.* to delete all files in that directory. Type **CD ** to switch to the
       root directory. Type **RD NWSERVER** to remove the NWSERVER
       directory.

       b.   Continue with Step 2 of the Case Study: Custom Installation for
            ACME listed earlier.

CASE STUDY: CLIENT INSTALLATION FOR ACME

Very good. Now that Albert and his gang have their servers up and running, it's time to activate the workstations. Your next mission, should you choose to accept it, is to install the ACME Labs clients. We're going to use the CD-ROM method, because we like it. Besides, it's the most common.

All right, here we go. Don't fall asleep at the wheel—remember, the fate of the whole world is in your hands. "No, not that key!" Just kidding.

1 • Install the CD-ROM drive. First, make sure that the CD-ROM drive is installed on the workstation as a DOS or network device, according to the manufacturer's instructions.

2 • Execute the INSTALL.BAT utility. Insert the NetWare 4 Installation CD-ROM disk in the CD-ROM drive. Type **D:** (or the appropriate drive letter) and press Enter to switch to the CD-ROM drive. Next, type **CD ** and press Enter to switch to the root directory. Finally, type **INSTALL** and press Enter to begin the automated installation process.

3 • Select the language. When you run INSTALL.BAT, you will be asked to choose the language to use during the installation process. Choose the Select this line to install in English option from the NetWare Install menu and press Enter if you want the installation instructions to be in English. Choose one of the other four languages (Deutsch, Español, Français, or Italiano) if you want the installation instructions to be displayed in another language. You will then be asked to indicate the type of installation desired. Choose the DOS/Windows Client Installation option from the Select the Type of Installation Desired menu and press Enter.

4 • Provide configuration information. Next, a data entry screen will be displayed requesting workstation configuration information, as shown in Figure 6.26.

a. In Step 1, you are asked to supply the destination directory for the client software. Press Enter twice to accept the default directory of **C:\NWCLIENT**.

b. In Step 2, you are prompted to indicate whether to allow the INSTALL program to make changes to your AUTOEXEC.BAT and CONFIG.SYS files. Select **Yes** and press Enter twice.

c. In Step 3, you are asked whether to install support for MS Windows. Select **Yes** and press Enter. You will also be asked to indicate the path to the MS Windows software. Press Enter twice to accept the default path of **C:\WINDOWS**. Press the Down Arrow key once to move down to Step 4.

d. In Step 4, you are asked to specify whether to configure the workstation to be backed up by the server running SBACKUP or other software. Select No and press Enter twice.

e. In Step 5, you are given the opportunity to select the appropriate LAN driver and associated settings. Press Enter to display a list of available LAN drivers. If the installation program detects an existing LAN driver in workstation RAM, it will display a screen similar to the one in Figure 6.27, advising you that it has detected an existing LAN driver and will install the newest version of the driver using the same options. If this is the case, press Enter to continue and skip to Step 6. If you do not already have a LAN driver loaded, indicate the appropriate LAN driver and related settings— making sure that the settings that you choose match those on the network board and do not conflict with other hardware. When you have finished entering your LAN driver settings, press Esc to continue.

F I G U R E 6.27

*Driver Detection
Notification*

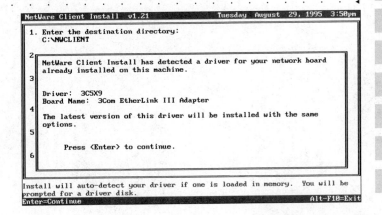

569

5 • Complete the installation process. When all of the information on the data entry screen is correct, press Enter to continue. At this point, the installation program automatically copies the appropriate client software to the directory you specified (which in this case is C:\NWCLIENT). When the installation process is complete, a screen similar to the one in Figure 6.28 is displayed.

F I G U R E 6.28

*Installation Completion
Notification*

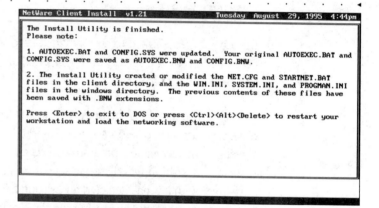

```
NetWare Client Install  v1.21                    Tuesday  August  29, 1995  4:44pm
The Install Utility is finished.
Please note:

1. AUTOEXEC.BAT and CONFIG.SYS were updated.  Your original AUTOEXEC.BAT and
CONFIG.SYS were saved as AUTOEXEC.BNW and CONFIG.BNW.

2. The Install Utility created or modified the NET.CFG and STARTNET.BAT
files in the client directory, and the WIN.INI, SYSTEM.INI, and PROGMAN.INI
files in the windows directory.  The previous contents of these files have
been saved with .BNW extensions.

Press <Enter> to exit to DOS or press <Ctrl><Alt><Delete> to restart your
workstation and load the networking software.
```

You'll notice that this screen provides you with information about files that have been created or changed such as AUTOEXEC.BAT, CONFIG.SYS, NET.CFG, STARTNET.BAT, PROGMAN.INI, SYSTEM.INI, and WIN.INI. After you review the information listed, press Enter to exit to DOS. If you allowed the installation program to make changes to your AUTOEXEC.BAT and CONFIG.SYS files, press Ctrl+Alt+Del to reboot the computer and load the LAN driver into workstation RAM.

"Why is there air?"

"How many properties does an external entity have?"

"What are the switches for NLIST?"

"How do I perform a server-to-server install of NetWare NFS?"

These are all great questions, and I know just the place to find the answers—DynaText. Now it's time to install NetWare 4's electronic documentation on a few of ACME's stand-alone workstations. Also, you can follow along at home with the CD-ROM included inside this book. Yippy, skippy.

Before you begin, make sure that your workstation meets the minimum hardware requirements listed earlier for DynaText. Because you will be installing the files on a workstation rather than into default directories on the server, you will need to use a manual installation method rather than an automated procedure. This is a little tricky, so follow along. Here we go.

1 • Install the CD-ROM drive. First, make sure that the CD-ROM drive is installed as a DOS or network device, using the instructions that came with the CD-ROM drive.

2 • Copy the DynaText viewer files. This step manually copies the DynaText viewer files from the \DOCVIEW directory on the CD-ROM to the \DOCVIEW directory on your workstation. The \DOCVIEW directory must be located in the root because of DOS pathname limitations. If your hard disk is the C: drive and your CD-ROM is the D: drive, type

```
XCOPY D:\DOCVIEW\DTAPPWIN\*.* C:\DOCVIEW\DTAPPWIN /S
```

and press Enter to copy the files to the workstation. When all of the files in the DTAPPWIN directory have been copied to the workstation, type

```
XCOPY D:\DOCVIEW\DTDATWIN\*.* C:\DOCVIEW\DTDATWIN /S
```

and press Enter to copy the DTDATWIN files to the workstation.

TIP

**The subdirectories in the \DTDATWIN directory contain language
support files for all available languages. The support files for each
language require approximately 2 MB of disk space. You can save disk
space by deleting the files for the languages that you don't need. Novell
uses a three-letter naming convention for language codes. These codes
can be found in the \DOCVIEW section of Appendix A of the *Novell
NetWare 4 Installing and Using Novell On-line Documentation* manual.**

3 • Copy the DynaText database files. To manually copy the DynaText database
files from the \DOC\language directory structure on the CD-ROM to your
workstation, type

```
XCOPY C:\DOS\ENGLISH\*.* C:\DOC\ENGLISH /S
```

and press Enter.

4 • Configure the DYNATEXT.INI file. The DYNATEXT.INI file will be located
in the C:\DOSVIEW\DTAPPWIN directory. It's used to reference private
(rather than public) collections, to indicate the location of the
SYSDOCS.CFG file, to specify the location of resource files, and to define
viewer presentation parameters. You can use any ASCII text editor to
modify it. When you look at the file, you'll notice that it is self-documenting,
with each parameter being explained in the file. You'll need to carefully
review the file, searching for any lines that are not commented out [that is,
that are not preceded by a semicolon(;)]. You'll need to change each line
that references a path to specifically reference the C: drive. For instance:

```
DATA_DIR=C:\DOCVIEW\DTDATWIN
SYSCONFIG=C:\DOCVIEW\DTAPPWIN\SYSDOCS.CFG
PUBLIC_DIR=C:\DOC\PUBNOTES
PRIVATE_DIR=C:\PRVNOTES
```

5 • Configure the SYSDOCS.CFG file. The SYSDOCS.CFG file will be located in the C:\DOSVIEW\DTAPPWIN directory and indicates the location of public collections. You can use any ASCII text editor to modify it. Make sure that the COLLECTION statement in the MS Windows section indicates the correct path to the documentation, language, and documentation set. For instance, if you want the on-line documentation to be displayed in English, the line should be changed to

```
COLLECTION=C:\DOC\ENGLISH\NW41=NetWare 4.1;
```

6 • Confirm existence of the SET NWLANGUAGE statement. Use any ASCII text editor to confirm that the following statement occurs in either your AUTOEXEC.BAT or STARTNET.BAT file:

```
SET NWLANGUAGE=English
```

If you performed an automated client install, the statement will be found in your STARTNET.BAT file.

7 • Create a DynaText icon in MS Windows. Run MS Windows by typing **WIN** and pressing Enter. Click on the Program Group icon containing your NetWare Tools. Select the New option from the File menu. Click on the Program Item option and then click on OK. Type **DynaText** in the Description field, and then click on the Command Line field. Click on the Browse button, and then double-click on the C: drive in the Drives window. Double-click on the C:\DOCVIEW\DTAPPWIN directory, and then use the scroll bar to locate the DTEXTRW.EXE file. Double-click on the DTEXTRW.EXE file, and then click on the Working Directory field and type **C:\DOCVIEW\DTAPPWIN.** (If the Working Directory field is not set properly, DynaText displays empty collections.) Finally, when all of the information listed on the screen is correct, click on OK.

NetWare 4 Migration

Ready for Migration!

It's Tuesday morning at 9:00 am. You carefully unlock your office door, and tiptoe across the ominous gray carpet. An eerie sense of destiny fills the room like low-flying fog over the Golden Gate Bridge. As you settle into the familiar Naugahyde™ of your office chair, you can't shake the frightening sensation from yesterday. It was at this very desk, yesterday, about this time, that your world turned upside-down. Your boss dumped *it* on your desk. You wonder if *it* is still alive. You can't torture yourself for another moment; you have to check. You launch from your Naugahyde and make a beeline for the computer room. Excitement swells as you turn the corner, your legs moving you faster then nerdly possible, then bam! It's there. The worm, a colon prompt (:) — aah, victory. Your NetWare 4 server is still alive!

Something magical happened yesterday — a new life was born. But that's only the beginning. Remember, ACME has 51 servers to install, and many of them are already breathing. Albeit, they're choking on NetWare 3.12. Now, it's Tuesday, and you approach each new day with a renewed vigor. You thirst for more installation. I think you're ready for *migration!*

ZEN

"Every day is a good day!"

Yun-Men

NetWare 4 migration is the ultimate achievement in "nerdiness." It's probably the most popular installation method for NetWare 4. After all, there are already 4 million NetWare servers out there, and nobody wants to start from scratch. With migration, existing CNEs can simply transfer bindery information to the new NDS "Cloud." They don't have to repopulate it.

Here's how it works:

- ▸ Installation (simple or custom) — Start from scratch and create a new NetWare 4 server with INSTALL.NLM.

- ▸ In-place upgrade (from NetWare 2 or NetWare 3) — Upgrade the server from an earlier OS (NetWare 2 or 3) to NetWare 4 using 2XUPGRDE.NLM and INSTALL.NLM.

▸ Migration (across-the-wire or same-server) — Migrate bindery information and files from a source NetWare 3 server to a destination NetWare 4 server using MIGRATE.EXE.

If you're starting from scratch (have never used NetWare on this equipment), you need to perform a complete installation. As you learned in Chapter 6, there are two types of NetWare 4 Installation: simple and custom. During the simple install, we relied on NetWare to make most of the tough decisions. The custom method, on the other hand, gave us total control during all 23 installation steps. This may be *too much* control for you — don't let it go to your head.

The NetWare 4 installation process assumes that you're starting with a "neoteric" server — no users, no files, no communications. NetWare 4 migration, on the other hand, jumps in midstream. In this case, we're migrating an existing server from NetWare 2 or 3 all the way to NetWare 4. *This is not an upgrade!* From coach to first class is an upgrade, Windows 95 is an upgrade, better carpeting is an upgrade. NetWare 3 to NetWare 4 is a "new frontier."

Welcome to Tuesday morning.

NetWare 4 supports two migration methods — in-place upgrade (an unfortunate name) and MIGRATE.EXE (a good name). The in-place upgrade enables you to move from NetWare 2 or 3 to NetWare 4 *on the same physical server.* This way, the data doesn't get bothered — only the NetWare OS and bindery/NDS information change. The majority of the migrating involves moving from NetWare 3 to NetWare 4. If you are using a NetWare 2 server (welcome to the modern age), then you must first "upgrade" it to NetWare 3 — using 2XUPGRDE.NLM.

The real NetWare 4 migration is handled by MIGRATE.EXE. It converts the NetWare 2 or 3 bindery information using an NDS workstation (running the NetWare DOS Requester). You can choose one of two types of NetWare 4 migration — across-the-wire or same-server. The across-the-wire migration transfers bindery information and data files from one server (NetWare 2 or 3) to another (NetWare 4). All information passes through, and is controlled by, the DOS workstation running MIGRATE.EXE. The same-server method, on the other hand, converts old bindery information into NDS on a single server. Migration is still controlled by the DOS workstation, but there's only one server involved. This is a little risky, as we'll see in just a moment.

> **REAL WORLD**
>
> There is, of course, another option. If you don't care about the server bindery information, you can simply COPY the files from one server to another. Start with a new server. Next, perform a NetWare 4 custom installation from scratch, then copy all the files from the old server to the new NetWare 4 machine. Using NCOPY *.* /S /E enables you to move virtually all data from NetWare 2 or 3 servers to NetWare 4. This is a quick-and-easy way of migrating to NetWare 4; no fuss, no muss. But be aware that the NetWare 2/3 user information, printing system, groups, and security are lost. Sometimes it feels good just to start all over.

So which one's for you? As you can see in Table 7.1, your choice depends entirely on your software (which version you're coming from) and available hardware (number of servers, and so on). Here are some examples:

- If you want to start from scratch, do a simple or custom installation using INSTALL.BAT and INSTALL.NLM.

- If you're moving from NetWare 2 to NetWare 4 on the same hardware, perform these two steps. First, upgrade to NetWare 3 using 2XUPGRDE.NLM. Second, upgrade from NetWare 3 to NetWare 4 using INSTALL.NLM.

- If you're running NetWare 3 or 4 and plan to use the same server machine, use the Upgrade option in INSTALL.NLM to do an in-place upgrade.

- If you plan to use new hardware, use the across-the-wire method.

TABLE 7.1

Comparing Different NetWare 4.1 Migration Methods

	SIMPLE INSTALL	CUSTOM INSTALL	ACROSS-THE-WIRE MIGRATION	SAME-SERVER MIGRATION	IN-PLACE UPGRADE
NetWare 2 to NetWare 4.1	X	X	X	X	X
NetWare 3 to NetWare 4.1	X	X	X	X	X
NetWare 4.1 to NetWare 4.1	X	X			X
Other network operating system to NetWare 4.1	X	X	X	X	

Before we dive into the detailed steps of in-place upgrade and migration, let's take a long, hard look at the advantages and disadvantages of each method. Study carefully. The choices you make today can irrevocably alter the path of your destiny — or not!

ZEN

"The clearest way into the universe is through a forest wilderness."

John Muir

Advantages and Disadvantages of Each Installation Method

Don't jump the gun. I know you're excited about diving into the ACME migration, but hold on for a second. We need to make a rational decision about which migration method is best for us. After all, it's only 9:23 am, and you have all day to get it done. Let's take a closer look at each of our six options:

- ▸ NetWare 4 Installation (Simple or Custom)

- ▸ NetWare 4 In-Place Upgrade (NetWare 2 or NetWare 3)

- ▸ NetWare 4 Migration (across-the-wire or same-server)

NETWARE 4 INSTALLATION

If you're starting from scratch, the simple or custom installation method is best. This assumes that you have sufficient hardware and know-how to pull it off. Refer to Chapter 6 for more details.

As you recall, the NetWare 4 installation process consists of six stages:

1 • Prepare the server hard disk.

2 • Run SERVER.EXE.

3 • Load the NetWare drivers.

4 • Load INSTALL.NLM.

5 • Install NetWare Directory Services (NDS).

6 • Create server startup files.

The NetWare 4 simple or custom installation method requires either two or three computers: the new server, a DOS client workstation, and the existing server (if applicable).

Following is a list of the key advantages for using the NetWare 4 installation method:

▸ You can design your NDS database and file system structure from scratch, for maximum efficiency.

▸ You can retain your existing NetWare 3.1x server while setting up and testing the new NetWare 4 server — pilot program.

But the NetWare 4 installation is not all "sugar and cream." It does have its disadvantages, including:

▸ It is more time-consuming than other methods because you have to create all network objects, security, and configurations from scratch.

▸ It requires additional hardware if you are upgrading from an existing server — namely, the new server. This ensures that you retain your old server while installing NetWare 4.

You should be an old pro at NetWare 4 installation by now. It's always a good idea to set up a pilot system whenever you migrate to a new frontier. For this reason, you may consider starting out with a few scratch installations. Then, when you have it all figured out, "migrate" the rest of your production servers by doing an in-place upgrade or using MIGRATE.EXE. Let's take a look.

NETWARE 4 IN-PLACE UPGRADE

If the NetWare 4 installation category isn't for you, there are still two more choices: in-place upgrade and migration. The in-place upgrade enables you to upgrade a NetWare 2 or 3 server to NetWare 4. If you're upgrading a NetWare 2 server, you'll need a stepping stone. First, upgrade the NetWare 2 bindery and files to NetWare 3 using 2XUPGRDE.NLM. Be careful, this involves reformatting the NetWare 2 partition — dangerous stuff. Now you're halfway there. Next, use INSTALL.NLM to perform a standard in-place upgrade from NetWare 3 to NetWare 4. No sweat.

The beauty of the in-place upgrade is that it's *in-place*. This means you only need one computer — the server. Later in the chapter, we'll walk through the six stages of an in-place upgrade. But for now, here's a peek:

1 • Prepare the server hard disk.

2 • Run SERVER.EXE.

3 • Load the NetWare drivers.

4 • Load INSTALL.NLM.

5 • Install NetWare Directory Services (NDS).

6 • View/modify the AUTOEXEC.NCF file.

Look familiar? The in-place upgrade process is similar to the "neoteric" custom installation. It performs roughly the same steps, but with a few changes. For example, the DOS partition isn't formatted, but the server boot files *are* updated. You get the idea.

I bet you're wondering how the in-place upgrade stacks up (pun intended) against the other two methods. Very well, here are some of its advantages:

▸ You are able to use your existing hardware if it meets the minimum requirements for NetWare 4.

▸ It can be used to upgrade NetWare 2, NetWare 3, and non-NetWare servers to NetWare 4 — extremely versatile.

▶ Bindery information such as login scripts, passwords, trustee assignments, and print configuration databases are written directly into the appropriate locations in the NDS database and are fully compatible with NetWare 4 — impressive.

▶ This method is faster than other methods because only the bindery has to be reformatted. The file system doesn't have to be moved or converted. Cool!

TIP

If you're upgrading from a NetWare 2 server that is using the native IDE disk driver and does not contain a DOS partition, you'll find that you'll be unable to add a DOS partition once it has been upgraded to NetWare 3. If you attempt to use the DOS FDISK utility to create a DOS partition on an upgraded IDE disk, it will cause the IDE disk driver to obtain head, sector, and cylinder information from the CMOS tables instead of from the disk drive. The resulting difference in parameters may cause data loss or corruption. This problem arises because the NetWare 2 IDE disk driver does not conform to DOS specifications.

If it looks too good to be true, it probably is. The in-place upgrade also has some shortcomings:

▶ If the existing server is running NetWare 2 using an IDE disk driver and does not have a DOS partition, you will be unable to add one when you upgrade to NetWare 3.1x. Hmmmm.

▶ This method does not allow you to change the volume size. If you need to change the volume size after the upgrade is complete, you'll need to save the information to tape, then delete and re-create the volume. Bummer.

▶ The in-place upgrade doesn't let you activate the suballocation feature for the file system. If you turn on suballocation after the upgrade, it will affect only files saved after the upgrade. That could be a problem.

▶ Passwords are not preserved during the upgrade of a NetWare 2 server to NetWare 3. (But they are from NetWare 3 to NetWare 4.)

▸ If the upgrade fails for any reason, you will need to restore the server to its original state before starting over. No way.

The in-place upgrade is a great way of quickly moving from NetWare 3 to NetWare 4 — on the same server. It also enables you to retain all files in their original, pristine state — without risky transfers. But, it doesn't allow you to move bindery information from NetWare 3 to a *new* NetWare 4 server. That's migration.

QUIZ

I'm in a poetic mood. There's a puzzle hidden in the following poem — all you have to do is pick a single letter from each line:

My first is in pansy, but not in rose.
My second in run, but not in goes.
My third is in daze, but not in muddle.
My fourth in haze, but not in puddle.
My fifth is in little, also in small,
My last in tumble, but not in fall.
My whole an amusement, so some guess,
To Others, nothing but a mess.

(Q7-1)
(See Appendix C for all quiz answers.)

NETWARE 4 MIGRATION

The final migration method enables you to move NetWare 3 bindery information and data to a new NetWare 4 server. You can approach it in one of two ways:

▸ Across-the-wire — migration over the LAN from one server to another

▸ Same-server — migration on the same server using a DOS client

Both migration methods use the same utility — MIGRATE.EXE — and they support the same operating systems (NetWare 2.1x; NetWare 2.2; NetWare 3.1x;

IBM PCLP 1.3 Extended Services; IBM LAN Server 1.0, 1.1, 1.2, and 1.3; and Microsoft LAN Manager 2.0).

Here's where they differ. The across-the-wire migration transfers bindery information and data from one server to another across the LAN. It requires three machines: two servers and one migration client. The same-server method, on the other hand, converts bindery information within a single server. It emulates the in-place upgrade to a point but operates at the migration client (MIGRATE.EXE) — unlike in-place upgrade, which uses INSTALL.NLM at the server. Let's take a closer look at the advantages and disadvantages of these two NetWare 4 migration methods.

Across-the-Wire Migration

As we saw earlier, the across-the-wire migration transfers bindery information and data from an existing NetWare 3 server to a NEW NetWare 4 machine. It uses a migration client and the MIGRATE.EXE utility to control the transfer. Here's how the three steps work:

1 • Migrates a copy of the bindery to the DOS Client workstation and translates it into NetWare 4 format — NDS.

2 • Migrates the translated bindery from the DOS Client workstation to the destination server using bindery services — LOGIN /B.

3 • Migrates the data files from the source server to the destination server — mostly copying.

Once you have confirmed that your migration was successful, you should immediately remove the bindery from the original server by deleting the NetWare partition or reformatting the hard disk. You can then either convert the original server into a NetWare 4 workstation or upgrade it to a NetWare 4 server.

Here's a list of some of the advantages of the across-the-wire migration:

▸ It is the safest upgrade method because the source server remains intact. This could prove to be especially useful if a power outage or connection loss occurs during the upgrade.

▸ You are given the option of determining whether to migrate all or selected information. We'll talk about this in more detail a little later.

▸ Multiple servers can be migrated to a single destination server. This enables you to consolidate the data from older servers to newer, more powerful computers. Great idea!

▸ Data can be moved from an 80286 server running NetWare 2 to a newer Pentium computer running NetWare 4, which is a good idea given the power of NetWare 4.

▸ Data from a non-NetWare network operating system can be moved to a NetWare 4 server. Look out, NT.

TIP

A Banyan Vines server can be migrated using a NetWare utility called BMIGRATE.EXE, which is a modified version of the MIGRATE.EXE utility.

Don't get too excited; across-the-wire migration does have its downside:

▸ Additional hardware is required — like an extra server.

▸ The DOS client workstation may require a large hard disk, depending on the number of users on the network.

What if you don't have any additional servers lying around, or you want to migrate a single server? Fortunately, there's same-server migration to save the day.

Same-Server Migration

The same-server migration uses the same utility (MIGRATE.EXE) as across-the-wire migration. It also upgrades the same operating systems. So what's different? Hardware. You only need two machines: one server and one workstation. Here's how to make it work:

1 • Back up the bindery information and data files on the existing server.

2 • Use MIGRATE.EXE to copy the bindery from the existing server to the DOS client workstation. Then, translate it into the NetWare 4 format — NDS.

3 • Use INSTALL.NLM to install NetWare 4 on the existing server. Use a modified custom installation method.

4 • Restore the data files from the backup media to the new NetWare 4 server.

5 • Use MIGRATE.EXE to move the translated bindery information from the DOS client workstation to the NEW NetWare 4 server.

It sounds pretty tricky to me, but all of this hard work will eventually pay off. Here are some advantages of the same-server migration method:

▸ No additional hardware is needed if the existing server meets the minimum requirements for NetWare 4.

▸ This method can be used to upgrade NetWare 2 servers and non-NetWare servers to NetWare 4.

Unfortunately, the same-server migration method has more disadvantages than advantages:

▸ Possible risk of bindery data loss during the conversion process. The original bindery is destroyed when NetWare 4 is installed on the server — oops.

▸ File attributes may not migrate.

▸ The DOS client workstation may require a large hard disk, depending on the number of users on the network — no problem.

▸ Not all tape units will work. Many of the new tape units do not look like a DOS device to the computer, thus they cannot be mapped to a DOS drive letter — blame SMS for this.

Well, there you have it: all the advantages and disadvantages of the four main NetWare 4 migration methods. Remember, we're not talking simple upgrade here — this is serious business. In the remainder of this chapter, we will explore the detailed steps of

NetWare 4 in-place upgrade and NetWare 4 migration. But first, let's take a quick look at some important setup tasks — namely, hardware requirements, prerequisites, and "getting ready. . . ."

ZEN

"Man's main task in life is to give birth to himself."

Erich Fromm

BEFORE YOU BEGIN

NetWare 4 migration is a little tricky and requires some critical preplanning. Before you begin a migration or in-place upgrade, you should verify that your hardware meets minimum requirements. In addition, you'll need to acquire a few prerequisites, including server information, new drivers, NDS data, and the Admin password. Finally, each migration method has its own set of preparation steps. For example, the across-the-wire migration process requires numerous preparation steps at all three machines — the source server, destination server, and migrating workstation.

Let's get prepared.

Hardware Requirements

Before you get too excited about the NetWare 4 migration, make sure your NetWare 2 or 3 hardware meets the following NetWare 4 requirements:

- ► An IBM-compatible architecture with an 80386, 80486 (SX or DX), or Pentium processor.

- ► A *minimum* of 8 MB of RAM for the basic NetWare 4 Operating System (OS) if you're migrating from CD-ROM or diskette. Also, at least 10 MB if you're migrating NetWare 4 using the across-the-wire method. (The additional 2 MB of RAM is used for loading STREAMS and CLIB NLMs.)

- ► A *minimum* of 90 MB of free disk space on the hard disk: 15 MB for the DOS partition and 75 MB for the NetWare partition (SYS: volume). If you copy all of the optional NetWare file groups to the server, you'll need an additional 25 MB for the SYS: volume.

- An additional 60 MB of free disk space to install the DynaText viewer and NetWare 4.1 documentation. Additional space will be needed if you want to install the documentation in more than one language. If you are low on disk space, you can view DynaText directly from the CD-ROM, rather than storing it on the server hard disk.

- At least one network interface card (NIC).

- The appropriate network cabling and related components (hubs, UPS, and so on).

- A CD-ROM drive that can read ISO 9660-formatted CD-ROM disks — only if NetWare 4 is being installed from CD-ROM.

REAL WORLD

The hardware requirements just listed are minimum, not recommended, standards. Realistically, you'll want a fast processor, more RAM, and a larger hard disk. You'll need to add additional memory based on the following:

- NetWare Loadable Modules (NLMs) used. You'll need to add an additional 2 MB of RAM if you use any of the following NLMs on this server: optional NetWare products (such as NetWare for Macintosh or NetWare NFS); print server software (PSERVER.NLM); or management NLMs such as BTRIEVE, INSTALL, MONITOR, or SERVMAN.
- The RAM required for disk caching (1 MB minimum, with 4 MB to 8 MB preferable).
- RAM that is calculated on the basis of disk size (that is, total disk size in MB multiplied by 0.008).

In terms of hard disk size, you'll need a disk that's large enough for all of your network needs, including the network operating system, optional NetWare products, applications, documentation, and the file system. Finally, if your server contains more than 16 MB of RAM, you'll need to use 32-bit AT busmastering or DMA boards (unless the driver supports more than 16 MB of RAM). Contact the computer manufacturer for additional information.

THE BRAIN

For more detailed information on calculating the RAM required for NetWare 4, refer to Appendix A of the *Novell NetWare 4 Upgrade* manual.

Prerequisites

Next, you'll need to acquire some important migration information before you begin. Following is a list of the stuff you'll need before you start a NetWare 3 to NetWare 4 in-place upgrade or migration:

- ► Server name

- ► IPX internal network number

- ► Locale information (country code, code page, and keyboard mapping)

- ► Filename format (DOS filename format recommended)

- ► Disk driver information (driver name, hard disk controller I/O port, hard disk controller interrupt setting)

- ► LAN driver information (driver name, location, frame type, network board I/O port address, network board interrupt, network address)

- ► Directory tree name

- ► Organization container name

- ► Directory tree context of server

- ► Admin username

- ► Admin user password

REAL WORLD

Novell introduced a new version of the NDS schema with NetWare 4.1. If you want to run a combination of NetWare 4.01, 4.02, and 4.1 servers in the same tree, you'll need to distribute the NetWare 4.1 schema to the 4.01 and 4.02 servers. To do this, you can either

- Install NetWare 4.1 on a new server or upgrade an existing NetWare 4.01 or 4.02 server to NetWare 4.1 — in which case the NetWare 4.1 schema is automatically updated on all NetWare 4.01 and 4.02 servers in your tree.
- Use the DSREPAIR utility to update the schema on your NetWare 4.01 and 4.02 servers.

Getting Ready . . .

Okay, now we're ready to start. Well, not quite ready. The first step in a NetWare 4 upgrade or migration is preparation. Before you begin anything, you'll need to prepare the NetWare 3 source server so that only necessary bindery objects and file system contents are upgraded. Here's a detailed list of the things you should do before starting your NetWare 3 to 4 upgrade or migration:

- Log all of the users out of the server. Confirm that all files (except bindery files) are closed.

- Back up your source server! In case you accidentally delete or change something you shouldn't have. Oops.

- Delete any objects and trustee rights that are no longer needed. If the source server is a NetWare 3 server, you can run SECURITY.EXE to obtain important information on account activity and possible security risks. Then, run BINDFIX.EXE to delete trustee assignments for users who no longer exist.

- Make sure that all bindery objects conform to NDS naming standards — the same ones you created in Chapter 4. Also, check for objects that have duplicate names (such as a groups and print queues). NetWare 4 won't migrate the second occurrence of an object with the same name.

▸ Check for users who have accounts on multiple servers. Remember, with NetWare 4, you log into the network itself rather than logging into each individual server. If you don't delete duplicate users prior to migration, the migration utility will give you the option of renaming the second and subsequent users (not recommended) or merging User objects with the same name into a single object with cumulative rights.

▸ Clean up the file system. Delete directories, files, and applications that are no longer needed. Rename any DOS directories and files that have long names. Modify your subdirectory tree so that it is no more than 25 levels deep.

▸ Make a backup of your server, then run the BINDFIX utility to clean up the bindery and remove MAIL subdirectories and trustee rights for users whose accounts no longer exist. Finally, make another backup of your system after BINDFIX is complete.

TIP

If you're running any third-party value-added processes (VAPs) on your NetWare 2 server, you'll want to contact your vendor or the manufacturer for information on possible solutions, because NetWare 4 uses NLMs instead of VAPs.

Next, if you're performing a migration specifically (rather than an upgrade), you'll want to prepare your NetWare 4 destination server for the migration process. Here are some things to think about:

▸ Make sure that you have the latest version of LAN and disk drivers.

▸ Log out all users.

▸ Create volumes into which data will be migrated.

▸ Make at least two full server backups.

THE BRAIN

For more information on updated LAN drivers and disk drivers:

▸ **Contact your Novell Authorized Reseller or call 1-800-NETWARE for a list of currently supported drivers.**

▸ **Download a list of currently supported drivers from the NetWire Forum on CompuServe.**

▸ **Call Novell Labs at 1-801-429-5544 for a list of drivers that have been certified as "Yes, Tested and Approved" with NetWare 4.1.**

Also, you'll want to prepare the migrating workstation:

▸ Make sure that the workstation meets the following minimum hardware requirements:

  ▸ Fast CPU (preferably 486/33 or better) for better transfer speed

  ▸ 640 KB of RAM, with 480 KB of free memory

  ▸ 5 MB free disk space on the workstation hard disk or a network drive

▸ If you're doing a *migration*, confirm that your CONFIG.SYS file contains the following command:

```
FILES = 20
```

(Don't forget to reboot the workstation if you have to add this command.)

▸ If you're doing a *migration*, confirm that the NET.CFG files contain the following lines:

```
PROTOCOL IPXODI
IPX RETRY COUNT = 60
```

▸ Make sure that you have the most current version of NetWare 4 LAN drivers and client files on your workstation.

▸ Log into the source and destination servers as SUPERVISOR — using bindery emulation. Here's how it works:

```
LOGIN LABS-SRV1/SUPERVISOR /B
```

If you're not logged in when you start MIGRATE.EXE, the utility will automatically log you in. Also, if you are using an NDS attachment, MIGRATE.EXE won't work correctly. Remember, use bindery emulation on the new destination NetWare 4 server.

QUIZ

Where is Podunk, anyway?

(Q7-2)

Well, there you have it. We're ready to go. Now, it's time to start our journey through the forest of NetWare 4 migration. "Watch out for that tree!" In the rest of this chapter, we'll explore the detailed steps of NetWare 4 in-place upgrade (from NetWare 2 and 3), across-the-wire migration, and same-server migration. For more information on NetWare 4 installation, refer to Chapter 6.

Remember, it's Tuesday morning and we have a whole new attitude. Life is our oyster, and it's time to polish the pearl. So, without any further ado — ready, set, go!

Netware 4 In-Place Upgrade

Here's where we start. Welcome to the in-place upgrade forest. This method enables us to migrate NetWare 2 or 3 servers to NetWare 4 without additional hardware. All bindery information is transferred to NDS, while the data stays right where it is — on the NetWare partition. That's the "in-place" part. It's pretty easy to comprehend.

However, starting from NetWare 2 is a little bit trickier. In this case, you have to first translate the NetWare 2 bindery and file system to NetWare 3. This is accomplished using 2XUPGRDE.NLM.

Once you have a NetWare 3 source server, you can start the six stages of an in-place upgrade:

1 • Prepare the server hard disk.

2 • Run SERVER.EXE.

3 • Load the NetWare drivers.

4 • Load INSTALL.NLM.

5 • Install NetWare Directory Services (NDS).

6 • View/modify the AUTOEXEC.NCF file.

I hope these stages look familiar to you. They follow the same general path as the NetWare 4 custom installation. First, you prepare the server hard disk, then run SERVER.EXE. Next, you upgrade the disk and LAN drivers to NetWare 4 equivalents. Then the fun begins. You load INSTALL.NLM and install NDS. Finally, you transfer the new NetWare 4 SYSTEM and PUBLIC files to SYS: and modify the server configuration files. No sweat.

This section explores each of these stages in detail — and their respective 18 steps. But first, let's take a quick look at 2XUPGRDE.NLM and the stepping stone from NetWare 2 to NetWare 3.

GETTING STARTED WITH NETWARE 2 TO NETWARE 3

If you're still using NetWare 2, you may want to consider joining the 20th century. In order to upgrade to NetWare 4, you'll first need to get the server up to NetWare 3. This is accomplished in five simple steps:

1 • Analysis of the file server

2 • Analysis of the disks

3 • Modification of the disks

4 • Creation of a NetWare 3.1x bindery

5 • Preparation of the DOS partition

Step 1 inventories the disks on the server and approximates how much memory is needed to complete the upgrade. Step 2 locates critical parts of the disk and upgrades a portion of the file system. Step 3 upgrades the partition table on track zero and writes the NetWare 3 files to the system area. Step 4 upgrades and writes the NetWare 2 bindery to NetWare 3 format. Finally, Step 5 prepares the disk partition for NetWare 3 upgrade. Let's explore each step in detail.

By the way, you deserve kudos for recognizing the limitations of NetWare 2 and attempting to move to NetWare 4. I guarantee your life will get better — busier, but better.

Step 1: Analysis of the File Server

In the first step, we must gather information about the NetWare 2 server and start the upgrade process. To accomplish the upgrade, the NetWare 2 server must have at least 50 MB of free disk space in the SYS: volume and space for a 5 MB or 10 MB DOS partition on the same hard drive. Begin the data-gathering process by booting the NetWare 2 server as a server. Type **CONFIG** at the console prompt. Record the server name, network address, and disk channel information. Once you've gathered the information you need, type **DOWN** at the console prompt to bring down the NetWare 2 server.

Next, boot the NetWare 2 server as a workstation with a DOS boot diskette. Insert the NetWare 3 SYSTEM_1 diskette in the A drive. Change to the A drive and type **SERVER**. Then, press Enter. Enter your NetWare 2 server name and an eight-digit IPX internal network number. The system will respond with the NetWare 3 colon prompt.

Next, load the NetWare 3 version of your NetWare 2 disk driver type (*.NLM). This driver will be loaded from the NetWare 3 SYSTEM_1 diskette. Other third-party disk drivers can be found on the NetWare 3 SYSTEM_4 diskette.

Then load the Macintosh name space NLM from the SYSTEM_1 diskette. This is accomplished by typing **LOAD A:MAC**. This may seem like an odd step at this time, but loading the Macintosh name space ensures that all volumes are mounted properly during Step 4.

Finally, you can start the fun stuff. Begin the NetWare 2 to NetWare 3 in-place upgrade by loading 2XUPGRDE.NLM at the server console. Type **LOAD A:2XUPGRDE** at the console prompt and press Enter. A warning displays, informing you that you could lose all of your data if there is a hardware failure during the upgrade. Of course, you've created a current backup, so press Enter to continue.

Screens will display, outlining each phase of the upgrade. Press any key to continue. Enter 15 at the prompt to create a 15 MB DOS partition for the system boot files. Step 1 is completed. Notice the Systems Analysis screen as it displays volume information and indicates how much memory the upgrade will require.

Step 2: Analysis of the Disks

Step 2 locates the critical parts of the disk—hot fix area, File Allocation Tables (FATs) and Directory Entry Tables (DETs). The FATs and DETs are translated, and directory and file attributes are upgraded. Macintosh files will also be upgraded. Remember, we've already loaded the MAC name space module.

Step 2 also ensures that the computer has enough memory to complete the upgrade. If not, NetWare will display an error and stop the upgrade. You can restart the process after adding more memory to the server. Step 2 disk analysis is automatically performed when you press the Spacebar at the Step 1 System Analysis screen.

ZEN

"Water which is too pure has no fish."

Ts'ai Ken T'an

Step 3: Modification of the Disks

Step 3 upgrades the partition table on track zero and writes the NetWare 3 files to the system area. Data blocks are moved to their new locations on the disk. If a power failure occurs during this step, you will need to restore the NetWare 2 system files from the backup and begin the upgrade process again.

A warning message will appear during this step stating that the NetWare 2 file system will be overwritten and the files cannot be reconstructed. Type **Y** to proceed with the disk modification step. A status screen appears indicating that Step 3 is completed.

Step 4: Creation of a NetWare 3.1x Bindery

Step 4 upgrades the NetWare 2 bindery to the NetWare 3 format. Then, later the NetWare 3 bindery will be translated to NDS. You are taking some major steps here — NetWare 2 bindery to NetWare 4 NDS.

First of all, passwords are not upgraded. Instead, you are given the option of creating random passwords or not assigning passwords. If you select random passwords, passwords are copied to a text file named NEW.PWD in the SYS:SYSTEM subdirectory. Passwords will be 26 alphanumeric characters and seemingly impossible to memorize. I highly recommend that you allow your users to create their own passwords once the upgrade process is completed.

After all disks have been upgraded, volume SYS: is mounted and the bindery is upgraded. The bindery step updates bindery objects, properties, and values such as user accounts and security.

Congratulations! The in-place upgrade is complete. Well, almost. A screen confirms that the upgrade has occurred and displays appropriate messages. Press any key to continue, and a status screen displays information on how to finish the upgrade process. Press any key to return to the console prompt. Type **MOUNT ALL** to activate the new NetWare 3 volumes.

Now, we can prepare the new DOS partition for NetWare 4 upgrade.

Step 5: Preparation of the DOS Partition

At this point, you have upgraded the NetWare 2 operating system to NetWare 3. You moved and overwrote the NetWare 2 files, loaded the disk drivers, and mounted the NetWare 3 volumes. You're not quite done. The remainder of the NetWare 2 to NetWare 3 in-place upgrade consists of a few NetWare 3 cleanup procedures. These tasks should be accomplished in order:

1 • Copy the NetWare 3 SYSTEM and PUBLIC files to the SYS: volume using INSTALL.NLM.

2 • Load the LAN driver from the console prompt.

3 • Define the NetWare 3 server startup files — STARTUP.NCF and AUTOEXEC.NCF. You can also do so using INSTALL.NLM.

4 • Create a DOS partition using the FDISK utility in exactly the same way as outlined in Step 1 of the NetWare 3 installation process. The only difference is when you create the DOS primary partition, it will automatically allocate all available space. Instead of choosing No, you want to choose Yes at this point because there are only 15 MB left. Finally, make sure to activate the DOS partition and make it bootable by using the FORMAT /S command.

5 • Copy server boot files to the DOS partition using the INSTALL.BAT utility in much the same way as outlined in Step 1 of the NetWare 3 installation process. The only difference is you should select Upgrade NetWare 3.1x from the INSTALL Options screen instead of Install New Server.

All right, then, you've done it! You've magically transformed a NetWare 2 LAN into a NetWare 3 masterpiece. I'm sure you'll agree this process is more complex than you had imagined — but you've accomplished a great deal in a short period of time. Speaking of accomplishments, now it's time to warp speed ahead to NetWare 4. This is accomplished in six stages, and I can't think of a better place to start than stage 1.

ZEN

"Life is what happens to you while you're busy making other plans."

John Lennon

STAGE 1: PREPARE THE SERVER HARD DISK

Now, you can start the NetWare 3 to 4 in-place upgrade process with hard disk preparation. In this first stage, we will perform two full system backups (including both network security and file system information), configure the CD-ROM as a DOS device, run the INSTALL.BAT utility, copy the server boot files to the DOS partition, and select the server locale and file system format. Let's get started.

Step 1: Make Full System Backups

The first step in the upgrade process is to boot your NetWare 3 server — nice idea. Next, you should make at least two full server backups on tape or another storage medium. When you perform your backups, make sure to include network security information (such as the bindery) as well as the file system. Remember, you *will* want to restore your server back to its original state if something goes wrong.

Step 2: Configure the CD-ROM Drive

Next, we should install your CD-ROM as a DOS device — use the directions that came with it. Don't forget to reboot the server if you make any changes to AUTOEXEC.BAT or CONFIG.SYS. Next, insert the NetWare 4 Installation CD-ROM in drive D. At the DOS prompt, type **D:** (or the appropriate drive letter) to switch to the CD-ROM drive, then **CD ** to switch to the root directory.

Step 3: Run INSTALL.BAT and Select the Server Language

The next upgrade step involves INSTALL.BAT. It hangs out in the root directory of the NetWare 4 CD-ROM. As you learned in the previous chapter, INSTALL.BAT automates most of the installation and upgrade steps. Start it by typing **INSTALL.**

▶ . . . . ◀

FIGURE 7.1

*Choosing a NetWare 4
Server Language*

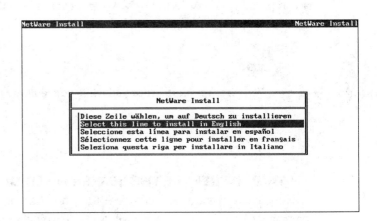

NetWare responds with a server language screen like the one in Figure 7.1. If you want the installation instructions displayed in English, choose the Select this line to install in English option. Otherwise, choose one of the other four language options (Deutsch, Español, Français, or Italiano). Next, you'll be asked which type of installation you'd like; select NetWare Server Installation option and press Enter. Now we're cooking! Next, select NetWare 4.1 from the Choose the Product You Want to Install menu and the final Installation Utility menu will appear, as shown in Figure 7.2. As your last configuration task, choose Upgrade NetWare 3.1x or 4.x from the Select the Type of Installation You Are Performing menu. Now we're ready to start the upgrade for real by copying server boot files.

FIGURE 7.2

*The NetWare 3 to 4
 Upgrade Screen*

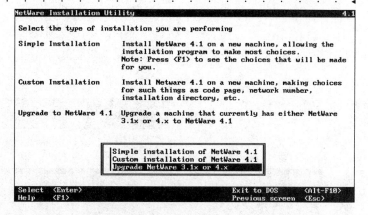

```
NetWare Installation Utility                                            4.1

Select the type of installation you are performing

Simple Installation      Install NetWare 4.1 on a new machine, allowing the
                         installation program to make most choices.
                         Note: Press <F1> to see the choices that will be made
                         for you.

Custom Installation      Install Netware 4.1 on a new machine, making choices
                         for such things as code page, network number,
                         installation directory, etc.

Upgrade to NetWare 4.1   Upgrade a machine that currently has either NetWare
                         3.1x or 4.x to NetWare 4.1

                         ┌────────────────────────────────────────┐
                         │ Simple installation of NetWare 4.1      │
                         │ Custom installation of NetWare 4.1      │
                         │ Upgrade NetWare 3.1x or 4.x             │
                         └────────────────────────────────────────┘

Select   <Enter>                              Exit to DOS        <Alt-F10>
Help     <F1>                                 Previous screen    <Esc>
```

Step 4: Copy the Server Boot Files to the DOS Partition

The first "real" upgrade step involves copying the server boot files to the existing DOS partition. Because NetWare 3 and NetWare 4 use the same partition type, you don't need to create a DOS partition. You just need to copy the NetWare 4 server boot files there. First, INSTALL.BAT asks for the DOS destination; it defaults to C:\NWSERVER. This is bad (see the discussion in the Real World). To change it, type **C:\SERVER.41**, then select Yes when asked whether to create the C:\SERVER.41 directory. Then, you must verify the source path; retain D:\NW410\INSTALL\ENGLISH if you're installing from an English CD-ROM.

Next, you'll be asked to enter the path for the existing SERVER.EXE file. Type **C:\SERVER.312**. INSTALL will copy a number of server boot files from the CD-ROM to the C:\SERVER.41 directory, including SERVER.EXE, disk drivers, LAN drivers, INSTALL.NLM, NWSNUT.NLM, and more. As you can see in Figure 7.3, not all the existing files are updated. Once the files have been copied, a message pops up listing the drivers that were not changed. Make sure you are using the latest version of these drivers. If not, copy the new ones to the C:\SERVER.41 directory.

F I G U R E 7.3

Drivers Not Updated by
INSTALL .BAT

REAL WORLD

During the NetWare 4 simple or custom installation, INSTALL.BAT copies the server boot files to C:\NWSERVER on the DOS partition. During the in-place upgrade, however, you should identify a different destination path, like C:\SERVER.41. Why, you ask? Because the original NetWare 3 server already has a directory called C:\SERVER.312 that contains the NetWare 3.12 server boot files. By all means, encourage coexistence and stay consistent. This way, when NetWare 5 comes along, you can create a similar DOS directory called C:\SERVER.5. Then, you'll be the only CNE on the block with all three major NetWare OS versions on your server. Very cool!

Step 5: Select the Server Locale and Filename Format

The final disk preparation step focuses on server-specific formatting — namely Locale and Filename Format. It starts with the Locale Configuration screen. You'll notice that the default values are set up for the United States. If you reside in a different country, here's your chance to modify the country code, code page, and keyboard mapping parameters. When the values listed are correct, press Enter to continue.

Next, is Filename Format. As you can see in Figure 7.4, you have two choices — DOS and NetWare. The DOS format forces all extended filenames to adhere to strict DOS rules (eight-character names with three-character extensions, all uppercase). The NetWare format, however, gives you move flexibility (lowercase characters). Because most applications and DOS utilities only support DOS filenames, you should select DOS Filename Format (recommended) and press Enter. Remember, we're performing an upgrade, and therefore, the file system already exists. If you switch from NetWare to the DOS filename format, all extended attributes will be changed once the volumes are mounted. Good. Now you're ready to start SERVER.EXE and switch control to the NetWare partition.

F I G U R E 7.4

Selecting a Filename
Format in INSTALL .BAT

STAGE 2: RUN SERVER.EXE

During Stage 1, we made a minimum of two full server backups (including network security and file system information), configured the CD-ROM as a DOS device, ran the INSTALL.BAT utility, copied the server boot files to the DOS partition, and selected the server locale and filename format. Now it's time for Stage 2.

In Stage 2, INSTALL will automatically execute SERVER.EXE from the C:\SERVER.41 directory. This turns upgrade control over to the server. Let's take a quick look at the only step in Stage 2.

Step 6: Start the Server

Once the server disk has been prepared, INSTALL.BAT automatically activates SERVER.EXE from the NetWare 4 directory — C:\SERVER.41. The server performs a warm boot to flush out DOS and load NetWare 4. Once the colon prompt appears, INSTALL.BAT automatically loads INSTALL.NLM. Now we can load the existing disk and LAN drivers. That's Stage 3.

STAGE 3: LOAD THE NETWARE DRIVERS

In Stage 2, INSTALL automatically executed SERVER.EXE and shifted control from DOS to NetWare 4. In Stage 3, you'll load and configure existing disk and CD-ROM drivers, reconfigure the internal CD-ROM, and update existing LAN driver(s). Let's take a look.

Step 7: Load and Configure Existing Disk and CD-ROM Driver(s)

After executing SERVER.EXE, INSTALL.BAT automatically loads INSTALL.NLM. The first Upgrade task is to display the currently loaded disk drivers, as seen in Figure 7.5. You can add additional disk drivers if necessary, but you should make sure to use one driver per controller. Also, verify that the hardware configurations (interrupt and address values) are correct. When everything's cool, select Continue installation and press Enter. The Upgrade program will then load the selected disk drivers from C:\SERVER.41. If you have updated drivers, place them in C:\SERVER.41 during Step 4.

Step 8: Configure the CD-ROM as a DOS or NetWare Device (Conditional)

At this point, a warning message may appear indicating a possible conflict with your internal CD-ROM driver. If it happens, calm down, everything is all right. Simply choose Continue accessing the CD-ROM via DOS and press Enter. You should be able to continue normally despite the warning. If not, your keyboard will lock up — oops. Reboot the server and start the Upgrade again. This time mount the CD-ROM as a network device.

Step 9: Update LAN Drivers

Next, another message pops up, this time concerning Ethernet frame types. Read the warning carefully and press Enter to continue. Remember, NetWare 4.1 uses a different default frame type (Ethernet_802.2) than NetWare 3.11 (Ethernet_802.3). Choose one. Then INSTALL.NLM will copy a number of LAN drivers and name space utilities to your hard disk. Once the files have been copied, a message appears with a list of the LAN drivers that weren't updated during the upgrade process. Read the message carefully and press Enter to continue. All is well. Are you ready for Stage 4?

QUIZ

Before we move on to Stage 4, let's take a little mental break. I'd like you to meet Guinevere's sister — she's quite an odd bird. She will ride in a cab, but not a taxi. She will talk to your neighbor, but not to you. She will eat pasta, but not rice. She will turn left or right but not around. Will she like tulips or roses?

(Q7-3)

STAGE 4: LOAD INSTALL.NLM

In Stage 3, we configured the appropriate disk and CD-ROM driver(s), determined whether to continue using the CD-ROM as a DOS device, and updated the LAN driver(s). In Stage 4, you'll determine which optional file groups (if any) to copy, license the NetWare 4 OS, then reestablish a server-to-server connection (if applicable). This all happens with the help of INSTALL.NLM. Here's how it works.

Step 10: Copy Optional NetWare Files

Step 10 begins with a detailed list of optional NetWare file groups (see Figure 7.6). Initially, all of the file groups are selected. To deselect a group, arrow down to a specific line and press Spacebar. At a minimum, you'll want to copy the NetWare DOS Utilities and NetWare MS Windows Utilities. When the correct groups are marked, press F10 to continue.

F I G U R E 7.6

*Optional NetWare File
Groups*

```
NetWare Server Installation  4.1                    NetWare Loadable Module

Select Optional NetWare Files

INSTALL by default copies 20 MB of system files to this
server. Select additional optional file groups you want
installed. File groups marked with 'X' will be installed.

  [X] NetWare DOS Utilities (12 MB)
  [X] NetWare OS/2 Utilities (2 MB)
  [X] NetWare MS Windows Utilities (4 MB)
  [X] NetWare UNIX Utilities (1 MB)
  [X] Set up a Network Directory for Client Install (7 MB)

  "NetWare DOS Utilities" Help

   The DOS utilities are executables and associated files for server
   administration from a DOS client workstation.  These files are copied to
   SYS:\PUBLIC.
                    (To scroll, <F7>-up <F8>-down)
Accept marked groups and continue <F10>       Skip copying files <F9>
Mark/unmark a file group          <Enter>     Previous screen <Esc>
Help                              <F1>        Abort INSTALL <Alt><F10>
```

INSTALL.NLM then copies the so-called preliminary files from the CD-ROM to the SYS: volume. You're also given an opportunity to view the temporary AUTOEXEC.NCF file. Press F3 to view or modify the file. You should notice remarks regarding lines that have been temporarily deleted (commented out) during the Upgrade process. Press F10 to save and execute the temporary AUTOEXEC.NCF file — it loads and binds the existing LAN drivers.

Once this happens, you should see something like Figure 7.7. This graphic displays the currently loaded LAN driver(s). If you installed additional NICs, add the drivers now. Otherwise, select Continue installation and press Enter. INSTALL.NLM will temporarily store the LAN driver(s) on the DOS partition before they are loaded. At this point, it copies the optional file groups to SYS:, then loads the LAN driver and binds IPX (or IP) to it. If multiple LAN drivers have been selected, it will do this for each one. Gee, thanks.

F I G U R E 7.7

Selected Network Drivers

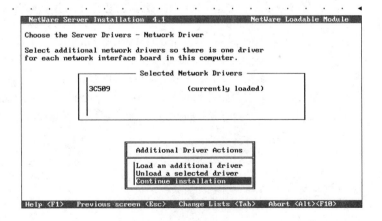

```
NetWare Server Installation  4.1                    NetWare Loadable Module

Choose the Server Drivers - Network Driver

Select additional network drivers so there is one driver
for each network interface board in this computer.

                    ── Selected Network Drivers ──
   3C509                    (currently loaded)



                    ┌─ Additional Driver Actions ─┐
                    │ Load an additional driver    │
                    │ Unload a selected driver     │
                    │ Continue installation        │
                    └──────────────────────────────┘

Help <F1>   Previous screen <Esc>   Change Lists <Tab>   Abort <Alt><F10>
```

Step 11: License the NetWare 4 Operating System

Now it's time to update the new server license. When you are prompted, insert the NetWare 4 License diskette ("SERVER CONNECTION LICENSE") in drive A. As you can see in Figure 7.8, a warning appears asking you not to install this license on another server. Doing so would cause a serious copyright warning violation — this is bad. Read the message carefully, then press Enter to continue. A greeting pops up stating that the Server Connection License was successfully installed. Press Enter to continue.

F I G U R E 7.8

NetWare 4 Server Connection License in INSTALL .NLM

TIP

Server connection licenses in NetWare 3 are embedded into the OS file, SERVER.EXE. If you use the same license on two servers, an annoying copyright violation appears on the server console and all workstations — but that's all. NetWare 4, on the other hand, relies on a Server License diskette, and its violations are a bit more disruptive. If you share a NetWare 4 license on two servers, the same warnings appear, but you also get an added little surprise: your total server licenses drop to *one!* That's just enough to revalidate the server. Be careful, the server might even put you under citizen's arrest and call in the bounty hunters.

Step 12: Reestablish the Server-to-Server Connection (Conditional)

If you're upgrading over a network, INSTALL might lose its connection to the host server at this point. If so, you'll need to reestablish the server-to-server connection by providing the correct password. Otherwise, ignore this step if you are running the in-place upgrade from CD-ROM.

Now it's the moment you've all been waiting for — NDS installation.

STAGE 5: INSTALL NETWARE DIRECTORY SERVICES (NDS)

In Stage 4, you determined which optional file groups to copy, licensed the NetWare 4 operating system, then reestablished a server-to-server connection (if necessary). Now it's time to build the Cloud. In Stage 5, you get a chance to install NetWare Directory Services and Time Synchronization. Of course, if you're upgrading a NetWare 4.0 source server, you can skip this step, because NDS is already installed.

Step 13: Install NetWare Directory Services (NDS)

This is where the fun begins, and it all starts with a simple question:

```
Is this the first NetWare 4 server?
```

You have two choices: Select Yes if this will be the first server in the NDS tree or No if this server will be inserted into an existing NDS tree. Let's assume this is the first NetWare 4 upgrade. Choose Yes, this is the first NetWare 4 server from the NDS installation menu in Figure 7.9. Next, you'll be asked for a new tree name. Choose something creative like Oak or Walnut.

F I G U R E 7.9

"Is This the First NetWare 4 Server?"

Next, a list of time zones appears. Choose yours and press Enter. INSTALL responds with the Time Configuration window (see Figure 7.10). This screen enables you to customize various Time Synchronization parameters, including Time Server type, offset from UTC (Universal Time Coordinated), and Daylight Saving Time options. These are critical NetWare 4 configurations. When you're done, press F10 to continue.

FIGURE 7.10

NetWare 4 Time Configuration Window

The final NDS configuration is Server Context. This defines where the server will appear in the new NDS tree. The CAMELOT server, for example, will be upgraded to the following context:

```
.OU=CHARITY.OU=CAMELOT.O=ACME
```

To create the above server context, you must supply the following information to INSTALL.NLM:

- ▶ Company or Organization: ACME

- ▶ Level-1 Sub-Organizational Unit: CAMELOT

- ▶ Level-2 Sub-Organizational Unit: CHARITY

- ▶ Level-3 Sub-Organizational Unit: (leave field blank)

Finally, you'll need to supply the Admin (central administrator) password. This NetWare 4 superhero controls access to all branches of the new NDS tree. If this is the first server in the tree, make up a password you'll definitely remember. When you are prompted, type the password a second time for verification. When you are asked whether to save the Directory information and continue, select Yes.

The in-place upgrade then installs NDS on the server. After the files have been copied, an informational screen appears with the Directory tree name, Directory context, and Administrator name. Note them for future reference, along with the Administrator password. Congratulations! The Cloud is alive. Now let's finish the rest of the sky with AUTOEXEC.NCF, NetWare 4 SYSTEM and PUBLIC files, Other Installation options, and Rebooting — they're Stage 6.

STAGE 6: VIEW/MODIFY THE AUTOEXEC.NCF FILE

Welcome to the final stage of NetWare 4 in-place upgrade. Now that NDS is in place, it's time to polish off the new server with AUTOEXEC.NCF, the NetWare 4 SYSTEM and PUBLIC files, and any optional products you may want. When we're done, we will down the server, reboot it, and welcome in a new era in computing — the birth of another NetWare 4 ACME server. Here are the final five steps.

Step 14: Create/Modify the AUTOEXEC.NCF File

INSTALL will scan the AUTOEXEC.NCF file to verify Ethernet frame type support, time synchronization parameters, and Directory context information. A message will appear regarding AUTOEXEC.NCF — check out Figure 7.11. Let it go through its gyrations, and eventually press Enter to continue. Remember, AUTOEXEC.NCF is a critical server configuration file. It supports LAN drivers, protocol binding, NDS information, and other management NLMs. If you want to manually edit the file, do so now. When you're done, move on to Step 15 — copying the new SYSTEM and PUBLIC files.

FIGURE 7.11

AUTOEXEC.NCF Update
Warning Message

```
NetWare Server Installation  4.1                    NetWare Loadable Module

            The AUTOEXEC.NCF will be scanned to verify that Ethernet 802.2
            frame support is loaded for Ethernet LAN drivers.  The AUTOEXEC.NCF
            file will be checked for time and Directory context information.
            You will be shown the changes that need to be made, if any.  See
            your written documentation to make sure you understand these items
            and can verify that the changes are correct.

            Press <Enter> to continue.
```

Step 15: Copy the NetWare 4 SYSTEM and PUBLIC Files to SYS:

Earlier, in Step 10, we copied Optional NetWare file groups to the new SYS: volume. Now we must copy the Required NetWare 4 SYSTEM and PUBLIC files to SYS:. They're placed in the existing LOGIN, SYSTEM, PUBLIC, MAIL, and ETC directories. Some of the required utilities include NWADMIN, NETADMIN, PCONSOLE, MONITOR.NLM, LOGIN.EXE, NLIST, and NDIR. Don't worry, INSTALL takes care of this step for you automatically.

Step 16: Other Installation Options

When the required SYSTEM and PUBLIC files have been copied, INSTALL jumps over to the Other Installation Options menu (see Figure 7.12). This screen lists the remaining NetWare 4 installation options, including Print Services, Client Support, NetWare for Macintosh, and so on. Simply choose one and press Enter. When you're ready to complete the upgrade, select Continue installation and press Enter. We're almost there. Can't you just feel it?

Step 17: Complete the Upgrade

Wow! You're done. A congratulatory message will appear indicating that you've successfully navigated the in-place upgrade forest. It looks something like the picture in Figure 7.13. Read the message carefully and let out a great big sigh. Now there's only one step standing between you and NetWare 4 bliss: Step 18.

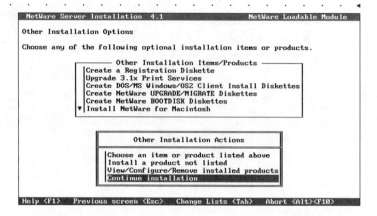

F I G U R E 7.12

*Other Installation Options
Menu in INSTALL .NLM*

Step 18: Boot the Server Using the New Startup Files

In order to enjoy the full glory of NetWare 4, you must first reboot the server. Remove the NetWare 4 license disk from drive A and store it someplace safe. Type **DOWN** to down the server, then **EXIT** to switch back to the DOS partition. Reboot the server.

Switch to the C:\SERVER.41 directory by typing **CD\SERVER.41**, then type **SERVER** to start the server. Make sure that all of the STARTUP.NCF and AUTOEXEC.NCF commands work properly. Step back and relish your masterpiece. All is well.

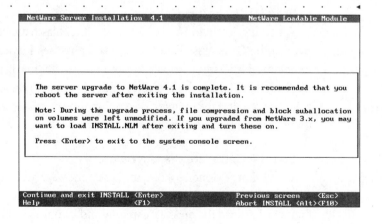

F I G U R E 7.13

*Congratulations — You're
Done!*

ZEN

"There is nothing either good or bad, but thinking makes it so."

Shakespeare

Just in case you missed anything along the way, here's a quick recap of the NetWare 3 to NetWare 4 in-place upgrade steps:

1 • Make full system backups.

2 • Configure the CD-ROM drive.

3 • Run INSTALL.BAT and select the server language.

4 • Copy the server boot files to the DOS partition.

5 • Select the server locale and filename format.

6 • Start the server (happens automatically).

7 • Load the existing disk and CD-ROM driver(s).

8 • Configure the CD-ROM as a DOS or NetWare device (conditional).

9 • Update LAN driver(s).

10 • Copy optional NetWare files.

11 • License the NetWare 4 operating system.

12 • Reestablish the server-to-server connection (if needed).

13 • Install NDS.

14 • View/modify the AUTOEXEC.NCF file.

15 • Copy the NetWare 4 SYSTEM and PUBLIC files to SYS:.

16 • Perform other installation options.

17 • Complete the installation.

18 • Boot the server using the new startup files.

There you are. Your boring NetWare 3 server is now a magnificent, sparkling NDS-enhanced NetWare 4 roadster. But what happened to your users? Don't worry they're okay. As you can see in Figure 7.14, they all started in a confining NetWare 3 bindery. All of the CHARITY_INC users were originally defined at the server level. Not anymore.

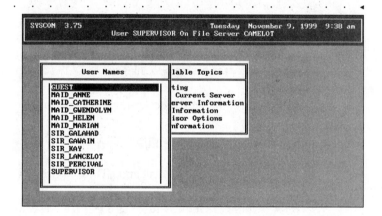

CHARITY_INC Users in
the Confining NetWare 3
Bindery (Before)

Your CHARITY_INC users have been magically transformed into NetWare 4 NDS objects. During the in-place upgrade, INSTALL dumps them into the same logical container as the CHARITY server. As Figure 7.15 shows, all the users, groups, volumes, printers, and print queues from CHARITY_INC have been placed in the OU=CHARITY.OU=CAMELOT.O=ACME container. Now they can log into the NetWare 4 Cloud and have immediate access to all resources in the ACME WAN (provided they have sufficient rights). But before you get too excited about this great new frontier, there's some housekeeping to be done.

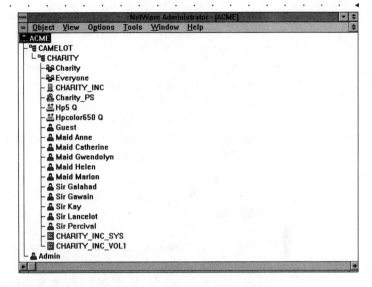

FIGURE 7.15

*CHARITY_INC Users in
Their New NetWare 4
Home (After)*

AFTER THE UPGRADE

After you complete the in-place upgrade and before you celebrate the birth of your new NetWare 4 server, there are a few housekeeping tasks that need to be accomplished. These tasks focus on object reorganization, login scripts, security, frame types, utilities, and printing. Here's a quick checklist:

▸ Reorganize upgraded objects into the appropriate NDS containers. Remember they all get dumped into a single container — the server's home OU. For help see Chapter 8.

▸ Assign NDS Object and Property rights to all your upgraded bindery objects; see Chapter 11.

▸ Change the Container and User login scripts to reflect any changes in the server name, directory paths, NO_DEFAULT, and so on; see Chapter 12.

▸ Modify upgraded objects so they fit your established NDS Naming Standard.

▸ Verify that User and Group file system rights are correct; see Chapter 11.

▸ Change the Ethernet frame type on each workstation to reflect the new NetWare 4 standard (Ethernet_802.2); see Chapter 12.

▸ Review the files in merged directories and reorganize them if necessary. Also, make sure to update directory and file attributes; see Chapter 11.

▸ Clean up the new printing system. You may want to run MIGPRINT.EXE to migrate the printing environment from NetWare 3 to NetWare 4. We'll talk about this a little later in the migration section.

▸ Verify that print queues are working properly. Assign print queue and print server operators.

▸ Verify that applications are running properly.

▸ Copy the NetWare 4.1 LOGIN.EXE file to the SYS:LOGIN directory on all NetWare 2 or 3 servers throughout the WAN. This enables NetWare 4 login scripts to work with bindery emulation.

▸ Pick a test user and log in to check all security and configurations, including passwords, login scripts, NDS security, account restrictions, and drive mappings.

▸ Use SBACKUP (or other SMS application) to make a copy of all data on the NetWare 4.1 server; see Chapter 13.

▸ Check all workstation configurations, including NET.CFG, boot diskettes, and VLMs; see Chapter 13.

▸ Type **ENABLE LOGIN** at the server console to open the server for new NetWare 4 users.

QUIZ

Maid Marion was out on patrol in a strange section of Sherwood Forest and she came across a beautiful princess. The princess was distraught because she lived in the land of the Liars and the Truthtellers. The princess was herself a Truthteller and had no wish to marry a Liar. When a handsome young man from far away asked for her hand in marriage, she devised a simple test to find out whether he was a Liar. She said to him "Do you see that woman walking in the road? I've never seen her before, but I would like to have her as a maid—she looks very nice. Go and ask her if she is a Truthteller or a Liar." The young man returned and said, "She says she is a Truthteller," which solved the problem for the princess very nicely. Was there a happy ending?

(Q7-4)

Well, that just about does it for in-place upgrade. You've successfully traversed the grand upgrade forest. As you learned earlier, this method enables you to migrate NetWare 2 or 3 servers to NetWare 4 without additional hardware. All bindery information is transferred to NDS, and the data stays right where it is — on the NetWare partition. That's the "in-place" part. Hopefully, you gained an appreciation for the advantages of "in-place." Namely, there's little risk of data loss.

Now, let's take a closer look at the third and final NetWare 4 installation method — migration. This approach involves more hardware, more risk, and more heartache. But hey, we get to use a new utility: MIGRATE.EXE. Cool.

NetWare 4 Migration

The final installation method enables you to move NetWare 3 bindery information and data to a new NetWare 4 server through an NDS workstation. There's no "in-place" involved. You can approach migration in one of two ways:

▶ Across-the-wire: migration over the LAN from one server to another — two servers, one workstation.

▸ Same-server: migration on the same server using an NDS client — one server, one workstation.

The across-the-wire migration method transfers bindery information and data from one server to another across the LAN. It requires three machines: two servers and one migration client. The client runs MIGRATE.EXE. As you learned earlier, it is the safest upgrade method because the source server remains intact, and it enables you to migrate from multiple source servers to a single NetWare 4 destination. Also, you are given the option of determining whether to migrate all or selected information. This can be particularly useful, especially when you're dealing with the NetWare 3 bindery.

The same-server method, on the other hand, converts bindery information within a single server. It emulates the in-place upgrade to a point but operates at the migration client (MIGRATE.EXE) — unlike in-place upgrade, which uses INSTALL.NLM at the server. Same-server migration requires you to offload your data to a backup tape and then restore it later — no "in-place" here. Once you've backed up the source data, MIGRATE copies the bindery information to the DOS client and installs NetWare 4 over the existing server. Finally, the bindery information and data are copied back to the new NetWare 4 NDS destination.

The detailed migration steps for both methods are similar: You use the same utility (MIGRATE.EXE) and the same DOS client. The main difference is in the movement of data — across-the-wire or backup/restore. This section concentrates on the across-the-wire migration method — it's the most popular. But don't worry, we won't ignore the same-server method. It pops up now and again. Let's start our discussion with a look at the NetWare information that gets migrated.

ZEN

"The creation of a thousand forests is in one acorn."

Ralph Waldo Emerson

NetWare 4 migration enables you to choose the categories of information you'd like to migrate. Here are some important details about what *is*, *isn't*, and *should be* migrated:

▸ All information — This is the default category. It migrates everything except print services, system login scripts, and user passwords.

- Data files — Only DOS directories and files that conform to DOS naming conventions are migrated, and their security attributes are preserved. Also, existing directories and files with the same name are not overwritten. Good. Finally, subdirectories greater than 25 levels deep are ignored.

- Trustee assignments — User and group trustee rights are migrated (thank goodness). If you select this category, you should also select these other support categories: data files, users, and groups.

- Users — User names, user login scripts (LOGIN.), and print job configurations (PRINTCON.DAT) are migrated, but passwords are not. You are given the option of assigning randomly generated passwords or allowing users to log into the new system without a password. If you choose to use random passwords, the new passwords are stored in the SYS:SYSTEM directory as the file NEW.PWD. If you choose to have users log in without passwords, you should configure login restrictions so that they are forced to set a password the first time they log in. Existing information on the destination server will not be overwritten, although user rights will be merged.

- User restrictions — User login restrictions are migrated. These include account balance restrictions, expiration date, password restrictions, and time restrictions. Unfortunately, user disk restrictions are not migrated. Existing user restrictions on the destination server will not be overwritten. Lucky for us, I was worried about that. How about you?

- Groups — Group membership and file system rights are migrated. If a group of the same name exists on the destination server, the source and destination groups are merged.

- Default account restrictions — Default account restrictions are migrated and overwrite existing settings on the destination server. That's intense.

- Accounting information — NetWare 3 accounting services are migrated and overwrite existing information on the NetWare 4 server. This differs from the NetWare 4 auditing feature. Advice: Use auditing, it's much more powerful.

▸ Print queues and print servers — NetWare 3 print queues and print servers are migrated. If objects of the same name exist on the destination server, the information is merged. The printing environment itself is not migrated, however. To do so, you must use the MIGPRINT.EXE utility after the migration is completed — and we will.

TIP

The NetWare 3 system login script is not migrated to the new NetWare 4 server. You can move it manually, though, by following any of these strategies:

   ▸ **Use the NetWare Administrator (or NETADMIN) utility to type in the login script statements manually. They should be placed in appropriate Container login scripts.**

   ▸ **Copy NET$LOG.DAT to the NetWare 4 server, then use an MS Windows text editor to copy it to the Clipboard and paste it into the Container login script.**

   ▸ **Copy NET$LOG.DAT to the NetWare 4 server, then use an INCLUDE statement in the Container login script to reference it.**

Although user login scripts are migrated to the NetWare 4 server (that is, SYS:MAIL\USERID#), they're not imported into the NDS database. The migration utility creates two files in the SYS:SYSTEM directory called UIMPORT.CTL and IMPORT.DAT, however, that can be used by UIMPORT to integrate these login scripts into NDS.

NetWare 4 migration is pretty simple. It relies on a single utility and two or three machines. Here's how it works:

1 • Access the Migration utility.

2 • Select the type of migration.

3 • Configure the Migration utility.

4 • Perform the migration.

5 • Verify the migration.

Piece of cake. Wanna learn more? Follow me.

TIP

When you use MIGRATE.EXE, you must be logged into the source and destination servers through bindery emulation. For some reason, the Migration utility depends on bindery services to work properly. You can either log into the source and destination servers before you start or let MIGRATE do it for you. If you want to log into the two servers prior to starting the migration, follow these simple rules:

▸ **Log into the NetWare 3 source server normally — no NDS.**

▸ **Log into the NetWare 4 server using the "/B" option for bindery emulation:**

```
LOGIN ACME/SUPERVISOR /B.
```

STEP 1: ACCESS THE MIGRATION UTILITY

It all begins by configuring your CD-ROM drive. Make sure one is available on your migrating workstation. This is where we will run MIGRATE.EXE. Don't forget to reboot the workstation if you make any changes to your AUTOEXEC.BAT or CONFIG.SYS files. When the CD-ROM drive is operational, insert the NetWare 4 installation CD-ROM, and make it your default drive.

Next, we will run MIGRATE.EXE. It is located in the D:\MIGRATE directory on the CD-ROM. Type D: (or the appropriate drive letter) to switch to the CD-ROM drive, CD \MIGRATE to switch to the MIGRATE directory, then MIGRATE to execute the utility.

TIP

NetWare 4 uses a different utility to migrate Banyan VINES servers — BMIGRATE.EXE.

Now, we're ready for Step 2.

STEP 2: SELECT THE TYPE OF MIGRATION

The next step is to choose one of two migration types: across-the-wire and same-server. In this discussion, we'll select Across-the Wire migration from the main menu shown in Figure 7.16.

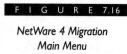

F I G U R E   7.16

NetWare 4 Migration Main Menu

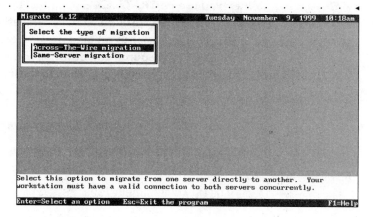

Next, choose the source LAN type from the approved list given here (also see Figure 7.17). I like NetWare 3.x; how about you?

- ► NetWare 2.x

- ► NetWare 3.x

- ► Microsoft LAN Manager 2.0

- ► IBM LAN Server 1.2 - 1.3

- ► IBM LAN Server 1.0 - 1.1

- ► IBM PCLP v1.3 Extended Services

F I G U R E 7.17

*Choosing a Source LAN
Type for NetWare 4
Migration*

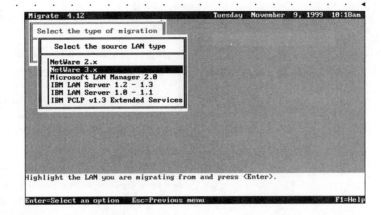

As you can see from this list, one of the main advantages of the NetWare 4 migration method is flexibility. Finally, choose a destination LAN type — NetWare 4.x. Once you've made all your choices, MIGRATE responds with a detailed configuration screen. This is where the fun begins.

STEP 3: CONFIGURE THE MIGRATION UTILITY

Most of the NetWare 4 migration tasks are integrated into Step 3. All activity centers around a single configuration form — that shown in Figure 7.18. As you can see it is broken into three main parts:

1 • Configure the migration utility.

2 • Define the NetWare 3.x source server.

3 • Define the NetWare 4.x destination server.

Each part has two or three fields that define critical migration parameters, including working directory, source server, destination server, and passwords. Let's take a closer look at the three parts of NetWare 4 migration.

The Main Configuration
Screen in MIGRATE .EXE

Part 1: Configure the Migration Utility

The top part of the migration form deals with general MIGRATE.EXE configurations — namely, working directory and error action.

It starts with the Working Directory field. Bindery information and migration settings, but no data files, are stored in this directory. It must have a minimum of 5 MB space, and the default location is D:\MIGRATE. Oops. This could be a problem. Remember, the CD-ROM drive is a read-only device — we're not storing any files here. You'll need to define a read/write device like C:\MIGRATE. If you forget to change the default, MIGRATE will respond with an error message — but not until you've completed almost all of the other steps. Please save yourself some time and change the default working directory to something writable.

TIP

The working directory is usually located on a workstation hard drive. If you choose to use a network drive instead, you will need to have the Read, Write, Create, and File Scan rights to that directory.

The second field enables you to define settings for errors and warning messages. In this field, you'll be asked whether to pause the migration after each error/warning. Although the default is to pause after each error, you might want to allow the migration to run unattended — because of the time element involved. After the migration is completed, you can review the migration log. It lists all the errors that were encountered during the migration.

When you're done with the TOP part of the migration form, continue to the MIDDLE section — source server.

ZEN

"Laugh, or I'll blow your lips off ...."

From the movie *Dead Men Don't Wear Plaid*

Part 2: Define the NetWare 3.x Source Server

The middle part of the migration form deals with the NetWare 3 source server — server name, information categories, and source volume.

These configurations begin with the name of the source server — typically a NetWare 2 or 3 server. In order for the migration to work properly, you'll need to be logged into both the source and destination servers as Supervisor. In the case of the NetWare 4 server, you'll need to use bindery services, so your entry reads LOGIN SUPERVISOR /B.

If you're not already logged in, Migrate will do it for you. Simply press Enter in the first field, and MIGRATE.EXE will display a list of servers that you are currently logged into. If the list is empty, press Ins, and MIGRATE.EXE will display a list of available servers (see Figure 7.19). Choose the source server and provide a valid username and password. If you're migrating multiple source servers, you have to define them one at a time.

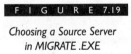

F I G U R E 7.19

Choosing a Source Server in MIGRATE .EXE

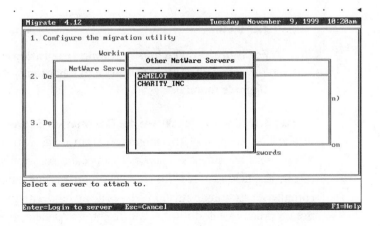

The second field in the middle section of the configuration screen deals with information categories. This option enables you to define the types of source information you want to migrate. If you press Enter, a detailed list appears (Figure 7.20), including data files, trustee assignments, users, user account restrictions, groups, default account restrictions, accounting information, print queues, printer servers, and non-Novell bindery objects. These categories were described earlier. To migrate everything, choose All information and press Enter.

F I G U R E 7.20

NetWare 4 Migration
Categories

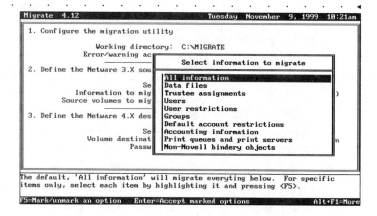

The final source field enables you to choose one or more source volumes for migration. Use F5 to mark multiple volumes. Once the source server, information categories, and volumes have been defined, it's time to move on to the destination server — NetWare 4.

THE BRAIN

For more detailed information on migrating a server running LAN Server or LAN Manager, refer to Chapter 3 of the *Novell NetWare 4 Upgrade* manual.

Part 3: Define the NetWare 4.x Destination Server

The bottom part of the migration form deals with the NetWare 4 destination server — server name, destination volume, and passwords.

The first field identifies the destination server. Remember, you must be logged into both the source and destination servers using bindery emulation. If you aren't logged in already, Migrate will do it for you. In the server field, press Enter to display a list of servers that you are currently logged into. If the destination server is not listed, it means you're logged in. Press Ins and choose a NetWare 4 machine from the Other NetWare Servers list — just like in Figure 7.19.

The next field deals with the destination volume. MIGRATE.EXE automatically tries to find a matching partner for your source volume — defined earlier. If you need a custom configuration, press F1 to display a list of available destination volumes and directories.

The final configuration field is for destination passwords. You need to determine whether you want MIGRATE.EXE to create random passwords or leave the new user objects without a password at all. If you choose to assign random passwords, they will be stored in the NEW.PWD file in the SYS:SYSTEM directory on the destination server. Only users and print servers that had passwords on the source server will be assigned passwords. Remember: Users will not be able to log into the destination server until they are told what their new passwords are, and those passwords will be long!

You're done. Press F10 when the information on the entire configuration form is correct. Now it's time to actually *perform* the NetWare 4 migration.

STEP 4: PERFORM THE MIGRATION

That's enough configuring, now it's time for action! To begin the NetWare 4 migration, select Start migration from the menu in Figure 7.21. While the migration is running, a log will be written to a report file in the working directory — and displayed on the screen. In addition, a message may be displayed warning that MIGRATE.EXE cannot create a SYS: volume on the destination server (because it already exists). If this happens, press Enter to continue — everthing's cool.

When the migration is over, an informational message will appear. Read it, then press Enter to return to the Select a Migration Action menu. Finally, another message will be displayed that reminds you to run the MIGPRINT.EXE utility to migrate your printing environment; that's described later.

That's it — well, not *quite* it. There are a few cleanup tasks, most notably verification. After all, you want to make sure everything migrated properly before you dump your old NetWare 3 server into the ocean.

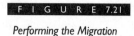

F I G U R E 7.21

Performing the Migration

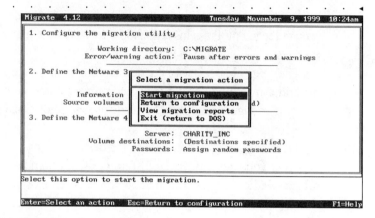

STEP 5: VERIFY THE MIGRATION

It's a good idea to verify the quality of the migration before you blow away your existing NetWare 3 server. First, you'll want to view the detailed migration report. Choose View migration reports from the Select a Migration Action menu. This report — a log file — is shown in Figure 7.22 and is an ASCII text file containing information on:

▸ The bindery import phase (migrating bindery data from the source server to the working directory)

▸ The bindery export phase (migrating bindery data from the working directory to the NetWare 4 destination server)

▸ A list of each item in each category that was imported from the source server

▸ A list of each item in each category that was exported to the destination server

▸ The number of errors that occurred during the migration — with luck, zero

*Viewing Migration Reports
in MIGRATE .EXE*

QUIZ

*In another area of Sherwood Forest, fierce winds blow all the time,
sometimes in one direction, sometimes in the other. A fast train — or
reasonably fast, depending on your ideas — can run under its own steam, if
forced — 100 MPH between Never-Never and Sometimes. This particular
day it picked up a strong favorable breeze that doubled its speed to 200
MPH, at which speed the train completed its 200-mile journey in 1 hour. At
the usual time, the train had to make the return journey. Unfortunately, the
same wind was still blowing in the same direction at the same speed. How
fast would the engineer have to push the train to make the journey home
in 4 hours?*

(Q7-5)

If all is well, you're done. Congratulations! You somehow pulled it off. The migration
was a little trickier than the upgrade, but certainly more entertaining. So your
next question is: "Where are my users?" Good question. Once again, they've been
transformed from boring NetWare 3 bindery users into magnificent NetWare 4 NDS
objects. Figure 7.23 shows a quick snapshot of the U.N. users BEFORE the migration.
Don't they look sad — all confined to a single server.

F I G U R E   7.23

U.N. Users Before *the
Migration — SYSCON*

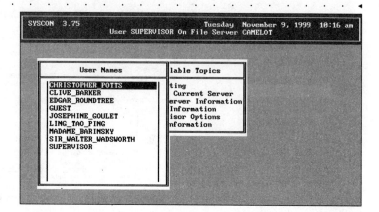

F I G U R E   7.23

U.N. Users Before *the
Migration — SYSCON*

Now, in NetWare 4, they are free to roam throughout the ACME Cloud. Their new home can be seen in Figure 7.24. Notice that they were all placed in the same container as the U.N. server. With the users firmly planted in their new homes, let's take a closer look at some migration housekeeping chores.

F I G U R E   7.24

U.N. Users After *the
Migration — NWADMIN*

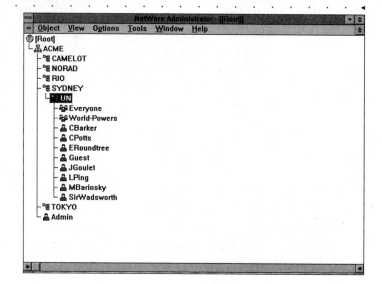

AFTER THE MIGRATION

After you complete the migration and before you celebrate the birth of your new NetWare 4 server, a few housekeeping tasks need to be addressed. These tasks focus on object reorganization, login scripts, security, frame types, utilities, and printing. Here's a quick checklist:

▶ Reorganize migrated objects into the appropriate NDS containers. Remember: They all get dumped into a single container — the server's home OU. For help see Chapter 8.

▶ Assign NDS Object and Property rights to all your upgraded bindery objects — see Chapter 11.

▶ Change the Container and user login scripts to reflect any changes in the server name, directory paths, NO_DEFAULT, and so on — see Chapter 12.

▶ Verify that user and group file system rights are correct — see Chapter 11.

▶ Change the Ethernet frame type on each workstation to reflect the new NetWare 4 standard (Ethernet_802.2) — see Chapter 12.

▶ Review the files in merged directories and reorganize them if necessary. Also, make sure to update directory and file attributes — see Chapter 11.

▶ Clean up the new printing system. You may want to run MIGPRINT.EXE to migrate the printing environment from NetWare 3 to NetWare 4. We'll talk about this in just a second.

▶ Verify that print queues are working properly. Assign print queue and print server operators.

▶ Verify that applications are running properly.

▶ Copy the NetWare 4.1 LOGIN.EXE file to the SYS:LOGIN directory on all NetWare 2 or 3 servers throughout the WAN. This enables NetWare 4 login scripts to work with bindery emulation.

> ► Pick a test user and log in to check all security and configurations, including passwords, login scripts, NDS security, account restrictions, and drive mappings.

> ► Use SBACKUP (or other SMS application) to make a copy of all data on the new NetWare 4 server — see Chapter 13.

> ► Check all workstation configurations, including NET.CFG, boot diskettes, and VLMs — see Chapter 13.

> ► Type **ENABLE LOGIN** at the server console to open the server for new NetWare 4 users.

Interestingly, MIGRATE.EXE doesn't transfer your source NetWare 3 printing environment. This requires another special migration tool — MIGPRINT.EXE. It's also found in the D:\MIGRATE directory on the NetWare 4 Installation CD-ROM.

To run MIGPRINT.EXE, you must have the following:

> ► A bindery connection from the DOS client to the source server

> ► An NDS connection from the DOS client to the NetWare 4 destination server

> ► Admin privileges to the destination printing container

> ► A search drive mapping to SYS:SYSTEM\NLS on the NetWare 4 destination server

Here's how MIGPRINT.EXE works:

```
MIGPRINT /S=source /D=destination
```

The source server is defined as *source* and the destination server is identified as *destination*. In addition, MIGPRINT supports various alternative switches, including:

/V=volume — an alternative volume (other than SYS:) for print queues

/O=output_file — an alternative output file for MIGPRINT messages

Finally, you'll definitely want to test your new printing system before allowing users to log in and use it. As you'll see in Chapter 14, there have been a number of changes to printing in NetWare 4, and things might not work as you expect them to. For instance, many third-party printing solutions don't support NDS, or they need to be reconfigured after migration.

Here's a quick review of the basic steps involved in a NetWare 4 migration:

1 • Access the MIGRATE.EXE utility.

2 • Select the type of migration.

3 • Configure the MIGRATE.EXE utility.

4 • Perform the migration.

5 • Verify the migration.

Yea, yea, yea! We made it. It's 4:59 p.m. on Tuesday afternoon, and we finished our two migrations. Boy, what a difference a day makes! Remember yesterday about this time, we were feeling a bit overwhelmed. Well, today we have a new attitude, and the migrations went much more smoothly.

Of course, NetWare 4 migration is the ultimate achievement in "nerdiness." And now you're an official member of "NLM" — Nerd Liberation Movement. Migration is the most popular NetWare 4 installation method, because there are 4 million NetWare 2 or 3 servers out there with already established binderies. As you learned in this chapter, NetWare 4 migration supports two methods:

▶ In-place upgrade — Enables you to move from NetWare 2 or 3 to NetWare 4. It does it on the same physical server. This way, the data doesn't get bothered — only the NetWare OS and bindery/NDS information is converted.

▶ Migration — Converts the NetWare 2 or 3 bindery using an NDS workstation (running the NetWare DOS Requester). You can choose one of two types of NetWare 4 migration — across-the-wire or same-server.

ZEN

"How many cares one loses when one decides not to be something but to be someone."

Coco Chanel

So there you have it. As an official member of "NLM," you can migrate servers anywhere in the world. And this is a good thing, because ACME spans the globe. Now, we're ready to take our new NetWare 4 servers to the next level: management. It's a good thing you have a new attitude. I wonder what Wednesday has in store for us?

Review the scenarios listed here, then answer the questions associated with each scenario.

SCENARIO 1

The Finance department currently has a 486/66 server with 16 MB of RAM that it wants to upgrade from NetWare 3.11 to NetWare 4. Because of the nature of the work, the finance manager is concerned that there be no loss of data or corruption during the upgrade. She also mentioned that the department has a new 120 MHz Pentium that just arrived that will take the place of the current server. The original server can then be used for a special project. The configuration of the current server is:

- A 20 MB DOS partition that currently has 11 MB of free space

- 98 MB of free space on the SYS: volume

- 149 MB of free space in the FINANCE: volume

- A 3C5X9 NIC

- An IDE disk controller

- A tape unit

- A CD-ROM drive on the workstation (the current server has no CD-ROM drive)

Your assignment:

1 • Indicate which upgrade or migration methods could be used to upgrade this server.

2 • Explain which method you would use to upgrade the new server and explain why.

3 • Explain which method you would use to upgrade the original server and explain why.

4 • Indicate what would be unusual about the method used to upgrade the original server and why it would be necessary.

SCENARIO 2

The Facilities department is currently using NetWare 2.2 on a 386/33 and would like to upgrade to NetWare 4. The facilities manager said that the department has no additional server hardware to use during the upgrade. The current configuration for this server is:

▸ 4 MB RAM

▸ 20 MB DOS partition

▸ 64 MB of free space in volume SYS:

▸ 56 MB of free space in volume VOL1:

▸ An NE1000 NIC

▸ An IDE disk controller

Your assignment:

1 • Indicate which method you would use to upgrade the server and explain why.

2 • Indicate what utility (or utilities) would be used for this method.

3 • Determine whether the current hardware configuration is appropriate for running the migration/upgrade method that you chose. If not, describe your recommendations.

4 • Specify whether the IDE disk controller would pose a problem in this situation and explain why.

SCENARIO 3

The Pollution department currently has a 486/50 commuter and is ready to upgrade from IBM LAN Server 1.2 to NetWare 4. The current configuration for this server is:

- 16 MB of RAM

- A 512 MB hard disk

- A 100 MB DOS partition with 62 MB of free space

- A CD-ROM drive

Your assignment:

1 • Indicate which upgrade or migration methods could be used to upgrade this server.

2 • Explain which method you would use if you learned that the department had no additional server hardware to use during the upgrade and explain why.

SCENARIO 4

The Marketing department has a 486/50 and is ready to upgrade from NetWare 3.12 to NetWare 4. The marketing manager is quite unhappy with the way the server is currently configured in terms of network security and would just like to start over. The current configuration for this server is:

- 16 MB of RAM

- A 15 MB DOS partition

- 25 MB of free disk space in volume SYS:

- 124 MB of free disk space in volume VOL1:

- An NE2000 network board

> ▸ An IDE disk controller and SCSI floppy controller

Your assignment:

1 • Indicate what methods could be used to upgrade this server.

2 • Indicate which method you would use to upgrade the server and explain why.

3 • Determine if the current hardware configuration is appropriate for running NetWare 4.1. If not, describe your recommendations.

4 • Explore whether the frame type of the source server would be a concern in this situation.

SCENARIO 5

The Nuclear department currently has a Banyan VINES server and would like to upgrade to NetWare 4 but would prefer not to start from scratch. The current configuration for this server is:

> ▸ 90 MHz Pentium

> ▸ 20 MB of RAM

> ▸ A 35 MB DOS partition

> ▸ 1.2 MB hard disk

1 • Indicate which upgrade or migration methods could be used to upgrade this server.

2 • Indicate which method you would use to upgrade the server and explain why.

In Chapter 6, we had the opportunity to install the new LABS-SRV1 server for ACME. Now, we need to upgrade a few servers for CHARITY. We'll start in CAMELOT and go from there. Following are the detailed steps for migrating the CAMELOT CHARITY_INC server. Follow them carefully and have a nice day.

STAGE 1: PREPARE THE SERVER HARD DISK

▶ Step 1: Make full system backups. First, boot your server using the version of DOS supplied with your computer. Then, make at least two full server backups on tape or another storage medium. Make sure to back up the network security information as well as the file system.

▶ Step 2: Configure the CD-ROM drive. Install the CD-ROM as a DOS device, according to the directions that came with the device. Reboot the server, then insert the NetWare 4 Installation CD-ROM in the CD-ROM drive. At the DOS prompt, type **D:** (or the appropriate drive letter) and press Enter to switch to the CD-ROM drive, then type **CD ** and press Enter to switch to the root directory of the CD-ROM drive.

▶ Step 3: Run INSTALL.BAT and select the server language. Type **INSTALL** and press Enter to execute the INSTALL.BAT file on the CD-ROM. When you run INSTALL.BAT, a screen will appear, enabling you to choose the language to use during the installation process. If you want the installation instructions to display in English, choose the Select this line to install in English option from the NetWare Install menu and press Enter. Choose one of the other four languages (Deutsch, Español, Français, or Italiano) if you want the installation instructions to be displayed in another language. You will then be asked to indicate the type of installation desired. Select the NetWare Server Installation option from the Select the Type of Installation Desired menu and press Enter. Next, select the NetWare 4.1 option from the Choose the Product You Want to Install menu and press Enter. Finally, select the Upgrade NetWare 3.1x or 4.x option from the Select the Type of Installation You Are Performing menu and press Enter.

▶ Step 4: Copy the server boot files to the DOS partition. Next, you will be asked to indicate the destination path for the server boot files. Type **C:\SERVER.41** and press Enter. You will then be asked whether to create the C:\SERVER.41 directory. Select Yes and press Enter. At this point, the source and destination paths for the server boot files should be correct. (For instance, if you're upgrading from CD-ROM in English, the source path should be D:\NW410\INSTALL\ENGLISH and the destination path should be C:\SERVER.41.) When the source and destination paths listed are correct, press Enter to continue. Next, you will be asked to enter the path to your existing SERVER.EXE file. Type **C:\SERVER.312** and press Enter. The system will then begin copying a number of server boot files from the CD-ROM to the C:\SERVER.41 directory on the DOS partition. After the files have been copied, a message will be displayed listing the drivers that were not updated during the installation process. Read the message carefully and press Enter to continue.

▶ Step 5: Select the server locale and filename format. Next, you will be asked to supply locale information. You'll notice that the default values are set up for the United States. If the system resides outside of the United States, you'll have to modify the country code, code page, and keyboard mapping parameters. When the values listed are correct, press Enter to continue. When asked to choose a filename format, select the DOS filename format (recommended) option and press Enter.

STAGE 2: RUN SERVER.EXE

▶ Step 6: Start the server. At this point, the SERVER.EXE file will automatically be executed by the Upgrade program. (The system essentially does a warm boot as it flushes the DOS operating system from server RAM and replaces it with the NetWare 4 operating system.)

STAGE 3: LOAD THE NETWARE DRIVERS

▸ Step 7: Load and configure the appropriate server disk and CD-ROM driver(s). The upgrade program will display the currently loaded disk driver. Add any additional disk drivers that are necessary. When all of the correct disk drivers have been loaded, select the Continue installation option from the Additional Driver Actions menu and press Enter.

▸ Step 8: Configure the CD-ROM as a DOS or NetWare device (conditional). At this point, a message may be displayed warning of a possible conflict with the CD-ROM driver. If this message is displayed, select the Continue accessing the CD-ROM via DOS option from the Select an Action menu and press Enter. (You'll probably be able to continue normally despite the warning.)

▸ Step 9: Update LAN drivers. Next, a message will be displayed regarding Ethernet frame types. Read the warning carefully and press Enter to continue. The upgrade program will then begin copying a number of LAN drivers and name space utilities to your hard disk. Once the files have been copied, a message will be displayed regarding the LAN drivers that were not updated during the upgrade process. Read the message carefully and press Enter to continue.

STAGE 4: LOAD INSTALL.NLM

▸ Step 10: Copy optional NetWare files. Next, a list of optional file groups will be displayed on the screen. Scroll down and make sure that only the following groups are selected:

1 • NetWare DOS Utilities

2 • NetWare MS Windows Utilities

To deselect a group that should not be selected, arrow down to that line and press Spacebar. When the correct groups are marked, press F10 to continue. The system will then automatically copy so-called preliminary files from the CD-ROM to the SYS: volume. You are then given a chance to view the temporary AUTOEXEC.NCF file. Press F3 to view the file — but don't change anything. You'll notice remarks in the file about lines that have been temporarily deleted (commented out) by the INSTALL.NLM utility. Press F10 to save and execute the temporary AUTOEXEC.NCF file, which will in turn load and bind the LAN drivers. The system will then display the currently loaded LAN driver. If you have additional network boards in the server, load a network driver for each board at this time. When the LAN drivers listed are correct, select the Continue Installation option from the Additional Drivers Actions menu and press Enter.

▶ Step 11: License the NetWare operating system. When you are prompted, insert the NetWare 4 License disk in drive A. A message will be displayed warning you not to try to install this license on another server — that to do so would cause a copyright warning violation to be issued. Read the message carefully and press Enter to continue. A message will then be displayed saying that the server connection license was successfully installed. Press Enter to continue.

▶ Step 12: Reestablish server-to-server connection (conditional). Ignore this step, because we are installing from a CD-ROM.

STAGE 5: INSTALL NETWARE DIRECTORY SERVICES (NDS)

▶ Step 13: Install NDS. You will be asked whether this is the first NetWare 4 server in the tree. Select Yes, this is the first NetWare 4 server and press Enter. You will then be asked for the name of the tree. Type **ACME_TREE** and press Enter. A list of available time zones will be displayed. Select the appropriate time zone for the server and press Enter. A time zone configuration information screen will be displayed.

Review the information on the screen and modify the parameters, if necessary. Press F10 to save the time parameters and continue. The server context screen will then be displayed. Type **ACME** in the Company or Organization field and press Enter. Type **CAMELOT** in the Level1 Sub-Organizational Unit field and press Enter. Type **CHARITY** in the Level2 Sub-Organizational Unit field and press Enter. Press Enter twice to move to the password field. Type a password that you are sure you will remember and press Enter. When you are prompted, type the password a second time for verification, and press Enter. When asked whether to save directory information and continue, select Yes and press Enter. At this point, NDS will automatically be installed on the server. After the files have been copied, a screen will be displayed listing the Directory tree name, Directory context, and administrator name. Note them for future reference (along with the Admin password used earlier) and press Enter.

STAGE 6: VIEW/MODIFY THE CONFIGURATION FILES.

▶ Step 14: Create/modify the AUTOEXEC.NCF file and STARTUP.NCF. Next, the AUTOEXEC.NCF file will be scanned to verify Ethernet frame type support, time, and directory context information. A message will be displayed regarding AUTOEXEC.NCF. Read the message, then press Enter to continue.

▶ Step 15: Copy the NetWare 4 SYSTEM and PUBLIC files to the SYS: volume. The system will then begin copying the main SYSTEM and PUBLIC files to the SYS: volume.

▶ Step 16: Other Installation options. A list of additional products that can be installed will be displayed. Do not install any additional products. Instead, select the Continue installation option from the Other Installation Actions menu and press Enter.

▸ Step 17: Complete the installation (migration). A message will be displayed on the screen informing you that the server upgrade to NetWare 4.1 is complete. Read the information carefully and press Enter to exit to the system console screen.

▸ Step 18: Reboot the server using the new startup files. Remove the NetWare 4 license disk from drive A. Type **DOWN** to down the server, then type **RESTART SERVER** to restart the server.

Oops, we keep forgetting about the U.N. This organization has committed to helping ACME save the world. Well, as part of that mission, we have to integrate the U.N.'s network technology into the ACME WAN. The first step in this process is migrating the NetWare 3 server to NetWare 4. Following are the detailed across-the-wire migration steps for the U.N. Thanks for all the help.

First, boot your server using the version of DOS supplied with your computer. If you were doing this in "real life," you'd then make at least two full server backups on tape or another storage medium, making sure to back up the network security information as well as the file system.

STEP 1: ACCESS THE MIGRATE.EXE UTILITY

▸ Configure the CD-ROM drive. Install the CD-ROM drive on your workstation as a DOS device, according to the directions that came with the device. Reboot the workstation if you have made changes to the AUTOEXEC.BAT or CONFIG.SYS configuration file, then insert the NetWare 4 Installation CD-ROM in the CD-ROM drive.

▸ Run MIGRATE.EXE. At the DOS prompt, type **D:** (or the appropriate drive letter) and press Enter to switch to the CD-ROM drive. Next, type **CD \MIGRATE** and press Enter to switch to the directory containing the MIGRATE.EXE utility. Finally, type **MIGRATE** and press Enter to execute the MIGRATE.EXE utility.

STEP 2: SELECT THE TYPE OF MIGRATION

▸ Indicate the type of migration desired. Choose the Across-the-Wire Migration option from the Select the Type of Migration menu and press Enter. Next, choose the NetWare 3.x option from the Select Source LAN Type menu and press Enter. Finally, choose the NetWare 4.x option from the Select a Destination LAN Type menu and press Enter. The Migration Utility Configuration form will then display.

STEP 3: CONFIGURE THE MIGRATE.EXE UTILITY

▸ Configure MIGRATE.EXE for the U.N. server. Press Enter in the Working directory field in order to be allowed to modify the default directory listed. Type **C:** and press Enter when you are prompted to specify the full working path. Next, press Down Arrow to accept the default listed in the error/warning action field (to pause the screen after warnings and errors).

▸ Define the NetWare 3.x source server.

1 • Select the source server. Press Enter in the server field to display a list of servers that you are logged into. Select your NetWare 3.12 server and press Enter, then skip to the next step. (If your NetWare 3.12 server is not displayed, press Ins to display a list of servers. Select your NetWare 3.12 server and press Enter. Type **SUPERVISOR** and press Enter when you are prompted for the username, then type the password and press Enter when you are prompted for the password. Finally, press Enter to return to the Migration Utility Conformation form.)

2 • Select the information to be migrated. Press Enter in the Information to migrate field to display your options. Select All Information as the category of information to be migrated and press Enter. A message will be displayed regarding migration of the printing environment to NetWare 4. Read the message carefully, then press Enter to continue.

3 • Select the source volumes. Press Enter in the source volumes to migrate field to display a list of available source volumes. Select each volume listed by marking it using F5. When all of the volumes are selected, press Enter to continue.

▸ Define the destination server.

1 • Select the destination server. Press Enter in the server field to display a list of servers. Select the destination server and press Enter, then skip to the next step. (If your NetWare 3.12 server is not displayed, press Ins to display a list of servers. Select your NetWare 3.12 server and press Enter. Type SUPERVISOR and press Enter when you are prompted for the username, then type the password and press Enter when you are prompted for the password. Finally, press Enter to return to the Migration Utility Confirmation form.)

2 • Select the volume destinations. Press Enter in the Volume destinations field to display a list of available volumes. Select the destination path of each source volume and press Enter. Press F10 when all of the information in the Destination path field is correct.

3 • Select password option. Press Enter in the Passwords field to list your options. Select Assign random passwords and press Enter. You are asked whether to assign passwords. (Because you have chosen to assign random passwords, they will be stored in the NEW.PWD file in the SYS:SYSTEM directory.)

STEP 4: PERFORM THE MIGRATION

▸ Begin the migration. Press F10 to display the Select a Migration Action menu. Select the Start the Migration option from this menu and press Enter. During the migration process, a log will be written to the MIG000.RPT file in the working directory (C:\MIG000.RPT) as well as being displayed on the screen. A message may be displayed warning that the MIGRATE.EXE utility cannot create a SYS: volume on the destination server (because it already exists). If this message is displayed, press Enter to continue.

▸ Complete the migration. A message will be displayed when the migration is complete. Read the message, then press Enter to return to the Select a Migration Action menu. Another message will be displayed reminding you to run the MIGPRINT.EXE utility to migrate your printing environment to NetWare 4. Read the message and press Enter.

STEP 5: CONFIRM THE MIGRATION

▶ View the migration reports. Select the View Migration Reports option from the Select a Migration Action menu and press Enter. Select the MIG000.RPT file and press Enter. Carefully review the migration report, then press Esc twice to return to the Select a Migration Action menu. Select the Exit (return to DOS) option from the Select a Migration Action menu and press Enter, then select Yes and press Enter. You are asked whether to exit.

▶ Verify that users were migrated properly. Using the NetWare Administrator, verify that the NetWare 3.12 users and their rights have successfully migrated to the NetWare 4 server.

NETWARE 4 INSTALLATION

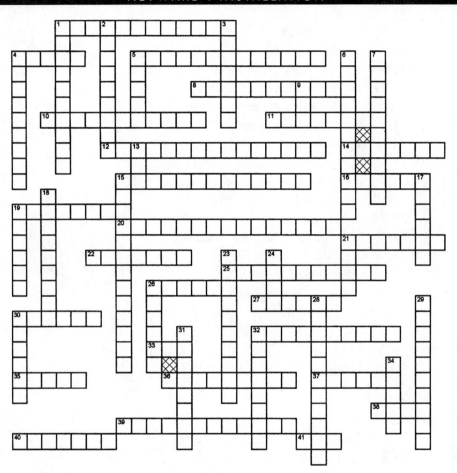

Across

1. The smaller of two server partitions
4. The first phase of DOS preparation
5. MIGRATE.EXE, a workstation, and two servers
8. Old NetWare 3 print job configurations are migrated
10. Printing migration

11. Default VLM directory
12. Default time provider
14. NetWare in Spanish
15. "Off" by default
16. NetWare 4 migration insurance
19. NetWare in French
20. Required for Japanese Kanji
21. NetWare 2 or 3 bindery preparation
22. NetWare in German
25. Automating the server at the NetWare partition
26. Server installation with all the bells and whistles
27. Most popular, built-in disk driver
30. Where NetWare lives
32. The tool of all great NetWare 4 installers
33. Default NetWare protocol
35. Minimum server RAM
36. The "brains" of NetWare 4
37. Random passwords
38. Not up
39. Approved by Novell Labs and bundled with NetWare 4
40. From NetWare 3 with INSTALL.NLM
41. Upgrade name space

Down

1. Communicating with the internal server disk
2. Are not migrated
3. A great on-line source of CNE tidbits
4. ETHERNET_802.2 in the NetWare environment
5. First NDS user
6. Automating the server at the DOS partition
7. Loads disk drivers
9. The great server communicator
13. New and improved DSK strategy
15. Built-in disk SFT with enhanced performance

17. User's playground created at installation
18. Communicating with the internal server NIC
19. The second phase of DOS preparation
21. Initializes LAN communications at the server
23. MIGRATE.EXE, a workstation, and a server
24. Activates server NLMs
26. In-place upgrade analysis
28. Automating the workstation
29. From NetWare 2
30. Admin's playground created at installation
31. "1234" on the cabling
32. BADCAFE at the server
34. Default NetWare 4 media

See Appendix C for answers.

Gardener

NETWARE 4 MANAGEMENT

I wandered lonely as a cloud
That floats on high o'er vales and hills,

When all at once I saw a crowd,
A host of golden daffodils;
Beside the lake, beneath the trees,
Fluttering and dancing in the breeze.

Continuous as the stars that shine
And twinkle on the milky way,
They stretched in never-ending line
Along the margin of the bay:

Ten thousand saw I at a glance,
Tossing their heads in sprightly dance.

William Wordsworth

You are a superhero.

You are a doctor.

You are a gardener.

As a NetWare 4 CNE, you are three people in one.

Today, you are a gardener. Welcome to the NetWare 4 garden—the last stop on your life-long CNE journey. When you first arrive, the garden is bare. You have a withering sapling (NDS tree), some soil (volumes), a greenhouse (server), and plenty of weeds. Not a promising site. Fortunately, you have plenty of fertilizer (this book) to get you started.

The first step is seeding. Be sure to segment your garden, because certain plants (users) require more attention than others. Once the seeds are in place, it's time for garden management. This is where the magic occurs. It's amazing how quickly your trees will bloom with the right combination of watering, love, sunshine, and weeding. Remember, balance is the key.

Gardening is a very rewarding experience, and your hard work will pay off in the form of productive users, organized resources, and peace on Earth. Good luck, and don't forget your green thumb.

CHAPTER 8

Managing NDS

"There is life in the ground: It goes into the seeds, and it also, when it is stirred up, goes into the person who stirs it."

Charles Dudley Warner

Welcome to the NetWare 4 garden!

This is the beginning of an exciting adventure for you—as the NetWare 4 gardener. You designed the "Cloud" (as a superhero), installed some servers (as a doctor), and now you get to breathe life into your glorious NDS tree (as a gardener). The next eight chapters will prepare you for the challenge of a lifetime—NetWare 4 CNE management. You'll adventure through partitioning, synchronization, the NetWare 4 file system, security, configuration, management, printing, and finally, optimization. However, the journey must start somewhere. Welcome to "point A." The challenge begins today—managing NDS.

In the beginning, the garden is bare. You have a withering sapling (NDS tree), some soil (volumes), a greenhouse (server), and plenty of weeds. Not a promising site. Fortunately, you have plenty of fertilizer (this book) to get you started. Once the soil has been prepared, you can start seeding. Be sure to segment your garden because certain plants require more attention than others. Once the seeds are in place, it's time for garden management.

Garden management is the fun part. This is where the magic occurs. It's amazing how quickly your trees will bloom with the right combination of watering, love, sunshine, and weeding. The trick is determining how much is enough. Just as in life, there is such a thing as too much. Too much water, for example, could lead to overhydration, while too much sunshine could cause dehydration. Gardening is a very tricky business— green thumb required.

ZEN

"Water is H_2O, hydrogen two parts, oxygen one, but there is a third thing, that makes it water and nobody knows what that is."

D. H. Lawrence

This is your life as a NetWare 4 gardener. You start with a sapling NDS tree, some default NetWare 4 files, and the Admin user. Now you must turn it into a thriving forest of communication and productivity. Good luck. To make matters worse, ACME's trying to save the world at the same time. Wow, you're going to need plenty of fertilizer!

Before you partition the tree, you must build it. Before you secure the tree, you must build it. Before you configure the tree, you must build it. Before you optimize the tree, you must build it. I see a pattern forming here. And finally, before you build the tree, you must understand the garden.

In this chapter, we'll help you discover your NetWare 4 garden and begin planting the seeds of connectivity. We'll learn everything there is to know about NDS objects, their properties, and how to effectively create/manage them. We will build ACME's tree, merge it with another, and even explore some controversial cross-breeding techniques for NetWare 3 and NetWare 4 trees—NETSYNCing. Here's a sneak peek at what's ahead:

▸ NDS Gardening—We will get acquainted with the garden, and learn how to browse ACME's NDS tree.

▸ Managing NDS Objects—We will explore the required and most commonly used NDS objects. We'll learn when to use each, and how to segment our garden for maximized productivity.

▸ Building the ACME Tree—We'll finally build ACME's tree and place all our leaf objects in their appropriate containers.

▸ DSMERGing—We will explore the DSMERGE utility and learn how to use it for merging two trees together.

▸ NETSYNCing—Finally, we will discover "crossbreeding" and learn how to make a rose that tastes like corn.

So, that's life in the NetWare 4 garden. Let's take a closer look.

NDS Gardening

The first rule of gardening is "know your garden." Know the quality of the soil, know the angle of the sun, and definitely, know the layout of the plants. The NetWare 4 garden is a haven for user connectivity. For that reason, you must understand the relationships between objects, and the general layout of the tree. That's where *browsing* comes in.

Browsing is a technical CNE term that means "to walk around the NDS tree looking at stuff." Browsing not only acquaints you with the tree, it also aids in NDS navigation. NDS navigation is required for a myriad of management tasks (such as creating users, adding security, configuring volumes, and partitioning). If you know what your tree looks like and how to navigate it effectively, you'll be well on your way to "green thumb-ship."

In this section, we will learn to browse the NDS tree using a variety of NetWare 4 utilities, including

- NWADMIN—An MS Windows-based utility called NetWare Administrator

- NETADMIN—A DOS-based version of NWADMIN

- CX—A command line utility for tree navigation

- NLIST—A command line utility for searching

- User Tools—GUI and menu utilities for user navigation

Hold your horses. Before we get too excited about browsing, let's take a quick tour of the NDS garden. Don't pick the flowers.

ZEN

"Anyone who has got any pleasure at all from nature should try to put something back. Life is like a superlative meal and the world is the maitre d'hotel. What I am doing is the equivalent of leaving a reasonable tip."

Gerald Durrell

THE GARDEN

NetWare Directory Services (NDS) is the garden. Instead of flowers and tomatoes, this garden organizes network resources (such as users, groups, printers, servers, volumes, and so on). As you can see in Figure 8.1, our garden organizes these resources into a hierarchical directory tree.

FIGURE 8.1

The ACME NDS Garden

NDS allows these resources to be managed in a single view. This is significant. It dramatically increases administrative flexibility, allowing you to manage the tree and its objects by using various properties and security capabilities. This contrasts with the earlier NetWare 3 bindery which was server-centric and inflexible. The Directory is network centric, that is, it's distributed and replicated on multiple servers throughout the WAN. This increases resource availability and fault tolerance.

All in all, our garden is a pretty amazing place. It seems as though it's been designed for gardening from the very beginning. Management in NetWare has never been so accommodating—notice I didn't say "easy." They're not the same thing. NDS accomplishes this with four main principles:

- ▸ NDS provides a single point of login.

- ▸ NDS provides easy administration.

- ▸ NDS is scalable.

- ▸ NDS allows tree walking.

Let's take a stroll through our new NDS garden.

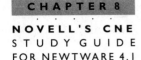

NDS Provides a Single Point of Login

NetWare 4 users log in to the network once—using one username and one password. Once there, they have instantaneous access to all authorized network resources. Very cool. NetWare 4 processes the server connections in the background and provides transparent access to resources, regardless of where they are physically located.

In contrast, NetWare 3 bindery users must log in to each server individually. This means that they must provide a different username and password for each additional server connection. Too much work.

A single user login also makes your job easier. You create each user account *once* for the entire NetWare 4 network. Multiple user accounts on multiple servers are no longer needed in NetWare 4. This feature alone will save you hours of work. As you can see, NDS serves as the central point of management, eliminating tedious duplication and reducing administrative costs.

NDS Provides Easy Administration

NetWare 4 consolidates all NDS administrative functions into a single, easy-to-use graphical utility that greatly reduces the time you spend administering the network. NWADMIN is your friend. It is a Windows-based utility that allows you to make changes to the Directory with the simple click of a mouse. It does virtually everything in NetWare 4—get used to it.

With NWADMIN, you can get information about an object simply by clicking on its icon. The icon explodes into a dialog box like the one in Figure 8.2. The main window shows current parameters for each of the 12 page buttons on the right of the screen. In this example, we're looking at the Identification page for George Washington in ADMIN.RIO.ACME.

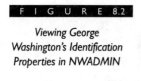

F I G U R E 8.2

*Viewing George
Washington's Identification
Properties in NWADMIN*

This object-oriented tool allows you to perform many routine NDS tasks more quickly. Users, directories, and server functions can be accomplished simply by dragging and dropping, or by clicking on icons. When a user changes departments, for example, you simply drag-and-drop the user to another location. I wish moving my house were so simple.

Adding directory or object rights in previous versions of NetWare involved multilayered menus and tedious processing. Now, all you have to do is drag the user's icon to the specific directory, and NetWare takes care of the rest.

Since all the network resources are represented in the NDS tree, managing many NetWare 4 servers is no more difficult than managing one NetWare 4 server. You don't have to concern yourself with the resources on any one server, but instead you can focus your efforts on managing *all* the network resources as a whole.

We explore NWADMIN in great depth later in this chapter. Also, don't miss the great ACME case study at the end of the chapter. It's fun, trust me.

NDS is Scalable

NDS is a global name service that can be split into pieces and distributed to any number of network servers. In contrast, the NetWare 3 bindery only supports operation from one server at a time. With NDS, the information is not only distributed, but also replicated. As we learned previously, this increases resource availability and fault tolerance. Figure 8.3 shows how NDS could be distributed across the ACME WAN.

FIGURE 8.3

Scalable NDS

The feature that distributes NDS is called *partitioning* and the characteristic that makes it redundant is called *replication*. These features makes NDS a powerful tool for storing, accessing, and managing resource information—regardless of where it is physically located.

This means that your NDS tree can easily grow to meet the demands of your environment. In addition, your tree can quickly transform to reflect the changes in your company's organization or functionality. We discuss NDS partition management and replication in great detail later in Chapter 9 (Partition Management and Synchronization). That chapter focuses on "pruning."

Finally, your entire NDS tree doesn't have to be stored on any one server. It can be distributed and replicated to multiple machines. How do the pieces find each other? Good question. NDS provides a mechanism for finding objects in the NDS tree even though they're scattered all over the WAN. This mechanism is called *tree walking*.

NDS Tree Walking
NetWare 4 tree walking refers to an automatic background process that locates physically separated resources. Basically, it means that NDS keeps track of objects even

if they're scattered from here to eternity. Tree walking allows users to access resources without having to know anything about them. They only need to know the name of the resource, and NDS figures out where it is.

Here's how it works. When a user requests an object, NDS searches the user's currently connected server first. If the server doesn't hold the object, NDS contacts all the other servers until it finds the object.

When the object is found, the user's server sends a list of host servers to the user's workstation. This is called a *referral list* and it includes all the servers with the requested object information. Then, the user's workstation determines where to get the information based on a least-cost algorithm. There's one last point. Before the workstation determines a cost for each server, it first checks to see if it's already connected to one of the servers in the referral list. If not, it bases its decision on cost. If the cost is the same, the workstation chooses the first server in the list.

With tree walking, users can always locate specific NDS information without having to worry about where it is. As a matter of fact, NDS uses tree walking to hold your hand while you're browsing. If you try to access resources outside of your server's partition, tree walking takes over immediately. You probably don't even notice what's going on. Very sneaky, and very cool.

Speaking of browsing, I'm ready for a tour of the NDS garden. How about you? As I mentioned, there are six utilities for NDS browsing. Let's start with the most fun one—NWADMIN. And remember, don't pick the flowers—yet.

QUIZ

There were a total of 229 matches played in our local open amateur knockout Tiddlywinks Championships last year. One player scratched out of the preliminary round because of illness and another from the third round because of holidays. Without doing any written calculation can you say how many players entered the competition?

(Q8-1)
(See Appendix C for quiz answers.)

BROWSING THE TREE WITH NWADMIN

NWADMIN (also known as the NetWare Administrator) is a Windows-based CNE tool that allows you to graphically manage all objects and properties in the NDS tree. You can also browse the tree by clicking on specific container objects and expanding their contents. Then, detailed resource information is just a double-click away. With this utility, you can view, create, move, delete, and assign rights to any object in the NDS tree. Of course, you can only mess around with the objects to which you have access rights.

TIP

You may restrict access to NWADMIN by moving it from SYS:PUBLIC into another, more restricted, subdirectory (such as SYS:SYSTEM). Everyday users don't need this powerful tree-browsing utility.

If you want to manage the NDS tree, you must load the NetWare DOS Requester or VLMs on your workstation. Once you've done so, you can perform any of the following functions with NWADMIN:

- Create and delete objects (such as users and groups).

- Assign rights to the NDS tree and file system.

- Set up NetWare 4 print services.

- Set up and manage NDS partitions and replicas.

- Browse object and property information throughout the tree.

NWADMIN runs as a multiple-document interface application. That means you can display up to nine different browsing windows at one time. The primary window is shown in Figure 8.4. It provides a background for viewing one or more secondary windows.

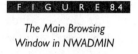

The Main Browsing Window in NWADMIN

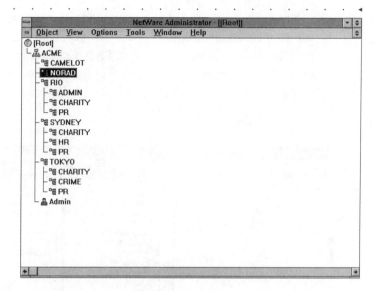

To open a secondary browser window in NWADMIN, select a container object from the primary window, and choose the Browse option from the Tools menu.

The new browser window displays all NDS objects within your new current context. You can now manage any of the objects, directories, and/or files in the window. Figure 8.5 shows a secondary browser window for the CAMELOT container of ACME. Notice all the resources (servers, users, volumes, and so on).

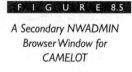

A Secondary NWADMIN Browser Window for CAMELOT

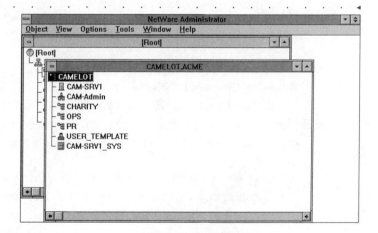

You can open up to nine browser windows at a time. To view multiple windows, select the Tile option from the Windows menu. Figure 8.6 shows three browser windows tiled for [Root], CAMELOT, and NORAD. Once again, notice how easy it is to view multiple ACME resources—regardless of their location. Finally, the title for each of the browser windows displays its context. This helps you track where all of your resources are—in the logical NDS world.

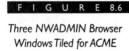

F I G U R E 8.6

Three NWADMIN Browser Windows Tiled for ACME

Now that we have the hang of general NWADMIN browsing, let's try a few special tasks (such as browsing containers, browsing properties, and searching). Ready, set, browse.

Browsing Container Objects

You can also browse the NDS tree by walking through container objects. Since they're glorified Tupperware bowls, containers can be opened and closed. Of the several ways to expand the contents of a container, here are just a few:

1 • Double-click on the container object. When you double-click on a container, it expands its contents. This also shows all subordinate container objects. If the container is expanded, you can collapse it by double-clicking again.

2 • Select a container object in the tree and choose the Expand option from the View menu. This will expand the contents of the container. You can collapse the container by using the Collapse option from the same menu.

3 • Select a container object and press the plus (+) key on the numeric keypad of your keyboard. The container object will expand and show its contents (sounds embarrassing). The plus (+) key above the equal sign (=) doesn't work. You must use the numeric keypad. You can collapse the container by pressing the minus (-) key on the numeric keypad.

4 • Select a container object and press the right mouse button. Select the Browse option from the pull-down menu that appears. This launches a new browser window with the contents of the container object. Figure 8.7 shows the short menu that appears when the right mouse button is pressed. By the way, this is a great shortcut feature. In this case, "right" is right. Draw your own conclusions.

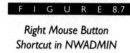

FIGURE 8.7

*Right Mouse Button
Shortcut in NWADMIN*

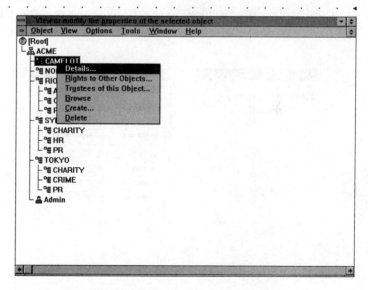

That's good for containers, now let's see what their contents have to offer.

Browsing NDS Properties

You can also browse the properties of any given object by choosing Details from the short menu in Figure 8.7. Or, here are a few other ways to browse NDS properties:

1 • Double-click on a leaf object. Remember, double-clicking on a container object expands and/or contracts it.

2 • Select the object and then choose the Details option from the Object menu. This works for containers as well.

3 • Select the object and press the right mouse button. Choose Details from the pull-down menu that appears. This works for containers as well.

The object dialog box is organized into pages that you can access with the buttons that run down the right side of the dialog. The Identification page always appears first and is shown in Figure 8.2. You can browse specific NDS properties by selecting the corresponding page button. Each object type has a different set of page buttons because each object type has a different set of properties. In Figure 8.2 above, we were browsing the user dialog window. Notice the difference in Figure 8.8—it shows the page buttons for the O=ACME container object.

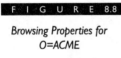

F I G U R E 8.8

*Browsing Properties for
O=ACME*

TIP

The Pages in the object dialog box are all part of the same dialog. When you select a different page, you are still in the same dialog. If you press OK or Cancel on any page, you are affecting the entire dialog box, not just the individual page. OK will save modifications to all the pages and Cancel will exit the dialog box without saving any changes to any page. In order to move between pages of the dialog box, select the desired page.

Searching for NDS Objects and Properties

You can find object and property information in the NDS tree by using the Search feature. You can perform this function without having to expand each of the container objects. It's much easier, trust me. The search operation will browse the entire tree, unless you narrow the search criteria.

For example, in Figure 8.9, the search criteria is configured to find all the users in the ACME tree who have a Department property equal to Charity. You can further narrow the search by starting at a subcontainer instead of the [Root]. Or, you can expand your searching criteria to include *all* Charity objects, not just users. As you can see, the NWADMIN searching engine is very sophisticated. Maybe you'll find what you're looking for.

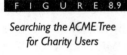

Searching the ACME Tree for Charity Users

ZEN

"What a man needs in gardening is a cast-iron back, with a hinge in it."

Charles Dudley Warner

That completes our brief tour through NWADMIN. You will quickly come to appreciate this utility—or not. Whatever your feelings are about Windows, you can't argue with NWADMIN's graceful interface and consolidated functionality. It does everything—even things its DOS-based cousin (NETADMIN) can't. Speaking of family, let's check out the other five browsing tools.

BROWSING THE TREE WITH OTHER TOOLS

NWADMIN is great, but it's not the only game in town. NetWare 4 provides a myriad of other browsing tools with a variety of different interfaces (GUI, DOS-based menu, and command line). If you're in a bind, or you just hate Windows, these tools are there for you:

- ▸ NETADMIN

- ▸ CX

- ▸ NLIST

- ▸ User Tools (NETUSER and NWUSER)

NETADMIN

NETADMIN is a DOS-based version of NWADMIN. The main difference is the "tunnel-vision" view it provides. Unlike NWADMIN, NETADMIN only displays one container at a time. If you remember from our earlier discussion, NWADMIN allows you to open multiple windows, or view multiple containers in a tree structure. No such luck in NETADMIN. For this reason, it's not a very good browsing tool, especially if you don't know what the garden looks like in the first place. Figure 8.10 shows the main screen of NETADMIN.

The Main Screen of NETADMIN

```
NetAdmin  4.55                          Friday  October  22, 1999  7:35am
Context: ACME
Login Name: Admin.ACME


                    ┌──────────────────────────────────┐
                    │         NetAdmin options         │
                    ├──────────────────────────────────┤
                    │ Manage objects                   │
                    │ Manage according to search pattern│
                    │ Change context                   │
                    │ Search                           │
                    └──────────────────────────────────┘




Press <Enter> to select an object to manage by navigating the directory
structure.
Enter=Select    Esc=Exit                                        F1=Help
```

In order to browse down the NDS tree with NETADMIN, select a container object from the browse window and press Enter. The container objects are marked with a plus sign (+) in front of the name (see Figure 8.11). Objects without a plus sign are leaf objects and do not contain other objects. In Figure 8.11, the CAMELOT, NORAD, RIO, SYNDEY, and TOKYO objects are containers. The Admin user is a leaf object.

To browse up the NDS tree to the parent container, select the double-dot (..) or parent marker. To view or edit the properties of the current container object, select the dot (.) or current container marker. Pretty fancy, huh? I guess it depends on your definition of "fancy."

Browsing in NETADMIN

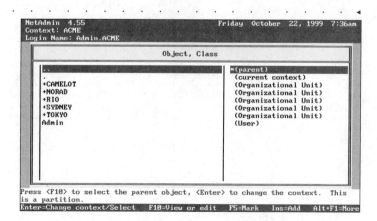

```
NetAdmin  4.55                          Friday  October  22, 1999  7:36am
Context: ACME
Login Name: Admin.ACME
┌─────────────────────────────────────────────────────────────────────┐
│                          Object, Class                                │
├─────────────────────────────────────────────────────────────────────┤
│ ..                              │ *(parent)                           │
│ .                               │ (current context)                   │
│ +CAMELOT                        │ (Organizational Unit)               │
│ +NORAD                          │ (Organizational Unit)               │
│ +RIO                            │ (Organizational Unit)               │
│ +SYDNEY                         │ (Organizational Unit)               │
│ +TOKYO                          │ (Organizational Unit)               │
│ Admin                           │ (User)                              │
└─────────────────────────────────────────────────────────────────────┘
Press <F10> to select the parent object, <Enter> to change the context.  This
is a partition.
Enter=Change context/Select   F10=View or edit   F5=Mark   Ins=Add   Alt+F1=More
```

THE BRAIN

For more information on using the NETADMIN utility, see the AppNote entitled "Using NETADMIN to Create and Administer NDS Objects" in the July 1993 issue of *Novell Application Notes*.

CX

Change Context (CX) is a DOS-based command line utility that allows you to navigate the tree by changing your current context. You can only use CX to view container and leaf objects in the tree. It doesn't provide any property information. Also, it's placed in the SYS:LOGIN subdirectory, by default. This way, your users can find themselves before they log in. Figure 8.12 displays the help screen for CX.

FIGURE 8.12

The CX Help Screen

```
CX                          Options Help                    4.20

Syntax:  CX [new context : /VER] [/R] [/[T : CONT] [/A]] [/C] [/?]

To:                                                    Use:
   View all container objects below the                /T
     current or specified context.
   View container objects at the current               /CONT
     or specified level.
   Modify /T or /CONT to view All objects              /A
     at or below the context
   Change context or view objects relative to root     /R
   Display version information                          /VER
   Scroll continuously                                 /C

For example, to:                                    Type:
   View directory tree below the current context     CX /T
   View containers within a specific context         CX .O=Novell /CONT

>>> Enter = More    C = Continuous    Esc = Cancel
```

Following is a brief description of the CX browsing options. If you want to learn more about using CX to change your current context, refer to Chapter 2 (Understanding NDS).

- /CONT—List just the container objects at the current context.

- /R—List all the container objects starting at the [ROOT] object.

- /T—List all the container objects below the current context.

- /A—List all the objects. This includes all the leaf objects.

Figure 8.13 displays the output of the CX /T command for the ACME tree when the current context is set to [Root]. Check out all of the interesting information. I sure hope it doesn't fall into the wrong hands—like the Alpha Centurions. Stay tuned for more information concerning security loopholes and CX—check out Chapter 11 (NetWare 4 Security).

F I G U R E 8.13

*Using the CX /T
Command at ACME*

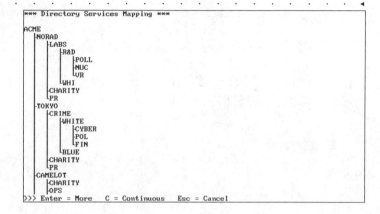

```
*** Directory Services Mapping ***

ACME
  ├NORAD
  │  ├LABS
  │  │  ├R&D
  │  │  │  ├POLL
  │  │  │  ├NUC
  │  │  │  └UR
  │  │  └WHI
  │  ├CHARITY
  │  └PR
  ├TOKYO
  │  ├CRIME
  │  │  ├WHITE
  │  │  │  ├CYBER
  │  │  │  ├POL
  │  │  │  └FIN
  │  │  └BLUE
  │  ├CHARITY
  │  └PR
  └CAMELOT
     ├CHARITY
     ├OPS
>>> Enter = More    C = Continuous    Esc = Cancel
```

NLIST

NLIST allows you to browse objects *and* properties in NetWare 4. It replaces a number of NetWare 3 utilities, including USERLIST, SLIST, SECURITY, and so on. NLIST works on most of the NDS objects (including Aliases, Computers, Directory Maps, Groups, Organizational Units, Printers, Profiles, Servers, Users, and Volumes). NLIST includes a multitude of options, and most of them are shown in Figure 8.14.

F I G U R E 8.14

NLIST Options

```
NLIST                        Basic Options Help Screen                    4.19

Purpose: Specify basic options for viewing objects.
Syntax: NLIST class type [= object name] [basic option]

To display:                                            Use:
  Active users or servers                                /A
  Objects throughout all subordinate contexts            /S
  Objects in a specified context                         /CO <context>
  Objects at [ROOT] context                              /R
  Continuously without pausing                           /C
  Bindery information                                    /B
  Version information                                    /VER
  Available Directory Services trees                     /TREE

For example, to:                            Type:
  See servers in all subordinate contexts     NLIST Server /S
  See logged in users (active)                NLIST User /A
  See volumes in the context O=My Org         NLIST Volume /CO "O=My Org"
  See servers in bindery mode                 NLIST Server /B
  See Directory trees in bindery mode         NLIST /Tree = *

C:\>
```

Please be sure to use the proper syntax for NLIST. It's kind of picky that way. Here's how it works:

```
NLIST [object type] [=object name] [/options]
```

Here are some examples:

- ▸ NLIST User /R /S—Searches for all user objects in the tree starting at [Root]

- ▸ NLIST Server /B—Displays all the servers

You can also use NLIST to view property information. In this case, you must use WHERE and SHOW, as follows:

```
NLIST [object type][=object name] [WHERE [property] [value]]

        [SHOW [property]]
```

Here are some great property examples:

- ▸ NLIST User=AEinstein /D—Shows all property details about a user named AEinstein

- ▸ NLIST User WHERE "Security Equal To" = CAM-Admin—Shows all the users that are security equivalent to the CAM-Admin Organizational Role

NLIST is a very powerful tool from the command line. The syntax is a little tricky, but once you get the hang of it, you'll love it.

User Tools

What about users? They like gardens, too. Well, my best advice to you is—watch them like a hawk. You never know what mischief they'll get themselves into.

Fortunately, NetWare 4 provides two gardening tools just for users—NWUSER and NETUSER. They provide the same functionality, except NWUSER is Windows-based and NETUSER is DOS-based. With these utilities, users can change their own context, manage server connections, manage the drive and search mappings, change their passwords, change login scripts, capture printers/print queues, and send messages.

In the case of NWUSER, it even does Windows (sorry). Refer to Figure 8.15 for a snapshot of the NWUSER browsing tool. In this case, we're mapping drives to the LABS-SRV1 server. Cool.

The Mapping Window in NWUSER

That completes our tour of the NetWare 4 garden. That was a rather nice, quiet stroll through NDS. We really should do this more often—stop to smell the roses. I especially enjoyed the browsing part, how about you?

Now that you're familiar with the garden, it's time to get down to business. To succeed in the NDS garden, you must be down-to-earth (literally), and focus on the NDS objects. Now it's time to put on our canvas gloves and dig in. Ready, set, garden.

ZEN

"Bees are not as busy as we think they are. They just can't buzz any slower."

Kin Hubbard

Managing NDS Objects

What does it mean to have a green thumb? Does it mean you're a Martian? No. Does it mean you should bathe more often? Probably not. Does it mean you get along well with plants? Bingo. The term green thumb implies that you understand the delicate balance of life in the garden. It means that you appreciate your chlorophyll-based friends and constantly nurture them. It means that you love the smell of fresh-cut flowers, dirt between your toes, and the hot sun beating down the back of your neck. To have a green thumb is to be blessed—and dirty.

As a NetWare 4 CNE, you need a red thumb. You must appreciate the delicate balance of life on the WAN. To have a red thumb means that you appreciate your users and their resources. It means that you like the smell of LaserJet toner, NDS objects between your toes, and disgruntled users breathing down the back of your neck. It means that you need to get a life.

So, what is garden management all about? It involves a combination of tools, knowledge, luck, and experience. You must know when to fertilize, when to water, and when not to spray pesticide. Similarly, NDS management is a combination of CNE tools (NWADMIN), knowledge of NDS objects, luck, and WAN experience. In this section, we will explore all the most important NDS objects and learn how to manage them effectively. This is the most important aspect of NetWare 4 gardening because after all— objects *are* NDS. Let's start by getting acquainted with NDS objects and learning what makes them tick.

GETTING TO KNOW NDS OBJECTS

Objects *are* NDS. In order to manage NDS, you must learn the intricacies of NDS objects. But you can't stop there. You must understand the relationships *between* objects as well. Sometimes it doesn't make sense to place a sunflower next to a rose. They're just not compatible.

In Chapter 2, we gained a fundamental understanding of NDS objects and their purposes. We learned about object classifications, and settled on two types: container objects and non-container (leaf) objects. The critical issue here is *containment*—that is, who contains whom. From a management perspective, it's important to understand how containment works. You must make sure that objects are correctly placed in the tree. Figure 8.16 shows how containers and non-containers interact with each other.

FIGURE 8.16

*Understanding Containers
and Non-Containers*

In general, containers are logical and non-containers are physical. This is another important distinction. It means the sole purpose of containers is to organize and store physical network resources—non-containers. So, if you think about it, the non-containers are doing all the work. They add productivity to the WAN. They are the sole reason you and I have a job. Wow, it sure puts things in perspective. Once you understand the relationships of these object types, it helps you better manage them. After all, roses are pretty, but tomatoes feed us—and, therefore, keep us alive.

The containment of an object specifies where it can appear in the Directory and which objects can be created underneath it. Table 8.1 provides a list of the NDS container objects and their containment rules. Notice the Locality container. It's there, but unavailable to the NetWare 4 utilities. That means you can't play with it. Also, refer to Figure 8.17 for a graphical representation of the NDS containment rules. This figure also includes non-container leaf objects.

TABLE 8.1

*Containers and Their
Containment*

OBJECT TYPE	CONTAINMENT
[Root]	Country, Organization
Country	Locality, Organization
Locality	Locality, Organization, Organizational Unit
Organization	Locality, Organizational Unit, Leaf Objects
Organizational Unit	Locality, Organizational Unit, Leaf Objects

F I G U R E 8.17

The NDS Containment Rules

You will quickly discover (if you haven't already) that some objects are more popular than others. The User object, for example, is the most commonly used leaf object because it defines everyone in your tree. On the other hand, you might never use an external entity or bindery queue. That's OK, your tree is unique, and it's nice to know that they're there for you if you ever need them.

Inside each object is a predefined subset of properties that describes characteristics about it. The User object, for example, has 55 different properties defining everything from First Name to Network Address. As a NetWare 4 CNE, it's your job to manage these properties and to make sure that the right people have access to the right information. Approximately 142 available properties are defined in the base NDS object definitions. Various combinations of these properties apply to all objects. You can easily view this information through any of the NWADMIN, NETADMIN, or NLIST tools. Take your pick.

ZEN

"Man is a complex being who makes deserts bloom and lakes die."

Gil Stern

For now, I'd like to take you on a magic carpet ride through some required and commonly used NDS objects. The more you learn about them, the better off you'll be.

Following is a list of the five required NDS objects. These containers and leaves are created automatically during first-server installation:

▶ [Root]—The top (or the bottom) of the tree, it depends on your point of view. [Root] is created during installation of the very first NetWare 4 server in the tree.

▶ Organization—Usually located directly under the [Root] (unless a Country or Locality is used). Think of it as the "trunk." The first server must exist somewhere, and it can't exist under the [Root], so here it is.

▶ User—You, me, them—leaves. The first, and only, default User is Admin and he or she is placed inside the first Organization container.

▶ Server—NetWare 4 must run somewhere. Regardless of what you might think, the NetWare garden still exists inside the server greenhouse.

▶ Volume—The soil.

Next, we must shift our focus from required to commonly used NDS objects. The following 11 object classes provide additional functionality to your tree. As a matter of fact, you'll probably use all or most of them. Remember, don't force the issue. Only use the object types that make sense for your unique situation. This is not a popularity contest.

▶ Bindery Object—Created by NDS for backward compatibility. It represents a bindery-based resource (such as an upgraded NetWare 3 print queue).

▶ Organizational Unit—The real branches of our tree. True geographic and organizational structure is provided through multiple OU layers.

▶ Organizational Role—Defines a role or position within the company. A useful tool for managing "turn stile" user objects.

- ▸ Group—A collection of unrelated users. Very useful management object.

- ▸ Directory Map—An independent pointer for automating application search drive mappings.

- ▸ Alias—Beware, they're not what they appear to be.

- ▸ Print Server—Serves printing.

- ▸ Printer—It prints.

- ▸ Print Queue—It queues.

- ▸ Profile—A special management group for sharing global, location, or special-function login scripts.

- ▸ Unknown—If all else fails....

Now, let's explore each of these required and commonly used objects in more detail. In each case, we will learn three important pieces of information: Purpose, Use, and Recommendations. *Purpose* describes what the objects do. *Use* provides some examples of how you might use the objects. *Recommendations* are provided to help you manage these objects in your own NDS tree. So, without any further ado, allow me to introduce NetWare 4's 16 most exciting NDS objects—starting, of course, with the [Root].

[ROOT]

Purpose   The [Root] object is at the top of our inverted tree structure. The [Root], from a visual standpoint, is the starting point of your tree and branches downward as shown in Figure 8.18. The name of the [Root] object is the name you give your tree. When you install the very first NetWare 4 server, you are prompted for a tree name. At this point you are actually naming the [Root] object. Each tree can have only one [Root] object. In our case, it's called ACME_TREE, but NWADMIN shows it as [Root].

The Beginning of ACME's Tree Structure in NWADMIN

The [Root] object's name is broadcast on the WAN using the Service Advertising Protocol (SAP). If you have multiple trees running on the same network infrastructure, you must ensure that the names are unique.

Use Choose a name for [Root] that will clearly identify your organization or company. Keep in mind that renaming the [Root] can only be done with the DSMERGE utility (discussed later in this chapter) and becomes more difficult the larger your tree becomes. This is because your entire NDS naming structure relies on the [Root].

Recommendations Most companies simply use the same name as their Organization object and add the extension _TREE. For example, our tree name is ACME_TREE, because the organization name is O=ACME. You must be able to recognize the tree name when you're monitoring server-to-server communications.

ZEN

"Spring has come when you can put your foot on three daisies."

Folk Wisdoms

ORGANIZATION

Purpose   This object class is used to define your company. An Organization is located directly under the [Root] object, and you are required to define at least one Organization in your NDS tree. Multiple Organization objects may be used directly below the [Root], if needed.

Use   As you learned previously, ACME's organization is O=ACME (see Figure 8.18). The Organization represents the name of your company and should be an overall descriptor of your business. If you are a nonprofit group or university, it can be the name of your campus (O=UCB, for example).

Recommendations   Most companies define only one Organization object in their tree. Our guideline for using multiple Organization objects is based on your network infrastructure. For example, if you are a large conglomerate with separate network infrastructures, you can use multiple Organization objects for each entity. In this case, each company is separately managed with a separate network infrastructure, and you create multiple Organization objects for each business unit under the [Root] object. If all business are connected with the same network, then a single Organization may more accurately represent your WAN. In the latter case, you would use Organizational Units to represent each business unit.

USER

Purpose   The most common object in your tree probably will be the User object. The NDS User object is similar to the bindery user in NetWare 3, but ours contains many more configurable attributes.

Use   During installation of the first NetWare 4 server, you are prompted to create the first user in the tree. This user, usually named Admin, has Supervisor rights to the entire NDS structure (see Figure 8.19). At this point, Admin is the only object with such complete and extensive access to your tree. The importance of maintaining Admin is well-documented—see Chapter 11 (NetWare 4 Security). If you delete Admin without making any backup contingencies, you lose all administrative control of the tree. Your options in this circumstance would be to reinstall NDS, or to call Novell Technical Support to provide you with reentrance to your tree. Be very careful with the Delete key.

*ACME's Required NDS
Objects*

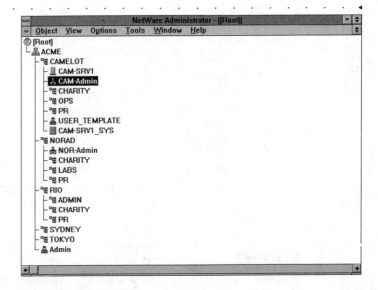

Recommendations   After you install the first couple of NetWare 4 servers, ensure
that the Admin password is protected. Follow these simple steps:

1 • Your first NetWare 4 server installation will prompt you for the Admin
password. Remember, this password is also assigned to the bindery
[Supervisor] object. If you change the Admin password at a later date, the
bindery [Supervisor] password does *not* change. Choose a secure password
and don't forget it. Change your passwords periodically for greater security.

2 • Create an Organizational Role at the Organization level and grant it
Supervisor rights to the [Root] object (see Chapter 11). In addition, create a
user called Backup and put him or her into the Organizational Role.
Whatever you do, don't make the Organizational Role object security
equivalent to the original Admin user. This creates a loophole. If the Admin
is deleted, the Organizational Role becomes useful—effectively, the security
equivalent to dirt! Again, refer to Chapter 11 for more in-depth security
analyses.

SERVER

Purpose   An NDS Server object will automatically be created for any server installed or upgraded to NetWare 4. The Server object holds key WAN information (such as the network address, NetWare version, and serial number). Refer to Figure 8.19 for an illustration of CAMELOT's first server (CAM-SRV1).

Use   The Server object is managed primarily by NDS and requires little or no attention from you. You may want to assign yourself Supervisor rights to the server for administrative purposes. Once again, see Chapter 11.

Recommendations   Be sure to follow the naming standards presented in Chapter 4 (NDS Design) when creating Server objects. Consistent and appropriate naming will help the tree walking process considerably.

VOLUME

Purpose   At least one server volume (SYS:) is created when you install a NetWare 4 server (see Figure 8.19). This is a logical representation of your physical server file system. It is possible to create multiple logical Volume objects, but they all must point to a physical file server disk.

Use   This object exists primarily to give you greater flexibility in volume management, if needed. It also increases file access by spreading the logical file system throughout the tree. It's important to note that the actual files always stay at the server—they are *not* distributed with the Volume object. That's NetWare 5.

Recommendations   NetWare 4 gives you the flexibility of placing print queues on any NetWare 4 volume. We recommend that you always create at least one other volume in addition to the SYS: volume so that your print queues will not fill up the SYS: volume. This can cause the server to shut down. In addition, use volume restrictions to limit the size of your volumes before they fill up completely. You can also limit the disk space occupied by user files with NWADMIN.

QUIZ

A Greek was born on the 260th day of 20 BC, and died on the 260th day of AD 60. How many years did he live?

(Q8-2)

That completes our discussion of the five required NDS objects. Refer to Figure 8.19 for a review of CAMELOT's subtree. Now, let's take a closer look at some commonly used NDS objects.

BINDERY OBJECT

Purpose   This leaf object represents any object created by bindery services and designated as such by the Directory. The Bindery object has the format of "Bindery Identifier + Object ID" and is used to provide backward compatibility for bindery-oriented applications or utilities.

Use   Bindery objects typically appear after a migration from NetWare 3 to NetWare 4. They only occur if NDS can't identify them. For applications that require the bindery, a Bindery object will be created. Although these objects appear in utilities such as NWADMIN, they are nonmanageable and are present for informational purposes only.

Recommendations   Do not delete a Bindery object until you verify its purpose with NDS. Some installation utilities create a Bindery object for specific purposes. If removed, they will cause problems for your applications. Also, some Bindery objects can't be removed at all, and may require the use of DSLOAD—a special "repo-man" for NetWare 4.

ORGANIZATIONAL UNIT

Purpose   Nearly all NDS trees will use Organizational Units. They are, however, optional. Organizational Units serve the purpose of subdividing the tree into functional units. As we learned in Chapter 4, this subdivision can be based on either location or organization—it's up to you.

Use   As shown in Figure 8.19, the ACME tree uses containers to make logical divisions in the tree. Notice that the first level of OU's represent geographic sites based on the network infrastructure. Subsequent levels are organized according to departments. Many trees will be designed in this fashion with several levels of nested organizational units. For more information on designing a NetWare 4 tree, see Chapter 4 (NDS Design).

Recommendations   Most companies use Organizational Units to represent geographic locations, divisions, and workgroups. You generally use an Organizational Unit to group common users and resources in the same container. Organizational Units should not be created to represent a single person or a single resource. They are used to provide access to a group of resources in a particular part of the tree.

·ORGANIZATIONAL ROLE

Purpose   An Organizational Role is typically used to define a functional position within the company. The role is extremely useful as an administrative tool because it acts as a holding cell for NDS and file system security. Once you place a user in an Organizational Role, that user immediately inherits the rights of the position.

Use   Organizational Roles can be used to create subadministrators. Users can be moved in and out of the role quickly to facilitate short-term assignments. For example, if the regular administrator is absent for any length of time, another user can be moved into the Organizational Role temporarily. While there, he or she can manage the network.

As shown in Figure 8.19, we have created an Organizational Role for each ACME location. Each Organizational Role will have complete administrator privileges to all resources within that city. This includes all containers and subcontainers.

Recommendations   Organizational Roles allow you to distribute access rights to various container administrators. It also allows you to switch occupants at a moment's notice (for instance, if an administrator goes on vacation, gets sick, or goes crazy). This system also allows you to easily track security by centralizing it all in one object. It sure beats assigning administrator rights to every user independently. Refer to Chapter 11 (NetWare 4 Security), for more information on NDS security.

GROUP

Purpose   Groups allow you to organize users from any part of the NDS tree. Groups function exactly the same way as they did in NetWare 3—they are primarily used for assigning rights. There is very little difference between Group objects and Organizational Units (OUs). As a matter of fact, containers are called natural groups because they naturally group all the users within their context. Both have the same function—placing common users close together.

It is true that users as members of both objects receive rights by security equivalence, but there are some differences. Because of security equivalency, any member of an OU will receive whatever rights the OU possesses, provided that there is not an intervening inherited rights filter (IRF) placed on that user. Users inside Groups also receive whatever rights the Group possesses, but there is no IRF provision.

OK, I can't hold out any longer. There is one major difference between OUs and groups—groups can contain users from separate parts of the tree. So here's the bottom line: If all the users are in the same container, use the OU. Otherwise, use a Group. Also, use a Group if you want to assign rights to a small subset of users *within* a container.

Use   In order to provide rights to a small subset of users in the CHARITY.SYDNEY.ACME OU, for example, you can use a Group. Figure 8.20 shows an Organizational Unit called OU=CHARITY and its populated users and resources. Within this OU are two sets of users—HP4SI and WP. Each group is accessing different software on the server and needs different rights assignments. Within the Container login script (known as the System login script in NetWare 3), the IF MEMBER OF GROUP statements are used to determine to which Group a user belongs for which rights assignments. When each user logs into the network, the login script determines if a user is a member of a Group, and sets the appropriate environmental variables. Very cool.

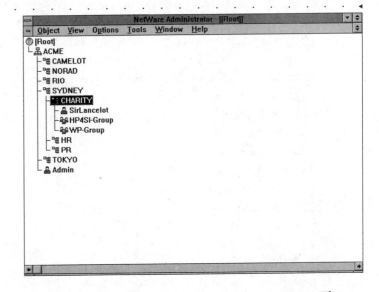

F I G U R E   8.20

*Understanding Groups in
the OU=CHARITY
Container of ACME*

Recommendations   Groups are great to use within or outside containers. They provide further differentiation of rights to a subset of users. We recommend that you create Groups within a container instead of creating more functional containers. If it's a geographically separated site, it's a different story. Limit your number of Groups to less than 15 in a Container login script, if possible. The more Groups, the longer the Container login script will be and the slower login will be. Also, if you have that many Groups, you should most likely create additional containers.

ZEN

"A plant is like a self-willed man, out of whom we can obtain all which we desire, if we will only treat him his own way."

Goethe

DIRECTORY MAP

Purpose The Directory Map object is a centralized pointer that refers to a directory on a NetWare volume. They're used in login scripts to point to applications. We'll explore them in much greater depth later in Chapter 10 (NetWare 4 File System).

Use Let's assume that you have WordPerfect installed in a directory called WP60. Then, let's assume you upgrade your software to WordPerfect 6.1—and rename the subdirectory WP61. You would also have to change every login script to reflect this change. Too much work. The Directory Map object allows you to centralize applications by pointing to the map object instead of the directory itself. Then, when you upgrade, all the login scripts remain the same and you only make one change—to the Directory Map object itself.

Recommendations Directory Maps are useful for providing a standard Container login script on multiple servers. We recommend that you have standard file structures for all your NetWare 4 volumes. There are also some security considerations when using Directory Maps, and we'll talk about them in Chapter 11 (NetWare 4 Security).

ALIAS

Purpose An Alias object points to any other object in the tree. It's NetWare 4 incognito—the object of a million disguises. An Alias object can point to either a container or leaf object.

Use An Alias object is a name containing at least one relative distinguished name (RDN). As a NetWare 4 CNE, you may want to use aliases to give users access to specific resources in other parts of the tree. You could create an Alias to reference a printer in another container, for example. The Alias can be considered a relay to another object in a different part of the tree.

You can also Alias an Organizational Unit to another OU. This basically gives all the objects in one container access to the resources in another.

The object being aliased is known as the *primary object*. When you create an Alias object, you may or may not name it with an Alias flag. For example, the name might include the word "alias," as in "AEinstein-Alias". You should use the Alias flag to distinguish between the primary and Alias object. Otherwise, they both use a mask and act the same. How do you tell who is who?

Recommendations   The Alias can be useful for some companies that create mobile users who do not want to remember their user contexts. The Alias can be created at the top of the tree below the Organization object to shorten the user's context. If user Dr. Watson in CRIME.TOKYO.ACME wants to log in to the network, he only has to remember that his context is Dr Watson.ACME because the Alias points to his actual context in the tree. This example is shown in Figure 8.21.

F I G U R E   8.21

Understanding the Alias Object with the Help of Dr. Watson

PRINT SERVER

Purpose The Print Server leaf object represents a server that takes print jobs out of a print queue and sends them to a network printer. This object is used in conjunction with the Printer and Print Queue objects. A Print Server object must be created for every actual print server that exists on the NetWare 4 network.

Use All NetWare 4 networks using printing will have at least one Print Server object. You can use this object to define to which printers to send printing. You can also define print server operators using this object.

PRINTER

Purpose Used in conjunction with the Print Server object, you use this object to manage a printer. The assignment for a print queue can be made within the object.

Use You can attach printers in several different ways to the network (for example, directly to the network, to a printer port of a NetWare server, or to a printer port of a PC).

Recommendations Place the Printer object along with the Print Queue object as high as possible in your NDS tree. This provides support for as many users as possible. If your printer is for this container only, then place the printer in this container. If more containers need access to the printer, place the object in the next higher level in the tree. We also recommend that you configure printers as network-direct printers in queue server mode.

PRINT QUEUE

Purpose This object represents a print queue defined on a NetWare 4 server volume. The queue actually represents the physical file system where the print jobs reside while they're waiting to be printed.

Use Place Print Queue objects along with the Printer objects at the highest level possible in your tree. This way they can service the most users.

Recommendations All NetWare 4 print queues should be placed on a volume other than the SYS: volume. This provides greater fault tolerance for the server. A Print Queue object must be created for NetWare 4 printing. A Print Queue object is assigned to a printer.

PROFILE

Purpose The Profile object is used as a special-purpose scripting object that executes a shared login script after the execution of your Container login script. The Profile script can contain special drive mappings or environment settings for a select group of people.

One of the properties of a User object is the Profile. When a user is first created, you can specify that the user participate in a Profile. You can also add a user to a Profile after the fact, through the user's login script property.

Use The three notable uses for a profile script are

- Global login scripts

- Location login scripts

- Special Function login scripts.

Global Login Scripts

NetWare 4 does not use a global System login script. Each Organizational Unit will have its own login script referred to as the OU login script. The order of execution of login scripts is

1 • OU container login script (if used)

2 • Profile login script (if used)

3 • User login script (if used)

4 • Default login script (if no other script is available)

Therefore, if you want to create a more global login script and include multiple Organizational Units, you could employ the Profile object for group-specific settings.

Location Login Scripts

A Profile can also be used for determining resource allocation based on location. For example, each department of a company may have three printers and three print queues. With a Profile, you have the ability to assign a particular group of users to a specific print queue. You can use a Profile login script to capture to a particular print queue and then automatically print to the right printer.

Special Function Login Scripts

A Profile can be used for a special-function script to assign access for applications and so on. For example, you can create a Profile script that will be used by administrators only. This script may give these users a specific drive assignment to a help desk utility. In this scenario, you would move the help desk utility out of the SYS:PUBLIC directory and into a new subdirectory you create called SYS:APPS\HELPDESK. When a user logs in to the network, the Admin Profile executes and assigns the user a drive mapping to the HELPDESK directory. Only the users executing the Profile script will be assigned appropriate rights.

Recommendations   Typically, the Profile is used as a global login script for an entire organization. Keep in mind that the Profile object will execute from one container, although users may be participating from other containers and may see some performance issues if the script is executing over a wide area connection.

UNKNOWN

Purpose   This class represents any restored object whose base class is currently undefined in the schema. Objects of this class type are only created by the NetWare 4 server. They usually occur when a mandatory property of an object has been lost.

Use   This object is automatically created by NDS. If you have an Unknown object appear in your tree, check to see if some other object has been deleted. In the case of a deleted Server object, the server's Volume objects will appear as Unknown objects and must be deleted by an administrator. In other circumstances, an Unknown object may appear temporarily as the NDS background processes work through a synchronization procedure.

Recommendations   Check before deleting an Unknown object as the object may resolve itself. If you have verified that the object is not needed, then remove it from your tree. There is no point in maintaining Unknown and unusable objects.

QUIZ

Very few of us now have dial (rotary) telephones, but the letter and number system is the same as it was when telephone dials were used for codes. Here is a coded message based on a telephone numbering system. For example, 2 would equal A, B, or C. All you have to do is select the correct letter from each group of three to solve the puzzle.

8447 47 4273 2322873 84373 273 84733 2464237 367 3224 686237

(Q8-3)

There you have it! Those are your NDS objects. Hopefully you have a better appreciation for the complexity of NDS gardening. There's a lot of diversity in life, and it seems there's an NDS object for every occasion. As a matter of fact, it's possible to customize the NetWare schema and create additional object types and properties. Once again, genetic engineering is put to good use.

However, before we get too excited about merging and crossbreeding, let's learn how to create these NDS objects. In the next two sections, we will explore NetWare 4's two main object creation tools:

▸ NWADMIN

▸ UIMPORT

Ready, set, create.

THE BRAIN

Check out these AppNotes for more information on creating and naming NDS objects: "Implementing Naming Standards for NetWare Directory Services" (February 1994) and "Understanding and Using NDS Objects" (January 1995).

CREATING NDS OBJECTS WITH NWADMIN

As we learned previously, NWADMIN is your friend. It allows you to create and manage NDS objects quickly and easily. We have discovered NWADMIN's browsing capabilities, now we're going to learn about its creating capabilities. Keep in mind that you can also use the DOS-based NETADMIN utility to accomplish these tasks.

After enabling NWADMIN from your Windows workstation, the main browsing screen appears. First, select a container in which to create your User objects. In our case, we're starting with OU=CAMELOT (see Figure 8.22).

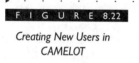

FIGURE 8.22

Creating New Users in CAMELOT

Once you have selected a container, you can choose the Create option from the Object menu (or use the shortcut menu by pressing the right mouse button). Next, you are presented with a list of objects (as shown in Figure 8.22). Select the User object and press Enter or double-click on it with the mouse.

If you want to create multiple users at once, the intermediate dialog window has a dialog box for this. Also, you can specify a home directory for the user at this point. Finally, if you're going to create many similar users, consider the special USER_TEMPLATE object. You'll find it in the Object menu of the main browsing screen. Figure 8.23 shows the default user template input window. Once you create a USER_TEMPLATE, future objects can inherit its properties (such as Group Membership, Trustee Assignments, or Time Restrictions).

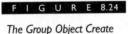

FIGURE 8.23

The USER_TEMPLATE Identification Page in NWADMIN

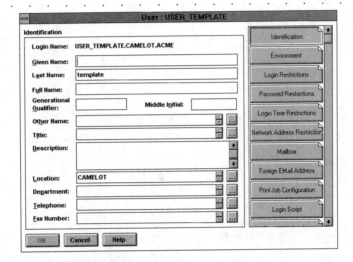

You can also create Groups with NWADMIN. Instead of selecting the User Object in the New Object window, simply choose Group. Next, the dialog window in Figure 8.24 appears. Follow this same process for any or all NetWare 4 NDS objects. As you can see, NWADMIN takes the pangs out of user creation.

FIGURE 8.24

The Group Object Create Dialog Window in NWADMIN

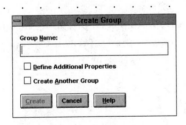

There is, however, another option. You can use UIMPORT to create large numbers of users from database records. Let's see how it works.

CREATING NDS USERS WITH UIMPORT

UIMPORT allows you to import users from a database application to NetWare Directory Services. This utility also can be used to create, delete, and update User objects and their existing properties. If you are using a database that has the ability to convert records to a comma-separated ASCII file, you can use UIMPORT to migrate this data to the NetWare Directory. Here's how it works:

1 • Create a data file based on your existing database.

2 • Create a control file to interpret and act on the data file.

3 • Just do it!

The UIMPORT utility consists of two files: the data file and the import control file. The creation of your data file is simply the generation of your ASCII comma-separated file from your previous database. The control file consists of some control parameters and field definitions. This defines where in NDS the information should be placed. Let's check them out.

THE BRAIN

To read more about UIMPORT, see the AppNote entitled "Importing User Information into NetWare Directory Services Using UIMPORT" in the April 1995 Novell Application Notes.

ZEN

"There is no season when such pleasant and sunny spots may be lighted on, and produce so pleasant an effect on the feelings, as now in October."

Nathaniel Hawthorne

The Data File

This is the easy part. The data file is created by your database application when you save the information in a comma-separated ASCII file (sometimes referred to as a *comma-delimited* file). A comma in the data file indicates a separation of fields in the NDS database. When a record is read through UIMPORT, a comma indicates the transfer of a new property. An example of the structure of your database might be as follows:

```
Last Name:
First Name:
Local Address:
Street:
```

```
City:
State or Country:
Zip Code:
Description:
Job Title:
```

After you have created a data file in delimited ASCII format, it should look something like this:

```
Madison,James,"111 Calle de Carnival","Rio de Janeiro",
Brazil,57775,Facilities,Administrator
```

We named our file ACMEDATA as we exited from the DOS editor. Next, we must define a control file so that UIMPORT can match field values with properties in the NDS database. Here's how it works.

The Control File

Next, you must create the import control file. This file actually controls how the data information is written to NDS. The control file can be created using any DOS text editor. You will enter a set of control parameters first, followed by a list of field definitions. Control parameters define how the information in the data file is separated. The field parameters define how the information is to be written to NDS. Table 8.2 displays a list of the control parameters, along with a brief definition of each.

T A B L E 8.2	CONTROL PARAMETER	EXPLANATION
UIMPORT Control Parameters	Separator	Defines the type of separator used in the data file (such as a comma or a semicolon).
	Quote	Defines the character used for string data in the data file.
	Name Context	Defines the NDS context where the users will be created.
	Replace Value	Enables you to overwrite or add data to multivalue fields (such as overwrite an existing telephone number in a user object).

CONTROL PARAMETER	EXPLANATION
User Template	Specifies the use of a user template in the creation of your users.
Import Mode	Defines how User objects will be created. C = Create, B = Create and Update, and U = Update data for existing objects.
Delete Property	Enables you to delete a property from a User object in NDS.
Create Home Directory	Allows the creation of a home directory for user objects.
Home Directory Path	Required if you create a home directory for users. The volume name is not necessary in the inclusion.
Home Directory Volume	Required if you create a home directory for users.

Next, the field definitions define which properties correlate with established user properties. These fields are listed below and can be selected based on your particular needs:

Name	Telephone	Location
Last Name	Fax Number	Group Membership
Other Name	Job Title	See Also
Postal Address	Description	Skip
E-Mail Address	Department	Login Script

Using our previous data file as an example, this is what our import control file would look like:

```
Import Control
Name Context="OU=FAC.OU=ADMIN.OU=RIO.O=ACME"
User Template=Y
Fields
Last Name
Other Name
Postal Address
```

```
Postal Address
Postal Address
Postal Address
Department
Job Title
```

That's our ACME control file and we've named it ACMECTRL. Notice the NAME CONTEXT line. This ensures that the users are imported into the correct container. If you don't specify one in the control file, UIMPORT places them into your current context—all users in the same container.

Now, there's only one step left—just do it!

Just Do It!

Once you've created your data and control files, you're ready to run UIMPORT. Type the following at your workstation command line:

```
UIMPORT <control file> <data file>
```

In our example, we would type:

```
UIMPORT ACMECTRL ACMEDATA
```

Off it goes. Keep in mind, you must have Supervisor access rights to the UIMPORT container in order to import users. This prevents random users from overpopulating your NDS database. Also, if an error should occur during the process, it will be displayed at the workstation command line. Consider using the redirect symbol to create an error log file:

```
UIMPORT ACMECTRL ACMEDATA > UIMPORT.LOG
```

That does it for NDS objects. I bet you didn't think gardening could be so much fun. It really pays off if you get to *know* your plants intimately. Put yourself in their roots, try to understand what makes them tick. Understand their dreams, their goals. Plants have feelings, too, you know.

In this section, we have done that with NetWare 4's NDS objects. We explored the 16 most interesting objects, and learned some valuable management lessons about each one. In addition, we explored object creation with NWADMIN and UIMPORT. Now I think you're ready for Prime Time. Now I'm gonna let you loose on ACME's tree. Now you get to pick the flowers!

Building the ACME Tree

Welcome to ACME's garden. Don't step on the daffodils. Now that you understand the fundamentals of NDS gardening, it's time to put your knowledge to the test. Did somebody say "test"?

Anyway, today's the *big* day. We finally get to build ACME's tree. Here's where we've been:

- ► In Chapter 2, we learned about NDS objects and their purposes.

- ► In Chapter 3, we learned all about ACME and the design process. We also discovered some key ACME design inputs, including the critical resource list.

- ► In Chapter 4, we designed ACME's tree with locations at the top and departments down below. In addition, we created a naming standards document and updated the ACME resource list to match.

- ► In Chapter 5, we started the ACME rollout with a testing lab and pilot program. We also practiced building the tree with DS Standard—but it's an off-line modeling tool, not the "real" thing.

- ► In Chapters 6 and 7, we installed and migrated most, if not all, of ACME's NetWare 4 servers.

With experience, NWADMIN, design inputs, and a little luck, you're ready to build ACME's tree. This consists of two stages. First, build the container structure as outlined in the ACME design in Chapter 4 (NDS Design). Then, place the leaf objects according to the resource list and managerial experience you gained earlier in this chapter. Are you ready? Go!!

THE NORAD SITE

At the NORAD site (as well as all other sites), we have placed a central server at the top OU=NORAD container (see Figure 8.25). This server will hold the Master replica of the NORAD partition and can also function as an e-mail server for internal and external communications. The same process is repeated at all five sites.

FIGURE 8.25

The NORAD Site at ACME

Notice the naming standards follow a very simple pattern based on our naming standards document. Servers are always defined by unique names across the entire tree because of the SAP requirement. Printers and print queues, however, can have the same name as long as they reside in different containers (such as HP4SI-P1 found in both the OU=CHARITY and OU=PR containers).

THE RIO SITE

Figure 8.26 shows the placement of resources in each of the Rio site's departments. It's not necessary to place all the users in your tree at this point. We have included a user in each location as an Administrative example. At the very least, you should include the container administrators, as we've done here.

FIGURE 8.26

The RIO Site at ACME

For the Rio location, as well as all other major locations, you should consider creating an Organizational Role object as the site administrator. Then, grant location-based Supervisor rights to the Organizational Role object. In our example (Figure 8.26), notice the RIO-Admin object at the top of the subtree. Finally, you should assign key administrators as occupants of the Role (in Rio that includes George Washington, Sir Percival, and Jeff Hughes).

THE CAMELOT SITE

Since Camelot is the center of ACME activity, you may want to maintain control over Admin from this location. Change the password frequently and limit the number of users who know it. Also, make Admin a member of the site Organization Role, CAM-Admin. See Figure 8.27 for an illustration of the CAMELOT subtree.

FIGURE 8.27

The CAMELOT Site at ACME

THE SYDNEY SITE

Use Directory Map objects to simplify administration of your users. For example, the Sydney office uses Directory Maps in all its Container login scripts. As versions of its specialized software change, the Sydney site administrator only changes the pointer of the Directory Map object to the new version of the software. This automatically enables all users in Sydney to see the new version of software, because all Container login scripts use the same Directory Map.

As you can see in Figure 8.28, we've placed the Directory Maps higher in the tree. This provides access to all users underneath. The Human Rights application, for example, is accessed from a Directory Map object in the OU=HR container (HR-APP). This way, all the HR employees can have access to the application. Follow this same conventions for all the other Sydney divisions.

F I G U R E 8.28

The SYDNEY Site at ACME

THE TOKYO SITE

The Tokyo office has traveling users (see Figure 8.29). We will create an alias for these users at the top of the ACME tree (at O=ACME). With the alias in place, a traveling user such as DHoliday in OU=THEFT can log in with the following simple context— DHoliday.ACME. This makes the login process much easier for users who travel, but do not carry their own laptop computers. For more information on these Nomads, refer to Chapter 4 (NDS Design).

F I G U R E 8.29

The TOKYO Site at ACME

Congratulations! You've taken a very big step today toward saving the world. ACME's garden is in place. Now all you have to do is water, fertilize, weed, and manage it. Be sure the users get enough sun, and whatever you do, don't let the snails get them.

This is the beginning of a wonderful friendship. This tree will follow you everywhere you go. In subsequent chapters, we will learn how to partition, secure, configure, and optimize it. You should be very proud of yourself. Also, if you want some hands-on practice building the tree, check out the case study at the end of this chapter. It explores three important creation utilities—NWADMIN, NETADMIN, and UIMPORT. Otherwise, you can practice off-line with DS Standard—a full-blown copy is included on the CD-ROM bound into this book.

So, what's next? In the remainder of this chapter, we will discuss two auxiliary NDS management responsibilities—DSMERGing and NETSYNCing. You never know when you're going to need a little genetic engineering to help your plants.

DSMERGing

Now, your gardening experience takes a strange scientific turn. In the next two sections, we will explore some "bizarre" ways of improving your NDS tree—through genetic engineering:

> ▸ Merging—DSMERGE allows you to combine two unrelated NDS trees. This functionality adds great flexibility to diverse and distributed organizations. It also doubles the size of your oak tree.

> ▸ Crossbreeding—NETSYNC allows you to cross-pollinate between NetWare 3 binderies and NetWare 4 NDS trees. It's a strange operation, but the result is mind-blowing—a rose that tastes like corn.

In this section, we will explore the details of DSMERGE. This utility allows you to combine multiple trees (two at a time) into a single, cohesive NDS WAN. Imagine what life was like before DSMERGE. Earlier versions of NetWare 4 forced CNEs to agree on a master plan before installing the very first server. Distributed organizations had to design and build the tree from a central location, or they had to *rebuild* the tree later.

DSMERGE has added an important level of flexibility by allowing CNEs to merge already existing trees once the organization agrees on a single NDS design. This way, distributed departments can implement NDS early, and merge into the parent tree at a later date.

DSMERGE occurs in the following four steps:

- ▶ Step 1—Check status of NetWare 4 servers.

- ▶ Step 2—Check time synchronization status.

- ▶ Step 3—Rename a directory tree (if necessary).

- ▶ Step 4—Perform the DSMERGE.

Let's explore each of these exciting steps. Refer to Figure 8.30 as you go. It shows the main screen of DSMERGE. Ready, set, merge.

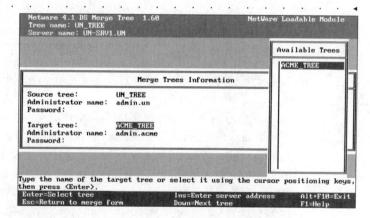

FIGURE 8.30

The Main Menu of DSMERGE

STEP 1: CHECK STATUS OF NETWARE 4 SERVERS

Before and after you merge two trees, it is important to check the status of your NetWare 4 servers. Before the merge, you want to check the versions of each NetWare 4 server and its current status. Table 8.3 shows the possible server status values and a brief description of each.

TABLE 8.3 *Understanding Server Status in NetWare 4*	SERVER STATUS	DESCRIPTION
	!DS Locked	The server responds with an error condition indicating that the NDS database is locked and inaccessible.
	!Inaccessible/Down	The server does not respond and is considered to be inaccessible.
	!Error <-N>	N is the Directory Services error code number. This status indicates that the server is not responding because of the error condition listed in the value N.
	!Wrong Tree	The server is responding with a tree name that does not match the tree name of the local server containing the Master replica of [Root].
	UP	The server is up and functioning.

The check phase of DSMERGE also ensures that the host DSMERGE server holds a replica of the [Root] partition. If it cannot find a replica of [Root], the operation will abort.

Next, the utility will attempt to find all NetWare 4 servers in the tree. DSMERGE will search an array of server IDs that are contained in the Master replica of the [Root] partition to collect the server name, version of NDS, and tree name. If a server in the list cannot be found, or has an incorrect tree name, the utility will issue an error code.

Once all the servers have been contacted, DSMERGE will display a list of servers and their respective statuses. Now, you're ready for Step 2—time synchronization check.

ZEN

"However much you knock at nature's door, she will never answer you in comprehensible words."

Ivan Turgenev

STEP 2: CHECK TIME SYNCHRONIZATION STATUS

The next important DSMERGE check involves time synchronization. Both trees must be synchronized and they must refer to the same time source. Once DSMERGE is loaded on a server containing a replica of the [Root] partition, you can initiate time synchronization as shown in Figure 8.31.

F I G U R E 8.31

Time Synchronization Status Screen in DSMERGE

DSMERGE will check the time status of all servers for the server name, NDS version, and the time synchronization status. If there is a time delta between a NetWare 4 server and the local server running DSMERGE, the difference is shown on the screen in hours, minutes, and seconds (see Figure 8.31).

Your merged directory tree must only have one Reference or Single-Reference time source. If more than one tree is a Reference or a Single-Reference server, you must assign all but one of them as a Secondary time server prior to initiating the merge.

STEP 3: RENAME A DIRECTORY TREE (IF NECESSARY)

Next, you should rename one of the trees—but only if necessary. You should use this option if you are merging two trees that have the same name. Keep in mind that this is the only NetWare utility that currently allows you to change the name of your NDS tree.

First, you load DSMERGE.NLM on the server that contains the Master replica of the [Root] partition and follow the previous checking steps.

Next, DSMERGE begins by changing the name of the local tree's [Root] object to the new tree name. If an error should occur during this process, the operation is aborted.

After the local server has changed the name of the [Root] object, a command is issued to change all servers in the local tree to the new tree name. Keep in mind that once this process has been completed, we're not finished. There are many more synchronization activities occurring in the background—you just can't see them. Once initiated, this process is irrevocable. After completion of the operation, you should check the status of the servers once again to verify that all servers have received the new name.

STEP 4: PERFORM THE DSMERGE

It's time! Once you have checked and verified the status of your NetWare 4 servers, along with time synchronization, you are ready to perform the merge. Get out your protective gloves. At the completion of DSMERGE, you will have a single tree with a common [Root]. Very cool.

Here's how it works:

▸ Phase 1: Merge Check

▸ Phase 2: Merge Preparation

▸ Phase 3: Merge Trees

▸ Phase 4: Merge Completion

THE BRAIN

A good reference on DSMERGE is "Using the DSMERGE Utility in NetWare 4.1" in the March 1995 *Novell Application Notes*.

Phase 1: Merge Check

The Merge Check ensures that your source server running DSMERGE.NLM contains the Master replica of the [Root] partition. If this check is successful, you will see a screen similar to the one shown in Figure 8.32. This screen asks for the tree name of both the source and target trees, along with their Admin names and passwords.

FIGURE 8.32

The Merge Tree
Information Screen of
DSMERGE

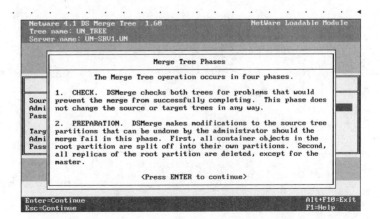

```
Netware 4.1 DS Merge Tree  1.60                 NetWare Loadable Module
Tree name: UN_TREE
Server name: UN-SRV1.UN




                            Merge Trees Information

    Source tree:          UN_TREE
    Administrator name:   admin.un
    Password:

    Target tree:          (Press <Enter> for a tree list)
    Administrator name:
    Password:



Enter the full Directory Services path (your complete name context). This user
needs the Supervisor object right to the Root object of the source tree.
 Enter=Edit this field            F10=Perform merge          Alt+F10=Exit
 Esc=Return to main menu          Down=Next field            F1=Help
```

Phase 2: Merge Preparation

This phase modifies the source tree partitions. The utility will remove all [Root]
replicas from any non-NetWare 4 servers. It will also split the [Root] partition from all
other objects in the tree, making a partition that contains only the [Root] object. Any
other Read/Write or Read-Only replicas of [Root] also will be removed from any servers
in the tree.

Once this operation is completed, DSMERGE can actually merge the two trees. Keep
in mind that the partitioning operations mentioned here also could be performed
beforehand with NWADMIN or PARTMGR. But why perform extra work if DSMERGE
is willing to do it for you? The first two phases are displayed (see Figure 8.33) before you
continue to Phase 3.

FIGURE 8.33

The First Two Phases of
DSMERGing

```
Netware 4.1 DS Merge Tree  1.60                 NetWare Loadable Module
Tree name: UN_TREE
Server name: UN-SRV1.UN
    ┌──────────────────────── Merge Tree Phases ─────────────────────────┐
    │                                                                     │
    │        The Merge Tree operation occurs in four phases.              │
    │                                                                     │
    │    1.  CHECK.  DSMerge checks both trees for problems that would     │
  Sour│  prevent the merge from successfully completing.  This phase does  │
  Admi│  not change the source or target trees in any way.                │
  Pass│                                                                   │
    │    2.  PREPARATION.  DSMerge makes modifications to the source tree │
  Targ│  partitions that can be undone by the administrator should the    │
  Admi│  merge fail in this phase.  First, all container objects in the   │
  Pass│  root partition are split off into their own partitions.  Second, │
    │  all replicas of the root partition are deleted, except for the     │
    │  master.                                                            │
    │                                                                     │
    │                    <Press ENTER to continue>                        │
    │                                                                     │
    └─────────────────────────────────────────────────────────────────────┘
 Enter=Continue                                              Alt+F10=Exit
 Esc=Continue                                                F1=Help
```

Phase 3: Merge Trees

Once the first two phases are completed, the merge operation begins. Once again, DSMERGE will gather the server IDs from the source server's replica list and check their statuses. Each server in the source tree will be contacted to obtain its server address and distinguished name in preparation for merging the source servers to the target tree.

The merge operation actually changes the name of the source tree [Root] object to match the [Root] object of the target tree. Once this process occurs, the source server receives a new name and issues a command to change the tree name of all servers in the source tree.

Phase 4: Merge Completion

The merge completion phase continues renaming source tree servers until all are done. A copy of the target tree's [Root] replica is then copied to each source server. This operation may take some time, depending on the size of the target's [Root] replica and the bandwidth of WAN links. Any objects that are no longer needed will be removed by the background synchronization process.

As with most gardening tasks, DSMERGing makes a mess. Some manual tasks may have to be completed after the two trees are merged:

1 • Place copies of the [Root] replica on strategic servers throughout the new tree.

2 • You may have to restore any objects that were deleted before the DSMERGE process.

3 • Because the source tree has had significant changes to its partitions below [Root], you will have to replace most of its child partitions. Refer to Chapter 9 (Partition Management and Synchronization) for more information.

4 • Finally, you may have to check workstations that have the PREFERRED TREE statement in their NET.CFG configuration file. Each workstation with the source tree name will have to be changed to reflect the target tree name. This can be accomplished through the use of batch files or a WSUPDATE program in each user's Container login script.

Figure 8.34 shows the DSMERGE display screen for the final two phases.

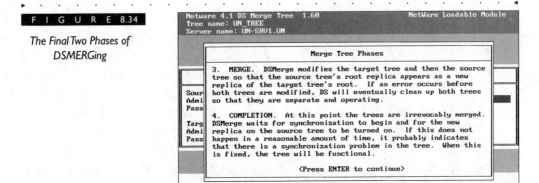

The Final Two Phases of DSMERGing

QUIZ

Some things are enough to scare anyone. You might be able to go from *warm* to *cold* quite easily, but how about from *cold* to *warm*? Can you change one letter at a time and make a proper English word with each step? You should be able to do it in four steps.

C   O   L   D

__ __ __ __

__ __ __ __

__ __ __ __

W   A   R   M

(Q8-4)

Voila! You're finished with DSMERGing. That wasn't so bad. How does it feel to be a full-fledged genetic engineer? Well, not quite yet. There's one more scientific experiment left—NETSYNCing. This is where it gets really weird.

NetSyncing

As promised, we now get to cross-pollinate NetWare 3 binderies and NetWare 4 trees. Don't forget your protective clothing. This is genetic engineering at its finest.

All of this scientific wizardry is accomplished by using NetSync—a special part of NetWare 4. It is a management utility designed to expand the benefits of NetWare Directory Services to NetWare 3 file servers. With NetSync, you can synchronize NetWare 3 users and groups with objects that are contained in a NetWare 4 Directory. Therefore, when you create or modify a user in the bindery context of a NetWare 4 server, the changes are synchronized with all NetWare 3 servers in the NetSync cluster.

A NetWare 4 server can have up to 12 NetWare 3 servers in its NetSync cluster. A *cluster* is simply a collection of NetWare 3 servers that are synchronized with a single NetWare 4 server—inside its bindery context. Because all servers in the cluster are synchronized, you only need to create a user once. That information is then automatically distributed to all NetWare 3 binderies in the cluster. This is amazing stuff! See Figure 8.35 for an example of a five-server NetSync cluster.

FIGURE 8.35

Creating a Five-server NetSync Cluster

You can also use NetWare 4 utilities to create and manage NetWare 3 users and groups (such as NWADMIN or NETADMIN). Printing is also manageable with the NetWare 4 versions of PCONSOLE and NWADMIN. Wow! So, how does it work? Smoke and mirrors—watch.

UNDERSTANDING NETSYNC

All great magic involves smoke and mirrors. NetSync is no exception. It is intended as a temporary solution for central administration of a mixed NetWare 3 and NetWare 4 environment. For those servers running versions of NetWare 3 that cannot immediately be moved to NetWare 4, NetSync provides a good (albeit, temporary) solution. Don't get too attached to this concept. Life would be much easier if you just upgraded your NetWare 3 servers to NetWare 4. But if you can't (or don't want to), NetSync is an option.

REAL WORLD

NetSync can also be used on WANs that are running Novell's NetWare Name Service (NNS) domain and cannot move all the servers in the domain to NetWare 4 immediately.

NetSync uses two NLMs. NETSYNC4 is loaded on a single NetWare 4 server, while NETSYNC3 operates on up to 12 NetWare 3 servers (once again, check out Figure 8.35). The NetSync NLM loaded on each server provides communication between the NetWare 3 binderies and the emulated bindery context of NetWare 4. From the NetWare 4 point of view, NetSync performs the following functions:

I • Holds bindery objects that are copied to its bindery context. When NETSYNC4.NLM is first enabled on the NetWare 4 server, it copies all users and groups from the NetWare 3 server's binderies into the bindery context of the NetWare 4 server.

2 • Downloads all objects in the NetWare 4 bindery context to the connected NetWare 3 servers. A combined bindery of NDS users and groups (along with the NetWare 3 binderies) is downloaded to each NetWare 3 server in the NetSync cluster. This process gives all servers (NetWare 3 and NetWare 4) a common, synchronized bindery. This is called a *Super Bindery*.

3 • Monitors any changes to the bindery context of the NetWare 4 server. The NetSync utility will monitor any user or group changes made on the NetWare 4 server, and synchronize these changes with all NetWare 3 servers in its cluster.

4 • Synchronizes bindery information of any NetWare 3 server that has been temporarily removed from the cluster. Any changes that may have occurred to the bindery during its absence will be sent down by the NetWare 4 server and redistributed automatically.

Genetic engineering is an amazing science. How do they do it? Now, let's find out how to install NetSync for ourselves. Ready, set, sync.

INSTALLING NETSYNC

Installing NetSync is not difficult. All of the components are already stored on your NetWare 4 file server. The SYS:SYSTEM directory contains the necessary NetWare 4 files and the SYS:SYSTEM\NETSYNC directory contains the NetWare 3 files. At least one NetWare 4 server is required, but you can have up to 12 NetWare 3 servers in the cluster. For authentication purposes, each NetWare 3 server will also need an available licensed connection to the NetWare 4 server.

As we learned previously, NetSync consists of two server modules:

- ▸ NETSYNC4—on the NetWare 4 server

- ▸ NETSYNC3—on each NetWare 3 server in the NetSync cluster

Let's take a closer look.

Loading NETSYNC4

To load NetSync at the host NetWare 4 server, simply type **LOAD NETSYNC4** at the server console. Always load NETSYNC4 first and authorize the NetWare 3 servers before loading NETSYNC3. If you don't, the NetWare 3 servers won't become part of the NetSync cluster. NETSYNC4 automatically creates the SYS:SYSTEM\NETSYNC directory—it contains log files and the other critical NetSync information.

Before activating NETSYNC3, you must authorize each NetWare 3 server on the NetWare 4 WAN. When you load NETSYNC4, you will see the screen shown in Figure 8.36. Select Edit Server List and press Enter to add NetWare 3 servers by name. This begins the authorization process. You can enter up to 12 NetWare 3 servers on the list.

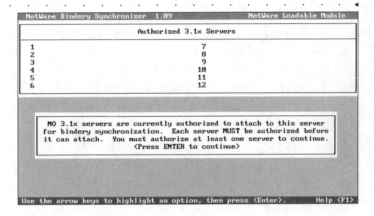

FIGURE 8.36

Authorizing NetWare 3 NetSync Servers with NETSYNC4

As an added measure of security you will also need to enter a NetSync password. This password will then be required as each NetWare 3 server requests entry into the NetSync cluster. The password is used only once.

TIP

You can use a different password for each NetWare 3 server. However, since this password is used only once, for simplicity we recommend the same password for all NetWare 3 servers in the cluster. Additionally, do not use your ADMIN or Supervisor password as your NetSync password—this may pose a security risk.

Next, you will be asked if you want to copy the NetSync files to the NetWare 3 server. This option appears when you first authorize a NetWare 3 server during installation. It sounds like a grand idea to me.

Loading NETSYNC3

Every NetWare 3 server that participates in the cluster must load the NETSYNC3 NLM. Again, be sure that you have completed the NetWare 4 installation steps before starting this phase. The first step is to reboot the NetWare 3 servers because they will need to execute some new files. These files were downloaded by the NETSYNC4 process previously. Once your NetWare 3 server is back up and running, you can now type **LOAD NETSYNC3** at the server's console.

Once loaded, you will be asked a couple of questions regarding NetWare Name Services (NNS). If you are not running NNS, select No to these questions and proceed. If you are running NNS, refer to Novell's NetSync documentation for more information.

The utility will ask you to enter the name of the NetWare 4 host server and the correct NetSync password. After successful entry, NETSYNC3 will upload the NetWare 3 bindery information to the NetWare 4 server's bindery context. The users and groups in the NetWare 4 server's bindery context, in turn, are loaded onto the NetWare 3 server.

For further NetSync configurations, you can use the NetSync Options menus within NETSYNC3.NLM and NETSYNC4.NLM. These include viewing or editing the log file, editing a server list, and other activities.

ZEN

"Earth laughs in Flowers."

Ralph Waldo Emerson

Now that NetSync is installed, it's time to explore NetSync management. You're off and running. Isn't this exciting?

MANAGING NETSYNC

Once you've successfully installed NetSync, you can manage your NetWare 3 bindery objects with the NetWare 4 NWADMIN or NETADMIN utilities. *Do not* go back and use SYSCON to modify user and group information on NetWare 3 servers. The use of SYSCON will not synchronize changes on NDS and should be avoided with this configuration.

NetSync will also provide printing support. After you have completed your installation of NETSYNC3 and NETSYNC4, all workstation print utilities are copied to the NetWare 3 servers. Also, PRINTCON and PRINTDEF databases are updated to the NetWare 4 formats. You can also choose to move your NetWare 3 print servers into a single print server on the NetWare 4 server. Your printers are moved into Directory Services where they can be managed from a single NetWare 4 print server.

In addition, NetWare 4 print utilities are immediately available for use in your NetWare 3. For more information on using print utilities with NetSync, refer to your Novell documentation.

Since NetSync synchronizes NetWare 3 users and groups with objects in the NetWare 4 bindery context, you must enable Bindery Services on the host NetWare 4 server. The NetWare 4 server will periodically download its bindery context changes to all the participating NetWare 3 servers in the cluster. If more than one NetWare 4 server is using the same bindery context, you will have all servers with the same context synchronizing with the NetWare 3 servers in the cluster. Although there is no theoretical limit to how many servers can be using the same bindery context, the NetSync operation is CPU-intensive. Thus, the more objects to synchronize, the more overhead placed on the server.

Finally, if you want to set multiple bindery contexts for a server, the process is also governed by the number of objects and the speed of your links during synchronization. Have a nice day!

ZEN

"When the oak is felled, the whole forest echoes with its fall, but a hundred acorns are sown by an unnoticed breeze."

Thomas Carlyle

Congratulations! You're tree is alive and well. It's been grown, browsed, accessed, fertilized, merged, and finally, cloned. Now there's only one thing left to do—chop, chop. T-I-M-B-E-R!

Just kidding. I wouldn't do that to you. It's a beautiful tree, and besides, this is only the beginning. Speaking of beginnings, let's review where we've been.

It all started with a brief tour of the garden. Then, we discovered a variety of tree browsing tools (including NWADMIN, NETADMIN, CX, NLIST, and various user tools). In the next section, we explored the purposes and uses of many required and commonly used NDS objects. As a matter of fact, most of these objects found their way into the ACME tree—it's a good thing we were paying attention.

Then, the chapter took a scientific turn into the realm of merging and crossbreeding. In the DSMERGing section, we learned the four steps for merging two unrelated NDS trees. Then, in the NETSYNCing section, we learned how to cross-pollinate NetWare 3 and NetWare 4 LANs. Scary.

Now what? Well, like I said before, this is only the beginning. In the next chapter, we will continue the gardening stint and learn about pruning (partitioning), grafting (replication), and pollination (time synchronization). And that's not all. In subsequent chapters, we'll file, secure, configure, manage, print, and optimize your NDS tree. You have so much more gardening to look forward to. I bet you can't wait. Go wash the dirt from under your fingernails. You're about to inherit a pair of green, uh, I mean red, thumbs.

ZEN

"To own a bit of ground, to scratch it with a hoe, to plant seeds, and watch their renewal of life—this is the commonest delight of the race, the most satisfactory thing a man can do."

Charles Dudley Warner

CASE STUDY: BUILDING ACME'S NDS TREE

Congratulations! You've built the ACME tree. The world is in very good hands with you on the job. In this exercise, we are going to explore building the ACME tree using three different utilities: ADMIN (a Windows-based utility), NETADMIN (a menu utility) and UIMPORT (a batch utility). This exercise assumes that you have completed the case study entitled "Custom Installation" in Chapter 6 and that the LABS-SRV1 server has been installed.

In this exercise, you will create the Organizational Unit, User, Printer, and Print Server objects in the CAMELOT, RIO, and SYDNEY branches of the tree shown in the Resource List in Chapter 4. (You can't create Server objects because they are created automatically when you install or migrate to NetWare 4. You also can't create the Print Queue objects listed because they require volume names for servers that haven't been installed.)

You will need the following additional information:

▸ The Location property for each container or leaf object should always contain the city or Location (such as Camelot, Rio, or Sydney). The Department should always be the full name of the container (such as Administration, Financial, Marketing, and so on).

▸ The address, phone, and fax information for the CAMELOT Organizational Unit and its subcontainers is:

London Road

Bracknell, Berkshire RG12 2UY

United Kingdom

Phone: (44 344) 724000

Fax: (44 344) 724001

▸ The address, phone, and fax information for the RIO Organizational Unit and its subcontainers is:

Alameda Ribeirao Preto 130-12 Andar

Sao Paulo 01331-000

> Brazil
>
> Phone: (55 11) 253 4866
>
> Fax: (55 11) 285 4847

▸ The address, phone, and fax information for the SYDNEY Organizational Unit and its subcontainers is:

> 18 Level
>
> 201 Miller St.
>
> North Sydney NSW 2060
>
> Australia
>
> Phone: (61 2) 925 3000
>
> Fax: (61 2) 922 2113

▸ Each Organizational Unit will have the following Intruder Detection/Lockout limits:

> Incorrect Login Attempts: 5
>
> Intruder Attempt Reset Interval: 10 days
>
> Intruder Lockout Reset Interval: 20 minutes

▸ User Templates and each User object should contain the following account restrictions, unless otherwise specified:

> Each user will be limited to logging in on one workstation at a time (that is, one concurrent login).
>
> Each user will be required to have a *unique* password consisting of 6 characters or more, and will be required to change their password every 60 days. Each user will be allowed six grace logins.

Each user will be restricted from logging in each day between
2:30 a.m. and 4:00 a.m. (whenbackups and system maintenance
are done).

Now that you know the plan, let's go ahead and implement it! Ready, set, build!!

PART I: NWADMIN

1 • Execute the NetWare Administrator utility through Windows.

a. The first thing to do is to log in to the network as .ADMIN.ACME by typing
LOGIN.ADMIN.ACME and pressing Enter, then keying in the appropriate
password and pressing Enter.

b. Next, execute MS Windows by typing **WIN** and pressing Enter. If the
NetWare Administrator icon has already been set up, double-click on it to
execute it, then proceed to Step 2.

c. If the NetWare Administrator has not been set up, create a program group
in MS Windows by selecting the New option from the File menu. A New
Program Object dialog box will appear. Be sure the Program Group radio
button is selected and click on the OK button. A Program Group Properties
dialog box will be displayed. Type **NetWare Tools** in the Description field,
then click on the OK button. (It's not necessary to fill in the Group File
field, because a .GRP file will automatically be created for the new group by
the Windows Program Manager.) The NetWare Tools group that you just
created will be opened.

d. To create a program item in the NetWare Tools group, select the New option from the File menu. Be sure that the Program Item radio button is highlighted, then click on the OK button. A Program Item Properties dialog box will appear. Type **NetWare Administrator** in the Description field. Click on the Browse button, then click on the arrow to the right of the Drives field. Click on the drive that points to the LABS-SRV1\SYS:PUBLIC directory (typically Z:). Use the scrollbar to the right of the filenames window to bring the NWADMIN.EXE filename into view, click on it, then click on the OK button. The Program Item Properties dialog box will be displayed. Click on the OK button to accept your changes. A message will be displayed saying that the specified path points to a file that may not be available during later Windows sessions. Click on the Yes button to indicate that you want to continue.

e. The message box will close and the new program item you created will appear in the program group. Double-click on the NetWare Administrator icon to execute the utility.

2 • Set the current context for the NetWare Administrator utility.

a. A portion of the NDS tree should be displayed. If not, select the Browse option from the Tools menu to open a browser window. Next, be sure that your current context for this utility is set to the [Root]. If the [Root] icon is displayed at the top of the screen, proceed to Step 3.

b. If the [Root] icon is not displayed at the top of the screen, set the context to the [Root] by clicking on the Set Context option in the View menu, typing **[Root]** in the New Context field, then clicking on the OK button.

3 • Create the CAMELOT Organizational Unit.

a. At this point, the [Root] icon and the ACME Organization icon should be displayed. Double-click on the ACME Organization to display its contents. The NORAD Organizational Unit icon and Admin User object icon should appear under the ACME Organization.

b. To create a CAMELOT Organizational Unit under the ACME Organization, be sure the ACME Organization is highlighted, then press the Insert key. (Alternately, you can select the Create option from the Object menu, or click on the ACME Organization with the right mouse button and choose Create from the pop-up menu that appears.) A New Object dialog box will appear. Choose the Organizational Unit object type by using the scroll bar on the right side of the dialog box to bring it into view, then double-clicking on it. (An alternate method would be to type the letter **O**, which happens to be the first letter in the term Organizational Unit. This would highlight the Organizational Role object class, since Organizational Role is the first object in the list that begins with the letter "O." You could then press the down-arrow key once to highlight the Organizational Unit object class, then double-click on it.) A Create Organizational Unit dialog box will be displayed. Type **CAMELOT** in the Organizational Unit Name field, then click the Define Additional Properties and Define User Default check boxes to select them. Finally, click on the Create button to create the new Organizational Unit called CAMELOT.

c. Because you selected the Define Additional Properties check box in Step 3b, a dialog box will appear. You'll notice that, by default, the Identification page button has been selected, allowing you to key in property information for that category. Key in the following fields in the Identification category:

> Other Name: **CAMELOT**
>
> Location: **CAMELOT**
>
> Telephone: **44 344 724000**
>
> Fax Number: **44 344 724001**

d. Next, Click on the Postal Address page button and fill in the following fields:

Street: **London Road**

City: **Bracknell**

State or Province: **Berkshire, United Kingdom**

Postal (Zip) Code: **RG12 2UY**

e. Then, click on the Intruder Detection/Lockout page button and fill in the following information:

Detect Intruders: **Yes**

Incorrect Login Attempts: **5**

Intruder Attempt Reset Interval: **10 days**

Lock Account After Detection: **Yes**

Intruder Lockout Reset Interval: **20 minutes**

f. Finally, click the OK button to return to the main browser window in the NetWare Administrator utility.

4 • Update the User Template in the CAMELOT container. If you double-click on the CAMELOT Organizational Unit to list its contents, you'll notice that a User Template object has been created under it because you selected the Define User Defaults check box when you created it. Double-click on the User Template. A dialog box will open.

a. Fill in the same location, telephone, fax, and address information as you did for the CAMELOT Organizational Unit in Step 3c.

b. Next, click on the Login Restrictions page button, then click on the box in front of the Limit Concurrent Connections property. The Limit Concurrent Connections property should then list a maximum connection value of "1."

c. To set password restrictions for this User Template, click on the Password Restrictions Page button, then do the following:

> (1) Click on the Allow User to Change Password property.
>
> (2) Click on the Require a Password property and type in password length of six.
>
> (3) Click on the Force Periodic Password Changes property and key in a Days Between Forced Changes value of **60.**
>
> (4) Click on the Require Unique Passwords property.
>
> (5) Click on the Grace Logins property and make sure that Grace Logins Allowed shows a value of "6."

d. Next, go ahead and restrict login privileges between 3:00 a.m. and 4:00 a.m. every day. Click on the Login Time Restrictions page button. A grid will be displayed on the screen showing days of the week along the left edge, and time of day across the top. Each box in the grid represents a half-hour period during the week. You'll notice that when you place the mouse cursor in a box, the day and time represented by that box is displayed. White boxes represent times during which the user is allowed to log in. Gray boxes indicate times that the user is prevented from logging in. Click on the 3:00 and 3:30 boxes for each day of the week. When you are finished updating the User Template, click on OK to accept the changes you made. Follow the same procedure for assigning User account restrictions to each of the User objects in this container.

e. Finally, click on the OK button to return to the main NetWare Administrator browser window.

5 • Create the CHARITY Organizational Unit under the CAMELOT container.

a. Use the same method listed in Step 3b to create a CHARITY Organizational Unit under the CAMELOT Organizational Unit, except that you'll highlight the CAMELOT Organizational Unit instead of the ACME Organization. Next, use the method described in Steps 3c and 3d to fill in the appropriate location, phone, fax, and address information. Finally, key in Login Restrictions, Password Restrictions, and Time Restrictions described in Steps 4c through 4e.

b. Create the SirGalahad User object by clicking on the CHARITY Organizational Unit and pressing Insert. A New Object dialog box will appear. Select the User object type by typing **U** and pressing Enter. The Login Name and Last Name fields are required properties for a User object. Key in a login name of **SirGalahad** and a Last Name of **Galahad,** and be sure that the Use User Template check box is selected. (Normally, you would also create a home directory for this user, but you can't at this time because the CAM-CHR-SRV1 server has not been installed yet.) Finally, click on the Create button to create the user by using the defaults in the User Template located in the Organizational Unit indicated.

c. Create the HP5-P1 Printer object by making sure the CHARITY Organizational Unit is highlighted and pressing Insert. A New Object dialog box will appear. Choose the Printer object type by using the scroll bar on the right side of the dialog box to bring it into view, then double-clicking on it. A Printer dialog box will be displayed. Key in a Printer object name of **HP5-P1** and click on the Define Additional Properties check box. A Printer dialog box will appear. Key in **HP5-P1** in the Other Name field, **CAMELOT** in the location field, **CHARITY** in the Department field, and **ACME** in the Organization field. Then press Enter to return to the main NetWare Administrator browser screen.

    d. Create the CAM-CHR-PS1 Print Server object by clicking on the CHARITY Organizational Unit and pressing Insert. A New Object dialog box will appear. Choose the Print Server object type by using the scroll bar on the right side of the dialog box to bring it into view, then double-clicking on it. A Create Print Server dialog box will be displayed. Key in a print server name of **CAM-CHR-PS1**, click on the Define Additional Properties check box, then click on the Create button. A Print Server dialog box will appear. Click on the Assignments page button, then click on the Add button. A Select Object dialog box will appear. The HP5-P1 printer you created in the previous step should appear in the Objects list box on the left side of the screen. Double-click on the HP5-P1 printer object, then click on the OK button to return to the main NetWare Administrator browser window.

6 • Create the .OPS.CAMELOT.ACME Organizational Unit using the method in Step 5a, then create the KingArthur User Object, the CANONBJ-P1 Printer object, and the OPS-PS1 Print Server object under it by using the methods listed in Steps 5b through 5d.

7 • Create the .FIN.OPS.CAMELOT.ACME Organizational Unit, then create the Guinevere User object, the HP4SI-P1 and HP4SI-P2 Printer objects and the CAM-FIN-PS1 and CAM-FIN-PS2 Print Server objects under it.

8 • Create the .DIST.OPS.CAMELOT.ACME Organizational Unit, then create the Merlin User object, the HPIII-P1 Printer object, and the DIST-PS1 Print Server object under it.

9 • Create the .PR.CAMELOT.ACME Organizational Unit, then create the CEttelson User object, the HP4SI-P1 Printer object, and the CAM-PR-PS1 Print Server object under it.

10 • To exit the NetWare Administrator utility, chose the Exit menu option from the File menu.

PART II: NETADMIN

1 • Execute the NETADMIN utility by typing **NETADMIN** at the DOS prompt and pressing Enter.

2 • Create the RIO Organizational Unit under the ACME Organization.

a. Select the Manage Object menu option from the NetAdmin Options menu. Walk the tree until you locate the ACME Organization. Highlight the ACME Organization using the up-arrow and down-arrow keys, press Enter to change context, then press the Insert key.

b. An Object, Class menu will appear. Highlight the Organizational Unit object class and press Enter. A Create Object Organizational Unit box will appear. Key in **RIO** in the New Name field and **Y** in the Create User Template field, then press F10 to continue. You will be informed that an Organizational Unit has been created. When asked whether to create another, select No and press Enter. The RIO Organizational Unit will be displayed in the appropriate position in the NDS tree.

c. Highlight the RIO Organizational Unit and press Enter to change context. Highlight the User Template and press F10 to select it. An Actions for Users menu will be displayed. Select the "View or edit properties of this object" option and press Enter. You'll see a list of property categories listed. Select the Identification menu option and press Enter. Key in the following information in the fields specified:

> Other Name: **Rio de Janeiro**
>
> Location: **Rio**
>
> Telephone: **(55 11) 253 4866**
>
> Fax Number: **(55 11) 285 4847**

d. When you are finished, press F10 to save, then select the Postal address menu option and press Enter. Key in the following information in the fields indicated:

Street: **Alameda Ribeirao Preto 130-12 Andar**

City: **Sao Paulo**

State or Province: **Brazil**

Postal (Zip) Code: **01331-000**

When you are finished, press F10 to save. Press Esc twice to return to the Object, Class window.

e. Highlight the period (.) representing the current context, then press F10 to select it. Select the View or edit properties of this object option from the Actions for Organizational Unit menu. Highlight the Intruder Detection option from the Viewer or edit Organizational Unit menu and press Enter. Fill in the following information:

Detect Intruders: **Yes**

Incorrect Login Attempts: **5**

Intruder Attempt Reset Interval: **10 days**

Lock Account After Detection: **Yes**

Intruder Lockout Reset Interval: **20 minutes**

Press F10 to save when you are finished. Press Esc three times to return to the Object, Class menu.

3 • Create the ADMIN, CHARITY, HR, and PR Organizational Units under the RIO Organizational Unit. Use the method listed in Step 2b to create the CHARITY, HR, and PR Organizational Units under the RIO Organizational Unit. When asked whether you want to create another Organizational Unit after creating the PR Organizational Unit, type **N** instead of **Y**.

4 • Create the FAC Organizational Unit under the ADMIN.RIO.ACME Organizational Unit.

5 • Create the MEDICAL, FOOD, and SHELTER Organizational Units under the HR.RIO.ACME Organizational Unit.

6 • Create the GWashington User object, the CANONBJ-P1 Printer object, and the ADMIN-PS1 Print Server object under the ADMIN.RIO.ACME Organizational Unit object. Walk the tree to find the ADMIN.RIO.ACME Organizational Unit, then highlight it and press Enter, then Insert.

7 • Create the SirPercival User object, the HP4SI-P1 Printer object, and the RIO-CHR-PS1 Print Server object under the CHARITY.RIO.ACME Organizational Unit.

a. Highlight the ADMIN Organizational Unit and press Enter, then Insert. The Select an Object, Class menu will appear. Type **U** to select the User Object class, then press Enter. A Create Object User box will appear. Type **GWashington** in the Login Name field and **Washington** in the Last Name field. (Normally, you would create a home directory for this user, but you can't at this time, because neither the ADMIN-SRV1 nor ADMIN-SRV2 servers have been installed.) Be sure that the Copy User Template Field has a value of Yes, then press F10 to continue. You will then be notified that the User has been created. When asked if you'd like to create another user, select No and press Enter.

    b. Try to create a Printer object and Print Server object in the same container. If you press Insert, the Select an Object Class menu will appear. You'll notice that the Print Server, Printer, and Print Queue object classes are not listed. This is because you cannot create or manage the printing environment using the NETADMIN utility. These objects can, however, be created with the NetWare Administrator and PCONSOLE utilities.

8 • Create the JMadison User object under the FAC.ADMIN.RIO.ACME Organizational Unit.

9 • Create the Gandhi User object under the HR.RIO.ACME Organizational Unit.

10 • Create the ASchweitzer User object under the MEDICAL.HR.RIO.ACME Organizational Unit object.

11 • Create the MTeresa User object under the .FOOD.HR.RIO.ACME Organizational Unit object.

12 • Create the FNightingale User object under the SHELTER.HR.RIO.ACME Organizational Unit object.

13 • Create the Buddha User object under the .PEACE.HR.RIO.ACME Organizational Unit object.

14 • Create the MClarke User object under the PR.RIO.ACME container.

15 • To exit the NETADMIN utility, press the Esc key repeatedly until the "Exit?" question is displayed, then select Yes and press Enter.

PART III: UIMPORT

1 • Before you can run the UIMPORT utility, you must have created two files: an ASCII control file and a comma-delimited ASCII data file. The data file is typically created by exporting user information from a database file. The control file consists of some control parameters and field definitions that define where information should be placed in the NDS. The UIMPORT utility can only be used to add users. It cannot be used to create other objects in the NDS tree. Because of this, before you run UIMPORT, you must create any Organization or Organizational Unit objects that you will need.

a. Since you don't have a database containing the information for the users in the SYDNEY subtree, you'll need to create a data file from scratch using an ASCII text editor. Let's try a very simple test case. Let's try importing the User objects for the network administrators for HR Organizational Unit and each of its four subcontainers into the HR container. To create the data file, key in the following lines into an ASCII file you create called ACMEDATA:

```
Gandhi,Gandhi,"Human Resources"
ASchweitzer,Schweitzer,Medical
MTeresa,Teresa,Food
FNightingale,Nightingale,Shelter
Buddha,Buddha,Peace
```

b. Next, create an import control file by keying in the following lines in an ASCII file you create called ACMECTRL:

```
Import Control
Name Context="OU=HR.OU=SYDNEY.O=ACME"
User Template=Y
Fields
Login Name
Last Name
Department
```

2 • Before you can import this data, you must create the NDS subtree structure using the NWADMIN or NETADMIN utilities.

   a. Use the utility of your choice to create the initial SYDNEY subtree structure, including:

       ▸ A SYDNEY Organizational Unit under the ACME Organization

       ▸ CHARITY, HR, and PR Organizational Units under the SYDNEY Organizational Unit.

       ▸ FOOD, MEDICAL, PEACE, and SHELTER Organizational Units under the HR Organizational Unit.

   b. When you create these containers, be sure that you create a User Template object for each. Don't forget to update both the containers and the User Templates with the property values listed at the beginning of this chapter.

3 • After you've set up the NDS subtree structure for the SYDNEY portion of the tree, you can execute the UIMPORT utility by typing **UIMPORT ACMECTRL ACMEDATA** at the DOS prompt and pressing Enter. To see the result of using this utility, type **CX .HR.SYDNEY.ACME /A / T**.

PART IV: SPECIAL CASES

Now that you've had an opportunity to build the basic ACME tree, let's explore some of their special conditions. Following is a list of some of ACME's more challenging NDS management requirements. Please help them out.

I • ACME needs a site administrator in each location. This will be a revolving position among each of the division heads. For example, the NORAD administrator (named NORAD-Admin), will have administrative access to all divisions of NORAD and the position will alternate among AEinstein, DClarke, and SirGawain.

2 • In addition, all of the site administrators will share a common login script. It will be a mechanism for global security, drive mappings, and special messaging.

3 • The Human Rights Tracking application is constantly being updated. Can you think of an easier way to manage its search drive mappings?

4 • Also, each of the Human Rights department administrators needs access to the Human Rights Tracking program. Security could be a problem.

5 • All of the employees in the Auditing department need easy access to all the resources in the Financial container—for auditing purposes. Also, the auditors don't want to have to navigate the tree to see them.

6 • In addition, the Auditing application is constantly being updated. Searching drive mapping is becoming a problem.

7 • As a matter of fact, the Financial database is due for some major changes as well. I see a pattern forming here. Please help us out.

8 • The following traveling users need a simpler context for accessing ACME from distributed locations: AEinstein, DHoliday, and MCurie.

9 • Everyone in the Crime Fighting division needs to share a common login script.

10 • Finally, Leonardo DaVinci believes in empowering his scientists. After all, he's a "labrat," not a bureaucrat. To distribute the administrative load evenly, he and his scientists take turns managing the R&D department—each scientist takes the helm for three months out of the year.

Partition Management and Synchronization

Pruning is an interesting phenomenon. You cut away branches in order to make them grow. You kill something so it may live. You break up the tree into little pieces so it can become whole again. Gardening is a strange science!

You are a NetWare 4 gardener now. It's time to take control of your horticulture— green thumb required. In the previous chapter you created the tree. Now you will get a chance to prune it as we take the bull-weed by the horns and implement ACME's partition design. Think of this as "tough love" for the chlorophyll set.

NetWare 4 pruning focuses on three important sciences:

1 • NDS Partition Management (pruning)

2 • NDS Replication (grafting)

3 • Time Synchronization (pollination)

In Chapter 2 we learned about partition boundaries and their purpose. Then, in Chapter 4, we discovered various guidelines for NDS partition design. Our first step here is partition management.

The next step is NDS replication—grafting. Once you have set the partition boundaries, you must scatter them around. This serves two purposes—fault tolerance and resource accessibility. In Chapters 2 and 4 we also learned about replica design. Now we get a chance to create ACME's replicas (using NWADMIN) and distribute them to servers throughout their global WAN.

The final step is time synchronization—pollination. Time is as important to NDS as seeds and sunlight are to daffodils. As a NetWare 4 gardener, it's your job to ensure accurate time throughout the WAN. In ACME's case, that's five time providers and 47 time consumers (see Chapter 4). In this chapter we'll learn how to implement and manage ACME's custom time synchronization design. Cool.

So there you have it—your agricultural future. NDS pruning is important business, and today we're going to learn all about it. Ready, set, prune.

ZEN

"Pressure is playing for ten dollars when you don't have a dime in your pocket."

Lee Trevino

NDS Partition Management

The beauty of NDS is its scalability and flexibility. NDS is *scalable* because it allows you to make the database as small, medium, or large as you want. NDS is *flexible* because it allows you to store the database (or pieces of it) anywhere you want. This beauty has a price, though—work. And guess who gets to do the work—*you*, the NetWare 4 CNE gardener.

NDS Partition Management deals with the daily tasks involved in scaling the database. In the next section, NDS Replication, you'll explore flexibility by distributing the database (or pieces of it) to distributed servers throughout the WAN. These scaling chores are your responsibility alone. Fortunately, they don't impact the user. As you can see in Figure 9.1, NDS partitioning provides two main benefits:

1 • NDS allows CNEs to break the database into smaller pieces and distribute those pieces to multiple servers—NDS partition management

2 • Regardless of how it's partitioned, NDS appears to users as a single, unified cloud—user transparency

F I G U R E 9.1

Benefits of NDS and Partitioning

Although portions of NDS can be distributed to multiple NetWare 4 servers, users see a single view of its resources. With NDS, the information is not only distributed, but also replicated multiple times to increase fault tolerance. In Figure 9.1, three of ACME's containers are distributed to location-specific servers. This is the best NDS partitioning approach for large multisite corporations such as ACME.

Smaller companies, on the other hand, can get away with centralizing the NDS database. In this case, all the network information can reside on a few central file servers. The benefit of centralized control is easier administration. Plus, synchronization operations are minimized. This will work as long as the total number of users and network resources remains small.

The bottom line is: YOU get to choose how NDS is partitioned and replicated. You are in control. Later in this section we'll discuss some key partition management strategies, including managing the [Root] partition, creating partition boundaries, and merging partitions. But first, let's spend a few moments reviewing NDS scalability and user transparency—also known as *partitioning*.

TIP

Small companies can greatly simplify partition management by placing all their objects in a single O=Organization NDS container.

UNDERSTANDING NDS PARTITIONS

NDS uses a hierarchical tree structure to organize network resources. As we've learned throughout the book, this tree consists of logical branches (container objects) and leaves (leaf objects).

NDS partitions are logical sections of the tree. Partitioning allows us to split a very large tree into smaller subtrees. These subtrees are easier to manage, and they provide users with better NDS accessibility and performance (see Figure 9.2). You can even distribute copies (replicas) of the subtrees to improve NDS fault tolerance. If all of this sounds too good to be true—it is! NDS partition management is hard work, and *you* get to do it.

FIGURE 9.2

NDS Partitioning at ACME

In earlier chapters we learned all sorts of interesting things about NDS partitions. In chapter 2 we discovered how they work, and in Chapter 4, we built a partition design for ACME. Now it's time to create them. Before we start, however, I want to point out three concepts that have an important impact on partition management:

1 • The Parent/Child Relationship

2 • Partition Transparency

3 • Partitioning Rules

Let's take a quick look.

QUIZ

All anagrams of animals:

(a) **CORONA**   (e) **SOMEDAY**

(b) **PAROLED**   (f) **ALPINES**

(c) **RETIRER**   (g) **ORCHESTRA**

(d) **LESIONS**   (h) **CALIFORNIA***

***two words**

(Q9-1)
(See Appendix C for all quiz answers.)

The Parent/Child Relationship

Partition boundaries follow the same logical, hierarchical flow as the NDS tree. If your tree looks like a pyramid, so does your partition map. This is called *natural partitioning*. As you can see in Figure 9.3, ACME's partition map includes five PARENT partitions and many CHILDREN.

▶ . . . . ◀

F I G U R E 9.3

Parent/Child Partition Map

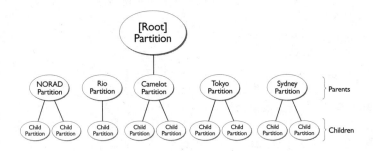

This relationship is known as the *parent/child partition relationship*. When the boundaries between two partitions meet, the partition closest to the [Root] is considered the parent; the one further away is the child. In Figure 9.3, the OU=*<location>* containers are parents to lower organizational containers. In fact, the OU=*<location>* partitions are also children of the [Root] partition. That's an interesting "double whammy."

As in life, partition parents have to manage their subordinate children. This is ensured in NDS through a concept known as *Subordinate References*. When new partitions are created under an existing container, their parent must maintain pointers to the new partitions. Therefore, any server holding a partition can end up with a large number of Subordinate Reference pointers to children of that container.

As a matter of fact, the [Root] is a very sensitive partition. Let me emphasize that NDS creates a Subordinate Reference pointer automatically when a server holding a parent partition creates a link to its child partitions. This is a big problem for the [Root] because it is a parent to all second-tier containers. For this reason I recommend that you make the [Root] partition very small, with only the [Root] and an Organization container inside. Later in the chapter we'll explore some special management strategies for the [Root] partition.

Partition Transparency

Partitioning is hard work. Fortunately, it's completely transparent to the user. In a nutshell, users can access the entire NDS tree, regardless of which server they are connected to. Furthermore, it doesn't matter how the tree has been partitioned and replicated. It appears as a single, unified cloud to the user.

How does this work? Well, NDS maintains a background connection between all parent and child partitions. Although a specific server may not contain the complete NDS database, users still have the ability to get the information from a variety of scattered sources. NDS pieces it together for them in the background. As a NetWare 4 gardener, you have to tell NDS where to put all the copies—that's work.

NDS partitioning is not foolproof, however. If there aren't enough distributed replicas, and a number of servers or WAN links crash, it is possible to temporarily (or permanently) lose access to NDS information. That's why I recommend at least three replicas of every partition. It's better to be safe than sorry.

NDS Partitioning Rules

Now let's review some of the more important NDS partitioning rules. It's as easy as 1-2-3-4.

1 • Each partition must be named and requires a single container object as the top (or root) of the partition (not to be confused with the [Root] partition). The container object used as the start of the partition is called the partition root object. Only one partition root object exists for each partition, and it is the top-most container object. In Figure 9.2 above, for example, OU=NORAD is the root object for the NORAD partition.

2 • Two containers at the same level cannot share a partition without a parent watching over them. Play nicely, children.

3 • Partitions cannot overlap with any other part of the NDS tree. This means that one object will never reside in two partitions.

4 • Each partition contains all of the information for the connected subtree, unless another subordinate partition is created underneath. For example, each location partition in Figure 9.2 includes all the NDS information for all resources in that ACME location.

Now that we know the rules, it's time to move on to NDS partition management. In the next two sections we'll explore some interesting partitioning tasks, including creating, merging, moving, and aborting NDS partitions. But first, let's learn a little more about the [Root] partition and discover why it's so special. Don't forget to bring your green thumb along.

MANAGING THE [ROOT] PARTITION

You know what they say about the first child—or, in this case, the first parent. In either case, it's a very special partition. The [Root] partition is created during the installation of the very first NetWare 4 server. And this server gets a Master copy of it.

In NetWare 4, the [Root] partition is the only default partition. For this reason, it is often called the *default partition*. All other partitioning is your responsibility. Since this

[Root] partition is the only partition created during installation, Figure 9.4 shows how INSTALL.NLM creates the [Root] partition. It happens when you provide the first server's context.

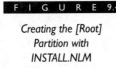

F I G U R E 9.4

Creating the [Root]
Partition with
INSTALL.NLM

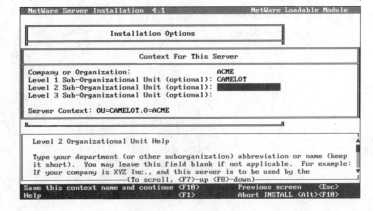

Once the first server has been installed, you can start adding your container and leaf objects. This process was outlined in the previous chapter. As you can see in Figure 9.5, ACME is starting to take shape. This is accomplished using any of the three NDS construction tools: NWADMIN, NETADMIN, or UIMPORT.

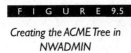

F I G U R E 9.5

Creating the ACME Tree in
NWADMIN

All the second-tier container objects in Figure 9.5 are held within the [Root] partition. Remember, it's the only partition that exists until YOU create some new ones. This is shown in Figure 9.6.

F I G U R E 9.6

A Single [Root] Partition at
ACME

In the beginning, there's only one copy of the [Root] partition. It exists on the very first server (CAM-SRV1) as a Master replica. When you install new NetWare 4 servers, you should immediately create a Read/Write replica of the [Root] partition on the new server (NOR-SRV1). This is accomplished using NWADMIN or PARTMGR (see Figure 9.7). In this figure, two copies of the [Root] partition have been placed on ACME's first two servers—CAM-SRV1 and NOR-SRV1.

Earlier we learned about parents, children, and Subordinate References. We also learned about the downfalls of a large [Root] partition. So, to keep things working efficiently, we need to "split" the [Root] partition so only two objects remain—[Root] and O=ACME. In order to accomplish this, we need to create five new partitions—one for each location (see Figure 9.8).

Now that ACME's [Root] partition is more manageable, we can concentrate on creating other child boundaries. But first, we must distribute one more copy (replica) of the [Root] partition—this time to the third ACME server (TOK-SRV1). For an illustration of this process, refer to Figure 9.22 later in the chapter. OK, done. Now we're ready to create, merge, move, and abort ACME's partitions. Ready, set, prune.

F I G U R E 9.7

*Distributing ACME's [Root]
Partition*

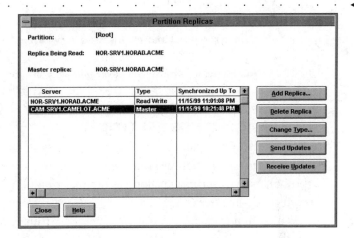

F I G U R E 9.8

*"Splitting" ACME's [Root]
Partition*

ZEN

"I have too much money invested in sweaters."

Bob Hope, on why he will never give up golf

MANAGING NDS PARTITIONS

With the [Root] partition in place, you can get on with the rest of ACME's pruning. This is hard work, but rewarding. And if you think the tree is screaming while you prune, it's just your imagination. It's not that painful. Besides, we're doing it for their own good—the trees know that.

NDS pruning requires special gardening tools; namely, NWADMIN (Windows-based) and PARTMGR (DOS-based). NWADMIN is a Windows-based GUI tool that allows you to manage all NDS objects in the tree. NWADMIN should be "old hat" by now.

In addition to tree management tasks, NWADMIN also has a set of special tools; namely, File Manager, RCONSOLE, and Partition Manager. Figure 9.9 illustrates the Partition Manager option under the Tools menu in the main menu of NWADMIN. The Partition Manager option controls NDS partition management. It is your friend.

▶ · ◀

FIGURE 9.9

*The Partition Manager
Option of NWADMIN*

As you can see in the figure, NWADMIN uses a small box icon to represent partitions. It appears to the left of the partition root object. In this case, we've partitioned OU=NORAD and OU=CAMELOT in the ACME tree.

PARTMGR is the other NetWare partition management tool. It's a DOS-based program that provides functionality similar to NWADMIN. As you can see in Figure 9.10, PARTMGR lacks a little grace in the user-interface realm. It is, however, a very effective partition tool for those of you who don't do Windows.

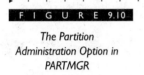

FIGURE 9.10

The Partition Administration Option in PARTMGR

In order to perform any partition management operation, you need to have access to the Master replica. It locks the partition before you start working. This ensures NDS database consistency and limits management to one partition at a time. In addition, all the replicas of a specific partition must be available in order to complete the entire operation. If one replica is missing, NWADMIN will wait until it is available.

Preparation is a virtue—especially in NDS pruning. Before you start a partition operation, you should check the status of its replicas. DSREPAIR is your friend. It provides valuable status reports on replicas and their synchronization process. Figure 9.11 shows a sample status check for the [Root] partition. Notice the default/replica status Edit Log File—SYS:SYSTEM\DSREPAIR.LOG.

*The Replica Status Edit Log
in DSREPAIR*

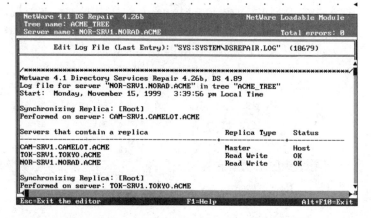

```
NetWare 4.1 DS Repair  4.26b                    NetWare Loadable Module
Tree name: ACME_TREE
Server name: NOR-SRV1.NORAD.ACME                        Total errors: 0

           Edit Log File (Last Entry): "SYS:SYSTEM\DSREPAIR.LOG"  (18679)

/*********************************************************************************/
Netware 4.26b Directory Services Repair 4.26b, DS 4.89
Log file for server "NOR-SRV1.NORAD.ACME" in tree "ACME_TREE"
Start:  Monday, November 15, 1999   3:39:56 pm Local Time

Synchronizing Replica: [Root]
Performed on server: CAM-SRV1.CAMELOT.ACME

Servers that contain a replica              Replica Type    Status
-----------------------------------------------------------------
CAM-SRV1.CAMELOT.ACME                        Master          Host
TOK-SRV1.TOKYO.ACME                          Read Write      OK
NOR-SRV1.NORAD.ACME                          Read Write      OK

Synchronizing Replica: [Root]
Performed on server: TOK-SRV1.TOKYO.ACME

Esc=Exit the editor              F1=Help              Alt+F10=Exit
```

Another pruning virtue is patience. Once you have started an NDS partition operation, you should wait for all the synchronization activities to complete. NDS is a "loosely consistent" database, and it takes time for partition changes to be reflected across the network. A partition with many objects and replicas will naturally take longer than one with just a few objects. In this case, DSTRACE is your friend. Among other things, it notifies you when replica synchronization is finished (see Figure 9.12). We will explore DSTRACE in great depth later in the chapter.

*Monitoring Replica
Synchronization with
DSTRACE*

```
NetWare 4.1 Directory Services  4.89,  8/30/1995

(99/11/15 15:43:19)
SYNC: Start sync of partition <[Root]> state:[0] type:[0]
 SYNC: Start outbound sync with (1) [030000C1]<CAM-SRV1.CAMELOT.ACME>
 SYNC: Start outbound sync with (2) [030000C2]<TOK-SRV1.TOKYO.ACME>
SYNC: End sync of partition <[Root]> All processed = YES.

(99/11/15 15:43:48)
SYNC: Start sync of partition <[Root]> state:[0] type:[0]
 SYNC: Start outbound sync with (1) [030000C1]<CAM-SRV1.CAMELOT.ACME>
 SYNC: Start outbound sync with (2) [030000C2]<TOK-SRV1.TOKYO.ACME>
SYNC: End sync of partition <[Root]> All processed = YES.
```

If possible, you should centralize your partition management operations. Only one person or a small group of people should be responsible for all of the partitioning and replication operations within your company. Typically, the central IS staff has control over initiating partition operations. This central management approach minimizes the chance that two CNEs are working on the same partition simultaneously. If this does occur, it can have unpredictable results—a bad thing.

In the following section, we will explore four key partition management operations:

1 • Creating Partitions

2 • Merging Partitions

3 • Moving Partitions

4 • Aborting Partition Operations

Creating Partitions

Creating a new partition is actually "splitting" a child partition from its parent. This sounds sad, but it really isn't. At some point all children must leave the nest and go out into the cruel world to find themselves. It just happens sooner for NDS partitions, that's all. We refer to partition creation as a *partition split*.

Normally partition splits occur on a single server, because the parent partition already resides there. Therefore, it doesn't generate any traffic and happens very quickly. The bottom line? A partition split divides one NDS database into two, with all the information staying on the same server. In addition, this split operation will create a new child partition on all the servers that contain a replica of the parent partition. This is an important point.

For example, in Figure 9.13, you can see that partitions have already been created for OU=CAMELOT and OU=NORAD. We are currently in the process of creating a partition for OU=TOKYO.

FIGURE 9.13

Creating OU=TOKYO's
Partition in NWADMIN

When we create the OU=TOKYO partition, copies of it (replicas) are automatically placed on all servers that already have a copy of TOKYO's parent ([Root] partition). As you can see in Figure 9.14, both OU=CAMELOT and OU=NORAD get replicas of the new OU=TOKYO partition. This ensures database reliability and NDS connectivity—mostly for tree walking.

FIGURE 9.14

Distributing OU=TOKYO's
Replicas in NWADMIN

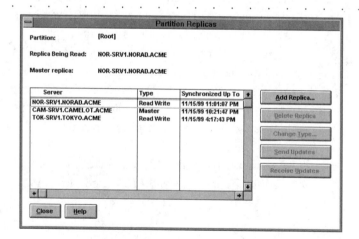

When the partition is created, it takes its name from the top-most container object (partition root object). All NDS objects in the new subtree become part of the new partition. This is always true, unless there's a previously defined partition lower in the tree. In that case, the old partition is unaffected. By partitioning the NDS tree, you can keep the location information in each location and still find and use the resources throughout ACME. Therefore, you should partition locally and replicate locally. As we add servers in TOKYO, we will place our recommended three replicas on servers in TOKYO. As you'll see in just a minute, it's not a good idea to partition or replicate over WAN links.

In order to perform the Create Partition operation, you need Supervisor object rights to the partition root objects—the highest container in the partition. You can also get away with the Write property right to the container's Access Control List (ACL) property. Both of these rights assignments will work. Figure 9.15 illustrates the NDS security necessary for AEinstein to create a partition at NORAD. In this case, OU=NORAD is the partition root object at the top of the new subtree.

F I G U R E   9.15

*AEINSTEIN Creates the
OU=NORAD Partition*

ZEN

"It's nice to look down the fairway and see your Mother on the left and your Father on the right. You know that no matter whether you hook it or slice it, somebody is going to be there to kick it back in the fairway."

Larry Nelson

Merging Partitions

Merging is the opposite of splitting. In partition management vernacular, merging combines a child partition with its original parent. This operation is sometimes called *partition join* —what a surprise! Typically, merging takes longer than splitting, and generates a great deal of WAN traffic, depending, of course, on the physical location of all servers in both partitions' replica rings.

In order to merge partitions, each server holding a replica of the parent partition must receive a copy of the child partition—before the merge can happen. In return, each server holding a copy of the child partition must receive a copy of the parent— before the merge can complete. The merge operation will attempt to move copies of either the parent or child partitions to the appropriate servers as needed. After the copies have been moved successfully, the merge operation will begin and ultimately join the two partitions together. Then, all servers will have copies of the new, larger partition.

To make your life easier, you should manually place copies of the parent partition on all the servers with a child partition before you initiate the merge operation. In turn, you should manually place copies of the child partition on the servers holding the parent partitions. This ensures a smooth merger—if there is such a thing. In order to accomplish this task, you must know where all of the replicas are stored. Use the Partition Manager tool in NWADMIN.

Here's an example. In Figure 9.16, we are rejoining the OU=OPS and OU=CAMELOT partitions. As you can see, NWADMIN forces you to confirm the merger. No mistakes here.

In order to perform the Merge operation, you must have Supervisor object rights (or Write property rights) to *both* parent and child containers. In this example, King Arthur is performing the merger, and his NDS access rights are shown in Figure 9.17.

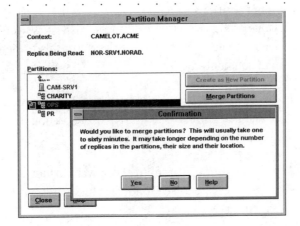

FIGURE 9.16

*Merging OU=OPS and
OU=CAMELOT Partitions*

FIGURE 9.17

*King Arthur's Partition
Merge Security*

Moving Partitions

Moving partitions is a tricky business. NDS allows you to move entire subtrees from one location to another. In order to perform this maneuver, you need to satisfy two important conditions:

1 • The moving container must be a partition root. This means that the source container must be at the *top* of an existing partition. You may need to create this partition if it doesn't exist.

2 • The partition (or subtree) you want to move cannot have any child partitions. You may be forced to merge child partitions with the above parent if they're currently split.

Moving containers (and their contents) is essentially moving a partition from one location in the NDS tree to another. This operation can generate *mucho* network traffic depending on where the source partition's replicas are.

Here's an example. In Figure 9.18, we're going to move the OU=OPS subtree to the OU=NORAD location. I don't know why, we just are. Also notice that NWADMIN gives you the option of leaving an Alias of OU=OPS behind. This recommendation is a temporary action that helps ensure continuity during the move. It's like leaving cardboard copies of your furniture behind when you move to a new house. For a while the neighbors think you still live there.

In order to perform the Move operation, you must have Supervisor object rights (or Write property rights) to all containers involved. In this case, that's OU=OPS (the source partition root), OU=CAMELOT (its parent partition), and OU=NORAD (the destination partition root). I see a pattern forming here. The more serious the work gets, the more security you need. Makes sense. Speaking of serious work, what happens if something goes wrong during the partition operation? Let's see.

Aborting Partition Operations

If something goes wrong during the pruning process, you can always stop and return the tree to its original state. This feature would really help the medical profession. It's important to note, however, that this is not an undo feature. It's just a way to back out of a partitioning operation that didn't complete.

*Moving the OU=OPS
Subtree to OU=NORAD*

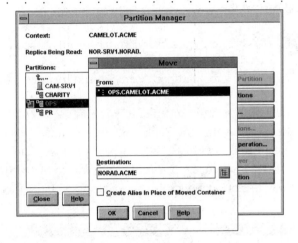

For example, only one partition operation can take place at a time. So, if you start an operation and it stalls, everyone else is stuck. No other operations can take place on that partition. You're probably wondering why a partition operation would stall. Typically, it's because one of the partition's replicas becomes unavailable—server crash, WAN link goes down, corrupted NDS database; take your pick. If this happens to you, you'll see a screen resembling Figure 9.19.

*Partitioning Stalls Because
a Replica Is Unavailable*

If you get this screen, you have two choices:

1 • Wait until the server comes back up or the WAN link is restored.

2 • Abort the partition operation and try again later.

To abort a partition operation, you can use NWAMDIN or PARTMGR. Select the Abort button within the Replica Status screen (see Figure 9.20). In this example, the operation stalled with a Change Type 0 message. This means that the [Root] replicas were trying to change types from Read/Write to Master (0 denotes a Master replica). By the way, it's not a good idea to mess around with the [Root] partition.

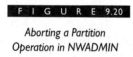

FIGURE 9.20

*Aborting a Partition
Operation in NWADMIN*

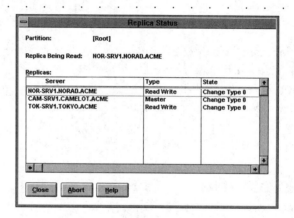

Once the partition operation has been aborted, the replicas will be turned back ON. This means all is well in the kingdom, and you can try again later.

All of this excitement can also be accomplished in DSREPAIR—there's something comforting in the term *repair*. From the DSREPAIR main menu, select Advanced Options. Then, select Replica and Partition Operations, and a list of all the partitions and replicas stored on this server will appear. Choose your troublesome partition and press Enter. The Replica Operations menu will appear, as shown in Figure 9.21. Finally, choose Cancel Partition Operation and press Enter.

Since you're running DSREPAIR from the server, you'll need to provide a valid username and password at this point. In addition, this user must have Supervisor object rights (or Write property rights) to all of the affected partitions. When you do, DSREPAIR takes care of the rest, and all is well again.

*Aborting a Partition
Operation in DSREPAIR*

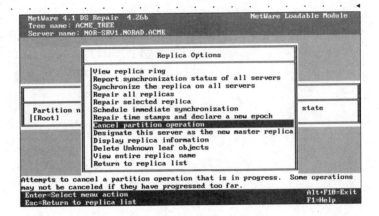

```
NetWare 4.1 DS Repair  4.26b                    NetWare Loadable Module
Tree name: ACME_TREE
Server name: NOR-SRV1.NORAD.ACME

                        ┌──────────────── Replica Options ────────────────┐
                        │ View replica ring                                │
                        │ Report synchronization status of all servers     │
                        │ Synchronize the replica on all servers           │
                        │ Repair all replicas                              │
        ┌───────────────┤ Repair selected replica                         ├──────────┐
        │ Partition n   │ Schedule immediate synchronization               │  state   │
        │ [Root]        │ Repair time stamps and declare a new epoch       │          │
        │               │ Cancel partition operation                       │          │
        │               │ Designate this server as the new master replica  │          │
        │               │ Display replica information                      │          │
        │               │ Delete Unknown leaf objects                      │          │
        │               │ View entire replica name                         │          │
        │               │ Return to replica list                          │          │
        └───────────────┴──────────────────────────────────────────────────┴──────────┘
Attempts to cancel a partition operation that is in progress.  Some operations
may not be canceled if they have progressed too far.
Enter=Select menu action                                          Alt+F10=Exit
Esc=Return to replica list                                        F1=Help
```

You're done. That's all there is to NDS pruning—a piece of cake. In this section, we learned about [Root] pruning; creating, merging, and moving partitions; and how to back out when something goes wrong. This has been an invaluable lesson to all you aspiring NDS gardeners out there. But it's just the beginning. The *real* fun is in grafting. "Spread the partitions," that's what I always say. Let's see how.

ZEN

"Golf is a good walk spoiled!"

Mark Twain

NDS Replication

NDS grafting is almost as intriguing as pruning. As if cutting up the tree weren't enough, now we have to piece it back together somewhere else. They say it's good for the tree. They say it adds years to the tree's life. Do you buy it? I don't know.

NDS grafting is a similar prospect. They say it's good for the NDS tree. They say it adds years to the life of your network. Do you buy it? Well, you have to. The good news is that NDS Replication makes more sense than grafting. Replication is the process of "spreading the partitions" around the WAN. This serves three purposes:

1 • Fault tolerance—Replication increases the availability of partitions—it spreads them around. This also increases reliability. For example, if a server holding a replica of your partition goes down, you can simply use another copy for authentication and updates.

2 • Performance—Distributed replicas increase NDS performance. Replication enables you to distribute partition copies to local servers throughout the WAN. Having a local replica decreases the time needed for certain NDS tasks, including authentication, NDS changes, searches, and data gathering. This does not imply that replicas should be used for mobile users. Having a replica locally means on the server, where the majority of the users need the information.

3 • Name Resolution—Replication enhances name resolution because users requesting NDS information first have to locate a server with the data's information on it. Replication spreads the data around. If the requested information is not found on the server that the user is already authenticated to, then NDS will automatically connect the user to the proper server through the process of name resolution. This connection process is simplified when there are more replicas to choose from. It also happens faster and more reliably.

The main difference between NDS partitioning and NDS replication is the difference between "logical" and "physical." NDS partitions are logical boundaries that split the hierarchical database into subtrees. A partition doesn't actually "exist" until you place a COPY (replica) of it on a server—replication. NDS replicas are physical pieces of the NDS database. They have mass. In Figure 9.22, for example, three physical copies of the logical [Root] partition have been placed on the physical NOR-SRV1 server.

So how does it work? The NetWare 4 installation program gets things started for you by creating three replicas for each partition. When you install a new server, NDS places a Read/Write replica of the server's home partition on it by default. It does this three times, then stops. If you want more than three replicas of any given partition, you have to create them yourself using NWADMIN or PARTMGR.

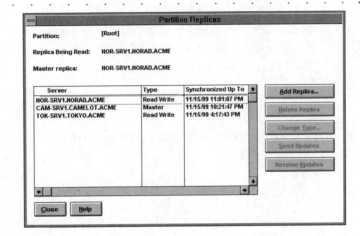

FIGURE 9.22

NDS Replication for the
[Root] Partition

In this section, we will explore three important aspects of Replica Management:

▸ Managing NDS Replica Types

▸ Managing NDS Replica Operations

▸ Managing NDS Replica Synchronization

Let's take a closer look at NDS Replication. This is a very important part of NDS gardening, so try to stay awake. Ready, set, replicate.

MANAGING NDS REPLICA TYPES

Replication is important business. It dramatically affects the speed and reliability of your NDS tree. The NetWare 4 server is the focal point. A server can contain any number of replicas, as long as they're from different partitions. On the other hand, a server doesn't have to contain any replicas at all. It's up to you.

In order to understand where and when to place NDS replicas, you must understand the different types of replicas and their characteristics. Certain replica types react differently in certain circumstances. It's your job to know when to hold them and when to fold them. Here's a list of the replica types:

- ▸ Master—King of the hill. There's only one Master replica per partition.

- ▸ Read/Write—Second in command. Allows users to make changes to the NDS database.

- ▸ Read-Only—For browsing the tree only.

- ▸ Subordinate Reference—A special replica created by NDS when the parent partition exists but the child does not.

As I said, each of these replica types has its own strengths and weaknesses. In the next section we will explore all four types and provide some management insight for each. Let's begin at the top with the Master replica.

Managing Master Replicas

The Master replica is king of the hill. It's the first replica created during initial partition creation. Although the first replica is always designated as the Master, it can be changed as other replicas are added. There can be only one Master replica for each partition. In short, the Master replica is in charge—it controls all partitioning operations. The Master essentially locks the partition for the duration of any partition operation. This ensures that only one operation happens at a time.

For example, if you want to create or merge a partition, you must have access to its Master replica. The master then works with the other replicas to complete the operation. As we learned earlier, you must also have Supervisor object rights or Write property rights to the partition root container.

It's important to note that the Master replica is equal to all other replicas during replica synchronization. This is a peer-to-peer mechanism, not a master-to-slave. In addition, the Master replica provides complete access to the object and property information within the partition. This means users can log in through this replica and make changes to the database—such as adding, deleting, renaming, and modifying NDS objects. Of course, they'll need sufficient NDS rights to do so.

Figure 9.22 shows the Master replica for the [Root] partition. It's stored on the CAM-SRV1 server. Notice that there is only one Master replica, but multiple Read/Write replicas. Makes sense. As a matter of fact, the Read/Write replica is probably the most popular type. Let's see why.

Managing Read/Write Replicas

The Read/Write replica is the most popular because there can be any number of them for any given partition. Although there is no limit to the number of Read/Write replicas, you shouldn't go hog wild. Keep the number manageable for the sake of synchronization traffic and managerial overload. Remember, replicas are distributed to increase fault tolerance and accessibility—not for the fun of it.

Like the Master, Read/Write replicas provide complete access to NDS object and property information. Users can log in to the cloud and manage objects with this replica type. Refer to Figure 9.22 for an illustration of ACME's replica strategy for the [Root] partition. Notice the single Master and multiple Read/Write replicas. I told you they were popular. As a matter of fact, the Master and Read/Write replicas are the only ones that can support authentication and Bindery Services. Read-Only and Subordinate References don't provide much management help. They do, however, provide a purpose. Let's discover what it is...together.

ZEN

"We have 51 golf courses in Palm Springs. He never decides which course he will play until after his first tee shot."

Bob Hope, on Gerald Ford

Managing Read-Only Replicas

The Read-Only replica, as its name implies, will not accept changes from users. The only way it discovers changes in the database is through synchronization with other replicas; namely, Masters and Read/Writes. Since the Read-Only replica can't be updated, it can't support login authentication or Bindery Services. All you can do is browse the tree. Boring.

TIP

When a user logs into NDS, three of his/her properties are updated—Network Address, Last Login Date, and Last Login Time. In order for users to change or update these three properties, they must log in to a Master or Read/Write replica. The Read-Only replica cannot accept user logins because these properties cannot be updated.

Here's an idea. Suppose you want to provide read access to the NDS database, but not allow updates. Then the Read-Only replica is for you. For example, you want to build an off-site disaster recovery center for your servers. You could place a Read-Only replica there. This way, the server would be updated through replica synchronization, but users couldn't bother it; that is, there would be no login activity. I know I'm stretching it, but it's a good example. Actually, now is a good time to move on to Subordinate References.

Managing Subordinate References

A Subordinate Reference pointer contains only one object, the partition root object. This container stores partition information linking it to other containers in the tree. The bottom line? Subordinate Reference replicas provide tree connectivity by acting as a link between the parent partition and child partitions.

Subordinate Reference replicas are completely managed by NDS and NetWare 4 servers. You do not need to manage them. You should understand them, though. NDS will place a Subordinate Reference on any server that contains a replica of its parent partition, but not the child. In summary, where the parent is but the child is *not*. Refer to Figure 9.23 for a graphical summary.

A lot of interesting replication is going on in Figure 9.23. As you can see, some servers have Subordinate References because they have a copy of the parent partition ([Root] partition in this case), but not the child. For example, NOR-SVR1 holds a copy of the [Root] Partition and itself, but no other partitions. Since all the location partitions are children of the [Root], NOR-SRV1 gets a Subordinate Reference of them all (except itself and the [Root]).

In a similar example, CAM-SRV1 also has a copy of the [Root] and itself. But it additionally holds a Read/Write replica of RIO, TOKYO, and SYDNEY. Therefore, the only child (of the [Root]) it doesn't have a replica of is NORAD, so NDS gives it a Subordinate Reference. How kind.

FIGURE 9.23

Understanding Subordinate
Reference Replicas

Subordinate References are visible in NWADMIN and DSREPAIR. They are not visible in NETADMIN or PARTMGR. Check out the CAM-SRV1 replicas in Figure 9.24. Since Subordinate References are just pointers, they don't actually contain any object information. Therefore, users can't log in, manage, or view NDS objects with this replica type. It's basically a tree-walking nuisance.

FIGURE 9.24

The Different Replica Types
for CAM-SRV1

TIP

Do not add Read/Write replicas to a server for the sole purpose of eliminating Subordinate References. You will increase synchronization traffic to that server.

That completes our first phase of Replica Management. How do you like it so far? Aren't replicas fun? Now that you have a new understanding of the four different replica types, let's spend some time learning what to do with them; namely, Add, Remove, Change, and Rebuild. Funny, it looks a lot like Add, Subtract, Multiply, and Divide. Maybe I learned this stuff somewhere else. Maybe in a previous life. You never know...

QUIZ

Without changing the order of the digits, insert four plus signs, one division sign and three minus signs between them to make the calculation correct:

9 8 7 6 5 4 3 2 1 = 0

(Q9-2)

MANAGING NDS REPLICA OPERATIONS

There are a lot of interesting things you can do to NDS replicas. First, you can create them—that's a good place to start. And, of course, anything you can create you can delete. But that's not all—you can also change and rebuild replicas. Wow, all this and so much more. Let's review the four options:

1 • Add Replicas—To distribute partitions throughout the WAN.

2 • Remove Replicas—If you change your mind, or the synchronization traffic is too much to bear.

3 • Change Replicas—To upgrade or downgrade existing replica types. This is also a great troubleshooting aid if the Master gets corrupted.

4 • Rebuild Replicas—Just in case.

Adding Replicas

Adding replicas is how we distribute partitions throughout the WAN. All you need is an existing partition and a host server; NWADMIN takes care of the rest. When you add replicas to other servers, all the NDS data is copied to the new server over the WAN. This operation causes significant network traffic. It depends, though, on the size of the replicated partition and the speed of the WAN links. It's a good idea to schedule replication operations when the network isn't very busy.

Figure 9.25 shows the NWADMIN screen for adding NDS replicas. First, choose a partition ([Root] in this case) and then choose a server, NOR-SRV1.

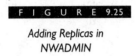

F I G U R E 9.25

Adding Replicas in NWADMIN

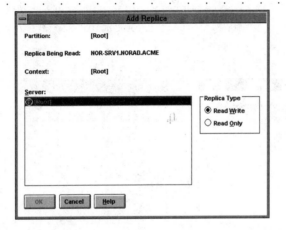

Removing Replicas

Whatever you create you can also destroy. Such power. NWADMIN also allows you to remove NDS replicas from specific servers. This operation is not as simple as it looks. When you remove a replica from a NetWare 4 server, NDS creates an external reference pointer to every object in the original partition. The external reference points to another reference. The creation of all these external references may take some time, depending on the size of the partition. Be careful.

ZEN

"I figure practice puts your brains in your muscles."

Sam Snead

Changing NDS Replica Types

NDS also allows you to change a replica's type. This is particularly important when you want to manage NDS partitions or log in to the cloud. Here's a quick summary:

- ▸ Partition Management—As we learned earlier, NDS requires access to the Master replica of a partition for any management operation. If the Master is unavailable, you can temporarily change an existing Read/Write or Read-Only replica into the Master.

- ▸ Login Authentication—We also learned that you need access to a Read/Write replica of your home partition in order to log in. If no Master or Read/Write replicas are available, you can upgrade an existing Read-Only replica. Cool.

The Change Replica Type Window

Figure 9.26 shows the Change Replica Type window in NWADMIN. It's pretty simple. You first select a partition, then a server, and finally, a new Replica Type. In this case, we're upgrading the [Root] partition on NOR-SRV1 from Read/Write to Master.

Rebuilding Replicas

Stuff happens. Some good, some bad. If your replicas lose their accuracy or become corrupted, you can always rebuild them. NWADMIN provides two methods for rebuilding replicas:

1 • Send Updates

2 • Receive Updates

The Send Updates option synchronizes all other replicas with the one you have selected. You would perform this operation when the partition information on some of the other servers is inaccurate or has become corrupted. This way you can control the source replica. Just make sure you select the best one—the one with the most recent, most accurate information. Figure 9.27 shows an example of the Send Update operation. In this example, CAM-SRV1 has a Master replica of the [Root] partition. It has been chosen as the source replica server. With the click of a button, we will update all other replicas in this replica ring.

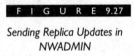

FIGURE 9.27

Sending Replica Updates in NWADMIN

The Receive Updates operation synchronizes selected replicas with information from the Master replica. You would perform this operation when the partition information on one of your servers is not as complete as the Master. You can perform this task in either NWADMIN or DSREPAIR. Figure 9.28 shows an example of the Receive Updates operation in DSREPAIR. In this example, the NOR-SRV1 server is receiving replica updates from the Master [Root] replica.

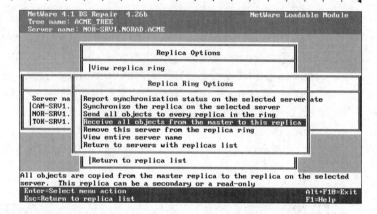

FIGURE 9.28

Receiving Replica Updates in DSREPAIR

That completes the second phase of Replica Management. We're cruising now. The final topic deals with a very important replica operation—synchronization. Replica synchronization affects NDS management more than any other partitioning task. Your goal is to maximize replica efficiency and minimize replica synchronization. It's a tough balancing act, and I'm here to help. So without further ado, let's synchronize.

MANAGING REPLICA SYNCHRONIZATION

Life is full of synchronization. We synchronize our watches; everybody wants synchronicity; the world even tolerates synchronized swimming. So, it's no surprise that NDS synchronizes too.

Why? Because the database is distributed, and all pieces need to be updated. Synchronization takes place within a special group of replicas called a *Replica Ring*. The Replica Ring is a list of all servers with replicas of a given partition. For example, Figure 9.29 illustrates the Replica Ring for the [Root] partition—CAM-SRV1 (Master), NOR-SRV1 (Read/Write), and TOK-SRV1 (Read/Write). Replica Rings are important because they dictate the speed and efficiency of synchronization. If a Replica Ring spans slow WAN links, updates are going to be cumbersome and slow. On the other hand, if you keep a Replica Ring local, synchronization will be no sweat.

In addition, NDS replica synchronization is said to be loosely consistent. This means that changes within a replica ring are not always instantaneous and consistent. One server may get updated while the others hang out in the dark for a few more minutes. This loose consistency is caused because NDS receives updates from a variety of places, including itself, users, and CNE gardeners. As we'll see in just a moment, a variety of events activate synchronization updates. However, to ensure the integrity of the database, NDS will over time automatically synchronize all the replicas within the ring. Some just take longer than others. Figure 9.29 illustrates the "real" ACME Replica Ring for the [Root] partition. Notice all the traffic generated when the servers try to synchronize.

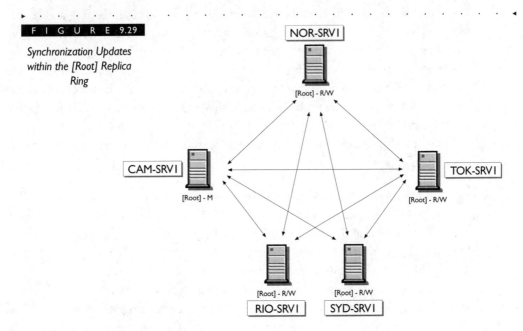

FIGURE 9.29

Synchronization Updates within the [Root] Replica Ring

This synchronization process introduces a new level of complexity to WAN traffic efficiency. Fortunately, the information passed between replicas is limited to only updates, so this reduces the total amount of network traffic created by synchronization. But as you can see in Figure 9.29, it's still quite significant. So, as the NetWare 4 gardener, it's your job to minimize replica synchronization traffic. How do you do this? Well, here are three issues to consider:

1 • The total number of replicas per partition—Replica Ring

2 • The total number of replicas per server

3 • Subordinate Reference replicas

In general, you should avoid both having too many replicas in the ring and having too many total replicas per server. These two factors go hand-in-hand in minimizing the workload of replica servers and the background network traffic generated by synchronization. Also, Subordinate References have a big impact because they are automatically created, generating more background traffic. Finally, consider controlling the types of replicas you create. Master and Read/Write replicas initiate synchronization, while Read-Only replicas don't.

Now, let's dive a little bit deeper into the scary world of replica synchronization management. Boo.

Total Number of Replicas per Partition—Replica Ring

The amount of replica synchronization for any given partition depends on the size of the partition (the number of objects), the number of updates or changes to the object information, the number of replicas or servers participating (Replica Ring), and the speed of the network (LAN and WAN links).

I encourage you to keep the size of the partitions small—no more than 5000 objects per partition. This way the synchronization process can efficiently update all the replicas as needed. If a partition grows too large, consider splitting it to minimize large periodic updates.

Next, the level of partition activity impacts synchronization traffic. A lot of changes means a lot of traffic. Makes sense. Also, if the object information changes in one replica, it needs to change in all the replicas of the ring. Finally, remember that the NDS database is loosely consistent. This means that not all of the replicas are instantaneously updated. For example, each user login initiates synchronization because changes are made to three of the user's properties: Network Address, Last Login Date, and Last Login Time. When the user logs in, these changes are automatically written to the replica on the server that authenticated the user. Of course, updates of these changes need to be synchronized to all other replicas in the ring. You can see that if a particular partition is active with logins and changes it will generate an inordinate amount of background traffic. In addition, you can increase replica synchronization traffic by simply having more objects in the partition and more replicas in the ring.

ZEN

"This suit is so stiff. I can't do this with two hands, but I'm going to try a little sand trap shot here."

Alan Shepard, on the first golf shot on the moon

Total Number of Replicas per Server

Another synchronization consideration is the total number of replicas per server. A server cannot hold two replicas of the same partition. A server *can*, however, hold multiple replicas of different partitions. Many multiples, in some cases.

You should always place NDS replicas on high-end servers, so they can keep up with the other servers in the WAN. The synchronization process between all replicas in a ring is only as fast as the weakest link. The bottom line is: don't place active replicas on a low-end server because it negatively affects all servers in the replica ring.

The total number of replicas per server varies according to the server's purpose. For example, an application/data server shouldn't hold more than 10–15 replicas. An e-mail server, on the other hand, can hold up to 20–25 replicas because it's not as disk-intensive. Finally, a dedicated NDS replica server can hold up to 100–150 replicas.

There is also an extreme case. Suppose, for example, you brought in a Super Server as a centralized NDS replica server. It could possibly maintain up to 200 replicas, but I wouldn't want to go much higher than that. Of course, this assumes an incredibly large NDS tree with at least 200 distributed partitions.

Subordinate Reference Replicas

There is a special consideration when it comes to the distribution of Subordinate Reference replicas. They are created like crazy all over the system, and do participate in daily synchronization activity. In some cases, this one event can impact a WAN so severely that it effectively shuts everything down. So what can you do about it? Well, Subordinate References are the end product of poor partitioning. If you design natural partitions according to a pyramid design, the number of Subordinate References will automatically fall.

Don't be too hard on Subordinate References. Remember, they're good in that they provide tree connectivity by linking parent partitions with their children. Using this mechanism, NDS operates more efficiently because it does not have to place a full replica (Master, Read/Write, and Read-Only) to provide tree connectivity. As we learned earlier, NDS will place a Subordinate Reference replica on a server that contains a replica of the parent but does not contain a replica of the child. In summary, where the parent is, but the child is not.

Since NDS manages Subordinate Reference automatically, you can only sit on the sidelines and watch. But, if you're perceptive and diligent, you can discover ways to change your partition design and minimize the number of Subordinate Reference pointers. The only way to reduce Subordinate References is to reduce the number of replicas of the parent partition. This can be done by reducing the number of servers that contain a copy of the parent partition. Let's see how it works.

QUIZ

One candle was guaranteed to burn for six hours, the other for four hours. They were both lit at the same time. After some time one was twice as long as the other. For how long had they been burning?

(Q9-3)

Let's return to ACME—but this time we've "phased" into a parallel universe (accidentally, of course). This new, weird ACME has 200 locations, all placed directly below the [Root] partition (see Figure 9.30). Assume that this new ACME follows the same partitioning strategy as our original ACME—that is, a partition in each of its locations. So as you can see in Figure 9.30, there's one [Root] partition and 200 location partitions directly below it.

FIGURE 9.30

ACME's Partition Strategy in a Parallel Universe

200 CITIES OR LOCATIONS

Consider what would happen each time you place a replica of the [Root] partition on a server. NDS would be forced to create 200 Subordinate References on that server, one for each of the [Root]'s child partitions. From the server perspective, it now has to participate in each of the 200 partitions' synchronization processes. This amount of work will probably overload the server entirely, unless they have special super-fast servers in the parallel universe. So how would you solve this problem?

The simplest way to minimize Subordinate References is to create a more pyramid-like partition design. In ACME's case, you could simply add another layer of regional partitions directly under the [Root] partition. This would help distribute Subordinate References across more NetWare 4 servers. Figure 9.31 illustrates this simple solution.

TIP

Be sure to place Regional OU replicas on separate servers from the location replicas. This will distribute the load of Subordinate References across the ACME WAN.

FIGURE 9.31

Adding Regional Containers
to Spread-Out Subordinate
References at ACME

Partitioning also affects the placement of Subordinate Reference replicas. By the way, welcome back to the correct ACME universe. During any partitioning operation, all the replicas in the ring must be available. This includes the Subordinate Reference replicas. If for any reason one of them isn't available, the partition operation will not complete. The total number of Subordinate References could affect the efficiency of partitioning operations because each Subordinate Reference is part of the replica ring. This increases the chances of a failure. In this case, more is *not* merrier.

REAL WORLD

You may wonder why a Subordinate Reference replica is contacted during a partition operation. Even though Subordinate References do not contain any NDS partition information, they do contain the partition root container. This container changes during the partition operations. Bummer.

THE BRAIN

For more guidelines on working with **NDS** partitions and replicas, see "Management Procedures for Directory Services in NetWare 4" in the March 1994 *Novell Application Notes*.

OK, that's enough synchronization. I am fully synchronized at this moment. Synchronicity has been achieved. Now I'd like to introduce you to a pal of mine. He's a swinging NDS utility from downtown. His name is DSTRACE.

ZEN

"I don't answer the phone. I get the feeling whenever I do that there will be someone on the other end."

Fred Couples

USING DSTRACE

DSTRACE is your friend.

This is NetWare 4's version of TRACK ON—an old NetWare 3 SAP and RIP tool. DSTRACE allows you to track NDS activity between NetWare 4 servers. DSTRACE will provide you with information on how NDS is functioning and whether or not the NDS synchronization processes are complete. DSTRACE will also assist you in diagnosing NDS errors.

The DSTRACE screen can be enabled at the NetWare 4 server console by typing:

```
SET DSTRACE = ON
```

Once DSTRACE is on, you can switch back and forth using the Alt-Esc keys. At some point, settle on the Directory Services console—this is DSTRACE. NetWare 4 displays the major synchronization activities in color to help you identify the most important information. If a problem pops up, NDS errors will be displayed as well. In a few moments I'll provide you with a detailed NDS Error Code listing. This will be a big help when something unexpected happens to the NDS database.

There are plenty of DSTRACE commands that can assist you in capturing trace information for further review. This feature is handy because on a very busy server your information may scroll across the screen too fast. The default report file name is SYS:SYSTEM\DSTRACE.DBG. To save screen output to this disk file type

```
SET TTF = ON
```

To stop screen output to disk file type

```
SET TTF = OFF
```

To change the name of the report file you can type

SET NDS TRACE = <filename>

DSTRACE filter settings allow you to view specific NDS activity. They are activated by typing

SET DSTRACE = <name>

Notice that some of the filters must be preceded by a plus sign (+). To disable the filters, type

SET DSTRACE -<name>

Other commands are preceded by an asterisk (*) and will be noted where necessary. For your reading pleasure, I have listed the more useful DSTRACE filters in Table 9.1. And if that's not enough fun, Table 9.2 lists the most popular DSTRACE Error Codes. They may seem superfluous now, but believe me, these codes will save your hide some day.

THE BRAIN

For a complete list of DSTRACE commands and codes, refer to Novell's Guide to NetWare 4.1 Networks by Novell Press.

T A B L E 9.1	COMMAND	DESCRIPTION
DSTRACE Filter Commands	ALL	View all DSTRACE activity.
	+AUDIT	View audit messages that may be created while using the AUDITCON utility.
	+AUTHEN	View authentication time stamp information as users are logging into the network.
	+BACKLINK	View backlink information processing from server to server (BLINK also works).
	+COLLISION	View NDS timestamp collisions (COLL also works).
	+JANITOR	View the janitor process which cleans up deleted entries (J also works).

	COMMAND	DESCRIPTION
TABLE 9.1 *DSTRACE Filter* *Commands*	+LIMBER	View a server's verification of name, network address, replica placement for that server.
	OFF	Disable the DSTRACE screen.
	ON	Enable DSTRACE minimal tracking.
	PART	View NDS partition information as an operation occurs.
	+SYNC	View the synchronization process for replicas stored on this server.
	SCHEMA	View the schema synchronization process.
	+VC	View virtual client (server to server) activity as replicas synchronize.
	*H	Begin synchronization process immediately.
	*L	Begin the limber process immediately.
	*R	Reset the DSTRACE.DBG file to 0 length.
	*U	Reset all servers in the replica list to "Up."

You can use DSTRACE to track replica management and synchronization activity as well. When you do so, it lists the replica type according to the following codes:

▸ Master is replica type 0

▸ Read/Write or Secondary is replica type 1

▸ Read-Only is replica type 2

▸ Subordinate Reference is replica type 3

TABLE 9.2

DSTRACE Error Codes

HEX CODE	ERROR	DESCRIPTION
FFFFFFFF	-001	Insufficient space
FFFFFF89	-119	Buffer too small
FFFFFF88	-120	Volume flag not set
FFFFFF87	-121	No items found
FFFFFF86	-122	Connection already temporary
FFFFFF85	-123	Connection already logged in
FFFFFF84	-124	Connection not authenticated
FFFFFF83	-125	Connection not logged in
FFFFFF82	-126	NCP boundary check failed
FFFFFF81	-127	Lock waiting
FFFFFF80	-128	Lock fail
FFFFFF7F	-129	Out of handles
FFFFFF7E	-130	No open privilege
FFFFFF7D	-131	Hard I/O error
FFFFFF7C	-132	No create privilege
FFFFFF7B	-133	No create delete privilege
FFFFFF7A	-134	Read-only create file
FFFFFF79	-135	Create file invalid name
FFFFFF78	-136	Invalid file handle
FFFFFF77	-137	No search privilege
FFFFFF76	-138	No delete privilege
FFFFFF75	-139	No rename privilege
FFFFFF74	-140	No set privilege
FFFFFF73	-141	Some files in use
FFFFFF72	-142	All files in use
FFFFFF71	-143	Some read-only
FFFFFF70	-144	All read-only

	HEX CODE	ERROR	DESCRIPTION
TABLE 9.2	FFFFFF6F	-145	Some names exist
DSTRACE Error Codes	FFFFFF6E	-146	All names exist
	FFFFFF6D	-147	No read privilege
	FFFFFF6C	-148	No write privilege
	FFFFFF6B	-149	File detached
	FFFFFF6A	-150	Target not a subdirectory
	FFFFFF6A	-150	No allocated space
	FFFFFF6A	-150	Insufficient memory
	FFFFFF69	-151	No spool space
	FFFFFF68	-152	Invalid volume
	FFFFFF67	-153	Directory full
	FFFFFF66	-154	Rename across volume
	FFFFFF65	-155	Bad directory handle
	FFFFFF64	-156	No such extension
	FFFFFF64	-156	Invalid path
	FFFFFF63	-157	No directory handles
	FFFFFF62	-158	Bad file name
	FFFFFF61	-159	Directory active
	FFFFFF60	-160	Directory not empty
	FFFFFF5F	-161	Directory I/O Error
	FFFFFF5E	-162	I/O locked
	FFFFFF5D	-163	Transaction restarted
	FFFFFF5C	-164	Rename directory invalid
	FFFFFF5B	-165	Invalid open create mode
	FFFFFF5A	-166	Already in use
	FFFFFF59	-167	Invalid resource tag
	FFFFFF58	-168	Access denied

(continued)

HEX CODE	ERROR	DESCRIPTION
FFFFFF42	-190	Invalid data stream
FFFFFF41	-191	Invalid name space
FFFFFF40	-192	No accounting privileges
FFFFFF3F	-193	No account balance
FFFFFF3E	-194	Credit limit exceeded
FFFFFF3D	-195	Too many holds
FFFFFF3C	-196	Accounting disabled
FFFFFF3B	-197	Login lockout
FFFFFF3A	-198	No console rights
FFFFFF30	-208	Queue I/O failure
FFFFFF2F	-209	No queue
FFFFFF2E	-210	No queue server
FFFFFF2D	-211	No queue rights
FFFFFF2C	-212	Queue full
FFFFFF2B	-213	No queue job
FFFFFF2A	-214	Unencrypted not allowed
FFFFFF29	-215	Queue in service
FFFFFF29	-215	Duplicate password
FFFFFF28	-216	Queue not active
FFFFFF27	-217	Queue station not server
FFFFFF27	-217	Maximum logins exceeded
FFFFFF26	-218	Queue halted
FFFFFF25	-219	Queue maximum servers
FFFFFF25	-219	Node address violation
FFFFFF24	-220	Log account expired
FFFFFF22	-222	Bad password
FFFFFF21	-223	Password expired

TABLE 9.2	HEX CODE	ERROR	DESCRIPTION
DSTRACE Error Codes	FFFFFF20	-224	No login connection available
	FFFFFF18	-232	Password expired
	FFFFFF17	-233	Member already exists
	FFFFFF16	-234	No such member
	FFFFFF15	-235	Property not group
	FFFFFF14	-236	No such value set
	FFFFFF13	-237	Property already exists
	FFFFFF12	-238	Object already exists
	FFFFFF11	-239	Illegal name
	FFFFFF10	-240	Illegal wildcard
	FFFFFF0F	-241	Bindery security
	FFFFFF0E	-242	No object read rights
	FFFFFF0D	-243	No object rename rights
	FFFFFF0C	-244	No object delete rights
	FFFFFF0B	-245	No object create rights
	FFFFFF0A	-246	No property delete rights
	FFFFFF09	-247	No property create rights
	FFFFFF08	-248	No property write rights
	FFFFFF07	-249	No property read rights
	FFFFFF06	-250	Temporary remap
	FFFFFF05	-251	Unknown request
	FFFFFF05	-251	No such property
	FFFFFF04	-252	Target already has message
	FFFFFF04	-252	No such object
	FFFFFF04	-252	Message queue full
	FFFFFF03	-253	Bad station number
	FFFFFF02	-254	Trustee not found

(continued)

T A B L E 9.2

DSTRACE Error Codes
(continued)

HEX CODE	ERROR	DESCRIPTION
FFFFFF02	-254	Spool delete
FFFFFF02	-254	Directory locked
FFFFFF02	-254	Bindery locked
FFFFFF01	-255	Target not logged in
FFFFFF01	-255	Target not accepting messages
FFFFFF01	-255	No trustee change privileges
FFFFFF01	-255	No spool file
FFFFFF01	-255	No files found
FFFFFF01	-255	Must force down
FFFFFF01	-255	Miscellaneous error
FFFFFF01	-255	I/O bound
FFFFFF01	-255	Hard failure
FFFFFF01	-255	File name
FFFFFF01	-255	File exists
FFFFFF01	-255	Close FCB
FFFFFF01	-255	Bad spool printer
FFFFFF01	-255	Bad parameter
FFFFFDA7	-601	No such entry
FFFFFDA6	-602	No such value
FFFFFDA5	-603	No such attribute
FFFFFDA4	-604	No such class
FFFFFDA3	-605	No such partition
FFFFFDA2	-606	Entry already exists
FFFFFDA1	-607	Not effective class
FFFFFDA0	-608	Illegal attribute
FFFFFD9F	-609	Missing mandatory
FFFFFD9E	-610	Illegal DS name

	HEX CODE	ERROR	DESCRIPTION
TABLE 9.2	FFFFFD9D	-611	Illegal containment
DSTRACE Error Codes	FFFFFD9C	-612	Can't have multiple values
	FFFFFD9B	-613	Syntax violation
	FFFFFD9A	-614	Duplicate value
	FFFFFD99	-615	Attribute already exists
	FFFFFD98	-616	Maximum entries exist
	FFFFFD97	-617	Database format; the database format is invalid
	FFFFFD96	-618	Inconsistent database
	FFFFFD95	-619	Invalid comparison
	FFFFFD94	-620	Comparison failed
	FFFFFD93	-621	Transactions disabled
	FFFFFD92	-622	Invalid transport
	FFFFFD91	-623	Syntax invalid in name
	FFFFFD90	-624	Replica already exists
	FFFFFD8F	-625	Transport failure
	FFFFFD8E	-626	All referrals failed
	FFFFFD8D	-627	Can't remove naming value
	FFFFFD8C	-628	Object class violation
	FFFFFD8B	-629	Entry is not leaf
	FFFFFD8A	-630	Different tree. No information is available
	FFFFFD89	-631	Illegal replica type
	FFFFFD88	-632	System failure
	FFFFFD87	-633	Invalid entry for [Root]
	FFFFFD86	-634	No referrals
	FFFFFD85	-635	Remote failure
	FFFFFD84	-636	Unreachable server

(continued)

TABLE 9.2

DSTRACE Error Codes
(continued)

HEX CODE	ERROR	DESCRIPTION
FFFFFD83	-637	Previous move in progress
FFFFFD82	-638	No character mapping
FFFFFD81	-639	Incomplete authentication
FFFFFD7F	-641	Invalid request
FFFFFD7E	-642	Invalid iteration
FFFFFD7D	-643	Schema is nonremovable
FFFFFD7C	-644	Schema is in use
FFFFFD7B	-645	Class already exists
FFFFFD7A	-646	Bad naming attributes. Invalid naming properties were used.
FFFFFD79	-647	Not Root partition
FFFFFD76	-650	Ambiguous containment
FFFFFD75	-651	Ambiguous naming
FFFFFD74	-652	Duplicate mandatory
FFFFFD73	-653	Duplicate optional
FFFFFD72	-654	Partition busy
FFFFFD71	-655	Multiple replicas. No information is available.
FFFFFD70	-656	Crucial replica. No information is available.
FFFFFD6F	-657	Schema sync in progress
FFFFFD6E	-658	Skulk in progress
FFFFFD6D	-659	Time not synchronized
FFFFFD6C	-660	Record in use. The requested record is already in use.
FFFFFD6B	-661	DS volume not mounted
FFFFFD6A	-662	DS volume I/O failure
FFFFFD69	-663	DS locked
FFFFFD68	-664	Old epoch. This is an NDS time stamp error.

HEX CODE	ERROR	DESCRIPTION

TABLE 9.2

DSTRACE Error Codes

HEX CODE	ERROR	DESCRIPTION
FFFFFD67	-665	New epoch. This is an NDS time stamp error.
FFFFFD65	-667	Partition root. The object being manipulated is the root of a Directory Services partition
FFFFFD64	-668	Entry not container. An illegal function was attempted on a leaf object
FFFFFD63	-669	Failed authentication. The Directory database is locked on the server; an invalid password was sent; authentication failed
FFFFFD61	-671	No such parent. A parent was specified that does not exist
FFFFFD60	-672	No access. The client does not have sufficient results to perform the requested operation.
FFFFFD5F	-673	Replica not on
FFFFFD5A	-678	Duplicate ACL. No information is available.
FFFFFD59	-679	Partition already exists
FFFFFD58	-680	An attempt was made to use a reference that is not a Subordinate Reference.
FFFFFD57	-681	Alias of an alias. An attempt was made to use an alias of an alias.
FFFFFD56	-682	Auditing failed
FFFFFD55	-683	Invalid API version
FFFFFD54	-684	Secure NCP violation. No information is available.
FFFFFD45	-699	Unknown. An unrecoverable error has occurred and the operation cannot be completed. Action: Contact your Novell Authorized Reseller.

(continued)

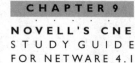

	HEX CODE	ERROR	DESCRIPTION
TABLE 9.2	FFFFFD44	-700	Obsolete API
DSTRACE Error Codes (continued)	FFFFFD43	-701	Synchronization disabled
	FFFFFD42	-702	Invalid Parameter
	FFFFFD41	-703	Duplicate template
	FFFFFD40	-704	No Master replica
	FFFFFD3F	-705	Duplicate containment

This completes our discussion of NDS grafting. Good work. In this section, we explored the three main aspects of replica management: replica types, replica operations, and replica synchronization. There's much more to replication than meets the eye. The good news is, we've made it through two of the three main NDS gardening tasks: pruning and grafting. That leaves pollination. I wonder if we have enough time to finish?

ZEN

"If you think it's hard to meet new people, try picking up the wrong golf ball."

Jack Lemmon

Time Synchronization

No matter how you look at it, time controls everything. This is especially true in NDS. Time impacts every aspect of your NetWare 4 life—NDS partitioning operations, replica synchronization, and resource access to name just a few. For this reason, time synchronization becomes a priority.

In Chapters 2 and 4 we learned all about what makes NDS time synchronization "tick." We learned that it coordinates and maintains consistent time for all the servers in your NDS tree. We also learned that NetWare 4 provides two different time configuration options: default (small trees) and custom (large trees).

The *default* time synchronization option works best for small networks with few servers in a single location. This configuration is commonly referred to as the *single reference* configuration because it uses a Single Reference time provider. The *custom* time synchronization option provides more flexibility for larger networks with multiple servers in distributed locations. It uses a special time provider group. The time provider group is designed to provide greater fault tolerance and efficiency for communicating time across multiple servers and wide area networks.

In this section, we will explore the realm of time management. This deals primarily with the custom time configuration method. We will re-introduce ACME's time provider group and learn everything there is to know about TIMESYNC.CFG. But first, let's take a quick stroll down memory lane and review some key time concepts.

UNDERSTANDING TIME SYNCHRONIZATION

Time synchronization provides NetWare 4 servers with a mechanism for coordinating NDS time stamps. NetWare 4 uses the TIMESYNC NLM to coordinate time stamps between all servers on the WAN. TIMESYNC.NLM maintains each server's Universal Time Coordinate (UTC)—a fancy name for Greenwich Mean Time (GMT).

All NetWare 4 servers are time servers of some type, either providers or consumers. Time providers provide time to time consumers. Makes sense. NetWare 4 supports three different time providers: Primary server, Reference server, and Single Reference server. On the other hand, there's only one type of time consumer: Secondary server. The majority of your NetWare 4 servers will be time consumers.

All NetWare 4 time servers perform three functions in relation to time synchronization:

1 • They provide UTC time to any NLM or requesting client workstation.

2 • They provide status information regarding the synchronization of UTC time.

3 • They adjust their clock rates to correct for time discrepancies and maintain UTC synchronization.

Time management operates on two important principles: time configuration and time communication.

Time configuration defines how your time servers are distributed. In addition, it outlines which servers are providers and which servers are consumers. As we learned earlier, NetWare 4 supports two basic time configuration designs:

1 • Default: Single Reference

2 • Custom: Time Provider Group

Whatever you do, make sure to choose the correct configuration method for your WAN. If your network is distributed over multiple sites and there are WAN links to consider, definitely use the custom method. A time provider group gives your network greater fault tolerance by distributing the time servers to multiple locations. Then determine if your network has less than 30 servers. If so, use the default configuration method.

THE BRAIN

For more information on NDS time synchronization, see the following
Novell Application Notes: **"An Introduction to NetWare Directory**
Services" (April 1993) and "Time Synchronization in NetWare 4"
(November 1993).

In Chapter 4 we learned that ACME will be using the custom time configuration approach. They will place a Reference time server in CAMELOT and Primary time servers in the other four hubs: NORAD, TOKYO, SYDNEY, and RIO. The next question is, How will these time servers communicate with one another?

Time communication occurs in two instances. First, when time providers "vote" with one another to determine the network's correct time. And second, when Secondary time servers "poll" time providers for the correct time. This occurs at regular polling intervals. Since ACME is using the custom time communication design, we'll need to create Configured Lists for server-to-server communications.

That's enough review for now. Let's dive into time management with a comprehensive exploration of TIMESYNC.CFG and ACME's time synchronization strategy.

REAL WORLD

Occasionally it may be necessary to change the time on a NetWare 4 server. Never change time at a server by typing TIME at the server's console and entering a new value. You can change a server's time by following these steps:

1. After hours, bring the NetWare 4 server down.

2. At the DOS prompt, type **TIME** and enter the new time value.

3. Restart NetWare 4 by typing **SERVER.EXE.**

NDS will get the new time value from DOS and the server's CMOS. This is the sole source of time for this server, unless it's getting time from an outside source. Also, remember to change the time zone information in SERVMAN if necessary.

MANAGING TIME SYNCHRONIZATION WITH TIMESYNC.CFG

NetWare 4 time synchronization is activated by default. It uses a Single Reference server configuration and SAP (Service Advertising Protocol) communications. You can start with this design if you'd like—just to test out the waters. But pretty soon you'll need greater flexibility and synchronization control. That's where time management comes in. Time management is the process of customizing two important time synchronization principles:

▸ Time Provider Group—determines which servers are providers. Also determines who gets to be the Reference time server and who are Primaries.

▸ Configured Lists—determines who gets time from whom. For providers, this list determines the voting patterns, and for consumers, this list determines where Secondary servers go for the correct network time.

Most time management tasks are accomplished using the Time Parameters option in SERVMAN. You can load this tool by typing **LOAD SERVMAN** at the file server console. Figure 9.32 shows the main Time Parameters window. This window, and subsequent screens, lists 17 different time management options. These options help us define time provider groups and build Configured Lists for every server. Let's check them out.

F I G U R E 9.32

The Time Parameters
Screen in SERVMAN

ZEN

"They call it golf because all the other four-letter words were taken."

Raymond Floyd

TIMESYNC Add Time Source

This option allows you to add the name of a server to your Configured List. The server name that you enter here will eventually find its way to the TIMESYNC.CFG configuration file. TIMESYNC.CFG is updated if you choose the Update TIMESYNC.CFG option after exiting the Time Parameters screen. In most cases you will only use this option if you are adding a new source time server to the Configured List. Again, the default is Empty.

TIMESYNC Configuration File

The TIMESYNCE.CFG configuration file is the default name given to the file that stores all the settings for time management. There is little if any need to change the name of this file, and I recommend you accept the default TIMESYNC.CFG. This file can easily be copied to multiple NetWare 4 servers if needed. Again, the default value is TIMESYNC.CFG.

TIMESYNC Configured Sources

This option activates the Configured List strategy. It is also shown in Figure 9.32. This option must be set to ON if you are using Configured Lists. When activated, this server only communicates with servers in its configured list—SAP broadcasts are deactivated. The default is OFF.

If you need to view your server's Configured List, you can type the following command at the server console:

```
SET TIMESYNC TIME SOURCE =
```

TIMESYNC Directory Tree Mode

This option specifies that SAP packets from other Directory trees can influence the time synchronization on this server. Do not change this parameter if this server is a time source. The default is ON.

TIMESYNC Hardware Clock

This option controls the hardware clock synchronization and instructs the server to read its hardware clock at the beginning of each polling loop (see Figure 9.33). A Single server or Reference server will read its hardware clock at the start of each polling loop. A Primary server or Secondary server will not read its hardware clock during each polling loop. They will adjust their software clocks during each polling interval. The default is ON.

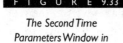

FIGURE 9.33

The Second Time
Parameters Window in
SERVMAN

TIMESYNC Polling Count

This option sets the number of times the polling packets should be exchanged. Typically, the default of three works adequately. In cases where you may have a long delay of communications between two time servers, you may want to increase this option by a few.

TIMESYNC Polling Interval

Each 10 minutes (600 seconds) a server will poll for time. After initial installation of your NetWare 4 servers, you may want to increase this value to 20 minutes or even one hour. The time polling process does not generate an inordinate amount of traffic on your network, so the default setting does not create large problems. The default is 600 seconds.

TIMESYNC Remove Time Source

This option allows you to remove a server from your list of configured time sources. The server name entered in this field will be removed from the TIMESYNC.CFG configuration file if you exit and choose Yes to update TIMESYNC.CFG. You can also use EDIT to change an entry in the TIMESYNC.CFG file.

TIMESYNC Reset

This option will return all values in your TIMESYNC.CFG configuration to the default values. If you issue a reset and write the configuration file after exiting, any changes made previously to the TIMESYNC file will be lost. Be careful with this paramter. The default is, kindly, OFF.

TIMESYNC Restart Flag

This option will cause the time synchronization process to restart using the parameters found in the TIMESYNC.CFG configuration file. These parameters will cause the TIMESYNC.NLM to reload without bringing down the server.

TIMESYNC Service Advertising

This parameter enables the Service Advertising Protocol (SAP) as the communication mechanism. If you are using Configured Lists, turn this parameter OFF. The default is ON.

TIMESYNC Synchronization Radius

The synchronization radius is the amount of time that a server's clock can vary and still be considered synchronized. The default of 2,000 milliseconds works well for most installations. This time parameter can be increased if more time is required for travel across satellite links or congested WAN links. The default polling interval is shown in Figure 9.33.

TIMESYNC Time Adjustment

This parameter is used to schedule adjustments to the server's network time. Use caution when executing this command because changing time can disrupt network operations. For example, entering the command

```
+00:00:01 at 11/17/99 08:59:00 PM
```

will adjust the time ahead three hours and one minute before midnight on November 17, 1999. Use this field only when a significant one-time correction must be made to the network time.

TIMESYNC Time Source

This parameter is used to add time sources to your TIMESYNC.CFG file. The same functionality is provided through the field ADD Timesync Time Source at the top of the screen. To reduce confusion, leave this field alone.

TIMESYNC Type

This field allows you to specify a type of time server to be configured. You will only need to modify the parameter when creating a Time Provider Group (as in ACME's case). You specify which type it is by typing Reference, Single, or Primary.

Write Parameters

This parameter is used to write changes to the TIMESYNC.CFG file. Use EDIT rather than this parameter. The default is OFF.

Write Value

This is used to modify the TIMESYNC.CFG file. Use EDIT rather than this parameter for making modifications.

If you are using the SERVMAN utility to make edits to TIMESYNC.CFG, you can save those edits when you exit the Time Parameters screen. The main SERVMAN screen will prompt you to save the changes as shown in Figure 9.34.

F I G U R E 9.34

Saving Time Parameters in SERVMAN

You can easily view the status of TIMESYNC.CFG by typing **SET** at the file server console. You can then select list option 9 to give the settings for all Time Parameters as discussed above. Finally, TIMESYNC.NLM supports a debug mode for time troubleshooting. This is helpful for determining if the servers are contacting one another during the expected intervals. Here's how it works:

```
SET TIMESYNC DEBUG = 7     (enables debug)

SET TIMESYNC DEBUG = 0     (disables debug)
```

That's everything you need to know about managing TIMESYNC.CFG. Now you're ready to attack ACME's time synchronization design. Ready, set, time.

QUIZ

Without changing the order of the digits, form a calculation equal to 100. Only four plus and/or minus signs can be inserted between the digits:

9 8 7 6 5 4 3 2 1 = 100

(Q9-4)

TIME SYNCHRONIZATION FOR ACME

Now it's "time" (pun intended) to implement ACME's time synchronization design. As you may remember from earlier discussions, their corporate headquarters are in CAMELOT. Furthermore, they have a Reference time server there that is linked to an external time source. This source provides time for both the NetWare server clock and the PC hardware.

Primary servers are located in each of the other WAN hubs; namely, RIO, NORAD, SYDNEY, and TOKYO. These time sources will work together to determine the actual network time during each polling interval. The ACME tree uses customized Configured Lists for time communication. The following information shows what it takes to make time work at ACME.

Reference Server in CAMELOT

TIMESYNC.CFG (CAMELOT)

- ▸ Configured Sources = ON

- ▸ Directory Tree Mode = ON

- ▸ Hardware Clock = ON

- ▸ Polling Count = 3

- ▸ Polling Interval = 10

- ▸ Service Advertising = OFF

- ▸ Synchronization Radius = 2000

- ▸ Type = REFERENCE

Configured List (CAMELOT)

- ▸ Time Source = RIO

- ▸ Time Source = TOKYO

- ▸ Time Source = SYDNEY

- ▸ Time Source = NORAD

- ▸ Time Source = CAMELOT

Primary Servers in RIO, TOKYO, NORAD, and SYDNEY

TIMESYNC.CFG (TOKYO as example)

- ▸ Configured Sources = ON

- ▸ Directory Tree Mode = ON

- ▸ Hardware Clock = ON

- ▸ Polling Count = 3

- ▸ Polling Interval = 10

- ▸ Service Advertising = OFF

- ▸ Synchronization Radius = 2000

- ▸ Type = PRIMARY

Configured List (TOKYO as example)

- Time Source = CAMELOT

- Time Source = RIO

- Time Source = TOKYO

- Time Source = NORAD

- Time Source = SYDNEY

Secondary Servers

TIMESYNC.CFG (Secondary Servers)

- Configured Sources = ON

- Directory Tree Mode = ON

- Hardware Clock = ON

- Polling Count = 3

- Polling Interval = 10

- Service Advertising = OFF

- Synchronization Radius = 2000

- Type = SECONDARY

Configured List (depends on location—NORAD as example)

- Time Source = NORAD

- Time Source = RIO

▸ Time Source = SYDNEY

▸ Time Source = CAMELOT

▸ Time Source = TOKYO

Congratulations! Your green thumb is shining brightly. You're going to be a great NetWare 4 gardener. Today, we added an in-depth knowledge of pruning to our agronomic repertoire. We learned about NDS partition management (pruning), NDS replication (grafting), and time synchronization (pollination). Doesn't it feel wonderful to be in the great outdoors?

This is not only the end of a chapter, this represents the end of an era. An era in NDS gardening that started seven chapters ago—way back in Chapter 2. In the beginning...we learned all about the "Cloud" and what it meant to live there. We learned about objects, naming, partitions, replicas, and time synchronization. Our innocence and naivete was only eclipsed by our insatiable curiosity.

Then, we took this rudimentary knowledge and used it to save the world. In Chapter 3 we discovered ACME and promptly designed their tree in Chapter 4. NDS design consisted of naming standards, tree design, partition design, replica placement, and time synchronization design. There are those topics again. But this time, we expanded our understanding of NDS into the realm of design and implementation. Tricky stuff.

We took a well-deserved rest from NDS until Chapter 8. Then bang! It hit us—NDS management. We brought our design to life with tools such as NWADMIN, CX, NetSync, and so on. We learned about special NDS objects, naming rules, Bindery Services, and management tricks. I never knew NDS had such a complex personality. Then things got even weirder in this chapter. We expanded our gardening skills into the realm of pruning—you know, kill a tree so it can live. Strange stuff.

So here we are. We've learned all there is to know about NDS. Of course, we're not done learning. There's a plethora of NetWare 4 Management tasks left; namely, the file system, security, configuration, management, printing, and optimization. And the good news is, NDS permeates them all.

I wonder if there's life after gardening. Something tells me that NDS will always be there—like a guardian "cloud" floating above our heads. Of course, it's especially beautiful at sunrise. Tomorrow is a new dawn.

NETWARE 4 FILE SYSTEM

Just when you think you have NetWare 4 and NDS figured out, a little voice inside your head whispers, "There is another...."

Another what? Listen more closely, "...directory structure."

Another directory structure? How could that be? You may think that there's only one NetWare directory structure and it's the foundation of NDS. Well, that's where you're wrong. If you look closely at Figure 10.1, you'll see *two* directory trees—one above the server and one below it.

F I G U R E   10.1

The Two NetWare 4
Directory Trees

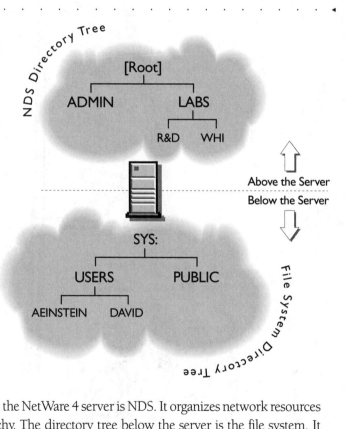

The directory tree above the NetWare 4 server is NDS. It organizes network resources into a logical WAN hierarchy. The directory tree below the server is the file system. It organizes network data files into a functional application hierarchy. Pretty simple, huh? The important thing is to separate the two in your mind. NDS handles resource data and the file system handles application data. Think of it as the "File Cabinet of Life."

ZEN

"To me, if life boils down to one significant thing—it's movement. To live is to keep moving. Unfortunately, this means that for the rest of our lives we're going to be looking for boxes!"

Jerry Seinfeld

In the past, cave-LANs relied on "sneakernet" for file sharing. First, they copied files to a diskette, then ran them down the hall to a coworker's machine. Finally, the coworker transferred the files from diskette to their own directory structure. Voilá!

With the advent of NetWare (and coaxial cabling), society experienced the dawning of a new age—the file server. The file server became the central repository of shared data and applications. Life was good.

Then, NetWare 4 came along. Once again, society experienced the dawning of a new age—NDS. The file server suddenly became a small fish in a very large, global pond. Volumes took on a life of their own. People started treating them as independent objects; free from the servers that house them. Is this progress? I'm not so sure. It underemphasizes the importance of the file server. Let's be honest. It's still the most important resource in the WAN. And what do file servers do? They serve files. How? Through the NetWare 4 file system.

Let's check it out.

Understanding the NetWare 4 File System

Every NetWare 4 file server contains a hierarchical directory structure for storing shared data files and applications. It is called the file system. The file system organizes internal disks into one or more volumes. Volumes are then divided into directories that contain subdirectories or files. On the surface it looks a lot like DOS. But don't be fooled; it's a whole new world. Check out Figure 10.2!

TIP

In earlier versions of NetWare, the file system was referred to as the directory structure. In NetWare 4, it is referred to as the file system to distinguish it from the NDS directory structure.

Earlier we called the NetWare 4 file system the "File Cabinet of Life." It fits. See Figure 10.3. In such an analogy, the file server is the filing cabinet, and the volumes are the drawers. Also, the directories are hanging folders, the subdirectories are file folders, and the files become individual sheets of paper. Pretty nifty, huh?

With this analogy in mind, let's explore the key components of NetWare 4's exciting new file system: volumes and directories. In the first section, we will re-discover the volume, and learn about its dual personality as a logical NDS object and physical disk resource. Then, we'll focus our journey even further into the Netware 4 directory structure—starting with system-created directories, which are defined automatically within the SYS: volume during NetWare 4 server installation (see Chapter 6). Next, we'll expand our horizons beyond default directories and into the realm of DOS, application, configuration, home, and shared directories. Finally, you'll get a taste of two different directory designs—shallow and deep.

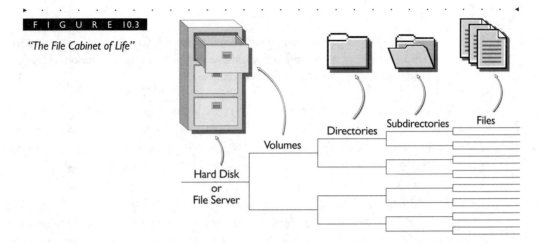

FIGURE 10.3

"The File Cabinet of Life"

And that's only the first section. Later in the chapter, we'll explore file system management and the land of drive mapping. Wow! So much to learn and so little time. So without any further interruptions, let's get on with the show.

UNDERSTANDING NETWARE 4 VOLUMES

Volumes are cool—mostly because they're so unique. They can span multiple disks, or they can be subdivisions of a single disk. They are physical storage units within the file server, but also independent logical objects that stand alone. They are neither here nor there—they are everywhere!

The volume represents the highest level in the NetWare 4 file system. It is the root of the server directory structure. Volumes can also be leaf objects in the NDS directory tree. Because of this unique position, they act as a bridge between NDS and the file system. The first volume on each NetWare 4 server is named SYS:. It is created automatically during NetWare 4 installation. In addition, an NDS leaf object is created in the server's home container. For our example, this is called WHITE-SRV1_SYS—a logical representation of the physical SYS: volume on WHITE-SRV1.

None of this is set in stone, of course. You can change the context of a Volume object using NetWare Administrator (NWADMIN) or NETADMIN. You can also rename volumes. To rename a physical volume, you'll need to change its server definition with INSTALL.NLM. To rename a logical volume, on the other hand, you can use either NWADMIN or NETADMIN. Finally, you can create a special pointer to a different physical volume using the Alias object type.

ZEN

Infobit—An individual item of information, such as a recipe or a description of a place, that meets the requirements for inclusion in a databank. Also used to describe properties of NDS objects.

So what are they? NetWare 4 volumes are fixed units of hard disk storage. They can be formed from any hard disk that contains a NetWare partition. Think of it as NetWare formatting. You can place 64 volumes on a NetWare 4 server, and each one can span up to 32 hard disks. Do the math. That means a NetWare 4 server can support 2048 disks—wow!

How does it work? Volumes are divided into physical volume segments. Different segments can be stored on one or more hard disks. Each volume can support 32 segments, and/or each hard disk can support 8 volume segments from one or more volumes. Because of this, a volume can:

▸ Contain a portion of a hard disk

▸ Occupy an entire hard disk

▸ Span multiple hard disks

The simplest configuration is, of course, one hard disk per volume. The advantage of spreading a volume across multiple hard disks is performance. It allows the server to read from or write to different parts of the same volume simultaneously—thus speeding up disk input/output. The disadvantage of such a technique, however, is fault tolerance. If you span volumes across multiple disks, it increases the chances that something will go wrong. If any disk fails, the entire volume fails, and you lose all your data. Consider protecting your volumes with mirroring, duplexing, or RAID (Redundant Array of Inexpensive Disks).

TIP

RAID provides numerous performance and SFT (System Fault Tolerance) advantages. From a performance standpoint, it uses *data striping*, which means that files are stored across multiple disks. Read

and write performance is enhanced dramatically because blocks can be accessed simultaneously. In addition, RAID employs a parity algorithm that protects volumes even when a disk crashes. Cool.

NetWare 4 volumes are further organized into *directories* and *files*. Directories are logical volume subdivisions that provide an administrative hierarchy to network applications and data files. They allow you to further organize your data into content-specific file folders. Directories can contain other directories (called subdirectories) or files.

Files are individual items of data. They represent the bottom level of the file-server food chain. Files can be valuable user data or network applications. It doesn't matter. What does matter is their location. Files should be stored in logical subdirectories according to their purpose and security level. That's the ultimate goal of the NetWare 4 file system—organize the user's data so that it's secure and easy to find.

To accomplish this goal, you must follow specific file syntax and naming rules. As with NDS object naming, filenames define the data's name and location:

```
Server\Volume:Directory\(Subdirectory)\Filename
```

Standard directory names and filenames support eight characters and an optional three-character extension. Special non-DOS filenames can extend as far as 32 characters (Macintosh) or even 255 characters (OS/2 and Windows 95). These special files require an additional volume feature called *name space* (see Chapter 13). Also, make sure to support the path conventions of standard or special filenames. NetWare allows 255 characters in a directory path (counting the drive letter and delimiters), whereas DOS only allows a maximum of 127 characters. Refer to Table 10.1 for more NetWare 4 file system naming rules.

T A B L E 10.1	PATH COMPONENT	RULES
NetWare 4 File System Naming Rules		
	File Server	Name is limited to 2 to 47 characters.
		First character in name cannot be a period.
		Name cannot contain spaces or special characters such as * + , \ / | : ; = < > [ ].

(continued)

TABLE 10.1

*NetWare 4 File System
Naming Rules
(continued)*

PATH COMPONENT	RULES
Volume	Name length is limited to 2 to 15 characters.
	Physical name must end with a colon (:), which is added automatically.
	First volume on server must be SYS:.
	Two physical volumes on the same server cannot have the same name.
	Name cannot contain spaces or special characters such as * + , \ / | : ; = < > [ ].
Directory	Name length is limited to a maximum of 11 characters (a directory name consisting of 1 to 8 characters plus an optional directory name extension of up to 3 characters).
	A period (.) is used to separate the directory name from the (optional) extension.
	Directories should be limited to functional groups.
	Name cannot contain spaces or special characters such as * + , \ / | : ; = < > [ ].
Subdirectory	Name length is limited to a maximum of 11 characters (a directory name consisting of 1 to 8 characters plus an optional directory name extension of up to 3 characters).
	A period (.) is used to separate the directory name from the (optional) extension.
	Subdirectories share common functionality.
	The size of subdirectories is limited by disk size.
	Name cannot contain spaces or special characters such as * + , \ / | : ; = < > [ ].
Files	Name length is limited to a maximum of 11 characters (a filename consisting of 1 to 8 characters plus an optional filename extension of up to 3 characters).
	A period (.) is used to separate the directory name from the (optional) extension.
	Name cannot contain spaces or special characters such as * + , \ / | : ; = < > [ ].

Before you get too carried away with NetWare 4 configuration and management, you should design the basic structure of the file system. This is just as important as designing the NDS tree. In both cases, you need to consider a number of important WAN factors, including security, administration, and accessibility. Except this time we're working below the server, not above it.

ZEN

Nonchaotic attractor—A pattern of movement in a system with motion that settles down to an easily describable and predictable pattern such as a pendulum or NetWare 4 volume. This can also be thought of as a normal attractor in that it is the opposite of a "strange" attractor.

Because volumes are at the top of the file system tree, they should be planned first. Here are a few things to think about:

▶ The simplest strategy is one-to-one. That is, one volume for each internal disk. In this scenario, stick with the default SYS: volume and let it occupy your entire internal disk. Then rely on directories and subdirectories for file organization and security.

▶ If the one-to-one strategy isn't for you, make sure to reserve the SYS: volume for files needed by the NetWare 4 operating system. Additional volumes can be created for applications, data files, and print queues.

▶ Create a separate volume for each client operating system that allows long filenames. For instance, if you have both Macintosh users and DOS or OS/2 users, you might want to create a separate volume for the Macintosh files. This is particularly important because it enhances administration, backup procedures, and disk space usage. Also, name space adds performance overhead to ALL files on the host volume. So, minimize the files on that volume.

▶ If fault tolerance is more important than performance, create one volume per disk. If performance is more important than fault tolerance, span one NetWare volume over multiple hard disks (with one segment of the volume on each hard disk). If fault tolerance and performance are equally important, you can still spread volumes across multiple hard disks, but you should make sure that they are duplexed or RAIDed.

Once the volumes are in place, it's time to shift your focus to directories. This is when it gets interesting. Fortunately, NetWare 4 gives you a big head start with system-created directories and files. Let's check them out.

SYSTEM-CREATED DIRECTORIES

With the NetWare 4 server installation, you get a default user (Admin) and two directory trees:

- The default NDS tree (server context)

- The default file system on SYS:

In our discussion of the NetWare 4 file system, we will explore the default tree and go a few steps beyond:

- System-created directories

- DOS directories

- Application directories

- Configuration directories

- Home directories

- Shared data directories

System-created directories contain NetWare 4 operating system files, NLMs, and utilities. They are divided into two main categories: Admin directories and User directories. This is a security issue. The Admin directories (SYSTEM, for example) are reserved for administrators only—they require Supervisor access rights. User directories, on the other hand, contain public utilities and are open to all users throughout the WAN (PUBLIC, for example). Next, with the system-created directories as a platform, you will spring forward into the world of file-system creativity.

DOS directories are optional. They are required only if you want users to access DOS from the server instead of from their local drives. Application directories contain third-party application programs such as word processing, spreadsheet, or database programs. Configuration directories hold user- or group-specific configuration files. These files help you manage network applications. Home directories hold special user files and create a cozy, productive network environment. Finally, shared data directories contain global files for all users throughout the WAN.

Let's start our discussion with a detailed look at the nine system-created directories. Refer to Figure 10.4. Here they are:

LOGIN   ETC
SYSTEM   QUEUES
PUBLIC   DELETED.SAV
MAIL   DOC
NLS

FIGURE 10.4

The System-created Directory Structure

LOGIN

LOGIN is your doormat to the WAN. From there you can knock on NetWare's door and provide the secret password for entrance. This is all accomplished with the help of LOGIN.EXE. In addition to logging in, there are other administrative tasks you (and users) can perform from the LOGIN directory—such as changing context (CX), viewing the NDS tree structure (NLIST), and mapping drives (MAP).

LOGIN is the only directory available to users prior to login. Be careful which programs you place there, because they are available to users without any security. Finally, there's an additional subdirectory under LOGIN, called OS2, which contains login programs for OS/2 clients.

Once you login and pass through the magic NDS gates, the rest of the world opens up to you—namely the other eight system-created directories.

SYSTEM

SYSTEM is Admin's workroom. This directory contains special administrative tools and utilities, including OS files, NLMs, and dangerous NDS programs. For this reason, SYSTEM should be kept out of the reach of users and small children. Fortunately, it contains a "child-proof cap" in the form of Supervisor access rights. Only Admin can gain access by default.

PUBLIC

PUBLIC, on the other hand, is the user's playground. This directory contains general user commands and utilities, such as NWADMIN, NETADMIN, NWUSER, and MAP. By default, all users in the server's home container have access to PUBLIC—but only after they've logged in. In addition, a subdirectory under PUBLIC, called OS2, contains NetWare programs and utilities for OS/2 users.

MAIL

MAIL is left over from the old days when NetWare shipped with an e-mail application. Well, guess what, it does again (see Chapter 12), but it doesn't use the MAIL directory. Go figure. Instead, it's a repository for old user-specific system configuration files, like bindery login scripts (LOGIN.) and print job configurations (PRINTCON.DAT). Of course, these files are now properties of each user object. Ah, NDS.

Oh yeah. MAIL is sometimes used by third-party e-mail applications, but not very often.

NLS

NLS is NetWare 4's translator. It stands for NetWare Language Support (or something like that). Each of the main system-created directories has its own NLS subdirectory. These NLS directories contain message and help files for multilingual NetWare 4 utilities. If multiple languages have been installed, each language has its own subdirectory under NLS.

Later in Chapter 13, we'll learn how multiple languages are supported in NetWare 4. But here's a quick preview: Each utility and message file has a general language pointer. The workstation determines which language the user wants and tells the pointer where to go for the language-specific modules (that is, which NLS directory). Then, NLS displays the utility or message in the appropriate language. It is very cool.

ETC

ETC is aptly named. It contains a bunch of other stuff, like sample TCP/IP configuration files and, you know, other stuff.

QUEUES

QUEUES is one of the great advancements in NetWare 4. Earlier versions stored print queues on the SYS: volume only. This caused serious problems if the print job was large and SYS: ran out of space—namely, the server crashed. Now, CNEs can offload print queue storage to any volume they want. When you do, NetWare 4 automatically creates a QUEUES directory off the root of the host volume.

DELETED.SAV

DELETED.SAV is file heaven. This is where files go when they die. You see, files can be brought back to life in NetWare 4—it's called *salvaging*. But the files must be salvaged from their parent directory. If, in some horrible plane crash, their parent directory was also deleted, the children files can also be salvaged from DELETED.SAV. This directory is only created when it's needed.

DOC

Welcome to NetWare 4's electronic documentation—DynaText. The interesting thing about DynaText is that it becomes available *after* you need it. For example, the NetWare 4 installation instructions are available once you install DynaText—*after* the server's been installed! Life has a funny way of surprising you. Remember, Murphy's law number 142: "I'm an optimist."

Anyway, NetWare 4 DynaText is installed in the DOC directory using INSTALL.NLM. Refer to Chapter 6 for specific details.

ZEN

"Pioneers took years to cross the country. Now people will move thousands of miles just for the summer. I don't think any pioneers did that, 'Yeah, it took us a decade to get there, and we stayed for the summer. It was nice, they had a pool, the kids loved it. And then, we left about ten years ago and we just got back. We had a great summer, it took us twenty years, and now our lives are over!'"

Jerry Seinfeld

```

That completes our brief pilgrimage through the NetWare 4 system-created directory structure. Make sure not to accidentally delete, move, or rename any of these system-created directories—especially LOGIN, SYSTEM, PUBLIC, MAIL, and NLS. These directories are critical to the server and bad things will happen if they're removed.

O.K. We're cruising now. Next, let's expand our horizons beyond the default directory structure and explore the land of additional directories. You'll be amazed at what you can find there.

## EXPANDING BEYOND THE DEFAULT DIRECTORY STRUCTURE

NetWare 4 provides you with a big head start by building the above default directory tree (see Figure 10.4). The next step is to add some productive DOS, user, application, and data directories. Think of it as a transition from Figure 10.4 to Figure 10.5. It boils down to five suggested directory components:

▸ DOS directories

▸ Application directories

▸ Configuration directories

▸ Home directories

▸ Shared data directories

Let's take a closer look.

FIGURE 10.5

*Beyond the Default
Directory Structure*
```

DOS Directories

DOS directories are vital because they provide support for various workstation operating systems (namely DOS and OS/2). They are, however, optional. You can choose to have users execute DOS commands and utilities from their local workstation drives or from a shared DOS directory on the server—it's up to you.

If you choose to have users run DOS from the server, you'll need to make a separate subdirectory for each version of DOS. It is preferable, of course, to have all users run the same version of DOS, but dream on—it'll never happen. Here's the trick: You'll need to somehow interrogate each workstation and point the user to the correct version of DOS. Fortunately, NetWare 4 supports login script identifier variables for this very purpose. We'll explore them in more depth in Chapter 12 (NetWare 4 Configuration).

For now, you'll need to create a DOS directory structure that supports all the different types of machines and DOS versions on your WAN. As you can see in Figure 10.5, the DOS structure starts under SYS:PUBLIC because users already have access there. Next, you'll need to create a subdirectory structure for each of the following three components:

- ▸ MACHINE—IBM_PC, DELL, or other

- ▸ OS—MSDOS, NOVDOS, OS2, and so on

- ▸ OS VERSION—V7.01, V6.22, or whatever version you're using

So why should you bother? Many users simply access DOS utilities from their local drives. Well, if you're using a diskless workstation, you'll need to get DOS somewhere else—such as the server. Also, some users get better performance from the server because of file caching and a slow local disk channel. Finally, a centralized DOS structure allows you to update DOS once (on the server), instead of hundreds of times on each distributed workstation. The bottom line is that it's your choice, DOS central or DOS local—whatever you do, just DOS it!

Application Directories

A subdirectory structure should be created under SYS:APPS for each network application. For security's sake, restrict this structure to application files only—no data. Users can store their data in home directories, group areas, or SYS:SHARED—a global data directory (see Shared Data Directories section below).

Configuration File Directories

What about application configuration files, such as templates, interface files, and style sheets? It depends on the type of configuration file it is. Application-specific configuration files, like style sheets, should be placed in a CONFIG directory under the application. User-specific configurations, on the other hand, such as interface files, should be placed in user home directories. Let's take a closer look.

Home Directories

Each user needs a place he/she can call home. A special subdirectory under SYS:USERS gives each of them a private, secure retreat for his or her own stuff. User directories serve two functions: security and organization. From a security viewpoint, they provide a secure place for private user files—a place away from coworkers' prying eyes (of course, you can look at their files because you are a NetWare 4 CNE). From an organizational viewpoint, user directories become the parent of a complex user-specific directory strucutre—a place for personal games and applications.

Each user's home directory should exactly match their login name—or at least be very close. This simplifies administration and makes them easy to find. Also, make sure to give users sufficient access rights to move around in there (see Chapter 11).

Shared Data Directories

The proper organization of network data strongly impacts user productivity. Let's be honest—the sole purpose of the NetWare 4 file system is to organize data efficiently. This is accomplished in three ways:

- Personal data—should be stored in user home directories

- Group-specific data—should be stored in special group data directories under SYS:SHARED

- Globally shared data—should be stored in the SYS:SHARED directory off of the root of SYS:

There you go. That's the NetWare 4 file system. So the only question that remains is, "What should it look like?" You have two choices: shallow or deep. Check it out.

QUIZ

I'm on this numbers kick. Numbers have an unavoidable fascination. Try this one on for size:

What is the five-digit number, no zeros, in which the first number is one-fourth of the second, the second is twice the third, the third is two-thirds of the fourth, and the fifth is half of the fourth, with the sum of all the digits being twenty-three?

(Q10-1)
(See Appendix C for quiz answers.)

DESIGNING YOUR DIRECTORY STRUCTURE

Now that you know what the file system is made of, you need to decide what it's going to look like. You can either create a flat tree with many directories stored off the root of the volume, or you can have a deep directory structure with many levels of subdirectories (see Figure 10.6). Novell recommends that for ease of administration, you design a directory structure that is no more than five levels deep.

FIGURE 10.6

Directory Structure Design Options

SYS:

• Flat Structure
• One Volume
• Small Organization

SYS:

• Deep Structure
• Multiple Volumes
• Large Organization

A flat directory structure, such as the one in Figure 10.7, could be used for a very small company with few users. In this example, all home directories are stored in the root of the volume—not recommended, but easy to use. On the up side, this design limits file storage to a single volume, and the path names are very short. Also, the application programs are separated from data files.

On the down side, the SYS: volume shares its space with everyone else. Sometimes it just needs to be alone. Also, home directories are located in the root of the volume, and there is no shared data area.

FIGURE 10.7

A Flat Directory Structure

A deeper directory structure is shown in Figure 10.8. In this design, system-created directories and applications share SYS:, while all other components have their own volumes. On the up side, the SYS: volume is more stable, because files are not added or deleted very often. Also, applications are more secure because they hang out with SYS:. Finally, you can consider using a different file system administrator for each volume.

On the down side, this design places users on different volumes, which makes security much more difficult to administer. Also, you may run out of room on a given volume, even though you have sufficient disk space on the server.

FIGURE 10.8

A Deep Directory Structure

So, there you are. The "other" NetWare 4 directory structure. It's not so bad. A lot easier than those crazy leaf objects and distinguished names. As you can see, the NetWare 4 file system provides a simple, straightforward structure for sharing valuable WAN files. But what about management? How do you keep it running on a daily basis? I'm so glad you asked. That's the next topic.

Managing the NetWare 4 File System

Once you've designed your file system, you'll need to develop a plan to maintain it—every day! You'll need to ask yourself the following questions:

▸ How much disk space is left on each volume?

▸ How much disk space is still available to users with volume space restrictions?

▸ How much room is being taken up by files that have been deleted but not yet purged?

▸ Which files have not been accessed in a long time?

▸ Are there any directories or files with no owner?

For the most part, the NetWare 4 file system looks like DOS. For this reason, you can perform a lot of DOS file management tasks in NetWare 4 as well. In addition, DOS tools such as DIR, COPY, and the MS Windows File Manager work just fine in the NetWare environment.

This is not nearly enough, however. Networking, in general, puts a great strain on file management. Fortunately, NetWare 4 includes a number of file management utilities that are specifically designed to work in a network environment, such as:

▸ FILER—A text-based utility that is used to manage directories and files, display volume information, and salvage and purge deleted files.

▸ FLAG—Allows you to view or modify directory and file attributes. It can also be used to modify the owner of a directory or file and to view or modify the search mode of executable files.

▸ NCOPY—Allows you to copy network files from one location to another.

▸ NDIR—Lets you view the files once they've been copied. In addition, this utility allows you to view a plethora of information about volumes and directories—but you can't modify anything with it.

▸ NLIST—A new NetWare 4 NDS utility that displays information about NDS objects and/or properties. It can be used to display information about volumes, as long as they're represented as Volume objects in NDS.

▸ NWADMIN (runs under MS Windows) and NETADMIN (runs under DOS)— NDS-based tools that can be used to perform a variety of file management tasks such as creating, deleting, renaming, copying, or moving directories and/or files. You can also use them to assign trustee rights, determine effective rights, and modify inherited rights filters. In addition, they display Volume object information and, finally, allow you to purge and salvage deleted files. Wow!

It's a good thing you have so many friends to help you out. In this section, we will explore these and other NetWare 4 file management tools. But we're going to approach them in a slightly unique way. Instead of talking about each utility alone, we are going to explore how they combine to help you manage three key file-system components:

▸ Volumes

▸ Directories

▸ Files

In each area, we will explore all the file management tools that apply to that component. Also, we'll provide some examples of how they can be used to simplify your life. This makes sense, because we're managing volumes, directories, and files—not utilities. So without further ado, let's start out with NetWare 4 volumes.

ZEN

"My parents live in Florida now. They moved there last year. They didn't want to move to Florida, but they're in their seventies now and that's the law!"

Jerry Seinfeld

MANAGING NETWARE 4 VOLUMES

Volumes are at the top of the file-system food chain. They also represent a bridge between physical files on server disks and logical leaf objects in the NDS tree. For your managing pleasure, NetWare 4 includes five key tools for managing volumes:

- ▸ FILER

- ▸ NWADMIN

- ▸ NETADMIN

- ▸ NLIST

- ▸ NDIR

Let's check them out.

FILER

The FILER DOS-based menu utility can be used to display a variety of volume information including:

- ▸ Volume statistics relating to space usage, directory entries, and compression

- ▸ Volume features such as volume type, block size, name space, and installed features (such as compression, migration, suballocation, or auditing)

- ▸ Date and time information, including creation date/time, owner, last modified date/time, last archived date/time, and archiver

To view information relating to the current volume, choose the View volume information option from the Available options menu, as shown in Figure 10.9. A Volume menu will appear that gives you the option of viewing volume statistics, features, or dates and times.

F I G U R E 10.9

Available Options Menu in FILER

If you select the Volume statistics option, a screen will appear that is similar to the one in Figure 10.10. This screen lists statistics relating to volume space usage, maximum and available directory entries, and file-compression space usage.

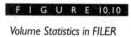

F I G U R E 10.10

Volume Statistics in FILER

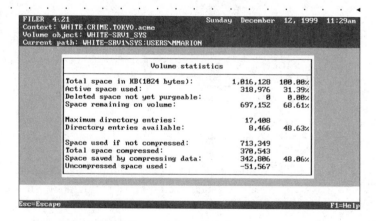

If you select the Volume features option, a screen will appear that is similar to the one in Figure 10.11. This screen includes information about the volume type (that is, non-removable), the block size, the name space(s) installed, and installed features (such as compression, migration, suballocation, or auditing).

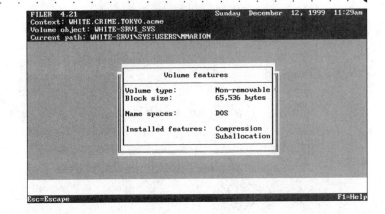

F I G U R E 10.11

Volume Features in FILER

THE BRAIN

Some of the most exciting NetWare 4 volume features are file compression, data migration, and block suballocation. Learn them, use them, live them. Refer to Chapter 1 for an introduction to these features and Chapter 15 for details on how to optimize volumes using them.

Finally, if you choose the Dates and times option, a Volume dates and times window will be displayed. This window displays information such as the volume creation date/time, owner, the last modified date/time, the last archived date/time, and the archiver.

FILER is the most useful non-NDS file management tool. It focuses on volumes, directories, and files as physical storage units within the NetWare 4 server—no NDS nonsense to confuse you. This is appealing to many CNEs. If you want fancy NDS footwork, refer to NWADMIN.

Hey, good idea!

NWADMIN

The NetWare Administrator (NWADMIN) tool treats volumes as NDS objects. It displays roughly the same information as FILER but from a slightly different point of view:

▸ Identification

▸ Dates and Times

- ▸ User Space Limits

- ▸ Trustee Security

- ▸ Attributes

To display volume information using NWADMIN, walk the tree until you find your desired volume—in our case it's .CN=WHITE-SRV1_SYS.OU=WHITE. OU=CRIME.OU=TOKYO.O=ACME. When you select a volume, the Identification page button activates by default. Because of this, a screen similar to the one in Figure 10.12 magically appears. It's marginally interesting, containing information on volume name, host server, NetWare version, host volume, and location.

F I G U R E 10.12

*Identification Page for
Volumes in NWADMIN*

The Statistics page is the really interesting NWADMIN volume page (see Figure 10.13). It displays statistical information relating to the volume type (non-removable), deleted files, compressed files, block size, name spaces, and installed features (such as suballocation, data compression, and data migration). Colorful pie charts are also displayed, showing the percentage of disk space and directory entries used. Very cool.

F I G U R E 10.13

*Statistics Page for Volumes
in NWADMIN*

In addition to Identification and Statistics, NWADMIN provides numerous other volume-related page buttons:

▸ Dates and Times—Displays values for the volume creation date and time, owner, last modified date, last archived date, and "user last archived by." The latter option offers valuable information for managing data backup (see Chapter 13).

▸ User Space Limits—Displays information regarding user space limits imposed on particular users (if any). This is an effective way of controlling "disk hogs."

▸ Trustees of the Root Directory—Displays security information concerning the trustees of the root directory, their effective rights, and the directory's inherited rights filter. You should be careful about who gets access rights to the root directory of *any* volume—especially SYS:.

▸ Attributes—Displays directory attributes for the root directory of the given volume. This is another security option (see Chapter 11).

▸ See Also—Displays who and what is related to the volume object. This is basically a manual information record for tracking special volume details.

NETADMIN

NETADMIN is the DOS-based version of NWADMIN for those of you who break out into hives every time you touch a mouse. It provides the same type of information as NWADMIN but in a slightly (or greatly) less user-friendly way. That means it's very hard to use.

To view volume information with NETADMIN, you have to find the volume first. This involves a labyrinth of tree-walking through three menu choices: Manage Objects, Object class, and View or edit properties of this object. Once you arrive at your destination, it looks something like Figure 10.14.

FIGURE 10.14

View or Edit Volume Menu in NETADMIN

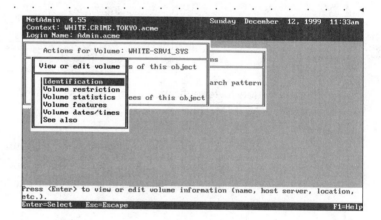

If you select the Identification option from this menu, a screen appears showing the same type of NDS information as the NWADMIN Identification page, including volume name, host server, NetWare version, host volume, and location. Once again, the really interesting data is in the Volume statistics screen (see Figure 10.15). This screen lists numerous statistics related to volume space, maximum and available directory entries, and file-compression space. As a matter of fact, it looks a little familiar—like the Statistics screen in FILER. It's exactly the same data, just a different DOS-based menu tool. Hmmm.

F I G U R E 10.15

*Volume Statistics
in NETADMIN*

```
NetAdmin  4.55                          Sunday  December  12, 1999  11:33am
Context: WHITE.CRIME.TOKYO.acme
Login Name: Admin.acme

                              Volume statistics

Total volume space in KB (1024 bytes):      1,016,128  100.00%
Active space used:                             318,976   31.39%
Deleted space not yet purgeable:                     0    0.00%
Space remaining on volume:                     697,152   68.61%

Maximum directory entries:                      17,408
Available directory entries:                     8,466   48.63%

Space used if not compressed:                  713,349
Total space compressed:                        370,543
Space saved by compressing data:               342,806   48.06%
Uncompressed space used:                       309,265


This is information pertaining to the physical volume.  These fields can't be
changed.  Press <Esc> when done.
Esc=Escape                                                          F1=Help
```

In addition to Identification and Statistics, NETADMIN provides a combination of options from both NWADMIN and FILER, including:

▶ Volume restrictions

▶ Volume features

▶ Volume dates/times

▶ See also

NLIST

As we learned earlier, NLIST is a special NetWare 4 NDS command line utility. It displays all related property information for any NDS object—including volumes. For our purposes, NLIST gives us access to:

▶ Object class

▶ Current context

▶ Volume name

▶ Host server name

> ▶ Physical volume name

> ▶ The number of Volume objects in the NDS tree

> ▶ Property values for Volume objects

NLIST can only be used to display information about NDS objects—it cannot be used to modify NDS information. Some of the most common commands used to display NDS volume information are included in Table 10.2. Check it out.

TABLE 10.2	COMMAND	RESULT
Partial List of NLIST Options	NLIST VOLUME	Lists information for all volumes in the current context
	NLIST VOLUME /D	Lists detailed information about a specific volume in the current context
	NLIST VOLUME /N	Lists the names of the volumes in your current context

Output from the NLIST VOLUME /D command is shown in Figure 10.16. Notice the detailed volume-based information you can view from the command line.

FIGURE 10.16

Results of the NLIST VOLUME /D Command

```
Object Class: Volume
Current context: WHITE.CRIME.TOKYO.acme
Volume: WHITE-SRV1_SYS
        Name: WHITE-SRV1_SYS
        Name: SYS
        Object Trustees (ACL):
                Subject: [Root]
                Property: Host Resource Name
                Property Rights: [ R    ]
        Object Trustees (ACL):
                Subject: [Root]
                Property: Host Server
                Property Rights: [ R    ]
        Host Resource Name: SYS
        Host Server: WHITE-SRV1
        Object Class: Volume
        Object Class: Resource
        Object Class: Top
        Revision: 1
--------------------------------------------------------------

One Volume object was found in this context.

One Volume object was found.
>>> Enter = More    C = Continuous    Esc = Cancel
```

NDIR

NDIR, as its name implies, is mostly a directory and file utility. It does, however, offer a few statistics for NetWare 4 volumes, namely:

▸ Volume space statistics

▸ Directory entry statistics

▸ Compression space statistics

Figure 10.17 shows an example of the type of information that can be displayed by typing:

```
NDIR /VOL
```

You'll notice that it lists a variety of volume information, including space used, space remaining, deleted space not yet purged, space available for use by you, maximum and available directory entries, as well as compression statistics such as space used by compressed files, space saved by compressed files, and uncompressed space used. It's amazing that all this information can be viewed from such a small utility!

Results of the NDIR /VOL Command

```
F:\USERS\MMARION>NDIR /VOL

Statistics for fixed volume WHITE-SRV1/SYS:
Space statistics are in KB (1024 bytes).

Total volume space:                      1,016,128   100.00%
Space used by 4,888 entries:               318,976    31.39%
Deleted space not yet purgeable:                 0     0.00%
                                         ----------
Space remaining on volume:                 697,152    68.61%
Space available to Admin.ACME:              697,152    68.61%

Maximum directory entries:                   17,408
Available directory entries:                  8,466    48.63%

Space used if files were not compressed:    713,349
Space used by compressed files:             370,543
                                         ----------
Space saved by compressing files:           342,806    48.06%

Uncompressed space used:                    -51,567

F:\USERS\MMARION>
```

There you go. That's everything you wanted to know about volume management but were afraid to ask! Now that you've gotten cozy with some of NetWare 4's finest file system tools, let's see what they can do with directories and files. Who knows, you might even meet some new tools along the way.

ZEN

"If professional wrestling didn't exist, could you come up with this idea? Could you envision the popularity of huge men in tiny bathing suits pretending to fight?"

Jerry Seinfeld

MANAGING NETWARE 4 DIRECTORIES

Volumes are important, but directories win the prize. These are the true organizational containers of the NetWare 4 file system. As we learned earlier, a logical directory design can save hours of security and file management. In this section, we will explore many of the same utilities as above, but from a totally different point of view:

- ▸ FILER

- ▸ NWADMIN

- ▸ NDIR

- ▸ NCOPY

- ▸ RENDIR

So let's get started.

FILER

FILER is NetWare 4's most comprehensive directory and file management tool. Earlier we learned about its volume savvy, but you ain't seen nothing yet. In its natural element, FILER can:

- ▸ Create, delete, and rename directories

- ▸ Copy and move entire subdirectory structures

- ▸ View or change directory information such as owner, directory creation date/time, directory attributes, trustees, inherited rights filter, and space limitations

- ▸ View your effective rights for directories

- ▸ Set up search and view filters (include and exclude options)

The first step is to select the default directory. If you look at the top of the screen, you'll notice that it lists the current path. To choose a different directory, choose the Select current directory option from the Available options menu, as shown in Figure 10.18. You can either modify the path manually or walk the tree by pressing Insert. If you walk the tree, don't forget to press Esc when you're done selecting directories. When the correct directory is selected, press Enter to return to the Available options menu.

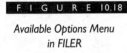

F I G U R E   10.18

Available Options Menu in FILER

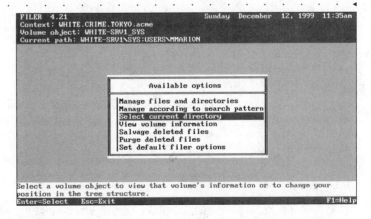

The next step is to determine if you want to use any search or view filters to limit the directories that are displayed. If so, select the Manage according to search pattern option from the Available options menu. As you can see in Figure 10.19, a screen appears with the directory include and exclude patterns. You can also specify Hidden and/or System directories. After you've made your selections, press F10 to return to the Available options menu.

F I G U R E 10.19

*Set the Search Pattern and
Filter Menu in FILER*

```
FILER  4.21                              Sunday  December  12, 1999  11:35am
Context: WHITE.CRIME.TOKYO.acme
Volume object: WHITE-SRV1_SYS
Current path: WHITE-SRV1\SYS:USERS\MMARION

          ┌──────────────────────────────────────────────┐
          │        Set the search pattern and filter       │
          │                                                │
          │   Pattern: *.*                                 │
          │                                                │
          │   Exclude directory patterns: ↓  <empty>      │
          │   Include directory patterns: ↓  *            │
          │                                                │
          │   Exclude file patterns: ↓  <empty>           │
          │   Include file patterns: ↓  *                 │
          │                                                │
          │   File search attributes: ↓  <empty>          │
          │   Directory search attributes: ↓  <empty>     │
          └──────────────────────────────────────────────┘

Type a pattern (for example: *.EXE) to search by, or press <Enter> to edit the
pattern.
Enter=Select    Esc=Escape    F10=Continue                         F1=Help
```

Now you're ready to go exploring—inside the selected directory. Select the Manage files and directories choice from the Available options menu. You'll notice that the subdirectories and files in the current directory appear as well as a double-dot (..), representing the parent directory, and a dot (.), representing the current directory.

You can do a number of different things with this screen. For instance:

▸ If you want to make another directory the current directory, you can walk the tree again.

▸ If you want to create a new subdirectory, press Insert and type in the name.

▸ If you want to delete a subdirectory, press Del. If you want to delete multiple directories at once, mark them all using F5 before pressing Del.

▸ If you want to rename a subdirectory, highlight it and press F3, then enter the new name.

To display information about this directory, highlight the period (.) and press F10. The Subdirectory options menu will be displayed. Press Enter to select the View/Set directory information option. A directory information screen will pop up, similar to the one in Figure 10.20. This screen lists information about the directory such as the owner, the creation date/time, the directory attributes, the inherited rights filter, the trustees of the directory, the directory space limitations, and your effective rights for this directory.

If you have the appropriate rights, you can change any parameter listed, except for effective rights, which are a calculation completed by NetWare 4 (as you'll see in painstaking detail in the Chapter 11). Go ahead and press Esc twice to return to the Directory contents screen.

If you highlight a subdirectory and press F10, a Subdirectory options screen will be displayed, as shown in Figure 10.21. Two of the most interesting options allow you to move or copy an entire branch of the tree at one time. Cool.

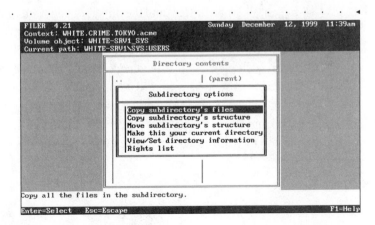

That does it for FILER; now let's see what NWADMIN can do for NetWare 4 directories.

QUIZ

Here's another numbers game:

Find the product of (x–a)(x–b)(x–c)...(x–z), where *x* is any number between 22 and 42.

(Q10-2)

NWADMIN

NWADMIN is primarily an NDS-management tool; however, it offers a few directory-related functions, such as:

- ▸ Create, delete, and rename directories

- ▸ Copy and move entire subdirectory structures

- ▸ View or change directory information such as owner, attributes, trustees, inherited rights filter, or space limitations

- ▸ Set up search and view filters (include and exclude options)

First of all, walk the tree until the directory you want to work with is in view. Click on the directory, then click on the Object menu. If you look at the options in the Object menu, you'll notice you can perform the following file management tasks: create a directory; delete a directory; rename, copy, and/or move a directory. You can also select the Details option to view information about your directory.

If you select Details, the Identification page button is activated by default. As you can see in Figure 10.22, this page includes two important pieces of information: the directory name and the name spaces available on the volume.

F I G U R E 10.22

*Identification Page for
Directories in NWADMIN*

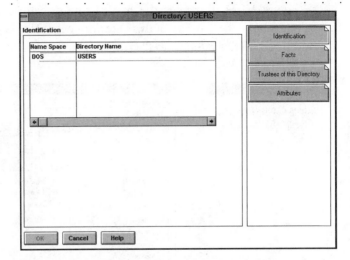

If you select the Facts page button, as shown in Figure 10.23, another screen appears
with more detailed directory information, including the owner, the directory creation
date/time, the last modified date/time, the last archived date/time, and the archiver. It
also lists the volume space available on this directory and the space limitations (if any).

F I G U R E 10.23

Facts Page in NWADMIN

Figure 10.24 illustrates the first of two directory-specific security options in NWADMIN—the Trustees of this Directory page. This page allows you to list trustees and their effective rights as well as the inherited rights filter for this directory.

*Trustees of this Directory
Page in NWADMIN*

The second NWADMIN file system security option deals with Attributes (see Figure 10.25). Don't worry, you'll get plenty of chances to work with security in Chapter 11.

*Attributes Page in
NWADMIN*

That's enough of NWADMIN for now. As you can see, it augments the FILER functions in a prettier Windows-based user interface. Now, for something completely different. Let's go back to the command line—starting with the forest moon of NDIR.

NDIR

NDIR gives us limited functionality at the volume level—because it's not a volume utility; it's a directory/file utility. NDIR opens a new world of directory information to you, including:

▶ Owner, creation date, attributes, and archive information

▶ Subdirectories/files

▶ Inherited rights filter

▶ Effective rights

In addition, directory information can be sorted according to almost any criteria (owner, creation date, attributes, and so on). If you don't specify any formatting options, NDIR lists the following information about each directory: the directory name, inherited rights filter, your effective rights, the creation date/time, and the owner.

By default, NDIR lists all subdirectories and files in the specified directory (unless otherwise noted). You can display directory information selectively by using wildcards, and/or display options. For example, use /C to scroll continuously or /SUB to include subdirectories and their files. You can also list directories that contain (or do not contain) a specific directory attribute.

The beauty of NDIR is its logic searching capabilities. NDIR also supports date options such as AFT (after), BEF (before), and EQ (equals); size options such as LE (less than), EQ (equal to), and GR (greater than); and sorting options such as /REV SORT (reverse order), /SORT CR (creation date), /SORT OW (owner), and /UN (unsorted).

Some of the more common NDIR directory commands are listed in Table 10.3.

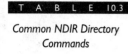
T A B L E 10.3	COMMAND	RESULT
Common NDIR Directory Commands	NDIR	Displays subdirectories and files in the current directory
	NDIR /DO	Displays directories only
	NDIR /DO /SUB	Displays directories and subdirectories only
	NDIR /SPA	Displays space limitations for this directory
	NDIR /DO /C	Displays directories only—scrolls continuously when displaying information
	NDIR /DO CR AFT 10/01/99	Displays directories only—those created after 10/01/99
	NDIR /DO /REV SORT CR	Displays directories only—sorts by directory creation date, with newest listed first

Figure 10.26 shows an example of output from the NDIR /DO command. Use it or lose it.

F I G U R E 10.26

The NDIR /DO Command

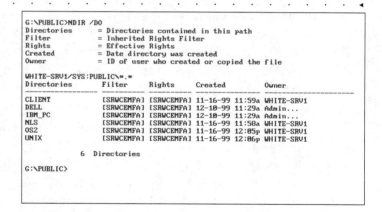

```
G:\PUBLIC>NDIR /DO
Directories    = Directories contained in this path
Filter         = Inherited Rights Filter
Rights         = Effective Rights
Created        = Date directory was created
Owner          = ID of user who created or copied the file

WHITE-SRV1/SYS:PUBLIC\*.*
Directories      Filter       Rights       Created          Owner
-----------------------------------------------------------------------------
CLIENT           [SRWCEMFA]   [SRWCEMFA]   11-16-99 11:59a  WHITE-SRV1
DELL             [SRWCEMFA]   [SRWCEMFA]   12-10-99 11:29a  Admin...
IBM_PC           [SRWCEMFA]   [SRWCEMFA]   12-10-99 11:29a  Admin...
NLS              [SRWCEMFA]   [SRWCEMFA]   11-16-99 11:58a  WHITE-SRV1
OS2              [SRWCEMFA]   [SRWCEMFA]   11-16-99 12:05p  WHITE-SRV1
UNIX             [SRWCEMFA]   [SRWCEMFA]   11-16-99 12:06p  WHITE-SRV1

            6  Directories

G:\PUBLIC>
```

NCOPY

NCOPY is the NetWare version of COPY. Can you guess what it does? Very good—it copies stuff. NCOPY is similar in function to the DOS XCOPY command and allows the use of the same wildcards. Benefits of using NCOPY include:

▸ Directory/file attributes and name space information are automatically preserved.

▸ Read-after-write verification feature is ON by default. (You must use the /V switch to use verification if you're copying files on local drives.)

▸ NetWare volume names can be specified in a path.

TIP

Because NCOPY is a NetWare utility, it accesses the NetWare file allocation table (FAT) and directory entry table (DET) more efficiently than the DOS COPY or XCOPY commands. It is faster than COPY and XCOPY if the files are being copied from one directory to another on the server, because it works within server RAM rather than copying the directories and/or files to and from workstation RAM. It is also a safer method because it uses the NetWare 4 read-after-write verification fault tolerance feature by default.

Some of the more common NCOPY commands are listed in Table 10.4.

COMMAND	RESULT
NCOPY G:REPORTS C:REPORTS	Copies the REPORTS directory from the G: drive on the server to the default directory on your workstation C: drive
NCOPY F:DATA C:DATA /S	Copies the DATA directory from the F: drive to the C: drive, including subdirectories
NCOPY G:1995 ..\ARCHIVE /S /E	Copies the 1995 directory on the G: drive (as well as its subdirectories and their files, including empty subdirectories) to an ARCHIVE directory under the current directory's parent directory
NCOPY .TEMP /V	Copies the current directory to the TEMP directory and verifies that the procedure was accurate (only needed if copying files on a local drive)

T A B L E 10.4

Common NCOPY Commands

RENDIR

RENDIR allows you to rename directories—what a surprise. Wildcards can be used, as well as a period (.) to represent the current directory or a colon followed by a forward slash (:/) to represent the default drive and volume. Check out Table 10.5 for some examples of the more common RENDIR commands in Netware 4.

TABLE 10.5	COMMAND	RESULT
Common RENDIR Commands	RENDIR REPORT REPORTS	Renames the directory called REPORT under the current directory to REPORTS
	RENDIR U:USER USERS	Renames the directory on Drive U: called USER to USERS
	RENDIR S: SAMPLES	Renames the directory to which drive S: is mapped as SAMPLES
	RENDIR . DATA	Renames the current directory to DATA
	RENDIR :/QTR1 95QTR1	Renames the directory called QTR1 on the current drive and volume to 95QTR1
	RENDIR /?	Displays on-line help for the RENDIR command

TIP

If you rename a directory, don't forget to modify any configuration files that reference it—like login scripts.

That completes our discussion of directory management. Wasn't that fun? There's only one more file system component left—and we've saved the best for last. Hold on to your hats; we're entering the file management zone.

ZEN

Sick-building syndrome—A condition found in humans, caused by a substance that pollutes the environment becoming trapped in a building, especially as a result of poor design or hazardous materials being used in construction. How are you feeling? Need some fresh air?

MANAGING NETWARE 4 FILES

Earlier, I said that directories win the prize—I lied. Files are really the most important components. After all, what's the ultimate goal of the NetWare 4 file system? File sharing. What do users ask for when they log in to the Cloud? Files. Why are we here?

Anyway, file management looks a little like directory management, and it uses the same tools. But that's where the similarities end. Directories are for organization; files are for productivity. And what's more important? Here's a list of the tools we'll explore in this section:

- ▸ FILER

- ▸ NWADMIN

- ▸ NDIR

- ▸ NCOPY

Don't just sit there; get moving. There are only a few utilities left. Ready, set, go.

FILER

Let's visit our old friend FILER just one last time. Now we're focusing on real file management, including:

- ▸ Creating, deleting, renaming, copying, and moving files

- ▸ Managing files attributes

- ▸ Setting up search and view filters (include and exclude options)

- ▸ Salvaging and purging deleted files

As before, the first FILER step is to select the default directory. Refer to the directory management section for more details. Once you're there, you can alter the include and exclude filters for specific files or even check out Hidden and/or System documents. After you've made your selections, you can press F10 to return to the Available options menu.

In addition to the search/view filters, FILER presents Copy and Delete options when working with files. First, select the Set default filer options choice from the Available options menu. A Filer settings screen will appear, as shown in Figure 10.27. You can set a number of defaults for copying and deleting files, including confirmations and messaging help. When all of file management settings are correct, press Esc to return to the Available options menu.

Now you're ready to display your files. Select the Manage files and directories option from the Available options menu. You'll notice a plethora of subdirectories and files in the current directory, as well as a double-dot (..) for the parent directory and a dot (.) for the current directory. Now, you're ready to get busy:

▶ Walk the tree to select another directory as the current directory.

▶ Delete a file by highlighting it and pressing Del. If you want to delete multiple files at once, mark them all with the F5 key before pressing Del.

▶ Rename a file by highlighting it and pressing F3.

Next, select a particular file to work with by highlighting it and pressing F10. The File options menu appears. This menu gives you the option of copying, viewing, or moving the file; displaying trustees of the file; or viewing/modifying file information. If you select the View/Set file information option from the File options menu, a file information screen pops up similar to the one in Figure 10.28. This screen lists information about the file such as the owner; access, archive, creation, and modification dates; file attributes; the inherited rights filter; the trustees of the file; the owning name space; the file size and EA size; as well as your effective rights.

If you have appropriate rights, you can change most of the parameters listed, except for effective rights, owning name space, file size, and EA size. Press Esc three times to return to the Available options menu.

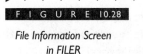

F I G U R E 10.28

File Information Screen in FILER

There are two more choices in the Available options menu that relate to files, namely Salvage deleted files and Purge deleted files. Salvage allows you to recover deleted files that have not yet been purged. Purge is the process of permanently removing deleted files from the system.

If you choose Salvage Deleted Files, you will be given three options:

- ▸ Salvage files from an existing directory

- ▸ Salvage files from DELETED.SAV (because the parent directory has been deleted)

- ▸ Set salvage options (that is, indicate whether to sort the list by filename, file size, deletion date, or deletor)

If you choose Purge Deleted files from the Available options menu, you can specify the filename pattern to be used when selecting purged files. It will also allow you to choose whether to purge files in the current subdirectory only or to purge the files in the entire subdirectory tree structure. Be very careful when purging files: You can never recover these files.

That completes our discussion of FILER all together. It's been a wonderous journey, and I hope you have learned to appreciate how helpful it can be for volume, directory, and file management. Now, let's visit NWADMIN one last time.

QUIZ

I like these number brainiacs so much, I thought I'd try another one:

What is the five-digit number in which the first digit is two-thirds of the second, the third is one-third of the second, the fourth is four times the last, and the last is one-third of the first. The digits total 28.

(Q10-3)

NWADMIN

NWADMIN is another important file management tool. It allows us to perform any of the following functions from a friendly Windows-based interface:

- ▸ Create, delete, and rename files

- ▸ Copy and move files

- ▸ View or change file information such as owner, attributes, trustees, and inherited rights filter

- ▸ Set up search and view filters (include and exclude options)

- ▸ Salvage and purge deleted files

First of all, walk the tree until the desired file is in view. Click on the file, then click on the Object menu. If you look at the options in the Object menu, you'll notice file management options that allow you to delete the file, rename it, copy and move it. The same options can be accessed from the Details menu as well.

If you select the Facts page button, a screen appears with the file's owner, size, file creation date/time, last modified date/time, last archived date/time, and archiver. If you have the appropriate rights, you can modify all of these parameters except for the size and creation date.

If you select the Trustees of this File page button, you will be allowed to view, add, or modify trustees and display their effective rights as well as view or change the inherited rights filter for the file. Similarly, if you select the Attributes page button, you can view the attributes that have been set for this file, and you can change them if you have the appropriate access rights (see Chapter 11).

In addition to the usual file management stuff, NWADMIN allows you to salvage or purge deleted files. Interestingly, both of these functions are handled by the same menu option: Choose Salvage from the Tools menu (see Figure 10.29).

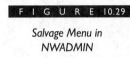

FIGURE 10.29

Salvage Menu in NWADMIN

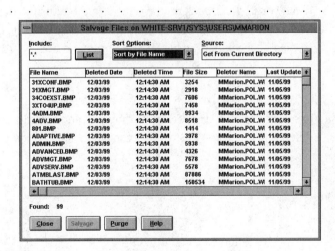

You can set three sets of options from the Salvage menu:

- ► Include pattern using wildcards or filenames

- ► Sort options (deletion date, deletor, filename, file size, or file type)

- ► Source (current directory or deleted directories)

When all of the options are set correctly, click on the List button to list the files indicated. As with other MS Windows utilities, to select the desired files, you can:

- Select a single file by clicking on it.

- Select sequentially listed files by clicking on the first file, holding down the Shift key, then clicking on the last file in the range.

- Select nonsequentially listed files by holding down the Ctrl key while selecting files.

When you have selected all of the desired files, you can click on either the Salvage or Purge button at the bottom of the screen to salvage or purge the selected file(s). Finally, when you're done, click on the OK button to return to the NWADMIN browse screen.

From there you can bid the utility one last fond farewell. It's time to leave this Windows scene and check out the NetWare 4 command line. NDIR awaits!

NDIR

As we discussed earlier, NDIR is a very versatile command line utility that allows you to selectively list a large variety of directory and file information, sorted by a number of different parameters. From a file management standpoint, NDIR displays:

- Filename

- Owner

- Creation date and time

- Last modified date and time

- Size

- File attributes

- Access rights

- Macintosh files

▸ Version information for application files

▸ Extended details

If you don't specify any formatting options, NDIR lists the following information about each file: the filename, size, last update (modified) date, and owner. You can customize the output by specifying one of the following formatting options: /COMP (compression statistics), /DA (Dates), /D (detail), /L (long names), /M (Macintosh), and /R (rights).

By default, NDIR lists all subdirectories and files in the current directory, unless otherwise noted. You can selectively list the information by specifying a particular file, using wildcards, or by indicating a display option such as /C (scroll continuously), /FI (list every occurrence within your current directory and path), /FO (list files only), /SUB (include subdirectories and their files). You can also list files that contain (or do not contain) a specific file attribute.

NDIR also lets you restrict files by specifying date options such as AFT (after), BEF (before), and EQ (equals); size options such as LE (less than), EQ (equal to), and GR (greater than); and NOT (all except).

NDIR lists files in alphabetical order by default. You can change the order files are sorted in by specifying one of the following options: /REV SORT (reverse order), /SORT AC (access date), /SORT AR (archive date), /SORT CR (creation date), /SORT UP (update date), /SORT OW (owner), /SORT SI (size), or /SORT UN (unsorted).

THE BRAIN

For further information on the options available with the NDIR command, refer to the NDIR section of the *Novell NetWare 4 Utilities* manual.

Get to really know the NDIR command by checking out Table 10.6.

COMMAND	RESULT
NDIR /FO	Displays files only—those in the current directory
NDIR /FO /C	Displays files only—scrolls continuously
NDIR /FO /SUB	Displays files only—those in the current directory and its subdirectories
NDIR /FO /REV SORT SI	Displays files only—sorts by size, starting with the largest file
NDIR /FO /SORT UP	Displays files only—sorts by last modified date
NDIR /FO /SORT OW	Displays files only—sorts by owner
NDIR /FO OW EQ DAVID	Displays files only—where the owner is David
NDIR R*.*/FO	Displays files only—those that begin with the letter R
NDIR *.BAT /FO	Displays files only—those in the current directory with an extension of .BAT
NDIR /FO /AC BEF 06-01-99	Displays files only—those not accessed since 06/01/99
NDIR \WHOAMI.EXE /SUB /FO	Displays files only—lists all occurrences of the WHOAMI.EXE file, starting the search at the root of the volume
NDIR Z:*.EXE /VER	Displays the version number for those files on the Z: drive with an .EXE extension
NDIR *.* /R /FO	Displays files only—lists your effective rights for each file
NDIR Z:NWADMIN.EXE /D	Displays detailed file information for the Z:NWADMIN file
NDIR SYS:SHARED*.* /RO	Displays those files in the SYS:SHARED directory that have the Read Only attribute set
NDIR *.* /FO /NOT RO	Displays files only—those that do not have the Read Only attribute set
NDIR F:*.* /FO /REV SORT AC	Displays files only—sorts by access date, listing the file with the most recent access date first
NDIR /FO DA	Displays files only—lists access, archive, creation, and update date

T A B L E 10.6

Common NDIR Commands

Output from the NDIR /FO command is shown in Figure 10.30. And that does it for NDIR. Now, let's explore the final NetWare file management tool—NCOPY.

```
F:\ETC>NDIR /FO
Files              = Files contained in this path
Size               = Number of bytes in the file
Last Update        = Date file was last updated
Owner              = ID of user who created or copied the file

WHITE-SRV1/SYS:ETC\*.*
Files                     Size Last Update      Owner
-------------------       ---- --------------   ---------------
ATTYPES.CFG                237  9-23-93  6:56p  WHITE-SRV1
BUILTINS.CFG             9,951  8-26-94 10:19a  WHITE-SRV1
GATEWAYS                   500  9-24-93  1:06p  WHITE-SRV1
HOSTS                      441  9-11-92  2:31p  WHITE-SRV1
NETWORKS                   288  9-11-92  2:31p  WHITE-SRV1
PROTOCOL                   370  9-11-92  2:31p  WHITE-SRV1
SERVICES                 1,570  9-11-92  2:31p  WHITE-SRV1
TRAPTARG.CFG             1,697  3-17-93  8:50a  WHITE-SRV1


      15,054  bytes (when the files are not compressed)
       8,192  bytes (disk space used by compressed and non-compressed files)
           8  Files

F:\ETC>
```

NCOPY

NCOPY can be used to copy files as well as directories. What a surprise. As we discussed earlier, NCOPY is similar in function to the DOS XCOPY command, except that directory attributes and name space information are automatically preserved. Refer to Table 10.7 for an exploration of NCOPY from a file management point of view.

THE BRAIN

For further information on the options available with the NCOPY command, refer to the NCOPY section of the *Novell NetWare 4 Utilities* manual.

T A B L E 10.7

Common NCOPY Commands

COMMAND	RESULT
NCOPY JULY.RPT F:	Copies a file in the default directory called JULY.RPT to the F: drive
NCOPY F:PHONE.NUM C:	Copies the PHONE.NUM file from the F: drive to the C: drive
NCOPY F:*.RPT A: /A	Copies files with a *.RPT extension that have the archive bit set (and thus, need to be backed up) from F: to A:
NCOPY DOC1.WP TEMP1.* /C	Copies the DOC1.WP file and renames the new version TEMP1.WP, without preserving extended attributes and name space information
NCOPY F:R*. G: /F	Copies files beginning with the letter R: from the F: drive to the G: drive, forcing the copying of sparse files
NCOPY *.DOC A: /I	Copies files with a .DOC extension from the current directory to the A: drive and notifies you when extended attributes or name space information cannot be copied because the target volume doesn't support these features
NCOPY F:*.DOC A: /M	Copies files with the *.DOC extension that have the archive bit set (and thus need to be backed up) from F: to A:, then turns off the archive bit of the source files (This allows NCOPY to be used for backup purposes.)
NCOPY C:FRED.LST C:TOM.LST /V	Copies FRED.LST to TOM.LST on the C: drive using the verify option
NCOPY /?	Displays online help for the NCOPY utility

Well, there you have it—the wonderful world of NetWare 4 file system management. Aren't you a lucky camper? Now you are an expert in gardening NDS and non-NDS trees. In this section, we focused on the three main components of the NetWare 4 file system—volumes, directories, and files. We discovered a variety of tools and learned how they help us manage each of these components. The important thing is to focus on the file system, not the tool—a unique, but effective approach.

I guess we're done then, huh? Wrong! We haven't journeyed into the mysterious land of drive mapping yet. I'm sure you'd rather not go there, but buck up soldier, you're a CNE—you can handle it. But can your users?

ZEN

"Fear of success is one of the newest fears that I've heard about lately. I think it's definitely a sign that we're running out of fears. A person suffering from fear of success is scraping the bottom of the fear barrel."

Jerry Seinfeld

Drive Mapping

Drive mapping is one of the great mysteries of life. Forget about the pyramids, alien cornfields, or quarks—drive mapping has them all beat.

It doesn't have to be this way. As a matter of fact, drive mapping is really pretty simple. The problem is that it requires you to unlearn the fundamentals of DOS. Let me explain. In the DOS world, drive letters point to *physical* devices. In Figure 10.31, the A: and B: letters point to floppy drives, C: and D: point to hard drives, and the E: drive is a CD-ROM. Pretty simple, huh? Well, it works fine on workstations, because they typically use multiple storage devices.

F I G U R E 10.31

*Drive Mapping to Physical
Local Devices*

So how does this theory apply to NetWare drives? If we extrapolate from the local theory, we would use 21 different drive letters (F–Z) to point to 21 physical devices— not very likely. So Novell returned to the proverbial drawing board and came up with a slightly different approach. Just different enough to confuse you, me, CNEs, and especially users. Here's how it works:

NetWare 4 drive letters point to logical directories instead of physical drives.

This is also pretty simple; a little too simple (see Figure 10.32). As a matter of fact, users treat the NetWare drives just like local drives—*mistake*. The first time they use the CD command, all heck breaks loose. Let me tell you a little story—ironically, about Little John.

F I G U R E 10.32

*Drive Mapping to Logical
Network Directories*

SYS:

F:\LOGIN

USERS   SHARED   APPS   MAIL   PUBLIC   SYSTEM   LOGIN

G:\SHARED\FIN

WHITE   POL   CYBER   FIN

DELL   IBM-PC

NLS

RHOOD   FRTUCK   LJOHN   MMARION   WP70   SS30   DB50   MSDOS   NOVDOS

U:\USERS\LJOHN

V6.22   V3.30   V5.00

One seemingly innocent summer day in August, Little John was working on his financial files in the SYS:SHARED\FIN directory. For his convenience, you have mapped this directory to drive letter G: (see Figure 10.32). He suddenly realizes that his report templates are at home, that is, SYS:USERS\LJOHN (drive map U:). Any other time he would simply type U: and press Enter to get home, but not today. Today he confuses his network and local drives. Today is a bad day for Little John.

Instead of using the existing U: drive mapping, Little John types CD\USERS\LJOHN from the G: drive. This would work fine in the DOS world, but it's unforgivable in the NetWare world. What has he done? Correct. Little John has inadvertently re-mapped his G: drive to SYS:USERS\LJOHN. Remember, NetWare drive letters are logical pointers to NetWare directories, not physical devices. As you can see in Figure 10.33, Little John now has two letters mapped to his home directory. Of course, he doesn't realize this. Let's return to the story.

FIGURE 10.33

Re-mapping Drives with the CD Command

Oblivious to the changes in his world, Little John searches the G:\USERS\LJOHN directory for his report templates. He can't find them. "Ah," he thinks. "They're in my home directory. That's drive U:." He quickly switches over to U:\USERS\LJOHN, unaware that this is the same directory. Remember, he thinks the G: and U: drives are different hard disks. He searches in vain and doesn't find the report templates on the U: drive either—he wouldn't. This is where it gets interesting.

Disgruntled, Little John decides to return to his financial directory and continue work without the missing templates. Naturally, he types G: and presses Enter to return to the G:\SHARED\FIN directory—it doesn't work. "That's odd," he thinks. "It's always worked before." Much to his dismay, all of the financial files have been removed from the G: drive and replaced by a duplicate copy of his home files. At least that's how it appears to Little John. Remember, he thinks the G: and U: drives are different hard disks. In actuality, Little John has re-mapped the G: drive to G:\USERS\LJOHN with the CD command. Oops.

In a panic, Little John deletes the duplicate copy of his home files—hoping it will clear enough space for his financial files to return. Of course, he has inadvertently deleted *all* his home files, because they are *not* duplicates. It's simply a duplicate drive mapping. He comes rumbling down the hall to your office, screaming at the top of his lungs, "Somebody has deleted my financial files!" Incidentally, Little John is not a little man. After picking yourself off the floor, you proceed to explain to him that the NetWare CD command doesn't change directories as it does in DOS. Instead, it *cancels data*. Of course this is a lie, but it stops him from using the CD command in the future. Fortunately, you're a CNE and you can save the day! Use SALVAGE to undelete his files, and MAP to return G: back to G:\SHARED\FIN where it belongs. Just another day in the life of a NetWare 4 CNE.

ZEN

"I once had a leather jacket that got ruined in the rain. Now why does moisture ruin leather? Aren't cows outside a lot of the time?"

Jerry Seinfeld

This story has been brought to you by NetWare 4 and your local neighborhood DMV (Drive Mapping Vehicle). It's a great example of what can happen when users get local and network drive mappings confused. For this reason, you have a choice to make: Do you perpetuate the myth or tell your users the truth? If you perpetuate the myth that NetWare drives point to physical disks, you'll need to use the MAP ROOT command to make them appear as such. This will also nullify the effects of CD. If you decide to tell your users the truth, consider that knowledge is power. Also consider that they may not want to know the truth. Either way, NetWare 4 provides you with three different approaches to drive mapping:

▸ Network Drive Mapping

▸ Search Drive Mapping

© Directory Map Objects

Network drives use a single letter to point to logical directory paths. The above example used network drives. Search drives, on the other hand, provide additional functionality by building a search list for network applications. Finally, Directory Map objects are centralized NDS resources that point to logical directory paths. They help ease the transition from one application version to another. Let's take a closer look.

NETWORK   DRIVE   MAPPINGS

Network drive map-ings have a singular pur-ose—convenience. They provide simple directory *navigat*ion for accessing data files. As we learned earlier, NetWare 4 supports 21 network drives by default: F–Z. *In* Figure 10.32, the F: drive points to SYS:LOGIN and the U: drive points to SYS:USERS\LJOHN. These mappings make it easy for users to find their stuff—as long as they don't use the dreaded CD command. Little John simply types U: followed by Enter to get home to U:\USERS\LJOHN. Without drive mappings, movement t**HROUGHOUT THE DIRECTORY** tree would be cumbersome and time consuming. It would involve long path names and confusing directory searches. Yuck!

TIP

The availability of network drives is dictated by the NetWare DOS Requester configuration at the workstation. By default, the VLMs specify F: as the first network drive. You can change this by removing the FIRST NETWORK DRIVE = F statement from NET.CFG. As a matter of fact, you can use 26 network drive letters by overwriting all existing local drives. Cool!

Network drive mappings are user-specific, temporary environment variables. Each user has a different set of drive mappings within his or her workstation RAM. These mappings are **CREated each time the user logs in. When the user logs out or turns off the machine, these mappings are lost. For this reason, you'll want to automate the creation of drive mappings in System and Profile login scripts (see Chapter 12).**

Network drive mappings are created using the MAP command. We'll explore this command in depth later in this chapter. For now, consider creating any or all of the following drive mappings for your users:

▸ U:—each user's home directory (for example, SYS:USERS\LJOHN)

▸ F:—SYS:LOGIN

▸ G:—group-specific data directories (for example, SYS:SHARED\FINAN)

▸ H:—global shared directory (for example, SYS:SHARED)

Now let's expand our understanding of NetWare 4 drive mapping with search drives. They help us build an internal search list for network applications.

SEARCH DRIVE MAPPINGS

Search drive mappings extend one step beyond network mappings by helping users search for network applications. When a user executes an application, NetWare searches two places for the program file:

1 • The current directory.

2 • The internal NetWare search list. Search drive mappings build the internal search list. They are the NetWare equivalent of local PATH statements.

The beauty of the NetWare search list is that it allows you to prioritize application directories. NetWare searches for programs in the order in which they are listed. The list can be a combination of local and network directories. For example, the following search list would find Windows on the local drive first; otherwise, it would use the network version in SYS:APPS\WINDOWS:

```
S1:=SYS:PUBLIC
S2:=SYS:PUBLIC\IBM_PC\MSDOS\V6.22
S3:=C:\WINDOWS
S4:=SYS:APPS\WINDOWS
S5:=SYS:APPS\SS30
```

Because search drive mappings are primarily used to build search lists, you should be more concerned with the order of the list than with the letter assigned to each directory. As you can see from the above list, NetWare assigns search drive mappings in search order—and each is preceded by the letter S. As a matter of convenience, NetWare automatically assigns a drive letter to each search directory—in reverse order (to avoid using network drive letters). For example, the first search drive (S1:) inherits the letter Z:, the second mapping (S2:) gets the letter Y:, and so on (see Figure 10.34). This allows you to navigate through search directories if necessary, although I don't recommend it. You are limited to a total of 16 search drives that inherit network drive letters. That is, you can have more than 16 search drives, but the extra ones will have to point to already-existing drive letters—such as C:.

Building a NetWare 4
Search List

SYS:

S1:=SYS:PUBLIC
Z:

USERS   SHARED   APPS   MAIL   (PUBLIC)   SYSTEM   LOGIN

WHITE POL CYBER FIN

DELL   IBM_PC   NLS

RHOOD   FRTUCK   LJOHN   MMARION   WP70 (SS30) DB50   MSDOS NOVDOS

V6.22   V3.30 V5.00

S5:=SYS:APPS\SS30
W:

S2:=SYS:PUBLIC\IBM_PC\MSDOS\V6.22
Y:

TIP

If a search drive encounters an existing network letter, the drive skips the letter and inherits the next one. For this reason, you should always assign network drive mappings first.

Because the NetWare search list and DOS PATH statements accomplish the same thing, there's a little conflict of interest. As a matter of fact, the NetWare search list systematically eliminates directories in the DOS path. To avoid this problem, consider incorporating your DOS path into the NetWare search list. This is accomplished using the MAP INSERT command (see Drive Mapping section).

That completes our discussion of network and search drive mappings. Refer to Table 10.8 for a summary of how they work.

T A B L E   10.8

*Comparing Network and
Search Drive Mappings*

FUNCTION	NETWORK DRIVE MAPPING	SEARCH DRIVE MAPPING
Purpose	movement	searching
Assignment Method	as the letter	in search order
Letter Assignment	by you	by NetWare
First Letter	F:	Z:
Directory Types	Data	Applications

Now, let's take a moment to explore Directory Map objects before we dive into the MAP command.

DIRECTORY MAP OBJECTS

In earlier chapters, we learned about a special NDS leaf object that helped us deal with drive mapping in the NetWare 4 file system—the Directory Map object. This special-purpose object allows us to map to a central logical resource instead of to the physical directory itself, mainly because physical directories change and logical objects don't have to.

This level of independence is very useful. Let's say, for example, that you have a central application server in the TOKYO container that everybody points to. On the server is an older copy of WordPerfect (WP5). You have two options for adding this application to your internal search lists:

1 • Search Drive Mapping—Use a traditional search drive mapping in each container's login script (five of them). This mapping points to the physical directory itself—TOKYO-SRV1\SYS:APPS\WP5.

2 • Directory Map Object—Create a central Directory Map object in TOKYO called WPAPP. Then, each of the five search drive MAP commands can point to the logical object instead of the physical APPS\WP directory. Finally, here the WPAPP object points to the physical directory as TOKYO-SRV1\SYS:APPS\WP5.

Both of these scenarios accomplish the same thing: They create a search drive mapping to WordPerfect 5 for all users in the Tokyo location. But, once you upgrade WordPerfect, you'll find the second option is much more attractive. In the first scenario, you'll need to change five different search drive statements in five distributed login scripts on five different servers. This is a lot of work!

In the second scenario, however, you'll only need to change the one Directory Map object reference, and all the other MAP statements automatically point to the right place. Amazing! In the next section, we'll explore the MAP command and learn how it can be used to reference Directory Map objects.

ZEN

"The movie ad I don't get is this one: 'If you see only one movie this year....'
Why go at all? You're not going to enjoy it—there's too much pressure. You're
sitting there, 'Alright, this is it for 51 more weekends, this better be good!'"

Jerry Seinfeld

USING THE MAP COMMAND

So, now that you know everything there is to know about network, search, and NDS drive mappings, the next logical question is, How? It's simple—the MAP command. The NetWare 4 MAP command allows you to:

- ► View drive mappings

- ► Create or modify network or search drive mappings

- ► Point to Directory Map objects

- ► Map drives to a fake root—to fool users or install special applications

- ► Change mappings from one type to another

- ► Integrate the network and local search lists

- ► All sorts of other stuff

As I'm sure you've probably guessed, the MAP command is the heart and soul of NetWare 4 drive mapping. Now, let's take a closer look at some fun and exciting MAP commands—starting with plain, old MAP. Also, there's a MAP summary table at the end of this section for your review. Ready, set, MAP!

MAP

You can use the MAP command without any options to display a list of your current drive mappings. As you can see in Figure 10.35, the local drives (A: through E:) are listed first, followed by the network drives, and finally, the search drives. Also, note the cool dashes in the middle. They separate the network drives from the search drives.

F I G U R E 10.35

The Plain Old MAP
Command

```
U:\USERS\MMARION>MAP

Drives A,B,C,D,E map to a local disk.
Drive F: = WHITE-SRV1_SYS.WHITE.CRIME.TOKYO: \LOGIN
Drive G: = WHITE-SRV1_SYS.WHITE.CRIME.TOKYO: \SHARED\FIN
Drive U: = WHITE-SRV1_SYS.WHITE.CRIME.TOKYO: \USERS\MMARION
------   Search Drives   ------
S1: = Z:. [WHITE-SRV1_SYS.WHITE.CRIME.TOKYO: \PUBLIC]
S2: = Y:. [WHITE-SRV1_SYS.WHITE.CRIME.TOKYO: \PUBLIC\IBM_PC\MSDOS\V6.22]
S3: = C:\WINDOWS
S4: = X:. [WHITE-SRV1_SYS.WHITE.CRIME.TOKYO: \APPS\WINDOWS]
S5: = W:. [WHITE-SRV1_SYS.WHITE.CRIME.TOKYO: \APPS\SS30]

U:\USERS\MMARION>
```

TIP

NetWare 4 does not track information on local drive assignments. Even though a map list will show that drives A: through E: are assigned to local drives, that doesn't necessarily mean they point to real devices. If you really want to mess with your users, map network drives to local devices. Or, even better, map local drives to network directories.

MAP G:=WHITE-SRV1\SYS:SHARED\FINAN

You can use the MAP command followed by a drive letter (A: through Z:) to create network drive mappings. In this case, the G: drive is assigned to the SYS:SHARED\FIN directory on the WHITE-SRV1 file server.

TIP

We also could have used the relative distinguished name or distinguished name for the volume instead of using the physical volume name. For instance, we could have typed :

```
MAP G:=WHITE-SRV1_SYS:SHARED\FIN
```

or

```
MAP G:=.WHITE-SRV1_SYS.WHITE.CRIME.TOKYO.ACME:SHARED\FIN
```

If the G: drive already exists, it will replace the existing assignment without displaying a warning. If you attempt to re-map a local drive (that is, Drive A: through Drive E:), however, you will receive a warning that the drive is currently assigned to a local device. NetWare 4 is polite and asks you if you want to assign it to a network drive anyway.

MAP NP E:=SYS:MAIL

Using the NP parameter allows you to overwrite local or search drives without being prompted. It must be listed first or second. In this example, the E: drive would be re-mapped without the usual warning:

```
Warning: You are attempting to re-map a local drive.
```

MAP S3:=SYS:APPS\WP70

You can use the MAP SEARCH command followed by a search drive number (S1: through S16:) to map a directory to a specific search drive. The number in the search drive defines the pointer's place in the search list (that is, its priority).

TIP

Search drive mappings share the same environment space as the DOS path. As a result, if you assign a NetWare search drive number using the MAP SEARCH command, it will overwrite the corresponding pointer in the DOS path. (For instance, if you use the MAP S1: command, it will overwrite the first pointer in the DOS path.) The only way to retain existing pointers in the DOS path is to use the MAP INS or MAP S16: commands (listed below), which insert new search drives into the DOS path rather than replacing existing ones.

In this example, the SYS:APPS\WP70 directory will be assigned as search drive S3:, which is the third item in the search list. It will also map the directory to the next available drive letter, starting with Z: and moving backward. Review the Search Drive Mappings section above.

TIP

There is a way to specify which network drive letter is assigned when creating a search drive. In the above example, if you want to assign network drive letter W: to the S3: search drive, you can use the following command:

```
MAP S3:=W:=APPS\WP70
```

REAL WORLD

A very interesting thing happens if you re-map an existing search drive number. NetWare assigns the new directory, as specified, without warning you that an existing search drive with the same number already exists. It does not, however, overwrite the network drive letter that was originally associated with the search drive number. Instead, it assigns a new network drive letter to the new directory and converts the old network drive letter into a full-fledged network drive mapping—thus stripping away its searching ability. Conversely, if you attempt to re-map the network drive associated with a search drive, you will receive a warning that the drive is already in use as a search drive and will be asked if you want to overwrite it. If you say Yes, both the network drive and its associated search drive will be mapped to the new directory. Weird, huh?

MAP INS S1:=SYS:PUBLIC

The MAP INSERT command can be used to insert a new search drive into the search list, at the number specified, without overwriting an existing drive mapping. All existing search drives below the new pointer are then bumped up one level in the list and renumbered accordingly.

In this example, we are inserting a new drive as S1:. Therefore, NetWare bumps up and renumbers all other search drives in the list. Then, it inserts the new drive at the top of the list as search drive S1:.

The interesting thing about this scenario is that it has no effect on existing network drives. All previous drives retain their original drive letters, even though they change positions in the search list.

Earlier, we learned that both the MAP INSERT and MAP S16: commands could be used to preserve the DOS path. This way, when you log off the network, your NetWare search drives will be deleted, but your local PATH statements will remain intact. Remember, DOS PATH drives don't count toward your limit of 16 network search drives.

TIP

So what happens when you mix the MAP INSERT and MAP S16: statements? You create a strange "genetic" breed. The resulting command, MAP INSERT S16: places your search drives in the NetWare search list but AFTER the DOS PATH directories. Weird.

QUIZ

One final numbers game: This is one of my personal favorites (see if you can figure out why). Change the position of only *one* number to make this a palindromic sequence:
1, 4, 2, 9, 6, 1, 5, 10, 4

Hint: When in Rome...

(Q10-4)

MAP DEL G:

The MAP DEL command deletes an existing drive mapping. This command can be used with both network and search drive pointers. The MAP REM command performs the same function. Network drive mappings and search drive mappings are deleted automatically if you log off the network or turn off your workstation.

MAP ROOT H:=SYS:ACCT\REPORTS

You can use the MAP ROOT command to create a false root. This command solves user problems like the one we had above with Little John. The user sees this drive as if it was the root directory; therefore, he can't wander off too far with the dreaded CD command.

MAP ROOT can also be used for application programs that need to be installed in the root directory. For security reasons and administrative purposes, you should never install applications in the actual root, so here's a great compromise. The install program thinks it's installing WordPerfect, for example, in the root directory, when it's actually a false root pointing to SYS:APPS.

To determine if a drive mapping is actually a false root, use the MAP command alone. As you can see in Figure 10.36, the H: drive is shown differently than are the other network drives. Instead of showing a blank space between the volume name and the directory name, it shows a blank space followed by a backslash following the directory name. This clues you in that we're dealing with a different breed—a false root.

F I G U R E 10.36

The MAP ROOT Command

```
U:\USERS\MMARION>MAP

Drives A,B,C,D,E map to a local disk.
Drive F: = WHITE-SRV1_SYS.WHITE.CRIME.TOKYO: \LOGIN
Drive G: = WHITE-SRV1_SYS.WHITE.CRIME.TOKYO: \SHARED\FIN
Drive H: = WHITE-SRV1_SYS.WHITE.CRIME.TOKYO:ACCT\REPORTS \
Drive U: = WHITE-SRV1_SYS.WHITE.CRIME.TOKYO: \USERS\MMARION
 -----    Search Drives    -----
S1: = Z:. [WHITE-SRV1_SYS.WHITE.CRIME.TOKYO: \PUBLIC]
S2: = Y:. [WHITE-SRV1_SYS.WHITE.CRIME.TOKYO: \PUBLIC\IBM_PC\MSDOS\V6.22]
S3: = C:\WINDOWS
S4: = X:. [WHITE-SRV1_SYS.WHITE.CRIME.TOKYO: \APPS\WINDOWS]
S5: = W:. [WHITE-SRV1_SYS.WHITE.CRIME.TOKYO: \APPS\SS30]

U:\USERS\MMARION>
```

MAP N SYS:DATA

You can use the MAP NEXT (N) command to assign the next available drive letter as a network drive mapping. It doesn't work, however, with search drive pointers.

TIP

Although the MAP NEXT command doesn't work with search drives, there is another technique that you can use to achieve the same effect, namely the MAP S16: command. The MAP S16: command assigns the next available search drive number to the specified directory. Because search drives update the DOS Path, NetWare 4 does not allow you to

assign search drive numbers that would cause holes to exist in the DOS path. For instance, if only search drives S1: through S4: exist, NetWare would not let you create search drive S7:. Instead, it would just assign the next search drive number in the list (S5:, in this example).

MAP C I:

The MAP CHANGE (C) command can be used to change a regular NetWare drive to a search drive, or vice versa. In this example, Drive I: will still point to the same directory to which it was originally assigned, but it would also be added to the end of the NetWare search list. Conversely, if you use the MAP CHANGE command with a search drive, the search drive number is deleted from the search list, but the network drive letter originally associated with it is retained as a network drive mapping.

MAP S5:=.WPAPP.TOKYO.ACME

You can also map a drive to a Directory Map object (WPAPP) instead of to the directory itself. This is especially useful if the directory name changes from time to time—such as every time you upgrade WordPerfect or Microsoft Word—but you don't want to change every MAP statement in every login script.

In this case, you only need to change the reference in the central Directory Map object. All other drive mapping commands will reflect that change instantly. It's fun at parties.

MAP /?

The MAP /? command displays on-line help for all variations of the MAP command.

MAP /VER

The MAP /VER command lists the version of the MAP utility that you are using as well as the files the utility needs to execute. If you use the /VER option, all other parameters will be ignored.

Table 10.9 provides a quick summary of all the really amazing MAP commands you've learned today.

T A B L E 10.9

Getting to Know the MAP Commands

COMMAND	RESULT
MAP	Displays a list of current drive mappings.
MAP G:=WHITE-SRV1\SYS:SHARED\FINAN	Maps the G: drive as a network drive that points to the SHARED\FINAN directory on the SYS volume of the WHITE-SRV1 server (using the physical volume name).
MAP G:=.WHITE-SRV1_SYS.WHITE.CRIME.TOKYO.ACME:SHARED\FINAN	Maps the G: drive as a network drive that points to the SHARED\FINAN directory on the SYS volume of the WHITE-SRV1 server (using the Volume object name).
MAP NP E:=SYS:HR\EVAL	Maps the E: drive to the HR\EVAL directory, suppressing the warning that you are about to re-map a local drive.
MAP S3:=SYS:APPS\WP70	Maps the S3: search drive to the SYS:APPS\WP70 directory and assigns the next available drive letter in reverse alphabetical order as a network drive.
MAP S3:=W:=SYS:APPS\WP70	Maps the S3: search drive to the SYS:APPS\WP70 directory and assigns W: as the associated network drive.
MAP INS S1:=SYS:PUBLIC	Inserts a new S1: search drive at the beginning of the search list, renumbering all existing search drives accordingly. Also assigns the next available drive letter in reverse alphabetical order as a network drive.
MAP DEL G:	Deletes the G: network drive (see MAP REM command below).
MAP REM G:	Deletes the G: network drive (see MAP DEL command above).
MAP ROOT H:=SYS:ACCT\REPORTS	Maps the H: drive as a false root pointing to the ACCT\REPORTS directory.

T A B L E   10.9

Getting to Know the MAP Commands

COMMAND	RESULT
MAP N SYS:DATA	Maps the next available network drive letter to the SYS:DATA directory.
MAP C I:	Changes the I: network drive to the next available search drive number.
MAP C S4:	Changes the S4: search drive to a network drive.
MAP S5:=WPAPP	Maps the S5: search drive to a Directory Map object called WPAPP.
MAP /?	Displays on-line help information for the MAP command.
MAP /VER	Displays version information about the MAP utility, including the files it needs to execute.

In the beginning...there was the NDS directory tree. We discovered the [Root], leaf objects, proper naming, and Read/Write replicas. We learned how to name it, partition it, design it, install it, manage it, and groom it. Just when we thought we understood the true meaning of NetWare 4 life, another tree appeared—the non-NDS directory tree.

This strange new tree is very different. Instead of a [Root], it has a root; instead of leaves, it has files; and instead of replicas, it has duplexing. But once you get past its rough exterior, you'll see that the non-NDS tree shares the same look and feel as the NDS one. And they approach life together with a similar purpose—to logically organize user resources, except this time the resources are files, not printers.

In this chapter we learned everything there is to know about our non-NDS friend. We learned how to name it, partition it, design it, install it, manage it, and groom it. All in a day's work.

ZEN

Megatrend—A far-reaching or widespread change in society such as the advent of computers and the information revolution, aerobics and physical fitness, microwave ovens and convenience food, or, most importantly, CNEs becoming florists.

So what does the future hold? Well, now that we've learned everything about NDS and non-NDS trees, we can expand our minds to the rest of NetWare 4 management. We will combine our "treeologist" skills and forge ahead into the great CNE abyss:

- ► Security

- ► Configuration

- ► Management

- ► Printing

- ► Optimization

During your journey through the rest of this book, look back to the fun times you had in gardening class. Count on your NDS and non-NDS gardening skills—because you will need them. Oh yes, you will.

Good luck, and by the way...thanks for saving the world.

You're ready to create the basic file system directory structure for the WHITE-SRV1 server. Using the scenario listed below, design the directory structure on paper first, then use the DOS MD command or the NetWare 4 FILER utility to create the directory structure on the system.

As you know, initially, the Crime Fighting division, the White-Collar Crime department, and the three White-Collar Crime units (Cyber Crime, Financial Crime, and Political Crime) will all be sharing the same server (WHITE-SRV1.WHITE.CRIME.TOKYO.ACME). Although there will be some sharing of programs and data, each group will essentially function as an independent workgroup with a separate network administrator.

Because the WHITE-SRV1 server has already been installed, the system-created LOGIN, SYSTEM, PUBLIC, MAIL, and ETC directories already exist.

The USERS directory should be created in the root of the volume. It will serve as the parent directory for the home directories for each user. (The home directories will be created when you actually create the users at a later time). Each of the workgroups will have access to the SHARED directory, which will be located in the root of the volume. This directory will be used for the sharing of files between workgroups. In addition, each workgroup will have exclusive access to its own group directory under the SHARED directory (called WHITE, CYBER, FIN, and POL, respectively).

The users in the various workgroups will be running different versions of DOS. Although each user will normally run DOS off his/her local workstation, there will also be a copy of each DOS version stored on the server in case anything happens to the copy on a particular workstation. Because the DOS versions differ in manufacturer, type, and version, you will want to use the standard DOS directory structure recommended by Novell (that is, a three-level directory structure under the SYS:PUBLIC directory: the machine type on the first level, the DOS type on the second level, and the DOS version on the third). So far, you know that there will be:

▸ Two types of machines (DELL and IBM_PC)

▸ Two types of DOS (MSDOS and NOVDOS)

▸ Three versions of MSDOS (v3.30, v5.00, and v6.22).

The first three applications that will be installed on the server include:

- ▸ A word processing application (in the WP70 directory)

- ▸ A spreadsheet application (in the SS30 directory)

- ▸ A database application (in the DB50 directory)

Each of these subdirectories will be stored under the APPS directory, which will be located in the root of the volume.

EXERCISE 10-1: UNDERSTANDING DRIVE MAPPING

Follow the steps listed below to create sample drive mappings for the directory structure that was created in the case study titled "Creating a Directory Structure for ACME."

1 • Display on-line help information for the MAP command.

2 • Display your current drive mappings.

3 • Map drive F: to the USERS directory. (Normally, it would point to each user's individual home directory, but they have not been created yet.)

4 • Map drive G: to the POLIT subdirectory under the SHARED directory, using the physical name of the volume.

5 • Map the J: drive to the same directory as the F: drive.

6 • Map drive S: to the SHARED directory, using the Volume object name.

7 • Map the S1: search drive to the SYS:PUBLIC directory without overwriting the existing pointers in the DOS path.

8 • Map the S2: search drive to the V6.22 directory without overwriting the existing pointers in the DOS path.

9 • Map the S3: search drive to the SS30 subdirectory.

10 • Map the S4: search drive as a false root to the DB50 subdirectory.

11 • Display your current drive mappings again. How does the system indicate a false root?

12 • Map the S5: search drive to the WP70 subdirectory, specifying that W: be assigned as the associated network drive. Did it work?

13 • To view the effect of the CD command on search drive mappings, switch to the Z: drive. Type CD .. and press Enter to switch to the root directory. Type the MAP command to list your current drive mappings. What happened? What should be done to fix the problem? Fix the problem.

14 • Delete the J: drive.

15 • Delete the S3: search drive using a different command than you did in Step 14. What happened to your other search drive mappings? What happened to the network drive associated with those search drives?

16 • Change the S4: drive from a search drive to a network drive. What happened to the search drive itself? What happened to the network drive associated with it?

See Appendix C for answers.

CHAPTER 11

NetWare 4 Security

"You won't find a more secure system anywhere."

Security is an interesting thing. Everyone wants it but how much are you willing to pay? On the one extreme, you could live in a titanium vault—secure but very uncomfortable. On the other extreme, you could live in a 1960s Woodstock fantasy—fun but way too risky. No, I believe you live somewhere in between. Whether you know it or not, your security requirements fall in a spectrum between a titanium vault and the 1960s. The key to security is gauging the range of your boundaries.

Goal: *Let the good guys in and keep the bad guys out!*

Security in the information age poses an even more interesting challenge. Computers and communications have made it possible to collect volumes of data about you and me—from our last purchase at the five-and-dime to our detailed medical records. Privacy has become a commodity to be exchanged on the open market. Information is no longer the fodder of afternoon talk shows. It has become *the* unit of exchange for the 21st Century, more valuable than money.

A recent study has shown that 92 percent of the Fortune 500 companies think security is important enough to do something about. Even the government is getting involved with the "clipper chip" and other anti-theft policies. I bet you thought you left cops and robbers behind in childhood. Well, this is a variation on the game and the stakes are very high. As a CNE, it is your responsibility to design, install, and manage the NetWare 4 network. But, most importantly, you must protect it. You need a brain filled with sophisticated security strategies and a utility belt full of advanced protection tools. Think of this chapter as your impenetrable network armor.

NetWare security, in general, is pretty good. But for many of today's WANs, it's not good enough. As a matter of fact, most of NetWare's security features need to be "turned on." It's not secure right out of the box. A truly *secure* network protects more than just user data—it protects everything! So what is "everything"? The definition of everything has changed in NetWare 4. Now the world exists in a nebulous cloud full of Tupperware containers and User objects. As the NetWare universe becomes more open and interconnected, security becomes more and more important.

So what is "security"? Simply stated, security is freedom from risk. Therefore, network security can be considered as any effort you take to protect your network from risk. Of course, it's difficult to protect your network from things you cannot see or understand. So the first thing you need to do in developing a security model is to learn about risks.

So what is "risk"? Risk is a combination of value and threat. The value you determine is the cost of your network resources should you lose them. Value extends well beyond monetary value—it encompasses data integrity, confidentiality, and the value of data to competitors. The threats are more difficult to define. Threats come from a variety of different sources including people, technology, and the environment. The very nature of computer networks puts them at continual risk. In summary, sharing data makes it harder to protect data. Of course, you don't have a choice. The first step toward true network security is *risk analysis*.

The goal of risk analysis is to define your network security principles and identify the threats against them. A threat is a person, place, or thing that poses some danger to a network asset. Threats can be physical (file servers and workstations), topology (wire tapping), network-related (back/trapdoors, impersonation and piggybacking), data (logic bombs and Trojan horses), and people (intentional sabotage or unintentional bumbling).

The goal of your threat-based security model is to determine how likely your network is to experience any of these threats. What are the chances, for example, that your system has a back/trapdoor in place? Is wiretapping a possibility? How about impersonation or, even worse, logic bombs? The best approach is to make a realistic judgment of each threat's probability on your WAN. This becomes the foundation of your network's risk index. You can then use this index to develop a successful system of security countermeasures.

Countermeasures are actions that create a protective barrier against network threats. In many cases, countermeasures can reduce the probability of serious threats. In addition, vulnerability decreases as countermeasures increase. There is, however, never a vulnerability level of zero because countermeasures themselves have vulnerabilities built in. The bad news is countermeasures cost money. As a matter of fact, the more serious the threat, the higher the cost of the countermeasure. And it's difficult to quantify the decrease in threat probability due to countermeasures. Therefore, cost justification becomes a challenge. But all in all, countermeasures are necessary to keep your network running and therefore money needs to be spent on them. After all, money makes the world go 'round.

As a CNE, it's your job to identify the network's threats and implement appropriate countermeasures to eliminate them. This isn't easy. You have many factors working against you—including money, office politics, and user productivity. But there are some quick and easy countermeasures that can dramatically improve your network security:

▶ Restrict physical access to file servers. In Chapter 13, we'll learn a few strategies for physical file server protection.

- One of your network's most insecure entry points is through virtual links.

- Consider using dial-back systems with multilayered password protection. Remember, anyone with a modem and phone line can gain access to your network.

- Background authentication and NCP packet signing protect data packets as they travel over topology lines. In addition, data is encrypted for further protection.

- Many advanced routers allow you to filter SAPs, RIPs, and specific frame types. Consider filtering non-essential packets to increase performance and keep out the bad guys.

- Don't use the Supervisor or Admin accounts—use an equivalent instead. Also, don't delete the original Admin account once you have made yourself equivalent. There's some existentialist ramifications in there somewhere.

- Always create a backdoor. Consider using Alt+255 as a null character. It's hard to track. The beauty of null characters is they appear as spaces. Intruders will see a username or password with a space and never assume it's a null character. Also, many times you can't tell how many null characters are involved—especially when they're sequentially added to the end of a username.

- NetWare 4 includes an extensive auditing system which allows you to audit Login events as well as file/directory events. Use it!

- Consider restricting the following file server access rights—Supervisory, Access Control, and Modify [SAM].

- Track rights carefully and make sure you know what you're doing before you get started. Calculating effective rights can be very tricky, especially if you use an inherited rights filter (IRF). Many times users end up with rights they shouldn't have.

▸ Classify people into security levels and identify the highest security risks. Then implement countermeasures against these people including training sessions, tracking, or extensive auditing.

▸ Be careful when assigning distributed administrative responsibility. Remember, power corrupts and absolute power corrupts absolutely.

Well, there you go. Risk analysis and countermeasures. These are key factors in protecting your NetWare 4 WAN. Sometimes NetWare security isn't good enough. You need to develop appropriate countermeasures for ALL network threats, not just a few. After all, the 60s was a great decade but welcome to the 90s. This is the information age and your data is a valuable commodity.

Fortunately, NetWare 4 has a dramatically improved security model for creating and maintaining your impenetrable network armor. This model allows us to perform risk analysis at five different levels. It also includes numerous countermeasures for dealing with "bad guys." Whatever you do, don't let this information fall into the wrong hands. Let's take a closer look.

ZEN

As you progress through this chapter, you'll find that "true security" is a mystery. What is it? How do you get it? Many times, it's not what it seems. You'll find it in the least likely places. As an example, let's rewind a few years to one of the greatest mysteries of our time—"Who shot Mr. Burns?" It all started with a simple question, from a key witness: "Who shot who in the what, now?"

Old Man

NetWare 4 Security Model

NetWare 4 improves on earlier NetWare security models by adding supplemental front-end barriers for filtering unauthorized users. Once again, the same security goal applies:

Let the good guys in and keep the bad guys out!

As you can see in Figure 11.1, the NetWare 4 security model consists of five different barriers. They are:

1 • Login/Password Authentication

2 • Login Restrictions

3 • NDS Security

4 • File System Access Rights

5 • Directory/File Attributes

The NetWare 4 Security Model

As you can see, each layer creates an increasingly strong barrier against user access. Each time you pass through a door, you are greeted with an even stronger barrier. This works much the same way as the opening to the TV show *Get Smart*. Maxwell would have to travel through numerous barriers until he finally reached the telephone booth.

After entering the correct code, he was allowed access to Control headquarters. Users pass through similar barriers on their way to the ultimate prize—data.

Let's take a quick look.

LAYER ONE—LOGIN/PASSWORD AUTHENTICATION

As you can see from Figure 11.1, it all starts with login/password authentication. Remember, users don't login to NetWare servers anymore—they login to the "Cloud." First, the user requests access by typing LOGIN followed by a valid username. Once this occurs, authentication begins. There are two phases:

▶ Initialization—The server and workstation authenticate the session with an encrypted key. You are required to enter a valid password to decrypt the key.

▶ Background—NetWare continues to attach the key to all messages to ensure data integrity. This process is known as *background authentication*. In addition, you can enhance background security with a related feature called *NCP packet signing*. We'll explore both features later in this chapter. In addition to authentication, NetWare 4 accepts passwords up to 127 characters. This is a substantial improvement over earlier versions. The limit is decreased significantly, though, for Macintosh clients. Once you have been authenticated, NetWare matches you against a list of global and personal login restrictions. These restrictions allow for conditional access according to a variety of criteria. That's Layer One.

LAYER TWO—LOGIN RESTRICTIONS

Once you provide a valid login name and password, you are authenticated. Congratulations! NetWare responds with conditional access and NDS rights take over. At this point, I stress the word *conditional* access. Permanent access is made possible by a variety of login restrictions. These login restrictions include:

▶ Account Restrictions—Includes anything from Account locked to Force periodic password changes.

▶ Password Restrictions—Includes Minimum password length and Force unique passwords.

▶ Station Restrictions—Limits users to specific workstation node IDs.

▶ Time Restrictions—Determines when users can and cannot use the system.

▶ Intruder Detection/Lockout—A global feature that detects incorrect password attempts and locks bad guys out.

Each of these restrictions are configured by *you* using a variety of NetWare 4 tools, including NWADMIN and NETADMIN. We'll learn all the details of how and why later in this chapter.

LAYER THREE—NDS SECURITY

Once you enter the "Cloud," your ability to access leaf and container objects is determined by a sophisticated NDS security structure. At the heart of NDS security is the Access Control List (ACL). The ACL is the property of every NDS object. It defines who can access the object (trustees) and what each trustee can do (rights). The ACL is divided into two types of rights:

▶ Object Rights—Defines an object's trustees and controls what the trustees can do with the object.

▶ Property Rights—Limits the trustees' access to only specific properties of the object.

Here's a great example (see Figure 11.2). Let's say the Group object WHITE-GROUP has rights to the User object MMarion. WHITE-Group has the Browse object right, which means that any member of the group can see MMarion and view information about her. But Maid Marion is shy. She wants to limit what the group can see (reasonable enough). She only wants them to see her last name, postal address, and telephone number. So MMarion limits the group's rights by assigning the Read property right to only these three properties: Last Name, Postal Address, and Telephone Number. No sweat.

Object and property rights are designed to provide efficient access to NDS objects without making it an administrative nightmare. You be the judge. Users can acquire object rights in a variety of ways, including trustee assignment, inheritance, and security equivalence. Property rights, on the other hand, are a bit trickier. Global property rights can be inherited, but rights to specific properties must be granted through a trustee assignment. Trustee assignments occur when an object is given explicit access to any other object or its properties. These trustee assignments are administered by adding the user to a host object's ACL property. This is accomplished using NWADMIN or NETADMIN menu utilities.

Inheritance is a little simpler. If rights are granted at the container level, they are inherited for all container and leaf objects within. This means that rights assigned to the [Root] object, for example, are inherited by every object in the NDS tree. Be very careful. Fortunately, NetWare 4 includes an inherited rights filter (IRF), which blocks inherited rights.

Finally, there's *security equivalence*. This means objects can absorb rights by being associated with other objects. Sometimes the associations are obvious, but most of the time, they're not. In reality, users can inherit rights ancestrally from containers, groups, organizational roles, and [Public].

Regardless of how you acquire object and property rights, the concept of *effective rights* still applies. This means the actual rights you can exercise with a given object are the combination of explicit trustee assignments, inheritance, and the IRF. The mathematical product of this mess is known as *effective NDS rights*—"modern math." And that effectively ends our discussion of NDS security and moves us on to Layer Four of the NetWare 4 security model—file system access rights.

LAYER FOUR—FILE SYSTEM ACCESS RIGHTS

Well, here we are. Congratulations! You've finally made it to NetWare Nirvana. You've passed through three very difficult barriers of network armor and the search is over—your files await you. Ah, but not so fast! Before you can access any files on the NetWare 4 server, you must have the appropriate file system access rights. Once again, another barrier pops up to bite you. Following is a list of the eight rights that control access to NetWare 4 files (they almost spell a word):

▸ W—Write: Grants the right to open and change the contents of files.

▸ (O)—Doesn't exist but is needed to spell a word.

▸ R—Read: Grants the right to open files in the directory and read their contents (or run applications).

▸ M—Modify: Grants the right to change the attributes or name of a file or directory.

▸ F—File Scan: Grants the right to see files and directories.

▶ A—Access Control: Grants the right to change trustee assignments in the IRF.

▶ C—Create: Grants the right to create new files and subdirectories.

▶ E—Erase: Grants the right to delete a directory, its files, and subdirectories.

▶ S—Supervisor: Grants all rights to a directory and the files and subdirectories below. This right cannot be blocked by the IRF.

Holy anatomical nematodes, Batman! That spells WoRMFACES. It's not a pretty sight but certainly a name you will not forget. NetWare 4 file system access rights are administered in much the same way as NDS object rights. They are granted with the help of trustee assignments, inheritance, and ancestral inheritance. In addition, file system rights are subject to the same rules as NDS effective rights. All in all, NDS and file server security parallel one another—one operating in the clouds (NDS) and one with its feet firmly planted on the ground (file system).

Well, that completes the majority of the NetWare 4 security model. There's only one layer left, and it is seldom used—directory/file attributes. Let's take a closer look.

LAYER FIVE—DIRECTORY/FILE ATTRIBUTES

Directory and file attributes provide the final and most sophisticated layer of the NetWare 4 security model. These attributes are rarely used but provide a powerful tool for specific security solutions. If all else fails, you can always turn to attribute security to save the day.

NetWare 4 supports three different types of attributes:

▶ Security Attributes—The main attribute category. Some attributes apply to both directories and files.

▶ Feature Attributes—Applies to three key features: backup, purging, and the Transactional Tracking System (TTS).

▶ Disk Management Attributes—For file compression, data migration, and block suballocation.

QUIZ

There's a hidden message in everything. The following coiled sentence contains a profound truth. Start at the correct letter, move to any touching letter, and you will find a mystery unfold.

V	E	O	E	T
E	U	Y	L	P
R	Y	S	L	A
H	T	R	O	M
I	N	A	A	D
G	E	X	R	T
E	C	O	E	I
P	O	T	F	D
T	H	W	O	L

(Q11-1)
(See Appendix C for quiz answers.)

Well, there you have it. That's a brief snapshot of NetWare 4's five-layered security model. Now we'll take a much closer look at each of these layers and learn how they can be used to create your impenetrable network armor. Of course, if somebody should get lucky enough and break through your network armor, it would be nice to know what they're doing there. That's where NetWare 4 auditing comes in. And, yes, we'll discuss it, too. But not yet. Now it's time to attack the first layer of NetWare 4 security—login/password authentication.

REAL WORLD

In October 1967, a task force was assembled by the Department of Defense to address computer security safeguards that would protect classified information and computer networks. The task force was formed primarily because networks were just beginning to make an impact on all the world's computers. Of course, they had no idea what they were in for the next 30 years. The DOD now explores security alternatives through the National Computer Security Center (NCSC). In December 1985, the DOD published a document affectionately known as "the Orange Book." Yes, I've seen it—it is orange. The document was entitled *The Department of Defense Trusted Computer System Evaluation Criteria* or TCSEC. The Orange Book was designed to provide security guidelines for both developers and administrators. The major goal of the document is "to encourage the computer industry to develop trusted computer systems and products making them widely available in the commercial marketplace." The book basically consists of a spectrum of evaluation criteria for differing levels of security. It lists basic requirements for very low and very high levels of security.

In order to be truly secure, your system must satisfy six fundamental requirements:

1 • It must have a clear and well-defined security policy enforced.

2 • All system elements must be associated with access control labels.

3 • All individuals accessing the system must be identified.

4 • Audit information must be selectively kept and protected so that all security actions can be traced.

5 • The computer system must contain hardware/software mechanisms that can be independently evaluated.

6 • The countermeasures that enforce these basic requirements must be continuously protected against tampering and/or unauthorized changes.

So there you have it. Is your system truly secure? Well, in addition to these six requirements, the Orange Book includes evaluation criteria for four different divisions of security—A through D. Just like in school, A is good and D is bad. Working your way from the bottom, Division D is simply the bottom of the totem pole. This classification is reserved for those systems that have been evaluated but have failed to meet the requirements for a higher evaluation class.

(continued)

REAL WORLD *(continued)*

Division C, on the other hand, provides security on a "need to know" basis. Division C security includes auditing and accountability. The Orange Book further classifies Division C into two classes—C-1 and C-2. Most of today's network operating systems, including NetWare 4 and NT, vow to meet C-2 requirements at the very minimum (the Government requires it). Class C-2 is entitled "Controlled Access Protection." Systems in this class enforce a more finely-grained discretionary control than C-1 systems. C-2 users are individually accountable for their actions through login procedures, auditing of security-related events, and resource isolation. The idea here is to permit or refuse access to any single file.

The bottom line is NetWare 4.1 satisfies C-2 security. Some of the new features that were implemented to meet this classification include login authentication, distributed NDS administration, and auditing. While you may yearn for level B or A security, you don't want to pay the price. C-2 should be fine.

Layer One—Login/Password Authentication

When you login to a NetWare 4 server, the world changes. Suddenly you have access to a plethora of resources that weren't available before—printers, files, users, and e-mail. Whatever you do, don't take the login process for granted. It's a complex series of sophisticated communication steps between your client and the server.

As you'll see in the next two chapters, logging in involves ODI drivers, VLMs, context, and STARTNET.BAT. But the real goal of logging in is security. After all, this is the only way to differentiate between real users and "bad guys." Now let's take a closer look at how hard it is to get into a NetWare 4 server.

GETTING IN

The first two layers of the NetWare security model are concerned with gaining access to the network, that is, "getting in." Once you're in, the bottom three layers take over. They control what you can do once you get there—access to NDS resources and the file system. As you can see in Figure 11.3, there's a lot going on during the login process.

Also notice that there are three ways to be denied and only two ways to be granted access to a NetWare 4 Cloud. This is because of authentication. Let's take a closer look at the flowchart in Figure 11.3.

It all starts with the LOGIN command. NetWare responds with a username prompt. You'll need to provide your login name with complete NDS context. This is so that NetWare 4 can match you against specific user properties in the NDS database. Once you enter a username, NetWare goes to the nearest Read/Write replica of your parent partition to verify that you exist. If you don't exist in the context specified, you'll be denied access and the following two error messages will be displayed:

```
LOGIN — 4.12 — 895: The user does not exist in the specified
   context.
LOGIN — 4.12 — 130: Access has been denied and you have been
   logged out.
```

If you do provide a valid username and context, the system continues to decision two—login restrictions. Using the information provided by the Read/Write replica, NetWare 4 checks all your major login restrictions including time restrictions, station restrictions, and account lockout. If you try to login from an unauthorized workstation or during the wrong time of day, access will be denied and the following error message appears:

LOGIN - 4.12 -860: You have tried to login during an unauthorized time period.

If you pass login restrictions, NetWare moves on to the final two decisions—passwords. First, it uses your NDS information to determine whether a password is required. If the password is not required, you are authenticated automatically and access is granted. Bad idea. If a password is required, you are prompted for it. Good idea. That brings us to the final login decision: Does the password you provided match the one in the NDS database? If not, access is denied, Intruder Detection is incremented and the following brief error message appears:

LOGIN - 4.12 - 100: Access has been denied.

If you provide the correct password, NetWare 4 uses it to decrypt the private authentication key. This completes the initialization phase of login authentication and access is granted. We'll discuss the two phases of authentication in just a moment.

In summary, the NetWare 4 login process consists of four decisions:

1 • Are you using a valid username?

2 • Do you pass login restrictions?

3 • Is a password required?

4 • Does your password match?

If all these conditions are met, access is granted. As you can see in Figure 11.3, there are three ways to be denied access—invalid username, you don't pass login restrictions, or you provide the incorrect password. Now you should have a new appreciation for all the work that's involved when you type that one magic word: **LOGIN**.

ZEN

"Nancy Drew says that all you need to solve a mystery is an inquisitive temperment and two good friends."

Lisa Simpson

INITIAL AUTHENTICATION

From a security standpoint, the entire login process points to one goal—authentication. This is the only way you can gain access to a NetWare 4 network. Authentication involves the username, the password, the client, NDS, and the NetWare 4 server. There sure are a lot of cooks in the kitchen. Once you've been initially authenticated, NetWare 4 activates a secondary authentication scheme—background authentication. Background authentication keeps the user validated throughout the current session. An additional feature, called NCP packet signing, validates *every* user packet as they're sent from workstation to server. This also applies to the active session only. We'll take a look at background authentication and NCP packet signing in just a moment.

In both cases, NetWare 4 authentication guarantees the following:

▶ Only the purported sender built the message.

▶ The message came from the workstation where the authentication data was created.

▶ The message pertains to the current session.

▶ The message contains no information counterfeited from another session.

▶ The message has not been tampered with or corrupted.

▶ You are who you say you are.

▶ You're doing what you say you're doing.

NetWare 4 authentication is based on the RSA (Rivest Shamir and Adleman) scheme. This is a public key encryption algorithm that is extremely difficult to break. In addition to RSA, authentication uses a independent private key algorithm as well. One key is public (which means that all users on the network can have access to it) while the other is kept private (which means only a designated user knows about it). If a message is encrypted with a private key, it can be decrypted with a public key and vice versa. As you can see in Figure 11.4, initial authentication consists of four sophisticated steps. Let's take a closer look.

F I G U R E 11.4

NetWare 4 Initial
Authentication

Step One: Client Requests Authentication

NetWare 4 authentication requires the NetWare DOS Requester. It uses a special VLM to control the encryption and decryption of public and private keys—RSA.VLM. In Step One, Admin logs in by providing his or her full NDS context. The client requests authentication from the NetWare 4 server. The request is handled by a special program within the core OS—Authentication Services.

Step Two: Server Returns Encrypted Key

Once the authentication request has been accepted, NetWare 4 matches the user information with an encrypted private key. This private key can only be decrypted by the user password. That's Step Three.

Step Three: Client Decrypts Private Key

In Step Three, the user provides a valid password to decrypt the private key. The password is then erased from memory to prevent a hacker from obtaining it illegally. This is where the fun begins. With the private key, the client creates an *authenticator*. This credential contains information identifying the user's complete name, the workstation's address, and a validity period (the duration of time the authenticator is valid). In addition, there are other undocumented values that make up the authenticator.

The client then creates an encryption called a *signature* using the authenticator and private key. The private key is then removed from memory while the authenticator and signature remain in workstation RAM throughout the login session. The signature is used for background authentication and validates all packets sent during this session.

Finally, the client requests authentication using a *proof*. The proof is constructed from the signature, the request for authentication, and a random-generated number. It is further encrypted by the user's private key. The proof is sent across the WAN instead of the signature to prevent anyone from illegally obtaining the valuable signature. An internal client random number generator ensures that each message sent from this workstation includes a different proof. The proof also assures NetWare 4 that the message has not been modified. This is the goal of background authentication and NCP packet signing.

Step Four: The User is Authenticated

During the final step, authentication services validates the proof as an authentic construct of the authenticator, the private key, and the message (request for authentication). Once the proof has been validated, the user is granted conditional access to the NDS Cloud. Permanent access is granted once you successfully pass Layer Two of the NetWare security model—login restrictions.

Table 11.1 summarizes the key concepts in initial authentication. Here's a madcap recap: Admin logs in by providing his/her complete name. The client (RSA.VLM) requests authentication from the server (authentication services). The server returns an encrypted private key. Admin enters a valid password and the private key is decrypted. The client then creates an authenticator with the private key which includes Admin's complete name, the workstation address, a validity period, and other undocumented values. Next, the client creates a signature by encrypting the authenticator with the private key. Finally, a proof is constructed from the signature, private key, and a random number for traveling over the WAN. The proof is sent to authentication services which validate it and grant Admin access to the NDS Cloud. All of this magic occurs in less than a second. Wow!

T A B L E 11.1	AUTHENTICATION ELEMENT	DESCRIPTION
Understanding NetWare 4 Authentication	Client	Participates in initial authentication on behalf of the user. Controlled by special RSA .VLM.
	Authentication Services	Participates in initial authentication on behalf of the server. Consists of features built into the core NetWare 4 OS.
	Username	Initiates initial authentication through login request. Also is used by the server in combination with the user password to create an encrypted private key.
	Encrypted Private Key	A specific key for each user, which can be decrypted only with the valid password.
	RSA Public Key	Used by authentication services to validate user information.
	Password	Entered by the user to decrypt the private key. Once this occurs, the password is removed from workstation RAM for security purposes.
	Authenticator	A special credential created by the client with user- and session-specific information including the user's complete name, the workstation address, a validity period, and other undocumented values.

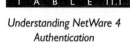 Understanding NetWare 4 Authentication	AUTHENTICATION ELEMENT	DESCRIPTION
	Signature	A background authentication credential created by the combination of the authenticator and encrypted private key. The signature is used to validate all packets sent during this session. It is also the foundation of the proof.
	Proof	A temporary encryption created for traveling over the WAN. It is constructed from the signature, a message, the user's private key, and a randomly generated number. The random number generator ensures that each message contains a unique proof.

THE BRAIN

If you feel inspired to delve more deeply into the mysteries of NDS authentication, check out the AppNote entitled "Understanding the Role of Identification and Authentication in NetWare 4" in the October 1994 issue of *Novell Application Notes*.

Once you have been initially authenticated, the second phase begins—background authentication. In this phase, the signature and proof are used to continually authenticate all packets during the current session. Let's take a closer look.

BACKGROUND AUTHENTICATION

Welcome to the second phase of NetWare incognito. Background authentication and NCP packet signing are designed to protect the WAN from experienced hackers who forge data packets or pose as unauthenticated clients. In earlier versions of NetWare, hackers could use protocol analyzers to capture server requests and forge their own instructions. For example, I could request something simple like login as Guest, then capture the packet and add something harmful like, "While you're at it, please make me Supervisor Equivalent." This is a bad thing. NCP packet signing solved this problem by requiring a unique signature on all messages. The signature is represented as a *unique proof,* which is the combination of the workstation signature and a random number.

If a message doesn't have the correct proof attached, it is discarded. When this occurs, an error message is sent to the error log, the affected workstation, and the server console. The alert message contains the login name and the station address of the invalid client.

NCP packet signing occurs at both the workstation and the server. NetWare 4 contains a default level of packet signing—the client signs only if the server requests it and the server signs only if the client requests it. Therefore, signing doesn't occur. You can customize NCP packet signing by using the SET server console command and NET.CFG client configuration file. Here's how it works:

▸ At the server—Use the following SET command:

SET NCP PACKET SIGNATURE OPTION=n

▸ At the workstation—Add the following statement to the NETWARE DOS REQUESTER section of NET.CFG:

SIGNATURE LEVEL=n

In both cases, n represents a signature level from zero to three: 0 deactivates NCP packet signing and 3 creates the highest level of protection available. Table 11.2 shows some common client-server combinations (this is not an exhaustive list). Notice what happens when either the client or server uses packet signing levels of zero and three. This can cause havoc on the WAN. Consider activating minimal packet signing —client (one) and server (two).

Finally, packet signing does have a cost. This background protection scheme causes a slight decrease in server performance because of the overhead involved. Not only is the header of each packet marginally larger, but the workstations perform additional processing for each packet transmitted. The server must also perform processing to validate each signed packet. That's okay; your security is worth it.

You've been authenticated. How does it feel? Isn't it nice to know that your life has a purpose? We all need a little validation. But we're not done yet. Remember, we just have *conditional* access to the WAN. In order to become a permanent resident of the NDS Cloud, we must successfully pass through the second layer of the NetWare 4 security model—login restrictions. Login restrictions offer much more administrative flexibility because you can limit users according to a large number of criteria including time of day, workstation, intruder detection, and so on. Let's get restricted.

REAL WORLD

NCP packet signing and background authentication recently became necessary because of the overzealous activities of a group of students at Lieden University in the Netherlands. These mischievous students are considered "the Netherlands hackers." This means they expose security loopholes as a means of plugging them. A few years ago, they discovered a simple piggyback intrusion mechanism for NetWare 2.2 and 3.11 servers. The NCP packet signing feature was implemented in NetWare 3.12 and all future versions as a way of slamming this backdoor. Way to go team.

T A B L E 11.2 *Understanding NCP Packet Signing Options*	CLIENT LEVEL	SERVER LEVEL	DESCRIPTION
	0	3	The client does not sign packets and the server requires it; therefore, the workstation cannot login to this server.
	3	0	Packet signing is required by the workstation, but the server does not support it. Workstations with this level will not communicate with unsigning servers because they consider them to be unsecure.
	1	1	This is the default. The client signs only if the server requests it, and the server signs if the client requests it. Therefore, signing doesn't occur.
	1	2	Client signs only if the server requests it and the server does request packet signing. This is the minimal setting for activating background authentication.
	3	3	Client always signs and requires server to sign. Server always signs and requires clients to sign. Therefore, everybody signs and all is well. This is the maximum level of packet signature protection.

Layer Two—Login Restrictions

Login restrictions further scrutinize WAN access by matching the login name with a variety of NDS qualifications:

- Is this user authorized to login during this time period?

- Is this user authorized to login from this particular workstation?

- Is this user authorized to login on this date?

- Will this user ever get the password right?

- Will this user ever change the password?

- Who shot Mr. Burns?

- What is the meaning of life?

The first layer of NetWare security (login authentication) restricts INVALID users. Login restrictions, on the other hand, restrict VALID users. At this point, NetWare assumes a valid username has been provided and authentication can probably be guaranteed.

As you can see in Figure 11.5, NDS supports a variety of login restriction properties. A quick scan of the right side of Figure 11.5 shows four obvious user restrictions— login, password, login time, and network address. In addition, NetWare 4 supports a password tracking feature called Intruder Detection/Lockout. This security feature tracks unauthorized login attempts and automatically locks accounts when the attempts exceed a given bad login threshold count. The user account can only be unlocked by an administrator.

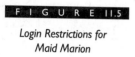

FIGURE 11.5

*Login Restrictions for
Maid Marion*

In summary, NetWare 4 login restrictions fall into five different categories:

▶ Account Restrictions

▶ Password Restrictions

▶ Time Restrictions

▶ Station Restrictions

▶ Intruder Detection/Lockout

Account restrictions apply only to specific users. Maid Marion, for example, can have her account expired, concurrent connections limited, or access disabled altogether. Password restrictions impact login authentication. In this screen, we can define a variety of Maid Marion's password settings including allowing her to change her password, requiring a minimum password length, forcing periodic password changes, requiring unique passwords, and limiting grace logins. Remember, the password is used by the client to decrypt the authentication private key.

The next option is time restrictions. These limitations simply apply to when users can be connected to NDS. Time restrictions are not login restrictions per se, they are *connection restrictions*. This means users cannot login or be connected to the tree during inactive time periods.

Similarly, station restrictions do not allow users to login or attach from unauthorized stations. NWADMIN calls this network address restrictions because it allows you to limit user access to a specific protocol, LAN address, or node ID.

Finally, Intruder Detection/Lockout is a global feature that is activated at the container level. All objects within the container are tracked according to a variety of parameters including Incorrect Login Attempts, Intruder Attempt Reset Interval, and Account Lockout. If, for example, Maid Marion logs in with her correct context and an incorrect password seven times within an hour, intruder lockout activates. Once her account has been locked, she has two options—wait the Intruder Lockout Reset Interval or have an administrator unlock her account. This feature allows you to sleep better at night knowing that NetWare 4 is doing all it can to keep intruders out of your WAN.

All of the above restrictions, except Intruder Detection/Lockout, are activated at the user level. This means you have to set them for each individual user—too much work. Fortunately, NetWare 4 includes a USER_TEMPLATE object for global configurations. If, for example, you'd like to set a minimum password length for all users in the WHITE container, you could create a USER_TEMPLATE object with the correct settings. Then all users created from this point forward will inherit the properties of the USER_TEMPLATE. This applies to all properties, not just login restrictions. Figure 11.6 shows a sample USER_TEMPLATE configuration screen for the WHITE container. Notice all the page buttons listed on the right-hand side. I'm a big believer in the theory "Less work and more play makes life worth living." And the USER_TEMPLATE object is right up my alley. Use it or lose it.

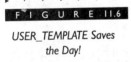

F I G U R E 11.6

USER_TEMPLATE Saves the Day!

ZEN

"And when he tried to steal our sunlight, he crossed over that line between everyday villainy and cartoonish super-villainy."

Mr. Wayland Smithers

Now let's take a much closer look at each of the five NetWare 4 login restrictions, starting with account restrictions.

ACCOUNT RESTRICTIONS

NetWare 4 account restrictions provide a method for controlling and restricting user access to the NDS tree. Account restrictions can be found in the Login Restrictions screen of NWADMIN (see Figure 11.7). As you can see, there are four main options:

▸ Account Disabled

▸ Account Has Expiration Date

▸ Limit Concurrent Connections

▸ Last Login

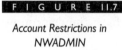

FIGURE 11.7

Account Restrictions in NWADMIN

Account Disabled

This option is pretty self explanatory. The account is either disabled or not. This option is not related to Intruder Detection/Lockout. It is possible for an account to be locked but not disabled. In both cases, the effect is the same—the user can't login. In order to disable a NetWare 4 account, you have two choices—manually check this box or use an expiration date.

Account Has Expiration Date

This option is a useful tool for temporary employees or students in an academic environment. It allows you to lock an account after a specific date. As you can see in Figure 11.7, the default is inactive. If you check the Account Disabled box, NOW appears as the default date and time. This means as soon as you exit NWADMIN, Maid Marion's account will be disabled. Make sure to increase the value before you leave. In Figure 11.7, Maid Marion's expiration parameters have been set to just before midnight on January 1, 2000. At this point, she will either be gone or celebrating the success of ACME.

Limit Concurrent Connections

Let's face it, users are nomadic. They like to migrate throughout the WAN and login from multiple workstations. You can limit a user's concurrent connections by changing the inactive parameters in Figure 11.7 to something greater than zero. As you can see, an ideal setting is three concurrent connections. This means that Maid Marion can only login from three workstations simultaneously. That's plenty. This account restriction works in conjunction with station restrictions. You can enhance a user's concurrent connection limitation by combining it with a specific physical workstation address. In this case, Maid Marion can only login from three specific machines simultaneously.

Last Login

The last login parameter allows users to track activity on their login account. You should train users to periodically check this parameter for intruder logins. If, for example, Maid Marion was gone for a week but saw that the last login was three days ago, she would have reason to believe an intruder had used her account.

That does it for login restrictions. Now let's take a closer look at password restrictions.

PASSWORD RESTRICTIONS

The next set of login restrictions properties deal with passwords. As you can see in Figure 11.8, there are five main options:

- ▶ Allow User to Change Password

- ▶ Require a Password

- ▶ Force Periodic Password Changes

- ▶ Require Unique Passwords

- ▶ Limit Grace Logins

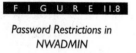
F I G U R E 11.8

*Password Restrictions in
NWADMIN*

Password restrictions directly impact login authentication. As we learned in Figure 11.3, NetWare 4 access can be granted in one of two ways—by providing the correct password if one is needed or automatically if no password is required. Requiring a password is absolutely mandatory. Otherwise, authentication is crippled. Once you require a password, the question remains, "Who manages it?" If you place the burden of password management on the user, the other four password restriction parameters become important. Let's take a closer look

Allow User to Change Password

If you allow users to change their password, you're opening a can of worms. On the one hand, it shifts the burden of password management from you to them—this is a good thing. On the other hand, it allows them to mess around with an important authentication parameter—this is a bad thing. Most annoying user complaints deal with password management and printing. Well, one out of two ain't bad. If you don't allow users to change their password, all the work falls on you. It's your call—a balance between security and practicality.

Require a Password

By default, NetWare 4 does not require a password—this is bad. This should be the very first parameter that you change when creating user accounts. If you activate Require a Password and Force Periodic Password Changes, the system will ask for a password the very first time users log in. Once you activate the Required Password parameter, it's a good idea to set a minimum password length of more than five characters. There are many password hacking routines that can guess a five-character password in less than 20 minutes. On the other hand, you want a password length that doesn't intimidate fragile users. Consider most users can't easily remember strings in excess of seven to ten characters. The last thing you want to do is force large passwords so that users have to write them down on a piece of paper and tape them to the front of their monitors. NetWare 4 supports passwords up to 127 characters in length. It also supports any alphanumeric and ASCII characters. Consider creating passwords that join two unrelated words with a punctuation mark such as

- ▸ DOOR!GROUND

- ▸ SHOE;QUARK

- ▸ LATCH PURPLE

Note the last example did not use a space—it used a null character (Alt+255). Funny, it looks like a space—that's the whole point. Intruders will assume it's a space. Also, it's even trickier when used in succession at the end of a password or username. I bet you can't tell there are seven successive null characters at the end of the second example. Once you've required a password, all the other restrictions light up.

Force Periodic Password Changes

Once a password has been required and a minimum password length of seven characters has been set, you should explore using the Force Periodic Password Changes restriction. This parameter forces users to change their passwords at periodic intervals. If you activate the option, NetWare asks you to input the days between forced changes. The default is 40 days. This is a little short and can become a nuisance very quickly. Remember, users love to complain about password problems. A periodic password interval of 90 days seems to be optimal.

Password expiration seems to be a touchy topic for users and administrators alike. We want the interval to be short for better security and they want the interval to be long for less interference. Either way, somebody has to track it. You can train your users to check NWADMIN periodically and view the Date Password Expires property within Password Restrictions. This will tell them exactly on what date and at what time their password will expire. Once the password interval has expired, the user is required to change his/her password. This is where grace logins come in. We'll talk about them in just a second.

REAL WORLD

Many times password expiration and grace logins cause unneeded friction between CNEs and users. Especially when users abuse the privilege and CNEs ultimately have to change the passwords anyway. Consider making password expiration a big "event." Use the PASSWORD_EXPIRES login script identifier variable to count down the number of days until password expiration (see Chapter 12). Then when the day arrives throw a party, bring in balloons and cake, and have everybody change their passwords at once. Turning this event into a party makes password transition every 90 days fun and unobtrusive. It's also a great excuse to have four parties a year.

Require Unique Passwords

The Require Unique Passwords restriction works in conjunction with forcing periodic password changes. When the periodic password interval expires and the user must change his or her password, unique passwords forces him/her to enter a new *different* value. If you're going to endure the effort of forcing periodic password changes, do yourself a favor and make them unique. It doesn't make sense to have users change their password every 90 days if they're going to use the same one. NetWare 4 only tracks the last 20 passwords. Don't let your users learn this. They will create numerical intervals such as FIFI1, FIFI2, FIFI3, and so on. Also, I've seen users change their passwords 20 times in succession so they can reuse the original one. Perpetuate the myth that NetWare keeps track of all passwords forever.

Limit Grace Logins

When the periodic password interval has expired, NetWare responds with the following statement during login:

```
Your password has expired. Would you like to change it now?
```

This provides the user with an opportunity to change their password right away. If they do not, the system will lock their account. The problem with the above message is the words "Would you like." It should say something like "You better change your password now or your computer will explode." Unfortunately, this message is not configurable. So many users see it as a choice and decide to move on using their existing password. This is where *grace logins* come in. Grace logins allow the user to login without changing their password. This is a temporary situation because even grace logins expire. As you can see in Figure 11.8, we're giving Maid Marion six grace logins. This means she can login six times without changing her password. But then her account will be locked. Once again, encourage your users not to rely on grace logins. There's a convenient Change Password button on the Password Restrictions screen for user access. Otherwise, they can use the SETPASS command at the NetWare prompt.

QUIZ

Even numbers have a certain mystery. Try to find the five-digit number, no zeros, in which the first digit is the sum of the last two digits, the second digit is twice the first digit and three times the fourth digit, and the total of all five digits is sixteen.

Hmmm.

(Q11-2)

That completes our discussion of password restrictions. Aren't they fun? As you can see, there's much more to NetWare 4 passwords than meets the eye. Remember, this is the foundation of our login authentication strategy. Don't underestimate the importance of passwords. Use them or suffer the consequences.

TIME RESTRICTIONS

The next two login restrictions deal with *when* and *where* you get to login. Time restrictions determine *when*. How many of you have suffered from the curious custodial syndrome (CCS)? Let's see a show of hands. Ah, just as I thought—just about all of you. CCS is a problem that afflicts most of today's modern businesses. It's caused by the simple fact that the network stays up 24 hours a day and you don't. Since nighttime janitors have access to your equipment, they can easily hack your networks. One simple solution is time restrictions. Deactivate the network after 9:00 at night and before 6:00 in the morning. This way, no matter how curious the custodial staff is, they can't access the network after hours.

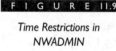

F I G U R E 11.9

*Time Restrictions in
NWADMIN*

Each square in Figure 11.9 represents a 30-minute interval. The shaded area represents inactive time periods. The white area shows that users can login any time between 6:00 a.m. and 9:00 p.m. Time restrictions go beyond login restrictions and become connection restrictions. Not only can they not login but they can't be connected. If Maid Marion is using the network at 8:55 p.m., she will receive a message:

```
Time expires in five minutes. Please logout.
```

She will get this message at five- and one-minute intervals. When a time restriction is encountered and the user connection is cleared, the system does not perform a proper logout. The system simply *clears* the connections without saving the file. This is a very serious problem. Clearing Maid Marion's connection could result in bindery corruption, hardware failure, or even worse, data loss. When you see a five-minute or one-minute message, make sure to pay attention and logout.

Here are some common time restriction strategies:

▸ Restrict After Hours—ACME doesn't expect employees to work between the hours of 9:00 p.m. and 6:00 a.m. They want to avoid burnout. Setting a time restriction during this period protects them from curious custodians.

▸ Restrict Weekends—Also to avoid burnout, ACME restricts anybody from accessing the network during the weekend. Remember, all work and no play....

▸ Activate Backup Periods—One down side of time restrictions is that it doesn't allow a window for backup. If you're backing up the system late at night, you'll have to activate a backup time window. Test your backup to determine how long it takes and give the system a large enough window— let's say from 11:00 p.m. till 1:00 a.m.

▸ Restrict Specific Users—Remember, time restrictions are a user configuration. You can restrict everybody in a container using the USER_TEMPLATE object or specific users individually. If temporary users, for example, only work on Tuesdays and Thursdays, consider deactivating their accounts on other days.

Don't go crazy with time restrictions. Intelligent time restrictions increase network security but careless time restrictions can significantly hinder user productivity. You want to give users time to work but not leave the network susceptible to CCS.

STATION RESTRICTIONS

Station Restrictions are the other half of the when/where dynamic duo. They deal with *where*. Now that we've solved our CCS problem, another one will arise—Nomadic User Syndrome (NUS). NUS hinders network security for a variety of reasons. First, nomadic users take up multiple network connections and block access to other users. Secondly, NUS implies that users are logging in from workstations other than their own. And, finally, NUS impairs your ability to limit intruders from accessing physical workstations.

Station restrictions solve NUS. They allow you to virtually chain users to specific machines. Instead of restricting them with passwords, disk restrictions, or time slots, you're physically restricting the workstation from which they can log in. As you can see in Figure 11.10, NetWare 4 station restrictions go a few steps farther:

- ▸ Protocol Restrictions

- ▸ Network Address Restrictions

- ▸ Node Restrictions

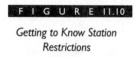

FIGURE 11.10

Getting to Know Station Restrictions

First you pick a protocol. NetWare 4 defaults to the IPX/SPX protocol. Other options include OSI, SDLC, TCP/IP, AppleTalk, and Ethernet/Token Ring. Each protocol treats network address restrictions differently. The IPX/SPX address format consists of an eight-digit external network address and 12-digit hexadecimal node ID. The network address identifies an external LAN segment while the node ID identifies a specific workstation. Maid Marion, for example, is restricted to any workstation (FFFFFFFFFFFF) on the 1234 LAN. We could further refine her restriction by listing one or more physical node IDs on the 1234 LAN.

The TCP/IP address format expresses logical and physical IDs in the dotted-dash decimal notation. In this case, you can also restrict to all workstations on a logical network or a specific physical machine. Finally, the Ethernet/Token Ring address format uses a SAP (Service Access Point) address, block ID, and PU ID (physical unit). Once again, these values specify all stations on a LAN segment or a specific workstation.

Unfortunately, NWADMIN doesn't dynamically interrogate the LAN to determine addresses for you. You must use other NetWare or third-party utilities to gain network and node ID information. As a word of warning, don't go hogwild with station restrictions. Use it only if you suffer from NUS. Like other login restrictions, if it's abused or mishandled, station restrictions can significantly impede user productivity. What happens, for example, when Maid Marion travels to another location? Or what if we restrict her to one workstation and the machine goes down? These are all important considerations. Although station restrictions are a useful security tool, they can also be detrimental to user relationships.

That completes our discussion of what, when and where. Now only one question remains: who?

ZEN

"If you've ever handled a penny, the government's got your DNA. Why do you think they keep them in circulation?"

Scientist Smith

INTRUDER DETECTION/LOCKOUT

Welcome to Whoville. This is not so much a restriction as it is a security tracking feature. Intruder Detection/Lockout tracks invalid login attempts by monitoring users who try to login without correct passwords. As you recall from Figure 11.3, this feature increments every time a valid user provides an incorrect password. It also leads directly to Access Denied! Once Intruder Detection has reached a threshold number of attempts, the account is locked completely.

There's one very important thing you need to know about this final login restriction—it's a container-based configuration. All the previous restrictions have been user based. As you can see in Figure 11.11, intruder detection is activated at the Organization or Organizational Unit level. Once an account has been locked, it must be reactivated at the user level. There are two main configuration elements:

- ▸ Intruder Detection Limits

- ▸ Lock Account after Detection

Once Intruder Detection/Lockout has been activated at the container level, all users in that container are tracked. Let's take a closer look.

FIGURE 11.11

Intruder Detection for
WHITE

Intruder Detection Limits

Intruder Detection is turned off by default. In order to activate it, you simply check the Detect Intruders box. Once you activate Intruder Detection, it begins tracking incorrect login attempts. This parameter is set to seven by default. As soon as the incrementing number exceeds the threshold, account lockout occurs. Finally, the Intruder Attempt Reset Interval is a window of opportunity, so to speak. The system uses it to increment the incorrect login attempts. It is set to 30 minutes by default.

Here's how it works. Assume the Incorrect Login Attempts parameter is set to seven and Intruder Attempt Reset Interval is set to one day, 12 hours (see Figure 11.11). The system will track all incorrect login activity and lock the user account if the number of incorrect login attempts exceeds seven in the 36-hour window. Pretty simple, huh? Now let's take a look at what happens once Intruder Detection is activated.

Lock Account After Detection

This is the second half of Intruder Detection/Lockout. After all, the feature wouldn't be much good if you didn't punish the intruder for entering the wrong password. When you activate the Lock Account After Detection Parameter, NetWare asks for an Intruder Lockout Reset Interval. By default, this value is set to 15 minutes. Doesn't make much sense, does it? This invites the hacker to come back 15 minutes later and try all over again. Typically a value equal to or exceeding the Intruder Attempt Reset Interval is adequate. As you can see in Figure 11.11, we're locking the account for two days, therefore giving you enough time to track down the intruder.

So what happens to the user when the account is locked? As you can see in Figure 11.12, NetWare tracks account lockout at the user level. The Intruder Lockout screen provides three important pieces of information:

- Incorrect Login Count—A dynamic parameter that tells the user how many incorrect login counts have been detected during this reset interval. If the account is locked, the incorrect login count should equal the lockout threshold.

- Account Reset Time—Informs the user how much time is remaining before the account is unlocked automatically.

- Last Intruder Address—Shows the network and node address of the workstation that attempted the last incorrect login. This parameter provides you with valuable information regardless of whether the account is locked or not. This is pretty undeniable evidence that somebody tried to hack this account from a specific workstation. You don't have to worry about disputed evidence or planted gloves.

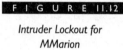

F I G U R E II.12

*Intruder Lockout for
MMarion*

So who's going to unlock Maid Marion's account? You! Only Admin or distributed administrators can unlock accounts that have been locked by the Intruder Detection feature. But what about Admin? After all, Admin is the most commonly hacked account— with good reason. If you don't have an Admin equivalent user to unlock the Admin account, consider using ENABLE LOGin at the file server console. It's always nice to have a back door.

There you have it. That completes our discussion of Intruder Detection/Lockout and login restrictions in general.

Congratulations, you are in! You've successfully navigated the first two layers of the NetWare 4 security model—login/password authentication and login restrictions.

In login/password authentication, we discussed the first two phases of WAN access— initial authentication and background authentication. Initial authentication is a sophisticated four-step process that develops a user-specific, session-specific signature and proof. This signature is then used by background authentication to validate incoming workstation packets. Once you've been authenticated, NetWare grants you conditional access to the WAN. Permanent access relies on login restrictions.

Login restrictions are the second layer of the NetWare 4 security model. They define what, when, where, and who gets access to the system. What is account and password restrictions, when is time restrictions, where is station restrictions, and who is Intruder Detection/Lockout.

NetWare has never been more secure. And we haven't even accessed any resources yet. The first two layers get us in but what we do inside the "Cloud" relies on NDS and file system security. How secure do you feel now?

NDS Security

Welcome to the Cloud!

The NDS park is a great place to hang out. It has trees, swings for the kiddies, a bike trail, and external entities. Feel free to look around. Browse all day if you'd like. But don't touch anything. You haven't been secured yet.

Access to the tree is one thing; being able to do anything there is another. Until you've been granted sufficient NDS access rights, all the pretty objects are useless to you. No trees, no swings, no bike paths. Once you enter the NDS park, your ability to access leaf and container objects is determined by a sophisticated NDS security structure. At the heart of NDS security is the Access Control List (ACL). The ACL is a property of every NDS object. It defines who can access the object (trustees) and what each trustee can do with it (access rights).

This strategy poses two important questions:

► What rights do I need to do stuff?

► How do I get these rights?

These are good questions. Fortunately, I have some simple answers. First, NDS supports two types of access rights—object and property. Object rights define an object's trustees and control what they can do with the object. Property rights, on the other hand, further refine NDS security by limiting access to only specific properties of the object. Fortunately, these rights are pretty self explanatory. Browse, for instance, allows you to see an object. Hmmmm, no "brain drain" there.

So that leaves us with an answer to the second question: "How do I get these rights?" It's a simple three-step process:

▸ Step One: Assigning Trustee Rights—Somebody gives you specific rights to specific objects through trustee assignments, inheritance, and/or security equivalence.

▸ Step Two: Filtering IRF Rights—Somebody else can filter certain rights if they want to.

▸ Step Three: Calculating Effective Rights—The result is effective rights, which define what you can actually do to the object.

As easy as A-B-C. And you thought NDS security was going to be hard—nope. It can get weird, though. As I'm sure you can imagine, the potential combination of object/property rights can be staggering—almost infinite. So you're going to want to try to keep it under control. In this section, we'll talk about default NDS rights and how you can use the simple three-step method for limiting potential loopholes. Finally, we'll talk about NDS administration and explore Admin, distributed administrators, and "special" cases. So, without any further ado, let's get on with the show—starting with NDS access rights.

QUIZ

While establishing the credibility of Mr. Smithers' testimony, we learned a few interesting things about him: he prefers pneumonia to a cold. He likes sequoias, but not pine trees. He is facetious, but not amusing. So the question remains, is he abstemious or sober?

(Q11-3)

UNDERSTANDING NDS ACCESS RIGHTS

Access to NDS objects is controlled by ten different NDS access rights—sounds reasonable. These ten rights are organized into two functional groups:

▸ Object rights

▸ Property rights

Let's use the famous "box analogy" to understand the difference between these two different sets of NDS access rights. Think of an NDS object as a box. Like any other three-dimensional rectangloid, the box has external characteristics. You can look at the box and describe its color, size, and shape. By describing the outside of the box, you have a good idea of the type of box it is. But you don't know anything else about it, especially what's inside the box. With object rights, you can look at the box, destroy the box, relabel the box, or create a new one. But you can't get specific information about what's inside the box—that requires property rights.

The contents of the box are similar to what's inside an NDS object—properties. In most cases, the contents of different boxes will vary. One box may contain caviar while the other contains video games. In order to see what's inside the box, you need permission to open it and look inside. With the proper rights, you can compare properties in this box with properties in other boxes, you can read the packing list or change the contents of the box altogether. It all depends on which property rights you have.

If you're feeling a little boxed in, that's okay. We'll try and take it slow. But before we can move on to the three-step NDS security model, we need to explore each of these ten rights in depth plus you'll need to have a firm understanding of default NDS rights before you start changing things around. The default rights in NetWare 4 are very sophisticated. In many cases, they're good enough. Let's start with a closer look at object and property rights.

Object Rights

Object rights control what a trustee can do with any object. As you can see in Figure 11.13, the five object rights spell a word—BCDRS. So what do NDS object rights have to do with dinosaurs? Absolutely nothing but it's an easy way to remember the five rights. Just visualize *Jurassic Park* and all the sick dinosaurs. What would they do without dinosaur doctors?

*A Jurassic Set of Object
Rights*

Object Rights

B	Browse
C	Create
D	Delete
R	Rename
S	Supervisor

Following is a description of the five object rights and their functions:

▶ Browse—Grants the right to see objects in the directory tree. With this right, you can see the outside of the box.

▶ Create—Grants the right to create a new object within this container. Obviously, the Create right is only available on container objects. With this right, you can create a new box.

▶ Delete—Grants the right to delete the object from NDS. With this right, you can throw away the box.

▶ Rename—Grants the right to change the name of the object, in effect changing the naming property. This is the only object right which has any impact on properties except Supervisor. With this right, you can relabel the box.

▶ Supervisor—Grants all access privileges. Anybody with Supervisor rights to an object has access to all its properties. The Supervisor right *can* be blocked with the Inherited Rights Filter (IRF). In effect, anybody with Supervisor rights owns the box.

Except for a few minor exceptions, object rights have no impact on properties. Remember, we're dealing with the outside of the box at this point. If you want to have control over the contents of the box, you'll need to be granted property rights.

Property Rights

Property rights control access to the information stored within an NDS object. They allow users to see, search for, and change the contents of the box. At the very minimal level, you must be a trustee of an object in order to be granted rights to its properties. As you can see in Figure 11.14, the property rights almost spell a word—SCRAW(L). In order to cure the dinosaur, you'll have to write a pretty big prescription. This involves that unique medical skill known as SCRAWling—wait till you see my signature.

F I G U R E II.14

Scrawling the NDS
Property Rights

Property Rights

S   Supervisor

C   Compare

R   Read

A   Add Self

W   Write

Here's a description of the five NetWare 4 property rights:

- ▸ Supervisor—Grants all rights to the property. The Supervisor right CAN be blocked by an object's inherited rights filter (IRF).

- ▸ Compare—Allows you to compare any given value to the value within the property. This is analogous to saying, "I'm not going to tell you what my phone number is, but I'll let you guess at it." With the Compare right, an operation can return True or False but will not give the value of the property. Compare is automatically granted when users have the Read property right.

▸ Read—Grants the right to read values of the property. This is better than Compare because it actually allows you to view the value.

▸ Add Self—Allows you to add or remove yourself as a value of a property. This right is only meaningful for properties that contain object names as values such as group membership lists and mailing lists. This right is automatically granted with the Write right.

▸ Write—Grants the right to add, change, or remove any values of the property. This is better than Add Self because it allows you to change any value, not just yourself.

▸ (L)—This is not a property right but is needed to spell a word.

Property rights can be assigned in one of two ways—All Properties and/or Selected Properties. As you can see in Figure 11.15, NWADMIN provides two choices. The All Properties option assigns the rights you choose to *all* properties for the object. A list of these properties is displayed in the Selected Properties window. The Read All Properties right selection, for example, would allow you to view the value of all the properties for a given object.

The Selected Properties option, on the other hand, allows you to fine-tune NDS security for specific properties. Simply choose the right you want to assign and highlight one or more properties from the Selected Properties window. It's important to note that the list will change for each object type. Users, for example, have 55 properties, whereas groups have only 23. Finally, granting rights to selected properties overwrites anything granted through the All Properties option. This is very powerful because it allows you to get very specific with certain properties even though a general assignment already exists.

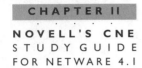
FIGURE 11.15

Assigning Selected Property Rights in NWADMIN

TIP

Later in Step One of the NDS security model, we're going to learn about a concept called inheritance. Inheritance is based on the concept that object and property rights flow down the NDS tree from container to container to leaf objects. It's a pretty simple concept, but there's one exception you need to be aware of. Object rights and All Properties rights are inherited, but Selected Properties rights are not. This means rights you assign to selected properties work with the specific object only—they do not flow down the tree. Keep this in the back of your mind when we get to inheritance later.

Now that you understand the ten different NDS access rights, it's time to start our three-step model. Before we do, however, let's take a detailed look at default NDS security. This discussion will help you determine when, where, and if you need to assign additional object and property rights.

Default NDS Rights

You've got to start somewhere and default NDS rights are a great place. As I said earlier, default NetWare 4 security is extremely sophisticated. In many cases, it's enough. Every time a Server and/or User object is created, NetWare 4 assigns a variety of object and property rights to them. Before you move on to the three-step model, you'll want to learn what these defaults are in case you can use them. There's no sense in re-inventing the wheel. Use NetWare 4's default NDS rights as a foundation and build from there.

NetWare 4 assigns default NDS rights during three major events:

- Initial NDS installation

- File server installation

- User creation

Let's take a closer look.

Initial NDS Installation

When NDS is installed on the very first server, two key objects are created—[Root] and Admin. [Root] represents the very top of the NDS tree (the Earth) and Admin has Supervisor control over the entire network. Incidentally, Admin is placed in the Organization level of the first server's context. The following default rights are granted when NDS is first installed:

- Admin—Granted Supervisor [S] object rights to [Root]. This allows the first user object to administer the entire NDS tree. Distributed administrators can be created using supplemental rights. We'll take a look at this later in the chapter.

- [Public]—A special system-owned trustee object also created at initial installation. Every object in the NDS tree inherits the rights of [Public]. This is analogous to the EVERYONE group in NetWare 3. By default, [Public] is granted Browse [B] object rights to [Root]. This allows every object in the NDS tree to see every other object.

REAL WORLD

A special trustee called [Public] is created during initial NDS installation and granted Browse [B] object rights to the [Root]. This trustee establishes a global assignment for all objects. Think of it as a minimum trustee assignment. There's one problem, though—users do not have to be logged in to inherit the rights of [Public]. They simply need to be ATTACHED.

(continued)

REAL WORLD *(continued)*

Therefore, any hacker with a notebook and VLMs can attach to your network and download the entire NDS tree. Consider removing [Public] as a trustee of the [Root] object and assign each Organization or Organizational Unit container Browse [B] rights to itself. This will allow users to see their portion of the NDS tree and not the entire tree. But, more importantly, users must be logged in (not just attached) to inherit these rights.

Server Installation

When a new file server is installed in NDS, default rights are given to the creator of the server object, the server itself, and [Public]. Remember, in order to create a server object, you must have Supervisor object rights to that portion of the tree. By default, INSTALL.NLM asks for the Admin password. If Admin doesn't exist or has been locked out of this portion of tree, a container administrator's username and password is sufficient. In either case, this person is known as the *Creator*. Let's take a look at the default rights assigned during server installation.

- ► Creator—Either Admin or a container administrator. By default, this user is granted Supervisor [S] object rights to the server. This allows Admin or the container administrator to manage the server object.

- ► Server—The server itself is granted Supervisor [S] object rights to itself. This allows the server to modify the parameters of its own object. Of course, in order for this to occur, the server would have to sprout arms.

- ► [Public]—Granted the Read [R] property right to a specific server property—Messaging Server. This allows any network client to identify the messaging server assigned to this file server. As you'll see in Chapter 12, this is required for MHS Services for NetWare 4.

TIP

Layers Three and Four of the NetWare 4 security model are completely independent. This means rights assigned at the NDS level do NOT apply to the file system. These rights only apply to network resources like printers, users, and servers. There is, of course, one exception. If you grant anybody Supervisor [S] object rights a Server object, they also inherit Supervisor file system rights to the [Root] of all volumes on that server. Therefore, by default, the creator of a server gets all rights to its NDS properties and file system. If you're lucky, this could be you.

User Creation

When you create a new User object in NDS, certain necessary rights are granted automatically. These rights are granted to provide the user with some degree of access to WAN resources. Remember, default NDS rights provide a very good beginning. In many cases, these rights are enough for users to be productive. In general, the User object receives enough rights to modify its own login script and print job configurations. If you don't like this idea, consider revoking these rights. Let's take a closer look:

▸ User—Each user is granted three sets of property rights by default. First, he/she is granted the Read [R] right to All Properties. This allows users to view information about themselves. Next, he/she is granted the Read and Write [RW] property rights to two selected properties—Login Script and Print Job Configuration. This allows users to execute and change their own user script and/or print job configurations. As you will learn in Chapter 12, this is a moot point since User login scripts are avoided at all costs. Finally, an obvious object right assignment is missing—Browse [B] rights to yourself. While this is not explicitly granted at user creation, the right is inherited from initial NDS installation. Remember, [Public] is granted Browse [B] rights to the [Root], and therefore all users can see all objects including themselves.

▸ [Root]—Granted the Read [R] property right to two specific user properties—Network Address and Group Membership. This allows anybody in the tree to identify the user's network address, location, and any groups he/she belongs to.

▸ [Public]—Granted the Read [R] property right to a selected user property—Default Server. This allows anyone to determine the default server for this user. The difference between the [Public] and [Root] assignment is that [Public] rights are granted upon attaching where [Root] rights imply a valid login authentication.

That completes our discussion of the default NDS rights. Refer to Table 11.3 for a summary. Hopefully, you've gained an appreciation for the sophistication of NetWare 4 default security. As you can see, users and servers are well taken care of. The only additional security you'll need to add are for special container administrators, traveling users, or groups. We'll discuss these special NDS circumstances later in the chapter.

But for now, let's put our understanding of object, property, and default rights to the test. Let's learn the simple three-step model for assigning NDS security:

▸ Step One: Assigning trustee rights

▸ Step Two: Filtering IRF Rights

▸ Step Three: Calculating effective rights

ZEN

"When I took your father's name, I took everything that came with it—including his DNA!"

Marge Simpson

TABLE 11.3	NDS EVENT	TRUSTEE	DEFAULT RIGHTS
Default NDS Security Summary	Initial NDS installation	Admin	[S]—Supervisor object rights to [Root]
		[Public]	[B]—Browse object rights to [Root]

TABLE 11.3	NDS EVENT	TRUSTEE	DEFAULT RIGHTS
Default NDS Security Summary	File server installation	Creator	[S]—Supervisor object rights to server
		Server	[S]—Supervisor object rights to self
		[Public]	[R]—Read right to selected server property (Messaging Server)
	User creation	User	[R]—Read right to All Properties
			[RW]—Read and Write rights to selected user property (Login Script)
			[RW]—Read and Write rights to selected user property (Print Job Configuration)
		[Root]	[R]—Read right to two selected user properties (Network Address and Group Membership)
		[Public]	[R]—Read right to a selected user property (Default Server)

STEP ONE: ASSIGNING TRUSTEE RIGHTS

I keep talking about how simple the NDS security model is—easy as 1-2-3. Well, now I get a chance to prove it. A lot has been written about NDS security and most of it is intimidating. Granted, there are a lot of complexities involved, but if you approach it with an open mind, everything falls into place. So far we've talked about object and property rights. Understanding these rights is a prerequisite to building an NDS security model. But it's certainly not enough. Now you have to learn how to implement these rights in the ACME NDS tree.

Step One deals with assigning these rights. In many cases, this is enough. You only need Steps Two and Three under special circumstances. NDS rights can be assigned in one of three ways:

- ▸ Trustee assignments

- ▸ Inheritance

- ▸ Security equivalence

Trustee assignments involve work—this is bad, of course, since our goal is to minimize the amount of work we do. But you have to start somewhere. Trustee assignments are granted using NWADMIN, NETADMIN, and/or RIGHTS. Inheritance, on the other hand, doesn't involve work—this is good. Inheritance happens automatically when you assign trustee rights at the container level. Just like water flowing down a mountain, trustee rights flow down the NDS tree—from top to bottom. The beauty of this feature is that you can assign sweeping rights for large groups of users with a single trustee assignment.

Finally, security equivalence gives us the added flexibility we need in today's modern world. There are a variety of security equivalence strategies including ancestral inheritance (AI), Organizational Roles, groups, and Directory Map objects. You'll learn that security equivalence is a way of augmenting the other two trustee assignment strategies. Let's take a closer look at Step One, starting with trustee assignments.

Trustee Assignments

You have to start somewhere and Step One starts with work. A trustee is any NDS object with rights to any other object. Trustees are tracked through the ACL (Access Control List) property. Every object has an ACL property, and the ACL lists the trustees of that object and the rights they have. NetWare 4 supports a variety of trustees including:

- ▸ User—A leaf object in the NDS tree. It represents a person with access to network resources. Individual users can be assigned specific NDS rights through the User trustee type.

▸ Group—A leaf object with a membership list. The membership list includes users from anywhere in the NDS tree. When NDS rights need to be assigned to unrelated users (in different containers), the group object is a great option. Rights granted to a group object are passed to all members of the group.

▸ Container—All container objects are considered "natural groups" and can be used to assign NDS rights to multiple trustees. If you make any container object a trustee of any other object, all users and subcontainers inherit those same rights.

▸ Organizational Role—A leaf object much like groups, except users are identified as occupants. This object is used to specify a particular role in the organization and not a group of unrelated users. Container administrators, for example, inherit the rights from the Organizational Role they occupy.

▸ [Public]—A special system-owned trustee. Rights granted to [Public] are passed to every object connected to the network. This means users do not have to be logged in in order to inherit [Public] rights. Be very careful when using the [Public] trustee.

Once you identify *who* is going to get the rights, you have to determine *what* rights you're going to give them and *where* the rights will be assigned. *What* consists of any of the ten object and property rights—simple. *Where* can be any object in the NDS tree—also simple. Take Figure 11.16, for example. As you can see, Sherlock Holmes is granted all object rights to the .OU=TOKYO.O=ACME container. In the figure, we have satisfied all three of the trustee assignment elements—who, what, and where.

So how is this accomplished in NWADMIN? It depends on your point of view. You
have two choices:

▸ Rights to Other Objects—This is from Sherlock Holmes's point of view.

▸ Trustees of this Object—This is from OU=TOKYO's point of view.

It really doesn't matter which option you choose. You can either assign rights from the user's point of view or the object's point of view. In the first example, we assign security from Sherlock Holmes' point of view. In NWADMIN, highlight SHolmes and click on the right mouse button. An abbreviated dialogue box appears. As you can see in Figure 11.17, there are two security options. In this case, we're interested in Rights to Other Objects.

F I G U R E II.17

*NWADMIN Security
Window for SHolmes*

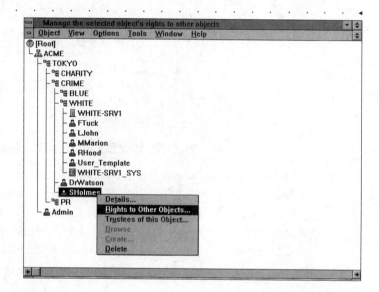

The SHolmes menu appears. Figure 11.18 shows the security window from Sherlock Holmes' point of view. As you can see, he has been granted all object rights to the TOKYO Organizational Unit. Specifically, the Supervisor object right implies the Supervisor property rights to All Properties. This was accomplished using the Add Assignment button.

FIGURE II.18

*Assigning NDS Rights from
the User's Point of View*

The second option allows you to assign NDS rights from TOKYO's point of view. In this case, you would select OU=TOKYO.O=ACME from the Browse window and click on the right mouse button. The same window will appear (as shown in Figure 11.17). This time, though, choose Trustees of this Object. Figure 11.19 shows the NDS security window from TOKYO's point of view. Notice the default trustees. In addition, SHolmes has been added with all object and property rights. This was accomplished using the Add Trustee button.

FIGURE II.19

*Assigning NDS Rights from
the Object's Point of View*

There you have it. As you can see, it doesn't matter how we assign trustee rights. Both methods accomplish the same thing—Sherlock Holmes (who) is granted [BCDRS] object rights (what) to .OU=TOKYO.O=ACME (where). I told you trustee assignments would be simple. Now that we've explored the "work" part, let's take a closer look at inheritance—the "no work" part.

Inheritance

NDS rights can also be assigned through inheritance. This is an automatic side effect of trustee assignments. As you can see in Figure 11.20, Sherlock Holmes got a lot more than he bargained for. When you assigned him the [BCDRS] object rights to .OU=TOKYO.O=ACME, he actually inherited these rights for all containers and objects underneath TOKYO as well. Now he has all object rights to all containers and all objects in that portion of the tree—this might not be a good thing.

F I G U R E 11.20

NDS Inheritance for Sherlock Holmes

As you recall from our ACME overview in Chapter 3, Sherlock Holmes heads up the Crime Fighting division. He probably shouldn't have Supervisor object rights to Charity and PR. Fortunately, we can rectify the situation. NetWare 4 provides two methods for overriding inheritance:

▶ New trustee assignment—Trustee assignments override inherited rights. If we assigned SHolmes Browse [B] rights to Charity and PR, he would lose his inheritance in these containers. The new trustee assignment would become his effective rights and inheritance within these containers would reflect the changes.

▶ Inherited Rights Filter (IRF)—The IRF is much more serious. It overrides inherited rights for all objects in the tree. A [B] filter on Charity and PR wouldn't allow anybody to inherit [CDRS] including SHolmes. So who manages these containers? What about SirKay and BThomas? Stay tuned for the answer.

Inheritance is a great thing. It allows you to assign sweeping NDS object rights with minimal effort. Remember, as a CNE, work is a bad word. As far as property rights go, only one type is inherited. Remember, there are two ways of assigning property rights— All Properties or Selected Properties. The rights assigned using the All Properties option are inherited. Rights assigned to Selected Properties are not. Combine this with what we learned about trustee assignments and we could have an effective strategy for property customization.

Here's an example. Remember, Maid Marion is shy. She's a user in the .OU=WHITE.OU=CRIME.OU=TOKYO.O=ACME container. She doesn't want Sherlock Holmes to see any of her properties except Telephone and Postal Address. This can be a problem since he inherits all rights from his [BCDRS] assignment to the TOKYO container. Fortunately, as a CNE, you have a solution. You simply assign SHolmes the Read [R] property right to Maid Marion's Selected Properties—Telephone and Postal Address. This trustee assignment overrides his inheritance through All Properties. Voilà, Maid Marion is safe. (See Figure 11.21.)

*Protecting Maid Marion
with a New Trustee
Assignment*

Trustee assignments and inheritance are the two main strategies of Step One. But special situations may arise when you need something more. This is where security equivalence comes in. Let's take a closer look.

Security Equivalence

If trustee assignments or inheritance aren't quite getting the job done, security equivalence may be the answer. Security equivalence simply states "one object is equivalent to another with respect to NDS rights." Users, for example, are security equivalent to their parent container. Security equivalence is different from inheritance in that it operates at the trustee assignment level. Please do not confuse the two. Security equivalence applies when an object is made equivalent to another object's explicit trustee assignments. Therefore, security equivalence overrides the IRF.

NetWare 4 provides four strategies for security equivalences:

- Ancestral inheritance (AI)

- Organizational Role

- Groups

- Directory Map objects

Ancestral Inheritance (AI)

Ancestral inheritance (AI) is a very cool term. But, before you get too caught up in it, you should know a little secret—it doesn't really mean anything. AI simply implies that an object is security equivalent to its ancestor (parent container). This means any rights you assign to an NDS container are absorbed by all the objects in the container. This is not inheritance; this is security equivalence. Therefore, AI can get very strange. Earlier we learned that containers can be trustees and they're thought of as "natural groups." This is true. But, remember, any rights that you assign to a container are implicitly assigned to all objects within the container. For example, suppose we assigned OU=CRIME [BCDRS] rights to TOKYO instead of SHolmes (see Figure 11.20). Now, both users in OU=CRIME—Sherlock Holmes and Dr. Watson—gain the same trustee assignments and inheritance shown in Figure 11.20. Pretty simple.

Well, that's not all. Not only do the objects in OU=CRIME absorb its trustee assignments, but all objects underneath CRIME as well! This means Maid Marion, Robin Hood, and all their friends would get the same trustee assignments as Sherlock Holmes and Dr. Watson. Wow. This concept is also called implied security equivalence. However tempting it is, avoid AI unless you know what you're doing.

Organizational Role

Organizational Roles are another type of security equivalence. These special NDS objects are designed as task identifiers. Jobs that require multiple temporary users are excellent candidates for Organizational Roles. Postmaster, for example, is a job that can be assigned to multiple users on a rotating basis. When a user is performing the Postmaster duties, he/she will need special NDS and file system rights. Let's say the White Collar Crime Division has a Postmaster Organizational Role that changes occupants every three months. This person needs special NDS security to e-mail objects and the file system.

Instead of continually moving trustee assignments around, you can define security once for the Organizational Role. Then switch occupants. Let's say it's Little John's turn, for example. When you remove Maid Marion from the Postmaster OR and replace her with LJohn, he immediately absorbs the NDS security of that object. Suddenly, Little John has all the security he needs to perform Postmaster duties. An elegant solution. Later we'll explore the Organizational Role as one solution for creating distributed administrators. For now, let's move on to the next security equivalence option—Groups.

REAL WORLD

AI allows you to make broad trustee assignments at high levels in the tree. For example, you could place a mail server at O=ACME and grant the container rights to it. Because of AI, all objects in the ACME organization will have immediate access to the mail server. This also applies to file system rights. You could place all the CRIME files on a single server in the OU=CRIME container. Then assign appropriate file system rights to OU=CRIME. Because of AI, all users in the CRIME division will have immediate access to the central server.

Groups

As we learned earlier, groups were another trustee type for assigning NDS rights. This allows us to distribute similar rights to unrelated users. That is, users not within the same area of the NDS tree. First, create a group, then assign it rights, and finally add members. This is similar to the Organizational Role object in that it works on the security equivalence concept. Members of any group absorb (not inherit) rights assigned to the host group object. Groups also differ from AI containers in that they don't involve "implied inheritance." Rights assigned to groups only apply to specific members of the group. And, as we all know, users can be easily removed from groups.

Directory Map Objects

In very special circumstances, security equivalence can be used to facilitate Directory Map objects. As we learned in Chapter 10, these objects allow us to map directory paths to a centralized object instead of to a physical location. To accomplish this, you must first create a Directory Map object that points to a physical location in the file system. Then create a logical drive pointer to the Directory Map object using the MAP command. There's one problem with this scenario: the drive mapping doesn't work until the user is assigned explicit or inherited file system rights to the physical directory. This involves a lot of planning, a lot of work, and some careful tracking. An easier solution would involve assigning the file system rights to the Directory Map object itself, then making each user a security equivalent of the NDS object. This makes security assignments much clearer.

In summary, when you create a Directory Map object, make sure to assign adequate file system rights to its physical directory. Then when you use the MAP command to create logical pointers, make sure to assign the host user security equivalence to the Directory Map object. Believe me, this will make drive mapping and security much easier to manage. Really!

There you have it—Step One. Don't get discouraged—this is the tricky part. Once you assign NDS rights, the rest takes care of itself. In Step One, we learned there are three different ways of assigning rights to NDS trustees—trustee assignments, inheritance, and security equivalence. We also learned there are a variety of different trustee types and to be aware of ancestral inheritance (implied security equivalence). The good news is, most of your work stops here. Only in special cases do you need to go on to Steps Two and Three. Of course, you remember Murphy's Law Number 342—special cases will appear just when you least expect them. So in honor of Murphy and to decrease your stress level, let's take a quick look at Steps Two and Three.

ZEN

"DNA.... Positive ID.... Those won't hold up in any court. Run Dad!"

Bart Simpson

STEP TWO: FILTERING IRF RIGHTS

Earlier we learned there are two ways of blocking unwanted inherited rights:

- ▸ New trustee assignments

- ▸ Inherited rights filter (IRF)

We propose a problem with Sherlock Holmes's inheritance. Since he's been assigned [BCDRS] object rights to .OU=TOKYO.O=ACME, he becomes distributed administrator of that entire section of the tree—this is bad. Sherlock Holmes is responsible for the Crime Fighting division. He has no authority over Charity or PR. However, his inheritance model shows [BCDRS] object rights to both OU=CHARITY and OU=PR (see Figure 11.20). We're going to have to do something about this right away.

Welcome to planet IRF. NetWare 4 includes an inherited rights filter which blocks inherited rights at any point in the tree. Right off the bat, you're going to need to understand two very important points about how the IRF works:

- It's an inclusive filter, which means the rights that are in the filter are the ones that are allowed to pass through.

- The IRF applies to everyone in the NDS tree. Once you've assigned an IRF to a container, everybody is blocked, including Admin.

TIP

The Supervisor object right can be blocked by an NDS IRF. It cannot be blocked, however, by an IRF in the file system. If you attempt to block the Supervisor [S] right with an IRF, NWADMIN will first require you to make an explicit Supervisor [S] trustee assignment to someone else (assuming, of course, that one does not already exist). This is so that access to that portion of the tree is not permanently removed. Imagine how much fun it would be if the Supervisor object right was filtered for everybody. Does the term *reinstall* mean anything to you?

The IRF can be used to block inheritance of either object rights or property rights assigned through the All Properties option. Remember, Selected Properties aren't inherited. Figure 11.22 shows how the IRF can be used to solve our Sherlock Holmes problem. We create an inclusive IRF of [B] to block everything but the Browse right. His inheritance in OU=CRIME, however, remains unaffected.

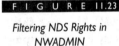

Blocking NDS Rights with
the IRF

So how do we assign an IRF? Once again, NWADMIN is our friend. Earlier we learned that trustee assignments can be assigned in one of two ways—"Rights to other objects" and "Trustees of this object." IRFs are accomplished using one of these two choices. Can you figure out which one? Correct—it's "Trustees of this object." Remember, IRFs are host object specific. They work from the host's point of view and apply to every object in the NDS tree. Figure 11.23 shows the IRF input screen for OU=PR. Notice the downward arrows that appear next to each option box. These differentiate IRF rights from trustee assignments. Anywhere you see a downward arrow, you can assume it's an IRF filter.

F I G U R E 11.23

Filtering NDS Rights in
NWADMIN

REAL WORLD

Even though the IRF input window in Figure 11.23 gives you the option of choosing Selected Properties, it's not a feasible configuration. Why? Because Selected Properties are *not* inherited. Therefore, the IRF is useless. Please don't let the utility confuse you. That's my job.

If the IRF applies to all objects in the tree, who is going to administer the OU=CHARITY and OU=PR containers? As you can see in Figure 11.22, nobody can have the [CDRS] object rights. Fortunately, trustee assignments override the IRF. Remember, the *I* in IRF stands for inherited. It only works on inherited rights. Figure 11.24 introduces two new players—SirKay (the administrator of OU=CHARITY) and BThomas (the administrator of OU=PR). We will simply assign BThomas the [BCDRS] object rights to OU=PR. Now he is the container administrator for this section of the tree and everybody else, including Sherlock Holmes and Admin, have been locked out. The same holds true for SirKay and OU=CHARITY.

FIGURE 11.24

Covering the IRF with New Trustee Assignments

So let me ask you—which activity occurs first? The IRF or the new trustee assignment? Correct, the new trustee assignment. Remember, NWADMIN will NOT allow us to set an IRF for OU=PR until somebody else has explicitly been granted Supervisor privileges. So first we assign BThomas [BCDRS] privileges, then we set the IRF to [B].

Good work.

So what's the bottom line? What can Sherlock Holmes *really* do in the TOKYO portion of the tree? "It's elementary, my dear Watson, elementary." More accurately, it's Step Three: calculating effective rights.

STEP THREE: CALCULATING EFFECTIVE RIGHTS

Effective rights are the bottom line. This is the culmination of our three-step process. In Step One, we assign the rights. In Step Two, we filter the rights. In Step Three, we calculate exactly what the rights are.

Calculating effective rights is about as simple as modern math. Any object's effective rights are the combination of NDS privileges received through any of the following:

▶ Trustee assignments made to the user

▶ Inheritance minus rights blocked by the IRF

▶ Rights granted to the special [Public] trustee

▶ Security equivalences to parent containers, groups, or Organizational Roles

I don't know if you've ever done modern math, but it's ugly. It would be easy if any of the assignments shown above canceled out the others. But, unfortunately, life isn't easy. These assignments work in combination with each other. Consider it modern math in the 7th Dimension.

Let's start with a simple example. Refer to Figure 11.25. In this first example, Sherlock Holmes is assigned [BCDRS] object rights to OU=CRIME. On the right side of the Figure, we've created an effective rights calculation worksheet. This is an *effective* (pun intended) tool for helping you get through modern math. You can create one at home with paper, a pencil, and a ruler.

FIGURE 11.25

Calculating Simple NDS Rights

CRIME		[BCDRS]
↓	IRF	—
	Inheritance	—
	SHolmes-TA	[BCDRS]
	Effective Rights	[BCDRS]
↓	IRF	[BC R]
	Inheritance	[BC R]
	SHolmes-TA	—
WHITE	**Effective Rights**	[BC R]
↓	IRF	—
	Inheritance	[BC R]
	Group-TA	[CD]
WHITE-SRV1	**Effective Rights**	[BCDR]

It starts with SHolmes' trustee assignment to OU=CRIME. Since there's no inheritance or IRF involved, his effective rights in this container are the same. Those effective rights become inherited rights in all subcontainers—one of which is OU=WHITE. To further complicate things, there's an IRF of [BCR] on the WHITE container. Since the IRF blocks [DS], Sherlock Holmes's inherited rights become [BCR]. With no other trustee assignments, his effective rights in OU=WHITE are the same—[BCR].

Finally, we arrive at the WHITE-SRV1 server object. It has no IRF so SHolmes' inherited rights are equal to the effective rights of the WHITE container—[BCR]. In addition, one of Sherlock Holmes's groups is assigned the [CD] object rights to the WHITE-SRV1 server. These rights combine with his inherited rights to create ultimate effective rights of [BCDR] for the server object. You see, that wasn't so hard. In this simple example, we had a limited number of different elements—one user trustee assignment, one group trustee assignment, and one IRF. Of course, the world is not always this simple. Now let's take a look at a more complex example.

Just when you think you understand it, they throw something like this at you. In this example (see Figure 11.26), there's one user assignment, one group trustee, an Organizational Role equivalent, AI, and three IRFs. Hold on to your hat!

FIGURE 11.26

Calculating Complex NDS Rights

Once again, we're going to use the effective rights calculation worksheet in Figure 11.26. As before, it begins with Sherlock Holmes at the OU=CRIME container—trustee assignment of [R]. In addition, the container is granted [CD] rights to itself. Since Sherlock Holmes lives in this context, he gains an ancestral inheritance of [CD]. This, combined with his user assignment, gives the effective rights [CDR]. In this case, the IRF is useless—simple window dressing. Remember, trustee assignments override the IRF.

Sherlock Holmes's effective rights in OU=CRIME become his inherited rights in OU=WHITE. The IRF, however, blocks [CDS] so his inheritance becomes [R]. This combines with a group trustee assignment of [CD] to give the effective rights [CDR]. But, wait a minute, we're not done. Remember, [Public] is granted [B] rights to the [Root]. Assuming no other IRFs, these rights are inherited throughout the tree. Since the OU=WHITE IRF allows [B], SHolmes gets it as well. Therefore, his real effective rights in OU=WHITE become [BCDR].

The above effective rights pass through the [R] filter at WHITE-SRV1. These inherited rights combined with his OR equivalence give effective rights of [BCR] at the WHITE-SRV1 server object. Piece of cake.

As you can see, effective rights get very hairy very quickly—just like modern math in the 7th Dimension. This is probably because there're so many forces at work. Remember, effective rights are the combination of trustee assignments, inheritance, [Public], and security equivalence. The default NDS rights are looking better and better all the time.

There you have it. The simple three-step NDS security model:

▸ Step One: Assigning NDS Rights—through trustee assignments, inheritance, and/or security equivalence.

▸ Step Two: Filtering IRF Rights—The inclusive filter allows you to block inherited rights. Remember to avoid isolating sections of the tree by using new trustee assignments with IRFs.

▸ Step Three: Calculating Effective Rights—just like modern math in the 7th Dimension.

Now I bet you're glad you made it through the simple steps of NDS security. Fortunately, there's a sophisticated foundation of NDS default rights to start from. And Steps Two and Three are optional. Your security system doesn't need to be this complex but in case it is, you have *Novell's CNE Study Guide for NetWare 4.1* to fall back on.

THE BRAIN

For more expert tips on NDS rights, see "Designing NetWare 4.x Security" in the November 1993 *Novell Application Notes*.

Before we move on to the Fourth Layer of the NetWare security model (file system access rights), let's spend a few moments exploring NDS administration. These are some supplemental strategies to help you deal with the daily grind of NDS security management.

QUIZ

OK, Bart. To prove your innocence, tell me: What is the English word most often pronounced wrong?

(Q11-4)

NDS ADMINISTRATION

NDS security is a daunting task. Don't feel like you have to accomplish it all alone. The advantages of NDS are that it enables you to section off certain areas of the network and delegate network administration tasks. You can, for example, delegate portions of the tree to distributed container administrators. On the other hand, what if it's a very highly secured government installation? You may only be involved in setting up the network. The daily administration tasks may be accomplished by a high-security work group.

NDS allows you to approach administration in one of two ways:

▶ Central administration

▶ Distributed administrators

Central administration means you have only one user (Admin) with Supervisor rights to the entire tree. This is the NetWare 4 default. Distributed administration, on the other hand, allows you to designate users with Supervisor rights to branches of the directory tree. This container administrator can either work in conjunction with Admin or replace him/her for that portion of the tree. Let's take a closer look.

Admin

The user Admin is created during installation and initially has all rights to manage NDS. As you saw in our earlier discussion, Admin is granted the [S] object right to [Root] by default. He/she consequently inherits all rights to the rest of the tree unless an IRF is applied. These rights also extend into NetWare 4 file systems unless blocked by an IRF in the NDS tree.

Centralized administration is appropriate for small organizations or large implementations with a central MIS department. Some tasks that could easily be centrally administered include:

▶ Naming the Directory tree

▶ Installing the first server

▶ Creating the top layers of the NDS tree

▶ Partition management and synchronization

▶ Assigning container administrators

It may be difficult for one person to administer the entire tree. A central Admin may not be able to meet the daily requests of user creation, file system rights, login scripts, and so on. Therefore, you may consider assigning container administrators for busy portions of the tree.

TIP

The Admin user has few special properties beyond [S] rights to the [Root]. This user can be deleted, replaced, or generally abused. This is unlike the special Supervisor account from previous versions of NetWare. The moral of the story is, "Don't get delusions of grandeur if you login as Admin."

Distributed Administrators

Distributed administration means that designated users are given enough NDS rights to manage distributed branches of the NDS tree. This special user is often referred to as a container administrator. Distributed administration tends to allow you to respond to users' needs more quickly, especially in a large implementation. The following tasks can be distributed:

▸ Creating user accounts

▸ Creating and configuring print services

▸ Backing up and restoring data

▸ Assigning file system trustees

▸ Installing additional servers

▸ Creating work group managers

Of course, the optimum administrative strategy combines a central Admin with a few distributed administrators. As we saw in our earlier discussion, there are two ways of creating distributed administrators—IRF/new trustee assignments and Organizational Role. If only one person will administer a container, consider using the first option. Otherwise, Organizational Roles can act as a host to rotating administrators. Remember our Postmaster example.

> **REAL WORLD**
>
> There is a third way of creating distributed administrations—security equivalence. You can create a single container administrator and then make other users security equivalent to that object. This is not recommended, however. If you happen to delete the host administrator, all security equivalent users lose their rights. If the host was an exclusive container administrator, you've just lost all administrative control over a section of the tree. Does the term *reinstall* mean anything to you?

As we saw in an earlier example, it's possible to create an exclusive container administrator. Refer back to Figure 11.24. When the IRF was used to block all rights in the PR container, all administrators, including Admin, were locked out. Then BThomas was granted [BCDRS] object rights—thus making him an exclusive container administrator. Remember, NWADMIN requires you to make the trustee assignments first, then the IRF.

There are two other distributed administrators in addition to Admin and the container administrator:

- ▸ Print server operator—Responsible for managing print services. This role is often incorporated into the role of the container administrator.

- ▸ Print queue operator—Can assist the print server operator or container administrator in managing print jobs.

Table 11.4 summarizes the actions and requirements of central and distributed administrators. For now, suffice it to say—you don't have to do it alone. No matter who you are, there will always be some special circumstances to deal with. Let's take a look at some clever solutions for Profile login scripts, Directory Map objects, mailing list administrators, and traveling users.

T A B L E 11.4

Summary of Distributed Administrators

ROLE	ACCOUNT INFORMATION	FUNCTIONS
Admin	Default Admin User Object [S] object rights to [Root] (by default).	Name the Directory tree; install the first server; create the top levels of the NDS tree; handle partition management and synchronization; assign distributed administrators; issue initial auditor password; and upgrade servers, clients, and applications.
Distributed Administrator	Exclusive container administrator or Organizational Role. Requires [BCDRS] object rights to appropriate container.	Install supplemental servers; perform data backup and restoration; create and configure print services; write and maintain login scripts; monitor file server performance; track errors; monitor disk space usage, assign file system security; and upgrade spective servers; clients, and applications.
Print Server Operator	Print Server Operator object or Organizational Role. Must be added to "Print Server Operator" property of the respective print server object.	Load and bring down the print server, manage and maintain print server configurations.
Print Queue Operator	Print Queue Operator object or Organizational Role. Must be added to the "Print Queue Operator" property of the respective print queue.	Delete print jobs, change the order of print jobs, change queue status.

"Special" NDS Security

If you only learn one thing in this crazy chapter, I hope it's this:
Expect the unexpected.

ZEN

"Doh!"

Homer Simpson

There are many special circumstances that require a unique approach toward NDS security. Certain objects in the tree, for example, require additional NDS rights beyond the defaults. This usually occurs when a user is defined in a different container than the resource he/she is trying to access. Also, there are special considerations for traveling users and mailing list administrators. Here are some proven solutions for dealing with special security circumstances:

- ▶ Profile Login Scripts—As you'll learn in Chapter 12, NetWare 4 provides a facility for group login scripts—the Profile object. In order for a user to access a Profile script, he/she requires special rights. If the User and Profile objects are in the same container, no additional rights are required because he/she gets them by default. If, however, the User is in a different container, the Read [R] right to the Profile Login Script property is required.

- ▶ Directory Map—In Chapter 10, we discovered the Directory Map object as a way of reducing redundant network administration. It allows you to map logical pointers to NDS objects instead of physical volume locations. In order to access Directory Map objects, users need two sets of rights. First, NDS rights (Read [R] to the "Path" selected properties of the Directory Map object) and, second, file system rights to the volume in question. If the user resides in the same container as the Directory Map object, no additional NDS rights are required. Otherwise, you'll need to make the above NDS assignment.

▸ Mailing list administrator—postal workers are special people, too. Mailing list administrators need special NDS rights to manage certain user properties. Specifically grant him/her Read and Write [RW] properties rights to the following Selected Properties of each user in the mailing list—Telephone, Street, City, State or Province, Postal (Zip) Code and other postal office box properties. Whatever you do, don't use the All Properties option. This would give the mailing list administrator unintended power. Remember, if you grant anyone the Write [W] property right to a user's ACL property, he/she can change the user's security. This is a bad thing.

▸ Traveling user between two offices—As we learned in Chapter 4, traveling users can cause havoc on NDS administration. These users typically bounce from location to location demanding access to distributed and centralized resources. Several of the NDS security issues you should consider when working with traveling users include access to applications, file storage in a central volume, access to distributed files, access to local and distributed printers and e-mail, login authentication, and the type of computer they're using (notebook or desktop). The user who divides his/her time between two offices needs similar resources in two different locations. The easiest way to approach this problem is create two User objects, one in each location. Give appropriate rights to any resources needed in the local location. Then give him/her the Read [R] property rights to Profile Login Script and Directory Map objects (as shown above).

▸

Traveling users between various locations—users who travel to various locations on a regular basis require a slightly different type of NDS security. In this case, you may want to create an Alias object in each location. You can also use groups or Organizational Roles. Then assign the appropriate rights to the Alias for access to directories and network resources. Finally, don't forget the Profile Login Scripts and Directory Map objects. This strategy can also be used for traveling users who find themselves stuck in a remote location for a temporary period of time.

Wow. That's NDS security! In this section, we've explored the simple three-step model for configuring NDS access rights. We've learned about trustee assignments, inheritance, and security equivalence. The IRF came along to help us lock inherited rights and quickly became the foundation of "modern math" in the 7th Dimension—calculating effective rights. That's all there is to it. Finally, we learned you don't have to do it alone. You can share all this fun with distributed administrators.

At the beginning of the chapter, we learned that security is "freedom from risk." At this discussion, you're probably thinking NDS security is freedom from sanity. Don't worry—it's not as crazy as you think. We've provided a detailed exploratorium at the end of the chapter for your enjoyment. And in the next section—file system access rights—you'll get a chance to review the three-step approach. Here's the good news. File system security is very similar to NDS security. Let's check it out.

QUIZ

So you wanna be the next Sherlock Holmes? Let's see if you've got what it takes. Each of the following six words is the odd one out for a different reason.

ABORT

ACT

AGT

ALP

OPT

APT

Can you find all six answers? If so, you are well on your way to answering the question, "Who shot Mr. Burns?"

(Q11-5)

Layer Four: File System Access Rights

NetWare 4 security exists on two functional planes:

- ▸ Above the server

- ▸ Within the server

In order to understand the two functional planes of NetWare 4 security, use the server as a midpoint (see Figure 11.27). NDS security occurs above the server—the "Cloud." In this plane, the server is at the bottom of the tree. It is treated as any other leaf object just like users, printers, and groups. NDS security applied above the server ends when it gets to a leaf object. There's no transition into the file system.

Above
(NDS Security)

Within
(File System Security)

VOL 1:   SYS:

File system security, on the other hand, occurs within the server. In this case, the server is the top of the tree. The server contains the volumes that contain the directories which house the files. Again, file system security ends once it gets to the server. There's no transition into the NDS security structure. Understanding the server's point of view will help you understand NDS and file system security.

The good news is NDS and file system security have a lot in common. You don't have to learn a whole new model. The same simple three-step approach applies. There're trustee assignments, inheritance, and security equivalence. The file system uses an IRF and calculating effective rights is still ugly. There are, however, a few minor differences between NDS and file system security:

- ▸ NDS has 10 access rights broken into two groups—object and property. The file system uses eight access rights.

- ▸ Rights do not flow from NDS into the file system except in one special instance—Supervisor [S] object rights to the Server object. This grants the trustee Supervisor file rights to the [Root] of all the server's volumes.

- ▸ The Supervisor NDS right can be blocked by the IRF. The Supervisor file system right, on the other hand, can NOT be blocked by the IRF.

That does it. As you can see, the file system and NDS have a lot more in common than you think. Let's start our discussion of security *within* the server by describing the eight file system access rights.

UNDERSTANDING FILE SYSTEM ACCESS RIGHTS

Welcome inside the server. It's kind of dark and cold in here but very secure. Before you can access any files, though, you must have appropriate file system access rights. As you can see in Figure 11.28, they also spell a word—WoRMFACES (the "O" is implied). Holy anatomical nematodes, Batman! It's not a pretty sight but certainly a name you will not forget. Let's check them out.

- ▸ W—Write: Grants the right to open and change the contents of files and directories.

- ▸ (O)—Doesn't exist but is needed to spell a word.

- ▸ R—Read: Grants the right to open files in the directory and read their contents or run applications.

File System Access Rights

W	Write
O	
R	Read
M	Modify
F	File Scan
A	Access Control
C	Create
E	Erase
S	Supervisor

▸ M—Modify: Grants the right to change the attributes or name of a file or directory. As we'll learn in just a second, the Modify right has a dual personality.

▸ F—File Scan: Grants the right to see files and directories.

▸ A—Access Control: Grants the right to change trustee assignments and the IRF.

▸ C—Create: Grants the right to create new files and subdirectories.

▸ E—Erase: Grants the right to delete a directory, its files, and subdirectories.

▸ S—Supervisor: Grants all rights to a directory and its files and subdirectories. This right *cannot* be blocked by the IRF (unlike NDS security).

In the above list, there are three rights you may want to steer clear of—[SAM] (and they also spell a word). The Supervisor right grants all privileges to files and directories and it cannot be filtered. Users with the Supervisor right can make trustee assignments and grant all rights to other users as well. Access Control also allows users to make trustee assignments but they can only grant the rights they possess. In addition, these users can modify the IRF. Finally, the Modify right has a split personality—Dr. Jekyll and Mr. Hyde. As Dr. Jekyll, Modify allows users to rename files and directories. Many applications require this. As Mr. Hyde, Modify allows users to change file and directory attributes. As we'll see a little later, attributes constitute the fifth layer of the NetWare 4 security model. I don't think you want users messing around with it.

REAL WORLD

The Supervisor access right is just as dangerous in the file system as it is in NDS. The tricky part is it can leak its way into the file system without you knowing it. Any user with the Write [W] property right to a server's ACL will implicitly receive Supervisor file rights to the Root of all volumes on the server. And to make things worse, the user will not appear on any file or directory trustee list. There's a variety of ways to get the Write [W] property right to a server's ACL including Supervisor object rights, Supervisor All Properties rights, and security equivalence. You may consider blocking these rights with a server IRF.

Recognizing the eight file system access rights is only the beginning. In order to effectively configure and manage file system security, you need to understand what they do. Individually, the rights are useless. But in combination, they become valuable security tools. Table 11.5 summarizes the file system rights requirements for common network tasks. Believe me, this will be an invaluable aid when it comes time to configure application and data security. Use it or lose it.

T A B L E 11.5	FILE SYSTEM TASK	RIGHTS REQUIREMENTS
Rights Requirements for Common File System Tasks	Open and read a file	Read
	See a filename	File Scan
	Search a directory for files	File Scan
	Open and write to an existing file	Write, Create, Erase, and Modify
	Execute an .EXE file	Read and File Scan

T A B L E II.5	FILE SYSTEM TASK	RIGHTS REQUIREMENTS
	Create and write to a file	Create
	Copy files *from* a directory	Read and File Scan
	Copy files *to* a directory	Write, Create, and File Scan
	Make a new directory	Create
	Delete a file	Erase
	Salvage deleted files	Read and File Scan for the file and Create for the directory
	Change directory or file attributes	Modify (Mr. Hyde)
	Rename a file or directory	Modify (Dr. Jekyll)
	Change the IRF	Access Control
	Change trustee assignments	Access Control
	Modify a directory's disk space restrictions	Access Control

So where do you begin? As with NDS, file system security starts with the defaults. NetWare 4 provides a sophisticated set of default file system access rights. These rights should become the foundation of your application and data security strategies. They aren't, however, as comprehensive as NDS defaults. You'll need to assign security whenever you create new application and data directories. Let's take a quick look at the NetWare 4 defaults:

▸ User—A unique User directory is created under SYS:USERS during User object conception. By default, the user gets all file system rights except Supervisor to the directory—[RWCEMF]. This directory will exactly match the User object name unless otherwise specified. Its location is also configurable.

▸ [Supervisor]—The Bindery Services Supervisor object is granted Supervisor [S] file rights to the [Root] of all volumes. This user performs special bindery functions using the Admin password.

▶ Creator—Whoever creates the file server object (usually Admin) automatically gets Supervisor [S] file system rights to all volumes. This can be blocked by filtering the Supervisor [S] object right with a server IRF.

▶ Container—The server's parent container is granted Read and File Scan [RF] access rights to SYS:PUBLIC. This way all users and objects in the server's home container can access NetWare 4 [Public] utilities.

That completes our discussion of file system access rights. As you can see, there's a lot more than meets the eye. Make sure to use Table 11.5 when assigning rights to new application and data directories. Also test these rights before you let the users loose. Many times, applications have strange unobvious requirements. Now that you know what to do, let's learn how to do it. Remember, the NetWare 4 file system behaves exactly the same as NDS:

▶ Step One: Assigning Trustee Rights

▶ Step Two: Filtering IRF Rights

▶ Step Three: Calculating Effective Rights

Ready. Set. Go!

ZEN

"I am Melvin Van Horn, and this is my associate Hershel Krustovsky. Officers, you have arrested an innocent man!"

Krusty's Sidekick

FILE SYSTEM THREE-STEP SHUFFLE

This gives us an opportunity to review the three-step NDS security model. Fortunately, file system security imitates it to the letter. Remember, NetWare 4 security starts with two simple questions:

▶ What rights do I need to do stuff?

▸ How do I get these rights?

Well, so far we've learned about the eight file system access rights and what rights are needed for common network tasks. Now we get to answer the question, "How do I get these rights?" As with NDS, file system security is as easy as 1-2-3:

▸ Step One: Assigning Trustee Rights—You assign the access rights through trustee assignments, inheritance, and/or security equivalence.

▸ Step Two: Filtering IRF Rights—In special circumstances, you can filter inherited rights at the directory level.

▸ Step Three: Calculating Effective Rights—The result is effective rights; that is, what users can actually do to directories and files.

Once again, it's as easy as A-B-C. Except in this case, we're assigning access rights to files and directories, not NDS objects. Let's take a closer look at this simple three-step model from the file system's point of view.

Step One: Assigning Trustee Rights

You have to start somewhere, and Step One starts with work. A trustee is any NDS object with rights to directories or files. Trustees are tracked through the DET (directory table). The file system supports the same trustee types as NDS—users, groups, containers, Organizational Roles, and [Public]. Once you identify who is going to get the rights, you have to determine what rights you're going to give them and where the rights will be assigned. This is shown in Figure 11.29. MMarion is granted all rights except [SAM] to the SYS:SHARED directory. These rights are then inherited for all subdirectories underneath. As you can see, the *who* is MMarion, the *what* is [RWCEF], and the *where* is SYS:SHARED. This is an explicit trustee assignment.

FIGURE 11.29

Understanding File System Security

So how is this accomplished in NWADMIN? Once again, it depends on your point of view and you have two choices:

▸ Rights to Files and Directories—This is from Maid Marion's point of view.

▸ Trustees of this Directory—This is from SYS:SHARED's point of view.

It really doesn't matter which option you choose. You can either assign rights from the user's point of view or the directory's point of view. In the first example, we assign security from Maid Marion's point of view. In NWADMIN, double-click on Maid Marion and her User Information window appears. Choose Rights to Files and Directories from the right-hand list and voilà—Figure 11.30 appears.

Figure 11.30 shows the security window from Maid Marion's point of view. As you can see, she has been granted [RWCEF] access rights to SYS:SHARED. In addition, she's also a trustee of SYS:\USERS\POLIT\MMARION—by default. You can create trustee assignments by using the Add... button.

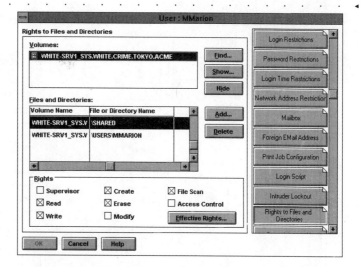

*Assigning File Rights from
the User's Point of View*

REAL WORLD

The Security Information window shown in Figure 11.30 only displays trustee assignments for a single volume at a time. By its very nature, NDS allows you to view information about multiple volumes throughout the WAN. In order to bring up the trustee assignments for a different volume, use the Show... button. You can also explore for other volumes by using the Find... button. In Figure 11.30, we're only looking at Maid Marion's trustee assignments for WHITE-SRV1_SYS.

The second option allows you to assign access rights from SYS:SHARED's point of view. In this case, you would double-click on WHITE-SRV1_SYS from the Browse window of NWADMIN. All of its directions should appear. Then highlight SHARED and click the right mouse button. A pull-down menu will appear—choose Details. Once the SYS:SHARED Details window appears, choose Trustees of this Directory from the righthand list (see Figure 11.31). In this screen, NWADMIN gives you the choice of adding trustees or setting the IRF (Inherited Rights Filter). Notice that MMarion has been added with the [RWCEF] access rights. You can create other trustee assignments for SYS:SHARED using the Add Trustee... button. Also notice the IRF allows all rights to flow through—this is the default.

F I G U R E II.3I

*Assigning File Rights from
the Directory's Point of
View*

There you have it. As you can see, it doesn't matter how we assign access rights. Both methods accomplish the same thing—Maid Marion (who) is granted [RWCEF] trustee rights (what) to SYS:SHARED (where).

Now that we've explored the "work part," let's take a closer look at inheritance—"no work."

As we learned earlier, access rights are also assigned through inheritance. This is an automatic side effect of trustee assignments. As you can see in Figure 11.29, Maid Marion inherits [RWCEF] access rights in all subdirectories of SYS:SHARED. Inheritance is a great thing. It allows you to assign sweeping file system access rights with minimal effort. Remember, as a CNE, work is bad.

But many times, inheritance gets out of hand. Fortunately, NetWare 4 allows you to override inheritance using a new trustee assignment or an IRF. We'll explore these topics in just a moment.

If trustee assignments or inheritance aren't quite getting the job done, security equivalence may be the answer. Security equivalence simply states "one object is equivalent to another with respect to file system access rights." As we learned earlier, users, for example, are security equivalent to their parent container. We also learned that security equivalence operates at the trustee assignment level—this is NOT inheritance. Therefore, security equivalence overrides the IRF.

NetWare 4 provides four strategies for security equivalence:

▶ Ancestral Inheritance (AI)—Any object is security equivalent to its ancestors (parent containers). This means any rights you assign to an NDS container are absorbed by all the objects in the container. This is not inheritance—this is security equivalence.

▶ Organizational Role—Our special NDS objects designed as task identifiers. Jobs that require multiple temporary users are excellent candidates for Organizational Roles. Simply assign file system access rights to the Role and they are absorbed by all occupants of the Role. Once again, this is not inheritance.

▶ Groups—Allows you to distribute similar rights to unrelated users. That is, users not within the same area of the NDS tree. Members of any group absorb (not inherit) rights assigned to the host group object.

▶ Directory Map—In very special circumstances, security equivalence can be used to facilitate Directory Map objects. When you create a Directory Map object, make sure to assign adequate file system rights to its physical location. Then when you use the MAP command to create logical pointers, make sure to assign the host user's security equivalence to the Directory Map object.

That completes Step One of the file system security model. Remember, this is the hard part. Steps Two and Three are optional. Step Two allows us to filter inherited rights and Step Three combines all rights assignments into a single mathematical formula—math in the 7th Dimension. Let's keep rolling!

Step Two: Filtering IRF Rights

Earlier we learned there are two ways of blocking unwanted inherited rights: new trustee assignments and the inherited rights filter (IRF). The IRF blocks inherited rights at any point in the tree. There are, however, two very important points you need to understand about how the IRF works:

▶ It's an inclusive filter, which means the rights that are in the filter are the ones that are allowed to pass through.

▸ The IRF applies to everyone in the NDS tree. Once you've assigned an IRF to a directory, everybody is blocked *except* Admin.

This is the only place where file system and NDS security differs. The NDS IRF blocks the Supervisor right. The file system IRF, on the other hand, *cannot* block the Supervisor right. As you can see in Figure 11.31, the IRF is assigned using the Trustees of this Directory option. Also notice that the Supervisor right has been grayed out. This means it cannot be removed. Also notice the downward arrows that appear next to each option box. These differentiate IRF rights from trustee assignments. Anywhere you see a downward arrow, you can assume it's an IRF filter.

When you assign an IRF, all sorts of crazy things happen. My word of advice is: Avoid them at all cost. But if you can't, you'll need to deal with Step Three—calculating effective rights.

Step Three: Calculating Effective Rights

As we learned earlier, effective rights are the bottom line. This is the culmination of our three-step process. In Step One, we assign the rights. In Step Two, we filter the rights. In Step Three, we calculate exactly what the rights are. We also learned that calculating effective rights is as simple as modern math—in the 7th Dimension! Any object's effective rights are the combination of file system privileges received through any of the following:

▸ Trustee assignments made to the user

▸ Inheritance minus rights blocked by the IRF

▸ Rights granted to the special [Public] trustee

▸ Security equivalences to parent containers, groups, or Organizational Roles

As we learned earlier, calculating effective rights for NDS can be mind-boggling and fun. The file system is no different. Let's use Maid Marion as an example. Suppose we're concerned about users making changes to our political database. To protect it, we assign an [RF] filter to SYS:SHARED\POL. This will block MMarion's inherited rights of [RWCEF]. Therefore, her effective rights must be Read and File Scan [RF]. But as you can see in Figure 11.32, her effective rights in SYS:SHARED\POL are, in fact, [RWF]. How did this happen? She must be getting the [W] right from somewhere else. Ah, I remember. She's a member of the POL-Group and they've been granted Write privileges to SYS:SHARED\POL. Therefore, her effective rights become inherited rights minus the IRF *plus* group trustee assignments.

F I G U R E 11.32

Calculating Effective Rights for Maid Marion

NWADMIN provides an excellent tool for viewing effective rights—check out Figure 11.32. All you have to do is identify the user (MMarion) and the directory (SYS:SHARED\POL)—NWADMIN does all the rest.

There you have it. The simple three-step file system security model:

▸ Step One: Assigning NDS Rights—Through trustee assignments, inheritance, and/or security equivalence.

▸ Step Two: Filtering IRF Rights—The inclusive filter allows you to block inherited rights.

▸ Step Three: Calculating Effective Rights—Just like modern math in the 7th Dimension.

That was a fun review. It's fortunate for us that NetWare 4 uses the same model for both NDS and file system security. Even though these two layers apply to dramatically different network elements, they approach security in a similar way. Hopefully now you've got a firm handle on access rights, default assignments, trustees, inheritance, the

IRF, and effective rights. They all work together as a synergistic solution for risk management. Of course, there's always that isolated exception when four layers of security aren't quite enough. You never know when a hacker will show up with armor-piercing bullets. Fortunately, NetWare 4 has one more layer for just these emergencies—file/directory attributes. Let's check it out.

ZEN

"Shot...by you? I'm afraid not my primitive friend. Your kind has neither the cranial capacity nor the opposable digits to operate a firearm."

Mr. Montgomery Burns

Layer Five: File/Directory Attributes

Welcome to the final layer. I bet you never thought you'd get here. Directory and file attributes provide the final and most sophisticated layer of the NetWare 4 security model. These attributes are rarely used but provide a powerful tool for specific security solutions. If all fails, you can always turn to attribute security to save the day.

Attributes are special assignments or properties that are assigned to individual directories or files. Attribute security overrides all previous trustee assignments and effective rights. Attributes can be used to prevent deleting a file, copying a file, viewing a file, and so on. Attributes also control whether files can be shared, mark files for backup purposes, or protect them from data corruption using the Transactional Tracking System (TTS).

Attributes allow you to manage what users can do with files once they have access to them. Attributes are global security elements that affect all users regardless of their rights. And they override all previous levels of security. Let's say, for example, Maid Marion has all rights except [SAM] to the SYS:APPS\WP directory—[RWCEF]. You can still restrict her from deleting a specific file by assigning it the Read-Only attribute. Therefore, the true effective rights for Maid Marion in this directory are the combination of her effective file system rights *and* file attributes.

NetWare 4 supports two types of attributes: directory and file. Directory attributes apply to directories only whereas file attributes can be assigned to files. In both these cases, attributes fall into one of three categories:

- ▶ Security attributes

- ▶ Feature attributes

- ▶ Disk management attributes

Security attributes affect users' security access—what they can do with files. Feature attributes, on the other hand, affect how the system interacts with files. That is, whether the files can be archived, purged, or transactional tracked. Finally, disk management attributes apply to file compression, data migration, and block suballocation.

Let's take a closer look at NetWare 4 attribute security starting with security attributes.

SECURITY ATTRIBUTES

Security attributes protect information at the file and directory level by controlling two kinds of file access—file sharing and file alteration. File access security controls not so much *who* can access the files but *what kind of access* they have. Once users have been given the proper trustee assignments to a given directory, they're in the door. Security attributes tell users they what he/she can do with the files once they're there. Here's a list of NetWare 4's security attributes and a brief description. An asterisk (*) indicates any attribute that affects both directories and files.

- ▶ Copy Inhibit (Ci)—Only valid on Macintosh workstations. Prevents users from copying the file. Even if users have been granted the Read and File Scan [RF] rights, they still can't copy this specific file. Macintosh users can, however, remove the Ci attribute if they have been granted the Modify [M] access right.

- ▶ Delete Inhibit (Di)*—Prevents users from erasing the directory or file.

▸ Execute Only (X)—This is an extremely sensitive attribute and provides a very high level of NetWare security. Only the Supervisor, Admin, or anyone with the Supervisor [S] right can set this file attribute and it *cannot* be cleared. The only way to remove X is to delete the file. The Execute Only attribute can only be assigned to .EXE and .COM files. These files cannot be copied or backed up—just executed or deleted. You should note that many applications don't work on files with the Execute Only attribute attached.

▸ Hidden (H)*—Valid on both DOS and OS/2 machines. Hidden is reserved for special files or directories that should not be seen, used, deleted, or copied over. However, the NDIR command shows the directory if the user has File Scan [F] access rights.

▸ Normal (N)*—No directory or file attributes have been set. This is the default. Normal files are typically flagged non-sharable, Read/Write automatically.

▸ Read-Only (Ro)—No one can write to the file. When Read Only is set or cleared, NetWare 4 also sets or clears the Delete Inhibit and Rename Inhibit attributes. Consequently, a user can't write to, erase, or rename a file when Read Only is set. A user with the Modify access right can remove the Di and Ri attributes without removing Ro. In this case, the file can be deleted or renamed but not written to.

▸ Read/Write (Rw)—Allows users to change the contents of the file. This attribute is assigned automatically through Normal (N).

▸ Rename Inhibit (Ri)*—Prevents a user from renaming the file or directory.

▸ Sharable (Sh)—Allows the file to be accessed by more than one user at a time. This attribute is usually used in combination with Ro for application files. The default "Normal" setting is non-sharable.

▸ System (Sy)*—Applies to DOS and OS/2 workstations. The NetWare 4 OS assigns this attribute to system-owned files and directories. System files are hidden and cannot be deleted, renamed, or copied. However, the NetWare NDIR command shows the file if the user has File Scan access rights.

That does it for security attributes. Now let's take a closer look at feature attributes.

FEATURE ATTRIBUTES

Feature attributes provide access to special NetWare functions or features. These features include backup, purging, and transactional tracking. As a matter of fact, there are only three feature attributes in NetWare 4 and one of them applies to both directories and files (P). Here's how they work:

▸ Archive Needed (A)—A status flag set by NetWare. Indicates that the file has been changed since the last time it was backed up. NetWare sets this attribute when a file is modified and clears it during SBACKUP full and incremental sessions. We'll learn more about this in Chapter 13.

▸ Purge (P)*—Tells NetWare to purge the file when it is deleted. The file then cannot be salvaged with FILER. Purge at the directory level clears all files and directories from the salvage table once they're deleted. This attribute is best used on sensitive data.

▸ Transactional (T)—Indicates that the file is protected by NetWare 4's internal Transactional Tracking System (TTS). TTS prevents data corruption by ensuring that either all changes are made or no changes are made when a file is being modified. The Transactional attribute should be assigned to TTS-tracked database and accounting files.

That does it for NetWare 4 feature attributes. Now let's take a quick look at disk management.

DISK MANAGEMENT ATTRIBUTES

The remaining seven file and directory attributes apply to NetWare 4 disk management—file compression, data migration, and block suballocation. File compression allows more data to be stored on a volume by compressing files that are not being used. Once you enable this disk management feature, volume capacity increases up to 63 percent. Data migration is the transfer of inactive data from a NetWare volume to an external optical disk storage device—called a jukebox. The process is transparent to the user because files appear to be stored on the volume. Data migration is made possible because of NetWare 4's internal High Capacity Storage System (HCSS). Finally, block suballocation increases disk storage efficiency by segmenting disk allocation blocks. Suballocation is also automatic, and you can turn it off using one of the following seven attributes. Here's a quick look at NetWare 4's disk management attributes:

▸ Can't Compress (Cc)—A status flag set by NetWare. Indicates that the file can't be compressed because of insignificant space savings. To avoid the overhead of uncompressing files that do not compress well, the system calculates the compressed size of a file before actually compressing it. If no disk space will be saved by compression or if the size difference does not meet the value specified by the "Minimum Percentage Compression Gain" parameter, the file is not compressed. This attribute is shown on attribute lists but cannot be set by users or CNEs.

▸ Compressed (Co)—A status flag set by NetWare. Indicates that the file has been compressed by the system. Once again, this attribute is shown on attribute lists but cannot be set by the user or CNEs.

▸ Don't Compress (Dc)*—Marks a file or directory so that it is never compressed. This is your way of managing file compression. This attribute is used in combination with Ic (immediate compression). We'll check this out in just a moment.

▸ Don't Migrate (Dm)*—Marks a file or directory so that it is never migrated to a secondary storage device. This is the only way you can directly manage data migration. Otherwise, all files are automatically migrated once they exceed the timeout threshold.

▸ Don't Suballocate (Ds)—Prevents an individual file from being suballocated even if suballocation is enabled on the volume. This is typically used for files that are huge or appended to frequently—databases. This attribute is your only tool for managing suballocation once it's been activated.

▸ Immediate Compress (Ic)*—Marks a file or directory for immediate compression. NetWare 4 will compress the file as soon as it can without waiting for a specific event to initiate compression—such as a time delay. As a CNE, you can use Ic to turn on compression and Dc to turn it off. Both attributes operate at the file and directory level.

▸ Migrated (M)—A status flag set by NetWare. Indicates that the file has been migrated. This attribute is shown on an attribute list but can't be set by the user or CNE.

TIP

Any of these attributes can be modified using the FLAG command line utility or NETADMIN menu utility and/or NWADMIN graphical utility. In addition, they can be viewed using the NDIR command line utility, FILER menu utility and/or NWADMIN graphical utility.

These file and directory attributes when used in combination can create effective security tools to control who has access to do what with specialized NetWare files. The default attribute combination for all files is Normal—nonsharable Read/Write. There are special instances, however, when you can justify customizing these attributes such as:

▸ Stand alone applications that are not to be shared should be flagged nonsharable Read-Only.

▸ Data files that are shared but not written to simultaneously should be flagged nonsharable Read/Write.

▸ Data files that are part of larger multiuser applications can be flagged Sharable Read/Write only if the application supports internal record locking is activated.

- Application files that are accessed by simultaneous users should be flagged Sharable Read-Only.

- Large important database files should always be flagged with the Transactional (T) attribute.

- Sensitive archive files should be flagged with the attribute Hidden. These include records that are only accessed once a month.

- All System files owned by NetWare should be flagged System. This is an attribute assigned by NetWare, not you.

- Sensitive application files that cost lots of money should be flagged Execute Only by the network administrator.

Congratulations! You've completed the NetWare 4's five-layered security model. Wow, what a wild ride. It all started with risk analysis and countermeasures. We learned the absolute goal of NetWare 4 security:

Let the good guys in and keep the bad guys out.

We also learned that NetWare 4's five-layered security model is an increasingly more secure series of barriers against network threats—users. In Layer One, they login to the "Cloud" with initial and background authentication. Then login restrictions take over. This barrier controls the user's conditional access through five different types of restrictions—account, password, station, time, and Intruder Detection/Lockout. Once the user passes through the first two barriers, their ability to access leaf and container objects is determined by a sophisticated NDS security structure. At the heart of NDS security is a simple three-step process—trustee assignments, IRF, and effective rights.

But what about security *within* the server? NDS security isn't enough. Now we must protect the file system. File system security operates in much the same way as NDS object rights. They're granted with the help of trustee assignments, inheritance, and security equivalence. We learned how the eight different access rights can be used to protect NetWare 4 files and directories. But sometimes this isn't enough. That's where attributes come in. The final barrier allows you to override previous security with three different attribute types—security, feature, and disk management.

Well, there you have it. The NetWare 4 five-layered security model. Of course, we're not quite done. Should somebody get lucky enough to break through your network armor, it would be nice to know what they're doing there. That's where NetWare 4 auditing comes in. Fortunately, NetWare 4 includes a sophisticated suite of event tracking services called auditing. Will this chapter ever end?

NetWare 4 Auditing

Have you ever had the feeling you're being watched? Paranoia is a good thing. Especially when it comes to NetWare 4 security. Auditing allows you to track network events from three different angles:

- From NDS

- From the volume

- From the user

Container auditing allows you to track a variety of interesting events including changes to the ACL, security equivalence, enable/disabling user accounts, intruder lockout, partition management, replication, and time stamp repairs. Volume auditing allows you to track numerous events according to three key elements—files, print queues, and servers. Finally, user auditing allows you to track logins, logouts, trustee assignments, connection termination, and disk space restrictions.

Wow. As you can see, NetWare 4 auditing gives you everything you need. So why do you need to audit? For any of the following reasons:

- To monitor any changes in network security

- To know who is accessing certain files

- To track the activities of selected users

- To keep a record of login and logout activity by date and time

- To justify the addition of new resources

Any of these activities justify the creation of an independent auditor. The beauty of NetWare 4 auditing is that auditors can audit—and nothing else. In addition, auditors can track Admin without his/her interference. Too bad we didn't have this facility around during the S&L days of the late 1980s.

QUIZ

This mystery doesn't seem to have any "rhyme or reason." Speaking of which, each of the following six "rhymes" provides clues to a word. When you've uncovered the mysterious list, use the first and last letters of each word to discover the "reason" for our journey. Ready, set, go.

A tiny note, it's in quick time,
All you need to solve this rhyme?

Cry to Mark, it's so abrupt,
Delight or horror will erupt.

Set a course to steer the ship,
Plot the route when off you trip.

Just a drop to come apart,
Joy perhaps, or sad at heart?

Describe a lad who now is striving,
One day his hopes may be arriving.

Sculpture of freedom and all is well,
Here's independence and the marching bell.

Good luck. You're going to need a lot of mental energy to solve this mystery.

(Q11-6)

It all starts by enabling auditing on a NetWare 4 volume or NDS container. Check it out.

ENABLING AUDITING

You can't audit anything until you turn it on. Enabling NetWare 4 auditing is accomplished in seven simple steps. As you can see in Figure 11.33, these steps are split between two key administrators:

▸ Admin—enables auditing and creates the initial audit password

▸ Auditor—configures auditing parameters and generates reports

FIGURE 11.33

NetWare 4 Auditing Steps

Admin

1. Activate AUDITCON

2. Enable Auditing

3. Assign Password to Volume or Container

Auditor

4. Login as Auditor with Appropriate Passwords

5. Change Password

6. Auditing Confuguration

7. Auditing Reports

The key to NetWare 4 auditing is its password strategy. Unique passwords are required at multiple stages throughout the auditing process. These passwords are kept independent from Admin and other administrative users. Because of this, auditors can track network resources without actually having any other rights to the network's resources. Auditors can only audit! This functionality is analogous to the independent auditors who audit banks—assuming, of course, that the bank is not a Savings & Loan. Here's how it works:

▸ Step One: Activate AUDITCON—The Admin user gets things rolling by
activating the AUDITCON utility from SYS:PUBLIC. The system responds
with a screen similar to Figure 11.34.

*Creating the Auditor
Password*

▸ Step Two: Enable auditing—Next, Admin enables auditing for a specific NDS
container or volume. Only Admin or a distributed administrator can enable
auditing. Once auditing is enabled, only the auditor can disable it.

▸ Step Three: Assign auditor password—When Admin chooses "Enable
Volume Auditing" from the Available Audit Options menu, a password
prompt appears. This is Step Three. Note: You can only enable auditing at
the volume or container level. Auditing does not extend to subcontainers.
This is almost like logging in with Bindery Services. Earlier, we learned the
key to NetWare 4 auditing: its multilayered password strategy. Each volume
and container maintains its own independent password. This way,
distributed auditors can track different areas of the tree simultaneously.
When you assign an auditor password at this point, you're only assigning the
password to a specific volume or container. In Figure 11.34, the password
will be assigned to the SYS: volume on the WHITE-SRV1 server. Once you
assign a password, it's time to transfer control over to the independent
auditor.

▸ Step Four: Auditor login—Now control shifts from Admin to the new auditor. Once auditing has been enabled, he/she can Login to AUDITCON using the new password. This activates volume or container auditing and expands the Available Audit Options menu—see Figure 11.35. A few new choices have been added including Audit files maintenance, Auditing configuration, Auditing reports, and Reports from old offline file. The auditor is in! The next step is to protect the auditor's independence by assigning a new password.

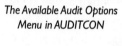

FIGURE 11.35

The Available Audit Options Menu in AUDITCON

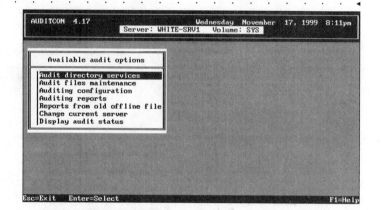

```
AUDITCON  4.17                            Wednesday  November  17, 1999  8:11pm
                        Server: WHITE-SRV1   Volume: SYS

        ┌─────────────────────────────────┐
        │    Available audit options      │
        │ ┌─────────────────────────────┐ │
        │ │Audit directory services     │ │
        │ │Audit files maintenance      │ │
        │ │Auditing configuration       │ │
        │ │Auditing reports             │ │
        │ │Reports from old offline file│ │
        │ │Change current server        │ │
        │ │Display audit status         │ │
        │ └─────────────────────────────┘ │
        └─────────────────────────────────┘

Esc=Exit   Enter=Select                                              F1=Help
```

▸ Step Five: Change auditor password—In order to maintain independence from Admin, the auditor should first change the auditing password. This is accomplished using the Auditing configuration option from the main menu. Remember, any changes made to this password take effect for the current volume or container only. Once the password has been changed, the setup phase of auditing has been completed and it's time to get to work—Steps Six and Seven.

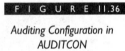

REAL WORLD

Whatever you do, DON'T forget the auditor password. If you do, nobody can deactivate volume or container auditing. This is a bad thing. Audit files can get large and generate all sorts of problems for NDS and the file system. Especially if you configure Event Lockout. Stay tuned.

▸ Step Six: Auditing configuration—This is where the auditor earns his/her pay. The Auditing Configuration window is shown in Figure 11.36. From here, the auditor can activate tracked events, change configuration options, or disable auditing. Nothing happens until the auditor switches on Tracked Events—they're all off by default. We'll take a much closer look at auditing configuration in just a moment.

FIGURE 11.36

Auditing Configuration in AUDITCON

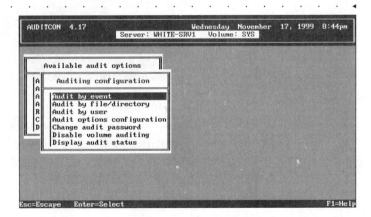

▸ Step Seven: Auditing reports—This is the pinnacle of NetWare 4 auditing. It doesn't do us any good to track volume and NDS events unless we generate reports on them. After you've configured tracked events, you'll have to determine which ones you want to include in the report. And what the reports are going to look like, and finally how often the reports should be printed. Auditing reports are based on a filtering concept. AUDITCON generates so much information it would be impossible to wade through all the tracked entries. Report filters allow you to print out only the information you're interested in. This includes date and time, specific container and volume events, include and exclude users, files or directories. We'll take a closer look at generating audit reports a little bit later.

That's it. Enabling auditing is as simple as 1-2-3-4-5-6-7. Of all these events, the final two are the most important. Auditing configuration involves activating tracked events, and Auditing reports gives you something to turn into Admin. Let's take a closer look at these last two tasks and learn how they can be used to audit NDS volumes and users.

AUDITING CONFIGURATION
Auditing configuration focuses on three main categories:

▸ NDS

▸ Volumes

▸ Users

NDS auditing tracks events at the container level. Remember, we can only audit a single container at a time. Every container needs its own distinct password. Volume auditing allows you to track file events, queue management, server events, and/or specific files and directories in the file system. Finally, user events allow you to track specific users as they navigate through the NDS Cloud. By default, all auditing events are turned off. Once you enable auditing, the auditor must login and activate specific events. This is accomplished using the Audit Configuration Option in Figure 11.35. Let's take a closer look at each of these important auditing categories.

Auditing NDS
Container auditing is activated by selecting the Audit Directory Services option from the main menu (see Figure 11.35). All you have to do is highlight the container you're interested in and press F10. Once you enter the auditor password, a screen similar to Figure 11.37 appears. As you can see, all NDS events are OFF by default.

FIGURE 11.37

Auditing NDS Events in
AUDITCON

```
AUDITCON  4.17                              Sunday  November  21, 1999  5:26pm
                        Session context: white.crime.tokyo.acme

                                   Audit by DS events

    Abort partition                                          off
    Add entry                                                on
    Add partition                                            on
    Add replica                                              off
    Change ACL                                               on
    Change password                                          on
    Change replica type                                      off
    Change security also equals                              off
    Change security equivalence                              on
    Change station restriction                               off
    Disable user account                                     off
    Enable user account                                      off
    Intruder lockout change                                  off
    Join partitions                                          off
    Log in user                                              off
  ▼ Log out user                                             off

Esc=Escape   F8=Toggle all   F10=Toggle audit                       F1=Help
```

We've turned on 10 important auditing events including:

▶ Add entry—Tracks when any entry is added to the NDS database.

▶ Add partition—Tracks when a new partition is created.

▶ Change ACL—Tracks changes to the Access Control List (ACL) of any property. This is a critical indication that security rights have been changed.

▶ Change password—Tracks when someone changes a password in the NDS database.

▶ Change security equivalences—Tracks changes to security equivalences in NDS security.

▶ Rename object—Tracks when an object is renamed. This can be particularly disruptive especially if container objects are renamed.

▶ Repair time stamps—Tracks when time stamps are repaired. This could indicate problems with time synchronization.

▶ Send replica update—Tracks when Master Replicas of partitions send updates to Read/Write replicas. Useful when checking the integrity of NDS over a WAN.

▸ Split partition—Tracks when a partition is split. This is a useful parameter to track when trying to coordinate the creation of partitions. Generally, only one central administrator should be creating partitions and replicas within the NDS tree.

▸ User locked—Tracks when a user account has been locked. Could be an indication that the Intruder Detection/Lockout system has been activated.

Auditing Volumes

Volume auditing is accomplished using one of the first two choices in Figure 11.36. Audit by Event allows you to track parameters according to three different events—file events, QMS events, and/or server events. This choice is shown in Figure 11.38. The other choice, Audit by File/Directory, allows you to track all activity on specific files and directories. This is a useful strategy for monitoring valuable database files. Once again, all volume events are turned off by default.

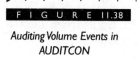

F I G U R E 11.38

Auditing Volume Events in AUDITCON

Following is a list of some file, QMS, and server events you may consider turning on:

▸ Delete directory—A file event that tracks directory deletions. You probably want to know who is deleting your valuable NetWare data and when.

▸ File delete—Similarly, you want to track the deletion of valuable NetWare files.

- ▶ File salvage—A file event that monitors the recovery of deleted files. This is particularly useful if nonauthorized users are accessing sensitive deleted files.

- ▶ Queue destroy—A QMS event that tracks deleted print queues.

- ▶ Queue detach server—A QMS event that indicates a print server being disconnected from a queue. This typically happens when the print server goes down and is something you probably want to track.

- ▶ Queue set job priority—A QMS event that tracks changes to the service sequence of print jobs. You can monitor when print queue operators move other jobs ahead of yours. If this is happening too often, you may want to speak with the print queue operator.

- ▶ Change date/time—An important server event that tracks any change of the date or time from the file server console. NetWare 4 time synchronization doesn't take kindly to this type of tampering.

- ▶ Down server—Another important server event which tracks when and why servers go down. Obviously, this is an indication of abnormal WAN activity.

- ▶ Volume dismount—A server event that tracks volume dismounts. Also a harmful activity.

- ▶ Volume mount—A server event that tracks volumes being mounted and remounted. This and the previous option are useful in tracking CD-ROM usage on the server. If you notice an excessive number of mounts and dismounts, consider adding a second CD-ROM unit. Or transferring the files to an internal disk.

Auditing Users

The final auditing category deals with users themselves. This option allows you to hook onto specific users and watch what they do with their time. This is especially important for suspect hackers and disruptive administrators. NetWare 4 tracks user events from two different angles—NDS and volumes. NDS tracks user logins and user logouts from the DS configuration screen (see Figure 11.37). Volume configurations, on the other hand, track bindery users. You can track bindery logins, logouts, account disabling, and disk space restrictions. In either case, user auditing is off by default.

So there you have it. NetWare 4 auditing has been activated for key NDS volume and user activities. But your auditing configuration duties are not finished. Now you must maintain configuration options to keep things running smoothly. These include threshold management, archiving, error recovery options, audit file maintenance, and status. Let's take a closer look at daily auditing configuration options.

Configuration Options

Auditing is serious business. NetWare 4 uses a variety of secure audit files to track NDS, volume, and user events. As I'm sure you can imagine, these files get very large very quickly. And like any database system, their configurations require daily maintenance. In addition to audit files, you'll need to configure the auditor, error recovery options and overall audit status. Most of these tasks can be accomplished on a single screen—shown in Figure 11.39. Other options are found elsewhere throughout AUDITCON.

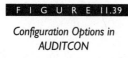

F I G U R E 11.39

Configuration Options in AUDITCON

Let's take a closer look at the daily grind of an auditor's life.

- ▶ Audit files—NetWare 4 uses two audit files to track all this crazy information—NET$AUDT.DAT (the current audit database) and AUD$HIST.DAT (the audit history file). Both of these files are kept in the root of each volume and perpetually flagged in Open. This ensures that non-auditors stay away from these two important files. As you can see in

Figure 11.39, AUDITCON provides a variety of configuration options for NET$AUDT.DAT. The first two parameters deal with the audit file's maximum size and threshold size. Once the files exceed the threshold, warning messages appear on the file server console. These messages continue until the file reaches its "maximum size." When this occurs, the Error Recovery Options activate. As we'll see in just a moment, you have three options: archive the file, dismount the volume, or disable event recording.

By default, the maximum audit file size is a little over 1 MB. This is approximately one week's activity on a busy network. You may consider increasing the audit file's maximum size. In addition, automatic archiving allows us to deal with NET$AUDT.DAT without causing too much chaos on the WAN—like dismounting volumes. As you can see in Figure 11.39, automatic archiving is set ON with seven days between archives. The file will be archived and reset at midnight and AUDITCON keeps the latest two backups. Finally, the audit history file (AUD$HIST.DAT) is used to audit the auditor. It simply tracks what the auditor does in AUDITCON and when the audit file is reset. This allows Admin to keep the auditor in check. Sounds like a good idea to me.

▶ Auditor—Figure 11.39 also includes a few configurations for the auditor. First, it allows you to manage concurrent auditor logins. This is necessary if different people are simultaneously auditing different parts of the tree. Remember, AUDITCON includes a sophisticated multilayer password system. For even better security, you can force dual-level audit passwords. This implements a second password that must be entered to save configurations or change settings. The second password is used in addition to entering the first volume login password. This way, the main auditor can create distributed auditors but keep them out of important AUDITCON configuration options. Finally, Figure 11.39 allows us to broadcast errors to all users. This means audit file threshold warnings extend beyond the file server console and to every connected workstation. Not bad.

▶ Error Recovery—When NET$AUDT.DAT gets full, you have three options—archive it, dismount the volume, or disable event recording. If Automatic Archiving is ON, the file will be backed up every seven days. But sometimes it'll fill before the seventh day. This option allows us to automatically archive it at that point. Otherwise, you can do something drastic like dismount the volume. If you're worried that users will access the system without being audited, you can dismount the volume when auditing stops. This can only happen in two instances—a full audit file with no archiving or AUDITCON corruption. Otherwise, the opposite reaction would be to disable event recording. This says, "I don't care if anybody logs in without auditing." It's your choice.

▸ Audit Status—AUDITCON allows you to display audit status at various points throughout the utility. For example, this choice appears in Figures 11.34, 11.35, and 11.36. The Audit status window displays current statistics about audit files and records. It displays the current audit file size, the maximum size, and the threshold size. It also tells you the current size of the audit history file. In addition, it tracks the number of records in both files. At any point throughout AUDITCON, the audit can get a quick snapshot of audit file maintenance.

We're getting close to the end. Can't you feel it? NetWare 4 auditing has now been enabled and configured. Only one task remains—audit reports.

AUDITING REPORTS

...Three weeks later.

Well, auditing has been running along smoothly for the last three weeks. And now it's time to generate a report. After all, all this rigmarole doesn't do us a hill of beans without some way of analyzing the results. Fortunately, AUDITCON includes a comprehensive reporting feature. It centers around two key concepts:

▸ Filters

▸ Reports

Filters are important because NET$AUDT.DAT tracks everything. If you displayed the entire file, it would include pages and pages and pages of seemingly meaningless information. Report filters allow you to display only the information you're interested in. As you can see in Figure 11.40, AUDITCON provides an editing facility directly from the Auditing Reports menu.

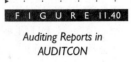

F I G U R E 11.40

Auditing Reports in AUDITCON

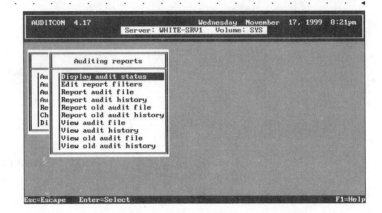

Once you've filtered the information, it's time to generate a report. Reports can be sent to a file (Report) or sent to the screen (View). As you can see in Figure 11.40, AUDITCON allows you to report and view current and archived audit files. Let's take a closer look at the two elements of auditing reports.

Filtering

You can create report filters by selecting the Edit Report Filters option from Figure 11.40. These filters allow you to display only the information you're interested in. AUDITCON includes four main filters:

- ▸ Date/time—This filter allows you to set up a report by date, time, or both. You can specify a starting and ending date or report only the events recorded on a certain day. This allows you to zero in on specific information.

- ▸ Event—You can also report on one or more specific auditing events. If, for example, you're auditing NDS activity, you could generate a report of only user logins and logouts.

- ▸ Paths/files—If you're auditing the NetWare 4 file system, you may be interested in only specific areas of the volume. This filter allows you to either include or exclude specific paths and files.

▸ Users—Finally, AUDITCON allows you to filter your report according to specific users. You can either include or exclude NDS and bindery users.

Once you've edited the Report filters, you can move on to Step Two—reporting.

Reporting

With the report filters in place, you can immediately send the report to either a file or the screen. If you choose the Report option from Figure 11.40, AUDITCON prompts you for a filename. You can accept the default name of AUDITDAT.TXT or choose another. The auditor must have [RWCEM] file access rights in the current directory to store temporary files during report creation. The report is a simple text file stored in whatever directory the auditor chooses. Since it is a text file, you may consider hiding it from curious users. It's not a good idea, for example, to place the reports in SYS:PUBLIC. It's best to print the text file once you've created it, then delete and purge it from the file system.

Once you choose a destination and file name for the report, AUDITCON asks you for a filter. The default is _no-filter_. Of course, you created filters in the previous step so now's the time to use them. Choose your filter and AUDITCON generates the report. Hakuna matata!

That completes our discussion of NetWare 4 auditing and security in general. Let me ask you a simple question:

So how secure do you feel?

QUIZ

Here's another doozy:

"Who shot Mr. Burns?"

Now that you have all the clues, let's see if you have what it takes to be a "Silicon Sleuth."

(Q11-7)

Now that you know everything about NetWare 4 security, how much are you willing to pay? Are you going to place your server in a titanium vault or live in a 1960s Woodstock fantasy? Remember, the key to security is gauging the range of your boundaries:

Let the good guys in and keep the bad guys out!

THE BRAIN

If you just can't get enough of NetWare security and auditing, Novell has devoted an entire special edition of *Application Notes* to the subject. It's the April 1994 issue, entitled "Building and Auditing a Trusted Network Environment with NetWare 4." Check it out.

As a NetWare 4 CNE, it is your responsibility to design, install, and manage the NetWare 4 network. But most importantly, you must protect it. Hopefully now you've gained a new appreciation for the value of an impenetrable network armor. We've filled your brain with sophisticated security strategies and given you a utility belt full of advanced protection tools—like NWADMIN and AUDITCON.

So where do you go from here? The world is your oyster. It's amazing what a little security can do for your fragile psyche. Once all your risks are in check, there's no limit to what you can do. So far you can manage NDS, synchronize time, map drives, and secure the WAN. I'd say you're becoming a full-fledged "NetWare 4 gardener"! But what about the big picture? Now I think you're ready to journey through the life-span of a LAN—starting with childhood (NetWare 4 configuration) and continuing through adulthood (NetWare 4 management). It all starts with a single seed.

CASE STUDY: ACME SECURITY

In this exercise, we are going to explore the exciting world of NetWare 4 NDS and file system security. In order to complete this exercise, you will need to install a server called WHITE-SRV1 in the WHITE.CRIME.TOKYO.ACME container.

Initially, the Crime division, the White-Collar Crime department, and the three White-Collar Crime units (Cyber Crime, Financial Crime, and Political Crime) will be sharing the same server (.WHITE-SRV1.CRIME.TOKYO.ACME)—but not the same data. The Users in the Crime division office will be located in a container called CRIME.TOKYO.ACME. The White-Collar Crime department and its three Crime units will be located in a subcontainer called WHITE.CRIME.TOKYO.ACME.

You will need to create Group objects for each of these workgroups (namely, CRIME-Group, WHITE-Group, CYBER-Group, FIN-Group, and POL-Group).

Temporarily, the managers of each workgroup will act as network administrators for their respective workgroups. Because these administrator assignments are temporary, you will need to create an Organizational Role for each (called CRIME-Admin, WHITE-Admin, CYBER-Admin, FIN-Admin, and POL-Admin, respectively).

Each workgroup will be given rights to the SYS:SHARED directory as well as to its own subdirectory under the SYS:SHARED directory (namely, SYS:SHARED\CRIME, SYS:SHARED\WHITE, SYS:SHARED\CYBER, SYS:SHARED\FIN, and SYS:SHARED\POL). The SHARED directory will contain those files that are shared by the entire division, whereas the individual subdirectories will contain those files that are shared by each workgroup. An inherited rights filter will be placed on each of the subdirectories under SHARED, so that users from one department cannot see the files from another.

Everyone in these five workgroups will have access to the word processing program (stored in SYS:APPS\WP70). In addition, the Financial Crime unit will have access to the spreadsheet program (stored in SYS:APPS\SS30) and the Cyber Crime unit will have access to the database program (stored in SYS:APPS\DB50). Each workgroup is currently generating a list of other applications that they'd like on the server.

User Templates will be used for consistency in creating User objects and will contain the following account restrictions:

- ▸ Each User will be limited to logging in on one workstation at a time (that is, one concurrent login).

▸ Each User will be required to have a *unique* password consisting of seven characters or more and will be required to change their password every 45 days. Each User will be allowed six grace logins.

▸ Because employees in this division work long hours and travel a lot, there will be no time restrictions on anyone's account except between 3:00 a.m. to 4:00 a.m. daily (when system backups and network maintenance are done).

▸ Intruder detection will be set to lock for 24 hours after seven incorrect attempts in 24 hours. Intruder detection statistics will be kept for 10 days.

Now that you know the plan, let's go ahead and implement it!

1 • Execute the NetWare Administrator Utility. Log into the network as .ADMIN.ACME and double-click on the NetWare Administrator icon in MS Windows.

2 • Change the current context to [Root]. You'll want to get a visual perspective of where these containers are located in the NDS tree. If the [Root] is not displayed on the screen, set the context by clicking on Set Context in the View menu, typing in [Root] as the new context, and clicking on OK. To display the portion of the tree that we will be working with, double-click on the ACME container, then double-click on the TOKYO container, then double-click on the WHITE container.

3 • Create the basic file system directory structure. Double-click on the WHITE-SRV1_SYS Volume object in order to display the directories under it.

   a. Press the Insert button to display the Create Directory window. To create the USERS directory, type **USERS** in the Directory Name field, then click on the Create Another Directory box, then click on the Create button.

   b. To create the SHARED directory, type **SHARED** in the Directory name field, then click on the Create Another Directory box to de-select it, then click on the Create button.

c. To create the CRIME subdirectory under the SHARED directory, click on the SHARED folder icon. Type **CRIME** in the Directory Name field, then click on the Create Another Directory box, then click on the Create button. Follow the same procedure to create the WHITE, CYBER, FIN, and POL directories under the SHARED directory.

d. Finally, use the same procedure to create a SYS:APPS directory, then create the following directories under it: DB50, SS30, and WP70.

4 • Set Intruder Detection/Lockout defaults for the CRIME and WHITE containers. Click on the CRIME container with the right mouse button and select the Details option from the menu displayed. Click on the Intruder Detection page button. (You'll have to use the scroll bar on the right side of the screen to bring it into view.) Click on the Detect Intruders box, then type the following Intruder Detection limits:

Intruder Attempt Reset Interval: **10 days, 0 hours, 0 minutes**

Next, click on the Lock Account After Detection box and type in the following information:

Intruder Lockout Reset Interval: **1 days, 0 hours, 0 minutes**

Use the same procedure to set the Intruder Detection/Lockout parameters for the WHITE container.

5 • Create a User Template for TOKYO container. As you know, changes to a User Template object affect only those Users created after the changes are made. Since no Users have been created yet, this will not be a problem. In actuality, a User Template is just a User object with the name USER_TEMPLATE. Make sure the TOKYO container is highlighted, and press Insert. The New Object window will be displayed. Use the scroll bar along the right side of the window to bring the User icon into view, then double-click it to select it. Type **USER_TEMPLATE** in the Login Name *and* Last Name fields, then click on the Define Additional Properties box.

Finally, click on the Create button at the bottom of the Window to create the User Template. The object dialog will be displayed. You will notice a set of page buttons along the right side of the screen. Select the page buttons listed below and make the changes indicated.

a. Identification page button. You'll notice the Identification Page button is selected by default. Type the following information on this screen:

> Location: **Tokyo, Japan**
>
> Telephone: **813-5481-1141**
>
> Fax Number: **813-5481-855**

b. Environment page button. Click on the Environment page button. Walk the tree to select the following Home Directory information:

> Volume: WHITE-SRV1_SYS.WHITE.CRIME.TOKYO.ACME
>
> Path: USERS

c. Login Restrictions page button. Click on the Login Restrictions page button.

Click on the Limit Concurrent Connections box. A value of 1 will be displayed in the Maximum Connections field.

d. Password Restrictions. Click on the Password Restrictions page button, then perform the following tasks:

Click on the Allow User to Change Password box.

Click on the Require a Password box.

Indicate a Minimum Password length of 7.

Click on the Force Periodic Password changes box.

e. Indicate a value of 45 for Days Between Forced Changes.

Click on the Require Unique Passwords box.

Click on the Limit Grace Logins.

Accept the default of 6 Grace Logins Allowed.

Click on the Change Password button. Change the password to one that you will remember, so that no one can actually login to the network using this account.

e. Login Time Restrictions page button. Next, go ahead and restrict login privileges between 3:00 a.m. and 4:00 a.m. every day. Click on the Login Time Restrictions page button. A grid will be displayed on the screen showing days of the week along the left edge and time of day across the top. Each box in the grid represents a half-hour period during the week. You'll notice that when you place the mouse cursor in a box, the day and time the box represents is displayed. White boxes represent times during which the User is allowed to log in; gray boxes indicate times that the User is prevented from logging in. Click on the 3:00 and 3:30 boxes for each day of the week. (Alternately, you can click on the box corresponding to 3:00 a.m. Sunday, and while holding down the mouse button, drag the mouse cursor to the rectangle representing 3:30 a.m. Saturday before releasing the mouse button.)

f. Postal Address page button. Click on the Postal address button and fill in the following information:

Street: **Toei Mishuku Building; 1-13-1, Mishuku**

City: **Setagaya-ku, Tokyo 154**

State or Province: **Japan**

When you have finished updating the User Template, click on the OK button at the bottom of the screen to accept the changes that you have made.

6 • Copy the TOKYO User Template to the CRIME and WHITE containers. Click on the CRIME container. Select the User Template menu option from the Object menu. Click on the Yes button when asked whether you want to copy the properties of the User Template from the TOKYO.ACME container. The Identification screen for the new User Template will be displayed. Click on the Cancel button since you don't need to make any changes at this time. Follow the same procedure for copying the User Template to the WHITE container.

7 • Create Group objects. Before you can create Users, you will need to create the Group objects that they will be members of. Click on the CRIME container and press Insert. The New Object window will appear. Double-click on the Group icon to select it. Type **CRIME** in the Group Name field, click on the Define Additional Properties box, and click on the Create button. The Group Object Identification screen will be displayed. Fill in the following information:

> Location: **Tokyo, Japan**
>
> Department: **Crime-Fighting**
>
> Organization: **ACME**

Click on the OK button when you are done. Follow the same procedure for creating the WHITE, CYBER, FIN, and POL groups in the WHITE container.

8 • Create User objects. Next, you need to create the SHolmes and DrWatson User objects in the CRIME container and the RHood, LJohn, MMarion, and FrTuck User objects in the WHITE container.

a. Click on the CRIME container and press Insert. Double-click on the User object icon. Type **SHolmes** for the Login name and Holmes for the Last Name. The Use User Template and Create Home Directory boxes should already be checked. Click on the Define Additional Properties box. The Identification screen for the SHolmes User object will be displayed.

b. Click on the Group Membership button, then on the Add... button. Double-click on the CRIME Group in the Objects box on the left side of the screen. Click on OK to accept the changes to the properties of this User object.

c. Follow the procedure listed above for adding the DrWatson User Object to the CRIMES container and the RHood, LJohn, MMarion, and FrTuck User objects to the WHITE container, indicating the WHITE, FIN, POL, and CYBER groups, respectively.

9 • Create Organizational Role objects. Your next task will be to create an Organizational Role object for each workgroup manager. Create an Organizational Role object for SHolmes by clicking on the CRIMES container, then pressing Insert. Double-click on the Organizational Role icon, then type **CRIME-Admin** as the Organizational Role Name. Click on the Define Additional Properties box, then click on the Create button. The Identification screen for the Organizational Role object will be displayed. Click the browser button to the right of the Occupant field, then click on the Add... button. Double-click on the SHolmes icon in the Objects list box on the left side of the screen, then click on the OK button in the Occupant Window. Click on the OK button at the bottom of the screen to accept the changes you've made to this Organizational Role object. Using this same technique, create Organizational Roles for the following Users in the WHITE container: RHood (WHITE-Admin), FrTuck (CYBER-Admin), LJohn (FIN-Admin), and MMarion (POL-Admin).

10 • Now that you've created the Organizational Roles for container administration, let's give them the rights they need. In this section, we will create an exclusive container administrator for CRIME (SHolmes) and

WHITE (RHood). As you remember, an exclusive administrator has all NDS rights to a container and blocks most rights (especially S) from everyone else.

a. To start, assign SHolmes as the administrator for .CRIME.TOKYO.ACME. Click on this container, and press the right mouse button. Choose Trustees of this Object from the dialog box. Click on the Add Trustee... button and walk the tree to select SHolmes.

b. Next, we'll need to assign SHolmes' object rights. Click on Supervisor, Create, Delete, and Rename, because the Browse box is already selected. With all rights in place, he's well on his way.

c. Finally, click on the OK button on the bottom of the screen. Good work.

11 • You have successfully made SHolmes an administrator of the .CRIME.TOKYO.ACME container. He currently shares this role with Admin. Now comes the "exclusive" part. We need to create an IRF of [B] for the CRIME container. This will block Admin, but not SHolmes.

a. The CRIME container should still be highlighted in the NWADMIN Browser. Press the right mouse button, and choose Trustees of this Object again. Click on the Inherited Rights Filter.... button. Currently, the defaults are selected—that is, all five object rights [BCDRS].

b. To make SHolmes an exclusive administrator, click on all rights except Browse. This will leave an IRF of [B]. Then click on OK twice to return to the browser window.

c. Very good work. Now, repeat these steps (10 and 11) to make RHood the exclusive container administrator of .WHITE.CRIME.TOKYO.ACME.

12 • Assign file system rights to the file system. You are now ready to start assigning rights to the file system.

a. Assign rights to the SHARED directory. Because all five workgroups will have the same level of access to the SHARED directory, you can grant these rights at the container level rather than at the Group level. Click on the SHARED folder, then select the Details option from the Object menu. Click on the Trustees of this Directory page button, then click on the Add Trustee button. Walk the tree until the CRIME container is displayed in the Objects list box on the left side of the screen, then double-click on it. You'll notice that the container is automatically granted the Read and File Scan rights. Click on the Write, Create, and Erase rights, then click on the OK button to accept this trustee assignment. (You don't need to make the same trustee assignment to the WHITE container, because the rights will be inherited by the members of the WHITE container from above.)

b. Assign rights to the CRIME directory under the SHARED directory. Double-click on the WHITE-SRV1_SYS volume. (Use the scroll bar on the right side of the screen, if necessary, to see the subdirectories under the SHARED directory.) Double-click on the SHARED directory, then click on the CRIME directory under it. Select Details from the Object menu, then click on the Trustees of this Directory page button. Next, click on the Add Trustee button, then select the CRIME-Group and click on OK. Finally, click on CRIME-Group.WHITE.CRIME.TOKYO.ACME in the Trustees box.

c. As you can see, Read and File Scan rights are assigned by default when you create a trustee. Click on the Write, Create, and Erase rights, then click on OK. Next, you'll want to change the Inherited Rights Filter for this directory so that rights are not inherited from above. Click on each of the rights, except for the Supervisor right, in order to de-select them. The net effect will be to assign an IRF of [S].

13 • Assign trustee rights for the APPS subdirectories. Now that you know how to grant trustee rights for directories to containers and Group objects, use the same techniques to make the trustee assignments. If you'd really like a challenge, see if you can make these assignments from the trustee's perspective (that is, container or Group) rather than the directory's perspective. (Hint: You can use the Rights to Other Objects option in the Object menu.)

a. Grant the CRIME container [RF] rights to the SYS:APPS\WP70 directory (since all five workgroups will have access to the Word Processing application).

b. Grant the FIN Group [RF] rights to the SYS:APP\SS30 directory.

c. Grant the CYBER Group [RF]rights to the SYS:APPS\DB50 subdirectory.

14 • Assign trustee rights to Organizational Role objects. Grant the trustee rights list below to the Organizational Roles indicated:

a. All five Organizational Roles should be granted all rights to the SHARED directory.

b. Each Organizational Role should be granted all rights to their corresponding workgroup's subdirectory under the SHARED directory.

c. Each Organizational Role should be granted all rights to the home directories of each User in their workgroup.

15 • Verify effective rights. You can verify an object's effective rights to a directory from the object's perspective or the directory's pespective.

a. To verify an object's effective rights from the directory's perspective, you can click on the object with the right mouse button, then select the Details option from the menu that is displayed. Next, click on the Trustees of this Directory page button, then click on the Effective rights... button. An Effective rights window will be displayed. Click on the Browser button to the right of the Trustee field. Walk the tree until the desired object is displayed in the Object list box on the left side of the screen. Double-click on the object to select it. The Effective rights screen will again be displayed. This time, the effective rights for this object will be displayed in black. (The rights they do not have will be displayed in gray.)

b. Practice verifying the effective rights of different objects for various directories that we worked with in this exercise from the directory's point of view.

c. Practice verifying the effective rights of different objects for various directories that we have worked with in this exercise from the object's point of view. (Hint: Use the Rights to Other Objects menu option.)

EXERCISE II.I: CALCULATING NDS EFFECTIVE RIGHTS

OK, now that you're a pro with NetWare 4 security, let's experiment with "modern math." Earlier in the chapter, we explored NetWare's version of calculus—calculating effective rights. We learned that both NDS and the file system have their own versions of effective rights—and they work exactly the same:

Effective Rights = trustee assignments + inheritance – IRF (inherited rights filter)

In this exercise, we'll begin Calculus 101 with NDS access rights. Then, in Exercise 11.2, you'll get an opportunity to explore file system access rights. Also, we've included some beautiful graphic worksheets to help you follow along. You can create your own at home with a pencil, some paper, and a ruler.

So without any further ado, let's get on with CASE #1.

CASE #I

In this case, we are helping Sherlock Holmes gain administrative rights to the Crime Fighting division. Refer to Figure 11.41. It all starts at .CRIME.TOKYO.ACME. He is granted [CD] NDS privileges. Also, he ancestrally inherits Browse rights from the special [Public] trustee. There is no IRF or inheritance in CRIME.

In the next container, WHITE, SHolmes gets [S] from his "CRIME-Group" group. Also, there's an IRF of [D]. Finally, these privileges flow down to the WHITE-SRV1 server object and become inherited rights. But the server's IRF is set to [BR], so some of them are blocked. Also, SHolmes has an explicit trustee assignment of [D] to the WHITE-SRV1 server. Finally, Sherlock's home container, WHITE, is granted [C] privileges to the server object.

*Calculating NDS Effective
Rights—CASE #1*

CASE #2

After careful consideration, you decide that the above rights are inappropriate. So let's try it one more time. But in this case, we're going to use the WHITE-Admin Organizational Role instead of the "WHITE-Group" group. This gives us more administrative flexibility and narrows the scope of rights assignments. For this case, refer to Figure 11.42.

As before, it starts in the .CRIME.TOKYO.ACME container. Sherlock Holmes is granted the [BR] rights to the container. Also, he ancestrally inherits [B] from [Public]. Finally, there is no inheritance in CRIME, but the IRF has been set to [CD] anyway.

In the next container, WHITE, SHolmes gets [BCD] through his CRIME-Admin Organizational Role. Also, there's an IRF of [CDRS]. Finally, the container's effective rights flow down to the WHITE-SRV1 server object and become inherited rights. But the server's IRF is set to [BR], so some of them are blocked. In addition, SHolmes has an explicit trustee assignment of [CD] to the WHITE-SRV1 server. Finally, Sherlock's home container, WHITE, is granted [B] privileges to the server object. Now, let's see what he ends up with.

CASE #3

In this final case, let's bounce over to the .BLUE.CRIME.TOKYO.ACME container and help out Wyatt Earp—their administrator. Refer to Figure 11.43. As with most NDS trees, it actually starts much higher up—above TOKYO. Wyatt Earp inherits [BCDR] to .TOKYO.ACME. The IRF is identical, so all rights are allowed to flow through. In addition, he's granted Rename privileges as a user and Browse privileges through his home container—BLUE.

▶ · ◀

F I G U R E 11.43

Calculating NDS Effective Rights—CASE #3

		[BCDRS]
⬇	IRF	[ ]
	Inheritance	[ ]
	BLUE-TA	[ ]
👤	WEarp-TA	[ ]
TOKYO	**Effective Rights**	[ ]
⬇	IRF	[ ]
	Inheritance	[ ]
	OR-TA	[ ]
	BLUE-TA	[ ]
CRIME	**Effective Rights**	[ ]
⬇	IRF	[ ]
	Inheritance	[ ]
👤	WEarp-TA	[ ]
	BLUE-TA	[ ]
BLUE	**Effective Rights**	[ ]

In the next container, CRIME, WEarp gets all object rights through his BLUE-Admin Organization Role. This overshadows the Browse privileges he ancestrally inherits from BLUE. Also, don't forget the CRIME IRF of [BCD]. Finally, all rights flow down to the BLUE container and become inherited. But the Organizational Unit's IRF is set to [DR], so most of them are blocked. In addition, WEarp has an explicit trustee assignment of [C] to BLUE. This assignment is enhanced by the Browse privilege he inherits from BLUE. Good luck.

Well, there you have it. Great work. Now that you're a security guru, let's dive into file system access rights. Rustle on over to Exercise 11-2.

Good luck, and by the way, thanks for saving the world!

See Appendix C for the answers.

EXERCISE 11-2: CALCULATING FILE SYSTEM EFFECTIVE RIGHTS

Here you are. In case you're lost, here is modern math, part 2. In this exercise, we're going to explore the wonderful world of file system effective rights. Now that you've helped "administrate" Sherlock Holmes and Wyatt Earp, it's time to "liberate" the rest of the crime-fighting team, namely Robin Hood, Maid Marion, Dr. Watson, Little John, and Friar Tuck. Ah, a CNE's job is never done.

CASE #1

FrTuck has been made a trustee of the SYS:SHARED directory and granted Read, Write, Create, and File Scan rights. The IRF for the SYS:SHARED directory contains all rights; the IRF for the SYS:SHARED\CYBER directory contains Supervisor, Read, and File Scan; and the IRF for the CYBER.DOC file contains Read, Write, Create, and File Scan. Calculate FrTuck's effective rights in the SYS:SHARED directory, the SYS:SHARED\CYBER directory, and the CYBER.DOC file, using the worksheet in Figure 11.44.

FIGURE 11.44

Calculating File System Effective Rights—CASE #1

SYS:SHARED	S	R	C	W	E	M	F	A
Inherited Rights Filter								
Inherited Rights-User								
Inherited Rights-Group								
Trustee Assignment-User								
Trustee Assignment-Group								
Effective Rights								

SYS:SHARED\CYBER	S	R	C	W	E	M	F	A
Inherited Rights Filter								
Inherited Rights-User								
Inherited Rights-Group								
Trustee Assignment-User								
Trustee Assignment-Group								
Effective Rights								

CYBER.DOC	S	R	C	W	E	M	F	A
Inherited Rights Filter								
Inherited Rights-User								
Inherited Rights-Group								
Trustee Assignment-User								
Trustee Assignment-Group								
Effective Rights								

CASE #2

LJohn was made a trustee of the SYS:SHARED\FIN directory and granted all rights except Supervisor and Access Control. The FIN group, of which he is a member, was granted the Read, Write, Create, and File Scan rights to the SYS:SHARED directory. In addition, the FIN group was granted Read rights for the 99QTR4.RPT file. The IRF for the SYS:SHARED directory contains all rights; the IRF for the SYS:SHARED\FIN directory contains the Supervisor right; and the IRF for the 99QTR4.RPT file contains Supervisor, Read, Write, and File Scan rights. Calculate LJohn's effective rights in the SYS:SHARED directory, SYS:SHARED\FIN directory, and 99QTR4.RPT file, using the worksheet in Figure 11.45.

F I G U R E 11.45

*Calculating File System
Effective Rights—CASE #2*

SYS:SHARED	S	R	C	W	E	M	F	A
Inherited Rights Filter								
Inherited Rights-User								
Inherited Rights-Group								
Trustee Assignment-User								
Trustee Assignment-Group								
Effective Rights								

SYS:SHARED\FIN	S	R	C	W	E	M	F	A
Inherited Rights Filter								
Inherited Rights-User								
Inherited Rights-Group								
Trustee Assignment-User								
Trustee Assignment-Group								
Effective Rights								

99QTR4.RPT	S	R	C	W	E	M	F	A
Inherited Rights Filter								
Inherited Rights-User								
Inherited Rights-Group								
Trustee Assignment-User								
Trustee Assignment-Group								
Effective Rights								

CASE #3

DrWatson was granted the Read, Write, Create, and File Scan rights to the SYS:SHARED directory. The CRIME Group, of which he is a member, was granted Read, Write, Create, Erase, Modify, and File Scan rights to the SYS:CRIME directory. The CRIME Group was also granted Read and File Scan rights to the CRIME.DB file. The IRF for the SYS:SHARED directory is all rights; the IRF for the SYS:SHARED\CRIME directory is Supervisor and Access Control; and the IRF for the CRIME.DB file is Supervisor, Read, Write, Create, and File Scan. Calculate DrWatson's effective rights in the SYS:SHARED directory, the SYS:SHARED\CRIME directory, and the CRIME.DB file, using the worksheet in Figure 11.46.

SYS:SHARED	S	R	C	W	E	M	F	A
Inherited Rights Filter								
Inherited Rights-User								
Inherited Rights-Group								
Trustee Assignment-User								
Trustee Assignment-Group								
Effective Rights								

SYS:SHARED\CRIME	S	R	C	W	E	M	F	A
Inherited Rights Filter								
Inherited Rights-User								
Inherited Rights-Group								
Trustee Assignment-User								
Trustee Assignment-Group								
Effective Rights								

CRIME.DB	S	R	C	W	E	M	F	A
Inherited Rights Filter								
Inherited Rights-User								
Inherited Rights-Group								
Trustee Assignment-User								
Trustee Assignment-Group								
Effective Rights								

CASE #4

MMarion was granted the Modify and Access Control rights to the SYS:SHARED\POL directory. In addition, the POL Group was granted the Read, Write, Create, Erase, and File Scan rights to both the SYS:SHARED and SYS:SHARED\POL directories. The IRF for the SYS:SHARED directory contains all rights; the IRF for the SYS:SHARED\POL directory contains the Supervisor right; and the IRF for the CRIME.RPT file contains all rights. Calculate MMarion's effective rights to the SYS:SHARED directory, the SYS:SHARED\POL directory, and the CRIMEP.RPT file, using the worksheet in Figure 11.47.

SYS:SHARED	S	R	C	W	E	M	F	A
Inherited Rights Filter								
Inherited Rights-User								
Inherited Rights-Group								
Trustee Assignment-User								
Trustee Assignment-Group								
Effective Rights								

SYS:SHARED\POL	S	R	C	W	E	M	F	A
Inherited Rights Filter								
Inherited Rights-User								
Inherited Rights-Group								
Trustee Assignment-User								
Trustee Assignment-Group								
Effective Rights								

CRIME.RPT	S	R	C	W	E	M	F	A
Inherited Rights Filter								
Inherited Rights-User								
Inherited Rights-Group								
Trustee Assignment-User								
Trustee Assignment-Group								
Effective Rights								

CASE #5

SHolmes was granted all rights to the SYS:SHARED directory. The CRIME Group, of which he is a member, was granted Read, Write, Create, and File Scan rights to the SYS:SHARED\CRIME directory. The CRIME Group was also granted Read and File Scan rights to the CRIME.DB file. The IRF for the SYS:SHARED directory contains all rights; the IRF for the SYS:SHARED\CRIME directory contains the Supervisor right; and the IRF for the CRIME.DB file contains Supervisor, Read, and File Scan rights. Calculate SHolmes' effective rights to the SYS:SHARED directory, the SYS:SHARED\CRIME directory, and the CRIME.DB file, using the worksheet in Figure 11.48.

SYS:SHARED	S	R	C	W	E	M	F	A
Inherited Rights Filter								
Inherited Rights-User								
Inherited Rights-Group								
Trustee Assignment-User								
Trustee Assignment-Group								
Effective Rights								

SYS:SHARED\CRIME	S	R	C	W	E	M	F	A
Inherited Rights Filter								
Inherited Rights-User								
Inherited Rights-Group								
Trustee Assignment-User								
Trustee Assignment-Group								
Effective Rights								

CRIME.DB	S	R	C	W	E	M	F	A
Inherited Rights Filter								
Inherited Rights-User								
Inherited Rights-Group								
Trustee Assignment-User								
Trustee Assignment-Group								
Effective Rights								

CASE #6

RHood was made a trustee of the SUMMARY.RPT file and granted the Read, Write, Create, Erase, and Modify rights. He was also made a trustee of the SYS:SHARED\WHITE directory and granted all rights. [PUBLIC] has been granted the Read and File Scan rights to the SYS:SHARED directory. The IRF for the SYS:SHARED directory contains the Supervisor, Read, File Scan, and Access Control rights; the IRF for the SYS:SHARED\WHITE directory contains the Supervisor, Read, and File Scan rights; and the IRF for the SUMMARY.RPT file contains the Supervisor right. Calculate RHood's effective rights for the SYS:SHARED directory, the SYS:SHARED\WHITE directory, and SUMMARY.RPT file, using the worksheet in Figure 11.49.

FIGURE 11.49

*Calculating File System
Effective Rights—CASE #6*

SYS:SHARED	S	R	C	W	E	M	F	A
Inherited Rights Filter								
Inherited Rights-User								
Inherited Rights-Group or [Public]								
Trustee Assignment-User								
Trustee Assignment-Group or [Public]								
Effective Rights								

SYS:SHARED\WHITE	S	R	C	W	E	M	F	A
Inherited Rights Filter								
Inherited Rights-User								
Inherited Rights-Group or [Public]								
Trustee Assignment-User								
Trustee Assignment-Group or [Public]								
Effective Rights								

SUMMARY.RPT	S	R	C	W	E	M	F	A
Inherited Rights Filter								
Inherited Rights-User								
Inherited Rights-Group or [Public]								
Trustee Assignment-User								
Trustee Assignment-Group or [Public]								
Effective Rights								

The answers to all of these cases are in Appendix C.

CHAPTER 12

NetWare 4 Configuration

5. E-Mail

4. Network Applications

3. Menu System

2. Login Scripts

1. Workstation
Connectivity

The birth of a LAN.

There are many different definitions of life. The one that you choose depends entirely on your point of view. Regardless of your choice, the fundamental question remains—is your LAN alive? Judging from the following guidelines, I think so:

- Carbon-based organic life form—Silicon is close enough.

- Consumes food—Your LAN processes valuable information.

- Propagates—Most NetWare 4 WANs include multiple servers.

- Self-awareness—Many times your network has a mind of its own.

There you go—your LAN must be alive. And as a living, breathing life form, it must pass through the three phases of "life span"—birth, childhood, and adulthood. This evolution (that we all experience) can be both painful and rewarding. But there's nothing more exciting than watching it happen and being involved from Day One.

During birth, the NetWare 4 server is installed. In the grand scheme of things, this event is theoretically quick and painless (although I don't know about the latter part). In Chapter 6, you learned about the six stages of NetWare 4 installation and how they can be automated using the STARTUP.NCF and AUTOEXEC.NCF files. Decisions you make during installation may have an irrevocable impact on the server, LAN and WAN. Birth is especially important in NetWare 4 because of the importance of the NDS infrastructure.

Once the server has been installed, you are left with a simple directory structure, some workstations, and a few users—a LAN version of a cute little baby girl. Over time, this adorable little monster will learn to walk, talk, and start getting along with others. She will go to school and learn some valuable skills—ranging from how to climb the social ladder to how to deal with integral calculus. Finally, at some point, she will make an abrupt transition to adulthood—buy her first car, get her first job, and move into her first apartment.

In NetWare 4, childhood is dominated by *NetWare 4 Configuration*. During configuration, your server undergoes five important steps:

1 • Workstation connectivity—Leia takes her first steps. In NetWare 4, workstation configuration files provide an initial attachment to the server and NDS. This is accomplished using CONFIG.SYS, AUTOEXEC.BAT, STARTNET.BAT, and NET.CFG.

2 • Login scripts—Leia finally begins to talk (and doesn't stop for 85 years). In NetWare 4, login scripts enable you to customize user connections and establish important login settings.

3 • Menu system—She learns how to share and begins getting along with others. In NetWare 4, the menu system provides a vital interface between users and the network. Just as Leia learns to get along with others, your users learn to get along with NetWare 4.

4 • Network applications—Leia goes to school and learns important (and not so important) skills. In NetWare 4, applications are productivity tools that give the network value. These tools are undeniably bound to the aforementioned menu system—just like Leia is likely to make most of her friends in school.

5 • E-mail—Leia makes a quick transition into adulthood by getting her first car, first job, and first apartment—all in the same week. In NetWare 4, e-mail provides a vital link between applications, interface, and management. Think of it as "the force which binds the network together."

ZEN

"Life is like a ten-speed bike. Most of us have gears we never use."

George Schultz

The third and final phase of "life span" is adulthood. At this point, your LAN is secure in its new purpose and the goal shifts from conception to "keeping it going." These are the golden years. During adulthood, your LAN will get married, have children of its own, plan for the future, and finally retire. Where do I sign up? This phase is controlled by *NetWare 4 Management*. It goes something like this:

▸ Server management—Your LAN gets married and becomes part of a team. Remember LAN synergy—the whole is greater than the sum of its users. In NetWare 4, marriage takes the form of startup management, NDS configuration, internationalization, internetworking, and server protection. In addition, you'll learn to use console commands and NLMs as parent tools.

▸ Workstation management—The family grows larger with the addition of three little "rug rats"—aka, children. Life suddenly takes on a whole new meaning. Your thoughts switch from "me" to "them"—cute little people who rely on you. In NetWare 4, these cute little people are represented by users and workstations. Workstation management relies on ODI files, the NetWare DOS Requester, non-DOS support, virus prevention (colds), and diskless workstations. You'll never truly understand the frustration and joy of running a network until you have children of your own.

▸ Storage Management Services (SMS)—With the family firmly in place and your children advancing through childhood, focus shifts to the future. You need to develop disaster recovery plans and begin saving for retirement. This is life's little backup (insurance) policy. In NetWare 4, backup management ensures job security. Remember Murphy's Law Number 107—the network WILL crash!

▸ Remote Management Facility (RMF)—Your children leave home and are off to a LAN of their own. Now it's time for you to take it easy. Through remote management, you can retire to Happy Acres and enjoy the good life. There's no reason to be involved in the daily grind anymore. In NetWare 4, RMF enables you to manage the central server from the comfort of your own office. And if you really want luxury, you can attach to the server from the comfort of your own sofa.

Wow, I bet you didn't think becoming a CNE would be such a life-changing experience! So far, the LAN has been relatively quiet—this will change. Remember, babies are cute until they learn to walk and talk and eat furniture. The daily bustle of humming workstations and crazed users will quickly take its toll on an unorganized NetWare LAN. That's why it's important to carefully configure it now—while things are still under control. It's imperative for you to establish workstation connections, write login scripts, and develop menu systems before the network goes into hyperactivity—configuring an active network is like tuning a moving car.

Consider this scenario: Guinevere walks into her office every morning, eager to begin a new day. She hangs up her coat, turns on the radio, and shifts her focus to the center of worklife—the computer. She gracefully reaches for the on/off switch and gives it a gentle nudge. Voilà! The day begins! During the booting process, Guinevere takes an opportunity to slip out for a quick cappuccino. When she returns, the machine displays a friendly network menu and her e-mail for the morning.

Magic! Although Guinevere doesn't pay much attention to what occurs while she's sipping her cappuccino, the LAN has undergone an entire childhood in only an instant. As a CNE, it's your responsibility to configure the system so that Guinevere doesn't have to worry about connectivity software, login scripts, VLMs, NMENU.BAT, or MHS. As a parent, it is your responsibility to make childhood as painless as possible.

Let's start our journey through the life span of a LAN with the first step—workstation connectivity.

Step 1: Establishing Workstation Connectivity

Leia begins to walk.

The first step is always the most exciting. I hope you have your camcorder. While Leia's taking her first step, the network begins life anew as well. During this step, the client computer boots and activates a variety of configuration files. These configuration files establish the client environment and attach Guinevere to the network. All of this magic occurs with the help of just four simple files:

▸ CONFIG.SYS—The first configuration file loaded during the boot process. Because DOS and the NetWare DOS Requester share drive table information, CONFIG.SYS must include the LASTDRIVE command.

▶ AUTOEXEC.BAT—This autoexecuting batch file is modified to activate STARTNET.BAT from the default C:\NWCLIENT subdirectory.

▶ STARTNET.BAT—Automates the workstation connection. By default, it resides in the C:\NWCLIENT subdirectory and initializes the workstation-specific ODI and VLM drivers.

▶ NET.CFG—The final workstation configuration file is used to customize ODI and VLM settings.

ZEN

"In walking, just walk. In sitting, just sit. Above all, don't wobble."

Yun-Men

Once the first step of configuration has been taken, Leia is well on her way toward childhood and Guinevere is well on her way toward LAN productivity. Let's take a closer look at these respective first steps, starting with CONFIG.SYS.

CONFIG.SYS

CONFIG.SYS is the first configuration file loaded when Guinevere turns on her computer. It is used by DOS for registering devices, managing memory, and establishing local drives. In addition, the NetWare DOS Requester uses CONFIG.SYS to identify a range of letters available for network drives. Here's how it works.

Because the NetWare DOS Requester and DOS share drive table information, we need a convention to determine where the local drives end and the network drives begin. Fortunately, the NetWare 4 VLMs do this for us. They read the workstation hardware configuration and determine where the local drives end. From that point forward, they make all remaining drive letters available to the network. The key is determining exactly which drive letters are available. This is accomplished using the LASTDRIVE command.

If you place the following statement in each workstation CONFIG.SYS file, all drive letters from A through Z will be available for local and network drives:

```
LASTDRIVE=Z
```

Remember, you don't have to determine where the network drives begin because VLMs do it for you. For example, most standard workstations have a single floppy drive (A:), an internal hard disk (C:), and a CD-ROM (D:). This means that the first available network drive is E:. Similarly, if you have only a local floppy drive (A:—a more simple configuration), your first network drive will be B:. Undoubtedly, this sounds strange because you're used to pointing to F: as the first network drive. Fortunately, NetWare 4 includes a statement in NET.CFG (by default) that ignores drives A: through E: and treats F: as the first network drive regardless of what your workstation thinks.

Once CONFIG.SYS is loaded and the LASTDRIVE statement has been activated, control shifts over to AUTOEXEC.BAT.

TIP

The LASTDRIVE statement works a little bit differently when used with NETx. In the NETx universe, the LASTDRIVE statement identifies local drives only—which means that the LASTDRIVE=Z command has an entirely different effect. In such a case, users are left with no network drives at all.

This is not entirely true because NetWare 4 reserves certain ASCII characters for emergencies. If you use the LASTDRIVE=Z statement with NETx, the first available network is [: (a smiley-face). It really works. Try it—it's fun at parties.

AUTOEXEC.BAT

AUTOEXEC.BAT is a DOS configuration file used for activating a variety of workstation parameters including PATH statements, the PROMPT command, SET parameters, and internal TSRs (terminate-and-stay-resident programs). By default, the NetWare 4 client installation creates a file called STARTNET.BAT and places it in the C:\NWCLIENT subdirectory. It then adds the following line to the top of AUTOEXEC.BAT:

```
@CALL C:\NWCLIENT\STARTNET.BAT
```

This is a great way to automatically load workstation connectivity files while separating them from normal DOS operations. There is, however, one problem with this strategy. By placing this line at the top of AUTOEXEC.BAT, none of the other DOS statements load until STARTNET.BAT is finished—which is never. Remember, the goal of workstation connectivity is to load the drivers, automatically execute login scripts, and leave Guinevere in a menu system. This means NetWare will never execute the remaining statements in AUTOEXEC.BAT. A better solution is to move the @CALL C:\NWCLIENT\STARTNET statement to the end of AUTOEXEC.BAT.

Speaking of STARTNET.BAT, let's take a closer look.

STARTNET.BAT

As you recall from Chapter 1, NetWare 4 workstation connectivity consists of two main components:

▶ Communications—ODI drivers

▶ NetWare DOS Requester—VLM files

STARTNET.BAT automates the loading of these files—isn't that special. By default, it consists of the following commands:

```
C:
cd \NWCLIENT
LSL.COM—the first ODI file
NE2000—or other MLID driver
IPXODI.COM—or other communications protocol file
VLM.EXE—loads the NetWare DOS Requester
F:—switches to the first default network drive
LOGIN Guinevere—or other username
```

By default, this file is stored in the C:\NWCLIENT subdirectory. This is also where the NetWare 4 client installation process stores ODI drivers and VLMs. The beauty of this scenario is that it enables you to separate workstation connectivity files from other DOS programs. Also, it gives you a central point of workstation management. Once STARTNET.BAT has loaded and the workstation connectivity files are initialized, control shifts from the workstation to server login scripts.

QUIZ

Here's an easy one to warm up your gray matter. Twenty-four red socks and 24 blue socks are lying in a drawer in a dark room. What is the minimum number of socks I must take out of the drawer that will guarantee that I have at least two socks of the same color?

(Q12-1)
(See Appendix C for quiz answers.)

But not so fast. Before we move on to Step 2, you need to learn a little bit more about how these workstation connectivity files are configured. That is, you need to learn more about NET.CFG.

· ·

REAL WORLD

As a CNE, you'll decide how transparent the login process should be. Do you want Guinevere to input her login name and password or have the system do it for her? While the latter is not the most secure alternative, it certainly removes the burden from Guinevere. The following line inputs Guinevere username and password automatically:

```
LOGIN GUINEVERE < C:\NWCLIENT\PASSWORD.TXT
```

This statement logs Guinevere into the network and redirects her password from a text file on the C: drive. In order for this to work, make sure to place only her password (followed by a carriage return) in the text file. Although this isn't great security, you can deter would-be hackers by placing the text file in a hidden directory or on a secure boot disk. Remember, there's always a compromise between user transparent and security.

NET.CFG

The final workstation connectivity file is NET.CFG. This file is not executed, it's simply used as a support file for customizing ODI and VLM settings for STARTNET.BAT. By default, NET.CFG must be stored in the same subdirectory as the other workstation connectivity programs. You only need to create a NET.CFG file if you plan to deviate from the established ODI/VLM defaults. You can create NET.CFG with any DOS text editor, and it must follow these general conventions:

- ▸ Left-justify section headings

- ▸ Place options under each section heading and indent them with a tab or at least one space

- ▸ Use upper- or lowercase for section headings and options

- ▸ Precede comments with a semicolon (;) or pound sign (#) for documentation purposes

- ▸ End each line with a hard return

- ▸ Write all numbers in decimal notation except where noted

NET.CFG is your friend. Use it to customize ODI and VLM parameters as well as to automate the login process. In this section, we will explore NET.CFG as a CNE workstation management tool. You'll have a lot of parameters to think about, but keep in mind that many times the defaults are just fine. All in all, NET.CFG configurations fall into three categories:

- ▸ LINK DRIVER section

- ▸ NETWARE DOS REQUESTER section

- ▸ Other NET.CFG parameters

LINK DRIVER

LINK DRIVER is the section heading for ODI support. You use this section to name the MLID driver and specify hardware and software settings for items such as interrupt, memory address, and frame type. Recall that ODI is a modular communications strategy that relies on NET.CFG for specific hardware settings. The IPX.COM file used in earlier versions of NetWare had these settings hardcoded into it during WSGEN configuration. This is not the case with ODI. LINK DRIVER enables you to specify nondefault MLID settings and incorporate a variety of different frame types at the NetWare workstation. Following is a sample format for Guinevere LINK DRIVER heading:

```
LINK DRIVER 3C5X9
        INT 3
        PORT 300
        MEM D0000
    FRAME Ethernet_802.2
```

Refer to Table 12.1 for a complete listing of the NetWare 4 LINK DRIVER parameters.

T A B L E 12.1 *LINK DRIVER Parameters for NET.CFG*	PARAMETER	RANGE	DESCRIPTION
	INT	2 to 15	Interrupt value for the NIC (in decimal notation).
	PORT	240 to 4AFF	I/O port address for the NIC (in hexadecimal format).
	MEM	8000 to EFFF	Memory address for the NIC (in hexadecimal format).
	DMA	1 to 7	Direct memory access (DMA) channel number for the NIC.
	NODE ADDRESS	000000000000 to FFFFFFFFFFFE	Physical address for the NIC. This parameter enables you to override the physical address that is burned into each NIC at the factory. This is especially important for ARCNet.
	SLOT	1 to 8	A MicroChannel and EISA parameter that identifies the NIC slot.
	FRAME	Ethernet_802.2, Novell_RX-Net	Determines the frame type for workstation communications. By default, NetWare 4.1/3.12 use Ethernet_802.2, whereas NetWare 3.11/2.2 use Ethernet_802.3.

NetWare DOS Requester

The majority of NET.CFG customization occurs under the NETWARE DOS REQUESTER section heading. Here you get an opportunity to specify configurations for VLM operations. Some of the activities you can control include preferred trees, preferred servers, name context, first network drive, and packet signing. In addition, you can use NET.CFG to specify which VLMs are loaded and their order of execution. Here's a sample NETWARE DOS REQUESTER section for Guinevere NET.CFG file:

```
NETWARE DOS REQUESTER
    Preferred Tree=ACME
    Name Context="OU=FIN.OU=OPS.OU=CAMELOT.O=ACME"
    First Network Drive=F
    PB Buffers=10
    Signature Level=3
```

QUIZ

What is Bullwinkle Moose's middle initial? You have a 1 in 26 chance of guessing it correctly!

(Q12-2)

Refer to Table 12.2 for a list of some of the most important NETWARE DOS REQUESTER parameters. Remember, this is the best way to customize the workstation attachment.

T A B L E 12.2

*NETWARE DOS
REQUESTER Parameters
for NET.CFG*

PARAMETER	RANGE	DESCRIPTION
PREFERRED TREE	Any tree name	Forces the workstation to attach to a specified tree. By default, it will find the tree defined by the nearest available server.
PREFERRED SERVER	Any server name	Forces the workstation to attach to a specified server. By default, NET.CFG will find the nearest available server.
NAME CONTEXT	Any NDS container	Places the workstation in a specified container once a connection is established. By default, the system will use the [Root] as the workstation context.
FIRST NETWORK DRIVE	A to Z	F by default. Establishes the first available network drive provided that the command LASTDRIVE=Z appears in the workstation CONFIG.SYS file. This is used for convenience and convention.
PB BUFFERS	0 to 10	3 by default. This sets the number of buffers used by packet bursting. Larger values increase performance but occupy additional workstation RAM.
SIGNATURE LEVEL	0 to 3	1 by default. Sets the level of packet signing at the workstation. Higher values increase security but decrease performance.
USE DEFAULTS	ON or OFF	ON by default. If set to OFF, you must specify which VLMs are loaded using the VLM parameter.
VLM	Complete VLM filename	Enables you to load specific VLMs in a specific order. Be forewarned: Most VLMs are load-order dependent.
CONNECTIONS	2 to 50	8 by default. This represents the maximum number of connections available to the workstation. You may need to increase this value if your NetWare 4 WAN has many active servers.

(continued)

T A B L E   12.2 *(continued)*

PARAMETER	RANGE	DESCRIPTION
LOAD LOW CONN	ON or OFF	ON by default. When set to OFF, this parameter causes the CONN.VLM to load in upper memory. This saves workstation RAM but degrades performance.
LOAD LOW IPXNCP	ON or OFF	ON by default. When set to OFF, this parameter causes IPXNCP to load in upper memory.
MESSAGE TIMEOUT	0 to 10,000	0 by default. This controls how long the workstation waits before clearing broadcast messages. The default of 0 means users must type Ctrl+Enter to clear a broadcast message. If you want these messages to clear without user intervention, increase the value up to 6 hours—where each number equals 1/18th of a second.
NETWORK PRINTERS	0 to 9	3 by default. This sets the number of printer ports the workstation can capture. Setting the value to 0 will cause PRINT.VLM not to load and disable network printing at the workstation.
CACHE BUFFER SIZE	512 to 4096 bytes	512 by default. This parameter sets the size of each cache buffer and can be used to increase performance. The size should be equal to (or at least an increment of) the maximum packet size.
CACHE BUFFERS	0 to 64	5 by default. This parameter sets how many cache buffers are available for sequential network files. Increasing this value speeds the movement of files across the LAN.

TIP

One important aspect of logging in is "context." In order for you to log in, the Cloud must be able to differentiate you from everybody else in the NDS tree. This means you have to tell the system where your home container is. In addition, most users access resources in their home container and therefore should be guided there during login. You can specify a user's context during login in one of two ways. You can include the context with the login statement

```
LOGIN .CN=Guinevere.OU=FIN.OU=OPS.OU=CAMELOT.O=ACME
```

Alternatively, you can use the NAME CONTEXT parameter to specify the user's context before logging in:

```
NAME CONTEXT="OU=FIN.OU=OPS.OU=CAMELOT.O=ACME"
```

Note that the NAME CONTEXT line specifies a full distinguished name without a preceding period. This is one of those exceptions that Murphy keeps talking about.

Other NET.CFG Parameters

In the past, CNEs used SHELL.CFG to define parameters for the old IPX/NETx connectivity files. Fortunately, NetWare 4 supports these parameters by enabling you to include them at the top of NET.CFG. Following is a list of some of the most useful of these parameters, and remember—they must be left-justified.

- ▶ IPX RETRY COUNT—The IPX/SPX protocol uses this parameter to determine how many times to resend packets. This setting should be increased for an active network with heavy traffic and WANs that cover long distances. It works in conjunction with the SPX ABORT TIMEOUT parameter.

- ▶ SPX ABORT TIMEOUT—Adjusts the amount of time SPX waits without receiving any response from the other side. If this timeout value is exceeded, SPX aborts the connection. SPX ABORT TIMEOUT should be combined with IPX RETRY COUNT, for instance, if the workstation is using RPRINTER over routers. The default SPX ABORT TIMEOUT should be increased from 540 to about 1080 and the IPX RETRY COUNT should be doubled from 20 to 40.

▶ LONG MACHINE TYPE—You should use this parameter to specify the value returned by the %MACHINE login script variable. The default is IBM_PC. This parameter can be up to six characters long and should specify the type of machine being used—Altima, Compaq, Dell, NEC, and so on. This is a very important part of configuring the workstation DOS settings (as shown in Chapter 10 and Step 2: Creating Login Scripts in this chapter).

▶ SHOW DOTS—Enables you to emulate the "dot" (.) and "double dot" (..) graphics in directory entries. The default is OFF but should be set to ON for Windows support.

In addition to the above SHELL.CFG settings, NET.CFG supports one more section heading—LINK SUPPORT. This section is used for configuring receive buffers, the size of memory pools, and the number of boards and stacks for TCP/IP support. The BUFFERS option configures the number and size of receive buffers that LSL maintains. Because the IPX protocol stack does not use LSL communication buffers, this heading is rarely configured. TCP/IP, on the other hand, requires at least two link support buffers.

As a CNE, you can create NET.CFG files in one of two ways:

▶ Edit NET.CFG *after* client installation

▶ Edit INSTALL.CFG *before* client installation

After installing the NetWare DOS Requester, you will need to customize each user's NET.CFG file with additional settings. You can use any DOS text editor or the Windows WRITE application. Regardless of how you do it, each user's NET.CFG must be configured individually.

On the other hand, you can edit INSTALL.CFG before client installation and the system will automatically create a special NET.CFG for each user. During the NetWare 4 server installation, INSTALL.CFG is placed in the SYS:PUBLIC\CLIENT\DOSWIN subdirectory. You can use any DOS text editor to change the NetWare DOS Requester settings in INSTALL.CFG. The client installation program will then recognize INSTALL.CFG and create an identical NET.CFG for each user.

ZEN

"If you gaze for long into the abyss, the abyss also gazes into you."

Nietzsche

BRAIN

For additional information on configuring the NetWare DOS Requester and NET.CFG settings, see these Novell Applications Notes:"Using the DOS Requester with NetWare 4.0" (April 1993),"The Functions and Operations of the NetWare DOS Requester v1.1" (June 1994),and "Support Issues for the NetWare Requester (VLM) 1.2" (March 1995).

This completes our discussion of NET.CFG and workstation connectivity files in general. Now the first step of configuration has been completed. Leia is well on her way to toddlership and Guinevere is well on her way to LAN productivity. At this point, the workstation computer has booted, the connectivity software has been activated, and Guinevere has been logged in. The next step is to customize Guinevere's network connection via login scripts. Let's dive in.

Step 2: Login Scripts

Chatterbox.

The next step in Leia's development is learning to talk. One day your LAN's mindless babbling will begin to form words. Of course, we all know her first word will be "Daddy." Embrace these early days because soon she'll begin to form sentences and "Daddy" will become "Daddy, where're the car keys?" or "Daddy, I'm getting married" or, even worse, "Daddy, I want to be a CNE." Aah, the innocence of youth!

ZEN

"But the Emperor has nothing on at all!," cried the little child.

Hans Christian Andersen

Login scripts are an expression of your LAN's vocal cords. Once Guinevere has been authenticated with a valid username and password, NetWare 4 greets her with login scripts. In short, login scripts are batch files for the network. They provide a simple configuration tool for user customization—drive mappings, text messages, printer redirection, and so on.

Login scripts are one of your most important configuration responsibilities. From one central location, they enable you to customize *all* users or just specific groups of users. Many of the configurations we've talked about are session-specific and disappear when users log out. Login scripts give you the ability to reestablish these settings every time Guinevere logs in. Don't underestimate the power of NetWare 4 login scripts.

NetWare 4 supports four types of login scripts, which are executed in systematic progression. As you can see in Figure 12.1, there's a flowchart logic to how login scripts are executed. Here's a quick look:

- *Container login scripts* are properties of Organization and Organizational Unit containers. They enable you to customize settings for all users within a container.

- *Profile login scripts* are properties of the Profile object. These scripts customize environmental parameters for groups of users. This way, users who are not directly related in the NDS tree can share a common login script.

- *User login scripts* are properties of each user object. They are executed after the Container and Profile scripts and provide customization all the way to the user level.

- *Default login script* are—is executed for any user who does not have an individual User script. This script contains some basic mappings for the system and a COMSPEC command that points to the appropriate network DOS directory.

Login scripts consist of commands and identifiers just like any other program or batch file. In addition, login script syntax must follow specific rules and conventions. Let's start our discussion with a more detailed look at the four login script types and then explore the commands that make them productive.

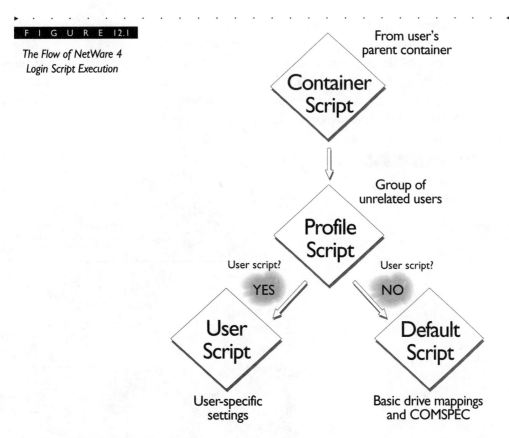

The Flow of NetWare 4
Login Script Execution

LOGIN SCRIPT TYPES

We just saw that there are four types of NetWare 4 login scripts—Container, Profile, User, and Default. All four work in concert to provide LAN customization for containers, groups, and users. As you'll quickly learn, login scripts are an integral part of your daily CNE grind. Let's start with a description of the four different login script types.

Container Login Script

Container login scripts are properties of Organization and Organizational Unit containers. In previous versions of NetWare, there was one System login script that was executed for all users. In NetWare 4, it is possible for every container to have its own login script. As you can see in Figure 12.1, the container is the first login script executed— Profile and User scripts follow.

There is one important difference between the NetWare 4 Container login script and earlier System login scripts. A container script only executes for users *within* the container. As you can see in Figure 12.2, the Admin user executes the ACME Container login script. SHolmes, on the other hand, doesn't execute any Container login script because the CRIME Organizational Unit doesn't have a script. Similarly, RHood executes the WHITE Container login script, whereas AEinstein executes none.

FIGURE 12.2

*Understanding NetWare 4
Login Script Types*

This is an important point because many CNEs assume that container login scripts can be inherited by lower containers. This is *not* the case. If you wish to have one login script for all users to share, you have three options: (1) You can create a Profile login script and have all users point to it; (2) you can use the cut-and-paste feature within NWADMIN to copy one script to all containers; or (3) you can use an INCLUDE statement in each container login script, which executes a text file containing these commands. Regardless, the moral of the story is NetWare 4 no longer provides a single script for all users.

As you plan login scripts for your network, keep in mind that at some point you'll need to maintain them. Use Container login scripts to provide access to network resources, Profile scripts for a specific group's needs, and User login scripts only in special circumstances. Following are the types of things you might do within a Container login script:

- ▶ Send messages to users within a container.

- ▶ Establish the first search drive mapping to SYS:PUBLIC.

- ▶ Establish the second search drive mapping to DOS directories.

- ▶ Create other search drive mappings for application directories.

- ▶ Establish a network drive mapping U: to each user's home directory.

- ▶ Connect users within a container to appropriate network printers.

- ▶ Use IF...THEN statements for access to specific resources based on times, group memberships, and other variables.

- ▶ Transfer users to an appropriate container-based menu system.

Profile Login Script

The Profile login script is a property of the Profile object. This script customizes environmental parameters for groups of users. Each user object can be assigned a single Profile script—that's all. This way, users who are not directly related in the NDS tree can share a common login script. For example, Figure 12.2 shows how the AEinstein and R Hood can share the LABS-Profile login script even though they live in different parts of the tree. Also note how the Profile login script executes after the Container script and in Mr. Einstein's case, the Profile login script is the only script that executes.

Figure 12.3 shows an example of how the Profile login script is created in NWADMIN. Once the script has been defined, two things must happen so you can use it. One, each user must have the Browse right to the object and the Read property right to the Profile object's login script property. Two, the complete name of the Profile object must be defined in the user's Profile login script property. See the case study at the end of this chapter.

▶ · ◀

F I G U R E 12.3

Creating the LABS Profile
Script in NWADMIN

TIP

Remember, users can be assigned to only one Profile object but other Profile login scripts can be specified at the command line. For example, the following line would allow RHood to execute the "WHITE-Profile" script in addition to his default "LABS-Profile" script:

```
LOGIN RHOOD
/P.CN=WHITE-Profile.OU=WHITE.OU=CRIME.OU=TOKYO.O=ACME
```

Wasn't that fun?

Profile login scripts should be used to customize specific group configurations. Some tasks you can accomplish with Profile login scripts include

▶ Send messages to users within a group.

▶ Establish network drive mappings to special data directories, report files, or other servers that contain critical group information.

▶ Establish search drive mappings to group application directories.

▶ Connect to group-specific printers such as high-resolution LaserJets, plotters, or faxes.

· · · · · ·

User Login Script

The User login script is a property of each User object. The User script is executed after the Container and Profile scripts and provides customization all the way down to the user level. Although User scripts are a nice feature, they can quickly become a maintenance nightmare—imagine hundreds and hundreds of User login scripts constantly screaming for attention. Nope, one baby is enough. A better strategy is to use Container and Profile scripts as much as possible and eliminate the User scripts altogether.

The primary purpose of the User login script is user-specific customization. This level of customization can be accomplished in the Container and Profile scripts by using IF..THEN logic commands. But if you absolutely have to create a user-specific script, it's nice to know that it's there.

User login scripts should be created only in special circumstances. Remember, you have to *maintain* any scripts you create. Some instances when a User script might be justified include

> ▸ Establish network drive mappings to specific user directories, provided that these directories do not correspond with the drive mappings made in the Container script

> ▸ Connect to commonly used printers in addition to the ones selected in the Container and Profile scripts

> ▸ Send weekly messages to remind the user about time-sensitive tasks

> ▸ Activate a special user-specific menu system

Default Login Script

The Default login script is executed for any user who does not have an individual User script. This poses an interesting dilemma. Earlier we said it's a good idea not to have a User script. This means the Default script will automatically execute. Oops. This is a problem because the default script typically corrupts already-established drive mappings and COMSPEC settings. Fortunately, Novell has recognized this problem and provides you with the means to disable the Default login script using the following statement:

```
NO_DEFAULT
```

This command must be placed in a Container or Profile login script.

TIP

The Default login script cannot be edited because it is included in the LOGIN.EXE command code. It can, however, be disabled by including the NO_DEFAULT command in a Container or Profile script.

QUIZ

So you think you're so smart? Let's see if you can think in three dimensions. A man is 100 yards due south of a bear. He walks 100 yards due east, then faces due north, fires his gun due north, and hits the bear.

What color was the bear?

Don't underestimate this one. The answer is much more involved than you think.

(Q12-3)

This completes our discussion of the different login script types. In leaving this little discussion, consider the factors that determine how you use login scripts and which types you'll need. These factors include the needs of users, their knowledge level, the size of your network, the complexity of the WAN, the type of groups, and access requirements for different containers. Remember, login script design can go a long way toward increasing your CNE quality of life and decreasing your daily workload. This is your first shot at parenthood (system customization); don't underestimate it.

LOGIN SCRIPT COMMANDS

Login scripts consist of commands and identifiers just as any other program or batch file. In addition, login script syntax must follow specific rules and conventions. The syntax for login script programming is quite simple, but you must make sure to organize identifier variables and commands with appropriate grammar—much like learning to talk. For example, consider the following line:

```
MAP U:=SYS:USERS\%LOGIN_NAME
```

This line uses proper login script syntax—it starts with the login script command MAP and uses appropriate identifier variable grammar—%LOGIN_NAME. The cool thing about this line is that it changes for each user. For example, when Dr. Watson logs in, the system creates a U: drive for him, and it points to SYS:USERS\DRWATSON. On the other hand, when SHolmes logs in, his U: drive points to SYS:USERS\SHOLMES. Cool!

Another good example of login script vernacular is the WRITE command. Consider the following statement:

```
WRITE "Good %GREETING_TIME, %FULL_NAME!"
```

Depending on the time of day and user who logs in, this single statement will provide a custom message. For example, Guinevere gets the following message when she turns on her machine in the morning:

```
"Good Morning, Guinevere Wannamaker!"
```

This can go a long way in making users feel warm and fuzzy about the LAN. As a matter of fact, some users get the perception that NetWare actually *cares* about them and is personally wishing them a nice day. Regardless of the LAN's motivation, the point is that users feel good about using the network!

All of this configuration magic is made possible because of two login script elements— identifier variable and commands. Let's take a closer look at how they work.

Identifier Variables

Identifier variables enable you to enter a variable (such as LAST_NAME) rather than a specific name (Wannamaker). When the login script executes, it substitutes real values for the identifier variables. This means you can make your login scripts more efficient and more flexible. In addition, it makes the concept of a single Container script feasible. As we saw in earlier examples, identifier variables are preceded by a percent sign (%) and written in all uppercase. This is the ideal syntax for identifier variables because it allows you to use them anywhere in the script, including inside quotation marks (" "). Table 12.3 lists all the identifier variables available in NetWare 4. Learn them. These cute little guys can go a long way in customizing Container and Profile scripts.

CATEGORY	IDENTIFIER VARIABLE	DESCRIPTION
Date	DAY	Day number 01 through 31
	DAY_OF_WEEK	Day of week (Monday, Tuesday, and so on)
	MONTH	Month number (01 through 12)
	MONTH_NAME	Month Name (January, February, and so on)
	NDAY_OF_WEEK	Weekday number (1 through 7, where 1 equals Sunday)
	SHORT_YEAR	Last two digits of year
	YEAR	All four digits of year
Time	AM_PM	a.m. or p.m.
	GREETING_TIME	Time of day (morning, afternoon, or evening)
	HOUR	Hour of day on a 12-hour scale
	HOUR24	Hour of day on a 24-hour scale
	MINUTE	Minutes (00 through 59)
	SECOND	Seconds (00 through 59)
User	CN	User's full common name as it exists in NDS
	ALIAS_CONTEXT	Y if REQUESTER_CONTEXT is an Alias
	FULL_NAME	User's unique full name as it appears in both NDS and the bindery
	LAST_NAME	User's last name in NDS or full name in bindery-based NetWare

TABLE 12.3

CATEGORY	IDENTIFIER VARIABLE	DESCRIPTION
	LOGIN_CONTEXT	Context where user exists
	LOGIN_NAME	User's unique login name truncated to 8 characters
	MEMBER OF "*GROUP*"	Group object that user is assigned to
	NOT MEMBER OF "*GROUP*"	Group object that the user is *not* assigned to
	PASSWORD_EXPIRES	Number of days before password expires
	REQUESTER_CONTEXT	Context when login started
	USER_ID	Unique hexadecimal ID assigned to each user.
Workstation	MACHINE	Type of computer (either IBM_PC or other name specified in NET.CFG)
	NETWARE_REQUESTER	Version of Requester being used (NetWare Requester for DOS or OS/2)
	OS	Type of operating system on the workstation (MSDOS, OS/2, and so on)
	OS_VERSION	Operating system version loaded on the workstation
	P_STATION	Workstation's 12-digit hexadecimal node ID
	SHELL_TYPE	Version of the workstation's DOS shell for NetWare 2 and 3 users
	S_MACHINE	Short machine name (IBM, and so on)
	STATION	Workstation's connection number

(continued)

	CATEGORY	IDENTIFIER VARIABLE	DESCRIPTION
T A B L E 12.3 *(continued)*	Miscellaneous	FILE_SERVER	NetWare server name that workstation first attaches to
		NETWORK_ADDRESS	IPX external network number for the cabling system (8-digit hexadeci-mal number)
		ACCESS_SERVER	Shows whether the access server is functional (true or false)
		ERROR_LEVEL	An error number (0 equals no errors)
		%n	Replaced by parameters entered after the LOGIN command (starting with %0)

In addition to these identifier variables, you can use any NDS property name within a NetWare 4 login script. Just make sure to use the same syntax—that is, uppercase and preceded by a percent sign.

REAL WORLD

Here's a list of things to think about when creating NetWare 4 login scripts. It's always a good idea to have a few guidelines in mind before you begin exploring all the possibilities:

▶ Minimum—None. All four login script types are optional. Of course, if no User script exists, the default will run. So at the absolute minimum, you must have one User script with one command—EXIT.

▶ Case—Not case sensitive except for identifier variables in quotations. They must be uppercase and preceded by a percent sign.

▶ Characters per line—150 maximum, although 78 is recommended for readability.

▶ Commands per line—one. Also press Enter to mark the end of each line. Lines that automatically wrap are considered one command.

▶ Blank lines—have no effect. Use them to visually separate groups of commands.

▶ Documentation—use any version of the REMARK command to thoroughly document what's going on.

These identifier variables have to be used with valid login script commands. As you can see in Figure 12.4, NetWare 4 includes a plethora of commands that can be used in various configurations. In this discussion, we'll present the commands as part of a productive NetWare 4 Container login script. In each case, refer to Figure 12.4 for appropriate syntax.

A. WRITE and REMARK

Login scripts should always start with documentation. This is accomplished using the REMARK command. Any line beginning with REMARK is ignored. It does, however, provide a useful tool for documenting the many different sections of your Container and Profile scripts. Besides the word REMARK, NetWare 4 supports three other uses—REM, an asterisk (*), and a semicolon (;). As you can see in Figure 12.4, all possibilities have been used. Another use of documentation is edit tracking. When multiple supervisors are maintaining the same container login script, it's a good idea to document who does what when. Finally, documentation is necessary for CNEs who follow you. After all, you do plan on winning the lottery, don't you?

ZEN

Miami Beach is where neon goes to die.

Lenny Bruce

One of the most popular login script commands is WRITE. With it, you can display a variety of friendly messages during login script execution. One of the friendliest is shown in Figure 12.4. Other identifier variables you can use with the WRITE command include:

```
Your password expires in %PASSWORD_EXPIRES days.
Today is %MONTH_NAME %DAY.
At the tone, the time is %HOUR:%MINUTE %AM_PM.
You're connected as workstation %STATION.
You're attached to %FILE_SERVER.
```

Don't underestimate the power of communication. Goodwill flourishes with a quick note to your users now and again.

▶ · ◀

F I G U R E 12.4

*A Typical NetWare 4 Login
Script*

A {
```
REMARK Greetings for users
WRITE "Good %GREETING_TIME, %FULL_NAME!"
WRITE "Your Password Expires in %PASSWORD_EXPIRES DAYS"
```

B {
```
REM Network Drive Mappings
MAP DISPLAY OFF
MAP ERRORS OFF
MAP U:=SYS:USERS\%LOGIN_NAME
MAP G:=SYS:GROUPS\"%Group Membership"
```

C {
```
*Search Drive Mappings
MAP INS S1:=SYS: PUBLIC
MAP INS S2:=SYS: PUBLIC \%MACHINE\%OS\%OS_VERSION
MAP INS S16:=SYS: AAPPS\WINDOWS
MAP DISPLAY ON
MAP
```

D {
```
; Command Specifier
COMSPEC= S2: COMMAND.COM
```

E {
```
SET PROMPT= "$P$G"
SET TEMP= "U:\USERS\%LOGIN_NAME\TEMP"
```

F {
```
IF DAY_OF_WEEK= "Friday" THEN BEGIN
   MAP R:=.REPORTS.LABS.NORAD.ACME
   DISPLAY R:FRIDAY.TXT
   PAUSE
END
```

G {
```
IF MEMBER OF "OPS-Group" THEN #CAPTURE P=HP4S1-P1 NT T1=10
IF MEMBER OF "ADMIN-Group" THEN #CAPTURE P=HP5-P1 NFF NT
IF MEMBER OF "LABS-Group" THEN #CAPTURE P=CANONBJ-P1 NB
```

H {
```
NO_DEFAULT
```

I {
```
PCCOMPATIBLE
DRIVE U:
EXIT "Start"
```

B. NETWORK DRIVE MAPPINGS

The next section in Figure 12.4 establishes user-specific and group-specific drive mappings. Drive mapping is the single, most important purpose of login scripts. Mappings are essential to NetWare navigation and provide a facility for representing large directory paths as drive letters. The problem with mapping is that it's both session specific (meaning drive pointers disappear when users log out) and user specific (meaning they're unique for each user). The temporary nature of drive mappings makes them particularly annoying—because complex MAP commands must be entered each time a user logs in. Fortunately, this process can be automated using NetWare 4 login scripts.

Before you get too excited about network and search drive mappings, it's a good idea to turn off the display of drive mapping and drive mapping errors. MAP DISPLAY OFF stops complex mappings from displaying during execution, and MAP ERRORS OFF avoids confusing users with mappings to directories they don't have rights to. Don't worry, we'll turn them back on later.

The MAP command is most useful when combined with identifier variables. This way, you can accomplish user-specific and group-specific mappings with only one command. Notice the second network drive mapping in Figure 12.4. Here we're using the Group Membership property from NDS. The trick is getting the quotes in the right place.

C. SEARCH DRIVE MAPPINGS

Once the network drive mappings have been established, it's time to shift your attention to search drive mappings. By default, the first two should always be SYS:PUBLIC and the network DOS directory structure. Notice our creative use of identifier variables in search mapping 2. This single statement intelligently maps every workstation to the appropriate version of DOS. Of course, these statements must be combined with the exact DOS structure outlined in Chapter 10. The three key identifier variables are

- %MACHINE—Identifies the machine such as IBM_PC, Dell, NEC, and so on. These values are established using the LONG MACHINE TYPE parameter in NET.CFG.

- %OS—Identifies the operating system as MSDOS, OS/2, PCDOS, DRDOS, and so on.

- %OS_VERSION—Identifies the specific version of DOS running on the workstation (for example, v5.00, v7.01, v6.22).

Next, you should create a search drive mapping for every application users are likely to access. In these cases, you can use MAP INS S16 to systematically create mappings in order. In each case, S16 will drop to the next available search number. Finally, turn MAP DISPLAY back on and issue one final MAP command to show the user what he/she has available.

TIP

Remember from Chapter 10 that NetWare search mappings systematically replace the DOS path statement. Also remember that using MAP INSERT eliminates this problem by adding the DOS path to the end of the NetWare search list. In addition, an interesting thing happens when you use "MAP INS S16." The NetWare search drives are added *after* the DOS path. This means users will execute local applications before network ones. Sometimes, this is a good thing!

QUIZ

What is the name for the upper portion of the brain? You know, the part that really hurts right now.

(Q12-4)

D. COMSPEC

The next step is to create a COMSPEC for the new DOS directory mapping. COMSPEC stands for Command Specifier, and it helps NetWare find COMMAND.COM when it's lost. This happens all the time when TSRs and Windows applications need extra space. If COMMAND.COM cannot be found, your users will get one of these messages:

```
Invalid COMMAND.COM
COMMAND.COM cannot be found
Insert Boot Disk in Drive A
```

Interestingly, this causes the hair to stand up on the back of your neck—especially if it happens all day. This must be a kinetic reaction.

COMSPEC solves the "lost DOS" problem by telling the system where to search for appropriate COMMAND.COM files. Keep in mind that each version of DOS on each of your workstations supports a different type of COMMAND.COM. You must make sure to point to the correct file. This is accomplished by using the S2: drive mapping we created earlier. Remember, it points to the correct DOS directory structure for each workstation.

TIP

Sending **COMSPEC** to a network directory for **COMMAND.COM** has its advantages. However, many **CNEs** still insist on pointing to a local drive such as **C:\DOS**. It's your choice. Here are some reasons to use the **NetWare 4 DOS** directory structure:

▶ **Speed (with file caching)**
▶ **Central management (all workstations point to the file server)**
▶ **Diskless workstations (it's required)**

E. SET

The SET command enables you to configure DOS environment variables within the login script. You can use the SET command exactly the same as you would in DOS (except that you'll need to surround the values with quotation marks). Otherwise, most SET variables are configured in the user's AUTOEXEC.BAT file. In Figure 12.4, we've included two important SET variables:

```
SET PROMPT="$P$G"
```

This configures the local and network prompt to display the current directory path. We want users to feel like they're at home.

```
SET TEMP="U:\USERS\%LOGIN_NAME\TEMP"
```

This points the Windows TEMP directory to a NetWare drive under the user's area.

Whatever you do, don't use the SET PATH command in a container login script; it overwrites local and network search drives.

F. IF...THEN...ELSE

The IF..THEN command enables you to use script programming logic. It checks a given condition and executes your command only if the condition is met. In addition, you can add the ELSE statement to selectively execute another command only when the condition is *not* met. For example, you can have the system display a fancy message and fire phasers whenever it is the user's birthday (using MONTH and DAY identifier variables). Otherwise, display a message pointing out that it's not his/her birthday the other 364 days of the year.

The IF...THEN command is the most versatile login script tool. Learn it, use it, be it. IF...THEN effectively enables you to execute any command based on condition, including login name, context, day of the week, or group membership. As you can see in Figure 12.4, we are executing these three commands only on Friday:

▸ MAP—Maps the R: drive to a Directory Map object.

▸ DISPLAY—Displays a text file that is stored on the R: drive.

▸ PAUSE—Temporarily stops execution of the login script to allow the user time to read the display. Just as with the DOS PAUSE command, execution resumes when the user presses any key.

Also notice the use of BEGIN and END. If you plan on including multiple commands within a nested IF...THEN statement, you must use BEGIN to start and END to mark the bottom of the nest. As a sidenote, IF...THEN statements can be nested up to 10 levels.

You can do anything with an IF...THEN statement. Don't be shy. Before you resign yourself to creating Profile and User login scripts, explore the use of IF...THEN statements in Container scripts.

G. # (DOS Executable)

The DOS executable (#) command has been included by Novell to support external programs. Because NetWare 4 has a limited number of login script commands, you might run across a case where you need to run a non-login script program. The most obvious oversight that comes to mind is CAPTURE. CAPTURE is a NetWare 4 printing command that redirects local ports to shared network printers. This command should be included in Container and Profile scripts for user and group automation. You can do so with the following command:

```
#CAPTURE P=HP4SI-P1 NT TI=10
```

There is one problem with this scenario. While CAPTURE is running, the entire login script and LOGIN.EXE is swapped to workstation RAM. Once the # command is finished, NetWare reloads the login script from memory. But what if the external program is a TSR or never returns stolen RAM to the workstation? In both of these cases, you run the risk of wasting 70 to 100 KB of workstation RAM. This is a bad thing. By default, NetWare 4 swaps login scripts and LOGIN.EXE into extended or expanded memory.

Fortunately, CAPTURE is not one of those misbehaving # commands. As you can see in Figure 12.4, we've combined the #CAPTURE program with IF...THEN statements to customize group-specific printing captures within a single container login script. Once again, the goal is to satisfy all your users' needs from within a single centrally managed login script.

H. NO_DEFAULT

Here's another command that helps you avoid conflicts between a central Container script and the Default login script. As you remember from our earlier discussion, the Default login script is contained in LOGIN.EXE and cannot be edited. In addition, it conflicts with drive mappings and the COMSPEC command from Container and Profile scripts. Finally, the Default login script executes only if there is no User script. And this conflicts with our goal of having one centrally managed Container login script. Fortunately, by using the NetWare 4 NO_DEFAULT command you can skip the Default login script even without a User script. Simply place it toward the end of your Container or Profile script and everything will be fine. Sometimes life can be so easy.

I. EXIT

Congratulations, you've made it to the end of our mammoth Container login script. Don't forget Guinevere. She's counting on finding a menu system and e-mail somewhere in her future. As a CNE, it is your job to orchestrate a smooth transition from Guinevere's login script to her menu system. Fortunately, you have the EXIT command.

EXIT terminates any login script and executes a specific network program. The program can be an .EXE, .COM, or .BAT file and must reside in the default directory. When combined with the DRIVE command (as shown in Figure 12.4), EXIT can facilitate a smooth transition from login script to menu system. In the case of Figure 12.4, we're exiting to a START batch file residing in either SYS:PUBLIC or the user's home area. Here's what START looks like:

```
ECHO OFF
CLS
CAPTURE P=HP4SI-P1 NFF NT
TSA_SMS /SE=CAM-FIN-SRV1 /P=RUMPELSTILTSKIN /D=C /B=30
NMENU GUINEVER.DAT
```

In this scenario, the DRIVE command dumps Guinevere into her own home directory where the menu system resides. Otherwise, she would be placed in the first available network drive (by default). In addition, the PCCOMPATIBLE line ensures that her clone workstation returns a %MACHINE value of IBM_PC.

It's important to note that the EXIT command skips all other login scripts. For this reason, you'll want to be careful where you place it. Only use EXIT in a container login script if you're convinced there are no Profile or User scripts, or if you'd rather not execute those scripts because they've been created by nonauthorized managers. All in all, this is a great strategy for skipping unnecessary login scripts and making a smooth transition to Guinevere's menu system.

ZEN

"When love and skill work together, expect a masterpiece."

John Ruskin

Before we move on to Step 3: Menu System, let's take a quick look at some other powerful login script commands.

Other Login Script Commands

In addition to the commands shown in Figure 12.4, NetWare includes a potpourri of other login script commands. For a complete listing, refer to the Brain Icon after this discussion.

- ▸ BREAK—If "BREAK ON" is included in a login script, you can press Ctrl+C or Ctrl+Break to abort the normal execution of a login script. This is not a good thing, especially in the hands of users. The default is BREAK OFF.

- ▸ CLS—Use CLS to clear the user's screen during login script execution.

- ▸ CONTEXT—This command changes the workstation's current NDS context during login script execution. It works similarly to the workstation CX utility.

- ▸ FDISPLAY—Works the same as DISPLAY, except it filters formatting before showing the file on the screen. It can be used to display the text of an ASCII file without showing all the ASCII formatting codes.

▸ FIRE PHASERS—Beam me up, Scotty. FIRE PHASERS can also be combined with identifier variables to indicate the number of times the phaser sound should blare. For example, FIRE PHASERS %NDAY_OF_WEEK will fire five phasers on Thursday.

▸ GOTO—This command enables you to execute a portion of the login script out of regular sequence. GOTO jumps to login script labels—text followed by a colon (TOP:, for example). Do not use GOTO to enter or exit a nested IF...THEN statement. This will cause the keyboard to explode. You can go through a lot of users this way.

▸ INCLUDE—As if one login script isn't enough. The INCLUDE command branches to subscripts from anywhere in the main Container script. These subscripts can be text files with valid login script syntax or entire login scripts that belong to different objects in the NDS tree. Once the subscript has been completed, control shifts to the next line in the original script. Now we're really getting crazy. Consider using INCLUDE subscripts with IF...THEN statements to ultimately customize Container login scripts. Now there's no excuse for using Profile, User, or Default scripts. As a matter of fact, everyone in the WAN can share the same Container script by distributing INCLUDE statements to all Organizational Units. Think of the synergy.

▸ LASTLOGINTIME—As you've probably guessed, displays the last time the user logged in. This can be combined with WRITE statements to ensure that nobody is logging in as *you* while you're on vacation. When the cat's away, the mice will play.

▸ SWAP—As you recall from our earlier discussion, the # command swaps 100 KB of stuff into workstation RAM and doesn't always give it back. The SWAP command can be used to force the 100 KB out of workstation RAM onto the local or network disk. Simply identify a path with the SWAP command and LOGIN.EXE will bother you no more. When the # command is completed, LOGIN.EXE continues on its merry way. If this bothers you, NOSWAP will force LOGIN.EXE into conventional workstation RAM.

THE BRAIN

For a complete list of NetWare 4 login script commands and identifier variables, refer to page 187 of Supervising the Network I. Another good reference is "Using NDS User Object Properties in NetWare 4.1 Login Script" in the May 1995 *Novell Application Notes*.

That completes our discussion of NetWare 4 login scripts. I hope you've gained an appreciation for how these cute little tools help you customize user and group connections. Once the Container and Profile scripts have been executed, NetWare 4 automatically loads Guinevere's menu. As we saw, this is accomplished by using the EXIT login script command.

QUIZ

Now that you're warmed up, let's try something a little more interesting. Besides, Guinevere could solve it—how about you?

Alice, Brett, Catherine, and Deirdre went to school together. They became, but not necessarily respectively, an author, a biologist, a cartoonist, and a doctor. Years before, they belonged to A, B, C, and D sororities, and they came from Australia, Brazil, Canada, and Denmark. The letters of each woman's house, the initial letters of her profession, her home, and her name are all different from each other. The doctor had never been to Brazil, and the biologist had never been to Canada. Back at school, Catherine, the girl from Australia, and the biologist used to spend all their spare time together.

What was the profession, the home, and the house of each of them?

Good luck.

(Q12-5)

She can walk, she can talk; your LAN is an unstoppable bundle of joy. Now that all of the fundamentals have been accomplished, it's time to put her to the test—preschool. It's time for your LAN to learn how to get along with others.

Step 3: Creating the Menu System

Leia goes to preschool.

One of the most rewarding aspects of a child's development is watching how she gets along with others. You can't beat the thrill of discovery and the sight of two toddlers bonding. Of course, this peaceful picture hinges on the ability of children to "share"—a lesson the world hasn't quite caught onto yet. Although with Barney the dinosaur as our ambassador of sharing, I can understand why some people have resorted to violence. Not my baby! Leia's going to learn how to share without resorting to Barney-isms.

Social interaction is a valuable skill on any level. It's how the world works. Learning to get along with others is as practical a skill as tying your shoes or signing your name. As a matter of fact, you'll run into questions on your CNE job application that deal with this very topic.

Social interaction is also important to our NetWare 4 LAN. In order for Guinevere to get anything done, she needs a friendly menu interface for all her network applications and e-mail. A turnkey custom menu environment provides transparent access from "point A" (turning on the computer) to "point Z" (accessing her e-mail with cappuccino in hand). Fortunately, NetWare 4 has a built-in menu system that provides custom NetWare-looking menus. This system uses a simple script format and is versatile enough to support large groups of users with a single menu file.

Menus are a good thing. They provide a comfortable, friendly interface for Guinevere and eliminate the need to learn NetWare command line utilities. They present information in multiple layers instead of all in one place. But let's be honest. You're probably using MS Windows. On the most fundamental level, MS Windows is a simple graphical menu. It controls what kind of information is presented and enables users to launch applications from a single place. If you're using MS Windows, you don't need this menu system. However, it does have merits as a simple network-oriented interface for small NetWare 4 LANs. So with that in mind, you're prepared to learn about it.

TIP

The NetWare 4 menu system is a partial version of the Saber Menu System. This software acquisition falls into the Novell category of "if you can't build it, buy it." As a partial version, NetWare 4 menus have limitations. For example, you can't specify the location of menus on the

screen nor avoid the default color palette—blue and gold. In addition, NetWare's internal menu system is limited to 11 cascading screens—1 main menu and 10 submenus. Finally, there's limited security and many missing features. So if you're intrigued by what you learn here, consider contacting Saber and buying the full-blown version.

NetWare 4 menus are built using two simple command types:

▸ Organizational commands—providing the menu's look and feel

▸ Control commands—doing the work

In addition, NetWare 4 has specific rules about how menus are executed and what rights are necessary to get at them. These are the topics we're going to discuss in this section—starting with organizational commands.

ORGANIZATIONAL COMMANDS

It all starts with organizational commands. They provide the menu's look and feel. NetWare 4 supports two organizational commands:

▸ MENU—Identifies the beginning of each menu screen and provides a title.

▸ ITEM—Defines the options that appear within the menu and includes a variety of built-in "squiggly" options.

As you can see in Figure 12.5, the MENU command is left-justified and followed by a number. The menu number is then followed by a comma and the title of the menu. Next, options are listed under the MENU command using the organizational tool—ITEM. Items can be specific applications or other submenus—it doesn't matter. Using Figure 12.5 as a guide, let's explore these two organizational commands.

FIGURE 12.5

Guinevere's Menu System

```
MENU 01, Guinevere's Main Menu
    ITEM  ^AApplications
          SHOW 10
    ITEM  ^EE-Mail {BATCH}
          EXEC WIN WMAIL
    ITEM  ^FFun Stuff
          SHOW 15
    ITEM  ^MAdmin Menu
          LOAD G:\GROUPS\ADMIN\ADMIN.DAT
    ITEM  ^LLogout
          EXEC LOGOUT

MENU 10, Guinevere's Applications
    ITEM  ^1Windows '95 {BATCH}
          EXEC WIN
    ITEM  ^2Network Utilities
          SHOW 20
    ITEM  ^3Word Perfect {CHDIR}
          EXEC WIN WPWIN

MENU 15, Guinevere's Fun Stuff
    ITEM  Pick your Doom
          GETO ENTER THE VERSION OF DOOM (1-3):{DOOM}1,1,{}
          EXEC
    ITEM  Solitaire {BATCH}
          EXEC WIN SOL

MENU 20, Network Utilities
    ITEM  NetWare User Tools {BATCH}
          EXEC WIN NWUSER
    ITEM  Network Copy {PAUSE} {SHOW}
          GETP ENTER SOURCE FILE(S):{}80,,{}
          GETP ENTER DESTINATION FILE(S):{}80,,{}
          EXEC NCOPY %1 %2
```

Menu

MENU identifies the beginning of each menu screen. It is left-justified and followed by a number. A single NetWare 4 menu file can support 255 different menus—1 through 255. The menu number is then followed by a comma and the title of the menu. As you can see in Figure 12.5, the first menu displays the title "Guinevere's Main Menu." Subsequent menus have systematically higher numbers (10, 15, and 20). Each menu number identifies the beginning of a new submenu for branching purposes (using the SHOW control command). Menu titles are limited to 40 characters.

REAL WORLD

The first menu defined in the source file is always the first menu displayed—no matter what number it uses. Subsequent submenus are referenced by their numbers. In Figure 12.5, the first menu has the number 01. This will be the first menu displayed for Guinevere—not because it's menu 01 but because it's the first menu shown in the source file. Branching to other submenus is accomplished with the SHOW command, not their numeric order. Bottom line: Menu numbers are for reference only; they don't have any systematical significance (there's a mouthful).

Item

Options are listed under each menu title using the ITEM command. Each item is preceded by a letter (from A through Z) and appears in the exact order in which it is written. If you'd like to force a different letter for any option, simply precede the text with a caret (^) and the desired letter. For example, refer to menu 01 in Figure 12.5. Notice how the five items are each preceded by a caret and a letter. This forces the letter E, for example, to appear in front of "E-mail." Otherwise, it would get the letter B. Numbers can also be used as shown in Menu 10 of Figure 12.5. NOTE: If you force the letter assignment of one item, you should force the letter assignment of every item—but you don't have to. The menu program does not track forced assignments and might duplicate letters—this is a bad thing.

ITEM options can be customized using one of four built-in parameters. These are called "squiggly options" because they live inside cute "squiggly" brackets. Let's take a look:

- {BATCH}—Shells the menu to disk and saves 32 KB of workstation RAM. See Figure 12.5.

- {CHDIR}—Returns the user to the default directory upon completion of the item.

- {PAUSE}—Temporarily stops menu execution and displays the message

```
Press any key to continue.
```

ZEN

"Where's the Any key?"

Guinevere

▸ {SHOW}—Displays DOS commands in the upper left-hand corner of the screen when they're executed.

Once you've created the "look and feel" of your menus, it's time to move on to the real workhorses of NetWare 4 menuing—control commands.

CONTROL COMMANDS

The second NetWare 4 command type is control commands. These little wonders are the workhorses of the menu system. They execute menu instructions and enable branching to internal and external submenus. The NetWare 4 control commands are

▸ EXEC—Executes any internal or external program.

▸ SHOW—Branches to another menu within this menu file. This is used for submenuing.

▸ LOAD—Branches to a completely different external menu file (with the .DAT extension).

▸ GETO—Supports optional user input.

▸ GETR—Supports required user input.

▸ GETP—Assigns user input to a programmable variable.

As you can see in Figure 12.5, the EXEC and SHOW control commands are the most popular. In Guinevere's main menu, for example, she has the option of branching to one of two submenus. This submenuing strategy continues throughout her complex menu file. Let's take a closer look at how these little dynamos work.

EXEC

EXEC is the most popular NetWare 4 control command. It executes internal or external commands. These commands can be either an .EXE file, a .COM file, a DOS internal command, or one of four special EXEC options:

▸ EXEC CALL—Runs a batch file and returns to NMENU.

▸ EXEC DOS—Returns to the NetWare command line temporarily. Users must type EXIT to return to NMENU.

▸ EXEC EXIT—The only way to exit a NetWare 4 menu. Don't lock yourself in—use this command.

▸ EXEC LOGOUT—Exits NMENU and logs the user out. Guinevere is left at the DOS prompt without access to the network.

Make sure to include at least one of these EXEC commands toward the bottom of your main menu. As you can see in Figure 12.5, we're giving Guinevere the option of logging out. If you don't include one of these special EXEC options, the user will be trapped in the menu forever. This might not be a bad thing.

SHOW

SHOW is the second most popular NetWare 4 control command. Because you can create 255 submenus within a single script file, you need a way of getting to them. SHOW branches to another menu number from within any item. This is a way of submenuing from WITHIN the same script file. Notice in Figure 12.5 how the SHOW command is used with the Applications and Fun Stuff submenus. Also notice how Network Utilities is called as a submenu from within the Applications submenu.

TIP

Try not to confuse the SHOW control command with the SHOW squiggly option. It's unfortunate they share the same name. The SHOW control command is used for submenuing whereas the SHOW squiggly option displays executed DOS commands in the upper left-hand corner of your screen.

LOAD

LOAD performs exactly the same function as SHOW but in a slightly different way. Instead of executing submenus within the same script file, LOAD branches to submenus in completely different files. Refer to Figure 12.5 for an example of how the LOAD command is used. The Admin Menu item includes a branch to ADMIN.DAT. This external menu file must be in the default directory or specified with an exact path.

There is no limit to the number of menus that you can LOAD at any one time. But remember, you can only display 11 cascading menus simultaneously.

GETO

The final three control commands allow for user input. This feature was previously not available in NetWare menus and is hard to find in MS Windows. GETO, GETR, and GETP are powerful tools but their syntax is a little tricky:

```
GETx prompt{PREPEND}length,prefill,{APPEND}
```

- ► *x* is replaced with the type of GET command you wish to use—O for optional, R for required, and P for programmable user input.

- ► *prompt* is replaced by the message you want to send to the user. For example, in Figure 12.5, the last item asks Guinevere to "Enter source file(s):". This is the prompt.

- ► {*PREPEND*} data is attached *before* the user input. This works oppositely from {*APPEND*}. For example, in Figure 12.5, refer to the Pick your Doom item. The user is asked to enter the version of Doom he or she wish to play. The number these choose is prepended by the DOOM command, and it executes a batch file to load the appropriate game. This is a {*PREPEND*}. If no {*PREPEND*} is necessary, use the braces without any characters between them. Refer to the last item in Figure 12.5.

- ► *length* is the maximum number of characters the user can enter. Again, a length is required and the maximum is 80 characters. In the DOOM example, users can only enter a one-character answer.

▸ *prefill* displays a default response if none is given. It is separated from *length* by a comma and no spaces. Again, in the DOOM example of Figure 12.5, you're forcing a 1 to appear if no input is given. This will run the original game.

▸ {*APPEND*} defines a value that will always be appended to the user input. Once again, these braces are required, and if no data are needed, type the brackets without any characters. Refer to the last item in Figure 12.5.

TIP

Wow, what a mind-boggling collection of NetWare 4 control commands. Don't GET too excited about using GETx. But if you have to, here are a few things to think about:

- ▸ **The GETO, GETR, and GETP commands must be entered between the ITEM line and the EXEC command associated with them.**

- ▸ **You can have a maximum of 100 GET commands per ITEM, although you want to limit each prompt to 1 line.**

- ▸ **Commands can be entered in either upper- or lowercase.**

- ▸ **You can enter up to 10 prompts in each dialog box. If you want a prompt to appear in its own dialog box, type a caret (^) at the beginning of the prompt text.**

- ▸ **During execution, the Enter key accepts input but does not cause the command to execute. To activate the appropriate EXEC command, you must press F10.**

Now it's time to GET on with the show.

GETO allows for optional user input. As you can see in Figure 12.5, the Pick your Doom item uses an optional GET control command. If the user does not enter any input and simply presses Enter, NetWare executes the {*PREPEND*} and {*prefill*}, which is "DOOM1."

ZEN

"The computer is a great invention. There are just as many mistakes as ever. But now they are nobody's fault."

Anonymous

GETR

GETR requires user input. The menu will not continue until some valid information has been entered. However, the user can press Esc to return to the main menu.

GETP

GETP assigns user input to a programmable variable. If you need a variety of inputs from the user, assign each to a GETP prompt. The corresponding EXEC command can then use these prompts in combination with some valid external commands. As you can see in the final item of Figure 12.5, two GETP prompts are shown. The first input is assigned to %1 and the second to %2. The EXEC NCOPY command then uses these variables to satisfy the user's request. In addition, the {PAUSE} squiggly option enables the user to view the results as long as necessary.

Well, wasn't that fun? If you're feeling a little dizzy, now's a good time to put down the book and grab a soda . . . welcome back. Now that we've conquered the NetWare 4 menu syntax, let's take a look at how these babies execute.

MENU EXECUTION

So how are NetWare 4 menu files executed? Good question. It all starts with the source file. Menu source files are created using any text editor, and they must have the .SRC extension. As you can see in Figure 12.6, these source files are then compiled into .DAT files using MENUMAKE.EXE. The compiled files are smaller, more flexible, and easily swapped to and from the local disk. You cannot, however, edit .DAT files. You must edit the source file and recompile it for testing.

The smaller, more flexible .DAT file is finally executed using NMENU.BAT. This step finally brings Guinevere's menu to life. (See Figure 12.7.)

That's not all—NetWare 4 also supports older menus. NetWare 3.11 menu files (with the extension .MNU) can be converted into NetWare 4 source files using MENUCNVT.EXE. These .SRC files are then compiled and displayed using

MENUMAKE.EXE and NMENU.BAT. However, this is not the end of menu conversion. You must also edit some of the .SRC syntax changes including invalid commands (such as SYSCON), preceding letters or numbers from the old menu system, and the conversion of "@1" variables into newer GETP statements.

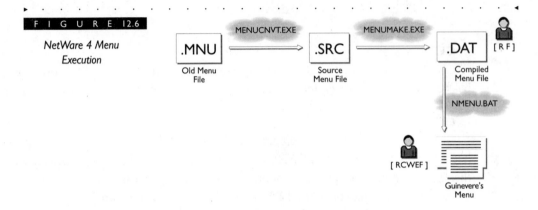

F I G U R E 12.6

NetWare 4 Menu Execution

So what about security? The NMENU.BAT program is stored in SYS:PUBLIC so it can be accessed from anywhere by any NetWare user. In addition, there are access right issues concerning the location of .DAT files. Here's a summary:

▸ Users must have the Read and File Scan (RF) access rights to directories that hold the .DAT files. This is typically their home directory or a shared area such as SYS:PUBLIC.

▸ The NetWare 4 menu system creates many temporary files. For this reason, users need special rights in the current default directory when executing NMENU.BAT. These rights are Read, Create, Write, Erase, and File Scan (RWCEF). Typically, this is the user's home or temporary directory. Recall that in the previous discussion, you used EXIT to bail out of the container login script and automatically accessed NMENU.BAT. You did this from Guinevere's home directory (with the DRIVE command) for security purposes. I knew there was a reason.

▸ If the menu file is going to be used by multiple users, it should be flagged as Sharable.

Once again, refer to Figure 12.6 for a summary of the access rights required at different points of menu execution.

F I G U R E 12.7

Looking at Guinevere's Menu

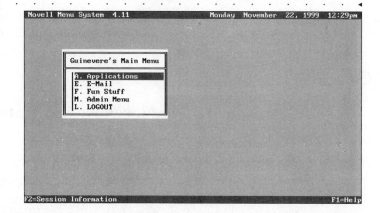

So what does Guinevere's menu look like? Check out Figure 12.7. As it shows, the NetWare 4 menu program creates an extremely NetWare-looking interface. As a matter of fact, it's difficult to tell the difference between Guinevere's main menu and NETADMIN. I just hope Guinevere can tell the difference. Let's review. NetWare 4 menu source files are created using any text editor. Their names contain the .SRC extension. These files are then compiled using MENUMAKE.EXE into a .DAT file. The smaller, more flexible .DAT file is then executed using NMENU.BAT. Piece of cake.

ZEN

"Never eat more than you can lift."

Miss Piggy

Remember, "wherever you go, there you are." With that in mind, let's take a moment to reflect on our LAN's brief, but exciting, life so far. First, she was born (installation), and then she took her first step (workstation connectivity). Once she learned to talk (login scripts), we sent her off to preschool to learn how to get along with others (menu system).

Now, it's time for our talented toddler to scurry off to kindergarten. There she'll start her long and winding journey down the road known as "SCHOOL"! During this journey, Leia will expand her body and mind to new levels—gaining valuable skills in the process. She'll make friends, buy clothes, ignore you, go to the prom, and, finally, graduate. This all leads to one inevitable climax—adulthood. Where did all the time go?

Step 4: Installing Network Applications

Leia goes to school.
Aah, school:
   "The chalice of wisdom, to drink once more from thee."

I don't know what's more memorable, school or all the extracurricular activities that surround it. Regardless, this is the fire in which we forge our personalities. So many memories—my fourth grade music teacher, recess, stomach-churning school lunches, mind-boggling math homework, field trips, sports, and the junior prom. As we help Leia through this phase of her childhood, we get an opportunity to live our own school days all over again. This is probably one of the most rewarding and excruciating experiences for any parent.

In addition to life lessons, school teaches you a few academic things. With knowledge comes productivity and wisdom. Suddenly, Leia's eyes open to the wonders and possibilities of calculus, art, and prepositional phrases. And sometimes the lessons aren't so obvious. I'm sure you'll never use algebra again in your life, but consider the problem-solving skills it taught you—skills that you'll put to good use as a NetWare 4 CNE.

As your LAN learns more and more from school, your users' productivity will increase as well. After all, a network is only as useful as the users who use it (that's a triple-word score). In Step 4 of NetWare 4 Configuration, you will give Guinevere all the productivity tools she needs to get her job done. That includes network applications, utilities, and a consistent user environment. Don't underestimate the value of the latter. This means if Guinevere wants to use MS Windows, her application should be in Windows. However, if she breaks out in hives every time she touches the mouse, consider giving her DOS-based applications. Please try not to mix interfaces—it gets ugly fast.

Network applications are the productivity tools of your LAN—and NetWare 4 has great support for them. This is accomplished with the help of a simple seven-step model. For the most part, these seven steps help you foster synergy between user productivity and shared application software—I learned those big words in school.

1 • Make sure your applications are NetWare compatible *before* you buy them.

2 • Ensure the software is truly multiuser.

3 • Create an appropriate directory structure for the applications and all their support components.

4 • Install them.

5 • Establish file attributes for Sharable and Nonsharable network applications.

6 • In addition to file attributes, assign user access rights to network application subdirectories.

7 • Customize the workstation for specific application needs.

This is just a general discussion. Most network applications include specific instructions for making them work on a LAN. However, these guidelines are a great place to start.

STEP 1: ENSURING NETWARE COMPATIBILITY

It is important to determine whether your applications are NetWare compatible before you buy them. Approximately 5,000 software packages are compatible and registered with Novell. This compatibility information is important because NetWare makes demands on application software that can cause it to corrupt data or at least impede users' productivity. Information about NetWare compatibility and registration are available on NetWire or from your local Novell sales office. You should also consider contacting the software vendor directly, but be forewarned, the company might not have the full story.

THE BRAIN

For more detailed information about Novell-certified hardware and software, consult the vendor forums on NetWire. In addition, the NSEPro CD-ROM has detailed results from Novell certification testing labs.

STEP 2: CHECKING MULTIUSERNESS

For the best results and highest level of user productivity, all applications should support multiple users simultaneously. If your application is designed to run on a stand-alone computer, don't assume it will work fine on the LAN. The good news is, most large software manufacturers routinely create multiuser versions of popular applications. Two signs of true multiuser capabilities are file sharing and multiuser access. Again, it is important to determine the level of multiuserness *before* you purchase the application. Also, be aware that almost all single-user software works in a NetWare environment—NetWare supports any DOS application. But don't expect these applications to offer data- or resource-sharing capabilities.

STEP 3: CREATING THE DIRECTORY STRUCTURE

Before you can install the application and configure its components, you must create an intelligent directory structure for it. As you learned in Chapter 10, the application directories need to support software data as well as program files. Each application should have a specific subdirectory under the main SYS:APPS directory to avoid cluttering the root. This also organizes network applications for easy, efficient security implementation.

In addition, some applications create their own directory structure during the installation process. Unfortunately, these programs attack the root directory. That's fine in a local environment but doesn't work well in the NetWare-shared directory structure. Consider "MAP ROOTing" a network drive before installation. This way the system will think that it's installing in [Root] when in fact it's installing under the SYS:APPS directory.

STEP 4: MANAGING THE INSTALLATION

The installation process is typically left up to the application. Many install programs perform file decompression as well as application customization. This is especially true in the MS Windows environment. Make sure not to simply copy the files from the source diskette or CD-ROM. You haven't lived until you've had to manually customize the 342 .INI files configured by Windows 95. Let the application do it—that's what you paid for.

Once the network software has been installed, three more steps help define its special configurations.

STEP 5: ASSIGNING FILE ATTRIBUTES

Network applications must have the correct file attributes so programs can share them without being locked out. Follow these simple guidelines:

▸ Shared application files—Sharable, Read-Only

▸ Shared data files—Sharable Read-Write

▸ Nonshared data files—Nonsharable Read/Write

Most of today's multiuser application programs provide detailed documentation about specific file attributes. I don't usually say this, but you might consider "reading the manual."

STEP 6: ASSIGNING ACCESS RIGHTS

In addition to file attributes, you'll need to assign user/group rights for access to network application directories. By default, users have *no* rights to the new directory structure you've created. If you install the application and walk away, users end up spinning their wheels trying to get work done. This also applies to NDS rights if you need access to other network resources, including printers and messaging objects.

As you recall from Chapter 11, most applications work fine with the Read and File Scan (RF) access rights. Also recall that these access rights can be inherited by all subdirectories under SYS:APPS. Next, you may consider assigning all rights except SAM (Supervisor, Access Control, and Modify) to data directories. Finally, consider these security guidelines:

► Application data should be stored under each application subdirectory (SYS:APPS\WP\DATA, for example).

► User-specific data should be stored in each user's home directory.

► Group-specific data should be stored in a corresponding SYS:GROUP subdirectory.

► Globally shared data should be stored in the SYS:DATA directory.

STEP 7: PERFORMING CUSTOMIZATION

The seventh and final step in network application support is workstation customization. Many programs require special DOS configurations in order to run properly. The most notable tool is CONFIG.SYS, which customizes the DOS environment. For example, device drivers might be loaded for programs that use a mouse. Here are a few other things to think about:

► You may need to increase environment space using the SHELL command:

```
SHELL=C:\COMMAND.COM /p /e:1024
```

► You may want to load HIMEM.SYS to activate the high memory area (HMA). Then you can use the following command in CONFIG.SYS to free 60 KB of conventional workstation RAM:

```
DOS=HIGH
```

► Many programs require special SET parameters for environment variables and temporary directories. Consult the application's documentation.

Once the application software has been installed, your LAN is well on its way to enlightenment: "sipping from the chalice of knowledge." In addition, the menu interface can provide a friendly, centrally managed arena for application launching. I know this is a lot of work, but "warm and fuzzy" is a good thing. Customization increases productivity by giving users the tools they need and decreasing their LAN-phobia—not to be confused with parent-phobia!

ZEN

"Actually I'm 18. I've just lived hard."

Clint Eastwood

Speaking of phobia, Guinevere is growing up way too fast. In the blink of an eye, the prom is over and she's ready for the fifth and final step of NetWare childhood—moving out.

Step 5: E-mail

The time has come. Your LAN becomes a woMAN (metropolitan area network).

It's inevitable. At some point, your child grows up and becomes an adult. The transition to adulthood is a scary time for everybody. She gets her first car, her first job, and her first apartment. Suddenly, the chalice of knowledge takes on a whole new importance. Her ability to survive depends on how many business classes she slept through. Suddenly all those nights you spent helping her with math homework equate to food on the table. Suddenly, Mom and Dad aren't so wrong anymore. It's weird how that happens—and it always does.

With adulthood comes new challenges and a new level of communication. To succeed, it's vital that you develop a high level of LAN synergy. All of your users, configurations, workstations and applications must work together as one cohesive unit. This is made possible through e-mail. The final step in NetWare 4 configuration focuses on tying all of these components together.

E-mail has become one of the most critical LAN services, next to filing and printing. That's because it

▸ Improves communication—E-mail enables employees to communicate even when business meetings, travel schedules, and distributed locations prevent them from seeing each other.

▸ Increases productivity—E-mail improves the success rate for communications because unlike other forms of communication, messaging does not require conversing participants to be available at the same time. No more "telephone tag."

▸ Maximizes the use of existing resources—E-mail leverages file, printing and connectivity services by providing a way of tying them altogether. Much the same way as time ties together the fabric of our universe. (Is that *esoteric* enough for you?)

QUIZ

Speaking of esoteric, here's a doozy for you. There are five men—A, B, C, D, and E—each wearing a disc on his forehead selected from a total of five white, two red, and two black. Each man can see the colors of the discs worn by the other four, but he is unable to see his own.

They are all intelligent people, and they are asked to try to deduce the color of their own disc from the colors of the other four whom they can see. In fact, they are all wearing white discs. After a pause for reflection, C, who is even more intelligent than the others, says, "I reckon I must be wearing a white disc."

Huh? How did he do that?

(Q12-6)

E-mail in NetWare 4 relies on an integrated messaging platform called MHS Services for NetWare 4. MHS (Message Handling Service) stores, forwards, and routes user messages. These messages can be text, binary graphics, digitized video, or audio data. MHS Services is integrated with NDS and uses many NDS objects to accomplish these magic messaging tasks.

Let's take a closer look.

UNDERSTANDING MHS SERVICES

MHS Services for NetWare 4 is an "engine" that provides messaging capabilities. Various messaging programs can now take full advantage of this technology. In the simplest terms, this "engine" takes input from various e-mail applications and routes it to any user on the internetwork running any other type of e-mail interface. This is much like THE WAY NetWare 4 file services stores a variety of different types of files from various network applications. However, unlike file services, MHS deals actively with the communication interactions between computer users. Instead of simply storing data files, MHS moves the data from point to point and notifies the user of waiting messages.

All of this magic is accomplished with three key components:

▸ Messaging server

▸ User mailboxes

▸ MHS applications

Messaging Server

The *messaging server* is NetWare 4's implementation of the MHS "engine." The server accepts data from a variety of user e-mail packages and delivers it to any type of mailbox (as Figure 12.8 shows). The server can deliver messages to local user mailboxes or route them through the internetwork to other messaging engines for eventual delivery. The main point is—MHS Services supports a variety of e-mail applications and can deliver to a variety of other engine types. Also, messages can be composed of text, graphics, video, or audio data.

All of this fancy footwork occurs within the messaging server. Each network server that has MHS Services installed is called a *messaging server.* A *message routing group* is a group of messaging servers that communicate with each other directly—to transfer messages. In a large WAN such as that in Figure 12.8, for example, this would be all the NetWare 4 servers that share a common backbone. Each message routing group has one or more *Postmasters General*. This special user is automatically granted the privilege to modify message routing groups and configure all of the messaging servers. In addition, each of these servers has one or more *Postmasters* that configure and manage user mailboxes.

User Mailboxes

A *user mailbox* is a physical location on the messaging server where messages are delivered. You can use any MHS application to send messages to any NDS object that can be assigned a mailbox. This includes Users, Groups, Organizational Roles, and Organizational Units. Also, you can send mail to special *Distribution List* objects, which in turn copy the mail to multiple mailboxes. This reduces network traffic throughout the message routing group by creating and routing only one copy of the message and then replicating it for every mailbox on the list. Finally, user mailboxes can be configured and managed using either NWADMIN (MS Windows) or NETADMIN (DOS). Once again, refer to Figure 12.8 for an illustration of the relationship between messaging servers and user mailboxes.

MHS Applications

All of this NetWare 4 messaging magic is made possible through a front-end e-mail application. Without these applications, there's no way to create or read MHS messages. Just your luck, NetWare 4 includes two rudimentary MHS applications—FirstMail for DOS and FirstMail for Windows. Both starter MHS applications are automatically installed in the SYS:PUBLIC subdirectory on each messaging server. The good news is, FirstMail automatically imports all user and group information from NDS. You don't need to lift a finger. This means that as soon as you install MHS Services, users can begin sending messages via FirstMail.

The bad news is, you get what you pay for. Although FirstMail for Windows has a nice interface (as shown later in Figure 12.12), it doesn't include any advanced messaging features. FirstMail is a simple starter application that can tide you over until you buy a real MHS front-end. Think of it as Guinevere's first broken-down VW or her one-room apartment under the train tracks. Even though it's not the Taj Mahal, it does represent her first shot at freedom. For this reason, you'll probably never forget FirstMail or that adorable VW Bug.

F I G U R E 12.8

*Understanding MHS
Services for NetWare 4*

There you have it. MHS Services in a nutshell. Even though I'm sure you absorbed it all the first time, let's take a quick review—just for the heck of it. Table 12.4 is your friend.

MHS COMPONENT	DESCRIPTION
MHS Services for NetWare 4	"The Product"
MHS engine	Implementation of "The Product"
Messaging server	Each NetWare 4 server running "The Product." Also the central communications point and storage location of user mailboxes
Message routing group	A collection of interconnected messaging servers.
Postmaster general	Manages the message routing group.
Postmaster	Manages the messaging server
User mailboxes	Physical storage location for MHS messages. They hang out on messaging servers
MHS applications	E-mail front-ends that send and receive MHS messages
Distribution list	A special NDS object that forwards messages to numerous user mailboxes

T A B L E   12.4

Getting to Know MHS Services for NetWare 4

Now that you're a pro with MHS Services, let's explore the details of installing and managing it. Don't have any illusions; nobody said moving out would be easy.

INSTALLING MHS SERVICES

A complete set of MHS Services software is included on the NetWare 4.1 CD-ROM. It has no mailbox limit, which means you can identify as many user mailboxes as you wish. However, MHS Services for NetWare 4 does have a concurrent connection limit. This means the maximum number of users who can send simultaneous messages is limited by your NetWare 4.1 user license. If you need greater access, consider creating a centralized messaging server with a 500- or 1,000-user copy of NetWare 4.1 on it. This is a popular strategy for large organizations such as ACME.

Following is a brief list of prerequisites needed for installing MHS Services. Once you've digested these, we'll dive into the detailed installation steps themselves.

MHS Prerequisites

The NetWare 4.1 server where you install MHS Services is called the *host server.* The host server prerequisites differ for small-scale and large-scale implementations. A small-scale installation can handle about 10 users and 100 messages per day. Here's a list of the small-scale hardware prerequisites:

- 80386 processor or later.

- 12 MB of RAM for the server plus 500 KB for MHS Services.

- 65 MB hard disk space for the default NetWare 4.1 installation plus 2.5 MB of disk space for MHS programs.

- Additional disk space requirements for user mailboxes. This number varies depending on how active users are.

- CD-ROM (required during installation only).

A large-scale MHS installation, on the other hand, can handle hundreds, even thousands, of messages per day. Following are the minimum hardware prerequisites for a large-scale MHS installation:

- 80386 processor or later.

- 16 MB of RAM plus any additional memory required to maintain more than 30 percent free cache buffers. Use MONITOR.NLM to determine availability of cache buffers.

- 65 MB of hard disk space for the default NetWare 4.1 installation plus 2.5 MB for MHS programs.

- An additional 5 MB of hard disk space for each user mailbox.

- CD-ROM (required during installation only).

► . . . . ◄

REAL WORLD

Many large-scale MHS sites opt to create a centralized MHS server for delivery of all user messages. Following is a sample configuration that can easily handle 5,000 messages per hour:

- ► 80486-66 MHz processor
- ► 16 MB of RAM
- ► Two or three concurrent users
- ► No other server activities.

Remember, the central MHS server doesn't provide file or printing services; it simply delivers mail.

Once you've established your minimum MHS prerequisites, it's time to get on with the installation. Here we go.

QUIZ

Which "Star Trek" character waited until the second season to beam aboard the Starship Enterprise?

(Q12-7)

MHS Installation Steps

You can install MHS Services during the custom NetWare 4.1 installation or afterwards. In either case, it consists of four simple steps:

1 • Running INSTALL.NLM. Load INSTALL.NLM at the server console if you're not already there. Select Product Options and press Enter. Then select Choose an item or product listed above and press Enter. Finally, select the Install NetWare MHS option. You can accept the default path by pressing Enter or specifying your own directory. The product will most likely reside on the NetWare 4.1 installation CD-ROM.

TIP

If the MHS Services software is located on a different server, you'll need to log into that server at this point. After you've been authenticated, you can continue with MHS Services installation.

2 • Assigning the Postmaster General. Next, the Postmaster General Authentication window will appear. In the Name field, enter the complete name of the user who will be Postmaster General. This is typically Admin. For example, ACME's Postmaster General is

```
.CN=Admin.O=ACME
```

Next, enter the Postmaster General's password in the Password field and press Enter to continue.

3 • Selecting the host volume. MHS Services is typically installed on the SYS: volume of the host server. If you wish to specify a different volume, do so now. Also, you are given options for installing additional products at this point. When you're finished, exit INSTALL.NLM.

4 • Revising AUTOEXEC.NCF. To automatically activate MHS Services for NetWare 4, add the following line to the host server's AUTOEXEC.NCF file:

```
Load MHS
```

For a more detailed walk-through of MHS installation, refer to the messaging case study at the end of this chapter. When you're done, a series of default MHS events will occur as if by magic. Table 12.5 lists the MHS objects that are created by default and actions that occur during installation. Note that Admin is assigned as the default owner of the Message Routing Group and Postmaster of the default messaging server. If you delete Admin, all heck breaks loose. In addition to 100 other NDS problems, you'll need to reassign these two MHS properties:

▶ Message Routing Group owner

▶ Messaging Server Postmaster

You will also notice that two FirstMail applications are copied to the SYS:PUBLIC directory on the host server—FirstMail for Windows and FirstMail for DOS. Later in this section, we'll take a closer look at using FirstMail and explore the steps for sending and receiving mail. For now, let's be content to bask in the glory of Table 12.5 and move on to MHS management.

T A B L E 12.5	NDS OBJECT	ACTION
Life After MHS Installation	Default message routing group is created as MHS_ROUTING_GROUP	(1) This object is placed in the home container of the host server object.
		(2) Admin is assigned as the default owner.
	Messaging Server object is created	(1) This object is also placed in the home container of the host server object.
		(2) Postmaster is assigned to Admin.
		(3) Admin mailbox and ID are assigned to the default Messaging Server.
		(4) Default Messaging Server is assigned to default Message Routing Group and vice versa. Also, their respective MHS properties are updated.
		(5) Host server is assigned to Messaging Server and vice versa. Also, their respective MHS properties are updated.
	FirstMail	FirstMail for Windows and FirstMail for DOS are copied to the SYS:PUBLIC directory on the host server.

MANAGING MHS SERVICES

So you've learned about it and installed it. Now what do you do with it? Moving out can be such a traumatic experience. One morning you wake up and bam! It hits you that you're on your own. A thousand questions pop into your head: Who's going to make breakfast? What am I going to do with my life? Where's the laundry machine? In order to survive in this cruel and exciting world, you must have a plan and, above all, you must have friends.

Managing MHS Services is not so different. One day you'll come into work and bam! It hits you that you're using e-mail. Then a thousand questions pop into your head: Who's the Postmaster? Where's my mailbox? What's a Distribution List? Fortunately, NetWare 4 provides numerous NDS objects especially for MHS Services—your friends. They are:

- ▸ Message Routing Group

- ▸ Messaging Server

- ▸ Distribution List

- ▸ External Entity

In addition to these MHS-only objects, you'll need to create and manage various mailbox owners—Users, Groups, Organizational Roles, and Organizational Units.

Now let's take a closer look at how these MHS "friends" can help you get along in the cruel and exciting world of NetWare 4 messaging.

Message Routing Group

As you remember from our earlier discussions, the MHS Message Routing Group is a collection of interconnected messaging servers. As an NDS object, it represents a cluster of messaging servers that communicate directly with each other for transferring messages. A default Message Routing Group object is created during the installation of MHS Services and placed in the same container as the host NetWare 4 server. Subsequent messaging servers are defaulted to this group.

There are only a few important properties for the Message Routing Group object. They are

ACL	Full name
Bindery property	Login script
CA private key	Mailbox ID
CA public key	Mailbox location
CN	Member
Description	Owner
E-mail address	See also

Also recall that the Postmaster General manages the Message Routing Group (through NW ADMIN–see Figure 12.9). This is usually the Admin user but can be assigned a unique name during initial MHS Services installation.

Messaging Server

In earlier discussions, you learned that the messaging server is the central communications point and storage location of MHS Services for NetWare 4. As an NDS object, it identifies the host NetWare 4 server and the location of the MHS directory structure (SYS:MHS). The SYS:MHS directory houses all user mailboxes assigned to this messaging server.

During a standard MHS Services installation, the Messaging Server object is created automatically and placed in the same container as the Host NetWare 4 server object. As you can see in Figure 12.10, the Messaging Server object includes various interesting NDS properties, including

ACL	Messaging Server type
Bindery property	Network address
Certificate revocation	Postmaster
Certificate validity interval	Private key
CN	Public key
Cross certificate pair	Reference
Description	Security equals to
Full name	Security equals to
Message Routing Group	See also
Messaging database location	Status
	Supported services

F I G U R E 12.10

Properties of the MHS
Messaging Server Object

In order for numerous messaging servers to communicate with one another, they must be part of the same message routing group. Once these first two MHS objects have been created, you're well on your way to e-mail paradise. With the groundwork in place, it's time to turn our attention toward the people who will be sending and receiving MHS messages. Look out, Guinevere.

Distribution List

As you recall, the Distribution List is a special NDS object that forwards messages to numerous user mailboxes. It accomplishes this in an interesting way. Only one copy of the message is delivered to the Distribution List mailbox. The message is then replicated for every mailbox in the Distribution List. This decreases network traffic between messaging servers because multiple messages are routed with only a single packet.

Group objects can also be used for messaging but they *do* increase network traffic. Unlike Distribution List, Group objects generate a packet for every message routed between Messaging Servers. Distribution List also differ from Groups in that membership can be nested. In other words, a Distribution List can contain other distribution lists. This is not true for group NDS objects. As you can see in Figure 12.11, the Distribution List object only contains a few properties:

Name	Mailbox ID
Full name	Foreign mail aliases
Owner	List members
Description	See also
Mailbox location	

F I G U R E   12.11

Properties of the MHS Distribution List Object

That completes our discussion of the three main MHS management objects—Message Routing Group, Messaging Server, and Distribution List. For a more practical hands-on approach toward MHS management, consult the case study at the end of this chapter. Now let's take a quick look at the final two management objects: External Entity and Mailbox objects.

ZEN

"The only Zen you can find on the tops of mountains is the Zen you bring up there."

Robert M. Pirsig

External Entity

The *External Entity* object represents nonnative NDS MHS objects. It's basically an NDS placeholder that enables you to send messages to users who are not part of the NDS tree. External Entity objects are not created during MHS Services installation; they are normally imported from special gateway software. This gateway software allows MHS to interface with other non-NDS systems.

Mailbox Objects

The discussion so far has focused on the key MHS management objects you need to deal with in order to make MHS Services work. But all of this lexicon doesn't mean a hill of beans if you don't have anyone to send the messages to. MHS Services for NetWare 4 supports four types of Mailbox objects:

- ▸ User

- ▸ Group

- ▸ Organizational Role

- ▸ Organizational Unit

Each of them can send and receive MHS mail with varying degrees of sophistication. In the exercise at the end of the chapter, we will explore how to assign mailboxes to each of these objects and use them in the grand MHS scheme of things. For now, suffice it to say that you probably fall into one of these four categories—maybe more.

USING FIRSTMAIL

As you learned earlier, MHS Services for NetWare 4 includes a rudimentary e-mail application called FirstMail available by default in two versions (DOS and Windows) that are copied to the SYS:PUBLIC directory on each Messaging Server.

FirstMail for Windows is an intuitive messaging application with simple icons for sending, receiving, and reading e-mail. As seen in Figure 12.12, FirstMail lists all of your new messages and enables you to open, reply, forward, move, copy, or delete them. In addition, the Button Panel provides five management tasks:

- Send mail

- Read new mail

- Mail folders

- Address books

- Distribution Lists

The greatest thing about FirstMail (other than it being free) is the fact that it's NDS-aware. This means you don't have to bother with user configurations; FirstMail gets everything it needs from the NDS database. Otherwise, if you're using an MHS-compatible application that's not NDS-aware, you have to register it with Directory Services and add the e-mail name to each user's list of applications. Too much work.

For a more extensive discussion of using FirstMail, refer to Exercise 12.3 at the end of the chapter. This will give you some valuable hands-on experience with NetWare 4 messaging.

F I G U R E 12.12

FirstMail for Windows

ZEN

"Ring the bells that still can ring.
Forget your perfect offering.
There is a crack in everything.
That's how the light gets in."

Leonard Cohen

THE BRAIN

For more information on using MHS Services in NetWare 4, see the AppNote entitles "Integrating MHS Services with Other Novell Products" in the October 1995 issue of *Novell Application Notes*.

Well, there you have it. That completes the final step of NetWare 4 configuration. Childhood isn't so bad. Let's quickly review where we've been.

It all started with Leia's first step (workstation connectivity). Once she became connected to the network, Step 2 took over—Leia learned to talk. This involved Container, Profile, and User login scripts.

Leia went to preschool. The next stage in your network's development was dominated by a friendly NetWare 4 menu system. The menu system acted as a central repository for user interface, network applications, and e-mail. In Step 4, you installed and configured the network applications as Leia went to "real" school. This was the most important phase of the child's development. After all, without school (or network applications), there would be no productivity and purpose to life.

Finally, in Step 5, Leia moved out. She got her first car, her first apartment, and her first job. Although it seemed like a difficult time for everyone, moving out represented an important stage in Leia's life. She made a smooth transition from childhood to adulthood. In much the same way, your network needs a smooth transition from NetWare 4 configuration to management.

In a side story, we were tracking Guinevere as she started her day with a computer and cappuccino. As a CNE, it's your responsibility to establish the configuration so that Guinevere never knows what's happening while she's sipping her cappuccino. In an ideal world, Guinevere never suspects that when she turns on her computer, it initializes workstation connectivity files, runs login scripts, establishes a menu system, and provides transparent access to network applications and e-mail—just like a child never understands what her parents go through while she's growing up. Of course, life doesn't end there; this is only the beginning. Now that you've made it through childhood in one piece, it's time to move on to the third and final phase of life—adulthood.

Get out of the way, we're coming through!

EXERCISE 12-1: WORKSTATION CONNECTIVITY FOR NETWARE 4

1 • Ensure that the NetWare 4 connection files are not currently loaded in workstation memory. Display the TSRs currently in workstation memory by typing: **MEM /C /P.** Make sure that LSL.COM, a LAN driver such as NE2000, IPXODI.COM, and/or VLM.EXE are not loaded. If they are, you must either unload them manually, boot off a "clean" bootable floppy, or comment out the @CALL STARTNET.BAT and related statements in your AUTOEXEC.BAT file and reboot. To manually unload these files, you must unload them in the reverse order from which they were loaded, namely by typing (pressing Enter after each line)

```
C:
CD \NWCLIENT
VLM /U
IPXODI /U
NE2000 /U (or the appropriate LAN driver)
LSL /U
```

2 • Load the NetWare 4 connection files

a. Switch to the C:\NWCLIENT directory by typing (and pressing Enter after each line)

```
C:
CD \NWCLIENT
```

b. Load the Link Support Layer software by typing)

```
LSL
```

What happens? Can you tell from the screen what the purpose is of LSL.COM? See Figure 12.13.

```
C:\NWCLIENT>lsl
NetWare Link Support Layer v2.14 (941011)
(C) Copyright 1990-1994 Novell, Inc. All Rights Reserved.

The configuration file used was "C:\NWCLIENT\NET.CFG".
Max Boards 4, Max Stacks 4


C:\NWCLIENT>3c5x9
3Com EtherLink III MLID w/ DME  v1.51 (941003)
(C) Copyright 1994 3Com Corp.  All Rights Reserved

Int 10, Port 360, Node Address 20AFE84943 L
Max Frame 1514 bytes, Line Speed 10 Mbps
Board 1, Frame ETHERNET_802.2, LSB Mode

C:\NWCLIENT>ipxodi

NetWare IPX/SPX Protocol  v3.01 (941031)
(C) Copyright 1990-1994 Novell, Inc.  All Rights Reserved.

Bound to logical board 1 (3C5X9) : Protocol ID E0

C:\NWCLIENT>
```

c. Load the LAN driver by typing

    NE2000 *(or appropriate LAN driver)*

d. Load the IPX communications protocol by typing

    IPXODI

What happens? Does IPXODI begin workstation communications, or do you have to wait for VLM.EXE?

e. Load the NetWare DOS Requester (and display the maximum amount of related information) by typing

    VLM /V4

The "/V4" parameter defines the highest level of driver verbosity. This will display all loaded VLMs and some additional troubleshooting information. Refer to Figure 12.14 for more information. What does this tell you about the relationship between IPXODI and VLM?

```
Patent pending.

The VLM.EXE file is pre-initializing the VLMs..............
The VLM.EXE file is using extended memory (XMS).
CONN.VLM       - NetWare connection table manager   v1.20 (941108)
IPXNCP.VLM     - NetWare IPX transport module   v1.20 (941108)
TRAN.VLM       - NetWare transport multiplexor module   v1.20 (941108)
SECURITY.VLM   - NetWare security enhancement module   v1.20 (941108)
NAME CONTEXT "WHITE.CRIME.TOKYO.ACME"
NDS.VLM        - NetWare directory services protocol module   v1.20 (941108)
BIND.VLM       - NetWare bindery protocol module   v1.20 (941108)
PREFERRED SERVER LABS-SRV1
PNW.VLM        - Personal NetWare protocol module   v1.20 (941108)
NWP.VLM        - NetWare protocol multiplexor module   v1.20 (941108)
FIO.VLM        - NetWare file input-output module   v1.20 (941108)
GENERAL.VLM    - NetWare general purpose function module v1.20 (941108)
FIRST NETWORK DRIVE F
REDIR.VLM      - NetWare DOS redirector module   v1.20 (941108)
FIRST NETWORK DRIVE F
PRINT.VLM      - NetWare printer redirection module   v1.20 (941108)
NETX.VLM       - NetWare workstation shell module   v4.20 (941108)
FIRST NETWORK DRIVE F
You are attached to server LABS-SRV1

C:\COLLDOS>
```

f. Switch to your first network drive by typing

   F:

3 • Log onto the network.

a. Display the servers currently available on your network by typing

   NLIST SERVER /B

b. Log into the network by typing

   LOGIN .ADMIN.ACME

   Notice that we're logging into the NDS tree and not the server. This is the fundamental advantage of NetWare 4. Why does it still reply with a "Servername"?

c. Display your login name and connection number by typing

   WHOAMI

d. Display users in your container that are currently logged into the network by typing

   NLIST USER /A

EXERCISE 12-2: UNDERSTANDING NET.CFG

The ACME R&D department has special WAN requirements. Also, it's made up of the most advanced—even sometimes dangerous—users. For these reasons, they've asked you to customize their workstation NET.CFG files. Fortunately, the hardware and software have already been sufficiently standardized. Now, you need to review their accessibility requirements and build an appropriate NET.CFG.

Be forewarned, it's not as easy as it looks. Following is a list of the R&D accessibility criteria. Good luck.

- ► A comment should be inserted at the top of the file indicating that it is the standard NET.CFG file for the R&D department It should also list the author of the file (who is you) and the date it iss created.

- ► Each workstation will consist of a Dell 133 MHz Pentium using ODI drivers and a 3COM C35X9 network card set to use interrupt A, I/O port 320, and Ethernet frame type 802.2.

- ► The ACME_TREE will be the only NDS tree accessed by the R&D department at this time.

- ► R&D-SRV1 will be the primary server used by the R&D department

- ► Users should have a default context of

OU=R&D.OU=LABS.OU=NORAD.O=ACME

prior to login.

- ► The first network drive will be F:.

- ► Packet Buffers should be set to 10 to increase performance.

- ► The Signature Level for the NCP Packet Signature feature should be set to 3 for maximum security.

- ► The connection files should be loaded in low memory for better performance and stability.

▸ Users should be allowed to connect up to 10 servers simultaneously.

▸ Users should be allowed to capture to a maximum of five printing ports.

▸ Microsoft Windows will be used on the workstations.

▸ The LONG MACHINE TYPE variable should be set to DELL.

For hints and a complete solution, refer to Appendix C. No cheating!

CASE STUDY: CONFIGURING ACME'S LOGIN SCRIPTS

Just as the day was winding down swimmingly at ACME (at 4:50 p.m.), FDR came cruising into your office. "I'm sorry it's so late," he said, "but something's up with the Net. Can you take a quick look?" Grudgingly (because that's how you do things at 4:59 p.m.), you agree to check it out. "Oh right," he adds, "I want all the public relations managers to share some applications and report files—any ideas?"

Of course you have ideas; after all, you are a CNE! Quickly you discover that the PR Container script has been destroyed—fortunately, you have notes from the old one in your NetWare Log book.

1 • Here's the PR Container login script notes:

   a. Insert a comment at the top of the login script indicating the purpose of the login script, the author (who is you), and the date the file was created.

   b. Set the DOS prompt to display the drive and directory name.

   c. Display a greeting that is displayed each time a user in this container logs in, including the username, day, and date.

   d. Turn off the display of drive mappings and assign the following regular drive mappings:

      (1) Drive U: should point to the User's home directory.

(2)   Drive G: should point to the user's shared group directory.

e. Assign the following search drive mappings, making sure not to overwrite
   existing drive mappings in the DOS path:

(1)   S1: pointing to SYS:PUBLIC

(2)   S2: pointing to the DOS directory on the network

(3)   S3: pointing to the SYS:APPS\WINDOWS directory

f. Insert a COMSPEC command that points to the DOS directory on the
   network.

g. Prevent the Default login script from executing when a user logs in that has
   no User login script.

h. Set up a printer capture of the HP4SI-P1 printer, specifying no tabs, no
   banners, and a timeout of 20 seconds.

i On Wednesdays, fire phasers and display a reminder to members of the
   PR-Group that the weekly Manager meeting is at 9:00 a.m. in Conference
   Room 3-D.

j. Every time a user logs onto the network, display a file called G:PR.NEW
   containing the important news of the day for the public relations
   department.

k. Set the default drive to U:.

l. Execute a custom menu called G:PRMAIN.DAT (which you will create in
   the next exercise).

m. General notes:

(1)   Whenever you display a message, don't forget to insert a PAUSE
       statement so that the message doesn't scroll off the screen before the
       user has a chance to read it.

(2) Insert appropriate remarks through the login script so that someone else that looks at it can easily understand what you have done.

2 • Next, you decide to create a PRMGRS-Profile login script for the public relations managers. Then, you discover, astonishingly enough, that one already exists in the ACME container! Hmmmm. Must be those crazy ACME fairies again. Anyway, you might as well make FDR a member of the PRMGRS-Profile login script while you're there. (See Appendix C for hints on the basic steps involved.)

3 • Log in FDR to check things out:

```
LOGIN .FDR.ADMIN.RIO.ACME
```

Watch the screen as the Container and Profile login scripts are automatically executed. Fix any errors that occur.

CASE STUDY: CONFIGURING THE ACME MENU SYSTEM

Well, the fun never stops. It seems as though FDR has opened Pandora's box. Now, for some unexplainable reason, the ACME gremlins have hit—the PR menu system has disappeared. If you don't get home soon, you're gonna miss "Friends." You'd better hurry.

Once again, the NetWare Log book has saved the day. Using the criteria outlined here, create a custom menu for the Public Relations department.

a. PR Main Menu

(1) Applications (which displays an Applications submenu)

(2) E-mail (which runs the Windows version of First Mail)

(3) NetWare Commands (which displays a NetWare Commands submenu)

(4)   Log off network (which exits the user from the menu and logs him/ her off the network)

b. Applications Menu (submenu called by option in the Main Menu)

(1)   Database (where executable file is DB)

(2)   Spreadsheet (where executable file is SS)

(3)   Word Processing (where executable file is WP)

c. NetWare Utilities Menu (submenu called by an option in the Main Menu)

(1)   File Management

(2)   NCOPY

(3)   NETUSER

(4)   User Tools

(5)   WHOAMI

Next, you'll need to quickly compile and debug the new menu. Once you're done, you can place it in the default SYS:PUBLIC subdirectory and test it. Make sure that the new login script can automatically find and execute the menu system. After all, you don't want another visit from FDR tonight.

Sweet dreams.

CASE STUDY: CONFIGURING ACME E-MAIL

Communication is the key to success in any business. It's even more important for ACME, considering the pressure the group is under—saving the world is a tough business.

One of the most important ACME divisions is R&D. This is where the ACME "brain trust" develops new technologies for making the Earth a better place. We can't do without antipollutants or NDS (Nuclear Disarmament Squads). To ensure that their critical WAN messaging works optimally, Leonardo Da Vinci has asked you to personally install MHS Services for NetWare 4 and assign mailboxes to all of his scientists. Also, he wants you to add another user to the R&D Container—"Nostradamus." The fate of the world (or at least its pollution) rests in your hands. Good luck.

Let's begin by installing MHS Services after the NetWare 4 server has been installed.

1 • Activate the INSTALL.NLM utility. At the file server console, type **LOAD INSTALL** and press Enter. First, select Product Options from the Installation Options menu and press Enter. Then, select the Choose an item or product listed above option from the Other Installation Actions menu and press Enter. Finally, select the Install NetWare MHS Services option from the Other Installation Items/Products menu and press Enter.

2 • Specify the source path. Next, you will be asked to specify the source path for the MHS Services software. Press F3 if you want to change the default path listed. Indicate the correct path and press Enter. If the path specified is on another server, you will be asked to log in to that server. Next, a warning message may be displayed advising that there might be a conflict with the CD-ROM driver. If this message is displayed, select the Continue to Access the CD-ROM option and press Enter. (You'll probably find that you are able to continue despite the warning.) The installation program will then begin copying the appropriate files to the SYSTEM and PUBLIC directories on the SYS: volume.

3 • Specify configuration information. The Postmaster General Authentication window will then be displayed. In the User Name field, indicate **.ADMIN.ACME** as the full name of the user that will act as Postmaster General and press Enter. Enter the password for the Postmaster General in the Password field and press Enter. After indicating the password, select the Press Enter to Continue field and press Enter. You may then be prompted to indicate whether this is the first MHS install in the NDS tree. If this is the first server, select Yes and press Enter; otherwise, select No and press Enter. Next, if the server chosen has multiple volumes, you will be prompted to indicate the destination volume for the MHS subdirectory, which will contain the MHS Services database and mailboxes. Before doing so, make sure the volume selected meets the minimum space requirements for MHS Services. When you have indicated the correct volume and pressed Enter, the installation program will continue the installation of MHS Services.

When the process is complete, a message will be displayed saying that the installation was completed successfully. When this message is displayed, press Enter to continue. An Installation Status Messages screen will be displayed. Press Enter to return to the Other Installation Items/Products menu. You can then continue installing optional products or exit from the INSTALL.NLM utility.

4 • Activate MHS Services. After you've installed the MHS software on the server, the next step is activate MHS Services by loading MHS.NLM and MHSLIB.NLM. To manually load MHS Services, type **LOAD MHS** and press Enter. You'll probably want to add this statement to the server's AUTOEXEC.NCF file so that MHS Services will be automatically activated each time the server is booted. Once MHS Services is activated, it will provide message-delivery services to all users with mailboxes.

5 • Manage MHS mailboxes. After you load the MHS software and activate MHS services, you'll need to assign an MHS mailbox to each User, Group, Organizational Role, and Distribution List in the LABS division. You cannot assign MHS mailboxes to Organizations or Organizational Units. To assign a mailbox to a user, you'll need to define two properties for that user: the Mailbox Location (which indicates the messaging server on which the user's mailbox is located) and the Mailbox ID (which identifies the name of the subdirectory in which the user's incoming messages are stored). For performance reasons, you should always locate a user's mailbox on the server that contains his/her home directory or the server where the user stores most of his/her directories and files. In order to assign an MHS mailbox to an Organizational Role, Group, or Distribution List, you'll need to specify a mailbox location for the object's Mailbox Location property that identifies the MHS messaging server. The MHS messaging server has the ability to identify members or occupants of an object and make a copy of a message for each one.

a.   Assign a mailbox to a User by using the Messaging Server object.
      From a workstation, log into the network as Admin by typing
      LOGIN .ADMIN.ACME and pressing Enter. Run MS Windows, then
      execute the NetWare Administrator utility by double-clicking its icon.
      Expand the tree view by double-clicking the NORAD Organizational
      unit, then double-clicking the LABS container, then double-clicking
      the LABS-SRV1_MSG Messaging Server object. Click the Users
      property button on the right side of the screen, then click the Add
      button at the bottom of the screen. An Object selection screen will be
      displayed. Double-click the R&D Organization Unit icon on the right
      side of the screen to display the contents of the R&D container, then
      click each of the members of the R&D department listed on the right
      side of the screen (such as Leonardo Da Vinci, Charles Darwin, Sir
      Isaac Newton, and Marie Curie). You'll find that if you hold down the
      Ctrl key while making your selections, you can make multiple
      selections at one time. When you've finished choosing the Users in
      the R&D container, click the OK button at the bottom of the screen.
      Then, click the OK button at the bottom of the next screen to return
      to the main NetWare Administrator screen.

b.   Create a new User object in the R&D Organizational Unit container
      called Nostradamus and assign him a mailbox. Click the R&D
      Organizational Unit container. Select the Create option from the
      Objects menu. Select the User icon and click the OK button at the
      bottom of the screen. Click the box in front of the Define additional
      Properties field. Type **Nostradamus** in the Login Name field and
      Smarty-Pants in the Last Name field, then click the CREATE button
      at the bottom of the screen. Click the Mailbox property screen button.
      Click the Browse button to the right of the Mailbox location field.
      You'll need to walk the tree to find the correct Messaging Server
      object. First, double-click the first entry in the Directory Context
      section on the right side of the screen (as indicated by two side-by-
      side periods), then double-click the LABS-SRV1_MSG icon in the
      Objects section on the left of the screen. Finally, click the OK button
      at the bottom of the User screen to return to the main NetWare
      Administrator menu.

c.   Create a Distribution List object named R&D-DL. Click the R&D
Organizational Unit container. Select the Create option from the
Objects menu. Select the Distribution List icon and click the OK
button at the bottom of the screen. Because this will be a distribution
list for the members of the R&D department, type **R&D-DL** in the
Distribution List Name field, then click the Browse button to the right
of the Mailbox Location field. You'll need to walk the tree to find the
correct Messaging Server object. First, double-click the first entry in
the Directory Context section on the right side of the screen (as
indicated by two side-by-side periods), then double-click the LABS-
SRV1_MSG icon in the Objects section on the left of the screen.
Finally, click the CREATE button at the bottom of the Create
Distribution List screen to return to the main NetWare Administrator
menu. Next, highlight the Distribution List object you just created
and click it with the right mouse button. Click the Details option in
the object menu. Click the Members screen button along the right
edge of the screen, then click the ADD button at the bottom of the
screen. While holding down the Ctrl key, click each User in the R&D
department that is listed in the Objects section on the left side of the
screen. When all of the Users in the R&D department are highlighted,
click the OK button at the bottom of the screen, then click the OK
button at the bottom of the next screen in order to return to the
NetWare Administrator main menu.

EXERCISE 12-3: USING FIRSTMAIL

Congratulations. You've successfully installed MHS Services for Leonardo Da Vinci and the R&D department. Now it's time to test FirstMail for Windows and make sure it's operating correctly. Follow these simple rules.

1 • Execute FirstMail.

    a. MHS and FirstMail must be installed on your server in order to be able to complete this exercise. Although these products are bundled with NetWare 4, they are not automatically installed during the installation process.

    b. Log into the network as NOSTRADAMUS.R&D.LABS.NORAD.ACME.

    c. Run MS Windows, then double-click the FirstMail icon. (If there is no FirstMail icon, you may want to create one in the Windows Program Group that contains your other NetWare tools, such as NetWare Administrator, DynaText, and User Tools. The executable file is called WMAIL and is located in the SYS:PUBLIC directory.)

2 • Create a message and send it to a user.

    a. Select the New Message option from the File menu [or click the first icon (pen and paper) on the button bar].

    b. Type **LDAVINCI** in the To: field and **Reporting for Duty** in the Subj: field.

    c. Click the message area and type **I'm looking forward to working with the R&D team, Regards, Nostradamus**, then click the SEND button on the left side of the window when you're done.

    d. Exit FirstMail and MS Windows.

3 • Log in as LDAVINCI.R&D.LABS.NORAD.ACME, then read the message and save it.

    a. Run MS Windows, then double-click the First Mail icon. Select the Read New Mail from the File menu [or click the second (envelope) icon on the button bar], then double-click the message to read it.

    b. Make sure that the message is highlighted. Click the Move button in the New mail folder button bar. Select the Mail Folder. Your message will be stored in this folder.

NetWare 4 Management

"As a NetWare 4 CNE, I consider them part of the family."

Welcome to adulthood.

An interesting thing happens on the way to adulthood—we grow up. All through childhood we look forward to the days when we can drive our own car, eat junk food, and play loud music 24 hours a day—freedom!

Then it happens! What a shock. Once we grow up and become adults, we yearn for the days when life was simple. We dream of the simplicity and innocence of childhood. Wow, we need therapy. Well, you're an adult now, so deal with it. But being an adult doesn't mean you have to lose the child within. It just means the toys get bigger.

So you have a new car, a new job, and a new apartment. Now your focus shifts from starting the "lifespan" (configuration) to keeping it going (management). As a CNE, you move into LAN adulthood with a new focus on NetWare management. Once the network is up and running, you can step back and shift your attention to the long term. Suddenly, your mind is filled with thoughts of a family (servers and workstations), a pension (SMS), and retirement (RMF). Aah, adulthood is a many-splendored thing.

NetWare 4 management is the most time-consuming aspect of being a CNE. Think about it: NetWare configuration occurs only once, but management dominates your life forever. In NetWare 4, network management occurs through four strategies:

- ▶ Server management

- ▶ Workstation management

- ▶ Storage Management Services (SMS)

- ▶ Remote Management Facility (RMF)

Server management is marriage. It involves daily tasks for protecting and maintaining your relationship with the NetWare 4 server. This includes startup management, NDS maintenance, internetworking, and console management. At this point, monitoring the server involves more than just walking by it once a day and making sure the green light is on.

Workstation management is like having children. It can be even more challenging than the other three strategies because you're dealing with the NetWare users (your children). And we all know that the user's primary purpose in life is to make CNEs miserable. In addition to battling users, our workstation management duties involve connectivity strategies, virus prevention, and diskless workstations. Finally, like it or not, you'll have to set up the LAN to support diverse client environments—DOS, Windows 95, OS/2, Macintosh, and UnixWare.

As the old adage goes, "you never miss anything until it's gone." This holds especially true for NetWare data. Welcome to your pension plan. One of the most important things you can do as a NetWare 4 CNE is plan for the future using backups. Storage Management Services (SMS) is a NetWare 4 backup engine that provides data storage and retrieval from various front-end applications to numerous back-end storage devices. In this chapter, you'll learn about the fundamental architecture of SMS and explore the many features of SBACKUP.NLM.

Finally, RMF (Remote Management Facility) enables you to manage the server console from anywhere in the world—including Happy Acres. You've worked hard, and now it's time for retirement. RMF will become the cornerstone of your server maintenance schedule. Of course, it's hard to maintain the server when it's chained up and locked away in a hidden closet. Fortunately, using RMF you can access the server console from any distributed workstation.

ZEN

"Every wakeful step, every mindful act is the direct path to awakening. Wherever you go, there you are."

Anonymous

Like adulthood, NetWare 4 management doesn't always come naturally. You have to work at it. Children have their parents to rely on, but now (as an adult) you're on your own. So, to help guide you through the minefield of CNE adulthood, I suggest these few management strategies.

First, build a NetWare Log book. Although few CNEs have one, it should become the foundation of your daily management life. The NetWare Log book is a detailed, step-by-step log of all activity from LAN conception to the present. It includes worksheets, floor plans, security restrictions, file management, pictures of LAN hardware, pictures of your mother, cabling layouts, application information, and weekly management tasks. It's vital that you take the Log book seriously because you never know when you might need it.

Next, use the worksheets provided with NetWare 4 documentation. The *Installation* manual includes various worksheets that can help you document LAN details including file server hardware, workstation hardware, configuration files, NetWare directories, users and group information, default login restrictions, trustee assignments, and login scripts. Then put these worksheets in your NetWare Log book for future reference. I see a pattern forming here.

Reference material is the fodder of creative minds. I don't know what that means, but it sounds good. The bottom line is, you can't know everything. Create an extensive library of reference material so you don't have to know everything. Some of the best sources include Novell Press books, Novell Application Notes, NSEPro CD-ROM, Web Pages, documentation, and, of course, this book. Don't forget your library card.

Finally, your mindset has an important impact on NetWare 4 management. Psychologically, you need to be committed to the network and recognize management as an important aspect of your daily life. Take time to embrace these management tasks and make sure that everyone in the organization recognizes that you need time to do them. Many times, users and management don't understand why the network needs to be down for VREPAIR or SMS backup. Educate them gracefully.

With these strategies in mind, let's now dive into the wild and wacky world of NetWare 4 management. Remember, this is the foundation of your daily life as a CNE. NDS design happens once, installation happens once, and NetWare 4 configuration happens once. On the other hand, management happens every day until you win the lottery. So without any further ado, let's start our jaunt through LAN adulthood, starting with marriage.

▶ · ◀

Server Management

Eventually you will find Mr./Ms. Right. Your eyes will meet across a crowded dance floor, you will feel that wonderful flutter in the pit of your stomach. Your knees will buckle and then bang—you're married! Marriage changes everything. Suddenly, your focus shifts from "me, me, me" to "the family." Your spouse becomes the center of your life. It's like sharing a lifeboat with that "special someone" while careening down the whitewater rapids of love. Yuck.

Similarly, the NetWare 4 server is at the center of your LAN. At some point, your focus shifts from "users, users, users" to "the server." After all, the entire WAN will crumble if your servers aren't running correctly.

NetWare 4 server management consists of five components:

- Startup management

- "Special" server management

- Server protection

- Console commands

- NetWare Loadable Modules (NLMs)

It all begins with startup management. As a CNE, you must separate the server startup tasks that occur once (during installation) from those that occur every time the server is turned on. Startup management includes SERVER.EXE, disk drivers, LAN drivers, NDS, and external network addressing. In addition, you must learn how to automate this process using AUTOEXEC.NCF and STARTUP.NCF.

Next, your server focus shifts to NDS and internetworking. As you learned earlier, NDS is a complex relational database distributed on all NetWare 4 servers. You also learned how to protect and manage this database through various server tasks, including NDS repair, partitioning, database replication, and server time synchronization. I guess sometimes the Cloud comes down to Earth. In this chapter, we'll discuss NDS maintenance from the server's point of view. In addition, we'll explore internetworking and server support for internationalization.

Because the server is at the heart of your WAN, you want to take any means possible to protect it. This includes locking up the server, preventing access to the keyboard with MONITOR.NLM, using the SECURE CONSOLE command, and adding a password for RMF. Also, don't forget to use The Club™. Server protection is a serious management task because of the vulnerability of the console—users can cause a lot of damage there. Many times, this security feature is overlooked and CNEs discover their inadequate security measures when it's too late—in the unemployment line.

The colon (:) prompt is the server console. This is where you'll spend most of your server management time. The colon prompt accepts two kinds of commands—console commands and NLMs. NetWare 4 includes numerous console commands for various server management and maintenance tasks, including NDS management, time synchronization, bindery services, sending messages, activating NLMs, server protection, and network optimization. This chapter explores most of the NetWare 4 console commands and gives you some hints on how to use them.

All remaining server activity is accomplished using NLMs. NLMs are modular Legos that provide supplemental functionality to the NetWare 4 server. There are four kinds of NLMs: disk drivers, LAN drivers, name space modules, and management utilities. In this chapter, we'll explore each of these and some key server management tools—INSTALL.NLM, MONITOR.NLM, SERVMAN.NLM, and DSREPAIR.NLM. You can think of NLMs as network management applications at the server.

ZEN

"What is the sound of one hand clapping?"

Zen Koan

As you can see, marriage takes a lot of work. Fortunately, the rewards greatly outweigh the pain. As a CNE, you must work hard at your network marriage to keep the server running and in peak condition (and with luck the rewards will also outweigh the pain). In both marriage and server management, communication is the key. Let's begin with a quick "walk down the aisle" of server startup management.

STARTUP MANAGEMENT

As you've heard previously, the NetWare 4 server is based on the Legos architecture model. It starts with a base foundation (SERVER.EXE) and colon prompt (:). Then added functionality is provided by supplemental Lego pieces (NLMs). NLMs use a "plug-and-play" architecture, which means they can be loaded and unloaded as needed. Some critical server NLMs include disk drivers (*.DSK), LAN drivers (*.LAN), and management utilities (MONITOR.NLM). We'll explore all of them a little later.

As you learned in Chapter 6, the NetWare 4 internal server hard disk contains two partitions: DOS and NetWare.

The server startup process begins when you activate the DOS partition and load SERVER.EXE. As Figure 13.1 shows, this process transfers control to the all-important NetWare partition. In addition, the colon prompt (:) appears. Now the Lego base is ready to accept NLMs. But wait: The NetWare 4 server is still on life support. Next, you must load disk drivers to activate internal files and LAN drivers to activate LAN communications. Now we're cooking. Finally, to round out the server startup process, you'll need to activate certain NDS configuration parameters such as the time zone, default time server type, and bindery context. All of these actions can be summed up in five simple steps:

1 • Load DOS.

2 • Start SERVER.EXE.

3 • Load the disk driver.

4 • Activate the LAN driver.

5 • Configure NDS.

FIGURE 13.1

NetWare 4 Server Startup Process

Of course, this is a lot of work to perform every time the server is booted. Fortunately, NetWare 4 includes two server configuration files that automate the startup process: STARTUP.NCF and AUTOEXEC.NCF.

In addition, you might want to perform a few other optional startup activities, such as customizing SET parameters, activating console commands and loading management NLMs. Let's take a closer look at the NetWare 4 server startup process, beginning with Step 1.

Step 1: Load DOS

As Figure 13.1 shows, the NetWare 4 server disk consists of two partitions—DOS and NetWare. It all starts at the DOS partition. You activate it by booting the server with COMMAND.COM (from either the C drive or a diskette). Once COMMAND.COM is loaded, the machine looks for two DOS configuration files—CONFIG.SYS and AUTOEXEC.BAT. Because this is the server, you shouldn't use elaborate configuration files. As a matter of fact, the CONFIG.SYS file should be nonexistent and AUTOEXEC.BAT should contain a few simple commands:

```
;Automate the NetWare 4 server startup process
CD \NWSERVER
SERVER.EXE
CD \
;NetWare 4 startup process completed
```

This script will automate the server startup process and jump to Step 2—SERVER.EXE. As you recall from Chapter 6, all server boot files are automatically copied to C:\NWSERVER. These include SERVER.EXE, disk drivers, LAN drivers, and other NLMs. The DOS partition should be 15 to 35 MB in size and is created using the FDISK DOS utility. In contrast, the much larger NetWare partition occupies the rest of the server disk and is created using INSTALL.NLM.

Once you've activated the server using DOS, it's time to shift control to NetWare. That's Step 2.

TIP

On a normal DOS workstation, CONFIG.SYS would play an important role in activating memory management, defining local and network drives, and loading resource drivers. On the NetWare 4 server, however, CONFIG.SYS can only do harm. Drivers such as HIMEM.SYS can severely impact the server startup process. Whatever you do, stay away from CONFIG.SYS on the server machine.

Step 2: Start SERVER.EXE

NetWare 4 is a strange bird because it doesn't have its own "cold boot loader." This means the operating system must be activated by SERVER.EXE. Most other network operating systems boot into their own native environment—NetWare 2.2, Windows/ NT, AppleShare, or OS/2 LAN Manager, to name a few. NetWare 4, on the other hand, starts with DOS and then shifts controls over to the NetWare partition. This is accomplished automatically using AUTOEXEC.BAT (see Step 1). As you can see in Figure 13.1, the result of this procedure is the colon prompt (:). At this point, the NetWare 4 server is alive but you can't do anything with it. Files cannot be accessed and communications cannot be initiated.

In order for SERVER.EXE to establish a unique foundation for this server, it needs two important pieces of information: a server name and IPX internal network number. The server name uniquely identifies this server for communications with all other servers on the WAN. The IPX internal network number performs the same function but uses an eight-digit hexadecimal address instead (not very friendly). Once you provide these two server identifiers, SERVER.EXE displays some informational messages and finally offers the colon prompt (:). Notice that the prompt includes the server name. This can be turned off if you like.

Here's a slight loophole—when SERVER.EXE is executed and command shifts to the NetWare partition, COMMAND.COM is still loaded in memory. Any would-be hacker can EXIT NetWare 4 and return to the DOS partition. This is not good. In order to eliminate this security loophole, you may consider removing COMMAND.COM from server RAM. This is accomplished using one of two console commands: REMOVE DOS or SECURE CONSOLE.

Once the NetWare 4 server has been activated, it's time to bring it to life. That's Step 3.

QUIZ

Here's a nice easy one to warm up with. Two U.S. coins add up to 30 cents, yet one of them is not a nickel. What coins are they? Don't spend it all in one place.

(Q13-1)
(See Appendix C for quiz answers.)

Step 3: Load the Disk Driver

With SERVER.EXE in position and the colon prompt activated, it's time to start up the internal resources—disk and NIC. As you can see in Figure 13.1, we kickstart the server by loading a disk driver. Disk drivers are identified by the .DSK extension and provide important communications between NetWare 4 and the internal disk. Until you load the disk driver, nothing else is available (except SET commands). For this reason, the disk driver resides on the DOS partition. Once loaded, it mounts the internal NetWare volume and shifts file control to the much larger NetWare directory structure. But until then, we're out of luck.

NetWare 4 supports various disk architectures, including SCSI, IDE, EIDE, and generic ISA. The disk driver Lego is loaded into memory and attached to SERVER.EXE by using the following LOAD command:

```
LOAD C:\NWSERVER\IDE.DSK
```

In this example, we're using the IDE disk driver. If you're using SCSI or Enhanced IDE, substitute your manufacturer-specific driver. Once it's been loaded, NetWare automatically mounts the default system volume, SYS:. Any other volumes need to be mounted using the MOUNT console command. Because all NetWare files and utilities reside on these volumes, this is a vital step.

When you load the disk driver, you'll also need to specify various hardware configurations including interrupt and port address. Typically, the defaults work fine, but in some instances, you'll have to come up with your own custom parameters. Consult the disk drive manufacturer's documentation or the Microhouse Technical Library (MTL) for specific settings.

Now that your NetWare 4 server is alive, it's time for it to start talking. That's Step 4.

Step 4: Activate the LAN Driver

Your server's not very useful until it begins communicating with workstations and other servers. This is accomplished by activating the LAN driver. LAN drivers control communications between NetWare 4 and internal NICs. NetWare 4 supports myriad LAN drivers, including NE2000, Intel EtherExpress, 3COM 3C5X9, TOKEN, and RXNET. LAN driver Legos are activated and attached to the SERVER.EXE foundation in much the same way as disk drivers:

```
LOAD 3C5X9
```

Notice that we didn't have to specify a location for the LAN driver. This is because NetWare automatically searches the SYS:SYSTEM subdirectory once the SYS: volume is mounted. With the disk driver in place and all NetWare files available, you now have access to the SYS:SYSTEM subdirectory. This is where you'll get the rest of your server startup utilities. If NetWare 4 doesn't have a LAN driver for your specific NIC, you'll need to get one from the manufacturer. Most NICs come with a LAN driver diskette. When you find the correct .LAN file, either copy it to SYS:SYSTEM or C:\NWSERVER on the DOS partition.

Like the disk driver, you'll have to provide specific hardware configurations when you load the LAN driver. These include interrupt, port, memory address, and frame type. Once again, the defaults usually work fine, but if you run into any problems, consider referencing the manufacturer documentation.

You're not quite done yet. Once the LAN driver is loaded, you need to initialize internal communications by *binding* a specific protocol to it. During the binding process, you'll need to provide two important pieces of information:

- ► Communications protocol

- ► External network address

The default communications protocol for NetWare LANs is IPX/SPX. NetWare 4 supports various other protocols including TCP/IP and AppleTalk. In addition to the protocol, you'll need to specify an external network address for each NIC. The network address uniquely identifies this cabling segment from any other on this or other LANs. It is typically an eight-digit hexadecimal number established by you—the network administrator. Be careful not to confuse the EXTERNAL network address with the IPX INTERNAL address. The external address identifies the cabling segment, whereas the internal address identifies the server.

TIP

In order to clearly separate **IPX** internal addresses from external network addresses, follow this simple convention—make the internal number contain only letters and the external address contains only numbers. Because they're both hexadecimal numbers, you can get creative with the letters A–F: **BAD, CAFE, BADCAFE,** and so on. Another option is to use the **NetWare 4** serial number as the internal **IPX** address. This number is always unique and many people find it easy to reference. Finally, you can always accept the randomly generated internal number but whatever you do, *write it down!*

Here's how it works. You initialize IPX communications and establish the external network address using the following command at the console prompt:

```
BIND IPX TO 3C5X9 NET=007
```

Once the LAN driver has been loaded and initialized, your NetWare 4 server is well on its way to social prominence. Now it can accomplish its two most important tasks—communicating with users and storing files. But we're not out of the woods yet. NetWare 4 servers have special startup requirements because of NDS and time synchronization. No matter how hard you try, you just can't get away from NetWare Directory Services. That's Step 5.

REAL WORLD

Frame types are a tricky issue. This is complicated by the fact that NetWare 4 IPX/SPX, NetWare 3 IPX/SPX, and other communications protocols default to different frame types. Here's a brief list:

- ► NetWare 4 IPX—Ethernet_802.2
- ► NetWare 3.11 IPX—Ethernet_802.3
- ► TCP/IP—Ethernet_II
- ► AppleTalk—Ethernet_SNAP

With this complexity comes management nightmares. You'll need to configure the NetWare 4 server to support packets from multiple frame types over the same NIC. Following is a list of LOAD and BIND statements that support NetWare 4, NetWare 3.11, and TCP/IP communications:

```
LOAD 3C5X9 Int=3 Port=300 Frame=Ethernet_802.2 NAME=NetWare_4

BIND IPX to NetWare_4 Net=1234

LOAD 3C5X9 Int=3 Port=300 Frame=Ethernet_802.3 NAME=NetWare_311


BIND IPX to NetWare_311 Net=4321

LOAD 3C5X9 Int=3 Port=300 Frame=Ethernet_II NAME=TCPIP

BIND IP to TCPIP Net=567
```

Notice that in all three cases, we used a different network address to specify the same NIC over the same cabling segment with a different frame type. This is because communications occur simultaneously using different frame types on the same cabling segment. Therefore, each frame type is set to occur in a different logical network. In addition, when you load the second and third frame type, you'll get an informational message acknowledging that a new frame type was loaded and that it will be using an existing LAN driver (reentrantly). This means that it will be binding an additional frame type to the same LAN driver in memory. I know it's a little tricky, but this sophisticated approach should make server communications with multiple protocols much easier.

THE BRAIN

For more tantalizing details about frame types and NetWare, see "Migrating Ethernet Frame Types from 802.3 Raw to IEEE 802.2" in the September 1993 *Novell Application Notes*.

Step 5: NDS Configuration

In addition to the standard startup steps, NetWare 4 requires special NDS SET parameters. They activate two important aspects of NDS—time synchronization and bindery services. Time synchronization ensures that all NetWare 4 servers agree what time it is. This is accomplished using time zone and time server SET parameters. Bindery services, on the other hand, provide non-NetWare 4 clients access to this server's resources. This is accomplished using a "bindery context" SET parameter. Let's take a closer look at NDS startup configuration, beginning with time synchronization.

Time Synchronization

As you learned earlier, time synchronization is an integral part of NetWare 4 and NDS. It can be configured using the Service Advertising Protocol (SAP) or custom configuration methods. In either case, five important SET parameters must be activated during server startup:

► SET Time Zone—This identifies the standard and Daylight Savings Time abbreviations and offset from the Universal Time Coordinated (UTC) standard (Greenwich Time). In Figure 13.3 (later), you'll see that the ACME time zone is MST7MDT. This means the standard abbreviation is MST (Mountain Standard Time) and the Daylight Savings abbreviation is MDT (Mountain Daylight Time). In addition, the center number means we're seven hours behind UTC time.

► SET Daylight Savings Time Offset—This parameter determines how far to adjust for Daylight Savings Time. ACME will "spring" one hour forward in April and "fall" one hour back in October.

► SET Start of Daylight Savings Time—This line identifies the date and time upon which to activate Daylight Savings Time. In almost all areas, it's the first Sunday in April at 2:00 a.m.

► End of Daylight Savings Time—This parameter identifies the date and time when Daylight Savings Time offset should end. In most areas, this is the last Sunday in October at 2:00 a.m.

► SET Default Time Server Type—This line configures this server for one of four time server types: Single-Reference, Reference, Primary, and/or Secondary. In Figure 13.3 (later), you'll see that the ACME server is configured as a default Single-Reference server. This means all other servers in the NDS tree must be Secondary time servers.

Refer to Chapters 2 and 8 for a more detailed discussion of NetWare 4 time server types.

Bindery Services

The next NDS startup configuration involves support for non-NDS clients. Workstations running NETx or any other non-NDS software can access NetWare 4 servers but only under bindery emulation. This means their maneuverability is limited to one container at a time. The single bindery services container is identified during startup using the following SET parameter:

```
SET Bindery Context =
```

As you'll see in Figure 13.3 later, the ACME bindery context has been set to OU=LABS.OU=NORAD.O=ACME. This means any NETx user attaching to the LABS-SRV1 server will see only resources in the OU=LABS container. Fortunately, NetWare 4 enables you to set the bindery context to multiple containers (up to 16). This creates a "superbindery" so that non-NDS clients can access multiple resources without having to log in again. Multiple containers are separated by spaces in the SET Bindery Context parameter.

These aren't the only NDS SET parameters that you can use but they're the only ones required during server startup. In Chapter 15 we'll explore all of NetWare 4's SET parameters and how they can be used for server customization and optimization. For now, let's review the NetWare 4 server startup process:

1 • Load DOS—The DOS partition is made active and COMMAND.COM is loaded into memory.

2 • Start SERVER.EXE—The NetWare 4 foundation is loaded into RAM as SERVER.EXE from C:\NWSERVER. Control shifts from the DOS to the NetWare partition.

3 • Load the disk driver—The server file system is activated by loading the .DSK driver from C:\NWSERVER. The default SYS: volume is also mounted automatically.

4 • Activate the LAN driver—The internal server NIC is activated and communications are initialized using the BIND command.

5 • NDS configuration—Required NDS parameters are established to activate server time synchronization and bindery services.

QUIZ

Speaking of time, at the next minute, it will be exactly twice as many seconds after the half-hour as it was minutes before the same half-hour last time the two hands were at right angles this afternoon. Hmmmm, help me out here—what time is it?

(Q13-2)

As you can see, the NetWare 4 server startup process, although flexible, is tricky. It would be a drag if you had to implement all of these steps every time the server was brought down and back up again. And we don't need any more work, do we? Fortunately, NetWare 4 provides the facility for automating all of these steps. This is done with the help of two server configuration files:

▸ STARTUP.NCF

▸ AUTOEXEC.NCF

Each of these startup files is activated automatically once SERVER.EXE is started. STARTUP.NCF begins by loading the disk driver and activating the SYS: volume. Then AUTOEXEC.NCF takes over and performs Steps 4 and 5. Let's take a closer look at these all-important, time-saving server startup files.

STARTUP.NCF

Once SERVER.EXE is executed, it searches for the configuration file STARTUP.NCF in the same DOS directory where SERVER.EXE resides. STARTUP.NCF has one purpose: to load the disk driver. Once the disk driver has been activated, control shifts to the SYS: volume and AUTOEXEC.NCF. As you can see in Figure 13.2, STARTUP.NCF includes other important SET parameters, namely:

SET Reserved Buffers Below 16MB=200 *(required for ASPI disk driver support)*

SET Maximum Subdirectory Tree Depth=10 *(decreases the default subdirectory tree depth from 25 to a more manageable 10)*

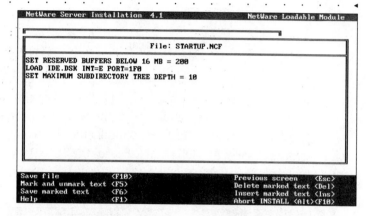

FIGURE 13.2

ACME's STARTUP.NCF
Server Configuration File

STARTUP.NCF is generated automatically by INSTALL.NLM during NetWare 4 simple or custom installation (See Chapter 6). It can be edited using the same utility. You can also boot with an alternative STARTUP.NCF using the following syntax:

```
SERVER -S C:\NWSERVER\filename
```

Or you can boot without a STARTUP.NCF file at all using the -NS switch. Once STARTUP.NCF has activated the internal disk and mounted the SYS: volume, we can continue with AUTOEXEC.NCF and the rest of the server startup process.

AUTOEXEC.NCF

Steps 4 and 5 of the NetWare 4 server startup process are accomplished with the help of AUTOEXEC.NCF. This file executes automatically after STARTUP.NCF and is located in the SYS:SYSTEM subdirectory. You can automate just about any NetWare 4 server task using AUTOEXEC.NCF, including:

- Time zone information

- Bindery context

- File server name

- IPX internal network number

- Calls to other .NCF files

▸ SET parameters

▸ Activating repair and management NLMs

As you can see in Figure 13.3 (finally), there's a lot more going on in AUTOEXEC.NCF than there was in the earlier STARTUP.NCF. The first six statements establish NDS configurations including time zone, time server type, and bindery context. The next two deal with SERVER.EXE—specifically, the file server name and IPX internal network number. Finally, AUTOEXEC.NCF loads the 3C5X9 LAN driver and binds it to the IPX protocol. Pretty nifty, huh?

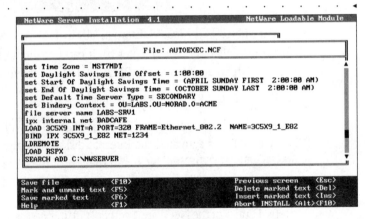

F I G U R E 13.3

ACME's AUTOEXEC.NCF
Server Configuration File

```
NetWare Server Installation  4.1                    NetWare Loadable Module

                            File: AUTOEXEC.NCF

set Time Zone = MST7MDT
set Daylight Savings Time Offset = 1:00:00
set Start Of Daylight Savings Time = (APRIL SUNDAY FIRST  2:00:00 AM)
set End Of Daylight Savings Time = (OCTOBER SUNDAY LAST  2:00:00 AM)
set Default Time Server Type = SECONDARY
set Bindery Context = OU=LABS.OU=NORAD.O=ACME
file server name LABS-SRV1
ipx internal net BADCAFE
LOAD 3C5X9 INT=A PORT=320 FRAME=Ethernet_802.2  NAME=3C5X9_1_E82
BIND IPX 3C5X9_1_E82 NET=1234
LDREMOTE
LOAD RSPX
SEARCH ADD C:\NWSERVER

Save file            <F10>              Previous screen    <Esc>
Mark and unmark text <F5>               Delete marked text <Del>
Save marked text     <F6>               Insert marked text <Ins>
Help                 <F1>               Abort INSTALL <Alt><F10>
```

As a NetWare 4 CNE, you can get creative with AUTOEXEC.NCF. You can skip it altogether using the SERVER-NA command or make it bigger with one of two server editing utilities—INSTALL.NLM and EDIT.NLM. Let's assume you're in a creative mood and want to add additional material to AUTOEXEC.NCF. What should you add? Following is a list of NLMs and console commands that are guaranteed to spice up even the most standard server AUTOEXEC.NCF file.

NLMs

In addition to the standard disk drivers and LAN drivers, NetWare 4 provides various exciting NLMs to help customize server startup:

▸ LOAD REMOTE and LOAD RSPX—Installs NetWare 4's internal Remote Management Facility (RMF). We'll talk about this later in the chapter.

▶ LOAD INSTALL—Provides a plethora of server configuration options, including hot fix redirection, disk duplexing, NDS configuration, and (last but not least) .NCF file editing.

▶ LOAD MONITOR—The mother of all server utilities. MONITOR enables you to monitor, manage, and optimize the NetWare 4 server, all from a single place. It's also been known to pitch a no-hitter and cook a mean breakfast.

▶ LOAD SERVMAN—The other great server management utility. It provides a centrally managed interface for customizing server SET parameters.

▶ LOAD EDIT—Enables you to edit server batch files including STARTUP.NCF and AUTOEXEC.NCF.

Console Commands

In addition, NetWare 4 provides various server console commands for AUTOEXEC.NCF:

▶ VOLUMES—Displays mounted volume information.

▶ CONFIG—Displays server NIC configuration data.

▶ MODULES—Displays all loaded NLMs and configuration parameters.

▶ SEARCH—Creates a search path other than SYS:SYSTEM for loading NLMs.

▶ REMOVE DOS—Removes COMMAND.COM from background server memory.

▶ SECURE CONSOLE—Increases server access security by removing DOS and limiting NLM loading.

▶ SET REPLY TO GET NEAREST SERVER=ON—Allows this server to respond to workstation connection requests. It supports both NDS and non-NDS clients.

► SET DISPLAY LOST INTERRUPT ALERTS=OFF—Removes annoying interrupt alerts from the server console. Keep in mind that alerts only happen if there's a reason, so ignoring them doesn't make the problem go away.

► SET ALLOW UNENCRYPTED PASSWORDS=OFF—Enhances workstation server security from non-NDS clients and older print servers.

Server configuration files are cool, but why stop with STARTUP.NCF and AUTOEXEC.NCF? You can create various other server batch files using the LOAD EDIT command. All you have to do is give them the .NCF extension. For example, REBOOT.NCF could include the following three commands for automating server reboot:

REMOVE DOS

DOWN

EXIT

► RMF.NCF—Activates the two NLMs needed for NetWare 4 remote management.

► OPTIMIZE.NCF—Initializes a preselected group of SET parameters for server optimization.

► UP.NCF—Brings the server back UP after DOWN.

In addition to server batch files, LOAD EDIT can be used to customize DOS configuration files like C:\AUTOEXEC.BAT. Just make sure to specify the correct paths and give the complete filename with extension.

ZEN

*"I know it is wet
And the sun is not sunny.
But we can have
Lots of good fun that is funny!"*

Dr. Seuss

"Start me up!" Consider the NetWare 4 server started. It's a comforting feeling knowing the server came up smoothly—seeing the familiar "WORM" prance around the screen (assuming that MONITOR.NLM is loaded), hearing the constant hum of NetWare workstations, and following the NetWare 4 packets as they bounce merrily along the cabling segment. A successful server startup is one of your most rewarding experiences. And so is marriage. Just like anything—if you work at it, the rewards greatly outweigh the pain.

Now that the NetWare 4 server is up and running, let's shift our focus from "starting" it to "managing" it. Daily NetWare 4 server management consists of four important components:

▶ "Special" server management strategies—these include NDS maintenance, internetworking, and internationalization

▶ Server protection—keep users away from the server console

▶ Console commands—keep the server running at peak performance

▶ NetWare Loadable Modules—everything else

Let's start our discussion of daily server management with a few "special" NetWare 4 strategies.

"SPECIAL" SERVER MANAGEMENT

There's only one guarantee in marriage—anything goes! There's never a dull moment on Sunday afternoons—one of you wants to watch the football game while the other is more interested in the mooshy showing of *On Golden Pond* at the local matinee. Circumstances like these call for "special" strategies. For example, the problem is easily solved with a miniature television and headphones (football game) at the movie theater.

Many times a NetWare 4 marriage is equally as interesting. Once the server is started, the fun begins. This is when you'll need all of your savvy and a tool belt filled with special server management strategies. In this section, we'll explore three important "special" circumstances:

- ▸ NDS maintenance

- ▸ Internetworking

- ▸ Internationalization

NDS maintenance issues involve monitoring server independence, ensuring synchronization, monitoring disk space for NDS files, and ensuring that the server's DOS clock is accurate. Next, there's internetworking. NetWare 4 ships with a full version of MPR 3.0 (NetWare MultiProtocol Router). MPR allows the WAN to "speak different languages" and transport messages across different communication protocols. Internetworking extends the boundaries of your NetWare 4 WAN. Finally, this extension requires that you support users who "speak different languages." This is accomplished with the help of built-in NetWare internationalization. Language enabling and special keyboard support ensure that international users can access resources in their native languages. I have a feeling there's a lot of fun ahead for us, so let's get started.

NDS Maintenance

NDS is a "sticky wicket." (I don't know what that means, but doesn't it sound great?) As a sticky wicket, NDS requires special precautions to make sure everything runs smoothly. If anything bad happens to NDS, it's only a matter of time before it starts to happen to you. That's karma.

As you learned in Chapters 8 and 9, many different bad things can happen to NDS. The network begins to wig out when replicas are unsynchronized, the NDS database gets corrupted, servers crash, or containers get moved around too much. You also learned some strategies for dealing with these unwanted realities. Now, let's take a look at a few additional NDS maintenance strategies that can help us deal with, or even prevent, NDS crises:

▶ Server independence—Downing a NetWare 4 server can have a dramatic effect on all other servers throughout the network. Remember, these servers have replicas of distributed partitions and often participate in time synchronization activities. If you don't remove replicas before downing a server for an extended period, partition operations (such as split and join) can't function on other servers because all replicas aren't available. Make sure to establish server independence before you remove a server from the NDS tree.

▶ Server synchronization—This is a critical, ongoing process and ensures that all distributed replicas have the latest information. If NDS can't synchronize with your server, first make sure it's running NDS properly. Next, check the communications hardware, routers, and bridges to make sure connectivity has not been affected. And, finally, check the server with the master replica of this partition. If it's not operating correctly, assign a new master replica so synchronization can occur normally.

▶ Server modifications—Before you rename a server or change the IPX internal network address, make sure the replicas of that server are synchronized. Also make sure that the server contains a replica of the partition in which the server object is contained. Also be careful when you change the server's bindery context. This can have a dramatic impact on availability of resources to non-NDS clients.

▸ SYS: volume—So where does NDS live? Off the [Root] of the SYS: volume. It is crucial that this volume *not* run out of space. If it does, NetWare automatically disables TTS, and all updates to the directory are deactivated. This will normally return a -621 error by the DSTRACE utility. Here are some precautions you can take to make sure SYS: doesn't run out of space—set Minimum Disk Space Alerts at the server console, store user files, applications, and print queues on volumes other than SYS:, and add the SET AUTO TTS BACKOUT FLAG=ON command to STARTUP.NCF. This allows TTS to back out all transactions that are incomplete when the server failed. That includes NDS.

▸ Server's clock—To eliminate confusion, make sure that the DOS clock is set correctly on the server so that when you update a file, the correct date and time will be stamped on it. This also impacts time synchronization.

These strategies should help you sleep better at night by decreasing the chances that something bad will happen to your NDS database. Now that your LAN is more stable, you can consider expanding its boundaries with NetWare MPR.

ZEN

Luis Ponce de Leon, returning to his university after five years imprisonment by the leaders of the Inquisition, resumed his lectures with the words: "As we were saying yesterday . . ."

REAL WORLD

So, where do the NDS files really live? Like I said, off the [Root] of the SYS: volume. NDS lives in a hidden system-owned directory called _NETWARE. You can view the files and their size through RCONSOLE. Simply choose Directory Scan from the Available Options menu and use the following path: SYS:_NETWARE. It's amazing what you can learn in a book these days.

Internetworking

As shown in Figure 13.4, NetWare 4 includes a suite of programs that provide internetworking among dissimilar workstations and servers. This suite runs on standard PC hardware and enables you to integrate various LANs regardless of the communication protocols being used. In short, NetWare 4 includes a full version of NetWare MultiProtocol Router (MPR).

F I G U R E   13.4

Internetworking with MPR

NetWare MPR provides the following services:

▸ It connects dissimilar media, frame types, and transports at all levels in the ODI model.

▸ It offloads routing tasks from busy servers to dedicated machines.

▸ It provides security by isolating traffic on LAN segments.

NetWare MPR for 4.1 includes routing capabilities for three communications protocols—NetWare IPX/SPX (default), Unix TCP/IP, and Macintosh AppleTalk. Like most other additional products, MPR is installed using INSTALL.NLM. Once it's installed, you can manage and configure MPR using a server application called INETCFG.NLM. INETCFG is a menu-driven utility that simplifies routing and bridging configuration. It also provides an extensive list of configurable parameters for IPX, TCP/IP, and AppleTalk (see Figure 13.5). When you load INETCFG for the first time, it performs two important initialization tasks:

▸ AUTOEXEC.NCF—INETCFG saves your old AUTOEXEC.NCF file as SYS:SYSTEM\AUTOEXEC.BAK. Then it prompts you to transfer five important commands from the old AUTOEXEC.NCF to the new file— LOAD, BIND, LAN driver, protocol, and route access commands. Answering YES to the prompts will enable INETCFG to automatically initialize AUTOEXEC.NCF for the new internetworking suite.

▸ CONLOG—Next, INETCFG inserts three commands into the new AUTOEXEC.NCF file in this order: First, LOAD CONLOG enables the server to begin a log file of all messages that appear during the initialization. These messages are stored in SYS:ETC\CONSOLE.LOG. Second, it loads INITSYS.NCF to configure server communications using the INETCFG database. Finally, the utility unloads CONLOG and startup is complete.

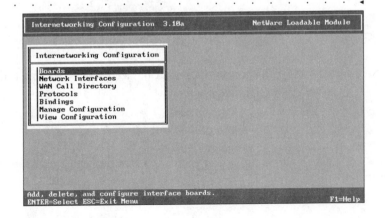

Once INETCFG has been initialized, you're ready to configure and manage your new multiple protocols. Figure 13.5 shows the INETCFG main menu. In general, these choices are selected systematically from top to bottom during protocol configuration. It all starts with the Boards option. Here, you configure LAN and WAN boards so INETCFG can place the correct LOAD commands in AUTOEXEC.NCF. You can also customize hardware parameters for internal NICs. The next two INETCFG menu choices are somewhat optional. That is, they're required if needed. The Network Interfaces option enables you to configure ports on multiport boards. Each port can be configured for a different WAN protocol such as PPP, frame relay, or X.25. Also, the WAN Call Directory option provides further customization for PPP WAN protocols.

The next step in INETCFG customization is accomplished using the Protocols menu choice. This option enables you to configure routing protocol operation such as IPX, RIP, and NLSP. Once again, INETCFG.NLM will build the correct LOAD commands for AUTOEXEC.NCF. On to Step 3.

The Bindings menu choice enables you to initialize MPR by binding protocols to each NIC as needed. For example, one interface could bind IPX RIP and another could initialize NLSP. Configuring the bindings in INETCFG builds the correct BIND statements for AUTOEXEC.NCF. Once you have configured network boards, protocols, and bindings, MPR is ready to go. The final two INETCFG options deal with managing SNMP, remote access, and viewing LOAD and BIND statements. This falls under the category of daily multiprotocol management.

THE BRAIN

Here are some good AppNotes on MultiProtocol Router, NLSP, and other NetWare internetworking topics: "Optimizing NetWare Wide Area Networks" (May 1994), "Wide Area Networking with Frame Relay and NetWare MultiProtocol Router" (February 1995), and "Configuring Asynchronous Connections with the NetWare MultiProtocol Router 3.0 Software" (July 1995).

Now that we've extended the boundaries of our WAN, let's explore NetWare 4 support for international languages.

Internationalization

If you're going to extend the boundaries of your WAN to "span the globe," you're going to need to speak everybody's language. And we're not just talking protocol languages—we're talking humans' written and spoken languages. This falls under the category of "knowing what your spouse means" when he/she says something crazy. For example, "you should've known I meant 'yes' when I said 'no.'" Once again, we find ourselves in a sticky wicket. Understanding spouses and NetWare 4 internationalization can be the difference between sweet dreams and a night on the sofa. Imagine waking up to Figure 13.6. Language support in NetWare 4 includes:

- ► Text displayed in non-English languages for utilities and system messages.

- ► Alternate display formats for numbers, dates, times, and other parameters that differ around the world.

- ► Double-byte character support for Asian languages as part of the UniCode specification. (I'm sorry, did somebody say unicorn?)

- ► Non-English filename characters and path separators.

F I G U R E   13.6

Viewing MONITOR.NLM in German

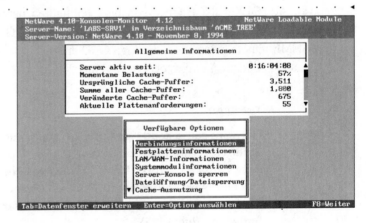

Here's the deal. Language support will enable you to use NetWare in your native language, but it won't translate messages for you. Sorry, we're not quite there yet—that's NetWare 7.2. So, how does it work? Language enabling in NetWare 4 is possible because message strings have been separated from the source code and placed in separate files called "language modules." If message strings were in the source code, for example, you'd have to recompile and relink the code every time you wanted to change the language.

Having the language modules separate enables us to switch languages on the fly. Pretty cool, huh?

Language modules use the same file naming as English utilities but have an .MSG extension. For example, the language module for MONITOR.NLM is MONITOR.MSG. Here's the kicker: Language modules for different languages all have the same name (MONITOR.MSG, for example). Therefore, they must be kept in separate directories. If you mix language modules, you'll end up with something like Figure 13.6. This is fine if you happen to live in Germany. But it's a little confusing any other place in the world.

In order to keep language modules separated, NetWare 4 creates a numbered subdirectory under the SYS:SYSTEM\NLS directory structure. Each subdirectory corresponds with the "languages designator"—there are 16 of them (German is number 7). Fortunately, you don't have to worry too much about this because INSTALL automatically puts each language module in an appropriate NLS subdirectory each time a new international version is installed. NetWare 4.1 currently ships with five different languages by default—English, French, German, Italian, and Spanish. NetWare 4 will create an NLM search hierarchy based on the default language designator. For example, you can have all utilities appear in English, but if that's not available, the system will default to Canadian French. And if that's not there, maybe Chinese would be nice. You get the idea.

Earlier I said language support is enabled using INSTALL.NLM. Here's how it works. First, load INSTALL at the server console. Then choose Product Options from the Installation Options main menu. Next, select Choose an Item or Product listed above and INSTALL will bounce over to the Other Installation Items/Products menu. In there, you'll see a detailed list of all available additional products. Refer to Figure 6.7 in Chapter 6 for a list. In this case, we're interested in the following option—Install an additional server language. From there, you'll get a list of available languages and their corresponding size. In order to create Figure 13.6, we had to choose NetWare 4.1 German Language-specific Files (5 MB). There you go, that's all there is to it.

REAL WORLD

Keep in mind, all of this international activity only allows us to view utilities, system messages, and display formats in alternative languages. It doesn't do much for the core operating system. If you want NetWare 4 itself to operate in a different language, replace SERVER.EXE in C:\NWSERVER with the appropriate SERVER.MSG language module.

Once you've installed the languages you need, changing the server language is a snap. This is accomplished using the LANGUAGE console command and an appropriate language designator. Remember, the language designator directs the utility to the correct NLS subdirectory for the .MSG language module. To change to German, for example, issue the following command at the server colon prompt:

LANGUAGE 7

Table 13.1 lists the 16 default language designators included with NetWare 4.1.

T A B L E 13.1	DESIGNATOR	LANGUAGE	DESIGNATOR	LANGUAGE

DESIGNATOR	LANGUAGE	DESIGNATOR	LANGUAGE
0	Canadian French	8	Italian
1	Chinese	9	Japanese
2	Danish	10	Korean
3	Dutch	11	Norwegian
4	English	12	Portuguese
5	Finnish	13	Russian
6	French	14	Spanish
7	German	15	Swedish

NetWare 4.1 Language Designators

Now that all of your server utilities are appearing in German, there are two other parameters you might want to configure—keyboard type and locale format. International server keyboard types are activated using KEYB.NLM. To define a German keyboard, for example, you would type the following at the server colon prompt:

LOAD KEYB GERMANY

Here's a more complete list of the NetWare 4.1 international keyboard types:

United States   Denmark
Germany   Norway
France   Sweden
Italy   Latin America
Spain   Netherlands
United Kingdom   Swiss German

Portugal   Swiss French
Belgium   Russia
                                 Canadian French

Also note that keyboard types are dependent on the code page set by DOS. Code pages are available to NetWare 4 only if you have the correct UniCode files that match your code page number and country code. These settings are defined during Stage 1 of the NetWare 4 installation process. For more information, refer to Chapter 6.

You may also want to define the Locale Format for international languages. Locale determines how time, dates, and numbers are formatted. This information is stored in C:\NWSERVER\LCONFIG.SYS. Once again, locale formatting is defined during Stage 1 of the NetWare 4 installation process.

So that's what happens at the server. But what about the workstation? After all, you have international users to think about as well. Fortunately, NetWare 4 clients can access the same NLS language modules as the server. You just need to designate the name of the language. This is accomplished using the following SET parameter at the workstation DOS prompt:

```
SET NWLANGUAGE=Deutsch
```

This line would setup the workstation for German utilities. NetWare 4 also includes support for English, Español, Français, and Italiano. This SET parameter tells the client to look for specific messaging files in specific NLS subdirectories. If no message files exist, the default English message files are used.

QUIZ

My first is in day, but not in night.
My second, in flame, but not in light.
My third is in milk, but not in tea.
My fourth in slip, but not in plea.
My last in yellow, not in whale.
My whole for love will tell a tale.
What am I?

(Q 13-3)

Well, there you have it. NetWare 4 is a great operating system for our global electronic village. Now that we've installed, configured, activated, maintained, internetworked, and internationalized our server, it's time to "protect" it. In the next section, you'll learn how to create a maximum security server. If we do it right, our server will be more impenetrable than Alcatraz. Interestingly, we're trying to keep the users from breaking *in*, not *out*.

SERVER PROTECTION

If the server is at the heart of your NetWare 4 WAN, it makes sense to take all measures you can to protect it. As we saw in Chapter 11, NetWare 4 has an elaborate security system that protects NDS and data files from would-be hackers. This system does nothing, however, to protect the server console itself. Any user with mischievous intent and a little bit of knowledge can cause a lot of harm at the NetWare 4 server console. For this reason, you should take extra measure to install an impenetrable network armor at the file server console. Following are four scenarios that can go a long way in protecting your server:

- ▸ Physical—lock up the physical server

- ▸ MONITOR.NLM locking—use the password feature

- ▸ SECURE CONSOLE—restrict access to the DOS partition

- ▸ REMOTE.NLM—add a password to the built-in RMF facility

Now, let's take a closer look at how to create a "maximum security server."

Physical

No matter what security locks you put in place, somebody's going to break them if they have physical access to the server. It's amazing how much information can be stolen from the physical server console including SERVER.EXE, NLMs, optimization data, and company secrets. The first step in creating a maximum security server is locking up the physical machine itself. This involves three steps:

- • Lock the server into a wiring closet or other restricted room.

2 • Remove the keyboard to discourage physical access to the console.

3 • Remove the server monitor and leave the hacker "in the dark."

Although this is a great plan, you're probably wondering, "How am I supposed to manage server operations from within a locked closet and with no keyboard or monitor?" That is a good question. Fortunately, NetWare 4 includes a built-in Remote Management Facility (RMF) that provides virtual access to the file server console—from a direct workstation or asynchronously remote machine. Later in this chapter, we'll explore RMF and show you how it can be used to supplement the server protection plan. For now, let's move on to the next protection scenario—MONITOR.NLM.

MONITOR.NLM Locking

If locking up the server is not an option or you want to increase your level of server protection, consider "locking" the console with MONITOR.NLM. This way, even if somebody does get physical access to the machine, he/she can't access the console unless he/she has the MONITOR.NLM password. First, load the MONITOR.NLM utility by typing

```
LOAD MONITOR
```

at the file server console. Next, choose the Lock Server Console option from the main menu. NetWare will ask for a password. Enter a unique password and press Enter. All done. Now anybody accessing the server console will have to first enter the MONITOR.NLM password.

By default, NetWare 4 accepts the bindery supervisor's password for unlocking the server console. As you learned earlier, this is the first password assigned to the Admin user when you installed the first server in this NDS tree. Even if you delete Admin or change his/her password, the supervisor bindery password remains the same. You should specify a different password when you lock the monitor—just in case. You can also automate monitor locking by placing the following command in the server's AUTOEXEC.NCF configuration file:

```
LOAD MONITOR L
```

In this example, only the supervisor bindery password can be used to unlock the server console. Next, let's expand our server protection scheme to include the SECURE CONSOLE command.

TIP

If intruder detection/lockout disables either the bindery supervisor or Admin account, the password won't unlock MONITOR. This is a bad thing. The only way to reactivate the accounts is to issue the ENABLE LOGIN console command at the server—but we can't get there! So as a backup measure, consider issuing a different MONITOR locking password.

SECURE CONSOLE

To further enhance server protection, you can use the SECURE CONSOLE command at the colon prompt (:). This command accomplishes four things:

▸ Path specifiers are disabled. Only the SYS:SYSTEM search path remains in effect. This means NLMs can only be loaded from the SYS:SYSTEM directory. SECURE CONSOLE provides protection against Trojan horse modules that are loaded from DOS partitions or diskette drives. These modules enter the core OS and access or alter valuable server information. Remember, anybody can load an NLM at the server from diskette unless he/she is restricted from physically accessing it or the SECURE CONSOLE command has been used.

▸ Keyboard entry into the NetWare 4 OS debugger is disabled. This stops super-nerdy hackers from altering the OS itself.

▸ This command prevents the server date and time from being changed by an intruder. This closes a loophole in the intruder detection/lockout feature. Without SECURE CONSOLE, users whose accounts have been disabled can simply access the server colon prompt and manually expire their lockout period. Bad user.

▸ COMMAND.COM is removed from server memory. This protects files on the DOS partition by preventing access to it. Remember, one of your most important NetWare 4 files (SERVER.EXE) resides on the DOS partition.

I'm feeling more secure already. With the server locked up tight as a drum, there's only one more back door to close—RMF access.

REMOTE.NLM

The final server protection strategy involves restricting access to RMF—NetWare 4's built-in remote management facility. As you recall from our first protection strategy, we've already locked the server in a closet and removed the keyboard and monitor. Now the only way to perform daily monitoring tasks is RMF. We'll talk more about the details of RMF later in this chapter, but here's the "Cliff Notes" version.

RMF enables you to access the server console from a local or remote workstation. In either case, it relies on two key components—REMOTE.NLM at the server and RCONSOLE.EXE at the workstation. It's reasonable to assume that if *you* can access the server console from a remote workstation, so can any malevolent hacker. So, let's take measures to protect REMOTE.NLM.

When you activate REMOTE at the server console, you can specify a password using the following syntax:

```
LOAD REMOTE password
```

Replace *password* with any alphanumeric name you can remember. With the password in place, RCONSOLE prompts you for it before enabling access to the server console. Here's the catch—you'll probably want to automate this step by placing REMOTE in the AUTOEXEC.NCF file. Because AUTOEXEC.NCF is a text file in the SYS:SYSTEM subdirectory, it's reasonable to assume that any hacker worth his/her salt would be able to view the REMOTE password. Oops. But we have a solution. You can use null characters in the password or, better yet, encrypt it. Null characters appear as spaces but are actual, valid, alphanumeric characters. You can issue a null character by pressing the Alt+255 keys simultaneously. When hackers view AUTOEXEC.NCF, they'll never know the difference between a null character and a space. Or, better yet, you can encrypt the REMOTE password using LDREMOTE. For more details, see the Real World that follows.

REAL WORLD

In previous versions of NetWare, REMOTE.NLM accepted the supervisor's bindery password in addition to its own. This meant you could issue the LOAD REMOTE command in AUTOEXEC.NCF without having to disclose the password. This has changed in NetWare 4.1. Now the REMOTE password is required and the supervisor bindery password no longer works. Fortunately, Novell has included an encryption scheme that enables you to encrypt what appears in AUTOEXEC.NCF. Here's how it works:

1. Load REMOTE.NLM at the server console by typing LOAD REMOTE and pressing Enter. NetWare 4 will prompt you for an RMF password. Enter it now (for example, Cathy).

2. RMF is now active, but your password is not protected. Next, you can encrypt the password by typing REMOTE ENCRYPT at the server console and pressing Enter. Once again, NetWare will ask you for a password. Enter the same one from above (Cathy).

3. NetWare 4 then responds with an encrypted LOAD statement such as:

```
LOAD REMOTE -e 14572BFD3AFEAE4E4759
```

This is the encrypted representation of the password Cathy.

Next, REMOTE will ask you a simple question:

```
Would you like this command written to SYS:SYSTEM\LDREMOTE.NCF?
```

You should probably answer Yes.

4. Now you're ready to add the REMOTE statement to AUTOEXEC.NCF without any concerns about giving away the password. Simply enter these two commands toward the end of AUTOEXEC.NCF:

```
LDREMOTE
```

```
LOAD RSPX
```

There you have it! We've increased server protection by requiring an RMF password and closed a loophole by encrypting it. In summary, use LOAD REMOTE with the password, then issue the REMOTE ENCRYPT command to encrypt the password. Provide the same password again and have NetWare create the LDREMOTE configuration file. Finally, automate RMF by placing LDREMOTE in the AUTOEXEC.NCF file.

Don't you feel much better now, knowing that you have a maximum security server? Just like Alcatraz, it should be almost impossible for NetWare criminals to "break in." Now let's return to the final two stages of NetWare 4 marriage—console commands and NLMs. These are the tools that make a marriage work.

ZEN

"We could tell you what it's about. But then, of course, we'd have to kill you."

From the movie *Sneakers*

CONSOLE COMMANDS

To be successful in anything, you need the right tools. Marriage is no exception. In order to make any marriage work, you both have to bring the right tools—love, compassion, understanding, respect, flexibility, truth, and a spirit of compromise. But more important than anything is communication. You need to work together as a team and develop synergy. This strategy revolves around the single most important tool—"honey-do's." Honey-do's make the world go around. "Honey, do this," "honey, do that." As long as you pay attention to honey-do's, you'll never have to miss another Sunday football game or "mushy" movie like *On Golden Pond*. Don't forget those compromises.

NetWare 4 marriage is not any different. In order to develop server management synergy, you must bring along the right tools—console commands and NLMs. Console commands are internal management tools that enable you to perform various server management maintenance tasks including NDS management, time synchronization, bindery services, sending messages, activating NLMs, server protection, and network optimization. NLMs, on the other hand, are the modular Legos that provide supplemental functionality to the core OS. NetWare 4 includes four kinds of NLMs—disk drivers, LAN drivers, name space modules, and management utilities. Let's start our discussion of NetWare 4 honey-do's with a look at some important console commands.

Console commands enable CNEs to interact directly with the NetWare 4 OS core. These commands are internal to SERVER.EXE and do not require any other support commands. One of the most powerful NetWare 4 console commands is SET. This utility enables you to customize the OS core with almost 100 advanced parameters. These parameters are organized into 11 categories ranging from communications to file system to time synchronization. Warning: don't mess around with SET unless you've been adequately trained and you're wearing protective gloves. We'll discuss server management and optimization with SET parameters in Chapter 15.

The syntax of console commands is relatively straightforward. The command itself is entered at the colon prompt and is followed by an Enter. Also, NetWare supports various command switches that customize their execution. Anybody can execute a console command as long as he/she has physical access to the file server console. This is a good reason to severely limit access to the machine and implement many of the protection schemes we discussed earlier. Also, console tools can be hazardous to the server if not handled correctly. You should ensure that they are kept out of the reach of small children and NetWare users. Fortunately, they have their own childproof cap (by being placed in the SYS:SYSTEM subdirectory by default).

Let's take a closer look at NetWare 4's top 15 console commands (provided here in alphabetical order). For a complete list of the console commands, refer to the *Novell NetWare 4 Utilities Reference Manual*.

TIP

Console commands are internal operating system tools similar to DOS's internal commands. They are built into SERVER.EXE just like CD or CLS is built into COMMAND.COM. You don't need to have any searching or NetWare directories available to access console commands.

BIND

BIND is an installation console command. As we saw earlier, it links LAN drivers to a communications protocol. Once the LAN driver is loaded, BIND must be issued to activate LAN communications. The default NetWare 4 communication protocol is IPX. Here's the syntax for activating communications on the 3C5X9 NIC:

```
BIND IPX to 3C5X9
```

When you issue the BIND statement at the server console, you'll be asked for the external network number. This is explained in more detail above in the Server Startup section.

BROADCAST

BROADCAST is an administrative console command that enables CNEs to send brief alert messages to all attached workstations. Another related command (SEND) enables you to broadcast messages to specific users or groups of users. In both cases, the message appears at the bottom of the workstation monitor and prompts the user to press Ctrl+Enter to clear it from the screen. Only users who are currently logged in will receive these messages. BROADCAST messages can be up to 40 characters, whereas SEND supports larger messages (55 characters maximum). Here's the syntax:

```
BROADCAST message
```

The downside of BROADCAST and SEND is that they lock up the destination computer until Ctrl+Enter is pressed. This lockup can create harmful effects if the computer is being used for unattended backups. To avoid having messages lock up unattended machines, consider issuing SEND with the following parameters:

/A=C—accept messages only from the server console

/A=N—accept no messages (dangerous)

/A=P—stores the last message sent until you poll to receive it

/P—polls the server for the last stored message

/A=A—accept all messages.

CLEAR STATION

CLEAR STATION is an administrative console command that enables you to abruptly clear a workstation's connection. Be forewarned—this command removes all file server resources from the workstation and can cause file corruption or data loss if it is executed while the workstation is processing transactions. This command is only useful if workstations have crashed or users have turned off their machines without logging out. Here's the syntax:

```
CLEAR STATION n
```

The n specifies the connection number of the workstation you want to clear. These connection numbers can be viewed from MONITOR.NLM or with the help of NLIST.

Connection numbers are incrementally allocated as workstations attached to the server and are not the same from one session to another.

CONFIG

CONFIG is a maintenance console command. It displays hardware information for all internal communication components. Figure 13.7 shows the CONFIG information for ACME's first LABS-SRV1 server, and Table 13.2 describes CONFIG parameters.

*The CONFIG Console
Command*

```
LABS-SRV1:CONFIG
File server name: LABS-SRV1
IPX internal network number: 0BADCAFE
    Node address: 000000000001
    Frame type: VIRTUAL_LAN
    LAN protocol: IPX network 0BADCAFE
Server Up Time:  1 Minute 38 Seconds

3Com EtherLink III 3C5X9 Family
    Version 4.01b   October 19, 1994
    Hardware setting: I/O ports 320h to 32Fh, Interrupt Ah
    Node address: 0020AFE28F2D
    Frame type: ETHERNET_802.2
    Board name: 3C5X9_1_E82
    LAN protocol: IPX network 00001234

Tree Name: ACME_TREE
Bindery Context(s):
    LABS.NORAD.ACME

LABS-SRV1:
```

*Understanding CONFIG
Parameters*

PARAMETER	VALUE	DESCRIPTION
File server name	LABS-SRV1	The name of the server.
IPX internal network number	BADCAFE	The eight-digit hexadecimal number used to uniquely identify this server.
Node address	000000000001	
	0020AFE8B8B5	The internal server node and unique factory address for internal 3C5X9 NIC.
Frame type	VIRTUAL_LAN	
	Ethernet_802.2	Modular communications within the server and external communications for this NIC.

T A B L E 13.2	PARAMETER	VALUE	DESCRIPTION
Understanding CONFIG Parameters (continued)	LAN protocol	IPX 1234	Identifies the internal IPX address as BADCAFE and external cable segment as 1234.
	Board name	NetWare_4	The unique board name given to this NIC's frame type and external address.
	Tree name	ACME_TREE	The name of the NDS tree in which this server participates.
	Server Up Time	4 minutes 49 seconds	The amount of time the server has been active.

DOWN

DOWN is a dangerous administrative console command. It completely shuts down file server activity and closes all open files. This is probably one of the most dramatic and potentially harmful NetWare 4 console commands so treat it with kid gloves. Before DOWN deactivates the server, it performs various tasks including clearing all cache buffers and writing them to disk, closing all open files, updating appropriate directory and file allocation tables, dismounting all volumes, clearing all connections, and closing the operating system. Once DOWN has been entered at the file server console, you have various options:

▸ Type **EXIT** to return to the DOS partition.

▸ Type **RESTART SERVER** to bring things back up again.

▸ Type **UP** to reactivate the server console (really—take a look at the following Real World section).

REAL WORLD

In many of my trials and tribulations with the world of NetWare 4, I've seen frustrated users trying to reactivate the server by typing "UP." I've come to the conclusion that Novell missed the boat in creating a cure for the DOWN command. Because turnabout is fair play, I offer this simple solution: Create a server batch file named "UP.NCF." In it, place a single command: "RESTART SERVER." Then add the following line to the end of your AUTOEXEC.NCF file:

```
SEARCH ADD C:\NWSERVER
```

Finally, copy UP.NCF to the C:\NWSERVER directory. Now whenever the server is brought DOWN, you can simply type UP to reactivate it. I just love it when a plan comes together.

ZEN

"Unformed people delight in the gaudy and in novelty. Cooked people delight in the ordinary."

Mao Pau Zen

DSTRACE

DSTRACE is a maintenance console command. It enables CNEs to monitor NDS replica-related activities including advertising, synchronization, and replica-to-replica communications. As you can see in Figure 13.8, DSTRACE provides various statistics concerning ACME partitions and replicas. Here's a snapshot of some of the more interesting messages:

> ▶ Date and time—The date and exact second of replica synchronization is shown in parentheses.

▶ SYNC:Start sync of partition [CAMELOT.Acme]—This indicates the start of a synchronization interval. A state of [0] indicates a normal synchronization check. A value greater than [0] (like [30]) shows replica activity like a partition being created or a partition being merged back into its parent.

▶ SYNC:End sync of partition—This line indicates the end of the synchronization interval. The message All processed=YES indicates that all updates were successfully incorporated into the master replica of this partition.

F I G U R E 13.8

Getting to Know DSTRACE

```
(99/12/24 03:24:06)
SYNC: Start sync of partition <RIO.ACME> state:[0] type:[1]
 SYNC: Start outbound sync with (1) [010000BC]<WHITE-SRV1.WHITE.CRIME.TOKYO.ACME
>
  SYNC: sending updates to server <CN=WHITE-SRV1>
  SYNC: update to server <CN=WHITE-SRV1> successfully completed
SYNC: End sync of partition <RIO.ACME> All processed = YES.

(99/12/24 03:24:06)
SYNC: Start sync of partition <SYDNEY.ACME> state:[0] type:[1]
 SYNC: Start outbound sync with (1) [010000BC]<WHITE-SRV1.WHITE.CRIME.TOKYO.ACME
>
  SYNC: sending updates to server <CN=WHITE-SRV1>
  SYNC: update to server <CN=WHITE-SRV1> successfully completed
SYNC: End sync of partition <SYDNEY.ACME> All processed = YES.

(99/12/24 03:24:06)
SYNC: Start sync of partition <TOKYO.ACME> state:[0] type:[1]
 SYNC: Start outbound sync with (1) [010000BC]<WHITE-SRV1.WHITE.CRIME.TOKYO.ACME
>
  SYNC: sending updates to server <CN=WHITE-SRV1>
  SYNC: update to server <CN=WHITE-SRV1> successfully completed
SYNC: End sync of partition <TOKYO.ACME> All processed = YES.
```

DSTRACE can be activated at the NetWare 4 server console by issuing the SET DSTRACE=ON statement.

THE BRAIN

For more information on using DSTRACE and its parameters, consult the SET discussion in the *Novell NetWare 4 Utilities Reference Manual* or Chapter 5 of the *Novell NetWare 4 Manual Supervising the Network* l Also, check out Chapter 9.

ENABLE/DISABLE LOGIN

ENABLE LOGIN and its counterpart are both maintenance console commands. DISABLE LOGIN enables you to prevent access to the server for troubleshooting or maintenance activities. DISABLE LOGIN is particularly useful when you are working on the NDS database, backing up filing, loading software, or dismounting/repairing volumes. Keep in mind that DISABLE LOGIN does not affect users who are currently logged in. You may consider combining this command with the CLEAR STATION statement.

As I'm sure you've probably guessed, ENABLE LOGIN enables file server logins if they've been disabled. It also provides one other facility—supervisor unlocking. If the Supervisor bindery account has been locked due to intruder detection, ENABLE LOGIN will unlock it. This only works on the Supervisor bindery or Admin accounts.

EXIT

EXIT is an administrative console command. It enables you to return to the DOS partition once the file server has been brought DOWN. You may want to EXIT the file server console to prevent any other commands from being activated or to reissue SERVER.EXE with new parameters. In addition, EXIT can be used in conjunction with REMOVE DOS to remotely reboot the file server. Of course, this facility has already been integrated into RESTART SERVER or our new UP.NCF utility. Who needs EXIT when you've got UP?

HELP

HELP is definitely an administrative console command. Many times when you feel the CNEship is weighing you down, simply type HELP at the server console and NetWare will come to your rescue. You can view help about a specific console command by identifying it with the HELP command or view a short description of all console commands by typing:

HELP ALL

Press Enter after each description to view the next command. Then press Esc to exit altogether.

LOAD/UNLOAD

LOAD is an installation console command. It is used to activate NLMs and attach them to the core OS. As you recall, the NetWare 4 architecture consists of two pieces— core OS and NLMs. The LOAD console command is used to activate these NLMs and bring them to life. You can also UNLOAD NLMs when you're done with them and free up valuable server RAM.

MODULES

MODULES is a maintenance console command. It displays a list of currently loaded NLMs and some brief information about each including the module short name, a descriptive string for each module, and the version number if it's a disk driver, LAN driver, or management utility. MODULES can be an important part of your NetWare 4 optimization strategy in that it enables you to identify which modules are occupying valuable server RAM. Also, it displays support NLMs you might not have known you're using.

MOUNT

MOUNT is an installation console command. It activates internal NetWare 4 volumes. The MOUNT command makes volumes available to users and can be used on specific volumes or all of them:

```
MOUNT ALL
```

MOUNTing and DISMOUNTing volumes can be used as a security feature for volumes that are rarely accessed. MOUNT them during access hours and DISMOUNT them when they are not in use. No matter how clever the hacker is, nobody can access a dismounted volume. Murphy's Law Number 142—never say "nobody."

REMOVE DOS

REMOVE DOS is an administrative console command. As you learned earlier, REMOVE DOS eliminates COMMAND.COM from background file server RAM. This memory is then returned to NetWare 4 for file caching. REMOVE DOS can also be used to increase file server security. When DOS is removed, NLMs cannot be loaded from the DOS partition—it doesn't exist any more. Also, users cannot EXIT to the DOS partition. If they try, the file server is automatically rebooted back to the NetWare partition. Recall that the SECURE CONSOLE command automatically removes DOS from file server RAM.

RESTART SERVER

RESTART SERVER is an administrative console command. It can be used to reactivate the server after it has been DOWNed. This is most useful when your troubleshooting duties require that you frequently DOWN the server. RESTART SERVER is not one of your normal daily activities. This command also has a couple of interesting parameters that improve its troubleshooting value:

-NS—restart the server without invoking STARTUP.NCF.

-NA—restart the server without invoking AUTOEXEC.NCF.

Remember, this console command is the foundation of our earlier server UP scheme.

TRACK ON

TRACK ON is a maintenance console command. It activates the RIP tracking screen. This screen displays router information protocol (RIP) traffic on the NetWare 4 server. Keep in mind that NetWare 4 NDS activities do not rely on RIP and therefore broadcast their own information over separate channels. In addition, it's possible to filter RIP activity using additional products like Novell's MultiProtocol Router (discussed earlier). As you can see in Figure 13.9, TRACK ON fills up the server console very quickly. You can bounce between this and other screens by pressing the Alt+Esc keys simultaneously or using Ctrl+Esc to view a list of all active console screens.

F I G U R E 13.9

Getting to Know
TRACK ON

```
Router Tracking Screen
OUT  [0BADCAFE:FFFFFFFFFFFF]  3:13:49 pm   00000DAD  2/3      00001234  1/2
OUT  [00001234:FFFFFFFFFFFF]  3:13:49 pm   0BADCAFE  1/2
IN   [0BADCAFE:000000000001]  3:13:56 pm   LABS-SRV1      1
IN   [00001234:0020AFE8B8B5]  3:13:56 pm   ACME_TREE___   1  ACME_TREE___   1
     WHITE-SRV1   1    WHITE-SRV1   1      WHITE-SRV1     1
IN   [00001234:0020AFC055F3]  3:14:07 pm   Get Nearest Server
OUT  [00001234:0020AFC055F3]  3:14:07 pm   Give Nearest Server LABS-SRV1
IN   [00001234:0020AFC055F3]  3:14:07 pm   Route Request
IN   [00001234:0020AFC055F3]  3:14:07 pm   Route Request
OUT  [00001234:0020AFC055F3]  3:14:07 pm   0BADCAFE  1/2
IN   [0BADCAFE:000000000001]  3:14:16 pm   ACME_TREE___   1
OUT  [0BADCAFE:FFFFFFFFFFFF]  3:14:19 pm   ACME_TREE___   2  ACME_TREE___   2
     WHITE-SRV1   2    WHITE-SRV1   2      WHITE-SRV1     2  ACME_TREE___   1
     LABS-SRV1    1
OUT  [00001234:FFFFFFFFFFFF]  3:14:19 pm   ACME_TREE___   1  LABS-SRV1      1
     LABS-SRV1    1
OUT  [0BADCAFE:FFFFFFFFFFFF]  3:14:19 pm   LABS-SRV1      1
IN   [0BADCAFE:000000000001]  3:14:23 pm   LABS-SRV1      1
IN   [0BADCAFE:000000000001]  3:14:25 pm   LABS-SRV1      1
IN   [00001234:0020AFE8B8B5]  3:14:26 pm   00000DAD  1/2
<Use ALT-ESC or CTRL-ESC to switch screens, or any other key to pause>
```

TRACK ON information is formatted according to whether the file server is receiving the information (IN) or broadcasting the information (OUT). Figure 13.9 shows the format of TRACK ON for the ACME LAB server and provides information about the many components it tracks including sending file server's network address, node address, name, hops from that file server to this one, network addresses known by the sending file server, and the number of tics it takes to traverse the WAN. Refer to Table 13.3 for a more detailed discussion of these TRACK ON components. Finally, you can activate the RIP tracking screen by issuing the following command at the server colon prompt (:):

```
TRACK ON
```

If you haven't figured it out yet, almost every ON switch in the world has an OFF. TRACK ON is no exception. To deactivate the RIP tracking screen, simply issue the command:

```
TRACK OFF
```

THE BRAIN

For more information on using TRACK ON and other server console commands, see the AppNote entitled "Using TRACK and Other Console Utilities in a Mixed NetWare Environment" in the October 1995 issue of *Novell Application Notes*.

That completes our discussion of NetWare 4 marriage tools. With this knowledge, comes responsibility. Remember, wield these tools wisely. Power corrupts and absolute power corrupts absolutely. Now let's complete our journey through the world of NetWare 4 server management with a final discussion of "honey-do's."

ZEN

"The story of a girl who gets mad, gets big, and gets even."

From the movie *Attack of the 50 Foot Woman*

T A B L E 13.3

Understanding TRACK ON
Parameters

PARAMETER	VALUE	DESCRIPTION
IN	IN [network address] 3:14:07 PM	Indicates inbound information originating outside this server and the time at which it was accepted.
OUT	OUT [network address] 12:44:59 PM	Indicates outbound information originating from this server and going across the WAN.
[network address]	[0BADCAFE:000000000001]	Identifies the IPX internal network address and node address of the internal virtual LAN. This is the server's unique internal network address.
	[00001234:FFFFFFFFFFFF]	The outbound network and node address for packets being sent from this server. The odd node address indicates this packet is meant to be broadcast to all workstations and servers on the 1234 external cabling segment.
	[00001234:0020AFC055F3]	Indicates a packet arriving from a specific machine — in this case, a workstation.
SAP Information	LABS-SRV1	Service advertising protocol information. This includes server names and a number. The number represents how many hops the server is from this server. Each router counts as a hop. Servers displaying SAP information include file servers, print servers, and mail servers, and so on.
	WHITE-SRV1 2	SAP information showing the WHITE-SRV1 server as 2 hops from LABS-SRV1. Internal Parameter Value Description IPX routing does count as a hop.

T A B L E   13.3

(continued)

PARAMETER	VALUE	DESCRIPTION
RIP information	00001234 1/2	Routing information protocol data. The number 00001234 indicates the destination network address for this packet. The values 234 1/2 indicate the number of hops and ticks it will take to reach the network. A tick is 1/18th of a second and typically one more than the number of hops. If you're sending packets over a large WAN, the ticks could take much longer.
GET NEAREST SERVER	GET NEAREST SERVER	This is a broadcast from a client seeking a connection from any server. If you do not get this message, it indicates that the workstation is having trouble communicating with the server.
GIVE NEAREST SERVER	GIVE NEAREST SERVER LABS-SRV1	This server's response to the GET NEAREST SERVER request.

NETWARE LOADABLE MODULES

NLMs are NetWare 4 honey-do's. If you ever need any help, it's nice to know NLMs are there for you. These cute little server dynamos attach to the core OS and provide additional NetWare 4 functionality. As you can see in Figure 13.10, NetWare doesn't have much to offer without NLMs. The core operating system provides these basic network services:

- ▶ NetWare Directory Services (NDS)

- ▶ File server

- ▶ Security

- ▶ Authentication

- ▶ Routing

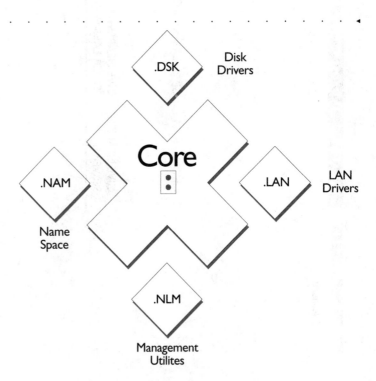

*NetWare 4 Server
Architecture*

But none of these facilities are available until NLMs activate internal communications and mount the file system. In addition to saving the day, NetWare 4 NLMs have the following advantages:

▸ NLMs free up RAM by enabling CNEs to remove inactive modules.

▸ NLMs can be loaded and unloaded without bringing down the server— hence the Lego analogy.

▸ NLMs provide an easy method for outside developers to write their own modules for NetWare 4.

From Figure 13.10, you can see that NetWare 4 supports four NLM types: disk drivers, LAN drivers, name space, and management NLMs. Disk drivers are primarily responsible for the interface between NetWare and the internal hard disks. LAN drivers initiate communications with the internal NIC, whereas name space modules provide support for non-DOS naming schemes. Management NLMs are the real stars of the show. They're used for monitoring, maintenance, and configuration of the NetWare server environment. Let's take a closer look at each of these NLM types and explore how they can improve your quality of life—or at least your marriage.

Disk Drivers

As I just mentioned, disk drivers control communications between NetWare 4 and the internal shared disk. You can load and unload disk drivers as needed. You learned earlier in this chapter that disk drivers activate the NetWare partition. They have the .DSK extension and are stored in the C:\NWSERVER directory. During the installation or startup process, your first task (after running SERVER.EXE) is to activate .DSK NLMs. This mounts the NetWare file system and makes all other utilities available from the SYS:SYSTEM directory. Some common .DSK drivers include ISADISK.DSK, IDE.DSK, and DCB.DSK for disk coprocessor boards. Newer disk modules written to the NetWare Peripheral Architecture (NPA) come in pairs and have the .CDM and .HAM extensions. For more details, see Chapter 6.

LAN Drivers

LAN drivers, on the other hand, control communication between NetWare 4 and internal network interface cards (NICs). You can load and unload these drivers as needed to make communications available to all LAN users. Bear in mind that when you load the LAN driver, you must specify hardware configuration options such as interrupt, port address, memory address, and frame type.

Although disk drivers are automatically activated from STARTUP.NCF, LAN drivers reside in AUTOEXEC.NCF. This is because they are available from the SYS:SYSTEM directory once the NetWare partition has been activated. LAN drivers have the .LAN extension and include NE2000.LAN, TOKEN.LAN, 3C5X9.LAN, and TRXNET.LAN for ARCNet. For a more detailed list, see Chapter 6.

Name Space

Name space modules enable non-DOS naming conventions to be stored on the server, directory, and file system. Name space is important so that Macintosh, Unix, and OS/2 names can be supported in cooperation with the default DOS environment. Name space modules have the .NAM extension and are stored in the SYS:SYSTEM directory with all other NLMs. Some common name space modules include MAC.NAM for Macintosh users and OS2.NAM for OS/2 users. Later in this chapter, we'll explore non-DOS workstations and review how name space works. For now, be aware that one other console command is required when you activate name space—ADD NAME SPACE.

INSTALL.NLM

This is where the fun begins. INSTALL.NLM is the first of a slew of management NLMs that help you install, manage, maintain, troubleshoot, and optimize the NetWare 4 server. As you can see in Figure 13.11, INSTALL consists of 10 options.

These 10 INSTALL steps systematically walk you through the server install process beginning from SERVER.EXE. Once the core OS has been activated, you load the disk driver and create the NetWare partition. Next, you create the default SYS: volume and activate the server license. Once you copy SYSTEM and PUBLIC files to the new volume, it's time to install NDS. This is the trickiest of the 10 installation options. Once time synchronization and server context have been established, you can automate the whole kit and caboodle with AUTOEXEC.NCF and STARTUP.NCF files. Finally, Product Options provides support for installing other products, and Server Options gives you the choice of starting all over again. Of course, like any management NLM, if things get too hairy, you can always EXIT.

F I G U R E   13.11

*Checking Out
INSTALL.NLM*

This INSTALL.NLM utility is a dramatic improvement over earlier versions. In the past, the installation process wasn't nearly as systematic or organized. Also, you can jump to any point in the journey from the main menu. Some of the tasks you might want to perform after the NetWare 4 installation include:

- ▸ Disk duplexing

- ▸ Adding drives and volumes

- ▸ Redefining the hot fix redirection area

- ▸ Editing server configuration files

- ▸ Loading an upgraded NetWare 4 license

- ▸ Installing and configuring additional products, including DynaText, MHS Services, Macintosh, or Unix support

For a more detailed walkthrough of the NetWare 4 installation process, refer to Chapter 6.

MONITOR.NLM

MONITOR.NLM has always been the "mother of all server utilities." It provides a plethora of information about key memory and communication processes. The types of resources that can be tracked using MONITOR.NLM include file connections, memory, disk information, users, file lock activity, and processor usage. Of course, with the advent of SERVMAN, there's some competition at the top of the mountain.

ZEN

"My grandfather once told me that there are two kinds of people: those who do the work and those who take the credit. He then told me to try to be in the first group, there was much less competition there."

Indira Gandhi

As you can see in Figure 13.12, MONITOR.NLM consists of two main menu screens—General Information and Available Options. Like most MONITOR windows, General Information contains dynamic statistics that change every second or so. Some of the most interesting General Information statistics include:

▸ Utilization—Reflects CPU utilization. This number is roughly the amount of time the processor is busy. For a more accurate reading of CPU utilization, use the histogram displayed from the processor utilization option from the main menu.

▸ Total cache buffers—The number of blocks available for file caching. This number decreases as modules and other server resources are loaded. Because file caching has the most dramatic impact on server file performance, you want this number to remain high. For a more accurate measure of available cache buffers, use the Resource Utilization option from the main menu.

▸ Dirty cache buffers—The number of file blocks in memory waiting to be written to disk. If this number grows large, you may have a bottleneck problem with the internal file system. A server crash at this point would corrupt saved data.

▶ Current service processes—Indicates the number of task handlers NetWare allocates to service incoming requests. This can dramatically impact server performance, because requests have to wait in line when service processes are busy. Consider what happens at the grocery store around 5:00 p.m. each evening. The default maximum number of service processes is 20, with a possible range of 5–100.

▶ Current licensed connections—The number of active licensed connections the server currently recognizes. This number will always be less than the maximum number of licensed connections your server supports. If this number approaches the maximum, consider upgrading your license using INSTALL.NLM.

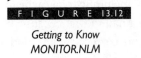

F I G U R E 13.12

Getting to Know
MONITOR.NLM

In addition to these general information statistics, MONITOR.NLM includes a plethora of Available Option submenus. Each submenu focuses on a specific subcomponent of the NetWare 4 server architecture. Here's a quick look:

▶ Connection information—Lists all active connections and tracks their current activity. CNEs can use this option to clear specific user workstation connections.

▶ Disk information—Lists all available internal disks and valuable hot fix redirection statistics. CNEs can use this option to activate, deactivate, or modify internal disks.

▸ LAN/WAN information—Lists LAN driver configurations and statistics as well as node and network addressing.

▸ System module information—Lists all loaded modules by name, size, and version. In addition, you can track resource "tags" and memory usage for each module.

▸ Lock file server console—As you learned earlier, enables you to protect the console by specifying a password.

▸ File open/lock activity—Monitors files, lock activity, and status. It also enables you to view which stations have open files and general information about mounted volumes and directory structures.

▸ Cache utilization—View detailed caching statistics, including total cache block requests, the number of times a block request had to wait because there were no available cache blocks, long- and short-term cache hits, and dirty cache hits. This option enables you to assess the efficiency of server RAM and take corrective actions.

▸ Processor utilization—Provides a detailed histogram of all selected processes and their CPU usage.

▸ Resource utilization—View memory usage statistics for cache buffer pool, allocated memory, and movable and nonmovable memory pools, and code/data memory. You can also view resource tags and determine which NLMs are "hogging" valuable server RAM.

▸ Memory utilization—View detailed memory statistics such as percent of allocated memory in use, memory blocks and bytes in use, and free blocks. This option also enables you to activate garbage collection routines. You never know when you might need it.

▸ Scheduling information—View and change the priority of a process by delaying CPU execution until a later time.

▸ EXIT—Sounds like a good time for this.

You could spend a lifetime exploring MONITOR.NLM and we probably will in Chapter 15. Stay tuned.

SERVMAN.NLM

Look out, there's a new superhero in Gotham. He is faster than a speedy microprocessor, has more storage than a CD-ROM, and is able to search huge databases in a single second. He's SERVMAN!

SERVMAN, the new SERVer MANager, is at the core of NetWare 4's new server utility strategy. It is the most exciting and versatile new server utility. SERVMAN provides a menu interface for SET parameters and displays valuable NetWare configurations. As you can see in Figure 13.13, SERVMAN includes two windows—Server General Information and Available Options. Each of the statistics in the Server General Information window is updated every second. Here's a quick look:

- Server uptime—Length of time the server has been running since it was last booted.

- Processor utilization—Percentage of time the server CPU is busy.

- Processor speed—Speed at which the processor is running based on CPU clock speed, CPU type, and the number of memory wait states. For example, the LABS-SRV1 server has a rating of 6576. This is an average setting for a Pentium 120 MHz machine.

- Server processes—The number of tasks handlers currently available to handle incoming user requests.

- Loaded NLMs—The number of modules currently loaded on the server.

- Mounted volumes—Number of volumes currently active on the server.

- Active queues—Number of active print queues currently servicing user print jobs.

- Logged in users—Number of users logged into the server.

▶ Loaded name spaces—Number of name spaces loaded on the server, and yes, DOS counts as one.

REAL WORLD

The processor speed rating is a measurement of the server's processing capabilities as determined by the CPU clock speed (such as 120 MHz), the CPU type (such as Pentium), and the number of memory wait states (for example, 0). For instance, a 386/33 machine should get a rating of about 320, a 486/50 should get a rating of around 1370, and a Pentium/120 should get a rating of approximately 6576.

F I G U R E 13.13

*SERVMAN—The New
NetWare 4 Superhero*

As you can see, there's a little overlap between MONITOR.NLM and SERVMAN.NLM. This is not where the similarities end. Throughout SERVMAN, you'll see references back to statistics displayed in INSTALL.NLM and MONITOR.NLM. And, of course, you'll see some new configurations not available anywhere else. The idea is this: With SERVMAN, you get a single management utility for all server maintenance and customization tasks. Although it doesn't provide a facility for *all* server management tasks, SERVMAN does help you accomplish *many* of them. Murphy's Law Number 342—never say "all."

QUIZ

I was out house-hunting the other day, and this one really bothered me. There was this odd house, on which the two halves of the roof were unequally pitched. One half sloped downward at an angle of 60° (left) and the other half at an angle of 70° (right). I wondered, if a rooster layed an egg on the exact peak, where would the egg roll—left or right? Help.

(Q13-4)

The Available Options menu within SERVMAN offers some valuable management capabilities, including:

- Server parameters—You can view and configure "almost all" NetWare 4 operating system parameters. This includes SET parameters automated by AUTOEXEC.NCF and STARTUP.NCF. Changes you make in SERVMAN will automatically be reflected in the server configuration files. Cool! Plus you can view a quick description of each SET parameter and its default settings from within a menu interface.

- Storage information—View adapter, device, and partition information similar to INSTALL and MONITOR.

- Volume information—View information about volumes mounted on the file server (similar to INSTALL).

- Network information—View network information such as number of packets received and transmitted. This is a summary screen of the detailed LAN statistics provided by MONITOR.NLM.

All in all, SERVMAN is a great superhero. Remember, never tug on Superman's cape.

DSREPAIR

It's nice to know that if SERVMAN can't save the day, you can rely on DSREPAIR.NLM. This replaces the BINDFIX utility used in previous bindery-based versions of NetWare. DSREPAIR makes repairs and adjustments to the NDS database and solves inconsistencies with time and replica synchronization. Figure 13.14 shows the main menu of DSREPAIR and both synchronization options. In addition, the Advanced Options menu enables you to set advanced repair configurations such as Log File Management, Pause on Errors, Validation, Scheme of Rebuilding, Remote Server ID List, and Scheduling. Finally, the Unattended Full Repair option attempts to repair corrupted databases with no interruption. If you're not sure you have a corrupted NDS database, consider the following symptoms:

▶ You cannot create, delete, or modify objects even though you have sufficient rights.

▶ You have unknown objects appearing in the tree that do not disappear after all servers are synchronized.

▶ You cannot create, merge, or modify partitions.

F I G U R E 13.14

*If Only I Knew
DSREPAIR.NLM*

Once DSREPAIR is completed, you can read through the DSREPAIR log as the file DSREPAIR.LOG in the SYS:SYSTEM subdirectory. Remember, DSREPAIR is your friend but should only be used in emergency situations.

ZEN

"Computers come in two varieties: the 'prototype' and the 'obsolete.'"

Anonymous

Well, there you have it—the tools of a good marriage. No matter what you do, remember: Communication is the key. And if you work hard at it and develop a synergistic team, I guarantee the rewards will greatly outweigh the pain. Speaking of pain, nothing grows a marriage more strongly than nine months of pregnancy.

Workstation Management

So you're cruising along through life, minding your own business, and wham—it hits you. Suddenly, your family is twice as big as it was a few years ago. It's an abrupt wake-up call when you finally realize *you're* not the child anymore. A strange thing happens when children have children. Even though Leia is 27 years old—firmly planted in adulthood—she's still our little baby. We were there through the rough years—login scripts, menu system, and e-mail. Now Leia's having children of her own. Suddenly her focus shifts from marriage to her baby.

Now is a good time for your focus to shift as well—from the server to your NetWare children (workstations). As a CNE, you will spend just as much time managing the workstations as you will managing the server—probably more. In addition, managing workstations can be even more challenging because it encompasses a much more diverse collection of users, applications, and operating systems. And we all know users can act like babies sometimes.

In order to fully optimize the client connection and keep things running smoothly, you'll have to employ a stern, yet caring, workstation management strategy. Here are a few things to think about:

- ▶ ODI—As with most family matters, it all starts with communications. Using ODI, all your diverse clients can coexist on the same NetWare 4 LAN. As we saw in Chapter 12, ODI consists of three layers: MLID communications, the LSL switchboard, and various protocol stacks. Finally, ODI relies on NET.CFG for LAN driver configurations.

▶ NetWare DOS Requester—The NetWare DOS Requester is a connection point between the workstation operating system (WOS) and NetWare 4 services. It lies between the WOS and ODI to make transparent network communications obtainable. This is Leia making sure that Anakin doesn't get in any trouble. In addition, the NetWare DOS Requester is required to support NDS Services at the workstation. In this case, NETx just doesn't cut the mustard. The NetWare DOS Requester is implemented through a series of Virtual Loadable Modules (VLMs). These modular client Legos provide specific services for communications to file server and printing. All of these diverse VLMs are connected through VLM.EXE and NET.CFG.

▶ Non-DOS support—NetWare prides itself on its ability to transparently support a multitude of workstation environments. In addition to DOS, NetWare 4 supports Windows 95 (Windows 95 Requester), OS/2 (NetWare Client for OS/2), Macintosh (NetWare for Macintosh and MacNDS), and Unix (NetWare NFS). In addition, DOS workstations can share non-DOS files through an internal server naming scheme—name space. The bottom line is this: any happy family is made up of many different kinds of children.

▶ Virus prevention—There will come a day when Anakin gets a cold. While it may seem like the end of the world, these things get better with time. The little one will just have to drink plenty of liquids and stay in bed (sounds like a cure for anything that ails you). Similarly, workstations can get hit by a virus and impart chaos on your WAN. It's paramount in network security to set standard procedures for protection against network viruses. In developing a workstation virus prevention strategy, consider limiting file server rights, monitoring the server disk, flagging executable files as Read-Only, and using virus scanning software. If none of this works, go see the doctor. Unfortunately, our discussion of workstation management won't enable us to explore virus prevention in much depth. Please reference the Service and Support course or other NetWare 4 documentation for hints.

▶ Diskless workstations—Clients without a floppy or hard disk. This strategy can dramatically improve your quality of life by enhancing virus prevention, saving money, and, of course, centralizing NetWare administration. If you're one of the lucky people who convinces management to install diskless workstations, you'll need to set up the NetWare server for remote booting. Remote booting relies on two things—a remote boot PROM chip on the internal NIC and a booting configuration file in the F:\LOGIN subdirectory. Once again, these details are in the Service and Support course or NetWare 4 documentation.

ZEN

"If my heart can become pure and simple like that of a child, I think there probably can be no greater happiness than this."

Kitaro Nishida

Children aren't so bad. Once you get the hang of it, I think you might even enjoy adulthood. Having servers and workstations enables you to relive a little bit of your own childhood and adds years to your life (yeah, right). Of course, all the while you need to be thinking about the future and what happens when your children get children of their own. What a disaster. But let's not get ahead of ourselves. Now, we're going to explore the three main aspects of workstation management—ODI, the NetWare DOS Requester, and non-DOS support.

ODI

Of all the places you'll go in your life, few will be as interesting as the NetWare 4 client. There you'll find fun, adventure, and Virtual Loadable Modules (VLMs). The client is one of the most important aspects of a NetWare 4 system because it's where the users meet the network. Someday, I guarantee you'll get the question, "Where's the ANY key?" In order to help you sleep at night, the interface should be as transparent as possible—avoid confusion and unnecessary support calls. In order to achieve client transparency, NetWare 4 breaks the workstation into two key components:

▸ NIC—The internal network interface card that provides communications between the local workstation operating system (WOS) and the NetWare server. This hardware device is managed by a series of workstation connectivity files called ODI (Open Datalink Interface).

▶ Workstation operating system—the WOS manages all local workstation services. It coordinates among local applications (word processing, spreadsheets, and databases) and local devices (file storage, screens, and printers). All of these local activities must be somehow orchestrated with network services. This is accomplished using the complex suite of workstation Legos called VLMs.

So let's start with the NIC. As you can see in Figure 13.15, the internal workstation NIC attaches directly to network cabling. On the other end, it must somehow coordinate message transfer with the internal WOS. "So, how does it do this?," you say. Easy. With the help of our next superhero—ODI.

FIGURE 13.15

The Two Main Components of Workstation Connectivity

ODI stands for Open Datalink Interface. Interestingly, it's also the name of an old TV character and a cartoon dog. What does this mean? Using ODI, your network can run multiple protocols on the same cabling system. This enables devices that use different communication protocols to coexist on one WAN, thus increasing your network's functionality and flexibility. For example, both IPX and TCP/IP can run on the same workstation using the same NIC. This means that a user may concurrently access services from a NetWare server using IPX and a Unix host using TCP/IP. In general, ODI provides the following benefits:

▸ Concurrent communication with various workstations, servers, and main frame computers that view different protocols

▸ Communication through any network board designed to meet ODI specifications

▸ Fewer hardware components to support

▸ Flexible configurations using NET.CFG file

As you can see in Figure 13.16, the workstation ODI architecture consists of three main components:

▸ MLID (the Multiple Link Interface Driver)— This component interfaces with the internal NIC.

▸ LSL (the Link Support Layer)—Acts as a switchboard to route packets between MLID and the protocol stack.

▸ Protocol stack—One of three protocol-specific files used to translate and negotiate network communications. This is the real star of the ODI show.

Let's take a closer look.

MLID

It all starts at the bottom of the ODI picture—MLID. Each physical NIC has its own specific MLID driver. MLIDs accept any type of packet and either send them up to LSL or down to the NIC. In either case, MLIDs handle workstation communications. In NetWare 4, MLIDs come in various shapes and sizes—each matching the specific NIC. The MLID driver NE2000.COM, for example, handles communications for the Novell NE2000 NIC. Similarly, the MLID driver 3C5X9.COM handles communications for the popular 3COM 3C5X9 NIC. The beauty of the modular ODI approach is that MLID drivers can be loaded and unloaded as needed. Also, their configuration settings are handled by a single text file—NET.CFG.

FIGURE 13.16

*Understanding ODI
Architecture*

Link Support Layer

The Link Support Layer (LSL) is the next point in the ODI picture. It acts as a switchboard to route packets between the MLID driver and appropriate protocol stack. LSL identifies the packet and then passes it to either IPX/SPX, TCP/IP, or AppleTalk. At the DOS workstation, LSL is implemented as LSL.COM. A NetWare 4 client can use any of the three protocols shown in Figure 13.16 because LSL directs information to the appropriate one. Think of it as your client traffic cop.

Protocol Stack

The final ODI layer contains protocol stacks such as IPX/SPX, TCP/IP, and AppleTalk (see Figure 13.16). Once a packet arrives at the specific protocol stack, it either passes through and communicates with the NetWare DOS Requester or is sent back down to another network. One of the main features of ODI is that it supports multiple protocols on the same cabling segment. This enables devices that allow different communication protocols to coexist on one network, thus increasing your WAN's functionality and flexibility. This is particularly important in NetWare 4 because it is the foundation of a multiprotocol, multinational, and multilingual operating system. Protocol implementation for the default IPX/SPX LAN is handled by IPXODI.COM whereas TCP/IP implementation works through TCPIP.EXE.

ODI loading at the workstation works a little bit differently from the way the picture shows it. Although the MLID layer is the bottom and is the first point of contact for incoming packets, it is not the first ODI driver loaded—go figure. Here's how it works:

- LSL.COM

- 3C5X9.COM (or other *MLID*)

- IPXODI.COM (or other *protocol stack*)

As you learned in Chapter 12, customization and configuration of the ODI files is implemented using NET.CFG. So how do you unload them? It's easy. Simply type the name followed by a /U. Make sure, however, that you unload the drivers in reverse order, because they build on top of each other. And always unload the NetWare DOS Requester before unloading ODI drivers.

ZEN

"Dishes. Relationships. Wind. This guy breaks everything!"

From the movie *Drop Dead Fred*

Once the packet finds its way up through the correct protocol stack, it's time for the WOS to take over. WOS connectivity at the NetWare 4 client is handled by VLMs—the NetWare DOS Requester.

As a quick side note, let's talk frankly about the current state of ODI drivers and VLMs. They are relatively new additions to the NetWare 4 puzzle, but they have been around for a few years. Fortunately, these workstation connectivity strategies have been tested at great length in NetWare 3.12. The good news is the kinks have pretty much been ironed out. Chances are good that the latest release of ODI/VLM drivers will work just fine. This has not always been the case. If you're still a little bit skittish about introducing unproven technology into your workstations, consider a stepping stone— ODI drivers and NETX.EXE. Eventually, however, you will have to go to the VLMs, because they are required for NDS and the committed future of Novell client software. Go ahead, take the plunge—the water's fine. Really!

REAL WORLD

The ODI drivers have some interesting command line switches. Although these are not widely known, they can help you in special circumstances:

- ▸ IPXODI /C—indicates an alternate filename for configuration information. This way, you can specify a different NET.CFG for ODI settings. The /c parameter also works with LSL and VLM.
- ▸ IPXODI /A—eliminates the diagnostic responder and SPX communications. Although this reduces the memory size by 9 KB, it does eliminate support for RCONSOLE and dedicated print servers. Be careful when you use this option.
- ▸ IPXODI /D—eliminates the diagnostic responder only reducing memory size by 3 KB.
- ▸ IPXODI /F—forcibly unloads IPXODI from memory even if other modules are loaded above it. Use this only in extreme circumstances, because it might cause the system to hang.
- ▸ IPXODI /?—all the ODI and VLM drivers have detailed help screens.

NETWARE DOS REQUESTER

The NetWare DOS Requester is a connection point between your WOS and network services. A DOS workstation, for example, is typically a standalone computer. It uses a local operating system to provide basic local services. These services include file storage to local disks, screen display access, printer access, and communications. DOS itself and most WOSs are not capable of communicating with the network. Therefore, they need a little help.

VLMs to the rescue! As you can see in Figure 13.17, the NetWare DOS Requester is a marshmallow-looking thing which surrounds DOS and provides transparent connectivity between user applications and the network. Interestingly, it looks as though it's two fingers squishing the life out of DOS. If I didn't know better, I would say this is a philosophical statement from Novell. Maybe I'm wrong.

At the most basic level, think of the NetWare DOS Requester as your workstation's conscience. It takes requests from the user and decides whether they should be handled by the WOS or the NetWare server. If your request is destined for a server, the Requester will send it down through the ODI layers. If not, it will allow DOS to process the request and send it back to the user. In addition, valuable information about your network

FIGURE 13.17

*The NetWare DOS
Requester Architecture*

connection is stored in the Requester, such as environment variables and drive mappings. It's important to note that this information is virtual and session-specific, which means when you log in, log out, or disconnect from the network, all reference to your information is deleted from the VLMs.

As you can see in Figure 13.17, the NetWare DOS Requester is oriented as a vise-like architecture that surrounds DOS. It shares drive table information with DOS, therefore reducing memory usage. The Requester performs such tasks as file and print redirection, connection maintenance, and packet handling. This is all made possible through various modular files, VLMs. Each VLM performs a specific function including PRINT.VLM for printer redirection, CONN.VLM for connectivity, FIO.VLM for file services, and NETX.VLM for backward compatibility to NETx. Of course, none of this could be possible without the conductor of our orchestra—VLM.EXE.

All of the VLMs work together in synergy to provide a myriad of connectivity services including:

▶ Modularity—Enables adopting third party and future functionality and takes advantage of expanded and extended memory in the form of protected-mode DOS extenders.

▶ Memory swapping—Enables efficient memory usage because the unnecessary items are not loaded. Also, VLMs can be placed in either conventional, expanded, or extended memory.

▶ DOS redirection—Eliminates the duplication of effort between VLMs and DOS. This also allows for direct communications between the local workstation operating system and NetWare 4 shells.

▶ System optimization—Includes packet bursting and large internetwork packet support.

▶ Compatibility with other versions of NetWare—Provides compatibility with previous versions of NetWare through NETX.VLM and current NetWare 4 features through NDS.VLM.

As you can see in Figure 13.17, the vise-like architecture consists of two main components—VLMs and NETX.VLM. The VLMs themselves have an interesting load-order architecture. As you can see in Figure 13.18, this model consists of three layers:

▶ Transport protocol

▶ Service protocol

▶ DOS redirection

CONN.VLM is used for connectivity among these three layers. Also, it's important to note that the NetWare DOS Requester supports two types of VLMs—parents and children. Parent VLMs route requests to applicable children. Parent VLMs or "multiplexers" incorporate the services of multiple children. Children, on the other hand, handle a particular implementation of a logical group of functions. Let's take a closer look at the happy VLM family.

Transport Protocol VLMs
The Transport Protocol Layer maintains server connections and provides packet transmission and other transport-related services. As you can see in Figure 13.18, it consists of one parent and two children. The main parent, TRAN.VLM, is responsible

for routing transport protocols to either of the two children—IPXNCP.VLM for IPX services or TCPNCP.VLM for TCP/IP services. In this example, the protocol-specific children are loaded before the TRAN.VLM parent.

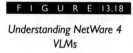

F I G U R E 13.18

Understanding NetWare 4 VLMs

Service Protocol VLMs

The Service Protocol Layer handles requests for specific services such as broadcast messages, file reads and writes, and print redirection. Service protocol VLMs are the heart and soul of NetWare 4 client connectivity. Here's a list of some of the more important NetWare 4 service VLMs:

- ▶ NWP.VLM—The NetWare protocol multiplexer. It establishes and maintains connections, logins, and logouts. As a parent, it also handles network service implementations through the following children—NDS.VLM for NDS support, BIND.VLM for bindery services, and PNW.VLM for Personal NetWare.

- ▶ FIO.VLM—The file input/output module that implements basic transfer protocols for files. This VLM handles cached or non-cached reads and writes and burst mode reads and writes for the client.

- ▶ PRINT.VLM—The print module provides printing services using the FIO module for its file writes. Print redirection is handled in various ways, including noncached, cached, via packet burst protocol, or via file services.

▸ RSA.VLM—Provides system-level background authentication for NetWare 4 workstations.

▸ AUTO.VLM—Reconnects a client workstation to a server and rebuilds the workstation's environment to its original state prior to losing the connection. Although this is an optional VLM, it certainly has its merits.

TIP

In case you never knew, RSA is an acronym named for the three developers of the Public Key Encryption scheme—Rivest, Shamir, and Adleman. Now you can sleep at night.

DOS Redirection VLMs

REDIR.VLM is responsible for DOS redirection services. The Requester makes a NetWare server look like a DOS driver to the user by having REDIR.VLM make decisions about client requests. This is analogous to the major functionality of NETX.EXE.

QUIZ

The "Puzzler" strikes again:
What will you break even if you name it?
What fastens two people yet touches only one?
What grows larger the more you take away?
What grows larger the more you contract it?

(Q13-5)

So who's in charge here? The VLM manager—VLM.EXE. When you run it, it oversees the loading and sequencing of VLM files. Because VLMs are load-order dependent, you have to make sure VLM.EXE activates them in the correct order. In addition, the NetWare DOS Requester supports two types of VLMs—core and optional. Core VLMs are activated automatically in a specific order when you execute VLM.EXE. There are 13 of them shown in Table 13.4—and they're listed in respective load order. Optional VLMs, on the other hand, can be activated by issuing the following command under the NetWare DOS Requester section heading of NET.CFG:

```
NETWARE DOS REQUESTER
        VLM=C:\NWCLIENT\AUTO.VLM
        VLM=C:\NWCLIENT\RSA.VLM
        VLM=C:\NWCLIENT\NMR.VLM
```

As you can see in Table 13.4, these are the three most popular optional VLMs. In addition, you can exclude core VLMs from loading, but only if you follow these two steps: First, add the following statement to the NetWare DOS Requester section of NET.CFG—USE DEFAULTS=OFF. Then, second, specify every VLM you do want to load in correct order. The bottom line is, you either load all 13 core VLMs or specify the ones you want in correct order.

T A B L E 13.4	LOAD ORDER	VLM	DESCRIPTION
Load Order for Core VLMs	1	BIND.VLM	NetWare protocol implementation using bindery services. This is an optional core VLM for NetWare 4 NDS. (Child)
	2	CONN.VLM	Connection table manager. Communicates between the three layers of VLM architecture. (Parent)
	3	FIO.VLM	File input and output services. (Parent)
	4	GENERAL.VLM	Miscellaneous functions for NETX.VLM and REDIR.VLM. (Child)
	5	IPXNCP.VLM	Transport protocol using IPX/SPX. (Child)
	6	NDS.VLM	NWP implementation using NDS support. This VLM is required for NetWare 4 NDS. (Child)

(continued)

	LOAD ORDER	VLM	DESCRIPTION
T A B L E 13.4	7	NETX.VLM	NetWare shell compatibility for previous versions of NetWare. (Parent)
Load Order for Core VLMs (continued)	8	NWP.VLM	NetWare protocol multiplexer. This parent VLM overlooks key NetWare 4 client services. (Parent)
	9	PNW.VLM	NWP implementation for Personal NetWare. (Child)
	10	PRINT.VLM	Printer redirector that provides CAPTURE capabilities for the DOS workstation. (Parent)
	11	REDIR.VLM	DOS redirector. This VLM performs most of the tasks of earlier NETx. (Parent)
	12	SECURITY.VLM	NetWare-enhanced security. (Parent)
	13	TRAN.VLM	The transport protocol multiplexer that oversees IPX and TCP/IP communications. (Parent)

The Requester supports DOS 3.1 and above and works with extended, expanded, and conventional memory. VLM.EXE, by default, tries to load all VLMs in extended memory first. Expanded memory is the second choice, and if extended or expanded memory is unavailable, conventional memory is used. VLM.EXE itself can be loaded in high memory, but this is not the default state. In addition to memory support, VLM has various switches that customize its activities.

▶ /?—Displays the help screen.

▶ /Mx—Loads VLM.EXE and associated files in conventional (C), expanded (E), or extended (X) memory.

▶ /Vx—Displays the detailed level of messaging where x runs from 0 to 4. Verbosity can display copyright messages and critical errors (0), warning messages (1), program load information (2), configuration information (3), or everything including diagnostics (4).

▶ /PS—Specifies the preferred server during connection.

▶ /PT—Specifies the preferred tree during connection.

▶ /D—Displays file diagnostics such as status information, memory type, current ID, and VLM manager functioning.

Well, that just about does it for the NetWare DOS Requester and ODI. Both of these workstation connectivity strategies rely on workstation-specific configuration files for implementation and customization. As you learned in Chapter 12, NET.CFG enables CNEs to increase user transparency and pinpoint communication problems. In summary, here's what it does for ODI and VLMs:

▶ ODI—NET.CFG provides vital information for NIC configuration. It includes a section heading called LINK DRIVER for ODI support. CNEs can use this section to name the MLID file and specify hardware and software settings including interrupt, I/O port, memory address, and frame type. Fortunately, you only need to use NET.CFG if you plan on deviating from the established ODI defaults.

▶ VLMs—NET.CFG can also be used to customize default VLM settings. As we saw earlier, it includes a NetWare DOS Requester section heading for defining workstation connections, the first network drive, and activating specific core and optional VLMs.

I bet you never thought the marshmallow man could be so much fun. Well, that's connectivity in a nutshell. I wonder if Leia is enjoying parenthood yet. If you thought that was fun, wait till you see what NetWare 4 looks like from a non-DOS WOS. The future's so bright, you better wear shades!

NON-DOS SUPPORT

NetWare 4 prides itself on the ability to transparently support a multitude of workstation environments. After all, NetWare 4 was designed to provide centralized WAN connectivity for diverse LANs spanning the globe. In other words, NetWare 4 lets lots of different people talk to each other. So how does it do it? As you can see in Figure 13.19, NetWare 4 supports five workstation environments: three on the client side and two on the server side. If you access the network from a DOS, OS/2, or Windows 95 client, the connectivity software resides on the workstation. On the other hand, if you access the network for a Macintosh or Unix client, the connectivity software resides on the NetWare 4 server. Once again, I wonder if Novell is making a subtle statement here.

F I G U R E 13.19

NetWare 4 Support for Diverse Clients

Either way, the goal is to allow all of these five diverse clients to coexist on the same WAN. In addition, file and print services appear to each client using their native interface. Cool! This means DOS users operate with the C:\, and GUI users (Windows 95, Macintosh, and OS/2) hang out in folders. This may seem magic to the user, but it requires a great deal of work for you, the CNE.

Let's take a quick look at life beyond DOS, including Windows 95, OS/2, Macintosh, and Unix.

ZEN

"If I have the belief that I can do it, I shall surely acquire the capacity to do it even if I may not have had it at the beginning."

Mahatma Gandhi

Windows 95

NetWare 4 supports Windows 3.11 through the NetWare DOS Requester. This is because earlier versions of Windows relied on the same 16-bit architecture as MS-DOS. Windows 95, however, is a completely different animal. Finally, the GUI world is integrated into a 32-bit operating system. Windows 95 is more complex and much more powerful than its earlier siblings. For this reason, both Novell and Microsoft have developed sophisticated client drivers to optimize the Windows 95 client in the NetWare 4 world. This software is loosely coined the Windows 95 Requester and operates at the client to allow for various services including GUI login, printer sharing, and access to NetWare 4 graphical utilities.

MS Windows takes on a whole new meaning in NetWare 4 because most administrative utilities are graphically based. The standard DOS Requester support for Windows still works with Windows 95 but eliminates some of the more advanced features. This basic Windows support is loaded as part of the NetWare DOS Requester installation process. During client install, two sets of files are copied to the Microsoft Windows directories, and one set of files is modified. Whatever you do, let Windows do the work. I can't think of anything worse than trying to manually modify Windows .INI configuration files. Here's how it works:

1. • The following files are copied to the \WINDOWS\SYSTEM subdirectory:

   NETWARE.DRV, NETWARE.HLP, NWPOPUP.EXE, VIPX.386, and VNETWARE.386.

2. • The next set of files are copied to the \WINDOWS subdirectory:

   NWADMIN.INI, NETWARE.INI, NWUSER.EXE, and NWUTILS.GRP.

3. • Finally, the client installation modifies three important Windows configuration files:

   SYSTEM.INI, WIN.INI, and PROGMAN.INI. Note that when these files are modified, a backup copy with the .BNW extension is placed in the appropriate directory.

One of the best features provided by NetWare 4 Windows support is NWUSER.EXE—NetWare User Tools for Windows. This GUI user utility provides a single graphical interface for driver mappings, printer redirection, server connection, and simple messaging. As you can see in Figure 13.20, NetWare User Tools provides just enough information for users to be productive, but not enough for them to be dangerous. Sending messages is one of the most useful facilities within NetWare User Tools for Windows (see Figure 13.20). You simply click on a user or group object, type in the message, and select Send. Piece of cake.

F I G U R E 13.20

*NetWare User Tools for
Windows*

THE BRAIN

If you're interested in **NWUSER**, there's a whole **AppNote** dedicated to the topic in the June 1995 issue of *Novell Application Notes*. It's called "Using Novell's NetWare User Tools (NWUSER.EXE) for MS Windows Clients" and it's great training material for users.

That does it for NetWare 4 support for Windows 95. Bear in mind that the prettier the software looks and the more productive it is for users, the more difficult it is for you to administer. Speaking of difficult administration, let's take a closer look at NetWare 4 support for OS/2.

OS/2

NetWare 4 client support for OS/2 is provided through a new system called NetWare Client for OS/2. Makes sense. The client software runs on the OS/2 workstation and is included with the NetWare 4 operating system. File service support for OS/2 is provided through NetWare's own IPX protocol stack. So, what do OS/2 clients gain from NetWare 4 services? Here are some benefits:

▸ Long names—OS/2 supports much longer names than those used by DOS. DOS restricts a filename to eight characters plus a three-character extension, whereas OS/2 can use names up to 255 bytes.

▸ Extended attributes—In addition, OS/2 attaches extended attributes to files that describe them and provide better management capabilities.

▸ GUI utilities—NetWare Client for OS/2 supports NDS utilities in OS/2's native, graphical Presentation Manager interface. This is a critical feature because most of NetWare 4's administrative tasks are performed in graphical utilities.

The bottom line is that OS/2 clients running the NetWare connectivity software have equal access to NetWare 4 services including NDS, file management, printing, and communications. In this discussion, we're going to explore the two main requirements for providing NetWare 4 support to OS/2 clients: OS/2 name space and OS/2 client installation.

OS/2 Name Space

OS/2 workstations use HPFS (High Performance File System) to store data with long names and extended attributes. NetWare 4 support for HPFS is provided through the OS/2 name space. As you learned earlier, name space NLMs have the .NAM extension and provide non-DOS support to the NetWare 4 file server. Once you've loaded the OS/2-specific name space, you must use the ADD NAME SPACE command to configure the volume. The following example would prepare the default SYS: volume for OS/2 files:

```
LOAD OS2
ADD NAME SPACE OS2 TO SYS:
```

You only need to execute the ADD NAME SPACE command once during initial configuration. After a volume has been configured for a new name space, you only need to load the appropriate NLM. This can be automated by placing the LOAD OS2 statement in STARTUP.NCF. Incidentally, Macintosh name space can also be configured on NetWare 4 volumes using a similar approach.

OS/2 Client Installation

Once the NetWare 4 file system has been prepared to accept OS/2 filenames, it's time to install the client software. The NetWare Client for OS/2 software provides access to the NetWare file system and print services. The OS/2 client installation software can be found on the NetWare 4 installation CD-ROM or in the SYS:PUBLIC\CLIENT\OS2 directory. In addition, you can create installation diskettes with the "MAKEDISK" utility—also found on the CD-ROM or in the OS2 subdirectory.

ZEN

"If you watch a game, that's fun. If you play it, that's recreation. But if you work at it, that's golf."

Bob Hope

Well, there you go. OS/2 has been configured and installed. Now we have three client platforms accessing the same NetWare 4 files—DOS, Windows 95, and OS/2. Anybody for a foursome?

TIP

To remove OS/2 or Macintosh name space, you must load VREPAIR.NLM. This repairs the volume and strips away any unused name space. But what if you want to run VREPAIR without removing name space—to repair volumes maybe? Fortunately, NetWare 4 includes protective shields that prevent name space stripping when VREPAIR is loaded. For OS/2, it's V_OS2.NLM and for Macintosh it's MAC_OS2.NLM.

Macintosh

Macintosh connectivity is provided through NetWare for Macintosh. This is an add-on product that runs at the NetWare server. As you can see in Figure 13.19, both Macintosh and Unix clients require special software at the NetWare 4 server. This is because both of them have their own internal networking capabilities—Chooser for Macintosh and NFS (Network File System) for Unix.

Unfortunately, Macintosh and Unix workstations don't understand NDS yet. In order to access to NetWare 4 Cloud, you'll need to install some special software at the Macintosh client—MacNDS. In either case, the NetWare for Macintosh server component provides NetWare file, print, and routing services to Macintosh computers using the AppleTalk filing protocol (AFP). Future support for the new System 8 is currently in the works.

In Chapter 6 we explored the detailed steps for installing NetWare for Macintosh. As you recall, this installation process consisted of three basic stages:

1 • Install NetWare for Macintosh on the server.

2 • Configure NetWare for Macintosh on the server.

3 • Install Macintosh client software on workstations.

In Stage 1, you begin the installation process by loading INSTALL.NLM. Then you choose NetWare for Macintosh from the Product Options menu. A message displays, informing you that files are being copied to the SYS: volume on the host server. And an electronic questionnaire appears asking for the name space volume, AUTOEXEC.NCF information, and whether to install client support files. After you've completed the server installation stage, the NetWare for Macintosh configuration window shows up. That's Stage 2.

Once you've installed the NetWare for Macintosh software, you must configure and activate it. This involves the following tasks in the configuration window:

▸ Configure and enable AppleTalk.

▸ Customize file services.

▸ Set up print services with ATPSCON.

The final installation stage involves the Macintosh workstation. As soon as the server has been configured, Macintosh workstations are granted limited access to NetWare 4. This is because the Chooser only recognizes bindery services. In order to log in as an NDS client, you'll need to install the NetWare for MacNDS client software on each Macintosh workstation. These files are typically copied to the server during the NetWare for Macintosh installation. You should find them in a self-extracting archive file called MACNDS.SEA in the PUBLIC\MAC folder. A dialog box will be displayed asking you to identify the destination directory for these files. If you accept the default, the installation program creates a MACNDS folder within your language folder.

For a more detailed discussion of NetWare for Macintosh installation, refer to Chapter 6. Now let's move on to the final non-DOS client: Unix.

Unix

In much the same way as do Macintosh clients, Unix workstations have internal networking functionality for attaching to NetWare 4 servers: NFS. NFS is the Unix network file system. It coordinates file storage and communications between Unix clients and hosts. Using a special server component called NetWare NFS, Unix clients can attach to NetWare 4 servers and use its file, printing, and connectivity services.

NetWare NFS can be used with NetWare's native IPX protocol or the Unix TCP/IP. However, if you want your NetWare 4 server to hang out on a TCP/IP-only network, you'll need another product—NetWare IP. Finally, support for NetWare 4 DOS clients accessing Unix hosts is provided through another Novell product—LAN Workplace for DOS.

As you can tell, it's not easy to incorporate various workstations into one cohesive, happy WAN. Although NetWare 4 provides a facility for transparent connectivity, some serious massaging is required in order for it to work smoothly. Once again, it may appear as magic to the user, but it's no mystery to you (the CNE)—just hours and hours of hard work. Don't get discouraged, though. It's ultimately rewarding when all the diverse users come together into one big happy family.

ZEN

"In dwelling, live close to the ground.
In thinking, keep to the simple.
In conflict, be fair and generous.
In governing, don't try to control.
In work, do what you enjoy.
In family life, be completely present."

Tao Te Ching

Speaking of family, ours is growing quickly. We watched Leia go through a childhood of her own and now she's experiencing the growing pangs of parenthood. Of course, one of our most important parent responsibilities is the family. And we can learn an important lesson from the Girl Scouts of America—be prepared! Let's continue our journey through adulthood with a detailed look at the "second half" of life—pension and retirement.

Storage Management Services

Call it a pension, a "nest egg," or whatever you like, planning for the future is important business. With a family comes serious financial concerns—college education, emergency fund, and retirement. And these financial decisions aren't as simple as they used to be. You must choose among IRAs, annuities, mutual funds, pension plans, and (my old favorite) the "sock in the bedpost." Regardless of what you do, it's critical that you plan for the future.

One of the most exciting things about life is that you never know what's around the corner. To be prepared, you must have a backup plan. Also, as your network grows in complexity, the value of its services grows as well. And we all know nothing becomes more valuable until it is lost. That's Murphy's Law Number 193.

Welcome to NetWare 4 backup. Backup provides both a prevention and maintenance strategy:

▶ Prevention—Backup is a proactive strategy toward disaster recovery. You don't want to be wondering what to do *after* the data is lost.

▶ Maintenance—Backup doesn't always prevent a disaster from occurring; it simply expedites recovery.

As soon as your network data is lost, file backup should be the first thing that pops into your mind. In many cases, having current backups can spell the difference between a successful and prosperous CNE career and the unemployment line. *Never* neglect your NetWare backup duties. Fortunately, NetWare 4 includes a versatile new backup feature called Storage Management Services (SMS).

SMS is a combination of related services that enable data to be stored and retrieved. The SMS backup process involves a *host* server and a *target*. The host server is the NetWare 4 machine on which the backup program resides. The target is the NetWare server or client that contains the data needing to be backed up. In addition, SMS uses an application on the host server to communicate with modules on target devices—SBACKUP.NLM is included for free. This discussion first explores the fundamental architecture of SMS. Then we'll take a closer look at backing up and restoring data using the default SMS application—SBACKUP.NLM. What are we waiting for? Let's go.

SMS ARCHITECTURE

As you learned earlier, SMS is a combination of related services that enable you to store and retrieve data from various targets—Target Service Agents (TSAs). SMS operates as a backup engine that is independent from the front-end application and back-end device. As you can see in Figure 13.21, SMS supports various TSA front-ends, including NetWare file systems, NDS, DOS and OS/2 file systems, and BTRIEVE databases. Any or all of these resources can be backed up to various back-end devices including DOS read/write disks, tape, and optical drives.

FIGURE 13.21

SMS Architecture

There are three main components to the SMS architecture model:

▶ Device drivers

▶ SBACKUP.NLM

▶ Target Service Agents

You can see the interaction among these components in Figure 13.22. The device drivers interface between SBACKUP.NLM and the internal host device. Then, SBACKUP uses Target Service Agents to activate source file systems. Let's take a closer look.

Detailed SMS Components

Device Drivers

Device drivers lie at the bottom of the SMS model. They control the mechanical operation of the host storage device. In addition, they must be specifically configured for each backup device and interface with the SBACKUP.NLM application. When device drivers are loaded, SBACKUP recognizes the storage device.

Device drivers are loaded at the host server and therefore must be NLMs. The following files are included with NetWare 4.1—TAPEDAI.DSK (Novell's generic tape driver for most ASPI-compatible SCSI controllers), MNS*.DSK (Mountain Backup devices), PS2SCSI.DSK (for IBM PS2 SCSI controllers), and AHA*.DSK (Adaptec SCSI devices). Before SBACKUP.NLM recognizes the host device, you must register it with NetWare 4 using the following command:

```
SCAN FOR NEW DEVICES
```

SBACKUP.NLM

The backup application (SBACKUP, in our case) communicates with device drivers through SDI—the Storage Device Interface. It is loaded as an NLM on the host server. Once the backup device is activated, you can enter the SMS application-SBACKUP.NLM. This utility works within the SMS architecture to route data requests from the source and to the device through SDI. Interestingly, we are now backing up clients from the server—isn't this backward? Later in this section, we'll explore the ins and outs of using SBACKUP.NLM.

Target Service Agents

The final component in the SMS architecture model is TSAs—Target Service Agent. TSAs must be loaded on target servers or workstations. SBACKUP.NLM recognizes TSAs through the Storage Management Data Requester (SMDR). It is an NLM running on the host server. NetWare 4 supports various TSAs including:

- NetWare 4 server—TSA410 or TSA400

- NetWare 3 server—TSA312 or TSA311

- DOS workstation—TSADOS and TSASMS

- OS/2 workstation—TSAPROXY and TSAOS2

- NDS database—TSANDS

Remember, if you're backing up data on the host server, you still have to load TSA410 and TSANDS. Finally, SBACKUP.NLM only recognizes targets which have loaded the appropriate TSA module.

ZEN

"Don't hurry, don't worry. You're only here for a short visit. So be sure to stop and smell the flowers."

Walter Hagen

Now that you understand the fundamental SMS architecture, let's explore SBACKUP.NLM in more depth. Keep in mind, any third-party backup application can be used with SMS as long as it follows this fundamental design.

USING SBACKUP

At the heart of the SMS model is the backup application. NetWare 4 includes a starter program called SBACKUP.NLM. You can use any server application as long as it's SMS compliant. SBACKUP, for example, is an NLM that operates at the NetWare 4 server and communicates directly with the host backup device. Running SBACKUP at the server has its advantages. First, it supports multiple file server connections at one time. Also, it operates faster because it doesn't cause an additional communications load on the network. Because the tape unit is connected directly to the file server, SBACKUP doesn't route packets over the LAN. Finally, SBACKUP supports a wide variety of backup devices because of their independent *.DSK device drivers.

Just like any application, you'll have to learn the SBACKUP "lingo" to use it efficiently. Following are a few terms you should be aware of:

▶ Host—The NetWare 4 server running SBACKUP.NLM. Also, the backup device is attached to it.

▶ Target—Any NetWare 4 server, workstation, or NDS database that has a TSA loaded. This is where the backup source material resides.

▶ Parent—A data set that may have subordinate data sets. In NetWare 4, a parent would be a directory, a subdirectory, or a container.

▶ Child—A data set that has no subordinates. In NetWare 4, for example, a child would be a file or leaf object.

Let's explore SBACKUP.NLM by first learning about its four main backup strategies. Then we'll discuss some guidelines before diving into the detailed steps of SMS backup and restore.

Backup Strategies

So how does it work? SBACKUP provides four strategies that can be used for backing up and restoring data. Each strategy provides a different balance of performance and efficiency. In Figure 13.23, you can see the three main strategies—full, incremental, and differential. Here's how they work.

As you can see in Figure 13.23, the full backup option is the most thorough. It is, however, not practical. During a full backup, all data is copied, regardless of when or if it has been previously backed up. While this option employs a slow backup performance, it does allow for very fast and easy restores—you only have to restore the latest full backup. During a full backup, the "modified bit" is cleared—we'll discuss why a little later.

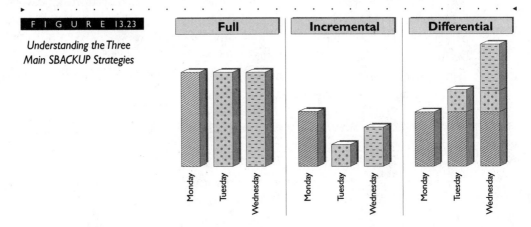

FIGURE 13.23

Understanding the Three Main SBACKUP Strategies

The second option (incremental) backs up only the files that have changed since the last backup. Although this option offers a quick backup, restoring can be quite a nightmare. In order to get all the data, you must restore the last full and every incremental backup since then *in order*. If one is missing or doesn't work, you're up a creek. During an incremental backup, the "modified bit" is cleared so SBACKUP skips it the next time. Only modified file activate the "modify" bit.

The differential backup is a new and interesting strategy. It backs up all the data that has been modified since the last full backup. Differential backup is the best balance of efficiency and performance because it minimizes the number of restore sessions. You only need to restore the last full and the latest differential. Also, the backup session is optimized because only the files that have changed are being copied.

The main difference is the state of the "modified bit"—it is *not* cleared. This way, all the files that have changed since the last full backup are copied each time. This is why the full backup strategy clears the modify bit. Notice in Figure 13.23 how the volume of data systematically increases. One word of warning, however—since the "modified bit" is also cleared during an incremental backup, this can mess up your differential strategy. Make sure never to perform an incremental backup between differential and full backups.

The fourth and final SBACKUP strategy is "custom." The custom method enables you to specify which files are backed up and whether the "modified bit" is cleared. This provides the ultimate level of flexibility.

Table 13.5 shows a comparison of the four SBACKUP strategies. The best combination is:

► Every day—differential

► Once a week on Friday—full

► Once a month—custom

Once you've chosen your backup strategy, you must follow some simple SBACKUP guidelines during backup and restore sessions. Let's take a look.

TABLE 13.5 Understanding the Four Main SBACKUP Strategies	SBACKUP STRATEGY	BACKUP	RESTORE	MODIFIED BIT
	Full	Slow	Easy	Cleared
	Incremental	Quick	Hard	Cleared
	Differential	Quick	Easy	Not cleared
	Custom	Whatever	Your choice	Doesn't matter

Guidelines

You've gotta have rules. Without rules, the world would be a very wacky place. Let me rephrase that—the world would be an even wackier place. SBACKUP is no exception. Here are a few guidelines you must follow when using this SMS application:

► Make sure you have enough disk space on the host server's SYS: volume for temporary files and log files (1 MB should be sufficient). Run the SBACKUP.NLM from a NetWare server and attach the backup device to the same host server. Also, make sure to run updated support NLMs such as STREAMS, SPXS, TLI, CLIB, and NWSNUT.

▶ Limit access to SBACKUP to maintain the security of your NetWare server and to ensure data integrity. Also be aware that security can be compromised if a delayed backup session does not fit on inserted media. If you are prompted to insert another tape, the program pauses at that point and does not exit. To reduce this risk, set APPEND to NO.

▶ When you are entering a filename that has a non-DOS format, use the DOS equivalent naming scheme. SBACKUP does support OS/2 and Macintosh naming schemes but the application interface doesn't. So even though you're backing up long filenames (September99, for example), they appear in their DOS equivalent (September, for example). You can track this by using the SBACKUP error and backup log files. They display both the DOS equivalent and the name space version of each directory or file.

▶ Monitor the size of SBACKUP temporary files. SBACKUP creates temporary files on the target server as well as the host machine. These temporary files may become quite large if you have extended attributes or linked Unix files.

▶ Do not mount or dismount volumes or unload drivers during a backup session. You may corrupt data or abend the host server—duh!

Know the passwords assigned to target servers and workstations.

ZEN

"Don't wait for your ship to come in; swim out to it!"

Anonymous

Backup Steps

Once you understand these guidelines, you're ready to perform your first SMS backup using SBACKUP.NLM. I can hardly contain my excitement. Follow the bouncing ball as we outline the seven steps of an SMS backup. For a more detailed walkthrough, try it yourself. C'mon in, the water's fine.

I • Load the backup device driver on the host server.

2 • Load appropriate TSA drivers on all target devices. This includes the host server, if you plan on backing it up. When you load the TSAs, all support modules are activated automatically.

3 • Load SBACKUP.NLM at the host server. Once you've activated SBACKUP, certain support modules are automatically loaded, including SMDR. The SBACKUP main menu is then displayed, as shown in Figure 13.24.

FIGURE 13.24

*NetWare 4
SBACKUP.NLM Main
Menu*

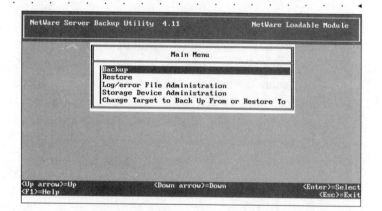

4 • Select a target to be backed up from the TSA list. Note: targets will only appear if the appropriate TSAs have been loaded properly. You can get to the TSA list by choosing Change Target to back up from or restore to from the main menu of SBACKUP.NLM. If you choose a remote server, you'll be asked for a valid username and password for authentication. Recall you can only back up files matching that user's access rights.

5 • Select the backup device from an Available Options list. The list should reflect all devices that are attached to the host server and have appropriate drivers loaded. If only one backup device driver is loaded, SBACKUP automatically selects this device. The list appears when you choose Storage Device Administration from the main menu of SBACKUP.NLM.

6 • Perform appropriate SBACKUP administration including selecting a location for the log and error file, selecting the type of backup, and providing a session description. All of these tasks are accomplished using the Log/Error File Administration option within the main menu.

7 • Finally, you're ready to back up. You can either proceed "now" or "later." If you choose later, you'll be prompted for a date and time. If you choose now, you'll be asked to insert the backup media and enter a unique label for it.

You're done. That wasn't so hard. Whatever you do, don't *trust* your backup. Always test SBACKUP tapes by selectively restoring them at regular intervals. This might involve restoring random files to a secondary volume or the entire SBACKUP session. Whatever you do, don't discover SBACKUP doesn't work after you've lost your disk.

Restore Steps

This is where "Murphy" comes in. If you need to restore, something bad happened. Let's hope you never have to implement the following seven steps. But before you begin, make sure the target server or workstation has enough free disk space. It must have approximately 20 percent *more* than the amount needed to restore. The overhead space stores temporary files and additional name space information. Here's a brief outline of the SBACKUP restore steps:

1 • Load the backup device driver on the host server (same as Backup Step 1).

2 • Load the appropriate TSA software on all targets you wish to restore to. This includes the host server if you plan on restoring to it.

3 • Load SBACKUP.NLM at the host server (same as Backup Step 3).

4 • Select a target to restore to. The Available Options within SBACKUP should reflect all devices which have loaded the appropriate TSA. Once again, this is accomplished using the Change Target to Backup From or Restore To option from the main menu of SBACKUP. Once you choose a TSA, a list of recognized restore sessions will appear. Select one.

5 • Perform SBACKUP administration including selecting a location for the log and error file and inserting the backup media.

6 • Select a restore device from the Available Options list. This list should match all attached devices and loaded drivers. If only one backup device driver is loaded, SBACKUP automatically selects this device.

7 • Now we finally get to restore. First select the type of restore from the following list of three—One File or Directory, An Entire Session, or a Custom Restore. Second, choose the files and objects you wish to restore. Finally, select one of the following restore options—Proceed now or Later.

There you have it. Let's hope you never have to perform a "real" SBACKUP restore. You should practice, though—every week.

ZEN

"Learn not to sweat the small stuff."

Dr. Kenneth Greenspan

THE BRAIN

When backing up NDS with SBACKUP, there are a number of issues to be aware of. These are covered in detail in an AppNote entitled "Backing Up and Restoring Netware Directory Services in NetWare 4" in the August 1995 *Novell Application Notes*.

Well, that wasn't so hard, was it? That's SBACKUP.NLM in a nutshell. After you've completed the SBACKUP steps each day, you'll find a certain peace of mind knowing that you have these hot little tapes in your hands. It matches the peace of mind knowing that your children can go to college and someday you'll finally get to retire to the beaches of Tahiti. But that time is not now so stop daydreaming and move on to the final section of NetWare 4 SMS—other SMS considerations.

OTHER SMS CONSIDERATIONS

We're not quite done yet. In order to take full advantage of NetWare 4's SMS feature, you'll need to explore a few other considerations. They are:

► Who does it?

► Workstation backup

► SMS management

So who's the lucky person? Probably you. Count your blessings because you're the lucky person chosen to be the SBACKUP administrator. Remember, you wanted to be a CNE. In addition to understanding the rights needed for SMS duties, you'll need to understand the special drivers which load at the SMS workstation. Finally, there are a few SMS management issues which can help you troubleshoot and optimize SBACKUP duties. Any questions? Good, time to move on.

Who Does It?
Being assigned SBACKUP responsibility is a dubious distinction. Although it has its status in the NetWare 4 management realm, it does also have a price. You don't want to mess up here. The person you assign to back up your network must have certain qualifications and access privileges, including:

▸ The backup administrator needs Read and File Scan (RF) access rights to the files he/she plans to backup. The administrator will also need additional rights for restoring—(RWCEMF).

▸ The backup administrator will need the Browse Object Write and Read Property right for backing up NDS information.

▸ The backup administrator must know the password on all servers and workstations that act as hosts and targets. A standard naming scheme would be a great idea at this point.

If you're the lucky soul chosen as SBACKUP administrator, continue with the next two considerations. If not, go grab a soda.

Workstation Backup
As if by some inspiration, Novell finally allows workstation backup from the server. This long-awaited feature has been implemented in the new SMS. SMS uses SBACKUP.NLM to back up and restore information from local DOS disks or OS/2 workstations. You can back up certain directories or the entire workstation including floppy and hard drives.

The DOS workstation TSA is a TSR (terminate-and-stay-resident) program that you can run on any target workstation. Some DOS TSA TSR options include /P for password, /T for no password, and /D for drive designation. Here's how the TSA works:

1 • Load TSADOS.NLM at the server for DOS workstations and TSAPROXY.NLM for OS/2.

2 • Load TSASMS.COM at the DOS workstation and TSAOS2.COM at the OS/2 workstation. This is where you specify the TSA parameters we just discussed. One additional parameter you may want to employ is /N to give the workstation a unique name. This name will appear in the TSA list of SBACKUP.NLM.

3 • Select the appropriate DOS TSA from the SBACKUP target list. The name that appears should match the name given in Step 2.

Workstation backup is a cool feature but make sure that you use the correct parameters with the DOS TSA TSR and that you remember to load the appropriate NLMs at the host server. And if those are not enough to worry about, check out the next discussion.

SMS Management

A few SMS management issues can help you journey through the SBACKUP jungle. Let's start with performance. The speed of SBACKUP varies depending on the configuration and location of the data being backed up. If a file server backs up its own data, for example, it runs about four times faster than if it backs up data from a remote server. This sluggishness is because communications are required between the host server and the target servers. The speed of communications also depends on the availability of packet receive buffers at the host server; see Chapter 15.

Next, let's talk about SBACKUP session files. Session files are "backup logs" that contain information to help you effectively manage SMS backups. The information also facilitates the restore process and helps you to troubleshoot anything that goes wrong. The two most important session files are the backup log and error log. The backup log consists of all data backed up during the session and the media ID, session date and time, session description, and location of data on the storage media.

The error file, on the other hand, is generated on the host server when a particular group of data is initially backed up. It contains the same header data as the backup log but also provides error information such as the names of files that were not backed up, files that were not restored, who accessed the NDS database, and error codes. As you recall from our earlier discussion, we identified the location of these session files during Step 6 of the backup process.

Now we're really done. Congratulations: You've been made SBACKUP administrator. I hope you understand the responsibility that accompanies this honor. But if you perform your duties admirably, everybody's going to treat you like a hero.

Pension planning works much the same way. Although it's a dubious honor to be responsible for the family's financial future, many times the rewards greatly outweigh the pain. I see a trend here. All I know is, retirement in Tahiti is sounding better and better all the time.

QUIZ

Here's a quick brain stretching exercise before you tackle NetWare 4 retirement:

A common English word can be made from the letters on the top row of a standard typewriter. For those of you who do not have a typewriter keyboard handy, the letters are Q, W, E, R, T, Y, U, I, O, P. Not all letters must be used and some letters may be used more than once.

(Q13-6)

Remote Management Facility

The final step in our life journey is retirement—RMF. Our life's been an exciting adventure and now it's time to kick back and put it in cruise control. Welcome to Happy Acres!

Now, nobody is saying that retirement has to be boring. Quite the contrary: It provides us with an opportunity to enjoy all the adventures we never had time for in the past. You can learn to scuba dive, hangglide, golf, and even bungee jump. And the best part is, you get to do it on your own terms. It sure sounds appealing—where do I sign up?

RMF is the final step in NetWare 4 configuration and management. It enables you to manage all your NetWare file servers from one central location. This is particularly useful because file server security states that the machine should be locked away in a cabinet with no monitor or keyboard. Also, NetWare 4 prides itself on managing multiple servers spanning wide geographic boundaries. In both cases, you'll spend more time trying to access the servers than doing the important stuff—maintaining and managing them.

Now let's take a moment to explore the details of RMF and learn how it can help you enjoy your new NetWare 4 retirement.

RMF ARCHITECTURE

So how does it work? As you can see in Figure 13.25, RMF supports access from both the workstation and a modem. In either case, it consists of two main components: server NLMs and RCONSOLE.EXE.

F I G U R E 13.25

RMF Architecture

The RMF server NLMs are broken into two functions—REMOTE and connection services. The REMOTE.NLM module manages information exchange to and from the workstation and the server. In addition, REMOTE.NLM enables you to specify an RMF password.

Connection services are a little bit trickier. As you remember from our earlier discussion, RMF supports access from both a direct workstation or from a modem. In either case, the connection NLM is different. When you access RMF from a direct workstation, connection services are provided by RSPX.NLM. This module provides communication support and advertises the server's availability for remote access. On the other hand, when you access RMF from an asynchronous modem, connection services are provided by RS232.NLM. This module initializes the server modem port and transfers screen and keystroke information to REMOTE.NLM.

Let's take a closer look.

ZEN

"Millions long for immortality who do not know what to do with themselves on a rainy Sunday afternoon."

Susan Ertz

SPX

The most popular RMF connection approach is direct—through SPX. Direct connection services are provided through the RSPX.NLM module. When you load RSPX, you have the option to require packet signatures—this ensures security. The default is ON, which means that packet signatures are required. However, packets with signatures are not compatible with NetWare 3.11. If your NetWare 4 server coexists with NetWare 3.11 machines, you'll need to deactivate packet signing by using the SIGNATURES OFF switch with RSPX.

In summary, the server modules required for a direct RMF connection are:

```
LOAD REMOTE
LOAD RSPX
```

Finally, a quick note about REMOTE passwords. As you learned earlier in the chapter, REMOTE.NLM includes a password facility that enables you to restrict access to the server console. As a matter of fact, in NetWare 4.1, a REMOTE password is required. This creates a security loophole when the command is placed in AUTOEXEC.NCF. To work around this weakness, consider using LDREMOTE and encrypted passwords. See the earlier Server Protection discussion for more details.

TIP

If you use the IPXODI /A parameter to deactivate SPX and same workstation RAM, RCONSOLE won't work. I wouldn't want you to be surprised at a bad time.

Asynchronous

In addition to a direct connection, RMF supports asynchronous connectivity. As you can see in Figure 13.25, the remote workstation can be attached to the server via a modem. This means you really can manage the NetWare 4 server from Tahiti. In this case, connection services are provided by the RS232.NLM module. When you load RS232.NLM, NetWare will ask you for some simple modem configurations, including the communications port number, baud rate, and an option for callback.

A callback list enables you to create a list of authorized modem numbers that can be used to access the server. When a connection attempt is made, the server notes the number of the modem that is calling and then terminates the connection. The server then compares the number to the numbers in the call-back list. If the number is in the list, the server calls the modem at that number and reestablishes the connection. If it is not, the server ignores the call. This is another security feature that limits "hacker" access to your server console.

In summary, the following NLM command entries must be given at the NetWare 4 server to activate asynchronous RMF:

```
LOAD REMOTE
LOAD RS232 1 9600 C
```

In this example, 1 is the comm port, 9600 is the modem speed, and C activates the call-back option. The authorized list is defined as CALLBACK.LST in the SYS:SYSTEM directory.

Table 13.6 summarizes these two RMF options.

T A B L E 13.6	DIRECT SPX	ASYNCHRONOUS MODEM
Understanding RMF	REMOTE.NLM	REMOTE.NLM
	RSPX.NLM	RS232.NLM

Whether you're accessing RMF from a direct workstation or asynchronous modem, you're going to need RCONSOLE.EXE.

USING RCONSOLE

RCONSOLE is the front-end for NetWare 4 RMF. It provides direct access to the NetWare server console screen and enables you to perform any task as if you were standing right in front of it. In addition, RCONSOLE provides an Available Options menu with supplemental tasks including changing screens, scanning server directories, and performing a remote install. All in all, RCONSOLE is your friend because it enables you to enjoy the good life without having to run around like a chicken with your head cut off.

Like most NetWare 4 utilities, RCONSOLE has both DOS and Windows versions. The DOS version is executed as RCONSOLE.EXE at any workstation DOS prompt. RCONSOLE.EXE resides in the SYS:SYSTEM subdirectory or any local hard disk.

Whether you access RCONSOLE from DOS or Windows, you'll get the same main screen asking the same simple question: What connection type do you want? The available choices are SPX for a direct connection or Asynchronous for a modem connection. The SPX option brings up a list of available servers as shown in Figure 13.26. Once you choose a server, the password prompt appears. Upon entering the correct password, you'll find yourself staring at the all-too-familiar colon prompt (:).

F I G U R E 13.26

Available Servers Option in RCONSOLE.EXE

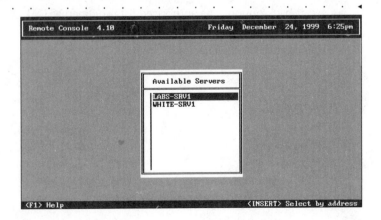

On the other hand, if you choose the asynchronous connection type, a different menu appears. The Asynchronous Options menu provides two choices: Connect to Remote Location and Configuration. From here, you can either dial a remote server or configure your local modem. Once your connection is established, a callback list will be activated and/or the password prompt will appear. Once again, after you enter the correct password, you'll find yourself staring down the barrel of the NetWare 4 console.

ZEN

"Go ahead: Make my day!"

Clint Eastwood

Once the RCONSOLE session is established, you can perform any available server task as if you were standing in the wiring closet yourself—closed quarters. In addition to standard console activities, you can perform various special RCONSOLE tasks including:

- ▶ Change screens

- ▶ Scan server directories

- ▶ Transfer files

- ▶ Shell to DOS to view network directories

- ▶ View your local workstation address

- ▶ Configure keystroke buffering

- ▶ Copy NetWare files to the server

All of these fun-filled activities are accomplished using the RMF Available Options menu. This menu is activated by pressing the Alt+F1 keys simultaneously and can be seen in Figure 13.27. Also, a list of RCONSOLE function keys can be found in Table 13.7.

F I G U R E 13.27

Available Options Menu in
NWADMIN

```
                    NetWare Administrator - [[Root]]
 Object  View  Options  Tools  Window  Help
 [Root]
 └ ACME
      ├ CAMELOT
      ├ NORAD
      ├ RIO
      ├ SYDNEY
      ├ TOKYO
      └ Admin



                         Remote Console
LABS-SRU1:load monitor
Loading module MONITOR.NLM
  NetWare 4.10 Console Monitor
  Version 4.12     October 21, 1994
  (c) Copyright 1989-1994, Novell, Inc.  All rights reserved.
LABS-SRU1:load install
Loading module INSTALL.NLM
  NetWare 4.1 Installation Utility
  Version 2.23     October 27, 1994
  Copyright 1994 Novell, Inc.  All rights reserved.
LABS-SRU1:load monitor
Loading module MONITOR.NLM
  NetWare 4.10 Console Monitor
  Version 4.12     October 21, 1994
  (c) Copyright 1989-1994, Novell, Inc.  All rights reserved.

12-24-99  2:48:41 pm:     RSPX-4.10-23
       Remote console connection cleared for 00001234:0020AFE84943
```

T A B L E 13.7

NetWare 4 RCONSOLE
Function Keys

KEYS	TASK
Alt+F1	View the RMF Available Options menu.
Alt+F2	Exit RCONSOLE.
Alt+F3	Move forward through the server console screens. Similar to Alt+Esc at the physical server console itself.
Alt+F4	Move backward through the server console screens.
Alt+F5	Show your workstation address.
F1	Display remote console help from within the Available Options menu.
Esc	Resume remote session with server.

Whenever a remote session is granted to RCONSOLE, the file server broadcasts a message to the error log and console prompt. This indicates that a remote session was attempted at a particular node address and that it was, in fact, granted or not. This is useful information if you like to track who's accessing the file server colon prompt using RMF—good idea!

REAL WORLD

RMF is cool. RMF is so cool, in fact, that it enables you to remotely install NetWare. Talk about extended vacations! This means you can actually install a NetWare 4 server in Camelot from Tahiti. Think of it. Sand between your toes and SERVER.EXE bouncing through your head. Just make sure to copy the public files locally or you're in for an unhappy phone bill!

Well, that does it. Your life in a nutshell!

We've brought our LAN from birth through childhood and the rewards of adulthood. Through NetWare 4 configuration and management, we've transformed a relatively limp and lifeless LAN into a powerful and productive business tool. How did we do it?

In NetWare 4 configuration, we walked Leia through the five steps of childhood. She learned to walk (workstation connectivity), talk (login scripts), and get along with others in preschool (menu system). Then she enjoyed the many splendors of school (network applications) and finally moved out (e-mail).

In NetWare 4 management, Leia continued her "lifespan" through marriage (server management) and children of her own (workstation management). Now, in her later years, Leia planned her pension (SMS) and finally retired to Tahiti (RMF).

QUIZ

This pretty much sums up NetWare childhood and adulthood:

"Individuals who are completely devoid of sapience in all respects indicate a propensity to cast themselves without hesitation onto those areas where beings of a heavenly nature would reflect seriously and be timorous about proceeding."

(Q13-7)

It was a long and winding road but certainly an adventure for all of us. No matter how much you might want to, you can't just set up the server and walk away. You're a CNE and as one, your life is irrevocably bound to the childhood and adulthood of NetWare 4.

Before we can go on our NetWare 4 exploratorium ride, you must pass a little test. Don't worry, you're tall enough. Segregate and order the following Server Startup steps into two groups—"Happens Once" and "Happens Often." One set occurs only once during initial NetWare 4 installation, and the other set occurs every time you start the server. Good luck.

Happens Once	Happens Often
1.	1.
2.	2.
3.	3.
4.	4.
5.	5.
6.	6.
7.	7.

Create STARTUP.NCF

Start SERVER.EXE

Define server context

Establish IPX internal network number

Run FDISK

Load AUTOEXEC.BAT

Load LAN driver

Define bindery context

Copy SYSTEM and PUBLIC files

Define volume block size

Create server name

Define locale format

License the server

Activate RMF

EXERCISE 13–2: THE NETWARE WORKSTATION ARCHITECTURE

Not so fast. You passed the server test, but what about the workstations? You won't be able to enjoy ACME's exploratorium until you've studied the NetWare 4 workstation architecture model. Review Figure 13.28 and identify the correct components. I know it's painful, but this is for your own good: "tough love."

The NetWare Workstation Architecture

![Black banner] CASE STUDY: SERVER MANAGEMENT AT ACME

Let's go on an "incredible journey" through one of ACME's most exciting servers—CAM-CHR-SRV1. Don't blink; you might miss something. This NetWare 4 exploratorium is packed with console commands, NLMs, NDS, and pixie dust. Hold on tight!

Let's start at the beginning. As you know, before you can log into the network, you need to load the client connection files. When you originally installed these files during the ACME case study in Chapter 6, you instructed the NetWare 4 client installation program for DOS and MS Windows to update your AUTOEXEC.BAT and CONFIG.SYS configuration files. Because of this, you'll find that these connection files are automatically loaded each time you boot your workstation. Let's investigate how this is accomplished.

First, take a look at your AUTOEXEC.BAT file. You'll notice that the Client Installation program added two lines: one to call the STARTNET.BAT batch file and the other to add C:\NWCLIENT to the path. Next, review the STARTNET.BAT file. You'll see that it designates the language to be used and loads the connection files and the NetWare DOS Requester. Finally, examine the CONFIG.SYS file. You'll find that the client installation program added a LASTDRIVE statement that is used by the DOS Requester to determine what drives are available to be used as NetWare drives.

Now that you understand how these files are loaded, try to accomplish the following tasks:

1 • First, check to see if the files are currently loaded in workstation RAM by typing:

MEM /C /P

2 • Next, unload the connection files in the reverse order from which they were originally loaded, using the /U (that is, unload) switch with each command. (See the STARTNET.BAT file if you want to see how they were originally loaded.)

Question 1: What commands did you use to unload the connection files from workstation RAM?

3 • Finally, load all four of the connection files manually, specifying "maximum verbosity" for VLM.EXE. (If you don't remember which switch to use, use the command line help method for viewing options that can be used with VLM.EXE.)

Question 2: What command did you use to list the options available for use with VLM.EXE?

Question 3: What command did you use to load VLM.EXE with maximum verbosity?

As soon as you execute VLM.EXE with the appropriate switch, various information will be displayed on the screen. Use the information displayed to answer the following questions:

Question 4: What version of VLM.EXE are you running?

Question 5: What type of RAM is being used to load the VLMs?

Question 6: Which is the first VLM loaded by VLM.EXE? Which is the last?

4 • Once you have successfully loaded the connection files, log into the network by typing:

```
F:
LOGIN .ADMIN.ACME
```

5 • The next thing you want to do is to explore the Remote Management Facility (RMF). As you know, RMF is a wonderful feature you can use to access the file server console screen from your workstation. Because security is a concern, we will load this utility using an encrypted password.

The first thing you need to do is to activate the RMF on the server by performing the following tasks at the server console, ending each entry by pressing Enter:

a. Load the REMOTE.NLM utility by typing:

```
LOAD REMOTE
```

NetWare 4 will prompt you for an RMF password. Enter it now:

```
CATHY
```

b. RMF is now active, but your password is not protected. You can encrypt the password by typing:

```
REMOTE ENCRYPT
```

Once again, NetWare will ask you for a password. Enter the same one:

```
CATHY
```

c. NetWare 4 then responds with an encrypted LOAD statement such as: LOAD REMOTE -e 14572BFD3AFEAE4E4759. (The number will be different every time you try this.) This is the encrypted representation of the password CATHY. Next, when you are asked whether you'd like for this command to be written to SYS:SYSTEM\LDREMOTE.NCF, type:

```
Y
```

d. Load RSPX.NLM by typing:

```
LOAD RSPX
```

e. Now that you've activated the RMF on the server, you need to run the RCONSOLE utility on the workstation by typing:

```
RCONSOLE
```

Read the message that is displayed regarding the fact that MS Windows may cause RCONSOLE to behave erratically, then press Enter. Because our workstation is connected to the server via cable rather than via modem, select SPX when you are asked to choose the connection type. Next, choose the NetWare 4 file server from the Available Servers menu by selecting CAM-CHR-SRV1.

Finally, when you are asked to provide the password, type:

```
CATHY
```

At this point, the same information that is displayed on the file server console screen should be displayed on your workstation screen.

Question 7: How can you tell that you are viewing the file server console screen?

Question 8: What type of warning is displayed at the bottom of the screen? Why is this important?

Because you are running the RCONSOLE utility, you can now execute console commands at your workstation rather than having to type them at the file server console.

6 • Next, let's take a look at the INSTALL.NLM utility. This utility is used for various functions such as installing the NetWare operating system and additional products, creating NetWare partitions and volumes, mirroring the hard disk, copying SYSTEM and PUBLIC files to the SYS: volume, and creating/editing AUTOEXEC.NCF and STARTUP.NCF configuration files. To load the INSTALL.NLM utility, type:

```
LOAD INSTALL
```

The first thing you want to do in this utility is to add the RMF commands to the AUTOEXEC.NCF file so that it will be activated with the encrypted password every time you boot the server. Select the NCF Files options choice from the Installation Options menu and press Enter, then Select the

Edit AUTOEXEC.NCF file option from the Available NCF Files Options menu and press Enter. The AUTOEXEC.NCF file will then be displayed on the screen. Add the following two lines to the end of the file:

```
LDREMOTE
LOAD RSPX
```

Go ahead and save the file and return to the Available NCF Files Options menu. Next, choose the appropriate options to view (edit) the AUTOEXEC.NCF and STARTUP.NCF configuration files so that you can answer the questions listed here:

Question 9: Which configuration file loads the LAN driver? Which one loads the disk driver?

Question 10: What time server type is designated for this server?

Question 11: If you have an Ethernet network board, what frame type is being used?

Next, press Esc once to return to the Installation options menu. Choose the appropriate options from this menu to answer the following questions:

Question 12: What percentage of the NetWare partition is reserved for the hot fix area?

Question 13: Is this disk mirrored?

Question 14: What volume block size is being used for SYS:, and why? On the SYS: volume, are file compression, block suballocation, and data migration turned on or off?

Question 15: For how many connections is this server currently licensed?

Question 16: Which menu choice would you select to install DOS/ Windows Client files?

7 • Let's leave INSTALL.NLM and move onto the MONITOR.NLM utility. To load the MONITOR.NLM utility, type:

```
LOAD MONITOR
```

Press the Tab key to expand the General Information window.

Question 17: How long has your server been up and what do the four sets of numbers separated by colons represent? At what level is your CPU processor utilization? What is the total number of cache buffers currently being used? What is the number of current service processes in use? How many licensed connections are available at the moment? Press Esc to contract the General Information window.

Question 18: What is the server's hot fix status? Have any blocks been redirected to the hot fix area?

Question 19: What protocol(s) is/are currently supported on your server?

Question 20: What is the load filename of the NetWare 4.1 Directory Services Module? What is the size of this file?

Question 21: Finally, cruise over to Processor Utilization. Which NetWare 4 process occupies the most server CPU time?

8 • Now let's exit MONITOR and warp ahead to SERVMAN. To load SERVMAN, type:

```
LOAD SERVMAN
```

Question 22: Which general statistics overlap MONITOR functionality?

Question 23: Explore some SET parameters. What console command could be used instead of SERVMAN to change SET parameters?

Question 24: Next, switch to the server console without exiting SERVMAN. What method did you use? Next, check out the RMF Available Options menu. What method did you use to activate it?

Question 25: Which option is similar to one found in INSTALL.NLM? How is this one different?

Question 26: Press Esc to switch back to the server console. Use the appropriate console command to activate the RIP tracking screen. What command did you use? What's ACME's tree name? How about the IPX internal network number of CHARITY_INC? Where else can you get this information?

Question 27: Switch to the server console and send yourself a message. What command did you use? Acknowledge receipt of the message. How did you do so? Aren't such messages annoying? How can you set your workstation so that it does not receive messages from other users?

9 • Turn off the RIP tracking screen and exit the SERVMAN utility.

Question 28: What method could you use to review a quick list of NetWare 4 console commands that are available?

Question 29: Use a console command to see what NLMs are currently loaded. Which console command did you use? What NLM would give you a count of the NLMs that are currently loaded?

10 • Exit RCONSOLE, log off the network, and call it a day! Very good, you lived through the exploratorium without a scratch. Now, wasn't that fun?

See Appendix C for answers.

CHAPTER 14

NetWare 4 Printing

Adding users to NetWare 4 printing is like putting Godzilla in a mosh pit.

Now that you've lived through the life span of a LAN, I think you're ready to discover one of the greatest mysteries of life—printing. The meaning of life?—Nah. The Great Pyramids?—Nah. The Sphinx?—No chance. Printing has them all beat. More brain cells have been lost pondering NetWare printing than any other philosophical question.

Why? It's not that printing itself is so puzzling. As a matter of fact, the concept of printing is fairly easy to comprehend—you click a button on the workstation, and a piece of paper comes out of the printer down the hall. No rocket science here. It's true, the fundamental architecture of NetWare 4 printing is solid—rock solid. So why is it such a mystery? One word—users! It's the users' fault. They introduce so much complexity to printing, it's a wonder the paper finds its way anywhere, let alone to the correct printer. And to make matters worse, users expect too much:

- ▸ They want the page to be formatted correctly every time.

- ▸ They want their print jobs to arrive at the "correct" printer (when they don't even know what that means).

- ▸ They always want their jobs to come out first.

So how do you possibly satisfy the lofty expectations of your users while maintaining a rock solid NetWare 4 printing architecture? That's the greatest mystery of them all. Fortunately, Novell is on your side, and they've come up with some answers. The NetWare 4 printing system has been improved dramatically in several ways—easier setup, better management, more flexibility. They certainly haven't solved your mystery entirely, but they've given you some great tools to help you crack the case—and we're gonna learn all about them.

In this chapter, we're going to explore this great printing mystery and discover some startling answers. You're going to learn about the four steps of printing setup, all the great tools available for printing management, and the future of NetWare printing through NDPS. But first, we need to spend a few moments meditating on the true essence of printing. You must become one with the printer. It works, trust me.

The Essence of Printing

Now, repeat after me—I *am* a printer, I *am* a printer. The best way to handle NetWare 4 printing is to *be* NetWare 4 printing. This is the essence of printing.

Actually, the essence of printing is a little more technical than that. It is a wondrous journey from the user's workstation to the network printer down the hall. Here's how it works:

- ▶ Capturing—The job moves from the local workstation to the NetWare 4 server.

- ▶ Moving to the queue—It waits in line (first come; first served).

- ▶ The print server—The brains behind the process.

- ▶ At the printer—Finally, the print job arrives at the printer and prints correctly (fingers crossed).

This is the Printing Journey. But before we take a closer look at the Journey, let's take a history lesson in network printing. Get out your notebooks.

ZEN

"School, thank God for school. I need those seven hours of personal time. I mean, how can I continue to be the bright, vivacious Nanny everyone knows and loves if I have to spend all day with the kids?"

Nanny Fine

GETTING STARTED

We already know what a great job NetWare does with its file services, but printing is just as important to users. Initially, all users need access to file storage and shared print services to get the most out of NetWare.

Setting up and using printing services under NetWare can be a challenging part of setting up the network, but printing isn't as difficult as it seems—especially if you understand the system's essence. This chapter will give you some insight into the overall architecture of network printing, and in the process should make print services setup a whole lot easier.

Printing By Yourself

Most people are familiar with printing from a local workstation. In this scenario, a PC or other station has a standalone printer (a LaserJet, dot matrix, or other type of printer) that is dedicated to that station. With a dedicated printer, you have much less to worry about when it comes to printing documents. Issues such as *print drivers* or notification when the print job is complete do not apply. You can see the printer on your desk or nearby at least, and hopefully the correct print driver (with the proper version) has already been set up. When the document is printed, you need only reach over and grab it from the printer.

To better understand network printing, it helps to have a solid foundation of how local printing works. Starting from the beginning, the workstation has one or more local ports. Most PCs have at least one *parallel* port, labeled LPT1, LPT2, and so on. Many PCs also have a *serial* port as well. Serial ports typically are used as communication ports (that is, for modems), because they work faster than do parallel ports.

When you begin printing (if a printer is attached), the default output for printing is LPT1. LPT1 outputs to parallel port one, LPT2 outputs to parallel port two, and so on. Serial output is not enabled by default. If you print something, the software program you are using will usually default to LPT1. Otherwise, it may ask you which port you prefer (LPT1–LPT*n*).

Once you have hit the magic button to print something, the machine takes over. If you are running strictly DOS (no Windows in sight), then the machine may halt while printing. This is because DOS is set up to do only one thing at a time, but there are ways to trick DOS into not halting your machine, for example, by using the PRINT command. This command will take the print data and store it locally on the hard disk while it feeds the data to the printer in the background. This will allow you to do other things while the system is printing (for more information on the PRINT command, see your DOS reference manual). If you don't trick the computer, you'll have to wait for the document (or other print job) to finish printing before the machine will return control back to you (just like the old *Outer Limits* program, huh!).

If you are printing to a serial port under DOS, you'll need to do a bit of preparation. First, you must *redirect* the LPT output from the parallel port to a serial port. This is done using another DOS command called MODE. The MODE command works similarly to how network printing works in general. MODE simply takes LPT1 output and redirects it to the serial port. The program *thinks* it's sending to the LPT port. DOS takes the output, however, and streams it to the serial device (see Figure 14.1).

F I G U R E 14.1

Printing By Yourself

If you are using Windows (3.x or Windows 95), there is a neat little program called Print Manager. Print Manager can be used to manage local printing from Windows. It also provides the same capabilities as the DOS PRINT program—such as the ability to spool the print data locally and feed it to the printer. Print Manager has a few more features than PRINT. For example, it will allow you to view the current printing job, delete it, or postpone it.

Typically, when you are printing to the network, those features are already provided by NetWare utilities, thereby making Print Manager functions unnecessary. Many users will disable Print Manager when using NetWare for this reason. Print Manager can actually slow network printing because the print job will be spooled once locally and then again to the network queue.

Instead of disabling Print Manager, you can select the Print Net Jobs Direct option (select Options and then Network Settings from the Print Manager). This will enable any network print jobs to spool directly to a NetWare queue and bypass local hard disk spooling. Check out the screen in Figure 14.2.

F I G U R E 14.2

*Network Printing in
Microsoft Windows*

Once you attach a workstation to a network, the rules change a little. Some considerations are:

1 • Does the workstation have the proper driver for the network printer?

2 • How will you know when the document has completed printing?

3 • How does the server know when you have stopped sending print data?

4 • What if the printer runs out of paper? How will you or the administrator be notified?

Printing on a Network

The flow for network printing works something like this: The user has enabled printing to a network device from the workstation, or the administrator has automatically enabled it via a batch file (AUTOEXEC.BAT) or a login script (Container, System, Personal, and so on). This is similar to using the MODE command under DOS except that when an application prints, the output gets redirected to a queue on a server somewhere. The workstation command line utility to enable printing is called CAPTURE.

When CAPTURE is executed, the local LPT port that is being redirected to the network is specified. By default, this is usually LPT1. With this approach, the application may send output via LPT2 and the NetWare shell knows to capture data coming from the LPT2 port and redirect it to the appropriate queue. As a default, the CAPTURE command automatically assumes that data will be sent via LPT1. Most applications also assume that this is the default port on which to send data. Remember, the LPT port is merely a channel, port, or stream as far as the application knows. It may *point* at a parallel port, a serial port, a file, or the network queue. This concept is shown in Figure 14.3.

F I G U R E 14.3

Printing on a Network

Understanding Print Queues Now that capturing is on, the user starts to print via the application, DOS, or Windows. The output can be an existing file (such as DATA.TXT) or raw data from a word processing program (such as WordPerfect). The data being printed will be sent to an area on a specified server called a *queue*. Queues are nothing more than a subdirectory with a *.QDR extension. The data will be spooled into an automatically created file. When the user signals that he/she is done sending data, the file is closed and prepared for printing.

Understanding Print Servers Now that the data file is closed and ready, it can be serviced from the QUEUE directory. A *print server* is a device that is assigned to watch a particular queue or queues. When it sees a job waiting to be serviced, it will open the job (file) and start to read from it. The print server will then print the data in the file to a printer attached to the print server. *Which* printer it sends the file to depends on the setup of the print server (see "NetWare 4 Printing Setup" section). See Figure 14.4 for a quick preview.

FIGURE 14.4

Understanding Print Servers

Understanding Printers   As the print server services the request, it attempts to print the data to a locally attached printer (physically attached to the print server) or a remotely attached printer (perhaps a printer attached to a workstation but remotely attached via software to the print server). If the printer is a remote printer, the print server *thinks* it is attached locally, when in fact the data is being sent across the network to where the remote printer physically resides.

Once the contents of the data file have been printed, the data file residing in the queue will be deleted to recover the disk space. In addition, if it has been set up to do so, a notification will be sent to the user (and possibly others) that the job has been successfully printed and is ready to be picked up.

QUIZ

**Let's begin our NetWare "sleuthing" with a simple one. Here goes....
At a college reunion, a group of men and women were discussing their lives after they had received their undergraduate degrees. It turned out that everybody in the group had gone on to receive an advanced degree, so each of them had two degrees. Each degree holder had both a B.A. and an M.S., an M.A., an M.B.A., or an M.F.A. Half of them had an M.S., one quarter had an M.A., one sixth had an M.B.A., and just one had an M.F.A. How many were there in total?**

(Q14-1)
(See Appendix C for all quiz answers.)

THE PRINTING JOURNEY

This is the beginning of your printing journey. Hold on to your hat.

Now, we will cover the details of printing under a NetWare environment from a PC workstation perspective. Two areas will be covered: printing from DOS and printing from Windows. This discussion assumes the reader has some knowledge of DOS and Windows in order to understand the elements of network printing.

This section also assumes that a printing system has already been set up (print server, print queue, and remote/local printer) and that the user has been granted access. If not, you can jump ahead to the section "NetWare 4 Printing Setup" and then return to this section.

Capturing

To enable network printing, you must first tell the network client (for example, VLM or NETX) that you wish to print to the network. You can do this by using the DOS command CAPTURE or by using the Windows tool NWUSER (see Figure 14.5).

FIGURE 14.5

Capturing a Local Port

FILESERVER

Queue

Capture

WS

Workstation   Printer

Capturing with DOS The CAPTURE command is included with NetWare and allows you to start and end network printing. It can be used in a DOS-only environment, or it can be executed *before* starting Windows 3.x to allow capturing under Windows. In Windows 95 environments, you can use the Win95 Print Manager or NWUSER (a NetWare tool).

CAPTURE has several command line options that allow you to customize how the network capture will work. These options include:

▸ /?—This option will show help for the CAPTURE command if you need it. You can also use CAPTURE /? ALL to show every possible option and explanation for CAPTURE.

- ▶ /SH (Show)—This is a very useful command to see how you are currently captured to the network. CAPTURE /SH will show all LPT ports currently enabled for network printing as well as other flags such as banners, copies, and so on. The Show parameter will *not* initiate a print capture. It is for informational purposes only.

- ▶ /S (Server)—This option allows you to specify the server to which you want to print. In NetWare 4 environments, this is usually unnecessary because the user is oblivious to servers per se. When capturing, the user can just specify the printer name using a distinguished name (for example, HP5-P1.CRIME.TOKYO.ACME), and the server will automatically be found and attached. In a NetWare 3 environment, however, /S can be used to point to a server with a particular printer/queue that you wish to use. If you are not logged in/attached to that particular server, then the CAPTURE command will attempt to login as GUEST. If the GUEST account does not exist, printing on that server will be denied to the user. This is a good reason (in an open environment) to keep the GUEST account around on a public NetWare 3 server.

- ▶ /Q (Queue)—This command line option allows the user to specify the queue to which data should be sent. In a NetWare 3 environment, it can be combined with the /S option to specify a server name and queue name that the user desires. In a NetWare 4 network, the queue name can be a relative distinguished name (for example, HP5-PQ1) or a distinguished name (for example, HP5-PQ1.CRIME.TOKYO.ACME). If a distinguished name is used, there is much less of a chance of ambiguity between printer and queue names. For example, if the user is in context CYBER.WHITE.CRIME.TOKYO.ACME, and he/she wishes to print to a queue in BLUE.CRIME.TOKYO.ACME, there is a chance that the relative distinguished name HPIII-PQ1 may exist in both locations (and it does). In such a case, if a user types in the command CAPTURE /Q=HPIII-PQ1, the printer captured will be the one in CYBER.WHITE.CRIME.TOKYO.ACME.

▸ /AU (AutoEndCap)—This option allows the application to decide if the user is done sending capture data. For example, when a user sends data, how does the network shell know when the application/user is done sending data? There are three ways:

1. The user stops sending capture data (via the CAPTURE command—discussed later).

2. The application sends a NetWare-specific command to signal the end of capture data (this is the case with network-aware applications such as WordPerfect).

3. The shell assumes you are done via AutoEndCap or timeouts. When AutoEndCap is enabled, the shell assumes you are done sending data if you leave the application that began sending capture data. Consider a user who enables capture (via the CAPTURE command), sends a print job via the application (such as WordPerfect), and then exits the application. The shell can safely assume that since the user exited, he/she was done sending data. If AutoEndCap were *not* enabled, the user would still have to terminate CAPTURE to signal the end of capture data.

▸ /TI (TimeOut)—This option is similar to the AutoEndCap command, except that the user does not need to exit the application. Instead, a timeout is specified when capture was started (such as CAPTURE TI=8). This means the network shell will assume that once capture data has been sent, if no more data has been sent after 8 seconds, the job will automatically be completed and scheduled for printing. The only problem with this command is what happens when an application pauses between spurts of data. For example, if a database program were sending data and then paused 10 seconds before sending page totals, the first data would be sent as one print job and the page totals would be sent as a second, thereby violating the integrity of the job.

▶ /K (Keep/No Keep)—This option tells the shell what to do if something interrupts the flow of data from the workstation to the queue on the server. For example, if a print job were started and then interrupted when the workstation lost power, all data sent to the queue up to that point would be lost if Keep were not enabled. If Keep is enabled, any data sent up to that point will be printed.

▶ /T (Tabs)—The Tabs option was included from the earlier versions of NetWare when printing documents was not always done through the application. As a result, when a document was printed, the proper spaces were not inserted for a tab character. Therefore, the NetWare shell was enabled to observe a tab character during the print process, remove it, and send the proper amount of spaces to the printer. This option was enabled in versions of NetWare 3.11 and below. The default amount of spaces per tab character was eight. Current versions no longer support this as a default. This is because most applications now format their own printing and convert tabs to the proper spaces. This option, if enabled, can cause printing problems since some graphics programs or other raw text may have characters that signify a tab. If T is enabled, the shell will strip the tab, send the spaces, and you'll end up with garbled print output. NT (No Tabs) is the default.

▶ /C (Copies)—This option specifies the number of copies you want of the printout. The default is 1.

▶ /B (Banner)—This option (enabled by default) will send a print banner at the beginning of the print job. You can specify the name of the person that submitted the document as well as the name of the job itself (B=<user name> and N=<job name>). If nothing is specified, then the document will either be the name of the file being printed (if an existing file is being printed) or PRN: if the print job is output from an application. The name will be the username of the person that submitted it.

▶ /NB (No Banner)—This option disables the Banner option. It is usually used when a small office is involved or with a local workgroup.

▶ /NFF (NoFormFeed)—This option prevents an additional page from being sent at the end of the print job. This may be necessary with some applications that do not send a form feed after a print job has been submitted.

▶ /FF (FormFeed)—This option sends a form feed after the job has been completed (default). This is necessary when the application doesn't do this automatically, since the last page of the document may not be ejected by the printer (especially when using a LaserJet printer). NFF (No Form Feed) turns off form feed.

▶ /L=n (Local Port Number)—DOS provides several channels for print output. The first and primary channel is LPT1. There can be more than one, however. Many applications today can output print data on LPT2–LPTn. Most default to LPT1. If your application is outputting on LPT2, you need to use this command to tell NetWare which LPT port is being used. For example, you might have a local printer attached to LPT1 and you want network printing to go out via LPT2. The CAPTURE command would look like this: CAPTURE /L=2. That way, through the application, you can print to LPT1 and the output will go to the local printer. If you print out to LPT2, however, the output will go to the network.

▶ /F (Form)—Forms allow network users to share the same printer for a variety of functions. When (and if) forms are defined, a user can submit a job of a particular form type and the print server will ensure that the printer being used is ready to accept a print job of that form type. For example, this option would allow one user to submit a purchase requisition (that requires a preprinted form), while another user could submit an invoice (also requiring a preprinted form). When the job is submitted, a form name or number is used to specify which form is to be used when printing the job. Form names and numbers are defined using the PRINTDEF utility.

▸ /CR (Create)—This option allows the user to send output to a file instead of to a print queue. When this option is specified, the user must also specify the filename to which output should be directed. If the file does not exist, it will be created automatically. After the first print job output has completed, subsequent print jobs will be sent to a normal queue. For example, if we typed **CAPTURE /CR=SYS:TEST.TXT /Q=.HP5-PQ1.CRIME.TOKYO.ACME**, the data will be captured to the printer HP5-P1, but the initial output will go to file TEST.TXT. We then submit data for print (through the application or an existing file). The data will go into the file TEST.TXT instead of being printed! If we print again, the data will be spooled to HP5-P1 and printed on the physical printer. This parameter is useful when you need to encapsulate an entire print job (printer escape codes and all) into a file. Another user could merely submit the entire file for printing (without the source application being available), and the data will print successfully.

▸ /NOTI (Notify)—With this option, provided the print server has been created to support it, a message will be sent to the user *after* the job has been printed successfully. In addition, the print server can be created to notify the user or other responsible parties (such as Admin or the print server administrator) if any problems arose (for example, if the printer ran out of paper or if it went off-line). NNOTI disables notification.

▸ /EC (EndCapture)—This option is used to return LPT output to the local port (usually the local parallel port). Since the CAPTURE command could have been started for LPT2, LPT3, and so on, ENDCAP can be used with the L=n switch to turn off CAPTURE on a specific port.

A sample CAPTURE command might look like this:

```
CAPTURE /NB /L=2 /K /Q=HP5-PQ1.CRIME.TOKYO.ACME /TI=10
```

For this print job:

▸ No banner will be prefixed to the print job.

▸ Output will be via LPT2.

▸ Data will be kept and printed *if* the capture is not formally closed.

▸ The queue to be used is HP5-PQ1.CRIME.TOKYO.ACME.

▸ A timeout of 10 seconds will be used.

Capturing with Windows   There are two options for enabling CAPTURE under Windows:

▸ Use the CAPTURE command, and then start Windows.

▸ Use the NWUSER utility.

Since we have already covered CAPTURE, let's look at the NWUSER utility. To start NWUSER, you may find the icon under the NetWare Tools Program Group. This is installed as part of the NetWare client that was installed on your NetWare workstation. NWUSER is simply a launcher for the Novell Driver for Windows. Another option is to launch File Manager and choose Disk/Network Connections. This will also launch the NetWare Tools utility.

TIP

If you have a sound card, choose the NetWare Settings option from the button bar (the one that has a key) and click once over the Novell icon in the upper left-hand corner!

Once the tool is running, choose the printer icon (third icon from the left on the Button Bar). This will display all the printers available to you in the browser window to the right. You can also walk the tree to find other printers and queues in your network. You will also see any queues available for any 3.x/2.x servers that you are logged into.
To capture to a printer, you may do one of two things:

▎•   Select the printer/queue you want and then select Capture or merely drag and drop the chosen printer from the right window to the desired LPT port on the left. Once completed, you can double-click on the newly captured printer and select printing options. These options correspond to the flags used under CAPTURE at the DOS prompt (see Figure 14.6).

*Capture Settings in
NetWare User Tools for
Windows*

One other note: You can select the Permanent option after capturing a printer. This will automatically recapture the printer every time you start Windows. If it is a 3.x/2.x printer/queue, you may be required to login to the server again before capture is complete.

Note: Printers and queues are referred to in the same context here since they are so closely related. More will be explained later, but for clarification's sake, a print job always must be submitted to a queue before it can be serviced by a printer via a print server. To minimize complexity, Novell allows you to choose a printer by name and you will be captured automatically to the queue that services that printer. This way, you don't need to know which queue services which printer.

To end CAPTURE under Windows, you can drag the printer mapping from the left window to the right. You can also select the desired printer/queue and choose End Capture from the lower button bar.

ZEN

*"Don't underestimate the power of these adenoids. I had next-door
neighbors move closer to the airport."*

Nanny Fine

Moving to the Queue

Once capturing has been started, data is sent either in the form of an existing file or by sending print output via an application.

Before the data is sent, however, a subtle thing may be happening. If you analyze the anatomy of a print stream (see Figure 14.7), there are three parts: the print header, the print body (data sent), and the print tail. The purpose of these other data become important when drivers are involved.

FIGURE 14.7

The Anatomy of a Print
Stream

Print Stream

Header
1. Reset (<ESC>E)
2. Bold
3. Landscaped

DATA

Tail
1. Re-initialize
Printer

Print Queue

Workstation

NetWare allows the user to specify escape codes that can be sent before the print data reaches the printer (*a print header*). And at the end of the print data, *a print tail* sends the proper escape codes to reset the printer to a default state. This leaves the printer ready for the next user. To use this feature of NetWare, two things must have been created: a PRINTDEF database, which includes escape code information for printers and modes of operation made up of these escape codes, as well as a Print Job Definition, which specifies details about how the capture should be handled. Remember the options for CAPTURE? Well these can be incorporated into a file stored in NDS that gets read and utilized when the user begins a CAPTURE. Any command line options used when executing the CAPTURE command will override the Print Job Definition options.

The print server's job is to control the flow of the print job from its beginning until it is finally printed on a printer *somewhere*. That somewhere is dictated by the queue typically.

Several server elements are involved in printing: the queue (which always resides on a server volume somewhere), the print server (which may reside on a file server, NetWare router, any other NLM platform, or even inside the printer itself), and finally the printer (which prints the data and notifies the print server of completion and any problems that may arise).

NetWare queue services are designed to provide more than just support for printing. Other applications can take advantage of the queue API under NetWare to service jobs based on a queuing mechanism. As a result, not all queue characteristics look related to printing.

A queue is basically comprised of a subdirectory stored on a volume of a server somewhere. Since the queue is there to hold files waiting to be printed, it must be on a storage area (volume) on a file server. Where the subdirectory exists is up to the person who created it. In NetWare 3 and below, the directories always existed under the SYS:SYSTEM subdirectory. NetWare 4 allows them to be placed on any volume at any level.

Once a print job has begun from the client, the queue servicing the request (selected by the user via CAPTURE, Print Job Settings, or NWUSER) will create a temporary file inside the queue's subdirectory. This file is used to keep track of the job as it flows through the system. One of the data kept in the file is the *Job Entry Record,* which contains information such as:

- ▸ When the job was submitted

- ▸ Who submitted the job

- ▸ Size of the data

- ▸ Whether the job can be printed immediately

- ▸ How many copies to print

And more. This information can be called up via NWADMIN or PCONSOLE. See Figure 14.8 for an example of the Print Job Detail screen in NWADMIN.

The queue also has security assigned to it. During setup, we can designate users, groups, or containers that may submit jobs to the queue. We can also restrict which print servers may service jobs from our queue. Finally, there is a security designation called Queue Manager. This entity, when designated, may delete jobs submitted by other users. In this manner, print queue administration may be delegated to other users.

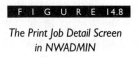

The Print Job Detail Screen
in NWADMIN

There are some utilities available that allow users and administrators to manage and view the flow of printing: These include PCONSOLE (under DOS) and NWADMIN (under Windows).

The Print Server

Once the print server is loaded and functioning, it must then login to the servers it is servicing in order to poll the queues it has been assigned. It is a very good idea to password-protect all the print servers in the network to minimize security problems.

Once the server is fully initialized, it will begin polling the queues it has been assigned and service print jobs within those queues. Some factors may affect which queues get serviced first. They include:

▸ Queue priorities—When a queue is assigned to a print server, a priority can be assigned. This priority tells the print server that if any jobs are waiting in the highest priority queue, it must service them once the currently serviced job has completed. This can be set up as part of security, allowing certain users to have better access to a printer than others. This would be the case if two queues were servicing the same physical printer: Users having access to the higher priority queue will have their jobs completed before the users that submitted jobs to a lesser priority queue.

▸ Forms servicing—This topic will be covered later in the chapter, but the Print Server Manager can designate how forms are serviced. As such, a print server may be required to service all forms of a particular type within a queue before it can move to the next queue. Or it may have to print all jobs that have a certain designated Form Type across all queues it is assigned to, before servicing jobs with a different form type.

TIP

Suppose print server Alpha were supporting Q1 and Q2. And further, assume it must service all jobs using a particular form before moving to the next form. If User1 submits a job of form type 0 into Q1 and User2 submits a job with form type 5 thereafter, User2 will have to wait if User3 submits a job of form type 0 into Q2 even if User3 submitted it *after* User2. Once User3's job is complete, the print server can begin to service jobs using form type 5.

Much like a print queue, print servers can have security designated.

▸ Print server users—These are users, groups, and containers that can view current jobs that are being serviced. Print server users can also abort their jobs if they wish.

▸ Print server operators—These are users, groups, and containers that can abort anyone's job currently being serviced. They can also view the status of any currently printing job.

Other things that can be controlled on print servers include how often the print server polls the assigned queues looking for jobs. As mentioned earlier, you can modify the queue priority and how forms get serviced using Admin utilities described later in this chapter.

When setting up print services, you should know the options available. The relationship of queues and print servers to printers can be:

▸ one to many

▸ one to one

▶ many to many

▶ many to one

At the Printer

Print servers usually reside at the file server, although they may reside as NLMs elsewhere, such as in a special third-party printer or NetWare router. Print servers, when created, are assigned the queues they are to service and which printers they will support. Unlike queues, print servers do not require disk storage; therefore, they can reside just about anywhere.

Once a print server has been initialized, it will first attempt to find any printers it is supposed to support. Print servers support two types of printers: local and remote. The print server software, in NLM form, is called PSERVER.NLM. PSERVER.NLM by itself does not know how to talk to a printer; therefore, a separate printer support module must be provided.

Local Printers   If the printer is local (as defined during print server creation), then the PSERVER.NLM loads a local NLM called NPRINTER.NLM. NPRINTER.NLM has a bidirectional communication with the print server, as well as a communication to the local port it is servicing. The local port is usually either a parallel or serial port.

This design has several advantages, including that:

▶ PSERVER can theoretically talk to devices other than serial and parallel ports.

▶ By design, NetWare SFTIII has two parts: one that talks to hardware (IOEngine) and one that is common to both servers. Using this method, the PSERVER resides in the shared engine and NPRINTER resides in the IOEngine.

Remote Printers   If the designated printer is a remote printer, PSERVER.NLM attempts to contact it using SPX as the communications method. This necessitates loading the NPRINTER.EXE module on a workstation that has the desired remote printer attached to it. Once NPRINTER.EXE has been loaded, a communication will be established and remote printing can be supported.

ZEN

"Some people say Yoga is a great way to keep your energy up. For me, it's a Snickers and a Diet Coke."

Nanny Fine

Just when you think you're at the end of your journey, the tour guide throws in a few side stops. Don't you just hate that? In our case, it's time to explore third-party printing solutions.

Third-party Printing Solutions

Several good add-ons are available for the NetWare printing system. These usually can augment the services already provided within the printing infrastructure.

For example, in a generic NetWare environment using remote printers, the job must go from the user to the queue, to the print server, and finally to the remote printer. Using a device that encapsulates these functions into one subsystem can greatly reduce the network traffic required to print. Two of these devices are the HP JetDirect Card and Intel's NetPort.

HP JetDirect This device resides in a printer (such as an HP LaserJet4M or 4SI) and acts as a peer device on the network. It can be configured either as a print server or as a remote printer.

Ideally, the JetDirect card will be configured as a print server. This would reduce the flow of network printing since the print job only has to go from the user to the queue, and then to the JetDirect card in the printer. The challenge is when you are running a system that the JetDirect card can't login to, for example, with an older JetDirect card and NetWare 4.

The other option is to set up the JetDirect as a remote printer. In this scenario, the JetDirect will have a name assigned to it when configured. This name must correspond to the name given to the remote printer when it was defined under NetWare. This way, the print server knows how to communicate with the JetDirect card. The down side is that you still have the same traffic, but you do not need a machine dedicated to support the remote printer.

Intel NetPort Intel's solution is similar to HP's, except an Intel NetPort can also be just a peer device on the network. It plugs into an Ethernet cable just like another node on the network. It can then have a standard parallel cable attached to it, enabling it to communicate with a standard printer (unlike the HP JetDirect card, which only plugs into HP printers).

The other options typically apply to the NetPort. Both modes can be supported, either as a remote printer or a print server.

These solutions also come with management software that allows the administrator to manage the print devices remotely. This software provides peer-to-peer communication with the print device.

Now, we're really at the end of our journey. They say, "A well-traveled person is an enlightened person." Do you feel well traveled? Do you feel enlightened? You should feel *something* right about now.

So, that's the essence of printing. It's not so bad. I think NetWare printing gets a bad rap. It's not very mysterious—you click a button on the workstation and your document comes out of the printer down the hall. Assuming, of course, that you set it up correctly. Now would be a good time to explore that aspect of NetWare 4 printing.

NetWare 4 Printing Setup

Welcome to NetWare 4 printing setup. Now that you understand the essence of printing, it's time to do something about it. This is where the mystery begins to unfold. This is where the clues appear. This is "Sherlock Holmes 101."

Creating print services for a NetWare 4 network requires a little bit of planning. In a simple environment, NetWare allows you to create a basic printing system by using the DOS utility PCONSOLE.

Under Windows, you must create the items separately and associate them. This is a relatively simple process—once you understand how printing works under NetWare. If you have read the previous section, this should appear relatively obvious.

As you recall, there are three elements to the printing system that must be present in order to print. They are:

▸ The queue—Used to store the print jobs on the way to the printer

▸ The print server—Polls the queue for jobs and prints them on assigned printers

▸ The printer—Defines whether the printer is local to the file server or remotely attached

You can use NWADMIN to create the NetWare 4 printing system. NWADMIN is a Windows-based graphical utility that integrates several aspects of managing NetWare, including rights assignments and user creation, into one easy-to-use application.

The order in which you create the print system items (queue, print server, and printer) really makes no difference. The most efficient way is to start with the queue since it is central to the printing system under NetWare. Here's how I like to do it:

▸ Step 1: Create the print queue

▸ Step 2: Create the printer

▸ Step 3: Create the print server

▸ Step 4: Activate the printing system

There you have it. Four simple steps. No mystery here. Let's take a closer look, and don't forget your NetWare magnifying glass.

ZEN

"I've often wondered how the British know what everyone's feeling. They all must wear mood rings."

Nanny Fine

STEP 1: CREATE THE PRINT QUEUE

It is important to remember that when you create a queue, it should be central to the users that are going to use it. When using NDS, you usually want to keep the queues and print servers proximal to each other.

TIP

NetWare 4 Printing Setup is closely related to NDS and partitioning. It is more efficient to have the area where the jobs get stored (Queue Volume) as close to the users as possible. If you reside in Camelot, it makes no sense to print something to a queue in Tokyo (unless you *want* the print job to print in Tokyo). See Chapter 9 for more information on replica distribution.

The first step is to choose the context where you create the queue. This is usually in the container where the users reside who will be using the queue the most.

To create the queue under NWADMIN, select Object/Create or select the container and press Insert. You'll be presented with a dialog box asking for the type of object you wish to create. Choose Print Queue and press Enter (see Figure 14.9). The items you need to define next are shown in Table 14.1 and Figure 14.9.

FIGURE 14.9

Step 1: Create the Print Queue

TABLE 14.1	PROPERTY	DESCRIPTION
Important Print Queue Properties	Directory Queue vs. Bindery Queue	If you are creating a regular queue (and we are), choose Directory Services Queue. A Bindery Reference Queue can service jobs out of a queue that resides on a 2.x or 3.x server. This can be useful if you have a mixed environment and need to support queues from a single location.
		In addition, you can submit a job to Bindery Reference Queue and it will be sent automatically to the reference queue on the 3.x server.

TABLE 14.1	PROPERTY	DESCRIPTION
Important Print Queue Properties	Print Queue Name	Usually you want to name a queue descriptively. It is easier to find a queue named CANONBJ-PQ1 than just Bubbble Printer.
	Print Queue Volume	This is the physical space where the job will be stored as it is spooled and when it is serviced. Therefore, this property must reference a volume somewhere in the NetWare 4 tree.
		In addition, the container in which the queue is created must have rights to that volume in order to create print jobs there.

REAL WORLD

In previous versions of NetWare, the queue was *always* stored under SYS:SYSTEM in the volume SYS:. In NetWare 4, the NWADMIN utility will create a subdirectory off of the root of the volume chosen (which can be other than SYS: now!) and call it QUEUES. This is where the data will be stored for the queue.

At this point, you can choose to define other queue properties (which will be brought up in a dialog box) or let NetWare create the queue and allow you to create another. For our example, let's click the Define Additional Properties check box, then click on Create.

Data added to the Print Queue Identification page (such as Other Name and Location) can be useful when searching for queues under NWADMIN. This allows the user to find a queue based on unique information entered here, but the additional data is purely optional (see Figure 14.10 and Table 14.2).

*The Print Queue
Identification Page in
NWADMIN*

Print Queue : HP5-PQ1

Identification

Name:	HP5-PQ1.CRIME.TOKYO.ACME
Volume:	WHITE-SRV1_SYS.WHITE.CRIME.TOKYO.ACME
Other Name:	Canon BubbleJet Print Queue
Description :	Really cool print queue.
Location:	Sherlock Holmes' Office
Department:	Crime-Fighting
Organization:	ACME

Operator Flags
☒ Allow Users To Submit Print Jobs
☒ Allow Service By Current Print Servers
☒ Allow New Print Servers To Attach

Buttons: Identification, Assignments, Operator, Users, Job List

Buttons: OK   Cancel   Help

*Additional Print Queue
Pages*

PRINT QUEUE PAGE	DESCRIPTION
Assignments	The Assignments page is a view-only screen used to show which printer(s) the queue is servicing and which print server is servicing this queue.
Operator	The Operator page contains some of the most important information for the queue. Print queue operators can do several valuable management items, such as: Create new jobs in the queue Delete jobs submitted by other users Affect the availability of the queue Place holds on their own submitted jobs Place holds on jobs submitted by other users Grant access to other users to use the queue By default, the user that created the queue is the queue operator. You can add other users if necessary.

TABLE 14.2	PRINT QUEUE PAGE	DESCRIPTION
Additional Print Queue Pages	Users	The Print Queue Users page is the most important item for the queue because it is where you designate who may use the queue (that is, who may submit jobs via CAPTURE or through Windows). By default, anyone in the container where the queue was created as well as any containers below this container may submit print jobs to this queue. To limit this, you can assign other objects such as Groups, Organizational Roles, or specific users the ability to submit print jobs to the queue.
	Job List	Job List is a management function available to users and operators alike. It allows a user to view the current jobs in the queue as well as change details about the job. If you are a print queue operator, you can change aspects of jobs submitted by other users in addition to your own. To do this, highlight the job you wish to change and click on Job Details. If the job is not actively being serviced, you can change aspects of the job such as number of copies, form feed after print, and so on.

A print queue operator can change the priority of a job by changing it's *sequence number*. For example, changing a job from sequence 3 to sequence 1 bumps the first job to sequence 2, 3 to 4, and so on. More of this function will be covered in the section "NetWare 4 Printing Management." |

STEP 2: CREATE THE PRINTER

The next step is to create a printer that will be serviced by the queue. Creating the printer is similar to creating the queue. Choose the container where the printer will be stored by selecting it with your mouse and pressing Insert (or choosing Create from the Object option on the toolbar). Choose Printer and give it a descriptive name. Click on Define Additional Properties and choose Create.

TIP

You don't have to create the printer, print server, and queue in the same container. You can locate them in three different areas and then associate them. For our example, it is easier to create them all in the same container.

You can use the Printer Identification page to provide information that NDS can use for searches as well as to provide more descriptive information for users and other administrators. Check out Figure 14.11 and Table 14.3.

FIGURE 14.11

The Printer Identification Page in NWADMIN

```
┌─────────────────────── Printer : CANONBJ-P1 ──────────────────────┐
│ Identification                                                     │
│                                                      ┌─Identification─┐
│   Name:          CANONBJ-P1.WHITE.CRIME.TOKYO.ACME   ├─Assignments──┤
│   Other Name:    Canon BubbleJet Printer         [▼][…] ├─Configuration─┤
│   Description :  Really cool printer.            [▲]  ├─Notification──┤
│                                                 [▼]  ├─Features─────┤
│   Network Address:                              [▼]  ├─See Also─────┤
│   Location:      Sherlock Holmes' Office     [▼][…]  ├─Printer Status─┤
│   Department:    Crime-Fighting              [▼][…]  └──────────────┘
│   Organization:  ACME                        [▼][…]
│
│  [ OK ]  [ Cancel ]  [ Help ]
└───────────────────────────────────────────────────────────────────┘
```

TABLE 14.3

Additional Printer Pages

PRINTER PAGE	DESCRIPTION
Assignments	This page is where you tell the printer which queue(s) it will be servicing. You may have one printer that services multiple queues or multiple printers servicing one queue. If you have more than one queue per printer, you can assign a *priority*, the highest being 1. Any jobs submitted to a higher-priority queue will get serviced before any waiting jobs in a lower-priority queue (see Figure 14.12).

T A B L E 14.3	PRINTER PAGE	DESCRIPTION
Additional Printer Pages	Assignments (continued)	The default queue is used when a user chooses to capture to the network by using a printer name instead of a queue name. When you choose a printer name, the job will be sent to the default queue.

For this option, choose the queue that you just created. |
| | Configuration | This option determines whether the printer is physically attached to the print server or remotely attached to a workstation.

The first option, Printer Type, determines what kind of printer this is. Typically, it is either serial or parallel. The other options (such as AppleTalk and XNP) are configured and used with additional software.

The Communication option specifies the local port that will be used. If the printer is polled, it will be sent printer output in a polled fashion instead of using interrupts to control print flow. Manual Load indicates that the remote printer software (NPRINTER.EXE) will be loaded instead of the local NPRINTER.NLM. If you choose Auto Load, the print server will know to load the NPRINTER.NLM at the server to service a locally attached printer.

Another security feature of remote printers is the ability to limit the network address that the remote printer can use. This way, only the allowed address can load NPRINTER.EXE and support the print server as a remotely defined printer. |
| | Notification | The Notification page is where you determine who will be notified in the event the printer has a problem. This is different than notifying the user when the print job submitted is complete. |

(continued)

T A B L E 14.3	PRINTER PAGE	DESCRIPTION
Additional Printer Pages (continued)	Notification (continued)	The default user is whomever submitted the print job. In a small office, this setting works just fine, but in a larger network, this setting is usually deleted and an IS group or person is added instead. This makes servicing the printer (for example, when it is out of paper) the job of such a person.

You can also specify how often (in minutes) the person gets notified. First indicates how long before the first message is sent, and Next is the interval at which subsequent messages will be sent. |
| | Features | This page allows more descriptive data to be placed in NDS, which allows for better searching. For example, a user/administrator could search for printers supporting PCL with 4 MB memory and a fax card. This search could occur network-wide or could be limited to a subarea of the directory tree. |

F I G U R E 14.12

The Printer Assignments Page in NWADMIN

REAL WORLD

The Printer Configuration page in NWADMIN is where you configure options for third-party printer support such as HP JetDirect cards or Intel's Netport. These devices can act either as a remote printer or as a print server to a NetWare server. Older versions of these products may only be used as remote printers and not as print servers in a NetWare 4 environment.

STEP 3: CREATE THE PRINT SERVER

To create a print server, use the NWADMIN utility. Select the container that will store the print server and press Insert while the container is highlighted. Choose Print Server off of the list and then choose OK.

First, you need to give the print server a name. Once again, descriptive names work best (such as WHITE-PS1). This will help you search for print servers later.

After entering the name, click on the Define Additional Properties check box and choose Create. The Print Server Identification page will appear (see Figure 14.13). Table 14.4 lists the basic information you will need to provide to complete print server creation.

F I G U R E 14.13

The Print Server Identification Page in NWADMIN

T A B L E 14.4	PRINTER	DESCRIPTION
Additional Print Server Pages	Assignments	This page allows you to tell the print server which printers it will be servicing. Note that it may support several (up to 128) for one print server. Naturally, not all the printers can be attached physically to the print server; the rest would be attached remotely. Select the printer you just created by choosing Add (see Figure 14.14). The printer will be added with a *Printer Number*. Usually this number will not be referenced on a day-to-day basis. One or two NetWare utilities still require it, such as Print Server Control (PSC), which is covered in the "NetWare 4 Printing Management" section.
	Users	Users information is not necessary for a user to print, even if this print server is servicing jobs in queues where the user has submitted a print job. This page is provided so that users can check the status of a print server using the management utilities (such as PSC or NWADMIN). If the user never needs to do this (for example, if printer management is handled by IS), then the user doesn't need the print server user status. By default, all users in the container where the print server was created are given the print server user status.
	Operator	Print server operators are similar to queue operators in that they can manage the print server. For example, print server operators may take printers off-line remotely, shut down the print server, and abort jobs in process.
	Auditing Log	This page allows you to enable an auditing function for the print server. You can limit the size of the audit file as well as how many jobs it will keep in its auditing log. The file can be printed or it can be viewed under NWADMIN.
	Print Layout	This is a very handy function in that you can graphically see the printing layout in one screen. This function works for all printers and queues associated with this print server.

TABLE 14.4	PRINTER	DESCRIPTION
Additional Print Server Pages	Print Layout (continued)	An additional function called Status allows the print server operator to view the status of all elements in the printing hierarchy. Simply select one of the printing components and click on Status. Figure 14.15 shows an example of the Print Server Status screen.

FIGURE 14.14

The Print Server Assignments Page in NWADMIN

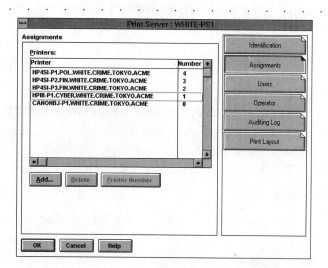

FIGURE 14.15

Monitoring Print Server Status in NWADMIN

When you create a print server, you should set a password for the print server for security reasons. You can set a password under the Print Server Creation screen by pressing the Change Password button. You will be asked for the password at server load time.

ZEN

"Danny bought me some lingerie for my birthday. It was so inappropriate. It's a good thing my mother's birthday was two days later or I'd still be stuck with the thing."

Nanny Fine

STEP 4: ACTIVATE THE PRINTING SYSTEM

Now that the configuration is set, the last step is to start the print server. This is done either at the server or remotely using RCONSOLE.

To start the print server, load PSERVER.NLM at the console by typing:

LOAD PSERVER

This will bring up the menu for PSERVER. It will show the context that the server is in within the directory tree. If you need to change where the print server is, you can either type in the new context or browse by pressing Enter. Selecting ".." moves up in the tree or you can select another container by choosing a container name and hitting enter. Once you have found the print server, load it by highlighting it and pressing Enter.

Three things will happen:

1 • The print server will load. Any printers that are locally defined for this print server will be supported by NPRINTER.NLM. NPRINTER.NLM is loaded automatically if it is needed by local printers. The local printers will have a status of "Waiting for Jobs" once this is complete.

2 • Remote printers defined for this server will attempt to find a remote printer. If they cannot, they will wait for remote printer software to contact them (either NetWare's NPRINTER.EXE or a third-party solution such as HP's JetDirect card or Intel's Netport).

3 •   The print server will ask for a password before loading. Passwords are desirable especially in larger networks. If you need to add or change a print server password, use NWADMIN and select the print server. PCONSOLE also allows you to change passwords as well.

The print server Main Menu provides you with two options: Printer Status and Print Server Information.

Printer Status

This option allows you to view status of all printers defined for this print server (see Figure 14.16). You can also execute some printer management functions such as:

▶ Abort currently printing jobs

▶ Stop printer output

▶ Start printer output

▶ Eject a page (form feed)

In addition, you can change how forms (discussed later) get serviced on the selected printer. All of these functions can also be done via NWADMIN and PSC (a DOS utility).

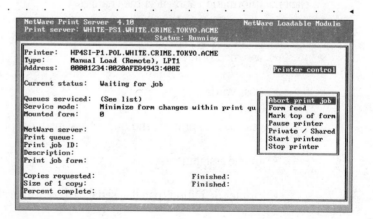

F I G U R E 14.16

The Print Server Status Window

Print Server Information

The Print Server Information screen has two functions:

▸ Allows you to view print server information such as version and name

▸ Allows the print server to be shut down gracefully

Ideally, the print server should be shut down either remotely (via NWADMIN or PCONSOLE) or at the server using this option.

To shut down the print server, choose Current Status and press Enter. You can then shut down the print server in one of two ways:

1 • Immediately—With this option, any currently running jobs are suspended. They will continue when the print server is restarted.

2 • Unload after active print jobs—This allows any printing jobs to complete before the print server terminates.

In either case, the print server will advertise that it is no longer available and then terminate. Let's take a look at how changes to print servers take effect.

When you make the following changes, the print server must be unloaded and reloaded at the file server/router where the print server is running. This way, NetWare can read the new information and effect the changes:

Changes made directly to a print server:

▸ assigned printers

▸ passwords

Changes made to printers and queues assigned to a print server:

▸ queue assignments

▸ printer definition (parallel, serial, remote, or local)

- ▸ forms servicing

- ▸ notification of service alerts

Changes to the following take place immediately:

- ▸ queue users

- ▸ print server users

- ▸ queue operators

- ▸ print server operators

Understanding that some changes take place immediately and others take place after loading/reloading will help you avoid frustration when the print server appears to accept changes but does not effect them immediately.

CUSTOMIZING NETWARE 4 PRINTING

Forms and devices add another dimension of printing for the NetWare printing system. You should be able to determine now if forms or device definitions are needed in your network.

The first step is to determine where in the tree the devices need to exist. If forms or devices do not exist in a particular context, the printing system will look into the next higher context until it finds a definition. This would allow an administrator to create forms and devices at the Organization level of the tree, and all users in the entire organization would benefit.

Users will always use the forms and devices in their own contexts if they exist. If they do exist within the context, then the users cannot see any others above their own context.

Creating forms and definitions can be done either under NWADMIN (graphically under Windows) or using the DOS menu command PRINTDEF. Once they have been created, you can assign forms or devices to users with either NWADMIN (under Windows) or PRINTCON (under DOS). This is accomplished by creating a print job configuration for the user or container.

Building Forms

1 • Choose the context where you wish the form or forms to exists. This could be at the root or deep within the directory.

2 • Select the Organizational Unit (container) and click the right mouse button.

3 • Choose Details.

4 • Choose Printer Forms.

5 • Choose Create.

6 • Give the new form a descriptive name. Typically form 0 is the first form. Therefore, it should be the most commonly used form. This might be labeled BLANK or WORDPROC.

7 • The form number is used from the command line under CAPTURE, although CAPTURE can now use form names as well. Usually the form is referenced by name not by number.

8 • Choose OK.

This will create the form desired within the selected context. The next step is to assign it to a user. This can be done two ways:

► Setup a *print job configuration*. This is a collection of printing attributes that the user can select by a given name. One of the attributes can be the form name used when submitting jobs.

► Select a form name when capturing a printer under NWUSER (Windows 3.1). This is usually chosen by the user before printing, as opposed to using a preset configuration such as print job configurations.

Creating print job configurations will be covered later (see the section "Tying It All Together").

Building Devices

Creating devices requires two steps:

▸ Step 1: Creating functions—These are printing specific. They would include codes for things like Reset, Landscape, Portrait, Letter-size, Graphics mode and so on. To get these codes you must refer to the manual that came with your printer.

▸ Step 2: Creating modes—These are made of up one or more functions. They allow you to send a series of functions to the printer before your job prints. For example, you can:

  ▸ Reset the printer

  ▸ Change to landscape

  ▸ Change to A4 format

Together, functions and modes constitute a *device* definition. The idea is that when you start to print to the network printer, NetWare will send these codes to the desired printer and properly initialize it for you.

TIP

As stated before, it is much more desirable to allow the application (such as WordPerfect) to send its own codes. If that is not possible, then NetWare can send them for you via this interface.

To create functions and modes, you must decide where you want them to be available. As with forms, you can create them once at the root of the tree and make them globally available, or deeper in the directory tree. Also as with forms, when looking for devices, NetWare looks in the current container, and if none are found it continues to looks into superior containers until one is found. If none are found, no devices will be available.

REAL WORLD

NWUSER allows you to choose a form when capturing under Windows. However, NWUSER doesn't look into superior containers for other forms is none exist in the current context. Therefore, you may need to create a form in the users' context anyway, or change contexts.

To create a device, first choose the container where the device will be stored. As noted above this will have an impact on who will be able to see and use the device. Then create the device as follows:

1 • Click the right mouse button on the desired container.

2 • Choose Details.

3 • Choose Print Devices.

4 • Choose Create.

5 • Next, we need to create a device name (such as HP4SI). To do this, put in a name under Name and press Enter.

6 • Next, we'll need to create functions since modes are created from one or more functions. As a sample, we'll create a reset function. Choose Modify.

7 • Choose Create Function (see Figure 14.17).

8 • First you need to give the function a name. This should be descriptive of the function. As described above, you can obtain the function codes from your printer manual. There are some codes that you cannot type in (such as ESCAPE). These codes are typed in within delimiters to tell NetWare that a special character is needed. For example, you can indicate ESCAPE in other ways:

 ▸   <ESC>

 ▸   <ESCAPE>

To represent reset string of Escape E, you would represent it as <ESCAPE>E.

9 • Once you have created one or more functions, you can now create a mode. To create a mode, choose Create Mode. There is a default mode that is automatically created called *reinitialize*. This mode can be populated with the reset function (created earlier) for the print device you are defining. To add the reset function we just created, choose Add Above or Add Below.

TIP

Above and *Below* **will make a difference in how the mode works. Naturally, you would want to send a reset function before you send the function for Landscape. It the functions were reversed, it wouldn't do you any good (setting Landscape, then reset!). Add Above and Add Below allow you to place functions where they need to be in the mode list.**

10 • Be sure to give the mode a name. This should be descriptive of what the mode needs to do. In our case, the mode name Reset is perfect. You may also want to add the reset function to the predefined mode reinitialize.

FIGURE 14.17

Creating a New Function in NWADMIN

Importing Devices   A nice capability is importing predefined devices defined by someone else into the system. This does not include device drivers from application manufacturers. Only NetWare-defined devices can be imported (and exported).

An example might be where another administrator already went through the pain of creating a print driver for a new device. They can export that device (see "Exporting Devices" section below) into a file that can then be imported into your system.

To do this follow these steps:

1 • Choose the container where you wish to import the device.

2 • Click the right mouse button and choose Details.

3 • Choose Print Devices.

4 • Choose Import.

5 • Under filename, type **Z:\PUBLIC** and press Enter (this step is shown in Figure 14.18).

6 • Choose a device name, such as HPLJ4.PDF (PDF stands for Printer Definition File), then choose OK.

7 • The file will now be imported into NDS as a new device. To verify, check the modes and functions defined for this device.

F I G U R E   14.18

Importing Devices in NWADMIN

Remember that to utilize these forms and devices, you must create a print job configuration for a user and either make it a default for the user or allow the user to activate the configuration via a batch file or command line.

Exporting Devices   This option is similar to import. The steps are as follows:

1 • Choose the container where the device exists.

2 • Open Details on the container.

3 • Choose Print Devices.

4 • Choose Export.

5 • Choose a filename and directory where you wish to store the exported device in the form of a file.

6 • Choose OK.

NWADMIN will then export all functions and modes for the device and store them in a file. At that point, you may copy it to a diskette, e-mail it or otherwise make it available for other administrators.

QUIZ

Let's test your mystery-solving abilities. What English word can have four of its five letters removed and still retain the same pronunciation?

(Q14-2)

Tying It All Together

You now know how to create forms and devices, but how do you assign them to users? That is the next step. NetWare 4 has a method for integrating a series of printing options together into a named grouping of items. This is called a *print job configuration*. Print job configurations can be used in several ways:

▶ They can be created for a particular user.

▶ They can be created for a container. Then all users/objects in the container can use it.

▶ You can use a print job configuration defined for another user and assign it to another user in lieu of creating a duplicate configuration.

▶ You can make a print job configuration *default*. This means if the user issues a CAPTURE command (under a Login Script or command line), then the items defined in the job will take effect.

To create a print job (either for a user or a container):

1 • Choose the item in NWADMIN and select Details.

2 • Choose Print Job Configuration.

3 • Choose New.

4 • Give the job a name.

5 • You must choose a print queue for this job. Other options (for example, banners, copies, and form feed) are at the discretion of the creator. You can also assign a device, mode, and form (if they are created and within the scope of the configuration being created (see Figure 14.19).

6 • Choose OK.

FIGURE 14.19

Creating Print Job Configurations in NWADMIN

After creating the print job configuration, you can now optionally make it a default. For obvious reasons, there can be only one default. You can make other configurations the default if you wish.

To use a configuration other than the default, use the /J option with the CAPTURE command on the command line (or when using CAPTURE in a Login Script).

To select the default, highlight the configuration desired and click on Default. You should see a small printer icon next to the chosen configuration.

Congratulations! You've passed the first test. You successfully set up NetWare 4 printing. Now comes the fun part—keeping it running. This is the *real* mystery of life.

NetWare 4 Printing Management

NetWare 4 printing setup was a breeze. And now the system is working flawlessly. You've tested a few documents, and they printed fine. You're probably getting a little over-confident right about now. Be careful, it happens to the best of us.

Now for the real test—letting the users loose on your new, clean, "working" printing system. You know it can print in a vacuum, but what about in a war zone? Welcome to NetWare 4 printing management. In this section, we will explore six key management responsibilities, and learn about six key printing management tools. They are:

- ► Managing printing with PCONSOLE

- ► Managing printing with NWADMIN

- ► Managing print servers with PSC

- ► Configuring print jobs with PRINTCON

- ► Customizing printing with PRINTDEF

- ► Printing with NETUSER

With the release of NetWare 4, many of the DOS-based administration utilities that have been around since the beginning of NetWare were replaced by new utilities that support NDS. Even though the new NDS utilities have the same C-worthy look and feel, most of them have changed entirely—much to the dismay of some of us old NetWare junkies! Fortunately for those who prefer to work under DOS, the DOS-based printing utilities under NetWare 4 survived the cut with a few minor changes.

This section describes how NetWare print services can be managed in a distributed environment. We'll also cover some common printing issues and how to resolve them. The main areas that can be managed are shown in Table 14.5. Take a look.

TABLE 14.5	COMPONENT	HOW YOU CAN MANAGE THIS COMPONENT
NetWare 4 Printing Management Components	Print Servers	If you are a print server operator, you can: 　Unload the print server 　View auditing records
	Queues	For queue operators and users, the queue allows for great flexibility in what can be seen and changed remotely (under NWADMIN and PCONSOLE). For example, you can: 　Delete a job (NWADMIN and PCONSOLE) 　Create a job (PCONSOLE) 　Suspend a queue from receiving new jobs (NWADMIN and PCONSOLE) 　Suspend servicing of jobs (NWADMIN and PCONSOLE) 　Place an operator hold on a job (NWADMIN and PCONSOLE) 　Place a user hold on a job (NWADMIN and PCONSOLE)
	Printers	For printers, you can: 　View how much of a job has been completed (NWADMIN and PCONSOLE) 　Mount a new form (NWADMIN and PCONSOLE) 　Pause and restart a printer (NWADMIN and PCONSOLE) 　Abort a currently printing job

Some of the same general-purpose utilities that you use to create print services are the same ones that you use for management. Some special-purpose utilities (such as PSC) are only used for management. Table 14.6 summarizes these utilities.

TOOL	FUNCTION
NWADMIN	Used to do most print system component management. This includes: Deleting jobs / Changing mounted forms / Stopping and starting printers / Checking the status of jobs in the queue / Placing holds on jobs / Aborting currently printing jobs
PCONSOLE	This is a DOS/MENU utility and encompasses most of the queue and print server creation and management functions. These include: Deleting jobs from a queue / Submitting a new job (not possible under NWADMIN) / Placing holds on a job / Stopping and starting printers / Aborting currently printing jobs
PSC	This is a command line utility that can be used to manage print servers from a command line. This includes: Mounting new forms / Stopping and starting printers / Aborting currently printing jobs

T A B L E 14.6

NetWare 4 Printing Management Tools

For the most part, users are more interested in getting information about jobs than they are in completing particular tasks. Most of the time, users need to know when a job will complete or if the printer is available. They might need to delete a submitted job, but otherwise, they probably don't need to be able to do too many things to a printer or print job. The double-X's in Table 14.7 show the minimum rights needed to complete certain tasks.

TABLE 14.7

NetWare 4 Printing Management Administrators

FUNCTION	QUEUE OPERATOR	QUEUE USER	PRINT SERVER OPERATOR	PRINT SERVER USER
View any submitted job		XX		
Delete a submitted job (personal)		XX		
Delete another user's jobs	XX			
Create a new job		XX		
Prevent users from submitting jobs to a queue	XX			
Suspend servicing of print jobs	XX			
Abort a printing job on a printer			XX	
Stop a printer			XX	
Restart a printer			XX	
Mount a new form for a printer			XX	
Check printer status			XX	
Place a user hold on a job (personal)		XX		
Place an operator hold on a job	XX			
Check printer status				XX
Check percentage of the job printed				XX

Now that you've got your battle plan, let's arm you with some powerful printing management weapons. Starting with the strongest of them all—PCONSOLE.

ZEN

"Men can't be rushed. They're like children. You cook them too fast, they get tough. Whereas, you take your time, let them simmer for awhile, they fall apart in your hands."

Nanny Fine

MANAGING PRINTING WITH PCONSOLE

PCONSOLE is the general of printing utilities. NetWare 4's print console allows for the configuration and administration of NDS printing objects. Let's take a look at the PCONSOLE main menu (see Figure 14.20).

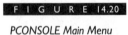

F I G U R E 14.20

PCONSOLE Main Menu

Before we begin exploring the PCONSOLE menu options, you need to be aware of a few important things about PCONSOLE. First, notice the top of the screen. In addition to the version of PCONSOLE that is running and the date and time, you will see your current context. This is very important because any menu option we choose at this point will affect this context only. For example, if we were to choose Print Queues, we would see the print queues configured in the current context only. A common mistake when using PCONSOLE is to be in the wrong context, select one of the menu items and then find yourself wondering, "What happened to all of my printing objects?" So, before beginning your printing administration, be sure you are in the proper context.

The default PCONSOLE context will be whatever context you were in when you ran PCONSOLE.EXE. Generally, this will be the context you were placed in at login. If your current context isn't correct, you can use the Change Context option to move to the proper context. Let's do that now. When you select Change Context you are prompted to either type the context you desire or to use the Insert key to browse for the desired context. Using the Insert key is the easiest, most foolproof method since it eliminates any guessing. When you press Insert, you will be presented with the container object below your current context.

By selecting the Organizational Unit you can move deeper in the tree. Just like in a DOS file system directory structure, the two dots indicate "parent," so if you press Enter at the two dots, you'll move up the tree to the parent container. When you have finished browsing for the desired context, press F10 or Esc to save the new context.

The second important item to notice on the PCONSOLE main menu is the menu bar at the bottom of the screen. Most of the options are self-explanatory: Enter to select, F10 or Esc to exit, F1 for help, but the one you should pay close attention to is F4=Switch To Bindery Mode. This option is a toggle switch. By pressing F4, PCONSOLE will change the display from NDS objects to Bindery objects. This option is normally used when you are logged into a bindery-based NetWare server (that is, NetWare 3 or NetWare 2). It can also be used if you are logged in as a user who is in the bindery context of the server to which you are authenticated. If you are not, when you press F4, you will receive a bindery context error message.

This option is useful in a mixed NetWare 3 and NetWare 4 environment because it allows you to toggle back and forth between NDS and bindery and easily manage network printing in both environments.

Using Quick Setup

Before we get into the details of PCONSOLE, let's take a look at the best part of the utility—Quick Setup. One of the most frustrating parts of configuring network printing is trying to remember the next step in the process. Administrators frequently create all of the necessary printing objects correctly but miss one step in the process of linking print queues to printers and printers to print servers. The result: hours of trying to figure out why jobs go to the print queue but never print.

Quick Setup allows you to set up a print server, printer, and print queue very quickly (hence the name), making all of the necessary assignments for you. This option is great for the administrator who doesn't like to hop back and forth between menus, trying to remember the next step in the print setup process.

If you choose Quick Setup from a context that does not have print services configured, the system will present you with default print object names as shown in Figure 14.21.

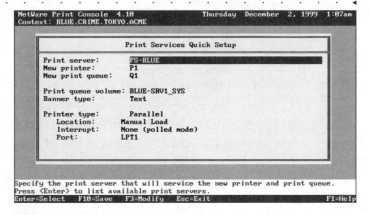

FIGURE 14.21

The Print Services Quick Setup Screen in PCONSOLE

Print servers will be named PS-<*Container_Name*>, the first printer will be named P1, and the first print queue will be named Q1. These defaults can be changed as necessary to match the naming standards of your organization.

Default assumptions will also be made about the print queue volume, banner type and printer configuration. These defaults can also be changed as necessary.

To change the printer configuration, arrow down to Printer type and press Enter. Select the appropriate printer type—Parallel, Serial, or other printer type—and press Enter. You will also need to specify whether this printer is an Auto Load printer (directly attached to the print server) or a Manual Load (workstation or network attached).

Generally, the Interrupt field can be left at the default of None (polled mode). If you choose to use an interrupt method, this field can be configured to indicate the interrupt of the port hardware. This field must match the port hardware if an interrupt is used. The Port field must match the port that this printer is physically attached to—LPT1, LPT2, and so on.

Quick Setup is the foolproof method for configuring NetWare 4 printing. Unfortunately, this option is only available in PCONSOLE, not NWADMIN. So, for those of you who are die-hard GUI administrators, if you find yourself caught in a DOS utility, this is the easiest way to set up NetWare 4 printing.

Quick Setup is not the only way to create printing objects in PCONSOLE—it's just the easiest! The objects can also be created using the individual Print Queues, Printers, and Print Servers options from the PCONSOLE main menu as described in the following sections.

Managing Print Queues

By selecting the Print Queues option from the PCONSOLE main menu, you are shown a list of print queues currently configured in the current context. By pressing Insert, a new print queue can be created. When creating a new print queue, you will be asked for two pieces of information: print queue name and print queue volume.

The name assigned to a print queue can be any hexadecimal name from 1 to 64 characters, including spaces and underscores. Even though this gives us tremendous flexibility, it is recommended that you keep your print queue names short and descriptive. For example, a print queue that is serviced by an HPIII LaserJet printer might be named HPIII-PQ1.

The second piece of information that will be required when creating a new print queue is the print queue volume. This is the volume where the print jobs sent to this queue will be spooled. Since the volume name entered here must be the full NDS name of the volume, use the Insert key to browse the tree to find the appropriate volume. When you have found the volume on which you want to create this queue, press Enter or F10 to accept your selection.

Remember, before any new print queue created can be used, all of the proper printing assignments must be made, including assigning a print server to service this queue and attaching a printer. This process is described below.

By selecting Print Queues from the PCONSOLE Available Options menu you can also manage existing NDS print queues. The left side of Figure 14.22 shows the print queues configured in the context .BLUE.CRIME.TOKYO.ACME.

FIGURE 14.22

The Print Queue Information Screen in PCONSOLE

When you select an available print queue, you will see the available information about this print queue displayed on the right side of the screen (see Figure 14.22). Table 14.8 summarizes the information found in each menu option listed.

TABLE 14.8

Print Queue Information Parameters

MENU OPTION	PURPOSE
Print Jobs	Allows you to view the current print jobs in this queue. Also allows a print queue operator to delete jobs from the queue, reorder jobs in the queue and put an operator hold on the jobs in the queue. Regular users (non-operators) can only modify jobs that they have submitted.
Status	Allows you to view the status of this print queue, including number of jobs, number of print servers servicing this queue and operator flags.
Attached Print Servers	Shows a list of active print servers servicing this print queue. The print server must be loaded in order to be active.
Information	Allows you to view the print queue identification number, and the server and volume in which this queue is created on. The print queue ID number is the subdirectory name of this print queue plus a .QDR extension. This subdirectory will be in the QUEUES directory of the indicated volume.

	MENU OPTION	PURPOSE
T A B L E 14.8 *Print Queue Information Parameters*	Users	Shows a list of users and groups who are authorized to submit jobs to this queue. Also allows you to add new users.
	Operators	Shows a list of users and groups who are authorized to manage this queue. Also allows you to add new operators.
	Print Servers	Allows you to view the print servers authorized to service this queue. Also allows you to authorize additional print servers to service this queue.

Viewing Jobs in a Print Queue   By selecting Print Jobs from the Print Queue Information menu, you can see all of the print jobs in this queue waiting to be serviced. Print queue operators will be shown all jobs in the queue. Regular users, or non-operators of the queue will only be shown the jobs that they submitted. By selecting a specific print job, you will see information about that job, as shown in Figure 14.23.

F I G U R E 14.23

The Print Job Information Screen in PCONSOLE

```
NetWare Print Console  4.10                     Saturday  December  2, 1995  6:51am
Context: BLUE.CRIME.TOKYO.ACME
┌──────────────────────────── Print Job Information ────────────────────────────┐
│ Print job:        0033A001           File size:          5797                   │
│ Client:           WEarp[7]                                                      │
│ Description:      J:USERS\WEARP\BLUCRIME.RPT                                    │
│ Status:           Print job is ready and waiting for the print server.          │
│                                                                                 │
│ User hold:        No                  Entry date:         12-3-1999             │
│ Operator hold:    No                  Entry time:         10:13:21 pm           │
│ Service sequence: 1                                                             │
│                                       Form:               Reports               │
│ Number of copies: 1                   Print banner:       Yes                   │
│                                       Name:               WEarp                 │
│ File contents:    Byte stream         Banner name:        LPT1                  │
│ Tab size:                                                                       │
│                                       Defer printing:     No                    │
│ Form feed:        Yes                 Target date:                              │
│ Notify when done: No                  Target time:                             │
└─────────────────────────────────────────────────────────────────────────────┘
Enter up to 49 characters to describe the print job.

Esc=Exit                                                                  F1=Help
```

This screen shows the print job ID number, who submitted the job, the filename, and the status of the job. This screen also allow a user or operator hold to be placed on the job. If the job is placed on hold, it will stay in the queue until the hold is removed.

The Service sequence field allows you to reorder jobs in the queue. In our example, there is only one job currently in the queue, so the service sequence is 1—indicating that this job is next in line to be serviced by the print server. If there were jobs in the queue ahead of this one, we could change the service sequence number, thereby moving it up in the queue. Only print queue operators can place one user's job ahead of another's. Users can only reorder their own jobs.

If you look closely at the remaining options, you'll notice that these are all of the parameters used with CAPTURE. So, if you send a print job with CAPTURE parameters and would like to change the parameters after the job is sent, you can do that here.

The last option on this screen is Defer printing. If this option is set to Yes, you will be able to specify the date and time for which you would like this job to print. This option is useful if you are printing large jobs that you would like to defer until a later, less busy, time.

Putting Print Queues on Hold   Using the Status option of the Print Queue Information menu, a print queue operator can put the select print queue on hold. There are three hold options in this menu:

▸ Allow users to submit print jobs— When set to No, this option prevents users from placing additional jobs in the queue. Any jobs already in the queue will continue to be serviced by the print server. This is useful when you are planning to do maintenance on a printer or if you are planning to change print queue definitions.

▸ Allow service by current print servers— This option, when set to No, will allow users to continue to place jobs in the queue, but those jobs will not be printed until this flag is removed. Again, this option is useful when doing printer or print server maintenance.

▸ Allow new print servers to attach— This option prevents new print servers from attaching to this queue.

Assigning Print Queue Users and Operators   The Users option of the PCONSOLE Print Queue Information menu allows you to authorize users and groups to place jobs in this queue. When you select this option, you are presented with a list of current print queue users. Use the Insert key to browse the tree and then authorize new users, groups, or containers as users of this print queue by highlighting an object and pressing F10. Multiple objects can be selected by using the F5 key to mark them and F10 to select. To remove print queue users, highlight the object in the user list and press Delete.

Assigning print queue operators is done is a similar fashion. Select the Operators menu option and use the Insert key to browse and F10 to select.

Attaching Print Servers to a Queue   To assign a print server to service a queue, select the Print Servers option from the Print Queue Information menu. You will be shown a list of the print servers currently assigned to service this queue. Use the Insert key to browse the NDS tree to find the print server you would like to service this queue. To add a print server to the list, highlight the server name and press F10 or Esc. Before the print server will actively service this queue, it must be loaded at a file server.

ZEN

"Big hair makes your hips look smaller."

Nanny Fine

Managing Printers

When you select the Printer option from the PCONSOLE main menu, you will be shown a list of print queues configured in the current context. Use the Insert key to create a new printer. When you create a printer in PCONSOLE, the only information you are asked for at this point is the printer name. This can be a little deceiving because additional steps are required to complete the printer setup.

Once the printer is created, you will need to select the printer by pressing Enter and configure it from the resulting Printer Configuration screen (shown in the background of the screen in Figure 14.24).

This default configuration assumes that you are configuring a parallel printer attached to LPT1 of a remote workstation. So, in order to complete the configuration you will need to provide the following information if the default configuration is not correct.

► Printer type—Whether this printer is a parallel, serial, or other type of printer.

► Configuration—Which port this printer is attached to (LPT1, LPT2, and so on). The location of this printer [locally (directly) attached or remotely (workstation) attached].

► Interrupt—NetWare defaults to a polled mode when checking a print queue for new print jobs. If you choose to use an interrupt mode instead, this field can be configured to indicate the interrupt of the port hardware. This field must match the port hardware if an interrupt is used.

► Address restriction—This optional field allows you to restrict this printer to being loaded on the specified workstation or network.

To complete the printer configuration, you must assign a print queue for this printer to service and link a print server.

To manage NDS printing objects with PCONSOLE, select the Printers option from the PCONSOLE main menu. This allows you to manage NDS printer objects in the current context. By selecting an available printer, you can see the current configuration of this printer (see Figure 14.25).

Printer Configuration Screen for an HPIII LaserJet Printer

```
NetWare Print Console  4.10                    Thursday  December  2, 1999  1:12am
Context: BLUE.CRIME.TOKYO.ACME

                        Printer HPIII-P1 Configuration

        Print server:           BLUE-PS1
        Printer number:         3
        Printer status:         (See form)
        Printer type:           Parallel
        Configuration:          (See form)
        Starting form:          0
        Buffer size in KB:      3
        Banner type:            Text
        Service mode for forms: Minimize form changes within print queues
        Sampling interval:      5
        Print queues assigned:  (See list)
        Notification:           (See list)


Specify the logical number (0-254, inclusive) assigned to this printer.

Enter=Select   F10=Save   F8=Port Driver Name   Esc=Exit                  F1=Help
```

Table 14.9 summarizes the information found in Figure 14.25.

TABLE 14.9	PARAMETER	FUNCTION
Printer Configuration Parameters	Print server	Specifies the active print server currently servicing this printer.
	Printer number	Displays the logical printer number assigned to this printer.
	Printer status	Displays the status of this printer and the active print job. Also allows a print server operator to change the queue service mode, change the currently mounted form, and issue printer control commands.
	Printer type	Displays the configured printer type. Available printer types include: parallel, serial, UNIX printer, AppleTalk printer, Other/Unknown, XNP and AIO.
	Configuration	Displays the configuration information about this printer, including port, location, and interrupt. For serial printers this field also includes COM port configuration information such as baud rate, stop bits, data bits, and parity.
	Starting form	Indicates the PRITNDEF form that the print server will assume is mounted on the printer when the print server starts.
	Buffer size in KB	Indicates the size of the print server's internal buffer for this printer. Increasing this number may improve printer performance if the printer stops and restarts in the middle of a print job.
	Banner type	Specifies the default banner type for this printer. Options are Text or Postscript.
	Service mode for forms	Specifies how the print server will service jobs in the queue when forms are used.

(continued)

PARAMETER	FUNCTION
Sampling interval	When the printer is idle, this number specifies how often, in seconds, that the print server will poll the queue assigned to this printer for new print jobs. When the printer is active the print server will automatically service the next job in the queue.
Print queues assigned	Allows you to view the print queues this printer is assigned to service. Also allows you to add new print queues to be serviced.
Notification	Displays the users and groups assigned to be notified if there is a problem with this printer. Also allows to add users or groups to the notification list.

T A B L E 14.9

Printer Configuration Parameters (continued)

Assigning a Print Queue   Assigning a print queue to a printer can be done through the Printer Configuration screen as well. To do so, select the Print queues assigned option and press Enter. You can then use the Insert key to browse the directory tree for the print queue to which you would like to assign this printer. Once you have located the desired print queue, press Enter or F10 to select it.

When you assign a print queue to a printer, you can also set the priority level and default status of the queue. After you select the print queue, a Priority Configuration screen appears. The priority of this queue can be set to any number between one and ten. Priority one is the highest, ten is the lowest.

If this printer is servicing multiple queues, you can use the Make this the default queue option to define the default queue for this printer. When network users capture to this printer instead of a queue assigned to it, print jobs will be spooled to the default queue assigned here.

In the background you will see the priority this queue is set to and the state. As shown at the bottom of this screen, a printer's state can be one of the following:

- ▸ [A]: Active

- ▸ [C]: Configured

▸ [AC]: Active and configured

▸ [D]: Default

Using Forms   If you have defined print forms using NWADMIN or PRINTDEF, the Printers option under PCONSOLE will also allow you to configure how those forms are used. Referring back to the Printer Configuration screen (Figure 14.25), there are a number of areas that affect forms.

Under the Printer status option, there are two forms options. The first is Service mode. This option determines how the printer will service the print queue when forms are being used. The next option is Mounted form. This is the form that is currently mounted at this printer. You would use this option to change the currently mounted form through PCONSOLE. The currently mounted form can also be change through NWADMIN, PSC, and at the print server console.

The next option that affects forms from the Printer Configuration menu is Starting form. This option defines the default starting form to be used when the printer starts up. This form number should represent the most commonly used form on this printer.

Finally, there is the Service mode for forms option. When you select this option, you are presented with the screen in Figure 14.26. Take a quick peek.

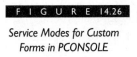

F I G U R E   14.26

Service Modes for Custom Forms in PCONSOLE

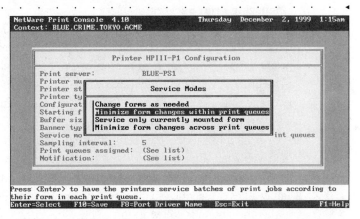

The first option, Change forms as needed, requires you to mount a new form at this printer each time a print job with a different form number is submitted to the queue. The print jobs in the queue will be serviced based on priority (on a first-in, first-out basis). So, if many different form types are used, this option may require you to change forms often.

To minimize the number of times form changes occur, you may consider leaving the default (Minimize form changes within print queues) enabled. With this option enabled, all of the print jobs with the same priority submitted to the queue with the currently mounted form requested will be serviced first. Lower priority jobs with a different form requested will require a form change before being serviced.

The next option, Service currently mounted form, will only service jobs submitted with the mounted form type. If this option is enabled, the print server will not prompt for a form change if a job with a different form type is submitted to the queue. These jobs will never be printed unless this option is changed to one of the other options above.

The final option on this menu, Minimize form changes across print queues, is similar to the default option above, except in this case, all jobs with the currently mounted form will be serviced first, regardless of priority.

ZEN

"If it ain't half off, it ain't on sale."

Nanny Fine

Managing Print Servers

When you select the Print Servers option from the PCONSOLE main menu, you are shown a list of print servers configured in the current context. When you press Insert, a prompt appears, at which you enter the print server name.

The print server can be any hexadecimal name from 1 to 64 characters, including spaces and underscores. Even though this gives you tremendous flexibility, you should keep your print server names short and descriptive. For example, the second print server created to service printers in the BLUE division might be named BLUE-PS2. When you press Enter to create the print server, a message appears on the screen indicating that it may take up to 60 seconds for the print server to be created. Though it rarely takes 60 seconds to create a new print server, this message is just to reassure you that the system is still working.

Once the print server is created, to complete the configuration you will need to assign this print server to service printers and print queues.

To manage NDS print servers with PCONSOLE, select the Print Servers option from the PCONSOLE main menu. By selecting Print Servers you can create new NDS print server objects or view existing print servers in the current context. The left side of Figure 14.27 shows the print servers configured in the current context.

F I G U R E 14.27

The Print Server Information Screen in PCONSOLE

After you select an available print server, all of the available information about that server will be displayed on the right side of the screen, as seen in Figure 14.27. Table 14.10 summarizes the information found in each menu option.

T A B L E 14.10

Print Server Information Parameters

MENU OPTION	PURPOSE
Printers	Displays the printers assigned to be serviced by this print server and their state. Also allows printers to be assigned or removed from this print server.
Information and status	Displays print server type, status, version, number of printers serviced, and advertising name. If the print server is running, this option also allows it to be taken down.
Users	Displays users and groups who are authorized to view the print server's status and active configuration. Allows print server users to be added or removed.

(continued)

T A B L E 14.10	MENU OPTION	PURPOSE
Print Server Information Parameters (continued)	Operators	Displays users and groups who are authorized to manage the print server's status and active configuration. Allows print server operators to be added or removed.
	Description	Allows an optional text description to be entered for this print server.
	Password	Allows a print server password to be entered. This prevents unauthorized users from loading the print server.
	Audit	Allows you to view or modify this print server's auditing information.

Assigning Printers to be Serviced   To assign printers to this print server, select Printers from the Print Server Information menu. A list of the printers currently being serviced by this print server will be displayed. Pressing Insert will allow you to browse the directory tree for the desired printer.

The Printers option will also show you the state of the attached printers. A printer's state can be one of the following:

▶ [A]: Active

▶ [C]: Configured

▶ [AC]: Active and configured

Selecting a configured printer from this screen will take you to the same Printer Configuration screen we saw when we were creating and configuring printers (see Figure 14.25). This is a nice short cut when you are setting up printing services with this utility.

Assigning Print Server Users and Operators   Print server users are network users who have the ability to view the information and status of a print server. Print server operators have the ability to actually change that information. Selecting the Users option from the PCONSOLE Print Server Information menu allows you to authorize users and groups as print server users. You do not have to be a print server user to have print jobs routed by a particular print server, but you do to view its configuration and status.

When you select the Users option, you will be presented with a list of current print server users. Use the Insert key to browse the tree for users, groups, or containers to be authorized as print server users. To select an object, highlight the object and press F10. Multiple objects can be selected by using the F5 key to mark them and then using F10 to select. To remove print server users, highlight the object in the user list and press Delete.

Assigning print server operators is done in a similar fashion. Select the Operators menu option and use the Insert key to browse and F10 to select. To remove a print server operator, use the Delete key.

Using the Auditing Feature

To keep track of printing transactions, print server auditing can be enabled. When auditing is enabled, information about each completed print job will be logged in an audit file called PSERVER.LOG. This log file can be viewed using PCONSOLE or NWADMIN. Also, because PSERVER.LOG is a text file, it can be viewed with any text editor.

To enable auditing or to view or delete the audit file for a particular print server, choose Audit from the Print Server Information menu. Figure 14.28 shows the resulting screen.

F I G U R E 14.28

Print Services Auditing in PCONSOLE

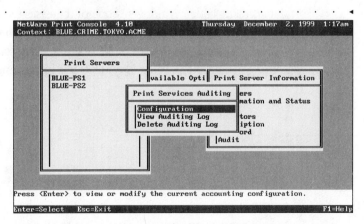

To enable auditing, choose Configuration and set the Enable auditing field to Yes. When you enable auditing, you are given the option of limiting the size of the audit file. If you do not limit this file's size, it could grow to the maximum of the available disk space. To prevent the file from getting out of hand, you may want to limit its size. When the file size is limited, the print server will log entries until the maximum size is reached and then it will stop until the file is deleted or this field is changed.

Anytime a change is made in the Auditing Information screen, the print server will need to be taken down and restarted before the changes will take place.

QUIZ

To be a crack sleuth, you have to know your codes. Decode the following:

C V C C V C V ! C V C   V C V C V C V C   V C   C V C V C V C .
18 2 99   3 4 11 2   10 2 1515 1   5 2   15 2 22 5   15154 5   9920   3 2 2 4 3 2 3
(Q14-3)

That completes our in-depth exploration of PCONSOLE. As you can see, it provides a lot of printing management punch. But for those of you who still prefer a GUI world, NWADMIN provides some printing management capabilities as well, albeit, not as many as PCONSOLE. Let's check it out.

MANAGING PRINTING WITH NWADMIN

Management under Windows is one of the easiest ways to track jobs and status of print servers. NWADMIN and NWUSER are the main tools for doing this. Even though NWADMIN is primarily an administrator's tool, users can benefit from it as well.

Printing management under NWADMIN is broken into two sets of tasks:

- ▸ CNE tasks

- ▸ User tasks

Let's take a closer look.

CNE Tasks

As a manager of printers and queues, you will need to do several things:

- ▸ Mount new printer forms

- ▸ Stop/start printers

▶ Unload the print server

▶ Place a hold on a job

▶ Delete a job

Remember, you must be an operator (printer or queue) to carry out these management functions. Table 14.11 shows the steps required to accomplish these functions. This assumes you are already in NWADMIN and at the context where the objects resides.

T A B L E 14.11	TASK	STEPS INVOLVED
CNE Printing Tasks in NWADMIN	Mount new printer forms	1 • Choose the printer (highlight and double-click).
		2 • Select Printer Status.
		3 • Select Mount Form.
		4 • Choose the form name (or number).
	Stop/start printers (see Figure 14.29)	1 • Choose the printer.
		2 • Select Printer Status.
		3 • Select Pause to stop or Start to resume printer output.
	Unload the print server	1 • Choose the print server.
		2 • At the lower middle of the screen, choose Unload.
		3 • Choose Immediately or After Jobs based on whether you wish current jobs to complete before the print server terminates.
	Place a hold on a job (see Figure 14.30)	1 • Select the queue that is servicing the job.
		2 • Select Job List.
		3 • Select Hold Job.

(continued)

TABLE 14.11	TASK	STEPS INVOLVED
CNE Printing Tasks in NWADMIN (continued)	Release a job hold	**1** • Select the queue that is servicing the job.
		2 • Select Job List.
		3 • Select Resume.
	Delete a job	**1** • Select the queue that is servicing the job.
		2 • Select Job List.
		3 • Highlight the specific job.
		4 • Select Delete.

▶ • ◀

FIGURE 14.29

The Printer Status Screen in NWADMIN

User Tasks

Some user management functions are similar to operator functions. Typically, they are basic view functions to check on the status of a job. These functions include:

▶ Viewing status of a job in a queue

▶ Viewing amount of job printed on a printer

▸ Deleting a job submitted

▸ Placing/releasing a user hold on the job

*The Print Queue Job List
Screen in NWADMIN*

These functions require that you have at least user access on the print server or queue in question. Refer to Table 14.12 for a quick review.

*User Printing Tasks in
NWADMIN*

TASK	STEPS INVOLVED
View job status	**1** • Select the queue that is servicing the job.
	2 • Select Job List.
	3 • Locate the job in question.
	4 • Scroll right to view status (Active, Held, Ready).

(continued)

TASK	STEPS INVOLVED
View percent completed	1 • Select printer that is printing the job.
	2 • Select Printer Status.
Delete a job	1 • Select the queue that is servicing the job.
	2 • Select Job List.
	3 • Highlight the chosen job.
	4 • Select Delete.
Place/release a user hold (see Figure 14.31)	1 • Select the queue that is servicing the job.
	2 • Select Job List.
	3 • Select the job to hold/release.
	4 • Select Hold Job to hold and Resume to release.

ZEN

"Ma has plastic on the furniture. I think she's preserving it for the afterlife!"

Nanny Fine

That's completes our discussion of general printing management with PCONSOLE and NWADMIN. These two tools are the cornerstone of your arsenal. But you never know when you might need a special utility. So, the next four topics deal with less common printing management components—like print servers, print job configurations, and print forms customization. Ready, set, explore.

MANAGING PRINT SERVERS WITH PSC

Print Server Control (PSC) is the first of the printing specialty tools. To use PSC, you need the following information:

1 • The print server name—This could be either the name of the print server on a Bindery (3.x, 2.x server) or an NDS name (such as WHITE-PS1. WHITE.CRIME.TOKYO.ACME).

2 • The name of the printer to manage—This could be P1, HP4SI-P1, and so on. The names were defined under PCONSOLE or NWADMIN.

3 • The command desired (for example, STATUS, MOUNT, DISMOUNT)

One of the more helpful options is the /? option, which will show all the options available for the PSC command. The next section covers some of the fun things that you can do with PSC.

Get Status of All Printers

This option shows all printers for the print server and their status (see Figure 14.32). Following is the syntax:

```
PSC PS=WHITE-PS1.WHITE.CRIME.TOKYO.ACME P=ALL STAT
```

F I G U R E 14.32

*Getting Printer Status
with PSC*

```
Z:\PUBLIC>PSC PS=.WHITE-PS1.WHITE.CRIME.TOKYO.ACME P=ALL STAT
Printer CANONBJ-P1 (printer number 0)
        Status:Not connected

Printer HPIII-P1 (printer number 1)
        Status:Not connected

Printer HP4SI-P3 (printer number 2)
        Status:Not connected

Printer HP4SI-P2 (printer number 3)
        Status:Not connected

Printer HP4SI-P1 (printer number 4)
        Status:Printing job
        Off-line
        Print job name: LPT1
        Print job ID: 212001
        Complete: 93%

Z:\PUBLIC>
```

Mount a New Form in a Printer

This option will make the desired form number the currently mounted form. Here's the syntax:

```
PSC PS=WHITE-PS1.WHITE.CRIME.TOKYO.ACME P=CANONBJ-P1 Mount
Form=Reports
```

You may also indicate the printer and/or form by number:

```
PSC PS=WHITE-PS1.WHITE.CRIME.TOKYO.ACME P=0 Mount Form=1
```

Stop/Start a Printer from Servicing Jobs

This option will tell the printer to stop printing once it's local buffer is empty. This would be useful if it's necessary to change paper or fix a problem without deleting jobs in the queue.

In this example, we'll assume that we're already in the context WHITE.CRIME.TOKYO.ACME. Therefore, we only need to specify the name of the print server.

```
PSC PS=WHITE-PS1 P=CANONBJ-P1 STOP
```

To restart the printer, type:

```
PSC PS=WHITE-PS1 P=CANONBJ-P1 START
```

Show Print Server Configuration

This option will show you the printer layout for the specified print server. This includes all printers and queues assigned to the print server. The syntax for this option is:

```
PSC PS=WHITE-PS1 List
```

This option helps you to find the name of the printers attached to the print server so that you can use the above options to get more specific details (see Figure 14.33).

F I G U R E 14.33

Showing Print Server Configuration

```
F:\SYSTEM>PSC PS=WHITE-PS1 LIST

WHITE-PS1                              (NetWare Server: WHITE-SRV1)
    ├─HP4SI-P1.POL                     (#4 - Waiting for job)
    │   └HP4SI-PQ1.POL                 (Volume: WHITE-SRV1_SYS)
    ├─HP4SI-P2.FIN                     (#3 - Not connected)
    │   └HP4SI-PQ2.FIN                 (Volume: WHITE-SRV1_SYS)
    ├─HP4SI-P3.FIN                     (#2 - Not connected)
    │   └HP4SI-PQ3.FIN                 (Volume: WHITE-SRV1_SYS)
    ├─HPIII-P1.CYBER                   (#1 - Not connected)
    │   └HPIII-PQ1.CYBER               (Volume: WHITE-SRV1_SYS)
    └─CANONBJ-P1                       (#0 - Not connected)
        └CANONBJ-PQ1                   (Volume: WHITE-SRV1_SYS)
F:\SYSTEM>
```

That's it for PSC. The next specialty printing tool is PRINTCON.

CONFIGURING PRINT JOBS WITH PRINTCON

Back in the days before NetWare supported Windows, the only way to capture printers was with the CAPTURE command, either through a login script or a batch file. To make this process easier, PRINTCON was used to create print job configurations that consisted of common user CAPTURE statements. Then, rather than having to enter long and cryptic CAPTURE statements, the CAPTURE command was simply:

```
CAPTURE J=<job_configuration>
```

Today, with the NWUSER Windows utility, we have an easier option: Just drag and drop to capture a printer once and select the Permanent option. But, even with this easier option, PRINTCON is still around for those who would like to use it. Figure 14.34 shows the PRINTCON main menu.

F I G U R E 14.34

PRINTCON Main Menu

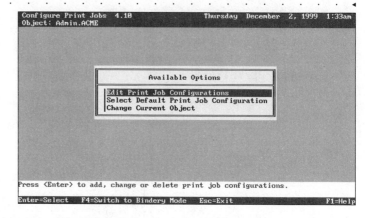

The first thing to notice in the PRINTCON main menu is the object at the top of the screen. Any print jobs configured during this session will be for the .Admin.ACME object. If we would like to set up print job configurations for another user, we can use the Change Current Object option. When we select that option, we are prompted to enter the object name. This can be done by either typing the full NDS name or by using the Insert key and browsing.

Print job configurations can be created for users or container objects. If a print job configuration is created for a container object, all of the users in that container can use it. This is an improvement over the PRINTCON of yesterday. In previous versions of NetWare, there was no way to assign print job configurations to groups of users—each user had an individual PRINTCON database. The database itself was a file called PRINTCON.DAT, which was located in each user's individual SYS:MAIL directory. In NetWare 4, the PRINTCON job configurations are not separate databases but rather are part of the NDS database and are properties of each user or container object.

To create a print job configuration, select Edit Print Job Configurations from the Available Options menu. A list of the current job configurations will be displayed. To create a new job configuration, press the Insert key and enter the job configuration name. The name can be just about anything you wish, but it should be descriptive of the configuration type. For example, if you are creating a job configuration to be used when you are printing letters on company letterhead, you may want to name the job configuration "letters."

After you name the job configuration, select it by pressing Enter. The Job Configuration screen will appear. If you look closely at the job configuration's options you'll notice that they are essentially all of the CAPTURE parameters. Since CAPTURE was covered previously, we won't cover each of these options in depth.

The only options listed that aren't regular CAPTURE options are Device and Mode. These options represent print devices and modes defined in the PRINTDEF utility. Print devices and modes generally are used when the application you are using doesn't support the print mode you want. However, most of today's applications support print modes for common printers. When selecting print devices and modes, be sure that you have selected a print queue first. Otherwise, the devices and modes defined in the user's context will not appear.

If you have more than one print job configuration defined, you can choose one of them as the default. The benefit of having a default job configuration is that you can use the CAPTURE command without other parameters and the default job configuration will be used. To change the default job configuration, choose Select Default Print Job Configuration, highlight the desired job configuration, and press Enter. To remove the default job configuration, press Delete.

CUSTOMIZING PRINT DEVICES AND FORMS WITH PRINTDEF

Now that everything is set up and running smoothly, we need to shift our printing focus to customization. These are the advanced tasks that separate NetWare 4 CNEs from pretenders. PRINTDEF is our friend. This DOS-based printing utility allows us to customize two important printing components:

- Print forms

- Print devices

Multiple print forms can be supported by attaching special instructions to specific print jobs. In addition, customized formatting is allowed with special print devices. All of this is accomplished using PRINTDEF.

The PRINTDEF utility is used to define and store printer definitions or command strings and printer form definitions. It's probably the least frequently used of all of the NetWare printing utilities, but it comes in handy when you have multiple paper types used on a single printer or you wish to exploit printer functionality that your application doesn't support. Let's take a look at the PRINTDEF main menu (see Figure 14.35).

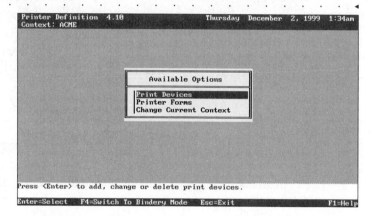

F I G U R E 14.35

PRINTDEF Main Menu

As with the other DOS-based print utilities, it's important to notice the context at the top of the screen before creating or modifying devices or forms. When creating or modifying devices or forms, the context shown at the top of the screen is where they will be created. Any user under the context where the forms or devices are defined will have access to them.

Devices and forms will flow down through the NDS tree until another definition is defined at a lower level. For example, if a print form is defined in ACME, all users in all Organizational Units below ACME will have access to that form. If forms are then defined in the .WHITE.CRIME.TOKYO.ACME container, users in that container will get only those forms and not the ones defined in ACME.

ZEN

"My Aunt Miriam always says, 'The more the merrier, unless you're talking about chins.'"

Nanny Fine

Using Custom Forms

In certain cases, a printing environment may require the use of preprinted forms for print jobs such as invoices, paychecks, return forms, and purchase orders. If this is the case, the administrator and the network must ensure that submitted print jobs get printed on the proper forms. Imagine if a paycheck were printed on an invoice form. The person on the receiving end of the paycheck wouldn't be too happy.

One way around this is to have a dedicated printer for every type of possible print job that requires the form. In fact, in companies that require high-volume print services, this is usually the case. This means the printers seldom have to be reset except to add new forms when they run out.

In environments where the volume is lower, preprinted forms may be required, but multiple form types may need to be consolidated to a single printer. This is where forms are used (see Figure 14.36).

F I G U R E 14.36

Understanding Print Forms

TIP

In the situation where you have dedicated forms printers, you can ignore forms altogether. Configuring forms where not needed just adds another layer of complexity.

A good example would be where the company ACME needs to print invoices and purchase requisitions on the same printer. ACME needs to have two forms defined plus a potential third if normal draft printing is also done on the same printer. In our example, we have defined three forms:

- INVOICE (0)

- PURCHASE (1)

- DRAFT (2)

Notice that each form also has a number. When referencing forms, you can use either a form name or a reference number—NetWare doesn't care which.

To specify the form to use, when the workstation is initially captured you can use the /F option under the CAPTURE command, or a form may be specified under a user's print job configuration. The administrator may also have more than one print job configuration per user specifically for that reason. That way the workstation will default to the standard print configuration for the user (perhaps using a draft form—standard blank paper, for instance), but the user can still choose a print job that specifies a particular form.

Ideally, form selection could be set via a batch file, login script, or Windows PIF file. This would eliminate the burden on the user of choosing the right print job configuration.

Servicing Print Forms   Once a user has submitted a print job with a specific form, the form number (and the name) will be kept as part of the Job Entry Record. If you recall, a Job Entry Record is kept for every print job submitted to the NetWare print system.

When the print server first comes up, it defaults to form type 0 even though form 0 may be undefined. Typically, most administrators make form 0 the most used form in a multiple-forms environment.

REAL WORLD

NetWare needs only the form number and not necessarily the form name. Therefore, when any print server initializes, it will default to form 0 for all printers serviced by that print server.

Once the print server has found a job in the queue to service, it will look to see what form type the job requires. It then decides whether to service the job immediately or to hold it temporarily for efficiency reasons. We'll assume for now that the print server will service jobs on a first come, first served basis.

The print server then opens the data file associated with the print job and checks the form type currently being used for the printer. Remember that the print server usually initializes the printer with form 0 (the default can be set when the printer is defined with NetWare 4). If the print server notes that the job submitted requires a different form that the currently mounted type, then the server halts the printer and sends a message to the designated persons that a new form needs to be mounted.

The printing administrator or whoever is designated to manage the print server can then take several steps to continue printing:

- ▸ remove the current paper type in the printer

- ▸ feed in the required form type

- ▸ use a server set command to indicate that the proper form is now in the printer

- ▸ restart the printer

If the next print job requires a different form type, the process must be repeated.

Changing Print Forms As you can see, changing forms can become quite tiresome if many different types of jobs are passing through, all with different form types. To minimize the number of form changes, NetWare allows you to optimize how forms get serviced.

By default, a print server services form types on a first come, first served basis. But if you're in a multi-form environment, you may want to change this default. When the print server is configured, you can specify how to handle forms when the print server encounters them. Options include:

- Minimize form changes within queues—This option will ask you to change form types only when all of the currently mounted forms have been serviced within the queue. If there were one form 0, three form 3, and five form 4 print jobs, here's what would happen: Assume that form 0 is currently mounted. First, the form 0 job would be printed, then the three form 3 jobs, followed by the five form 4 jobs, regardless of their submission order. When all jobs were completed, if there were another queue being serviced by the printer, the print server would rotate to the next queue and do the same.

- Minimize form changes across queues—This option is similar to the previous, except the print server will do all the form 0 print jobs across all queues being serviced by the one printer, then move on to the next form and so on, until all print jobs had been serviced. This is used only when more than one queue services a single printer.

- Service only the currently mounted form—This option allows the print server operator to control when jobs with forms get printed. The currently mounted form type will be the only type serviced until the operator changes the printer's mounted form. Then the print server will only service that form. This is useful in an environment where the main form (invoices, for example) are being printed all day long, and the other form(s) only need to be batch printed at intervals (like at the end of the day).

Remember, in an ideal situation, each preprinted form should have its own dedicated printer, in which case, no forms definition is necessary. If forms are necessary (more than one form printed per printer), then there are two ways to configure forms: CAPTURE (discussed earlier) and NWADMIN (discussed below).

Under NWADMIN, you may define forms under a container to service the objects (users, for example) of that container. To do this:

1 • Start NWADMIN and locate the container where the desired print server resides.

2 • Place the pointer over the container icon and click the right mouse button once.

3 • Choose Details.

4 • Choose Forms.

In most cases, applications send all the formatting information needed by a plotter or a printer via their own native print drivers. In addition, Windows has support for every major printer available today.

In certain cases, NetWare may need to send printer formatting functions along with the actual print data. This is accomplished through the printer definition database (PRINTDEF), which can be defined by the administrator.

To review, every print job has three parts in the actual data stream; a print header, the print data, and the print tail. When you are using the PRINTDEF database, you are telling NetWare what to put in the print header. The header information reaches the printer first and will format it properly before the data starts to print. The print tail is used normally to reset the printer to its initial state so that it's ready for the next print job.

Once you have assigned a user either a form or a device (or both) using PRINTCON or NWADMIN, when the user prints, the device information will get appended to the print job data. For example, if you have chosen HPLaserJet4 and Landscape as a function, the proper escape codes will be part of the print header. In addition, if the function for printer reset (under the reinitialize mode) has been set, NetWare will automatically send the reset string after the job data has been sent. This way, NetWare can ensure that the printer is left in a reset state after a function has been used.

Using Print Devices

To define a new print device, select Print Devices from the PRINTDEF main menu. Print devices can be created manually by using the Insert key and entering each escape sequence that represents your printer's command strings. The easiest way to define a new printer definition is to take advantage of the 57 predefined print devices that come with NetWare 4. Those print devices are stored in the SYS:PUBLIC directory of each

NetWare 4 file server. These print devices can be imported into your current context by selecting Import Print Devices from the Print Device Options menu.

If the printer you are using is not on the list, check your printer manual because your printer may emulate a printer that is on the list.

PRINTDEF print devices consist of two parts: print devices and print modes. *Print devices* are the various printer command strings that you often find in the back of printer manuals. *Print modes* are made up of one or more print functions and represent the various modes a printer supports. For example, the reinitialize mode will reset the printer after each print job. Another example of a common printer mode is landscape mode.

QUIZ

Try this one on for size. A man is walking his dog on a leash towards home at a steady 3 mph. When they are 7 miles from home, the man lets his dog off the leash. The dog immediately runs off towards home at 8 mph. When the dog reaches the house, it turns round and runs back to the man at the same speed. When it reaches the man it turns back for the house. This is repeated until the man gets home and lets in the dog. How many miles does the dog cover from being let off the leash to being let into the house?

(Q14-4)

That pretty much finishes our journey through printing management LANd— otherwise know as the NetWare "war zone." The final utility deals with everyday, run-of-the-mill user printing. NETUSER is a pacifier for troublesome users. Use it or lose it (your mind, that is).

PRINTING WITH NETUSER

NWUSER makes network printing easier for Windows users, but what about DOS users? Are they limited to capturing from the DOS command line? Well, there is an option to simplify printing for the DOS user—NETUSER. Figure 14.37 shows the NETUSER main menu.

F I G U R E 14.37

NETUSER Main Menu

Just like with the other DOS utilities, it's important to note the context at the very top of the NETUSER screen. Anything done in NETUSER from this point will be from the .WHITE.CRIME.TOKYO.ADMIN context.

You should also notice the box above the Available Options menu, indicating current user and capturing information. In Figure 14.37, we are currently logged in as Admin and LPT1 is captured to the queue servicing the Canon Bubble Jet.

Managing Print Jobs

When you select Printing from the Available Options menu, you are shown a list of the available LPT ports. If you select an LPT port, you are given two options: Print Jobs and Change Printers. Since we have already captured LPT1 to the CANONBJ-PQ1 queue, we can select the queue by pressing Enter and view a list of print jobs currently in the queue. If you select a print job, you are presented with the Printing Management menu.

Does this screen look familiar? It happens to be the same screen we saw when we selected a print job in PCONSOLE and also when we were setting up print job configurations in PRINTCON. The parameters shown here are the flags used with CAPTURE when the job was sent to the queue.

Capturing with NETUSER

To capture a printer port with NETUSER, under the Printers option, select the port you wish to capture and choose Change Printers. You are then presented with a list of printers and print queues in your current context.

To capture to a printer, use the arrow keys to highlight the printer you want (or the print queue assigned to it) and press Enter. Any capturing done through NETUSER will remain active during the current login session only. One disadvantage this utility has in comparison with its Windows counterpart is that there is no way to make the capturing permanent.

ZEN

"I just can't tame this darn charisma. Can I help it if I effervesce?"

Nanny Fine

That completes our discussion of NetWare 4's printing management tools. Wow, there's a lot to work with. We learned about PCONSOLE, NWADMIN, PSC, PRINTCON, PRINTDEF, and NETUSER. With all of these tools, it should be easy to keep NetWare printing running smoothly. It is...until somebody tries to print something! That's when it gets a little out of hand.

I hope you've enjoyed this in-depth exploration of NetWare 4 printing as it is today. But what about tomorrow? The good news is—the future's so bright you've got to wear shades. And it's all because of a little four-letter acronym called NDPS. Check it out.

The Future of Printing—NDPS

Ask any network administrator what the most frustrating part of managing their network is and nine times out of ten the answer will be printing. In an average networking environment, 80 percent of all support calls are printer related.

NetWare today provides the best network printing services available on the market. But, even with the robustness and flexibility of NetWare's print services, a number of challenges still exist for network users and administrators when it comes to network printing.

Users often can't find the printer they want to print to, and when they do, chances are likely they won't have the necessary driver for it. So, they just do the best they can at guessing. The result is generally pages and pages of wasted paper with a bunch of printer error codes.

Network administrators face complex configuration and management with network printing today. Earlier in the chapter we looked at how to set up network printing, and for the first-time NetWare user, it's not a simple task. Just to add a new printer to the network, there are many steps involved. After the new printer hardware is installed and configured, the administrator must create a print queue and a print server to service that printer. Then, after the printer is set up, each user may need to have the correct driver installed on his/her desktop. The whole process of installing a new printer is quite time-consuming.

These reasons alone were enough for Novell to stop and take a good hard look at NetWare's printing services. Recognizing these issues and others, Novell partnered with Xerox and Hewlett-Packard to develop an entirely new printing architecture called NetWare Distributed Print Services (NDPS). NDPS will be delivered with the next release of NetWare and, at the time of this writing, is still largely in development.

The goal of NDPS is to take the guesswork out of managing and using network printing. NDPS will provide simple plug-and-print configuration of network printers, eliminating the need to spend hours configuring network printing. NDPS will also take advantage of the intelligence built in to many of today's printers, giving users more information about network printers and more control over their print jobs than ever before.

NDPS will provide many benefits to users and to CNEs. Those benefits are described below. Ready, set, print.

ZEN

"My hair. The outer shell is hair spray. Inside, there's gel, mousse, volumizer—a whole infrastructure. The only difference between me and the Kingdome is Astroturf!"

Nanny Fine

MAKING LIFE EASIER FOR USERS

Did you ever notice that just about every time you send a print job to the network something unexpected happens? Unfortunately, that unexpected something is usually bad. You accidentally sent a PCL print job to a postscript printer, or somebody else did something weird and your print job is stuck behind about 15 others, so you go to lunch and come back an hour later to find that your job still hasn't printed! And, through all of this, the network never once gave you any indication that there was a problem.

NDPS solves these network printing problems by providing the following capabilities:

- ► Bidirectional communication

- ► Print job move/copy options

- ► Automatic driver download

- ► Job-to-printer matching

- ► Multifunction printer and device support

Bidirectional Communication

NDPS takes advantage of the intelligence built in to today's network printing by providing bidirectional information exchange between network users and printers. This exchange provides feedback so that users always know the state of their print jobs. When something is wrong with the printer that a user has selected, the user can be notified of the problem and how to fix it. For example, if the selected printer is out of paper, the user can be notified and given the option of either adding paper and resuming the job or rerouting the job to another printer. Administrators can also be notified of critical printer problems such as low toner or printer failure. This notification can be in the form of an on-screen pop-up message, an e-mail message, a telephone call, or a pager beep.

Print Job Move/Copy Options

Users have complete flexibility when it comes to rerouting print jobs after they have been submitted to the network for printing. With the current NetWare printing services, once a print job has been submitted to the queue, there is not a whole lot a user can do with it except delete it or put it on hold. NDPS will provide users with the option to move or copy print jobs to other printers after they have been submitted to the network for printing.

As mentioned above, the bidirectional communication functionality allows for printers to notify users of the state of their print jobs. Users can then take action based on that information. For example, let's say you have 20 minutes to get to a meeting that's all the way on the other side of town. And, of course, you need to print a document to take to that meeting. So you think, "20 minutes...no sweat, it'll take 5 minutes to print the job and I'll be on the road in 10." (Yeah, right.) So you submit the job to the network for printing.

Now, in today's printing environment, when your job doesn't print right away, you run around like a chicken with its head cut off trying to figure out where the problem is. With NDPS, you'll get a nice little message right at your desktop that says something like, "The printer you selected is not available. Would you like to reroute the job?" Of course you would, so the job is routed to another printer that meets the requirements of your job (for example, postscript printing), and you're on your way as planned. Sounds like a dream, huh?

Automatic Driver Download

Another big area of frustration for users is never having the right driver for the printer they'd like to use. With NDPS, if a user selects a printer that he/she does not have a driver for, the system will automatically download that driver to their desktop. Also, when installing new printers on the network, the administrator can specify an automatic driver download for the users who will be using that printer. This saves a tremendous amount of time since the administrator no longer has to go to each workstation to physically install the driver.

Job-to-Printer Matching

With NDPS, the user is presented with a "best fit" printer that meets the requirements for the print job he/she is sending, whether the requirements are locality, resolution, color, or speed. Also, if the user sends a print job to the incorrect type of printer, such as a PCL job to a postscript printer, NDPS will notify the user of the problem and provide him/her with a list of printers he/she is authorized to use and that match the job requirements. And if the user doesn't have a driver for the selected printer, the driver will be downloaded to his/her workstation automatically. Users also are able to filter the available printers based on which ones are most important to them.

Multifunction Printer and Device Support

The current NetWare printing architecture isolates applications from network printers. When a user sends a print job from within an application, that job is directed to a local LPT port. NetWare then captures that print job and redirects it to a print queue at the file server. The print server then routes the print job to the appropriate network printer. Since applications can't access network printers directly, they cannot take advantage of new network printer functionality that is emerging today, such as gluing, stapling, or duplex options.

NDPS provides an open integration platform for both hardware vendors and software developers. The architecture is fully extensible, increasing user and application awareness of printer capabilities. Hardware vendors can expose their printer capabilities to users through standard NDPS APIs. Through the NDS and NDPS APIs, software developers can create desktop applications that let users select printer capabilities from within applications.

This extensible design will also accommodate add-on printer functionality, such as gluing and stapling, that can be provided through third-party drivers and extensions or through embedding of NDPS functionality into a variety of print devices and products.

The NDPS architecture also supports fax, scan, and multifunction devices. As nontraditional types of devices such as these become integrated into the network, the NDPS functionality will extend to support them.

ZEN

"Fourteen is a very vulnerable age. I remember once my mother picked me up from school in a halter top and pedal pushers. I'm still looking for the right support group."

Nanny Fine

That's great for the users, but what about us?! Fortunately, NDPS includes a myriad of great features for CNEs as well. Check them out.

MAKING LIFE EASIER FOR CNES

The usability features of NDPS alone make administrators eager for the next release of NetWare. But it gets better. NDPS also provides a number of administration features that make creating and administering NetWare 4 printing quick and easy. These features include:

- ▸ Streamlined configuration

- ▸ Plug-and-print

- ▸ Reduced network traffic

- ▸ Event notification

Streamlined Configuration

NDPS streamlines printing configuration by eliminating print servers and print queues found in previous versions of NetWare. NDPS contains a logical print management agent that acts as an intelligent, simplified print server, spooler, and print queue all in one. This agent maintains information about specific physical printers and accepts operations from print clients. These agents appear as NDS objects and take advantage of NetWare services such as management and security. These agents can be physically embedded on NDPS enabled printers or can be run as an NLM at a NetWare 4 file server. This allows for support of both NDPS-enabled and legacy printers.

NDPS also allows all printers to be managed remotely from within NWADMIN. Printer manufacturers can write NWADMIN snap-ins that provide printer management from within the utility. The administrator can then control a printer remotely without ever leaving his/her desk. For example, if the administrator would like to issue a form feed on an NDPS printer, he/she simply clicks on the NDS object that represents the printer and is presented with a graphical representation of the device. The administrator then checks the status, issues a form feed or performs any other function that would normally be done at the printer.

Plug-and-Print

Adding new printers to a Novell network has never been easy. Not only do you have to set up and configure the hardware, but you also have to deal with the NetWare printing setup, which we've just spent an entire chapter trying to teach you. NDPS's plug-and-print feature will eliminate the time and frustration of adding printers to the network. When a new NDPS-enabled printer is added to the network, you will be able to plug it in and begin printing.

Plug-and-print is where Novell's partnership with HP and Xerox comes in. In addition to teaming up with Novell to develop the NDPS architecture, these printer vendors will be delivering NDPS-enabled printers with the logical NDPS management agent embedded in them. This eliminates the need for the administrator to set up printers, queues, and print servers in NDS. When the printer is plugged into the network, it will automatically register with NDS as an available printer and no other configuration will be required.

HP and Xerox will be the first printer manufacturers to provide NDPS-enabled printers. After the initial release of NDPS, other printer manufactures will begin providing NDPS-enabled printers.

Reduced Network Traffic

Currently, when network attached printers are used, they immediately begin advertising their availability to NetWare users as soon as they are plugged in. This advertising is done through NetWare's Service Advertising Protocol (SAP). These devices will send a SAP broadcast out on the network every 60 seconds, which results in increased network traffic. With NDPS, when a network-attached printer is added to the network, it will register once with NDS, and NDS will take care of the rest. This will greatly reduce network traffic because network-attached printers will no longer be required to advertise their availability.

Event Notification

NDPS not only provides event notification for users, but also for administrators. An administrator can be notified of important events such as emergency breakdowns or other out-of-service conditions. They can also receive advance notice of when service will be required, such as a low-toner situation. This notification can be received in a number of different ways: as an on-screen pop-up message, an e-mail message, a fax, or even a pager beep. With Novell's promise of workflow management within NetWare, NDPS could send an e-mail to the administrator to indicate that the toner is low on a specific printer and at the same time place an order for a new toner cartridge. Other information can be kept and communicated on demand, such as printer utilization statistics and accounting information.

NDPS is scalable from the smallest network to the largest enterprise. With features like plug-and-print, organizations won't require printing experts to install and maintain printers. This benefits small and large organizations alike. For enterprise environments where centralized security and control are required, NDPS provides the distributed management capabilities and security necessary. And for the small company, anyone can add a new printer to the network without having to be a NetWare guru.

QUIZ

Here's the ultimate numbers mystery. Let's see if you're up to the task. Fill the grid below with the numbers 1 to 16 to form a magic square so that each vertical and horizontal line, each corner to corner diagonal line, the four corner numbers, each block of four corner squares and the middle four block of numbers each add up to 34. The number 7 has been filled in for good luck. Ready, set, calculate.

7			

(Q14-5)

Congratulations! Mystery solved. The answer to the question of life is a four letter acronym—NDPS. And it doesn't stand for "Never Darn Purple Socks" or "Neanderthal's Don't Purchase Spaghetti." NDPS is Novell's answer for the current state of NetWare 4 printing. But you can't have it yet, sorry. Patience is a virtue—and whoever said that never had to deal with NetWare users.

I enjoy a good mystery, how about you? NetWare 4 printing is a great place to start. We discovered a lot of interesting things about it today, and I think you're definitely ready to attack it on your own. But if you're still feeling a little skittish, here's a quick review:

It all started with the essence of printing. In the old days, we used to print by ourselves. Now, we get to share this honor with hundreds of strangers. Network printing is has probably had a major impact on the social fabric of humanity—we just don't notice it. We went on a little journey through the life of a print job—starting with CAPTURE, then to the queue, print server, and ultimately the printer. Wasn't that fun?

Then, we learned all the steps involved in printing setup. It's not so bad. There are only four steps and they're not very hard. First, you create the print queue, then the printer, and finally the print server. Then, to top it all off, you activate the print server. No sweat. We also discovered a few secrets about customizing NetWare 4 printing with print forms and devices.

Once it's up an running, the fun part starts—keeping it running. NetWare 4 printing management focused on six CNE and user tools, namely PCONSOLE, NWADMIN, PSC, PRINTCON, PRINTDEF, and NETUSER. We learned how to configure, manage, and customize the NetWare 4 printing system. I bet you didn't realize how much help there is out there! Don't worry—you're not alone.

Finally, we took a peak at NetWare's printing future—NDPS. I'm excited, how about you. It's great to know there's help around the corner—if you need it. NDPS provides a myriad of benefits for both using (users) and managing (CNEs) NetWare 4 printing. Look for it soon at a printing store near you.

ZEN

"I was thinking about the Pilgrims. How'd they know what to pack? I mean, you're going to a new world. Is it hot, ...cold, ...rainy? There are no brochures! So they all wear the same thing and what a mistake. Very few people look good in a bit hat, a big collar, AND a big buckle. What were they thinking?"

Nanny Fine

So how do you feel now? A little better? Did all that wisdom from Nanny Fine soothe your brain? Well, if you're still a little worried about going out on your own, I have a surprise for you—exercises! You want practice, I've got practice. A bunch of hands-on exercises are just the cure for printing cold feet. Once you've cruised through the following seven exercises, you'll be a printing pro. You'll be ready for anything...except a shopping spree with Nanny Fine—ouch! Go get them, and I'll see you in the final frontier.

This exercise will walk you though the creation and loading of a basic print system using the NWADMIN (Windows) graphical interface. This assumes you have already created ACME's NDS tree. We'll be working in the Crime Fighting department today. Seems appropriate since we're trying to solve a mystery. Where's Sherlock Holmes when you need him?

For the exercise, we will assume the following names:

- *Print server:* WHITE-PS1

- *Print queue:* CANONBJ-PQ1

- *Printer:* CANONBJ-P1

First we will create the queue.

QUEUE CREATION

1 • Select the container WHITE.CRIME.TOKYO.ACME with the mouse.

2 • With the container WHITE selected, press Insert or choose Object/Create from the menu bar.

3 • Choose Print Queue and click on OK.

4 • Enter the queue name CANONBJ-PQ1.

5 • Click on the browser button and select your server's volume SYS.

6 • Click on the Define Additional Properties option.

7 • For Other Name, type in **MainQ.**

8 • For Location, type in **Downtown.**

9 • Select Users.

10 • Who is/are the existing queue users? Why?

11 • Remove the allowed users and add yourself as the only queue user.

12 • Select OK.

13 • Go to a DOS box (under Windows). Type in **DIR Q*.*** and notice what you see.

14 • CD into the directory found. Count how many subdirectories exists with a QDR extension.

Next, we need to create the printer.

PRINTER CREATION

1 • Return to NWADMIN.

2 • Select the WHITE.CRIME.TOKYO.ACME container again.

3 • Press Insert again (or Object/Create), and choose a printer this time.

4 • Name the printer as noted above.

5 • Click on Define Additional Properties and then on OK.

6 • Under Other Name, type **Booking Printer**.

7 • Click on Assignments.

8 • Add the print queue just created.

9 • Click on the Configuration button, then the Communication button, and choose the Auto Load button.

10 • Choose OK.

11 • Click on Notification.

12 • Click on Notify Print Job Owner (deselect the option). Note what happens.

13 • Click on Notify Print Job Owner again to reselect, and note what happens.

14 • Click on Features.

15 • Under Supported Cartridges, type **Fingerprint.**

16 • Select OK.

Finally, it's time to build the print server.

CREATING THE PRINT SERVER

1 • Select the WHITE.CRIME.TOKYO.ACME container again.

2 • Press Insert again (or Object/Create), and choose a print server this time.

3 • Name the print server as noted above.

4 • Click on Define Additional Properties and click OK.

5 • Click on Change Password.

6 • Enter the password **Secret,** and reconfirm. Then press OK.

7 • Click on Assignments.

8 • Add the CANONBJ-P1 printer.

9 • Click on Users.

10 • Who is the current print server user? Why?

11 • Delete the current print server user and add yourself only.

12 • Click on Operator. Who is the operator and why?

13 • Click on Auditing Log.

14 • Click on Enable Auditing.

15 • Click on OK in the lowest left-hand corner (to save all changes).

16 • Double-click on the print server WHITE-PS1.

17 • Click on Print Layout.

18 • Note the exclamation point next to the print server. Why do you think this is?

19 • Click on the print server to select it and then click on Status. Note what you see.

20 • Click on Close.

21 • Click on Cancel to leave this screen.

Congratulations! You've built ACME's printing system. Now all you have to do is find the right printer and load the print server. Ready, set, print.

FINDING THE PRINTER

1 • Click on the very [root] of the tree.

2 • Choose Object/Search from the menu bar.

3 • Click on Search Entire Subtree.

4 • Under Search For choose Printer.

5 • Under Property, choose Cartridge.

6 • Under the blank entry box (to the right of Equal To), type **Fingerprint.**

7 • Select OK.

8 • Select Yes (Continue).

9 • Note the results from the search.

10 • Double-click on the printer to verify it's correct.

LOADING THE PRINT SERVER

1 • At the server console, ensure you are at the colon prompt.

2 • Type **LOAD PSERVER** and press Return.

3 • Enter in the context where the print server resides (WHITE.CRIME.TOKYO.ACME) and press Return.

4 • Choose the print server we've defined (WHITE-PS1).

5 • What happens next?

6 • Take steps to allow loading to continue.

7 • Choose Printer Status.

8 • Choose CANONBJ-P1.

9 • Note status of the printer.

10 • Escape back to the Available Options screen.

11 • Choose Print Server Information.

12 • Choose Current Status.

13 • Choose Unload. What happens?

14 • Reload the print server again.

See Appendix C for answers.

CASE STUDY: USING ACME'S PRINTING SYSTEM

This section assumes that you have two users setup in the WHITE.CRIME.TOKYO.ACME container. This will allow us to test capturing data and enabling print job configurations. You should have already completed the previous exercise.

You will log in as two different users in this exercise:

- ▶ Robin Hood (RHood)

- ▶ Maid Marion (MMarion)

You should also be created as yourself and currently logged in as such. You should not be currently captured.

1 • Go to a DOS box under Windows.

2 • Type **CAPTURE SH** and note the results.

3 • Type **CAPTURE** and note what happens.

4 • Change to the context where the CANONBJ-PQ1 exists. How do you do this?

5 • CAPTURE to the CANONBJ-PQ1 using the Q option. What does the command look like?

6 • End the capture using CAPTURE. How do you do this?

7 • Return to Windows.

8 • Run the NWUSER utility.

9 • Click on the printer icon.

10 • Use the browser on the right to locate the context WHITE.CRIME.TOKYO.ACME. Then click on the printer icon located on the top button bar.

11 • Drag either the printer or the queue to the left onto LPT1:.

12 • Double-click on the new printer mapping.

13 • Note the default settings for the capture.

14 • Leave the NWUSER utility.

15 • Logout as the user and re-login as RHood. Before you do this, ensure Sspeeders has at least Read and File Scan access to the volume SYS:.

16 • From a DOS box, change to the WHITE.CRIME.TOKYO.ACME container using the CX command.

17 • Attempt to CAPTURE to the CANONBJ-PQ1 queue. What happens and why?

18 • Re-login as yourself again. How would you grant access to the user RHood?

19 • Change to the context WHITE.CRIME.TOKYO.ACME and reenable capture to the network queue CANONBJ-PQ1. How can you do this?

20 • Start NWADMIN.

21 • Choose Object/Print from the NWADMIN menu bar and print the current NWADMIN screen.

22 • Ensure the capture is working. Where can you look in NWADMIN to verify this?

23 • Return to a DOS box and ensure capture is working. What is the command to do this?

24 • Print a DOS text file to the network. How can you do this while capture is activated?

25 • End the capture.

26 • Return to Windows.

27 • Create a print job configuration for the container WHITE.CRIME.TOKYO.ACME and call it Main. Where would this be done?

28 • Grant the container WHITE.CRIME.TOKYO.ACME access to the print queue CANONBJ-PQ1. How would you do this?

29 • Login as RHood.

30 • Under DOS, type **CAPTURE** and note what happens.

31 • Login as yourself to modify the queue.

32 • Return to NWADMIN and again select the configuration under the container WHITE.CRIME.TOKYO.ACME. Highlight the configuration Main and click on Default. Note the printer icon that now appears next to the configuration. Note also the options for the configuration (copies, queue, notification). Press OK to save.

33 • Login as RHood again.

34 • Return to a DOS box and execute **CAPTURE**. What happens now?

35 • Type **CAPTURE SH.** What do you note about the settings?

See Appendix C for answers.

This assumes you have a printer attached to the print server ready to print (on-line, with paper). It also assumes the print server is running on the NetWare server.

1 • Login as yourself, start Windows, and run NWADMIN.

2 • Select the printer CANONBJ-P1 by double-clicking.

3 • Select Status for the printer.

4 • Select Pause. What changes with the printer?

5 • Send two jobs to the queue CANONBJ-PQ1.

6 • Go to the queue CANONBJ-PQ1. Double-click on it and choose Job List. What do you see?

7 • Select the first job and choose Details.

8 • Click on the User Hold option. What does the status display?

9 • Return to the printer CANONBJ-P1 and choose Status again.

10 • Choose Resume to reenable the printer. What happens?

11 • Place the printer off-line after the job has completed printing. Use the printer's on-line/off-line button for this.

12 • View the printer CANONBJ-P1's status under NWADMIN.

13 • Note the status of the printer.

14 • With the printer status up (viewing percentage and such), place the printer back on-line and watch what happens.

15 • Once the job has completed printing, select the print server WHITE-PS1 by double-clicking on it.

16 • Select Print Layout.

17 • Select each item and click on status one at a time. What do you see?

18 • Select the Identification button on the top right. Near the bottom is another button labeled Unload. Select it.

19 • Choose Unload Print Server Immediately. Monitor the file server if you can. What happens?

20 • Choose Cancel to leave the Print Server Detail screens.

21 • Reselect the print server WHITE-PS1. Choose Print layout.

22 • What do you notice that is different? What do you think this means?

23 • Choose WHITE-PS1 and click on Status. Does this verify your assumption?

24 • Submit another job to CANONBJ-PQ1.

25 • Choose the CANONBJ-PQ1 and select Job List.

26 • Select any job other than the first (Seq 001) and choose Job Details.

27 • Locate Service Sequence on the middle left-hand side.

28 • Change Service Sequence to 001.

29 • Select OK.

30 • What looks different?

See Appendix C for answers.

EXERCISE 14-1: USING QUICK SETUP IN PCONSOLE

The following exercise will walk you through the process of creating NetWare 4 printing objects using the Quick Setup option of PCONSOLE. Before beginning this exercise, be sure you are in the context that you wish to create new printing objects in and logged in as a user with sufficient rights to create objects.

1 • From the DOS command line, run the PCONSOLE utility by typing **PCONSOLE** and pressing Enter.

2 • Use the arrow keys to select Quick Setup and press Enter.

3 • From the Print Services Configuration menu, modify the print server, printer, and print queue name to match the naming standards of your organization.

4 • Verify the volume you wish this print queue to be created on. If necessary, use the Insert key to browse the tree and select the appropriate volume.

5 • Specify the banner type. This should be based on the type of printer you are using. PCL printers use text banners.

6 • Specify the printer type (parallel, serial, or other), location (manual load—workstation or network attached; or auto load—locally attached).

7 • Specify the interrupt or polled mode (recommended). If interrupt is chosen it must match the configuration of the physical printer port.

8 • Specify the port to which this printer is attached.

9 • When configuration is complete, press Esc and Yes to save.

EXERCISE 14-2: MANUAL PRINTING SETUP IN PCONSOLE

The following exercise will walk you through the process of creating NetWare 4 printing objects using the individual print queues, printers, and print server options of PCONSOLE. Before beginning this exercise, be sure you are in the context that you wish to create new printing objects in and logged in as a user with sufficient rights to create objects.

1 • From the DOS command line, run the PCONSOLE utility by typing **PCONSOLE** and then pressing Enter.

2 • From the Available Options menu select Print Queues.

3 • Use the Insert key to create a new print queue.

4 • Enter a print queue name that matches the naming standards of your organization.

5 • Enter the print queue's volume. Press the Insert key and browse the NDS tree to choose the appropriate volume and press Enter to select.

6 • Press Esc to return to the Available Options menu.

7 • Choose Printers.

8 • Press the Insert key to create a new printer.

9 • Enter a printer name that matches the naming standards of your organization.

10 • Select the printer by pressing Enter.

11 • Under Printer Configuration specify the port to which this printer is attached.

12 • Specify the printer type (parallel, serial, or other) location (manual load— workstation or network attached; or auto load—locally attached).

13 • Specify the interrupt or polled mode (recommended). If interrupt is chosen it must match the configuration of the physical printer port.

14 • Specify an address restriction, if desired.

15 • When configuration is complete, press Esc.

16 • If forms are being used, specify the starting form number.

17 • Specify the banner type. This should be based on the type of printer you are using. PCL printers use text banners.

18 • If multiple form types are being used, specify the forms service mode you desire.

19 • Press Enter at *Print queues assigned* and use the Insert key to add a print queue to service this queue.

20 • Use the arrow keys to select the queue you created above and press Enter to select. When you have finished, press Esc.

21 • Optional: Press Enter at Notification to add users or groups to be notified of printer problems. Use the Insert key to browse the NDS tree.

22 • When you have completed the printer configuration, press Esc to save the changes.

23 • Press Esc to return to the Available options menu and select Print Servers.

24 • Use the Insert key to add a new print server.

25 • Enter a print server name that matches the naming conventions of your organization.

26 • Under the Print Server Information menu, select Printers.

27 • Use the Insert key to select the printer you created above.

28 • Press Esc twice to return to the Available Options menu.

This exercise will walk you through the process of creating a print job configuration for the user you are currently logged in as.

1 • From the DOS command line, run the PRINTCON utility by typing: **PRINTCON** and then pressing Enter.

2 • Select Print Job Configurations.

3 • Press the Insert key to create a new print job configuration.

4 • Enter a name for this new print job configuration.

5 • Press Enter to select the job configuration.

6 • Use the arrow keys to select Local printer.

7 • Enter the printer port you wish to capture (1=LPT1, 2=LPT2, and so on).

8 • Use the arrow keys to select print queue.

9 • Press Insert and browse the NDS tree to find the desired print queue. Press Enter to select it.

10 • Specify other desired options such as form feed, banner, and form number.

11 • When you have finished, press Esc and Yes to save changes.

12 • Press Esc to exit.

Optimization

Optimization...the final frontier. This is the voyage of the starship NetWare 4. Its continuing mission is to explore strange, new NDS trees. To seek out new users and new wide area networks. To boldly go where no CNE has gone before!

Congratulations! You made it. Welcome to the next generation of NetWare 4. And more important, welcome to the end of this book. It's been a long and winding road, but we struggled through it together. We designed the cloud, built the tree, secured the users, configured the WAN, and managed the printers. It's all in a day's work for a CNE superhero/doctor/gardener.

Now, we've reached the final frontier of NetWare 4—optimization! This is the last great journey. A journey of self-realization; learning to be the best you can be; reaching for the stars; expanding your horizons; and so on. But don't stop there; NetWare 4 optimization is more than just a collection of trite phrases, it is "warp" speed!

Before you can cruise the intergalactic information highway, you need to make a few last-minute adjustments to your server's warp drive. It will need to operate at peak performance in order to handle the demands of strange aliens and NetWare 4 users. Fortunately, you're Captain CNE, and you know how to optimize the warp drive. You know that it consists of two important tasks:

▸ Monitoring

▸ Optimization

Monitoring involves periodic interrogation of key performance components, like file cache buffers, packet receive buffers (PRBs), and disk allocation blocks. NetWare 4 CNEs use MONITOR.NLM for daily performance monitoring. *Optimization* is the next step. Now you must proactively fine-tune each of these components so the server operates at peak performance. NetWare 4 CNEs use SERVMAN.NLM and SET parameters for optimization tasks.

Balance is the key. Balance among server performance, reliability, and security. They all live in cohesive harmony. If you exaggerate any component over the others, it could throw the server out of balance—this is not a good thing. The bottom line is this: Don't optimize the server in a vacuum. Consider the impact of your actions on the server as a whole. Believe it or not, that extra nanosecond of performance isn't always worth it overall—consider the big picture.

Speaking of the big picture, let's start our journey with a discussion of optimization components. They are the "di-lithium crystals" that make up your NetWare 4 server. We need to understand them before we start fiddling around. Warp speed ahead.

ZEN

"Victory belongs to the most persevering!"

Napoleon

▶ · ◀

Optimization Components

There are many factors that affect your network's overall performance. Most of them center around the file server. It is a source of great misunderstanding and confusion. Administrators from the mainframe world tend to overemphasize the importance of file server processing. The bottom line is: This is a distributed computing system, not a centralized one. The file server handles only 5 percent of the network's overall processing. The majority of the work is handled by the workstation—it says so right there in the name.

If the file server CPU isn't the most important optimization component, then what is? Well, that depends on your bottlenecks. *Bottlenecks* are optimization hot spots that slow down file server performance. They can exist anywhere—server NIC, disk channel, memory, workstation, cabling, and so on. The best place to start is the server network interface card (NIC).

The file server NIC sees the most network traffic. It should be fast—at least 16-bit, but hopefully 32-bit. Also, consider bus-mastering NICs and disk controllers to alleviate chatter from the CPU. Finally, some LANs benefit from splitting the network segment and placing two NICs in the file server. This is called Internal Routing.

The next bottleneck is created by the disk channel. It relies on controller and hard drive speed. If the hard drive channel is slow it won't matter how much memory or processor power you put in the server. You can make an 80386 server (with a fast hard drive) run just as fast as an 80486 server (with a slow hard drive). Remember, the

NetWare 4 server is simply serving files. You also need to be aware of what sorts of tasks you're asking the server to perform. If most users access a customer database for reading information, then you need to optimize the file system for fast "reads." If the same users spend all day changing the database you'll want to optimize for fast "writes."

Third, take a long hard look at your client workstations. Because NetWare 4 distributes processing to clients, the quality of your workstations makes a big difference. You could have a super fast file server but if your clients are running on 80286 workstation with 1 MB RAM, they're going to complain that the network is slow. Remember, distributed applications are running at the speed of the client station. While you're upgrading the clients, upgrade their NICs as well. No sense leaving an 8-bit card in a PC when you can essentially double the network throughput with a 16-bit card.

Fourth, explore the bottlenecks created by local operating systems. If your users are using Windows, consider adding local bus video to their workstations. Windows bottlenecks are frequently screen redraws. Speeding up that process sometimes compensates for other slow components. As new versions of Windows are released, you'll also want to increase the amount of memory and hard disk space at the desktop.

ZEN

"We are here and it is now. Further than that, all knowledge is moonshine."

H. L. Mencken

There are a few good bottlenecks to explore before you get too wrapped up in NetWare 4 optimization. Many times these simple fixes make the world of difference. But, no matter how you slice it, optimization focuses on three main components:

- ▶ Blocks and Buffers

- ▶ Tables

- ▶ Memory Management

A *block* is an allocation unit on the server disk. They store files permanently. *Buffers* are allocation units in server memory. They store files temporarily. Block and buffer sizes dramatically affect memory utilization, and therefore network performance.

Tables, on the other hand, transcend blocks and buffers. Some tables are stored on disk, then copied into memory as needed. Some are only memory constructs, and are created and discarded as needed, but never saved. We care about server tables because they use up file server memory and impact read/write performance.

Finally, *memory management* impacts every facet of NetWare 4 optimization. In earlier versions of NetWare, the server relied on a fragmented memory pool architecture that was inefficient and slow. NetWare 4 uses the same architecture, but memory utilization has improved—now it's more efficient and not as slow (faster). In addition, NetWare 4 memory management relies on a new memory protection scheme for fault tolerance and reliability. After all, performance is REALLY bad when the server crashes.

Let's take a closer look at these three main optimization components and prep ourselves for the onslaught of MONITOR.NLM (monitoring) and SERVMAN.NLM (optimization).

BLOCKS AND BUFFERS

As we learned earlier, blocks are storage allocation units on disk and buffers are storage allocation units in server memory. Since the file server is primarily involved in serving files, performance optimization relies on the efficient management of blocks and buffers. Also, you'll find that many of the monitoring tasks in MONITOR.NLM and optimization tasks in SERVMAN.NLM focus on special blocks and buffers—such as file allocation blocks, file cache buffers, packet receive buffers, and directory cache buffers. Refer to Figure 15.1 for an illustration of NetWare 4 blocks and buffers.

When a volume is created (initial installation or when a new disk is added), the file allocation blocks are created as well. One of your most important installation decisions is block size. Valid answers are 4 KB, 8 KB, 16 KB, 32 KB, and 64 KB. There will be a default, and it will vary with the size of the volume itself. For example, a 100 MB volume will default to 4 KB blocks, while a 10,000 MB volume defaults to 64 KB.

The trade-off between a small and large block size is speed and space. Each file takes up at least one block—suballocation works only on excess data; the first file segment always reserves an entire block. This fact argues for a small block size. At the other extreme, a large file can be read far more efficiently if its blocks of data are contiguous. So a 64 KB file in one block provides much better performance than the same file stored in sixteen 4 KB blocks scattered around the disk (see Figure 15.2).

FIGURE 15.1

Blocks and Buffers in
NetWare 4

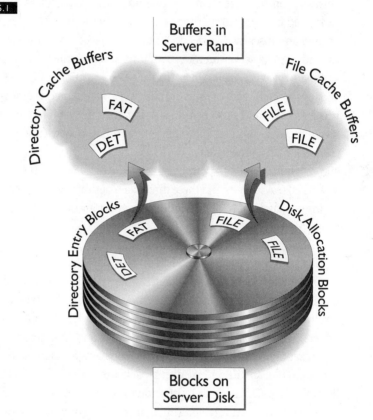

If there is only one volume on the server, then the default is almost always fine especially if you've activated the block suballocation feature. On the other hand, if the server supports multiple volumes, it is often worth the effort to find the optimal block size and standardize it across all volumes. This makes file cache memory utilization far more efficient. Let me explain.

File cache buffer sizing doesn't have as dramatic an effect on performance as file allocation block sizing. But there is one hard and fast rule: File cache buffer sizing must be consistent across all volumes on a server. (NetWare does this for you.) And, the size must match the smallest file allocation block size on any volume. NetWare will not mount a volume whose file allocation block size is smaller than the file cache buffer size.

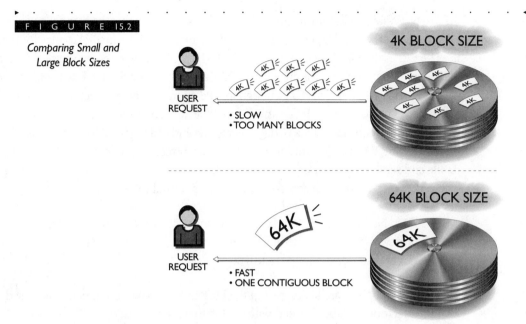

This means that a server with several large volumes and a single small one will be forced to use smaller buffers—this is less efficient. The defaults will set a small block size for the small volume, and then force the file cache buffers to match that small allocation size. This will have a negative impact on the performance of the larger disks with their larger blocks. To tune dissimilar hardware properly, you should increase the size of the smaller volume's allocation units to match the size of the large disk's blocks. Easy as pie.

That completes our discussion of blocks and buffers. Don't worry; we'll explore them in more depth throughout the chapter. Now let's take a look at NetWare 4 tables.

TABLES

Tables are involved in every facet of file reads and writes. NetWare 4 relies on two file system tables to store location and configuration information about internal files and directories. To understand them, let's review the steps the server goes through in accessing a user's data file.

First, NetWare checks the directory table (DET) to make sure that the user has sufficient rights to access the file. Then it looks at the DET entry to find the first FAT entry for that file. The FAT is the File Allocation Table. The FAT has an entry for every physical sector on the disk. Every time a file is created, the FAT entry for that cylinder, head, and sector address is updated. If the file is big enough to take up more than one sector, the first FAT entry also points to the next FAT entry for that file, and so on.

When a user requests a block of data toward the end of a big file, NetWare reads all of the intervening FAT entries until it has found the correct file, then it actually retrieves the file and sends it to the user.

In order to speed up data access, NetWare does several things:

▸ First, NetWare keeps files in RAM as long as it can. This way, files are retrieved from file cache buffers, thus avoiding disk access. This can increase server read performance up to 100 times!

▸ Second, NetWare keeps part of the DET in RAM, so that frequently accessed directories can be checked without first having to go to disk.

▸ Third, NetWare keeps the entire FAT in server memory to speed up the FAT scanning time.

▸ Fourth, and finally, NetWare creates an index of the FAT entries (for large files only). This index is called the "Turbo Fat." It is created when the file is first accessed, then maintained as long as any client has the file open. It is discarded a short time after the last user closes it—five and a half minutes is the default; it can be changed with a SET command.

Table 15.1 summarizes NetWare 4 file and directory hashing (indexing) and caching. As you can see, the FAT is held in memory (cached), as are the most recently accessed files. Furthermore, parts of the FAT are indexed (hashed). Files themselves are not indexed. It would be rather useless to have the system alphabetize all of the words in your memos, for example.

T A B L E 15.1		CACHING	HASHING
A Summary of File/ Directory Hashing and Caching options	FAT	Yes	Yes
	File	Yes	No

MEMORY MANAGEMENT

Memory management has the most dramatic impact on NetWare 4 server optimization. After all, everything happens there. Of course, disk and NIC optimization run a very close second. Memory management operates in two important spheres:

▸ Memory Utilization

▸ Memory Protection

Let's take a closer look.

Memory Utilization

NetWare 4 includes a substantially improved memory utilization strategy. In order to best understand it, let's take a moment to explore our roots—NetWare 3.

When NetWare 3 arrived, everyone applauded its new memory utilization scheme. That was appropriate because it was a vast improvement over the strategy used in NetWare 2. As experience with NetWare 3 accumulated, certain minor problems became apparent. The most troublesome of them was memory pool inefficiencies. It turned out that memory pools grew as needed, but never contracted. They never returned unused RAM. In some cases, this could result in the loss of a significant portion of file server memory.

The designers of NetWare 4 decided to fix this, and reengineered the memory pool concept. It still uses the memory pool architecture, but unused RAM is returned. The biggest change is that memory pools can both request and free memory. In NetWare 3, there were some pools, most notably Permanent Memory and Alloc Short-Term Memory, that would take memory as needed, but never return it when finished. The only cure for this problem was to periodically down and restart the server. This reset all the memory pools to their default (smaller) sizes. In NetWare 4, memory is still assigned to pools, but they return RAM to the file cache pool when they're done.

So why do we need the memory pools at all? To off-load memory resource tracking from SERVER.EXE. You see, when a particular resource requests a buffer of RAM (for an NLM, LAN driver, or console screen image), NetWare takes it from file caching. Therefore, SERVER.EXE can ignore the pooled chunk of memory. If it wasn't "pooled," SERVER.EXE would have to track all its memory-related parameters—too much work for one little file.

SERVER.EXE does, however, track other memory-related events—such as dirty. If the contents of a memory buffer change, the file cache buffers marks the buffer as "dirty"—who washes them? You can track dirty cache buffers in MONITOR.NLM.

ZEN

"Look, I really don't want to wax philosophic, but I will say that if you're alive, you got to flap your arms and legs, you got to jump around a lot, you got to make some noise, because life is the very opposite of death."

Mel Brooks

The process of recovering available memory is called Garbage Collection. NLM programmers can tell the operating system that they no longer need a particular block of memory via the FREE command. Once freed, those blocks are ready for collection. Note: Can't you just see the little garbage trucks running about inside file server memory looking for discarded bits and collecting them together to make new pools? I can see you're going to have strange dreams tonight.

The garbage collection process is a low-priority process that runs in the background when the file server is experiencing periods of low activity. Nevertheless, there are three SET parameters that control the process. Table 15.2 lists the commands, their default, minimum and maximum settings, and their meanings. In use, they provide three different triggers for garbage collection. In other words, if either 15 minutes have elapsed, or 5000 FREEs have been issued, or 8000 alloc memory bytes are available, then garbage collection will begin.

We'll explore SET commands and SERVMAN later in the chapter. But here's a quick preview. SET is a NetWare 4 console command. The great news about SET is that once you select a category, the current values for each parameter are displayed on the screen. In addition, the range of parameters is also displayed so you know how high or low you can go. Beats looking it up in a manual.

COMMAND	DEFAULT	MIN.	MAX.	MEANING
Garbage Collection Interval	15 min.	1 min.	60 min.	The interval between times that the collection process is initiated
Number of FREEs for Garbage Collection	5000	100	100,000	Number of FREEs that will trigger the collection process
Minimum Free Memory For Garbage Collection	8 KB	1000	1 MB	The minimum number of bytes that must be available in Alloc memory for successful collection

T A B L E 15.2

SET Parameters for Garbage Collection

In addition to SET, MONITOR.NLM provides numerous memory utilization statistics. Most of them are found under the Resource Utilization option. Figure 15.3 illustrates the NetWare 4 memory pools and their current utilization statistics. Later in the chapter, we'll use this screen to determine how our server resources utilize available RAM. For now, let's move on to memory protection.

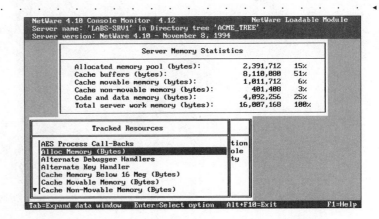

F I G U R E 15.3

Memory Utilization in MONITOR.NLM

Memory Protection

Ever since Intel released the 80286 chip in 1986, PC-based processors have had the capability to protect various areas of memory. *Protected* means that if a program wants to use a chunk of RAM it asks the operating system for an allocation, then it can do whatever it wants to do within that allocated space. If, however, it tries to access or manipulate storage areas outside of its allocated range, the CPU gets mad (and even).

As you might imagine, asking the CPU to watch every memory access command for every task running on the server would seriously impact performance. On the other hand, there are times when some tasks or resources need to be watched very closely. Well, good news: You have the best of both worlds with NetWare 4. It has the capability to monitor tasks—NLMs—if and only if necessary.

Here's how it works. Intel designed its 80286 chip with four logical *rings*. Ring 0 is where the operating system lives. Nothing can interrupt the operating system without its permission. Ring 1 surrounds Ring 0 and can be interrupted by the operating system running in Ring 0. Ring 2 surrounds Ring 1 and can be interrupted by both Rings 0 and 1. Finally, Ring 3 surrounds Ring 2 and can be interrupted by any of the other three rings. Refer to Figure 15.4 for more details.

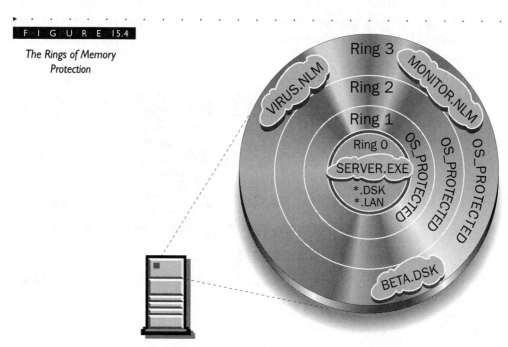

F I G U R E 15.4

The Rings of Memory Protection

A well-behaved, polite program in a multitasking environment will, from time to time, stop and see if any higher priority program is waiting for execution. If so, it will suspend itself and defer to the other task. A program that does not give up the processor can cause the server to appear dead—aka SERVER CRASH! This rudeness cannot be allowed. When the operating system, running in Ring 0, detects that some other program is hogging the processor, it can intervene and kick that program out. Similarly, when a program running in Ring 3 accesses memory that has not been allocated to it, the Ring 0 program can detect it and deal with it harshly; for example, unload the NLM from memory altogether.

NetWare 4 allows developers to create programs that can run in Ring 3 and gives administrators the ability to load them there. If you get a new NLM and you want to run it on a mission-critical server, you're taking a risk that the NLM will be well-behaved and not interrupt the core operating system—SERVER.EXE. To prevent this, use DOMAIN.NLM to run new NLMs in Ring 3 for a while. This Ring 3 domain is referred to by Novell as the Operating System Protected Domain (OS_PROTECTED in Figure 15.4). If the NLM proves safe, you can move it to Ring 0 with the rest of the operating system and get a little better performance.

DOMAIN monitors NLMs running in Ring 3 for time or data violations and will abort those processes when a violation occurs. To enable this Miss Manners of the operating system, DOMAIN must be loaded before the operating system loads any other NLMs. Therefore, it has to be loaded via STARTUP.NCF. Next, you're ready to place specific NLMs in Ring 3. To do so, type the command DOMAIN 3 before loading the new NLM. This switches console control to the OS_PROTECTED Ring 3. Then load the NLM. Finally, when you're done, return console control to the OS domain (Ring 0) by typing DOMAIN 0. Table 15.3 summarizes the DOMAIN command.

T A B L E 15.3	COMMAND	DESCRIPTION
Protecting Server Memory with DOMAIN.NLM	LOAD DOMAIN	Loads the DOMAIN. NLM
	DOMAIN	Provides a list of the available domains
	DOMAIN HELP	Provides a list of the DOMAIN help screens
	DOMAIN = <domain name>	Switches console control to a specific domain for loading new NLMs

REAL WORLD

In previous versions of NetWare, NLMs sometimes were responsible for fatal ABEND errors. ABEND stands for Abnormal End—every CNE's nightmare. If the software developer made a mistake when writing the program, the NLM might allocate a system resource that the operating system does not have available, and thus the server comes crashing to its knees, only capable of one last ABEND message.

By loading the DOMAIN.NLM and using the DOMAIN=OS_PROTECTED command, NLMs can be loaded into an area of memory that will protect the server from ABENDing. If the NLM fails, the memory that the NLM had allocated is locked up, but the rest of the server's resources are still available. The idea is to test out new NLMs in protected memory and later let them run in unprotected memory.

Unfortunately, not just any NLM will successfully load into protected memory. In fact most NLMs will not. The EDIT NLM is one NLM that will load into protected memory. Use the DOMAIN command to confirm which NLMs are in protected and unprotected memory.

That's it. Everything you need to know about optimization components. Now I think you're ready for prime time. The rest of this chapter is dedicated to the two main stages of NetWare 4 optimization:

- Monitoring with MONITOR.NLM

- Optimization with SERVMAN.NLM

In addition, we'll explore some other optimization strategies, including file compression, block suballocation, packet burst protocol, and large internet packets (LIPs). Wow, I had no idea NetWare 4 has so much to offer. But wait, that's not all. We'll throw in a lengthy discussion of optimization and troubleshooting. Now how much would you pay?

I'll see you on the other side.

QUIZ

**Five men had a race at the annual picnic of the Associated Widget and
Dingbat factory. They were, not in order, Tom, John, Bill, Pat, and Kevin.
Pat was neither first nor last. Kevin was four behind the winner. Bill beat
Pat, John came in after Tom, but ahead of Pat. Bill was neither first nor
second. Tom was not second or third. Give the rankings.**

(Q15-1)

(See Appendix C for all quiz answers.)

Monitoring with MONITOR.NLM

It all starts with MONITOR.NLM. I know you're good, but not even a CNE Superhero
can fix problems he/she doesn't know about. Monitoring is important because it allows
you to create an Optimization Plan. Your plan should include weekly server statistics
and threshold values. You check the numbers every week, and if they eclipse a certain
value, you perform an optimization task (usually in SERVMAN.NLM).

Having said that, it's interesting that many people claim NetWare 4 is "self-tuning."
While there is some truth to this statement, it still takes hands-on work and good
optimization techniques to get a finely tuned server.

In this section, we'll take a closer look at NetWare 4 monitoring with
MONITOR.NLM—the grandfather of NetWare server tools. We will start with a quick
view of the main screen, and then dive into its most useful options:

▶ Memory Utilization

▶ Cache Utilization

▶ LAN/WAN Information

▶ Processor Utilization

You'll spend most of your monitoring time in the four areas listed above. But MONITOR doesn't stop there. To get a jump on NetWare 4 optimization, you'll need to explore ALL aspects of this great utility. That's what the ACME Exploratorium is for at the end of the chapter. Don't miss it. So, without any further ado, let's get on with the show!

THE MAIN SCREEN

It all starts with the main screen of MONITOR.NLM. From there, the NetWare 4 server can be watched, prodded, tweaked, and cooed at. Yes, it's the last of the great NetWare utilities.

To get to the main screen, type LOAD MONITOR at the file server console prompt. You're greeted with a screen similar to the one in Figure 15.5. You can spend days going through all the detailed information provided in this handy dandy tool. There is one serious limitation, though. There is no convenient way to print out all the information available— no reporting function. For that you need to look at some third-party products. Bummer.

FIGURE 15.5

The Main Screen of MONITOR.NLM

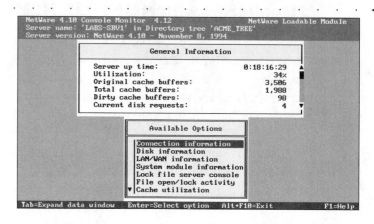

If you're familiar with NetWare 3, MONITOR will look and feel familiar. It has undergone some major and some minor changes, though. Among the minor changes is a small tweak to the main screen. When you first start the program, or while you're changing from one subscreen to another, the box at the top shows six important items. If you hit the Tab key, or wait ten seconds, the box will expand to show seven more items. In its expanded state, it nearly covers the Available Options menu. Figure 15.20 (in the ACME Exploratorium) shows the main screen in full view. Also, refer to Table 15.4 for a description of all 14 server parameters.

	ITEM	MEANING
TABLE 15.4 *Monitoring Parameters on the Main Screen of MONITOR.NLM*	Server Up Time	Days:hours:minutes:seconds since server last started.
	Utilization	Percentage of time the CPU is working (vs. idle).
	Original Cache Buffers	Number of cache buffers measured just after the OS Kernel (SERVER.NLM) is loaded.
	Total Cache Buffers	Number of currently available buffers. This number is reduced as other memory pools convert cache buffers for their use; it increases when they return it.
	Dirty Cache Buffers	Number of buffers that have updated data not yet written to disk.
	Current Disk Requests	Number of disk I/O requests currently pending.
	Packet Receive Buffers	Pool of buffers set aside for incoming network packets
	Directory Cache Buffers	Pool of buffers set aside for volume directory tables.
	Maximum Service Processes	Ceiling on the number of service processes that will be allocated.
	Current Service Processes	Number of service processes currently allocated.
	Maximum License Connections	Total of all licenses applied to this server. Up to 10 licenses can be "stacked" on top of each other.
	Current License Connections	Number of license connections currently in use.
	Open Files	Number of files currently being accessed by both the server itself and any connected workstations.

MEMORY UTILIZATION

NetWare 4 introduced several new subscreens to MONITOR. One of them is the Memory Utilization screen. From this screen, you can choose any of the NLMs loaded on your system and see that it is using server memory. If you add a new NLM, perhaps as a result of purchasing a new server-based program (SMS Backup, for example), you might want to track its supporting resources through Memory Utilization.

A well-behaved NLM will take the memory it needs and then free it after use. Let's explore our new SMS backup NLM. When you activate the backup program, the application NLM will begin to swell in size. Once it finishes, the NLM should release nearly all of the memory it had allocated, leaving just enough for it to be accessed and started again at the appropriate time.

RCONSOLE is another good example. Figure 15.6 shows the Memory Utilization screen for RCONSOLE when it's being used. At this moment, it is using ten blocks of 4 KB each, with about two-thirds in use and the remainder freed. These freed blocks will be picked up by garbage collection the next time it is activated.

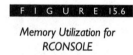

F I G U R E 15.6

Memory Utilization for
RCONSOLE

CACHE UTILIZATION

NetWare 4 has also reintroduced an old friend to the MONITOR family—cache utilization. These terrific statistics were available in NetWare 2, but were removed from view in NetWare 3. Now they're back. Check out Figure 15.7.

TIP

Several third-party programs are in circulation that provide Cache Utilization statistics for NetWare 3 servers.

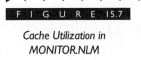

F I G U R E 15.7

Cache Utilization in MONITOR.NLM

Having enough cache memory is essential to the health and well-being of any NetWare file server—especially NetWare 4. The good news is that you can easily increase available cache by installing more memory in your server. However, as a frugal CNE, you don't want to add memory needlessly. This screen gives you all the information you need to make the right decision. Here's how it works.

Cache hits occur when a workstation requests data, and the server gets the data from RAM instead of from disk. NetWare 4 uses an LRU (Least Recently Used) algorithm to determine which data stays in memory and which data goes. Cache hits are broken down into two parts: short-term hits and long-term hits.

Short-term hits are those that have occurred within the last second. *Long-term hits* include all cache requests since the server was last booted. The short-term numbers should be over 98 percent and the long-term numbers over 90 percent. If not, add more memory. If the numbers are lower than that, Novell suggests performing some short-term fixes, such as unloading unneeded NLMs or removing DOS from memory. These actions won't hurt, but please remember that they treat a symptom of a problem (not enough memory) rather than the problem itself.

In addition, cache utilization can be optimized during volume creation. How? Well, performance is best when cache size equals buffer size. If you have volumes with different sizes, it is impossible to optimize. If you remember from our earlier discussion, NetWare requires that you select a buffer size equal to the smallest block size mounted. If you are installing multiple volumes, you would do well to choose the same block size (bigger is usually better if they're close) for all volumes and then set cache buffer size to match. No sweat.

OK, so what can you do about cache utilization? Well, NetWare 4 includes a few important SET parameters that allow you to manage file reads and writes. If your server is performing a lot of small writes, consider optimizing these parameters as shown in Table 15.5.

	COMMAND	DEFAULT	MIN.	MAX.	MEANING
TABLE 15.5 *SET Parameters for Write-Intensive Servers*	Dirty Disk Cache Delay Time	7 sec.	0.1	10 sec.	Minimum amount of time the system waits before writing a not-completely-dirty disk cache buffer
	Maximum Concurrent Disk Cache Writes	50	10	4000	Maximum number of disk cache writes that will be scheduled on one pass of the read/write head
	Dirty Directory Cache Delay Time	2 sec.	0	10 sec.	Minimum amount of time the system waits before writing a not-completely-dirty directory cache buffer
	Maximum Concurrent Directory Cache Writes	25	5	50	Maximum number of directory cache writes that will be scheduled on one pass of the read/write head

On the other hand, if your server performs a lot of read operations, consider optimizing cache utilization parameters according to Table 15.6.

	COMMAND	DEFAULT	MIN.	MAX.	MEANING
TABLE 15.6 *SET Parameter for Read-Intensive Servers*	Maximum Concurrent Disk Cache Writes	10	10	4000	Maximum number of disk cache writes that will be scheduled on one pass of the read/write head
	Maximum Concurrent Directory Cache Writes	5	5	50	Maximum number of directory cache writes that will be scheduled on one pass of the read/write head
	Directory Cache Buffer Non-Referenced Delay	1 min.	1 sec.	5 min.	Minimum time to hold a directory block in cache after it was last accessed

LAN/WAN INFORMATION

All network interface cards (NICs) maintain a set of statistics about themselves. Items like Packets Received and Packets Sent are common to every protocol and are reported for every board. Others like Collisions or Beacons are particular to one protocol or another (Ethernet and Token Ring, respectively, in this example). Those statistics are stored in counters called registers, and are accessible via special commands to the NIC itself. The manufacturer of the board writes the LAN driver, which MONITOR uses to access and interpret the statistics. There are whole shelves of third-party programs that access these registers on every station on the LAN, and produce pretty reports that help identify dead or dying NICs. Check them out; they're fun at parties.

ZEN

"To change one's life: Start Immediately! Do it flamboyantly. No exceptions."

William James

Welcome to the WAN. MONITOR has an internal mechanism that allows it to access NIC registers. You can view these statistics on the LAN/WAN Statistics screen (see Figure 15.8). When you first select this item, you will be presented with a list of all your LANs. If you happen to have two protocols loaded for a single LAN card (the default for Ethernet) that card will be listed twice, since it represents two logical LANs. Don't worry; the data will be identical—you can pick either one.

Figure 15.8 shows the registers for ACME's Ethernet card—a 3COM 3C5X9. As you can see, there are several pages of statistics you can look at, and they're all explained in the NIC's Reference Manual. Remember, different manufacturers write different LAN drivers and capture different statistics. You might find a register called Enqueued Sends Count for an NE2000, but not find it for our 3C5X9—even though they're both Ethernet cards. By the way, the NE2000 Enqueued Sends Count field represents the number of times the server wanted to send something, but the NIC was still busy dealing with the previous packet. The solution is to get a faster NIC.

FIGURE 15.8

The LAN/WAN Statistics Screen in MONITOR.NLM

```
NetWare 4.10 Console Monitor  4.12              NetWare Loadable Module
Server name: 'LABS-SRV1' in Directory tree 'ACME_TREE'
Server version: NetWare 4.10 - November 8, 1994

      3C5X9_1_E82 [3C5X9 port=320 int=A frame=ETHERNET_802.2]

  Version 4.1
  Node address: 0020AFE28F2D
  Protocols:
     IPX
        Network address:   00001234

  Generic statistics
     Total packets sent:                               868,601
     Total packets received:                         1,029,808
     No ECB available count:                                 0
     Send packet too big count:                              0
     Reserved:                                   Not supported
     Receive packet overflow count:                          0
     Receive packet too big count:                           0
     Receive packet too small count:             Not supported
     Send packet miscellaneous errors:                       0
     Receive packet miscellaneous errors:                    2

Esc=Previous list   Alt+F10=Exit                            F1=Help
```

There is one particular statistic you should always look for (regardless of the card)—the No ECB Available statistic. This register gets updated whenever an incoming packet has to be rejected because there is no available packet receive buffer, or PRB. We'll discuss PRBs in just a second. If this figure is above zero and climbing, then the number of buffers allocated has reached the maximum and many more are needed.

Another important set of statistics deals with collisions. Ethernet packets are subject to collisions, and when they occur, packets have to be retransmitted. If there is a high number of collisions, it is usually due to a very busy segment (too busy). And the retransmissions only make it worse. On the second page of statistics (not shown here), MONITOR lists collision count registers. On our test server, with 1.3 million packets sent since it was brought up, there were 26 collisions. Any number under 2 percent is acceptable. When it climbs above that, the proper remedy is to split or segment the LAN.

PROCESSOR UTILIZATION

Under most conditions, the server CPU is not taxed. In fact, most servers have far more CPU power than they really need. MONITOR's Utilization percentage is often well under 30 percent, and on many machines it is in the single digit range. On the off chance that you have a server with a significant CPU load, there are a few things you can do about it.

The first thing you have to do is find the process or task that is using the most CPU power. It would be a waste of your time, for example, to move the print server NLM to another machine if, in fact, the print server was taking only 5 percent of the CPU's time. However, if it was taking 35 percent of the computer power in your server, then moving it might be a great idea.

Refer to Figure 15.9 for a snapshot of the Processor Utilization screen in MONITOR.NLM. To get to this screen, choose Processor Utilization from the menu, then press F3 to see utilization statistics for all tasks. If there are just a few tasks to monitor, choose them with the F5 key.

```
NetWare 4.10 Console Monitor  4.12              NetWare Loadable Module
Server name: 'LABS-SRV1' in Directory tree 'ACME_TREE'
Server version: NetWare 4.10 - November 8, 1994

  Process Name                        Time      Count      Load

  Idle Loop                         31,346        18      32.75%  ▲
  MakeThread                             0         0       0.00%
  Media Manager                          0         0       0.00%
  MONITOR main                           0         0       0.00%
  Remirror                               0         0       0.00%
  Remote                             2,880         2       3.00%
  RSPX                                   0         0       0.00%
  Sync Clock Event                       0         0       0.00%
  TimeSyncMain                           0         0       0.00%
  Interrupt  0                         651         5       0.68%
  Interrupt  1                           0         0       0.00%
  Interrupt  2                           0         0       0.00%  ■
  Interrupt  3                           0         0       0.00%
  Interrupt  4                           0         0       0.00%
  Interrupt  5                           0         0       0.00%
  Interrupt  6                           0         0       0.00%
  Interrupt  7                           0         0       0.00%  ▼
Esc=Previous list   Alt+F10=Exit                              F1=Help
```

The four columns in the Processor Utilization screen are:

▶ Name—The name of the process. Some processes spawn other subtasks (the PSERVER process on this screen is an example). and so they get numbered sequentially in order to distinguish them.

▶ Time—The amount of time the CPU spent executing this process since the last sample was taken.

▶ Count—The number of times this process was executed at all during the sample period.

▶ Load—The percent of CPU load attributable to this task. The total of this column equals 100 percent, so if you have a CPU Utilization (from the opening screen) of 75 percent and a load of 33 percent for Task-A, then Task-A is using 25 percent of the CPU's capacity (a third of 75 percent = 25 percent).

One of the tasks always listed is the Idle Loop. When the CPU has nothing to do, it simply hangs out for one tick—there are 18.2 ticks per second on every Intel-based CPU. Then it checks again for something to do. This checking, idling, and checking again is called the Idle Loop Process. Its load will vary inversely with CPU utilization.

Bus Mastering can also help. These special SCSI and LAN cards have 80188 CPUs on them. So they can handle some of the workload that usually has to be passed to the main processor. If your processor utilization statistics point to a system that has a lot of disk activity taking the CPU's time, then get a bus mastering SCSI card. Similarly, if your CPU is busy handling LAN traffic, then a bus mastering NIC will offer significant help.

QUIZ

Let's test *your* monitoring capabilities. Three men are standing in front of you. Each is either a Truthteller or a Liar. You ask if any of them is a Truthteller. The first one says, "There are three Truthtellers here." The second says, "No, only one of us is a Truthteller," and the third one answers, "The second man is telling the truth." Well, what are they: Liars, Truthtellers, or a mixture, and how many of each? Note: You can't use MONITOR.NLM to help you.

(Q15-2)

Well, that does it for monitoring. Are you getting the feeling someone is watching you? Is it paranoia, or does MONITOR.NLM extend to your living room? Regardless, we can all agree it's a great server monitoring tool.

Now that you're comfortable with the first phase of NetWare 4 optimization, let's move on to the second phase—SERVMAN.NLM. In the next section, we'll explore the details of proactive optimization with SERVMAN.NLM. Move over Batman; there's a new Superhero in town.

Optimization with SERVMAN.NLM

Novell has performed countless market analysis studies and found that most LANs still have fewer than 20 workstations per server—very surprising. They've also found that LANs with over 50 workstations per server also have at least a part-time LAN administrator (CNE). Taking these two factors into account, Novell designed a server that would have default tuning parameters covering the 20 to 50 workstation range.

For example, we'll discuss something called packet receive buffers later in this section. Without even defining them, let's look at their defaults. NetWare sets an initial size of 50 packet receive buffers, and allows the operating system to allocate up to 50 more (a ceiling value of 100). They even tell you that a good rule of thumb is two per workstation plus 10 for the server. This default calculation is perfect for that 20 to 50 workstation range. After that, Novell expects the LAN administrator to make adjustments.

You can make similar adjustments with respect to NetWare 4's three most popular optimization components:

- ▶ Memory

- ▶ LAN

- ▶ Disk

To check the current status of these three areas use MONITOR. If you need to make changes to the items reported in MONITOR, you'll use the SET parameters listed in SERVMAN. It's that easy—a one-two punch. First, check it out in MONITOR, then fix it in SERVMAN.

In this chapter, we've already explored a few different SET parameters. As you've seen, NetWare provides several scores of tuning parameters that can be changed in environments that demand it. Some, like the minimum and maximum packet receive buffer parameters, are essential in all but the smallest LANs. Others, like the ones that adjust the volume log file size, are almost never changed. In this section, we'll look at the SERVMAN screens that pertain to memory, LAN, and disk optimization.

MEMORY OPTIMIZATION

There are three separate SERVMAN screens that deal with memory. The first is called Directory Caching and is shown in Figure 15.10. The second is simply called Memory and is shown in Figure 15.11. And finally, the File Caching parameters are shown in Figure 15.12.

Let's check them out.

Optimizing Directory Caching in SERVMAN

NetWare file servers keep a part of the Directory Entry Table (DET) in memory at all times. The DET contains information such as ownership, attributes, dates, and times about the files and directories on each volume. As files and directories are added, updated, deleted and even accessed, the respective DET entry needs to be updated. These SET parameters adjust how much file server RAM should be allocated to the DET, how often to make new buffers (up to the limit), and how long to keep old ones around after they're no longer being referenced. The only parameter most CNEs are likely to modify is the one that is highlighted in Figure 15.10:

```
SET MAXIMUM CONCURRENT DIRECTORY CACHE WRITES
```

FIGURE 15.10

*Directory Caching
Parameters in SERVMAN*

In Figure 15.12 there is a related SET parameter called Maximum Concurrent Disk Cache Writes. This is similar to the SET command for directory cache writes, in that it tells NetWare how many updated file cache buffers can be written to disk at once.

When requests to write to the disk are made, they are placed in a queue. Each time the read/write head on the disk swings in or out, a list of clusters to read or write is given to the controller. The size of the list is different for each controller. For some, it is as low as 100 entries; for others there's room for a thousand.

By default, up to 20 of them can be DET buffer writes, and 50 can be file cache buffers. As a CNE, you can increase this number, but it will be at the expense of potential read requests. For controllers that can only handle a few at a time, these numbers are too high. For those that are capable of handling a thousand at a time, feel free to increase these values. You'll know if they need to be increased by looking at the Cache Utilization Monitor screen and examining the too many dirty cache buffers count. If it is non-zero, you need to take action.

ZEN

"The most incomprehensible thing about the world is that we think it's comprehensible."

Albert Einstein

Optimizing Memory in SERVMAN

Figure 15.11 focuses on the general Memory window in SERVMAN. In this case, we've highlighted AUTO REGISTER MEMORY ABOVE 16 MB. On EISA-, MCA-, and PCI-based machines, NetWare will be told the exact amount of available RAM. You can set this to ON so that the server knows about and uses all of the memory you have installed. While it seems obvious that everyone would always want to use all the available memory, this isn't the case.

F I G U R E 15.11

*The Memory Screen in
SERVMAN*

There are many drivers that are written in such a way that they have to be loaded in the first 16MB of RAM. If they are located at a higher address, they won't be able to function properly. NetWare defaults to loading drivers (both LAN and disk) at the highest available memory address while it loads other NLMs just above the operating system itself. (It does this because drivers are very seldom unloaded, so loading them together at the top of memory reduces RAM fragmentation.) If this parameter is set to ON and you use these low-memory-only drivers, your network will bog down. The solution is to set the parameter to OFF, then load the drivers, then tell NetWare about the additional memory after the drivers are loaded. (Use the REGISTER MEMORY console command.)

Optimizing File Caching in SERVMAN

SERVMAN also allows you to optimize file caching. Check out Figure 15.12. In this case, we've highlighted Read Ahead LRU Sitting Time Threshold. When buffers are in such high demand that they are reused after being idle only ten seconds, the server is seriously short on memory. Leaving data in RAM for extended periods reduces demands for disk activity. If the buffers have to be used again in such a short time, it is likely that additional read requests will be made for data that was just recently overwritten.

FIGURE 15.12

The File Caching Screen in SERVMAN

Statistically speaking, when a block is read the most likely next read request will be for the adjacent block. NetWare takes advantage of this possibility by reading the next block right away, thus saving the time it takes for the controller to position the head over the right cylinder and track. When memory is tight, NetWare forgoes this potential time-saver.

As a CNE, you probably understand your server much better than the NetWare designers. If most access is random, then increase this parameter because it will be better to retain already read data than to read adjacent blocks. On the other hand, if the data is often searched in a sequential manner, then a decrease is in order. Read-ahead is far more important than retention. Note, though, that either choice merely treats a symptom of too little file server RAM. The only real solution is to install more memory.

That completes our discussion of memory optimization. Now let's take a look at the LAN itself.

LAN OPTIMIZATION

Data is transferred across the LAN in small chunks known as packets. As you might imagine, the server sends and receives far more of these packets than do normal workstations. When a packet arrives, it is likely that the server will be busy servicing a previously sent packet. When this is the case the newly arrived packet has to wait in an area known as the packet receive buffer pool (sometimes called the PRB pool).

If a packet arrives when there is no more room in the PRB pool, it gets dropped. Packets are normally received in the memory area of a LAN card, then transferred to the PRB pool, then erased from the card's memory so that the card is ready for the next incoming packet. If the PRB pool is full, then it is erased immediately after it is received, without the transfer. LAN architectures are able to recognize missing packets and so the sender will just send another one, but this wastes LAN capacity, or bandwidth.

On the other hand, if the pool is much larger than ever needed then precious server RAM is wasted. Why reserve a big chunk of memory for the PRB pool if it just sits idly by in case a flurry of incoming packets should arrive? Better to have that memory available for file caching or an NLM task.

Novell's surveys of its customers show that the average LAN still has fewer than 20 workstations, so the default number of PRBs is just 50, with permission to grow to a maximum of 100. A good starting rule of thumb is two buffers per workstation, plus 10 for the server. Go back and look at Figure 15.5, the MONITOR main screen. Around the middle of the list you'll see the number of currently allocated PRBs. For this server, the number allocated is the minimum. No more than 50 have been needed so far. If the number was 100, it might mean that this was the high water mark, or it might mean that more were needed but couldn't be allocated because the server did not have permission to do so.

If your server is consistently using all the allocated PRBs then you should raise the ceiling by typing the SET command **SET MAXIMUM PACKET RECEIVE BUFFERS=200**. Wait to see if the number climbs to the new maximum. Repeat this command until the ceiling is high enough that you don't hit it. Then type a similar line **SET MINIMUM PACKET RECEIVE BUFFERS=nnn** in the STARTUP.NCF file so that the server will start out with the proper number to begin with. Nnn is the observed high water mark, maximum should be a hundred or two higher.

Another way to solve the problems of too many packets and high bandwidth utilization is to increase the size of the packets themselves. We'll discuss this in more detail at the end of this chapter—it's an optional optimization strategy known as Large Internet Packets, or LIP.

Don't give me any lip; it's time to move on to the final optimization component—the disk.

DISK OPTIMIZATION

Now we get to optimize the Disk. SERVMAN provides two screens for this task:

- ► File System Parameters (see Figure 15.13)

- ► Disk Parameters (see Figure 15.14)

Let's check them out.

Optimizing the File System in SERVMAN

Figure 15.13 shows the SERVMAN parameters for optimizing the NetWare 4 File System. We've highlighted a key parameter Immediate Purge Of Deleted Files. Normally, this parameter is set to OFF, so that files can be salvaged or recovered long after they've been deleted. There is one time, however, when you might consider setting the parameter to ON.

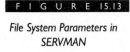

F I G U R E 15.13

File System Parameters in SERVMAN

When a disk is new, all files written to it are placed on the disk in never-before-used blocks. Files and directories that are deleted are simply marked as deleted and otherwise left alone. When the system runs out of this never-used space, it begins reusing it, taking first the space that has been deleted the longest. The only exception is that space from files that have been purged (either manually or because of the purge attribute) will be reused before space from the file deleted for the longest time. Normally, this scheme works to keep recently deleted files available for recovery as long as possible. However, there is one case in which it doesn't work as planned.

When a disk is more than half full, and a full restore from the backup tape is being done, you'll want to turn this parameter to ON temporarily. Otherwise, the files will be restored from the backup tape and as they are created, they will automatically delete the version already on disk. By the time the restore is finished, nearly all of the files that were on the disk before the restore will have been deleted. Those files that happened to have been deleted before the restore will no longer be salvageable (and remember, as deleted files they weren't backed up). By setting the parameter to ON, NetWare will immediately reuse the space taken by files deleted during the restore process. When finished, the old deleted files will still be salvageable.

Optimizing the Disk in SERVMAN

Figure 15.14 shows the SERVMAN parameters for optimizing the NetWare 4 Disk. We've highlighted a key parameter Enable Disk Read After Write Verify.

FIGURE 15.14

The Disk Screen in SERVMAN

One of NetWare's fault-tolerance features is its habit of rereading every block of data just after writing it, just to make sure that it was written correctly and that it can be read from disk. This is a holdover from days when disks were not nearly as reliable as they are today. In fact, many of today's disks (all IDEs and some SCSIs) are automatically reread by their controller before the operating system is told that the write is complete. If you have one of these disks in your server, then leaving this parameter ON wastes resources for no valid reason.

QUIZ

What is the five-digit number in which the last number is the product of the first and second, the last number is twice the second, the fourth is the sum of the third and the last, and the sum of all the digits is 24?

(Q15-3)

That completes our brief, but informative, journey through SERVMAN. You should really explore this wonderful optimization tool whenever you get a chance. We've given you a big headstart here, but there's so much more to learn. As a matter of fact, there are a few miscellaneous parameters I'd like to leave you with. Check them out.

MISCELLANEOUS OPTIMIZATION

SERVMAN and SET parameters are primarily used for memory, LAN, and disk optimization. But there are a few other cases where they can be very helpful, namely:

- ▸ WatchDog

- ▸ Bells and Whistles

- ▸ Saving Your Work in SERVMAN

Let's explore these miscellaneous optimization strategies before we leave SERVMAN and enter the realm of packet bursting—sounds painful.

WatchDog

As much as we tell them otherwise, users often fail to log out. Sometimes they just turn off their machines and then leave, sometimes they wind up having to reboot. In either case, the server has no way of knowing that the workstation is no longer actively using its connection.

NetWare 4 has a series of SET parameters, shown in Table 15.7, that are collectively known as WatchDog. You can tell NetWare to contact workstations that it has not heard from in a while, and if they don't respond after several such contacts, to assume that they're no longer around and to clear their connection. As an administrator, you have to balance the need to avoid wasting connections with the possible data loss from an improperly cleared connection. The SET parameters control how long to wait before checking to see if a workstation is still there, how many times to check, and how long to wait between tries. With these defaults, it takes 15 minutes for the WatchDog to clear a connection. The minimum would be 65 seconds; the maximum is almost 15 days.

T A B L E 15.7	COMMAND	DEFAULT	MIN.	MAX.	MEANING
WatchDog SET Parameters	Delay Before First WatchDog Packet	5 min.	15 sec.	14 days	The length of time that has to elapse before the server will send the first WatchDog packet
	Number Of WatchDog Packets	10	5	100	The number of packets to send without a response from the workstation before clearing the connection
	Delay Between WatchDog Packets	1 min.	10 sec.	10 min.	The amount of time to wait before sending the next WatchDog packet

Bells and Whistles

Of all the things you can do for the system, there is one parameter that's primarily useful to you—the NetWare 4 CNE. When the server issues an alert, it displays a message on the screen and rings the "bell" (sounds a tone on the server's speaker). If you are dealing with a problem in the computer room, the last thing you need is a beep going off every few seconds. At those times, the SET parameter shown in Figure 15.15 will be especially useful.

Saving Your Work in SERVMAN

Whenever a change is made via SERVMAN, it is in effect immediately (except those changes that have to be issued from STARTUP.NCF). To save you the trouble of entering them over and over again, SERVMAN offers to write them to the STARTUP.NCF and AUTOEXEC.NCF files for you when you exit the SET Parameters section. Figure 15.16 shows how changes are written to the STARTUP.NCF and AUTOEXEC.NCF files.

Now it's time to explore a few additional optimization strategies, including file compression, block suballocation, Packet Bursting, and Large Internet Packets. These are the "other" topics people keep talking about. They are primarily unique to NetWare 4, and are very cool. So let's not waste any time. Ready, set, optimize!

FIGURE 15.16

Saving Your Work in
SERVMAN

Other Optimization Strategies

So what's left? After MONITOR and SERVMAN, it's hard to believe that there are more ways to optimize NetWare 4. Well, prepare yourself—there's a lot more! As a matter of fact, NetWare 4 includes four more optimization strategies beyond what you've already seen. They are:

- ▶ File Compression

- ▶ Block Suballocation

- ▶ Packet Burst protocol

- ▶ Large Internet Packets

There are two keys to optimizing disk space: file compression and block suballocation. For users of DOS, compression is old news. Programs like Stacker and DoubleSpace have been around for a few years. Adding it to the NetWare operating system was a bold step forward. Suballocation is an entirely new concept. We'll take a closer look at both.

In addition, NetWare 4 offers two ways of optimizing LAN/WAN communications: packet bursting and large internet packets (LIPs). Packet bursting sends more packets per session, while LIPs send bigger packets each time. We'll also take a closer look at these.

What are you waiting for, Ensign—let's optimize.

OPTIMIZING FILE COMPRESSION

Some files are read and reread every day, or even every few minutes (LOGIN.EXE, WP.EXE, and so on). These files are always stored in their fully expanded form. Other files, however, are only read a few times and then sometimes left untouched for months or years. Think of the last memo or letter you wrote. While composing and editing it, you probably saved and retrieved it several times, but after printing and mailing, you saved for the last time. That memo will live on the disk forever. Other examples of files that stay idle for extended periods are on-line documentation for many applications, NetWare's own Electrotext or Dynatext files, prior years' accounting data, and so on.

With NetWare 4, you can enable compression. After a file is left idle for several days (the default is seven, but you can change it), it will be compressed. Reading it once in any day won't change that, but if it's accessed more than that, it will be stored back in expanded form. Even when it's compressed, if it's accessed it will be expanded in file server memory before being delivered to the requester. Except for a small delay for decompression, this whole process is invisible to the user.

If there are files that you want to compress right away and leave compressed or, alternatively, if there are files that you never want compressed, NetWare has a solution. NetWare 4 contains some new attributes. Use FLAG or FILER or NWADMIN to set the IC (Immediate Compress) or DC (Don't Compress) attributes on any file or directory and NetWare will comply.

Figure 15.17 shows a screen from the INSTALL program, indicating that both compression and suballocation are turned on. It is important to note that once on, they cannot be turned off, but if they are off, they can be turned on (once).

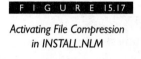

Activating File Compression in INSTALL.NLM

ZEN

"An atom (and thus all matter) is mostly empty space. Therefore, things are not what they appear."

Encyclopedia Britannica

Figure 15.18 shows the File Compression statistics in NWADMIN. These statistics are also available via the NDIR program (NDIR /VOL) and through FILER. The volume has 992 MB of space, of which 640 MB are free, yet there are 981 MB of data already stored on it. Apparently, you can get six pounds of sand into a two-pound bag, if you have a good compression program.

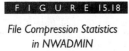

FIGURE 15.18

File Compression Statistics in NWADMIN

When compression is enabled, NetWare will scan the volumes each night looking for files that have been idle for seven days. Those files will be compressed. If they are accessed once in any day, they will remain compressed, but if they are accessed a second time, NetWare will write them back to disk in expanded form. If the disk is nearly full, however, NetWare will leave them compressed to avoid running out of disk space. If NetWare tries to compress a file and it doesn't save at least 2 percent of the file's space, it will leave it in its fully expanded form, and will set the Can't Compress (CC) attribute to remind itself not to bother trying again. All of these defaults can be changed using SET commands described later.

You have some control over this situation. You can set the attribute of a file or directory to Immediate Compress (IC), which will cause NetWare to compress the file as soon as possible and to always leave it on disk in compressed form, no matter how many times it is accessed. On the other hand, you can set a Don't Compress (DC) attribute, which tells NetWare to always maintain a file or directory in fully expanded form. You might choose IC for large, infrequently accessed files, such as documentation, while choosing DC for infrequently accessed databases where retrieving a record from a large database would take quite a bit of time.

Figure 15.19 from the SERVMAN.NLM shows the compression-related SET commands. Table 15.8, which follows, explains these commands in detail.

FIGURE 15.19

File Compression Parameters in SERVMAN

OPTIMIZING BLOCK SUBALLOCATION

In most operating systems, including prior versions of NetWare, a small file takes an entire allocation block. In the typical NetWare 3 file system, that block size is 4 KB, so a one-byte file takes 4096 bytes of disk space. As it grows, the next 4095 bytes are "free." Byte 4097 gets a second allocation block and so on.

For most of today's hard disks, the minimum size chunk of data that can be read or written is 512 bytes, meaning that eight separate files might fit into that same 4 KB block.

To further complicate things, if a volume has large files, an even bigger block size is more efficient when reading and writing them, but the few small files on that volume can waste a tremendous amount of space.

	COMMAND	DEFAULT	MIN.	MAX.	MEANING
TABLE 15.8 *Description of the Compression SET Commands*	Compression Daily Check Stop Hour	6:00 a.m.	0	23	When system should stop scanning for compression candidates. If equal to start hour, then run until done.
	Compression Daily Start Hour	0	0	23	Time when system should start scanning for candidates to compress.
	Minimum Compression Percentage Gain	2%	0	50%	If a file compresses less than this percent (or expanded), then leave it expanded.
	Enable File Compression	ON	OFF		If OFF, then don't scan for compression and queue all IC flag requests.
	Maximum Concurrent Compressions	2	1	8	Number of volumes that can be scanned for compression at once. NetWare still only compresses one file per volume. Novell does not recommend increasing the default.

	COMMAND	DEFAULT	MIN.	MAX.	MEANING
TABLE 15.8 *Description of the Compression SET Commands*	Convert Compressed to Uncompressed	1	0	2	0 = leave it compressed; 1 = store uncompressed after second access in "untouched" period; 2 = store uncompressed after a single touch.
	Uncompress Percent Disk Space Free to Allow Commit	10%	0	75%	The minimum percentage of free space that must exist before a compressed file will be rewritten uncompressed. An updated file is always written uncompressed.
	Uncompress Free Space Warning Interval	31 min., 18.5 sec.	0	29 days	Frequency of warning alerts when volume has too little space to write decompressed files. Setting of 0 disables messages.
	Deleted File Compression Option	1	0	2	0 = Don't; 1 = Compress next day; 2 = Compress immediately.
	Days Untouched Before Compression	7	0	100,000	Number of days to wait before an unmodified file becomes a candidate for compression.

NetWare 4 solves these problems through a technique called block suballocation. When a new file is created, it always gets assigned to a new block. As it grows into a second block, the suballocation process begins. NetWare takes a block and breaks it into 512 byte segments. When the 4097th byte is written (on a volume with 4 KB blocks), the file takes a full block, plus one suballocation chunk. If it grows by another 512 bytes, then it gets a second suballocation chunk. Since multiple files are being managed this way by the operating system, it's possible that these two suballocation chunks might, for a moment, be in separate blocks. In its spare time, NetWare rearranges the suballocation units so that the pieces are moved to contiguous spaces. In that way, by the time the file grows to 8192 bytes (8 KB) it will occupy two full 4 KB blocks. If the file continues to grow, the process is repeated.

Since this saves so much space that would otherwise be wasted, NetWare now defaults to assigning larger block sizes when creating volumes. Depending on the size of the volume, NetWare will assign block sizes ranging from a low of 4 KB (volumes under 64 MB) to a high of 64 KB (volumes over 1 GB). During the volume creation portion of the installation, this number can be changed if the installer so desires.

OPTIMIZING PACKET BURST PROTOCOL

There is yet another way to improve packet transmittal performance, and that is to use the Packet Burst protocol. Normal NetWare procedure is for the receiver to acknowledge ("ack") the receipt of each packet. When the sender hears the ack, it sends the next packet. If it does not hear an ack for an extended period of time (occurs when a packet is dropped), it resends the same packet. This back-and-forth process is extraordinarily time consuming and wastes a tremendous amount of bandwidth. A much better alternative is to send a bunch of packets and then wait for an ack from the group. If one part of the group is received OK and another part is bad, the ack can simply indicate which part needs to be retransmitted. This is called Packet Burst. In the NetWare 3.x environment, it had to be added to both the workstations and the servers by the administrator. In NetWare 4.1 it is automatically turned on for both.

The largest packet size is 64 KB, but on a busy day it would be unfair to other waiting stations if the LAN permitted some stations to send that much. The server can decide how big the burst size should be, and that size is called the window size. Also, it is possible for a really fast sender to overwhelm a slower receiver. To prevent this, the receiver (usually a workstation) can dictate the burst gap time, which is a delay time between bursts that gives the slower station time to process the last burst. As the server dictates smaller window sizes, the workstation can reduce the burst gap time.

Using Packet Burst protocol has increased LAN performance by 10 to 300 percent, depending on such factors as bandwidth, memory, and file sizes.

You, as the NetWare 4 CNE, might choose to eliminate the use of Packet Burst for a station or group of stations. (For example, the administrator might know that the packets have to cross a router or bridge that does not know how to handle burst traffic.) To do that, all he or she has to do is alter (or add) a line to the NET.CFG file on the workstation that says PB BUFFERS = 0. To reverse that decision, changing the value to any non-zero number will turn it on. (It doesn't matter which non-zero number is used. For now, Novell recommends using 2 so that future enhancements might be implemented more easily.)

OPTIMIZING LARGE INTERNET PACKETS (LIPS)

When NetWare was first introduced, CPUs were slow (8MHz was a fast machine), memory was expensive, and there was plenty of extra bandwidth. The engineers at Novell quite properly decided to make IPX smaller and faster by eliminating the code that could break a large packet into smaller parts for retransmission (a process known as fragmentation). This meant that whenever a LAN had two segments of different sizes, packets from the larger capacity segment could not be retransmitted to the smaller unless, somehow, the larger packet size LAN was forced to issue smaller packets to begin with. To make matters worse, the servers couldn't be sure what size might be in use on any segment. The solution was to force all packets to the smallest packet size of any commonly available protocol whenever a server detected that there was more than one segment on that LAN.

The ARCnet protocol was one of the available protocols, and it uses 576 byte packets. Therefore, NetWare forces all packets to that size whenever it detects multiple segments. Since ARCnet's popularity has dwindled to almost nothing, this is a major waste of resources for most networks. The solution was to tell the server to use larger packets. It still could not fragment, but at least it could be told to operate at the smallest size in use on that LAN. Ethernet packets top out at 1514 bytes and both Token Ring and FDDI use 4202 byte packets. A mixed Ethernet/Token-Ring LAN would need to use 1514 as the maximum packet size; a Token Ring only or mixed Token-Ring/FDDI LAN could set its packet size at 4202. The SET command that tells the server what packet size to use is SET MAXIMUM PHYSICAL RECEIVE PACKET SIZE=nnnn.

One of the new features of NetWare 4.1 is a routing process called NetWare Link State Protocol (NLSP). Among its features is the capability to fragment and reassemble packets so that mixed LANs can exist. Very cool.

QUIZ

I love a good math problem—how about you? Aren't they wonderfully relaxing? Anyway, here's a doozy for your calculating pleasure: Using the figure "5" eight times together with any mathematical symbols, with the exception of the plus sign, write out a calculation to give the answer 110. Ready, set, calculate (hey, that rhymes).

(Q15-4)

"That's not all. It slices, it dices...." Oops, sorry. I was working on my latest infomercial. Check it out at 2 a.m. on any local access channel near you. What I was trying to say was "Optimization is not just for optimizing." It can also be used for troubleshooting. As a matter of fact, optimization and troubleshooting are forever tied together. Are you confused? Watch (I mean "Read")....

Optimization and Troubleshooting

Optimization and troubleshooting are forever tied together. Here's how it works. Optimization is a proactive strategy to increase server performance. True. Troubleshooting is a reactive strategy to fix a broken server. True. How optimized is your server when it's broken? Not very. So, it stands to reason that fixing your server increases its performance, and in some strange way, is a form of optimization. Hmmmm.

Let's begin our discussion of optimization and troubleshooting with a review of how the server works and how data flows.

HOW THE SERVER WORKS

By now it should be clear that memory plays a huge part in how well your file server responds to your users' requests. Every process that takes place on your file server requires memory. These processes are loaded into file server memory because you have loaded an NLM. While you may think the solution is to not load any NLMs, you would quickly find that you could do very little, including logging in. You can't log in unless your network card driver, which is an NLM, is loaded and bound to the right protocol stack.

This is the most basic of NLMs, but there are other essential NLMs you'll want to leave in file server memory. Many backup and virus protection programs are implemented as NLMs. You certainly don't want to do without these. You may want to leave the MONITOR.NLM loaded so you can view statistics on an ongoing basis. Many management utilities like inventory and metering programs require NLMs. All these processes may be essential to maintaining your file server. So after all the administrative trivia, how much memory do you have left for your users? Specifically how many file cache buffers do you have left?

Your job is to make sure there is enough memory left over for those pesky users. You can control how much memory will be allocated to various processes by using the SET command and the SERVMAN utility. SET commands can be issued directly at the file server console prompt except for those that can be issued only in STARTUP.NCF. The good news is that SET will tell you which ones have to be in STARTUP.NCF. You can't hurt the file server by accidentally issuing this subset of SET commands at the prompt. You'll just get a message that says you can only set the particular parameter in STARTUP.NCF. There are a couple of SET commands that can also be issued in STARTUP.NCF. You can use the INSTALL.NLM or SERVMAN to edit STARTUP.NCF to include the appropriate commands.

Note: If you change your STARTUP.NCF, the changes won't take effect until the next time you down and bring back up your file server. Some are parameters settable only in STARTUP.NCF, including:

▸ Minimum Packet Receive Buffers—This makes sense if you think about it. You want to make sure enough memory is set aside for incoming packets before all the other memory gets allocated.

▸ Maximum Physical Receive Packet Size—This works with the parameter above. Not only do you want to set aside memory buffers for incoming packets but you need to know how big each of those buffers needs to be.

Other parameters can be set in STARTUP.NCF but don't have to be, including:

- ▶ Garbage Collection Interval

- ▶ Number of Frees for Garbage Collection

- ▶ Minimum Free Memory for Garbage Collection

ZEN

"Life consists not in holding good cards but in playing those you hold well."

Josh Billings

Before you start tuning your file server you should figure out if it needs tuning. You do this by monitoring how well your file server is performing without tuning it. Obviously, if you bring up your file server and start watching what's going on, it will look like you don't need to do anything. The trick is to watch how your file server is doing when all your users are pounding on it. So wait until most everyone has logged in, say around 10:30 in the morning or after they come back from lunch but before they leave early to pick up their kids—say around 2:30 in the afternoon. These are generally considered peak times in most environments. Your environment may be different.

The process of tracking how your file server is doing on a regular basis is called *baselining*. You're establishing the baseline or most normal levels your file server operates at. By baselining, you can spot when the file server isn't behaving at its most normal level. It makes it much easier to figure out if something is wrong, or different, if you have some information to compare it to.

You know how to move around MONITOR, so you know how to find out the baseline parameters of your file server. Because MONITOR doesn't contain a print option you'll want to write down the parameters you're tracking. (The NetWare Log book would be a good place.) If you decide to use a third-party management utility that prints reports, make sure they make it to the log book instead of the trash can.

Despite the fact that we seem to be focusing exclusively on memory, you'll remember that we discussed how important the disk system is to optimal performance of a NetWare file server. The two are intimately related because everything you read or write from or to the disk goes through memory. So how well do you understand the path data takes through file server memory on its way to and from the file server disk? Time to learn.

HOW DATA FLOWS

When a workstation wants a data file from the file server it first has to ask permission to open it. This is different from actually reading the contents of the file, which depends on your trustee rights. So there you are at your workstation and you issue a command to open a file. What happens? First the DOS Requester wraps your request into a NetWare Core Protocol (NCP) request. NCP is the language the server speaks. The packet then travels across the cable to the file server where it sits in a packet receive buffer. Packet receive buffers are also referred to as event control blocks, or ECBs.

If no ECB is available, the packet is dropped into the euphemistic bit bucket. The more packets that get trashed into the bit bucket the higher the No Available ECB Count number gets. If there is an available buffer, the request gets parked in one. From the packet receive buffer, the request moves up to the appropriate protocol stack. If the request is for this server, the server looks around to see if a File Server Process, or FSP, is available to handle the request. Remember that FSPs are task handlers. They do the work. If the requesting packet is for another file server it will get routed appropriately. If no FSPs are available the packet will just twiddle its thumbs in the packet receive buffer until one becomes available.

Once an FSP starts to handle the request, it will look in the FAT for the location on the hard disk where the requested file blocks are located. If the requested file block is in file cache, the server sends a reply to the workstation that the file is available. If the file blocks are not in cache already, the server will read the file from disk into cache memory. Then the file server asks the workstation if it needs anything else.

If you want to write a file to the file server's hard disk, the first part of the process is the same—up until the FAT search. If no hard disk blocks have been allocated before (for example, this is a new file you want to save), then hard disk space and cache buffers are allocated for use. If the file is associated with previously allocated hard disk blocks the server checks to see if the relevant blocks are currently in cache memory. If they are cached then the data is written to the buffer. The buffer is then marked as "dirty." At this point the workstation ceases to worry about the data.

It's now up to the file server to keep track of the dirty buffers and get the data permanently stored on the file server's hard disk. Now we start the data count down. If the data has been in the dirty buffer for more than 3.3 seconds the file server sends it to the hard disk waiting line—the write queue—and frees up the buffer for other caching needs.

Now that you know the details of the read and write paths that data take through file server memory, it will be easier to understand why you may want to tune certain parameters like packet receive buffers. Let's look at some common performance symptoms, their possible causes, and what you might want to do to alleviate them. Now we're flying through the Troubleshooting Nebula at warp factor 12.

SYMPTOM: SLOW SERVER RESPONSE

The server seems really slow in responding to requests. A request might be running an NDIR *.* /SUB or just logging in and asking for a file. There are several possible solutions. Let's take them one by one.

Solution #1—High LAN traffic

It may be that you have truly outgrown how much traffic your network cable can handle. Your user population may have grown faster than you, or management, anticipated. You may have moved to more traffic-intensive applications like multimedia, or graphic design applications.

Redesign your network cable layout. You can do this by just segmenting what you have by putting another network card in your server and putting some of your users on the cable segment attached to this new card. Or you can upgrade your cable plant by moving to something faster.

Note: Sometimes the only problem is a bad network card. Amazingly, network cards can be deaf, dumb, or dead. Deaf cards can't hear and so they keep requesting stuff that drives the network traffic up. Dumb cards hear but don't speak—they send. Dead cards— well, they're just dead.

What parameters might you want to watch for trouble indicators?

▸ Utilization—If it's high you should probably add another server instead of just more cable.

▸ Dirty Cache Buffers—If they're consistently high, you may consider favoring Disk Cache Writes over reads. Refer to Table 15.5.

▸ Current Disk requests—This may indicate the problem is really with a slow disk system.

▶ Packet Receive Buffers—If they're maxing out, there could be a communications bottleneck between the server NIC and processor. Consider increasing the Maximum Packet Receive Buffers parameter as a short-term fix.

▶ Service Processes—If these are maxing out, you can either adjust them with SERVMAN or SET as long as there is enough memory left over for file caching. If not, consider adding more memory.

Solution #2—Packet Receive Buffers have maxed out

This one is easy. Check your baseline statistics for packet receive buffers. Next, down the server (your users won't notice, right?) and watch how quickly the buffers max out again. If it's just a matter of minutes you probably have a bad network board or network board driver somewhere. If it takes days or months to max out, then if you have enough memory left over for caching. Just increase the number of PRBs using SERVMAN or SET.

Solution #3—Not enough cache buffers

Do you have any NLMs loaded that you aren't using? Do you have the INSTALL.NLM loaded? If your server is up and running you don't need to leave INSTALL in memory. You also might be loading NLMs from products you aren't using, or aren't using anymore. Unload them. You can use the MEMORY console command to see if the server knows about all the memory you actually installed. You may need to use the REGISTER MEMORY command to make sure it realizes that there is more memory installed than it recognizes. Occasionally RAM chips go bad. A bad RAM chip may lower the amount of memory the server can access. Unfortunately bad RAM chips more likely will just crash your server.

Solution #4—Slow disk

We've talked about this in detail already. As a good CNE, you'll check to see if there is a hardware problem and if the disk driver is the correct one for your hardware. You may have to upgrade your disk driver by calling your disk manufacturer. Most vendors have bulletin boards or libraries on services like CompuServe where you can download the latest driver instead of waiting for a disk to arrive in the mail. Diagnostic software for your disk system should be provided by the vendor. They know their hardware the best.

If you have only one disk or disk channel in your file server, you should consider expanding. You can increase disk throughput by adding another disk controller and drive and Host Bus Adapter, or HBA. If one disk channel is busy performing a read or write, the next disk request in the queue (remember the disk request queue from above?) can use the other disk channel.

You could also just speed up the entire process by upgrading all the disk channel components to faster, newer components. If you have CD-ROM drives hanging off your file server disk channel, move them. There is no reason shared CD-ROMs need to be physically on the file server. They only need to be shareable somehow. Microtest in Arizona makes a whole range of sharable CD-ROM solutions that take advantage of NetWare performance features and off-load the CD-ROM processing from your file server.

Solution #5—The file server CPU is overburdened

In other words, the CPU utilization is consistently high and you've already added more memory and off-loaded or unloaded everything you can think of.

Buy a faster CPU. That's pretty obvious. Not so obvious is buying another CPU. Split the server tasks among multiple servers. This is called load balancing. To do this efficiently you need to know which processes are the most computer intensive. But you already know how to find that out, right? Use MONITOR to track which tasks are using most of the CPU's time. Also check for new NLMs that may not have read Miss Manners. Misbehaving NLMs frequently hog the CPU. Usually you can reconfigure the errant NLM. If not, you may have to get rid of it.

Solution #6—The Directory Tables aren't all cached

Remember that NetWare likes to cache the Directory Tables so that file lookups are faster. You'll especially notice this problem when running NDIRs of whole volumes or large parts of the directory structure.

Check if the directory cache buffers have reached their maximum. You know what to do. Increase the amount of memory that can be used for directory caching. You also know the impact this will have on file caching. There will be less memory for caching files. Feels sort of like robbing Peter to pay Paul.

Solution #7—File Service Processes (FSPs) are maxed out

Running out of task handlers is not a pretty picture and is usually caused by a misbehaving NLM. If that's not the problem, you may have too many users accessing the file server. Again, load balancing is the answer here. It is pretty common to see networks in which the user population outgrows the original design of the network. While every company likes to imagine itself growing, very few enjoy paying for hardware for the future. CNEs are responsible for recognizing when the future has arrived.

QUIZ

What is unique about the number 854,917,632? (Be careful, this is a tricky one!)

(Q15-5)

As you can see, there are lots of reasons users may be legitimately complaining about slow network response. Whichever solution works for your environment, be sure to document it in your network log book. Time for a new symptom.

SYMPTOM: ABEND (ABNORMAL END)

The NetWare 4 server can crash for a variety of reasons. But many times it ends up as an ABEND. This is a special kind a crash that can be caused by a variety of server problems, including NMI I/O and System Board parity errors. Let's check them out.

Solution #1—ABEND Due to NMI parity error (I/O)

The server console says ABEND and refers to an NMI parity error generated by I/O.

ABEND is short for Abnormal End of Operation. It's a bad thing. You'll know right away because your users will tell you the network is down. The NMI part refers to bad memory. Really. A memory chip someplace gave up the ghost. The I/O part points you toward an input output device instead of the memory on your mother board.

The tough part about this is that locating exactly the bad memory chip is tricky and takes time, which your users won't be happy about. The fastest solution is to replace the offending board containing the bad memory. It could be memory on any board in your system including your network card, HBA, or video card.

Sometimes memory chips go bad because of bad power. If you have had brownouts or blackouts, you'll probably notice because the lights will go out or dim perceptively. Spikes and surges are tougher to notice unless you disobey your mother and put your finger in a wall socket. The solution is a line-conditioning UPS.

It is also conceivable that the power supply in the file server, or disk subsystem, has decided to go on the fritz. You can check the power supply voltages but again the fastest solution is to replace the power supply. This is also a good reason to maintain a parts inventory.

Solution #2—ABEND Due to NMI parity error (System Board)

You get an ABEND error with an NMI parity error generated by the system board.

You guessed it! Bad memory on the system board. It is also conceivable that the system board has some other problem, but the NMI part almost always refers to memory-related problems.

Change your system board. Frequently you can get away with swapping memory chips until you find the faulty set. At least that way you don't have to order a new motherboard.

SYMPTOM: SERVER CRASH

If you server doesn't ABEND, it will probably just plain, old CRASH. This is a bad thing. Following are a few follow-up procedures for dealing with NetWare 4 server crashes.

Solution #1—Error message on server console

The server crashes. Any old crash. Now what? There may be an error message displayed to point you in the right direction.

If there is an error, try to figure out what process caused it. It is likely to be NLM related. If you can pinpoint the NLM, start the server up without the suspect NLM. If it's a newly installed NLM, unload the program, contact the vendor, and review any compatibility issues or installation configuration options that might cause problems and start again. If the error persists, get rid of the NLM. It could also be that the NLM doesn't get along with the other NLMs in the sandbox. You may have to reevaluate your older NLMs. You might have to upgrade them so they get along with the new kid (NLM). You may simply have to download a patch and install it. Now would be a good time to check your NSEPro or NetWire to find out about new patches for the operating system or other vendor's NLMs.

Solution #2—GPPE error

The server crashes (a technical term) with a GPPE error.

All the same problems with NLMs as described above PLUS you may have a corrupt SERVER.EXE.

Get a new copy of SERVER.EXE from your original disks or CD-ROM and copy it to your file server.

SYMPTOM: NLM WON'T LOAD

NLMs are usually pretty well behaved. But in some cases, they like to cause a fuss. Most of the time, they're missing a supporting NLM or the server is out of memory. Let's take a closer look.

Solution #1—Supporting NLMs didn't load

A pesky NLM just will not load. This happens more often than you would think, especially with third-party NLMs.

The good news is that this is a pretty easy problem to solve. Check for messages claiming that supporting NLMs, like CLIB.NLM or STREAMS.NLM, are not loaded. You might also see a message claiming a "...public symbol could not be found." You could also just flat be out of available memory for the NLM to load.

Check the NLM's documentation to find out what other NLMs have to be loaded first. If you got the "public symbol could not be found" message you need to load CLIB. If you have CLIB loaded and you're still getting this message, check the version. You may need to download a newer CLIB from NetWire and load it. Third-party NLMs can be very picky about which version of CLIB they run with. You'll need to pay special attention to the letter associated with the CLIB version (for example, CLIB version 3.12g, d, or e).

If there isn't enough memory available to load the NLM you know what to do—add more memory. But be sure. There are several NLMs for third-party developers who claim they don't have enough memory to load, and when you check with MONITOR you see megs and megs worth. Contact the NLM vendor and have a long heart-to-heart talk with them about what else could be going on.

Solution #2—Out of server memory

An NLM won't load because there really isn't enough memory available.

You may have installed plenty of memory but SERVER.EXE may not know about it. This can happen frequently with ISA machines and occasionally on EISA machines.

Time to dig out the REGISTER MEMORY command. It is possible that you manually issued this command at the console prompt. Then the server was restarted and the command was forgotten about. Of course, you made a note of the need for this command in your log book but to make your life even simpler you should put it in the STARTUP.NCF file so that it runs automatically each time the server comes up. If this isn't the solution, fall back on the old standby—add more memory.

SYMPTOM: CACHE ALLOCATOR IS OUT OF AVAILABLE MEMORY

The console displays an error message saying that the cache allocator is out of available memory.

One of the boards in the file server, most likely the HBA(s), may be trying to use memory above 16 MB but the driver for the board freaks out because it doesn't know how to work above the magic 16 MB line. To top it off, there probably isn't space available below the 16 MB line. Now how is the server supposed to give memory for this board?

Well, double-check with MONITOR to make sure there really isn't enough memory and double-check with your startup files to see if you're trying to load items "high" or "low." Then double-check with the vendor to see if they have a newer driver that can use any memory the cache allocator wants to give it. If none of that works you can reserve memory below 16 meg.

SYMPTOM: SERVERS ARE LOST IN RCONSOLE

You can't see any of your NetWare 4.x servers when you try to access them via RCONSOLE.

Guess what? You probably have an old version of RCONSOLE. Earlier versions of RCONSOLE did not support packet signing. It's a relatively new feature of NetWare. It's also possible that you neglected to load RSPX and REMOTE on the file server. Without them, you won't be able to get to the file server console via any version of RCONSOLE.

Check to make sure RSPX and REMOTE are loaded. Then check the version of RCONSOLE that you are running. Look at the very top of the screen when you bring it up. You can install the NetWare version 4.1 RCONSOLE.EXE on your NetWare 3.x servers by simply copying it to the SYS:SYSTEM directory on the 3.x servers.

If you find this odious and packet signature level security is of no consequence in your environment you can issue the following command:

```
LOAD RSPX SIGNATURE OFF
```

SYMPTOM: DRIVE DEACTIVATION ERROR

The users lose their connection to the file server. You race to the console and see a drive deactivation error message.

You definitely have a hardware problem with the disk channel. There may just be loose connections on the drive channel. Remember that a hardware problem may mean that the driver doesn't match the hardware setup.

Check all the connections. Unplug and replug all the drive channel cables. Then check the configuration, especially if you have SCSI drives. The addressing may be off or the final device in the chain may not be terminated. If you have recently upgraded the drivers, try to un-upgrade them. Check for compatibility issues with your existing firmware by calling the vendor.

Well, that should keep you busy managing your file server. It's amazing how simple things like slow network access can get so detailed when you start troubleshooting them. Understanding how the file server allocates memory and manages the disk processes helps a lot in determining where to start. If in doubt, start with the simple stuff like checking all the cable connections, power connections, and error messages. Sometimes the error message is right. Sometimes a pencil is just a pencil.

ZEN

"Any sufficiently advanced technology is indistinguishable from magic!"

Arthur C. Clarke

That completes our discussion of NetWare 4 optimization. As you can see, it's definitely the new frontier of NetWare 4 networking. Optimization is more important now than ever before, mostly because NDS taxes the server so much. In this chapter, we've learned everything there is to know about optimization components, monitoring with MONITOR, and optimization with SERVMAN. In just a few moments, you'll get to go on an Optimization Exploratorium through ACME's MONITOR.NLM.

Oh, my goodness! Would you look at the time—where has it all gone? I've just been rambling away here...sorry, if you missed your train or something. I guess I'm done. There's not much more that can be said about NetWare 4. Are you interested in golf? We could talk about that for awhile. Nah, I better save that for another book.

Before you leave, let's take a quick moment to review your journey. It's been quite a wild ride, and you should be very proud of yourself for surviving it in one piece—or so it seems. Do you still want to be a CNE? A NetWare 4 superhero, doctor, and gardener? Good. Because the world needs a few good CNEs, and you're a great place to start. Speaking of starting...

The journey began with a brief introduction into the next generation of NetWare 4. Chapter 1 was a preview of NetWare 4 and the entire book. Then, we focused on the fundamentals of NDS in Chapter 2. It's a whole new ball game. With all of that knowledge under our collective belt, we began the great journey of life—quest for NetWare 4 CNEship and saving the world.

Throughout this book we learned that NetWare 4 CNEs have three main tasks: design, installation, and management. First, you design the NDS tree—as a superhero. Second, you install the servers using an established design—as a doctor. And third, you get to configure and manage it—as an NDS gardener. Talk about split personalities! CNEs must excel in all three jobs, although each is very different. Fortunately, this book helped us every step of the way. First stop—NetWare 4 design.

In Chapter 3, we discovered ACME—A Cure for Mother Earth. We learned about its plight and helped develop the ACME project team. We gathered a large list of design inputs, including WAN layouts, an organization chart, and workflow diagram. Then, in Chapter 4, we explored the nuts and bolts of NDS design—a very important CNE task. We learned about tree design, partitioning, time sychronization, and most important, accessibility design. Things really started hopping right about now. Finally, with the design in place, we started NDS implementation—that's Chapter 5. With water, sunlight, and a little love, our seedling quickly grew into a fruitful, majestic tree. Next stop—NetWare 4 installation.

In Chapter 6, the network was born. During NetWare 4 installation, we followed 6 stages and 23 steps toward NetWare 4 Nirvana. It was a great place to start. Next, in Chapter 7, we discovered the miracle of NetWare 4 migration. NetWare 4 is so different from earlier versions, upgrading really is "migrating." It's a whole new frontier of networking. In Chapter 7, we outlined the steps of migrating from NetWare 2 or 3 all the way to NetWare 4. It seemed like a breeze next to installation. Final stop—NetWare 4 management.

Once the tree had been designed and installed, we entered the wonderful world of NDS gardening. We covered object naming, NWADMIN, object types, and Bindery Services—all the time trying to keep the dirt out from under our fingernails. As we learned in Chapter 9, the tree also needs to be pruned periodically. This provides better health and efficiency (distributed databases) as well as tree stability and longevity (fault tolerance). Also, we learned how to use time synchronization for better access to sunlight. That completed our journey above the server; next, we dove inside.

In Chapter 10, we learned that the file system represents NetWare life within the server. All of our focus shifted to NetWare 4's big, electronic filing cabinet. Chapter 11 continued this journey with a look at security. Information is now the new commodity—more valuable than money. We need to take new measures to protect our information. We discovered NetWare 4's five-layered security model—login/password authentication, login restrictions, NDS rights, file system access rights, and attributes. Think of it as your impenetrable network armor.

Once the LAN has been installed (born), it enters the second and third phases of its lifespan—configuration (childhood) and management (adulthood). In Chapter 12, the first of two related chapters, we walked through the five steps of configuration using Leia as an example. Then in Chapter 13, we discovered the final phase of LAN lifespan—adulthood. Here your network got married, had children, planned for retirement, and finally retired. How about you?

In the final two chapters, we ended the journey with NetWare 4 printing and optimization. Printing (Chapter 14) was the greatest challenge. NetWare 4 printing is simple, and works great until...you add users. In Chapter 14, we explored some time-proven methods for successful NetWare 4 printing installation, management, and troubleshooting. In addition, we learned about printing's future—NDPS. Then, we completed the journey with Chapter 15—the final frontier. Once you'd lived through the LAN lifespan and set up NetWare 4 printing, only one task was left—optimization.

ZEN

"All good things must come to an end!"

Q

Well, that does it! The End...Finito...Kaput. Everything you wanted to know about NetWare 4, but were afraid to ask. I hope you've had as much fun reading this book as I've had writing it. It's been a long and winding road—a life changer. Thanks for spending the last 1600 pages with me, and I bid you a fond farewell in the only way I know how:

"See ya' later, alligator!"

"After a while, crocodile!"

"Hasta la vista, baby!"

"Live long and prosper!"

"So long and thanks for all the fish!"

"May the force be with you..."

GOOD LUCK, AND BY THE WAY....
THANKS FOR SAVING THE WORLD!!

ツ

BEST WISHES,

David James Yorke IV

ACME EXPLORATORIUM: GETTING TO KNOW MONITOR.NLM

MONITOR is your friend. In this chapter, you've had a chance to explore some of its greatest assets. Now we get a chance to explore them all! This exercise will work its way through all the MONITOR screens and subscreens, sequentially. If you have a NetWare 4 server available, practice along the way. Also, you can use the World Wire service described in the Introduction. Otherise, I'll provide some sample screens for you as we go. Ready, set, explore.

MAIN SCREEN

We will start our tour with the MONITOR.NLM main screen. It initializes with two screens—a General Information statistics view and the Available Options menu. About ten seconds later, or upon pressing the Tab key, the main screen expands into full statistics view. You can repeatedly press the Tab key to switch between full and partial views. Figure 15.20 shows the MONITOR.NLM full statistics view.

F I G U R E 15.20

Full Statistics View in MONITOR.NLM

If any monitor screen is idle for ten minutes, a screen saver affectionately called "The Worm" is displayed. This is an intelligent screen saver, showing two important statistics— CPU Utilization and Disk Activity. The speed at which it moves around the screen indicates CPU utilization, and the length of its tail reflects disk activity.

CONNECTION INFORMATION

Our next stop is the first Available Options choice—Connection information. This option gives you a list of connected resources. Some, usually most, of them will be users. A few will be other server processes such as print servers and connected, but not-logged-in, workstations. Any connected but not authenticated (logged in) station will be marked with an asterisk (*). Users can browse the tree from these stations but cannot access any of its resources.

Connections can be monitored and cleared from this screen. Pressing Delete will remove the connection from the list. But be careful. If the connection represents a user actively working on the system, that user will need to log back in before continuing. This usually means that the user can't save current work, which leads to an unhappy user. On the other hand, if the connection represents a user who has just rebooted or powered off his/her machine, clearing the connection might be just the thing to do in order to allow the user to be able to log back in. Some organizations limit the Current licensed connections to 1, in order to prevent users from logging in from multiple stations. Clearing the connection will decrement the current connection count, and thus let these users back on.

In order to check if a particular connection is the one you think it is, just press Enter with the highlight over the username. If the user has any open files (open is not equal to locked, which we will look at later in this exercise) they'll be displayed here. In addition, it shows other identifying information such as connection time, network address, and so on. An example of the Connection Information screen is shown in Figure 15.21. It looks as though Admin.ACME has been attached for only 10 minutes.

DISK INFORMATION

The next item on the Available Options list is Disk information. In this context, the word *disk* is taken very loosely. In addition to internal hard disks, MONITOR tracks backup devices and CD-ROM drives as disks as well. Acording to MONITOR, anything attached to a SCSI board that loads a .DSK driver is a disk.

The Disk Information screen shows a myriad of statistics, including hot fix redirection parameters, disk channel information, and total blocks. Check it out.

LAN/WAN INFORMATION

The next stop on our MONITOR odyssey is LAN/WAN information. Each frame type loaded for a particular board shows up as a separately selectable item, although the statistics are merged. In other words, one board may have two LAN/WAN items, but the statistics are the same. After all, it's just one board.

Each server NIC provides detailed statistics. As we learned earlier, some are different than others. The most popular statistics include Total Packets Sent/Received, Protocols, Node Address, No ECB Available Count, and Packet Collision statistics. Use this screen to diagnose an overburdened or failing server NIC.

SYSTEM MODULE INFORMATION

The fourth item on the Available Options screen of MONITOR.NLM is System module information. When you first enter this screen, a submenu at the lower left is displayed. Using the arrow keys, you can move to and select the module you wish to examine. In our example, we have selected MONITOR itself (NetWare 4.10 Console Monitor). Pressing Enter brings up the detail menu on the right, and the module size information box superimposed on the General Information window in the upper center of the screen (see Figure 15.22).

Looking at the module size information screen first tells us the total amount of memory in use by that module. An administrator might want to look only at this piece of data for a new NLM to see its initial impact on memory. Taking another look after the NLM has been running for a while will tell how much memory it uses. For example, consider looking at SBACKUP.NLM before, during, and after the backup has run. An NLM that retains memory or grows slowly will eventually have a strong negative (or disastrous) effect on the system.

FIGURE 15.22

System Module Detail
Information Screen in
MONITOR.NLM

From this detail menu screen, you can also select any of the displayed items and find out how many processes the NLM has spawned, or if any of them are maintaining locks, and so on. Stay tuned, because this option has a cousin—Resource Utilization. They work very well together.

LOCK FILE SERVER MONITOR

As we learned in Chapter 11, the first level of NetWare 4 security is physical: lock the door to the file server room. The second is to lock the console. Curiosity often leads otherwise nice people to do strange things on a file server keyboard "just to see what will happen."

That brings us to the next Available Options screen—Lock file server console. From this screen, you can type in any password. You'll be asked to key it twice to make sure that a simple keying mistake doesn't leave you with an unknown password. After you type it once, the phrase Enter a password changes to Verify your password.

To unlock the console, just type the password at the keyboard. Since others might have been keying in random letters, or someone might have just innocently picked up the keyboard and inadvertently pressed some keys in the process, start out with the Enter key to clear the keyboard buffer, then key the password. Finally, press Enter.

As we learned in Chapter 11, NetWare 4 supports two passwords for clearing the server keyboard: the one that was entered when it was locked and the [Supervisor] password. In NetWare 4, the [Supervisor] is a special bindery user, and his/her password is the same as the first Admin password entered during installation of the very first NetWare 4 server. Any later change to the Admin password won't affect the [Supervisor] password—this is an important point. If, by chance, the server has activated Bindery Services, you can always LOGIN with the /B parameter and use SETPASS to change the [Supervisor]'s password.

FILE OPEN/LOCK ACTIVITY

Next, stop—File open/lock activity. You can use MONITOR to find locked files and unlock them. When you activate this choice, you are presented with a list of all the mounted volumes on the file server. If there is only one volume, the server won't ask you to choose it. Pick the volume and then you'll be asked to navigate to the directory and file that you want to check.

This program works by checking any file you care to ask about. It will not scan for locked files—you'll have to make a specific request to check a specific file. Once the directory is selected, move to the selected file. The Locking Status screen will appear with a plethora of statistics, such as Use Count, Open Count, Deny Counts, and Lock Status.

CACHE UTILIZATION

The seventh choice in the Available Options screen of MONITOR.NLM is cache utilization. The Cache Utilization Statistics screen is shown in Figure 15.23. The most important numbers are Long term cache hits (should be over 95%), Short term cache hits (over 80% is good; over 90% is even better), and LRU sitting time. In our example, the LABS-SRV1 has been very busy; only 65% of the cache hits are long term. Short term is 100%, and the LRU sitting time is only 32 seconds—that's good.

Cache Utilization Statistics in MONITOR

PROCESSOR UTILIZATION

The next stop on our fascinating Exploratorium is Processor utilization. Typically, the server processor (CPU) is idle most of the time. However, there are a few servers where the CPU is overworked.

When you activate this choice, you get a sub-menu listing all of the processes and interrupts running at the file server. You can pick any one of them by pressing Enter, or pick a few by tagging them with the F5 key. A third choice is to select all of them at once by pressing F3.

Processor utilization in MONITOR.NLM is displayed according to a complex histogram. The histogram uses three columns of numbers—Time, Count and Load. Time represents the amount of time the CPU spent in this process (the screen is updated every second and there are about a million units of time available in every second). Count is the number of times that this process was initiated in that second. And Load is the percentage of the total time that this process occupied the CPU.

The important thing to keep in mind is that the numbers always total 100 percent (give or take a small amount of rounding error) and that the 100 percent figure is percentage of current utilization. To give an example, let's assume you have a server with 75 percent utilization and that you examine this screen to see what process you might be able to move to another server. You find the PSERVER process and notice that it is taking 33 percent of the load. Deciding that this process is a good candidate, you move it to a different server. You should expect that the new utilization percentage will be around 50 percent. That's because a third of 75 percent is 25 percent, and that's the amount of reduction that you'll get.

Finally, the idle-loop process activates when the CPU has no work to do. Idle-loop load varies inversely with CPU utilization.

RESOURCE UTILIZATION

The next item deals with file server memory. It's the Resource Utilization option. The Server Memory Statistics window shows each of the memory pools and its current utilization status. The first place to look is at cache buffers. In most environments, 50 percent or more of the total file server memory should be available for cache buffers. For a high-volume production server, that figure should never get below 20 percent.

If memory seems to be "leaking," that is, the file cache pool is shrinking while another is growing, it is possible to pick the growing pool and then look at the modules that have requested memory from it. Examining them one by one and then tracking their memory usage will quickly identify the culprit.

Earlier I said that the System Module Information menu had a cousin. This is it! The difference between the two is one of approach. Here in the Resource Utilization screen you pick the pool, then look at the memory usage of the modules in that pool. In System Module Information, you pick the module, then look at which pools it is using memory from. Since there are varying levels of detail available in each of these two screens, the numbers will be close, but not exact.

MEMORY UTILIZATION

As we approach the end of our tour, we come across the Memory Utilization screen. This screen, and its accompanying subscreens, indicate the memory used by modules loaded after SERVER.NLM, the operating system file.

Figure 15.24 displays two important Memory Utilization windows—Allocated Memory and System Modules. The Allocated Memory screen shows utilization statistics for all or specific NLM modules. In turn, the System Modules screen allows you to choose the module you're interested in. In our example, MONITOR is giving us the allocated memory of all modules, even though we've highlighted the 3Com NIC driver.

F I G U R E 15.24

Memory in Use by NLMs

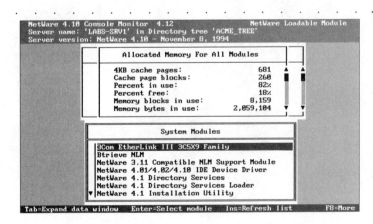

SCHEDULING INFORMATION

The final stop on our whirlwind tour is Scheduling Information. It is possible to adjust the scheduling delay of any particular server process. A delay of 0 means that a process has a normal priority. If this figure is increased to 2, the process would have half the normal processor access; a value of 3 would result in a third of the access. Press the plus (+) and minus (—) keys to increase and decrease the delay. For the curious, the first time + is pressed, the value skips from 0 to 2. It is not possible to select a value of 1—that would be the same as 0.

Well, there you have it. That's MONITOR.NLM in a nutshell. As a NetWare 4 CNE, you'll need to be intimately familiar with everything this server tool has to offer. This magic carpet ride is only the beginning. Practice, Practice, Practice. It's good for the soul. Goodbye, good luck, and thanks for saving the world!

NETWARE 4 MANAGEMENT

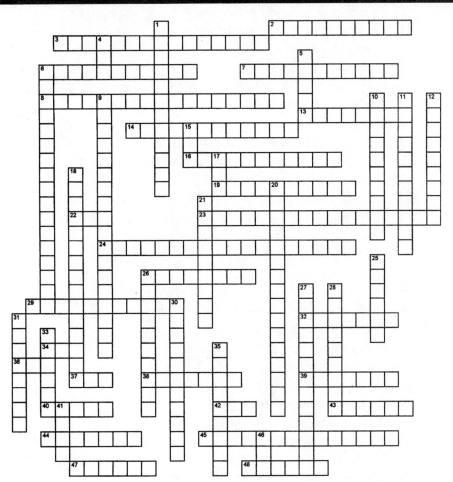

Across

2. Your password has expired, but c'mon in anyway
3. Timing is the key
6. Weapons in the new frontier
7. All your replication buddies
8. The second layer of NetWare 4 security
13. Managing from Tahiti

14. NDS pruning
16. #1 performance benefit in NetWare 4
19. Configuring ODI MLID in NET.CFG
22. Filing phone book
23. Who can do what with whom
24. Programming in NetWare 4 login scripts
26. Auditing in the new frontier
29. NLM test-bed
32. Where, oh where is my COMMAND.COM?
34. TCP/IP configuration files in the NetWare 4 file system
36. Optimization at the server console
37. NetWare 4 backup engine
38. Monitoring server SAP and RIP traffic
39. Where I live
40. Relating unrelated users
42. DynaText
43. The Dr. Jekyll and Mr. Hyde of WORMFACES
44. Maximum number of search drive mappings
45. One of the three reasons to replicate
47. A graceful exit from the NetWare 4 WAN
48. The king of the replica hill

Down

1. Central application control
4. "Don't give me any_____" (big packets)
5. Filing in a non-GUI world
6. Task handler
9. Don't mess with my packets
10. The Albert Einstein of server utilities
11. NDS cloning
12. Skipping the Default login script
15. Filtering effective NDS rights
17. The ODI "traffic cop"
18. A two-dimensional view of the 3-D NDS world
20. Group mail
21. A non-DOS client included with NetWare 4

25. Printing on a different volume

26. The final layer of NetWare 4 security

27. Better security at the file server

28. Protecting memory at the NetWare 4 server

30. Fixing a broken tree

31. Login script messaging without all the mess

33. Workstation configuration file

35. Speaking to the whole "Cloud"

41. High-capacity from a bunch of cheap stuff

46. NetWare 4 encryption

See Appendix C for answers.

PART V

APPENDIXES

Overview of Novell Education

"I WANNA BE A CNE!"

Novell's purpose is to advance human knowledge and effectiveness through innovative, networked information solutions. Novell and its partners are creating a world of pervasive computing that connects people with other people and the information they need, enabling them to act on it anytime, anyplace. By the year 2000, Novell networks will serve one billion people.

The mission of Novell Education is to drive global pervasive computing through quality education programs and products. To build the infrastructure to support Novell's goal of one billion users, Novell Education has developed authorized training partnerships throughout the world and certification programs for network support professionals. Today, Novell has more than 1,500 authorized education partners, including colleges and universities, and more than 75,000 certified support professionals worldwide.

This discussion gives you a brief overview of Novell's educational strategy by exploring the implementation of Novell's authorization and certification programs. In addition, we will briefly discuss the NetWare courses and alternative education methods. Let's begin with a brief discussion of Novell's educational philosophy.

Novell's Education Philosophy

Novell Education is the leading training provider in the network computing industry. Through the years, Novell Education has provided NetWare-oriented training to more than 2 million users. Novell Education is designed to help industry professionals develop network design, installation, and management skills. Novell-authorized courses provide comprehensive training in network performance, network functionality, and user productivity.

Novell's worldwide network of more than 1,500 authorized education partners can be categorized into two groups: NAECs and NEAPs. Novell Authorized Education Centers (NAECs) are private, independent training organizations that meet Novell's strict quality standards. Novell Education Academic Partners (NEAPs) are colleges or universities that meet the same strict guidelines. In addition, NEAPs provide Novell-authorized courses in a normal semester- or quarter-length format.

These Novell-authorized education partners offer more than 40 networking-oriented courses. Students can simply drop in for one or two courses or complete a rigorous technical certification curriculum.

Novell offers four certification programs:

- ▸ Certified Novell Administrator

- ▸ Novell Authorized CNE

- ▸ Novell Master CNE

- ▸ Certified Novell Instructor

The Certified Novell Administrator (CNA) program is designed for users or administrators who are responsible for the day-to-day operation of the network. The Certified Novell Engineer (CNE) program certifies service technicians or consultants to provide quality support for Novell networks, including systems design, installation, and maintenance. The Novell Master CNE program is designed to give CNEs an opportunity to achieve a higher level of certification, focusing on the support of enterprise-wide networks. Finally, the Certified Novell Instructor (CNI) program is a comprehensive training program for instructors who want to teach Novell-authorized courses. CNI candidates are required to attend courses, pass high-level tests, and perform satisfactorily at a rigorous instructor performance evaluation course.

Candidates who are interested in attaining any of these certifications must pass comprehensive Novell-authorized exams. These exams are designed to provide the most accurate and efficient measurements of a candidate's skill level. Novell currently offers three types of certification testing through its authorized testing partners. All tests are administered on a personal computer. They are "closed-book" and are graded on a pass/fail basis. For testing information, call a Novell authorized testing partner:

- ▸ Sylvan Technology Centers (1-800-RED-TEST or 1-410-880-8700)

- ▸ Drake Prometric (1-800-RED-EXAM or 1-612-820-5706)

Novell Education currently offers more than 40 courses that support its certification programs. For the latest course catalog, call 1-800-233-EDUC or 1-800-222-7800. You can also visit the Novell home page on the World Wide Web at http://www.novell.com.

In addition to instructor-led courses, Novell offers a variety of educational supplements, including self-study workbooks, computer-based training (CBT), and video-based training. These self-study materials diversify the delivery method of Novell-based education. Because these products are self-paced, you can focus on information you are unfamiliar with and reduce training time. You can also review course materials as often as necessary and refer to them as needed to learn specific skills.

Additional education supplements include Novell Press books, user's groups, conferences, NetWare Users International (NUI), the Internet, and seminars. As you can tell, Novell's educational philosophy is quite comprehensive. Whether you are interested in becoming a network expert or just want to learn the basics, you can count on Novell Education to meet your training needs.

This discussion provides information about how you can benefit from Novell Education. It's an excellent way to learn the ins and outs of Novell networking solutions.

Let's start with a quick look at education centers.

Education Centers

More than 1,500 Novell authorized training partners worldwide offer instructor-led courses and self-study education products to give you convenient access to a Novell-authorized education. You can count on the classes to be topnotch. Furthermore, Novell guarantees complete customer satisfaction for all Novell courses when they are taught at Novell-authorized training partners, which must meet four strict education guidelines:

▸ The facility must use Novell-developed course materials.

▸ The course must be taught within a recommended time frame.

▸ The facility itself must be Novell authorized. Authorization is based on a strict set of standards for equipment, instructional soundness, and student comfort.

▸ The course must be taught by a Certified Novell Instructor who is certified to teach the specific course.

Let's take a quick look.

NOVELL AUTHORIZED EDUCATION CENTERS

Novell Authorized Education Centers are private training organizations that provide Novell-authorized courses. While some NAECs are also Novell product resellers, many operate independent of Novell's reseller channels. The advantage of attending an NAEC is that these organizations typically have a great deal of experience in technology training and are driven to provide quality education. You can be assured of that because the success of the NAEC is dictated by the quality of the training—all courses are accurate, timely, and comprehensive. In order to become an NAEC, the private training organization must submit an extensive application to Novell Education. In addition, the applicant pays an initiation fee and annual licensing fees. NAECs are required to offer various courses in a consistent, timely matter.

For a list of NAECs in your area and the courses they are authorized to teach, call 1-800-233-EDUC in the US and Canada. In all other areas, call 1-801-222-7800 or contact your nearest Novell office.

NOVELL EDUCATION ACADEMIC PARTNER

The Novell Education Academic Partner program was created to provide quality Novell-authorized education through participating schools, colleges, and universities. NEAP implementation was driven by students who wanted to participate in Novell-authorized courses in a traditional education format and by colleges and universities that saw the value of network training. NEAPs must follow the same strict guidelines as NAECs and provide Novell courses as part of their standard curriculum. There currently are 150 colleges and universities authorized to teach NEAP courses—and the number is growing. For a list of participating schools, call 1-800-233-EDUC in the United States and Canada. In all other areas, call 1-801-222-7800 or contact your nearest Novell office.

Certification Programs

Novell Education's certification programs are designed to develop a high level of expertise in the management and implementation of Novell products. To ensure the availability of quality support professionals, Novell has developed the following certification programs:

- Certified Novell Administrator program

- Novell Authorized CNE program

- Master CNE program

- Certified Novell Instructor program

Those who certify are recognized by others in the network computing industry as competent, knowledgeable resources for network management, technical support, and training. Novell's instructor-led courses and self-study materials can help candidates prepare for the required certification tests. These tests are currently offered by Novell authorized testing partners throughout the world.

Novell strongly recommends that candidates seek as much hands-on experience with Novell products as they can before and during the certification process. In addition to on-the-job experience, candidates can gain valuable practice by attending hands-on training at Novell-authorized facilities. Novell's performance-based certification tests cover concepts learned from study, hands-on training and lots of practice.

Let's take a brief look at the four certification programs.

CERTIFIED NOVELL ADMINISTRATOR

The CNA program is designed for users who are responsible for the day-to-day operation of a network. System administrators typically perform tasks such as adding and deleting user accounts, backing up the server, loading applications, and maintaining security. CNAs are certified by passing one CNA test for the operating system they choose.

Successful completion of the certification test identifies CNAs as knowledgeable and trained NetWare or GroupWare administrators. It also serves as a valuable credential in the networking industry. If a CNA decides to go on to become a CNE, the knowledge gained in the courses will be useful and applicable. Also, CNAs can apply test credits toward CNE certification.

In addition to the CNA program objectives that are covered in the administration courses, CNA candidates should have a thorough knowledge of DOS and microcomputer concepts and user interface fundamentals. If you have anymore questions about Novell's CNA program, contact Novell Education at 1-800-233-EDUC in the United States or Canada. In all other locations, contact your local Novell office or call 1-801-222-7800.

NOVELL AUTHORIZED CNE

The CNE program certifies service technicians and consultants to provide quality support for Novell networks. This support includes NetWare and GroupWare design, installation, and maintenance. Once certification requirements are met, Novell stands behind its CNEs with technical support and up-to-date product profiles. CNEs must also meet continuing certification requirements to keep up with developing technologies and the latest Novell products.

MASTER CNE

Master CNEs are CNEs who take additional training and tests to provide support for connectivity issues and network administration problems. Master CNEs have advanced skills to provide solutions to complex networking problems that span several different platforms.

Master CNEs specialize in one of three technologies: Network Management, Infrastructure and Advanced Access, or GroupWare Integration.

CERTIFIED NOVELL INSTRUCTOR

The Cerified Novell Instructor program is designed for people who want to make a career of teaching others how to install, configure, and use Novell networking products.

In addition to attending Novell courses and passing proficiency tests at a higher level than other certification candidates, CNIs must successfully complete a rigorous Instructor Performance Evaluation. Novell also requires CNIs to meet continuing certification requirements, which include additional training and testing as Novell updates courses and releases new products.

Education Supplements

In addition to the instructor-led courses, Novell provides additional education methodologies: workbooks, computer-based training, video-based training, and Novell Press publications such as this book. Education supplements have been included so that professionals can train at their own pace in a more convenient manner. Self-paced education materials can be purchased through NAECs and authorized resellers. Following is a discussion of the most popular Novell Education supplements.

WORKBOOKS

Novell Education provides a series of self-study workbooks. These workbooks are designed to supplement existing instructor-led courses or provide additional details in areas of specialty that do not warrant an instructor-led course. Novell-authorized workbooks are intended to be completed at the student's own pace. Each section within the workbook includes objectives, a list of terms, and review questions. Following is a list of currently available Novell Education workbooks:

- *DOS for Network Users*

- *Microcomputer Concepts for Network Users*

- *LANalyzer for Windows*

- *NetWare SFT III 3.11*

- *Administering NetWare for Macintosh 3.12*

- *Administering NetWare for Macintosh 4.01*

- *Administering SNADS for NetWare Global MHS*

- *Administering SMTP for NetWare Global MHS*

COMPUTER-BASED TRAINING

A sophisticated series of computer-based training courses are available that supplement the more traditional Novell Education materials. These courses are fully graphical and interactive. Most are based on the Microsoft Windows interface. In addition to providing the technical information in an easy-to-understand format, the computer-based training courses include mastery tests and review questions. For more information on computer-based courseware, contact Novell's authorized course developer, CBT Systems at 1-800-929-9050 or 1-415-737 9050.

VIDEO-BASED TRAINING

For more information about courses on videotape, contact Novell's authorized course developer, J3 Learning Corporation at 1-800-532-7672 or 1-612-430-0330.

OTHER SUPPLEMENTS

In addition to Novell Education, other organizations provide supplements for network training. These organizations are primarily concerned with developing and distributing accurate technical information. The serious network professional can enhance his/her understanding of NetWare-related topics using the following educational supplements:

- Novell Press
- NetWare Users International
- Conferences
- Novell World Wide Web Page

Novell Press

Novell Press was created to provide technically accurate information about Novell products through the retail book channel. Novell Press books contain practical information about designing, building, and managing a diverse network. These books are invaluable tools for all levels of users. All books are written by experts and provide the kind of practical information that is highly prized by system administrators. This book itself, for example, is designed to provide supplemental discussions of key topics for CNE candidates. In addition, information in this book can be used toward the CNA, Master CNE, and CNI certifications.

NetWare Users International

NetWare Users International is an organization that was created in conjunction with Novell to provide support to NetWare users groups. These users groups meet monthly to discuss critical technology issues and provide short training seminars. Also, through NUI, NetWare users can present a united voice to Novell, giving vital feedback on improving products and services. In addition, NUI provides a supplemental education program to its members through regional NetWare users conferences; *NetWare Connection* magazine; and NUI-sponsored videos, products, and services. For more information about these resources or to join NUI, call Novell at 1-800-228-4NUI.

Conferences

Novell hosts BrainShare technical conferences for developers and instructors throughout the world.

Novell World Wide Web Page

Visit the Novell home page on the Internet at http://www.novell.com for the latest information about Novell products, education, and certification.

CNE Cross-Reference
to Novell
Course Objectives

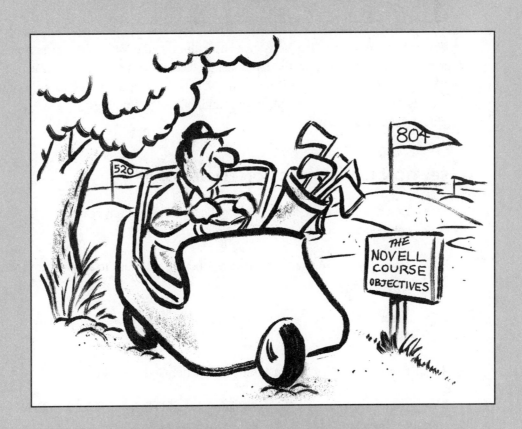

Following is a list of the Novell-authorized course objectives for the entire NetWare 4 CNE curriculum. These objectives are the foundation of the "new" NetWare 4 CNE program. Novell Education uses the objectives to write authorized courseware and to develop certification exams. In order to become a NetWare 4 CNE, you must be intimately familiar with every objective. *Novell's CNE Study Guide for NetWare 4.1* enables you to learn these objectives (see page numbers cross-reference) in conjunction with Novell-authorized courseware. This appendix clarifies that relationship by pointing you in the right direction.

Have fun and good luck!

Course 520: NetWare 4 Administration

This is the foundation of the NetWare 4 curriculum. In the *NetWare 4 Administration* course, you are introduced to the fundamental technologies of NetWare 4, namely NetWare Directory Services, the File System, NDS and Server Security, Backup, Login Scripts, the "new" Menu System, Messaging, and, of course, Printing.

This is a great place to start.

SECTION 1: INTRODUCTION TO NETWARE 4

1 • Describe a network, including its basic function and physical components...**14–17**

2 • List the NetWare 4 network services students will learn to administer in this course...**6–12**

3 • Describe NetWare Directory Services (NDS) and explain its role on the network...**14–17, 92–121**

4 • Describe the Directory, including its function and basic components...**17**

5 • Describe the Directory tree, including leaf and container objects...**92–121**

SECTION 2: CONNECTING TO THE NETWORK AND LOGGING IN

1 • Describe how a workstation communicates with the network, and list the files required to connect a DOS workstation to the network...**1055–1074**

2 • Describe the function of the software and hardware necessary to connect a workstation to the network, including local operating systems, NetWare DOS Requester, communications protocols, and network board...**1055–1074**

3 • Connect a workstation to the network by loading the appropriate DOS workstation files...**1201–1202**

4 • Explain and perform the login procedure...**1081–1083**

SECTION 3: ACCESSING DATA FILES AND APPLICATIONS ON THE NETWORK

1 • Explain the basic concepts of network file storage, including volumes, directory structures, network drives, and search drives...**801–819**

2 • Define NetWare command line utilities, describe how they are used, and activate Help information for them...**819–851**

3 • Display volume, directory, and file information...**819–851**

4 • Map a network drive to a volume using a Volume object and a Directory Map object, and navigate between the volumes...**851–867**

5 • Map a network drive to a directory using a Volume object and a Directory Map object and navigate the directories of a volume...**851–867**

6 • Map a search drive to a directory containing an application using a Volume object and a Directory Map object and run the application...**851–867**

SECTION 4: PRINTING TO A NETWORK PRINTER

SECTION 5: SETTING UP USER ACCOUNTS AND LOGIN SECURITY

8 • Describe and establish login security, including user account restrictions, time restrictions, station restrictions, and intruder detection...**898–914**

SECTION 6: SETTING UP THE NETWORK FILE SYSTEM

1 • Explain guidelines for planning and creating custom volumes and directories in the network file system...**803–810**

2 • List the system-created volumes and directories; describe their contents and function...**810–814**

3 • Identify the strengths and weaknesses of sample directory structures...**814–819**

4 • Design and create a directory structure based on a given scenario...**814–819**

5 • Explain guidelines for selecting and installing network applications...**1057–1061**

SECTION 7: MANAGING THE FILE SYSTEM

1 • Manage the file system directory structure by creating, deleting, renaming, and moving directories...**830–841**

2 • Manage files in the file system by copying, moving, deleting, salvaging, and purging files...**841–851**

3 • Manage the use of volume space by viewing volume usage statistics; restricting space usage by user and directory; changing file ownership; locating files based on usage, owner, and size; setting compression attributes; and setting data migration attributes...**821–830**

SECTION 8: SETTING UP FILE SYSTEM SECURITY

1 • Describe NetWare 4 file system security, including the concepts of directory and file rights, trustee assignments, inheritance, rights reassignment, Inherited Rights Filters (IRFs), security equivalence, and effective rights...**951–964**

2 • Given a scenario, calculate a user's effective rights...**998–1002**

3 • Perform basic security implementation tasks, such as assigning a trustee and granting rights, setting a directory IRF, creating a group object and assigning members, and making a user security equivalent to another user...**987–997**

4 • Describe guidelines for planning a directory structure based on security considerations...**814–819**

5 • Given a directory structure and the function of its directories, recommend the rights that should be granted and the trustee object that will make security implementation and management easiest...**987–997**

6 • Describe and set directory and file attributes that can be used to regulate access to files: Copy Inhibit, Delete Inhibit, Execute Only, Hidden, Purge, Read Only, Read Write, Rename Inhibit, Shareable, System, and Transactional...**964–971**

7 • Activate, navigate NDS and file systems with, and get help for, NetWare Administrator...**725–729, 987–997**

8 • Based on a scenario, create and implement a file system security plan that appropriately grants directory and file rights to container, Group, and User objects, and set directory IRFs...**987–997**

SECTION 9: ACCESSING AND PROTECTING THE NETWARE SERVER CONSOLE

1 • Describe the function of a NetWare 4 server and its interface...**1099–1101**

2 • Define console command and NetWare Loadable Module (NLM)...**1131–1155**

3 • Describe the function of the LOAD command...**1138**

4 • Describe remote console management; list the steps necessary to set up a server for both SPX and asynchronous remote connections...**1190–1194**

5 • Use RCONSOLE.EXE to remotely access the server console, change between console screens, and activate the RCONSOLE Available Options menu...**1194–1197**

6 • Describe security strategies for a NetWare 4 server, such as setting a password on the monitor, setting a password for Remote Console, and placing the server in a secure location...**1126–1131**

SECTION 10: SETTING UP NETWORK PRINTING

1 • Set up a network printing environment by creating and configuring related Print Queue, Printer, and Print Server objects...**1232–1247**

2 • Set up network printing hardware by bringing up a print server on a NetWare 4 server and connecting a printer to the network through a NetWare server or DOS workstation...**1241–1247**

3 • Regulate who can do any of the following: print to a print queue, manage print jobs in the print queue, be notified by a printer when a problem occurs, view the status of the print server, or manage the print server...**1256–1281**

4 • Manage the flow of print jobs into and out of a print queue by managing the status of the print queue...**1256–1281**

5 • Manage print jobs in a print queue by pausing, rushing, delaying, and deleting print jobs in the print queue...**1256–1281**

6 • Describe how to customize print jobs using print job configurations, printer definitions, and printer forms...**1247–1256**

SECTION 11: INSTALLING AND CONFIGURING NETWARE CLIENT ON A DOS WORKSTATION

1 • Describe the appropriate options needed in the CONFIG.SYS, AUTOEXEC.BAT, and NET.CFG files to automate the network connection and login processes...**1013–1024**

2 • Install NetWare Client for DOS and MS Windows using the NetWare Client installation software...**667–669**

3 • Create a custom network connection by modifying the INSTALL.CFG and NET.CFG files...**1017–1024**

SECTION 12: CREATING LOGIN SCRIPTS

1 • Describe the types of login scripts and how they coordinate at login...**1024–1032**

2 • Recommend procedures that should be executed during login...**1032–1046**

3 • Plan login scripts with correct login script command syntax, given an environment need...**1032–1046**

4 • Create, execute, and debug a login script...**1085–1087**

SECTION 13: CREATING USER MENUS

1 • Describe the process of creating menus...**1046–1057**

2 • Plan a simple menu using correct command syntax...**1046–1057**

3 • Build, compile, execute, and debug menus...**1087–1088**

4 • Describe the process of converting menus from previous versions of NetWare to the new menu system...**1054–1055**

SECTION 14: MANAGING NDS SECURITY

1 • Explain how access to the Directory is controlled by object trustees, object rights, and property rights...**914–950**

2 • List and explain the automatic rights assignments that can occur in NDS...**920–925**

3 • Explain guidelines and considerations for managing NDS security...**914–950**

4 • Implement NDS security by making trustee assignments; modifying Object, All Property, and Selected Property rights; and setting Inherited Rights Filters...**987–997**

SECTION 15: MANAGING RESOURCES IN THE DIRECTORY TREE

1 • Describe how the Directory tree structure affects network use and management skills...**657–663**

2 • Describe sample Directory structures and discuss basic guidelines for organizing resources...**700–707**

3 • Demonstrate correct object-naming techniques...**121–138**

4 • Change the current context and navigate the Directory tree with CX...**672–673**

5 • Log in, map network drives, and redirect print jobs to resources in other contexts...**664–675**

6 • Grant rights to file system and network printing resources in other contexts...**664–675**

7 • Create shortcuts to objects in other contexts using Directory Map and Alias objects...**688–689**

8 • Establish an initial context at login for a DOS workstation...**1019–1023**

9 • Edit login scripts to access resources in other containers...**1032–1046**

SECTION 16: BACKING UP SERVERS AND WORKSTATIONS

1 • Compare and contrast backup strategies...**1181–1183**

2 • Describe the process of backing up a NetWare server's file system with SBACKUP...**1177–1187**

3 • Describe the process of restoring lost file system information with SBACKUP...**1177–1187**

SECTION 17: PROVIDING MESSAGING SERVICES

1 • Determine appropriate use of messaging services through MHS Services for NetWare 4...**1062–1066**

2 • Describe the process of installing messaging services using MHS Services for NetWare 4...**1067–1071**

3 • Create a Distribution List object and assign members...**1088–1092**

4 • Assign mailboxes to User, Group, Distribution List, and Organizational Role objects...**1071–1078, 1088–1092**

5 • Send and receive e-mail with FirstMail...**1092–1093**

Course 525: NetWare 4 Advanced Administration

Your CNE education continues with *NetWare 4 Advanced Administration*. In this course, you explore the advanced topics which separate CNEs from pretenders. You learn all about Server Startup, advanced NDS Design and Management, Partitioning, more Messaging, and Optimization.

Pay attention to these objectives, because they can be a little tricky.

SECTION 1: SERVER STARTUP PROCEDURES AND CONFIGURATION FILES

1 • Identify and describe the server components...**1098–1100**

2 • Perform a server startup procedure...**1098–1100**

3 • Identify and describe server configuration files...**1110–1114**

4 • Identify commands and options used to customize the appropriate server configuration file...**1110–1114**

5 • Select the appropriate utility and edit the server configuration files...**1112**

6 • Create server batch files that perform specific tasks, such as remotely rebooting the server...**1114**

SECTION 2: DESIGNING AND ADMINISTERING NDS

1 • Identify the process for designing the Directory tree, which includes determining the Directory structure, naming conventions, and implementation method...**187–199**

2 • Create a structural design for an organizational, divisional, or departmental Directory tree implementation...**308–321**

3 • Merge small Directory trees in a department-to-organizational implementation...**706–713**

4 • Navigate the contexts of the newly-created Directory tree using CX and NetWare Administrator...**664–673**

5 • Demonstrate correct use of object names in utilities...**121–138**

6 • Create users with UIMPORT...**695–700, 734–736**

SECTION 3: SECURING THE DIRECTORY TREE

1 • Identify and explain the need for NDS security...**914–915**

2 • Perform steps to assign additional object and property rights...**925–943**

3 • Identify additional NDS rights users may require when using specific NDS objects: Alias of a User object, Profile Login Script, and Directory Map...**943–950**

4 • Given a Directory tree, determine effective rights for objects and properties and troubleshoot an NDS security scenario...**987–997**

5 • Set up an auditor User object and enable auditing...**971–986**

SECTION 4: PARTITIONING AND REPLICATING NDS AND SYNCHRONIZING TIME

I • Partition the Directory to allow proper replication and distribution to multiple servers...**739–759**

2 • Place replicas in a way that fosters network accessibility, performance, and fault tolerance...**333–354, 759–786**

3 • Anticipate what partitions and replicas are created by default when a server is installed in a Directory tree...**333–354**

4 • Move a container object and its subordinate objects within the Directory tree...**756**

5 • Configure servers to synchronize time in a NetWare 4 network...**788–800**

6 • Given a scenario that includes a WAN topology, choose between Service Advertising Protocol (SAP) and specified time sources to synchronize time among servers...**364–366**

SECTION 5: CREATING A DETAILED DESIGN AND TROUBLESHOOTING NDS

1 • Create a detailed design of the Directory tree that provides for securing NDS, partitioning the Directory, replicating partitions of the Directory, and synchronizing time...**291–294, 305–308**

2 • Identify NDS inconsistencies...**777–788, 1116–1118**

3 • Execute the procedures to prepare an NDS server for downtime...**766–775, 1116–1118**

4 • Execute the procedures to recover from a failed master replica...**768–770**

5 • Perform the steps to remove a server from the Directory tree...**566–567, 1116–1118**

SECTION 6: INTEGRATING AND MANAGING NETWARE 3

1 • Integrate NetWare 3.1x with NetWare 4 using bindery services...**29–31, 330–332**

2 • Manage NetWare 3.1x resources from NetWare Administrator using NetSync...**714–719**

SECTION 7: CONFIGURING NETWARE 4 FOR DIVERSE CLIENTS

1 • Configure the server to support diverse clients such as OS/2 and Macintosh...**1170–1176**

2 • Install the NetWare Client for DOS and MS Windows using the NetWare Client installation software...**568–570**

3 • Create a custom network connection by modifying the NET.CFG file...**1017–1024**

SECTION 8: MANAGING NETWORK SERVICES

1 • Define the purpose of the NetWare MultiProtocol Router (MPR) 3.0 and give an example of its function within a network...**1119–1121**

2 • Determine appropriate use of messaging services through MHS Services for NetWare 4...**1062–1066**

3 • Create a Distribution List object and assign members...**1088–1092**

4 • Assign mailboxes to User, Group, Distribution List, and Organizational Role objects...**1071–1078, 1088–1092**

5 • Send and receive e-mail with FirstMail...**1092–1093**

6 • Enable internationalization...**1121–1125**

SECTION 9: OPTIMIZING THE NETWORK AND SERVER

1 • Describe NetWare 4 memory management architecture, including memory allocation and memory protection features...**80–81, 1321–1332**

2 • Interpret the MONITOR Statistics screen...**1334–1335**

3 • Monitor and modify file and directory cache performance...**1336–1339, 1344–1347**

4 • View and modify server buffer and packet parameters...**1339–1341, 1348–1351**

5 • Define and enable memory suballocation...**1357–1360**

6 • List the steps to enable file compression...**1355–1357**

7 • Enable and manage the Packet Burst protocol...**1360–1361**

8 • Enable and manage Large Internet Packets (LIPs)...**1361–1362**

Course 526: NetWare 3 to NetWare 4 Update

This course is the Administration alternative for advanced NetWare 3 CNEs. Everything you learn in the *NetWare 3 to NetWare 4 Update* course is carefully hand-picked from the previous two Administration courses. Novell Education removed the NetWare 3 material with the assumption that CNE-3 students should already know it. The result is a fun-packed three days of insanity and NDS wizardry.

Don't forget your magic wand.

SECTION 1: PERFORMING NETWARE 3 TASKS WITH NETWARE 4

1 • Organize network resources using NetWare Directory Services (NDS) in NetWare 4...**92–121**

2 • View the NetWare 4 server startup components and compare them with NetWare 3. These components include server configuration files, the server startup process, server utilities (such as MONITOR and INSTALL), and commands (such as DISPLAY SERVERS and CONFIG)...**1100–1155**

3 • Connect and log in to a NetWare 4 server...**1081–1083**

4 • Manage objects in NetWare Directory Services (NDS) that have been migrated from the NetWare 3 bindery. Such objects include users, groups, servers, and volumes...**676–683**

5 • Manage the file system using the Volume object in the NetWare Administrator utility...**821–830**

6 • Control file system security using NetWare Administrator. View effective rights, assign rights to users and groups, and modify the Inherited Rights Filter (IRF)...**940–952, 987–997**

7 • Set up and manage printing using NetWare Administrator and the NetWare 4 DOS text print utilities...**1232–1281**

8 • Manage the server using the NetWare 4 server utilities and command line utilities...**1098–1155**

9 • Back up the server using the NetWare 4 SBACKUP server utility...**1180–1187**

SECTION 2: MANAGING THE USER ENVIRONMENT

1 • Create and modify user, Profile, and container login scripts...**1024–1046**

2 • Create users with UIMPORT...**695–699, 734–736**

3 • Create and compile menus...**1046–1057, 1087–1088**

4 • Identify the procedures for converting NetWare 3 menus using MENUCNVT...**1054–1055**

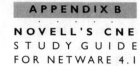

SECTION 3: INTEGRATING AND MANAGING NETWARE 3

1 • Integrate NetWare 3.1x with NetWare 4 using bindery services...**29–31, 330–332**

2 • Manage NetWare 3.1x resources from the NetWare Administrator using NetSync...**714–719**

SECTION 4: DESIGNING AND ADMINISTERING NDS

1 • Identify the process for designing the Directory tree, which includes determining the Directory structure, naming conventions, and implementation method...**187–199**

2 • Create a structural design for an organizational, divisional, or departmental Directory tree implementation...**308–321**

3 • Merge small Directory trees in a departmental-to-organizational implementation...**706–713**

4 • Navigate the contexts of the newly created Directory tree using CX and NetWare Administrator...**664–673**

5 • Demonstrate correct object naming...**121–138**

SECTION 5: SECURING THE DIRECTORY TREE

1 • Identify differences and similarities between NDS security and file system security in NetWare 4...**951–952**

2 • Identify and explain the need for NDS security...**914–915**

3 • Identify the default object and property rights using NetWare Administrator...**920–925**

4 • Given a Directory tree, design a security strategy using security design guidelines...**987–997**

5 • Perform steps to assign additional object and property rights...**925–943**

6 • Identify additional NDS rights users may require when using specific NDS objects: Alias of a User object, Profile Login Script, and Directory Map...**943–950**

7 • Define inheritance as it applies to object and property rights and create Inherited Rights Filters (IRFs) to manage the flow of security...**914–950**

8 • Given a Directory tree, determine effective rights for objects and Properties and troubleshoot an NDS security scenario...**987–997**

9 • Set up an auditor User object and enable auditing...**969–986**

SECTION 6: PARTITIONING AND REPLICATING NDS AND SYNCHRONIZING TIME

1 • Partition the Directory to allow proper replication and distribution to multiple servers...**739–759**

2 • Place replicas in a way that fosters network accessibility, performance, and fault tolerance...**333–354, 759–786**

3 • Anticipate what partitions and replicas are created by default when a server is installed in a Directory tree...**333–354**

4 • Move a container object and its subordinate objects within the Directory tree...**756**

5 • Configure servers to synchronize time in a NetWare 4 network...**788–800**

6 • Given a scenario that includes a WAN topology, choose between Service Advertising Protocol (SAP) and specified time sources to synchronize time among servers...**364–366**

SECTION 7: CREATING A DETAILED DESIGN AND TROUBLESHOOTING NDS

1 • Create a detailed design of the Directory tree that provides for securing NDS, partitioning the Directory, replicating partitions of the Directory, and synchronizing time...**291–294, 305–308**

2 • Identify NDS inconsistencies...**777–788, 1116–1118**

3 • Execute the procedures to prepare an NDS server for downtime...**766–775, 1116–1118**

4 • Execute the procedures to recover from a failed master replica...**768–770**

5 • Perform the steps to remove a server from the Directory tree...**566–567, 1116–1118**

SECTION 8: CONFIGURING NETWARE 4 FOR DIVERSE CLIENTS

1 • Configure the server to support diverse clients such as OS/2 and Macintosh...**1170–1176**

2 • Install the NetWare Client for DOS and MS Windows using the NetWare Client installation software...**568–570**

3 • Create a custom network connection by modifying the NET.CFG file...**1017–1024**

SECTION 9: MANAGING NETWORK SERVICES

1 • Define the purpose of the NetWare 4 MultiProtocol Router (MPR) 3.0 and give an example of its function within a network...**1119–1121**

2 • Determine appropriate use of messaging services through MHS Services for NetWare 4...**1062–1066**

3 • Create a Distribution List object and assign members...**1088–1092**

4 • Assign mailboxes to User, Group, Distribution List, and Organizational Role objects...**1071–1078, 1088–1092**

5 • Send and receive e-mail with FirstMail...**1092–1093**

6 • Enable Internationalization...**1121–1125**

SECTION 10: OPTIMIZING THE NETWORK AND SERVER

1 • Describe NetWare 4 memory management architecture, including memory allocation and memory protection features...**80–81, 1321–1332**

2 • Interpret the MONITOR Statistics screen...**1334–1335**

3 • Monitor and modify file and directory cache performance...**1339–1341, 1348–1351**

4 • View and modify server buffer and packet parameters...**1336–1339, 1344–1347**

5 • Define and enable memory suballocation...**1357–1360**

6 • List the steps to enable file compression...**1355–1357**

► . . . . ◄

Course 532: NetWare 4 Design and Implementation

With NDS comes great responsibility. Gone are the days when you could yank NetWare 3.12 out of the box and slam it into a server over lunch. Now, you need to fully understand the "purpose" of your WAN before installing the very first server. The good news is Novell Education has developed a special "new" course just for you — *NetWare 4 Design and Implementation*. In this thorough three-day journey, you'll grasp the fundamentals of Project Team creation, NDS Tree Design, Partitioning and Replica Design, Time Synchronization, and NetWare 4 Implementation.

This is the trickiest test of them all. Study hard.

SECTION 1: DETERMINING THE PROJECT APPROACH

. . . . .

SECTION 2: DESIGNING THE DIRECTORY TREE

1 • Given a case company, revise a naming standards document that specifies a unique Directory tree name and ensures consistent object names, property values, and other network names (such as IPX addresses)...**256–290**

2 • Given a case company's WAN topology and geographic location, draw the structure for the upper layers of the Directory tree...**308–320**

3 • From an analysis of corporate documents that include the organization chart, resource chart, and workflow chart, draw a first draft of the lower layers in the Directory tree...**321–323**

4 • Modify the Directory tree for a centralized or decentralized administration approach and login script maintenance strategy...**324–326**

5 • Given a draft Directory tree, verify that all containers are appropriately placed for efficient partitioning...**326–328**

6 • Given a draft Directory tree, place leaf objects in the Directory tree to facilitate efficient user access...**700–706**

SECTION 3: DETERMINING A PARTITION AND REPLICA STRATEGY

1 • Assess a company scenario (including WAN topology, a map of physical locations, numbers of servers, and server proximity) to determine where to draw partition boundaries in the Directory tree structure...**334–345**

2 • Given a scenario with new servers, upgraded servers, and merged Directory trees, determine how the default replica placement should be modified...**345–351**

3 • Given a company scenario, adapt the replica replacement plan to accommodate additional considerations...**352–354**

SECTION 6: DEVELOPING A MIGRATION STRATEGY

1 • Given a company scenario, create a client migration strategy that includes configuration parameters and plans for automating the migration process...**412–420**

2 • Given a company scenario with an existing network, create a migration strategy for existing servers to become NetWare 4 servers...**421–434**

SECTION 7: CREATING AN IMPLEMENTATION SCHEDULE

1 • Given a company scenario, give the proper sequence of tasks to implement a NetWare 4 network...**400**

2 • Set timelines and milestones for the implementation of a NetWare 4 network by matching available people with the required tasks...**399–441**

SECTION 8: CREATING AN IMPLEMENTATION SCHEDULE

1 • Given a company scenario, design a Directory tree structure with associated partition, replica, time synchronization, and accessibility plans...**399–441**

2 • Given a company scenario, develop a migration strategy and implementation schedule for NetWare 4...**399–441**

Course 804: NetWare 4 Installation and Configuration Workshop

The final NetWare 4 course is the most interesting. You get to spend two fun-filled days of "hands-on" bliss. The entire *NetWare 4 Installation and Configuration Workshop* course consists of exercise after exercise, including Installing NetWare 4 (seven times), Migrating from NetWare 3, Building NDS, Partitioning NDS, Time Synchronization, Securing Everything, and finally, Optimizing the File System and Server. As if that's not all, they even throw in a "NetWare for Macintosh" installation for good measure.

Your fingers sure are going to be sore after this one.

SECTION 1: UPGRADING NETWARE 3.1x TO NETWARE 4

SECTION 2: EXECUTING A SIMPLE NETWARE 4 INSTALLATION

1 • Compare the requirements of the NetWare 4 Simple Installation and the NetWare 4 Custom Installation...**479–484**

2 • Identify the major steps for installing NetWare 4...**485–494**

3 • Install a NetWare 4 server using the Simple option...**550–556**

SECTION 3: MIGRATING FROM NETWARE 3.1x TO NETWARE 4

1 • Identify the two types of upgrade available using the Migration utility...**617–620**

2 • Discuss which elements of the NetWare 3.12 environments will migrate and which will not...**617–634**

3 • Discuss the prerequisites of an Across-the-Wire Migration upgrade...**617–634**

4 • Identify the major steps to upgrading a NetWare 3.1x server using the Across-the-Wire Migration method...**617–634**

5 • Upgrade a NetWare 3.1x server using the Across-the-Wire Migration method...**645–648**

SECTION 4: EXECUTING A CUSTOM NETWARE 4 INSTALLATION

1 • Identify the major steps for installing NetWare 4 using the Custom Installation option...**495–531**

2 • Install NetWare 4 with multiple volumes and modify compression and suballocation...**557–565**

3 • Set up time synchronization with groups in different time zones...**523–526**

4 • Discuss the two methods used to install TCP/IP and AppleTalk protocols...**514–516**

SECTION 5: INSTALLING NOVELL ONLINE DOCUMENTATION

I • Identify the steps for preparing to install the Online Documentation on your server...**537–543**

2 • Set up and configure clients to view the Online Documentation...**571–573**

SECTION 6: CONFIGURING A NETWARE ENVIRONMENT

I • Set up network user accounts and configure property information...**721–737**

2 • Create file system structure and provide appropriate security for users...**870–871, 987–997**

3 • Set up a network printing environment by creating and configuring print queue, printer, and print server...**1304–1309**

SECTION 7: MERGING, CONFIGURING, AND TROUBLESHOOTING NDS

I • Merge two NetWare 4 Directory trees...**706–713**

2 • Given an NDS tree, create and merge partitions using Partition Manager...**748–759**

3 • Move an NDS container from one context to another...**756**

4 • Execute the procedures to recover from a failed master replica...**768–770**

5 • Set the bindery context for multiple servers in multiple contexts...**330–332**

6 • Manage NetWare Directory Services with multiple containers...**721–737**

SECTION 8: MANAGING THE NETWARE 4 SERVER

1 • Describe NetWare 4 memory components, memory requirements, and memory allocation...**1321–1332**

2 • View critical components to verify memory status and use commands to optimize memory allocation...**1321–1332**

3 • Describe the components that affect server and network performance...**1343–1373**

4 • Implement appropriate SET parameters for increased performance in a scenario setting...**1343–1362**

5 • Describe the maintenance utilities and use them to verify the integrity of the server data and hardware...**1362–1373**

SECTION 9: APPLYING STRATEGIES FOR NETWARE 4

1 • Identify strategies for designing, installing, and maintaining NetWare 4...**291–294, 1097–1098, 1126–1131, 1190–1197**

2 • Given scenarios, apply the strategies for designing, installing, and maintaining NetWare 4...**291–294, 1097–1098, 1126–1131, 1190–1197**

SECTION 10: INSTALLING NETWARE FOR MACINTOSH

1 • List the capabilities provided to Macintosh and non-Macintosh users by NetWare for Macintosh...**544**

2 • Identify the three major steps for setting up NetWare for Macintosh clients...**543–548**

3 • Install NetWare for Macintosh on a NetWare 4 server...**543–548**

4 • Identify the steps for configuring the NetWare for Macintosh services...**543–548, 1175**

5 • List the steps for installing Macintosh Client software...**543–548**

Solutions to Quizzes, Puzzles, Exercises, and Case Studies

"Scanner indicates no life forms, Captain...only the answers to CNE exercises."

NetWare 4 CNE—A New Frontier

Chapter 1: Introduction to NetWare 4

ANSWERS TO QUIZZES

Q1-1

The only available matching color for the large present is red. Next, the only contrasting color available for the small wrapping is silver. Finally, that leaves green wrapping and a gold bow for the medium-sized gift. Happy birthday.

Q1-2

15

APPENDIX C

. . . . .

S O L U T I O N S   T O
Q U I Z Z E S ,   P U Z Z L E S ,
E X E R C I S E S ,   A N D
C A S E   S T U D I E S

Q1-3
Decimal point.

Q1-4
$(7777 \times 7)/(\sqrt{7} \times 7)$ Told ya so.

Q1-5
It doesn't. It takes place "A long time ago...in a galaxy far, far away."

Q1-6
Assume that the total number of birds is 240—that is 6 trees with 40 birds, or 40 trees with 6 birds, or 3 trees with 80 birds, or 80 trees with 3 birds. Remember I said, "If you know the number of birds, you can figure out the number of trees." Therefore, it can't be 240, or any number that factorizes.

Now try prime numbers. A prime number is any number that can only be divided by 1 and itself. If 229 were the number, there would only be 1 tree with 229 birds in it, or 229 trees with only 1 bird each. Nope—there's more than one tree, and you have to have more than one bird per tree.

That leaves only the square of a prime number. Voilà, there's only one answer between 200 and 300—289. Therefore, there are 17 trees, each with 17 birds. Now, wasn't that fun!

Q1-7
The average is calculated as the total distance (240 miles) divided by the total time (2 hrs. + 3 hrs. = 5 hrs.). Therefore, it's not 50 mph, but 48 mph.

EXERCISE 1-1: GETTING TO KNOW DYNATEXT

1 • Greenwich Mean Time

2 • No

3 • 256

4 • Objects that are trustees of that object as well as the object's inherited rights filter

. . . . .

5 • Yes (for example, the Telephone property)

6 • Over 120 properties

EXERCISE 1-2: GETTING TO KNOW NETWARE 4

1 • D		**11** • A
2 • J		**12** • K
3 • O		**13** • H
4 • F		**14** • Q
5 • R		**15** • E
6 • B		**16** • P
7 • I		**17** • N
8 • L		**18** • M
9 • G		**19** • T
10 • S		**20** • C

EXERCISE 1-3: GETTING TO KNOW NDS—PART 1

1 • L		**4** • L
2 • C		**5** • C
3 • L		**6** • L

7 • L

8 • L

9 • L

10 • C

EXERCISE 1-3: GETTING TO KNOW NDS—PART II

1 • Container (Organizational Unit)

2 • Leaf

3 • Leaf

4 • Leaf

5 • Container (Organization)

6 • Leaf

7 • Container (Country or Organizational Unit)

8 • Leaf

9 • Organizational Unit

10 • Leaf

Chapter 2: Understanding NDS

ANSWERS TO QUIZZES

Q2-1
The only days the Lion can say "I lied yesterday" are Mondays and Thursdays. The only days the Unicorn can say "I lied yesterday" are Thursdays and Sundays. Therefore, the only day they can both say it is Thursday.

Q2-2
On no day of the week is this possible! Only on Mondays and Thursdays could he make the first statement; only on Wednesdays and Sundays could he make the second. So there is no day he could say both. Poor Alice is stuck in the Land of Forgetfulness forever.

Q2-3

This is a very different situation! It illustrates well the difference between making two statements separately and making one statement that is the conjunction of the two. Indeed, given any two statements X and Y, if the single statement "X and Y" is true, then it follows that X and Y are true separately; but if the conjunction "X and Y" is false, then at least one of them is false.

Now, the only day of the week it could be true that the Lion lied yesterday and will lie again tomorrow is Tuesday (this is the only day that occurs between two of the Lion's lying days). So the day the Lion said that couldn't be Tuesday, for on Tuesdays that statement is true, but the Lion doesn't make true statements on Tuesdays. Therefore, it is not Tuesday; hence, the Lion's statement is false, so the Lion is lying. Therefore, the day must be either Monday or Wednesday. Tricky little Lion.

Q2-4

A–4
B–5, 8
C–1
D–2, 6
E–3

The Hint (Synergy) means the whole is greater than the sum of its parts. This means we must be dealing with a whole number. Therefore, half of "What I'd be" must be a whole number. "What I'd be" must be an even number. "What I am" cannot end in 1. There are four possible arrangements of the three digits:

	(A)	(B)	(C)	(D)
What I am	1?3	13?	31?	?13
What I'd be	3?4	34?	43?	?34

"What I am" is "Nine less than half what I'd be." So ("What I am" + 9) × 2 = "What I'd be." Examination shows that only "A" fits the bill and "What I am" must be 183. No sweat.

EXERCISE 2-1: "TREE WALKING" FOR TODDLERS

1a. Answers will vary in terms of what objects are displayed when you activate the NetWare Administrator utility. Your current context is the topmost icon displayed on the screen. (You may need to use the scrollbar on the right side of the screen to get to the top of the screen.) When you first activate the NetWare Administrator utility, your current context is the one that was in effect last time you used the utility on this workstation. Your current context in the NetWare Administrator utility is utility specific. In other words, it is independent of your current context as displayed at the command line.

1b. Answers will vary for all questions in this section.

EXERCISE 2-2: UNDERSTANDING NDS NAMING

1 • .BMasterson.BLUE.CRIME.TOKYO.ACME

2 • .CN=RHood.OU=WHITE.OU=CRIME.OU=TOKYO.O=ACME

3 • CRIME.TOKYO.ACME

4 • CN=BLUE-SRV1.OU=BLUE.OU=CRIME.OU=TOKYO.O=ACME (since the default current context is the [Root])

5 • SHolmes

6 • LJohn.WHITE.CRIME

7 • CN=SirKay.OU=CHARITY.

8 • Admin...

9 • CN=BThomas.OU=PR..

10 • CN=BLUE-SRV1_SYS.OU=BLUE.OU=CRIME.OU=TOKYO.O=ACME....

11 • .BLUE.CRIME.TOKYO.ACME (since it's the context of the server)

LOGIN DHolliday.BLUE.CRIME.TOKYO.ACME

LOGIN DHolliday (since NetWare 4 searches the server's context by default)

12 • CX CHARITY..

13 • Add the following statement to his NET.CFG file:

NAME CONTEXT="OU=CHARITY.OU=TOKYO.O=ACME"

14 • LOGIN .CN=SHolmes.OU=CRIME.OU=TOKYO.O=ACME

LOGIN .SHolmes.CRIME.TOKYO.ACME

LOGIN SHolmes.

LOGIN CN=SHolmes.

LOGIN SHolmes.CRIME..

LOGIN CN=SHolmes.OU=CRIME..

LOGIN SHolmes.CRIME.TOKYO...

LOGIN CN=SHolmes.OU=CRIME.OU=TOKYO...

LOGIN SHolmes.CRIME.TOKYO.ACME....

LOGIN CN=SHolmes.OU=CRIME.OU=TOKYO.O=ACME....

15 • CX /R

EXERCISE 2-3:

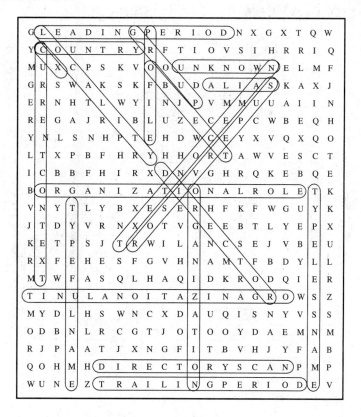

1 • ALIAS		11 • OBJECT	
2 • COUNTRY		12 • ORGANIZATION	
3 • CURRENT CONTEXT		13 • ORGANIZATIONAL ROLE	
4 • CX		14 • ORGANIZATIONAL UNIT	
5 • DIRECTORY MAP		15 • PROFILE	
6 • DIRECTORY SCAN		16 • SUPERVISOR	
7 • GROUP		17 • TRAILING PERIOD	
8 • LEADING PERIOD		18 • TYPEFUL NAME	
9 • LOCALITY		19 • TYPELESS NAME	
10 • NAME CONTEXT		20 • UNKNOWN	

Part 1: NetWare 4 CNE Basics

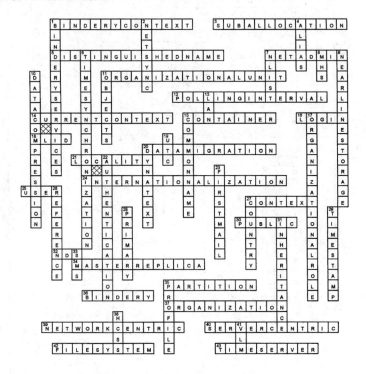

Chapter 3: Step 1: NDS Preparation

ANSWERS TO QUIZZES

Q3-1
* = asterisk (ass to risk)

Q3-2
William Shakespeare

Q3-3

It was raining.

"...country at the top of the Himalayas" = Nepal = PLANE

"...man from the Far East" = China = CHAIN

"...man from the Middle East" = Iran = RAIN

Q3-4

Necklace

Current context

Directory Map

Directory scan

Chapter 4: Step 2: NDS Design

ANSWERS TO QUIZZES

Q4-1

Certainty. The sum of the digits 1 to 8 is 36. Any number divides by 9 exactly when the sum of its digits are also divided by 9 exactly. It does not matter in which order the balls are drawn out as the sum will always be 36.

Q4-2

17 (seventeen). All numbers containing only "E" vowels.

Q4-3

The names are all anagrams:

> Zena le Vue = Venezuela (the Americas)
> Dr. A. Glebe = Belgrade (Europe)
> Rob E. Lumen = Melbourne (Australia)
> Ann Ziata = Tanzania (Africa)

That tricky Sherlock Holmes—got me again!

Q4-4

You = 4/7

Me = 2/7

Albert = 1/7

(Because you go first, you have twice the chance as I do. And since I go second, I have twice the chance that Albert does—therefore the chances are 4 to 2 to 1.)

Q4-5

$[(1.5 + 0.25) \times {}^{60}/_{50}]$ = 2 minutes 6 seconds

Q4-6

It helped me remember pi to 8 decimal places. The number of letters in each word represents the digits of pi: 3.141559265. I really had a "warped" childhood.

Q4-7

In a pack of 52 cards there are 32 cards of nine or below. The chance that the first card dealt is one of the 32 is ${}^{32}/_{52}$, for the second card the chance is ${}^{31}/_{51}$, and so on. The chance of all 13 being favorable is ${}^{32}/_{52} \times {}^{31}/_{51} \times ... \times {}^{20}/_{40} = {}^{1}/_{1828}$. The odds were strongly in Lord Yarborough's favor.

Chapter 5: Step 3: NDS Implementation

ANSWERS TO QUIZZES

Q5-1

You win $59.00. You will always win the same number of units that heads comes down in the sequence, as long as the final toss is heads.

Q5-2

12365

Q5-3

Yes, in 2.777 minutes.

```
54 seconds = 0.9 minutes, reciprocal(*) = 1.11

48 seconds = 0.8 minutes, reciprocal     = 1.25

                             Add           2.36

30 seconds 0.5 minutes, reciprocal       = 2.00

                          Deduct          0.36

                   Reciprocal    = 2.777 minutes
```

(*) A reciprocal is a number or quantity that, when multiplied by a given number or quantity, gives the product of 1, that is, 0.8 × 1.25 = 1. To find the reciprocal of 0.8, it is necessary to divide 1 by 0.8, which gives the reciprocal 1.25.

EXERCISE 5-1 THE NEXT GENERATION OF NETWORKING

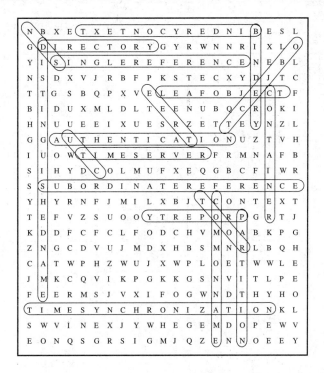

1 • NDS

2 • BINDERY CONTEXT

3 • OBJECT

4 • ROOT

5 • PARTITION

6 • DIRECTORY

7 • CONTAINER

8 • TIME SYNCHRONIZATION

9 • LEAF OBJECT

10 • COMMON NAME

11 • TREE

12 • SINGLE REFERENCE

13 • CONTEXT

14 • SUBORDINATE REFERENCE

15 • DISTINGUISHED NAME

16 • UTC

17 • TIME SERVER

18 • BINDERY

19 • AUTHENTICATION

20 • PROPERTY

Part II: NetWare 4 Design

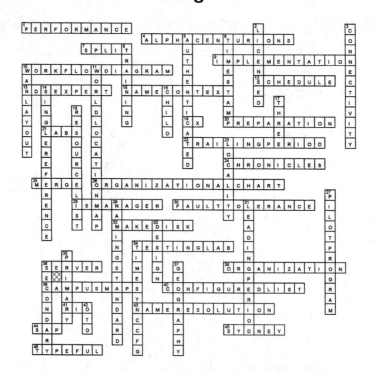

Chapter 6: NetWare 4 Installation

ANSWERS TO QUIZZES

Q6-1

Actually, the two trains will be at the *same* distance from Boston when they meet.

Q6-2

Linguists. *Mutual intelligibility* is when two people can understand each other without instruction.

Q6-3

The first answer from Dick cannot be true (if true, it is false). Therefore, Dick is not a Wotta-Wooppa. Because he has made a false statement, Dick can't be a Pukka either. Therefore, Dick is a Shilla-Shalla, and his second answer is true.

Because Dick's second answer is true, Tom is a Pukka. Therefore, Harry's second answer is false as is his first answer, which makes Harry a Wotta-Woppa.

So, Tom is a Pukka, Dick is a Shilli-Shalla, and Harry is a Wotta-Woppa. No sweat.

Q6-4

Mukluks are Eskimo boots made from seal or reindeer hide.

Q6-5

1 • Since the only one to predict correctly was the man who married Dana, John did not predict correctly (that Arthur would marry Dana). Therefore, Arthur did not marry Dana, and John did not marry Dana.

2 • Therefore, Arthur did not predict correctly. Therefore, David married Eve.

3 • Therefore, by elimination, Dana married George. Therefore, George and only George predicted correctly.

4 • Therefore, John did not marry Christine. Therefore, by elimination, Arthur married Christine and John married Rose.

Complete result: George married Dana; John married Rose; Arthur married Christine; David married Eve; Gallant Dancer did not win the race.

Q6-6

Thomas Jefferson, the head of ACME's Marketing department. Who would have thunk it?

Q6-7

Let's start with a quick summary of their comments.

> Andy: The number of Brad's house is even.

> Brad: 1. The number of my house is greater than the number of Doug's, and 2. My age is a perfect cube.

> Cole: 1. The number of my house is greater than the number of Andy's, and 2. Doug's age is a multiple of Andy's age.

> Doug: 1. Brad's age is either 27 or an even number other than 64, and 2. Cole does not live at number 19.

Now, here's my reasoning. The difference between age and house number is always 7; therefore, if house number is even, age is odd; and if house number is odd, age is even. Therefore, false remarks are made by those with odd ages and even houses; true remarks are made by those with even ages and odd houses.

If Brad2 is true, Brad's age is 27 or 64, but if his age is 27, the remark is false. Therefore, either Brad's age is 64 (and the remark true), or Brad's age is an odd number other than 27 (and the remark is false). Doug1 contradicts this; therefore, Doug1 is false.

Therefore, Doug's age is odd and his house number is even, and Doug2 is false.

Therefore, Cole lives at number 19, and Cole's age is 26 (it cannot be $19 - 7 = 12$).

Therefore, Cole's remarks are true, and from Cole1, Andy's house is number 16.

Therefore, Andy's age is 23 (it cannot be $16 - 7 = 9$).

Therefore, Andy's remark is false.

Therefore, Brad's house number is odd and Brad's age is even.

But we know that Brad's age is either 64 or an odd number other than 27. Therefore, Brad's age is 64.

Therefore, Brad's remarks are true.

Since Cole2 is true, Doug's age is a multiple of 23.

But Doug's age is odd (see above). Therefore, Doug's age is 69.

Brad1 is true. Therefore, the number of Brad's house is greater than the number of Doug's.

But Brad's age is greater than Doug's. Brad's house must be 64 + 7 (71), and Doug's house must be 69 – 7 (62).

Complete results: Andy is 23 and lives at number 16; Brad is 64 an lives at number 71; Cole is 26 and lives at number 19; Doug is 69 and lives at number 62.

Wasn't that fun—Jell-o brain!

EXERCISE 6-1: CHOOSING THE CORRECT INSTALLATION METHOD

1 • Simple Installation

2 • Simple Installation

3 • Custom Installation

▶ · ◀

Chapter 7: NetWare 4 Migration

ANSWERS TO QUIZZES

Q7-1
Puzzle!

Q7-2
Podunk is an unincorporated area in Massachusetts about six square miles in size. It houses about 100 families within East Brookfield town about fifteen miles west of Worcester.

Q7-3

Tulips. She only likes words in which two consecutive letters of the alphabet appear.

Q7-4

If the woman were a Liar, she would have said she was a Truthteller. If she were really a Truthteller, she certainly would have said she was a Truthteller. Therefore, the young man reported truthfully, proving he was a Truthteller. Happy ending.

Q7-5

If his top speed is 100 mph he'll never get there. He'll be going 100 mph and be pushed backward at 100 mph. He'll just have to wait until the wind dies down. Of course, if he could get the train up to 150 mph he could do it in four hours, but we've just said 100 mph is the top speed. Sorry.

EXERCISE 7-1: CHOOSING THE CORRECT MIGRATION METHOD

Scenario 1—Finance Department

1 • Across-the Wire migration, Same-Server migration, or In-place upgrade

2 • Across-the-Wire migration. The original server would still be intact if anything went wrong during the upgrade. Also, this method would be more convenient since the original server does not have a CD-ROM drive.

3 • Custom installation. Because the original server is going to be used for a special project, it is not necessary to retain any of the current information. Thus, when the new server is fully up and operational, you can delete the NetWare partition on the original server and do a Custom Installation of NetWare 4. Doing a Custom Install rather than a Simple Install would provide you with greater control of configurable parameters, such as specifying the container in which the server would be installed.

4 • Because the current server does not have a CD-ROM drive, you'd need to use the remote network installation area method for doing the installation. Using this method, you could mount the CD-ROM drive as a network drive on the new server, then login to the new server from the original server to do the installation.

Scenario 2—Facilities Department

1 • In-place upgrade. This method would allow you to upgrade the server from NetWare 2.2 to NetWare 4 without requiring a second server in the process.

2 • You would need to perform the upgrade in two steps: First, you'd have to use the 2XUPGRD.NLM utility to upgrade from NetWare 2.2 to NetWare 3.1x and then would use the Upgrade option in the INSTALL.NLM utility to upgrade from NetWare 3.1x to NetWare 4.

3 • There is too little RAM available. The Facilities department would need to purchase a minimum of 8 MB additional RAM (for a total of 12 MB) to use this migration method.

4 • The IDE.DSK driver would not be a concern because the DOS partition is already of sufficient size (that is, at least 15 MB) and, thus, would not have to be recreated.

Scenario 3—Pollution Department

1 • Across-the-Wire migration or Server-Server migration

2 • Server-to-Server migration. The Server-to-Server method would allow you to upgrade the server to NetWare 4 without requiring a second server.

Scenario 4—Marketing Department

1 • Simple Installation method or Custom Installation method

2 • Custom Installation. The Custom Installation method makes sense because the Marketing Manager wants to set up network security from scratch. Another reason for choosing the Custom Installation method is that you'd like to have more control over configurable parameters during the installation process than the Simple Installation method would allow.

3 • There is insufficient hard disk space available on the SYS: volume. You'd either need to delete files to free up an appropriate amount of free space or move files to the VOL1: volume.

4 • The frame type of the source server would not be a concern if the source server was using the default Ethernet frame type for NetWare 3.12. (The default Ethernet frame type for both NetWare 3.12 and NetWare 4 is 802.2.)

Scenario 5—Nuclear Department

1 • BMIGRATE.EXE

2 • The Nuclear Department Manager does not want to start from scratch and there are no other NetWare 4 upgrade or migration methods available that are compatible with Banyan Vines.

Part III: NetWare 4 Installation

Crossword puzzle solution containing the following answers:

DOS PARTITION, FDISK, ACROSS THE WIRE, PRINTCON DAT, MIGPRINT EXE, NWCLIENT, SINGLE REFERENCE, ESPANOL, DATA MIGRATION, BACKUP, FRANCAIS, KEYBOARD MAPPING, BINDFIX, DEUTSCH, AUTOEXEC NCF, CUSTOM, SERVER, INSTALL NLM, IPX, EIGHT, SERVER EXE, NEWPWD, DOWN, NETWARE READY, INPLACE, MAC

Chapter 8: Managing NDS

ANSWERS TO QUIZZES

Q8-1

232 entries—229 matches were played; therefore, there must have been 229 losers. Add the two who scratched out without playing and then add the winner of the championship and you arrive at the total number of entries—232.

Q8-2

79 years (there was not a year 0)

Q8-3

This is hard because there are three choices for each number.

Q8-4

COLD, CORD, WORD, WARD, WARM

CASE STUDY: BUILDING ACME'S NDS TREE

We need a little help building ACME's NDS tree. In addition to the normal network resources, they have some special needs. Here's a quick list.

1 • Each site needs a revolving administrator. This sounds like a job for Organizational Roles. Create an Organizational Role under each location OU. Use the following naming standard:

> NORAD-Admin in OU=NORAD.O=ACME
>
> RIO-Admin in OU=RIO.O=ACME
>
> CAM-Admin in OU=CAMELOT.O=ACME
>
> SYD-Admin in OU=SYDNEY.O=ACME
>
> TOK-Admin in OU=TOKYO.O=ACME

Then, assign the divisional administrator as the first occupant in each location OR—AEinstein, GWashington, KingArthur, Gandhi, and SHolmes, respectively.

2 • Next, create a common Profile Login Script object for all the administrators to share. It should be called ADMIN-Profile and placed in the O=ACME container. Remember, shared objects are placed higher in the tree. Finally, attach each Organizational Role to the shared login script by referencing the Profile object within each Organizational Role's Login Script property.

3 • The Directory Map object saves the day. If the Human Rights (HR) tracking program is constantly changing, consider creating a Directory Map object as a point of central control. Then, all the HR login scripts can point to the central object, not the physical application directory. In this case, create an HR Directory Map object called HR-App, and place it in the .OU=HR.OU=SYDNEY.O=ACME container. Then, place the following directory in the Directory Map object's Path property:

HR-SRV1/SYS:APPS\HRT

4 • In addition, each of the HR administrators need access to the Human Rights tracking application in HR-SRV1/SYS:APPS\HRT. Security could be a problem. The Group object is your friend. Create a Group leaf object called HR-Group, and place it in the .OU=HR.OU=SYDNEY.O=ACME container. Then, create a Group Membership list with each of the HR administrators—Gandhi, ASchweitzer, MTeresa, FNightingale, and Buddha.

5 • The people in the Auditing department need easy access to the Financial resources. There's a simple solution, and it allows the auditors to access these resources from within their home .OU=AUDIT container. Simply create an Alias object for .OU=FIN.OU=OPS.OU=CAMELOT.O=ACME, and place it in the .OU=AUDIT container. The Alias will point to the original objects from within the auditor's home context. Clever, huh?

6 • In addition, the auditors and financial accountants need access to the ever-changing financial database program. Once again, the Directory Map object saves the day. In this case, create a Directory Map object called FIN-App and place it in the .OU=AUDIT.OU=ADMIN.OU=RIO.O=ACME and .OU=FIN.OU=OPS.OU=CAMELOT.O=ACME containers. Then, place the following directory in the Directory Map object's Path property:

CAM-FIN-SRV1/SYS:APPS\FIN

7 • The same holds true for the auditing application, except this time only the auditors need access to the Directory Map object. In this case, create a Directory Map object called AUD-App, and place it in the .OU=AUDIT.OU=ADMIN.OU=RIO.O=ACME container. Then, place the following directory in the Directory Map object's Path property:

AUDIT-SRV1/SYS:APPS\AUDIT

8 • To accommodate traveling users, we will create corresponding Alias objects for them in the very top of the ACME tree. This way, they can login from anywhere with a very simple name context. For example, MCurie's alias becomes .MCurie.ACME. That's a big improvement over MCurie.NUC.R&D.LABS.NORAD.ACME. To accomplish this, create three user Alias objects (MCurie, AEinstein, and DHoliday), and place them in the O=ACME container. All done.

9 • Everyone in the Crime Fighting division needs access to a common login script. Simply create a global Profile Login Script property called CRIME-profile, and place it in the .OU=CRIME.OU=TOKYO.O=ACME container. Don't forget to add CRIME-profile to each user's Login Script property.

10 • To empower Leonardo's scientists, you'll need to create an Organizational Role called R&D-Admin. Place it in the OU=R&D.OU=LABS.OU=NORAD.O=ACME container, and give the Organizational Role Administrative rights over all R&D resources. Then, you can rotate the scientists through the Organizational Role, starting with LDaVinci. Make him the first occupant. It's as easy as 1-2-3.

Thanks for helping out. The world's in good hands with a CNE like you on the job!

Chapter 9: Partition Management and Synchronization

ANSWERS TO QUIZZES

Q9-1

(a) Raccoon

(b) Leopard

(c) Terrier

(d) Lioness

(e) Samoyed

(f) Spaniel

(g) Carthorse

(h) Africa lion

Q9-2
$9 + 8 + 7 + 6 \div 5 - 4 - 3 + 2 - 1 = 0$

Q9-3
Three hours. After x hours,

A had burned $x/6$ leaving $6-x/6$.

B had burned $x/4$ leaving $4-x/4$.

But after x hours, A was twice as long as B. Therefore, $6-x/6 = 2(4-x)/4$. Therefore, $x = 3$.

Q9-4
$98 - 76 + 54 + 3 + 21 = 100$

Chapter 10: NetWare 4 File System

ANSWERS TO QUIZZES

Q10-1
28463

Q10-2
It doesn't matter what *x* is, because at some time during the calculation you will be multiplying by (x–x), which equals 0; therefore, the product will be 0. Tricky!

Q10-3
69382

Q10-4
1, 4, 9, 6, 1, 5, 10, 4, 2
Now change to Roman numerals:
I, IV, IX, VI, I, V, X, IV, II
Very tricky, and I like it for that reason and because the Roman numeral IV appears in my name. Touché.

EXERCISE 10-1: UNDERSTANDING DRIVE MAPPING

1 • MAP /?

2 • MAP

3 • MAP F:=SYS:USERS

4 • MAP G:=SYS:\SHARED\POL

5 • MAP J:=F:

6 • MAP S:=.WHITE.SRV1_SYS.WHITE.CRIME.TOKYO.ACME:SHARED

7 • MAP INS S1:=SYS:\PUBLIC

8 • MAP INS S2:=SYS:\PUBLIC\IBM_PC\MSDOS\V6.22

9 • MAP S3:=APPS\SS30

10 • MAP ROOT S4:=SYS:\APPS\DB50

11 • MAP

In the map list, the false root has no space after the volume name but does have a space followed by a backslash after the name of the directory it points to.

12 • MAP S5:=W:=SYS:\APPS\WP70

Yes.

13 • The MAP command didn't work. To fix the problem, type **CD \PUBLIC**

14 • MAP DEL J:

15 • MAP REM S3:

The search drives with higher search drive numbers were renumbered accordingly.

The network drive associated with the search drive was deleted.

16 • MAP C S4:

The search drive was deleted.

The network drive associated with the search drive was moved to the top portion of the map list.

Chapter 11: NetWare 4 Security

ANSWERS TO QUIZZES

Q11-1
"A road map tells you everything except how to refold it." (Start at *A* in center.)

Q11-2
36421

Q11-3
He is abstemious. We discovered that he only likes words with all five vowels in them—an odd bird.

Q11-4
That's easy, man. It's "wrong."

Q11-5

ABORT: It is five letters long.
ACT: Last letter cannot be placed first to form another word.
AGT: Not an actual word.
ALP: Does not end with a T.
OPT: Does not start with A.
APT: Not in alphabetical order with rest.

QII-6
Here's the mysterious list:

MinutE
ExclamatioN
NavigatE
TeaR
AspirinG
LibertY

And, of course, the purpose of our journey is to generate as much "MENTAL ENERGY" as possible. Did we succeed?

QII-7
Maggie Simpson. That's what he gets for trying to steal candy from a baby. Mr. Burns certainly learned his lesson the hard way. Kudos to you, for figuring it out.

EXERCISE 11-1: CALCULATING NDS EFFECTIVE RIGHTS

CASE #1

See Figure C11.1 for answer to this case.

▶ • ◀

F I G U R E C11.1

*Calculating NDS Effective
Rights—CASE #1*

CASE #2

See Figure C11.2 for answer to this case.

*Calculating NDS Effective
Rights—CASE #2*

CASE #3

See Figure C11.3 for answer to this case.

FIGURE C11.3

*Calculating NDS Effective
Rights—CASE #3*

		[BCDRS]
⬇ IRF		[BCDR]
Inheritance		[BCDR]
Blue-TA		[B]
WEarp-TA		[R]
TOKYO	Effective Rights	[B R]
⬇ IRF		[BCD]
Inheritance		[B]
OR-TA		[BCDRS]
Blue-TA		[B]
CRIME	Effective Rights	[BCDRS]
⬇ IRF		[DR]
Inheritance		[DR]
WEarp-TA		[C]
Blue-TA		[B]
BLUE	Effective Rights	[BCDR]

EXERCISE 11-2: CALCULATING FILE SYSTEM EFFECTIVE RIGHTS

CASE #1

See Figure C11.4 for answer to this case.

F I G U R E C11.4

*Calculating File System
Effective Rights—CASE #1*

	S	R	C	W	E	M	F	A
SYS:SHARED								
Inherited Rights Filter	S	R	C	W	E	M	F	A
Inherited Rights-User								
Inherited Rights-Group								
Trustee Assignment-User		R	C	W			F	
Trustee Assignment-Group								
Effective Rights		R	C	W			F	

	S	R	C	W	E	M	F	A
SYS:SHARED\CYBER								
Inherited Rights Filter	S	R					F	
Inherited Rights-User		R					F	
Inherited Rights-Group								
Trustee Assignment-User								
Trustee Assignment-Group								
Effective Rights		R					F	

	S	R	C	W	E	M	F	A
CYBER.DOC								
Inherited Rights Filter	S	R	C	W			F	
Inherited Rights-User		R					F	
Inherited Rights-Group								
Trustee Assignment-User								
Trustee Assignment-Group								
Effective Rights		R					F	

CASE #2

See Figure C11.5 for answer to this case.

Calculating File System
Effective Rights—CASE #2

SYS:SHARED	S	R	C	W	E	M	F	A
Inherited Rights Filter	S	R	C	W	E	M	F	A
Inherited Rights-User								
Inherited Rights-Group								
Trustee Assignment-User								
Trustee Assignment-Group		R	C	W			F	
Effective Rights		R	C	W			F	

SYS:SHARED\FINAN								
Inherited Rights Filter	S							
Inherited Rights-User								
Inherited Rights-Group								
Trustee Assignment-User		R	C	W	E	M	F	
Trustee Assignment-Group								
Effective Rights		R	C	W	E	M	F	

99QTR4.RPT								
Inherited Rights Filter	S	R		W			F	
Inherited Rights-User		R		W			F	
Inherited Rights-Group								
Trustee Assignment-User								
Trustee Assignment-Group		R						
Effective Rights		R		W			F	

CASE #3

See Figure C11.6 for answer to this case.

SYS:SHARED	S	R	C	W	E	M	F	A
Inherited Rights Filter	S	R	C	W	E	M	F	A
Inherited Rights-User								
Inherited Rights-Group								
Trustee Assignment-User		R	C	W			F	
Trustee Assignment-Group								
Effective Rights		R	C	W			F	

SYS:SHARED\CRIME								
Inherited Rights Filter	S							
Inherited Rights-User								
Inherited Rights-Group								
Trustee Assignment-User								
Trustee Assignment-Group		R	C	W	E	M	F	
Effective Rights		R	C	W	E	M	F	

CRIME.DB								
Inherited Rights Filter	S	R	C	W			F	
Inherited Rights-User								
Inherited Rights-Group		R	C	W			F	
Trustee Assignment-User								
Trustee Assignment-Group		R					F	
Effective Rights		R					F	

CASE #4

See Figure C11.7 for answer to this case.

	FIGURE C11.7

Calculating File System
Effective Rights—CASE #4

SYS:SHARED	S	R	C	W	E	M	F	A
Inherited Rights Filter	S	R	C	W	E	M	F	A
Inherited Rights-User								
Inherited Rights-Group								
Trustee Assignment-User								
Trustee Assignment-Group		R	C	W	E		F	
Effective Rights		R	C	W	E		F	

SYS:SHARED\POLIT	S	R	C	W	E	M	F	A
Inherited Rights Filter	S							
Inherited Rights-User								
Inherited Rights-Group								
Trustee Assignment-User						M		A
Trustee Assignment-Group		R	C	W	E		F	
Effective Rights		R	C	W	E	M	F	A

CRIME.RPT	S	R	C	W	E	M	F	A
Inherited Rights Filter	S	R	C	W	E	M	F	A
Inherited Rights-User						M		A
Inherited Rights-Group		R	C	W	E		F	
Trustee Assignment-User								
Trustee Assignment-Group								
Effective Rights		R	C	W	E	M	F	A

CASE #5

See Figure C11.8 for answer to this case.

FIGURE C11.8

*Calculating File System
Effective Rights—CASE #5*

	S	R	C	W	E	M	F	A
SYS:SHARED								
Inherited Rights Filter	S	R	C	W	E	M	F	A
Inherited Rights-User								
Inherited Rights-Group								
Trustee Assignment-User	S	R	C	W	E	M	F	A
Trustee Assignment-Group								
Effective Rights	S	R	C	W	E	M	F	A
SYS:SHARED\CRIME								
Inherited Rights Filter	S							
Inherited Rights-User	S	(R)	(C)	(W)	(E)	(M)	(F)	(A)
Inherited Rights-Group								
Trustee Assignment-User								
Trustee Assignment-Group		R	C	W			F	
Effective Rights	S	R	C	W	(E)	(M)	F	(A)
CRIME.DB								
Inherited Rights Filter	S	R					F	
Inherited Rights-User	S	R	(C)	(W)	(E)	(M)	F	(A)
Inherited Rights-Group		R					F	
Trustee Assignment-User								
Trustee Assignment-Group		R					F	
Effective Rights	S	R	(C)	(W)	(E)	(M)	F	(A)

CASE #6

See Figure C11.9 for answer to this case.

*Calculating File System
Effective Rights—CASE #6*

SYS:SHARED	S	R	C	W	E	M	F	A
Inherited Rights Filter	S	R					F	A
Inherited Rights-User								
Inherited Rights-Group or [Public]								
Trustee Assignment-User								
Trustee Assignment-Group or [Public]		R					F	
Effective Rights		R					F	

SYS:SHARED\WHITE	S	R	C	W	E	M	F	A
Inherited Rights Filter	S	R					F	
Inherited Rights-User								
Inherited Rights-Group or [Public]	S	R	C	W	E	M	F	A
Trustee Assignment-User	S	R	C	W	E	M	F	A
Trustee Assignment-Group or [Public]								
Effective Rights	S	R	C	W	E	M	F	A

SUMMARY.RPT	S	R	C	W	E	M	F	A
Inherited Rights Filter	S							
Inherited Rights-User	S	(R)	(C)	(W)	(E)	(M)	(F)	(A)
Inherited Rights-Group or [Public]								
Trustee Assignment-User		R	C	W	E	M		
Trustee Assignment-Group or [Public]								
Effective Rights	S	R	C	W	E	M	F	A

CASE STUDY: ACME SECURITY

F I G U R E C11.10

*The .TOKYO.ACME NDS
Directory Tree*

F I G U R E C11.11

*The WHITE-SRV1_SYS File
System Directory Tree*

*Password Restrictions for
the USER_TEMPLATE in
.TOKYO.ACME*

Chapter 12: NetWare 4 Configuration

ANSWERS TO QUIZZES

Q12-1

The most common wrong answer is 25. If the problem had been, "What is the smallest number I must pick in order to be sure of getting at least two socks of *different* colors," then the correct answer would have been 25. But the problem calls for at least two socks of the *same* color, so the correct answer is three. If I pick three socks, then either they are all of the same color (in which case I certainly have at least two of the same color), or else two are of one color and the third is of the other color—so I have two of the same color.

Q12-2

J.

Q12-3

The bear must be white—it must be a polar bear. The usual answer is that the bear must have been standing at the North Pole. Well, this is indeed one possibility, but it's not the only one. From the North Pole, all directions are south, so if the bear is standing at the North Pole and the man is 100 yards south of him and walks 100 yards east, then when he faces north, he will be facing the North Pole again. I'll buy that.

But, there are many more alternative solutions. It could be, for example, that the man is very close to the South Pole on a spot where the Polar circle passing through that spot has a circumference of exactly 100 yards, and the bear is standing 100 yards north of him. Then if the man walks east 100 yards, he would walk right around that circle and be right back at the point he started from.

In addition, the man could be a little closer to the South Pole at a point where the polar circle has a circumference of exactly 50 yards, so if he walked east 100 yards, he would walk around that little circle twice and be back where he started. You get the idea.

Of course, in any of these solutions, the bear is sufficiently close to either the North Pole or the South Pole to qualify as a polar bear. There is, of course, the remote possibility that some mischievous human being deliberately transported a brown bear to the North Pole just to spite us—who's paranoid?

Q12-4

Cerebrum

Q12-5

1 • The biologist is not Catherine and not from Canada. Therefore, she belongs to C house (she must have one C).

2 • If Catherine were the doctor, then she would have to come from Brazil (we know she's not from Australia), and if she were the doctor, she couldn't be from Denmark. Therefore, the doctor is from Brazil—but we are told the doctor is not from Brazil. Therefore, Catherine is not the doctor. Therefore, she must be the author.

3 • The biologist is not from Australia and not from Canada. Therefore, she must be from Denmark.

4 • Since the biologist is from C house and from Denmark, she must be Alice.

5 • Therefore, the doctor is not Alice, and the doctor is not Catherine. Therefore, the doctor is Brett, and Deirdre must be the cartoonist.

6 • Since the doctor is Brett, she is not from B house. Therefore, the doctor is from A house (the only alternative left). Therefore, the doctor is from Canada.

7 • Since the cartoonist is Deirdre, she cannot be from D house. Therefore, she is from B house. Therefore, the cartoonist is from Australia.

8 • Therefore, Catherine, the author, is from Brazil and was in D house.

Complete solution:

Alice	Biologist	C	Denmark
Brett	Doctor	A	Canada
Catherine	Author	D	Brazil
Deirdre	Cartoonist	B	Australia

Q12-6

OK, here's what was going on inside the cerebrum of "C." If anyone were to see two red and two black, he would know that he was white. If anyone were to see two red, one black, and one white, he would know that he could not be black. If he were, the man with the white disc would see two red and two black and would know that he was white. Similarly, if anyone were to see one red, two black, and two white.

If anyone were to see one red, one black, and two white, he would know that he could not be black. If he were, either of the men wearing white would see one red, two black, and one white, and would argue as above. If anyone were to see two red and two white, he would argue that he could not be black. If he were, someone would see two red, one black, and one white and would argue as above.

If anyone were to see one red and three white, he would argue that he could not be black. If he were, someone would see one red, one black, and two white and would argue as above; similarly, he would know that he could not be red. Therefore, if anyone sees me wearing red or black, he can deduce his color. Therefore, I must be white.

C really needs to get a life.

Q12-7
Ensign Chekov

EXERCISE 12-1: WORKSTATION CONNECTIVITY FOR NETWARE 4

2B.   Look at Figure 12.13. You'll see that LSL.COM loads the Link Support Layer, provides version information, and activates the default NET.CFG file. From this, we can surmise that the Link Support Layer is in control of the client connection somehow. It's the traffic cop.

2D.   No. When IPXODI loads, it activates the internal NIC, but you still can't talk to the server without VLM.EXE.

2E.   IPXODI activates communications at the NIC level, whereas VLMs activate communications at the higher DOS level. Neither one is any good without the other.

3B.   Regardless of what you might think about the "logical" nature of NetWare 4 NDS, you still have to attach to a server. In this case, LABS-SRV1 is our host server for all NDS resource access. Any other necessary server attachments will be made for you automatically in the background. You only need to attach to the initial host server.

EXERCISE 12-2: UNDERSTANDING NET.CFG

```
; Standard R&D Dept. NET.CFG file
; Created for LDaVinci on 10/28/99

SHOW DOTS = ON
LONG MACHINE TYPE = DELL

LINK DRIVER C35X9
        INT A
        PORT 320
        FRAME Ethernet_802.2

NETWARE DOS REQUESTER
        PREFERRED TREE=ACME_TREE
        PREFERRED SERVER=R&D-SRV1
        NAME CONTEXT="OU=R&D.OU=LABS.OU=NORAD.O=ACME"
        FIRST NETWORK DRIVE=F:
        PACKET BUFFERS = 10
        SIGNATURE LEVEL = 3
        LOAD CONN TABLE LOW = ON
        CONNECTIONS = 10
        NETWORK PRINTERS = 5
```

Note: Make sure you don't put a preceding period (.) in the NAME CONTEXT statement

CASE STUDY: CONFIGURING ACME'S LOGIN SCRIPTS

1 • Create the Container login script for the PR Organizational Unit. (If you already did this step, proceed to Step 2.)

    a. Login in as the Admin user and run MS Windows. Switch to the first network drive on the server by typing **F:** and pressing Enter. Login to the network as the Admin user by typing **LOGIN .ADMIN.ACME** and pressing Enter. Run MS Windows by typing **WIN** and pressing Enter.

b. Execute the NetWare Administrator utility.

1) Locate the Program Group icon containing the NetWare Tools, and double-click on it. Then, double click on the NetWare Administrator Program Item icon to run the NetWare Administrator utility.

2) Double-click on the NORAD Organizational Unit using the right mouse button. A menu should be displayed. Select the Details option from the menu and press Enter.

3) Use the scroll bar along the right edge of the screen to display the Login Script button and click on it. Next, single click in the upper right corner of the window located in the center of the screen.

c. Create the System (Container) login script for the Public Relations department.

1) Key in the appropriate statements for the Public Relations department Container login script using the clues in the Chapter 12 case study. (If you need help with what each script should look like, see Figures C12.1 and C12.2 below.)

FIGURE C12.1

*PR Container Login
Script—Part I*

```
Login Script

Login Script:

* Public Relations Dept. Container Login Script
* Created by David James Clarke, IV on 10/28/99

* Set DOS prompt and display greeting upon login
SET PROMPT="$P$G"
WRITE "Good %GREETING_TIME, %FULL_NAME!"
WRITE "You have logged in on %DAY_OF_WEEK"
WRITE "%MONTH_DAY, %DAY, %YEAR"
WRITE "at %HOUR:%MINUTE %AM_PM"

* Assign network drive mappings
MAP DISPLAY OFF
MAP U:=SYS:USERS\%LOGIN_NAME
MAP G:=SYS:SHARED\"%GROUP MEMBERSHIP"

* Assign search drive mappings and COMSPEC command
MAP INS S1:=SYS:PUBLIC
MAP INS S2:=SYS:PUBLIC\%MACHINE\%OS\%OS_VERSION
MAP INS S3:=SYS:APPS\WINDOWS
COMSPEC=S2:COMMAND.COM
NO_DEFAULT
```

Buttons shown on right: Mailbox, Foreign EMail Address, Print Job Configuration, Printer Forms, Print Devices, Print Layout, Rights to Files and Directories, See Also, Login Script, Intruder Detection

OK   Cancel   Help

FIGURE C12.2

PR Container Login Script—Part II

2 • Make the FDR user a member of the PRMGRS-Profile login script. (The PRMGRS-Profile login script is located in the ACME container.)

a. Identify PRMGRS-Profile as the name of the Profile Login Script object in the Profile login script field of the FDR's User's login script screen (see Figure C12.3).

FIGURE C12.3

Adding FDR to the PRMGRS Profile Login Script Object

APPENDIX C
. . . . . .
SOLUTIONS TO
QUIZZES, PUZZLES,
EXERCISES, AND
CASE STUDIES

b. Grant the User the R property right to the Login Script property of the Profile. Also, make sure that the B right to the Profile Login Script object that was granted by default to [Public] at the [Root] has not been blocked by an IRF.

3 • Login as the FDR user by typing LOGIN .FDR.PR.RIO.ACME and pressing Enter. Watch as the Container and Profile login scripts are automatically executed. Fix any errors that occur.

CASE STUDY: CONFIGURING THE ACME MENU SYSTEM

1 • Create a custom menu:

```
; PR Main Menu
; Created by David James Clarke, IV on 10/28/99

    MENU 01,Public Relations Main Menu
        ITEM  ^AApplications
                SHOW 10
        ITEM  ^EE-Mail
                EXEC WIN WMAIL
        ITEM  ^NNetWare Commands
                SHOW 20
        ITEM  ^LLog off the network
                EXEC LOGOUT

    MENU 10,Applications
        ITEM  Database
                EXEC DB
        ITEM  Spreadsheet
                EXEC SS
        ITEM  Word Processing
                EXEC WP

    MENU 20,NetWare Utilities
        ITEM  File Management
                EXEC FILER
```

```
ITEM  NCOPY
        GETP Enter Source File(s): { }80,,{}
        GETP Enter Destination File(s): { }80,,{}
        EXEC NCOPY %1 %2
ITEM  NLIST
        GETO Enter Class Name and Option: { }25,USER/A,{}
        EXEC NLIST
ITEM  User Tools
        EXEC WIN NWUSER
ITEM  WHOAMI
        EXEC WHOAMI
```

2 • Compile and execute the custom menu (and debug any problems):

```
MENUMAKE PRMAIN.SRC <Enter>
NMENU PRMAIN.DAT <Enter>
```

(See Figure C12.4 for a sample of what the PR Main Menu should look like.)

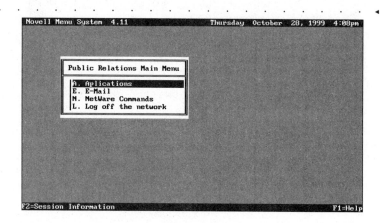

FIGURE C12.4

PR Main Menu

Chapter 13: NetWare 4 Management

ANSWERS TO QUIZZES

Q13-1
The answer is a quarter and a nickel. One of them (namely the quarter) is not a nickel.

Q13-2
Thanks—it's 3:31 p.m.

The only times that the hands of a watch are at right angles at an exact minute are 3:00 and 9:00. Since it was afternoon, we must be talking about 3:00 p.m. At 3:00 p.m. it was 30 minutes "before the half hour." Also, at the next minute it will be 60 seconds (twice as many seconds) after the same half hour. Therefore, it's 3:31 p.m.

Q13-3
DAISY

Q13-4
Nice try. Roosters don't lay eggs.

Q13-5
Silence, Wedding Ring, Hole, Debt.

Q13-6
TYPEWRITER

Q13-7
Fools rush in where angels fear to tread. Which one are you?

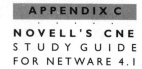
EXERCISE 13-1: MATCHING SERVER STARTUP STEPS

HAPPENS ONCE	HAPPENS OFTEN
Run FDISK	Load AUTOEXEC.BAT
Define locale format	Start SERVER.EXE
Define volume block size	Define bindery context
License the server	Create server name
Define server context	Establish IPX internal network number
Copy SYSTEM and PUBLIC files	Load LAN driver
Create STARTUP.NCF	Activate RMF

EXERCISE 13-2: THE NETWARE WORKSTATION ARCHITECTURE

1 • Protocol Stack—IPXODI.COM

2 • The NetWare DOS Requester—VLM.EXE

3 • Link Support Layer—LSL.COM

4 • MLID—3C5X9.COM

5 • Transport Multiplexer—TRAN.VLM

6 • File System Multiplexer—FIO.VLM

7 • Connectivity Module—CONN.VLM

CASE STUDY: SERVER MANAGEMENT AT ACME

1 • VLM /U

IPXODI /U

NE2000 /U (or appropriate LAN driver)

LSL /U

2 • VLM /?

3 • VLM /4

4 • v1.20 (answers will vary)

5 • Extended Memory (XMS)

6 • CONN.VLM; NETX.VLM

7 • The file server console prompt is displayed (that is, CHARITY_INC:)

8 • A message is displayed indicating that a remote (RCONSOLE) connection has been granted. This is important to know in case unauthorized personnel (or worse yet, a hacker) have gained access to your file server console through the RMF utility.

9 • AUTOEXEC.NCF; STARTUP.NCF

10 • Single

11 • 802.2

12 • 2 percent

13 • No, this disk is not mirrored.

14 • 4 KB. This server was migrated from a NetWare 3.12 server where the default block size was 4 KB. (Your block size may vary.) On the SYS: volume, file compression, block suballocation, and data migration are turned off.

15 • 10 (Answers will vary.)

16 • Product options

17 • 10 days, 2 hours, 6 minutes, and 34 seconds (answers will vary). The elapsed time since the server was last restarted is represented in the format DD:HH:MM:SS, where DD = number of days, HH = number of hours, MM = number of minutes, and SS = number of seconds. Current server utilization is at 8 percent (answers will vary). What is the total number of cache buffers currently being used? What is the number of current service processes in use? Eight licensed connections are available at the moment (10 minus 2 in use).

18 • Normal; no. (Answers may vary.)

19 • IPX

20 • DS.NLM; 598,515 bytes. (Size may vary.)

21 • Idle loop (that is, polling)

22 • Processor Uptime (called Server Up Time in MONITOR.NLM), Processor Utilization (called Utilization in MONITOR.NLM), Server Processes (called Server Processes in MONITOR.NLM), and Users logged in (called Connection Information in MONITOR.NLM).

23 • SET command

24 • Alt+F3; Alt+F1

25 • The Transfer files to server option in SERVMAN performs a similar function to the Copy SYSTEM and PUBLIC files option in INSTALL.NLM. The difference between the two is that the SERVMAN option copies the SYSTEM and PUBLIC files from the workstation's drive rather than the server's.

26 • TRACK ON; ACME_TREE; DAD; Server Information in SERVMAN, AUTOEXEC.NCF in INSTALL.NLM, and CONFIG console command.

27 • BROADCAST or SEND. You can acknowledge an incoming BROADCAST or SEND message displayed on the screen by pressing Ctrl+Enter. You can turn off receipt of incoming messages from other users by typing SEND / **A=N** at the workstation prompt after you exit RCONSOLE.

28 • HELP ALL

29 • MODULES; SERVMAN.NLM

Chapter 14: NetWare 4 Printing

ANSWERS TO QUIZZES

Q14-1
There were 12 friends in the group

Q14-2
QUEUE—pretty sneaky, huh?

Q14-3
V (vowel) 1 = A, and so on
C (consonant) 1 = B, and so on
"Well done! Message successfully decoded."

Q14-4

Like so many puzzles of its type, this looks much more complicated than it really is. In fact, it has a beautifully simple solution. The trick is to first work out how long it takes the man to walk home. You know that the dog has been running for all this time at its given constant speed, so it is then simply a matter of working out how many miles the dog has covered during this period.

In this case, the man walks for 7 miles at 3 mph, which means he takes $2 \frac{1}{3}$ hours or 2 hours 20 minutes. Therefore, the dog is running for $2 \frac{1}{3}$ hours at 8 mph, which means it covers $18 \frac{2}{3}$ miles.

Q14-5

This was a tough one. If you figured it out, you're definitely NetWare sleuth material. As a matter of fact, printing is a breeze compared to this brain puzzler.

7	13	4	10
2	12	5	15
9	3	14	8
16	6	11	1

CASE STUDY: BUILDING ACME'S PRINTING SYSTEM

Queue Creation

10 • The container where the queue was created. Because all users in the container usually need access.

13 • There is a QUEUES directory off the root.

14 • One or more.

Printer Creation

12 • The job owner as the person notified disappears.

13 • It reappears.

Creating the Print Server

10 • The context where the print server was created. Because everyone in the container usually has access.

12 • You are, because you created it!

18 • Because the print server hasn't been loaded yet. It isn't yet running.

19 • The print server is down.

Loading the Print Server

5 • It asks for a password.

6 • Enter the password **Secret.**

9 • It should be off-line or waiting for job if no printer is attached.

13 • The print server unloads back to a colon prompt.

CASE STUDY: USING ACME'S PRINTING SYSTEM

2 • All LPTs should be set to local ports.

3 • Error. Default Configuration cannot be found.

4 • CX .WHITE.CRIME.TOKYO.ACME

5 • CAPTURE Q=CANONBJ-PQ1

6 • CAPTURE Endcap

17 • Access not authorized. The only user authorized during print queue creation was the person doing the exercise.

18 • Use NWADMIN or PCONSOLE to give the entire container access to the queue as a queue user or give it specifically to Speeders.

19 • Either under NWUSER or CAPTURE in a DOS box.

22 • Click on the print queue and choose Job List.

23 • CAPTURE SH

24 • Use the DOS PRINT command. PRINT DOSFIL.TXT.

25 • CAPTURE Endcap

27 • Right-mouse click on the container WHITE.CRIME.TOKYO.ACME and choose Details. Choose Print Job Configuration. Choose Create. Choose the CANONBJ-PQ1 for the queue. Save the new configuration.

28 • Choose the print queue by double-clicking. Choose Users. Add the context WHITE.CRIME.TOKYO.ACME to the list of allowed users.

30 • CAPTURE still doesn't automatically set you up.

34 • The station is captured with the settings of the job configuration.

35 • They match the print job configuration.

CASE STUDY: MANAGING ACME'S PRINTING SYSTEM

4 • The printer shows Stopped in the status screen.

5 • Use NWUSER to drag and drop, then send a print out from NWADMIN under Object/Print twice.

6 • Two jobs submitted.

8 • Job shows Held.

10 • The second job now prints on the printer—the first is still held.

12 • Double click on the printer CANONBJ-P1 and view status.

13 • Off-line/paper out.

14 • The status screen shows the percentage of the job being printed as it prints.

17 • Each has a status that can be seen now that it's running.

19 • The print server unloads automatically.

22 • The print server has an exclamation point next to it. This means the server is not available.

23 • The print server should show that it's down.

24 • Use either CAPTURE or NWUSER to start network capture. Then print from NWADMIN using Object/Create.

30 • The jobs have reordered themselves to place the job just modified at the top of the queue.

Chapter 15: NetWare 4 Optimization

ANSWERS TO QUIZZES

Q15-1
Tom, John, Bill, Pat, Kevin

Q15-2
None of them can be a Truthteller. The first man's statement cannot be true. If the second says something to indicate the first man is truthful, he is a Liar. The first man cannot be right. The second man is a Liar, as demonstrated, so the third man, who says the second man is telling the truth, must be a Liar. It is possible that the second man is a Truthteller, but he can't really be because the third man says the second is telling the truth, and he is a proven liar. Therefore, the second man is also lying. Check each one's statements against the others. Good monitoring! You have a future yet.

Q15-3
24198!!

Q15-4
$5.5 - 5 \times 55 \times (5 - {}^5/_5)$
or
${}^{555}/_5 - {}^{55}/_{55}$

Q15-5
It contains the numbers 1 to 9 in alphabetical order.

Part IV : NetWare 4 Management

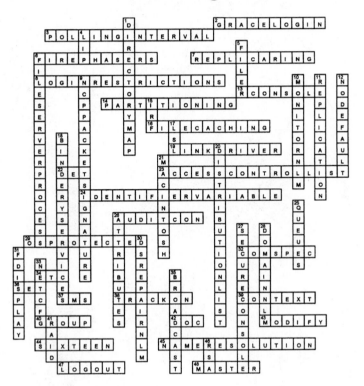

CD-ROM Contents

The Novell Press Advantage CD-ROM bound into this book contains a variety of tools that you will find useful as you prepare for your future career as a CNE. Check it out!

The Clarke Tests v2.0

The Clarke Tests v2.0 is a next-generation interactive learning system. It combines a colorful Windows-based interface with valuable text, 3-D graphics, sound clips, clues, and interactive answers. *The Clarke Tests v2.0* includes 70 tests covering 9 CNE courses and over 3000 study sessions. Each study session combines a variety of question types with interactive graphics, sounds, and clues. But the real stars of the show are the interactive answers. Each answer includes a full page or more of explanation and study material—plus page references to Novell-authorized courseware, NetWare documentation, *Novell's CNE Study Guide for NetWare 4.1*, and NUI's *So You Wanna Be A CNE?!* video series.

A special Novell Press version of *The Clarke Tests v2.0* has been included on the CD-ROM in this book (check out the directory D:\CNE4\CLARKE). Refer to the README.CNE file for installation instructions. If you would like to purchase the complete commercial version, call 1-800-684-8858 for more information.

World Wire

World Wire is an exciting, new global on-line information service. It provides myriad educational benefits, including "real-time" technical support, on-line technical databases, Internet access, fax response, networking files and information, on-line testing, career opportunities, a shopping mall, and access to a variety of networking authors and professionals.

But the really exciting part of World Wire is its on-line practice LANs. World Wire provides unlimited access to NetWare 3.1x and 4.1 LANs. System administrators and CNEs can use the World Wire LANs to get real-time hands-on experience before they attack their own production systems. Let's take a closer look.

The World Wire DOS graphical interface is on the CD-ROM bound into this book. It is in the directory D:\CNE4\WIRE. Just make a directory on your hard drive called WIRE and copy these files into it. Then, look for a file called README.WIR. This will give you last-minute instructions.

Also in the directory you will find an executable file called RIPTERM.EXE. Execute it. Follow the instructions for adding directories and initial configurations. Once the software is set up, you are ready to enter World Wire.

The first time you call World Wire you will need to fill out an on-line registration form. After you complete the form, let the system operator know you are in and need your security level upgraded. Now, you are ready to begin your journey.

In the New User Files area, you will find other software, updates and information to help you on your journey. This includes special Windows interface files for access to the GUI areas of World Wire.

Cyber State University

Join the on-line revolution at Cyber State University. Cyber State University uses World Wire to connect students from all over the world. They offer the most advanced and comprehensive training facility on-line. Using their exclusive *Synergy Learning System*, students traverse the electronic airwaves, taking virtual classes and learning nonvirtual skills.

The new *Synergy Learning System* combines video, Professor Wire lectures, interactive chats with students, reading from *Novell's CNE Study Guide for NetWare 4.1*, focused testing, *The Clarke Tests v2.0*, and extensive, hands-on World-Wire lab exercises. All of these features combine to create a dynamic multimedia training environment.

We've included a special Cyber State University package on the CD-ROM in this book. Check out the D:\CNE4\CYBER directory on the CD-ROM. You can sign up on-line or call 1-510-253-TREK.

NSEPro

Novell has kindly provided a special edition of the latest Network Support Encyclopedia, Professional Volume (NSEPro) on the CD-ROM included with this book.

NSEPro is a comprehensive networking information base with hundreds of megabyte of valuable text, graphics, questions/answers, application notes, and files. Plus, it operates with a sophisticated Folio search engine, which makes the information easy to find whenever you need it. Refer to the D:\NSEPRO directory on the CD-ROM, and be sure to check out the README.NSE file for installation instructions.

DS Standard

DS Standard was co-developed by Preferred System, Inc. (PSI) and Novell. It is a Windows-based design tool that allows you to model, analyze, and manage your NDS tree off-line, before and after moving it into production. Using DS Standard, you can practice all this great design stuff without threatening the viability of your company's NDS tree and once your tree is up and running, you can use DS Standard for ongoing day-to-day NDS management. A preview version of DS Standard NDS Manager is included on the CD-ROM bound into this book. To renew this license, or to purchase the product, please contact your PS representative at 1-203-937-3000.

To install DS Standard, use the following instructions:

1 • From Microsoft Windows, select File/Run, and then type D:\DSINST\SETUP.EXE, and click OK.

2 • Supply the DS Standard application subdirectory when prompted.

3 • Select NO when prompted to run the PSI License Manager. Because this preview version of DS Standard is preconfigured to access an unlimited number of NetWare servers for a limited time period, there is no need to run the PSI License Manager.

Just in Case...

If a replacement CD-ROM is needed, please return the CD with a written request to the following address: IDG Books Fulfillment Center, Attn: *Novell's CNE Study Guide for NetWare 4.1,* IDG Books Worldwide, 7260 Shadeland Station, Indianapolis, IN 46256, or call 1-800-762-2974 for more information.

INDEX

(continued)

(continued)

(continued)

G

(continued)

(continued)

O

(continued)

P

(continued)

(continued)

(continued)

T

The Network Support Encyclopedia™

Professional Volume (NSEPro™)

The NSEPro™ contains thousands of Technical Information Documents created and used by Novell support engineers. All information and product reference manuals are easy to search on the CD-ROM. It's compatible with MS Windows, DOS or Macintosh.

Use the CD in the front of this CNE Study Guide today. It's the next best thing to studying with someone from Novell.

Now special CNE pricing!
$295 for 12 monthly updates to the NSEPro™.

Call 1-800-377-4136 to order yours today.

About Novell Research

Novell Research is a program through which Novell publishes technical information about designing, implementing, and managing NetWare-based systems. Publications produced by Novell Research include Novell Application Notes, Novell Research Reports, and Novell Developer Notes.

Novell Research publications are written by Novell consultants and engineers, with the help of outside industry experts when necessary. The information contained in these publications is based on lab research and actual field experience of the authors, covering topics in the areas of network design and optimization, network management, operating system internals and theory of operations, product implementation, third-party integration, and programming.

This information is designed to benefit Novell's technical audience consisting of systems engineers, support engineers, consultants, programmers, network managers, and information systems personnel.

Novell Application Notes (AppNotes) is Novell's monthly technical journal for network design, implementation, administration, and integration. Each issue contains several articles that address different aspects of working with Novell products, including configuration, optimization, and management. The material is based on technical research performed by Novell personnel.

Novell Research Reports are in-depth treatments of key technical issues such as network backup, security, and integration with other vendors' products. These reports also represent technical research performed by Novell personnel. Cooperative research projects are planned for topics of general interest for which Novell cannot produce strategic research without outside assistance.

Novell Application Notes are available directly from Novell, by subscription only. The one-year subscription rate is $95 for orders within the United States, and US$135 for orders outside the U.S. AppNote subscribers also receive copies of selected Novell Research Reports as they become available. A discount is available for organizations desiring 10 or more subscriptions. For more information, contact the Novell Research Order Desk at 1-800-377-4136 or 303-297-2725.

N O V E L L   R E S E A R C H

Application Notes Order Form

Use this form to order subscriptions to Novell Application Notes (AppNotes). (Please type or print.)

Name: _____

Title: _____ Phone: _____

Company: _____

Address: _____

City: _____ State: _____

Country: _____ Postal code: _____

Fax: _____ Telex: _____

❑ Please enter my one-year subscription for US$95 (US$135 outside the United States).*

   *Shipping and taxes are included in subscription price. Prices subject to change without notice.

Payment *All orders must be prepaid.*
❑   My check or money order is enclosed.

❑ Please bill my credit card: ❑ VISA   ❑ MasterCard   ❑ American Express

Card number: _____ Expiration date: _____

Cardholder signature: _____

Cardholder name (printed): _____

Mail or fax the completed form to: **or call:**

Novell Research Order Desk
1601 Park Avenue West
Denver, CO 80216-5199
Fax (303) 294-0930

(800) 377-4136 (U.S. & Canada)
(303) 297-2725 (other locations)
Please have your order and
 credit card information ready.

Novell, Inc ✦122 East 1700 South ✦ Provo, Utah 84606 ✦ 801-429-7000   PCode=IDG195

Novell Research Publications

To obtain an updated list of Novell Application Notes (including those published prior to 1994 and Research Reports), download the APPNOT.LST file from NetWire. Prices for AppNote reprints are US$15 per copy in the United States, US$20 per copy in all other locations (price includes shipping and handling). For information on how to order these publications, call the Novell Research Order Desk at 800-377-4136. Outside the U.S. and Canada, call 303-297-2725.

Date / Part Number

Nov 95 / 164-000047-011
NetWare Link Services Protocol: An Advanced Theory of Operations
Guidelines for Implementing NetWare/IP
Tuning the Server Memory Calculation Worksheet

Oct 95 / 164-000047-010
Integrating the NetWare Client for DOS/MS Windows (VLMs) with Windows 95
Using TRACK and Other Console Utilities in a Mixed NetWare Environment
MHS Services' Role in Novell's Messaging Strategy
Using AppWare to Automate PerfectOffice Applications

Sep 95 / 164-000047-009
An Introduction to Novell's NetWare Client32 for Windows 95
Overview and Benefits of Novell Embedded Systems Technology (NEST)
Using UnixWare 2 to Set Up a Web Server: A Case Study
Comparing Novell's IPX-to-IP Connectivity Solutions: IP Tunneling, NetWare/IP, and IP Relay

Aug 95 / 164-000047-008
Backing Up and Restoring NetWare Directory Services in NetWare 4
SBACKUP Configuration and Usage Notes
Troubleshooting Tips for NetWare Directory Services

Jul 95 / 164-000047-007
Installing and Configuring UnixWare 2.0
Understanding the NetWare UNIX Client (NUC) NLM 2.0
Configuring Asynchronous Connections with the NetWare MultiProtocol Router 3.0

Jun 95 / 164-000047-006
Centralized Multiserver Backup over 100VG-AnyLAN Networks
Using Novell's NetWare User Tools (NWUSER.EXE) for MS Windows Clients
Anatomy of a Voice Processing NLM
ABEND Recovery Techniques for NetWare 3 and 4

May 95 / 164-000047-005
The Benefits of Using Intelligent LAN Adapters in NetWare Servers
Using the NTSWD Utility to Diagnose MS Windows Workstation Problems
Upgrading to NetWare 4.1 Across a LAN/WAN Using RCONSOLE
Using NDS User Object Properties in NetWare 4.1 Login Scripts

Apr 95 / 164-000047-004
Integrating the NetWare DOS Requester (VLMs) with Windows for Workgroups
Importing User Information into NetWare Directory Services Using UIMPORT
Unified Messaging: Paving the Road to Pervasive Computing
Using NetWare/IP Over Satellite Networks
Understanding NetWare HostPrint 1.1x
NetWare 4 Memory Architecture / Understanding Memory Fragmentation in NetWare
Using MONITOR to Track NetWare 4 Memory Allocation

IDG BOOKS WORLDWIDE LICENSE AGREEMENT

Important—read carefully before opening the software packet(s). This is a legal agreement between you (either an individual or an entity) and IDG Books Worldwide, Inc. (IDG). By opening the accompanying sealed packet containing the software disk(s), you acknowledge that you have read and accept the following IDG License Agreement. If you do not agree and do not want to be bound by the terms of this Agreement, promptly return the book and the unopened software packet(s) to the place you obtained them for a full refund.

1. License. This License Agreement (Agreement) permits you to use one copy of the enclosed Software program(s) on a single computer. The Software is in "use" on a computer when it is loaded into temporary memory (i.e., RAM) or installed into permanent memory (e.g., hard disk, CD-ROM, or other storage device) of that computer.

2. Copyright. The entire contents of the disk(s) and the compilation of the Software are copyrighted and protected by both United States copyright laws and international treaty provisions. You may only (a) make one copy of the Software for backup or archival purposes, or (b) transfer the Software to a single hard disk, provided that you keep the original for backup or archival purposes. The individual programs on the disk(s) are copyrighted by the authors of each program respectively. Each program has its own use permissions and limitations. To use each program, you must follow the individual requirements and restrictions detailed for each in the Appendix of this Book. Do not use a program if you do not want to follow its Licensing Agreement. None of the material on the disk(s) or listed in this Book may ever be distributed, in original or modified form, for commercial purposes.

3. Other Restrictions. You may not rent or lease the Software. You may transfer the Software and user documentation on a permanent basis provided you retain no copies and the recipient agrees to the terms of this Agreement. You may not reverse engineer, decompile, or disassemble the Software except to the extent that the foregoing restriction is expressly prohibited by applicable law. If the Software is an update or has been updated, any transfer must include the most recent update and all prior versions.

4. Limited Warranty. IDG warrants that the Software and disk(s) are free from defects in materials and workmanship for a period of sixty (60) days from the date of purchase of this Book. If IDG receives notification within the warranty period of defects in material or workmanship, IDG will replace the defective disk(s). IDG's entire liability and your exclusive remedy shall be limited to replacement of the Software, which is returned to

IDG BOOKS WORLDWIDE REGISTRATION CARD

RETURN THIS REGISTRATION CARD FOR FREE CATALOG

Title of this book: Novell's CNE Study Guide for NetWare 4.1

My overall rating of this book: ❑ Very good [1] ❑ Good [2] ❑ Satisfactory [3] ❑ Fair [4] ❑ Poor [5]

How I first heard about this book:

❑ Found in bookstore; name: [6]

❑ Advertisement: [8]

❑ Word of mouth; heard about book from friend, co-worker, etc.: [10]

❑ Book review: [7]

❑ Catalog: [9]

❑ Other: [11]

What I liked most about this book:

What I would change, add, delete, etc., in future editions of this book:

Other comments:

Number of computer books I purchase in a year: ❑ 1 [12] ❑ 2-5 [13] ❑ 6-10 [14] ❑ More than 10 [15]

I would characterize my computer skills as: ❑ Beginner [16] ❑ Intermediate [17] ❑ Advanced [18] ❑ Professional [19]

I use ❑ DOS [20] ❑ Windows [21] ❑ OS/2 [22] ❑ Unix [23] ❑ Macintosh [24] ❑ Other: [25]_____
(please specify)

I would be interested in new books on the following subjects:
(please check all that apply, and use the spaces provided to identify specific software)

❑ Word processing: [26]

❑ Data bases: [28]

❑ File Utilities: [30]

❑ Networking: [32]

❑ Other: [34]

❑ Spreadsheets: [27]

❑ Desktop publishing: [29]

❑ Money management: [31]

❑ Programming languages: [33]

I use a PC at (please check all that apply): ❑ home [35] ❑ work [36] ❑ school [37] ❑ other: [38] _____

The disks I prefer to use are ❑ 5.25 [39] ❑ 3.5 [40] ❑ other: [41]_____

I have a CD ROM: ❑ yes [42] ❑ no [43]

I plan to buy or upgrade computer hardware this year: ❑ yes [44] ❑ no [45]

I plan to buy or upgrade computer software this year: ❑ yes [46] ❑ no [47]

Name: _____ Business title: [48] _____ Type of Business: [49] _____

Address (❑ home [50] ❑ work [51]/Company name: _____)

Street/Suite#

City [52]/State [53]/Zipcode [54]: _____ Country [55] _____

❑ **I liked this book!** You may quote me by name in future
IDG Books Worldwide promotional materials.

My daytime phone number is _____

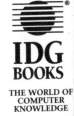

IDG BOOKS

THE WORLD OF COMPUTER KNOWLEDGE

❏ YES!

Please keep me informed about IDG's World of Compu
Send me the latest IDG Books catalog.

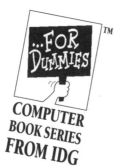

COMPUTER
BOOK SERIES
FROM IDG